OCT. 1 6 1997

LOS ANGELES A TO Z

LOS ANGELES

A to Z

An ENCYCLOPEDIA
of the CITY and COUNTY

LEONARD PITT and DALE PITT

UNIVERSITY OF CALIFORNIA PRESS

BERKELEY   LOS ANGELES   LONDON

The publisher gratefully acknowledges the contribution provided by the General Endowment Fund, which is supported by generous gifts from members of the Associates of the University of California Press.

University of California Press
Berkeley and Los Angeles, California

University of California Press, Ltd.
London, England

© 1997 by
The Regents of the University of California

Library of Congress Cataloging-in-Publication Data

Pitt, Leonard.
    Los Angeles A to Z : an encyclopedia of the city and
county / Leonard Pitt and Dale Pitt.
        p.   cm.
    Includes bibliographical references (p.   ).
    ISBN 0-520-20274-0 (cloth : alk. paper)
    1. Los Angeles (Calif.)—Encyclopedias.   2. Los
Angeles County (Calif.)—Encyclopedias.   I. Pitt,
Dale.   II. Title.
    F869.L84.P58   1997
    979.4'93—DC21   96-50261
                                                        CIP

The paper used in this publication meets the minimum requirements of American National Standard for Information
Sciences—Permanence of Paper for Printed Library Materials, ANSI Z39.48-1984.⊗

To our immigrant parents,
Dora and Selig Pitt — Dora and Jack Lash,
and our Angeleno children,
Michael, Adam, and Marni

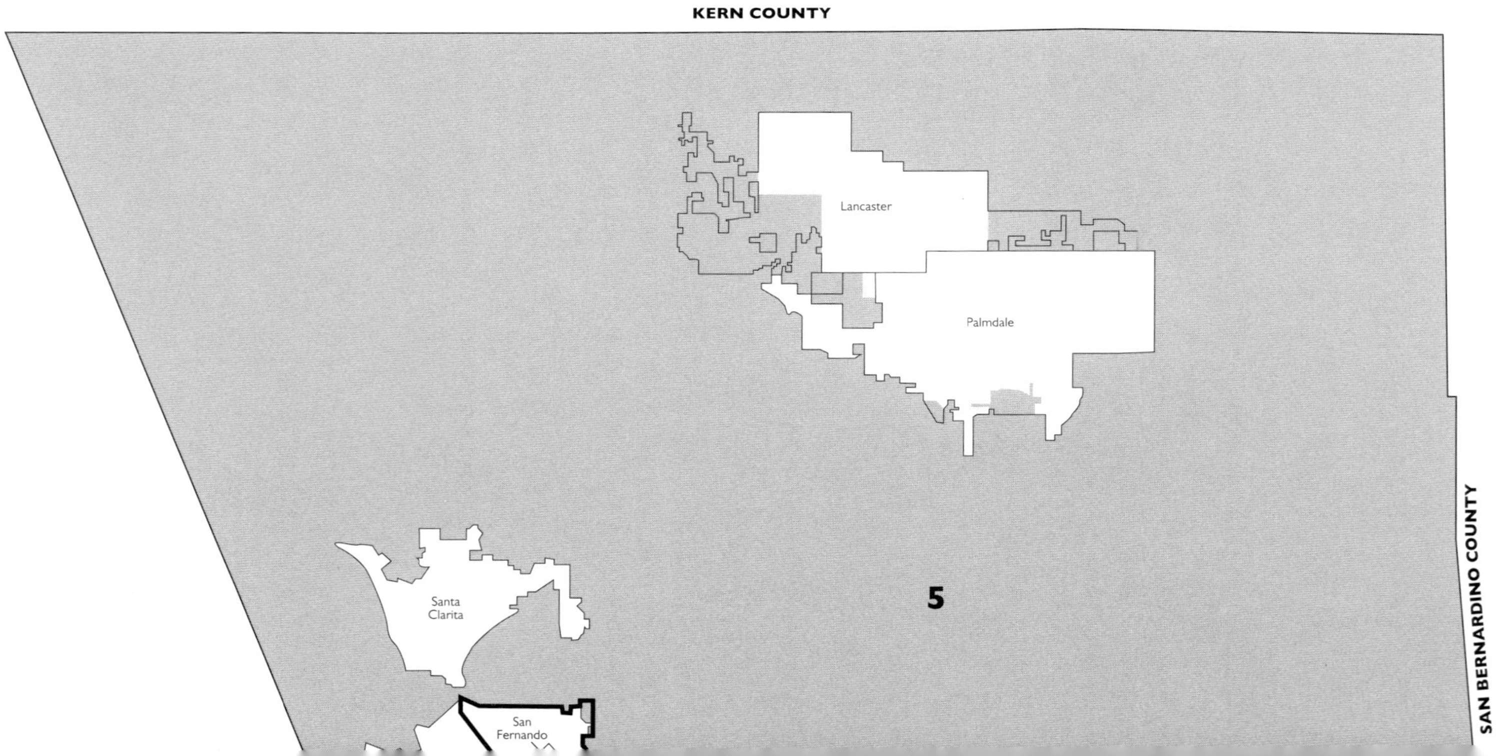
KERN COUNTY
Lancaster
Palmdale
5
Santa Clarita
San Fernando
SAN BERNARDINO COUNTY

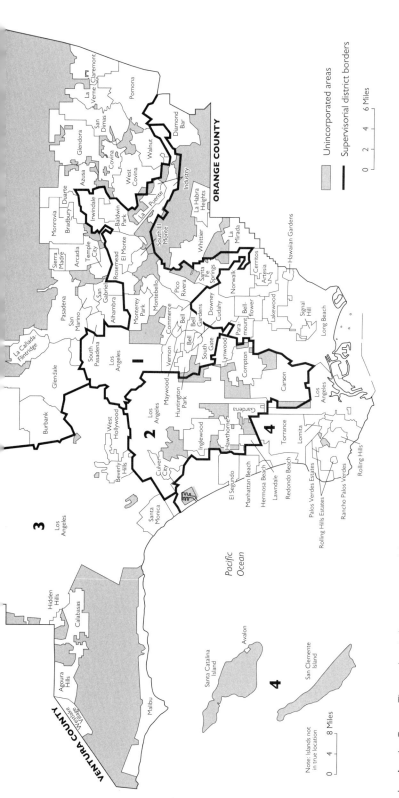

Los Angeles County. The numbers indicate supervisorial districts.

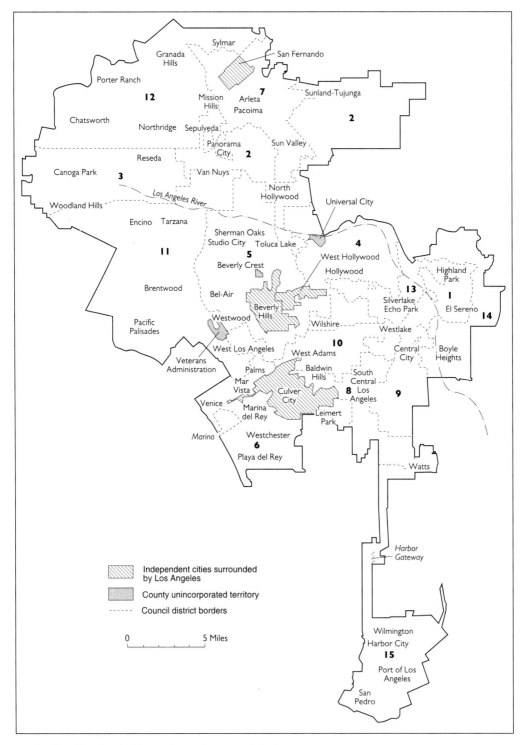

The City of Los Angeles. The numbers indicate council districts.

CONTENTS

PREFACE

An encyclopedia is intended to meet a variety of needs. It can supply specific information for anyone seeking the answer to a specific question. It can provide an overview to broader issues. And finally, it can satisfy the browser who searches at leisure for unexpected nuggets. We have tried to bear in mind these multiple purposes while preparing this first-ever encyclopedia about Los Angeles County.

The task has proven immensely challenging. The region, with the city of Los Angeles at its core, has had a short but dynamic history. In little more than 200 years, it has exploded from an isolated *pueblo* on the farthest reaches of European civilization to a major world metropolis at the heart of the Pacific Rim. Its population has expanded from the original 44 settlers in 1781 (excluding the indigenous Indians who witnessed their arrival) to 9.2 million in 1996. Its beaches, its freeways, its climate, its laid-back lifestyle, and its upheavals, springing from both natural causes and human conflict, make news headlines throughout the world. The movie and television industry is—for better or worse—the window through which most of the world thinks it knows us.

The idea for this encyclopedia came from several different directions. When we asked librarians specific questions about Los Angeles, they expressed frustration at the lack of reference books, especially those regarding smaller communities. At the same time we became aware of how little people knew about their own communities. With the influx of a huge non-native population, the knowledge gap has widened among Angelenos. More and more, college students confess that they have never visited Olvera Street, have no idea of the importance of the San Pedro and Long Beach ports, are unsure of where the Los Angeles River is, and are astonished to learn how recently it was that Los Angeles had been an agricultural area.

Looking to fill this need, we discovered that very few metropolitan areas have encyclopedias devoted to them, and that few authors have ever tried to cover all or most of Los Angeles County within the confines of a single volume. Among the early writings were James M. Guinn's *Historical and Biographical Record of Los Angeles and Vicinity* (1907), Harris Newmark's *Reminiscences* (1916), John Steven McGroarty's *History of Los Angeles County* (1923), and W. W. Robinson's *Ranchos Become Cities* (1939). In 1946 Carey McWilliams gave us *Southern California: An Island on the Land*, the first richly interpretive work, and in many respects the best. More recent efforts to present a broad panorama have included Robert M. Fogelson's *Fragmented Metropolis* (1967), Howard J. Nelson's *Los Angeles Metropolis* (1983), Andrew Rolle's *Los Angeles: From Pueblo to City of the Future* (1985; 2d ed., 1995), and David Gebhard and Robert Winter's *Los Angeles: An Architectural Guide* (1985; 2d ed., 1994). We took some comfort from their books and pressed on. At this point, two works proved especially helpful. James D. Hart's *Companion to California* (1987) provided us with an excellent model for a single-volume encyclopedia, and Doyce B. Nunis Jr.'s *Los Angeles and Its Environs in the Twentieth Century: A Bibliography of a Metropolis* (1973) offered us initial ideas for the list of entries.

Meanwhile, we had started collecting clippings on Los Angeles County from a variety of sources. We soon were reminded of the sorcerer's apprentice, as the clippings multiplied rapidly and came spilling out of our file cabinets. Around 1991 we began writing brief sketches, and by the time we completed the work in 1996, we had nearly 2,000 alphabetically arranged entries.

The entries fall into three categories. In the first group are general topics that make comprehensive statements, cover an extended period of time, or establish a framework for a broad understanding of a given subject. Among these listings are "Ethnic groups," "Earthquakes," and "Trade and commerce." This category also includes subjects such as religion, education, the movie industry, the natural environment, demographics, theater, and the history of the city of Los Angeles, to name but a few.

The second—and by far the largest—category concentrates on briefer and more specific topics. These include ethnic and religious groups under their individual names, rather than as general themes: African Americans, Presbyterians, Cubans, Mormons. The topics are wide ranging, with entries for the Northridge earthquake, the Downey Block, the Rose Bowl, the Los Angeles Dodgers, the peregrine falcon, the Long Beach Grand Prix, La Fiesta de Los Angeles, the Ridge Route, the Huntington Library, the Mediterranean fruit fly, and the Academy of Motion Picture Arts and Sciences. We have also tried to cover every geographical area in Los Angeles County for which information was available. Here the reader will find answers to what are probably the most frequently asked questions about Los Angeles. When did smog begin? Who really founded Los Angeles? Which trees are native to the area? How does the Los Angeles city charter distribute power? Who was the Black Dahlia? When was Los Angeles County formed? Many readers will be surprised to learn, for example, that the first discovery of gold in California occurred not at Sutter's Mill but in Los Angeles County, or that the County Board of Supervisors once had seven members rather than five.

The third group of entries consists of biographies. The majority describe historic figures, from Governor Pío Pico to author Helen Hunt Jackson, from bandido Tiburcio Vásquez to actor Clark Gable, from aqueduct builder William Mulholland to Olvera Street founder Christine Sterling, from *Los Angeles Times* publisher Harrison Gray Otis to philanthropist S. Mark Taper, from newspaper publisher Charlotta Spears Bass to Franciscan missionary Juan Crespi. All the mayors of the city of Los Angeles are included. The personal sketches, as a rule, are of people who have contributed to the community in some way or have been important to its history. Also included are influential contemporary figures, such as former mayor Tom Bradley, civic leader Dorothy ("Buffy") Chandler, basketball great Kareem Abdul-Jabbar, and community advocate Stewart Kwoh. We would have liked to add many more names to this list but were forced to set limits that would keep us within the bounds of a single volume.

Several other features of this book deserve mention. Sprinkled throughout the text are quotations from early settlers, famous visitors or residents, and contemporaries from various walks of life. Varying in tone from somber to lighthearted, they provide food for thought about Los Angeles and indicate the range of emotions the area has generated since its beginnings. In addition, some 335 carefully chosen illustrations, including maps, charts, and tables, complement the text. Further tables appear in Appendixes B, C, and D, while Appendix A presents a year-by-year chronology, intended not as a comprehensive listing of the city's history but rather as an insight into the sequence of events over its lifetime. Following the appendixes, the list of selected readings cites some of the sources of information used in preparing this work. By no means an exhaustive bibliography, it includes books and articles that we believe would be available to the general reader in a regional branch library, as well as novels about Southern California. Finally, we offer a list of selected films that depict the Los Angeles area over more than seven decades.

We intended this book to be user-friendly for a wide variety of readers. It should provide a valuable research tool to specialists in history, political science, urban planning, ethnic studies, law, architecture, and education, and a reference aid to librarians, students, scriptwriters, journalists, businesspeople, history buffs, and community activists. We believe it can be useful for anyone visiting, or planning to visit, the Los Angeles area. Certainly it should increase understanding of the cultural diversity of the metropolis. And finally, we hope that it will furnish hours of pleasure for the devoted browser who allows the book to fall open at random and the eye and mind to roam from topic to topic.

Every effort has been made to meet the most exacting criteria, but inevitably there will be errors of omission and commission, as well as differences of interpretation. We hope to correct any errors in future editions of *Los Angeles A to Z.* To this end we invite you to give us your own impressions of the book, and what you would like to see changed or added in the future. You may write us at P.O. Box 66712, Los Angeles, CA, 90066.

We are fascinated by Los Angeles's past and very optimistic about its future. It has become one of the most important, exciting, and controversial urban centers on the globe. The extent to which it influences world culture is staggering. In spite of its size, its complexity, and the criticism it has endured from time to time, Los Angeles continues to entice and seduce vast numbers of visitors and residents. We like to think that this book helps explain that fascination.

Enjoy!

Leonard and Dale Pitt

ACKNOWLEDGMENTS

In researching and writing this wide-ranging work, we have benefited from the generous assistance, insights, and knowledge of scores of people—scholars, librarians, artists, journalists, government officials, publicists, community activists, and friends and colleagues.

Three individuals deserve special mention for having read every word of the manuscript. They are Robert Blew, history scholar and teacher; Sidney Richman, emeritus professor of American literature; and Betty Wentworth Trotter, freelance writer and editor. Their critical reading was invaluable, and they are blameless for any errors that may remain.

Several scholars read parts of the manuscript. Among them were John Baur and Leonard Leader, both of whom died before the work was completed. We were greatly encouraged by the positive reactions of Kevin Starr and Robert Winter, who read parts of an early version. Nancy Meyers Wilkman and Jon Wilkman, filmmakers, historians, and friends, also encouraged us from the start. At various times we have gleaned information from fellow historians, including Rudy Acuña, Suzanne Borghei, Jacqueline Braitman, William Deverell, Michael Engh, Doug Flamming, Judd Grenier, Abraham Hoffman, Rodger Lotchin, Gloria R. Lothrop, Julian Nava, Merrie Ovnick, Martin Ridge, Antonio Rios-Bustamente, Andrew Rolle, Tom Sitton, Denise S. Spooner, and Arthur Verge. Many of these colleagues have presented papers or participated in discussions at the Los Angeles History Research Group at the Huntington Library.

We owe a collective debt to the many scholars whose published works we used (see the Selected Readings at the back of the book for a partial list). It is worth noting that the articles in the *Southern California Quarterly,* and other publications of the Historical Society of Southern California, have been particularly useful.

Three extremely able graduate students at the University of California, Los Angeles—Michael J. Gonzalez, Richard Lester, and Daniel Johnson—have allowed us to pick their brains or read portions of their dissertations. At California State University, Northridge, geographer James Allen offered maps and newly generated information regarding ethnicity, while Susan Henry guided us to data concerning newspapers.

Librarians, archivists, curators, and museum administrators ferreted out specific information, clarified disputed points, recommended works to read, and located photographs. Among them were Mary Artino of the Newport Harbor Art Museum; Edward R. Bosley of the Gamble House; Steven Branch of the Ronald Reagan Presidential Library; Walter Brem of the Bancroft Library at the University of California, Berkeley; Lonnie G. Bunch III of the National Museum of American History in Washington, D.C.; Ann Caiger, Octavio Olvera, and Simon V. Elliott of Special Collections in the Research Library at the University of California, Los Angeles; Kevin Cartright of the Richard Nixon Library and Birthplace; Suellen Cheng and Jean Bruce Poole of El Pueblo de Los Angeles Historic Monument; David Earle of the Lancaster Museum; Bettye Ellison and Carolyn Cole of the Los Angeles Public Library; Janet R. Fireman and William Mason of the History Division of the Natural History Museum of Los Angeles County; Leonard Gordon, formerly of the Kennedy Library, California State University, Los Angeles; Marcy Guzman of the Norton Simon Museum; Markrid Izquierdo of the Glendale Public Library; Alan Jutzi and Lisa Blackburn of the Huntington Library; Virginia Kazor of the Los Angeles Cultural Affairs Department; Jorge Lambrino of the Edward Roybal Institute for Applied Gerontology; Daniel Lewis of the *Los Angeles Times* History Center; Robert Marshall of the Urban Archives Center, California State University, Northridge; Rick Moss of the African American Museum of Los Angeles; Jeannette O'Malley of the Southwest Museum; Militza Savalas of the J. Paul Getty Museum; Dace Taube of the University of Southern California Doheny Memorial Library; Francis J. Weber of the Catholic Archdiocese Archives; and various staff members of the Rosemead Public Library. Paul J. Karlstrom, Regional Director of American Art for the Smithsonian Institution, provided his own writings, and those of others, on the history of painting.

We were pleased to encounter a great many well informed, resourceful, and courteous public servants in state, county, and city governments. For specialized information about the workings of government and the economy we are grateful to several people at the state level: Steven Gray-Barkan, Chief of Staff to Assemblywoman Debra Bowen; Javier O. Lopez of the California Commission for Economic Development; Dawn L. Rodrigues of the California State Library; and Margie Tiritilli, Duncan McIntosh, and Vincent Moreno of the California Department of Transportation.

In Los Angeles County government we would like to thank Michael D. Antonovich; Martin Barrera of the County Graphic Arts Department; Vivian Elliff of the Los Angeles Music Center; Judy Hammond of the County Public Affairs Department; Wendy Harn of the Sheriff's Department; Victoria B. Pipkin of Kenneth Hahn's office; Keith Rohrlick and Robert Schwartz of the Memorial Coliseum and Sports Arena; Ann Roubideaux of the Metropolitan Transit Authority; Charles Sifuentes of the Community Redevelopment Agency; Lee R. Stark and Norma Shanks of the Regional Planning Department; and Joanne Sturges and Angie Montes of the Board of Supervisors Executive Office.

In the offices of the city of Los Angeles we offer our appreciation to William R. Bamattre of the Los Angeles Fire Department; Jeff Beckerman, Frank Eberhard, Melanie S. Fallon, and Fae Tsukamoto of the Department of City Planning; Ernani Bernardi; Jackie Brainard of Councilwoman Joy Picus's office; Nancy Fernandez of the Los Angeles Cultural Heritage Commission; Cora Fossett and Joan Sewald of the Department of Airports; Robert B. Freeman of the Los Angeles City Archives; Howard Gantman of Councilman Michael Feuer's office; Kristin F. Heffron in the Election Division, City Clerk's Office; Nate Holden; Richard A. Lukas of the Bureau of Street Lighting; Sharyn Michelson and John M. Dunkin of the Los Angeles Police Department; Greg Nelson of Councilman Joel Wachs's office; Claire Rogger of Councilman Marvin Braude's office; Robert Schaefer of the Department of Water and Power; Rick Tuttle; Barbara T. Yamamoto of the Port of Los Angeles; and LaGronie Wyatt of the Bureau of Engineering.

We also owe a debt to other government offices in the city of Los Angeles as well as to the offices of other cities within the county: Lee N. Duer, City of Signal Hill; Greg Grammer, City of Bradbury; Betty Irwin, West Covina Redevelopment Agency; Diana Love, South Coast Air Quality Management District; Joann Lundgren, Public Relations Department of the Metropolitan Water District of Southern California; Pat O'Donoghue of the Burbank, Glendale, Pasadena Airport; Ria C. Parody, Los Angeles Unified School District; Kirk Pelser, Glendale Redevelopment Agency; Judy Rambeau, City of Commerce; and Don Waldie, City of Lakewood.

We received helpful information or graphics materials on higher education from Toni Beron and Barbara Parks, California State University, Long Beach; Anita Bonnell, California Institute of the Arts; Carlos Chavez, Occidental College; Felis Cintron, University of Southern California; Vicki

Dewar, California State Polytechnic University, Pomona; Donna Dixon and Bill Bennett, University of California, Los Angeles; John V. German, Claremont University Center and Graduate School; Pamela Hammond and Rich W. Turner, California State University, Dominguez Hills; Harvey D. Kern, Los Angeles County–University of Southern California Medical Center; Bill Meredith and Carol Selkin, California State University, Los Angeles; Patricia Orr, California Institute of Technology; Margaret Reeve, Southern California Institute of Architecture; Julie Richardson and Jeffrey C. Bliss, Pepperdine University; Norm Schneider and Angela B. Winston, Loyola-Marymount University; Bruce Smith, Santa Monica College; and Randy Thompson and Bruce Erickson, California State University, Northridge.

We are grateful to the chamber of commerce personnel who supplied useful written materials or photographs: Maurine Aldridge, Claremont Chamber of Commerce; Mary Lou Blackwood and Nancy S. Steiner, Malibu Chamber of Commerce; Veronica Calvillo and Judi Oberbillig, Pasadena Convention and Visitors Bureau; Bruce J. Cohen, San Fernando Chamber of Commerce; Lois Drake, Redondo Beach Chamber of Commerce; Carol Duff, Chamber of Commerce of Hermosa Beach; Julian Foreman, Avalon Chamber of Commerce; Aline Hausman, Canoga Park Chamber of Commerce; Virginia Hultman, Whittier Marketing Council; Paul Kreutzer, Santa Clarita Valley Chamber of Commerce; Barbara La Fata, Palmdale Chamber of Commerce; Che' R. Martinez, Venice Area Chamber of Commerce; John Maxon, Arleta Chamber of Commerce; Wendy Norell, Central City Association; Ann Pritchard, Pacific Palisades Chamber of Commerce; Carol Ritscher, Palos Verdes Peninsula Chamber of Commerce; John Robinson, Long Beach Area Convention and Visitors Bureau; Ursula Ruiz, Baldwin Park Chamber of Commerce; Marcia Sculatti, West Hollywood Convention and Visitors Bureau; Gary C. Sherwin, Carol Martinez, and Susan Ferrull, Los Angeles Convention and Visitors Bureau; Chris Volker, Los Angeles Area Chamber of Commerce; and Jan Wight, Chamber of Commerce of Duarte.

Equally helpful were individuals in corporate offices: Joe Amati, NBA Entertainment; Betsy Bartscherer, ARCO; Elizabeth A. Borsting, The Queen Mary; James Bray, Unocal Corporation; Dale A. Carlson, Pacific Stock Exchange; Barbara Casey, Casey & Sayre, Inc.; Ellen Castruccio, Lewitzky Dance Company; Sally Childs, The Citadel; Clifford Chin, Friar's Club; Bill Cohen, The Luckman Partnership; Elaine Cullen, Economic Development Corporation of Los Angeles County; Al Davis, The Magic Castle; Terri Dishman, Beverly Hills Hotel; Caryn Eaves, Tournament of Roses Parade; Vivian Leigh Edwards, Chevron Corporation; Robin Ellerthorpe, Ellerby Becket, Inc.; Tammy Fareed, Long Beach Opera; Tina Fields, Contrarian Group; J. C. Flores, East Los Angeles Community Union; Dick Friend and Denise King, Southern California Gas Company; Christina V. Godbey, *Los Angeles Times;* Jane Goldstein, Santa Anita Park; Audrey Hodges, Macy and Associates; Steven Koff, Southern California Grocers Association; Pamela Krolczyk, Southern California Automobile Club; Kristine Krueger, Academy of Motion Picture Arts and Sciences; Patti Kuczwaj, Century Plaza Towers; Kathy Lendech, Turner Entertainment; Lisa Lochanko, Sony Pictures Entertainment; Stephen Loew, Capitol Milling Co.; Janna Loosli-Valtrakis, Frank Gehry Associates; Paul McGuire, NBC; Lori Moizio, Copley Los Angeles Newspapers; Mike Murray, GTE California, Inc.; John Olguin and Jay Lucas, Los Angeles Dodgers, Inc.; Claire H. Peters, Sunkist Growers; Lon Rosen, First Team Marketing; Lisa Rosenfeld, Los Angeles Marathon, Inc.; Kevin Sinclair, Sabre Mortgage Co.; Jan Taylor, Fleishman Hillard; Julie Taylor, Pacific Design Center; Cecelia Vazquez, Ahmanson & Co.; Michael Woo, Corporation for National Service; and Jane Young, Janss Investment Corporation.

Private individuals were also generous with their time and expertise. David Cameron assisted with matters relating to railroads and historic preservation; musical legend Buddy Collette provided us with wonderful personal insights into the Los Angeles jazz scene; John Crandell helped us better understand the natural environment of the Los Angeles River; Tom Doyle supplied vital information about Malibu; Steven Erie gave us a copy of his paper on the city charter of Los Angeles; Jack Fromkin and Victoria Fromkin offered help in several areas, as did Richard Glickman; Simon Glickman and Nathan Kaproff helped us with music entries; attorney Robert Hertzberg gave us access to his private historical research collection; social workers Lillian and Nathan Horwitz shared information about county social services; Anna Kathleen Hull made available a research paper on Los Angeles journalism; Lynne T. Jewell of the *Daily News* helped us sort out details about newspaper ownership; George Laine gave us a copy of his research paper on the Newspaper Guild; Lorraine and Martin Lubner contributed their knowledge about painting; Elaine Rose clarified information about dance; and Jane Wilson provided a copy of her book on the law firm Gibson, Dunn, and Crutcher.

Additional information came from people in community organizations and religious groups: Al Albergate of Soka Gakkai USA; Elizabeth Bailey of the Weingart Center; Kenneth R. Brown of the Unitarian Universalist Church of Studio City; Lynn Brusseau of the American Friends Service Committee, Pacific Southwest Division; Greg Castillo of the California Labor Federation; Maricela Cueva-Quiroz of the Mexican American Legal Defense and Educational Fund; Martha Davis of the Mono Lake Committee; Estella Dobbie of the American Friends Service Committee of Pasadena; Karen Dardick of the Descanso Gardens Guild; Peggy S. Ebright of the Pasadena Playhouse; Rene Etienne of the Los Angeles Urban League; Harriet Glickman of the Southern California Association for Philanthropy; Betty Greenstein of the Wilshire Boulevard Temple; Chris Harrer of the Los Angeles Athletic Club; Nancy Hereford, Phyllis Moberly, and Ken Worther of the Mark Taper Forum; Stewart Kwoh of the Asian Pacific American Legal Center; Lora LaMarca of the Los Angeles Zoo Association; Andy Lipkis of TreePeople; Hugo Morris of the Teamsters Union; Cecil Murray of the First African Methodist Episcopal Church of Los Angeles; Susan Nelson of the Santa Monica Mountains and Seashore Foundation; Marge Nichols of United Way; Debra J. T. Padilla of Social and Public Art Resource Center; Toni Pogue of Heal the Bay; Cheryl Rhoden of Writers Guild of America, West, Inc.; Keith Scotnes of the United Auto Workers; Rebecca Shehee of the American Civil Liberties Foundation; Kris Vosburgh of the Howard Jarvis Tax Payers Association; Jeff Weber of the Zamorano Club; Susan Valerie Weight of Catholic Charities; and Suzanne Williams of the American Institute of Architects, Los Angeles.

Those in local history associations who supplied information or words of encouragement include Marie Adamson of the Altadena Historical Society; Thomas F. Andrews and Margaret Dickerson of the Historical Society of Southern California; David L. Clark, Joe Northrop, and Hynda Rudd of the Los Angeles City Historical Society; Cecelia Ditlefsen of the Alhambra Historical Society; Alice Stelle of the Calabasas Historical Society; and Gladys Waddington of the Inglewood Historical Society.

We relied on the *Los Angeles Times* and the *Daily News* for basic reports of current news about the metropolis. One newspaper columnist in particular deserves special commendation: Cecelia Rasmussen, of the *Times,* for her historical human interest column, "The City Then and Now." Nor should we fail to note that the computer database Lexis-Nexis provided us with an invaluable tool for digging out news and opinion on current affairs and recent history.

Excellent original contemprary photographs were taken by Marni Pitt and Michael Krakowiak and by Lori Shepler. Laurel Anderson of Photosynthesis helped with photo research; Margaret Bach provided leads to photographs; and Miriam Matthews and Julius Shulman supplied photos. The maps were drawn by Bill Nelson.

In the early stages of our work, Marcia Dunnicliffe, Kelly Sciortino, and Regina Lark-Miller of the History Department at California State University, Northridge, helped us with clerical matters. Supervised research papers created by history students at Northridge—Tamera Breckenridge, Ralph Easton, Edward T. Gomez, Denise Hamilton, David Kendrick, Sally Mendelsohn, Kathleen L. Miller, Jill Sciliano, Gail Stein, Christina M. Whitmore—yielded useful information on a variety of topics.

At the University of California Press, Eileen McWilliam was the first to champion our cause. She made an enthusiastic believer of Director James Clark. Subsequently Rose Vekony and Valeurie Friedman, who worked directly with us throughout this project, were always cooperative and accessible. We are grateful to them and to their colleagues Sam Rosenthal, Barbara Jellow, Anna Bullard, and Mary Bahr. They established a fine program of editing, graphic design, production, and promotion. We are also extremely thankful for the exacting work of copy editor Anne Canright, who made a thorough, word-by-word review of the entire manuscript. Her careful reading kept us on our toes.

Our deep gratitude and love goes to all of our friends and family, particularly Norman Pitt and Ed and Gloria Lash. They did not give up on us while we worked on the book but kindly put up with our absences and preoccupations. If we were inattentive, it was not for lack of caring.

Finally, we are particularly grateful to Vivian Weinstein for granting us permission to select from the extensive historic photo collection of her husband, the late Robert Weinstein. Bob was a dear and cherished friend of many years, as is his wife, and we miss him.

AAA. *See* Automobile Club of Southern California

ABDUL-JABBAR, KAREEM (1947–), basketball star. Born Lew Alcindor in New York City, he attended that city's Power Memorial High School, where his team had a 71-game winning streak. He was recruited to UCLA, and during his three-year tenure as a center the Bruins racked up an 88–2

Kareem Abdul-Jabbar in 1985 NBA playoffs. Photo by Andrew D. Bernstein, courtesy NBA Photos.

record; he also led the team to three NCAA titles with a 12–0 tournament record, and was named Outstanding Player of the NCAA tournament for all three years and College Player of the Year in 1967 and 1969. After graduation in 1969 he entered the National Basketball Association (NBA), playing for the Milwaukee Bucks. In 1971 he changed his name to Kareem Abdul-Jabbar. In 1975 the Los Angeles Lakers acquired him in a trade. During his career Kareem amassed an astonishing number of NBA records: he scored 37,639 points, appeared in 1,486 games, made 15,524 field goals, was the leading scorer in All-Star competition and the only player chosen to participate 18 times, was the only player to win six Most Valuable Player awards, and was the first to appear in 200 playoff games. Famous for his sky-hook shot, at the time of his retirement in 1988 the 7-foot 2-inch Kareem was the oldest player in the NBA.

ACADEMY OF MOTION PICTURE ARTS AND SCIENCES (AMPAS), film industry association established in 1927 to recognize and foster meritorious film work. It is best known to the public for its annual Academy Awards ceremony (originally known as Merit Awards). The perhaps apocryphal story is that the "Oscar" award was so named when Margaret Herrick, the AMPAS librarian, remarked that the bronze figurine resembled her uncle Oscar. These treasured statuettes are presented to the year's best film, actors, director, screenwriter, cinematographer, etc. The first awards (presented in 1929 for the 1927–1928 season) were held at the Roosevelt Hotel in Hollywood. Only three awards were given: to Emil Jannings and Janet Gaynor as best actors, and for *Wings* as best film. The ceremony has expanded over the years to include numerous artistic, technical, humani-

The Oscar. "Oscar" statuette. © AMPAS.™

tarian, and life achievement awards. In recent years it has been held at the Dorothy Chandler Pavilion and at the Shrine Auditorium. The awards have become an international event, viewed on television by hundreds of millions of people around the world.

The Academy maintains a research library and archives in a restored historic building on La Cienega Boulevard in Beverly Hills. The library's priceless collections of 12,000 films, 18,000 books, 5 million photos, and 5,000 scripts are open to the public.

ACLU. *See* American Civil Liberties Union of Southern California

ACQUIRED IMMUNE DEFICIENCY SYNDROME. *See* AIDS

ACTON, unincorporated county area in the mountainous reaches of the Santa Clara River. Located 20 miles from the urbanized Santa Clarita Valley and 6 miles from Soledad Canyon, the site was established in the 1870s as a railroad construction camp on the Saugus-to-Mojave line of the Southern Pacific Railroad (SP). The name first

appeared on an SP station between 1873 and 1876, possibly for one of the many cities named Acton in the eastern part of the country. For a short time during the 1880s thousands of people came to the area, drawn by the copper ore and gold-bearing quartz in nearby Soledad Canyon. After the turn of the century mining gave way to ranching. Acton experienced considerable growth in the 1970s and 1980s; in 1990 its population, combined with that of nearby Mint Canyon, was 9,200.

ACT UP/L.A. *See* Gay and lesbian movement

ADAMIC, LOUIS (1899–1951), author. A Slavic immigrant, Adamic lived in Los Angeles among the radical outcasts and socialist idealists of the 1920s. His autobiography, *Laughing in the Jungle* (1932), debunks the philistinism of the boosters and midwestern exiles who dominated the town during the Boom of the Twenties. His book *Dynamite: The Story of Class Violence in America* (1935) contains a plausible account of the bombings that racked Los Angeles in 1910 and their aftermath. Adamic was a friend of Carey McWilliams and other literati, and influenced their work.

ADAMS, HARRY (1919–1985), photographer. Adams was an important recorder of the African American scene in Los Angeles, working for a time on both the *California Eagle* and the *Los Angeles Sentinel* newspapers. He was mainly known for his later work, however, which included portraits of noted African Americans in entertainment, society, sports, and politics.

ADAMS, MARGARET Q. (1873–1974), first woman deputy sheriff in Los Angeles, and perhaps in the United States. She was appointed in 1912 and worked for 35 years in the Civil Division.

ADOBE, Spanish name for rough-hewn, sun-baked bricks. Widely used by Spanish and Mexican colonials, adobe is made by mixing clayey soil, water, and weeds. Adobe buildings were ideal structures for the local environment: cool in summer, warm in winter, cheap, and easy to construct. They had a striking appearance when whitewashed and combined with colored clay tiles and wooden beams. Several old adobes have been preserved or reconstructed, among them the Avila Adobe on Olvera Street (ca. 1822), Andrés Pico Adobe in Mis-

Adobe brick-makers, Glendale, 1920s. Courtesy Robert Weinstein Collection.

sion Hills (1834), Adobe de Palomares in Pomona (1834), Hugo Reid Adobe in Arcadia (1839), Feliz Adobe in Griffith Park (ca. 1853), and Catalina Verdugo Adobe in Glendale (1875). A strong candidate for reconstruction is the Lugo Adobe, which once stood on the east side of the Los Angeles Plaza.

ADVERTISING INDUSTRY, highly developed enterprise in Southern California since the 1880s. From 1885 to 1915, Los Angeles was the most advertised city in the United States. The promoters of real estate, railroad land, oil drilling, and tourism, as well as the chamber of commerce, newspapers, orange growers, and movies, made a virtual cult of the selling of Los Angeles. Mainly they extolled the magnificent climate.

Today the industry is a national trendsetter. It

Chiat/Day/Mojo Advertising Agency, Venice. Photo by Michael Krakowiak/Marni Pitt.

thrives on special local characteristics: a lifestyle highly involved with cars, outdoor recreation, health, diet and dining, the entertainment media, single-family homes, a multicultural population, and a consumer population with strong regional preferences. Angelenos as an advertising audience are sophisticated and heterogeneous, and often indifferent to campaigns that succeed in other parts of the country. Agency directors work to accommodate a "laid-back" attitude and more than a trace of eccentricity; they capitalize on the Angeleno's love of experimentalism and trendiness, and on a pattern of rapid style changes.

The enormous geographic landscape of the county also influences the industry's approach to advertising. Radio advertisers must adjust to the area's huge boundaries and ethnic diversity. The streets and highways, jammed with millions of cars and drivers, are a bonanza for billboard advertisers. In 1993, Los Angeles had 40,000 of the nation's 500,000 billboards, transit shelters, benches, and bus ads. As for newspapers, the potential readership is so vast that even the mighty *Los Angeles Times* cannot cover the entire scene. A major challenge for advertisers is to encourage the tens of millions of visitors and tourists who vacation in the city to buy and spend.

The industry has been highly profitable but, beginning around 1987, experienced a serious downturn when nine or so large firms closed their Los Angeles offices and moved elsewhere. New York remains the king of the industry, with $24.7 billion in annual ad billings in 1990, compared to $4.3 billion for Los Angeles. The largest Los Angeles–based ad agency is Chiat/Day/Mojo, headquartered in Venice. It does business in the $1 billion range and has acquired a reputation for bold and innovative advertising.

AEROSPACE INDUSTRY, a combination of firms producing missiles, spacecraft, aircraft, communications networks, and navigational instruments. It is an offshoot of the giant aircraft industry of World War II, and became the dominant feature of the Los Angeles economy beginning in the 1950s. The term *aerospace* entered into general use in 1959, after the formation of the National Aeronautics and Space Administration (NASA) in that year. The industry drew upon the combined efforts of several elements: a strong existing aircraft industry (Hughes, Douglas, Lockheed, etc.), a distinguished academic science institution (Caltech), a government rocket laboratory (Jet Propulsion Laboratory), and a private rocket-building firm (Aerojet-General). General Dynamics, Litton Industries, North American, and numerous small firms were also part of the scene. The heart of the missile industry of the non-Communist world was located just south of Los Angeles International Airport (LAX), with branches in the San Fernando Valley and Orange County.

The postwar industry underwent repeated rejuvenation during the Cold War, Korean War, and Vietnam War, when missiles increasingly replaced airplanes on the assembly lines. The industry was dominated by stellar physicists and engineers, notably Theodore von Karman, Simon Ramo, Clark Millikan, and Dean Wooldridge. Ramo and Wooldridge set up their own technological firm, later known as Thompson, Ramo, Wooldridge (TRW). The air force established its own aerospace think tank in Santa Monica, the nonprofit RAND Corporation, whose staff developed scientific strategies for the Cold War. In the late 1960s and early 1970s, the industry provided jobs for some half a million people—nearly 43 percent of the region's total manufacturing employment. Aerospace had become the area's most important manufacturing industry.

With the end of the Cold War and a decline in defense spending, the industry initiated a major restructuring and downsizing. Defense spending by NASA and the Department of Defense peaked in 1987, and thereafter fell sharply. Over 20 percent of the work force was let go in the ensuing three years. Even after downsizing, in 1991 aerospace accounted for 225,600 jobs in Los Angeles County,

or about 5 percent of the total employment, and 24 percent of manufacturing jobs. The largest dislocations occurred in Canoga Park, Lancaster, North Hollywood, Glendale, and Torrance.

Business leaders and elected officials have begun pursuing ways of converting the industry to peacetime pursuits. They seek new commercial markets and are exploring ways to recycle old production facilities and retrain and adapt the highly skilled work force. They have pressed for tax incentives and government supports for new research and development, and for an elimination of certain environmental regulations to stimulate growth.

Some astronauts in the space program are products of Los Angeles area high schools: Walter Cunningham (Venice High School), Sally Ride (Westlake School for Girls), and Kathleen Sullivan (Taft High School).

A. F. GILMORE COMPANY. *See* Gilmore Company, A. F.

AFI. *See* American Film Institute

AFL-CIO. *See* Labor union movement

AFRICAN AMERICANS were prominent in the first Spanish settlement of Los Angeles in 1781. Twenty-six of the 44 original settlers *(pobladores)* were of black or mixed ancestry. Most came from Sinaloa, Mexico, where two-thirds of the residents were *mulatos*. In the 1790s Francisco Reyes, an African American, received ownership of the San Fernando Valley and became mayor of the *pueblo*. Pío Pico, the last Mexican governor of California,

Detail from "Cecil," by Richard Wyatt, a public art mural in tribute to Cecil Ferguson, at the Watts Towers Art Center. © SPARC.

was of African-Mexican descent. The number of blacks was eclipsed by new immigrants in the early American years. Only about a dozen of the 1,600 county residents listed in the 1850 census were black, including a successful barber, Peter Biggs. In the second half of the century Robert Owens and ex-slave Biddy Mason became astute real estate investors and prominent landowners. In the 1880s Lucky Baldwin hired African American families from South Carolina to work on his ranch, some of whom bought land in Monrovia.

The African American community's political awakening came during the Progressive Era from 1900 to 1917. In 1903 Jefferson Lewis Edmond and other Progressive-leaning blacks at the First African Methodist Episcopal (AME) Church created the Los Angeles Forum to foster political debate. The statewide Afro-American Council and the Women's Civic League, along with two newspapers, the *Liberator* and the *California Eagle,* also worked for

---

This "City of the Angels" is anything else, unless the angels are fallen ones.
—John W. Audubon

---

social reform and the end of discrimination. Frederick M. Roberts was the first African American elected official. A Republican, in 1918 he represented the "Black Belt" district of Los Angeles in the state assembly. Although nominally associated with the party of Lincoln, most black Angelenos remained alienated from politics. Marcus Garvey's black nationalist movement was popular among working-class blacks in the 1920s. The swing to the Democratic Party occurred in the 1930s.

Although overshadowed by white immigration, the numbers of African Americans grew steadily: 188 in 1880, 1,200 in 1890, 2,800 in 1900 (2.5 percent of the total population), 15,500 in 1920, and 19,000 in 1929. By 1930 Los Angeles was home to the largest black community on the Pacific Coast. Although they faced discrimination, many families owned their own homes and had improved their previous living conditions in what has been called the Golden Era for blacks in Los Angeles. They operated their own churches, restaurants, businesses, nightclubs, insurance organizations such as Golden State Mutual Life, and civic groups. Distinctive African American neighborhoods

sprang up in Los Angeles. The Budlong district near downtown Los Angeles was a favorite area for sleeping-car porters, redcaps, and their families. "Sugar Hill" in the West Adams district was preferred by the small black middle class. Central Avenue, with its churches and businesses, was "Main Street" for black Los Angeles during the 1920s. It stretched as far as Slauson Avenue, where whites threw up an invisible racial barrier that endured until World War II. The color bar, maintained by enforceable racial covenants, was especially rigid in the beach cities, where black occupancy was restricted in the first part of the century; the only exception was Venice, where blacks lived while working at the amusement complex there.

Owing to employment opportunities in the aircraft industry, migration from the South quickened during World War II and continued after the war. The suburban farming town of Watts was one site transformed by this migration. By 1950, 218,000 blacks resided in Los Angeles County. It was a period of developing black organizations, one that influenced the careers of such future city leaders as Tom Bradley and Gilbert Lindsay.

The increase of the county's African American population has slowed considerably in recent decades. In the 1980s it grew by only 1 percent. At the same time, the black population has dispersed widely, more than doubling its numbers in 163 communities, though remaining a minority in most of them. In South Central Los Angeles the black population fell by 17 percent during that decade.

Leimert Park Village, a cluster of stores at 43rd Place and Degnan Boulevard in the Leimert Park area, serves a population in the surrounding area that was 92 percent African American in the early 1990s. The village has become a center for African American artists and professionals.

AFRICANS. According to the 1990 U.S. Census, 28,850 Africans live in Los Angeles. More than half of them immigrated between 1980 and 1990. Of the 52 nations of Africa, the ones with the greatest representation in Los Angeles County are Egypt, 10,271; South Africa, 3,363; Nigeria, 2,900; Ethiopia, 2,890; Morocco, 1,753; Kenya, 985; Ghana, 780; Senegal, 94; and other, 5,814. Their residences are dispersed throughout the Los Angeles region, although the most concentrated center of African businesses is on Degnan Boulevard in Leimert Park. The *African Times* newspaper is published for Africans living in Los Angeles.

AFRO-AMERICAN MUSEUM. *See* California Afro-American Museum

AFTRA. *See* American Federation of Television and Radio Artists

AGOURA, partly incorporated, partly unincorporated area in the far western part of the county 47 miles northwest of downtown Los Angeles. It was first inhabited by Chumash Indians, then by Spanish colonials. The Reyes Adobe, built between 1797 and 1820 on Rancho Las Virgenes, is still extant. In 1924 the area was known as Independence, and shortly afterward as Picture City because Paramount Studios bought 335 acres. The name was rejected in 1927 by the U.S. Post Office, which preferred one-word names. The town was finally called Agoure, after a local Basque rancher, the *e* soon being dropped in favor of an *a*.

From the 1960s to the 1980s Agoura hosted the annual Renaissance Pleasure Faire. Recently, most of the area was incorporated as Agoura Hills, except for a small portion on unincorporated county territory that still calls itself Agoura. The population of the city of Agoura Hills grew an astonishing 79 percent between 1980 and 1990, reaching a total of 20,400. It is governed by a council and city manager. The Las Virgenes Homeowners Federation has been instrumental in protecting the area from overdevelopment.

AGRICULTURE, primary source of wealth in Los Angeles County in the 19th century, and a significant factor throughout most of the first half of the 20th. From 1910 to the early 1950s Los Angeles was the leading county in the nation in farm production, with oranges the leading crop through much of that period.

Because the Gabrieleño Indians were gatherers rather than farmers, agriculture started in Spanish colonial days. The mission fathers recruited Indian laborers to plant grapes, wheat, barley, corn, and citrus trees and to herd cattle, horses, and sheep. From the 1780s the citizens of the *pueblo (pobladores)* who were farmers became successful by shipping their surpluses to the presidio at Santa Barbara. The rancheros raised cattle for hides and tallow to trade with Yankee outsiders. Grapes were cultivated for wine by Jean Louis Vignes and others, and William Wolfskill began growing citrus fruit commercially. Local cattle herds were driven north into the gold mining areas during the Gold Rush. In 1862 and 1865 a drought devastated thousands of head of cattle, leading to a breakup of the ranchos. For a time sheep raising became prevalent. In the 1870s the San Fernando Valley was given over to extensive wheat growing. Cattle growers now raised animals on enclosed pastures instead of the open range, improved their herds, and placed greater emphasis on dairying.

Agricultural jobs were associated with ethnicity. Indian neophytes cultivated the orchards, gardens,

Van Nuys Ranch, San Fernando Valley, ca. 1898. California Historical Society, Title Insurance and Trust Photo Collection, Dept. of Special Collections, USC Library.

and fields and, for cheap wages or in peonage, worked as vaqueros herding the cattle for the missions and ranchos. They were followed by other minorities, often migratory and poorly paid. Southern California crops such as lemons, strawberries, and tomatoes were labor intensive and dependent on cheap labor. The Chinese worked in orchards and truck gardens in the 1880s, and soon the Japanese were replacing them. Mexicans were also part of the local migratory labor pool.

In the peak agricultural year of 1942 over 318,000 acres were farmed in the county as a whole; by 1987 only about 32,000 acres were under cultivation. Farming survives mainly on land owned by electric power companies where other permanent structures are outlawed: nursery crops—trees, shrubs, and plants—are grown beneath high-tension power lines. In addition to raising chickens and horses, the county also produces eggs (West Covina), onions, sprouts, strawberries, alfalfa, and milk. In the past three or four decades farmers have taken refuge on the high desert in the Antelope Valley. About 77,000 acres of barley and other crops were farmed there in 1960, before the growers were beset by problems of drought, pests, and rising water prices. By 1990 the amount of cultivated land in that valley had dropped to 10,600 acres. Even so, 50,000 tons of onions were harvested in 1993, under the flight path of air force planes. At the same time, Antelope Valley land has become extremely valuable; farms bought 15 years earlier sold in 1993 for about 15 times their original price, or $30,000 an acre. The rapid rise in land costs in valley areas with such evocative names as Pearblossom and Almondale has been due largely to the development of housing tracts. No government policy has been established to save the region's farmland.

AGUA DULCE, unincorporated rural area of the county in the eastern Santa Clarita Valley. In the 1870s the area, which is completely surrounded by hills, became a hideout for the bandit Tiburcio Vásquez. The land has been ranch country since the late 19th century, with some mining taking place in nearby Soledad Canyon. Bawdy establishments secluded themselves along the old "Sierra Highway" connecting Los Angeles and Palmdale. Today the Antelope Valley Freeway runs just south of Agua Dulce.

AGUILAR, CRISTÓBAL, mayor of Los Angeles from 1866 to 1868 and again from 1871 to 1872. In 1868 he made a momentous decision by vetoing a city council proposal to sell off the city's water rights. Had he not done so the city would have rescinded exclusive ownership of water rights, thus forfeiting its ability to become a major metropolis.

AHMANSON, HOWARD (1906–1968), entrepreneur and philanthropist. An insurance broker since 1928, Ahmanson was considered an upstart in the savings and loan industry in 1947 when he bought the struggling Home Building and Loan Association for $162,000 and built it into the largest savings and loan in the nation. In 1988 his enterprise, renamed Home Savings and Loan (more recently shortened to Home Savings), had assets of $36 billion and employed 11,000. He donated money to establish the Ahmanson Theatre, which opened in 1957, and became a member of the governing board of the Los Angeles Music Center. Ahmanson also contributed to construction of the main gallery of the Los Angeles County Museum of Art and, as a trustee of USC, gave a substantial donation to its Center for Biological Research.

Howard Ahmanson. Courtesy H. F. Ahmanson & Co. Archives.

AIDS (ACQUIRED IMMUNE DEFICIENCY SYNDROME), fatal disease caused by HIV (Human Immunodeficiency Virus). The first diagnoses in the county occurred in 1981 when five cases of rare pneumonia were traced to the new disease. The spreading illness soon reached alarming proportions. By April 1995 over 29,100 cases and 19,200 deaths had been reported in the county. Homosexual or bisexual men accounted for 79 percent of the cases, intravenous drug users for 5 percent, and women for 4 percent. The remaining cases included babies born to infected mothers, people who had received tainted blood injections, etc. AIDS Project Los Angeles (APLA), with strong roots in the gay community, is the largest nonprofit social service agency dealing with the illness. Responding to public pressure, the county and city have created a task force to cope with the crisis. "Safe sex" has begun to reduce the rate of infection, social service agencies have become more responsive, and drugs are helping patients to live longer. In a major effort to prevent the spread of AIDS, the Los Angeles Board of Education authorized the distribution of condoms in city high schools.

AIN, GREGORY (1908–), distinguished architect. Born in Pennsylvania and educated at UCLA and USC, Ain first practiced with R. M. Schindler and Richard Neutra, and in 1935 opened his own firm. He was most active from the 1930s to the 1960s and became known for his modern style of residential design. He was one of the originators of the Case Study Houses.

AIRCRAFT INDUSTRY, established in Los Angeles before World War I. It became dominant during the Second World War and remained so throughout the 1960s. The combination of mild climate, abundant labor, venture capitalists, and creative engineering led by men such as Glenn Martin, Donald Douglas, Allan Loughead (Lockheed), and John K. Northrop fostered a thriving industry. The physical conditions were ideal for aircraft. Since planes could be manufactured and serviced outdoors throughout the year, costs remained low, and the abundance of cleared flat land and vigorous sea breezes helped loft the planes.

The first plane built in California was handcrafted in 1906 by Martin in Santa Ana. Four years later, the 1910 air show at Dominguez Hills attracted thousands of curious spectators and helped popularize the airplane. In 1920 Martin's chief engineer, Donald Douglas, formed his own company and set up shop in Santa Monica. Douglas developed the DC-2, the first all-metal commercial

Outdoor assembly line for Lockheed P-38 Lightnings, World War II. *Los Angeles Examiner,* Hearst Collection, Dept. of Special Collections, USC.

plane, and the workhorse two-engine DC-3 that still carries passengers and freight in remote parts of the world. By the 1920s Los Angeles was the terminus for all commercial air service to the West Coast.

The industry quickly spread to the urban fringes, where land was abundant—Burbank, Santa Monica, Hawthorne, Long Beach, and the area near Mines Field, now Los Angeles International Airport. In the following decades Southern California became a magnet for federal contracts. Government orders poured in on the eve of World War II for Lockheed P-38 fighters, Douglas C-47s (the military version of the C-3), and C-54 transports, as well as other warplanes. Hughes Aircraft became a major player during this period. By the 1940s the industry had spread throughout the metropolitan area, and in 1943 it employed about 250,000 in Southern California. The industry profoundly influenced the local economy. It stimulated urban growth, attracted middle-class families to the greater Los Angeles area, and provided a living for many thousands, in both wartime and peacetime.

AIR POLLUTION consists chiefly of carbon monoxide, nitrogen oxides, acid aerosols, and ozone, plus 200 or so other chemicals. Air pollution is a factor in the deaths of 80,000 Californians annually. The chief culprit is auto exhaust, but stationary sources such as factories share the blame. Dirty air was noted in the area as early as 1542, when the Portuguese-born Juan Cabrillo, exploring for Spain, sailed into San Pedro Bay and noticed smoke from Indian fires that rose several hundred feet and then stretched out horizontally. He consequently named the area the "bay of smokes." This early sight was a portent of things to come. Four centuries later, a steady increase in air pollution caused by factories and auto exhausts spilling chemicals into the air gave birth to "smog," a coined word combining *smoke* and *fog.* It was first identified in July 1940 when civic center workers complained of eye and throat irritation. The "abnormal" affliction appeared again in September 1942 and spread to outlying districts. It made the front pages in July 1943 when a streetcar strike increased downtown car traffic to an unprecedented peak, causing a reduction in visibility. The worst air seemed to collect in downtown tunnels. Investigations were ordered throughout the basin during the war years, and a rubber factory and a chemical plant on Aliso Street were pinpointed as the presumed offenders. But the severity of the problem was still misunderstood, and nothing was resolved.

Smog occurs particularly when air, trapped by the mountains surrounding Los Angeles, is capped by a temperature inversion layer. Light sea breezes are unable to sweep the sky clean. This is probably the same condition that kept the Indian smoke from dissipating. Hence Los Angeles, famous since the 1880s for its healthful climate, fell victim to its own success. As of 1989, Los Angeles, Houston, New York, and Chicago were the nation's smoggiest cities. In four Southern California counties—Los Angeles, Riverside, San Bernardino, and Orange—12 million people, 8 million motor vehicles, and 31,000 businesses spew 1,246 tons of noxious gasses into the air daily.

AIR POLLUTION CONTROL began in 1948 at the county level. With the increasing complexity of the issue and improved scientific understanding of air pollution, policy-making shifted to regional, state, and even federal agencies. In 1948 the county formed the Air Pollution Control District (APCD). Its first targets were stationary sources—refineries, foundries, smelters, steel mills, and other smokestack industries. In 1957 it banned open fires and the backyard incinerators that stood

in almost every backyard. Private industry spent an estimated $100 million on pollution control in one decade, measurably improving the environment. But still the problem persisted.

About 1950, Caltech professor Arie J. Haagen-Smit placed hydrocarbons and nitrogen dioxide in a laboratory flask and exposed it to sunlight, thus manufacturing smog. Now the spotlight shifted to automobile exhaust as the chief cause of bad air. At first the oil and auto industries vociferously denied responsibility, but by 1961 the evidence was so overwhelming that they agreed to join the struggle. In 1975, the APCD merged with similar bodies in Orange, Riverside, and San Bernardino Counties to become the South Coast Air Quality Management District (AQMD). This larger, regional body regulates all stationary commercial and industrial facilities; motor vehicles, meanwhile, come under the regulatory jurisdiction of the California Air Resources Board.

The AQMD, which enforces federal, state, and regional air pollution laws, hopes to bring the region's air quality into compliance with federal standards by the year 2010. In 1988 the U.S. Environmental Protection Agency (EPA) demanded that Los Angeles County impose stiff rules for reducing smog or suffer the loss of hundreds of millions of dollars in federal funds for sewer cleanup. These rules include special methods of fueling jets at Los Angeles International Airport and computerizing stoplights for smoother traffic flow. In 1989, too, the AQMD adopted tough regulations for large businesses that use or manufacture paint, aerosols, or lawn mower engines or engage in charcoal broiling, tire making, baking, brewing, or dry cleaning. It is hoped that these measures, plus increased use of electric cars, methanol fuel, carpooling, and public transportation, will lead to improvements in air quality. If not, the EPA could take over the job.

Pollution conditions vary widely across the Los Angeles Basin. The worst air in recent years has been recorded in Azusa, and the best in the coastal area from Inglewood to Palos Verdes. Efforts to improve air quality in Los Angeles, Orange, Riverside, and San Bernardino Counties succeeded in reducing pollution levels by 50 percent in the 10 years since 1981. In 1992, major smog alerts were down by 25 percent. Emission restrictions on both cars and factories have contributed to the dramatic decline. Car owners, for example, must have their cars smog-checked every two years.

In 1989 the California Air Resources Board approved the sweeping, 20-year AQMD plan for cleaning the air of Los Angeles by the year 2010. According to 1991 estimates, the cost may run as high as $10 billion. Many business interests find this unacceptable, though proponents of strict standards say that the benefits in terms of improved public health will more than outweigh the costs, but no one is optimistic about meeting those standards. Meanwhile, evidence of the harmful effects of bad air keeps mounting. An 11-year study by UCLA researchers found that respiratory deterioration is worst in areas where the air is dirtiest, and the damage seems to be irreversible. Los Angeles, however, is not alone in having to deal with this problem. Air pollution is now an environmental issue in virtually every metropolis in the world.

AIRPORTS numbered 11 in Los Angeles County as of 1989. They include Los Angeles International Airport (LAX), one of the world's largest airports, which in 1990 handled 45.3 million passengers and 1.2 million tons of freight. Next in size is the Burbank-Glendale-Pasadena Airport, located in Burbank. Other airports, which cater mainly to private planes, are Compton, El Monte, Hawthorne Municipal, Santa Monica Municipal, Torrance Municipal, Whiteman Airpark in Pacoima, and Long Beach Municipal, which also handles commercial flights. Van Nuys is the nation's busiest field devoted to noncommercial aviation. Ontario International Airport, although lo-

---

[**H**ollywood] is a mining camp in lotus land.   —F. Scott Fitzgerald

---

cated outside the county, was bought by the Los Angeles City Department of Airports in 1967 as a satellite to LAX. In 1990 it handled 5.4 million passengers, and plans are in the works to expand capacity to 12 million. The Department of Airports also owns Palmdale Regional Airport in the high desert. In 1969 it purchased 18,000 acres next to that field in the hope of someday expanding commercial service for the residents of the Antelope, Santa Clarita, and San Fernando Valleys. Owing to competition from Hollywood-Burbank Airport, commercial airline traffic never materialized in Palmdale. The 18,000 acres lie idle. In 1996,

however, the department estimated that LAX would handle as many as 98 million passengers by the year 2015. To meet the developing crisis, the Department of Airports began studying alternative plans either to create a new landing strip on fill dirt in Santa Monica Bay or to develop the Palmdale field as a satellite to LAX.

AIRPORTS, LOS ANGELES DEPARTMENT OF. *See* Los Angeles City Department of Airports

ALAMEDA CORRIDOR, narrow railroad right-of-way along Alameda Street that strategically links Los Angeles and Long Beach harbors to downtown Los Angeles. The city of Los Angeles has offered to purchase the land from its owner, Union Pacific Railroad, so as to upgrade the rail beds and add bridges and overpasses for vehicular cross-traffic, thereby improving the transit of goods to and from the harbors.

ALAMITOS BAY, estuary 18.5 miles south of downtown Los Angeles, adjacent to the mouth of the San Gabriel River at Belmont Shore and surrounding the oval island of Naples. Opened to settlement in 1905 when Henry Huntington extended a rail line from Long Beach, Alamitos Bay is now part of Long Beach.

ALARCON, RICHARD (1954–), Los Angeles City Council member representing the 7th District, a heavily Latino area in the northeastern San Fernando Valley. A native of the area, Alarcon is the first Latino to represent it in the council, occupying the seat vacated by Ernani Bernardi in 1993. He is a graduate in political science from California State University, Northridge.

ALATORRE, RICHARD (1943–), former state assemblyman and, since 1985, Los Angeles City Council member from the 14th District. A Latino born in Los Angeles, Alatorre attended public schools on the Eastside and earned a master's degree in public administration at USC. At age 25 he was elected to the California Democratic Party central committee. In 1971 he ran for and won a California assembly seat, serving six additional terms. While in the assembly Alatorre introduced landmark legislation on agricultural labor, bilingual education, prison reform, and child care services, and pressed for fair legislative apportionment for the Latino community.

ALCALDE, chief civil officer of a Spanish or Mexican *pueblo.* He was a member of the *ayuntamiento* (council), as well as a justice of the peace and mayor. The *alcalde*'s authority was granted from Governor de Neve's *Reglamento* of 1779 (the code governing California during Spain's rule). The *alcalde,* elected annually, presided over the *ayuntamiento* but was subordinate to the governor's military representative, the *comisionado.* Among the Mexican *alcaldes* of Los Angeles were José María Avila, Guillermo Cota, and José Antonio Carrillo. During the U.S. occupation from 1847 to 1849, the military installed ethnically mixed pairs of *alcaldes:* Stephen C. Foster and José del Carmen Lugo, followed by Abel Stearns and Juan Sepúlveda.

ALDER, native deciduous tree of the birch family. It grows widely throughout the region, especially near streams and in association with sycamores and other birch varieties. Early travelers and residents used the Spanish word *aliso* to designate this tree and the sycamore interchangeably. Jean Vignes called his vineyard El Aliso, and Charles Fletcher Lummis named his home El Alisal.

ALEXANDER, GEORGE (1839–1923), progressive mayor of Los Angeles from 1909 to 1913. Before being elected, the bewhiskered 70-year-old Iowan, who arrived in Los Angeles in the Boom of the Eighties, had been a grain dealer. He gained election as a reform candidate following the recall of the corrupt Mayor Harper. Wilmington, San Pedro, and Hollywood were annexed during his term in office. After the bombing of the *Los Angeles Times* building in 1910 he hired detective William J. Burns, who broke the case. The Los Angeles Aqueduct was completed during his administration.

George Alexander. Courtesy Photographic Collections, Los Angeles Public Library.

ALEXANDRIA HOTEL, historic downtown hotel at 5th and Spring Streets. Boasting 500 rooms, it opened in 1905 as "the first completely fire-proof building in Los Angeles" and the city's premier hotel. Its garage, capable of housing 200 cars, presaged the future of Los Angeles. The recently restored Palm Court Banquet Room on the first floor remains an architectural treasure. The Alexandria became the city's leading social center and was a favorite meeting place of silent screen stars. Presidents Theodore Roosevelt, William H. Taft, and Woodrow Wilson slept there. Today, it houses welfare families, including hundreds of children.

Alexandria Hotel Lobby (John Parkinson, architect), 1906. Pitt Collection.

ALHAMBRA, independent city 8 miles north of Los Angeles calling itself the "Gateway to the San Gabriel Valley." The town was founded by Benjamin D. Wilson, a Yankee pioneer who arrived in 1841, on land that was once part of San Gabriel Mission and, subsequently, Rancho San Antonio. Wilson acquired the property in 1854 from the widow of the Scottish pioneer Hugo Reid. He named the area after the Moorish castle in Spain, made popular by Washington Irving's book *The Alhambra* (1832), which his wife was reading at the time. The streets, called by such evocative names

---

Here if anywhere in America, I seem to hear the coming footsteps of the muses.   —William Butler Yeats, on a visit to Los Angeles in 1925

---

as Granada, Almansor, Vega, and Boabdil, also suggest the Spanish and Moorish influence. The Mississippian J. C. Wallace, arriving in 1871, built the first house, using Indian laborers who carried the lumber on their backs from Mt. Wilson. When Wilson died in 1878 the development passed to his son-in-law, James de Barth Shorb. By 1903 orange groves and vineyards were being subdivided, and on 11 July of that year the 600 residents incorporated Alhambra as a city. Pres. William Howard Taft visited Alhambra High School on 16 October 1911. In 1915 Alhambra became a chartered city.

Farming eventually gave way to single-family residential settlement; in recent decades many private homes have been replaced by apartments. A major rail artery bisects the town, though its tracks are set below street level. Braun Engineering, a firm with worldwide connections, is a major enterprise located in Alhambra. Between 1983 and 1990 the population grew from 68,300 to 82,106. The city's past is represented by the Alhambra Historical Museum, run by the Alhambra Historical Society, Inc., in cooperation with the city government. Preservationists have conserved numerous 19th-century residences.

ALIANZA HISPANO-AMERICANA, largest Mexican fraternal organization in the United States. Founded in Tucson in the 19th century, it had established 30 lodges in Los Angeles County by the 1930s and is now based in Covina. Offering life and health insurance and other financial services and social activities, it appeals chiefly to the Mexican middle class.

ALL YEAR CLUB OF SOUTHERN CALIFORNIA. *See* Los Angeles Convention and Visitors Bureau

ALMARAZ, CARLOS (1941–1989), Mexican-born painter. Almaraz, Frank Romero, Beto de la Rocha, and Gilbert Lujan together made up "Los Four." Their works were shown at the Los Angeles County Museum of Art in 1979, in one of the first major exhibits in the country to feature Chicano art. A graduate of Garfield High, he was married to the painter Elsa Flores. His paintings are said to combine a barrio aesthetic with a vision of Los Angeles that is at once funky and romantic. Almaraz died of AIDS in 1989. His epitaph, penned by fellow artist Jeffrey Vallance, says, "Here lies a chap quick as a cat and short one life."

ALONDRA PARK, unincorporated community 11 miles southwest of downtown Los Angeles. Surrounded by Lawndale, Hawthorne, Gardena, and Torrance, it is adjacent to El Camino College. The population in 1990 was 12,215.

ALTADENA, unincorporated area north of Pasadena and 11 miles northeast of downtown Los Angeles, located at the base of the San Gabriel Mountains. The name, combining *alta* (Spanish for "high" or "upper") and *Pasadena,* was adopted in 1887, having been in use for a year already by a local nursery. Pasadenans regarded the land as worthless because it was too high to be watered by the Arroyo Seco. The more far-sighted Woodbury brothers from Iowa, however, formed a syndicate and began subdividing a town on this "worthless" land in the boom year of 1886. Despite a planned railroad (which never materialized), the town developed handsome and valuable residences and thrived. Thirty-two business tycoons built summer homes on Altadena's foothill slopes, some as big as 12,000 square feet. Early residents also planted thousands of trees—pine, deodar, cypress, California live oak, and avocado, among others—on fields once blanketed by California poppies. Altadena was the gateway to the Mt. Lowe Railway, which climbed into Rubio Canyon from 1893 to 1937, and the Mt. Wilson Observatory, built in 1903.

The 8.8-square-mile area is under county jurisdiction and includes a Central Historic Area that attracts residents interested in restoring Victorian-era homes. Preservationists have identified 3,000 structures appropriate for placement on a state inventory of historic structures, and 60 that could qualify for the National Register of Historic Places. Altadena has long been a haven for writers and artists and is renowned for its high owner-occupancy rate and low crime rate. The official population count in 1990 was 42,658.

ALVARADO TERRACE, residential street noted for its Victorian architecture, located off Alvarado Boulevard near Bonnie Brae Street east of downtown Los Angeles. What was first a farm, and then a golf course, was developed as a haven for wealthy Angelenos between 1902 and 1904. The tract was originally named Windmill Links, after a windmill left standing on the farm. Seven stately homes atop a rise retain their Victorian charm. One of them, built for a lumber magnate in 1902, is today a bed-and-breakfast.

AMAT, TADEO (THADDEUS) (D. 1878), pioneer archbishop of Monterey who maintained a residence in Los Angeles. The Spanish-born theologian was serving in Philadelphia in 1853 when he was appointed to head the New California archdiocese covering 80,000 square miles. Arriving in Los Angeles in 1855, he established Roman Catholic schools for the Hispanic population and oversaw the work of priests and the Sisters of Charity. By his own assessment, Amat's greatest achievement was the construction of the Cathedral of St. Vibiana (1871–1876).

AMBASSADOR HOTEL, palatial lodging house built in 1919–1921 on a former dairy farm facing Wilshire Boulevard, a dirt road that did not yet connect with downtown. Constructed on a 24-acre site at a cost of $5 million, the hotel, with its lawns, fountains, and gardens, had accommodations for 3,000 guests and served as a catalyst for development of the Wilshire District. Such socialites as Doheny and Hancock family members dined there regularly, and presidents and other out-of-town celebrities stayed there. Jean Harlow held her wedding reception at the hotel. Its posh Coconut Grove ballroom attracted all the big bands of the 1920s and 1930s. The Ambassador was the site of the early Academy Award banquets. It was also where Richard Nixon, the 1952 Republican vice presidential nominee, trying to regain support after a financial scandal, wrote his famous televised "Checkers speech." In 1968 the hotel acquired unwanted fame when Robert Kennedy was tragically assassinated there after winning the Democratic presidential primary. The landmark closed in 1990 after 68 years of operation.

AMERICAN CIVIL LIBERTIES UNION (ACLU) OF SOUTHERN CALIFORNIA, nonpartisan constitutional rights organization providing legal, lobbying, and educational services in defense of civil liberties. The national ACLU was founded in 1920 and came to be regarded as the quintessential expression of the term *liberal.* The local affiliate emerged in 1923, during the strike of marine transportation workers in San Pedro, when police harassed pro-union speakers who defied an antipicketing ordinance. The writer Upton Sinclair, an ardent Socialist who had been arrested for reading the Constitution aloud on both public street corners and private property, was active in the chapter's formation. In the 1930s, Police Captain William Hynes "joked" that lawyers such as Southern California ACLU director Clinton J. Taft should be "thrown out of ten-story windows." Abe Lincoln Wirin, the feisty local director during the 1940s, angered many Angelenos by denouncing the forced evacuation of Japanese Americans in 1942 and defending the constitutional rights of Communists, Fascists, and pro-Nazis. Sometimes he defied the express wishes of the national ACLU. Wirin also challenged the Hollywood blacklist in the 1940s, and the attempt to prevent a rock 'n' roll concert from being staged in the American Legion Hall in El Monte in 1957. In 1967 local ACLU leaders denounced the Vietnam War as "unconstitutional." Today the Southern California affiliate, which claims 31,000 members, is headed by Ramona Ripston.

AMERICAN CONQUEST OF LOS ANGELES. *See* Mexican War, 1846–1848

AMERICAN FEDERATION OF MUSICIANS (AFM), AFL-CIO, LOCAL 47, predominant labor union in the Los Angeles music and entertainment industries. The AFM was formed nationally in 1896 and became the leading musicians union within the next decade when it organized stage musicians. By 1918 it was the strongest affiliate of the Los Angeles Central Labor Council, and by 1930 it ranked as the largest labor organization in the state.

In the 1920s, Local 47 represented live theater performers who were being replaced first by "canned" or recorded music and then by "talking pictures" in movie houses. It also sought, eventually with success, to represent studio musicians, who were increasingly important in the making of Hollywood films. In 1921, performers belonging to Local 47 struck 35 downtown theaters, including the Orpheum circuit. Beginning in 1925, the Los Angeles AFM affiliate also began organizing in radio broadcasting. Radio station KHJ, owned by the antilabor *Los Angeles Times,* was a prime target. The union also boycotted the Rose Parade because of its nonunion employment practices. By 1938 the union local had 5,600 members. It was headed by Jack Tenney, composer of "Mexicali Rose." Tenney later became a state senator, making a name for himself as a fierce opponent of "unfriendly" witnesses testifying before the House Un-American Activities Committee during the McCarthy period.

Struggling to protect musicians' pay, working conditions, and benefits in radio, recording, movies, and live performance, Local 47 made its strongest advances in the 1940s. James C. Petrillo of Chicago became director of the national union in 1940 and made his main targets the Hollywood-based recording industry giants RCA, Victor, and Columbia. These firms eventually signed with the union, agreeing to pay royalties to musicians.

In 1956 a dissident group within AFM formed the rival Musicians Guild of America, which began to function as a bargaining agent in the Hollywood studios. It was absorbed back into the main union in 1961. Today an AFM minority is represented by the International Conference of Symphony and Opera Musicians (ICSOM), founded in 1962. Local 47 still retains its central place in an industry shaped by the increasingly sophisticated and shifting technology of live performance and electronic sound reproduction.

AMERICAN FEDERATION OF TELEVISION AND RADIO ARTISTS (AFTRA), guild of broadcast artists. AFTRA was established on 17 July 1937 as the American Federation of Radio Artists, a branch of the Associated Actors and Artistes of America, after previous efforts at unionization led to the blacklisting of 21 radio performers. With Eddie Cantor as president and attorney Emily Holt

and actor George Heller as staff, eight locals were formed nationwide in major cities such as New York and Chicago. In 1938, the willingness of such radio stars as Cantor, Edgar Bergen, Jack Benny, and Fred Allen to go on strike, if necessary, led to the first agreements with NBC and CBS. In 1944 AFTRA won a landmark court battle against film producer-director Cecil B. De Mille, who had refused to pay a special lobbying assessment to protect the union shop. When television artists joined the organization in 1952, the name was altered accordingly. The guild endured bitter divisiveness during both the McCarthy blacklist era and a 1982 antitrust suit.

AMERICAN FILM INSTITUTE (AFI), nonprofit film society. AFI is devoted to preserving the heritage of film and television, identifying and training new talent, and increasing recognition and understanding of the moving image as an art form. It sponsors seminars and workshops on its Los Angeles campus on N. Western Avenue, sells and publishes books on film, and houses the outstanding Louis B. Mayer Library containing thousands of books and screenplays. Since 1983 it has also conducted an annual international film festival in Hollywood.

AMERICAN FRIENDS SERVICE COMMITTEE (AFSC), Quaker organization. Its Pacific Southwest Regional Office was established in Pasadena in the early 1940s to serve the cause of peace in a war-torn world. The moving force behind the local affiliate was John W. Dorland, a Pasadena dentist and overseas relief worker who had organized efforts to cope with the Russian famine in the early 1920s. Keeping "as its motivation the spiritual insight of the early Quakers that there is a God of Love available to all," the Pacific Southwest Regional Office serves Hawaii, Arizona, New Mexico, and Southern California. During the 1930s the committee founded an institute in Whittier devoted to peace education.

AMERICAN GI FORUM, short-lived civil rights organization created by Mexican American veterans returning from World War II. Their purpose was to battle discrimination and improve the status of Mexicans in the Southwest.

AMERICAN INDEPENDENT PARTY (AIP), a third party founded in 1967 during the presidential run of Gov. George C. Wallace of Alabama. It appealed mainly to white working-class voters who opposed court-ordered racial integration. In 1991 the AIP had 33,728 members registered in Los Angeles County, and 156,524 statewide. In the 1992 presidential election it supported Conservative Caucus leader Howard Phillips, a former Republican.

AMERICAN INSTITUTE OF ARCHITECTS (AIA), prestigious professional architects organization. Active since 1894, the Los Angeles chapter is the largest in the nation. It offers peer contact, publications, a job bank, and educational programs for its members, fosters historic preservation in the community, and awards annual "Oranges" and "Lemons" for the best and worst architecture. Lemons of the past several years include the Autry Museum of Western Heritage, the Beverly Center, the World Trade Center, Valley State Bank, Barrington Plaza, and the UCLA Medical Complex.

AMERICAN LEGION, veterans organization active locally since World War I. The first such organization formed in Southern California after the Spanish-American War in 1898, American Legion Post No. 8 became an important post nationally. It published a weekly bulletin in the 1920s, lobbied for social services for war veterans, collected funds for charitable activities, promoted patriotic causes, commemorated patriotic holidays, fostered an Americanism campaign among immigrants, sought restrictions for Japanese residents, and combated union organizers and others whom it considered radical and unpatriotic. Politicians sought members' votes and courted them for en-

dorsements, and members who ran for office in turn boasted of their legion association. In 1924 the county built Patriotic Hall, an imposing 10-story edifice at Washington Boulevard and 18th Street that housed all veteran groups and hosted their activities. Although far less influential than in the past, the American Legion today has 40,000 members in 153 posts in Los Angeles County.

AMITY-COMPTON HOUSING PROJECT. *See* Channel Heights housing project

AMUSEMENT PARKS AND PIERS first appeared locally in the 1880s as family attractions modeled after New York's Coney Island. Over time Los Angeles County has boasted five such parks, located in Venice, Ocean Park, Santa Monica, Long Beach (The Pike), and Redondo Beach. They featured roller coasters and other rides, carnival attractions, and fun houses. (In the 1930s and 1940s Tommy Dorsey's band played in the Aragon Ballroom in Venice; he was followed by Lawrence Welk, who played there for many years.)

The Pike opened in 1902 and included the Cyclone Racer, a sometime movie prop that outlasted the rest of the amusement park and operated until 1979. Early in the century three amusement parks were built on piers jutting into Santa Monica Bay. Ocean Park Pier, developed by Abbot Kinney in 1905 at the south end of Santa Monica, advertised itself as "A Vacation in a Day" and featured, among other attractions, a "scenic railway." That same year Kinney also built the Venice Pier as an adjunct to his Venice-of-America attraction, complete with a pavilion, auditorium, and ship-hotel. This pier burned and was completely rebuilt

Santa Monica Pier, ca. 1910. Pitt Collection.

after 1920 into a larger and more elaborate attraction. Santa Monica Pier was yet a third amusement park; it featured the Blue Streak Roller Coaster, a ballroom, and a carousel. The Redondo Beach park opened in the 1920s in what was then a summer resort.

Full-scale oceanfront amusement parks declined in popularity after World War II, although some of their rides and special features continued as independent attractions. Venice Pier disappeared in the late 1940s. Ocean Park Pier was refurbished and reopened in 1958 for a short time as Pacific Ocean Park (POP), but the owners filed for bankruptcy in 1967; the pier itself was demolished in 1974. Santa Monica Pier, built in 1909, still exists, with a carousel, food concessions, and arcade games, but minus the roller coaster.

Many of the piers, in disrepair because of age, storms, and fire, have been undergoing renovation. Badly damaged by a raging winter storm in 1983, Santa Monica Pier has been getting a $45 million face-lift since 1989. A grand reopening, complete with roller coasters and an 85-foot Ferris wheel, took place in 1996. Redondo's Municipal Pier, closed in 1988 when it was wrecked by storms and fire, was reconstructed with concrete pilings and deck and reopened in 1995. A new amusement pier featuring restaurants and musical entertainment is also scheduled for Malibu Pier, on the pile structure built in 1905 as part of the private domain of rancher Frederick Rindge. Venice Fishing Pier, closed in 1986 owing to falling pieces of concrete, is likewise being restored, with $3.2 million approved by the Los Angeles City Council. Finally, both Hermosa Beach and Manhattan Beach are planning improvements or restoration of their fishing piers.

The superstar of amusement parks, of course, is Disneyland, the "Happiest Place on Earth," which opened in Orange County in 1955 to worldwide acclaim. Knotts Berry Farm in Buena Park began as a roadside stand in the 1920s and became a major attraction soon afterward. Other popular attractions are Six Flags Magic Mountain, near Saugus; Universal Studios, in Universal City; and the ocean liner *Queen Mary,* in Long Beach.

ANDERSON, GLENN M[ALCOLM] (1913– 1994), lieutenant governor and congressman. The first baby born in the community that was later incorporated as Hawthorne, Anderson was rewarded 27 years later by being elected the town's mayor in 1940. After serving in World War II as an infantry sergeant, he returned to Hawthorne and became a builder. In 1958 he was elected lieutenant governor, serving under Gov. Edmund G. "Pat" Brown until 1966. During the Watts riot of August 1965, a delay in calling in the National Guard earned him a rebuke from the McCone Commission. Nevertheless, he remained popular in the South Bay and was elected to the U.S. Congress as a Democrat representing San Pedro in 1968. He served eight terms in the House, rising to the post of chair of the Public Works and Transportation Committee. As such he was instrumental in gaining federal authorization for the building of Interstate 105, later renamed the Glenn Anderson Freeway.

ANDRUS, ETHEL PERCY (1884–1967), a founder of the National Retired Teachers Association and of the American Association of Retired Persons (AARP). A permanent resident of Los Angeles after 1910, she was a teacher and principal of Manual Arts High and Lincoln High and earned a doctorate at USC for work in curriculum development for girls. A facility at that university is named for her.

ANGELES CREST HIGHWAY, road in the San Gabriel Mountains. It originates in La Cañada Flintridge and climbs above Pasadena, past the Mt. Wilson area, to Big Pines, providing access to Angeles National Forest. The highway is 66 miles long and reaches an elevation of 7,986 feet at Dawson Saddle, where construction crews resisted the temptation to add 14 feet of dirt to bring the number to an even 8,000 feet. A joint effort of the Pasadena Board of Trade, the Automobile Club of Southern California, the United States Forest Service, the State Highway Commission, and Los Angeles County, the road cost about $1 million a mile to build and was some 42 years in the making, between the first survey, made by Joseph Barlow Lippincott in 1919, and the opening of the final link in 1961. Some of the construction was done by prison labor.

ANGELES NATIONAL FOREST, 50-mile belt of forest and chaparral in the San Gabriel Mountains on the northern rim of Los Angeles. It was designated in 1892 by Pres. Benjamin Harrison as the first national forest in the state, and one of the earliest in the nation, its purpose being to protect the local watershed. Originally called San Gabriel

Timberland Reserve, it was renamed in 1907. The tallest peak, Mt. San Antonio ("Old Baldy"), rises to a height of 10,080 feet. The forest is a major year-round recreational area for camping, hiking, and skiing, and contains a profusion of plants and wildlife. The area, comprising 643,656 acres, also includes Mt. Wilson and a large reservoir, Castaic Lake.

ANGELINO HEIGHTS, housing tract near downtown. Framed by Sunset Boulevard to the north, the Hollywood Freeway to the south, Echo Park to the west, and Boylston Avenue to the east, this neighborhood has often been called the first of Los Angeles's suburbs. It was developed during the Boom of the Eighties on a hillside at the end of a streetcar line near Echo Park. Today the 1300 block of Carroll Avenue is lined by over a dozen Victorian homes, mostly Queen Anne/Eastlake in style, which form the largest such cluster in Los Angeles. They include two outstanding Queen Anne buildings by architect Joseph Cather Newsom and are lovingly cared for by current owners. In 1983 Angelino Heights became the first Los Angeles community to become a Historic Preservation Overlay Zone (HPOZ).

Angels Flight Railway, ca. 1910. Pitt Collection.

1901. It was the creation of New York–born Col. James Ward Eddy (1832–1914), who owned and operated it until 1912. The two cars of Angels Flight, Olivet and Sinai, crept 350 feet on a 33-degree slope along the eastern flank of Bunker Hill at 3rd Street. The line carried the residents of the fashionable Victorian hillside neighborhood to and from the stores and offices on the streets below. Each car carried ten people, on a one-minute trip costing 5 cents. Eddy sold the railway to the Funding Company of Los Angeles, in what proved to be the first of a number of sales. Although the line was designated a city cultural landmark in 1926, the Community Redevelopment Agency (CRA) dismantled it in the spring of 1969 to make way for the massive California Plaza office complex. The CRA warehoused the cars, promising eventually to restore them. In February 1996, amid a two-day festival honoring the occasion, the orange and black cars reappeared on Bunker Hill at a site one-half block from their original location. The funicular was restored under a contract with the Los Angeles Conservancy and is operated by a private nonprofit foundation. A one-way ride costs 25 cents.

Sessions House (1888), Angelino Heights. Photo by Michael Krakowiak/Marni Pitt.

ANGELS, CALIFORNIA. *See* California Angels baseball team

ANGELS FLIGHT, inclined cable railway on Bunker Hill that advertised itself as "The Shortest Paying Railway in the World" when it opened in

ANGELUS TEMPLE, mother church of the Foursquare Gospel Church, founded by Aimee Semple McPherson in 1923. The immense domed, circular concrete building with seating for 5,000

Angelus Temple. Photo by Lori Shepler.

people has tall stained-glass windows and an altar under a great proscenium arch. The main stage can accommodate choirs, orchestras, bands, and movable scenery. Situated on Glendale Boulevard overlooking Echo Park, the church grounds also contain the offices of the worldwide religious association, radio station KFSG, and a Bible college.

ANHEUSER-BUSCH, INC. *See* Beverage industry; Busch Gardens

ANIMAL SHELTERS are maintained by both the city and the county to control untold legions of dogs and cats. The first animal regulation was an 1836 law allowing no more than two dogs per household and requiring them to be securely tied. Los Angeles opened its first pound in 1863. The city charter of 1925 created a Department of Humane Treatment of Animals, renamed, in 1947, the Department of Animal Regulation. The department maintains shelters for impounded animals, issues licenses and permits, oversees ownership of wild animals, supervises a rabies control program, enforces state immunization and leash laws, and inspects medical research labs. It pioneered a public low-cost spay-and-neuter clinic program, and it also sponsors volunteer services and trains a corps of animal control officers.

In 1982 an estimated 423,500 dogs were living in the city, or about one for every seven persons. Not all of these are provided for in a stable home. Abandoned or lost pets create immense problems, particularly during economic downturns when many owners can no longer care for them. In 1990–1991 the city destroyed 22,552 of the 38,609 dogs it impounded (58.4 percent), and 27,019 of the 34,654 cats (78.0 percent). In the same period

the county destroyed 29,544 of the 47,035 dogs impounded (62.8 percent) and 32,983 of the 39,337 cats (83.8 percent). The county's Agoura shelter has the best record of returning lost pets to owners and destroying the fewest animals. In general, too many people neglect to spay and neuter their pets; meanwhile, budget cuts, equipment disrepair, and understaffing at the city animal shelters continue to exacerbate the problems associated with animal welfare.

ANNEXATION AND CONSOLIDATION of new territory was pursued vigorously by Los Angeles for many years. The city was originally 28.01 square miles (4 square leagues) in size. It tripled to 89.61 square miles by 1910. The greatest period of expansion, spurred by the introduction of the aqueduct, took place a few years later, and by 1920 the city covered 363.92 square miles. It reached its current 465 square miles by 1970.

Two processes have allowed expansion: (1) annexation, the addition of unincorporated areas, which requires a popular referendum both within and outside the city; and (2) consolidation, the addition of previously incorporated cities. Annexation proposals are required to meet basic conditions: the annexed property must be directly contiguous to the municipality; the owners of the annexed property must be assured of receiving better public services; annexation must improve "the free flow of commerce and industry"; and a majority of the voters in both the annexed area and the city as a whole must approve the proposal.

In the late 19th century, the needs of farmers for irrigation water in areas adjacent to the city limits led to the annexation of Highland Park, Garvanza, Sycamore Grove, and the area south of Slauson and

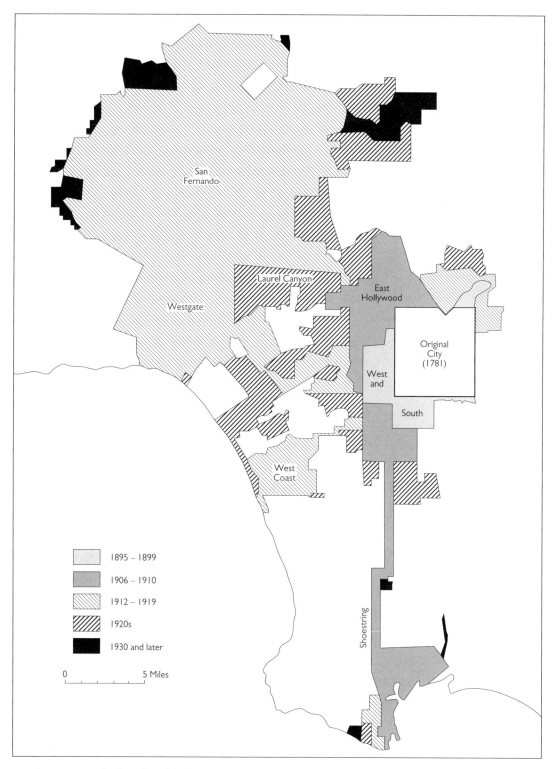

San
Fernando

Laurel Canyon

East
Hollywood

Westgate

Original
City
(1781)

West
and

South

West
Coast

1895 – 1899

1906 – 1910

1912 – 1919

1920s

1930 and later

0   5 Miles

Shoestring

Annexations to the City of Los Angeles

west of Arlington. By 1899 the city was almost double its original size. From 1906 to 1927 a rash of annexations occurred when existing cities and unincorporated areas realized that only by linking up with Los Angeles could they meet their future water needs. This brought in Colgrove, Hollywood, the Los Feliz district, Bairdstown, and Arroyo Seco, adding 24 additional square miles to Los Angeles. Gardena also wanted to become part of Los Angeles but was refused by Los Angeles voters, who feared that Gardena's tax base was inadequate. Wilmington and San Pedro were also added: in 1909, anncxationists forced the city to acquire a "shoestring strip," a narrow band of territory linking those two cities to Los Angeles proper.

With the coming of Owens River water, the process of expansion by annexation advanced rapidly. On one day, 22 May 1915, Los Angeles tripled its size with the addition of the San Fernando Valley and Palms (from Crenshaw to Overland). Between 1922 and 1928, 34 unincorporated areas and five cities merged with Los Angeles, among them La Brea, Sawtelle, Eagle Rock, Fairfax,

---

In 1922 and 1923 white-collar clerks in Southern California everywhere deserted good office jobs to become real estate salesmen.

—W. W. Robinson, writer

Venice, Sunland, and Mar Vista. Major annexations ceased in 1928, although Tujunga joined in 1932, and tiny areas have been attached since 1948. Minor detachments, or de-annexations, have straightened out existing boundaries. The net effect of the planless expansion was a city of grotesque shape, likened to "a charred scrap of paper" or "a one-legged, east-facing turkey with feathers ruffled."

From time to time, dissidents in outlying parts of the city have complained of city hall's indifference to their needs and have threatened to secede from Los Angeles. The strongest secession movements have arisen in the San Fernando Valley, in the 1970s and again in 1996. According to California law, however, secession requires the majority approval not only of the voters of the aggrieved area but also of the Los Angeles City Council, which has never shown the slightest inclination to approve such efforts.

ANTELOPE, graceful, swift-footed, pronghorn animal that is said to have ranged throughout the area during Indian, Spanish, and Mexican times. Eyewitness accounts and ethnographic information are sparse and conflicting, however. Some believe that Portolá saw them in 1769 and that they roamed in the Antelope and San Fernando Valleys and as far south as Orange County. What is certain is that an antelope herd was reintroduced into the county's northern desert area in the 1960s and is flourishing.

ANTELOPE ACRES, unincorporated area in the western Antelope Valley, 64 miles from downtown Los Angeles. Its sparse and stable population of 725 people led county planners in 1986 to designate the area as nonurban and agricultural.

ANTELOPE VALLEY, triangular-shaped valley in the northern part of the county. Situated between the Tehachapi and San Gabriel Mountains, parts of the valley merge into the Mojave Desert and extend into Kern County. It is named for the graceful animal herds that are said to have roamed there until being decimated by hunters and bad weather in the 1880s.

Indians once had settlements in the surrounding hills. The area's earliest Yankee pioneers, in the 1860s, ranched in the vicinity of Elizabeth Lake. In some locations they grew alfalfa, fruit, and vegetables and raised chickens. Cattle raising developed into a major enterprise between 1880 and 1910. The herds of antelope, numbering 30,000, were destroyed or driven from the area from 1882 to 1885, owing to unusually heavy snows.

The towns of Lancaster, Palmdale, and Rosamond (in Kern County) took form in the period 1876–1882, along newly established sections of the Southern Pacific Railroad. From around 1870 to 1914 numerous other colonies—Wicks, Manzana, Chicago, Kingsbury, John Brown, Old Palmdale, Almondale, and Llano—were established by outsiders. Miners flocked to the area when gold was discovered at Rosamond (Tropico Hill) in 1880, and farmers were lured into the valley in the 1880s by heavy rainfalls, only to face extreme drought and bitter disappointment between 1893 and 1904. Afterward, fortunes improved somewhat, and Lancaster established a high school and newspaper in 1912.

Activity at Edwards Air Force Base during World War II, and at USAF Plant 42 (between Palmdale and Lancaster) during the Cold War, brought many workers and military personnel to the Antelope Valley. Their presence transformed Palmdale and Lancaster into small cities.

Although some towns are growing rapidly, much of the Antelope Valley remains vacant or under cultivation. Among the smaller communities with stable populations and an agricultural or mixed residential-and-rural lifestyle are Acton, Elizabeth Lake–Lake Hughes, Lake Los Angeles, Leona Valley, Littlerock, Pearblossom, and Sun Village. Boron, Mojave, and Rosamond, in the same geographic region, are in Kern County.

ANTONOVICH, MICHAEL D. (1940?–), county supervisor representing the 5th District. Born to a family of Croatian background and raised in Los Angeles, Antonovich graduated from John Marshall High School and holds an M.A. degree from CSULA. While in college he became active in the Young Republicans; in 1973 he was elected to the state assembly, where he served six years. Antonovich first joined the Los Angeles County Board of Supervisors in 1980, helping to create a conservative majority, and was twice reelected to that body.

ANTS. Prevalent variety in the area is the Argentine ant *(Iridomyrmex humilis)*. Scientists believe they entered New Orleans in 1891 and California in 1905 and have thrived because of a combination of factors: the ants are extremely fertile, having many queens (as many as one per 1,000 workers); they are armed with a poison that kills rival varieties; they colonize rapidly; and they devour the nutritious "honeydew" excreted by aphids and numerous other common insects, which they farm for food. Humans can resort to pesticides, but so far the ants remain triumphant.

ANZA, JUAN BAUTISTA DE (1734–1788), Spanish soldier, explorer, and pioneer. Captain Anza led a party of 240 settlers along a new route from Sonora, Mexico, to Mission San Gabriel, arriving in the Los Angeles area on 22 March 1774, six years before the Pueblo de la Reina de Los Angeles was founded. The group continued through the southern San Fernando Valley, continuing north as far as San Francisco Bay—a trek of 1,200 miles. Anza traveled the same route a second time, again bringing a large party of settlers from Mexico. Bound for San Francisco, they passed through San Gabriel in January 1776. Diaries of these expeditions provide vivid descriptions of the native inhabitants and natural surroundings.

APLA (AIDS PROJECT LOS ANGELES). *See* AIDS

AQMD (AIR QUALITY MANAGEMENT DISTRICT). *See* Air pollution control; South Coast Air Quality Management

ARABS. With an estimated 200,000–300,000 Arabs and Arab Americans, the county qualifies as the second largest Arab community in the nation. Principal areas of settlement are Glendale, Arcadia, Pasadena, Burbank, Long Beach, Palos Verdes, Torrance, and Northridge. The *News Circle,* a monthly magazine founded in 1972, serves the community, supplying news of Arab homelands and community issues; the publisher also issues an almanac of Arab Americans nationwide. Palestinian Arabs have become more numerous since the war of June 1967, numbering as many as 50,000.

ARBORETUM, LOS ANGELES STATE AND COUNTY. *See* Arcadia; State historic parks

ARBUCKLE, ROSCOE ("FATTY") (1887–1933), silent film comedian whose career ended in scandal. A master of the two-reel slapstick comedy, Arbuckle was arguably, next to Chaplin, the most popular comedian of the silents. In 1921 he was tried in San Francisco for the rape and murder of starlet Virginia Rappe. Despite conflicting testimony and an acquittal after three trials, Arbuckle was blackballed as an actor. Buster Keaton, who acknowledged an artistic debt to Arbuckle, subsequently hired him as a director, giving him the pseudonym William Goodrich. His directorial career was short, however, and he died alone at 46. The episode was one of a series of scandals that led to the establishment, in 1930, of the Hays Office, a Hollywood self-censorship agency.

ARCADIA, independent city east of Pasadena, 13 miles northeast of downtown Los Angeles at the foot of the San Gabriel Mountains. Its first inhabitants were Gabrieleño Indians. The Scottish trader Hugo Reid, who married Victoria Bartolome'a Comecrabit, an Indian woman, received a Mexican land grant of 13,319 acres on the site in 1839. The town itself was platted and named by a railroad official in about 1888. Arcadia, to the ancient Greeks, recalled a place of beauty, bounty, and peace. In 1875 the flamboyant Elias J. "Lucky" Baldwin saw the land and exclaimed, "Egad, this is Paradise!" He bought a ranch and established a racehorse stable there. He was mayor when, on 5 August 1903, the town of 11 square miles was incorporated. Arcadia's most prominent features today are the famed Santa Anita Park, the racecourse established in 1934, and the Los Angeles State and County Arboretum, which was originally Baldwin's private estate. Hugo Reid's adobe has been preserved on the grounds. In 1990 the city had a population of 48,290.

ARCADIA BLOCK, first modern commercial structure in Los Angeles. Made of brick and sporting an iron balcony, it was built by Abel Stearns on Los Angeles Street in 1858 and named for Stearns's wife, Arcadia Bandini. It came down in 1939.

ARCHITECTURE, TO 1848. The Gabrieleño Indians who occupied the Los Angeles Basin for many millennia were the region's first home builders. They lived in small domelike huts made of boughs and reeds. Their structures were not emulated by Europeans. The Spaniards and Mexicans who supplanted them beginning in 1781 introduced Spanish and Mexican colonial influences. They preferred adobe construction and the architectural styles current in the more settled regions of New Spain. The missions, which were originally thatched lean-tos and huts, evolved into a simplified version of neoclassical Mexican churches. Mission San Fernando was conceived in majestic proportions, with sweeping horizontal lines and archways, and a tile floor. While the homes of most Californios were small and plain, patterned after those in Mexico, more affluent homes featured many rooms arranged around a patio. These outdoor spaces were adorned with fountains and flower beds. The adobe walls, usually 3 feet thick, were covered with a mud plaster. Some of the larger private homes doubled as public buildings; Abel Stearns's *palacio* in the *pueblo* was also the prefect's office. In the 1830s and 1840s, New England traders introduced some architectural features of their homeland, but the styles of colonial New Spain prevailed.

ARCHITECTURE FROM 1848 TO 1900 reflected the shift in taste toward American design following the Yankee takeover. Adobe increasingly gave way to wood and fired-clay brick as new buildings began to resemble those of the eastern United States. Carpenters, using lumber imported by ship to San Pedro from the Pacific Northwest and Mendocino coast, turned to the frame-construction building method. Increasingly in the 1860s and 1870s buildings were designed in a variety of styles: Greek Revival, Italianate, Eastlake, Romanesque, Shingle, Queen Anne, and Colonial Revival. Houses, hotels, and commercial structures built in these styles typically incorporated curlicues, pillars, gables, and mansard roofs. As a result, the towns that sprouted in the region during the Boom of the Eighties resembled Milwaukee, St. Louis, Albany, and other towns of equal size. The first structural steel building was the Homer Laughlin Building, riveted together in 1898.

ARCHITECTURE FROM 1900 TO 1945 went through vast changes in Southern California. But soon the region was drawing some of the world's leading architects, who experimented with new styles and materials. While the single most important innovation was Modernism, overall the styles were eclectic, flamboyant, and discordant.

Home builders in Southern California had the advantages of sizable lots, cheap land, and low construction costs. One notable introduction was the bungalow. It originated in the Far East but was adapted to the needs of the local inhabitants, especially middle-class families, and enjoyed a tremendous vogue. Usually a one-story home made of shingles or redwood siding, often with a front porch supported by a masonry pier, the bungalow was part of the Arts and Crafts, or Craftsman, movement that was very popular and influential early in the century. Architects Charles and Henry Greene raised it to a level of perfection in the Gamble House and other Pasadena homes.

As trained architects made their way west they introduced variations of the French, English, American Colonial, and Dutch Colonial styles. They also tried to preserve the old adobe buildings and to foster a Mediterranean look. The Mission Revival style greatly influenced the next several generations of architects and builders. The style flowered in Southern California from around 1915 and was widely adopted in the design of homes, city halls, churches, and railroad stations. It drew inspiration from the crude, simple style of the Spanish and Mexican era, but is not to be confused with the design elements of the earlier period, sometimes called Hispanic Traditional. Instead, Mission Revival featured the plain surfaces and elaborate ornamentation of Mexican churches.

The modern style found outstanding practitioners in Southern California. In a home built for Walter Dodge in 1916, for example, Irving Gill combined the walls, arches, and patios of a Spanish building with the simplicity, standardization, and technological innovation of a modern building. Another modernist, Frank Lloyd Wright, left his mark on Los Angeles in the 1920s with the Barnsdall House (1920) and other structures in the Los Feliz area. The modern school also was evident in the early 1930s in the work of Richard J. Neutra and R. M. Schindler and their followers.

The region had many examples of Art Deco and Streamline Moderne as well. Among the most successful were the downtown Richfield Building, Bullock's Wilshire Department Store, and the Pellisier tower on the corner of Western Avenue and Wilshire Boulevard.

Downtown Los Angeles featured buildings of fairly sedate and traditional style inherited from the latter part of the 19th century. The commercial skyline was dominated by traditional Beaux Arts architecture. With a healthy regard for the potency of earthquakes, and from a fear of resembling New York or Chicago, the city fathers imposed a 150-foot height limit. The only exception was the new City Hall, completed in the 1920s. City Hall was the only true skyscraper and would remain so for a generation. Another notable public building was the Los Angeles Central Library, designed by Bertram Goodhue. A city-county civic center was planned beginning in 1909 and replanned in 1923, but did not take shape for two more decades.

ARCHITECTURE SINCE 1945 has reflected the dominant influence of the modernist style in commercial design, although in recent decades the postmodernist trend and experimentalism among younger architects have made their mark as well.

Immediately after World War II speculative developers hired Los Angeles architects to build tens of thousands of moderately priced homes, mostly of wood and stucco, for aspiring young middleclass families moving into the suburbs. These structures incorporated various traditional elements as well as the Southern California "ranch style."

A few architects undertook experimental work, too. From 1945 to 1962 the avant-garde Case Study Houses of Craig Ellwood, Charles Eames, and others received wide recognition. John Lautner's Chemosphere House, perched UFO-like atop the Hollywood Hills, also attained the status of a "classic," even though its direct influence on domestic design was limited.

In the 1950s and 1960s the downtown Los Angeles civic center expanded and took on a new look. Older public buildings were torn down; the new County Court Building, County Administrative Center, State Office Building, and City Hall Annex achieved imposing sizes, though architectural critics rated their individual designs as stodgy and the overall space of the civic center as lacking in unity or distinction. A few public structures, such as the Department of Water and Power headquarters and the Dorothy Chandler Pavilion and Music Center theater complex, achieved high honors for design.

Downtown commercial architecture changed dramatically in the 1960s and 1970s, when Los Angeles lifted its 150-foot building height limit. Engineers promised that towering steel buildings, constructed with new technological know-how, could survive major earthquakes. This opened the way for the first true skyscrapers in Los Angeles. Tall spires sheathed in dark glass soon pierced the skyline as the older Beaux Arts style gave way to Modernism and the central business district began to resemble other major American cities. By 1981 many giant corporations had downtown office buildings: Union Bank, Security Pacific Bank,

Model of Walt Disney Concert Hall, Frank O. Gehry & Associates. Courtesy Frank O. Gehry & Associates.

ARCO Plaza Towers, United California Bank, Broadway Plaza, the Los Angeles County Convention Center, Crocker Bank, and Occidental Tower. New commercial centers in outlying areas, such as Century City and the Wilshire District, acquired a similar appearance.

Large and established architectural firms dominated the field of commercial architecture, leaving a strong imprint on the downtown skyline. Among them are Welton Becket Associates; Daniel, Mann, Johnson & Mendenhall; Gruen Associates; the Luckman Partnership, Inc.; Albert C. Martin and Associates; and William L. Pereira Associates.

In the 1980s, however, the bolder and more innovative imprints were being made by smaller firms, which strode to the forefront of American architecture, surpassing even New York City architects in renown. Jon Jerde, for example, created impressive designs for the 1984 summer Olympics. Local practitioners such as Eric Moss and Brian Murphy located themselves in outlying areas such as Culver City, Santa Monica, and Venice.

By the 1980s, architectural historians were characterizing the leading architectural trend of Los Angeles as "new wave" or "postmodernist." Practitioners were rejecting the stark glass-and-steel-box designs of the International style in favor of less massive and more supple and varied designs that incorporated older historical forms—Classical, Art Deco, Egyptian, or Bauhaus. In addition, the younger generation drew upon design motifs suggested by popular culture—sports cars, Nintendo games, and vernacular buildings. Following the lead of Frank Gehry, they used cast-off building materials, as well as such common materials as corrugated iron sheeting, particle board, wire mesh, and fiberglass, thereby introducing a playful or unfinished element in their designs. They also favored a bright palette. Gehry, a designer of museums, office buildings, and private homes, became the best known of these younger experimental architects, winning the coveted Pritzker Award in 1989. Among his followers are Michael Rotondi and Thom Mayne.

Many of the successful younger architects, of all stylistic predilections, were products of local training institutions: UCLA's School of Architecture and Urban Planning, USC's School of Architecture, or the Southern California Institute of Architecture (SCI-Arc).

Los Angeles's experimental designers have received widespread recognition in state and national competitions. In 1992 all eight awards of the California Council of the American Institute of Architects (AIA) for innovative design went to Southern California projects, including the Chiat/Day/Mojo Advertising Agency in Venice. Another eye-catcher was Hodgetts and Fung's temporary Powell Library Tent at UCLA, known on campus as the Towell. Despite such accolades, however, the avant-garde has also garnered some censure. Because of its reliance on computer-generated distortion, inversion, rotation, and fragmentation, the leading design approach of the 1990s has been termed "deconstructivist." Commentators cite buildings in this genre for contributing to a helter-skelter cityscape lacking in restraint.

ARCHITECTURE, STYLES OF, are locally so profuse that a full listing is impractical. While "pure" examples exist of all styles, most buildings represent a blend, and there is no consensus on terminology. The following is a brief summary of prevalent basic styles and notable local examples. The *Spanish Colonial/Mission Revival* features stucco surfaces, low-pitched tile roofs, a limited number of openings, decorative ironwork, and formal gardens (Adamson House, Malibu). The *Eastlake* style, named after the English architect Charles Eastlake, is characterized by thin vertical shapes, jigsaw and lath work in wood, ornamented porch posts, and decorative knobs (Arcadia Railroad Station, Pomona). The *Craftsman* or *Arts and Crafts* style highlights boxy shapes, low-pitched roofs, use of clapboard or shingles, some brick or river boulder, exposed roof rafters, and sun porches (Gamble House, Pasadena). The *Modernist* style observes the rule "form follows function" and is typified by smooth or stripped-down surfaces (Frank Lloyd Wright's Barnsdall House, Hollywood; John Lautner's Chemosphere House, Hollywood Hills). The *Beaux Arts* or *City Beautiful Classicism* style is characterized by formal, ponderous shapes, symmetry, columned domes, and monumental flights of stairs (Second Church of Christ, Scientist, Long Beach). *Art Deco*—or *Art Deco Moderne,* as architects prefer to call it—arose in the early 1920s and features heavy, formal volumes; ornamental zigzags, sunbursts, spirals, and stylized animals; glass brick; and flat roofs (El Rey Theater, Wilshire Miracle Mile). The *California Ranch-House* style, which appeared in the 1930s and was at its most popular following World War II (propelled most prominently by architect Cliff

May), features a single-floor dwelling with low-pitched roofs, broad windows, sliding glass doors, and open interior spaces. The *High Tech* style, developed in the 1970s, uses stock industrial systems and often exposes the ventilation ducts and framework (Student Placement and Career Planning Center, UCLA). *Pop Modernism* uses commonplace and even "throwaway" building materials (Frank Gehry's Temporary Contemporary is a prime example).

ARCHITECTURE, VERNACULAR, genre of zany landmarks that sprang up especially during the early automobile age (1920s–1950s) to startle motorists and lure them from their cars. Some roadside vernacular buildings, known to architects as "programmatic," were shaped to mimic their name or function. Among the best known were the hat-shaped Brown Derby Restaurant on Wilshire Boulevard (1926); the camera-shaped camera store known as the Dark Room on the Miracle Mile of Wilshire Boulevard (1938); the toad-shaped Toad Inn in Santa Monica Canyon; and the bowl-shaped Chile Bowl eateries (1930s), whose slogan was "We cook our beans backwards—you only get the hiccups." The Tail O' the Pup (1946), designed by Milton J. Black and looking like a mustard-smothered hot dog in a bun, was moved from its original location on La Cienega to San Vicente near Beverly Boulevard. Crossroads of the World on Sunset Boulevard (1936), an early shopping mall, has a central building shaped like a ship and a beacon tower with a revolving globe. The Tower of Wooden Pallets (1951) was assembled from discards of the Schlitz brewery on Magnolia Boulevard, in Sherman Oaks. The Malibu Castle, on a bluff near Webb Way and Pacific Coast Highway, has been seen in many films. The Coca-Cola Bottling Company (1936), located on Central Avenue, is shaped like an ocean liner. Some eye-catching structures in this genre are now gone, including downtown's 23-foot-high Chicken Boy and a 35-foot-tall woman's leg advertising nylon hosiery.

ARCHIVES, or historical records of institutions or organizations, exist in scattered locations throughout Los Angeles. The collections tend to be highly specialized and comparatively recently organized. Among business archives, the private collection of the Disney Corporation is extensive and valuable. Among government archives, the Los Angeles City Archives is a superior entity. Los Angeles County has begun a pilot program but has yet to make a full commitment to a comprehensive archival program. Among university archives, both UCLA and USC have substantial collections concerning the growth and development of those institutions. Los Angeles–based voluntary associations are well represented at the Urban Archives Center of CSUN. The most outstanding religious archives are the genealogical collection at the Mormon Library in Westwood and the Archives of the Catholic Archdiocese on the grounds of Mission San Fernando. The entertainment industry is represented at the library of the Academy of Motion Picture Arts and Sciences in Beverly Hills, the Louis B. Mayer Library of the American Film Institute in Hollywood, and the William Fox Research Library, a private collection at the 20th Century-Fox Studio. Many ethnic groups have begun collecting records; the Chinese Historical Society, with its 500 cubic feet of records, is but one example.

ARCO. *See* Atlantic Richfield Company

ARELLANO, MANUEL RAMÍREZ (1742–CA. 1800), Mexican-born soldier on Capt. Gaspar de Portolá's expedition of 1769. He returned with his wife, a member of the de Haro family, to Los Angeles, and in 1797 became an *alcalde*. His children (named Arellanes) also became prominent.

ARGÜELLO, JOSÉ DARIO (1754–1827?), *comisionado* at Los Angeles in 1781 and sergeant at Santa Barbara. His marriage to Ignacia Moraga joined two powerful colonial families. In 1814–1815 he served briefly as the Spanish governor of Alta California. Despite his many personal successes, his fortunes dwindled and he died destitute.

Pig Restaurant, 1934. Courtesy Robert Weinstein Collection.

ARLETA, residential area of Los Angeles located south of San Fernando and Pacoima in the San Fernando Valley. It is 17 miles northwest of downtown.

ARMAND HAMMER MUSEUM OF ART, in Westwood, built by oil magnate Armand Hammer to display his art collection. Paintings by Leonardo da Vinci, Rembrandt, Van Gogh, Goya, Monet, and Rubens have been on display since the museum opened in 1990. In 1994 the UCLA art department took over management of the 79,000-square-foot facility for 99 years, agreeing to oversee day-to-day operations, from exhibitions and education to fund raising and budgeting. The Wight Art Gallery and Grunwald Center for the Graphic Arts, formerly housed on the UCLA campus, were moved into the Hammer facility. The nine-member board of directors consists of three representatives from UCLA, three from Occidental Petroleum, one from the Armand Hammer Foundation, and two from the community.

ARMENIANS numbered about 100,000 in Los Angeles County in 1980 and 250,000 in 1990—the largest enclave outside Armenia. Although some Armenians have U.S. roots going back several generations, migration and settlement have been most intense since the 1970s, when the Soviet Union lifted immigration restrictions. Armenians tend not to live in concentrated areas, though the neighborhood between Hollywood and Santa Monica

---

My first picture had fifty-three scenes and it was freely predicted I would be fired for wasting so much time and film. . . . It took three days to make.
—Thomas Ince, silent film director, ca. 1911

Boulevards, and between the Hollywood Freeway and Vermont Avenue, is sometimes called "Little Armenia." The city of Glendale also has a large Armenian community. Armenians are united by communal memory of the genocide inflicted by Turkey in 1915, and by pride in the election of Gov. George Deukmejian in 1982. The *California Courier,* a Glendale weekly, serves the community, and the Armenian Evangelical Social Service helps immigrants find work and adjust to American life.

ARMET AND DAVIS, Los Angeles architectural firm responsible for many 1950s coffee shops and diners, such as Pann's on La Cienega and La Tijera Boulevards, and Norm's at Overhill Drive and Slauson Avenue. They drew inspiration from the angular forms used by Frank Lloyd Wright. Their trademark was the simple, low-slung hip roof and bright neon sign.

ARROYO CULTURE, loosely knit community of writers, artists, architects, and craftsmen (including potters, furniture makers, tile makers, printers, and book designers) who, from 1890 to 1920, clustered along the Arroyo Seco in Pasadena. Their focal point was the home of Charles F. Lummis, "El Alisal," in Highland Park. The devotees of this aesthetic gave expression to the ideas of the Englishman William Morris and the New Yorker Gustav Stickley, who rejected all that was machine-made, favoring instead the handmade. Wood was the preferred building material, together with clay and boulders from the arroyo. In architecture the members embraced the Arts and Crafts or Craftsman style, but also the English Tudor, Swiss Chalet, and Bavarian Hunting Lodge styles. The homes they designed were not massive in size and were intended to heighten an enjoyment of nature. Aspects of Hispanic and Indian cultures also influenced their work.

ARROYO SECO, Spanish for "dry watercourse, creek, or riverbed." In Los Angeles the name refers specifically to the bed that originates in the San Gabriel Mountains and flows past western Pasadena into the Los Angeles River. At the turn of the century the area was a favored community for wealthy individuals and artists and intellectuals. In 1903, conservation-minded Pres. Theodore Roosevelt praised the natural beauty of the area and urged residents to retain it as parkland. Pasadena's 61-acre Brookside Park, which includes the Rose Bowl, became the major preserve in the area. The Arroyo is crossed by the Colorado Street Bridge. The Pasadena Freeway was once called the Arroyo Seco Freeway.

ART. *See* Painting

ARTESIA, independent community in the southeastern part of the county, 16 miles from downtown. It was founded and named by the Artesia Company, which drilled artesian wells there in

1875. Some 50 farms were developed in the next few years, when land could be bought for about $15 an acre. By the time the town was incorporated in 1959 land prices had risen to $50,000 an acre. Most of the dairy farmers moved out shortly afterward, giving way to suburban home development. In 1990 Artesia's population was 15,464.

ART GALLERIES. *See* Painting

ASHER, BETTY (1914–1994), art collector, curator, and gallery owner. She moved from Chicago to Los Angeles in 1941, and began collecting art in the 1960s, especially the work of Pop Art painters. Roy Lichtenstein, Claes Oldenburg, and Edward Ruscha were early favorites. Her impressive collection also included abstract paintings and ceramic works, particularly cups and mugs, which can be viewed at the Los Angeles County Museum of Art (LACMA). Asher was an assistant curator at LACMA from 1966 until 1979, when she became a co-owner of the Faure Gallery in West Hollywood. It remained an important gallery up to its closure in 1990.

ASH GROVE, Melrose Avenue folk and blues club from 1958 to 1973. Many legendary performers got their start or developed there, including Lightnin' Hopkins, Mississippi John Hurt, Doc Watson, Lester Flatt and Earl Scruggs, Linda Ronstadt, Bonnie Raitt, Bob Dylan, David Crosby, Ry Cooder, and Jackson Browne. Founder Ed Pearl closed the club in 1973, reopening on the Santa Monica Pier in 1996.

ASIAN PACIFIC AMERICAN LEGAL CENTER OF SOUTHERN CALIFORNIA, founded by Stewart Kwoh in 1984, provides legal assistance, social and cultural orientation, and educational programs for low-income Asians and Pacific Islanders. It also works with groups in the African American and Latino communities. The center, located in a Methodist church on the outskirts of downtown Los Angeles, served 15,000 people in 1994, including several thousand who wished to become citizens. It was recognized by the Ford Foundation for its effectiveness.

ASIANS, SOUTHEAST ASIANS, AND PACIFIC ISLANDERS, comprising about 10 percent of the population of Los Angeles, make up the largest such concentration anywhere in the nation. Local Asians, once primarily American-born Japanese, are now largely immigrants from diverse ethnic groups. The new influx from across the Pacific began in earnest after the relaxation of foreign immigration quotas in a 1965 law that took effect in 1968. The major points of settlement in the county in the last 10 years have been in the San Gabriel Valley. In Monterey Park Asians constitute a clear majority, while in Alhambra, Cerritos, Gardena, and Walnut they are the largest ethnic minority. Significant settlement has also occurred in the Wilshire District, Long Beach, Torrance, and Glendale. By the same token, some older Asian ethnic communities, such as Jefferson-Crenshaw, Boyle Heights, and Sawtelle, have sustained losses in the past decade.

Of the three groups of Asian immigrants, mainlanders from Japan, China, and Korea are the largest in number and most clearly identified. All had established communities early in the century. The influx from the Southeast Asian peninsula brought Burmese, Malays, Thais, and nationals from the former French Indochina—Laotians,

---

It is a sort of island on the land.

—Helen Hunt Jackson

Cambodians, and Vietnamese—who arrived after the Vietnam War. Their total number is smaller, and their communities newer and therefore less well defined, than those of the Japanese, Chinese, and Koreans. Filipinos are the largest single group among the Asian Pacific Islanders; also included are native Hawaiians, Fijians, Marshall Islanders, Indonesians, Tongans, Aleuts, Samoans, Melanesians, and Guamanians.

In 1990 over 954,000 Asians, Southeast Asians, and Pacific Islanders lived in the county, out of a total population of 8.8 million, an increase from 250,000 in 1970 and 450,000 in 1980. They reflect varying degrees of acculturation, schooling, and income levels. A study made by the county revealed that 46 percent of the Asians living in Los Angeles County had limited capacity in English, and 21 percent lived in poverty. Asian Americans, moreover, have been relatively slow to participate in the political process. In 1993 they made up 11 percent of the city's voting-age population, but only 4 percent voted.

This population has diverse needs and is aided by numerous service organizations and volunteer associations. The Asian-Pacific Research and Development Council, for example, studies the overall conditions of the Asian-Pacific population; the Asian Pacific American Legal Center of Southern California provides legal aid to needy Asians and Pacific Islanders; and Asian-Pacific Americans for a New L.A., formed after the 1992 rioting, attempts to unify diverse groups of Chinese, Filipinos, Koreans, Japanese, Vietnamese, and Cambodians.

ASISTENCIA, branch of a Spanish mission serving a community that had no resident priest. During *pueblo* days, the Plaza Church was an *asistencia*.

ATCHISON, TOPEKA, AND SANTA FE RAILROAD COMPANY (AT&SF), or Santa Fe Railroad, has played a major role in Southern California's development since its arrival in March 1886. The AT&SF broke the transportation monopoly of the Southern Pacific Railroad (SP), slashed the price of rail tickets from Missouri River towns to Los Angeles, sparked a great influx of newcomers, and marked the beginning of the Boom of the Eighties in the region. Although they were fierce rivals, SP agreed to let the AT&SF enter Los Angeles on SP tracks from San Bernardino. This allowed AT&SF to bring thousands of passengers from the East. By 1887, between the city's eastern limits of the city and the San Bernardino County line, an AT&SF land development corporation had laid out 25 towns—an average of one every 1.5 miles, though not all of them survived the boom. Existing towns that had developed earlier now expanded rapidly. Claremont, Azusa, Glendora, Duarte, Monrovia, Arcadia, and Pasadena were all on the AT&SF's main line. From 1893 to 1933, the railway operated out of an eye-catching Moorish-style wooden depot at 2nd Street and Santa Fe Avenue. Damage from the Long Beach earthquake necessitated the building's demolition.

The railroad eventually expanded its tracks south to San Diego and as far north as San Francisco and Oakland. Still a major carrier in Los Angeles, the AT&SF handled 680,000 cargo containers in the Los Angeles Harbor in 1990.

ATLANTIC RICHFIELD COMPANY (ARCO), largest industrial employer in Southern California and the 15th largest industrial corporation in the world. The corporate offices are in the ARCO Plaza Towers in downtown Los Angeles. The company was formed by a merger of three corporations. The first, the Atlantic Refining Company, founded in 1870 in Philadelphia, was gobbled up by John D. Rockefeller's Standard Oil empire but became independent again when the Supreme Court fragmented the Standard Oil trust in 1911. The second, the Richfield Oil Corporation, began in 1905 as a western producer and merged with Atlantic in 1966. To this amalgam a third, the Anaconda Company, a copper giant formed in Montana in 1875, was added in 1977. Today ARCO has operations worldwide, including oil and gas, chemicals, copper, aluminum, and coal, with special strength in

Richfield Building (demolished in 1968). Courtesy ARCO Photo Collection.

First Santa Fe Railroad locomotive in Los Angeles.

ARCO Plaza Towers. Courtesy ARCO Photo Collection.

oil operations in Alaska, Indonesia, the Gulf of Mexico, and the North and China Seas. Professing a policy of corporate responsibility, ARCO stresses its involvement in education, the arts, the environment, and community affairs.

ATWATER VILLAGE, older blue-collar community in Los Angeles lying just east of the Los Angeles River and south of Glendale. Formerly on Rancho Eulalia, it was first developed in 1912 and named after a pioneer resident, Harriet Atwater Paramore. Walt Disney, Tom Mix, and Mack Sennett all had studios there for a time.

AUSTIN, MARY HUNTER (1868–1934), author associated with Arroyo culture, the literary circle of Charles Fletcher Lummis. Originally from the Midwest, she came to Tejón Ranch in 1888, but moved to the Owens Valley after marrying a rancher. When the marriage failed Austin went to live first in San Francisco and then, in 1899, at Lummis's home in Highland Park. *Land of Little Rain* (1903), generally considered her finest work, is a series of sketches on the desert. *The Ford* (1917) is an exposé of Los Angeles's despoilment of the Owens Valley to obtain its water. She wrote novels, essays, and short stories for 30 years, many of them dealing with Southern California. Austin was a noted feminist in her time.

AUTOMOBILE, a feature of the regional culture so dominant as to defy brief description. Historians trace the development of the modern car to 1919, when the self-starter replaced the front-end hand crank. The steering wheel, originally on the right side imitating the British model, already had been switched to the left. Within a decade most autos were enclosed and had glass windows, electric headlights, and metal tire rims.

Cars affected life in myriad and revolutionary ways. Owing to the mild climate and scenic attractions of Southern California, car touring met with instant success and by the 1920s was widely

Fording a stream in Eastlake (Lincoln) Park, ca. 1908. Courtesy Robert Weinstein Collection.

practiced. Middle-class families now had access to beaches, deserts, and mountains, often located hundreds of miles away. Domestic architecture changed to accommodate the car, such that the one- or two-car garage and driveway were soon all but universal. In 1928 Los Angeles averaged one automobile for every 2.9 persons. The cars of people who lived in outlying areas but drove downtown to work or shop created paralyzing traffic jams and all but insoluble parking problems. Thus the car and parking lot soon became central to planning strategy in the downtown area. The amount of city space paved over by asphalt and concrete for roads and parking was eventually great enough to affect local temperature and water drainage patterns. Over time roads were greatly improved, until by 1940 landscaped highways (freeways) were being designed that would displace rapid transit. Drive-ins were created for fast food, retail sales, and banking. Various car manufacturers were already assembling cars locally, and manufacturing peaked in the 1940s through 1960s. The hundreds of millions of dollars in credit carried by car dealers and car owners had a great impact on the economy. By the 1940s, moreover, air quality throughout the basin had been seriously compromised by the internal combustion engine.

At the turn of the century, speed limits for the new cars were 8 miles per hour in residential areas and a more sedate 6 miles per hour in business districts. Over time the police and judicial systems became increasingly involved with enforcing traffic regulations and prosecuting violators. Road construction and maintenance accounted for an enormous part of the public works budgets of state and local governments. Access to cars gave teenagers a mobility and sexual freedom that caused some people to predict the end of morality. Billboard advertising and radio broadcasting targeted the driver and passengers. Myriad gas stations, repair shops, and car accessory stores were needed to keep the cars rolling. The motel became a fixed part of the landscape. Even before the introduction of malls, shopping strips such as Wilshire Boulevard were designed to favor the customer arriving and departing by car.

Much of the real estate development and urban sprawl of the 1920s occurred expressly because of the suburbanite who commuted to work by private automobile. By the 1940s cars were considered a necessity, not a luxury, and it was common for families to own two of them. After the war, devel-

opment of the auto-fed suburbs continued. The Angeleno's love affair with cars led to the building of the freeways, which soon became the dominant pathway of travel in the basin. The last vestiges of the interurban Red Car lines were disbanded in 1961, and the bus system languished. By 1964, 3.2 million cars and 370,000 trucks traveled Los Angeles roads. Deadly smog attacks increased. Although innovations in air quality control have stemmed the deterioration of the air in recent years, the problem remains severe owing to the ever increasing number of cars.

Today traffic gridlock honors go to two intersections: Wilshire Boulevard and Veteran Avenue, and Highland Avenue and Sunset Boulevard. Each is crossed by 128,000 cars every 24 hours. Other heavily trafficked intersections are Century and La Cienega Boulevards, with 127,000 cars, and Century and Aviation Boulevards, with 113,000.

Whether the new Metrorail system will materially improve the picture remains to be seen. On balance, the automobile enhanced personal freedom, increased physical mobility, and reinforced access to recreation in Southern California, but it also damaged the environment.

AUTOMOBILE CLUB OF SOUTHERN CALIFORNIA (AAA), service association founded in

Touring Topics, Automobile Club Magazine, 1909. Seaver Center for Western History Research, Natural History Museum of Los Angeles County.

Los Angeles in 1900. It was formed as a social club by 10 auto enthusiasts at the dawn of the "horseless carriage" era. They undertook to improve road signs, stage races, and, starting in 1909, published a lively club magazine, *Touring Topics*. By 1920 the club had 30,000 members. Today AAA is a national organization involved in emergency road service, public safety, travel planning, automotive testing, insurance sales, and legislative advocacy. It lobbies actively for the freeway system and distributes maps and books. In 1989 the club answered 3 million calls for roadside aid. The Southern California affiliate is the largest AAA unit in the nation, with a headquarters serving 3.6 million members and employing 5,800. The magazine, retitled *Westways* in 1933, boasts excellent writing by outstanding regional writers on a range of topics. The headquarters, a Spanish Colonial Revival structure on Adams Boulevard designed by Hunt and Burns in 1923, is a city historic-cultural monument.

AUTOMOBILE INDUSTRY AND TRADE has prospered locally since the 1920s. The first person to drive a car in Los Angeles was J. Philip Erie, on 30 May 1897. He had a "motor wagon" privately built by S. D. Sturgis in a shop on 5th Street. Henry Ford was the first auto manufacturer to realize the potential of the regional California car market, establishing a branch assembly plant in 1917. He sent engines, body panels, frames, and other large components from Detroit to be assembled near the market. By 1915 there were 55,000 autos in the area, and by the 1920s, over 600,000. The building and selling of cars was by then well established: an entire urban culture was developing around the auto. In 1927 Ford moved his plant to a site in Long Beach, and still later to Pico Rivera. Other car makers followed suit: Willys-Overland opened a plant in Maywood in 1929; Chrysler established itself in the City of Commerce in 1931; and Studebaker settled in Vernon, and General Motors (GM) in South Gate, in 1936.

After World War II, Kaiser-Frazer opened in Long Beach, Nash in El Segundo, and Chevrolet in Van Nuys. More than 15,000 Southern California workers made 500,000 cars in a single year. Goodyear took advantage of the demand by manufacturing tires in Los Angeles beginning in 1920; Firestone Rubber followed suit in 1927, and United States Rubber in 1930. By then Los Angeles was second only to Akron in tire production.

Auto manufacturing peaked from the 1940s to the 1960s but then declined owing to Japanese competition. Assembly plants shut down from the 1970s to the 1990s, and thousands of workers were laid off. GM closed its South Gate facility with a loss of 2,500 jobs, Chrysler shut down its factory in the City of Commerce in 1971, and in 1980 Ford followed suit in Pico Rivera. In 1992 GM announced closure of the last auto plant in California, its assembly facility in Van Nuys, with a loss of 2,600 jobs.

Despite the contraction of manufacturing, Southern California remains a testing ground for industrial design. Japanese and American manufacturers maintained local design studios to study the habits of motorists by means of questionnaires, video cameras, and site visits to parking lots and highways. The Art Center College of Design in Pasadena is one of the institutions involved in these studies.

AUTOMOBILE RACING originated on a board track in Playa del Rey around 1908. Promoters also initiated a cross-country race from Los Angeles to Phoenix, mainly along unpaved roads. In the first such race, four cars sped away from a cheering crowd at the downtown Hollenbeck Hotel at 2nd and Spring Streets. The final cross-country race, in 1914, was won by one Barney Oldfield piloting a Stutz. Car racing came of age with the Vanderbilt Cup race in 1912, sponsored by philanthropist-sportsman William K. Vanderbilt. The contests took place on a triangular course involving Ocean Park, Wilshire (near the Soldiers' Home) and San Vicente Boulevards. In 1914 Ralph DePalma challenged Barney Oldfield on that course. From 1922 to 1924 the Beverly Hills Speedway occupied the current site of the Beverly Hilton Hotel. Its maiden race was witnessed by 90,000 spectators, including movie celebrities Tom Mix, Wallace Beery, Douglas Fairbanks, Charlie Chaplin, and Mary Pickford. The winner was Jim Murphy, star of the Hollywood feature film *Racing Hearts* (1922). The short-track oval built at the Firestone plant in South Gate, and the second one at Monterey Road in East Los Angeles, added to the racing vogue.

In the 1930s midget auto racing, a sport invented at Loyola High School in 1934, became popular. Races were held at Gilmore Stadium in the Fairfax area and in the Rose Bowl. Speedway motorcycle racing, an Australian import, was popularized by movie personalities Clark Gable and Hoot Gibson. Various types of races were held at the San Fernando Drag Strip and Lions Drag Strip in Wilmington. Other popular racing venues were in Riverside in the 1950s and the Ontario Motor Speedway in the 1970s.

AUTRY MUSEUM OF WESTERN HERITAGE, opened in Griffith Park in 1989. Established by the Texas-born "Singing Cowboy" of movie fame, Gene Autry, the museum explores the evolving culture of the territory west of the Mississippi through artifacts, photos, and published documents. The collections, varied and wide ranging, include an extensive holding of pistols and guns of the frontier era. A major emphasis is placed on interpreting myths and legends. Temporary exhibits are displayed in a 7,000-square-foot gallery.

AVALON, Santa Catalina Island's only town and Los Angeles County's only city not on the mainland. Avalon, which is slightly larger than 1 square mile, was named after the island paradise of Celtic legend, where King Arthur's knights went when they died. The town was founded by George Shatto, who purchased the island from the James Lick estate in 1887. Shatto subsequently sold it to the Banning brothers (the sons of Phineas Banning), who built the Hotel Metropole on Avalon Bay.

Incorporated in 1913, the town is governed by a five-member city council, which includes the mayor. It contracts with the Los Angeles County Sheriff's and Fire Departments for police and fire protection, has a 12-bed hospital operated by Memorial Medical Center of Long Beach, and is provided with energy and telephone utilities by Southern California Edison and Pacific Bell. The permanent population of 2,900 swells to 6,000–10,000 during the summer. Thirty percent of Avalon's land is privately owned, with the remaining 70 percent held by the Santa Catalina Island Company, which provides properties for sale or lease.

Summer sunbathers fill the small beach to capacity, but visitors' cars are forbidden on the island. The waterfront boardwalk, ballroom, pleasure-boat marina, and hillside home area are principal attractions of the town. Avalon was the only part of Catalina Island *not* owned by the Wrigley family, whose tenure began in 1919.

AVIATION. *See* Aerospace industry; Airports

AVILA ADOBE, city's oldest extant residence. Built in 1818 of adobe brick and located on today's Olvera Street, it was the home of one of the original *pobladores,* Francisco Avila, who was an *alcalde* in the early 1800s. The walls are over 3 feet thick; the floors, originally packed earth, were later covered with planks. The adobe fell into disrepair and was nearly destroyed in the 1920s, but preservationist Christine Sterling took up residence there and saved it. It is now a main feature of El Pueblo Park.

AVOCADO, or "alligator pear," commercial fruit cultivated in the basin beginning in the 1890s. Native to Mexico and South America, the avocado is sensitive to the sun and dry winds and grows best in mild, humid environments. Ranchers sometimes created windbreaks and sunshades to protect them. The fruit is picked when hard and must be harvested carefully to avoid bruising. The commercial possibilities became clear around the turn of the century, and in 1910 the Calavo cooperative marketing organization was formed to make a se-

Avalon Bay, Santa Catalina Island, 1995. Courtesy Catalina Island Chamber of Commerce.

Avocado packing plant. Courtesy Robert Weinstein Collection.

rious enterprise of avocado ranching. By 1940, huge groves flourished in the Puente Hills, but beginning in the 1950s the orchards gave way to suburban development.

AVOCADO HEIGHTS, unincorporated county area between the San Gabriel River and Workman Mill Road. In 1990 Avocado Heights and nearby Bassett had a population of 14,232.

AYUNTAMIENTO, governing body for Los Angeles during the Spanish and Mexican colonial era (1781–1850). The system drew its power from a 1779 declaration by Gov. Felipe de Neve, but was strengthened after 1835 when Los Angeles officially became a city. The members of the Los Angeles *ayuntamiento* served a single term and were chosen by elected *compromisarios* (electors). The body consisted of two *alcaldes* (mayors), a variable number of *regidores* (aldermen), a *síndico* (city attorney), and a secretary. It adopted a solemn and decorous manner, followed established bylaws, made decisions by majority vote, limited meetings to three hours, and left a written record of proceedings. The members regulated saloons, controlled Indians, recruited police, met with visiting dignitaries, distributed public land, established schools, straightened streets, managed refuse, and found new ways to improve the city. In addition, the *ayuntamiento* had the right to dictate private conduct.

AZALEA, flowering shrub with blooms varying from white and pale pink to deep red and magenta. Azaleas are available commercially in both sun and shade varieties and bloom profusely in Southern California gardens, mainly from March to June. A native variety grows wild along California streams and in the mountains.

AZUSA, town 19 miles east of downtown Los Angeles, nestled at the foot of the San Gabriel Mountains north of Claremont. Despite comedian Jack Benny's joke that the name Azusa means "everything from A to Z in the U.S.A.," a more likely derivation is the Gabrieleño Indian word *Asuksagna* or the Serrano Indian word *Ashukshavit,* which have been translated variously as "skunk-place" or "grandmother." Indians were living at the mouths of the local canyons when the Portolá expedition passed through in 1769. In 1874 the Yankee settler Henry Dalton developed an estate that he called Rancho Azusa. He imported, from Italy, the first foreign honey bees into the United States. For a quarter of a century Dalton fought doggedly to retain title to his land, ultimately without success. The land fell into the hands of the man who bankrolled him, Jonathan Sayre Slauson. The name of Dalton's ranch was soon applied to the town laid out by Slauson in the boom year of 1887. It became a citrus center, but the soil proved hostile to orchards and orange production. Owing to its location in the floodplain of the San Gabriel River, Azusa is a major source of sand and gravel. Beer, chemicals, and missile motors have been manufactured there as well. The population reached 41,333 in 1990, representing a 40 percent increase over 1980. The town's Cultural Heritage Landmark Commission has taken an active role in historic preservation.

B

BAHA'I FAITH, Middle Eastern religion founded in 19th-century Persia by Baha'ullah (1817–1892). The faith claims 110,000 adherents in the United States, and about 5,000 in Southern California. The Baha'i community of Los Angeles was established in 1909. Members of the faith believe that all religions are divinely inspired; they therefore accept Jesus Christ, Mohammed, Buddha, Moses, and Krishna as prophets. They also believe in racial and sexual equality.

BALDWIN, ELIAS JACKSON ("LUCKY") (1829–1909), developer of Santa Anita racetrack. The flamboyant San Francisco hotelier and stock market gambler bought the 13,000-acre Rancho Santa Anita in 1873 and devoted himself to the good life. Baldwin had made a fortune in 1872 in the Comstock mines by buying shares at $2 and

Lucky Baldwin Cottage, Los Angeles State and County Arboretum, Arcadia. Courtesy Los Angeles County Dept. of Public Affairs.

selling them for $1,800. At Santa Anita he built the biggest horse racing stables in the country, as well as a racetrack and a hotel to serve the patrons of the "sport of kings." His vineyards also attracted notice. When Baldwin subdivided some land parcels in 1881 he invented a new sales pitch: "Hell, we're giving away the land," he proclaimed. "We're selling the climate." He founded the town of Arcadia, hoping to turn it into the Monte Carlo of western America. To legitimize the racetrack complex to a skeptical public, he filed for town incorporation. Lacking the legal minimum number of residents, he borrowed Henry Huntington's "illiterate peon gang" and brought them to the site posing as permanent town dwellers. Baldwin then installed himself as Arcadia's mayor and drafted some of his employees as city council members. The 75-year-old Baldwin also provided a bevy of pretty women for the celebration of incorporation. A notorious roué and hedonist, he was involved in several sensational law cases involving extramarital relations.

BALDWIN HILLS, 5 square miles of unincorporated hillside near Culver City. Once a part of the 4,000-acre Rancho La Cienega granted to Vicente Sánchez in 1843, it was acquired by E. J. "Lucky" Baldwin in 1909. It was the site of the Olympic Village in 1932.

At about noon on 14 December 1963, the Baldwin Hills Dam, which held back 292 million gallons of water in the massive Baldwin Hills Reservoir, sprung a leak and burst. Within 77 minutes the gushing water had blanketed the hillsides and lowlands between Rodeo Road and La Cienega Boulevard, drowning five people, destroying hundreds of houses and apartments, and causing $12 million worth of damage and a water shortage for

500,000 people. The cause of the catastrophe was traced both to oil drilling that had undermined the dam structure and to a shift in the Newhall-Inglewood earthquake fault. The reservoir was subsequently filled with earth and, in 1984, landscaped with grass, trees, and shrubs, the gift of foreign nations participating in that year's summer Olympic games.

Baldwin Hills, the home of West Los Angeles College, has upscale homes with views of the San Gabriel Mountains. In 1990 it had a population of 30,000 people.

BALDWIN HILLS VILLAGE. *See* Village Green

BALDWIN PARK, San Gabriel Valley town 16 miles east of downtown Los Angeles. Incorporated in 1956, it stands on land once granted to Mission San Gabriel and subsequently to William Workman and John Rowland, as Rancho La Puente, in 1845. Workman and Rowland lost their holdings to E. J. "Lucky" Baldwin in 1867. The town was originally named Pleasant View, changed to Vineland, and again renamed, for Baldwin, in 1912. Southern California's first drive-through restaurant, In-N-Out Burger, was established there in 1948. Today Baldwin Park is a manufacturing and service community whose largest employers are the school system and United Parcel Service. It calls itself the "Hub of the San Gabriel Valley." Its population in 1980 was 62,000, and in 1990, 69,000.

BALLONA CREEK, small stream wending southwest through West Los Angeles and Culver City and emptying into Santa Monica Bay. Indians used to fish along its banks, and the Portolá expedition crossed it in 1769. At least once in historical times, somewhere around 1825, the Los Angeles River jumped its banks, flooded Ballona Creek, and used the creekbed as its path to the ocean. The name derives from the Ballona (or Paso de las Carretas) grant given to the Talmantes family in 1839, named after Bayona, a city in northern Spain, the ancestral family home. In August 1887 the Santa Fe Railroad and local promoters celebrated the opening of "Port Ballona," at the mouth of the creek, as the "Future Harbor of Southern California." The harbor never materialized.

Ballona Creek originates below ground in the Mid-City District, rises to the surface near Venice Boulevard and Cochrane Avenue as a concrete-lined flood channel, and from there proceeds 9.1 miles to the ocean. In a heavy rain it carries up to 10 billion gallons of water daily. This flood control project was carried out by the U.S. Army Corps of Engineers in the 1930s and 1940s. Since Ballona Creek drains 126 square miles of surface area and thousands of street gutters, freeway runoffs, and industrial overflows, its highly toxic waters constitute the most serious source of pollution for Santa Monica Bay. A new city sewer line in the 1980s alleviated some, but not all, of the problem.

BALLONA WETLANDS, one of the last remaining wetlands in Los Angeles County. The fragile, self-sustaining bog is located south of Ballona Creek, between Marina del Rey and Playa del Rey, and consists of 175–325 acres fed by both fresh and salt water. Before the turn of the century it was much larger, including the coastal area near Venice. This and other major wetlands, including Bixby Slough at the mouth of the San Gabriel River, have been filled in for urban development.

The Ballona wetlands are alive with fish, wildlife, and native plants. Birds, including the great blue heron and egrets, feed on clams, snails, crabs, worms, and shrimp. The land is owned by Maguire Thomas Partners, developers of the massive Playa Vista project, now in the planning stages and said to be the largest as yet undeveloped urban land in the county. From 1978 to 1989 environmentalists locked horns with the developers in an attempt to spare the marshy area from overuse. They reached a court-ordered agreement, with 270 acres to be set aside in a preserve for some 200 bird species; it is anticipated that as many as 900,000 visitors will visit the preserve's planned interpretive center each year.

BALLOON ROUTE EXCURSION, Pacific Electric Railway interurban tour that circled parts of Southern California early in the century in a figure-eight path. Along the way Red Car passengers could enjoy the lush landscaping of the Soldiers' Home in Sawtelle, stroll the beach at Santa Monica, ride a gondola car in Venice, and gather moonstones at Redondo Beach.

BANDINI, ARCADIA (1825–1912), daughter of Don Juan Bandini and Dolores Estudillo, of San Diego. When she was 14 she married Abel Stearns, who was then 40. The Yankee merchant built a spacious Los Angeles adobe, "El Palacio de Don Abel," at Main and Arcadia Streets, where they lived most

Arcadia Bandini. Courtesy Photographic Collections, Los Angeles Public Library.

of the year. The couple spent summers at Rancho Los Alamitos (now part of Long Beach and Seal Beach), which he purchased in 1842. Stearns was by then the biggest landowner and rancher in Southern California. After his death in 1871, Arcadia Bandini Stearns married Robert Symington Baker. The wealthy cofounder of Santa Monica tore down El Palacio and built the Baker Block on that valuable downtown site, then moved with his wife to Ocean Avenue in Santa Monica. When Baker died in 1894 his widow married John T. Gaffey of San Pedro. Upon her death in 1912 she left an estate of $8 million.

BANKING began slowly in the frontier period but has evolved to such an extent that some now regard Los Angeles as the banking capital of the United States. Southern California is an important international banking center and the nation's second largest center for bank deposits; its banks control billions in assets.

Commercial banking began informally before the Gold Rush era, when the hide-and-tallow traders lent money to the rancheros. The first bona fide chartered banking institution in the southern part of the state was Hayward & Co., formed by John Gately Downey and Alvinza Hayward, reputedly the richest man in the state. Other pioneer bankers were Isaias W. Hellman and William Workman. Downey and Workman also founded the Farmers and Merchants Bank in 1871, which subsequently became part of Security Pacific Bank.

Today, Los Angeles County is home to 6 of the 19 largest commercial banks in the state. They are, in order of total deposits and net income, First Interstate of California, Union Bank, City National Bank (Beverly Hills), Imperial Bank, Mitsui Manufacturers, and Mitsubishi Bank of California. Together they accounted for over $66 billion in deposits in 1987. Los Angeles–based Security Pacific merged with San Francisco–based Bank of America in 1992. Considering the importance of real estate development in the region, it is not surprising that the savings and loan industry has thrived. Most of California's 20 leading S&Ls have home offices in Los Angeles. In fact, the top five S&Ls *in the entire nation* are Home Savings of America (Irwindale), Great Western Bank (Beverly Hills), California Federal, Glendale Federal, and American Savings Bank. These five giants accounted for total deposits of $100.9 billion at the start of 1990. Historically, S&Ls were limited by federal law to making domestic investments only, which meant that their basic realm of interest was real estate. They now, like commercial banks, provide a wider range of services.

BANNING, PHINEAS (1830–1885), Yankee pioneer known as the "Father of Los Angeles Har-

Phineas Banning. Courtesy Photographic Collections, Los Angeles Public Library.

bor" for his efforts to build a port for landlocked Los Angeles. He started out in Wilmington and San Pedro in 1851 as a teamster hauling people and goods to Los Angeles. He soon replaced ox carts with stagecoaches and wagons. With contracts to supply government posts at Tejón, Yuma, and Tucson, he off-loaded boats tied up at the San Pedro and Wilmington mud flats. Devoting himself to harbor improvements, Banning began to buy up land in anticipation of developing a deep-water port for Los Angeles. He named Wilmington after his hometown in Delaware. With a state subsidy he constructed a rail line running from tidewater to Alameda Street near the Plaza in downtown Los Angeles. This first rail line in Southern California was later incorporated into the Southern Pacific system. The Banning residence, a handsome two-story Georgian structure built in Wilmington in 1864, is now a public museum.

BAPTISTS, denomination established locally in El Monte in the 1850s, when Los Angeles's population was 2,000. Baptists, who split off from the New England Congregationalists during the 18th-century Great Awakening, believe that baptism should be administered only to those who have made a confession of faith, and only by immersion. In the 1850s Baptists were the second largest Protestant denomination in the country but, faced by opposition, had only a small following locally. Rev. John Freeman, in answer to a clique of rowdies who

---

Critics of Los Angeles . . . abominate our architecture as the lowest form of high kitsch. . . . Having no schooling in architecture, I have always assumed they were right. But secretly I loved it all.   —Jack Smith, journalist

---

came to El Monte to disrupt a prayer meeting in 1853, placed a loaded pistol alongside his Bible and stationed his pistol-packing sons in the front pew. In 1869 the Baptists, who numbered 118 people in five churches in Southern California, convened in El Monte to adopt the New Hampshire Confession of Faith. A new congregation formed in Los Angeles began to conduct baptisms in the bed of the Los Angeles River. The first Baptist church in Los Angeles was built in 1881. California Baptists held their first state convention in 1892 and experienced an expansive period until 1920. At that time, the Southern California Baptist Convention was reorganized and revived. Baptists were shaken by the fundamentalist-modernist controversy that racked Protestantism in the 1920s, and after major organizational splits the movement declined in popularity. Billy Graham's Los Angeles religious crusade in 1949 had a tonic effect on Baptists and marked the beginning of a revival. By 1980, about 2 percent of religious adherents in Southern California were Baptists.

BARKER BROTHERS, upscale furniture chain, the oldest in Southern California. It was founded in 1880 by the Coloradan O. T. Barker and Otto Mueller, who had met a year earlier at a horticulture exhibit, when Los Angeles's population was 11,000. The first outlet was near Olvera Street. In 1926 the firm occupied a modern, imposing-looking 11-story showplace on W. 7th Street. In 1984 it abandoned the downtown area and expanded to 22 suburban stores. After a Wall Street takeover, the company faltered, filed for bankruptcy, and closed down in 1992.

BARLOW SANITARIUM, clinic for the county's indigent tuberculars, located in Chavez Ravine near Elysian Park. It was founded in 1902 when Isaac Lankershim sold 25 acres to Dr. Barlow for $7,000, forgiving $1,000 as a gift to the facility. The original buildings still stand.

BARNES, "PANCHO" [FLORENCE LEON-TINE LOEW] (D. 1975), adventurer, pilot, and rancher from San Marino. The estranged wife of a clergyman, Barnes acquired her nickname in 1927 as a gunrunner for Mexican revolutionaries. Her grandfather was the inventor Thaddeus S. C. Lowe. As a renowned pilot, Barnes appeared in movies about flying. In the 1940s and 1950s she established a 380-acre Antelope Valley dude ranch, which she called the Happy Bottom Riding Club. It was intended for the recreation of off-duty pilots stationed at Murdoc Army Air Base (now Edwards Air Force Base). The air force brass tried to close it down, citing it as a house of prostitution. Barnes sued for defamation and won an out-of-court settlement. The military finally put her out of business by co-opting her property for a runway. When she died alone of cancer in 1975, her body was found lying among her 55 dogs.

BARNSDALL, ALINE (1882–1946), theatrical impresario. Barnsdall was born to a wealthy Pennsylvania oil family. A theater enthusiast, she ran a professional company in Chicago. It was in that city that she heard a public address by Emma Goldman, the Russian-born anarchist, which influenced her thinking. Given to maverick ideas and bold political statements, she moved to Los Ange-

---

We were in the remote parts of the earth, on an almost desert coast, in a country where there is neither law nor gospel.
   —Richard Henry Dana, writer and seaman, recalling his visit to Los Angeles in 1835

---

les and built a billboard on her property that faced Vermont Avenue. On it she advertised her singular views to the motorists and pedestrians on the street below. During the 1932 Olympics, for example, the billboard implored the California governor to "Free Tom Mooney!" the labor leader imprisoned—falsely, Barnsdall believed—for a 1916 San Francisco bombing.

She continued her work as a theater impresario with producer Norman Bel Geddes and helped found the Hollywood Bowl, where she promoted the Easter sunrise concert. Although a freethinker, rather than a political radical, Barnsdall was tracked by the FBI for 27 years.

Her major legacy is Hollyhock House (1917–1920), a home on Olive Hill, in Hollywood, designed by architect Frank Lloyd Wright, whom she knew from her Chicago days and with whom she had an affair. Wright used Barnsdall's favorite flower as a design motif on exterior and interior surfaces of this nationally renowned architectural landmark. A theater designed for the property by Wright in 1916 was never built, owing to differences over the design between patron and architect. Barnsdall gifted the home and property to the city of Los Angeles in 1927.

BARNSDALL PARK, city-owned open space and cultural center in Hollywood. The facility is situated on land donated to the city by Aline Barnsdall, along with her home, Hollyhock House, designed by Frank Lloyd Wright. In keeping with the donor's wishes, the 11-acre preserve is devoted to a municipal art gallery and other cultural activities, and the house is preserved as a historic cultural monument.

BARRIO, Spanish word for "city ward" or "district," applied to Latino urban communities. The first such Los Angeles neighborhood was Sonoratown, near the Plaza, established in the 1850s. By 1940, most cities in the county had at least small barrios. East Los Angeles is clearly the largest in the metropolis—and in the United States—with Latinos making up over 90 percent of the population.

BARTLETT, DANA WEBSTER (1860–1942), preacher and settlement-house worker. Arriving from Maine in 1896, he settled in the slums around the Plaza and east of Alameda Street, determined to help the working poor. His base, the Bethlehem Institute, provided public baths, counseling, and social services for the poor. He worked with Mexican families in and around Sonoratown and the railroad yards. A passionate Los Angeles booster, Bartlett wrote *The Better City* (1907) during the City Beautiful movement early in the century. He later published a nature book, *The Bush Aflame* (1923).

BASEBALL, American pastime that cropped up locally in 1870. The first team was made up of high school girls. Other amateur groups were formed in private clubs, factories, schools, and colleges. In the 1880s a Saturday afternoon league was organized; it played in Agricultural (now Exposition) Park. In 1886 eastern professional teams began taking spring practice in Los Angeles, using 6th Street Park (Pershing Square) as a playing field. Louisville beat a local club that year. Phil Knell, by 1891 the greatest left-handed pitcher, got his start in Los Angeles. In 1892 the city entered a team in the California State Baseball League that ended the season having won 101 of 175 games.

Long before the Dodgers blew in from Brooklyn in 1958, the minor league had strong roots in Los Angeles. Founded in 1903, the Pacific Coast League (PCL) was minor in name only. Its clubs were drawing crowds of over 500,000 a year after the introduction of night games in the 1920s. The baseball season stretched from March to November, with 200 games a season—more than in the majors. The local PCL rivals were the Los Angeles Angels and Vernon Tigers. The former played at

Wrigley Field, at 41st Place and Avalon Boulevard, and the latter on a field in Vernon near Jack Doyle's saloon. In 1926 the Tigers moved to San Francisco. Soon, a Salt Lake City team moved to Los Angeles and was renamed the Hollywood Stars. Owned in part by motion picture notables, the Stars usually played in Wrigley Field, but in 1939 moved to Gilmore Stadium, adjacent to

---

I don't want to live here, but a stay here rather amuses me. It's a sort of crazy-sensible.

—D. H. Lawrence

Farmers Market in the Fairfax district. The team disbanded in 1957. The Angels, nicknamed the "Serifs," were a powerhouse in the 1920s and 1930s, with a .732 winning average in 1934. Arnold "Jigger" Statz played 18 seasons for the Angels, setting all-time records for most games played (2,790), most at bats, most hits, and most doubles, triples, and runs scored.

Eastern major league teams held spring training in Southern California and became a top drawing card for baseball fans. The Chicago Cubs practiced on Santa Catalina Island, the Pittsburgh Pirates in San Bernardino, and the Chicago White Sox in Pasadena. A separate nationwide Negro League was created for African American players, who were excluded from the majors by the color bar. Players from these teams sometimes came to Southern California; during the winter months they played pickup games against major league players wintering on their own in the Southland.

Today, of course, the Los Angeles Dodgers provide the county's major baseball excitement. On a nonprofessional level, the Little League is extremely active for youths, and colleges and universities, especially CSULB, CSUN, USC, and UCLA, have developed championship baseball teams while supplying the majors with key athletes. The related sport of softball is played in parks and playgrounds.

BASKETBALL is played locally by two professional teams, the Los Angeles Lakers and the Los Angeles Clippers; by several competitive National Collegiate Athletic Association (NCAA) teams; and at most high schools and innumerable playgrounds. The Lakers have won five National Bas-

ketball Association (NBA) championships (1981, 1983, 1984, 1986, 1989). At the university level, UCLA won 10 NCAA titles under the leadership of head coach John Wooden (1948–1975), more than any other school in the nation. It has also produced the most professional players. UCLA's all-time leading scorer, Kareem Abdul-Jabbar (formerly Lew Alcindor), played for the Lakers from 1975 until his retirement in 1988. In 1995, after a 20-year hiatus, UCLA was named the nation's number one college team and again captured the NCAA championship: led by their coach, Jim Harrick, the Bruins defeated Arkansas in the final game of the series. USC's basketball teams have won 14 Pacific Coast Conference championships. Long Beach State University and Pepperdine University are also active in men's basketball. Both UCLA and USC compete nationally in women's basketball as well. Local high schools have produced many college and professional players, and pickup games are played on hundreds of neighborhood playgrounds. The courts at Venice Beach attract players and spectators from all over the city.

BASS, CHARLOTTA SPEARS (1880?–1969), African American newspaper editor and civil rights activist who used the pages of the *California Eagle* (Los Angeles), which was owned by her husband, to crusade for racial justice. Bass was born in South Carolina, arriving in Los Angeles in 1910. She crusaded against the film *The Birth of a Nation* when it opened in Los Angeles in 1915, and battled the KKK in the 1920s. Bass took over management of the *Eagle* after her husband's death in 1934. A Re-

Charlotta Bass with Paul Robeson, 1949. Courtesy Dept. of Special Collections, University Research Library, UCLA.

publican, she supported Wendell Willkie in 1940, and in 1943 served on the Los Angeles County Grand Jury. After World War II her politics shifted to the left as she supported the Hollywood Ten and, in 1952, ran as the vice presidential candidate on the Independent Progressive Party ticket. Her memoir is entitled *Forty Years* (1960).

BAUM, L. FRANK (1856–1919), author of the utopian *Oz* books. A frequent visitor to Los Angeles, he took up residence there in 1909, building his estate, "Ozcot," on Cherokee, near Highland Avenue and Sunset Boulevard in Hollywood. He dedicated one volume of his series to fellow members of the Uplifters Club in Santa Monica Canyon. Literary historian Kevin Starr asserts that *The Wizard of Oz* is an archetypal Southern California story. During the 1950s Ozcot was demolished and replaced by an apartment complex.

BEACH BOYS, all-American Los Angeles rock group. Except for Alan Jardine, the brothers Brian, Carl, and Dennis Wilson and Mike Love were all Southern Californians. Their first recording was *Surfin' Safari* (1962), followed by others with both surfing and automobile themes. Wearing striped shirts and light trousers, they had a clean-cut, casual look. Their later songs, such as "Good Vibrations," retained their mainstream sound, but were more sophisticated.

BEACHES are a magnificent natural feature of Los Angeles County's 75-mile coastline. Beaches are created when rain washes the sand of coastal bluffs, hills, plains, and mountains into the sea, where the waves and currents distribute it along the coast. Beaches may appear empty of life, but actually they are populated by innumerable marine invertebrates and insects. Bivalve mollusks, crustaceans, and tube-building worms are common, with microscopic diatoms and zooplankton providing their food. Sand-burrowing flies and beetles are as natural to the environment as sunbathers. Gabrieleño Indians lived, fished, and hunted on or near the beaches. Until 1900 or so the beaches looked much the same as during prehistoric times.

The recreational development of beaches began around the turn of the century and has reached extraordinary levels. Los Angeles County has 25 distinct beaches, with ownership divided among state, county, municipal, and private jurisdictions. Owing to the construction of flood control dams and breakwaters, runoff has declined, halving the natural sand supply, and the beaches have become sand starved. New breakwaters and jetties have been constructed to divert sand from one place to another, but with only partial success.

Many beaches are public or have public access, but in some areas private property is so near the waterline that public access is virtually nonexistent. The largest state beach is Leo Carrillo State Beach, in northern Los Angeles County. The cities of Santa Monica, Los Angeles, Long Beach, Redondo Beach, Manhattan Beach, and Huntington Beach maintain their own beaches, realizing millions of dollars in revenue from a variety of sources such as parking fees, fairs, and other special attractions. Swimming is allowed at all 25 of the county beaches. Other activities include biking, boating,

Oceanfront property, Santa Monica, late 1800s.

Beach at Santa Monica, ca. 1910.
Pitt Collection.

camping, clamming, scuba diving, picnicking, volleyball, fishing, hiking, and surfing. Dockweiler State Beach in Playa del Rey is acknowledged to be the birthplace of the sport of hang gliding. The beaches express the hedonistic side of Southern California culture.

It was during the Boom of the Eighties that real estate promoters began touting the ocean as a selling point for homes. Hotel developers created seaside resorts that became popular tourist attractions. Since the 1920s movie people have built large beach homes and flocked to beach clubs from Malibu to Santa Monica. At the same time, young people created an outdoor subculture that scorned the adult conventions of urban life and celebrated the human body. This way of life, which was glorified by the music of the Beach Boys and the *Beach Party* films of the 1960s, is epitomized in the slogan "Life's a beach." It often involved the cult of surfing, a sport introduced from Hawaii in 1907 and popularized after World War II. Venice's Muscle Beach, famous for bodybuilders, attracts many aficionados. The only "clothing optional" beach advertised by the Visitors and Convention Bureau is Pirate's Cove, just north of Point Dume, though nudity is tolerated unofficially at Sacred Cove in Rancho Palos Verdes as well. The Venice–Santa Monica "boardwalk" has become a favorite strolling place for both tourists and Angelenos. Vendors, musicians, restaurants, and specialty shops line the beachfront stretch with its parallel bicycle path.

Pollution in Santa Monica Bay has, since early in the century, forced occasional closures of beaches, sometimes for months at a time. Los Angeles Hyperion sewage plant, oil refineries, and other industrial installations are among the major offenders. Awareness of the human and industrial threat to California beaches increased after the disastrous Santa Barbara oil spill of 1969. This led to passage of the Coastal Preservation Act of 1972, and creation of a coastal commission with local authority to control environmental degradation. In both 1989 and 1992, beaches had to be closed because of sewage spills. Another problem is the erosion of the bluffs, a natural process that is intensified by road building and housing development. Landslides along Pacific Coast Highway can be dramatic and lethal. The enormous numbers of beachgoers also have a tremendous impact on the environment. In 1988, 60 million people visited public beaches; half a million took to the beach on a single Sunday that August. There are only 14,500 parking places in beach lots, which means that on hot weekends thousands of cars inch along and fill the side streets of local communities. Santa Monica, with the most popular beaches, removes 1,500 tons of trash weekly. On a busy summer day as many as 300 lifeguards keep watch. In 1988 they rescued 5,000 swimmers.

BEACH PARTY FILMS, a series of seven movies made in the 1960s at Point Dume. These films portrayed teenage romance on the beaches of Southern California in a world undisturbed by parents, teachers, or other annoying realities. Frankie Avalon and Annette Funicello were the original mainstays of this fantasy world. The films were *Beach Party* (1963); *Muscle Beach Party,* which introduced Stevie Wonder (1964); *Bikini Beach* (1964); *Pajama Party* (1964); *Beach Blanket Bingo* (1965), generally considered the best of the series; *How to Stuff a Wild Bikini* (1965); and *Ghost in the Invisible Bikini* (1966).

BEALE, EDWARD FITZGERALD (1822–1893), federal official in the 1850s and 1860s. During the Mexican War, from 1846 to 1848, he served as a naval officer in Southern California. In the 1850s he was appointed U.S. Indian Affairs superintendent in the region and set about creating five small reservations, which he administered in a humane manner. The major one, Sebastian Reserve in El Tejón, was home to 2,500 Indians, who had some success growing farm crops. He was also asked to establish a wagon road along the 1,200 miles from Fort Tejón to New Mexico. Beale imported a herd of camels to handle the freight, but the project failed. He settled on a large ranch near the fort, and during the Lincoln administration served as surveyor general of California and Nevada. In the 1860s he was responsible for digging Beale's Cut through the San Fernando Mountains. His pick-and-shovel crew created this deep trench (still intact) to improve a turnpike connecting the Santa Clarita and the San Fernando valleys. Movie cowboys were often filmed spurring their horses on to make daring leaps across the great gap.

BEAT GENERATION, counterculture arts movement that began in San Francisco in the mid-1950s but had its innings in the coffeehouses of Venice. The "Beatniks" experimented with psychedelic drugs and alcohol and rejected Establishment fiction, poetry, painting, and sculpture. Their poetry readings and jazz attracted media attention. Poet Stuart Z. Perkoff and novelist Lawrence Lipton, a writer of popular detective stories and screenplays who hoped to be recognized as a poet and social critic, were the area's leading lights. Lipton's *The Holy Barbarians* (1959) is a memoir depicting the Venice cohort of the Beat generation.

BEAUDRY, PRUDENT (1818–1893), pioneer land developer and mayor of Los Angeles from 1874 to 1876. A Canadian by birth, Beaudry made a small fortune developing hillside lots downtown. He bought all the land on Bunker Hill for $51 in 1867 and piped water to its lots in the 1870s. During his term as mayor he pioneered welfare institutions, established hospitals, and fostered expansion of the city's water system.

BECHTEL CORPORATION (FORMERLY W. A. BECHTEL COMPANY, BECHTEL BROTHERS McCONE CORPORATION), a worldwide engineering and construction firm founded in 1898. It has maintained vital operations in Vernon and elsewhere in the region since the early 1940s. The company was a major contractor on Hoover Dam and designed hundreds of ships for the California Shipbuilding Corporation during the Second World War. The Vernon-based office was also involved in engineering and design for Southern California Edison in the 1960s, the Department of Defense, North American Rockwell at Seal Beach, and the Calabasas Park development on the Warner Ranch in 1963. It is strong in transportation, petroleum, space and defense, and environmental design.

BECKET, WELTON DAVID (1902–1969), architect whose firm designed the Music Center and Memorial Sports Arena. He created a master plan for UCLA and Century City and pioneered in the design of large shopping centers.

BEL-AIR, residential enclave in the Santa Monica Mountains west of Beverly Hills, founded by Alphonzo E. Bell in the 1920s. Its palatial homes are enhanced by huge pools, lavish gardens, and spectacular views of the city and the ocean. The community has no shopping area on the premises, and the only commercial enterprise is the Bel Air Hotel. The chaparral-covered slopes turn brown and dry in summer, posing a major fire hazard. On 6 November 1961 a wind-driven blaze destroyed $24 million worth of real estate. The 1990 population was 7,409.

Gateway to Bel-Air Estates. Photo by Leonard Pitt.

BELL, incorporated town about 6 miles south of downtown Los Angeles, founded by James George Bell, a cattle farmer from Kentucky, and his son, Alphonzo Bell. Originally called Obed, the town changed its name to Bell in 1898. Its population was 34,365 in 1990.

BELL, ALPHONZO E., SR. (1875–1947), farmer, oilman, and real estate developer. Bell was born in Los Angeles, graduated from Occidental College, and attended a theological seminary. In 1921, while digging a water well on his near-bankrupt 200-acre Santa Fe Springs ranch, he smelled gas and persuaded Standard Oil to drill for petroleum. A fountain of crude erupted in what turned out to be one of the most lucrative oil fields in the country. It also made Bell one of the wealthiest men in California: for some years the black gold earned him up to $300,000 *monthly.* He parlayed his profits into an even bigger fortune by developing Bel-Air, the Bel-Air Bay and Country Clubs, and properties in Castellamare, Miramar, and Eastridge. He was also a tennis champion, civic and religious leader, and philanthropist. His son, Alphonzo E. Bell Jr., was elected to the U.S. Congress from the Westside.

BELL, HORACE (1830–1918), local-color writer, adventurer, and humorist from Indiana who, after a stint in the gold fields, settled in Los Angeles in 1852. He soon left, first to seek adventure in Central America with journalist and adventurer William Walker, then to serve as a Union army scout in the Civil War. Returning to Los Angeles, Bell became a lawyer and edited the satirical paper *Porcupine.* In the 1860s he became the city's first subdivider by buying and selling town lots. His book *Reminiscences of a Ranger* (1881) is the first memorable piece of literature written about Southern California. It was followed by a posthumous collection, *On the Old West Coast* (1930). The local history presented in these works should be taken with a grain of salt, since Bell deliberately distorted real events for literary effect.

BELLA UNION HOTEL, located on Main Street, was the first and best Yankee-era hotel before being surpassed by the Pico House in 1870. Built in 1850 and owned by John Rains, the hotel was a center of social life. Bachelors took up residence in the rooms, businessmen made deals in the bar, weddings were celebrated in the dining hall, and politicians delivered orations from the iron balustrade of the front balcony.

Bella Union Hotel. Courtesy Robert Weinstein Collection.

BELLFLOWER, independent city 17 miles southeast of Los Angeles. It originated in 1905 on what was the Bixby family's Somerset Ranch, named for the Somerset Red Car—the first to arrive there. That name was rejected by the U.S. Post Office because a town named Somerset already existed in Colorado. Today's name comes from a variety of apple that was grown in the area around 1910. Now a residential and metropolitan region, Bellflower had a population of 61,815 in 1990.

BELL GARDENS, independent city 8.5 miles southeast of downtown Los Angeles. Incorporated in 1961, Bell Gardens was originally part of Rancho San Antonio, granted to Antonio María Lugo, a Spanish soldier. In the 1930s the area was called

Horace Bell. Courtesy Robert Weinstein Collection.

"Billy Goat Acres," a derisive reference to the many "Okies" who settled there during the Great Depression. Japanese farmers maintained extensive vegetable farms there during the same era. Its population of 42,355 in 1990 consisted mostly of blue-collar Latino families. After a recall campaign and a hotly contested election involving rent control, zoning, police services, term limitations, and child care issues, a Latino majority was established on the five-member city council.

BELMONT SHORES, residential and commercial section of Long Beach along Alamitos Bay. The town was established and house lots first sold in the 1920s, on 2 million cubic yards of sand dredged from the bay. The original Belmont Pier, a wooden structure built in 1915, was replaced in 1976 by a 1,400-foot concrete pier that is used for sport fishing.

BELVEDERE GARDENS, East Los Angeles neighborhood that emerged after 1910. By the late 1920s it was home to some 30,000 Mexicans, making it the most densely populated Latino neighborhood in the county to that time. The population of this unincorporated area south of City Terrace was 62,986 in 1991.

BENEDICT CANYON, ravine in the Hollywood Hills named by Edson A. Benedict, a storekeeper, who filed a claim to the canyon land in 1868. It was part of Rancho de las Aguas ("Ranch of the Waters"), which also included present-day Beverly Hills.

BERMAN, WALLACE ("WALLY") (1926–1976), Beat generation guru. Berman was raised in the Fairfax district in a middle-class Jewish home where the struggling young Sammy Davis Jr. was a boarder. He was, together with Ed Kienholz, a founder of the controversial Ferus Gallery. Convicted for displaying lewd art there in 1957, he scrawled on the courtroom blackboard, "There is no justice, only revenge." He moved to San Francisco, where he edited the underground magazine *Semina,* created collages, assemblages, and drawings, and wrote poetry. His friends included actors James Dean and Dennis Hopper (who gave Berman a bit part in the film *Easy Rider*) and poets George Herms and Hal Glicksman. A well-known member of the drug and counterculture movements, Berman is pictured on the cover of the Beatles' classic *Sgt. Pepper's Lonely Hearts Club Band* album. In 1961 he returned to Los Angeles, which he once called "the city of degenerate angels." Ironically, he was struck and killed near his Topanga Canyon home by a motorcyclist who was on drugs.

BERNARDI, ERNANI (1911–), former city council member, representing the 7th District in the San Fernando Valley. The Illinois native played saxophone with Benny Goodman, Tommy Dorsey, and Bob Crosby before coming to Southern California in 1939 with Kay Kyser's "Kollege of Musical Knowledge." After settling in Van Nuys he became a building contractor and sat on the city council for the first time in 1961. A Democrat, Bernardi was noted for his fiscal conservatism and hostility to big government. A lawsuit instituted by him against the Community Redevelopment Agency in 1977 capped the spending powers of the giant downtown building agency. He chose not to run again in 1993.

BERNSON, HAL (1930–), Los Angeles City Council member. He was born in Los Angeles in 1930, graduated from Roosevelt High, attended Los Angeles City College, served in the U.S. Navy, and worked in the retail clothing business for 30 years. He has lived in the San Fernando Valley since 1957. A conservative Republican, Bernson has represented the Valley's 12th District since 1979. He was active in BUSTOP, a movement to end busing for school integration, and is a member of the advisory board of the American Jewish Committee. On the council he helped to establish Stoney Point climbers' park, wrote landmark legislation to rehabilitate seismically unsafe buildings, and has backed the Porter Ranch project in his district.

BERRY, DANIEL M. (D. 1887), cofounder of the Indiana Colony and the town of Pasadena. He was greatly influenced by Charles Nordhoff's *California for Health, Pleasure, and Residence* (1872). When he and his party of 31 Hoosiers arrived in 1873 at Los Angeles, a *pueblo* of 5,700 people, they put up at the new Pico House. A widower, schoolteacher, and newspaper man, Berry was described as a "slender, pale, weak-looking, round-shouldered man, with a stove-pipe hat . . . a tender-foot." He and his fellow Indianans were captivated by Rancho San Pascual, at the foot of the San Gabriel Mountains along the Arroyo Seco, where they bought land. They nearly called the area Hoosier, but switched to the Chippewa Indian word *pasadena,* meaning "crown or key of the valley." Berry developed land and sold real estate throughout Los Angeles. Although the Indiana Colony was a financial failure, Pasadena prospered—but without Berry. He soon resumed his career in journalism, editing the Los Angeles *Daily Commercial* and later the *Herald,* and settled in San Fernando, where he died.

BET TZEDEK (THE HOUSE OF JUSTICE), nonprofit legal assistance service established in 1974 as a storefront operation, with legal work provided by volunteers. Two years later the Jewish Federation Council stepped in and donated $23,000 in seed money. It ministers not only to elderly and poor Jews, but to anyone in need, regardless of race, religion, or ethnic background. The most common cases involve equity fraud, tenant rights, nursing care establishments, and consumer protection. One of the largest funders is the State Bar Legal Service Trust Fund. In the first 20 years of its existence, Bet Tzedek handled 80,000 cases.

BEVERAGE INDUSTRY quenches the thirst of the 10.5 million people of the metropolis with scores of beer and soft drink facilities. With even greater brewing capacity than St. Louis or Milwaukee, Los Angeles is heir to the title "Beer Capital of the World." Brewery locations are dictated by brewery needs: a great deal of water, a railroad siding for handling barley and other ingredients, and truck-loading docks. Breweries have been located on North Main Street in downtown since the last century. Anheuser-Busch has its facility (one of 12 nationwide) on 51 acres in the San Fernando Valley. Completed in 1954 and greatly expanded in 1982, it employs 800 workers and produces 145 million cases of beer annually. It uses the most modern technology to conserve water and maintain air quality. The Joseph Schlitz Brewing Company, Miller Brewing in Azusa, and Pabst, a long-time tenant on North Main Street, are other large breweries in the county. Soft drink plants are also abundant. Pepsi-Cola Bottling Company employs 800 workers in its plants in Torrance, Baldwin Park, and Buena Park. Coca-Cola Company, bottlers of Coke, Tab, Fresca, Bubble-Up, Canada Dry, and Arrowhead, has a streamlined-looking plant on Central Avenue that was designed to resemble an ocean liner, with another branch plant in Downey.

BEVERLY CREST, area in the city of Los Angeles, on Beverly Crest Drive between Coldwater Canyon and the Trousdale Estates area of Beverly Hills. The hillside development with its panoramic views was established by developer George Read, who opened a 250-lot subdivision. In 1990 the area's average household income of $195,119 was the highest in the city of Los Angeles.

BEVERLY GARDENS, public park flanking Santa Monica Boulevard in Beverly Hills. It is renowned for its gardens, shaded pathways, fountain, and three stately churches: Catholic Good Shepherd, All Saints' Episcopal, and Beverly Hills Community Presbyterian. The green oasis was dedicated in the 1920s on property belonging to Rodeo Land and Water Company. Over the years, celebrity watchers have spotted many movie figures attending services on Sunday mornings.

BEVERLY GLEN, canyon community in the Santa Monica Mountains. Part of the city of Los Angeles, it lies above Bel-Air Estates and Beverly Hills along Beverly Glen Boulevard, an artery connecting Sunset Boulevard and the San Fernando Valley. Residential development began in the 1920s. Quito Lane, a sparsely populated cul-de-sac in Beverly Glen Canyon, was the subject of an appreciative book, *My Urban Wilderness in the Hollywood Hills* (1983), by the late Richard Lillard, professor of English at Cal State Los Angeles, who lived there in the 1970s and 1980s.

BEVERLY HILLS, independent city 10 miles west of downtown Los Angeles and entirely surrounded by Los Angeles. While not directly settled by Indians, the area was familiar to the native Tongva (Gabrieleño) people. In prehistoric times, abundant waters flowed out of Coldwater and Benedict Canyons during rainy seasons, creating lakes and

Beverly Hills Civic Center, 1995. Photo by Leonard Pitt.

swamps throughout the plains area below. The Portolá expedition marched through the area in 1769,
crossing dry streambeds lined with sycamores, and
skirting *cienegas* (swamps). They spent the night
of 3 August 1769 at the "Spring of the Alders of Es-
tevan," probably near today's La Cienega and
Wilshire Boulevards.

The area's first settler was María Rita Valdez de
Villa, an African American who was granted a
4,500-acre rancho, Rodeo de las Aguas ("Gathering of the Waters"). Arriving sometime before
1822, she lived in an adobe near today's Sunset
Boulevard and Alpine Drive. In 1836, her home had
29 residents. The main family occupation was
tending horses and cattle. For years María Rita
fought a running battle over water rights and cattle
ownership with a kinsman named Luciano. In 1844
the Los Angeles *ayuntamiento* decreed that she pay
Luciano a nominal sum; in return, he was to end
his harassment.

In 1854 de Villa sold the rancho for $3,000 to
Maj. Henry Hancock and Benjamin D. Wilson,
who subdivided portions of it. At various times,
new pioneers grew wheat, beans, and other vegetables, raised sheep and bees, planted walnut
trees, and pumped oil. In 1869 the "Town of Santa
Maria," a 36-block village surrounded by 75-acre
farm lots, was laid out in the vicinity. During the
Boom of the Eighties promoters planned a town
they called Morocco, which never materialized.
Other names applied to the area at one time or another were San Antonio, Villa Ranch, and Ham-
mel and Denker Ranch.

In 1906, Burton E. Green, a real estate man
from Beverly Farms, Massachusetts, and head of
Rodeo Land and Water Company, acquired part
of the former rancho and founded the town of
Beverly. A year later the name was changed to Beverly Hills. The Beverly Hills Hotel, built in the
middle of bean and grain fields in 1911–1912, immediately became a chic meeting place for film
people. When movie stars Douglas Fairbanks and
Mary Pickford chose to enlarge and live in what
was originally a hunting lodge on a picturesque
hillside lot in Beverly Hills, many in the film industry quickly followed their example, among
them Charlie Chaplin, Gloria Swanson, Will
Rogers, Charlie Ruggles, Fredric March, and
Harold Lloyd.

The city is noted for strict zoning, careful planning, and an absence of slums. Curb parking, real
estate sale signs, and billboards are closely regu-

lated. Utility poles are set back in alleys. Curbside
trees are planted and maintained by the city. Beverly Hills' distinctive civic center was elegantly reconstructed (1981–1982), at a cost of $110 million,
in accordance with plans developed by architect
Charles Moore. The business district, a triangle on
the map, features internationally known department stores, luxurious hotels, and offices of major
corporations and lending institutions. Rodeo
Drive's pricey boutiques attract wealthy customers
and window shoppers from all nations.

Beverly Hills boasts some of the most lavish and
costly residences in the nation. The most palatial
homes are on the hilly north side of town. Maps
locating movie stars' homes (both accurate and
inaccurate) have been a staple item in the tourist
trade since the 1930s, and are hawked at curbside
along Sunset Boulevard. Less pretentious dwellings
occupy the city's southern section. Surprisingly,
more than half of the city's housing units are
apartments. The population has hovered around
32,000 for the last two censuses, although the daytime population sometimes reaches 200,000.

In 1982 shoppers spent $662 million in Beverly
Hills—$143 million for clothing, $72 million for
cars, and $46 million for restaurant meals. More
books per capita are sold here than in any other
city in the world. It also has the most physicians
per capita of any city—550 medical doctors, or one
for every 60 residents (the U.S. average is one for
every 612). It also has 250 psychiatrists and 110 psy-
chologists—one for every 90 or so inhabitants.

BEVERLY HILLS HOTEL, famous lodging
house on Sunset Boulevard. Constructed in 1911–
1912 by Burton Green on 12 acres of land and at
a cost of $500,000, it is named for Green's home
in Beverly Farms, Massachusetts. The huge pink
Mission Revival–style structure originally had 325
rooms, as well as bungalows, gardens, pools, and
restaurants, including the famous watering hole,
the Polo Lounge. When it opened in 1912, the
"Pink Palace" was still surrounded by lima bean
fields. It soon attracted the likes of W. C. Fields,
John Barrymore, Gene Fowler, and Will Rogers,
who descended from their hillside homes to gather
in the lobby and bar. It continued to cater to luminaries during Hollywood's most glamorous
years. Howard Hughes paid $350,000 for the
year-round rental of Bungalow Three. In the
1940s the hotel underwent an important renovation under the supervision of architect Paul

Beverly Hills Hotel. Underwood Photo Archives, San Francisco.

Williams, who created the hotel's famous pink-and-green motif. In the 1950s a new east wing was built with New Orleans–style balconies. The latest owner, Muda Hassanal Bolkiah, sultan of Brunei (said to be the richest man in the world), purchased the hotel in 1987 for $187 million. After two years of planning, he shut the hotel down in 1992 for a major remodel, involving an additional $100 million, that included enlarging rooms and reducing their number from 252 (from a previous remodel) to 194. The festive reopening took place in 1995.

BEVERLY WILSHIRE HOTEL, rendezvous for affluent tourists and Hollywood notables since its opening in 1928. The striking façade with its arched openings and low-relief baroque ornamentation shows an Italian influence. A tradition of elegance was established by hotelier Hernando Courtright, whose family owned the property. Sold to a Hong Kong investment firm in 1985, it has been renamed the Regent Beverly Wilshire Hotel.

BEVERLYWOOD, incorporated residential community within the city of Los Angeles, south of Pico Boulevard between Beverly and Beverwil Drives, containing 1,370 homes. The community was incorporated in 1940. As a condition of home ownership, buyers had to join a homeowners' association, one of the first in the nation. Its purpose was to enforce conditions established by deed and conveyance regulations.

Beverly Wilshire Hotel. Courtesy Regent Beverly Wilshire Hotel.

BEYOND BAROQUE, nonprofit arts center in Venice. Founded as a literary magazine by George Drury Smith in 1968, the enterprise soon developed into a workshop and performance theater, and in 1972 moved to the two-story Venice City Hall, built in 1907. The facility conducts free poetry workshops, poetry readings, and performance art events. The city of Los Angeles allows Beyond Baroque management free tenancy in exchange for building maintenance. The center has a $200,000 annual budget, with funds from government grants, corporate and private foundations, and individual donations.

BICYCLES, popular since the 19th century, have had to fight cars for their place in the sun. The General Plan of the city of Los Angeles proposes 600 miles of bikeways along city streets, public utility rights-of-way, flood control channels, and other public property. The 19-mile coastal bikeway from Temescal Canyon to Palos Verdes Peninsula is nearly completed. Two other sites with off-street paths are in the Sepulveda Dam Basin and Tujunga Wash. A bicycle advisory committee appointed by the mayor works to improve conditions for bicyclists. Los Angeles bike owners must have a license.

"BIG FIVE" FILM STUDIOS. *See* Metro-Goldwyn-Mayer; Paramount Pictures Corporation; RKO Radio Pictures; 20th Century–Fox Studio; Warner Brothers Studio; Movie studios

BIG RED CARS. *See* Pacific Electric Railway Company

BIG TUJUNGA CANYON, steep gorge in the San Gabriel Mountains draining 87 square miles of upland country. The name is probably from an Indian word, *ti'anga* (mountain range). In much of the 19th century and earlier, grizzly bears roamed the area. Beginning in the 1870s a wagon road carried hunters, cowboys, outlaws, and prospectors into "Big T," some of whom discovered gold in 1889. The region's first known settler, in 1880, was the rancher José Ybarra. Winter rainwaters often raged down a "wash" onto the lowlands that now compose Pacoima, Arleta, Panorama City, Sepulveda, and North Hills. Big Tujunga Dam, completed in 1931 and maintained by the Los Angeles County Flood Control District, now tames the runoff. "Big T" has been ravaged by fire on numerous occasions.

BILINGUAL EDUCATION. *See* Education, bilingual

BILLBOARD REGULATION resulted from a 1960s struggle between environmentalists and planners. Restrictions vary from one jurisdiction to the next. Beverly Hills, Santa Monica, and Claremont have attacked "visual pollution" with stringent regulations. The county, in contrast, has quite lenient rules for unincorporated territory. The colorful and numerous signs advertising records and movies along the Sunset Strip in the city of West Hollywood are an integral feature of the cityscape. Since 1986 the city of Los Angeles has had stricter regulations than the county. Regulating signs that "constitute a hazard to the safe and efficient operation of a vehicle," its laws provide for a 600-foot interval between signs, protection for private homes from infringement, and use of the roof line as a maximum height.

East Side Club, a bicycling group in Boyle Heights, ca. 1896. Courtesy Henry E. Huntington Library.

Billboards on Sunset Strip. Photo by Michael Krakowiak/ Marni Pitt.

These laws apply only to new signs, not old ones, however, so billboards are still numerous in many places.

BILTMORE HOTEL, largest hotel in Los Angeles. This downtown landmark, built on a strategic location overlooking Pershing Square at a cost of $10 million, was opened in 1923 with 1,500 rooms. Presidents Franklin D. Roosevelt, Harry Truman, John

F. Kennedy, Lyndon Johnson, Gerald Ford, Jimmy Carter, and Ronald Reagan slept there. Royalty—including Queen Beatrix of the Netherlands and her husband, Prince Claus, and the Duke and Duchess of York—stop by from time to time. The 1960 Democratic National Convention, which nominated John Kennedy for president, was held there. During World War II the Biltmore was reserved mainly for military personnel. The Academy of Motion Picture Arts and Sciences has held some of its awards ceremonies there. One guest, Thelma Becker, a prominent figure in dress manufacturing, checked in in 1940 and was still there in 1988.

The three towers facing the park, with their reddish brick, cream-colored stone, and terra cotta roof, reflect a Spanish-Italian renaissance architectural style. The 1,700-seat Biltmore Theater (now defunct) was for many years the city's premiere venue for drama. The hotel has been a location site for over 250 TV shows and motion pictures, including *Chinatown, A Star Is Born,* and *Beverly Hills Cop.* In 1987–1988 the entire building underwent a $40 million face-lift that restored much of its original 1920s elegance. The main entrance has been shifted to Grand Avenue.

BIRDS inhabit the county in surprisingly large numbers. Of the approximately 9,500 species worldwide, some 450 species have been identified in Los Angeles County or off its coast. Half of these are migratory, flying north in spring and south in winter along the Pacific Flyway, a huge avian path.

Local seabirds live on the water but breed on offshore islands. Gulls, including the California, herring, and ring-billed, are among the most common local varieties, soaring and swooping into the water to catch fish, or loitering on the sand near the water's edge. Many spend winters locally, although only the western gull lives in the area. Ducks, once prevalent in the wetlands where they bred, and geese still skim the surface of some of the county's rapidly disappearing marshlands, reservoirs, and real and artificial lakes.

The perching birds—pigeons, larks, jays, crows, sparrows, and mourning doves—exist in the greatest numbers. The night-singing northern mockingbird, the Brewer's blackbird, and the scrub jay are among the most common local varieties. Various species of hummingbird hover and flit, most of them migratory, visiting the area for different lengths of time.

The county's most common birds of prey are the

Biltmore Hotel. Photo by Michael Krakowiak/Marni Pitt.

red-tailed hawk, great horned owl, golden eagle, and peregrine falcon. Naturalists attempted in the 1980s to establish falcons on high-rise buildings, with the hope that the predators would control the pigeon population. Of 1,000 pairs of eagles in all of California, only six pairs are known to live in the Los Angeles area, in the western end of the San Fernando Valley. They are the biggest birds in the region, with a wingspan of more than 6 feet. Scientists have made a concerted effort to save and increase the tiny stock of surviving California condors. Although these efforts have borne some fruit, attempts to return breeding pairs to the wild have had limited success.

The Audubon Society lists several prime bird-watching spots: Placerita Canyon, in the Santa Clarita Valley (for hawks, wrens, jays, finches, and bluebirds); Big Sycamore Canyon (orioles, goldfinches, flycatchers, and sparrows); Ballona Creek (cormorants, owls, and migrating ducks and geese); and Little Rock, in the Antelope Valley (thrashers, falcons, larks, and plovers).

BISCAILUZ, EUGENE WARREN (1883–1969), sheriff of Los Angeles County. Biscailuz was born in Los Angeles and attended USC's law school. Entering law enforcement in 1907, he rose through the ranks of the sheriff's department to become sheriff in 1932. He supervised 3,300 men when he retired in 1958. During his tenure Biscailuz realized a long-held goal of establishing an "honor rancho" at Castaic for juvenile offenders. A noted horseman and fancier of silver saddles, he was consistently a featured attraction at civic parades and festivals. Although the colorful Biscailuz identified with the Hispanic origins of California, in fact his father was of French Basque heritage and his mother was a Yankee. He was an Episcopalian and a member of the exclusive Jonathan Club.

BIXBY FAMILY, Yankee pioneers who arrived in the 1850s from Maine and acquired significant ranchlands in Los Angeles, San Luis Obispo, Monterey, and Orange Counties. The brothers Llewellyn, Amasa, and Jotham Bixby raised sheep, horses, and cattle, and acted occasionally as partners to I. W. Hellman. The city of Long Beach was laid out in 1880 on part of their property, Cerritos Rancho. In the 20th century, when the Bixbys were the largest landholders in the Los Angeles area, oil was discovered on their property at Signal Hill. Preserved ranch houses at Los Alamitos and Los Cer-

ritos in the Long Beach area, now open to the public, belonged to them. Sarah Bixby Smith, Llewellyn's daughter, wrote a delightful memoir of the early years of American rule, entitled *Adobe Days* (1925). Another family member, Susanna Bryant Dakin, produced a biographical sketch, *A Scotch Paisano: Hugo Reid's Life in California, 1832–1852, Derived from His Correspondence* (1939), with revealing insights into the Mexican era.

BLACK DAHLIA MURDER CASE, sensational homicide of aspiring actress Elizabeth Ann Short, nicknamed the Black Dahlia because of her fondness for dahlias and black dresses. Her severed body was found in the Crenshaw district on 15 January 1947. Over 500 people have "confessed" to the infamous crime, but the file remains open. The movies *Who Is the Black Dahlia?* (1975) and *True Confessions* (1981) are based on the case.

BLOCK, SHERMAN (1924–), sheriff of Los Angeles since 1982. Born in Chicago, he served in World War II under General Patton and moved to Los Angeles in 1953. He entered the sheriff's department in 1956 and became a protégé of Peter Pitchess, sheriff from 1959 to 1982. In 1962, Block made history by arresting stand-up comedian Lenny Bruce on an obscenity charge at the Trou-

Sheriff Sherman Block. Courtesy Los Angeles County Sheriff's Dept.

badour nightclub in West Hollywood. He was acting on the orders of his superiors; personally, he regarded the comic as a brilliant social commentator. Teased with the nickname "Sergeant Baldy," Block sometimes wore a toupée to cover his bald spot and avoid being recognized during undercover work. Low-key and self-effacing, he is nevertheless considered a shrewd media user and an able politician. He has managed to increase his department's budget from $345 million to $1.1 billion. In 1986 he won election with 85 percent of the vote, and in 1990 with 67 percent. Whereas LAPD chief Daryl Gates succumbed to charges of condoning police brutality, Block managed to finesse serious complaints of excessive use of force in the sheriff's department.

BLUE LINE, light-rail transit line running on the 22-mile corridor from Los Angeles to Long Beach. Operated by the Metropolitan Transportation Authority, it was the first of several lines—including

---

The thing a future historian will note about 20th-century America is immigration . . . and Los Angeles is the great place to look at what this America . . . will be.

—David Rieff, writer

---

the Green Line, Red Line, and Metrolink—that will eventually radiate throughout the Los Angeles Basin. The Blue Line opened in July 1990 and by 1995 was carrying 35,000 passengers daily, with trains running every 6–10 minutes during rush hour, and every 12–20 minutes at other times. Tickets cost $1.10. The Metro Blue Line offers connections with the Metro Green Line.

B'NAI B'RITH TEMPLE, first synagogue in Los Angeles, built at Broadway between 2nd and 3rd Streets in 1872. I. W. Hellman was the first president of the congregation, which included Harris and Joseph Newmark, early Jewish Los Angeles pioneers. The inaugural services in the new Gothic-style temple (designed by Ezra F. Kysor) were led by Abraham Wolf Edelman, the city's first rabbi, who also led the initial B'nai B'rith congregation, established in 1862. B'nai B'rith moved to a new build-

ing at Hope and 9th in 1894, and to its third (and current) site, on Wilshire Boulevard, in the 1920s. B'nai B'rith means "children of the covenant."

BOARD OF HARBOR COMMISSIONERS OF LOS ANGELES. *See* Los Angeles Harbor Department

BOARD OF SUPERVISORS, LOS ANGELES COUNTY. *See* Los Angeles County Board of Supervisors

BOARD OF WATER AND POWER COMMISSIONERS. *See* Los Angeles Department of Water and Power

BOBCAT *(LYNX RUFOUS)*, relatively small carnivore with a short tail, pointed ears, and spotted coat, also known as a lynx or wildcat. It ranges through various local environments from desert floor to timbered mountains. Primarily nocturnal, it feeds on rabbits, rodents, and other small mammals.

BODDY, MANCHESTER (1891–1967), newspaper publisher and editor. Born in Washington, D.C., in the 1920s he became a columnist and editorial writer for the *Los Angeles Daily News,* and later bought and published that paper. During the Great Depression Boddy at first supported the utopian political movement known as Technocracy, but later shifted his allegiance to Franklin Roosevelt's New Deal. He became a radio and TV commentator and Democratic committeeman. An avid horticulturalist, Boddy planted an extensive camellia garden with tens of thousands of plants on his estate, "Rancho del Descanso," in La Cañada Flintridge. After his death the estate was bought by the county and opened to the public as Descanso Gardens, and is now supported by a private foundation.

BOGARDUS, EMORY S., sociologist and director of the School of Social Welfare at USC. He conducted pioneer studies of Mexican immigration, labor, education, and settlement patterns in the Southwest from around 1913 to the 1930s.

BOLLENS, JOHN C[ONSTANTIUS] (1920–1983), UCLA political scientist. Born in Pittsburgh, with a doctorate from the University of Minnesota, his association with UCLA began in

1950. He authored 26 books on various aspects of local government, including a profile of Mayor Sam Yorty. Bollens served as a county civil service commissioner, a city zoning commissioner, and a member of a Los Angeles charter reform group appointed by Yorty.

BONELLI, WILLIAM ("BIG BILL") GEORGE (1895–1968), powerful politician accused of influence peddling. He started as a progressive politician in the 1920s, was elected to the city council and appointed by Gov. Frank F. Merriam to the State Board of Equalization in 1938. In 1951 Bonelli was grilled by the Kefauver crime committee of the U.S. Senate for alleged connections with organized crime, but used his charm and intelligence to circumvent the questioning. Through much of his career he was a crony of Harry Chandler of the *Los Angeles Times.* When Buffy Chandler took over operation of the *Times*-owned *Los Angeles Mirror* she gave the go-ahead for an exposé on "Big Bill." In October 1953 the *Mirror* ran the most explosive investigative series ever seen in Los Angeles publishing. In the series of five articles by reporter Art White, Bonelli was alleged to have developed a system of kickbacks in the sale of liquor licenses and run a "B-girl" operation among downtown saloons. An enraged Bonelli retaliated by publishing *Billion Dollar Blackjack: The Story of Corruption and the Los Angeles Times* (1954), a book ghost-written by journalist Leo Katcher. It presented a picture of a scheming Chandler family managing a half-billion-dollar empire with a $50 million yearly income and manipulating businesses and government officials all over the city. Threatened with an indictment, he fled to Mexico, where he died 15 years later.

BONTEMPS, ARNA WENDELL (1902–1973), African American writer who grew up in "Mudtown" (Watts) and evokes the life of the Los Angeles ghetto in the novel *Anyplace but Here* (1966).

BOOK COLLECTING, PUBLISHING, AND SELLING. Los Angeles has been a major center for the book trade since the early part of the century. According to a recent U.S. Department of Commerce report, residents of the Los Angeles–Long Beach area spend an average of $256 million on books annually. In 1984 an estimated $176 million worth of books were sold in Los Angeles alone, a figure topped only by sales in New York City. Fowler Brothers, established in 1888, was Los Angeles's oldest book store until it closed its doors in 1994; that distinction then went to Dawson's Bookshop on Larchmont Boulevard.

The book trade originated with the establishment of large private collections and libraries. With unlimited money at their disposal, wealthy individuals like Henry E. Huntington, William Andrews Clark Jr., and Estelle Doheny ransacked the world for rare books and manuscripts. They specialized in select themes: Spanish missions, Hispanic culture, English and Catholic culture, etc. Robert C. Cowan, scouting for Clark, and Henry Raup Wagner, for Huntington, established high standards for the pastime of book collecting. The most important book club, the Zamorano, was established in 1928. Independent scholars and journalists such as Phil Townsend Hanna, Paul Jordan-Smith, W. W. Robinson, and Carey McWilliams also pursued this cultural activity, as did wealthy movie people, among them Rudolph Valentino, Edward Everett Horton, and Cecil B. De Mille.

Book collecting and bookselling were associated with fine printing as well. Publishing was carried out not only by commercial publishers, but also by rare book dealers such as Jake Zeitlin, who set exacting standards. The Ward Ritchie Press was a nationally honored, distinguished small press. Ernest Dawson, Arthur Clark, and Zeitlin all created small runs of elegant special editions. Moreover, as with the coffeehouses of 18th-century England, the shops of these entrepreneurs became the gathering places of Los Angeles literati.

BOOM OF THE EIGHTIES, wildest and most memorable real estate boom in Southern California, lasting from 1886 to 1888, with its peak in 1887. It was sparked in March 1886 by the completion of the Santa Fe Railroad, which touched off a rate war with the Southern Pacific. Rail fares from the Midwest plummeted. Trains, sometimes as many as four daily, brought a flood of 120,000 people to Los Angeles. Fly-by-night operators handing out pictorial brochures with fanciful scenic views and imaginative names promoted new towns and tracts. An estimated 2,000 real estate agents sold off the old ranchos by promoting the blue ocean, the healthful breezes, the cheapness of land, the fertility of the soil, and the easy access to rail and water transportation. A brochure for several thousand lots in "Chicago Park," south of Monrovia, depicted steamers navigating the San Gabriel River.

Bird's-eye view of Los Angeles in 1887. Courtesy Robert Weinstein Collection.

With brass bands, free lunches, and excursion trains as bait, the inventive sales agents organized auctions and sales all over Southern California, hawking hundreds of tracts and establishing scores of towns.

Before the madness started, the total tax assessment of Los Angeles, city and county, was about $3 million. It jumped to $40 million in March 1886 and to $103 million by 1888. The railroad companies sited many towns. The Santa Fe laid out 25 towns just on the 37 miles of the eastern part of the county. Over 100 towns were mapped in the county, two-thirds of which disappeared in the planning stage. The boom's collapse left real estate flags fluttering uselessly all over the county and drove thousands of disheartened would-be settlers out of town; it also left a lasting residue of irrigation districts, railroad spurs, hotels, schools, colleges, and churches. It certainly hastened the "Americanization" of Los Angeles, and it established boosterism as a permanent feature of the cultural landscape. Interestingly, the banks survived

the bust, proving that the financial basis of the local agricultural economy remained sound.

Cities, towns, tracts, shopping centers, and neighborhoods dating from the Boom of the Eighties are still with us, if sometimes only in name. Among them are Alhambra, Arcadia, Avalon, Azusa, Belvedere, Buena Park, Burbank, Chino, Claremont, Corona, Covina, Cucamonga, Eagle Rock, Fullerton, Glendora, Hawthorne, Hollywood, Inglewood, La Verne, Monrovia, Puente, Redondo Beach, Rialto, Rivera, San Dimas, Sawtelle, Sierra Madre, South Pasadena, Sunland, Tujunga, Verdugo Hills, Vernon, Watts, and Whittier.

BOOM OF THE TWENTIES, dramatic upsurge in population and real estate growth in Southern California during the 1920s. For the first time, Easterners flocked to Los Angeles by car instead of by train. The completion of transcontinental highways, like completion of the rail lines from the Midwest in the 19th century, made access to the region easy. At the peak of land sales in 1923,

11,000 acres were subdivided, over 1,000 tracts put up for sale in the city, and hundreds of mercantile buildings and 25,000 one- and two-family dwellings erected. Much of the real estate activity was on speculation; humorist Will Rogers remarked that many lots were put through escrow with multiple copies of deeds because each purchaser "wouldn't have time to read it in the ten minutes he owned the lot." Not only real estate sales, as in the 1880s, but also oil speculation and movie production fueled growth. Nor was the influx altogether spontaneous or random: it was finely orchestrated by the All Year Club of Southern California, which promoted the region as a haven for summer tourism. Between 1920 and 1930 the city's population increased by 661,000, or 115 percent. Carey McWilliams calls the influx "the largest internal migration in the history of the American people."

In other parts of the county, too, the population swelled. New cities incorporated during those years were South Gate, Bell, Lynwood, Torrance, Hawthorne, Maywood, and Tujunga. The bubble burst in 1925 in a flurry of bankruptcies and foreclosures. Structures were abandoned, and mapped communities reverted to weeds or farmland.

BOUQUET CANYON, unincorporated area north of Saugus. The original name was given by a French sailor who settled there in the 1800s; he had sailed on a ship nicknamed *El Buque* (meaning simply "the ship"). Surveyors gave the town the new, official spelling in the 1980s.

BOWRON, FLETCHER E. (1887–1968), reform mayor of Los Angeles from 1938 to 1953. Bowron had worked as a Hearst reporter and as executive secretary to Gov. Friend W. Richardson, and he had served as a Superior Court judge. Respected for his honesty and Republican conservatism, he was the mayoral candidate of the recall coalition that toppled corrupt mayor Frank Shaw. The coalition consisted of the leaders of CIVIC (Citizens Independent Vice Investigating Committee) as well as the Municipal League. Although the *Los Angeles Times* opposed Bowron, he had broad support and won by a landslide. Bowron was appointed to finish Shaw's term and went on to serve three additional terms, for a total of 15 years, becoming the first to achieve that record. He is considered by some to have been the city's most effective mayor.

Mayor Fletcher Bowron, Nisei Week 1940. Courtesy Dept. of Special Collections, University Research Library, UCLA.

Bowron brought about dramatic changes. He asked all sitting commissioners to resign, and reconstituted the police, civil service, and fire commissions. He reappointed some holdovers, named many new commissioners, abolished the police Red Squad, and overturned the antipicketing ordinance that had effectively prevented labor strikes. The mayor also replaced the entire board of water and power commissioners and brought greater efficiency, economy, and accountability to the Department of Water and Power. Bowron appointed the first City Administrative Officer, Samuel Leask, who served ably for 10 years. Despite his GOP roots, Bowron was able to work with local Democratic leaders.

At the outbreak of World War II, Mayor Bowron urged the federal government to intern the Japanese for the duration, although in 1946, after witnessing the heroism of the nisei soldiers in the U.S. military, he publicly recanted. He also supported integrated public housing, in the face of withering opposition. For this Bowron received the undying hatred of the real estate lobby and the downtown establishment, who helped effect his defeat for reelection in 1952.

BOXING. In the 1920s and 1930s the town of Vernon was the center of organized fisticuffs in the western United States, where it thrived on the fringes of respectability. Prior to 1915, major fights lasted up to 20 rounds. James J. Jeffries, the future heavyweight champion known as "the Great White Hope," came to Los Angeles at age seven. He first gained prominence at the Manitou Club on Main Street in 1892. Jeffries fought 25 times from 1892 to 1905, and held and defended the world's heavyweight title from 1899 to 1905. He earned enough money to buy and settle on a stock ranch in Burbank. When California outlawed the sport in 1915, promoters kept it alive by scheduling exhibitions that offered no prizes and lasted only four rounds. Boxing was taught at the Hollywood Athletic Club, but the main fight venues were Naud Junction Arena (near Main, Alhambra, and Macy Streets), Jack Doyle's arena in Vernon (until it burned to the ground in 1927), and the posher 15,000-seat Olympic Auditorium, which opened in 1925. In these beery, smoke-filled arenas, movie stars Charlie Chaplin, Mabel Normand, Chester Conklin, and Fatty Arbuckle rubbed elbows with film extras, members of the social elite, and teamsters.

Fidel La Barba, a home-bred champion who had attended Lincoln High, became flyweight champion of the world at the 1924 Olympics in London. Ace "Nebraska Wildcat" Hudkins, middleweight, was also a popular figure; he fought a major match with Mickey Walker in 1928. The greatest of all local talents, however, was Henry "Homicide Hank" Armstrong. He came to live in Los Angeles during the Great Depression and went on to hold four different titles, three of them simultaneously. In a lackluster championship match in Wrigley Field on 17 April 1939, Joe Louis knocked out Jack Roper in the first round. Los Angeles has produced several Olympic boxing gold medalists, including Paul Gonzalez in 1984 and Oscar De La Hoya in 1992. The latter pair hail from Boyle Heights in East Los Angeles.

BOYLE, GREGORY J. (1954–), a pastor of Dolores Mission Church on the Eastside, the poorest Catholic parish in the city. Boyle was born into a middle-class Hancock Park family and was trained as a Jesuit. The *Times* has referred to him as "the patron saint of eastside gangs," while the members of the Clarence Street Locos, the Mob Crew, Cuatro Flats, and the East L.A. Dukes affectionately call him "G-Dog." By 1992 Father Boyle had, sadly, buried 26 youths killed in gang violence and gone on to another assignment.

BOYLE HEIGHTS, Los Angeles neighborhood just east of the river. It emerged in the 1880s as a streetcar suburb for Los Angeles artisans and white-collar workers. The Yankee pioneer William H. Workman named it after his father-in-law, Andrew Boyle, who built himself a spacious residence on the bluff in 1858. Some families along Echandia Street had Spanish surnames in 1887, but the Latino identification declined, and by the 1920s the community had a predominantly Jewish population of 70,000, which expanded to 150,000 by 1940. Since World War II, Boyle Heights has become predominantly Latino again—especially Mexican.

Community life centers around Hollenbeck Park, although freeway designers seriously damaged the neighborhood by building the Golden State Freeway adjacent to that public space. To the

Boyle Heights, 1885. Courtesy Henry E. Huntington Library.

north lies Brooklyn Heights, centered on Prospect Park. The city is studying rehabilitation plans for Boyle Heights and neighboring El Sereno. Councilman Richard Alatorre hopes to refurbish 5,400 acres in those communities, establishing a major shopping mall, creating a commercial or light-industrial area, removing auto wrecking yards, and improving existing housing. The population—94 percent Latino—stood at 94,558 in 1990.

BRADBURY, secluded independent city, 21 miles northeast of downtown. It is named for Lewis Leonard Bradbury of Maine, who made his millions at gold and silver mining in Mexico and came to Southern California in 1888. With an official population count of 829 in 1990, the city may have more horses than people. Its population has remained stable for the last two decades. Bradbury has no stores, gas stations, traffic lights, or apartment buildings. Most of its homes, priced from $500,000 to $7 million, are gated or guarded. The city is zoned for 10 horses per acre, and some equines from nearby Santa Anita racetrack are boarded there.

Bradbury City Hall. Photo by Greg Grammer, courtesy City of Bradbury.

BRADBURY, RAY (1920–), science fiction writer. Born in Illinois, Bradbury has made Los Angeles his home for most of his adult life. He has authored novels, plays, and movie scripts, some of them satirical. *The Martian Chronicles* (1950) is one of his most important story collections. In one tale, space travelers reach Mars only to find that it is really Los Angeles. Bradbury has a teasing admiration for the city. As "a Child of the Beast [Los Angeles]" he believes that "the wave of the Future, irrefutable, indomitable, irreversible, is to be found lodged in our sunlit high-tide TV aerial, rock-and-roll flood space symphony video cassette environ-

ment." A champion of space travel, he has never learned to drive a car.

BRADBURY BUILDING, downtown commercial edifice noted for its exquisite interior. It was built as a garment factory in 1893 by mining entrepreneur and real estate developer Lewis Leonard Bradbury. Legend has it that the designer, George Herbert Wyman, a $5-a-week untrained draftsman in the firm of Sumner P. Hunt, was inspired to take the job after receiving a message on a Ouija board. The structure is said to incorporate ideas from Edward Bellamy's novel *Looking Backward* (1887), which describes a utopian civilization in the year 2000. The building's plain exterior belies a breathtaking interior court with glass roof, open-caged elevators, iron grillwork, marble flooring, and wooden paneling. The Bradbury stands at 3rd Street and Broadway—a short walk from the original owner's Bunker Hill residence. It was designer Wyman's only success. The building has been featured in the movies *D.O.A.* (1949) and *Blade Runner* (1982), among others, and in TV series such as *Banacek.* It has recently undergone a $7 million renovation and is listed as a National Landmark.

BRADLEY, THOMAS (TOM) (1917–), Los Angeles mayor from 1973 to 1993. Bradley's Texas sharecropper family moved to Los Angeles when

Tom Bradley. Courtesy Tom Bradley.

he was seven. He excelled as a student and athlete at UCLA before attending law school. In 1940 Bradley became a police officer, retiring as a lieutenant in 1961. Elected to the city council in 1961, he served until 1969, when he ran, unsuccessfully, against Mayor Sam Yorty. Four years later he made a second bid, becoming the city's first African American mayor. His singularly low-key political style contrasted strongly with the flamboyance of his predecessor. Bradley's major backing came from a coalition of westside liberals, many of them Jewish; southside blacks; labor unions; and the downtown business establishment. To his backers he represented the legacy of Martin Luther King Jr. and Robert Kennedy. He envisioned Los Angeles as a "world-class city," the "gateway city to the Pacific Rim," with a thriving downtown boasting luxurious hotels, towering office buildings, and a rapid-transit subway.

While in office, Bradley strengthened the economy, helped reform the Los Angeles Police Department, initiated Community Redevelopment Agency low-income housing projects, brought minorities and women into the public work force, and presided over the start of a mass transit network. The successful 1984 summer Olympics was the mayor's greatest triumph. He could not, however, forestall the riot of 1992, prevent ethnic and racial balkanization, or cope with the growing traffic congestion and the threat of real estate overdevelopment. A Democrat, Bradley lost in two runs for the governor's seat to Republican George Deukmejian in 1982 and 1986. In 1993 he decided not to make another run for mayor.

BRAND, LESLIE CARLTON (1859–1925), St. Louis–born financier, land developer, and "Father of Glendale." Brand settled in Los Angeles in 1898 and made his fortune as head of the Title Guarantee and Trust Company. In 1902 he acquired 1,000 acres in the foothills of the Verdugo Mountains and below, much of which skirted both sides of the future Brand Boulevard, north of Casa Verdugo. He was a partner in the San Fernando Valley Land and Development Company, a key figure in banking and land development in the city of San Fernando, and a director of the Henry E. Huntington Land and Improvement Company. He convinced Huntington to extend his Pacific Electric Railway to Glendale. This project, completed in 1904, ensured the city's future. Brand was also a partner or full owner of a Glendale bank, hotel, and public utility company, and he was a prime mover in the incorporation of Glendale in 1906.

While an aerodrome he built on Mountain Avenue no longer exists, Miradero, his 1903 Glendale home, remains. The imposing residence, designed in a style inspired by the East Indian Pavilion at the 1893 World's Columbian Exposition in Chicago, overlooks much of Verdugo Valley. Brand willed the building and grounds, popularly known as "Brand's Castle," to Glendale, which maintains them as Brand Library, noted for its music and art collections. The grounds have a carefully cultivated Japanese tea garden. The upscale community around the estate, located on Glendale's northwest side, is called Brand Park.

BRASTOFF, SACHA (1918–1993), ceramicist and sculptor. Born in Cleveland, Brastoff entertained troops during World War II and afterward settled in West Los Angeles where he ran his own ceramics factory, creating fine lamps, china objects, and jewelry. His effort to bring refinements into private homes was funded by the Rockefeller Foundation. The 30-foot suspended cross and matching altarpiece at St. Augustine-by-the Sea Episcopal Church in Santa Monica are his most celebrated works.

BRAUDE, MARVIN (1920–), city council member from the 11th District. Formerly a businessman, Braude was a founder and board member of Scientific Data Systems, later incorporated into the Xerox Corporation. A strong conservationist, he cofounded and served as president of the Santa Monica Mountains Regional Park Association. He helped lead the rebellion of hillside community organizations against land developers of the Santa Monica Mountains, earning the title "sage of the slow growth movement." Since 1965 Braude has represented Pacific Palisades, Tarzana, Brentwood, Encino, and Woodland Hills.

BRAZILIANS, numbering about 10,000 in Los Angeles county in 1990, have located mostly on the city's Westside. Nearly all are recent immigrants from São Paulo, Rio de Janeiro, and Bahia. Favorite gathering places are cafés and restaurant-clubs that feature Brazilian cooking and performances of dance and music (Brazilian jazz, bossa nova, samba) and of martial arts *(capoeira)*. These South Americans have brought with them the *candomble* religion, a mixture of traditional folk and Catholic practices.

BREAKWATER, SAN PEDRO, early-20th-century engineering marvel, constructed between 1899 and 1910 using granite boulders barged in from Santa Catalina Island. The start of the project on 26 April 1899 was marked by a great barbecue attended by 20,000 celebrants. Originally 2 miles long, 200 feet wide at the base, 15 feet wide at the top, and as high as a four-story building, the breakwater transformed a mud flat of limited economic value into a roadstead safe for ocean vessels, thus helping to create one of the most important shipping centers on the West Coast. Beginning in 1928, the breakwater was extended to 8 miles and provided with a few openings. This made possible the development of the Long Beach outer harbor and the huge navy facility on Terminal Island that became headquarters for the U.S. Fifth Fleet.

BRENT, JOSEPH LANCASTER (1826–1905), lawyer from Maryland who in the 1850s helped Los Angeles rancheros confirm their land titles. He owned Rancho San Pascual, which included the site of Pasadena. A prominent Democratic politico and, from 1856 to 1857, state assemblyman, he left the city for the southeastern United States in 1861, serving as a general in the Confederate army and later settling in Louisiana.

BRENTWOOD, westside district on the south slopes of the Santa Monica Mountains, developed in the 1920s. While many of its expensive homes have lovely views of the city, they are also subject to landslides and fires. A particularly devastating blaze on 6 November 1961 raged over 6,000 acres and burned 484 dwellings. Brentwood is home to Mount St. Mary's College and the new Getty Center.

BRIDGE, NORMAN (D. 1925), pioneer physician who practiced during the Southern California "health rush" in the late 19th century. He originally practiced in Chicago but, after contracting tuberculosis, settled in Los Angeles in the 1890s. He treated many "lungers" and became an expert and prolific writer on lung diseases. A humane and intelligent man, he battled against "tuberculophobia," the paranoid fear of indigent sick people that spread throughout the otherwise sober community. Dr. Bridge made millions from investments and became a benefactor of the Southwest Museum, USC, and Caltech.

BRIDGES, though relatively few in Los Angeles County, are often recognized as historic monuments. In Pasadena, the Colorado Street Bridge, with its huge concrete arches, has been a stately landmark since 1912–1913, but is now closed to traffic. In Los Angeles, the Santa Fe Arroyo Seco Bridge (1895) is the oldest and highest bridge in the county; over 700 feet long and 100 feet high, it carries a single track over the Pasadena Freeway. Sunset Boulevard Bridge (1934), which crosses Silver Lake Boulevard, is a span with elegant romanesque arches and detailing. The Macy Street Viaduct (1926), crossing the Los Angeles River between Mission Road and Vignes Street, is recognized for its Spanish Colonial style; it features Ionic and Doric columns with unique street lights. The city bridge at 4th and

Colorado Street Bridge, Pasadena. Pitt Collection.

Lorena Streets (1928) is one of the few suspension bridges in Los Angeles. Fletcher Drive Bridge (1928), crossing the river near Larga Avenue and Crystal Street, is of reinforced concrete in the classical style. Long Beach has a unique bridge: the Commodore F. Heim Drawbridge, a little-known structure spanning Cerritos Channel. Probably the most impressive bridge in Los Angeles County is the Vincent Thomas Bridge, linking San Pedro and Terminal Island. It dates from the 1960s and features a toll booth. The Sam R. Kennedy Bridge, a single-arch span connecting the Sunland-Tujunga area and Antelope Valley, named after the head of the county road department, is another imposing structure.

BRIER, JULIET, pioneer Yankee settler. Brier was a member of the Jayhawker Party, which, in 1849, survived the harrowing journey across the wasteland they named "Death Valley." On the danger-

ous passage that nearly claimed all their lives, she tended cattle, cared for the children, and nursed the sick adults. After a stay in Soledad Canyon she and her husband, Rev. James Brier, moved to Los Angeles, where he conducted the first Protestant religious services ever held in the city.

BRITISH make up a community of over 50,000 in Los Angeles. Ever since the silent film era, Hollywood has had a close-knit colony of expatriate actors, directors, and writers from Great Britain, including actors Charlie Chaplin, Basil Rathbone, and Michael Caine and writers Christopher Isherwood and Aldous Huxley.

BROADWAY, major downtown street, featuring retail stores and movie theaters. The original dirt road led to a cemetery and was named, appropriately, Eternity Street. Eternity then became Fort

Broadway, ca. 1920. Pitt Collection.

Broadway, 1995. Photo by Michael Krakowiak/Marni Pitt.

Street and, in 1890, Broadway. The first department store to be built here, in 1896, was likewise called the Broadway. The department stores the City of Paris (then the largest in Los Angeles) and Hamburger's People's Store (later the May Company) soon relocated to Broadway from other locations. All sorts of brightly lit retail stores followed. They, together with the movie and vaudeville houses, brought lively crowds to the street.

In recent decades Broadway has become a Mexican *mercado* and is now the major shopping street of Latinos in Los Angeles. In fact, the stretch from 2nd to 9th Streets ranks as the busiest commercial street west of Chicago. Latin music pours into the street from small-appliance and gift shops. The Spanish-language movie theaters have a steady audience, and on Sundays, when entire families come to shop, the street pulses with activity. The string of theaters, officially designated as the Broadway Historic Theater District, is the largest remaining collection of old cinema and vaudeville houses in the country.

BROADWAY DEPARTMENT STORE, successful retail mart, opened in 1896 by British-born Arthur Letts at 4th Street and Broadway, a site that was then on the outskirts of town. Letts became wealthy from the store and, buying up ranchland, created Holmby Hills. In the 1940s the Broadway's president, Edward W. Carter, anticipating the city's expansion, transformed the business into a chain of suburban stores and laid the groundwork for a Los Angeles–based national network of retail outlets known as Carter Hawley Hale Stores, Inc.

BROADWAY HISTORIC THEATER DISTRICT, area along Broadway from 3rd Street to Olympic Boulevard containing 12 wonderful old vaudeville and movie houses, designated by the city as a historic district. The theaters are the Roxie, Million Dollar, Cameo, Arcade, Los Angeles, Palace, Loew's State, Globe, Tower, Rialto, Orpheum, and United Artists. Some of the greatest entertainers appeared live in these houses, and some of the most popular films ever made in Hollywood were shown there. The oldest theater opened in 1905. Many remain in an excellent state of preservation. They provide a good introduction to the architectural diversity of Los Angeles, and point up the importance of movies and vaudeville earlier in the century. The Los Angeles Conservancy offers an outstanding tour of the area.

BROADY, EARL C., SR. (1905–1992), lawyer, jurist, and philanthropist. A graduate of Jefferson High School, Broady worked as a janitor, mail carrier, and Los Angeles Police Department officer, where he served for 17 years, before passing the bar in 1944. Broady became a criminal defense attorney, primarily representing blacks accused of murder. He attained a high post in the district attorney's office and was named to the Superior Court bench by Gov. Edmund G. "Pat" Brown in 1965. He served on the McCone Commission investigating the August 1965 Watts riot. Judge Broady donated $1 million to Howard University.

BROWN, JOHN, American fur trapper, known as Juan Flaco, or "Skinny John." He is best remembered for riding horseback 500 miles through enemy territory in September 1846, at the outset of the Mexican War, to report the rebellion against American forces occupying the *pueblo* of Los Angeles. The journey from Los Angeles to Monterey, then the capital of California, took six days. A message scribbled on a piece of cigarette paper hidden in Brown's long hair stated cryptically, "Believe the Bearer." Upon hearing Brown's news, Commodore Robert Stockton dispatched help to the beleaguered troops.

BROWN BERETS, militant Chicano group. Established by David Sanchez in 1966 as Young Chicanos for Community Action, the interfaith East Los Angeles group formally adopted the nickname Brown Berets, a moniker first used by sheriff deputies. The group was nationalist, evangelical, and messianic. They participated in the high school demonstrations for educational reform ("blowouts") of the late 1960s, marched in the 1971 Chicano moratorium to end the Vietnam War, and sent a caravan to "reconquer" Arizona, New Mexico, and Colorado for Mexico. They even invaded Santa Catalina Island, claiming that it had not been formally transferred to the United States as part of the Treaty of Guadalupe Hidalgo. The group disbanded in 1972.

BROWN MOUNTAIN, peak in the San Gabriel Mountains. It is named for the two sons of the abolitionist John Brown, whose family moved to Pasadena after the Civil War.

BRYSON, JOHN, SR. (1819–1907), mayor of Los Angeles from 1888 to 1889. Bryson arrived in

1879 and, at the height of the Boom of the Eighties, bought a Spring Street property, for $120,000, that was located next to the new city hall. With George H. Bonebrake, a financier, he also built the Bryson-Bonebrake Building. Immediately following the boom, Bryson served as mayor. At the time, Los Angeles had an area of approximately 30 square miles and a population of 50,000.

BUDDHISM, religious system founded in India in the sixth century B.C. that has had a strong presence in Southern California's Asian communities since early in the 20th century. Around 1905, when there were but 500 Japanese in Los Angeles, the legendary Japanese Zen master Nyogen Senzaki lectured to an audience of 1,000 at a meeting hall on Turner Street. By the 1930s three temples existed in Chinatown and Little Tokyo. The oldest Buddhist temple in Los Angeles, Nishi (Hompa) Honganji, was built in 1925 in Little Tokyo. During World War II it was a storehouse for the belongings of Japanese internees. Today it is the Japanese American National Museum.

Although Buddhism now counts many converts from Western religions, most of its sects are divided according to national and ethnic background. Hsi Lai Temple in Hacienda Heights is the largest Buddhist monastery and temple complex in the Western Hemisphere and is the headquarters in this country of Fo Kuang Shan, a prominent Buddhist organization of Taiwan. The Korean-Buddhist Dharma Sah Zen Center, near Park La Brea, practices a rigorous old-world routine. Khemara Buddikaram, an old Cambodian temple, added a large complex in Long Beach in 1987. Wat Thai Buddhist Temple in North Hollywood serves the Thai community. Chua-Viet-Nam is the country's oldest and largest Vietnamese Buddhist temple. Nichiren Shoshu Buddhism, a secular branch stemming from Japan, has gained numerous American-born adherents in recent years, and is creating a university campus in the Santa Monica Mountains.

BUDGET OF LOS ANGELES COUNTY is the responsibility of the Board of Supervisors. It is funded principally from property taxes, with smaller amounts collected from vehicle license fees and sales taxes. In addition, the county receives considerable funding from the state and federal governments, and also exercises the authority to borrow funds. In the 1980s its borrowings increased greatly, with the total in 1994 standing at $7.9 billion.

Courts, hospitals, jails, welfare, and other services have utilized 89 percent of the budget in recent years. Many of these services are mandated by state and federal legislation. In fact, the board has direct control over less than 20 percent of the overall budget.

The 1990s produced a major financial crisis for the county of Los Angeles, the delayed by-product of the 1978 passage of Proposition 13, which sharply reduced property taxes. An economic slowdown that began in 1990 added to the county's financial woes by curtailing tax revenues even further. The state, faced with similar reductions in tax revenue, cut back its funding of county services, and federal subventions to the country also declined. Meanwhile, wage increases for county employees, the relatively lavish expenditures of the supervisors in the course of their own official duties, and generous pension benefits for top administrators crimped the budget. By 1993 the county found itself in its worst financial crisis since the 1930s. To fill a $600 million gap in a $13.1 billion budget, the supervisors made major cuts in services. In 1994 they faced a $1 billion deficit and made further cuts, finally approving a $14.2 billion budget. That year, the economic slump persisted, immigration—legal and illegal—continued at a high rate, and expected federal and state funding for health-care financing never materialized. The 1995 projected county budget deficit reached a staggering $1.2 billion; the only apparent recourse lay in massive staff reductions, sharp wage decreases, and cutbacks in basic social services so severe that even the closure of County USC Medical Center was up for discussion.

BUDGET OF THE CITY OF LOS ANGELES originates with the mayor, who produces it in the month of April. It begins with requests from city departments and recommendations by the city administrative officer. The mayor presents it to the city council by 1 June, which must rule on it by 28 June. The mayor has a line-item veto that can be overridden by a two-thirds vote of the council. The council has until 31 August to find the necessary sources of revenue. The general fund derives from property taxes (the major source of revenue), sales taxes, and income earned by council-controlled departments. Some funds may be specially earmarked. Budgets for such issues as bond redemption may not be altered by the council.

City Budget Dollars in Select Years
(as percentage of total)

Budget Item	1982/83	1990/91[a]	1993/94	1994/95
Source of Funds				
Proprietary				
departments	6.0	3.9	4.2	6.7
Utility users tax	9.8	11.3	11.0	10.5
Licenses, permits, fees,				
fines	16.5	23.0	25.1	26.1
Business taxes[b]	10.4	11.1	8.7	8.5
Sales tax	14.1	8.4	6.9	6.5
Local assistance trust				
funds	3.9	—	—	—
Grants and				
allocations	12.9	13.6	15.4	17.5
Property taxes	19.9	14.7	15.1	13.4
Reserve fund transfer	—	1.0	—	—
Miscellaneous	6.5	13.0	13.6	10.8
Use of Funds				
Community safety	47.2	36.8	36.6	37.4
Home and community				
environment	22.7	30.8	34.9	32.5
Transportation	12.4	14.0	12.1	13.1
Cultural, educational,				
recreational	6.0	5.1	5.6	5.0
Human resources,				
economic assistance	2.5	2.1	2.1	2.7
General administration	9.2	11.2	8.7	9.3

SOURCE: Los Angeles Controller.
[a]1990–91 figures are from proposed budget.
[b]Business tax, 1991–95, includes transient occupancy tax.

City revenues were adversely affected by the simultaneous approval in 1978 of Proposition 13 and the elimination of federal support for manpower in the Comprehensive Employment and Training Act (CETA). In 1992 the council adopted a recession-based budget of $3.8 billion, of which about 60 percent went for police, fire, and related services. The equally austere 1993 budget of $3.9 billion continued a hiring freeze in most departments. In April 1995 Mayor Richard Riordan produced a $3.9 billion budget for consideration. His plan for the fiscal year of 1995–1996 included expanding libraries, which had been cut back, putting more money into street repair, and cutting 1,200 city jobs, many of them administrative. Funds would be allocated to five different areas: Community Safety, including fire and police control, 39.5 percent; Home and Community, including sewage services, trash control, and street repair, 31.3 percent; Transportation, involving streets, highways, and traffic control, 11.9

percent; General Administration and Support, involving financial, legislative, administrative, legal, and executive services and care for public buildings, 8.5 percent; and Cultural, Educational, and Recreational Services, 5.4 percent of the budget. In May, the city council accepted the budget with a minimum of wrangling or changes, adding only some traffic officers and enlarging a domestic violence unit. Including a $9.7 million surcharge on business taxes, their proposals increased the proposed budget by only $30 million, a relatively small amount. The only real disagreement was over the surcharge.

BUFFUM'S DEPARTMENT STORE, Southern California mercantile chain founded in Long Beach in 1904. Los Angeles civic leader Dorothy Buffum Chandler is a descendant of the founders. During the recession of 1991 the parent firm, an Australian steamship company, closed all 16 Buffum's stores.

BUILDING AND SAFETY, DEPARTMENT OF. *See* Los Angeles City Department of Building and Safety

BUILDING HEIGHT LIMITS were not a problem before the turn of the century. The tallest building in town in 1869, the Pico House overlooking the Plaza, was only three stories high. From 1905 to 1957 the city maintained an official height limit of 150 feet, or 13 stories, on all buildings. This limit was the result of aesthetic concerns, according to architectural historian Paul Gleye, and had nothing to do with a fear of earthquakes: Angelenos simply sought to maintain "beauty and symmetry" in downtown architecture and wished to avoid the Manhattan look. The height maximum was reaffirmed in the charter of 1911. The tallest building at that time was the Continental Building on Spring Street, built in 1905. The only exception made to the rule was for 28-story City Hall, dedicated in 1928. The city finally lifted the traditional ceiling in 1957, chiefly to allow architects to incorporate parking spaces into new downtown office buildings. In 1989 the 73-story First Interstate World Center on 5th Street became the tallest structure, and is expected to remain so for some time to come.

BUKOWSKI, CHARLES (1920–1994), author and poet. Born in Germany, Bukowski came to

America with his family as a child. For many years he worked as a postal clerk at Terminal Annex, an experience that led to *Post Office* (1971), an autobiographical account of his alcoholic youth, which in turn inspired the movie *Barfly* (1987). An underground literary figure, he published poetry and short stories in such publications as the *Los Angeles Free Press* and *Hustler* magazine. Bukowski wrote about the seedy underside of Los Angeles and its people. He was called the "poet laureate of Los Angeles low-life."

BULLOCK, GEORGIA P. (MORGAN) (1878–1957), first woman judge in California. A graduate of USC Law School, Bullock was admitted to the bar in 1913, elected to the Los Angeles Municipal Court in 1926, and appointed to the Superior Court in 1931. The Chicago-born jurist was an accomplished public speaker on family law, among other topics, and served with distinction until she retired in 1956.

BULLOCK'S DEPARTMENT STORES, major regional mercantile chain founded in 1907 by the Canadian immigrant John G. Bullock and a partner. They used an investment by Arthur Letts, founder of Broadway Department Store, who then took Bullock's into his chain. The first Bullock's was located in the heart of downtown. In September 1929 a second, upscale store, Bullocks Wilshire, was opened, on a bean field near Vermont Avenue; some historians regard this as the first suburban department store in the nation. An estimated 300,000 people jammed the building on its opening day. This flagship Bullock's store, which eventually became I. Magnin/Bullocks Wilshire, is a remarkably fine showcase of the Art Deco architectural style of the 1920s and features elegant interiors, including murals and sculpture. Although the building itself remained in good physical condition, the store closed in 1992. At its height, the Bullock's chain had 22 outlets. It was purchased by R. H. Macy & Co.

"BUM BLOCKADE," misguided depression-era effort by the Los Angeles Police Department to stop poor migrants, who were streaming into California from the Dust Bowl, from entering the city. In February 1936 Chief James E. Davis, supported by the chamber of commerce, *Los Angeles Times,* and the city attorney, decided to deploy 136 officers to the state's borders with Arizona, Nevada, and Oregon. These forces were ordered to block the "bums" from entering California, and therefore Los Angeles. In a scene reminiscent of Steinbeck's *Grapes of Wrath,* they turned away unemployed and poor people traveling by car, truck, or railroad. The American Civil Liberties Union argued that the action violated constitutional rights, adding that if Jesus Christ had returned to earth he, too, would have been turned away. Although hundreds of potential newcomers retreated, the operation created resentment elsewhere in California and generally failed. Five years later, in a case arising in Texas, the U.S. Supreme Court declared such police action unconstitutional.

BUNCHE, RALPH J[OHNSON] (1904–1971), African American diplomat and Nobel laureate. Born in Detroit, Bunche came to Los Angeles with his family at an early age. He attended John Adams Junior High and Jefferson High, and received a B.A. from UCLA in 1927; he then served as a professor of political science at Howard University from 1928 to 1940, earning his Ph.D. from Harvard in 1934. Bunche became a career diplomat, working for the State Department, where he was the first African American to be a division head, and the United Nations. In 1950, for his work as secretary of the U.N. Palestine Commission, Bunche won the Nobel Peace Prize, the first African American to be so honored. He later served as a U.N. undersecretary. The social science building at UCLA is named for him.

BUNGALOW ARCHITECTURE, popular Southern California residential style early in the 20th century. It featured a simple one-story construction with wooden siding; a low-pitched, gabled roof and wide eaves; a front porch; and an airy interior. It was usually painted white or had stained natural wood. Derived from cottages common in India, bungalows had great appeal for middle- and working-class families owing to their low cost. The style was more or less invented by the talented Greene brothers with the 1903 Bandini house in Pasadena. The most outstanding example is the more elaborate Gamble House (1908) in Pasadena. Many of the thousands of bungalows built have since been bulldozed to make way for apartments, although clusters are still to be seen in Hollywood, Glendale, Pasadena, and other older communities. Nine hundred bungalows are protected in a six-block Pasadena historic district. The bungalow is

A California Log Cabin.

A California bungalow, ca. 1907. Pitt Collection.

considered part of the Craftsman aesthetic, which had a strong vogue in the region; it also spread to various other parts of the nation from Southern California.

BUNKER HILL, downtown promontory, now topped by office spires. Founded in the 19th century as a middle-class residential enclave, it is about the size of its Boston namesake. Builder Prudent Beaudry first developed the hill in 1869, and by the 1870s and 1880s doctors, merchants, and lawyers had built spacious Queen Anne and Eastlake mansions there. In the following decade, apartment buildings rose beside the private homes. Early Bunker Hill residents commuted to work on a one-stop railway, Angels Flight, which scaled the south slope of the hill. In 1900, at a cost of over $100,000, the city carved the 3rd Street Tunnel beneath the hill. Construction of the underpass took a year to complete and cost the lives of six work-

ers killed in cave-ins. As early as the 1920s, the hill had started to serve as a refuge for pensioners, transients, and derelicts. By the 1940s many Bunker Hill Victorian homes were seedy and run down.

After World War II, downtown business leaders began to clamor for extensive urban renewal on Bunker Hill. Some called for total removal of the old buildings, while others favored selective remodeling. In the 1950s the city opted for massive clearance and initiated the Bunker Hill Redevelopment Project, involving a dozen blocks on 130 acres. The work began in earnest in 1963. All existing structures and the Angels Flight railway were torn down. Bunker Hill eventually became home to the Dorothy Chandler Pavilion, the Museum of Contemporary Art, towering office buildings on California Plaza, and an apartment complex, with parking on the fringes. Although the Bunker Hill apartment complex at the northwest corner of the project did lure some white-collar workers from suburbia, the plan to create a residential neighborhood with a strong kinship to the rest of downtown failed.

BUNKER HILL STEPS, most imposing stairway in Los Angeles. The five-story climb between 4th and 5th Streets and Grand Avenue and Flower Street was designed to encourage pedestrian traffic in downtown Los Angeles by connecting the Los Angeles Central Library with the office towers atop Bunker Hill. It replaced an old eyesore and barrier, the 5th Street Wall. The stairway is graced by an inviting water fountain and terraces with outdoor cafés and sitting areas. Inspired by the Spanish Steps in Rome and designed by landscape architect Lawrence Halprin, the 103-step curved

Bunker Hill, 1885. Courtesy Robert Weinstein Collection.

Bunker Hill Steps, 1995. Photo by Michael Krakowiak/Marni Pitt.

stairway was built, and is owned, by Maguire Thomas Partners as a permanent public easement. The project was part of a brokered deal in which the city allowed the developer to break the zoning limit and add extra stories to its new Bunker Hill property, the First Interstate World Center, Los Angeles's tallest building. As part of the deal, Maguire Thomas also agreed to build the new wing of the Los Angeles Central Library building. The Bunker Hill steps were completed in 1990 at a cost of $12 million.

BURBANK, incorporated city 11 miles north of downtown Los Angeles in the eastern San Fernando Valley. It is on land granted to José María Verdugo, a retired Spanish soldier, in 1784. The name derives not from Luther Burbank, the naturalist, as some assume, but from Dr. David Burbank, a Los Angeles dentist who arrived in 1866 and became an early subdivider. A product of the Boom of the Eighties, the town of Burbank was founded in 1887 on part of Providencia Rancho. At that time a five-room home cost $400 to $500; by 1990, a small Burbank residence hovered around $239,000. Lockheed Aircraft located there early in the century, adjacent to an airport that is now a busy regional complex serving Burbank, Glendale, and Pasadena. Nearby are NBC's TV studios, the old Warner Brothers film studios (now Burbank Studios), and Disney Studios, making Burbank a major entertainment center. TV's Johnny Carson brought national fame to "beautiful downtown Burbank" on the *Tonight Show.* The city blends industry, commerce, and residential use. Its 1990 population of 93,643 had not changed greatly since the 1950s.

BURBANK AIRPORT, or more properly Burbank-Glendale-Pasadena Airport, is a regional facility in Burbank developed as a mail cargo stop and flying field for the Lockheed Corporation. By 1934, when it changed its name to Union Air Terminal, it was the busiest airport in Los Angeles. Lockheed bought it in 1940. The field experienced an active period during World War II, but traffic declined from 1945 to 1950, when Los Angeles International Airport came into its own. It received a lift from air cargo and commuter flights, especially from the fledgling PSA airline. In a quest to upgrade the airfield's image, the proprietor officially renamed it Hollywood-Burbank in 1967. During the 1970s it became an alternative to LAX for regional travelers and sparked a public controversy concerning noise pollution. In 1978 Lockheed sold the facility to the cities of Burbank, Glendale, and Pasadena. It now serves over 3 million passengers annually, with about 55,000 flights a year.

Burbank Airport, 1930s. Courtesy Robert Weinstein Collection.

BURBANK STUDIOS. *See* Warner Brothers Studio

BURKE, YVONNE WATSON BRATHWAITE (1932–), county supervisor. A Democrat and civil rights attorney, Burke was elected to the state assembly in 1966. She served briefly in Congress and was later appointed to a term as a county supervisor, becoming the first African American to hold that post. She lost an election bid to retain her seat in a contest against conservative challenger Deane Dana. Burke ran again in 1992 for the seat vacated by longtime supervisor Kenneth Hahn, and was elected.

BURKHARDT, HANS (1905–1994), painter. Born in Switzerland of German-Swiss background, he immigrated to New York in 1924, where he studied with Arshile Gorky, and made his way to Los Angeles in the 1940s. An Abstract Expressionist, he is known for his panels of social protest. He was a

---

The sun gave me a frightful headache and I have to wear smoked glasses all the time. In other words, phooey on Cal. . . .   —Nathanael West, writer, 1933

---

friend or colleague to Stanton MacDonald-Wright, Lorser Feitelson, Knud Merrild, Millard Sheets, Rico Lebrun, and Ed Keinholz. In 1992 Burkhardt won the Jimmy Ernst Award for lifetime achievement in art.

BURROUGHS, EDGAR RICE (1875–1950), adventure fiction writer. He authored *Tarzan of the Apes* (1914) and its sequels, about a boy who is reared by apes and grows to manhood in the African jungle. From 1919 Burroughs lived in the San Fernando Valley on his estate, "Tarzana." Burroughs's Tarzan novels were made into popular films that starred a variety of actors, the most famous being Johnny Weissmuller, the Olympic gold medal swimmer.

BUSCH GARDENS, popular theme parks with two separate incarnations. In 1903 the beer magnate Adolphus Busch built the first Busch Gardens on 30 acres of his fashionable estate on "Million-

aire's Row" in Pasadena. It consisted of formal gardens and natural woodland overlooking the Arroyo Seco. Amid the exotic plants and shrubs he installed pools, waterfalls, and miles of trails that drew tourists escaping midwestern winters. Also scattered in the greenery were sculptured tableaux of gnomes and other fairy tale characters. One group was seated around a table and drinking Busch beer. The gardens remained open to visitors until the late 1930s, when the land was subdivided.

August A. Busch Jr. created the second Busch Gardens in 1966 in Van Nuys, on land adjacent to the Anheuser-Busch Brewery, which had opened in 1954. He presented a 20-acre tropical paradise that featured 2,000 birds, many of them rare species, as well as a variety of animals. Adult visitors received free beer. When attendance plummeted from 1.2 million in 1975 to 950,000 a year later, Busch Gardens became the Busch Bird Sanctuary. Attendance continued to fall, however, and the preserve closed in 1986.

BUSING. The practice of transporting children to schools outside their own neighborhoods to promote desegregation was imposed by the courts on the Los Angeles Unified School District (LAUSD) in the 1970s. The 1970 court decision grew out of the *Crawford* case, initiated by the American Civil Liberties Union of Southern California. In 1963 Judge Alfred Gitelson found the district guilty of both intentional and unintentional racial discrimination. He required LAUSD to develop a plan whereby each school would have no more than 50 percent, nor less than 10 percent, minority representation. The judge's decision was upheld by the U.S. Supreme Court in 1976. In the twice-daily migration, hundreds of buses were used to transport hundreds of thousands of youngsters. A vigorous grass-roots anti-busing campaign that developed in the San Fernando Valley eventually impeded the program. Whether or not busing led to educational success became a moot point. It was discontinued by a California ballot measure in 1979.

BUSS, JERRY (1933?–), sports franchise owner. Buss is a graduate of the University of Wyoming with a Ph.D. in chemistry from USC. While working in aerospace he invested $1,000 in a West Los Angeles apartment building, the beginning of his multi-million-dollar real estate business. In 1979, in the largest single business transaction in sports

68   BUTTERFIELD STAGE

history, Buss bought the Los Angeles Lakers basketball team, Los Angeles Kings hockey team, and
the Forum, as well as a 13,000-acre ranch in Kern
County. He is a founding partner in Prime Ticket
Network, a regional sports cable television network. Buss has retired from the real estate business,
and his daughters are involved in managing tennis, volleyball, and special events at the Forum.

BUTTERFIELD STAGE, or Butterfield Over-
land Mail, first direct transportation link with the
East. It was established in 1858 by John Butterfield,
founder of American Express, to carry the U.S.
mail, with an annual federal subsidy of $595,000.
The "ox-bow" path stretched 2,700 miles from St.
Louis to San Francisco via El Paso, Texas; Tucson,
Arizona; and Los Angeles. The line employed 100
coaches, 800 workers, and 1,500 horses. In the Los
Angeles area, the coaches stopped at El Monte, Los
Angeles, Cahuenga, Mission San Fernando, and
Fort Tejón. The climb to Tejón was the most tor-
turous of the entire trip. When the newlyweds Mr.
and Mrs. H. D. Barrows set off for Los Angeles
by Butterfield stage in 1860, they rode day and
night for 18 days over a 1,900-mile route. The company went under in 1861, on the eve of the Civil
War and within four years of its founding. A
replica of a Concord stage is on permanent display at the Wells Fargo History Museum on Grand
Avenue.

CABLE CARS jolted their way along the streets on three separate lines from downtown to outlying areas during the Boom of the Eighties. The initial line, established in 1885, was the 1.5-mile-long Second Street Cable Railroad, running from City Hall and the Hollenbeck Hotel at 2nd and Spring Streets to the newly opened residential tract on Crown Hill. Cars ran every 12 minutes, 16 hours a day. At the end of the line they connected with the Cahuenga Valley Railroad, a short steam line to Colgrove, a town on the outskirts of today's Hollywood. Streams of mud from winter storms oozing onto unpaved streets destroyed the line within five years.

The second line, the Temple Street Railway, organized in 1886, ran parallel to the first, on Temple Street to Dayton Heights at Hoover Street, the city limits. By 1890 this successful venture had carried a total of 1.5 million riders.

The third line, the Los Angeles Cable Railway, formed a giant X on the city map, running from Westlake to Boyle Heights and from Jefferson to East Los Angeles. At one point it lumbered along a platform 20 feet high—the first elevated road in the county. Passengers never had to wait more than 2½ minutes for a car, and the fare was a nickel. All of the cable lines were established more as a way of selling real estate than as a public service.

CABLE TELEVISION has experienced unprecedented growth in recent years, catering to those who prefer to take their entertainment at home. The city is divided into 14 franchise areas, each served by a privately owned cable company that is loosely regulated by federal law. Los Angeles awards franchises on a competitive basis, granting companies the right to use the city's power poles for cables. A cable tax has been debated before the city council and in the state legislature, but is vigorously opposed by the cable companies themselves. The city's Telecommunication Department monitors consumer problems.

CABRILLO, JUAN RODRÍGUEZ (D. 1543), European discoverer of California, in 1542. Actually a Portuguese navigator (João Cabrilho), he was sailing under the flag of Spain when he commanded the first expedition along the California coast. As he passed Southern California he named several local features, including San Pedro Bay, and he visited Catalina Island and Santa Monica.

Juan Rodríguez Cabrillo. Courtesy California State Library.

CAFETERIAS were probably imported from New York or Chicago, but they became so popular in Los Angeles during the first half of the century that the city could have claimed the title "Cafeteria Capital of the World." The Mexican-era *cafetería* was a place for drinking rather than eating. The first local low-cost eatery serving hot meals on individual trays all day long, not just at meal time, was opened by Miss H. S. Mosher in May 1905. It appealed to tourists as well as locals. In time hundreds of cafeterias sprang up. Among the most popular were the Clifton Cafeterias (the name conflates those of the founder, Clifford E. Clinton), outfitted with palm trees, fountains, and separate rooms for intimate gatherings or business meetings. Clifton's served free food to the poor during the depression, dishing up 10,000 free meals in one three-month period. Six of the original chain remain in existence today. Cafeterias were a favorite meeting place for politicians and community activists. The famous Lincoln-Roosevelt League, which toppled the Southern Pacific Railroad in California in 1911, was organized in a Los Angeles cafeteria, and the meetings that led to the demise of the corrupt Mayor Shaw in the 1930s were similarly held in a cafeteria. During World War II, the largest cafeteria in the city, and possibly the county, of Los Angeles, with 6,000 seats, was located at Douglas Aircraft in Santa Monica.

CAHUENGA PASS, historically important canyon through the Santa Monica Mountains, connecting Hollywood and the San Fernando Valley. The Gabrieleño word *cahuenga* means "place of the mountain"; the canyon itself was a footpath for Indians who lived on the south side of the pass. It was also the site of a burial ground near today's Franklin and Sycamore Avenues. The Spanish explorer Gaspar de Portolá marched his men through the pass on his way north in 1769; the route then became part of El Camino Real, and was used by Spanish and Mexican colonials to drive ox carts, horses, sheep, and cattle over the mountains. In a skirmish that took place in the pass in 1831, local Californios defeated Mexican governor Manuel Victoria. In 1845 Juan B. Alvarado and José Castro fought a battle on the same site that nearly toppled Mexican governor Micheltorena. Near the end of the Mexican War, on 13 January 1847, the Mexican general Andrés Pico capitulated to John C. Frémont in an adobe situated in today's Universal City. In the Yankee era, Cahuenga Pass became a roadway for horse-drawn wagons, stagecoaches, mule teams, and even bicycles. In the 20th century

the Big Red Cars of the Pacific Electric rolled through the pass. The road was eventually paved as a highway for autos, trucks, and buses, and in 1954 it became a route for a modern freeway.

Cahuenga Valley on the south side of the pass was sold off and laid out as farmland in the late 1860s. The area along Foothill Road (now Santa Monica Boulevard) was particularly valuable because it was frost-free in winter. In 1869 John T. Gower settled on a 160-acre plot between Sunset Boulevard and Melrose Avenue. In the 1880s pineapples, dates, tomatoes, beans, oranges, lemons, and garden vegetables were grown locally. Two present-day landmarks at the bottom of the pass are the Hollywood Bowl and John Anson Ford Theater.

CAHUENGA VALLEY RAILROAD, short steam railway. It started running in the 1880s from Crown Hill to Colgrove, a town later incorporated into Hollywood. A passenger boarding at City Hall on Spring Street could ride a cable car to Crown Hill and then take the steam line to the south side of Cahuenga Pass.

CAIN, JAMES M. (1892–1977), author. He wrote *The Postman Always Rings Twice* (1934), *Double Indemnity* (1936), and *Mildred Pierce* (1941), the earliest underbelly crime novels depicting a brooding, cynical Southern California. They were all adapted into successful Hollywood *film noir* movies.

CALABASAS, county area 26 miles northwest of downtown, at the west end of the San Fernando Valley. The name is probably derived from the Spanish *cañada de las calabasas,* or "canyon of wild gourds or squashes." Capt. Gaspar de Portolá passed through, returning south from Monterey to San Diego, on 15 January 1770. Juan Bautista de Anza also passed through, once on 10 April 1774, on a trek north from Sonora, Mexico, to Monterey, and again on 22 February 1776, while traveling north with 240 settlers. After 1779 Calabasas became a way station of the Franciscan padres traveling along El Camino Real to and from Ventura and northern missions.

In the 1860s Calabasas was a stagecoach stop and the site of a tough frontier town, complete with a store, town hall, dance hall–saloon, and a cast of dangerous characters. From the limbs of Hangman's Tree, a massive live oak, vigilantes hanged members of the Tiburcio Vásquez gang. After the secularization of the missions, lands in Calabasas, including the colorfully named El Escorpion Rancho, were granted to three Native Americans. Some of the property later fell into the hands of the "King of Calabasas," the Basque settler Miguel Leonis. The Miguel Leonis Adobe, built in 1869, is now a historical landmark. During the 1930s, Warner Brothers maintained a 1,200-acre property in Calabasas that served as the location of scores of feature films.

CAL ARTS. *See* California Institute of the Arts

CALIFORNIA AFRO-AMERICAN MUSEUM, state-owned facility in Exposition Park documenting the African American experience in this country. Authorized in 1977, it began operation in 1981 and has become the largest museum of its kind in the nation. Its 44,000-square-foot site includes galleries, a library, and a theater for displaying permanent and temporary collections of cultural objects, books, historic documents, works of art, and photographs. The museum offers workshops, lectures, and public forums.

CALIFORNIA ANGELS BASEBALL TEAM, American League club franchised to Gene Autry in 1960. The team played its first seasons in Los Angeles from 1961 to 1965, when it was known as the Los Angeles Angels, a name transferred from a minor league team of the old Pacific Coast League. Nicknamed the "Halos," the new Angels held their first tryouts on the grounds of the Sawtelle Veterans Hospital in 1961. Three hundred hopefuls came, and six were hired. The team then signed with the city of Los Angeles to play at Wrigley Field. Spring training opened in Palm Springs, where President Eisenhower visited the team. In the Angels' first game Ted Kluszewsky hit two home runs and the team beat the Orioles at Baltimore 7–2. The Angels also played in Dodger Stadium briefly. In 1965 the team changed its name to California Angels and the next year settled into its own ball park, Anaheim Stadium in Orange County. In 1995 the Walt Disney Company bought 25 percent of the team, with an option to buy the entire organization should it come up for sale.

CALIFORNIA AQUEDUCT, state-owned water system. Since the 1960s it has delivered Feather River water to Los Angeles via the San Joaquin Valley. The water originates at Oroville Dam, courses through the 440-mile aqueduct, and is pumped through the San Gabriel Mountains on its way to San Diego. It is distributed by the Metropolitan Water District of Southern California, which transfers water over to the Los Angeles Department of Water and Power at their Jensen facility near Castaic.

CALIFORNIA CLUB, oldest and most exclusive men's social club in Los Angeles. It was founded in 1887 by Ben C. Truman, I. W. Hellman, H. Gaylord Wilshire, J. J. Mellus, James de Barth Shorb, and three other men in a room above a stable at 1st and Fort Streets. Since the 1930s it has occupied a large, stately building designed by architect member Robert David Farquhar, at 6th and Flower. The club has comfortable living, dining, meeting, and recreational facilities. Over the years, members of

California Club, former building at 5th and Hill Streets. Pitt Collection.

the downtown elite have entertained visitors and settled business matters over lunch or dinner at the California Club. It has been charged with strong bias on grounds of race and sex.

CALIFORNIA EAGLE, Los Angeles newspaper under African American ownership begun in 1910. During the Great Depression it became the major periodical for the black community. Edited by Charlotta Spears Bass and owned by her husband, the *Eagle* fearlessly reported instances of police brutality, housing segregation, and job discrimination. The newspaper reached its peak in the 1940s; it is no longer published.

CALIFORNIA FRUIT GROWERS EXCHANGE. *See* Sunkist Growers

CALIFORNIA HISTORICAL SOCIETY, the state's premier historical society. Although based in San Francisco since its founding in 1871, it has many members in Southern California and maintains a branch at El Molino Viejo in San Marino.

CALIFORNIA INSTITUTE OF TECHNOLOGY (CALTECH), a leading center of scientific and technological research located in Pasadena. Founded in 1891 by Amos G. Throop, a Chicago businessman who was attracted to the craft movement, it was first named Throop University, then Throop Polytechnic Institute, and finally, in 1920, Caltech. The institute's history was shaped indelibly by the work of astronomer and trustee George Ellery Hale, chemist and former Massachusetts Institute of Technology (MIT) president Arthur

Amos Noyes, and physicist and Nobel Prize winner Robert Andrews Millikan. This trio recruited the finest faculty, with special strengths in astronomy, biology (particularly molecular biology), chemistry, engineering and applied sciences, physics, and mathematics. Its offerings in the humanities and social sciences are less extensive. Caltech is the birthplace of modern earthquake science and molecular biology. It founded and operates the Jet Propulsion Laboratory (JPL) for NASA, and owns and operates Palomar Observatory, near Escondido in the southern part of the state. It also runs a radio observatory, a seismological laboratory, and a marine biology laboratory. Albert Einstein visited several times. A relatively small institution, Caltech has 272 full-time professors, 800 undergraduates, 1,000 graduate students, and 700 visiting professors and research fellows. Among its alumni and faculty are over 20 Nobel laureates and over 30 winners of the National Medal of Science. The campus comprises more than 100 buildings on 124 acres.

CALIFORNIA INSTITUTE OF THE ARTS (CAL ARTS), private art school created in 1961 by a merger between the Los Angeles Conservatory of Music, established in 1883, and Chouinard Art Institute, founded in 1921. The latter institute, founded by Madame Nelly Murphy Chouinard (1879–?), had trained 40,000 artists, including fashion designer Edith Head, painter Ed Ruscha, and sculptor Larry Bell, as well as animators who worked for Walt Disney in the 1930s. An endowment of $30 million from the Disney family enabled Cal Arts to build a 60-acre Valencia campus

West Gate, Caltech. Photo by Lori Shepler.

in the Santa Clara Valley, which opened in 1971. The school offers degrees in dance, film, video, theater, and in disciplines within art and music. It annually enrolls some 1,000 students, maintains some 200 visiting artists in residence, and sponsors 250 exhibitions and performances.

CALIFORNIA LANDMARKS CLUB, a historic preservation society founded in 1894 by Charles F. Lummis and others. Trailblazers in the area of architectural conservation, the club's members attended to the neglected and shabby Spanish mission buildings. Although well meaning, in some respects they distorted the original structural designs of Missions San Gabriel and San Fernando.

CALIFORNIA STATE MUSEUM OF SCIENCE AND INDUSTRY, complex of buildings in Exposition Park housing popular scientific and technological exhibits. The museum itself was founded in 1888. In 1912 the California legislature appropriated funds for a state exposition building and a state armory. The museum's mainstay has been hands-on exhibits relating to state water resources, recreation, parks, forests, and horticulture. The Aerospace Building, designed by Frank Gehry and opened in 1984, displays space-age hardware. In the Mitsubishi IMAX Theater, films are projected onto a five-story-high screen. The Kinsey Hall of Health presents exhibits on nutrition, drugs, and health, while Technology Hall focuses on energy use, trash recycling, electricity, mathematics, and earthquakes. Other facilities are the Howard F. Ahmanson Building and Mark Taper Hall of Economics and Finance. The Armory, no longer used for military purposes, is also part of the museum. The California Afro-American Museum, also located in Exposition Park, is a separate entity.

CALIFORNIA STATE POLYTECHNIC UNIVERSITY, POMONA, opened in the fall of 1938 on 153 acres in San Dimas, on property donated to the state by the Charles B. Voorhis family. Originally administered as the Voorhis Unit of the state agricultural college, California Polytechnic School, San Luis Obispo, the San Dimas site had an all-male enrollment of 80 students. In 1949 the breakfast cereal magnate W. K. Kellogg deeded to the college 813 acres of land in Pomona, 3 miles away from the campus. The land had been, since 1925, the site of his world-famous Kellogg Ranch and its prize-winning herd of Arabian horses, and Kellogg

stipulated that the horse breeding operation was to remain an integral feature of the campus. In 1956 the college's 550 male students and 30 faculty members moved to the Pomona site. Ten years later the state reorganized the school as Cal Poly Pomona, the 16th California State College campus; in 1972 the school was granted university status. In the 1990s the campus had some 2,300 faculty and staff and an enrollment of more than 19,000 students, with course offerings in agriculture, arts, engineering, science, and education.

CALIFORNIA STATE UNIVERSITY, DOMINGUEZ HILLS (CSUDH), one of 20 campuses of the California State University system. CSUDH was established in 1960 on a 346-acre campus on historic Rancho San Pedro, and enrolled its first students in 1965. It features multiethnic, multicultural programs and has gained national recognition for helping underrepresented minority students overcome educational barriers. About 62 percent of the students are women, and about 70 percent are 26 years or older. The university has accredited special fields in art and theater arts, music, chemistry, medical technology, nursing, and pubic administration. The School of Health has the largest enrollment.

CALIFORNIA STATE UNIVERSITY, LONG BEACH (CSULB), one of 20 campuses of the California State University system. It opened as Los Angeles–Orange County State College on 26 September 1949 in a converted apartment building on Anaheim Road in Long Beach. In 1991 the school's enrollment had reached 32,600, with 1,080 full-time faculty. The 322-acre campus includes a library with 1 million volumes. CSULB has the largest engineering school in the West, the largest fine arts

The Pyramid athletic stadium, CSU Long Beach. Photo by Lori Shepler.

school in California, and one of the top dance programs in the country. It also has a highly ranked public policy and administration program and is a leading center for the study of graphic design. The University Art Museum is one of the best of its kind in the nation. The campus participates in many intercollegiate sports.

CALIFORNIA STATE UNIVERSITY, LOS ANGELES (CSULA), one of 20 campuses of the California State University system. It opened its doors to 136 students in 1947, when it was known as Los Angeles State College and temporarily shared facilities with Los Angeles City College (LACC) on Vermont Avenue. Two years later it was renamed Los Angeles State College of Applied Arts and Sciences; meanwhile, a permanent site was un-

The Harriet and Charles Luckman Fine Arts Complex, CSU Los Angeles. Photo by Lori Shepler.

der construction in the San Gabriel Valley. In 1956 academic divisions began moving from the Vermont campus to the new location overlooking the San Bernardino Freeway; the formal opening occurred in September 1958. Los Angeles State College soon had eight divisions and 37 departments, most of them offering a master's degree: business and economics; education; fine arts; health and safety, physical education, recreation and athletics; language arts; science and math; social sciences; and technical sciences. Later it was accorded university status and the name changed accordingly. In the fall of 1995 CSULA had an enrollment of 18,385 students, 580 full-time faculty, and 367 part-time faculty.

CALIFORNIA STATE UNIVERSITY, NORTH-RIDGE (CSUN), one of 20 campuses of the California State University system. It was founded as the San Fernando Valley campus of Los Angeles State College in the fall of 1956. The legislature declared it a separate entity on 1 July 1958 and renamed it San Fernando Valley State College. It opened in temporary buildings on 350 acres in Northridge with 3,300 students and 104 faculty. Valley State was accredited as a university and renamed in 1972; by 1987 it had 29,689 students and 972 full-time faculty. CSUN is basically a liberal arts institution with programs also in technological and professional fields. It has eight schools: arts, business administration and economics, communication and professional studies, education, engineering and computer sciences, humanities, science and mathematics, and social and behavioral sciences. Like all the state colleges, it stresses a commitment to teaching, research, and public service, with undergraduate instruction as the first priority. Bachelor's degrees are given in 47 subject areas, and master's degrees in 37. In the January 1994 earthquake CSUN sustained over $250 million in damage to virtually all of its buildings. Classes continued to be held in temporary quarters on the campus.

Business Administration/ Economics and Education Complex, CSU Northridge. Publications Dept., CSU Northridge.

CALIFORNIOS, Mexicans born or living in California during the rule of Spain and Mexico, from 1781 to 1848, and also any of their offspring born following the Yankee takeover. The term is a local variant of the Spanish word *Californianos.*

CALL, ASA VICKERY (1892–1978), leading member of the downtown business elite in the 1950s and 1960s. Call was one of the small circle of conservative GOP leaders who hand-picked political candidates, thereby shaping city and state politics. Referred to as "Mr. Big" in California's governing circles, he worked to shape the political scene along with Kyle Palmer and Harry Chandler of the *Los Angeles Times.* Call helped quash Socialist

---

Unemployment is a crime in Sunny California. The state is advertised as a paradise, and when "come-ons" come and fail to get work they are jailed.

—Louis Adamic, writer, on the 1920s

Upton Sinclair's bid for governor in 1934, and progressive supervisor John Anson Ford's mayoral bid in 1937. In 1952 he helped elect Norris Poulson as mayor. In the 1950s, as CEO of Pacific Mutual Life, Call was a mover and shaker in Greater Los Angeles Plans Incorporated (GLAPI), an organization formed for downtown redevelopment. He also sat on the McCone Commission that investigated the Watts riot of 1965, and he was part of the "millionaires group" that organized Ronald Reagan's run for governor in 1966.

CAL POLY, POMONA. *See* California State Polytechnic University, Pomona

CALTECH. *See* California Institute of Technology

CAMBODIANS began arriving from their wartorn homeland in the 1980s. By 1990 they numbered some 50,000 in Southern California, the largest Cambodian community in the United States. Concentrated in the Long Beach area, many have established small, family businesses. In addition, they have organized social service agencies to assist the newly arrived. Most Cambodians are Buddhists.

"CAMEL CORPS," unusual U.S. government freight-hauling experiment that operated in Southern California in the 1850s and 1860s. A camel team was recommended by Gen. Edward F. Beale after reading the book *Travel in China and Tartary* by Abbe Huc. Acting on Beale's idea, Secretary of War Jefferson Davis authorized the corps' establishment as a way of hauling cargo from California to Arizona. In late 1857, 77 seasick animals arrived from Egypt and the Ottoman Empire at the docks of New Orleans. On 8 January 1858, Angelenos turned out en masse to greet the arrival of the first caravan. The procession had traveled from Fort Defiance in the New Mexico Territory en route to Fort Tejón in the northern part of Los Angeles County. The animals of the "lightning dromedary express" managed to swim across the Colorado River, but developed sore feet while walking the cactus-covered Arizona desert trails. Their unsympathetic handlers found them to be smelly and stubborn animals besides. The camel corps had made but few transits before it was disbanded in 1864; the "humpbacked brutes" were sold to private owners for pleasure riding and circus acts in San Francisco.

CAMERO, MANUEL AND TOMASA, Mexican *mulato* couple who were among the original 44 founders of the *pueblo* of Los Angeles in 1781. Manuel Camero, 31 years old in 1781, was born near Nayarit and moved as a child to Rosario. He married the 23-year-old Tomasa García, also from Rosario, in 1777. Manuel served a single term in the *pueblo* as *regidor* (alderman), in 1789. The couple, who remained childless, farmed and raised cattle but, for reasons unknown, had to give up their land by 1816. He died in Los Angeles in 1819, and she died ca. 1844.

CAMINO REAL. *See* El Camino Real

CANADIANS have shaped the city's history for over a century. In the 1870s the French Canadian Remi Nadeau operated 80 mule teams to haul goods to and from Los Angeles and the Inyo County silver mines. With the profits he built a new and thriving downtown hotel. The Canadian-born brothers George and William Chaffey established residential colonies at Etiwanda and Ontario in the 1880s, instituting innovative water and electrical systems for the local residents. Toronto-born Daniel Freeman founded the town of Inglewood in the same decade. The colorful Mack Sennett, "the King of Comedy," arrived from Canada in 1912 to make a splash in the movie industry. Two flamboyant characters of 1920s Los Angeles, oil speculator C. C. Julian and evangelist Aimee Semple McPherson, hailed from Canada.

Canadians live widely dispersed in the five Southern California counties and are said to number about 1 million in Los Angeles, making this the third largest city of Canadians. Since the 1970s Canadian corporations have come to own considerable property in downtown Los Angeles. Canada remains a major California trading partner.

CANOGA PARK, area in the San Fernando Valley about 25 miles northwest of downtown. The nearby hills are a source of the Los Angeles River. Albert Workman, an Australian, bought 13,000 acres in the 1860s and, during the next decade, became a major producer of wheat in the valley. He also imported thousands of eucalyptus trees. In 1912 the land was purchased and subdivided by the Los Angeles Suburban Homes Company in anticipation of the coming of water from the Owens Valley. The company bought up the vast holdings of Isaac Lankershim and his son-in-law, Isaac Newton Van Nuys, and subdivided it as Owensmouth—a name invented by Harrison Gray Otis because of the town's proximity to the terminus of the Owens River Aqueduct. The syndicate members were H. J. Whitley; Harrison Gray Otis and Harry Chandler of the *Los Angeles Times;* Otto Brant of Title Insurance Trust; and Moses H. Sherman of the Los Angeles Water Board. The name held until 1931, when it was changed to Canoga, after Canoga, New York (which in turn was named after an Indian village, Ganogeh, probably meaning "place of floating oil"). Canoga had already been the name of the Southern Pacific Railroad station in the 1890s. "Park" was added later. Sherman

Way was the center of town and the western terminus of the Pacific Electric Railway when the chamber of commerce organized in 1912. Topanga Plaza opened in 1964 as the first fully air-conditioned two-level enclosed shopping mall in western America.

CANYON COUNTRY, unincorporated community near Santa Clarita, 41 miles northwest of downtown Los Angeles.

CAPITOL MILLING COMPANY, historic flour mill on N. Spring Street in Chinatown. Built in 1831 with brick from Philadelphia and millstones imported from France, it is the oldest extant manufacturing establishment in Los Angeles. The wheels were originally driven by water flowing in the *zanja madre,* or "mother ditch," along Alameda and N. Spring. The mill, built by landowner Abel Stearns, was subsequently bought by Jacob Lowe and Herman Levi, who took over in 1883. The company, still owned by these two families, is said to be the oldest privately owned company in Los Angeles.

CAPITOL RECORDS TOWER, Hollywood office building designed by Welton Becket in 1954. He denied that the 12-story, circular structure on Vine Street was intended to resemble a stack of records topped by a needle, but it does. It was Los Angeles's first fully air-conditioned office building.

CAR CULTURE, popular movement of the 1950s and 1960s that took its inspiration from the hot-rod and motorcycle culture. Young people would customize their cars, air-brushing them in "kandy kolors" or having them pin-striped. On Saturday nights they cruised Van Nuys Boulevard to show their creations off, and young couples parked and "necked." Owners of dune buggies, mobile homes,

Capitol Milling Co., 1995. Photo by Michael Krakowiak/Marni Pitt.

and vans sometimes created elaborate interiors in the same aesthetic. Sleek-looking stretch limousines with darkened glass bearing rock stars such as the Beach Boys and other celebrities appeared on city streets. In the 1950s young painters incorporated these icons and color schemes in canvases that were shown in the Ferus Gallery on La Cienega Boulevard. What was by then called the "car culture" was also the subject of Kenneth Anger's cult film *Kustom Kar Kommandos* (1964–1965). *Rebel Without a Cause* (1955) and *American Graffiti* (1973) also depicted aspects of the car culture.

CAROLE AND BARRY KAYE MUSEUM OF MINIATURES, 1994 addition to Wilshire Boulevard's "Museum Row." The two-story, 14,000-square-foot facility is an expansion of the privately owned Petite Elite Miniature Museum, opened in 1992 in Century City by Carole Kaye, initially as a hobby and then as a business.

CARRILLO FAMILY was established in California by José Raimundo Carrillo, who arrived with the Portolá expedition in 1769. The family became prominent politically, establishing lines in Santa Barbara, San Diego, and Los Angeles. One son, José Antonio (1796–1862), was a captain and *presidio* commander in Santa Barbara, and later *alcalde* of Los Angeles (1828–1829). He joined his brother Carlos Antonio of Santa Barbara in attempting to overthrow Gov. Manuel Victoria in 1831. José Antonio married, in succession, two sisters of Pío Pico, the last Mexican governor, and was his political ally. The Hollywood character actor Leo Carrillo, a member of the Santa Barbara clan, played the role of the sidekick to the Cisco Kid in a series of films that romanticized and stereotyped Spanish California. Carrillo Beach State Park was named for Leo in 1953.

CARROLL AVENUE, historic district near downtown with the city's largest concentration of Victorian homes. It was the main street of Angelino Heights, a suburban tract development south of Sunset Boulevard built in the Boom of the Eighties. The street featured wooden buildings in the prevalent Queen Anne and Eastlake styles, with ornate scrolls, turrets, and porches. In 1960 Carroll Avenue was a dying neighborhood when a couple moved onto the 1300 block and began refurbishing their home in the original style. They were joined by others, who then spearheaded a founda-

tion and an active neighborhood organization that is responsible for much fine preservation work.

CARSON, independent industrial and commercial city 19 miles south of downtown Los Angeles on the site of the former Rancho Domínguez. Its history has been shaped by ranching, truck farming, and oil. Carson was incorporated in 1968 as an area of about 20 square miles. The 10,000 residents narrowly rejected the more historical name of Dominguez in favor of Carson, after George Carson, a pioneer of the 1850s. In assessed valuation, the city's biggest firms were Richfield Oil, Shell Oil, and the Watson Land Company, historically a dominant landlord, along with the Dominguez Estate Company. In 1990 the population reached 83,995.

CARTER, EDWARD (1911–1996), retail executive, philanthropist, and art patron. His family moved from Maryland to Los Angeles when he was a child. While a UCLA student he worked as a salesman at Silverwoods menswear chain and later at the May Company and Broadway department stores. In Horatio Alger fashion, he rose to become president of the Broadway in 1947 and revived the struggling chain in the postwar era by anticipating

---

What is so striking about Los Angeles after a period away from it is how well it works.   —Joan Didion

---

the growth of the suburbs. On a former golf course he designed one of the nation's first suburban malls, Crenshaw Shopping Center (today's Baldwin Hills Crenshaw Plaza), which featured a new Broadway store. He was soon coordinating the location of additional stores to coincide with the evolving freeway system. From 1972 to 1983 he directed the nationwide Carter Hawley Hale chain of 54 department stores.

Carter's many interests included education and the arts. He sat on the board of Occidental College and was a member of the University of California Board of Regents, on which he served from the 1960s to the 1980s. Instrumental as the principal fund-raiser for the Los Angeles County Museum of Art, he became its founding president. He was also a generous donor to the Music Center

Foundation. Edward Carter's valuable personal collection of 17th-century Dutch paintings is slated to go to LACMA. He and his wife, Hannah Carter, bestowed to UCLA a private two-acre Japanese garden in Bel-Air.

CARTER, VICTOR M. (1910–), Jewish leader who presided over the Jewish Federation Council in 1967–1968. He had been an executive in Republic Pictures and the O'Keefe and Merritt Corp. In 1961 Carter headed the fund drive of the United Jewish Welfare Fund.

CASA DE ADOBE, replica rancho home maintained on N. Figueroa Street as part of the Southwest Museum. Its patio is decorated with native shrubs, and the display rooms are furnished with genuine antiques.

CASE STUDY HOUSES, 36 innovative homes built between 1945 and 1962, featuring an open-space design, integration of indoor and outdoor living, and an exposed structural frame. The living area was placed at the rear. The experimental houses were inspired by John Entenza, editor of *Arts and Architecture* magazine, and designed by Craig Ellwood and other talented architects and designers, including Charles and Ray Eames, Richard Neutra, Raphael Soriano, Pierre Koenig, Gregory Ain, A. Quincy Jones, Ed Killingsworth, and Ralph Rapson. The avant-garde designs influenced domestic architecture nationwide.

CASTAIC, unincorporated town 50 miles from downtown Los Angeles in the northern part of the county. It is located in the San Gabriel Mountains on a former Indian *ranchería* and Spanish rancho known variously as Castec, Casteca, Castac, or Casteque, possibly from a Chumash Indian word designating a neighboring Shoshonean village and meaning "my eyes" or "our eye." A major oil field was developed nearby. The town is best known as an access point for Castaic Lake State Recreation Area and as a refreshment stop along I-5, where the Grapevine highway crosses the mountains. The population in 1990 was around 8,000, with an expectation of heavy future growth.

CASTELLAMMARE, Pacific Palisades neighborhood in the city of Los Angeles, west of Santa Ynez Canyon, 20 miles from downtown. The name, after a celebrated ancient Roman seaport and resort,

means "castle by the sea." The land was owned by a syndicate formed by oilman Alphonzo E. Bell, developer of Bel-Air, but was developed in 1925 by Frank Meline. The well-appointed homes, designed in the Mediterranean style, sold originally for $3,500. The first home built in Castellammare—and to this day a prominent landmark along Pacific Coast Highway—was Villa Leon, owned by Leon Kauffman, a Vernon manufacturer; this castlelike structure occupies six lots.

CASTILLO, AURORA (1914–), urban environmental activist. Castillo is affectionately known in her East Los Angeles Community as "La Doña." She is a cofounder and guiding light of the organization Mothers of East Los Angeles (MELA). Beginning about 1986, with the dedicated help of Fr. John Moretta and several hundred neighborhood women, MELA successfully blocked the construction of a prison, toxic waste incinerator, and hazardous waste site, all earmarked for their area. In 1995 Castillo was one of a select international group who received the Goldman Environmental Prize, considered "the Nobel Prize of environmental awards" and accompanied by a $75,000 grant. She was the first person from Los Angeles so honored.

CASTLE GREEN, tourist hotel in Pasadena, formerly called the Webster Hotel and the Green Hotel. Constructed by patent-medicine king G. G. Green, it opened on 1 January 1890, playing host to Pres. and Mrs. Benjamin Harrison the next year. The fashionable lodging on Green Street expanded over the years until it covered two city blocks, which included its own landscaped area, now Central Park. In 1964 the hotel was condemned as unsafe and renovated as a home for senior citizens

Castle Green (formerly the Green Hotel). Pasadena Convention & Visitors Bureau.

called Castle Green. Subsequently the historic structure was again reorganized to combine both subsidized low-income apartments and expensive condominiums.

CASTRO, SAL, public school teacher and Chicano activist. He led the first of the high school "blowouts" of 1968, protesting the perceived inferior education of Mexican youngsters and the racist attitudes of some educators.

CATHEDRAL OF ST. VIBIANA, first cathedral for the Roman Catholic Archdiocese of Monterey and Los Angeles. Ground was broken for the church at 2nd and Main Streets in 1869, the same year as the ground breaking for the more celebrated frontier cathedral in Santa Fe, New Mexico. Modeled after a church in Barcelona, Spain, it was constructed between 1871 and 1876, when the population of Los Angeles hovered around 5,500, of whom 3,000 were Catholic. The Baroque-style church, designed by architect Ezra F. Kysor, cost $75,000 to build and furnish. Bishop Tadeo Amat solicited and received funds from many non-Catholics, including Jews, for the project. The cathedral was extensively remodeled in 1922 and again in 1975, and was visited by the Pope on his tour of the western United States. Relics of the third-century martyr Vibiana, brought by Amat from Rome to California in 1856, are on display. In 1995 the archdiocese

Cathedral of St. Vibiana, 1877. Courtesy Robert Weinstein Collection.

announced that the landmark, severely damaged by earthquakes in 1971 and 1994, might be torn down and replaced with a church and conference center. In 1996 Cardinal Roger M. Mahony announced that a new cathedral would be built downtown to replace St. Vibiana.

CATHOLIC CHARITIES OF LOS ANGELES, INC., founded in 1919 as a nonprofit benefit corporation, provides services to the Archdiocese of Los Angeles, which embraces not only Los Angeles but also Ventura and Santa Barbara Counties. The organization is governed by a board of trustees, with the archbishop as chairman. Its 700 employees and 3,500 volunteers serve 300,000 people yearly. The organization's overall objective is to promote social justice, human dignity, and self-sufficiency. It offers a wide range of benefits, from food and shelter, to transportation and clothing, to emotional counseling, and serves all who are needy, regardless of race, sex, age, income, religion, or immigrant status.

Various internal divisions deliver specific services. The Family and Community Services Division operates 22 poverty programs, for the working poor and others. It also provides transportation to take homeless persons to shelters. Its youth outreach program serves teenagers, while an after-school program is intended for children in grades K–8. The Residential and Rehabilitative Services Division operates emergency shelters for homeless men, women, and children in the MacArthur Park/Wilshire area and Long Beach. The Immigration and Refugee Division offers supportive programs for newly arrived immigrants. The Clinical Services Division makes mental health counseling available on both a long- and short-term basis for those dealing with problems of anxiety, stress, depression, and grief.

In 1991 Catholic Charities disbursed $23.7 million, most of it stemming from government grants. Additional support and revenues came from private contributions and the United Way.

CATHOLIC CHURCH. *See* Roman Catholic Church

CATTLE were introduced to the hills and plains of Southern California during the expeditions of Portolá in 1769 and Anza in 1774 and 1775. The first herds were raised by the mission fathers and rancheros. The Spaniards and Mexicans consumed practically no dairy products, but they did eat beef, and, even more important, they sold the hides and tallow. Boston traders such as Alfred Robinson and Abel Stearns bought the hides, called "California bank notes," and shipped them to New England for use in shoe factories. The trade was described by Richard Henry Dana Jr. in *Two Years Before the Mast* (1840). The tallow, melted and stored in sacks made of hide, was used for candles.

Normally grazing on unfenced rangeland, the lean cattle were rounded up and branded in annual spring rodeos. Before the Gold Rush, California herds may have numbered 400,000 head, with each animal worth about $4. During the Gold Rush, when beef was in demand up north, the value rose to between $50 and $500 a head. At first the southern rancheros benefited tremendously, but in the late 1850s superior beef cattle were driven into California from the eastern United States, undermining the market. In the 1860s, high taxes, drought, land-title insecurities, squatters, and poor management bankrupted many of the old rancheros.

CAUGHEY, JOHN WALTON (1902–1996), UCLA history professor from 1930 to 1970, and an activist civil libertarian. During the McCarthy era, the Kansas-born scholar was fired for refusing to sign the special loyalty oath imposed by the university's board of regents. He fought his case as an infringement of First Amendment rights and eventually won full reinstatement. In the 1960s he and his wife, LaRee, conducted research supporting the Crawford case for public school integration. They published a pamphlet, "To Kill a Child's Spirit," and later an anthology, *Los Angeles* (1976). Professor Caughey's *California,* first published in 1940, was for many years the standard textbook in the field. He also authored a biography of Hubert Howe Bancroft (1946), and for many years was editor of the *Pacific Historical Review.*

CAWSTON OSTRICH FARM. *See* Ostrich farms

CBS, INC., since 1974 the official name of the former Columbia Broadcasting System, Inc. In addition to radio and television broadcasting, the company is involved in book and magazine publishing and in music recording. The New York–based firm gained a foothold in Los Angeles when it bought KNX radio station in 1936, the height of the

CBS Studios, Beverly Boulevard and Fairfax Avenue. Photo by Michael Krakowiak/Marni Pitt.

"Golden Age of Radio." It opened its Sunset Boulevard headquarters in 1938. Architecturally, the CBS Building, a five-story block at Sunset and Gower, was a monument to the International style. Many popular radio shows were broadcast from there. To accommodate the new medium of television, the corporation also built Television City, a 25-acre studio complex on Beverly Boulevard. It maintains yet another center in the San Fernando Valley. The CBS record division is based in Century City.

CEDARS-SINAI MEDICAL CENTER, major hospital facility near La Cienega and Beverly Boulevards, established in 1961 and funded by the Jewish community. Its predecessors were Kaspare Cohn Hospital, founded in 1910, whose name became Cedars of Lebanon Hospital in 1929; and Mount Sinai Hospital, established by the Bikur Cholim Society in 1922.

CEMETERIES provide a resting place for the dead, but they also often show, by their layout, sculptures, and interment policies, how living Southern Californians try to celebrate the good life.

The Roman Catholic Church consecrated several burial grounds, including one next to the Plaza Church on Main Street that was used from 1823 to 1844 for the remains of the neophyte Indians of Yangna. Other Indians were buried at the missions. Protestants had two graveyards, one burial on Fort Hill, the other near Figueroa and 9th Streets. Jews established their own cemetery in 1854 on land owned by José Andrés Sepúlveda. Meanwhile, some of the landed elite established private burial grounds, as when Phineas Banning established Wilmington Cemetery in 1857 to receive the remains of his family. By contrast, Chavez Ravine contained a potter's field. Evergreen Cemetery in

Boyle Heights, founded in 1877, did not discriminate by race or religion.

Today the county contains 58 cemeteries, including Forest Lawn, the enterprise that revolutionized the American cemetery business early in the century by offering elaborate services, burial, and perpetual care on finely manicured grounds. It is satirized in Evelyn Waugh's novel *The Loved One* (1948). Other well-known cemeteries are Hollywood Memorial Park, Holy Cross, Chapel of the Pines, and Rosedale. Some burial grounds are clustered together but segregated by religious preference, such as Home of Peace Cemetery, for Jews, and Calvary Cemetery, for Catholics. Some cemeteries receive thousands of visitors seeking out the burial sites of celebrities. Tucked in among the high

---

The African Americans, the Latinos, the Iranians, the Asians. I think in 10 years you're going to look back and you're going to see a lot of the new growth has been in companies started by these ethnic groups.

—Richard J. Riordan

---

rises of Westwood Village, for example, is Westwood Memorial Cemetery, containing the remains of Marilyn Monroe, Natalie Wood, Armand Hammer, Oscar Levant, Will and Ariel Durant, and Darryl Zanuck. Fanny Brice, Louis B. Mayer, Carl Laemmle, Harry M. Warner, and Charles Vidor are buried at Home of Peace. In Calvary Cemetery, consecrated in 1896, are the remains of Ethel and Lionel Barrymore, Gov. Henry T. Gage, and Ramon Navarro. In addition to mourning the departed in these cemeteries, visitors picnic on the grounds, study epitaphs and mausoleums, admire stained glass windows and statuary, and stroll through the manicured gardens.

Southern California has also developed a fondness for pet cemeteries. Los Angeles Pet Memorial Park, founded in Calabasas in 1928, now contains the remains of 40,000 animals, including Humphrey Bogart's dog Droopy and Hopalong Cassidy's horse Trooper. This pet interment park was depicted in Waugh's *The Loved One* as "Happier Hunting Grounds." Another such resting spot

is Pet Haven, in Gardena, with 30,000 animal remains.

CENTER THEATRE GROUP (CTG), theatrical management organization that operates the Mark Taper Forum and Ahmanson Theatre at the downtown Music Center. Gordon Davidson is its artistic director. Launched in 1967, CTG immediately shone as a star in the city's cultural firmament. By 1993, having produced hundreds of plays and attained a budget of $22.9 million, it had become the wealthiest nonprofit theatrical institution in the nation.

CENTINELA VALLEY, area partly in Los Angeles and partly in Inglewood. Its name is derived from Aguaje de la Centinela ("Spring of the Sentinel"), a land grant issued in 1844. A spring flowing in its midst empties into Ballona Lagoon. The area had its own post office from 1889 to 1895. La Casa de la Centinela Adobe, a historic house built in the early 1800s, is the oldest structure in the area.

CENTRAL AVENUE, center for African American life from the 1920s to the 1940s. This avenue paralleled the nearby Southern Pacific tracks in an era when the railroad was bringing African American families from the East to work on the dining cars of the western train runs. The main activity on Central was near the intersection of 12th Street. The avenue supported churches and newspapers, insurance companies and dentists, appliance and clothing stores, groceries and cleaners, hotels and restaurants, barber shops and beauty parlors. By World War I, restrictive homeowners' deeds in the rest of Los Angeles had created a "white wall" around the black ghetto, all but halting outward migration. The Jim Crow restrictions that barred black musicians from working in the film industry and prohibited mixed couples from dancing in many popular night spots only encouraged night life on Central Avenue. In the 1950s dozens of clubs were in operation, including the Jungle Room, Jack's Basket Room, Down Beat Club, Last Word, Club Alabam, Dunbar Grill, Memo Club, Ivy's Chicken Shack, Ritz Club, Parisian Room, and Plantation Club, among others. An enduring landmark, the Hotel Somerville, renamed Dunbar Hotel, opened in 1928, and is now preserved as a historic monument. In its initial year it hosted the first western convention of the NAACP, and musicians such as Louis Armstrong, Ella Fitzgerald, Lena

Horne, and Duke Ellington stayed there while performing at Los Angeles nightclubs.

CENTRAL BUSINESS DISTRICT (CBD). *See* Central City Association of Los Angeles; Central City East; Central City North; Central City West; Downtown Los Angeles, since 1945

CENTRAL CITY ASSOCIATION OF LOS ANGELES (CCA), business association promoting the interests of downtown. It was formed during the 1924 controversy over the creation of a union passenger railway station. The original name was Downtown Association of Los Angeles, altered to Downtown Business Men's Association of Los Angeles and, in the 1960s, to Central City Association of Los Angeles. During that decade it was led by such figures as department store executive Neil Petree, insurance company CEO Asa Call, Norman Chandler of the *Los Angeles Times,* and P. J. Winant of Bullock's Department Store. These men were all instrumental in the creation of the Music Center and Convention Center. The association's corporate members lobby government officials and educate the public on behalf of the business community regarding such issues as housing, land use, transportation, public safety, and economic and cultural development. In 1993 CCA unveiled a 25-year "Downtown Strategic Plan."

CENTRAL CITY EAST, as designated by city planners, is the downtown area east of Alameda Street. It has long been a center of industry and is the main wholesale distribution center of Los Angeles. It also incorporates part of Skid Row, though most of its numerous old transient hotels are being phased out.

CENTRAL CITY NORTH, as designated by city planners, is the downtown area that lies in the triangle delimited by the San Bernardino, Santa Monica, and Pasadena Freeways. It includes Chinatown, North Broadway, El Pueblo Park, Elysian Park, and an old industrial and rail yard section.

CENTRAL CITY WEST, as designated by city planners, is the downtown area immediately west of the Harbor Freeway and south of the Hollywood Freeway. This inner-city Latino neighborhood is slated for a significant development of offices, stores, and homes that could make it into "a second downtown." Facing eviction in an ongoing slum-removal process, local residents teamed up with public-interest lawyers and a parish priest to prevent the community's total annihilation. In 1991 Councilwoman Gloria Molina attempted to hammer out an agreement to provide affordable housing and social services to residents affected by the change.

CENTRAL PARK (PASADENA), established originally by patent-medicine king G. G. Green as landscaped gardens for Green Hotel, built in 1890.

CENTURY CITY, 176-acre high-rise community in West Los Angeles on the original site of the 20th Century–Fox motion picture studio. The developer, ALCOA, hired architect Welton Becket in 1957, and construction began in 1961, with heavy use made of aluminum. Century City's skyscrapers are visible from much of the city. The buildings include hotels with over 1,600 rooms altogether, offices, theaters, and shopping centers linked by pedestrian malls and served by the largest underground parking garage in the nation. Century City has its own hospital. Forty thousand people work in 10 million square feet of office space, and 4,000 more live in condos and town houses. Although its design is criticized by many architects and urban designers as being cold and forbidding, supporters maintain it is a "mature and vibrant symbol" of the city. Moviemakers have

Century Plaza Towers and ABC Entertainment Center. Courtesy Premisys Real Estate Services.

found the architecture photogenic. In *Conquest of the Planet of the Apes* (1972), Century City represented a metropolis of the future, and in *The Turning Point* (1977) it doubled for New York's Lincoln Center. Part of the old 20th Century studio remains in operation nearby.

CERRITOS, independent city 17 miles southeast of downtown Los Angeles. The original community was engaged largely in dairying, and was first incorporated as Dairy Valley in 1956 by dairymen pressing to protect their interests against suburban developers. In the mid-1960s it was still largely a backwater dairy town, with only 3,500 people and 100,000 cows. Inevitably the cows and chickens gave way to people, and a residential, commercial, and industrial community emerged. The name was changed to Cerritos in 1966. With its 13 distinct ethnic groups, Cerritos in the 1980s was, according to CSUN geographers James P. Allen and Eugene Turner, the country's most "ethnically diverse" city. The city comprises 8.9 square miles, and as of 1989–1990 the median household income was $52,870, the average home value was $265,763, and the median age was 30.1 years. Its population has remained relatively stable for the last twenty years, numbering 53,240 in 1990.

CERRO GORDO, silver mining region in the Inyo Mountains, 250 miles north of Los Angeles, which brought a flurry of commercial activity to Los Angeles from the 1860s to around 1875. Teamsters headquartered on Negro Alley, in what was becoming Chinatown, south of the Old Plaza, kept 1,200 mules in harness hauling goods and silver. Mule teams and skinners brought silver bars into town and down to San Pedro; returning from the port, they passed back through town and into the mountains with barley, fruit, nuts, potatoes, corn, whiskey, tools, clothing, and other supplies. Freight bills amounted to $500,000 a year, while business receipts rose as high as $5 million. A rail line, the Los Angeles & Independence Railroad, opened in 1875. It would connect Santa Monica with Los Angeles, and Los Angeles with Inyo, but only the first leg was completed.

CHALFANT, WILLIAM (WILLIE) ARTHUR (1868–1943), scrappy editor and publisher of an Inyo County newspaper who bitterly denounced Los Angeles's water imperialism. He argued his case fervently in a book, *The Story of Inyo* (1922).

CHAMBERS, STAN (1923–), pioneer television newscaster. Chambers started his career in 1948 when, for 27 straight hours, KTLA covered the tragic story of Kathy Fiscus, a three-and-a-half-year-old who fell into a well and died. His coverage on the new medium of television was carried worldwide. Later, microphone in hand, the Los Angeles–born Chambers conducted street interviews at the corner of Hollywood and Vine on the show "Meet Me in Hollywood," which aired for a decade. He made the announcement of President Kennedy's assassination, and in 1991 personally received George Holliday's home video of the beating of Rodney King. The handling of this tape earned KTLA a Peabody Award.

CHAMBERS OF COMMERCE have orchestrated local business development for over a century. The first chamber was formed in 1873 as the

Chamber of Commerce Building, 1913. Pitt Collection.

Board of Trade, and reorganized on a new footing as the Los Angeles Chamber of Commerce in 1888. The goal it established in 1890 has changed very little over the years: "to foster and encourage commerce; to stimulate home manufactures; to induce immigration and the subdivision, settlement and cultivation of our lands; to assist in the development of the material resources of the region; and generally to promote the business interests of Los Angeles city and county and the country tributary thereto." The Los Angeles Area Chamber of Commerce has been probably the most active and successful such organization in the nation. Other Southern California cities and many smaller subareas have chambers as well—the *Thomas Brothers Guide* for 1991 lists 117 of them.

CHANDLER, DOROTHY BUFFUM (BUFFY) (1901–), civic leader and *Los Angeles Times* mover-and-shaker who is recognized as the most powerful and influential woman in Los Angeles history. Born into an established Long Beach family (owners of Buffum's department store), in 1922 she married Norman Chandler, the eldest son of Harry Chandler, real estate tycoon and *Times* publisher. During the war years she took control of the paper's women's section and steered other corporate decision making as well. She later became involved in cultural affairs, saving the Hollywood Bowl

Dorothy Chandler. Courtesy Los Angeles Times History Center.

from financial collapse in 1951, and promoting cultural exchange with the Soviet Union in 1958.

Chandler exerted a strong influence over editorial matters, for example in promoting the presidential candidacy of Eisenhower over Taft in 1952 and of the Rockefeller wing of the GOP. As a member of the University of California Board of Regents, she generally sided with the liberal wing, as when she backed Franklin Murphy for UCLA chancellor. She helped William Knowland in his run for governor. Although refusing to be identified as a feminist, Chandler actively promoted women's interests. A political moderate, she pressed to soften the *Times*'s image as the last bastion of Cold War conservatism, anti-Communism, and rock-ribbed Republicanism. She assumed a leadership role in the *Times*-owned tabloid newspaper the *Mirror*, and helped her husband restructure and move the Times-Mirror Corporation into enterprises other than newspapers.

One of Chandler's major achievements was spearheading the 10-year fund-raising drive to establish the Music Center, which lasted from 1954 to 1964. She skillfully invaded the private coffers of many segments of society and their individual members: old-money families (Myford Irvine), the westside Jewish community (Eugene Wyman and Mark Taper), and the newly affluent (Howard Ahmanson). She made many enemies but achieved her goal. Her contribution to the arts was recognized and honored in the naming of the Dorothy Chandler Pavilion. It was her enormous influence over the music world that helped bring Zubin Mehta as conductor of the Los Angeles Philharmonic in 1965.

CHANDLER, HARRY (1864–1944), publisher of the *Los Angeles Times* from 1917 to 1941, real estate tycoon, and political kingmaker. Born in New Hampshire, Chandler came to Los Angeles to cure his "weak lungs" in 1883. He worked as a clerk in the *Times* delivery room, and in 1894 married Marian Otis, one of publisher Harrison Gray Otis's three daughters. He was elected to the city's Board of Freeholders in 1900 and backed direct legislation reforms. Aside from that, Chandler was old-guard Republican. No one ran for office under the GOP label without his approval. He shared his father-in-law's hatred of organized labor, and took an active role in the prosecution of the McNamaras for the 1910 bombing of the *Times*. He backed the fight for a free harbor, and was a major figure in

Harry Chandler. Courtesy California State Library.

the real estate syndicate that developed the San Fernando Valley, making a fortune in the process. Chandler took over the paper from has father-in-law in 1917, and was publisher until 1941. An avid Los Angeles booster, especially in the 1920s, Chandler devoted himself to encouraging the expansion of local industry, agriculture, tourism, population, and real estate development. He was a prime mover in the chamber of commerce and All Year Club. With investments in publishing (including printing and binding), ranching, timber, paper and woolen mills, water development, steamship lines, air express, and acreage in Mexico, his personal fortune was said to be between $200 million and $1 billion. At the time of his death he was probably the richest man in Southern California.

Chandler was a complex man. A tall, imposing figure with a baby face, he lived in a comparatively simple manner. He was a Congregationalist, a Mason, and a teetotaler. Yet he also dealt secretly with police spies, provocateurs, and seedy speculators.

CHANDLER, OTIS (1928–), publisher of the *Los Angeles Times* from 1960 to 1980. The son of Harry Chandler, he was born in Pasadena and attended Philips Academy in Andover, Massachusetts, and Stanford University. When he took over the reins of the *Times* at age 30, the paper was

highly profitable but still steeped in the tradition of yellow journalism and in narrow, Cold War politics.

Chandler fostered a vision of Los Angeles as a world-class city, and of the *Los Angeles Times* as a giant of journalism, second only to the *New York Times.* He hired experienced talent, formed a news syndicate with the *Washington Post,* expanded the foreign bureaus, editorialized against the conservative John Birch Society, and featured important articles on civil rights problems. He rebuffed the old-guard Republican leadership of Los Angeles, adopted a liberal Republican position, and hammered Mayor Sam Yorty editorially for his provincialism. Chandler's personal enthusiasm for outdoor recreation and sports was reflected in the *Times*'s coverage. Although he realized many of his goals, he suffered a bitter defeat when he failed to topple Yorty in the 1969 election.

CHANDLER, RAYMOND (1888–1959), Chicago-born detective fiction writer who first arrived in Los Angeles in 1912. After a stint in the Canadian army he returned in 1919 to a high-paying job in the oil industry. When he lost that job in 1932 he began writing for magazines such as *Colliers* and the *Saturday Evening Post;* he completed his first detective novel, *The Big Sleep,* in 1939 at age 51. His hard-boiled private eye, Philip Marlowe, immediately captured the imagination of the reading public. Most of Chandler's works are set in Los Angeles, a city he grudgingly admired. Also well known are *Farewell, My Lovely* (1940), *The Lady in the Lake* (1943), and *The Long Goodbye* (1954). These four novels were all made into films. Scores of places mentioned in his books are identifiable even today, including Marlowe's office on La Cienega and the Appian Way Hotel in Santa Monica, which he calls "Bay City."

CHANNEL HEIGHTS HOUSING PROJECT, model 1930s low-cost housing project. The units were designed originally, by modernist architect Richard Neutra, as a proposal for "Amity-Compton," a community of low-cost private homes to be built in Compton. The project evolved into multiple-unit wartime living for shipyard workers in the harbor area. The 600 units, costing $2,600 each, were located in either a two-story building accommodating four families or a one-story duplex. The 222 individual structures were arranged in three super-blocks. The units were described as sturdy, simple, and cheerful; they continued to serve for some years before they were emptied and abandoned. History professor Thomas Hines suggests that even today the basic concept of Channel Heights could provide a model for alleviating housing problems in South Central Los Angeles.

CHAPARRAL, plant community consisting of brush and low trees that cling to hillsides and mountains. The name derives from the Spanish *chaparro* (dwarf evergreen oak). Tree and plant species typical of chaparral are chamise, ceanothus, scrub oak, red shank, sagebrush, deerwood, greasewood, live oak, mesquite, manzanita, sumac, sugar bush, and buckwheat. The plants, which tend to be prickly and dense, have adapted to survive in very dry conditions, becoming dormant during the hot months and growing during the rainy season. They stand 4 to 15 feet high. In summers the chaparral becomes tinder-dry and burns readily, menacing human habitation. However, such fires promote reseeding and rapid regrowth. Animals that live in the chaparral include raccoons, deer, woodrats, opossum, ground squirrels, moles, foxes, skunks, and feral dogs and cats. Among reptiles are gopher snakes, alligator lizards, horned lizards, and the Pacific rattlesnake. Birds include California quail, red-tailed hawks, Anna's hummingbirds, crows, great horned owls, mockingbirds, thrashers, band-tailed pigeons, scrub jays, towhees, and Brewer's blackbirds. Among the insects noted there are ants; the sphinx moth and Gulf fritillary butterfly, together with their caterpillar larval stage; Jerusalem crickets; and bees. The environment is sensitively described by Richard Lillard in *My Urban Wilderness in the Hollywood Hills: A Year of Years on Quito Lane* (1983). Chaps, the leather leg shields worn by cowboys and vaqueros, take their name from the Spanish word *chaparajos,* indicating their origin as protection when riding through the chaparral.

CHAPLIN, CHARLIE (CHARLES SPENCER) (1889–1977), British-born actor, producer, and director who arrived in the United States in 1910. Hired by Mack Sennett of Keystone Studio, he made his first film appearance in *Making a Living* (1914). His second short film (he made 35 in his year with Sennett) was *Kid Auto Races,* in which he introduced the character of the "Little Tramp." Chaplin used the bowler-hatted persona, with variations, in many short films and features, becom-

ing established in such films as *The Kid* (1921), *The Gold Rush* (1925), *City Lights* (1931), *Modern Times* (1936), and *The Great Dictator* (1940). In 1919 Chaplin established his own studio, United Artists, in partnership with D. W. Griffith, Douglas Fairbanks, and Mary Pickford. He was attacked by the House Un-American Activities Committee in the 1940s for alleged Communist sympathies and for moral turpitude, and angrily moved with his family to Switzerland. In 1972, with the McCarthy era ended, he returned to a warm and emotional welcome in Hollywood. In 1975 he received a British knighthood, having never given up his citizenship.

CHAPMAN, JOSEPH ("PIRATE JOE") (1785–1849), first American in Los Angeles. In 1818, while on a pirate raid along the California coast, he was captured at Monterey. Don Antonio Lugo took the blond captive under his wing and brought him to Los Angeles on the promise that Chapman would supervise Indian neophytes in the building of a church at the Plaza. The Yankee sailor was a gifted woodworker, and he made good his promise by using timbers hefted in the mountains and carried to the Plaza by Indians. Chapman was baptized and in 1822 married a Señorita Ortega. He also had valuable basic medical skills and successfully treated Gov. Manuel Victoria, who was wounded in 1831 while fighting dissident Californios at Cahuenga Pass. In 1821 he built a grist mill for the Franciscan fathers at San Gabriel; most remarkably, he also constructed for them, again using mountain timbers, the 60-ton schooner *Guadalupe,* which he launched at San Pedro. He attempted commercial winemaking by setting out 4,000 vines taken as cuttings from San Gabriel Mission. When the enterprise failed, Pirate Joe and his family moved to Santa Barbara in 1839.

CHARTER AMENDMENTS, CITY OF LOS ANGELES. *See* Los Angeles City Charter; Los Angeles City Charter reform

CHARTER OAK, part of the city of Covina, developed in the 1890s. It was probably named for a large oak tree that reminded someone of the Charter Oak in Hartford, Connecticut. Over 200 Native American *metates* (concave stones used for grinding grain) still exist there near Reeder Street and Walnut Wash. The population in 1990 was 8,858.

CHATEAU MARMONT HOTEL, lodging house on the Sunset Strip associated with filmland personalities. Featuring bungalows and large rooms, it attracted such luminaries as Errol Flynn and Greta Garbo. Boris Karloff, Jean Harlow, and director Billy Wilder lived there in relative seclusion. It was at this hotel that John Belushi met his death from a drug overdose in 1982. Oliver Stone's film *The Doors* (1991) depicts rock star Jim Morrison lurching across the Marmont's roof in a drunken stupor. The Garden of Allah Hotel, another Hollywood watering place, once stood across the street. Humorist Robert Benchley, a famous hanger-on at the Garden, feared the car traffic on Sunset so much that he would hire a taxi to drive him to the Marmont.

Chateau Marmont Hotel. Photo by Lori Shepler.

CHATSWORTH, residential area near the Santa Susana Mountains in the northwestern corner of the San Fernando Valley. It is part of the city of Los Angeles, 31 miles from downtown. An Indian village existed at Stoney Point, on the east side of Topanga Canyon Boulevard. Homesteaders came to the site as early as 1870. The Chatsworth Historical Society preserves Homestead Acre, the only remaining homestead cottage in the area. Over 2,000 films have been shot in this locale, one of the earliest being Cecil B. De Mille's *The Squaw Man* (1913). Chatsworth, named after the estate of the duke of Devonshire, had about 35,000 residents in 1991.

Chatsworth Community Church, dating from 1903, is the oldest public building in Chatsworth. One of the few examples of New England–style architecture left in Southern California, it was built as a Methodist church and originally stood on Topanga Canyon Boulevard, but was moved to Lassen Street.

CHAVEZ RAVINE, location of Dodger Stadium. The steep canyon in downtown Los Angeles was named for Julian Chávez, a Mexican pioneer who served on the first County Board of Supervisors. It was a potter's field in the 1850s, the site of a smallpox infirmary in the 1880s, a tuberculosis sanitarium in the early decades of the 20th century, and a working-class barrio in the 1930s. The locals, some of whom kept goats and chickens on the steep hills, called it Palo Verde. In the late 1940s the ravine was slated to become an integrated federal housing project. After much political turmoil, the project was killed and the site preempted for a stadium for the transplanted Brooklyn Dodgers baseball team. Twenty longtime resident families resisted the move. The Archegas, who had owned a home in the ravine for 36 years and refused to be bought out, were evicted with all their belongings on 9 May 1959. Mrs. Aurora Archega was jailed for 30 days, ending the protest. The city then sold 300 acres to Walter O'Malley, who built the stadium that opened in 1962. The ravine is also the site of an old arboretum.

CHAVEZ RAVINE ARBORETUM, Southern California's first botanic garden, located in Elysian Park. It was established by the Los Angeles Horticultural Society in 1893 and still has many original and rare plantings. Among them are a double row of date palms, rubber trees, and a golden-leaf baphia, perhaps the only one of this species in cultivation in the United States.

CHESSMAN, CARYL (1921–1960), the "red light bandit," who was convicted and condemned to death in 1948. While on parole, and using a stolen car with a red light to fool his victims, he stalked couples in their cars on lover's lanes in Altadena and along Mulholland Drive. He robbed his victims and sexually assaulted some of the women. Because Chessman forced his victims to move from one car to another he was charged with violating the state's "Little Lindbergh Act." He was ultimately condemned to death, not for murder, but for "kidnapping with great bodily harm"; this irregularity made him the center of a movement to repeal the death penalty. A brilliant "jailhouse lawyer" and media star, he won repeated stays of execution for 12 years. His books, *Cell 2455* and

Death Row (both 1954), became best-sellers. Governor Edmund G. "Pat" Brown refused to intervene, and Chessman was sent to the gas chamber in 1960.

CHEVIOT HILLS, housing tract in West Los Angeles south of Pico Boulevard along Motor Avenue. Developed in the 1930s and 1940s, its large homes replaced orange groves and celery and bean fields. The name of the tract and many of its streets, such as Dumfries, Haddington, Wigtown, and Troon, reflect the Scottish background of the developers, Forrester and McConnell.

CHICAGO PARK, town mapped by developers south of Monrovia in the sandbed of the San Gabriel River. During the Boom of the Eighties fanciful brochures depicted steamers paddling "up the rippling waters of the San Gabriel" at Chicago Park. Buyers bought land to sell for quick profits, but the town followed the fate of many boomtowns and never materialized. In fact, at one time it had an estimated 2,289 lots for sale and only one lonely resident—who eventually left.

CHICANO MOVEMENT, militant political activity, originating in the 1960s, of young Mexican Americans attempting to improve educational and economic opportunities and to raise cultural identity and pride among Mexicans. The movement popularized the terms *Chicano* (a contraction of *mexicano*), and *la raza* ("the race" or "the people"). It emerged full-blown in 1967 both locally and in the Southwest and in March 1968 resulted in high school "blowouts"—staged walkouts. Most active in East Los Angeles, militants demanded an increase in the number of Spanish-speaking teachers in the public schools, instruction in Spanish for non-English speakers, courses in Mexican history and culture, and better access to higher education.

Manifestations of the movement on college campuses resulted in the establishment of Chicano studies programs at CSULA and CSUN. The movement also spearheaded a drive to end stereotypes in television broadcasting, to increase opportunities in the arts, and to end discrimination in jobs and housing. Activists also pressed for improved relations with police and sheriff's officers. This phase climaxed after the Chicano Moratorium, an antiwar demonstration in Belvedere Park in August 1970 that resulted in tragic violence, including the death of *Times* journalist Ruben Salazar. The Texas-born Raza Unida Party caused a flurry of excitement in 1971 but made little political headway. After achieving some improvements in affirmative action hiring, bilingual education, and Chicano studies programs, the movement subsided in the 1970s. The terms *Chicana* and *Chicano* survived, referring to Americans of Mexican ancestry.

CHICK, LAURA (1947–), councilwoman from the 3rd District. She holds a bachelor's degree in history from UCLA and an M.A. in social work from USC. Chick formerly worked as chief field deputy to Councilwoman Joy Picus. She has encouraged the establishment of a San Fernando Valley Economic Council to help develop new jobs.

CHIEF ADMINISTRATIVE OFFICER, LOS ANGELES COUNTY. *See* Los Angeles County Chief Administrative Officer

CHILDREN'S HOME SOCIETY OF CALIFORNIA, welfare society for homeless children in downtown Los Angeles. The society was formed in 1891 by Dr. and Mrs. J. R. Townsend, former missionaries to Jamaica who were grieving the loss of their only child, a son. Its first superintendent was Rev. R. Garten, an Iowan. Still headquartered in Southern California but with offices in many cities in California, the Children's Home Society now provides services in adoption, foster home care, child care, parent education, counseling of pregnant women, and shelter care for thousands of homeless children and their families.

CHILD WELFARE CONDITIONS have plummeted in recent years. Much of the blame is ascribed to a growing poverty rate in the population and shrinking public services. According to a 1987 city council report, in that year 400,000 of the city's 1.5 million youngsters were in need. (By 1990, according to the U.S. Census, the figure had risen to 483,000.) In 1989 the cost in Los Angeles of caring for two children under age five was $6,500 per year, an amount that many families were unable to provide. Some 455,000 to 545,000 youngsters—about 40 percent of the school-age population (4–16)—were latchkey children, and another 362,026 infants and preschoolers in the county had mothers who worked outside the home. The Washington-based Food Research and Action Center, which tracks hunger and under-nutrition, found that emergency food services for children rose 38 percent in Los Angeles in 1992 over 1991. In addition, in 1990 the Inter-Agency Council on Child Abuse and Neglect tallied 114,000 reported cases of abuse and neglect in the county, including one child murdered each week by a caretaker or parent. Social-work caseloads have reached an all-time high. Bored, alienated, and unemployed teenagers are increasingly involved in gang activity. Fatal shootings of young people under age 19, mainly gang-related, have risen annually, from 12 percent of all murders in 1970 to 26.5 percent in 1991.

Public services for children have declined materially since the 1950s and 1960s. In the post–Proposition 13 era, city-, county-, and board of education–supervised programs and activities that once existed for children from kindergarten through 12th grade, such as sports, arts and crafts, music, drama, and library story hours, have disappeared or been sharply curtailed. The same is true for such organizations as the Boy Scouts and the Girl Scouts, which today lack the volunteers who were once the mainstays of these programs. The inner cities, especially, lack the YWCA, YMCA, and 4-H programs and Little League teams that once provided recreation and guidance to urban youths.

In its approaches to these problems, which exist nationwide, Los Angeles County has actually been a leader in reform. The county was the first to establish, in 1978, teams to review child deaths. In 1995 the U.S. Advisory Board on Child Abuse and Neglect published the results of a 2½-year study. Shocking in its statistics, the report ended with a series of recommendations that included the institution nationwide of child death review teams modeled on those of Los Angeles County.

CHINATOWN has had three separate incarnations in Los Angeles. The first Chinatown arose in the 1870s on the east side of the Plaza, on a ramshackle street known as "Calle de los Negros" or "Negro Alley" (the present-day site of Union Station). It was inhabited by Chinese workers brought to Southern California after 1859 to construct a wagon route near Newhall, and later to build the railroads. In 1870 they numbered about 200, and by the 1880s and 1890s the area had become known as Chinatown. By 1900, thousands of Chinese, mostly males, lived in this ghetto, working as food peddlers, laundry and restaurant employees, and

Chinatown, 1995. Photo by Michael Krakowiak/Marni Pitt.

curio shop attendants. Much of the area consisted of overcrowded tenements, markets, shops, restaurants, native theaters, joss houses (temples), and opium dens—but there were no subterranean tunnels, despite persistent rumors to that effect. Prostitution and gambling flourished, often with the cooperation of city police. By the 1890s community leadership was centered in the Garnier Building on Los Angeles Street, which had been constructed expressly for Chinese businesses, offices, and residences and which still exists. This Chinatown was razed in 1933 to make way for the new rail terminal.

Several displaced Chinese families, led by developer Peter Soo Hoo, then created a second Chinese enclave, known as New Chinatown. It was located several blocks to the northwest, where land was cheap and the property privately owned. Opened in June 1938, the neighborhood immediately thrived.

"China City," a block-long reconstruction of a street in China—as imagined by Hollywood—also opened in 1938. Like Olvera Street, it was the spiritual godchild of ethnic romanticist Christine Sterling and was intended strictly as a tourist attraction. Decorated with pieces from various movie sets, the street featured an ornate gate, rickshaws, and a "pirate junk." Many members of the Chinese community were dubious about "China City," and no attempt was made to rebuild the street when fire destroyed it. Meanwhile, New Chinatown grew and prospered; it also began to cater increasingly to tourists, soon becoming a major downtown attraction.

In the mid-1990s some 14,000 people, most of them immigrants, lived in Chinatown. The area has suffered economic decline in recent decades, however, with the true center of Chinese life in Southern California shifting to Monterey Park and Alhambra. To offset stagnation, the Community Redevelopment Agency has maintained a project on 300 acres in Chinatown since 1980.

In 1995 the Chinese Historical Society of Southern California received a gift of 200,000 artifacts dating back to the early settlers. These objects were collected between 1989 and 1991 at 59 digs, supervised by archaeologist Roberta Greenwood, that took place during construction of the Metro Red Line station at Union Station, site of the original Chinatown. The objects, covering a range from fragile porcelain to Chinese coins, offer valuable insight into the daily life of those times. The Chinese Historical Society recently added another link to its regional past by saving a Chinese burial shrine that stood forgotten in Evergreen Cemetery in Boyle Heights. Chinatown's founders built the shrine, which consists of two 12-foot kilns connected by an altar, during the 1880s. The two-year restoration will cost $60,000.

CHINATOWN, 1974 Roman Polanski film starring Jack Nicholson, Faye Dunaway, and John Huston. It depicts a bizarre tale of incest, intrigue, and violence. Written in the vein of the hard-boiled mysteries of Dashiell Hammett and Raymond Chandler, the movie also portrays local political machinations concerning the development of Owens River water earlier in the century. Writer Robert Towne, a native Angeleno, received an Oscar for best screenplay.

CHINESE today number about 170,000 in the county. The first Chinese came via Northern California during the Gold Rush; they originated in the depressed Kwangtung region of southeastern China. In the Los Angeles area they were recruited as house servants, orchard hands, and railroad construction laborers. The 1850 census listed two male house servants—Ah Luce and Ah Fou—as the first Chinese residents in the city. Chinese laborers who were recruited in China by Chinese contractors and trapped into servitude for years afterward were considered "coolie slaves" by whites. Some 4,000 Chinese—mostly males from Canton—were recorded as living in the city in 1870. Many of the men farmed or peddled vegetables or swung picks and shovels laying the tracks for the Southern Pacific in the southern part of the state. From 1874 to 1876 they carved out the San Fernando railroad tunnel through the mountains, at a considerable loss of life.

In Los Angeles the Chinese endured vicious racial hatred, stemming from intense economic rivalries with whites. Norwalk, Burbank, Vernon, Pasadena, and other communities used the restrictive federal legislation of 1882, 1892, and 1902 to forcibly drive them out. Real estate developers incorporated restrictive covenants into deeds to prevent Chinese from owning residential property. These covenants lasted until the 1960s.

Today the community is more diverse than ever. Cantonese, Mandarin, and Szechwan dialects and cuisine are widely in evidence, and many Chinese have come from Vietnam, Hong Kong, Taiwan, and other parts of Asia. The community comprises rich and poor, supporters and opponents of the Communist regime, traditionalists and assimilationists. Older immigrant women work long hours in crowded, unsafe dressmaking shops. In the

Chinese in La Fiesta parade, 1901. Courtesy Robert Weinstein Collection.

1970s the young Chinese American realtor Frederic Hsieh began attracting Chinese businesses into the suburban community of Monterey Park; that town has since become the most affluent and expansive Chinese community in Southern California. Education tends to be a high priority among the Chinese.

A federal program instituted in 1991 gives legal-immigrant status to foreigners who promise to invest $1 million in a business that creates at least 10 full-time jobs. This program has attracted hundreds of millionaires from China, Taiwan, and Hong Kong. By the same token, 15 percent of the ethnic Chinese of Southern California live in poverty, according to the 1990 census.

A museum of Chinese American history is under development in the Garnier Building in Old Chinatown, on the Pico-Garnier block.

CHINESE MASSACRE, vicious assault on the Chinese of Los Angeles by an estimated mob of 500 whites, on 24 October 1871 in Calle de los Negros (a.k.a. Negro Alley) and at the Coronel adobe near the Plaza. The conflict was touched off by a dispute between two rival Chinese immigrant associations, known as tongs, said to involve a clash over a beautiful Chinese woman. A mounted policeman attempting to disarm the Chinese disputants was shot and killed. Sheriff James F. Burns and Robert Widney, a prominent resident, tried to calm tempers, but a mob gathered and in the next five hours murdered 19 Chinese men and boys, 15 of them by hanging. Of the 11 white men who risked life and limb attempting to protect the Chinese and restore order, one was shot. One of the white participants later wrote, "American blood had been shed. There was . . . that sense of shock that Chinese had dared to fire on whites, and kill with recklessness outside their own color set." The incident focused nationwide attention on the remote village of Los Angeles. Judge Ygnacio Sepúlveda and a grand jury pressed for justice. Seven rioters were convicted, but only one was punished. An "Anti-Coolie" Club, formed in May 1876, gave evidence that bigotry against the Chinese was not yet dead.

CHINESE THEATRE, Hollywood Boulevard movie palace built by Sid Grauman in 1927. The concrete slabs in the entry court displaying footprints, handprints, and congratulatory messages from movie stars were an immediate Hollywood attraction. The custom came about when Grauman accidentally stepped into wet cement in the courtyard. The first celebrity footprints belonged to Douglas Fairbanks, Mary Pickford, and Norma Talmadge. The prints remain a popular draw for both Angelenos and tourists. Grauman's Chinese has, since the 1970s, been known as Mann's Chinese.

CHINIGCHINICH, Indian prophet or god who originated among the local Indians, probably the Gabrieleños, though the Indians of the San Juan Capistrano area absorbed his legend as well. He was a creator and lawgiver who lived in the sky and created the world and all its creatures. Porpoises, crows, and other animals were said to have carried his messages to the people. He was associated with a jimson-weed cult. Fr. Gerónimo Boscana described him in an appendix to Alfred Robinson's

Mann's (formerly Grauman's) Chinese Theatre, 1995. Photo by Michael Krakowiak/Marni Pitt.

Life in California (1846). The deity's name appears in various spellings, often Chingichnich.

CHOUINARD ART INSTITUTE. *See* California Institute of the Arts (Cal Arts)

CHRISTIAN SCIENCE, American religion and system of healing founded about 1886 by Mary Baker Eddy in Boston. Its followers in Los Angeles met first in 1889 in the home of Mrs. Bixby, and they formed a church in the city in 1892. The leading founder was Lou Aldrich, a student of Mrs. Eddy's. Women, especially, were attracted to Christian Science as an alternative to established religion and medicine. Over the years the church was enveloped in doctrinal disputes and lawsuits and endured numerous reorganizations and reincorporations. It met at first on W. 7th Street but in 1910 occupied a spacious structure on South Alvarado, and soon afterward another on West Adams. Today it is housed in churches and reading rooms throughout the Los Angeles region.

CHRISTOPHER, WARREN M. (1925–), attorney and, from 1993 to 1997, U.S. secretary of state under Pres. Bill Clinton. A graduate of USC and Stanford Law School, he worked as a law clerk to Supreme Court Justice William O. Douglas. He joined the law offices of O'Melveny and Meyers in 1950 and, while a principal of the firm, served as vice chairman of the McCone Commission investigating the 1965 Watts riot. Pres. Jimmy Carter named him deputy secretary of state in 1977, in which capacity he served until 1981. Mayor Tom Bradley appointed him in 1991 to head a commission—subsequently known as the Christopher Commission—to investigate the Rodney King incident and excessive use of police force.

CHRISTOPHER COMMISSION, special panel established in 1991 to investigate brutality in the Los Angeles Police Department. Formed in the wake of the beating of motorist Rodney King, it was headed by attorney Warren M. Christopher. The members examined police records and found evidence of the use of excessive force, racism, and mismanagement at the top. It recommended that Police Chief Daryl Gates step aside and that reforms be instituted. Some of the proposed reforms were incorporated into Proposition F, a ballot measure approved by the voters in 1992. One of the reforms limited the position of police chief to a five-

year term, with an option of a second such term; in all, the tenure cannot exceed 10 years.

CHUMASH INDIANS, native people who occupied the Malibu coast and western Santa Monica Mountains, as well as other parts of California. They lived in the region for as long as 5,000 years before the coming of the Europeans, and adhered to a rather sophisticated system of governance. Their villages were the most populous in California. The Chumash, who built sturdy seaworthy craft, called their village at Malibu Humaliwu, meaning "the surf sounds loud." The explorer Juan Cabrillo encountered the Chumash on 10 October 1542, and the Franciscan fathers later absorbed the Chumash into their Indian mission system. The remains of many burial grounds have been uncovered, including one at Cypress Cove in 1991.

CHUNG, TONG SOO (T. S.) (1956–), Korean American leader. Born in Korea, Chung arrived in Los Angeles as a teenager, attended Hollywood High, Philips Academy in Andover, Massachusetts, Harvard, and Princeton. He took his law degree at UCLA. He founded the Korean-American Coalition, dedicated to fostering ethnic understanding inside and outside the Korean community. In the wake of the rioting that hit Koreatown in 1992, Chung organized a peace march to help focus the outrage and sadness of many Koreans.

CHURCH OF JESUS CHRIST OF LATTER-DAY SAINTS. *See* Mormons

CHURCH OF OUR LADY QUEEN OF THE ANGELS, oldest church in Los Angeles. Popularly known as the Plaza Church, it was originally called Church of Our Lady of the Angels ("Queen" was added in 1859) and stood on another location, perhaps at the junction of Sunset Boulevard and Upper Main Street, until damaged by a flood and vacated. The current structure, designed by José Antonio Ramírez, was built on the Plaza between 1818 and 1822, with money raised by the sale of donated wine and cattle, and the labor of Franciscan neophyte Indian laborers who hauled the beams from the San Gabriel Mountains. Joseph Chapman, the first American in Los Angeles, supervised the effort. The structure originally had a flat roof covered with *brea* (tar). The roof, façade, and interior have undergone periodic changes. The bells are solely decorative. In

Church of Our Lady Queen of the Angels, Los Angeles, late 19th century. Courtesy Robert Weinstein Collection.

1859 the church was the residence of Bishop Tadeo Amat. Always a parish church and never part of the Franciscan mission system, it has been administered by the Claretian Missionaries since 1910. It is one of the most actively used Catholic churches in the western United States.

CHURCH OF SCIENTOLOGY, religion based on the therapeutic belief system originated in the 1950s by science fiction writer L. Ron Hubbard. The belief system is also known as Dianetics, from a Greek word meaning "logical reasoning," as opposed to "intuition." Although the movement is based in New Jersey, it has a major branch in Los Angeles and owns considerable property in Hollywood.

CINCO DE MAYO, fifth of May festivity commemorating the 1862 victory of an outnumbered Mexican military force over the invading imperial army of Napoleon III at the city of Puebla, Mexico. The holiday is celebrated yearly in Lincoln Park and other public places in Los Angeles amid great fanfare—in fact, it attracts more celebrants in Los Angeles than in Mexico itself.

CIO. *See* Labor union movement

CITRUS FRUIT GROWING. *See* Oranges

CITY ARCHIVES, LOS ANGELES. *See* Los Angeles City Archives

"CITY BEAUTIFUL" MOVEMENT, high-minded early-20th-century progressive crusade to beautify and humanize the city. Inspired by the remodeling of Paris and the grand design of the Great White City at the Chicago World's Fair of 1893, it had counterparts in many large American cities.

Advocates pressed for parks, parkways, promenades, public squares, waterside boulevards, and grand architecture, as well as public comfort stations, baths, and other amenities. An enthusiastic advocate was the preacher and settlement house director Dana Bartlett, author of *The Better City* (1907). In Los Angeles the movement resulted in a comprehensive zoning ordinance in 1909 (the first in the United States), a city planning association in 1915, a city planning commission in 1920, and the county Regional Planning Commission in 1923, which influenced the design of Los Angeles, Long Beach, and Pasadena.

CITY CHARTER. *See* Los Angeles City Charter

CITY COUNCIL, LOS ANGELES. *See* Los Angeles City Council

CITY HALL, LOS ANGELES. *See* Los Angeles City-County Civic Center

CITY NEWS SERVICE (CNS), wire service syndicate founded in Los Angeles in 1928 by Marvin Willard and Welland Gordon. Its purpose was to feed local news to the United Press, the Scripps-owned national news syndicate, as well as to the *Daily News, Hollywood Citizen-News,* and other liberal or progressive rivals of the conservative *Los Angeles Times.* The service provided reliable, low-cost coverage of sensational aspects of the Hollywood film industry and covered corruption in city hall.

CITY OF COMMERCE, independent city located at the apex of the Santa Ana and Long Beach Freeways, 7 miles south of Los Angeles. It is on the main line of the Santa Fe Railroad and is home to

The Citadel Shopping Mall (former tire factory), City of Commerce, 1995. Courtesy The Citadel.

two of the county's three major freight rail yards. Plant closings in auto, steel, rubber, and other industries caused hardship in the area, but in recent years the shells of older factories and warehouses have been restored and put to new uses. Part of the old Uniroyal Tire and Rubber Company factory, built in 1929 and shut down in 1978, has been converted to a store-office-hotel-restaurant complex called the Citadel. The tire factory's landmark Assyrian-style wall, 1,700 feet of bas-relief panels, buttresses, towers, and stepped architecture, has been retained. The City of Commerce boasts of having no city taxes, utility taxes, or gross-receipts taxes. It was incorporated in 1960 to ensure a favorable environment for industry. The 6.6-square-mile city is home to more than 1,500 businesses, including dozens of Fortune 500 corporations, but has very few residents. In 1990 the population was only 12,135. The city provides many social services. The average small wood-frame home costs around $165,000.

CITY OF HOPE, independent, nonprofit, nonsectarian medical and research center in Duarte, 15 miles northeast of Los Angeles. It was founded in 1912 as a sanitorium by a few Los Angeles businessmen who formed the Southern California Jewish Consumptive Relief Association to assist victims of tuberculosis who were dying on the streets. With assets of $136.05 and a good deal of idealism, the founders bought 10 acres of barren desert, pitched two tents, and hired a nurse to tend the first two patients. Soon the enterprise was supported chiefly by the Amalgamated Clothing Workers and International Ladies Garment Workers Unions. Samuel H. Golter oversaw its early

growth as executive director until 1953. Since the introduction of antibiotics in the 1940s, which led to the decline of tuberculosis, the hospital has specialized in cancer treatment. Today, its corporate name is City of Hope National Medical Center and Beckman Research Institute of the City of Hope. It is recognized as one of the world's outstanding medical and research centers. In 1990 the hospital admitted 4,600 patients and had 2,209 full-time employees, including 88 physicians; its 100 buildings are spread over 102 acres.

CITY OF INDUSTRY, independent community 17 miles east of downtown Los Angeles. It snakes 14 miles through Puente Valley along railroad tracks and the Pomona Freeway, having a shape that is said to resemble "a sausage filled with toothpicks." A city virtually devoid of citizens, it has been called a "tax shelter for industry and warehouses." Five years after being incorporated in 1957, City of Industry had 10,000 employees in 27 industrial plants, but only a few hundred residents. Motels, hotels, and apartments were forbidden. In 1990 the population stood at 631, a net loss of 33 residents from the 1980 census.

CITY PLANNING COMMISSION. *See* Los Angeles City Planning Department

CITY TERRACE, unincorporated district east of Boyle Heights. Historically it has been, like its neighbor Boyle Heights, an entry place for immigrants to Southern California. The first wave of newcomers were East European Jews, who arrived in the 1920s and 1930s. Yiddish was frequently spoken on the streets, and business signs were in Yiddish, Hebrew, and English. The area was part of the largest Jewish settlement west of Chicago.

Since World War II, Mexicans have made up the majority of the population. Construction of the San Bernardino Freeway in the 1950s dissected the community and displaced thousands of people. The striking mural on the wall of the City Terrace Library is entitled "Mayan Offering." Two main thoroughfares are City Terrace Drive and Cesar E. Chavez Avenue (formerly Brooklyn Avenue). City Terrace now occupies the county area between the San Bernardino, Long Beach, and Pomona Freeways, and is often thought of as a part of East Los Angeles.

CITYWALK, Universal Studio's answer to Disneyland's Main Street. An idealized Los Angeles street, the two-block shopping mall is situated on the grounds of the popular hilltop tourist attraction in Universal City. Designed by architect Jon Jerde, and constructed at a cost of $100 million, CityWalk opened in 1993. It is projected as the core of a $3 billion "Entertainment City." In addition to the specialty shops, CityWalk features fanciful public icons, including 1950s-era "Googie"-style architecture, billboards, neon lights, three-dimensional murals, and a 70-foot light pole with a huge King Kong as its centerpiece.

CIVIC CENTER. *See* Los Angeles City-County Civic Center

CIVIL WAR ERA (1860–1865) found Los Angeles deeply divided over the issues of slavery and secession. Although California was a free state, an overwhelming majority of Angelenos favored the "Chivalry" (proslavery) wing of the Democratic Party, a result of heavy migration from southern and border states. The town's only newspaper, the *Los Angeles Star,* was rabidly hostile to California's antislavery senator, William Broderick, and Republicans represented a distinct minority. In the 1860 presidential election John C. Breckinridge (Democrat) collected 686 votes; Stephen Douglas (Democrat), 494; Abraham Lincoln (Republican), 350; and John Bell (Constitutional Union), 201. Union and Confederate partisans formed volunteer military companies that nearly came to blows. In 1861 U.S. dragoons had to be called in from Fort Tejón to quiet the scene.

With the outbreak of war, some 250 Angelenos went to fight for the Confederacy. Among them were Albert Sidney Johnston, who was appointed commander of the western front and would die at the battle of Shiloh. On the other side, Capt. Winfield Scott Hancock went east to serve the Union cause. The Confederate invasion of Arizona alarmed the Unionists of Los Angeles. As a precaution, Col. James H. Carlton took a force of Unionist volunteers to Fort Yuma. The Union Army also established Camp Drum (Drum Barracks) at San Pedro in January 1862 and maintained it for four years; it would become the only major landmark in Los Angeles from the Civil War period. That year, some Union forces arrested a batch of Confederate hotheads, including state assemblyman Edward J. C. Kewen, who appeared to be conspiring to seize the government. In 1863 the Democratic candidate for governor defeated the Union Party candidate, and California Union volunteers streamed across San Pedro Channel to seize Santa Catalina Island from Confederate sympathizers who had taken charge there. But the most dramatic events of the era had nothing to do with the Civil War: a drought in 1862–1864 devastated the cattle industry, and a deadly smallpox epidemic in the winter of 1862–1863 decimated the Indian and Mexican populations.

In the presidential election of 1864, "Father Abraham" Lincoln garnered 872 votes against 593 for McClellan (Democrat). Late in the war there was much jubilation in town over the Union victories. News of Robert E. Lee's surrender was received on 11 April, one day after the fact. Lincoln's death was publicly mourned. The outcome of the war altered the town's political complexion by emasculating the Democratic Party for years to come and giving the Republicans the upper hand.

CLAMOR PÚBLICO. See *El Clamor Público*

CLAREMONT, residential city 29 miles east of downtown Los Angeles in the lower foothills of the San Gabriel Mountains. Created by the Santa Fe Railroad in 1887, the city was incorporated in 1907. The name honors Claremont, Vermont, birthplace of a corporate director of the Pacific Land and Improvement Company, the railroad's land-developing subsidiary. Located on a site that once belonged to Mission San Gabriel, Claremont was founded by New Englanders who favored deciduous trees and wood-frame houses with wraparound porches. The city is graced by 240 acres of parks and gardens. Once famed for its citrus groves, today it is best known for its Oxford-style cluster of schools, the Claremont Colleges. The citizenry has established an exemplary record for historic preservation. In 1990 the population was 32,503.

CLAREMONT COLLEGES, loose association of private colleges in Claremont dubbed "the California Oxford." The complex, which flows together geographically, consists of six autonomous institutions devoted mostly to the liberal arts. Each has its own campus, faculty, student body, trustees, endowments, and curriculum, but together the colleges share common library facilities and services, such as security, maintenance, and health.

Pomona College, established in 1887, is the oldest college in the complex. In the 1920s it was faced with the pressure to grow, but rather than make it larger its trustees adopted a plan, borrowed from Oxford, England, to establish several adjacent colleges in Claremont. It is a coeducational liberal arts college with 1,300 students.

The Claremont Graduate School, established in 1925, is a coordinating body that offers master's and doctoral degrees in five academic centers. It now has 2,000 students who are taught by a separate faculty of about 70, in addition to the regular faculty of the associated institutions.

Scripps College was established in 1926. It is a women's liberal arts college with emphasis on the humanities. It enrolls about 600 students.

Claremont McKenna College was established in 1946. For nearly 40 years it was called Claremont Men's College. It is now a coeducational liberal arts college with an enrollment of about 500 men and 370 women.

Harvey Mudd College was established in 1955.

It is a coeducational college specializing in engineering and the physical sciences, with 600 students.

Pitzer College was established in 1963. A coeducational liberal arts college with some 800 students, its special strengths are the social and behavioral sciences.

The combined faculty at the Claremont Colleges numbers approximately 250. In somewhat looser affiliation is the School of Theology at Claremont, and several research institutes. Honnold/Mudd Library houses more than 2 million volumes. Students enrolled at one college may take courses at another; they therefore enjoy the social advantages of a small residential suburban college while having the academic benefits of a large university.

CLAREMONT McKENNA COLLEGE. *See* Claremont Colleges

CLARK, ELI P. (1847–1931), streetcar developer. Clark, with his brother-in-law Moses Sherman, organized the Los Angeles Railway Company in 1893. Within its first year the pair had built 38 miles of electrified railways covering seven routes.

CLARK, WILLIAM ANDREWS, JR. (1877–1934), philanthropist and cultural benefactor. His father, William Andrews Clark Sr., was a copper magnate and U.S. senator from Montana. Clark Jr. became an attorney and was also an accomplished amateur violinist. He founded the Los Angeles Philharmonic Orchestra in 1919 and became its major patron. A devoted book collector, Clark assembled a collection rich in 17th- and 18th-century English literature, the works of Oscar Wilde,

Harvey Mudd College, Claremont Colleges. Courtesy Harvey Mudd College.

and fine printing of the 19th and 20th centuries. The books are preserved today at the William Andrews Clark Memorial Library, named for his father and located on the younger Clark's former estate in the West Adams area. Upon Clark's death, the library and the estate were gifted to UCLA. The Mary Andrews Clark Memorial Home, a YMCA residence hall, was established by Clark Sr. in 1913 to honor his late mother.

CLARKE ESTATE, country home of Chauncy and Marie Clarke in Santa Fe Springs. The 8,000-square-foot home (ca. 1920) was designed by renowned architect Irving Gill on 60 acres of orange groves on Pioneer Boulevard. The entire property was recently purchased by the city of Santa Fe Springs from the descendants of the original owners.

CLARK MEMORIAL LIBRARY. *See* Clark, William Andrews, Jr.

CLELAND, ROBERT GLASS (1885–1957), Occidental College history professor. His writings include *Cattle on a Thousand Hills: Southern California, 1850–1880* (1941), *From Wilderness to Empire: A History of California, 1542–1900* (1944), *California in Our Time* (1947), and *The Place Called Sespe* (1953).

CLEMENTS, STILES OLIVER (1884–1966), architect. Stiles was born in Maryland and came to Los Angeles in 1911 after studying at Drexel Institute in Philadelphia and the Massachusetts Institute of Technology. In 1923 the firm of Morgan, Walls, and Morgan was reorganized to include him, becoming Morgan, Walls, and Clements. He was subsequently responsible for the design of many commercial structures, including the Bank of Italy Building, Pacific National Bank Building, Mayan Theater, Belasco Theatre, and *Los Angeles Evening Herald* Building.

CLIMATE in Los Angeles is a harmonious merging of latitude and the influences of seashore and mountains. The combination produces a nearly perfect human environment that over the years has attracted huge numbers of settlers and tourists from less hospitable climes. The latitude discourages the cyclonic effect that may bring storms further north. The ocean moderates the desert heat, especially in summer, and makes the sun bearable on the hottest days. The mountains shield the coastal area from interior heat and cold—though they also help create the conditions that foster smog. Southern California has two seasons: one is a long, dry, moderately warm spell from May to November, and the other is a wet, moderately cool, but never bitter spell from November to May. The many days of sun and comparative lack of rain have spurred numerous real estate booms and been primary reasons for the location of certain industries in California, such as aircraft and motion picture production.

Residents notice many differences in weather and climate within the basin itself, which sometimes baffles newcomers. Geographers speak of "desert," "near desert," "semiarid," and "Mediterranean" climate zones because of the variations. The days of summer can vary widely in temperature, depending on location. It may be noticeably cooler in Santa Monica (July averages 66°F), where the marine influence is strong, than in Pasadena in the San Gabriel Valley, which is 10 degrees warmer on average.

Paradise has its troubles, however. Prolonged droughts, flooding and mudslides from torrential rains, fires, and dust from Santa Ana winds are natural occurrences. In recent decades, summer smog has marred the atmosphere as well.

CLINTON, CLIFFORD E. (1900–1969), cafeteria operator and courageous fighter of vice in the 1930s. The son of Salvation Army ministers, Clinton was born in Berkeley, did missionary work in China, and came to Los Angeles during the Great Depression. He opened the first of a chain of seven cafeterias in July 1931, calling them Clifton's Cafeterias (a conflation of his first and last names) and giving each a distinctive design theme. Clifton's Pacific Seas cafeteria on Olive Street, for example, featured a real waterfall and lush tropical plants. Applying the Golden Rule, he allowed free meals to anyone who could not pay. Around 1940 his restaurants served 25,000 meals daily, with the motto "All you can eat for 45 cents." Determined to fight hunger, he worked with Caltech scientists to create a nourishing meal for 5 cents. Clinton established Meals for Millions, a foundation to combat world hunger.

In an era of rampant city hall corruption and wide-open vice and racketeering he organized CIVIC (Citizens Independent Vice Investigating Committee), a coalition of business, church, and community organizations, to combat crime and reform city government. Clinton sat on a county grand jury that investigated and implicated 27 men for racketeering and exposed a web of corruption in the administration of Mayor Frank Shaw. On 18 October 1937, Clinton's home was bombed, as was the car of the incorruptible Harry Raymond, a private investigator working with CIVIC. The *Times* dismissed the bombing as a cheap publicity stunt, but Police Captain Earl Kynette was later linked to the violence and served time for those crimes. In 1938 Shaw and other corrupt officials were forced out of office in a recall election, and Fletcher Bowron was elected mayor.

CLIPPERS, LOS ANGELES. *See* Los Angeles Clippers

CLUNES BROADWAY THEATER, silent movie house on downtown's Broadway, now called the Cameo. Dubbed a "nickelodeon" because of its 5-cent admission price, the theater was opened by showman Clunes in 1917.

COHEN, MICKEY (1913–1976), the "lovable racketeer." Born Meyer Harris, he was involved in bootlegging at age nine, became a prizefighter, and later ran nightclubs and a men's clothing store. He took control of the Mob in Los Angeles when Benjamin "Bugsy" Siegel moved to Las Vegas in 1945. Cohen had an expansive personal style, high public profile, and was not averse to using strong-arm tactics in public places. He served time twice for income tax evasion, from 1952 to 1955 and from 1961 to 1972. Somehow he managed to survive being shot in a restaurant, having his house bombed, and being beaten and crippled by a fellow convict in jail. Cohen died of cancer several years after his release from prison.

COHN, KASPARE (D. 1918?), German Jewish pioneer who arrived in Los Angeles in 1859. He worked for, and became a partner of, his uncle, Harris Newmark, mainly in the hide and wool business. He left the city for some years, returned in 1866, and married Hulda, the sister of M. A. Newmark. After he became wealthy in his own right—first through informal banking and then by establishing Kaspare Cohn Commercial and Savings Bank (which became Union Bank and Trust Company after his death)—his philanthropic donation helped establish Kaspare Cohn Hospital in 1910 (later, Cedars of Lebanon Hospital). By the time of his death he was, most probably, the wealthiest Jew in Los Angeles.

COLISEUM, LOS ANGELES MEMORIAL. *See* Los Angeles Memorial Coliseum

COLLEGES AND UNIVERSITIES number over 60 in the county, making Los Angeles a major center for higher education. Among private institutions the most distinguished are California Institute of Technology (Caltech), the University of Southern California (USC), Claremont McKenna College, and Occidental College. Among public universities the most renowned are the University of California, Los Angeles (UCLA), and the five campuses of the California State University: Cal Poly Pomona, Dominguez Hills, Long Beach, Los Angeles, and Northridge. Many municipalities have community colleges as well. These institutions, although independently administered, are linked by the provisions of the 1960 California Master Plan for Higher Education. Of the state institutions, UCLA (as part of the University of California system) is responsible for most graduate instruction, the California State University campuses focus on undergraduate and master's level instruction, while the community colleges cover the first two years of college.

Los Angeles also boasts many independent specialized schools, including, for the commercial and fine arts, Art Center College of Design, California Institute of the Arts (Cal Arts), Otis College of Art and Design, Southern California Institute of Architecture (SCI-Arc), and the Fashion Institute; for law, Southwestern; and for specialized health services, the Los Angeles College of Chiropractic and the College of Osteopathic Medicine. Colleges and universities cover a wide range of religious affiliations as well, and include Fuller Theological (nondenominational evangelical), Pepperdine (Church of Christ), Mount St. Mary's and Loyola-Marymount (Catholic), University of Judaism, and Soka (Soka Gakkai Buddhism). Proprietary business schools, such as Woodbury University, offer training in various fields.

COLORADO RIVER AQUEDUCT, 242-mile pipeline that has delivered Colorado River water to Southern California since 1941. Construction was financed by a bond issue of $220 million, approved in 1933 by the cities involved. The water is impounded at Parker Dam in San Bernardino County, southwest of Needles. The state then created a superutility, the Metropolitan Water District (MWD), to build the aqueduct and sell Colorado water at wholesale rates. The MWD serves Los Angeles, Anaheim, Beverly Hills, Burbank, Glendale, Pasadena, San Marino, Santa Ana, Santa Monica, Fullerton, Long Beach, Torrance, and Compton. Today Southern California's allotment from the Colorado is declining, owing to a 1964 U.S. Supreme Court ruling favoring the claims of the state of Arizona for more of the precious liquid.

COLUMBIA PICTURES INDUSTRIES, INC., movie studio founded in 1924 by Harry Cohn, a former salesman and short-subject filmmaker, who remained the studio head until his death in 1958. Columbia was one of the "Little Two" movie studios, along with Universal, during Hollywood's Golden Era. Columbia purchased a 40-acre lot in Burbank in 1934 and made many of its films at that location. The studio produced a host of popular films and created its share of stars, the greatest of whom was

---

A lot of people think there aren't Indians in the San Fernando Valley anymore. . . . We have been here a long time and we plan to stay here.

—Rudy Ortega, Fernandeño Indian

Rita Hayworth. Among Columbia's early movies were the Frank Capra comedies, including *It Happened One Night* (1934) and *Mr. Smith Goes to Washington* (1939). In the 1940s Columbia produced a string of important films, such as *All the King's Men* (1949), *Born Yesterday* (1950), *From Here to Eternity* (1953), and *On the Waterfront* (1954). *The Bridge on the River Kwai* (1957) was the studio's largest-grossing film to that time. *A Man for All Seasons* (1966) was another major achievement.

In 1972, after corporate restructuring within the industry, Columbia joined Warner Brothers to form Burbank Studios. In 1987 Dawn Steel became studio head, one of the very few women in such a position; she remained there until 1990, when the Japanese Sony Pictures Entertainment Company bought Columbia from Coca-Cola. Columbia then moved from Burbank and took up quarters at the old Metro-Goldwyn-Mayer location in Culver City. After Columbia left, Burbank Studios was renamed Warner Brothers Studio. The restructuring of the industry, and of Columbia, has continued. A Columbia subsidiary, Screen Gems, makes and distributes TV films, and in 1993 the head of Columbia Pictures ran both Columbia and TriStar Pictures, another Sony Pictures Entertainment concern.

COMEDY CLUBS, showcases for stand-up comics and aspiring television personalities, arose in the 1950s and 1960s along Sunset Strip and soon spread to outlying districts. Techniques include monologues as well as call-and-response improvisation. The clubs depend greatly on young, affluent audiences. Among the prominent graduates of Los Angeles venues are Mort Sahl, Bill Cosby, Shelly Berman, and Bob Newhart. The Ice House in Pasadena is the granddaddy of these clubs, the Comedy Store on Sunset is the largest; the Groundling Theater on Melrose has outstanding new talent, while Igby's Comedy Cabaret in West Los Angeles tends to attract established performers. The Improv on Melrose is part of a nationwide chain of comedy clubs. Most of the comics who appear on the *Tonight Show, Late Show with David Letterman,* and cable comedy shows got their start in these and similar clubs.

COMMERCE, CITY OF. *See* City of Commerce

COMMERCE AND INDUSTRY in Los Angeles are so vast and important that the county and surrounding area rank as a global marketplace. Southern California is home to the largest Latino and Asian/Pacific Islander markets in the nation, and some analysts accordingly consider Los Angeles the "hub of the Pacific Rim." In 1991 the ports of Los Angeles and Long Beach accounted for over 58 percent of the West Coast foreign import cargo. Most of the manufactured goods made in California, moreover, are produced within a 60-mile radius of the civic center. The Gross Regional Product surpasses the Gross National Product of all but 11 nations in the world. Around 1990, the area possessed more high-tech firms than any other county in California, ranked third in the United States as a supplier of jobs, and was the top manufacturing county in the nation. The economic downturn of the 1990s took its toll on the county, although by 1996 there were encouraging signs of a steady recovery.

COMMISSIONS OF THE CITY OF LOS ANGELES, which numbered 46 in 1993, are comparatively strong under the charter of 1925. They were instituted by progressive reformers who sought to dilute the power of the city council and mayor and to encourage the participation of civic-minded individuals in government. Commissioners are appointed by the mayor and approved by the council. Some, such as the Water Conservation Appeals Board, receive no fee; others receive a per-meeting fee, such as the Animal Regulation Commission ($25), the Water and Power Commission ($50), and the Employee Relations Board ($350). The only full-time city commissioners are the members of the public works commission, who in 1993 received an annual salary of $71,187. The number of members on a given commission varies from five to nine; the average term of service is five years.

The most powerful commissions—airports, harbor, water and power, and the Community Redevelopment Agency—have an independent budget and oversee a city department. Other commissions are basically advisory to the city council, the mayor, or a department. Thus, the planning commission has no real power over the Planning Department, but merely makes recommendations to the city council.

Some critics contend that the commission system has inherent dangers. They cite as an example the gridlock that resulted from the battle between the police commission and city council over the fate of Police Chief Daryl Gates in 1992.

City Government Commissions

	Function
Affordable Housing Commission	Advises mayor, council, and Housing Department on rent control.
Airport Commission	Manages and controls all airports; heads Department of Airports.
Animal Regulation Commission	Oversees Department of Animal Regulation.
Building and Safety Commission	Hears appeals resulting from enforcement of city building code.
Child Care Advisory Board	Advises County Child Care Coordinator on child care policy.
City Employees' Retirement System	Manages and administers City Employees' Retirement Fund.
City Ethics Commission	Enforces the charter and ordinances relating to campaign finances, conflict of interest, and governmental ethics.
Civil Service Commission	Establishes classes of employment and manages employment examinations.
Community Redevelopment Agency	Has authority over all matters relating to city revitalization projects.
Convention and Exhibition Center Authority	Advises general manager on management of the convention center. Constructs and leases convention center facilities.
Cultural Affairs Commission	Approves purchases or gifts of art to city; approves design of public structures; informs the council on matters in arts, science, and historic affairs.
Cultural Heritage Commission	Maintains a list of historic structures and promotes their preservation according to city ordinances.
Disability, Commission on	Advises mayor and council on issues relating to disabled persons and monitors programs of the Office for the Disabled.
El Pueblo de Los Angeles Historic Monument Authority	Controls the Pueblo de Los Angeles Historic Monument Authority Department; negotiates contracts with concessionaires.
Employee Relations Board	Manages collective bargaining elections and arranges labor relations mediation and fact finding.
Environmental Affairs Commission	Advises the mayor, council, and departments on environmental matters.
Fire Commission	Supervises, controls, and manages the City Fire Department.
Handicapped Access Appeals Board	Hears appeals regarding enforcement of state health and safety codes.
Harbor Commission	Manages, supervises, controls, and heads the Harbor Department.
Health Facilities Authority Commission	Issues bonds, enters contracts, leases lands, and receives funds and gifts for county health facilities.
Housing Authority, Board of Commissioners	Has jurisdiction over matters relating to city public housing.
Human Relations Commission	Manages an advisory committee, investigates human relations problems, and pursues public education in the human relations field.

City Government Commissions (continued)

	Function
Industrial Development Authority	Promotes industrial development by issuing development bonds.
Library Commission	Controls and manages the Library Department, appoints its head, and controls all monies.
Los Angeles Services Authority (joint county and city)	Provides services to the homeless.
Martin Luther King Jr. General Hospital Authority (joint county and city)	Issues revenue bonds, enters into contracts, leases land, and receives gifts pertaining to the hospital.
Metropolitan Transit Authority	Develops and manages mass transit in the county.
Metropolitan Water District of Southern California (city members)	Operating body of the MWD, a water wholesaler.
Native American Indian Commission (joint city and county)	Obtains funding, recommends public policy, and disseminates information for the American Indian community.
Pension Commission	Manages and administers the city's fire and police pension systems.
Planning Commission	Advises and recommends on matters relating to city planning, approves subdivisions, and approves the city's general plan and zoning actions.
Police Commission	Supervises, controls, regulates, and manages the Police Department.
Police Permit Review Panel	A subpanel of the Police Commission; it reviews hearing examiners' reports.
Productivity Commission	Reviews productivity of city workers and studies measures to improve efficiency and effectiveness.
Public Works Commission	Heads the Department of Public Works; supervises all city activity regarding sanitation, street lighting, and street maintenance.
Recreation and Parks Commission	Heads the Department of Recreation and Parks; leases property, makes rules, and appoints and removes the general manager.
Relocation Appeals Board	Hears appeals from residents relocated by city agencies.
Rent Adjustment Commission	Holds hearings, makes studies, and carries out intent of Rent Stabilization Ordinance.
Social Services Commission	Advises Social Service Department regarding solicitations for charitable donations.
Status of Women, Commission on the	Advises the city on equal opportunity in public employment and general welfare of women in the community.
Telecommunications Commission	Investigates franchises, establishes standards of quality and rates to be charged, and investigates complaints regarding franchises.
Transportation Commission	Advises the Department of Transportation on planning, coordination, and management.
Water Conservation Appeals Board	Appeals board for residential and nonresidential property owners that have been cited for violating city water conservation ordinances.
Water and Power Commission	Heads the Department of Water and Power; constructs, operates, maintains, and manages city water and electric energy.
Zoning Appeals, Board of	Hears appeals from the Zoning Administrator's decisions regarding variances and conditional uses.

SOURCE: City of Los Angeles, July 1994.

COMMITTEE OF 25, group of downtown business executives that in the 1950s and 1960s served as a sort of shadow government, choosing public officials for appointment or election and setting the agenda for public policy. The group included insurance executive and Republican leader Asa Call; James Lin Beebe, an attorney with O'Melveny and Meyers; USC's president Dr. Norman Topping; UCLA chancellor Franklin D. Murphy; Dan Bryant of Beacon Industries; Norman Chandler of the *Los Angeles Times;* and Justin W. Dart of Dart Industries. The group's power began to wane in the aftermath of the Watts riot of 1965.

COMMUNIST PARTY, Marxist-Leninist organization that peaked locally in the 1930s and 1940s. In 1933 its 700 members were mostly Jewish needle trade workers and house painters from Boyle Heights. In the following decade the party branched out into CIO unions, Hollywood film studios, and basic industries, forming alliances with left liberal and civil rights organizations. The party's most active period came immediately after World War II. The FBI estimated 4,500 members regionally in 1948–1949. Soon blacklisting, the anti-Communist provisions of the Taft-Hartley Act, and a pervasive red scare eroded its position. Dorothy Healey and Ben Dobbs were for many years the leaders of the Los Angeles Communist Party.

COMMUNITIES. *See* Neighborhoods

COMMUNITY COLLEGES are more numerous in Los Angeles than anywhere else in the country. The two-year institutions, formerly called junior colleges, exist in 11 Los Angeles County cities. They are by law closely articulated with the California State University system and the University of California. The first junior college in the area was established in 1929 by the city of Los Angeles on the downtown campus of the University of California, which that year moved to Westwood. The Los Angeles Community College (LACC) District, the largest such district in the nation, has nine campuses: East Los Angeles, Los Angeles, Harbor, Mission, Pierce, Southwest, Trade-Technical, Valley, and West Los Angeles. LACC has tried to work on the "open-door policy"—allowing entry to anyone wanting a college education. Recent budgetary cutbacks have curtailed this policy, however. The majority of LACC students are female, non-white, and attend both day and evening classes. The operating budget in 1990–1991 was $365 million, with an enrollment of over 111,000 students. Other community colleges are Cerritos, Citrus, Compton, El Camino, Glendale, Long Beach City, Mt. San Antonio, Pasadena City, Rio Hondo, and Santa Monica.

COMMUNITY REDEVELOPMENT AGENCY, LOS ANGELES. *See* Los Angeles Community Redevelopment Agency

COMMUNITY SERVICE ORGANIZATION (CSO), Mexican civic unity organization, one of the most important Chicano associations ever formed locally. Originally known as the Community Political Organization, it evolved in 1947 as part of Edward Roybal's unsuccessful bid for a seat on the Los Angeles City Council. The driving force behind the group was community organizer Fred Ross, a disciple of the Chicago activist Saul Alinsky and his Industrial Areas Foundation. The legwork was performed by Chicano steelworkers and other volunteers. CSO had an effective confrontational style that it used to combat discrimination. It registered voters in a drive that helped elect Roybal in 1949, and it helped train organizers such as Cesar Chavez.

COMMUTING, by automobile, is the way that most Angelenos get to work. In-depth surveys of car riders from 1990 to 1994 showed that, despite public efforts to popularize ride sharing, only 3 percent in 1990, 8 percent in 1992, and 5 percent in 1994 shared a ride on a full-time basis, while 19 to 21 percent did so irregularly. Both men and women drove alone about 80 percent of the time. The average round-trip commute distance remained constant, at about 32 miles. Despite congestion, riders seem to believe that their commute has been improving: 11 percent thought it was better in 1991 than in the year before; 12 percent thought so in 1992, 19 percent in 1993, and 31 percent in 1994, particularly after the improvements of the roads following the Northridge earthquake. In 1992 employers intensified efforts to encourage ride sharing by offering flexible work hours, guaranteed rides home in emergencies, and information and assistance in forming carpools.

The average monthly cost of commuting depended on the means of transportation: $92 for solo drivers, $68 for carpool riders, $51 for vanpoolers, $52 for bus passengers, and $97 for rail users.

COMPTON, incorporated city 11 miles south of downtown Los Angeles. It was a stop on the route of the Los Angeles–San Pedro Railroad, the first rail line in the region, completed in 1869. Located on the site of the former Rancho San Pedro, owned by the Domínguez family, the city was named for Griffith D. Compton, a temperance minister and founder of a local college. It is also where the region's first artesian well was discovered. Originally a farming community where land sold for 36 cents an acre, Compton blossomed into a residential and manufacturing town after World War II. In the 1930s an oil discovery turned it into a boomtown. In the 1960s Compton became the first California city with an African American majority, although today the Latino population is increasing. In 1990 Compton had 90,454 residents.

CONFEDERACIÓN DE UNIONES OBRE-RAS MEXICANAS (CUOM), anarchist Mexican labor union formed in East Los Angeles in 1927 to champion the cause of manual workers and establish a bond with Mexico's labor movement. Reorganized in the 1930s, its members participated in strikes in the berry, onion, and celery fields of El Monte, Venice, Culver City, and Santa Monica in the summer of 1933.

CONSERVATION. *See* Water conservation

CONTROLLER. *See* Los Angeles City Controller

COOK, BRUCE (1932–), a writer whose mystery books, *Mexican Standoff* (1988) and *As a Career Move* (1992), feature the unconventional Latino sleuth from Boyle Heights Antonio (Chico) Cervantes. The author is a Chicago-born Anglo.

COPTIC ORTHODOX CHURCH, Egyptian-based Christian faith, with an estimated worldwide following of 27 million. In 1996 Pope Shenouda II of Cairo appointed Bishop Serapion as the first bishop of Los Angeles. The appointment recognized the steady immigration of Egyptians to Southern California and the growth of the church from 13 to 30 congregations between 1980 and 1996. In the latter year the number of Coptic Christians in the region reached an estimated 10,000. The church, which according to tradition was founded by the apostle Mark in the first century A.D., uses both the Coptic language and Arabic in its services.

CORNERO (STRALLA), TONY, 1920s and 1930s bootlegger and gambler. During Prohibition his ships smuggled thousands of cases of illegal liquor into Southern California. In 1930, after a stint in jail, he anticipated repeal of the Eighteenth Amendment by operating four floating casino boats off the shore of Long Beach and Santa Monica. The *Rex* was an especially handsome ship that catered round-the-clock to as many as 2,000 people. Cornero evaded all efforts to close him down until the "Battle of Santa Monica Bay" in the summer of 1938, when lawmen raided the *Rex* and closed it down. In court the following year, Attorney General Earl Warren charged that Cornero's ships were a public nuisance and put an end to his operations. (The *Rex,* which later saw action in World War II, was eventually sunk by a German sub.)

CORONA, BERT (1918–), AND BLANCHE TAFF CORONA (1918–1993), community activists. Raised in Albuquerque, Bert Corona was recruited to USC on a basketball scholarship. He later worked as a longshoreman, and served as president of Local 26 of the ILWU from 1941 to 1943.

Blanche Taff Corona was born in Brooklyn, New York, but grew up in Los Angeles. She met her future husband on a strike of the UAW against North American Aviation. During World War II, while her husband was in the military, she organized Mexican, Jewish, and immigrant Russian workers doing salvage work. After the war the couple helped form Los Angeles chapters of Saul Alinsky's Community Service Organization, before establishing the Mexican American Political Association (MAPA).

CORONEL, IGNACIO (1796–1862), AND ANTONIO FRANCO CORONEL (1817–1894), prominent citizens of the Mexican and Yankee *pueblo.* Members of the 1834 Hijar-Padres colony, an unsuccessful plan of the Mexican government to colonize areas in Alta California, they came to Los Angeles shortly after the colony's collapse. Ignacio, a Mexican soldier, started the first school of consequence in Los Angeles in 1838, which lasted six years. He also became a storekeeper

Antonio F. Coronel with his wife, Mariana. Courtesy Photographic Collections, Los Angeles Public Library.

and a member of the *ayuntamiento,* on which he served as secretary. He was later appointed commissioner of streets. In 1843 he was granted Rancho La Cañada ("Mountain Valley Ranch").

Ignacio Coronel's son, Antonio, had an even more distinguished career. After his arrival in Los Angeles he became a justice of the peace and inspector of missions. Although he had backed Mexico in the Mexican War, Antonio Coronel took the Yankee side afterward, and held a succession of government posts, including city assessor, mayor in 1853 and 1854, county supervisor in the 1860s, and state treasurer. Helen Hunt Jackson visited him at his adobe near the river and later incorporated his stories into her novel *Ramona* (1884). A man of many interests and talents, Coronel was a noted exponent of the fandango, helped establish the Sisters of Charity in Los Angeles and the Historical Society of Southern California, and from 1872 to 1892 published the newspaper *La Crónica.* Coronel's cousin was Agustín Olvera, for whom Olvera Street is named.

COUNTRY CLUBS were initially established in the late 19th century by wealthy white Protestants to preserve the privileges of class. Golf was a major attraction. The largest club, organized in 1897 by banker Joseph F. Sartori and others as the Los Angeles Golf Club, changed its name a year later to Los Angeles Country Club. It opened on West Pico and moved to its present location on Wilshire Boulevard, just west of Beverly Hills, in 1911. In addition to nonwhites, the club excluded movie people and Jews, professing to cater only to "old Los Angeles"—a curious concept for a young city.

In the 1920s, upwardly mobile Jews, including Hollywood film moguls, responded by forming the Hillcrest Country Club. Groucho Marx, George Burns, Milton Berle, and others were invited to join. Berle recently described Hillcrest as "a dining club with golf."

The most fashionable club in its time, with an entry fee of $3,800, was the Midwick Country Club, begun largely by rich Pasadenans on a hill overlooking 200 acres of grounds in the San Gabriel Valley on the road to Los Angeles. It opened in 1912 and featured polo. The "Midwick Foursome" captured the national polo title in 1924, and King George V played a match at Midwick while on a visit to Los Angeles. Frequent players were an army team headed by Gen. George Patton Jr., the son of a pioneer Pasadena family, as well as such movie personalities as Will Rogers, Hal Roach, David Niven, Spencer Tracy, and Walt Disney. The club also had apartments, a swimming pool, tennis courts, and a golf course where Sam Snead and Bing Crosby played. During the Great Depression the club declined, and the grounds were sold to an Italian immigrant who would have been rejected for membership had he applied. Today, the acreage is occupied by homes; the only remaining traces of its past glory are the names of streets honoring the celebrities who once frolicked there.

Throughout the Los Angeles region, real estate developers have built country clubs to lure wealthy customers into new suburban residential tracts. The result is some 20 country clubs that serve as centers for social activities, business meetings, weddings and receptions, recreation, and sporting events, particularly golf and tennis tournaments. Polo is no longer played at any of the Los Angeles–area country clubs.

COUNTY OF LOS ANGELES. *See* Los Angeles County

COURT FLIGHT, funicular railway that carried passengers for one block from Broadway to Hill, from 1904 until it burned in 1944. Fares were five cents. It never rivaled in popularity the companion downtown funicular, Angels Flight.

COURT SYSTEM. *See* Judicial system

COURTYARD HOUSING, a style of apartment that flourished early in the century. Around 1910 these complexes were considered little better than slums—the Los Angeles version of East Coast tenements. In the 1920s they became more stylish, however, and charming and comfortable apartment complexes were built, each with a dozen units or fewer, never more than two stories high, and attractively landscaped. They evoked the romantic architecture of Mexico. Examples may be seen especially in the mid-Wilshire district and in West Hollywood. This style is the subject of Stefanos Polyzoides's book *Courtyard Housing in Los Angeles* (1992).

COVINA, incorporated city 23 miles east of Los Angeles. It was established in the 1880s on a subdivision of La Puente Rancho, an area of abundant wildflowers and rich alluvial soil whose first inhabitants were Shoshonean-speaking Gabrieleños. The land was part of Rancho San José, which was granted to Don Ygnacio Palomares and Don Ricardo Vejar in 1837, and of Rancho Azusa, granted to Don Luis Arenas in 1842. The name is thought to mean "place of vines," but, as main street Citrus Avenue indicates, it is oranges rather than wine that made Covina prosperous. Covina was first subdivided in 1884 into tracts of 10 or 15 acres, the optimum size for family orange growers. The Southern Pacific ran tracks there in 1895, allowing for fast shipment of fruit to eastern markets. By 1909 the city was the third largest orange producer in the world; as late as the 1950s it still raised "the best oranges in the world." Its motto was "A Mile Square and All There." Homes, many of them California bungalows built for $2,500 before World War I, now average $200,000. After the Second World War the city became a bedroom community. In 1991 its population stood at 43,207.

COYOTE (CANIS LATRANS), wild dog native to Southern California. Highly intelligent, swift, and resourceful, coyotes live in packs in rangeland, chaparral, and piñon-juniper woodlands. They have a distinctive yapping howl, often used in chorus as a means of keeping track of one another. Active at night in the Santa Monica Mountains, the nocturnal dogs have been known to interrupt

---

For the first time in American history, a frontier was developed by the sickly and invalid.

—John E. Baur, historian, writing of 1870–1900

Hollywood Bowl concerts. Coyotes are highly adaptable to the urban environment; they thrive in alleys around garbage barrels and feed on rabbits, rats, cats, bugs, birds, vegetables, and fruit. It is unlawful to feed coyotes. Each year, animal regulators document several hundred cases of coyotes biting or killing pets, and 12 to 15 cases of coyotes biting people. The only recorded human death by a coyote is that of a 3-year-old Glendale girl, in 1981.

CRA. *See* Los Angeles Community Redevelopment Agency

CRAFTSMAN ARCHITECTURAL STYLE, vogue for home design based on simple lines and a close relationship with nature. Intended chiefly for middle-class families, the style enjoyed popularity in the early part of the 20th century. Often a Craftsman house, or bungalow, was built on a site with a view and featured a courtyard with one or more native trees. Using wood or native boulders, the individual designers or builders frequently incorporated their own personal flourishes into the finishing touches. Hundreds of examples of homes designed in this mode still exist throughout the region. Among the most skilled practitioners were Charles and Henry Greene, Alfred Heineman, and Arthur Rolland Kelly.

CRAWFORD V. LOS ANGELES BOARD OF ED-UCATION. *See* Desegregation of public schools

CREATIVE ARTISTS AGENCY, Hollywood's most powerful talent agency. It was formed in 1975 by Michael Ovitz and four colleagues, all of whom were former talent agents for the William Morris Agency. Creative Artists developed the "package deal," whereby the agency represents the actor, director, and the writer on a given project. Ovitz, who is generally considered the most powerful person in Hollywood, as well as one of the wealthiest, is the agency's chairperson and main stockholder. He is credited with engineering some of the largest entertainment mergers of recent years, such as the sale of the Music Corporation of America and Sony Pictures Entertainment's purchase of Columbia Pictures. Ovitz, who is said to earn over $35 million yearly, has turned down offers to take over the helm of various mega-entertainment companies. Creative Artists Agency headquarters, at the corner of Santa Monica and Wilshire Boulevards in Beverly Hills, was designed by I. M. Pei.

CRENSHAW DISTRICT, Los Angeles neighborhood centered on Crenshaw and Martin Luther King Boulevards and a nucleus of the postwar African American community. Numerous Japanese Americans and Latinos live there as well. Its core is the Baldwin Hills Crenshaw Plaza, which rises on the site of the former Crenshaw Shopping Center, built in the 1940s as one of the first retail shopping malls in the nation. The new mall covers 54 acres and features 100 specialty shops. The $120 million renovation was completed as a Community Redevelopment Agency project in 1988.

CRESPI, JUAN (1721–1782), Franciscan missionary who served as chaplain and official diarist with the Portolá expedition in 1769. In August of that year Fra Crespi recorded earthquake occurrences; about the Los Angeles area he wrote: "This plain where the river runs is very extensive. It has good land for planting all kinds of grain and seeds, and this is the most suitable site of all that we have seen for a mission, for it has all the requisites for a large settlement." Crespi conducted the first Catholic mass in Southern California.

CRESTWOOD HILLS, planned community in Kenter Canyon in the Santa Monica Mountains. It opened in 1953 with about 100 homes and soon expanded fivefold. The development, located a mile north of Sunset Boulevard and designed by Quincy Jones, Whitney Smith, and Edgardo Contini, includes a playground, park, nursery school, outdoor theater, and community center. Community meetings are actively attended.

CRIME in Los Angeles has reached alarming levels in recent decades. Yet the public's perception of it as strictly a recent problem is somewhat misleading. As early as 1782 the Franciscan missionaries complained of an infestation of thieves in the *pueblo* of Los Angeles, and perhaps the worst crime wave occurred in the 1850s when the tiny cow town was marked by frequent bandit depredations, vigilante reprisals, and incessant homicidal brawls. Illegal activity such as gambling, prostitution, drug sales, and bootlegging also reached record proportions in the 1920s and 1930s.

While crime levels have risen throughout major cities in the United States, Los Angeles has had a *relatively* low overall ranking for murder, rape, robbery, aggravated assault, burglary, larceny, and other felonies. According to the FBI, in 1990 the city was 36th in the nation, at 92.3 crimes per 1,000 people—down two notches from 1989. Los Angeles has a crime rate comparable to San Francisco's (96.6) and New York's (97). One of the most disturbing trends in Los Angeles, as in the urban industrial world generally, is that most violent crimes are committed by males in their teens and early twenties, with ever more preteens becoming involved.

In 1987 the highest crime rate occurred in the Central Division of the Los Angeles Police Department, with an average of 499.2 offenses per 1,000 population. In 1991 the county coroner tallied 2,401 murders—more than 6.5 per day. Sometimes the record reaches even more alarming proportions. During the single weekend beginning on Friday, 21 August 1992, assailants bearing guns, knives, and other weapons committed 28 homicides. The bloodiest season for homicide generally is the summer months of July, August, and September. The Los Angeles County Sheriff's Department in 1991 reported one homicide every 21 hours, one forcible rape every 9 hours, one incident of arson every 7 hours, one robbery every 29 minutes, one aggravated assault every 21 minutes, one auto grand theft every 21 minutes, one burglary every 18 minutes, and one larceny theft every 11 minutes.

In 1994 the city of Los Angeles experienced a dramatic decrease in crime, attributable in part to community-based policing, a bigger budget for police work, and more police officers on the streets. Homicides, robberies, and auto thefts dropped 21 percent, 20 percent, and 15 percent, respectively, in the course of that year. Other violent crimes were also down considerably.

CRIPS AND BLOODS, rival African American gangs of South Central Los Angeles who have engaged in deadly turf warfare since the 1970s. They kill "to protect their neighborhood" and were said to be heavily involved in drug sales. In the aftermath of the 1992 riots, warring factions signed a pact in which they called off "payback" (revenge) fighting. This pact was modeled after a 1949 U.N. Middle East peace treaty, a copy of which a former gang member had found in the USC archives. By an ironic twist of fate, the earlier document had been drafted by Ralph Bunche, the African American United Nations undersecretary who grew up in Watts. To the amazement of even the most cynical observers, the Crips-and-Bloods pact had long-term beneficial effects.

CROSSROADS OF THE WORLD, Hollywood shopping center established in 1936. It was designed by Robert V. Derrah, master of the Streamline Moderne style. Like his best-known creation, the Coca-Cola plant on Central Avenue, Crossroads of the World incorporated a ship motif, to which the concept of a medieval European village was added. The ship is topped by a lighted world globe. Designed and intended originally as a shopping mall, one of the first in the region, it is now occupied mainly by offices.

CROWN HILL, residential tract at 2nd and Belmont Streets. It was opened during the Boom of the Eighties and was connected to downtown by a streetcar line.

CRUZ, RICHARD (1943–1993), Chicano rights attorney active in La Raza Unida, a political party of the 1960s and 1970s. Charging that the Catholic Church was unresponsive to Latino needs, he led a 1969 Christmas Eve demonstration against the newly constructed St. Basil's Cathedral on Wilshire Boulevard. He claimed that the clash, although regrettably violent, nevertheless caused

---

To the home of the orange blossom,
To the land of fruit and honey,
Where it does not take much money
To own a bungalow.
　　　　　—George Devereaux, ca. 1900

---

the church to appoint Latino bishops, support Cesar Chavez, and create new social agencies for the Latino poor. As an attorney, he won the dismissal of charges against a teenager wrongly convicted of murder.

CRYER, GEORGE E[DWARD] (1875–1961), mayor of Los Angeles from 1921 to 1929. During his tenure the city was in the throes of a major growth spurt, with the population rising from 570,000 to over 1 million and the metropolitan area expanding from 360 square miles to over 400. In his 1921 and 1923 campaigns Cryer's denunciation of public ownership of utilities won him the backing of *Los Angeles Times* publisher Harry Chandler. Cryer lost that support, however, when he shifted toward municipal water ownership, lost control of crime and vice, and proved unable to deal with police corruption. Cryer's right-hand man, Kent Parrot, was considered the "de facto mayor of Los Angeles." Despite intense *Times* opposition in 1925, the Cryer-Parrot administration won reelection by defeating the *Times*'s candidate, Judge Benjamin Bledsoe. During Cryer's last years as mayor the police chief's office became a revolving door as he appointed, in quick succession, Charles A. Jones, W. Everington, Louis D. Oakes, August Vollmer, and James Edgar Davis.

CRYSTALAIRE, unincorporated Antelope Valley community at the foot of the San Gabriel Mountains between Llano and Valyermo, east of Valyermo Road. By 1986, some 400 half-acre and one-acre lots had been subdivided. The rural area features a mobile home park, a country club, and a small airport.

CSULA. *See* California State University, Los Angeles

CSULB. *See* California State University, Long Beach

CSUN. *See* California State University, Northridge

CUBANS numbered 120,000 in the Los Angeles metropolitan area in 1990. Most arrived in the 1960s, when Fidel Castro lifted travel restrictions, and have established themselves in the Echo Park and Silver Lake areas, and to a lesser extent in Culver City, Long Beach, Inglewood, South Gate, and Glendale. They are a diverse community representing all classes and occupations. Cubans gather in social clubs and at events such as soccer games, debutante balls, and religious holidays.

CUDAHY, tiny independent town 12 miles south of Los Angeles. It was founded early in the century as a town for small farmers, on a ranch owned by meat packer Michael Cudahy. Even as late as the 1960s, residents lived in single-family homes on large lots and kept chickens, goats, and horses. Cudahy experienced a rapid 27 percent rate of growth in the 1980s. In 1990, with a population of 22,817 and a geographic area of 1.1 square miles, it was the most densely populated municipality west of the Mississippi, and with a per capita income of only $5,935, it also had the dubious distinction of being one of the poorest communities in the nation, with 27 percent living below the poverty line.

CULTS. *See* Religion

CULTURAL HERITAGE COMMISSION, LOS ANGELES. *See* Los Angeles City Cultural Heritage Commission

CULTURAL HERITAGE COMMISSION, PASADENA. *See* Pasadena Cultural Heritage Commission

CULVER, HARRY H. (1880–1946), founder of Culver City. Born in Nebraska, Culver enlisted in the Spanish-American War, then attended the University of Nebraska and worked as an entrepreneur and newspaperman in both the Philippines and St. Louis before arriving in Southern California in 1910. He hired on as a realtor for I. N. Van Nuys but soon struck out on his own. While watching filmmaker Thomas Ince shoot a scene on a barley field near Ballona Creek, he conceived the idea of developing a town specifically for filmmakers. Culver bought the land, laid out the town, and served on its board of trustees and as a bank director, before becoming president of the California Real Estate Association. He donated 100 acres of land as a site for Loyola University.

CULVER CITY, independent residential and industrial city 11 miles west of downtown Los Angeles. Tongva (Gabrieleño) Indians once fished along the banks of the meandering stream that was later named Ballona Creek. The area's earliest European settlement was on Rancho La Ballona and Rancho Rincón de los Bueyes, established by the Lugo and Machado clans in the Hispanic era.

The city was named in 1914 for realtor Harry H. Culver, who bought and subdivided part of the Ballona land grant. Culver induced movie maker Thomas Ince to found a studio there that later became the Metro-Goldwyn-Mayer Studio (MGM). The city deliberately maintained low tax rates to attract other production companies. In 1914 its voters—all 59 of them—rejected a strong annexation bid by the city of Los Angeles.

During the Roaring Twenties, Culver City became a wide-open town. It attracted crowds from neighboring Los Angeles, where prohibition was more strictly enforced. They came for gambling, in the form of craps and dog racing, as well as bootlegged whiskey, live jazz, and dancing. Most of the action took place at speakeasies and nightclubs along West Washington Boulevard, such as the Cotton Club and the Plantation Club, which featured alcoholic beverages brewed in nearby private homes. These nightspots, along with overt prostitution, tended to corrupt local government until they were phased out in the 1930s.

Archway, City Hall, Culver City, 1995. Photo by Leonard Pitt.

Culver City was home not only to MGM but also to the Hal Roach Studios and the Desilu television studios. Sony Pictures Entertainment now occupies the old MGM grounds, allowing Culver City to still call itself the "Heart of Screenland." Within the city limits is also a large parcel of land belonging to Hughes Aircraft Company.

Culver City's population was 503 in 1920, 8,996 in 1940, and 38,793 in 1990. Some of the increases came from 16 annexations during the 1950s and 1960s, including the unincorporated areas of Culver Crest, Baldwin Hills, and Fox Hills. The Fox Hills Mall, built in 1975, represented a major infusion of new tax dollars. By the same token, the city's older, central area began showing the signs of physical decay. To address this problem the city formed a redevelopment agency in the 1970s that set about preserving historic structures, refurbishing schools, constructing a new fire department headquarters, and redesigning the downtown traffic patterns. The crowing achievement was the new $30 million City Hall, designed by CHGC Architects and dedicated in 1995.

CUNNINGHAM, WALTER (1932–), astronaut. Although born in Iowa, he moved with his family to Los Angeles when he was young, attending Venice High and graduating from UCLA with a master's degree in physics. After serving in the navy in 1951, he worked first for the RAND Corporation in Santa Monica, and then, in 1963, joined NASA, participating in the earth-orbiting *Apollo 7* mission. A building has been named in his honor at his high school alma mater.

DACE, CATHERINE HUBBARD EGBERT (1886–1961), San Fernando Valley pioneer. Dace was born on the family homestead in San Fernando, the city founded by her grandfather, Charles Maclay. She was a friend, relative, or acquaintance of all the early valley families. Dace witnessed the evolution of the valley from its pastoral beginnings to its emergence as a vast suburban and commercial center. Her oral history memoir chronicles the evolution of the area from the perspective of her family.

DAILY COMMERCIAL NEWS AND SHIPPING GUIDE, Long Beach newspaper founded in 1911 by Charles A. Page focusing on the shipping and transportation industry of Southern California. The same publisher also issues the *Weekly Commercial News and Cargo* magazine.

DAILY NEWS OF LOS ANGELES, San Fernando Valley newspaper. It was founded in 1911 as the weekly *Van Nuys Call,* changed its name to the *Van Nuys News,* and in 1953 became the *Valley News and Green Sheet.* It slowly added days of publication, becoming a daily in 1981. It then changed its name to the *Daily News of Los Angeles*—modifying the name of the recently defunct *Los Angeles Daily News.* In 1985 the Jack Kent Cooke Media Group, Inc., purchased the paper, and two years later moved its editorial offices from Van Nuys to Woodland Hills. By achieving a circulation of over 200,000 in its primary service area—the San Fernando Valley and neighboring valleys—the *Daily News of Los Angeles* has given serious competition to the *Los Angeles Times.*

DAIRYING, business enterprise started locally by Americans and Europeans. Mexicans, who consumed few dairy products, raised cattle mostly for hides and tallow. The first major suppliers of milk, cream, butter, and cheese to the local metropolitan market were Swiss immigrants. One of the most prominent dairies in Los Angeles was Adohr Milk Farms. Occupying 600 acres, it was located at Encino's western border, facing Ventura Boulevard. The dairy was owned by the son-in-law and daughter (Rhoda: Adohr is her name spelled backward) of Frederick and May Rindge.

In the 1950s dairy owners, facing the increasing encroachment of residential development, began cutting back or closing down operations and moving out of Los Angeles County. In order to realize the highest prices for their land, they incorporated new cities. In 1955–1956, for example, the towns of Dairyland, Dairy Valley, and Cypress were created, with a combined population of 75,000 cows and 5,000 people. Later, the same dairy interests changed the zoning from agricultural to residential and sold out at favorable prices. The community of Cerritos emerged.

Dairy farming in Southern California shifted from Los Angeles to Riverside and San Bernardino Counties. By the 1980s, of the 223 dairy farms in the southern part of the state, only one remained in Los Angeles County—in Lancaster. The processing of milk and milk products continues within the metropolitan area, however, and is handled by major grocery chains.

DAKIN, SUSANNA BRYANT. *See* Bixby family

DALTON, EMMETT (D. 1937), member of the notorious Dalton Gang of Coffeyville, Kansas. After he was released from jail in 1907 he decided, having seen the amazing one-reeler *The Great Train Robbery* (1903), to come to Hollywood with his wife and become a movie actor. He failed as a performer, but found a good living as a building contractor. When Dalton died in 1937, upstanding citizens, including some in the movie industry, attended his funeral. Los Angeles was also the final home of the colorful sheriff Wyatt Earp (1848–1929) and train robber Al Jennings (1863–1961).

DAMS AND RESERVOIRS are maintained by the federal, state, county, and city governments as part of the intricate water system developed early in the century. The majority are meant to control floodwaters. Twenty large dams maintained by the county flood control district range in height from 33 to 365 feet. Devil's Gate Dam on the Arroyo Seco, Pacoima Dam, Big Tujunga Dam, and San Gabriel Dam were built in the mountains, while Hanson, Sepulveda, Santa Fe, and Whittier Narrows Dams were constructed further downstream in the floodplains. The first dam in the area was located in Bear Valley in 1884.

As far away as the distant Colorado River, dams affect the lives of Angelenos. Parker Dam collects water for the Colorado River Aqueduct that eventually snakes its way into thousands of Southern California homes, while Hoover Dam generates the electricity that lights Los Angeles. Once built, dams tend to attract most attention when they are too full, too empty, or about to burst. By all odds the most serious dam catastrophe was the collapse of the Francisquito Canyon Dam on the Santa Clara River in 1928, which killed some 400 people—about the same number as perished in the mammoth San Francisco earthquake of 1906. During the 1971 earthquake the Van Norman Dam neared a collapse that would have inundated the northern San Fernando Valley. It has since been completely redesigned and is no longer a threat.

DANA, DEANE (1926–), county supervisor for the 4th District. Before his election in 1980, Dana worked for Pacific Telephone for 28 years in marketing, administration, and engineering. He is a strong advocate of privatization. Until the early 1990s he joined with Pete Schabarum and Mike Antonovich to form a conservative majority on the County Board of Supervisors. Dana has served as president of the Coliseum commission and was reelected as supervisor in his large and diverse district in 1992.

DANA, RICHARD HENRY, JR. (1815–1882), Boston Brahmin who shipped out as a common seaman on the *Pilgrim,* a brig that sailed along the California coast in 1835 and 1836. He wrote of his experiences in *Two Years Before the Mast* (1840), now considered a classic American autobiography. He describes the hide-and-tallow trade, but mentions the Los Angeles area only in passing.

DANCE has played an important role among the peoples living the Los Angeles area for centuries. To the prehistoric Tongva and Chumash peoples, and through the mission era, dance was a critical part of ritual celebrations. In Spanish and Mexican colonial days, from 1781 to 1848, both music and dance figured strongly in home and family leisure time, and most people became proficient dancers. The popularity of dancing as recreation and formal celebration began to decline, however, once large numbers of Americans settled in Los Angeles.

In the 1930s and 1940s, dance studios opened, training young hopefuls who dreamed of breaking into the movies via the Hollywood musical. Films popularized the tap dance (an art form created by African Americans) through such performers as Bill "Bojangles" Robinson, Ruby Keeler, the Nicholas Brothers, Ann Miller, Fred Astaire, and Ginger Rogers. Tap dancing studios were especially popular, and public parks offered tap dancing classes to youngsters who lacked the means to pay for formal instruction. Astaire and Rogers also revitalized ballroom dancing and performed the Lindy, Charleston, and Cake Walk to the delight of film audiences. A new generation of dancers—Gene Kelly, Cyd Charisse, Jeanmaire, Leslie Caron—introduced ballet and modern dance into the mix. Astaire and Kelly choreographed much of their own work, and movie studios also hired choreographers such as Busby Berkeley, Hermes Pan, Michael Kidd, and Bob Fosse, most of them from Broadway.

Ironically, although Hollywood musicals popularized dance nationally and even internationally, and employed many of the greatest practitioners, dance did not take a strong hold in Los Angeles. Ballroom dancing did become something of a fad during the 1930s and 1940s in the casinos of Long Beach, Ocean Park, Hollywood, and Catalina, but it was the jitterbug that dominated the dance halls during these decades, in Los Angeles as in the nation as a whole. The introduction of modern dance in the 1940s, while limited, reached a high profes-

Impressions, No. 2, Bella Lewitzky, choreographer. Photo by Vic Luke.

sional level in the work of Lester Horton and some of his pupils, such as Alvin Ailey, Carmen de Lavallade, and Bella Lewitzky. From 1946 to 1959 Joseph Rickard, a white dance teacher in Los Angeles, organized and headed the nation's First Negro Classic Ballet. The company gave its premiere performance at Hollywood High School auditorium and traveled to other cities, receiving favorable reviews. As a performance art, dance continues to receive relatively little local support. Relative to San Francisco or New York, classical ballet in Los Angeles has never held a secure position. In the 1980s, the Joffrey Ballet had a disappointingly short residency at the Los Angeles Music Center. The Los Angeles Chamber Ballet was formed in 1981. Lewitzky maintains the only local dance company whose performers are contracted year-round, although it spends about half the year on the road.

The dance scene since the 1970s has been characterized as eclectic; groups tend to be avant-garde, traditional, experimental, and multicultural, and their audiences appear to be growing. Some of the companies that exemplify these trends are the Aman Dancers; the Inner City Dance Company; the L.A. Contemporary Dance Theater, an African American company founded by Lula and Erwin Washington; Loretta Livingston and Dancers, a modern dance company cofounded by Lewitzky protégée Loretta Livingston and her husband, David Plettner; the Francisco Martinez Dancetheatre, which merges classical and modern dance; and Danza Floricanto/USA, directed by Gema Sandoval, Los Angeles's oldest professional Mexican folk dance troupe. The Los Angeles Modern Dance and Ballet Company was founded by dancer and choreographer Naomi Goldberg in 1989. In addi-

tion to performing, the group has devoted itself to community involvement. The Performing Tree, a private nonprofit agency, attempts to foster the performing arts, including dance, among children by placing professional performers in school workshops. In the 1990s a dance called *quebradita* became the rage among young Latinos. A lively country-style dance that resembles a stomping Texas two-step, it enjoyed considerable popularity in local clubs.

Several of the region's universities, such as CSULA, CSULB, and UCLA, have become centers for the local dance scene. Increasingly, campus departments are hiring professional performers who not only choreograph and organize programs but also teach and train a new generation of dancers.

D.A.R.E. (DRUG ABUSE RESISTANCE ED-UCATION), nonprofit antidrug program established in the Los Angeles schools in 1983. It helps children from kindergarten through 9th grade resist drugs by fighting peer pressure and managing stress. It has since been established nationwide, although in some cities its effectiveness has been debated. An umbrella organization, D.A.R.E. America, provides financial support and coordination.

DARROW, CLARENCE S. (1857–1938), most celebrated trial lawyer and labor attorney in U.S. history. In 1911 he defended John J. and James B. McNamara, brothers accused in the 1910 bombing of the *Los Angeles Times* Building. After the brothers' dramatic confessions that ended the case, he was forced to remain in Los Angeles for years while defending himself against the accusation that he had bribed a prospective juror. Defended by his legal opponent in the McNamara case, Earl Rogers, Darrow was twice tried and twice released by split juries. During the ordeal, in 1912, he nearly died of an ear infection. The bribery cases spurred an ongoing debate among legal scholars and writers as to whether or not Darrow was guilty as charged.

DAVIDSON, GORDON (1933–), artistic director and producer of the Center Theatre Group (CTG) of the Los Angeles County Music Center. He graduated from New York City's Brooklyn College, where his father was a member of the theater faculty, and earned an M.A. degree in theater at Case Western Reserve University in Cleveland.

Shortly afterward he joined the famed Group Theater in New York, and in 1964 came to Los Angeles with John Houseman, who founded the theater group at UCLA. Hand-picked by Dorothy Chandler in 1967 to head the new theater organization at the Music Center, Davidson has, since 1989, also served as the producing director of the CTG/Ahmanson. He has gained a national reputation for his contributions to regional theater and for his direction of numerous productions from on and off Broadway. Among his many awards was a 1977 Tony for directing Michael Christofer's *The Shadow Box.*

DAVIS, ED[WARD MICHAEL] (1916–), former Los Angeles chief of police (1969–1978) and GOP state senator from Valencia (1980–1992). As a blunt-spoken, law-and-order police chief he once suggested that airplane hijackers be tried and hanged at airports. In the state senate he served on the judiciary, education, insurance, and banking and commerce committees and simultaneously was a member of the Police Task Force of the National Advisory Commission on Criminal Justice Standards and Goals. He served three terms in the Senate; on one occasion he won 72 percent of the vote, more than any other Republican in California history.

DAVIS, MARVIN HAROLD (1925–), entrepreneur and investor. The son of a dress manufacturer, Davis made his fortune in oil wildcatting and real estate. He once owned 20th Century–Fox studios. His estimated fortune of over $2.5 billion makes him one of the nation's wealthiest persons.

DAWSON'S BOOKSHOP, renowned rare book sellers. Ernest Dawson originated the business in San Luis Obispo in 1898 but moved it to downtown Los Angeles in 1905. He was encouraged in his endeavor when he bought 2,250 books from the Salvation Army at 1 cent apiece and resold one of them, a book on Indian basketry, for $2.50. Soon he was attending book auctions in Boston, Philadelphia, and New York and conducting worldwide searches on behalf of collectors. The business has been continued by his sons, Glen and Muir. The shop, which is now in the Larchmont district, is the oldest operating bookstore in Los Angeles.

DAY OF THE LOCUST, THE (1939), Nathanael West's gloomy, satirical study of Hollywood. Often considered the greatest novel of the genre, it was made into a film by Fred Zinnemann in 1975. Homer Simpson comes to Hollywood seeking fame and fortune and encounters others living on the shabby fringes of the film world. It is a tale of twisted values and the American Dream gone berserk.

DEADMAN'S ISLAND, rocky outcropping near San Pedro used, along with Rattlesnake Island, by the Army Corps of Engineers to create a jetty in the harbor. The purpose of the structure was to help the rushing tides scour and deepen the shallow channel so that ocean vessels could enter and leave the bay.

DEBS, ERNEST E. (1904–), Ohioan who became a county supervisor after serving in the legislature and the Los Angeles City Council. He fostered the establishment of CSULA. In 1958, after defeating Ed Roybal in a bitterly fought election, he represented the 3rd Supervisorial District, which ranged from Panorama City to Montebello. Associated with liberal policy in education, recreation, hospital care, community services, and senior citizens welfare, he retired in 1974. Ernest E. Debs Regional Park is located in Montecito Heights.

DE CELIS, EULOGIO (D. 1869), native of Spain who purchased the 117,000-acre former San Fernando Mission from Pío Pico in 1846 for $14,000. In 1853, after reselling half of those lands to Pico's brother, Andrés, he returned to Spain, and died 16 years later. His son, Eulogio F. de Celis, who remained in California, was administrator of the heavily mortgaged estate that remained; he also worked as editor of the newspaper *La Crónica.* The land was sold at a court-ordered sheriff's sale in 1873.

DEER, specifically mule deer *(Odocoileus hemionus),* are often seen in their native chaparral, oak woodland, and yellow-pine forest environments in Southern California. Although they nibble valuable shrubs in developed and near-wild areas in the Santa Monica and San Gabriel Mountains, the law protects them from being shot or trapped.

DE LA HOYA, OSCAR (1973–), boxer. In 1992, at 19 years of age, he won a gold medal in the lightweight division at the Barcelona Olympic Games and returned a hero to his Boyle Heights neighborhood. After turning professional, De La Hoya held the World Boxing Organization belt and in 1995 defeated Rafael Ruelas to become the International Boxing Federation lightweight champion.

DEL AIRE, small unincorporated enclave west of the 405 and south of the 105 freeways. It lies south of Los Angeles International Airport. Del Aire Park is its most distinctive feature. Its population in 1990 was 8,000.

DEL OLMO, FRANK (1948–), journalist. The Los Angeles native attended CSUN and Harvard University. A *Los Angeles Times* editor and columnist who specializes in community affairs, del Olmo won a Pulitzer Prize for a series on the Latino community in 1984.

DE LONGPRE, PAUL (1855–1911), French-born painter who settled in Hollywood. Unable to sell his traditional watercolor flower paintings in Paris or New York, he brought his wife and family to Los Angeles. Here he met Daieda Wilcox, the land-rich widow of the founder of Hollywood, who was bent on promoting culture in that town. She became his patron, turning over to him three lots facing east on Cahuenga Boulevard, just north of Hollywood Boulevard, and later adding yet another property—receiving three of his paintings as payment. An enterprising entrepreneur, De Longpre built a large Moorish-style mansion at Hollywood and Cahuenga in 1901, was elected president of the Hollywood Club, and became a bank director. He also developed his picture-postcard home and gardens into a major tourist attraction. Thousands traveled by trolley from Los Angeles to chat with the artist, admire the dazzling flower beds and compare them to his watercolors, and buy either original paintings or reproductions.

DE MILLE, CECIL B[LOUNT] (1881–1959), pioneer movie director and producer who specialized in lavish spectaculars in a career that spanned more than 45 years. He first came to Los Angeles from New York as a traveling actor in 1903. In 1913 De Mille rented a barn abutting an orange grove at Vine and Selma Streets, which he and his partners, Jesse L. Lasky and Samuel Goldwyn, used as a studio. Here he made one of the area's first feature films, *The Squaw Man* (1913). When De Mille scouted locations on horseback he wore a six-shooter, as protection against a possible attack by

agents of the New York Film Trust, which he was opposing. By 1920 he was earning $260,000 a year and lived in a mansion in Laughlin Park (on what is now De Mille Drive). He was indicted, but not prosecuted, in the C. C. Julian scandal, a financial scam that hit the town in 1927. De Mille's films include two versions of *The Ten Commandments* (1923, 1956), *The Crusades* (1935), and *The Greatest Show on Earth* (1956).

DEMOCRATIC PARTY emerged in the 1850s in Los Angeles by pushing aside the Whigs and maintaining an anti-abolitionist, pro-southern posture until the Civil War. Anglo-Catholic Democrats joined hands with Mexican Catholics to bring out the vote for the party; those who did were rewarded with political plums. In 1852 and 1853 Antonio F. Coronel was chair of the Democratic County

---

Los Angeles has replaced San Francisco as the dominant city on the Pacific Rim.

—John McMahan, investment adviser

Committee, and 38 Californios were elected or appointed to state or local office between 1850 and 1860. Perhaps the greatest triumph of the Los Angeles Democrats was the election of John Gately Downey, an Irish-born druggist, real estate speculator, and banker, as lieutenant governor in 1859. Downey later succeeded to the governorship, although in 1861 he was swept from office by Republican Leland Stanford.

The party, which split deeply over the slavery issue, had trouble regaining power during the Reconstruction era. It recovered some strength in 1893 when Stephen White, a progressive Los Angeles district attorney, was elected to the U.S. Senate as a Democrat. Democrats made a decent showing regionally during the reformist Progressive era, from 1906 to 1912.

The Great Depression brought a significant and long-term change in voter preference in Los Angeles. Between 1928 and 1940 Republican registration fell from 71 percent to 42 percent, while that of Democrats rose from 29 percent to 58 percent. All California governors since 1895 had been Republican, but in 1938 Los Angeles helped elect Democrat Culbert Olson. The Democrats have managed to maintain a strong voter registration advantage over the Republicans ever since, at least within Los Angeles city limits.

Despite the nonpartisan cast of California local politics, Democratic Party volunteer organizations have been active at the grass-roots level at least since the 1940s. The California Federation of Young Democrats, formed in 1949, set itself the task of recruiting younger voters, and the California Democratic Council, formed in 1953, had active chapters on the Westside and in the San Fernando Valley for over a decade. The Democratic grass-roots activity peaked in the 1960s and then declined, although remnants of the movement continued. In the 1970s, for example, the Campaign for Economic Democracy, formed by Tom Hayden with the support of his then wife, Jane Fonda, organized door-to-door canvassing and grass-roots involvement on issues such as housing, energy, health, and economic justice. Although short-lived, the organization helped elect Democratic candidates to local office in Santa Monica.

In recent decades liberal Los Angeles Democrats had strong representation in the Democrat-controlled U.S. House of Representatives. Edward Roybal was elected in 1962, the first Mexican American in the U.S. Congress; he served until his retirement in 1992 on committees dealing with the treasury and postal services, aging, immigration, welfare, and education. James Corman, from the San Fernando Valley, who served from 1961 to 1981, sat on the space and aeronautics committee and the judiciary committee, where he cosponsored the 1964 Civil Rights Act and the 1965 Voting Rights Act. Pres. Lyndon Johnson appointed him to the Kerner Commission, which investigated civil disorder in 1967–1968. Anthony Bielenson, repre-

senting the Westside and portions of the San Fernando Valley since 1976, has served on the rules, budget, and intelligence committees. He has championed legislation for the protection of natural resources and the environment, including the Santa Monica Mountains National Recreation Area. Howard Berman, after serving in the state assembly from 1973 to 1982, moved up to the U.S. Congress, also representing portions of the San Fernando Valley. He was a principal in the liberal "Berman-Waxman machine" of the 1980s, and served on the key foreign affairs, judiciary, and budget committees. Henry A. Waxman, elected in 1974 to represent the 24th District, which includes Beverly Hills, Hollywood, Santa Monica, and West Los Angeles, coauthored the Clean Air Act of 1990 and sponsored legislation for the aged. Julian Dixon, first elected in 1979, represents the 28th District. He has served on the House appropriations committee and is a former president of the congressional Black Caucus. His interests have included civil rights and strengthening the congressional code of conduct, and he was instrumental in obtaining funding for Metrorail. Congresswoman Maxine Waters, elected in 1990 from the 35th District, which covers parts of Los Angeles, Inglewood, and Gardena, has sat on the banking, finance, and urban affairs committees.

DE NEVE, FELIPE. *See* Neve, Felipe de

DEPARTMENT OF WATER AND POWER, LOS ANGELES. *See* Los Angeles Department of Water and Power

DEPARTMENT STORES, from 1896 to 1910, were centered on Broadway between 4th and 8th

The original Broadway Department Store, Courtesy California State Library.

Streets, providing an anchor for downtown commerce. The earliest were the Broadway, the City of Paris, Hamburger's People's Store (later the May Company), and Bullock's. This stretch of Broadway and parts of 7th Street remained the most exciting section of town for the next half century. Also represented downtown were Robinson's, F. W. Woolworth, J. J. Newberry, S. H. Kress, W. T. Grant, and innumerable apparel shops and cigar stores, as well as theaters and restaurants. With its bright lights and lively pedestrian traffic Broadway became the "Great White Way" of the growing metropolis.

DEPRESSION. *See* Great Depression era

DESCANSO GARDENS, 165-acre county-owned garden in La Cañada, originally part of Rancho San Rafael, granted in 1784 to José María Verdugo. When the northern section was inherited by his daughter, Catalina, she renamed it Rancho La Cañada. It was owned from 1939 to 1953 by Manchester Boddy, publisher of the *Los Angeles Daily News,* who called it Rancho del Descanso ("Ranch of Tranquillity"). He planted thousands of plants, including camellias and roses, that mixed well with the original yuccas, live oaks, and seasonal poppies. Some 100,000 camellias bloom each year between November and March. Other special features are a Japanese garden, a rose garden, and a bird sanctuary. The county acquired the property in 1954 and subsequently turned the daily operations over to a nonprofit foundation.

DESEGREGATION OF PUBLIC SCHOOLS erupted as a controversy in Los Angeles in 1963. That year the California Supreme Court ruled that segregation—whether de jure (established by law) or de facto (resulting from housing patterns)—was unconstitutional. Although segregation of black and Asian youngsters had been officially abolished in the 1880s, it still existed. The Board of Education of the Los Angeles Unified School District (LAUSD) acknowledged the problem but denied wrongdoing, asserting that the situation resulted from demographic factors beyond its control. The board refused to institute busing to adjust any imbalance.

In 1968 the ACLU and NAACP filed *Crawford v. Los Angeles Board of Education* to address segregation. The school board quickly took steps to encourage voluntary desegregation. In ruling on *Crawford* in 1970, Judge Alfred Gitelson called for an end to de facto segregation—but without mentioning busing. An assassination attempt on the jurist failed. The schools delayed acting on the decision but then made a partial move, assigning 85,000 youngsters, some 20 percent of the total affected, to schools outside their neighborhood districts. This precipitated a strong pattern of "white flight" to the suburbs. Many parents simply sent their children to private schools, while others resorted to strong political and legal challenges to busing. In 1978 the California Supreme Court again ruled against the LAUSD and ordered hearings, subsequently held by Judge Paul Egly, on the issue of busing. Egly forced the schools to adopt busing to achieve racial balance, but by 1981 the anti-busing forces had achieved legislative and court victories that overturned Egly and ended forced busing. Meanwhile, white flight had caused major changes in school populations; in effect, the schools remained largely racially segregated, and busing continued in order to relieve overcrowded schools.

DESERT BUTTES, unincorporated community east of Palmdale in the Antelope Valley. In 1967 the developers, Watt Industries, created an artificial 20-acre body of water called Lake Los Angeles—for which the community was at first named—but the cost of maintaining the small lake forced the residents to let it go dry in the 1980s. In 1993, the year in which the name was changed to Desert Buttes, the quiet, sun-baked residential community had between 15,000 and 18,000 inhabitants, most of them occupying homes on large lots. Immediately west of the community is Lovejoy Buttes, a protected wildlife area.

DESERT VIEW HIGHLANDS, an area in Antelope Valley. Its population in 1990 was 2,154.

DESILVA, JOSEPH (1931–1985), labor leader who created Local 770 of the Retail Clerks Union. Born in Italy and raised in New York, he originally hoped to become a movie actor in the Valentino tradition. DeSilva began labor organizing during the depression years of 1937–1938 when he worked as a buyer for a grocery chain. The average wage at the time was 50 cents an hour, with a 72-hour workweek. Militant union action soon reduced the hours to 54 and raised the wages. In 1942 he began organizing drugstore clerks and won a contract covering 9,000 members. DeSilva also championed the cause of equal pay for equal work for women, and battled the color barrier. During a work stoppage in 1947 he denounced teamster boss Dave Beck as "the number one strikebreaker in the nation" for maintaining a sweetheart agreement with management. He also attempted to reintegrate Japanese workers returning from the internment camps, pioneered a medical and hospital plan with the Kaiser Foundation, and, in 1956, won a $10 million judgment against the Food Employers Council. DeSilva was among the first in the labor movement to recognize the potential of television, producing a local program, "770 on TV," on Sunday afternoons. He was active in legislative lobbying and party politics, mainly endorsing Democratic candidates.

DETECTIVE FICTION, literary genre strongly associated with Southern California. Writers Willard Huntington Wright (a.k.a. S. S. Van Dyne), Raymond Chandler, James Cain, Erle Stanley Gardner, Ross Macdonald, and John Gregory Dunne have used Los Angeles as a setting, often with tough-guy detectives and fast dialogue. Chandler's private eye, Philip Marlowe, has a jaundiced view of both the tawdry underworld and the corrupt, glamorous establishment. Macdonald's more straightforward narratives feature P.I. Lew Archer and deal with family and generational conflicts around Southern California.

The locale seems to inspire the creation of fictional detectives, from police officers to nuns. To name but a few: John Ball's Virgil Tibbs is identified with Pasadena, G. G. Fickling's Honey West with Long Beach, and Elizabeth Linington's Ivor Maddox with Hollywood, while Los Angeles is home to Roger Simon's Moses Wine; Erle Stanley Gardner's Bertha Cool, Donald Lam, and Perry Mason; Joseph Hansen's David Bradstetter; Arthur Lyons's Jacob Asch; Anthony Boucher's (a.k.a. H. H. Holmes) Sister Mary Ursula; Del Shannon's Luis Mendoza; and Stuart Kaminsky's Toby Peters—and this is only a partial list of local crusaders. Many works, such as James Cain's *The Postman Always Rings Twice* and *Double Indemnity,* Chandler's *The Big Sleep* and *The Long Goodbye,* and Macdonald's *The Drowning Pool,* have been translated into feature films, and others, including Gardner's creation Perry Mason, have become successful TV series. Other Los Angeles–based television crime shows have included *77 Sunset Strip; Badge 714,* which was actually endorsed by the Los Angeles Police Department; and *Dragnet,* which made an easy transition from radio to the small screen.

DE TORO, JUAN, Mexican American editor and historian. In 1882 he published *A Brief Sketch of the Colonization of California and the Foundation of the Pueblo of Our Lady of Los Angeles.* He edited the newspapers *El Demócrata* (The democrat) and *La Fe en la Democracia* (Faith in democracy).

DEUKMEJIAN, [COURKEN] GEORGE [JR.] (1928–), 35th governor of California, who served from 1983 to 1990. In 1955, Deukmejian moved from New York to Long Beach, where he practiced law. Entering politics as a tough law-and-order advocate, he served in the assembly from 1963 to 1967, the senate from 1967 to 1979, and as attorney general from 1979 to 1982. A Ronald Reagan conservative, "Duke" backed agribusiness, took a hard line on crime, opposed environmental regulations as detrimental to business, and cut back many of the state's social welfare programs.

DIAMOND BAR, independent community near Pomona, 24 miles east of downtown Los Angeles. It registered a 91 percent population increase in the decade 1980–1990, reaching a total of 53,672 in 1990.

DIAMOND LANE, ill-fated and short-lived (five months) experiment on the Santa Monica Freeway conducted by Caltrans in 1976. The goal was to reserve the inside lane for buses and cars carrying three or more people so as to conserve energy and reduce air pollution. Cars overheated and slowed to a crawl in the other lanes, however, as irate drivers counted few carpoolers or buses in the reserved lane. Widespread protest erupted, and politicians took up the cause, finally killing the experiment. The remnant of the system is a diamond-marked lane on some on-ramps reserved for cars with two or more passengers, and a dedicated express lane on the San Bernardino Freeway. Caltrans's latest policy has been to double-deck some freeways.

DICKSON, EDWARD A[UGUSTUS] (1879–1956), Wisconsin-born newspaper publisher and progressive political reformer. Dickson published the *Los Angeles Evening Express* and was a cofounder of the Good Government and Lincoln-Roosevelt Leagues. He also served as a regent of the

University of California and championed the development of the UCLA Westwood campus.

DICK WHITTINGTON PHOTOGRAPHY, commercial photography firm, named after a legendary 14th-century mayor of London, established by Wayne Whittington in 1926. He passed the business to his son, Ed[ward], in the 1950s. The Whittingtons' snapshots of aircraft factories, oil installations, sporting events, public festivities, and sales promotions were seen the world over and helped foster the image of a prosperous, sunny, and glamorous Southern California. The company's photo collection is now housed at the USC library.

DIDION, JOAN (1934–), Sacramento-born novelist and essayist. She and her husband, novelist John Gregory Dunne, resided in Los Angeles for many years, and both have written extensively about the city. Her stark novel *Play It as It Lays* (1970), which was made into a film in 1970, depicts the Los Angeles *noir* of the 1960s. She and Dunne wrote a version of *A Star Is Born,* which starred Barbra Streisand (1976).

DINGBAT STYLE, boxlike, two-story walk-up apartment building with sheltered parking at street level but no space for outdoor amenities. The dingbat typifies Los Angeles apartment architecture at its worst. The term, coined by Francis Ventre while teaching architecture at UCLA and living in such a box, was popularized by writer Reyner Banham.

DIRECTORS GUILD OF AMERICA (DGA), professional association of movie directors that serves as a bargaining agent with producers. It was formed in 1935 by 10 directors who met in King Vidor's living room; they formally organized as the Screen Directors Guild (SDG) on 15 January 1936 with a membership of 29. Producers refused to recognize them until 1940, when they won their first Basic Agreement. It guaranteed directors advertising billing and screen credits—but, because they were considered "artists," did not grant them minimum salaries.

The first person to receive an Academy Award for "Best Direction" was Joseph L. Mankiewicz, for *A Letter to Three Wives* (1949); he also won an Oscar for the script. Television directors became guild members in 1950, when the name was changed to Screen Directors Guild of America. Five years later

the SDG merged with the Radio and Television Directors Guild to form the national Directors Guild of America, Inc. In 1963 the membership expanded to include assistant directors. In 1989 the DGA, which now counted 9,500 members, moved into its new, six-story headquarters in Hollywood.

DISNEY, WALT[ER ELIAS] (1901–1966), commercial artist and producer of animated films. Disney was born in Chicago, but lived in the farming community of Marceline, Missouri, whose main thoroughfare he later memorialized in Disneyland as Main Street U.S.A. He moved to Hollywood as a young man. His breakthrough came in 1928 when he presented Mickey Mouse—or as he

---

Never before had my passion for beauty been satisfied. This place did not seem like earth; it was paradise.
—Charlotte Perkins Gilman, writer, 1890s

---

was then known, "Steamboat Willie"—to the world, dubbing in his own voice. In 1936 he introduced Donald Duck. Disney's first full-length animated feature was *Snow White and the Seven Dwarfs* (1938). Many more animated movies followed, including *Pinocchio* (1939), *Bambi* (1943), *Cinderella* (1950), and *Lady and the Tramp* (1950). Disney's first nonanimated film was *Treasure Island* (1950).

He founded the Disney Studio, located in the Toluca Lake area of Burbank, in 1940. Fifteen years later he unveiled Disneyland in Anaheim in Orange County. His short cartoons, feature-length animations, live-action films, comic books, records, nature documentaries, television shows, and theme parks—not to mention a vast array of consumer products—have exerted global influence. While Walt Disney was much praised for his artistic and business acumen, he was also under frequent attack for his extreme hucksterism, sentimentalism, and anti-unionism.

Even in a period when the major studios were in decline, Disney remained one of the very few Hollywood moguls to maintain absolute control over his studio and his films. He also was able to enter prime-time television and became a major player. He received special Academy Awards for several of his short features, as well as one in 1940 for the innovative *Fantasia.* Disney bequeathed part of his fortune to the California Institute of the Arts in Valencia, where the art of film animation is taught.

DISTRICT ATTORNEY. *See* Los Angeles County District Attorney

DODGE HOUSE, private residence on Kings Road in West Hollywood. The architectural masterpiece, designed by Irving J. Gill in 1916, sat on unincorporated land and was unfortunately destroyed in 1969 to make way for an apartment complex. The event sparked the formation of the preservation movement in Los Angeles.

DODGERS, LOS ANGELES. *See* Los Angeles Dodgers

DODGER STADIUM, in Chavez Ravine, became the permanent home of the Los Angeles Dodgers in 1962, after the team played four years at the Los Angeles Coliseum. Because the site had been slated for a low-cost, integrated housing project, the transfer of the land to the Dodgers in 1959 caused political acrimony. The privately financed, 56,000-seat stadium opened on 2 April 1962, and 2.7 million people passed through the turnstiles in the first year. By 1990, 73 million people had attended Dodger home games. The 3.6 million attendance in 1982 was an all-time major league record.

The stadium is an excellent ballpark; cantilever construction allows for unobstructed viewing throughout what is considered one of the most beautiful arenas ever built in the United States. The center-field fence is 395 feet from home plate. The parking lot has room for 16,000 cars. Dodger stadium was the baseball site for the 1984 Olympics.

Dodger Stadium. Courtesy Los Angeles Dodgers, Inc.

DOGS AND CATS. *See* Animal shelters

DOHENY, EDWARD L. (1856–1935), Wisconsin-born Colorado miner who discovered oil in Los Angeles in 1892. Doheny's discovery made him immensely wealthy and sparked the city's first oil boom. He and a partner had been digging a well with shovels near the intersection of Glendale Boulevard and 2nd Street when they struck crude. Seemingly overnight the area bordered by Figueroa, 1st, Union, and Temple Streets became a forest of oil derricks. Doheny celebrated his prosperity by building himself a mansion in the University Park area.

In the 1920s Doheny was implicated in the Harding administration's Teapot Dome scandal as the man who offered a bribe to Interior Secretary Albert B. Fall to obtain drilling rights in the Elk Hills oil field in California. When Doheny died, his wife, Estelle, inherited a fortune. She created a fine book collection, funded various Catholic charities, and became a Papal Countess in the Catholic Church. The Doheny mansion at 8 Chester Place is one of the best preserved and most impressive late-Victorian residences in the West Adams district.

DOMÍNGUEZ, MANUEL (1803–1882), eldest son of Juan José Domínguez. Born in San Diego, he had little formal schooling but taught himself to read. He was married to María Engracia Cota, with whom he had 10 children. Don Manuel was a member of the Los Angeles *ayuntamiento,* was twice elected *alcalde,* served as a judge, represented Los Angeles in 1833–1834 in the legislative body that secularized the California missions, and became prefect of the Second District, that is, the top civilian government official in the southern part of Alta California. Don Manuel fought in the Battle of Domínguez Rancho in the Mexican War and was elected to the Constitutional Convention that met in Monterey in 1849–1850. In the mid-1850s his estate was divided among him, a brother, and two nephews. His portion was about 25,000 acres and included his home near San Pedro as well as Rattlesnake Island (today's Terminal Island). Oil was discovered on the family estate in 1922.

DOMINGUEZ AIR MEETS, a series of sporting events on Dominguez Hill, near today's city of Carson. The original spectacle, the country's first international aviation meet, occurred from 10 to

Dominguez Aviation Meet poster, January 1910.
Courtesy Seaver Center for Western History Research,
Natural History Museum of Los Angeles County.

19 January 1910, seven years after the Wright brothers' first successful airplane flight. The organizer, local promoter Dick Ferris, chose the 57-acre location for its favorable prevailing sea breeze, lack of obstructions, and railway access for transporting equipment. The mayor declared a city holiday, and the spectacle was attended by some 175,000 people, many of whom commuted via the Pacific Electric Red Cars. Each day saw the 20,000-seat grandstand packed with spectators. Aviator Glenn H. Curtiss broke a record with a 55-mile-per-hour flight. French pilot Louis Paulhan won a $50,000 prize for soaring to the breathtaking altitude of 4,165 feet, a new record. Georgia Broadwick became the first woman sky diver when she parachuted from a hot-air balloon. Except for minor mishaps, the 1910 air show proved an immense success. One spectator, teenager Jimmy Doolittle, who later became a famous flier in his own right, said the event changed his life forever. Dominguez Hill airfield was used for air meets in 1911 and 1912 before it was abandoned. Aviatrix Blanche Stuart Scott was one of the 1912 participants.

DOMÍNGUEZ FAMILY, prominent Southern California clan. Although Domínguez is a common name in early California, the most important Domínguez line goes back to Juan José (1736–1809), a Catalonian who arrived in Alta California as a soldier in the Portolá expedition. His mother was a Sepúlveda. In 1784 he received grants to Rancho San Pedro (the first rancho granted in the Los Angeles area) and Rancho Palos Verdes—some 76,000 acres, or 120 square miles, in all—which he stocked with cattle. His son Manuel, a signer of the first state constitution, took over the estates in 1827. Now located on the former rancho lands are the cities of Compton, Gardena, Carson, Torrance, and Redondo Beach, as well as additional property on the Palos Verdes Peninsula and in the harbor area.

Manuel Domínguez's daughters, Dolores Domínguez de Watson, Victoria Domínguez de Carson, and Susana Delfinia Domínguez del Ama y González, together with their husbands and offspring, managed their birthrights with great acumen. They resisted the temptation to sell land even when prices soared, and in the 1920s exploited the valuable oil strikes on their Torrance and Dominguez Hill properties to great advantage. Even today the family retains a large portion of the land and receives handsome revenues.

DOMINGUEZ HILLS, hilly area in Carson, near Avalon Boulevard and Victoria Street. The site was part of the former Rancho San Pedro, granted to Juan José Domínguez in 1784, and part of it is still owned by the Domínguez family. It is the location of California State University, Dominguez Hills. The highest point, Dominguez Hill, is 214 feet above the coastal plain. It is where air meets were once held and where, in 1985, Dominguez Properties, a family-owned enterprise, unveiled an industrial park known as Dominguez Technology Center.

DOO DAH PARADE. *See* Pasadena Doo Dah Parade

DOROTHY CHANDLER PAVILION, grand auditorium in downtown Los Angeles. The 3,200-seat hall is one of three theaters that make up the Music Center complex. It features one of the largest stages in the nation and is home to the Los Angeles Philharmonic, Los Angeles Music Center Opera, and Los Angeles Master Chorale. The

Pavilion is one of the sites for the Academy Awards ceremonies. The interior's deluxe furnishings include crystal chandeliers, full-storied windows, plush carpeting, 17th-century tapestries, and gold-leaf sculptures. The pavilion opened in 1965 bearing the name of the civic leader who spearheaded fund raising for construction.

DOUGLAS, DONALD WILLS (1892–1981), aeronautical engineer and airplane manufacturer. Born in Brooklyn and graduated from the Naval Academy and Massachusetts Institute of Technology in 1914, Douglas was hired by Glenn L. Martin to head a fledgling airplane company in Los Angeles. In 1920, when he was 28 years old, he put up $1,000 and formed his own company in the back of a Santa Monica barbershop. After obtaining greater backing he produced the Cloudster, the first airplane to lift a useful load exceeding its own weight. In 1924 two army pilots took off from Clover Field in a pair of Douglas World Cruisers and circled the globe in 371 hours. The flight put the Douglas Aircraft Company on the map. He then began building mail planes for Western Airlines. The firm developed the all-metal frame, controlled-pitch propeller, and retractable landing gear. In 1932 work began, for Trans World Airlines, on the DC-1, a 12-passenger plane that cruised at 145 miles an hour. The DC-3 was the best-known Douglas aircraft; during World War II, the company assembled more than 10,000 of these planes, also designated the C-47. The DC-4 became the first presidential airplane. From 1957 to 1972 the company's mainstay was the DC-8, a highly successful jet airliner built in Long Beach. Douglas also helped develop ballistic missiles.

In 1967 the Douglas Aircraft Company merged with the McDonnell Corporation to become the McDonnell Douglas Corporation, of St. Louis. By 1989 it was the nation's largest defense contractor.

DOUGLAS, HELEN GAHAGAN (1900–1980), actress and congresswoman. Heywood Broun called her "ten of the twelve most beautiful women in the world." The former Broadway actress and opera singer, and wife of actor Melvyn Douglas, was a Democratic National Committee member. She served three terms in Congress, from 1945 to 1950, representing a downtown Los Angeles district. In 1950 she became the first woman from California to win the backing of a major party for the U.S. Senate. A New Deal Democrat, she

Helen Gahagan Douglas and Congressman Jerry Voorhis. Courtesy Dept. of Special Collections, University Research Library, UCLA.

lost the race to Republican congressman Richard Nixon amid the growing Cold War atmosphere. His red-baiting campaign dubbed her the "Pink Lady . . . pink right down to her underwear." As the campaign heated up she was once stoned by children, and when she spoke on the USC campus fraternity boys doused her with seltzer water.

DOWNEY, independent city 13 miles southeast of downtown Los Angeles. It was named by former governor John Gately Downey in 1865 when he subdivided his 17,000-acre Rancho Gertrudis, located between Rio Hondo and the San Gabriel River. The laying of Southern Pacific tracks in 1873 initiated an era of growth and prosperity. Farmers in the vicinity grew grain, corn, castor beans, mustard, and deciduous fruit. County fairs were held in Downey (at the site of the present city hall) from 1884 to 1889, and in 1888 the county established a "poor farm" that eventually became Rancho Los Amigos Medical Center. After about 1940 the numerous farms, ranches, and citrus groves gave way to aerospace factories and suburban tract homes. Incorporated in 1956, Downey became a charter city in 1964, with an area of 12.7 square miles. In 1990 the population reached 91,444. Residents take special pride in an outstanding school system.

DOWNEY, JOHN GATELY (1826–1894), Irish immigrant who became a California governor. Arriving in Los Angeles during the Gold Rush as a poor 15-year-old, Downey made his initial fortune operating the only drugstore between San Francisco and San Diego. After being elected lieutenant governor on the Democratic ticket, at age 32 he was appointed governor, in which capacity he served from 1860 to 1862. Although he was a committed Union man, some perceived him as a Confederate sympathizer, and he was not reelected. Returning to private life, he poured his profits into ranching and real estate near the town he named for himself. Downey was also responsible for subdividing Norwalk and Santa Fe Springs, and he later joined Alvinza Hayward (the richest man in California, having staked a mine during the Gold Rush that yielded $25 million) and I. W. Hellman in the banking business. On 10 April 1871 he and Hellman opened Farmers and Merchants Bank. The enterprise prospered and later became part of Security Pacific Bank, which, in 1993, merged with Bank of America.

DOWNEY BLOCK, important Los Angeles commercial block at Spring, Temple, and Main Streets in the 1860s and 1870s. It was the site of the old Temple adobe and was developed by Gov. John G. Downey. The block contained a bank, dentist's office, marble cutting shop, restaurant, barbershop, the first public library in Los Angeles, and several photography studios. Eventually Downey Block became the site of a federal building.

DOWNTOWN LOS ANGELES, FROM 1890 TO 1945, was focused on Broadway and Spring Streets. Commercial activity had begun migrating southward from the Plaza, the first downtown core, in the 1870s. Building booms occurred in

1896–1917 and 1920–1929. The years 1896–1910 saw the building of several major department stores along Broadway, and of a clutch of theaters. By the 1930s Broadway and 7th seemed to mark the center of downtown, with West 7th aspiring to be the "Fifth Avenue of the Pacific Coast." By the same token, in the 1920s the city's banks, title and trust companies, stockbrokers, and savings and loan associations moved to Spring Street, between 3rd and 8th, giving Spring a reputation as the "Wall Street of the West."

The downtown skyline was comparatively low, the result of a 150-foot height limit. The towering 28-story City Hall, built in the 1920s, was the only exception. Before the 1920s downtown was fairly centralized, with the most important city functions —stores, factories, theaters, banks, and government offices—concentrated there. Tens of thousands of Angelenos lived downtown, and others commuted into the central district by interurban Red Cars. In the 1920s the automobile changed all that, enticing people to the suburbs and creating a multicentered urban environment. By the 1940s downtown street congestion had reached alarming levels, as streams of cars jostled with streetcars and Red Cars for space, further driving people away from downtown.

DOWNTOWN LOS ANGELES, SINCE 1945, has been defined as the area south and east of the four-level interchange of the Santa Monica and

Los Angeles skyline, looking west on Aliso Street, ca. 1899. Courtesy Robert Weinstein Collection.

Downtown skyline, 1994.
Courtesy Caltrans Photos.

Harbor Freeways. The area was much transformed in the 1960s by population increases, freeway construction, the lifting of the 150-foot building height limit, and federal and state laws that encouraged urban redevelopment. The core of downtown shifted to the area immediately east of the Harbor Freeway, between 1st and 8th Streets, an area known to planners as the Central Business District (CBD). It is a relatively small area, comprising 200 city blocks, about half of which is devoted to parking. The rest is home to real estate firms, corporate headquarters, law offices, accounting firms, travel and transportation companies, savings and loans, banks, brokerage houses, insurance companies, and government offices. Autos and freeways decentralized Los Angeles's downtown commercial activity and dispersed much of it to outlying districts.

The skyline burst upward in the mid-1960s, starting with the 36-story Union Bank Building. The tallest building today, First Interstate World Center, is 73 stories. The skyline is dominated by buildings bearing the logos of banks, savings and loans, and industrial corporations. Many were designed by leading architects in the modern style, and a few in the postmodern style. The corporate and law offices towering above Bunker Hill serve the commerce of the entire Pacific Rim. In comparison to other big cities, Los Angeles has fewer major hotels, department stores, restaurants, or theaters downtown, owing to the development of suburban shopping malls and business centers.

In the 1980s much of downtown's real estate came to be owned by foreign firms: Japanese, British, Canadian, Chinese, German, and Dutch. A 1986 *Times* survey revealed that two-thirds of the biggest downtown office buildings were foreign owned. In 1991, even amid the prevailing glut of offices, 16 new real estate construction projects, including 11 skyscrapers, were being planned—representing an additional 20 million square feet of office space over the next decade. The Community Redevelopment Agency (CRA) controls the future of much of the area. To offset the desolation of most downtown streets after dark, the

Tallest Buildings in the City		
	Feet	*Stories*
First Interstate World Center, 633 W. 5th Street	1,017	73
First Interstate Bank Tower, 770 Wilshire Boulevard	858	62
Southern California Gas Company, 555 W. 5th Street	755	54
Wells Fargo Center, 333 S. Grand Avenue	750	53
333 S. Hope Street	735	55
Two California Plaza, 350 S. Grand Avenue	723	52
Sanwa Bank Plaza, 601 S. Flower Street	719	52
777 Figueroa Street	716	53
ARCO Tower, 515 S. Flower Street	699	52
Bank of America, 555 S. Flower Street	699	52

SOURCE: Auto Club of Southern California, *Guide to Downtown Los Angeles*, 1993.

CRA has been trying to attract people into condos and apartments. About 30,000 people lived downtown in the 1980s. Although there was no longer any true residential area, the CRA planned to increase the resident population of the area of Bunker Hill, Civic Center, and the Figueroa Corridor by 100,000 over the next two decades.

DREAMWORKS, multimedia entertainment company formed in 1994 by three industry giants: Steven Spielberg, producer and director of several of the top-grossing films of all time; David Geffen, former record company mogul and a major stockholder in Music Corporation of America (MCA); and Jeffrey Katzenberg, former head of Walt Disney Studio. In 1995 Bill Gates announced that his company, Microsoft Corporation, would become a minor investor, injecting technical know-how into DreamWorks' future. Microsoft cofounder Paul Allen has also invested $500 million in the venture. Through other investments, bank loans, and cash infusions from the three partners, DreamWorks started out with a $2 billion operating base. With DreamWorks headquartered in Los Angeles, the city's position as a multimedia leader gained considerable strength.

DRUM BARRACKS, Civil War military post in Wilmington from 1862 to 1866 named for Richard Drum, assistant adjutant general of the Department of California. It is Southern California's only significant Civil War landmark. The federal government spent $1 million on its construction and processed more than 13,000 Union soldiers there. When decommissioned in the 1880s it became the campus of a denominational college; it is now a historic landmark and museum. Of the original 20 structures, only 2 remain.

DRUNKARD, THE, William H. Smith's Victorian melodrama, also known as *The Fallen Saved,* originally made famous by showman P. T. Barnum. A revival opened in Los Angeles in 1933 and by 1938 had broken the existing record for a long-run theater production, overtaking *Abie's Irish Rose,* which ran for 283 consecutive weeks in New York City. The amusing burlesque, interspersed with rollicking and sentimental Gay Nineties ballads, was still going strong decades later.

DUARTE, independent city in the San Gabriel Valley 13 miles northeast of downtown Los Angeles. It was named for Andrés Duarte, who received title to Rancho Azusa in 1841 and subdivided it in 1864–1865. Cattle, horses, and sheep ranged in the area until about 1880. The town was founded in the Boom of the Eighties and quickly became famous for its citrus groves and avocado trees. In 1912 Los Angeles Jewish merchants raised $136, bought a 5-acre plot, and erected two tents as a haven for tubercular garment workers. This was the beginning of the City of Hope. Band leader Glenn Miller lived in Duarte as a youngster. The town's orange groves gave way to residential tracts after World War II. Duarte was incorporated in 1957, and in 1990 its population stood at 20,688.

DUARTE, FRANK R. (1910–), East Los Angeles community leader, born in the Mexican state of Chihuahua. In 1923 Duarte witnessed the ambush shooting of Pancho Villa. His family moved to Los Angeles and settled near Union Station. In 1934 he was involved in the garment workers' strike. He later moved back to Mexico, returning to Los Angeles only after World War II. He has served on various city and county commissions, committees, and boards since the 1960s. Duarte

Wilmington's Drum Barracks, with camel, 1860s.

helped found the East Los Angeles Community Improvement Association and the East Los Angeles Job Clearing House. A widely respected community elder, he is employed by Los Angeles County as a liaison officer to recruit Latinos; as such he is the oldest county employee.

DUCOMMUN, CHARLES LOUIS (1820–1876), Gold Rush pioneer and respected merchant. A Swiss immigrant, he arrived in Los Angeles in 1849 after walking all the way from Arkansas. He established a jewelry store on Main and Commercial Streets that evolved first into a general store and then into a hardware and tool business, and he was a director of Farmers and Merchants Bank. Though greatly admired for his honesty, Ducommun was considered slightly eccentric. In the 1920s his enterprise, which was still family run, supplied building materials for the aircraft industry—including tubing for Charles Lindbergh's *Spirit of St. Louis.* Today the Ducommun Metals and Supply Company is the oldest continuously operating business in Los Angeles.

DUNBAR HOTEL, lodging house at 41st Street and Central Avenue, near the Coliseum. Built by an African American dentist, Dr. Alexander Somerville, it was originally called Hotel Somerville. The NAACP held its national convention there in 1928. When Somerville lost ownership during the Great Depression, Lucius Lomax Sr., a successful gambler, bought the place and renamed it for Paul Laurence Dunbar, the celebrated African American poet. (Lomax Sr.'s son was Lucius Lomax, a criminal lawyer, and his daughter-in-law, Almena Lomax, was a journalist and pub-

lisher of the *Los Angeles Tribune.* Their daughter, Melanie E. Lomax, is a prominent Los Angeles attorney.)

The Dunbar was frequented by black entertainers, musicians, and community leaders who were barred from hotels in Beverly Hills and Hollywood when Jim Crow laws held sway, and by whites who opposed segregation. Among the celebrated guests were W. E. B. DuBois, James Weldon Johnson, Arthur Spingarn, Lincoln Steffens, Duke Ellington, Count Basie, Bill ("Bojangles") Robinson, and Eddie ("Rochester") Anderson. There was no entertainment at the hotel, but it did provide lodging for musicians who worked next door at Club Alabam. Bernard Johnson bought the four-story structure in 1968 to save it from the wrecker's ball. With Community Redevelopment Agency help it has been converted into a senior citizens' home.

DUNN, WILLIAM ELLSWORTH (1861–1924), Michigan-born attorney and public official. Arriving in Los Angeles in 1885, Dunn married into the prominent Briggs family, and in 1887 became a member of the bar and an assistant city attorney. For a time he specialized in prosecuting prostitutes. Dunn and his close associate Albert Hodges "Handsome Billy" Crutcher, a former Kentuckian with whom he cofounded the prominent law firm of Gibson, Dunn, and Crutcher, were steady fixtures in city hall politics from 1888 to 1898. Assistant City Attorney Dunn was instrumental in changing elections from an annual to a biennial calendar, and in his first year in office he wrote a record 1,113 ordinances. A conservative Republican, he served on the welcoming committee for the railroad stopover of Pres. William Henry Harrison in 1891. Dunn was an important legal adviser and friend to railroad and real estate magnate Henry E. Huntington.

DUNNE, JOHN GREGORY (1932–), Connecticut-born writer who lived in Los Angeles for many years. His book *The Studio* (1969) is a nonfiction analysis of the movie industry, and his novel *True Confessions* (1977) concerns the relationship between two brothers, one a semitough Los Angeles cop, the other a prominent Catholic priest. The latter work is based, in part, on the Black Dahlia murder case. Dunne has also authored and coauthored film scripts with his wife, Joan Didion.

Dunbar Hotel, opened in 1928. Courtesy Miriam Matthews Collection.

DURANT, WILL[IAM] (1885–1981), teacher, philosopher, and historian. Durant was the greatest popularizer of philosophy in American publishing history. His 1926 work *The Story of Philosophy* was translated into a dozen languages and sold more than 1 million copies. Some volumes of his series titled *The Story of Civilization* (1935–1963) were written with his wife and former student, Ariel Durant (1898–1981). For many years they lived and worked in Hollywood, prompting the patrons of a Hollywood public library, in a popular contest, to rename their neighborhood branch the Will and Ariel Durant Library.

DUTCH came to Los Angeles chiefly in the 1920s and 1930s, finding work as tradesmen, artisans, and farmers in the burgeoning dairy industry centered in La Mirada, Norwalk, Bellflower, Artesia, Cyprus, and La Palma. Beginning with two settlers in 1850, the numbers from Holland had reached 50,000 a century or so later. The community once supported the *Holland News,* the only Dutch-language newspaper in the United States, as well as several congregations of the Reformed and Christian Reformed Churches. In the 1960s the pressure for suburban real estate development squeezed out the dairies, causing some migration of Dutch ethnics to Central and Northern California.

DWP. *See* Los Angeles Department of Water and Power

DYKSTRA, CLARENCE A[DDISON] (1883–1950), city reformer and political scientist. In the 1930s he argued against downtown development, favoring a horizontal growth pattern that would allow for many commercial and residential subcenters. Dykstra sat on the water and power commission and was a UCLA faculty member. After serving as president of the University of Wisconsin and in the government war effort, Dykstra returned to California as UCLA provost from 1945 to 1948 and as vice president from 1948 to 1950.

DYMALLY, MERVYN M. (1926–), former elected official from Compton. Born in Trinidad in the West Indies, Dymally came to the United States in 1949. He worked as a janitor, union organizer, and teacher, earning a B.A. in education from CSULA and an M.A. in government from California State University, Sacramento. Dymally became a Democratic assemblyman in 1962, and a state senator in 1966; he then served as lieutenant governor from 1975 to 1979, and as congressman from the 31st District from 1980 to 1992. He chaired the International Operations Subcommittee of the Committee on Foreign Affairs as well as the Congressional Caucus for Science and Technology.

EAGLE ROCK, massive sandstone outcropping on Figueroa Street, off the 134 freeway, whose profile resembles that of an eagle. A portion of the 20,000-foot-deep underground fissure known as the Eagle Rock fault passes through the base of the 50-foot boulder. In 1991, with the landmark threatened by vandals and developers, the city of Los Angeles bought the outcropping and surrounding land and gave it the protective status of a historic monument.

Eagle Rock is also the name of the surrounding neighborhood. This area, bordering on Pasadena, was incorporated as a city in 1911 but consolidated with Los Angeles in 1923. Occidental College moved to Eagle Rock from Highland Park in 1914.

EAMES, CHARLES (1907–1978), AND RAY EAMES (D. 1988), designers. Born in St. Louis, Charles Eames studied at the Cranbrook Academy of Art in Bloomfield, Michigan, whose distinguished director was Eliel Saarinen. There he met his future wife, Ray Kaiser, a Sacramento-born painter. The pair achieved instant fame in 1946 with a Museum of Modern Art exhibit of chairs made of molded plywood and fiberglass-reinforced plastic. In a converted warehouse in Venice known as the "Eamery," Charles and Ray Eames created designs in the modern style. The Eames chair, a dining chair made of plywood mounted on steel rods, became a classic, as did their leather-and-wood recliner. The Eames home and studio on Chautauqua Boulevard in Pacific Palisades, a Case Study House of prefabricated components that blended high technology and fine art, has been described as "one of America's great 20th-century houses."

EARL, EDWIN T. (1856–1919), successful entrepreneur, progressive reformer, and newspaper publisher. Born in Inyo County, he made his fortune in the fruit shipping business and by inventing a refrigerator car that could carry fresh fruit to the East. In 1900 he sold his fruit packing firm, the most successful in the state, for $2 million. He moved to Los Angeles, where he bought and published the *Los Angeles Evening Express* and *Los Angeles Tribune,* as a foil to Harrison Gray Otis and the *Los Angeles Times.* He supported Hiram Johnson for governor in 1911.

EARTHQUAKES, occurring as frequently as 30 times a day in Southern California, have been observed throughout recorded history. Essentially, they are caused by the grinding together of huge, 70-mile-thick rock plates floating on the semi-molten earth's mantle. The Pacific Plate is moving northward past the North American land mass at a rate of about 2 inches a year; in tens of millions of years, Southern California will slide past San

Major Earthquakes Felt in the County			
Epicenter	Year	Richter Magnitude	Time of Day
Tejon	1857	7.7+	8:00 A.M.
Northwest Los Angeles	1893	6.0+	11:40 A.M.
Long Beach	1933	6.3	5:54 P.M.
Brawley	1940	7.1	8:37 P.M.
Tehachapi	1952	7.7	4:52 A.M.
Sylmar	1971	6.6	6:00 A.M.
Imperial Valley	1979	6.4	4:16 P.M.
Whittier Narrows	1987	5.9	7:42 A.M.
Landers	1992	7.4	—
Northridge	1994	6.7	4:31 A.M.

SOURCE: *Los Angeles Times,* 10 July 1992.

Francisco and continue moving northward until it slips under the North American Plate at the Aleutian Islands.

Many of these sudden shifts of earth originate at depths of 10 to 30 miles, along lines of weakness—faults—which release shock waves that rumble for miles through the earth. Three major faults slice through the Los Angeles area: the San Andreas, San Gabriel, and Newport-Inglewood. Geologists have identified numerous lesser faults as well. The underwater Malibu Coast fault, for example, lies parallel to the shore about 2 miles south of Pacific Coast Highway and extends from Point Dume to the Malibu pier. Should the state officially designate it as "active"—that is, showing movement during the last 11,000 years—it would severely curtail further coastal land development.

The force of earthquakes has been measured in recent years on a logarithmic scale devised by Caltech seismologist Charles F. Richter. With the highest possible recorded earthquake an 8.9, Richter readings of major Southern California quakes include Long Beach, 6.3, in 1933; Sylmar, 6.6, in 1971; Whittier Narrows, 5.9, in 1987; and Northridge, 6.7, in 1994.

Degree of earthquake damage is affected by complex factors involving local terrain, surface irregularities in a given fault, and soil type. Liquefaction may occur in loosely packed, fine-grained soil, whether it is saturated with water or not, and may cause huge structures to literally hop off the ground.

Fra Juan Crespi, chronicler of the Portolá expedition that crossed the basin in the summer of 1769, wrote the first account of a Los Angeles quake. A temblor knocked a soldier from a horse as they crossed the Santa Ana River; it lasted "as long as half an Ave Maria." The members of the expedition felt additional quakes in the San Fernando Valley a few days later.

Seventy-five sizable tremors were recorded in the region from 1812 to 1971. On 9 January 1857 a terrifying earthquake in the Fort Tejón area, estimated at magnitude 8.0, shook the village of Los Angeles 40 miles away. The 7.8 quake that occurred in Owens Valley on 26 March 1872 was also felt in Los Angeles, over 200 miles away. There were fatalities in the Long Beach earthquake of 1933, the Sylmar quake in 1971, and the Northridge quake in 1994.

Talk of a "Big One"—a rupture in the San Andreas fault exceeding 8.0 on the Richter scale—has been heard for many years. The science of earth-

quake prediction is still primitive, but in 1992 a panel of earthquake scientists released a 42-page report called "Future Seismic Hazards in Southern California," which stated that, owing to the 1992 Landers quake centered in a sparsely populated desert area, the statistical probability of a major Southern California quake had been revised upward. The report asserted that a 5 to 12 percent possibility of a massive quake existed yearly, and

---

Hordes of Yankee emigrants . . . are cultivating farms, establishing vineyards, sawing up lumber, building workshops and doing a thousand things which seem natural to them, but which Californians neglect or despise to do. . . . Shall these incursions go unchecked until we shall become strangers in our own land? . . . I pronounce for annexation to France or England, and the people of California will never regret having taken my advice.

—Pío Pico, last Mexican governor, 1846

---

chances of it hitting within five years were 46 percent. The report also called for improved earthquake preparedness. Meanwhile, a U.S. Geological Survey–organized Ad Hoc Working Group on the Probabilities of Future Large Earthquakes in Southern California warned against giving too much credence to predictions that are based on past patterns. The report, they said, should be looked upon as "betting odds."

Because most earthquakes seem to occur near sunrise or sunset, a mythology has arisen that the sun's gravitational pull is involved. Experts dispute this, as well as the idea of "earthquake weather."

EAST COMPTON, county area east of the city of Compton. Its population in 1990 was 7,967.

EASTERN COLUMBIA BUILDING, at Broadway and 9th Street (now known as the 849 Building), is the best example of Art Deco (Zigzag) architecture in Los Angeles. It was built in 1929 to

Eastern Columbia Building, Broadway at 9th Street. Pitt Collection.

house two retail businesses, the Columbia and Eastern Outfitting department stores. The building, designed by Claude Beelman, is easily identified by its gold and blue-green terra-cotta façade and four-sided clock tower.

EASTERN RELIGIONS are widely represented in the general population of Los Angeles. Buddhism, which originated in India, has local adherents of various traditions and national backgrounds. Hsi Lai Temple in Hacienda Heights is the largest Buddhist monastery and temple complex in the Western Hemisphere. The Vedanta Society and Hare Krishna (founded in Los Angeles in 1966) draw upon Vedic beliefs in the Hindu tradition. Theosophy, which rejects Judeo-Christian beliefs, adopted tenets from Buddhism and Brahmanism and has had followers in the area since early in the century. Shintoism, a principal religion of Japan, also has numerous disciples, as does the Self-Realization Fellowship, a Southern California creation that finds inspiration in various Eastern religions.

EAST LA MIRADA, county area east of La Mirada. Its population in 1990 was 9,367.

EAST LOS ANGELES, unincorporated area 5 miles east of downtown that is the heart of the Los Angeles barrio. It is bounded by Boyle Heights on the west, Monterey Park on the north, Montebello on the east, and the City of Commerce on the south (between the Pomona and Santa Ana Freeways). The 15-square-mile area includes the localities of City Terrace, Maravilla, and Belvedere.

Community settlement, which began in the 1870s, expanded rapidly in the early 20th century when the construction of the civic center forced Mexicans out of downtown. They moved to the Maravilla district, east of the adjoining New Calvary and B'nai B'rith Cemeteries, and also to the Belvedere Gardens area, east of Evergreen Cemetery. The community grew even more rapidly in the 1920s, owing to massive immigration from Mexico. East Los Angeles at that time included distinctive settlements of Jews, Armenians, and Russians as well. In the 1950s, when the community still lacked proper representation, a consistent voice for fairness and equity was Alberto Diaz (d. 1989), publisher of the *Belvedere Citizen,* who was known as "Mr. Eastside."

The half-mile-square Belvedere Park became an important focus of community life. Tens of thousands gather there to celebrate Cinco de Mayo and Mexican Independence Day, on 16 September. Belvedere Park was the staging area for the anti–Vietnam War Chicano Moratorium demonstration of 29 August 1970, an event that ended tragically in the death of journalist Ruben Salazar, who was covering the story for the *Los Angeles Times.*

East Los Angeles Latinos who argue that they are underrepresented and politically powerless often advocate incorporating East Los Angeles as an independent city. Notable incorporation efforts occurred in 1961, 1963–1965, and 1974. Proponents argued that incorporation would abolish city taxes, possibly reduce property taxes, create a responsive city council–style government, stimulate business, improve social services, and generally empower Latinos. Opponents argued that the community's position would worsen, and defeated the moves.

The main surface streets are Cesar Chavez Boulevard (formerly Brooklyn Avenue) and Whittier Boulevard. The area is dissected by four freeways, whose construction in the 1950s and 1960s led to a major displacement of population and commerce. East Los Angeles's vibrant street scene, with pedestrians of all ages strolling and shopping along streets lined with restaurants, pastry shops, *discotecas, farmacias,* and other small businesses, reflects a zest that is typical of Latin America. The community, known locally as "East Los" or "ELA" and noted for its hundreds of outdoor murals, has appeared in films such as *Born in East L.A.* (1987).

For decades the community has struggled with the perennial problems of low income, joblessness, crime, underfunded and overcrowded schools, lack of recreational facilities for youth, and insufficient housing. Parts of the area have completed or are undergoing urban redevelopment. Some innovative

---

I sat down in an armchair in Los Angeles when I was 23, and when I got up I was 61.   —Orson Welles

---

community projects have been quite successful. The students of Belvedere Junior High's magnet program for Latin music, for example, achieved widespread recognition during the 1980s. A former principal of that school, Victoria Castro, was elected to the Los Angeles Board of Education in 1993.

Larger than Manhattan or Washington, D.C., in population, East Los Angeles is home to a million people, as many as 90 percent of them Latino. In fact, by 1970 East Los Angeles contained the greatest concentration of Mexicans outside of Mexico City.

EAST LOS ANGELES COMMUNITY UNION, THE (TELACU), Mexican-American economic development corporation formed in 1968. It arose as a grass-roots barrio movement demanding economic empowerment in the aftermath of the Watts riots. Venture capital was the main goal, to stimulate the sagging economy of the Eastside and relieve locally high unemployment. TELACU obtained grants from the United Auto Workers and Ford Foundation, as well as federal poverty agencies, the Model Cities program, and the Department of Labor. Under the leadership of David C. Lizarraga, the union dedicated itself to positive social change and community improvement, mainly within an 8-square-mile area east of downtown. In the 1980s it was forced to respond to allegations of

misappropriation of federal funds, but recouped its position and embarked on new and successful ventures. Among the projects it undertook were a bank (Community Thrift and Loan), industrial parks, malls, and low-cost housing (Casa Maravilla Housing Community and City View Terrace) in East Los Angeles, Hawthorne, and the City of Commerce. In 1994 TELACU's assets exceeded one-third of a billion dollars.

EASTMONT, unincorporated county area near Watts. In 1990 its population was 14,364.

EAST PASADENA, unincorporated county area east of Pasadena. Its population in 1990 was 5,910.

EAST SAN GABRIEL, unincorporated county area near San Gabriel. Its population in 1990 was 12,736.

EATON, FREDERICK (1855–1934), city engineer and Los Angeles mayor from 1898 to 1900. Eaton was born in Los Angeles, the son of a forty-niner who helped found Pasadena. A prominent Republican, he was elected mayor on a municipal water ownership platform. After leaving office Eaton became a key player in efforts to bring Owens River water to Los Angeles. He and William Mulholland traveled to the Owens Valley in 1904, where they concocted a visionary plan to deliver water more than 200 miles to the city of Los Angeles. Eaton then bought options on land that gave him personal water rights, which he later sold to Los Angeles for $450,000. His dream, the Los Angeles Aqueduct, was begun in 1908 and completed in 1913.

EATON, HUBERT LEWRIGHT (1881–1966), the builder of Forest Lawn Memorial Park. He was born in Missouri, trained as a chemist, and worked in copper mills in Montana and Mexico before arriving in Glendale in 1916. There he revolutionized the cemetery industry by creating Forest Lawn in 1917. Eaton belonged to the California Club and Jonathan Club, and was a Republican and a Baptist.

EATON CANYON, gorge in the San Gabriel Mountains located in the Angeles National Forest adjacent to Altadena. Formerly known as Cañon El Precipicio, the gorge now bears the name of Judge Benjamin S. Eaton, a native of Connecticut who came to Los Angeles in 1852 and served as district attorney in the 1850s. After a severe drought in 1864–1865, Eaton built an aqueduct to tap the canyon waters for the vineyards of his Fair Oaks Ranch, in the lowlands. The picturesque canyon, with its falls and scenic trails, is a favorite of hikers and campers.

EBELL CLUB, group formed to advance the cultural enlightenment of women, active in Los Angeles since 1894. It followed the educational philosophy of Dr. Adrian Ebell, a German scholar who had settled in Oakland. The Los Angeles Ebell Club chose as its first president the agriculturist and inventor Harriet Russell Strong. The club has occupied six different buildings, including, since 1927, the one at Wilshire and Lucerne Boulevards, which includes the Wilshire Ebell Theater, a concert hall. Active clubs have also existed in Long Beach and Highland Park.

EBONY SHOWCASE THEATER, African American repertory group founded in 1950 to allow local talent to gain professional training and experience in theater arts.

ECHO PARK, city park and its adjoining neighborhood. Situated near Glendale and Sunset Boulevards, close to downtown Los Angeles, the park is famous for its pond, which came into being as a reservoir catch-basin in the 1860s. A canal and reservoir company organized in 1868 threw up a 20-foot dam across the canyon where the park now lies. In 1895 the 15-acre pond cost the city $5,637 to dredge. The park was landscaped with willows, eucalyptus, and garden shrubs. In 1907 nearby wildcat drilling operations leaked so much

oil into the water that the lake caught fire and burned for days. The floating lotuses may have been planted by missionaries who brought the seeds from China in the 1920s and tossed them in the water. The geyser fountain was installed in 1984. Across the street is the Foursquare Gospel Church, built by Aimee Semple McPherson in the 1920s. A few blocks away, on Carroll Avenue, is Los Angeles's most noteworthy cluster of Victorian houses. Echo Park was the setting for many Keystone Kops movies.

ECOLOGY OF LOS ANGELES. Ecology is the study of animals and plants interacting in their natural communities, or biomes. Ecologists recognize a dozen or so natural zones in this region, which are shaped by elevation, temperature, and humidity:

The *Coastal (Cismontane) Rural Zone* is devoted to agriculture; much of the San Gabriel Valley was such a zone until transformed in the last half century.

The *Coastal (Cismontane) Urban Zone* is the ecologist's term for much of suburban Los Angeles.

The *Riparian (Streamside) Woodland Zone* is found along creeks and streams in mountains or areas between mountains and plains. Characteristic trees locally are spruce, alder, maple, sycamore, cottonwood, and willow. This zone may be accessed, for example, from Angeles Crest Highway in the San Gabriel Mountains and in the area of the Arroyo Seco.

Much of the *Coastal Salt Marsh Zone,* commonly known as wetlands, has evaporated in this century, though patches persist at the mouth of the Los Angeles River and at Marina del Rey.

The *Rocky Shore Zone* is typified by the surf-battered rocky beaches, shores, and sea cliffs near

Ebell Club, ca. 1909. Pitt Collection.

Malibu, Palos Verdes Hills, and Santa Catalina Island.

The *Chaparral Zone* features the hardy, dense, low shrubbery that clings to the slopes of the Santa Monica Mountains and Hollywood Hills. It is home to both people and wild creatures.

The *Oak Woodland Zone* is familiar to residents of the less populated areas of the San Fernando Valley. Oaks dot the open forest and grassland, and the wildlife includes deer, raccoons, foxes, squirrels, woodrats, and mice, as well as quail, woodpeckers, and jays.

The *Piñon-Juniper Woodland, Yellow Pine (Ponderosa) Forest,* and *Lodgepole Pine–White Fir Forest Zones* are found in the sparsest areas of the San Gabriels and other mountains and are familiar to campers.

The *Sagebrush Scrub* and *Desert Wash Zones* are characteristic of the Antelope Valley.

ECONOMIC DEVELOPMENT CORPORATION OF LOS ANGELES COUNTY (EDC), private nonprofit organization devoted to stimulating long-term economic growth and creating permanent jobs. Formed in 1981, it had, by 1995, a membership of 70 corporations, professional firms, and local and state government agencies. The city of Los Angeles was a major participant. The EDC gathers and disseminates information, advises in the placement of capital, provides technical assistance, and counsels prospective employers. With the shrinking of defense industries in the 1990s and the general economic downturn, the organization devoted particular effort to defense conversion and to stimulating other sectors. Its goal was to restore employment, wages, and salary to the peak levels of 1990.

EDELMAN, EDMUND D. (1930–), former county supervisor from the 3rd District. A native of Los Angeles, Edelman received his undergraduate and law degrees from UCLA. For a time he worked as a professional mediator. After serving on the Los Angeles City Council from 1965 to 1973 Edelman was elected supervisor in 1974; he was re-elected four times. As part of a liberal board majority, he helped create the legislation that established the Department of Consumer Affairs, improved the status of the handicapped and of women, benefited Native Americans, supported affirmative action, and created a Department of Children's Services. He has been active in Demo-cratic politics. Edelman chose not to run in 1994. Zev Yaroslavsky, a former member of the Los Angeles City Council, ran for, and won, the seat vacated by Edelman.

EDENDALE, southern part of Glendale, where filmmakers built the first movie studios before moving to the town of Hollywood.

EDSON, KATHERINE PHILLIPS (1870–1933), social reformer, feminist, and public servant. Edson was born in the Midwest but in 1890 moved to the Antelope Valley with her husband, Charles Farwell Edson, a prominent rancher. In 1900 she settled in Los Angeles where she agitated for woman suffrage, becoming the person most instrumental in the passage of the state suffrage amendment in 1911. A field agent for the Bureau of Labor Statistics in the administration of Hiram Johnson, Edson became a prominent activist in the Republican Party and League of Women Voters. Later named executive director of the California Division of Industrial Welfare, she was the first woman to hold a major appointive post in state government.

EDUCATION, BILINGUAL, special approach to teaching English to children who have little or no knowledge of the language. Under a 1981 state law, school districts with many non-English-speaking students must try to provide teaching in the children's native language. Bilingual proponents believe that youngsters must become literate in their mother tongue before learning English; that they must be well grounded in their parents' culture and history before they can understand and be a part of the larger culture; and that unless basics such as math and science are taught in the native language, the children will have fallen far behind in these subjects by the time they are English-proficient.

Opponents to bilingual instruction claim that the time spent on English instruction is too little; on average, they further maintain, children are transferred into English-only classes only after four to seven years have passed—far too late. They assert that children learn English more quickly in an all-English class and that, in any case, there are too few bilingual teachers to make the effort practical. In addition, they maintain, the cost, estimated at $360 per student per year ($400 million for the state as a whole), is unwarranted by the results.

Each side has presented studies and statistics to support its position. Meanwhile, California's non-English-speaking students represent more than one-third of all such students nationwide—and more than half of those are in the Los Angeles Unified School District. In 1994, of those children whose household language was not English, 80 percent spoke Spanish, followed by Vietnamese, Hmong, and Cantonese.

EDUCATION, HIGHER. *See* Colleges and universities

EDUCATION, HISTORY OF. Formal education in the *pueblo* of Los Angeles was, for most people, minimal under Spanish and Mexican rule. Mission Indians received manual training, and a few were fortunate enough to be granted private tutoring, but illiteracy remained the norm. A local *pueblo* school was begun in 1817–1818, languished, and was reopened in 1828. California governors, including José María Echeandía, José Figueroa, and Manuel Micheltorena, exhorted the Franciscan missionaries and *pobladores* to provide education to all children. Nevertheless, little educational progress had been made by the time of the Mexican War.

In 1848 Dr. William B. Osborn, an army hospital steward, established a school in Los Angeles, but it closed during the exodus of Angelenos to the gold fields. By 1850, when the state constitution mandated a public school term of three months, the only teachers were private tutors employed by the city. The city council then hired Francisco Bustamente to teach reading, writing, and "morals," in Spanish. The first school supported with public funds, School No. 1, was built in 1854 or early 1855 at the corner of 2nd and Spring Streets; it opened on 19 March 1855 with separate classrooms for boys and girls. In 1856 the Sisters of Charity opened a day school. In 1865, after the state cut off

Los Angeles High School, Olympic Boulevard, 1917. Courtesy Robert Weinstein Collection.

funding for parochial schools, the Catholic clergy opened St. Vincent's Academy on the Plaza. This was the first private preparatory school in Los Angeles. The first public high school was established in 1873. The earliest universities had religious roots: St. Vincent's College (Catholic, 1867), the University of Southern California (Methodist, 1879), Occidental College (Presbyterian, 1887), and Whittier College (Quaker, 1891). The state opened a normal school, or teacher training college, in Los Angeles in 1882, which later became UCLA. In 1887 and 1888, during the Boom of the Eighties, numerous public schools were established throughout the region, authorized by county voters in 21 bond elections and 15 special tax elections.

Beginning in the 1890s, education in Los Angeles burgeoned. The number of private schools increased after 1910 as well-to-do families founded and patronized exclusive college-prep institutions. The teacher-student ratio of these schools was as low as three-to-one, and their offerings in music, painting, languages, and physical education were generally superior to those of the public schools. The public school system also underwent enormous changes during this time. As a legacy of the political era from 1911 to 1916, the board of education was entirely separated from city government, in an effort to eliminate partisan politics from educational policy. In the 1920s and 1930s public schools were widely recognized for fostering the ideas of progressive educator John Dewey. In 1929 Los Angeles opened its first junior college. An eight-year study published in 1940 by the Progressive Education Association cited Eagle Rock High School as among the 32 best secondary schools in the nation. The board of education, meanwhile, remained a subdivision of state government, and was supervised by the state superintendent of public instruction. The board encompassed a score of neighboring districts as well as schools in some unincorporated areas.

Education since 1945 reflects changes arising from tremendous population growth, great ethnic and racial diversity, and, in recent years, declining revenues. In the immediate postwar boom, physical facilities expanded rapidly, barely keeping up with growth. By 1950 the Los Angeles Unified School District (LAUSD) encompassed close to 450 public schools, and it was still expanding. At the time, LAUSD included junior colleges as well, and had some 175,000 people enrolled in adult evening classes. The district was on its way to becoming one of the largest educational systems in the country, and the one with the most diverse student body. Successive waves of foreign immigration placed further demands on the curriculum, while the passage of the 1978 tax limitation measure, Proposition 13, caused a reduction in revenues. Racial balance became a major issue with the filing of the case of *Crawford v. Los Angeles Board of Education* over school desegregation. A 1970 decision called for an end to de facto racial segregation (as a consequence of housing patterns); it was finally implemented in 1978 after many delays.

In 1988 LAUSD pupils spoke over 80 different languages at home. In 1991 the ethnic distribution of students was 51 percent Latino, 26 percent Caucasian, 12 percent black, 10 percent Asian, and 3 percent other (some groups overlap); 71 percent of the teachers were Caucasian. In 1995 the proportions were 67.2 percent Latino, 14.3 percent black, 11.3 percent Caucasian, 4.6 percent Asian, 1.9 percent Filipino, 0.4 percent Pacific Islander, and 0.3 percent Native American.

Los Angeles has the highest student-teacher ratio of any major school system in the nation. Nor has its budget kept pace with growth. The dropout rate has reached alarming proportions, affecting many more African Americans and Latinos than Caucasians. It is of some comfort, perhaps, that the dropout rate has been declining countywide in recent years, dropping from 26.1 percent in 1991 to 23.7 percent in 1993; nevertheless, an estimated 1 million youths and adults in the county are functionally illiterate, only 4 percent of whom are being served educationally. Over half (56 percent) of recent adult immigrants lack fluency in English. The county has other school districts besides the LAUSD, and the level of expenditure varies from one to another.

EDUCATIONAL ACHIEVEMENT in the Los Angeles Unified School District has displayed an overall downward trend since the 1980s, as reflected in modest declines in scores on the Comprehensive Tests of Basic Skills (CTBS) for reading, mathematics, and language skills. This decline has generally been attributed to the vast influx of non-English-speaking youngsters, many of them from poor families, and to overcrowded classrooms.

By the same token, individual students from individual schools have often shown an impressive level of achievement. The most famous case was that of the students of mathematics teacher Jaime

Escalante at Roosevelt High School, who as a group attained extraordinary scores on the Scholastic Achievement Test (SAT) in the 1980s. Their story was portrayed in the movie *Stand and Deliver* (1987). In 1995 a team of nine students from Marshall High in the Los Feliz area won the Decathlon, a major academic contest of high school teams across the nation. The determined students, guided by their coach, Phil Chase, worked six days a week, eight hours a day, for 10 months—all after school hours. James Evrard, 17, was the top individual scorer. The other members of the team were Paul

---

At its best, looking forward, there is no more inspiring city in America.
    —*The Economist,* British weekly

Auerbach, Douglas Kleven, Elsie Lau, Masaki Miyagawa, Steve Na, Linda Siu, Ann Rose Van, and Sung Lee. In the end they set a new record, scoring 49,935 points of a possible 60,000 during the two-day event, which tests in ten academic areas. They topped the previous high score of 49,372, achieved by Woodland Hills' Taft High School in 1994. Marshall also won the Decathlon in 1987. Los Angeles teams have been victorious in the Decathlon five times in that contest's 14-year history.

Also in 1995, two Los Angeles high school students were among the handful, nationwide, to receive perfect scores of 1,600 on their SATs: Jennifer Koo, 16, a junior at the Math and Science Magnet School of Van Nuys High, and Dale Shuger, 17, a junior at El Camino Real High School. That same year a team of five students from Van Nuys High's Math and Science Magnet also won first place in the National Science Bowl. They were Scott Schneider (team captain), Michael Mazur, Jonathan Kirzner, Do Joon Ra, and Michael Chu.

EDWARDS AIR FORCE BASE, world-famous Antelope Valley military installation. Established in 1933 as Muroc Air Force Base at Muroc Dry Lake, it changed its name to Edwards in 1950. In 1942–1943 the first U.S. jet plane was tested at this base. It was also the testing ground for the P-38 Lightning fighter, the B-24 Liberator, and the B-25 Mitchell bomber used during World War II. In 1947 Capt. Charles Yeager, flying an XI Bell aircraft over the Antelope Valley, was the first pilot to break the sound barrier. A year later, Maj. Richard Johnson established a new world speed record of 670.98 miles per hour in a fully armed and equipped F-86 fighter plane from Edwards. The NASA space vehicles launched at the Kennedy Space Center in Florida normally land at Edwards because of the highly predictable and usually safe weather conditions.

EGYPTIAN THEATRE, 1,200-seat movie palace built by Sid Grauman on Hollywood Boulevard in 1922. Originally planned to resemble a Spanish hacienda, it was under construction when archaeologists made the sensational discovery of King Tutankhamen's tomb in Egypt. Ignoring the Spanish tile roof, Grauman shifted to an Egyptian motif, with hieroglyphics on the walls and bulrushes and lotus emblems. Charlie Chaplin's *The Gold Rush* (1925) and *Ben Hur* (1926) premiered at the theater. The Egyptian closed in 1992 after years of decline, but has been declared a city landmark by the Los Angeles Cultural Heritage Commission and may be reopened as a nonprofit center for the study of film and video.

EL ALISAL, home built by Charles Fletcher Lummis on the Arroyo Seco in what is now the Highland Park area of Los Angeles. Construction began in 1898, with eclectic materials—boulders from the arroyo, iron rails from the Santa Fe Railroad, telegraph poles, etc.—and design suggesting the spirit of the West. Construction was completed in 1903. The name, meaning sycamore or alder in Spanish, commemorated the trees growing in the canyon, a large specimen of which stood in the patio. From the windows Lummis could see part of the arroyo as well as the Southwest Museum, which he had founded. He deeded the property to the museum, but it later became city property and is occupied by the Historical Society of Southern California.

EL CAMINO REAL, "the king's or royal highway," which ran from Loreto (Baja California) to San Francisco. Originally the name referred to the coastal trail blazed by Capt. Gaspar de Portolá in 1769 that would eventually connect the Spanish missions and presidios. Charles Fletcher Lummis and Caroline Severance led a drive to plant signposts marking this path, and they were in place by 1906. El Camino Real was later rerouted several times to include Los Angeles and other major communities. In the 20th century the name was revived and applied to Highway 101, but this des-

ignation is faulty in that 101 goes nowhere near missions San Gabriel and San Fernando, two main stops on the original Camino Real. In the 1960s new guideposts shaped like mission bells were installed to replace the originals. Car drivers can see some of these signposts when they navigate the Ventura and Hollywood Freeways.

EL CAPITAN THEATER, historic theater on Hollywood Boulevard. Designed by Morgan, Walls, and Clements and featuring an ornate East Indian interior and a Spanish colonial exterior, it was built for live performances in 1926. Before it was converted to a movie house in the 1940s, Clark Gable and Rita Hayworth were among those who performed there. In 1989, Hillsman Wright of the Los Angeles Historic Theater Foundation took up the cause of restoring the house to its original glory. Los Angeles declared it a historic monument, and Buena Vista Pictures Distribution Company, an arm of Disney Corporation, and Pacific Theaters Corporation agreed to refurbish the theater according to its original design and use it as a movie palace. Historical architects and designers Joseph J. Musil, Martin Weil, and Ronald Reed carried the scheme to completion. The restoration has received an architectural award.

EL CLAMOR PÚBLICO (The public outcry), weekly newspaper from 1855 to 1859. It was the city's third newspaper and the first one published all in Spanish (though the *Los Angeles Star* had previously published a Spanish page titled "La Estrella de Los Angeles"). *El Clamor* went to press on Thursdays, and subscriptions cost $5 a year. Founded and edited by Francisco P. Ramírez, an 18-year-old native-born Angeleno, the paper reflected Ramírez's commitment to Republicanism and progress. He wrote on numerous topics ranging from prostitution to the rights of blacks, becoming the voice of the local Mexican community.

EL DORADO, rural area in the Antelope Valley. It is located on both sides of the Antelope Valley Freeway, between Avenues N and O. Many residents own horses and other farm animals and live on 2-acre lots. The community has private roads.

ELECTIONS. *See* Voting and elections

ELECTRICAL POWER is delivered to Angelenos by the municipally owned Department of

Water and Power (DWP), and to other municipalities by the privately owned Southern California Edison. The DWP system arose in 1908 as an offshoot of the amazing Los Angeles Aqueduct, which brought Owens River water to the Los Angeles Basin. The aqueduct was conceived of almost solely as a water conduit, but the movement of the water created cheap hydroelectric energy as a surprise bonus feature. The annual sale of the 100,000 horsepower of aqueduct-generated electricity would net $1.4 million—enough to pay off, in a

---

It is as if you tipped the United States up so all the commonplace people slid down there into Southern California.   —Frank Lloyd Wright

---

short time, the entire aqueduct project. In 1911, voters approved channeling this "excess" power into a municipally owned system. Despite considerable opposition from private utilities, the DWP began generating and distributing power the following year from Power Plant No. 1, near Saugus. This plant is still in operation. In 1922 Los Angeles bought Southern California Edison's distribution system within city boundaries, and in 1937 it bought out the Los Angeles Gas and Electric Corporation's properties, to became the sole electric power supplier in the city and the largest municipal electric utility in the country.

In 1955, 90 percent of the city's energy was from hydroelectric sources, but gradually it shifted over to other sources as well. Between the 1940s and 1960s Los Angeles built four giant plants that use a combination of natural gas (preferred for its low sulfur and low ash residues) and oil (used when gas is not available). In the 1970s the city contracted to purchase excess power from Pacific Northwest utilities through the creation of a special network. In 1986 it began accessing power from a coal-fueled station in Utah and a nuclear power plant in Arizona. The DWP also has some methane plants at retired landfills, and it is experimenting with solar and geothermal power. Its rates are the lowest of the four largest California electric utilities.

ELECTRICAL WORKERS UNION. *See* International Brotherhood of Electrical Workers

EL HERALDO DE MÉXICO, East Los Angeles Spanish-language newspaper published in the 1920s. Edited by Juan de Heras, it championed the rights of Mexicans in the United States.

ELIZABETH LAKE. *See* Lake Hughes–Elizabeth Lake

ELLROY, JAMES (1948–), mystery writer. Penned in the hard-boiled detective style, his books—*The Black Dahlia* (1987), *The Big Nowhere* (1988), *L.A. Confidential* (1990), and *White Jazz* (1992)—are sequentially set in Los Angeles from 1947 to 1959 and use historical events, including the zoot suit riots, the McCarthyite attacks on the film industry, and the arrival of the Dodgers, as background.

ELLWOOD, CRAIG (1910–1992), architect. Born in Texas, he migrated with his family to California, picking fruit for 12 cents an hour. After graduating as an engineer from UCLA, he participated in creating the experimental Case Study Homes, along with Charles and Ray Eames and others. The Security Pacific Bank Building at Wilshire Boulevard and Bedford Drive, the Art Center College of Design in Pasadena, and the 1950 Hale House in Beverly Hills are among his best-known designs. His trademark was the steel grid filled with glass. In the 1970s he grew disenchanted with architecture, moved to Italy, and took up painting, which he pursued until his death.

EL MONTE, independent city on the San Gabriel River 12 miles east of downtown Los Angeles. Founded in the summer of 1851 by a party made up mostly of Texans, who squatted the local rancho, it was the first community in the county settled by Yankees. The location was at the terminus of the Old Spanish Trail from New Mexico, which connected Southern California with the rest of western America. It was first called Lexington, after the town in Kentucky, then The Monte ("thicket" in Spanish) because of the willows that grew there, and finally, in 1905, El Monte. The "Monte boys" were predisposed toward vigilante activity and could be counted on to fight Mexican bandits. Politically the town was a Democratic stronghold, opposed to both Whigs and Republicans.

Incorporated in 1912, El Monte, with its walnut groves, strawberry fields, and dairy farms, was for many years a thriving agricultural community.

Most of the farm work was done by Mexicans who lived in barrios such as Hicksville. El Monte was the site of a major strike of berry pickers in 1933. The town grew rapidly after World War II, when suburban housing development and industry replaced agriculture. By 1990 it had 106,209 residents, a rise of 34 percent since 1980.

EL PORTAL THEATER, playhouse on Lankershim Boulevard in North Hollywood. Built in 1926 for vaudeville and silent films, the 1,200-seat house later fell into disuse, but was declared a historic-cultural monument in 1993. It is slated for remodeling.

EL PUEBLO DE LA REINA DE LOS ANGE-LES. *See* Los Angeles name, origin of

EL PUEBLO DE LOS ANGELES HISTORIC MONUMENT, city-owned preserve in downtown. The 44-acre park is located near, but not directly on, the 1781 birthplace of the *pueblo*. It contains 27 certified historic structures built between 1818 and 1926 (many of them now closed pending refurbishment), as well as Olvera Street, a Mexican-style marketplace. The driving force behind the park's creation was Christine Sterling. After 27 years of lobbying, the site was dedicated as a state park in 1953, to be governed by an entity representing the state, county, and city governments. When this arrangement proved unworkable, the state deeded the park to the city, which established the Pueblo de Los Angeles Historic Monument Authority, with powers to preserve the buildings and develop and lease commercial establishments.

Sepúlveda House, Main Street, 1987. Photo by Frank A. Serrano, courtesy El Pueblo de Los Angeles Historic Monument.

On the west side of the Pueblo monument stands the Plaza Church. Dating to 1818, it is the oldest church in the city and still one of the most active Catholic parish centers in the western United States.

On the park's north side is the Avila Adobe, the oldest residence in the city, also dating to 1818, and housing the park office. Pelanconi House, built in 1855, is one of the earliest brick buildings in Los Angeles; today it is used as a restaurant. The carefully renovated Sepúlveda House, built as a hotel in 1887, serves as the park's visitor center. Italian Hall, established in 1907–1908, was headquarters for the Italian community early in the century and contains a mural by the famed Mexican painter David Alfaro Siqueiros. Olvera Street, originally an alley filled with machine shops, was opened as a Mexican *mercado* in 1930 and has remained one of the city's most popular tourist attractions. The 1904 Plaza Substation was an electrical supply unit for streetcar lines; it may become a streetcar museum.

On the Pico-Garnier block, south of the Plaza, is another cluster of buildings, the most prominent of which is Pico House, a hotel built by Pío Pico, the last Mexican governor of California, in 1869. It opened in 1870 as the city's best and most modern hotel. Next door is the Merced Theatre, the town's first legitimate theater, also dating from 1870. The second floor featured a 12-by-5-foot stage. A façade on the top floor made the building appear higher than the Pico House. The proprietors, William and Merced Abbot, lived on the premises. The Garnier Building was built in 1890 as a commercial building, community center, and dormitory residence for Chinese in Los Angeles. Masonic Temple, opened in 1858, is one of the oldest structures in the city and is still used for Masonic lodge meetings. The Old Plaza Fire House was a station for horse-drawn equipment in 1884 and today is a museum of old fire-fighting memorabilia. Two other structures, the Old Chinese Building and 425 N. Los Angeles Street, complete the historic complex.

EL SEGUNDO, incorporated industrial and residential city south of Los Angeles International Airport (LAX) and 14 miles southwest of downtown Los Angeles. It bills itself as "the aerospace center of the world." The Spanish name, meaning "The Second," comes from the local Standard Oil refinery, which was the firm's second complex in California, built in 1910. The 1,000-acre petroleum complex still exists. Oil is off-loaded to waiting tankers by gravity flow from reservoir tanks submerged in the dunes. Pioneering aviation firms located in El Segundo, next to what would become LAX. Computer, electronic, and aerospace companies are El Segundo's major industries. In 1990 the population was 15,200.

EL SERENO, part of the city of Los Angeles near Alhambra. The name is Spanish, meaning either "serene," "night watchman," or "night air."

ELYSIAN HEIGHTS, hillside residential neighborhood in the Echo Park area. It is north of Sunset Boulevard, south of Riverside Drive, and next to Elysian Park. Having first emerged on the map during the Boom of the Eighties, its domestic architecture still displays arresting layers of history.

ELYSIAN PARK, downtown recreational area. Established on 5 April 1886, the park originally had 550 acres, ultimately growing to over 600 acres. Some have argued that it was the location of the Gabrieleño Indian village of Yangna. It is likely that Capt. Gaspar de Portolá crossed the river going west near the park bluff overhanging the river on 2 August 1769.

Over the years the park boundaries have shifted and been chopped away. In November 1937 the 400-foot cliff atop which the park sits slid, dumping millions of tons of boulders, trees, and earth onto Riverside Drive and destroying the Dayton Avenue Bridge and four homes. Later, a large portion of the park was turned over to the Police Department for a training academy. In 1940, 30 more acres were severed by the Pasadena Freeway, and in 1959 another 30-acre parcel was ceded to the Dodgers, in exchange for an equal segment located between Rose Hill and the Arroyo Seco.

EMBASSY THEATER, Los Angeles's oldest concert hall. Located in the Embassy Hotel, on S. Grand Avenue, it opened in 1914 with 1,600 seats. The Los Angeles Symphony Orchestra, precursor of the Los Angeles Philharmonic, made its home here from 1914 to 1920. The stage has been graced by such artists as Sergei Prokofiev, Efrem Zimbalist Sr., Gregor Piatigorsky, and the La Scala Grand Opera Company. Evangelist Aimee Semple McPherson preached there, and the Count Basie and Duke Ellington bands performed on its stage during the 1940s. Once a favorite venue for political meetings and lectures, the auditorium, along with the hotel, which is now a student residence, was purchased by USC in 1987.

ENCINO, historic west San Fernando Valley district 17 miles northwest of downtown Los Angeles. The large Tongva Indian village located there was spotted by Captain Portolá's expedition as it descended Sepulveda Pass in 1769. Fra Crespi's diary of that trek mentions beautiful oaks and bubbling springs. The Franciscans established their first headquarters near the village, before they built San Gabriel Mission. Pío Pico granted 4,460 acres of former mission land to Don Vicente de la Osa in 1845, and the land was subsequently owned by families named Garnier, Oxarart, Glass, and Amestoy. The name Encino (meaning "evergreen oak") was first used in the 1890s for a nearby Southern Pacific rail station. Wheat and barley were grown in the area around the turn of the century. By 1925 the local population was 1,300.

The Encino Chamber of Commerce was organized in 1927; later, movie mogul Darryl F. Zanuck bought an old golf course, created a polo field, and built a large stable there. Soon the popular Los Angeles community was home to such movie stars of the 1930s as Spencer Tracy, John Wayne, Dinah Shore, and W. C. Fields. It remains an affluent San Fernando Valley area.

In 1984 a construction crew working near Los Encinos State Historic Park unearthed over 2 million artifacts of a Tongva village perhaps 3,000 years old. The skeletons of some 20 people were included in the find.

ENDANGERED SPECIES of flora and fauna have been identified in some numbers in Los Angeles. Immediately west of Los Angeles International Airport is a habitat known as Airport Dunes in which are found the El Segundo blue butterfly, Lora Aborn's moth, and Henne's Eucosman moth, all endangered species. It is also a haven for the endangered scaly herb pholisma, five threatened insects, the Pacific pocket mouse, the coast horned lizard, and the California legless lizard. An endangered bird known as the California least tern is native to Terminal Island. Owing to the efforts of biologists, the endangered bald eagle is making a comeback on Santa Catalina Island.

END POVERTY IN CALIFORNIA (EPIC). *See* Sinclair, Upton

ENGINE HOUSE NO. 18, fire station in the West Adams area designed in the Mission Revival style in 1904 by John Parkinson. Declared a Historic-Cultural Monument of the City of Los Angeles in 1988, the structure was saved from demolition and refurbished as a community art center with funding from the Community Redevelopment Agency.

ENTENZA, JOHN (1905–1984), influential editor and publisher of *Arts and Architecture* magazine from 1940 to 1962. He was a great booster of modern architectural design, and conducted a salon in his own modern home in Santa Monica Canyon that included Charles Eames and Peter Krasnow. He helped stimulate the Case Study House movement and the International style of office building.

ENVIRONMENTAL MOVEMENT, consisting of grass-roots organizations working individually or in loose alliance, originated in Los Angeles in the 1960s. Citizens for a Better Environment concentrates on air, water, and pollution issues; the Tree People promote green education in the schools and plant trees; the Clean Air Coalition focuses on cleaning up the atmosphere; Heal the Bay, American Oceans Campaign, and Surfrider Foundation support efforts to clean up the polluted waters of

---

Hollywood is two things. It's a state of mind, and it's a particular place in Los Angeles.   —Robert Redford

---

Santa Monica Bay; Friends of Ballona Wetlands maintains a watch over that unique westside environment; the Santa Monica Mountain Conservancy is a state agency that acquires park land and transfers it to the state or national parks; the Mono Lake Committee is involved with Los Angeles environmental policy as it affects a place located hundreds of miles beyond city limits; and the Watchdog Organizing Committee of the Labor/Community Strategy Center battles polluters in working-class neighborhoods, as described in their 1991 pamphlet "L.A.'s Lethal Air."

In addition, national environmental organizations have taken up the cudgel for regional issues. The Los Angeles–based Santa Monica Mountains

and Seashore Foundation supports the interests of the Santa Monica Mountains National Recreation Area, as does the Sierra Club, while the Natural Resources Defense Council and American Lung Association have presented testimony before the Air Quality Management District.

Heat generated by environmental activists caused the city of Los Angeles to form the Environmental Affairs Commission and Environmental Affairs Department. The county has also entered the fray. In the aftermath of a suit filed jointly by the Sierra Club and Corral Canyon Homeowners Association, the county was required to establish a review board for the environmentally fragile area along the Malibu coast. At the insistence of Supervisor Ed Edelman, the county has designated 29 significant ecological areas (SEAs) since 1991, some of them privately owned. For purposes of planning, these sensitive districts are to be inventoried by a biologist and to receive close scrutiny before building permits are issued. Although a 1989 *Los Angeles Times* survey found that Angelenos were opposed to offshore drilling, favored restrictions on coastal development, and would pay taxes to clean up the water supply, those surveyed also expressed an unwillingness to pay for saving endangered wildlife.

EPISCOPAL CHURCH. The Diocese of Los Angeles has 80,000 members and 151 congregations in six Southern California counties (Los Angeles, Orange, Ventura, Santa Barbara, San Bernardino, and Riverside). Established in 1895, it owns and operates Good Samaritan Hospital, a 411-bed acute-care facility west of downtown. Other Episcopal institutions in the area include the Bishop Gooden Home for treatment of alcoholism, the Episcopal Home for senior citizens, Hillsides Home for abused children, and the Seamen's Church Institute in San Pedro. Each member church is part of the catholic and apostolic tradition but is independently governed and autonomous. The church recognizes the archbishop of Canterbury as its spiritual leader.

ETHICS COMMISSION, LOS ANGELES. *See* Los Angeles City Ethics Commission

ETHIOPIANS numbered almost 3,000 in Los Angeles County in 1990, of which two thirds lived in the city of Los Angeles. One block on Fairfax Avenue has four Ethiopian restaurants; it is called

Cross-cultural menu. Photo by
Michael Krakowiak/Marni Pitt.

"Little Addis," after Addis Ababa. A newspaper and
magazine are published in Amharic, the language
of Ethiopia, and two Pentecostal churches and two
Coptic Christian churches serve the community's
spiritual needs.

ETHNIC GROUPS are so varied as to make Los
Angeles the most ethnically diverse metropolitan
area in the world. In 1991 the city's population was
40 percent Latino, 37 percent Anglo, 13 percent
African American, and 10 percent Asian. Cerritos,
Hawthorne, Culver City, Carson, and Walnut display particular diversity. In fact, one study charac-
terizes Cerritos as the most ethnically diverse urban place in the United States.

Ethnic and racial concentrations in Los Angeles are constantly shifting. Since the 1980s African
Americans have been moving out of the South
Central area in favor of outlying parts of Los Angeles and Orange Counties. As they move, they
tend to be replaced by Latinos, a population that
continues to spread eastward in the basin. In the
decade of the 1980s, the county's Latino population increased by 1.5 million. The Asian distribution, meanwhile, remains fairly evenly distributed.

The Anglo population declined proportionately
by 8 percent in the 1980s, with the largest losses in
southeastern and South Central Los Angeles and
in the western San Gabriel Valley, but with declines
also in San Marino, Northridge, Panorama City,
Sun Valley, Westwood, Santa Monica, Beverly
Hills, and Brentwood. Meanwhile, the Anglo population has surged in the areas of Palmdale, Lancaster, Santa Clarita, Diamond Bar, Walnut, La
Verne, and Westlake. During the same period,

*County Ethnic and Racial Population, 1990
(estimated)*

African	unknown
African American	950,000
Arab	200,000 to 300,000
Argentinian	45,000
Armenian	250,000
Baltic	15,000
(Estonian, Latvian, Lithuanian)	
Brazilian	10,000
Cambodian	30,000 to 80,000
Chilean	16,000
Chinese	170,000
Cuban	120,000
Dutch	unknown
English	350,000
Filipino	350,000
French	45,000 to 50,000
German	30,000
Greek	100,000
Guatemalan	100,000
Gypsy (Roma)	50,000
Indian (Asian)	45,000
Iranian	300,000 to 400,000
Irish	55,000
Israeli	100,000 to 200,000
Italian	20,000
Japanese	200,000
Korean	145,000
Laotian	30,000
Mexican	2,519,514
Native American	50,000 to 200,000
(Indian)	
Nicaraguan	50,000
Palestinian	40,000 to 50,000
Peruvian	50,000 to 60,000
Polish	unknown
Russian	unknown

County Ethnic and Racial Population, 1990 *(continued)*	
Salvadoran	350,000
Scandinavian	100,000
Scots	unknown
Thai	100,000
Vietnamese	80,000 to 85,000
Yugoslav	30,000

SOURCE: Zena Pearlstone, *Ethnic L.A.* (Beverly Hills: Hillcrest Press, 1990); *Los Angeles Times*, 21 Feb. 1991, 23 July 1992, 21 Oct. 1993. Mexicans are estimated by U.S. Census.

towns such as Downey, Bellflower, North Long Beach, Arcadia, San Marino, Covina, and West Covina have become much more diverse.

Figures published by the U.S. Census and Los Angeles Unified School District revealed that in 1993 people from over 140 countries lived in Los Angeles County. The largest communities of Mexicans, Armenians, Koreans, Filipinos, Salvadorans, and Guatemalans outside their homelands are found in Los Angeles County, as well as the largest U.S. concentrations of Japanese, Iranians, and Cambodians. Some 1.1 million adults and children do not speak English at home, and of the 649,054 students in the schools in 1995, 44 percent have limited proficiency in English. Of the 80 or so languages other than English spoken, the most prevalent are Spanish, Vietnamese, Hmong, Cantonese, Tagalog, Korean, Armenian, Russian, Farsi, Cambodian, and Hebrew. Seventeen foreign languages could be heard on Los Angeles radio, and more than 50 foreign-language newspapers are published in the county.

The 1990s have seen a dramatic increase in aliens seeking naturalization in Los Angeles. In ceremonies held annually at the Los Angeles Convention Center or similar venues, as many as 10,000 people from 110 countries have been sworn in as citizens. The surge in citizenship applications has resulted from two factors: the 1989 federal amnesty law that allowed undocumented resident aliens to become citizens after a five-year waiting period, and Proposition 187, the 1995 ballot measure that denies undocumented aliens access to medical and educational benefits. The trend toward naturalization has helped Los Angeles maintain a high level of congressional representation.

EUCALYPTUS, tree known in its native Australia as "blue gum." Eucalypti were probably first imported into Southern California in the 1860s by William Wolfskill, who planted them on his farm near the Los Angeles River, east of today's Alameda Street. When the planted trees reached 30 to 40 feet, they were cut down, and new growth arose from the stumps. The eucalyptus was cultivated for windbreaks, shade, aromatic oil, firewood, and even lumber until the 1880s. In 1874, in the hope of making a substantial profit in the construction industry, the Forest Grove Association planted 100,000 saplings on 60 acres near Florence, south of Los Angeles. The group miscalculated, however: the twisted, irregular grain of the eucalyptus proved unsatisfactory for lumber.

EVANS COMMUNITY ADULT SCHOOL, largest and best known of the 27 adult education facilities operated by the Los Angeles Unified School District. Drawing on huge nearby immigrant communities, the complex, which has been at Sunset Boulevard and Figueroa Street since 1972, enrolls 13,000 students from 80 countries. It is the most populous adult school, and the most polyglot, in the nation. English classes are in the greatest demand. The school is named after E. Manfred Evans, the district's first superintendent of adult education, and traces its origins to a school formed in 1937.

"EVENING CONCERT SERIES," early radio classical music program. It began in 1940 on KFAC, airing weeknights from 8 to 10 P.M. Sponsored by the Gas Company, hosted by Thomas Cassidy, and highly acclaimed by musicians and music teachers alike, the program shifted to KKGO in 1989.

EXPOSITION PARK, state-owned public space on Exposition Boulevard containing major cultural facilities operated by both the state and county. The park houses the Memorial Coliseum, Sports Arena, Swimming Stadium, Natural History Museum, Museum of Science and Industry, California Afro-American Museum, and Aerospace Museum. It also contains a lovely 19,000-plant rose garden. The 160-acre site served as an agricultural fairground from 1872 until 1910 (hence its original name, Agricultural Park), but open soliciting by prostitutes on the grounds caused a judge to lobby for creation of a public park.

Before the turn of the century the area was a fashionable residential neighborhood. Mansions on

Entrance to the future
Exposition Park. Courtesy
Robert Weinstein
Collection.

nearby Chester Place and St. James Park housed some of the most affluent people in town, including the Dohenys. The University of Southern California was established across the street. By the 1920s signs of decay began to set in, becoming more apparent in subsequent decades. In an attempt to reverse the trend, the state has hired an architectural firm to draft plans for a $350 million face-lift. The proposal involves tearing out the excessive asphalt, installing new lawns and greenery, and improving the access roads. The plan, submitted by the Zimmer Gunsul Frasca Partnership of Newport Beach, would create a "green necklace"—a 30-foot promenade—to flank the streets surrounding the park.

FACTOR, MAX (1877–1938), Polish immigrant who settled in Los Angeles in 1908, four years after coming to America. He became a makeup artist for the film industry and gained fame glamorizing some of the best-known faces in the movies. He went on to establish a business in the manufacture and sale of cosmetics. The contents of the Max Factor Beauty Museum, a landmark Hollywood building on Highland Avenue, contains an extensive collection on makeup and will be donated to the Hollywood Entertainment Museum, now in the planning stages.

FAGES, PEDRO (1730–1794), Spanish explorer and colonial governor of California. Lieutenant Fages was a member of the Portolá expedition that passed through Los Angeles in 1769. In 1773 he had a serious falling-out with Fr. Junípero Serra, who traveled to Mexico City and had Fages removed to other posts. Fages eventually returned to California, however, where he served as governor from 1782 to 1791, the formative years of the *pueblo* of Los Angeles and the establishment of the ranchos.

FAIRFAX, neighborhood whose spine is Fairfax Avenue, stretching from Santa Monica Boulevard south to 6th Street. It is the oldest ongoing Jewish area in Los Angeles. Its history includes the presence of an oil field, the sprawling Gilmore estate and Gilmore Stadium, the Pan Pacific Auditorium, CBS Television City, and Farmers Market. José Antonio Rocha built the first structure in the area, an adobe residence that is still standing on the Gilmore property. The Fairfax district was initially composed of two unincorporated county tracts annexed by the city in 1922 and 1924, respectively. When Fairfax High School was built in the 1920s, the district was so rural that the school curriculum included landscape gardening, forestry, and agronomy.

The neighborhood's Jewish presence began around 1928 when the first synagogue was built, and grew in the 1930s as Jews began moving out

Fairfax Avenue. Photo by Michael Krakowiak/Marni Pitt.

of Boyle Heights and City Terrace. Post–World War II immigrants to the area included American Jews from various parts of the United States, European refugees, and Holocaust survivors. Canter's landmark deli moved from Boyle Heights to Fairfax Avenue in 1948. In its heyday during the 1950s the neighborhood had a wide variety of Jewish organizations—religious and secular, cultural and educational, and fraternal, political, and social. The population was largely middle class and reflected East European origins. In the 1960s the demographics showed an increasing concentration of older people. The area experienced a new wave of Jewish immigration from Israel, the Soviet Union, and the Middle East during the 1970s and 1980s.

FANTE, JOHN (1915–1983), novelist and screenwriter. Born in Colorado, the son of an Italian immigrant bricklayer, Fante dropped out of college and hitchhiked to Los Angeles at age 24. While busing tables in a barbecue joint, he wrote *Ask the Dust* (1939), the first of a cycle of novels about a poor Los Angeles poet, Arturo Bandini. Much of the book focuses on Main Street and Pershing Square. He wrote movie scripts with drinking partner William Faulkner in the 1940s, and was still active in the studios in the 1950s and 1960s. His reputation, however, rests on his novels, *Full of Life* (1952), *Brotherhood of the Grape* (1977), *Wait Until Spring, Bandini* (1938), and *Dreams from Bunker Hill* (1985), which, published posthumously, he dictated to his wife from his hospital bed. *Ask the Dust* was reissued in 1980 and has achieved the status of a literary classic.

FARMERS AND MERCHANTS BANK, pioneer bank chartered in 1871 by dry goods merchant and banking wizard Isaias W. Hellman and his partner, ex-governor John G. Downey. It stood at Temple and Main Streets and survived the statewide banking panic of 1875 to became a forerunner of Security Pacific Bank, now merged with Bank of America.

FARMERS MARKET, popular shopping mart at 3rd Street and Fairfax Avenue. Opened in July 1934 as a place for farmers to peddle their fresh produce, it was conceived by advertising writer Fred Beck and struggling entrepreneur Roger Dahljelm. They located the market on the property of the Gilmore Company (formerly part of Rancho La Brea), which once managed extensive oil drilling opera-

tions. The original 18 food stalls eventually expanded to 160 stalls, restaurants, and shops featuring a variety of merchandise, including ethnic, clothing, pet, jewelry, and gift items. The Farmers Market was the site of the city's first self-service gas station, known as "Gas-a-Thon," where customers saved 5 cents by serving themselves. As early as 1944 the Farmers Market was grossing $6 million. It now serves some 20,000 customers daily. Currently, the Gilmore Company is considering replacing Farmers Market with office buildings, a large shopping mall, and a hotel. Other farmers markets have sprung up in Santa Monica, Hollywood, Westwood, Venice, and other communities in recent years, generally operating one day a week and featuring locally grown flowers, fruits, and vegetables.

FAUNA. *See* Wildlife; Wildlife preservation; individual animals

FAWKES, JOSEPH WESLEY (1861–1928), Pennsylvania-born monorail inventor. He moved to Burbank, and around 1910 constructed a streamlined monorail machine. It was suspended from an overhead rail and used an air-cooled Franklin engine to power a front and a rear propeller. Fawkes then tried to develop the Aerial Trolley Car Company, a public monorail line that would carry passengers from Burbank to Los Angeles at 60 miles an hour. He had trouble selling the $100 stock certificates, and his machine lay rusting on his property until it was scrapped in 1940.

FEDERAL SUBSIDIES to Los Angeles were small in the 19th century but expanded after the Great Depression. In general, the city has received less in federal social services than its residents have paid out in federal taxes, although during World War II and the Cold War federal defense spending in Southern California was high.

Subsidies began with a small but crucial federal grant authorized in 1899 to create a breakwater and other improvements in San Pedro Harbor. In the 1930s, with the city treasury virtually bankrupt, Los Angeles received some federal dollars via the Work Projects Administration and other New Deal agencies, as well as modest support for public housing. Late in the decade, when war erupted in Europe, millions of dollars in federal contracts began pouring into the airplane industry. The government used the Reconstruction Finance Corporation to funnel $312 million into privately owned companies, such as Douglas Aircraft, and spent $142 million on building 1,000 new plants between 1939 and 1944. Shipyards, aluminum producers, and rubber plants also received significant wartime subsidies.

After World War II, the GI home loan program allowed many young families the luxury of purchasing new homes in the suburbs. The federal highway legislation of the 1950s and 1960s favored the freeway building program that has had a heavy and lasting impact on Southern California. The GI Bill of Rights provided subsidized education for veterans, resulting in a stimulus for the expansion of UCLA, USC, and other institutions of higher learning. Huge federal outlays for the B-1 bomber, the Saturn and Apollo space projects, the manned orbiting space laboratory, and Voyager planetary probes stimulated the local economy as well.

During the War on Poverty of the 1960s, Los Angeles received relatively little federal funding compared to other cities of similar size, in part because of a political feud between Mayor Sam Yorty and the Lyndon Johnson administration. This changed in the early 1970s, when a variety of grants began to pour in again, including block grants for housing improvements. In 1977 the city created a single,

---

On my first visit to Los Angeles I was conveniently prepared for almost anything except for what it really looked like—a quite beautiful place.   —Nathan Silver, British writer, 1969

---

consolidated agency, the Community Development Department, to allocate government grants. Federal support for private housing helped stimulate single-family home construction in the 1970s. A general falling-off of federal urban development funds and social services in the 1980s negatively affected housing subsidies and assistance to low-income groups, contributing to the growth of homelessness. A major problem for Los Angeles in the 1980s and 1990s has been the high impact of immigration on education and social services, and the simultaneous decline in federal grants for such services.

In the wake of the 1994 Northridge earthquake disaster, the federal government acted swiftly. The Federal Emergency Management Administration (FEMA) and the Small Business Administration provided major assistance to businesses, homeowners, and public agencies.

FEDERAL THEATRE PROJECT, division of the Work Projects Administration (WPA). Beginning in 1935, in the midst of the Great Depression, the WPA provided government subsidies for professional theater, and Los Angeles was a major participant. The thriving New Deal program had various subdivisions that sponsored radio and musical performances, marionette theater, vaudeville, Negro theater, Yiddish theater, and Shakespearean drama in the public schools. Christmas performances were staged in churches. Artists lived on government stipends, and tickets cost but a few cents, attracting audiences that had never before attended professional performances. Only New York had a greater level of theatrical activity than Los Angeles. The project died in 1939, a casualty of rising anti–New Deal sentiment in the Congress.

FEDERATION OF HILLSIDE AND CANYON HOMEOWNERS, umbrella group of westside neighborhood associations, including those of Brentwood, Bel-Air, and Beverly Glen. Inspired by the visions of environmental polemicist Richard Lillard, it was formed in the 1950s to fight development in the Santa Monica Mountains. Marvin Braude, an electronics entrepreneur from Crestwood Hills and later a city council member, was a leading figure in the movement. The federation clashed with giant land-developing corporations—Hilton Hotels, Lantain Corporation, Castle and Cooke, Gulf-America, and Tucker Land Company—over plans for a megadevelopment west of Sepulveda Pass. In alliance with the Sierra Club and other environmental groups, it succeeded in creating the Santa Monica Mountains National Recreation Area in 1978, thereby blocking much overdevelopment.

FEDERATION OF SPANISH-SPEAKING VOTERS, first political group formed expressly for Los Angeles Mexicans. No longer in existence, the group backed a losing slate of candidates for state and local offices in 1930.

FELIZ, VICENTE, veteran of the 1776 expedition led by Capt. Juan Bautista de Anza that passed through the basin. As acting corporal, Feliz escorted the original Spanish settlers to Los Angeles in 1781, and became a *poblador* there himself in 1785.

FERGUSON, CECIL (1931–), African American arts curator. A native Angeleno and graduate of Jordan High School in Watts, Ferguson started out as a janitor at the Natural History Museum in Exposition Park, eventually helping to mount exhibitions. Ferguson also worked in the community presenting exhibitions of African American art, dance, and music. His growing involvement in the arts led to his establishment of the Watts Summer Festival in the 1960s. To foster an appreciation of black culture, he and Claude V. Booker created the Los Angeles Black Arts Council. Ferguson was a curator at the Los Angeles County Museum and Los Angeles Southwest College until his retirement in 1985. His image appears in a giant mural outside the Watts Towers Art Center.

FERNANDEÑO INDIANS, generic name for Native Americans of Mission San Fernando. Unlike the Indians of Mission San Gabriel (Gabrieleños), all of whom were Tongvas, the Fernandeños consisted of many ethnic groups. Over a period of years the Spaniards brought together Tataviam Indians from the northern San Fernando Valley and areas northward; Tongvas from the Los Angeles River Basin and the region to the west; members of the Chumash nation from Malibu; and Serraños from the area east of the mission, including the Mojave River. Felled by disease and economically exploited, Fernandeños had apparently been completely eradicated by the early 20th century. Recently, however, Native Americans have begun to trace their ancestry back to these neophytes of Mission San Fernando.

FERNWOOD, unincorporated Topanga Canyon area, 3 miles from Pacific Coast Highway. County planners regard it as one of 14 "rural villages" that dot the mountainous portions of the Malibu coastal zone. However attractive to the eye, the hilly terrain with its scattered chaparral and eucalyptus trees is highly susceptible to wildfire. Some homes and cabins cradled in the steep canyon walls were lost during the wind-driven Calabasas blaze of November 1993.

FERRARO, JOHN (1924–), Los Angeles City Council member representing the 4th District, which includes Toluca Lake, Hollywood, Silver-

lake, and the Wilshire area. Ferraro was born in Maywood and attended USC, where he was a star athlete. After being appointed to the council in 1966, he was elected in 1967. Ferraro's main committee assignments have been intergovernmental relations, rules and elections, and commerce, energy, and natural resources. He has also served as council president.

FERUS GALLERY, La Cienega art salon owned by Walter Hopp. In the 1950s it promoted the work of a core of modernist artists, including Edward Kienholz, Billy Al Bengstrom, Ed Moses, Craig Kauffman, Robert Irwin, Larry Bell, and Ed Ruscha. During the next decade these young painters and sculptors broke the hold of academic art on the art scene. Their work, which epitomized the so-called L.A. Look, was distinctively "cool, semi-technological, [and] industrially pretty," embodying a strong folk art element.

FEUCHTWANGER, LION (1884–1958), émigré German writer. In 1933 he fled Hitler's Germany to France, only to be arrested by French authorities. In 1940 he escaped, came to the United States, and a year later settled in Pacific Palisades. His home, called Villa Aurora, was a favorite gathering place for European exiles. Since his death in 1958 Villa Aurora has become a center for the study of the German exile experience.

FEUER, MIKE (1959–), Los Angeles City Council member representing the 5th District. A graduate of Harvard University and Harvard Law School, he worked in the law firm of Hufstedler, Miller, Carlson, and Beardley, and he assisted Tom Bradley in his 1986 gubernatorial campaign. A public interest attorney, Feuer served as executive director of Bet Tzedek Legal Services from 1986 to 1995, spearheading advocacy campaigns on behalf of Holocaust survivors and elderly victims of home equity fraud. He was elected to the city council in 1995, filling the seat vacated by Zev Yaroslavsky.

FICTION ABOUT LOS ANGELES, TO 1950, began with Helen Hunt Jackson's *Ramona* (1884), a novel that drew upon the recollections of two Angelenos, Antonio and Mariana Coronel, and derived inspiration from Rancho Camulos, the Del Valle estate on the northwest fringes of the county. *Ramona* created a mystique that came to be associated with all of Southern California. Mark Sibley Severance was probably Los Angeles's first novelist. However, his sole book, *Hammersmith* (1876), was not about Los Angeles, and Severance later went on to become a real estate developer. Not until 1922, with Harry L. Wilson's humorous *Merton of the Movies,* did a work of fiction deal directly with a modern Los Angeles theme.

Fiction about Los Angeles per se can be divided into three groups: the detective novel, the Hollywood novel, and general works on a wide variety of themes having to do with Los Angeles. Many of the stories stress dissolution—they are peopled by the dishonest, the fraudulent, the unscrupulous, the tenaciously greedy and ambitious, and their victims. This decaying or degenerate society is depicted against the background of Southern California's hot beaches and rolling surf, picturesque canyons, lush growth, and laid-back style. In this literary world, violence occurs frequently, and a mood of irony, cynicism, and contradiction prevails. Dreams are born and die, solid façades turn out to be movie sets, people have destinations at which they never arrive, and money rules human conduct. Perhaps some of the alienation that pervades so many of these books is due to the prevalence of writers who first came to Los Angeles as adults and established an active-hate/reluctant-love relationship to it. Many were summoned by, or heard the siren call of, the movie studios. They came not only from different parts of the United States but also from England—Christopher Isherwood, Evelyn Waugh, Aldous Huxley—and Germany—Thomas Mann, Bertolt Brecht, Lion Feuchtwanger. An unusually high proportion of this era's fiction has met the test of time and falls into the "classic" category.

Interestingly, some of the most honored books about Los Angeles emerged during the same years as Hollywood's most honored movies: 1939 and 1940. They include Nathanael West's *The Day of the Locust* (1939), Aldous Huxley's *After Many a Summer Dies the Swan* (1939), Raymond Chandler's *The Big Sleep* (1939) and *Farewell, My Lovely* (1940), and John Fante's *Ask the Dust* (1939).

The mystery genre began in Los Angeles with James Cain's *The Postman Always Rings Twice* (1934); his *Double Indemnity* (1936) and *Mildred Pierce* (1941) also set high standards. They were, however, surpassed by the works of Raymond Chandler, which W. H. Auden regarded "not as escape literature, but as works of art." *Farewell, My Lovely* is considered his best novel. Among Chandler's other works are *The Big Sleep* (1939), *The High Window* (1942), *The Lady in the Lake* (1943), *Little Sister* (1949), and *The Long Goodbye* (1954). They all feature detective Philip Marlowe. Other mystery writers based their detectives in Los Angeles as well. They include Erle Stanley Gardner's Perry Mason; A. A. Fair's (a.k.a. Gardner) Donald Lam and Bertha Cool; Ellery Queen's detective, also called Ellery Queen, who was an occasional Hollywood resident; Barnaby Ross's (a.k.a. Queen) actor-turned-sleuth Drury Lane; and Craig Rice and her sophisticated creations, attorney John J. Malone and Jake and Helene Justis.

The Hollywood novel deals not with the town per se but with the film industry. In fact, the geographic scope is often large and varied, ranging from Malibu to Pasadena, from the beaches to the foothills, and from the mountains to downtown's Bunker Hill. Although the genre began with Wilson's *Merton of the Movies* (1922), the most highly acclaimed Hollywood novel remains Nathanael West's *The Day of the Locust.* Though now considered a classic, upon publication the book received poor reviews and by the end

---

As soon as we arrived, about eight heathen from a good village came to visit us; they live in this delightful place among the trees on the river. They presented us with some baskets of pinole made from seeds of sage and other grasses.
—Father Juan Crespi, Franciscan missionary and Portolá expedition diarist, 1769

---

of its first month had sold fewer than a dozen copies. Budd Schulberg's *What Makes Sammy Run?* (1941) depicts the climb from rags to studio-head riches of Sammy Glick, a name that has become synonymous with duplicity and ruthless ambition. F. Scott Fitzgerald's unfinished *The Last Tycoon* (1941), considered by many critics to be his best book, is based in large part on Irving Thalberg. Aldous Huxley's *After Many a Summer Dies the Swan* (1939) and Evelyn Waugh's *The Loved One* (1948) also deal, at least in part, with Hollywood.

The general novels render various aspects and attitudes about Los Angeles. Mark Lee Luther's *The Boosters* (1923) is an early example of East-West competition that sounds an optimistic note for Southern California. Upton Sinclair's *Oil!* (1927) opens with an account of the Signal Hill oil mania. Horace McCoy's *They Shoot Horses, Don't They?* (1935) is a deeply pessimistic novel of marathon dancers during the depression that takes place on a rundown amusement pier overlooking the Pacific. Waugh's satire *The Loved One* deals with Hollywood figures; its base of operations is the cemetery Whispering Glades, a send-up of Forest Lawn. *American Me* (1948), by Beatrice Griffith, contains short stories from the Mexican American barrio, many of them about young people. Huxley's *Ape and Essence* (1948) pictures Los Angeles in ruins in the early 21st century.

The era produced many lesser works, some by well-known writers. They include Vicki Baum's *Falling Star* (1934), P. G. Wodehouse's *Laughing Gas* (1936), John O'Hara's *Hope of Heaven* (1938), Peter Viertel's *The Canyon* (1940), and Budd Schulberg's *The Disenchanted* (1950).

FICTION ABOUT LOS ANGELES, SINCE 1950, is more diverse than in the earlier period, though detective and Hollywood novels still play a major role. The Cain-Chandler torch passed to Ross Macdonald and his private eye, Lew Archer, whose career stretched from *The Moving Target* (1949) to *The Blue Hammer* (1976). Writers like Mark Connelly (*Black Ice,* 1993) and Dianne G. Pugh (*Cold Call,* 1993) write convincingly about Los Angeles. Fictional detectives increasingly represent the changing face of Los Angeles: Michael Nava writes about the East Los Angeles barrio, as does Bruce Coo, whose detective is Antonio "Chico" Cervantes; Joseph Hanson's insurance-investigator detective, Dave Brandstetter, is gay; Roger Simon's hero, Moses Wine, is a Jewish P.I.; and E. V. Cunningham's detective is a Japanese American, Masao Masuto. Other prominent mystery and crime writers using the Los Angeles setting include Joseph Wambaugh, whose novels about the Los Angeles Police Department began with *The New Centurions* (1970); Elmore Leonard; M. J. Howe; and Thomas Pynchon. Examples of books that use the seamier side of life to highlight recent history are John Gregory Dunne's *True Confessions* (1977), which incorporates elements of the Black Dahlia murder case; Thomas Sanchez's *Zoot Suit Murders* (1978), dealing with events in 1943; James Ellroy's *The Big Nowhere* (1988), based on the 1950s Sleepy Lagoon case; and Walter Mosley's *A Red Death* (1991), which brings the red-baiting 1950s to the black ghetto. Mosley's reluctant sleuth, Ezekiel ("Easy") Rawlins, like Chandler's Philip Marlowe, covers Los Angeles of the 1940s, but Rawlins's beat is mainly the South Central area.

The third and more general group consists of novels depicting a variety of aspects about Los Angeles. A sampling of prominent books includes Gavin Lambert's *The Slide Area* (1959), dealing with counterculture Venice beach; Alison Lurie's biting social satire *The Nowhere City* (1966); Richard Vasquez's *Chicano* (1970), a description of contemporary East Los Angeles; Joan Didion's *Play It as It Lays* (1970), which follows Maria Wyeth as she tries to bring order to her life in a tangle of cars, freeways, motels, and despair; Charles Bukowski's *Post Office* (1971), a grim depiction of the city's underside; Oscar Zeta Acosta's

---

Local conditions are especially beneficial for pulmonary ailments, asthma, liver trouble, nervous disorders, and old age. The sunny skies, the delightful winter climate, and the beautiful walks all contribute to make Los Angeles a veritable sanitarium.

—Ludwig Salvator, Austrian archduke, 1878

The Revolt of the Cockroach People (1973), about Chicanos and the city; Marc Norman's unusual *Bike Riding in Los Angeles* (1973); Bret Easton Ellis's *Less Than Zero* (1985), which deals with alienated affluent high-schoolers; David Freeman's *A Hollywood Education: Tales of a Movie Dream and Easy Money* (1986), which was hailed by many reviewers as the best and most important book about Hollywood and its hangers-on since *The Day of the Locust;* Mona Simpson's *Anywhere but Here* (1986), which, while not about Los Angeles and Hollywood alone, describes well the continued fascination the city holds for so many people; Gore Vidal's *Hollywood: A Novel of America in the 1920s* (1990), his sixth fictional exploration of American history and politics, which serves up

Hollywood in the era of Fatty Arbuckle and friends; and John Gregory Dunne's Hollywood novel *Playland* (1994).

FIESTA DE LOS ANGELES. *See* La Fiesta de Los Angeles

FIFIELD, JAMES W., JR. (1899–1977), conservative pastor of the First Congregational Church from the 1930s to the 1950s. Born and ordained in Chicago, Fifield arrived in Los Angeles in 1935 and took over the helm of the 1,000-member church, which was deeply in debt. To counteract a growing liberal and progressive ecumenical trend within Congregationalism that embraced the New Deal, he founded the conservative Spiritual Mobilization movement, thus becoming a beacon for social conservatism and anticommunism in Los Angeles. Within eight years Fifield had built his congregation's membership to 21,000, retired the financial debt, and burned the mortgage. During his tenure the mid-Wilshire institution featured a radio broadcasting studio, gymnasium, children's chapel, music library, foreign language classes, and courses in piano and elocution. With a paid staff of 42, it was the biggest Congregational church in the nation.

FILIPINOS established a presence in Los Angeles beginning in the 1920s. With the passage of the 1924 federal immigration law excluding Japanese immigration, a vacuum developed in the agricultural labor market. Filipinos were the only Pacific Islanders who could legally enter the United States, even though under the law they were neither citizens nor aliens. Those who came to Los Angeles took up residence in the areas of Los Angeles and 1st Streets and near Grand Avenue and Hope Street. Most of the newcomers were young, single males who came as sojourners—"birds of passage"—intending to work temporarily as farm laborers or cannery workers and return eventually to their homeland. A few were students or merchant seamen.

The rampant racist sentiments originally directed against the Chinese and Japanese were now turned on the Filipinos, including a powerful organized movement for exclusion and repatriation. Resentment against them reached its apogee during the Great Depression. Those Filipinos remaining in Los Angeles found themselves isolated in the poorest slums. In one case, the county clerk

attempted to enforce the state's antimiscegenation law against a Filipino man and a white woman who planned to marry; the state supreme court overruled the clerk in 1933, but the legislature simply reinstituted the law in 1937. In the 1930s six taxi dance halls—where male customers paid hired hostesses to dance—on Main, 1st, and 5th Streets catered to Filipinos. Historian Carey McWilliams suggests that, at 10 cents a dance, this was the most expensive recreation in town.

In recent decades Los Angeles County has had the largest Filipino population outside of Manila. The 1950s saw a major exodus of professionals from the Philippines, and many of the more recent immigrants were in that group; they found work in medicine, nursing, law, dentistry, accounting, and engineering. A "Little Manila" community developed near the Los Angeles civic center, though it was displaced in the 1960s and 1970s by urban renewal projects. Some Filipinos then moved toward Temple Street and Beverly Boulevard.

Substantial Filipino communities also exist in Long Beach, Carson, Glendale, Eagle Rock, San Pedro, and West Covina. The Filipino population of the city of Los Angeles rose from 99,043 in 1980 to 219,653 in 1990, an increase of 122 percent. The overall Southern California Filipino community supports 300 voluntary organizations and four weekly newspapers, which in 1990 had a combined circulation of 120,000 readers. Voter registration and political participation of Filipinos has been relatively low, with few seeking elected office anywhere in California.

FIRE DEPARTMENTS. *See* Los Angeles City Fire Department; Los Angeles County Fire Department

FIRES. *See* Wildfires

FIRESTONE TIRE AND RUBBER COMPANY, 5-acre factory in South Gate built during World War II to produce gun mounts and barrage balloons. Used for civilian production afterward, it closed in the postwar era when heavy industry diminished in Los Angeles.

FIRST AFRICAN METHODIST EPISCOPAL (AME) CHURCH, oldest black religious institution in Los Angeles and a center for religious instruction and community improvement. The AME Church originated in the 1790s in the eastern part of the nation. In 1872, 12 charter members

Rev. Cecil L. ("Chip") Murray. Mikiholo Photos, courtesy First AME Church.

organized the Los Angeles congregation in the Spring Street home of Biddy Mason, a former slave. They purchased a lot at the corner of 4th Street and Grand Avenue for $700 and built a church. In 1903 the congregation completed a handsome Gothic edifice at 8th and Towne, and later relocated at S. Harvard Boulevard. The church, which counts 7,500 parishioners, is a major center for both worship and community action. Since the 1970s the pastor has been Rev. Cecil L. "Chip" Murray, a former combat pilot and a Claremont Ph.D. He is a respected leader in Los Angeles and was a leading figure urging calm and reason during the 1992 upheaval in Los Angeles. "Be cool," he urged. "Even in anger, be cool."

FIRST CONGREGATIONAL CHURCH, founded in 1867, is the oldest continuously functioning Protestant church in the city. In the 1960s membership was 5,000; today it stands at 1,200. The church has been located on New High Street, at 3rd and Hill, 6th and Hill, 9th and Hope, and, since 1932, on S. Commonwealth Avenue. The Gothic-style edifice is an architectural landmark.

FIRST INTERSTATE WORLD CENTER, tallest building on the West Coast and the eighth tallest in the nation. Completed in 1989, the 73-story cylindrical spire of gray granite is planted firmly on top of Bunker Hill. Henry Nicholas Cobb of I. M. Pei Partners of New York designed it for developer Maguire Thomas Partners.

The building, which soars 1,018 feet into the sky, encompasses 1.3 million feet of rentable space. Bunker Hill Steps, a staircase leading up to the building from 5th Street, designed by Lawrence

First Interstate World Center and Wells Fargo Building (right). Photo by Michael Krakowiak/Marni Pitt.

Halprin, gives the vicinity a welcoming air. First Interstate is located directly opposite the Central Library on 5th Street. The two buildings have a symbiotic relationship, as the city granted the developer a zoning variance for the supertower in exchange for financing the historic library's restoration following a 1986 arson fire.

FISCUS, KATHY, three-and-a-half-year-old child who fell into the pipe of an abandoned water well near her home in San Marino in 1949. The attempt to save the girl, which lasted 54 hours, was one of television's first live-coverage events and was watched by a huge audience nationwide. The child's lifeless body was finally recovered at the 95-foot level. The story was fictionalized in Billy Wilder's angry film *The Big Carnival* (1951), an early, prophetic look at the public exploitation of a tragic event.

FISHING, for food, fun, and profit, has long been part of the local lifestyle and economy. Many of the more than 500 fish species found in California's coastal waters have as their habitat the sprawling offshore kelp forest. Indians lived off of the ocean's harvest. In 1898 the first local person known to catch a tuna with a fishing rod was Charles Frederic Holder, originally of Lynn, Massachusetts, and a renowned naturalist. He developed the sport of deep-sea fishing off the local coast. Since then anglers have cast their lines from boats, piers, and beaches. The oldest big-game fishing club in the world, the Tuna Club on Santa Catalina Island, once included among its members British prime minister Winston Churchill, Gen. George Patton, and the western writer Zane Grey.

The black sea bass is the heaviest fish in local waters, weighing in at 450 to 500 pounds. Among the fishes caught in the kelp forest are various species of rockfish and perch. The law dictates that California grunion, the "fish that dance at the beach at the full moon," may only be caught by hand on the nights they swim ashore to spawn. Surfperch is a prized game fish, abundant in the surf zone along sandy beaches. Pacific mackerel is an important commercial and sport fish that swims in schools near the shore. Tuna is the basis of a major industry. Many fish species, such as Dover sole, white sea bass, and white croaker, have been seriously affected by pollution from sewage.

From time to time a red tide afflicts bay waters. The phenomenon is not a result of pollution but is caused by a profusion of microscopic plankton called dinoflagellates. These same plankton are the cause of paralytic shellfish poisoning (PSP) in humans, a condition of the summer months; poisoning can occur when a person eats clams, mussels, or other bivalves that feed on dinoflagellates.

FISH PACKING INDUSTRY had its beginnings around World War I at Fish Harbor on Terminal Island, where it thrived until the 1960s. At the peak

of operations 19 canneries, including Star-Kist Foods, Van Camp Sea Foods, and Pan Pacific Fisheries, employed as many as 17,000 workers. The fish were first delivered to Fisherman's Dock in San Pedro and sold either to the local retail trade or to Fish Harbor canneries on Terminal Island. The fishing and cannery workers were mainly of Japanese, Yugoslav, Italian, and Portuguese background. Japanese men living in Fish Harbor fished for tuna with poles from their boats in the North Pacific and, later, in South American waters. Their wives worked in the canneries. Yugoslav fishermen, in contrast, used nets. At one time Los Angeles Harbor berthed 700 tuna boats and was worked by 5,000 fishermen. The canneries processed 500 million pounds of fish each year.

In the 1970s, South American governments applied sanctions against the American tuna fishing fleet. At the same time, sardines, tuna, mackerel, and other fish species in California waters declined. A series of low-tariff agreements between the United States and Latin American nations further undermined the trade, which was reduced almost to the point of extinction.

FITTS, BURON (1895–1973), county district attorney from 1928 to 1941, after having served as lieutenant governor from 1926 to 1928. Fitts was an American Legion activist who in 1919 was appointed special district attorney to fight anarchists and labor radicals. He became a personal favorite of Harry Chandler and the *Times*. Although Fitts was appointed to office to clean up crime, he himself was suspected of bribery, and in 1934 a grand jury indicted him for perjury for protecting a prominent real estate businessman ac-

Abalone fishing in Los Angeles Harbor, pre–World War II. Pitt Collection.

cused of statutory rape. He survived that charge and defended Mayor Frank Shaw against charges of corruption.

FLAG of the city of Los Angeles was designed in 1931 by Roy E. Silent and E. S. Jones for the city's 150th anniversary. The colors are the same as in the flags of Mexico and Spain and are said also to represent vineyards (red), orange groves (golden yellow), and olive orchards (green). In the center is the official seal, adopted in 1905.

FLINT, FRANK PUTNAM (1862–1929), Republican attorney who served as U.S. senator from 1905 to 1911. Born in Massachusetts and reared in California, he became a prominent lawyer in Los Angeles. He supported Los Angeles's use of Owens River water. In a crucial meeting with Pres. Theodore Roosevelt, Senator Flint argued for the city's right to import water for agricultural development in the San Fernando Valley as a case of the "greatest good for the greatest number." Flintridge, a residential area on part of Rancho La Cañada that was subdivided in 1920, is named for him.

FLOOD CONTROL throughout the 4,000-square-mile Los Angeles Basin is handled by a vast network of dams, catch-basins, and canals that normally work very well. Water that runs off the mountains and canyons is channeled into major streams; in the event of heavy rain, spreading grounds and debris basins stand ready to handle water temporarily shunted from the main streams to keep them from jumping their banks. An underground empire of 2,370 miles of storm drains handles street runoff. The U.S. Army Corps of Engineers manages five dams, including the Sepulveda Dam. Sepulveda Basin, Santa Fe Basin, and Whittier Narrows Basin double as recreational areas in dry seasons and floodplains in wet seasons. The county's Department of Public Works, from its "war room" in an office building in Alhambra, operates 15 dams with a combined storage capacity of 116,000 acre-feet of water. In a storm involving the Los Angeles River, the flood control system can handle up to 146,000 cubic feet of water per second before the water overflows its channel and causes major damage.

FLOODS have drowned large parts of Los Angeles from time immemorial. An 1825 deluge permanently shifted the channel of the Los Angeles River from its westerly outflow into Santa Monica Bay to a southerly outlet into San Pedro Bay. This shift caused miles of natural marshes and lakes to dry up and vast stands of willow trees to die. In the winter of 1861–1862 a flood left the western part of the Los Angeles Basin looking like a chain of lakes dotted with islands. On that occasion the San Gabriel River overflowed its banks and joined the Los Angeles River to create the new channel known as Rio Hondo, and the Arroyo Seco became a raging stream which swept so much driftwood into the lowlands that firewood was plentiful for years. A flood in 1884 resulted from 40 inches of rain falling in downtown Los Angeles, with even more in the mountains. River water sloshed up to the intersections of 1st and Main (one-half mile from the river) and Maple and 24th Streets, and the San

Los Angeles River at flood stage, 1938. Courtesy Dept. of Special Collections, University Research Library, UCLA.

Fernando Valley was under water from Glendale to Chatsworth. The torrent washed out practically every bridge in town, destroyed many houses, and claimed numerous lives. Destructive floods also occurred in 1914, 1934, 1938, and 1969. Even now, with a vast flood control system in place, the basin is subject to damage from drenching rains. Cloudbursts caused flood damage in the Sepulveda Basin and elsewhere in early 1992, and again in the 1994–1995 rainy season.

FLORA. *See* Chaparral; Wildflowers; individual plants

FLORENCE, unincorporated county area 6 miles south of downtown. Originally a farming community, it is now residential. In 1990 the combined population of Florence and the Graham area, directly to the south, was 57,147.

FLORES, JOAN MILKE (1937–), former Los Angeles City Council representative from the 15th District. Born in Wisconsin but raised in Southern California, Flores worked as a stenographer and held other city hall jobs until elected to the council in 1981. She was reelected in 1985 and 1989, then lost an election bid to become California secretary of state, and was defeated for city council reelection in 1993. She was the only Republican woman ever to serve on the council.

FLORES, JOSÉ MARÍA, Mexican army captain in California who arrived with Gov. Manuel Micheltorena in 1842 and played a significant role in the Mexican War, from 1846 to 1848. He was Gov. José Castro's representative in dealings with U.S. commodore Robert Stockton. Flores organized a highly effective rebellion among the Californios of Los Angeles to fight the Americans, forcing Lt. Archibald Gillespie's U.S. dragoons, who had marched in to clear out rebel Mexican forces, to flee the *pueblo* en masse. He succeeded Gov. Pío Pico when the latter was forced to leave the province in 1846, revived the assembly, and assumed the role of *comandante general* over the region from San Luis Obispo to San Diego. After refusing to negotiate with Lt. Col. John Frémont, Flores left for Sonora, where he again headed a Mexican military force at the end of the war.

FLORES, JUAN (1836?–1857), Mexican bandit leader who terrorized Southern California communities from 1855 to 1857. Flores had been sentenced to San Quentin for horse theft in 1855, but escaped from prison and established a bandit group, mostly Mexicans seeking revenge against the now-dominant Yankees. In reaction to killings by Flores's men, over 100 vigilantes counterattacked, seizing and lynching not only many bandits but also some of their innocent allies. Flores was captured in Orange County (near a peak that is named for him), confessed to his crimes, and was hanged at Fort Hill, Los Angeles, on 14 February 1857.

FLORES MAGON, RICARDO (D. 1922), anarchist hero of the Mexican revolution of 1910 who for a time lived in Los Angeles in exile. An inveterate essayist, speaker, and organizer for the Mexican Liberal Party, Flores founded the newspaper *Regeneración* in this city. It boasted a circulation of 30,000. Convicted of violating U.S. neutrality laws, Ricardo was imprisoned along with his brother, Enrique, in Leavenworth Federal Penitentiary, where he died in 1922.

FLOWER MARKET, colorful wholesale center between 7th and 8th, and Maple and Wall Streets, in the central city. Since 1923 each weekday before dawn commercial flower growers and sellers have gathered at the two-block area to haggle over thousands of flowers of every variety grown by Southern California nurseries. Formerly established in nine barnlike sheds, the flower market has recently been relocated to a new two-story building. This is the largest wholesale cut-flower market in the nation, employing some 2,000 people and with the participation of 90 Southern California Flower Growers Association affiliates. The spectacular floral displays are sold by local retailers and flown to distant parts of the nation. Over $40 million changes hands in the market annually.

FOLTZ, CLARA SHORTRIDGE (1849–1932), California's first woman lawyer, and Los Angeles's first woman assistant district attorney. Foltz fostered legislation allowing women to practice law in the state and encouraged them to enter the profession.

FOOD FROM THE 'HOOD, cooperative enterprise organized after the 1992 riots. With the help of their biology teacher, Tammy Bird, 40 students from Crenshaw High School planted a quarter-acre plot behind their football field in flowers and vegetables. They were soon distributing the results of their labors to families in their South Central neighborhood. They also sold their produce to farmers markets, calling their enterprise Food From the 'Hood. Their success led to the production and market distribution of a salad dressing, Straight Out 'the Garden, using their own herbs. The student-owned cooperative expected to bring in $50,000 in 1995. Guidance has been provided by Bird and market consultant Melinda McMullen. The students do all the work in their garden, and manage all aspects of the business from distribution to public relations. The profits are set aside to fund student scholarships. As of 1995, ten of the seniors involved in the cooperative had been accepted by, and planned to attend, four-year colleges.

FOOTBALL, COLLEGE, has been dominated since the 1920s by the rivalry between the UCLA Bruins and the USC Trojans. In 1888, USC was the first local university to play the new American game, with teams of 11 players. It participated in the first Rose Bowl game, in 1916. The cross-town rivalry started in 1929, when USC crushed UCLA

So which is it: Do we live in Eden or in a hellhole?   —Patt Morrison, journalist

---

(then known as the University of California, Southern Branch) 76–0. The following year brought another lopsided USC victory of 56–0. Their next game, in 1936, ended in a 7–7 tie. In 1942 UCLA had its first taste of revenge, winning 14–7. That year quarterback Bob Waterfield took the team to the Rose Bowl.

A second rivalry attracts tremendous attention in Southern California, that between USC and Notre Dame—the oldest intersectional rivalry in the nation. The Trojan-Irish matchup traces its beginnings to 1926, when Knute Rockne brought his team to Southern California to play before a sellout crowd of 70,000 in the Coliseum. The Irish tend to dominate the series.

Between 1925 and 1975 California has nurtured more All-American football stars than any other state—many of them from Southern California.

FOOTBALL, PROFESSIONAL, started at the Los Angeles Memorial Coliseum in 1925 when Red

Grange's Chicago Bears triumphed over a pickup team called the Los Angeles Tigers. A 1926 match-up between the newly formed Los Angeles Wildcats and Los Angeles Buccaneers failed to kindle major interest in pro football, however. Further efforts in 1937 proved equally futile, but a 1945 game between the Washington Redskins and an army all-star team was more effective.

The first official National Football League (NFL) game was played on 6 September 1946 when the Los Angeles Rams, newly transplanted from Cleveland by owner Daniel F. Reeves, faced the Washington Redskins in an exhibition charity game sponsored by the *Los Angeles Times.* Also featured in local pro football that year were the Los Angeles Dons of the All-American Football Conference, who competed against the San Francisco Forty-Niners. The Rams won their first NFL championship game at the Coliseum in 1951, with a 73-yard pass from Norm Brocklin to Tom Fears, to beat the Cleveland Browns 24–17. In 1960 a new league was formed. The Rams later moved to Anaheim, and then, in 1995, to St. Louis. Meanwhile, Los Angeles briefly became the home of the Oakland Raiders, a team that under general manager Al Davis won three Super Bowls and became, for a time, the dominant team in professional football. The Raiders infuriated their new fans by returning to Oakland in 1995, leaving Los Angeles with no professional football team.

FORD, JOHN ANSON (1883–1983), progressive county supervisor from 1934 through 1958. A Wisconsin-born journalist and ad man, Ford moved to Los Angeles in 1920 and served on the grand jury formed in the aftermath of the C. C. Julian scandal in 1927. As a supervisor he helped cope with the poverty and joblessness of the depression years. He fought against city corruption during the Shaw administration, running unsuccessfully in 1937 to unseat the corrupt mayor. Ford oversaw the formation of the County Human Relations Commission to cope with racial bigotry in 1943. An avid Los Angeles booster, he supported welfare reform, racial integration, and improvement of cultural institutions, and helped change an inflexible state law that prevented the county from subsidizing musical, theatrical, and other cultural events. The Pilgrimage Play Amphitheatre in Cahuenga Pass was renamed the John Anson Ford Theater in 1978. He wrote a memoir about his career called *Thirty Explosive Years in Los Angeles County* (1961).

FORD MOTOR COMPANY opened an assembly plant at 7th and Santa Fe Streets in 1914, where 300 employees assembled Model T's. In 1930 the plant moved to Long Beach. The Detroit-based company also built a Lincoln Mercury factory in Maywood in 1948, moving it in 1957 to a 200-acre site in Pico Rivera. This shop remained active until 1979, when its 550 employees were laid off and the operation was moved to Ohio. A Long Beach bridge is named after Henry Ford.

FOREIGN TRADE AND COMMERCE. *See* Trade and commerce, foreign

FOREST LAWN MEMORIAL PARK, cemetery based in Glendale, with annexes in the San Fernando Valley and Long Beach. The concept of Baptist layman Hubert L. Eaton, a mining engineer from Missouri, it was created in 1917 specifically to make death seem peaceful, beautiful, and uplifting. Taking over a small and failing cemetery, Eaton revolutionized the industry through artful landscaping, the commissioning of elaborate artworks, re-creations of famous churches, and the elimination of tombstones and cemetery plots. The artworks included a glass replica of da Vinci's *Last Supper;* a depiction of the Crucifixion that, at 44 feet in height and 195 feet in width, is called the world's largest painting; and a replica of Michelangelo's *David*.

Eaton fought for legislation allowing cemeteries to have their own mortuaries. He also launched a successful advertising campaign that promoted complete "before need" sales, arranged for the bereaved to be served with "just one telephone call," and conducted enormously popular Easter sunrise services on the premises. The burial areas are named Slumberland, Vale of Memory, and Whispering Pines. The ground-level plaques scattered over several hundred acres make up a Who's Who of the greats and near-greats in industry, film, sports, art, science, and religion. They run the gamut from baseball manager Casey Stengel to Nobel physicist Robert A. Millikan, from cowboy-philosopher and entertainer Will Rogers to evangelist Aimee Semple McPherson, from novelist Theodore Dreiser to actor Humphrey Bogart. Novelist Evelyn Waugh based his biting satire *The Loved One* (1948) on Forest Lawn, which he calls "Whispering Glades."

FORT MacARTHUR, U.S. Army post poised on a bluff overlooking San Pedro harbor, established before World War I for coastal and harbor defense. It housed Battery Osgood, whose guns could fire projectiles 17 miles—farther than any battleship at the time. Those weapons were later replaced by anti-aircraft guns that stood poised on alert throughout World War II. The fort has three distinct segments: the topside, which is now a park; the 244-acre Middle Reservation, which houses the main facility; and the Lower Reservation, built during World War II and used since 1948 mainly as a reserve training center. The fort was named in 1914 for Lt. Gen. Arthur MacArthur, hero of the Spanish-American War and father of Gen. Douglas MacArthur, who became famous in World War II. A military museum is located at Leavenworth Drive and Gaffy Street.

FORT MOORE, site of an abandoned U.S. military post above the Plaza, in the civic center area. Designed during the Mexican War, it accommodated 200 soldiers whose job it was to protect the *pueblo*. The fort was dedicated by American troops on 4 July 1847 and named for Capt. Benjamin D. Moore, who was killed in the Battle of San Pascual, where in 1846 Brig. Gen. Stephen Kearny attacked Gen. Andrés Pico's Californio army. The site was formally deserted the following year. Today it is part of the headquarters complex of the Los Angeles Unified School District and is marked by a sculptured wall.

FORUM, THE, Roman-style columned circular arena in Inglewood that is home to the Los Angeles Lakers basketball team and the Los Angeles Kings hockey team. It is considerably larger than the Roman forum that inspired it. With 16,000 to 19,385 seats, depending on the occasion, the Forum also hosts tennis matches, rock concerts, track meets, ice shows, circuses, rodeos, boxing bouts, and political events. Built by sports promoter Jack Kent Cook in 1967 and unofficially dubbed "the House the Jack Built," the arena was purchased by Dr. Jerry Buss in 1979. It was officially named the "Fabulous Forum" at the start, and more recently the "Great Western Forum." By 1990 more than 52 million spectators had witnessed over 5,000 events there.

FOSTER, STEPHEN C. (1822–1898), *alcalde* in the Mexican period, from 1848 to 1849, and mayor of Los Angeles from 1854 to 1855, and again in 1856; he resigned from office during his first term to lead a lynch mob. Born in Maine, he taught school in the South, and in 1845 trekked to Santa Fe. During the Mexican War he was part of the Mormon Battalion, which arrived in Los Angeles in March 1847. Fluent in Spanish, Foster became an *alcalde* during the brief period of military rule, and married into the Lugo family. He rode with Dr. Alexander W. Hope's vigilante rangers, served as a school commissioner, and was elected twice as mayor, receiving an annual salary of $400. While he was mayor he faced down a lynch mob that was about to hang Dave Brown, a murderer. He persuaded the angry crowd to let the miscreant be tried in superior court, promising that if the court released Brown he would resign as mayor and personally head the lynchers. Brown was released, and Foster kept his promise. From 1857 to 1859 he served as a county supervisor.

FOSTER, THOMAS (D. 1863), physician and sixth mayor of Los Angeles from 1855 to 1856. A Kentuckian by birth, he was one of over a dozen physicians who settled in Los Angeles in the 1850s. Foster, whose wife was a teacher, lived and practiced medicine on Main Street, opposite Masonic Lodge No. 42, where he was a charter member. He took office as the city's mayor in May 1855, when Los Angeles's 2,000 people lived in an area of only 28 square miles. Foster tried to improve the city's education and water systems, and he helped raise funds to bring the Catholic Sisters of Charity to Los Angeles and to establish the first Protestant church, in 1859. He was lost at sea off the SS *Senator* on the way to San Francisco. Some people speculated that he committed suicide.

FOURSQUARE GOSPEL, INTERNATIONAL CHURCH OF THE. *See* Angelus Temple; McPherson, Aimee Semple

FOX, WILLIAM (1879–1952), Hungarian-born film producer. His success in New York with nickelodeon theaters brought him to Hollywood in the 1920s, where he became a producer, establishing Fox Pictures in Culver City in 1924. The 1935 merger of his Fox Film Corporation with Joseph Schenck and Darryl F. Zanuck's 20th Century Pictures brought the major Hollywood studio 20th Century–Fox Film Corporation into existence. Fox developed the careers of such stars as Theda Bara, pioneered Movietone's sound-on-film methods, and established a chain of movie palaces. Fi-

nancial troubles and a federal antitrust suit forced him into bankruptcy in 1936; the U.S. Supreme Court then ruled that Fox did not own the sound patents for the entire film industry. Charged with trying to bribe a judge, he served a jail term. Upton Sinclair wrote a biography called *Upton Sinclair Presents William Fox* (1933).

FOX HILLS, community in the southwest corner of Culver City, 12 miles from downtown Los Angeles. Unincorporated county territory until annexed to Culver City in the 1960s, the neighborhood features suburban housing, a major shopping mall, and an industrial park. The community is made up exclusively of apartment buildings and condominium complexes, with no single-family residences. The boundaries are Centinela and Slauson Avenues, Sepulveda Boulevard, and the Ladera Heights neighborhood. Its population in the early 1990s was approximately 5,000.

FOY, MARY EMILY (1862–1962), educator, librarian, and civic leader. Foy was born in Los Angeles and attended Los Angeles High School and the State Normal School (now UCLA), where she trained to be an English teacher. She was head city librarian from 1880 to 1884, and principal of Duarte School in 1886 and 1887. Foy was active in the Friday Morning Club and the Historical Society of Southern California. Democratic Party politics interested her, and she avidly supported woman suffrage and other feminist causes.

FRANKFORT, JACOB (1810–?), first recorded Jewish resident of Los Angeles. He was a German-born tailor and arrived with the Rowland-Workman party from New Mexico in 1841. He is mentioned as having been in Los Angeles in 1846, and is cited in the 1850 census, where his age is given as 40.

FRANKLIN CANYON, 3.5-mile gorge in the Santa Monica Mountains between Coldwater and Benedict Canyons above Beverly Hills. The canyon contains the Upper Franklin Reservoir—a lake that has impounded water imported from the Owens Valley since 1914. The water, carried by the Los Angeles Aqueduct, is no longer used for drinking purposes, but merely to maintain the lake and the lush pine trees in the surrounding area. This portion of the canyon is part of the Santa Monica Mountains National Recreation Area and is often used for film shoots. Most of the canyon is accessed by Franklin Canyon Drive.

FRATERNAL SOCIETIES, or fraternal orders, have been active ever since the Freemasons established a lodge and occupied Masonic Temple at the Plaza in 1858. These voluntary societies, which often have elaborate secret initiation rites, are established to provide insurance, perform charitable acts, and foster social improvement. They have obscure origins (Freemasons claim to go back to King Solomon's temple) but were prevalent in antebellum America and became popular in Los Angeles in the last half of the 19th century. The city directory of 1890 lists over a dozen Masonic lodges, including the Royal Arch, Coeur de Lion Commandery, Hugues de Payens Council, Robert Bruce Chapter, King Solomon Lodge of Perfection, Eastern Star, and Acacia. The directory also lists branches of the Independent Order of Odd Fellows, Ancient Order of United Workmen, Knights of Pythias, and Improved Order of Red Men. Currently the main orders are the Freemasons, Odd Fellows, Knights of Pythias, and Benevolent and Protective Order of Elks. Although still basically male organizations, the societies often have women's auxiliaries. Social theorists assert that the tremendous surge of fraternal organizations in 19th-century America reflected a male response to the breakdown of community in an increasingly urban society.

FREE CLINIC. *See* Los Angeles Free Clinic

FREE HARBOR CONTEST, fierce political battle to develop a harbor for Los Angeles that took place from 1890 to 1899. In 1890 Collis P. Huntington of the Southern Pacific (SP) tried to block the development of a harbor in San Pedro and instead built a long pier at Santa Monica, where the SP owned land and could be assured of a transportation monopoly. This move ignited the 10-year struggle known locally as the "Free Harbor Contest." Arrayed against Huntington and the SP, and favoring the San Pedro location, were the Los Angeles Chamber of Commerce, *Los Angeles Times,* downtown landowners, and the young, outspoken U.S. senator Stephen White. This alliance urged an investigation by the Army Corps of Engineers to study the viability of building a breakwater to protect the exposed landing at San Pedro and establishing a deep-water harbor there. The con-

Poster for Free Harbor Jubilee, 1899. Courtesy Seaver Center for Western History Research, Natural History Museum of Los Angeles County.

gressionally appointed investigatory board determined that the project was more feasible for the San Pedro site than for the Santa Monica one. Meanwhile, Huntington used his own friends in the U.S. Senate to block a congressional appropriation favoring San Pedro. Nevertheless, in 1899 Congress voted the money and the San Pedro breakwater construction began.

FREEMAN, DANIEL (1837–1918), Canadian who came to Los Angeles in 1873 after reading Nordhoff's popular book of travel and description, *California for Health, Pleasure, and Residence* (1872). He bought 25,000 acres of Rancho Centinela from the Scottish owner, Sir Robert Burnett, which he stocked with sheep. The 1875–1876 drought destroyed 22,000 of his animals. The farm was on the site of today's Inglewood.

FREEMASONS. *See* Fraternal societies

FREEWAYS, vast expressway network that has unified and defined the physical structure of the Los Angeles area since the 1960s. The sprawling and decentralized metropolitan region was once said to be "72 suburbs in search of a city." In the

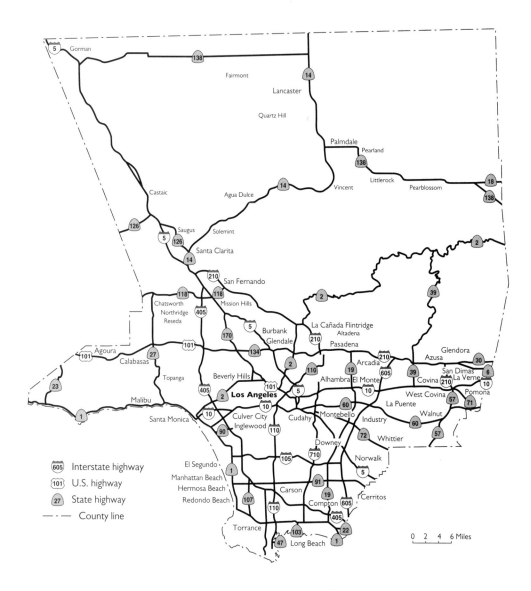

The state highway system in Los Angeles County.

1920s, officials began talking about creating a system of "motor parkways." The first such structure, the 6-mile Arroyo Seco Parkway (today's Pasadena Freeway), opened on New Year's Eve 1939—in time for the New Year's Day festivities at the Rose Bowl in Pasadena. The actual freeway system—four-to-six-lane concrete motorways with no crossings—resulted from studies drawn up by the Automobile Club of Southern California in 1937 and the city of Los Angeles Engineering Transportation Board in 1939, and from the 1947 County Regional Plan-

ning Commission's Master Plan of Highways. Farseeing engineers, alert to the burgeoning new suburbs and the record number of people and cars that were pouring into the area, proposed incorporating rapid transit facilities into the freeway system, but they were overridden. Creation of a complete freeway system became possible in 1947 when the state legislature increased highway taxes for that purpose and federal highway funds were made available.

Freeways were constructed in an overlapping

Los Angeles County Freeways at a Glance	Corridor No.	Miles Open	When Opened
Artesia	SR 91	17.6	1968–75
Foothill	I-210	41.2	1955–77
Glendale	SR 2	8.8	1958–78
Glenn Anderson	I-105	17.3	1993
Golden State	I-5	71.5	1956–75
Harbor	I-110	22.8	1952–70
Hollywood	U.S. 101	16.1	1940–48
Long Beach	I-710	20.4	1952–65
Marina	SR 90	1.9	1968–72
Pasadena	SR 110	8.0	1940–53
Pomona	SR 60	30.4	1965–71
San Bernardino	I-10	30.5	1943–57
San Diego	I-405	93.7	1957–69
San Gabriel River	I-605	27.7	1964–71
Santa Ana	I-5	43.0	1944–58
Santa Monica	I-10	16.2	1961–66
Terminal Island	SR 47	2.6	1948
Ventura	U.S. 101	80.4	1955–74

SOURCE: Caltrans Public Relations Department, 1996.
I = interstate highway; SR = state route; U.S. = federal highway

time sequence, with the most ribbon-cutting activity occurring in the 1960s and 1970s. They vary in length from 80.4 miles (Ventura) to 1.9 miles (Vincent Thomas). The first five freeways were begun in the 1940s and finished by the 1950s: the Pasadena (1940–1953), Hollywood (1940–1948), San Bernardino (1943–1957), Santa Ana (1944–1958), and the small Terminal Island Freeway (1948).

The Hollywood Freeway, completed in 1948, connected downtown with the film capital and the exploding San Fernando Valley, and was the first Los Angeles freeway designed with most new engineering elements built in from the outset. It satisfied the needs of both the downtown establishment, which still hoped to centralize the city on its own terms, and the aggressive valley developers, who had embarked on a heroic building spree. With four lanes in each direction for most of its length, the freeway had longer on-ramps, wider lanes, paved shoulders, and functional and banked curves to accommodate speeding vehicles. Although it was originally to be called the Hollywood Parkway (possibly a toll road), at its completion landscaping and most other scenic features had been eliminated. The artery plunged through crowded neighborhoods and provoked serious protests, most of which were discounted. As part

of the effort of building the Hollywood Freeway the highway commission moved or demolished almost 2,000 buildings. The agency was racked by scandal when right-of-way agents were convicted of conspiring to sell property at inflated prices for personal gain. The first segment of the Hollywood Freeway, a half-mile stretch through Cahuenga Pass, was completed in 1940. For a short time, the old Pacific Electric railway ran down the center of the freeway, but highway builders rejected the addition of a permanent transit lane. The Hollywood Freeway was soon jammed with 183,000 cars each day, causing Bob Hope to call it "the biggest parking lot in the world."

The carrying load on the Hollywood Freeway subsequently rose to 273,000 vehicles. Police were forced to crack down on motorists speeding at 85 miles per hour. Trucks were banned in the 1950s. Accidents were frequent, including a rather comic one in 1970 in which a load of chickens was strewn all over the freeway, some of whose offspring were still noted grazing happily in the adjacent shrubbery a decade later. The downtown "stack," or four-level interchange connecting the Harbor, Hollywood, and Pasadena Freeways, finished in 1948, soon was handling 350,000 cars in a 24-hour period.

During the 1950s construction began on five more freeways: the Long Beach (I-710, 1952–1965), Ventura (Routes 101 and 134, 1955–1977), Golden State (I-5, 1956–1975), Foothill (I-210 and Route 30, 1955–1977), and San Diego (I-405 and I-5, 1957–1969). These were followed in the 1960s by the Santa Monica (I-10, 1961–1966), Antelope Valley (Route 14, 1963–1974), Garden Grove (Route 22, 1964–1967), San Gabriel River (I-605, 1964–1971), Pomona (Route 60, 1965–1971), Simi Valley–San Fernando Valley (Route 118, 1968–1977), Artesia (Route 91, 1968–1975), and Marina (Route 90, 1968–1972) Freeways. By 1968 the city of Los Angeles alone had 138 miles of freeway, with 270 total miles projected upon completion of the system.

Most freeways are named after cities, natural landmarks, or prominent political figures, but at least two of them took their original names from a literary work: the Ramona and Alessandro Freeways were both named for central characters in Helen Hunt Jackson's popular novel *Ramona*. Some freeway names have been changed from the original—including Ramona and Alessandro, which today are known by the more mundane names San Bernardino and Glendale—altered by the highway

Average Daily Freeway Traffic in Select Years (24-hour count)

Intersection	1972	1982	1991
101 at 110	165,000	192,000	232,000
101 at 405	187,000	238,000	273,000
405 at 10	208,000	201,000	313,000
10 at 405 (west to east)	127,000	166,000	218,000
10 at 210 (west to east)	75,000	116,000	181,000
5 at 10	127,000	164,000	228,000
5 at 605	122,000	139,000	192,000
605 at 210	58,000	77,000	95,000
605 at 5	133,000	165,000	222,000
605 at 405	12,000	28,000	35,000

SOURCE: Caltrans, 1995. Figures are for the number of cars entering the specified intersection.

commission to eliminate driver confusion or to adjust to political realities. Thus the picturesquely named Arroyo Seco Parkway became the Pasadena Freeway; the Olympic Freeway became the Santa Monica; the Sepulveda Freeway, named after the boulevard whose path it parallels, is now the San Diego; and the Redondo Beach Freeway became the Gardena Freeway. The Slauson Freeway was given the name Richard Nixon but, after the Watergate debacle, received yet a third designation, the Marina Freeway. The Century Freeway is officially called the Glenn Anderson Freeway, after the San Pedro congressman who fought for the funds to build it. The Los Angeles River Freeway was renamed the Long Beach Freeway. Part of the Ventura Freeway was originally called the Riverside Freeway because it followed the course of the Los Angeles River, but this was confused with the city of Riverside and had to be revised.

By 1970 most of the planned freeway construction in the Los Angeles Basin was completed—including the Vincent Thomas Bridge Freeway, which was finished that year. Recent exceptions are the Century Freeway, begun in the 1980s and completed in 1993, and a project to double-deck the Harbor Freeway and add lanes to the Ventura Freeway, launched in the 1990s. The heaviest traffic is borne by the Santa Monica, San Diego, Harbor, Hollywood, Santa Ana, and Ventura Freeways—each with a daily traffic count of over 200,000 cars in 1979, and rising.

Five interchanges carry in excess of 500,000 vehicles each day. The busiest is the Santa Monica–Golden State–Pomona–Hollywood interchange in East Los Angeles, with 547,500 cars and trucks, followed by the Santa Monica–San Diego interchange, in West Los Angeles; the Santa Monica–Harbor, in central Los Angeles; the Century–San Diego, near the airport; and the original four-level downtown stack. The latter cost $5.5 million to build (compared to $134 million for the Century–San Diego)—and took the life of one construction worker. The symmetrical curving lines of the downtown freeway "stack" immediately became the city's most familiar symbolic image, akin to the Empire State Building in New York City.

Freeways can handle 4 to 5 million cars, but increasing slowdowns and stoppages in the 1980s sparked renewed interest in rapid transit. Ironically, studies indicate that Angelenos today spend as much time behind the wheel and have as many accidents as 20 years ago, even with a lower speed limit of 55 miles per hour. (In December 1995, the speed limit of some stretches of specified freeways was raised to 65 miles per hour, while others remained at 55. Trucks and trailers were held to the 55 limit.)

The California Department of Transportation (Caltrans), which is charged with ensuring a balanced mass transportation system involving highways, airports, and maritime and rail facilities, is responsible for the building and maintenance of the freeways. In the 1990s, Caltrans continued to make major improvements in the Los Angeles freeway system, erecting sound walls to muffle the roar of traffic in densely populated areas, continuing work on an 8.1-mile upper deck of the Harbor Freeway, adding new lanes to the Ventura Freeway, and improving harbor area access roads. In 1993, after 11 years of construction, the agency completed the 17.3-mile Century Freeway (I-105), connecting the cities of Norwalk and El Segundo. At a cost of $2.2 billion, the Century was Los Angeles's most expensive new highway, and possibly the last one to be built. Following the 1989 Loma Prieta earthquake in Northern California and the 1987 Whittier Narrows earthquake, Caltrans also undertook an extensive program to retrofit as many as 456 Los Angeles freeway support columns. However, a Santa Monica Freeway column collapsed in the Northridge quake of 1994 before it could be strengthened, causing a months-long traffic tie-up, the worst in the auto age. Reconstruction took place swiftly.

While public acceptance of freeways has been

An East Los Angeles freeway interchange. Courtesy Caltrans Photos.

high, resistance does flare up and occasionally blocks the road builders. Older maps still show the paths of freeways planned but never built when public pressure rose to the boiling point: the Pacific Coast Freeway, a projected shoreline causeway; the Laurel Canyon Freeway, planned to penetrate the Hollywood Hills; and the Beverly Hills Freeway. The most persistent case of resistance to a freeway has been in South Pasadena, where for several decades residents have fought the completion of the Long Beach Freeway, arguing that it would sever an older residential community and lead to the destruction of many historic homes and neighborhoods.

FREEWAY SOUND WALLS, masonry structures that reduce traffic noise in homes adjacent to freeways. First built in 1969, they have proven very successful and popular. Costing $1.2 million per mile, by 1992 the barriers lined 112 miles of freeway in the county. Householders who can prove that they experience 67 decibels of freeway noise are entitled to a place on the Caltrans waiting list, which is 10 years long.

FRELENG, ISADORE ("FRIZ") (1906–1995), film animator. Freleng was employed by Walt Disney for two years before moving to Warner Brothers in 1930, where he cofounded their animation

section and where he worked for much of his career. He created Warner's first Looney Tunes cartoon, *Sinkin' in the Bathtub,* in 1930, and helped develop such favorites as Bugs Bunny, Tweety and Sylvester, and Daffy Duck. In 1935 he introduced Porky Pig in *I Haven't Got a Hat.* As director of animation at Warner Brothers he synchronized music with the visual action in the Merry Melodies cartoons. Freleng won four Academy Awards as well as a special Oscar for creating the character of the Pink Panther. He received many awards, national and international, including one from the British Film Institute.

FRÉMONT, JOHN CHARLES (1813–1890), adventurer, army officer, U.S. senator from California, and U.S. presidential candidate in 1856. He appeared briefly in Los Angeles during the Mexican War when Commodore Robert F. Stockton appointed him lieutenant colonel and ordered him to march south from Monterey with 400 American riflemen (participants in the Bear Flag Rebellion) to clear rebel Mexican forces from Los Angeles. Actually, this feat was accomplished from the south by a force led by a marine, Lt. Archibald Gillespie, on 10 January 1847. One day later the tardy Frémont entered the San Fernando Valley. He accepted the capitulation of Mexican general Andrés Pico on 13 January at a brush hut in Cahuenga

Pass (now a state historic site) and entered the *pueblo*, taking up residence briefly in the Avila Adobe on the Plaza. Later he revisited Los Angeles with his wife, Jesse Benton Frémont.

FRENCH settlers in Los Angeles have tended to keep a low profile and to shed their separate identity. The first Frenchmen in the area were wine growers: Louis Bouchette, who in 1830 established himself on what is today Macy Street, and Jean Louis Vignes, who settled on what is now Vignes Street a year later. On a 2-acre plot near the Plaza the community established French Hospital in 1868. The outbreak of the Franco-Prussian War (1870–1871) brought prosperous merchants to town. By 1883 the number of French settlers warranted the publication of a French-language newspaper, *Le Progrès.* The romantic painter Paul de Longpre was a celebrated local figure in Hollywood around the turn of the century. The French community, which has included many restaurateurs and merchants, today numbers around 45,000.

FRIARS CLUB, prominent private show business club in Beverly Hills. It was founded when the New York Friars Club, led by Milton Berle, granted a franchise. Its first officers were George Jessel, Bing Crosby, Robert Taylor, Bob Hope, and Jimmy Durante. Berle became the club's leading light when he moved to California. He was succeeded as head (abbot) by Steve Allen, in 1992.

Friars Club founder Milton Berle with actor Burt Reynolds. Courtesy the Friars Club.

The Friars Club, which also includes such Angelenos as Gloria Allred and Tommy Lasorda, is famous for its star-studded award dinners and infamous stag roasts. It also offers gymnasium facilities, arranges sporting events, and engages in charitable activities, including dinners for underprivileged children at Thanksgiving and Christmas.

FRIDAY MORNING CLUB, women's association inaugurated in April 1891 by Caroline Severance and her associates. Its 200 members campaigned for better kindergartens, helped to establish training for teachers, increased involvement of women in educational programs, improved treatment of juvenile offenders, and better housing for working women. They elected the first woman to the board of education. Their method of raising funds by holding flower festivals soon became a popular community activity in its own right.

FRIENDS OF THE RIVER, environmental group founded in the 1980s by Lewis MacAdams and others to restore the Los Angeles River. They urged the development of areas along the stretch from the Sepulveda Basin to Long Beach that would revive the riverine ecology and allow for fishing, swimming, picnicking, and strolling among alder and sycamore trees and along grassy paths.

FRIENDS OF WESTWOOD, slow-growth watchdog group formed in 1984 by local residents Sandy Brown, Jackie Freedman, Laura Lake, and a coalition of local homeowners. They monitor government meetings and helped institute a city ordinance requiring all major new real estate developments to submit environmental-impact reports. They have been responsible for the creation of a Westwood Village Specific Plan.

FULLER THEOLOGICAL SEMINARY, in Pasadena, the largest nondenominational evangelical school of religion in the world. Founded in 1947, it teaches the Scriptures as "the utterly reliable and authoritative Word of God." The curriculum focuses on theology, the arts, economics, and social justice. Half of its 3,700 students represent Pentecostal or charismatic denominations in mainstream churches worldwide. The founder, Charles E. Fuller (1887–1969), was a pioneer radio evangelist who broadcast his weekly "Old-Fashioned Revival Hour" from Long Beach Municipal Auditorium, beginning in the 1930s and continuing into the post–World War II era. He is credited with helping to restore the declining fortunes of revivalism in America. The seminary's current head is Dr. Richard J. Mouw, a member of the Christian Reformed Church.

FURLONG TRACT, African American neighborhood established in 1905. James Furlong, an Irish farmer, owned acreage between 50th and 55th Streets, and Long Beach Avenue and Alameda. He subdivided this land and sold lots to black families, who were restricted to limited areas by racial laws. The working-class district had decent transportation and soon became a cohesive neighborhood of small, neat homes, served by small businesses, three churches, and a school. The 51st Street School, built in 1910, was Los Angeles's first all-black school. Bessie Bruington, the school's first African American teacher, became its principal in 1919. A fire destroyed the school in 1922, and it was rebuilt as the Holmes Avenue School. The 1933 Long Beach earthquake damaged many homes in the Furlong Tract, and families began moving out; thereafter the neighborhood slid into decline. The buildings were all torn down in the 1940s and replaced by a low-income housing project, Pueblo del Rio.

FURNITURE INDUSTRY AND TRADE employed 47,000 people in the county in 1983, mostly in small factories with fewer than 500 workers. The industry manufactures many types of furniture, for office, kitchen, living room, dining room, bedroom, and terrace. The wholesale trade that caters to retail stores is centered at the Los Angeles Mart, at Broadway and Washington.

G

GABLE, CLARK (1901–1960), movie superstar. Named "King of Hollywood" in a 1938 poll conducted by Ed Sullivan, he remained "the King" to his death. Born in Cadiz, Ohio, Gable was the son of an itinerant oilfield worker. In Hollywood, he was rejected by Warner Brothers after Jack Warner, seeing him in a screen test, declared that his ears were too big for a movie star. So he signed on with MGM. In 1934 he won an Oscar for *It Happened One Night* (his personal favorite film), was earning $3,500 weekly, and was one of Hollywood's top ten film stars. He was also nominated for best actor for *Mutiny on the Bounty* (1935), and for his role as Rhett Butler in *Gone with the Wind* (1939). The death of his wife, Carole Lombard, in a plane crash while on a World War II bond-selling tour in 1942 ended one of Hollywood's most famous marriages. Gable, though overage, enlisted; he became an aerial gunner and emerged from the war a major. He

Clark Gable and wife, Carole Lombard. *Los Angeles Examiner,* Hearst Collection, Dept. of Special Collections, USC.

died of a heart attack shortly after completing *The Misfits* (1960), also Marilyn Monroe's last picture.

GABRIELEÑO INDIANS. *See* Native Americans; Tongva Indians; Yangna

GALANTER, RUTH (1941?–), New York–born councilwoman representing the 6th District, which covers Baldwin Hills, Crenshaw, Del Rey, Mar Vista, Playa del Rey, Venice, and Westchester. Galanter has a degree in urban planning and has

---

A great place to live if you're an orange.   —Fred Allen, comedian

---

lived in Los Angeles since 1970. As a member of the Coastal Commission in 1977 she worked hard to preserve wetlands and the Santa Monica Mountains. In 1985 she survived a brutal stabbing by a neighbor. Galanter was elected to the council in 1987, ousting an 18-year incumbent, and was re-elected in 1995. She has a special interest in fighting crime and improving public safety, boosting economic development, preserving and restoring the environment, and improving housing and human services.

GAMBLE HOUSE, beautiful home on Westmoreland Place, Pasadena, designed by architects Charles and Henry Greene. It was built in 1908 as a private residence for an heir of the Procter and Gamble fortune. An example of a California bungalow in the Craftsman style, it features handcrafted wooden interiors and furniture, and tile and brick exterior accents. The house and grounds

Gamble House, east elevation, Greene & Greene, 1908. Photo by Tavo Olmos.

now belong to the city of Pasadena and are maintained as a museum by the USC Department of Architecture.

GAMBLING has had a seesaw career in the county. It was openly practiced in pre-Yankee days by Gabrieleño Indians and Mexicans, outlawed in the American period, illegally practiced from the 1920s to the 1940s, and is today legally permitted in specified casinos and at racetracks. During the 1920s and 1930s, Chinatown gamblers paid for police protection to operate illegal games of keno, pan, mah-jongg, and *pai gow,* with payoffs as high as $400,000 passing into the hands of officials.

People who wanted to gamble could easily indulge in roulette, craps, blackjack, and slots. If the gambling was not in speakeasies, it might be on floating casinos—ships anchored in coastal waters from Long Beach to Santa Monica. The fleet included the *Johanna Smith, Monte Carlo Monfalcone, Rex,* and *City of Panama* (later, *City of Hollywood*). Federal statutes controlled only crooked gambling, not the gambling itself. (Raymond Chandler's detective Philip Marlowe visits such a ship in the 1940 mystery novel *Farewell, My Lovely.*)

In the 1930s mobster Tony Cornero ran a fleet of gambling ships, refurbishing the *Rex* with expensive appointments costing $250,000. Expert chefs onboard served fine food to as many as 1,000 guests daily. Wealthy gamblers, including Hollywood celebrities, wagered on bingo, roulette, and dice. On a given day passengers might bet as much as $400,000, of which the house kept a hefty portion. Reformers railed against the gambling, and District Attorney Buron Fitts prosecuted the operators, but the courts rejected the feeble argument that the ships, anchored close offshore, were operating in state waters and so should be closed down under state antigambling laws. The state attorney general, Earl Warren, took a different tack, arguing that the floating casinos constituted a public nuisance. In 1939 his lawmen simply boarded the boats and tossed the gambling equipment overboard.

Today California operates a state lottery, and sustains a local option for certain types of gambling. Gardena, Bell, Bell Gardens, City of Commerce, and Huntington Park have poker casinos where gamblers play seven-card stud, lo-ball, pan, *pai gow* poker, and super-pan nine. The Bicycle Club in Bell Gardens is the largest gaming establishment in the county, with $82 million in revenues in 1991.

GANGS. Before World War II gangs were usually just groups of rambunctious but harmless city youths, mostly male. In recent decades they have turned lethal. Since the late 1960s gangs have been associated with drugs, guns, turf wars, drive-by shootings, and revenge killings. Police estimate that some 3,500 lives have been lost in the last 10 years in gang-related violence. In 1985 there were an estimated 400 gangs and 45,000 gang members operated in the county; by 1991 those numbers had risen to 950 and 100,000, respectively. Whatever the figures, the totality of confrontations and deaths, mainly involving young people, is alarming. In 1990 law enforcement agencies tallied 650 gang-related homicides, up from 554 a year earlier.

While the majority of gangs are Latino or African American, they are also made up of Asians, Pacific Islanders, and Anglos. The two main African American gangs are the "Crips" and the "Bloods" (also called "Pirus," after Piru Street in Compton). Gangs are turf-oriented by neighborhood or housing project, and their graffiti serve to mark the extent of their turf. Most gangs are subdivided into cliques and sets, and they are self-segregated. Gang members recognize one another by the color or style of their jackets, caps, bandannas, or sweatbands (the Crips, for example, wear blue; the Bloods wear red), as well as by hand gestures.

While a hard-core leadership is in charge, the gang allows for associates and peripheral members. The role of gangs as surrogate family gives many members a sense of belonging.

The Los Angeles County Sheriff's Department allocates some $10 million yearly to combat gangs. Their main program, Operation Safe Streets, encourages reporting and evaluation of gang activity. The program is in operation in East Los Angeles, Lennox, Lynwood, Pico Rivera, Carson, Firestone,

---

During the Depression . . . even the names of the theaters—Palace, Majestic—conjured up a fantasy. When a person went to the movies in those days it was like being king for a day.　　　　—Joe Spencer,
long-time Los Angeles resident

City of Industry, Lakewood, Norwalk, and Walnut. In 1992 it employed some 50 uniformed personnel working in teams and maintained a file of 100,000 names. Following the 1992 riots the county supervisors pledged $2.9 million and the city pledged $2.5 million to Hope in Youth, a coalition of religious organizations made up of 160 family teams whose task it is to help 10,000 families a year cope with the issue of gangs.

Gang violence reflects, in part, the instability of neighborhoods rife with a sense of hopelessness due to unemployment, broken homes, alcoholism, and drug addiction and trafficking, where cocaine and other drugs can produce earnings of $200 to $300 a day. It is aggravated by the increasing availability of guns.

New assessments of gang activity were made after the 1992 riots. In that year, the district attorney blamed gangs for the dramatic upsurge in murder since 1984. Yet an FBI investigation determined that although gang members had participated in the mass disturbance, there was no proof of organized gang plots. In the riots' aftermath, the Crips and Bloods signed a formal truce, agreeing to work together to bring peace to the streets, and they began to be described as a "new political force in Los Angeles." Some communities started enforcing curfews and barring gang members from public parks. The sense of community outrage against

gang activity continues throughout all parts of the city of Los Angeles and Los Angeles County.

GARBAGE COLLECTION originated in 1902 when the city used wagons to collect and burn food waste. Around 1915 the city began selling the garbage for chicken and hog feed and for fertilizer, instead of burning it. In the 1920s Los Angeles shipped huge quantities of garbage by rail to Fontana Farms in San Bernardino County. Fontana Farms was the largest hog-feeding operation in the world, with 40,000 to 60,000 porkers being fattened at any given time. Since the pork ended up as food in Los Angeles and the waste was used as fertilizer, the recycling system was ecologically sound. Fontana Farms closed in 1950, along with similar farms in Buena Park, Palmdale, and Saugus, defeated by concerns about trichinosis, the popularity of the in-sink disposal unit, and the stench they produced. While the new conditions eliminated the long-distance movement of garbage, it also created new burdens for the sewage system and destroyed the efficient and environmentally sound process of recycling organic materials through hogs.

Householders then used small cement incinerators to burn papers and other trash in their backyards, until these omnipresent devices were banned in the 1950s in an effort to curb air pollution. More recently, giant high-tech commercial incinerators have been proposed for low-income residential and industrial parts of the city. Neighborhood coalitions opposed them, however, and they have been rejected by the voters. Despite partial recycling of household garbage, public dumps located in mountain and desert sites continue to fill quickly.

GARCETTI, GIL (1942–), Los Angeles County district attorney. Both his parents grew up in Boyle Heights, though his father was born in Mexico, and Garcetti himself was born and raised in South Central Los Angeles. After graduating from USC with a bachelor's degree, Garcetti attended UCLA Law School. He joined the district attorney's office in 1968, becoming chief deputy D.A. in 1984. It was his responsibility to supervise the day-to-day management of more than 900 prosecutors and 1,000 support staff. He was elected county district attorney, a four-year term, in 1992 and 1996. The department's budget is in excess of $130 million.

GARCIA, DANIEL P. (1947–), East Los Angeles–born attorney. After graduating from Loyola

University and USC Graduate School of Business, he took a law degree at UCLA. A trusted adviser to Mayor Tom Bradley, he served on the planning commission from 1976 to 1988 and had a brief stint on the police commission in 1990–1991, in the course of which he developed a keen understanding of city hall politics and bureaucracy. He is a vice president at Warner Brothers for real estate development and public relations and has been president of the Los Angeles Area Chamber of Commerce.

GARDENA, independent city 14 miles west of downtown Los Angeles. It was established when the cities of Strawberry Park, Moneta, and Western City merged in the 1930s. Bones and artifacts near the meandering stream Laguna de los Domínguez attest to Indians having used the area for hunting and fishing. The town originated in the 1880s with a general store at Figueroa and 161st Streets. By 1906 the center of commerce had moved to Vermont Avenue and Gardena Boulevard, a junction of the Pacific Electric railway on the lines running from Redondo Beach and San Pedro. Incorporation came in 1930.

Gardena has long been the major site of Japanese American settlement in Southern California. Historically the community was rooted economically in agriculture, nurseries, and gardening. In recent decades many major industrial firms from Japan have located in Gardena.

Since the late 1940s the town has allowed burlesque shows and poker parlors to operate legally. The two clubs, the Normandie and the Eldorado Card Casino, have Las Vegas–style entertainment and reportedly produced $4.9 million in tax revenues in 1991.

In 1981 the city conducted an extensive historical survey in which it listed scores of homes, schools, stores, and restaurants going back as far as the turn of the century. The population in 1990 was 49,800.

GARDEN OF ALLAH, Hollywood hotel and watering place on Sunset Boulevard. It was built in 1921 by actress Alla Nazimova, who maintained financial control until the depression. Its opening was marked by a lavish party. In the 1930s, F. Scott Fitzgerald, Robert Benchley, Dorothy Parker, and other literary notables drank, partied, and lived there while they worked in Hollywood writing film scripts. Other frequent visitors were Somer-set Maugham, Leopold Stokowski, Clara Bow, Dashiell Hammett, and S. J. Perelman. It is where Ernest Hemingway is reputed to have first met Gary Cooper. By the 1940s the Garden of Allah had sustained so many incidents of robbery, murder, drunkenness, and suicide that it closed under a cloud in 1953, and was replaced by a mini-mall.

GARDENS, PUBLIC, have flourished in Southern California since the 19th century. The Spanish and Mexican colonists planted flowers, but few trees, near their adobes and mission buildings. Enchanted newcomers found that almost every plant and flower thrived in the mild climate and fertile soil. Colorful exotic plants imported from elsewhere—including coral trees, palms, bougainvilleas, poppies, impatiens, and bird of paradise—have become symbolic of the area. Flowers bloom in all seasons, and plant nurseries are a major business in a metropolis of private homes. Landscape

---

Music, dancing, singing, slaughtering cattle, or gambling are the usual pastimes of the inhabitants.   —John Ford, after a visit to Los Angeles in 1850

---

architects have long been in great demand, designing both public and private gardens that enhance adjoining buildings. Some public gardens were once part of vast private estates. Both Henry E. Huntington and E. J. "Lucky" Baldwin employed landscape architects who planned magnificent gardens, and hired large crews to maintain them. (Baldwin's estate is now the Los Angeles State and County Arboretum, in Arcadia.) The Virginia Robinson Gardens in Beverly Hills include an extraordinary 2-acre plot devoted to palms and ferns. The Descanso Gardens, a former private estate in La Cañada Flintridge, features 100,000 camellias in a 30-acre oak forest. Other flowering enclaves, such as UCLA's Mildred Mathias Botanical Garden and Exposition Park's Rose Garden, were conceived and always functioned as public places.

GARLAND, WILLIAM MAY (1866–1948), Los Angeles booster and attorney. A native of Maine, Garland came to California in 1890 and became a successful real estate man and president of the California Chamber of Commerce. He helped bring the Olympic Games to Los Angeles in 1932.

GARMENT INDUSTRY. Since the 1940s Los Angeles has been second only to New York City in production, volume, and profits in the manufacture of clothing. In 1990 the sector was second only to aircraft equipment as the largest manufacturing employer in the county. Manufacturing operations exist in many areas, including Chinatown, City of Commerce, Montebello, Fullerton, and Van Nuys. The industry has traditionally relied on poorly paid immigrant workers to do piecework, and much of today's labor force consists largely of Latina and Asian immigrant women, legal and illegal, often working at below minimum wage in small, nonunion factories, substandard garages and warehouses, or their homes, as well as in modern factories.

The main garment manufacturing center is the 20-square-block area between 7th and 10th Streets and Broadway and San Pedro in downtown Los Angeles. It contains the city's largest concentration of cutters, pressers, and sewing machine operators, who make the garments; buyers, who place the orders; "factors," who deal with the banks; accountants and bookkeepers, who track the money flow; and truckers, who carry off the goods. Anything necessary to the trade—from a dozen zippers to a thousand pearl buttons to a million dollars—is available in the immediate vicinity. California Mart, the world's largest apparel mart, occupies 3 million square feet.

As of 1991 the biggest apparel-marketing firms in Los Angeles County, with annual sales of over $100 million, were L.A. Gear, Cal-Togs/Breton, Jonnathan Martin, E-Z Sportswear, Catalina Cole, and Chorus Lines. The main stock-in-trade is sportswear and swimwear, but every category of attire is represented.

Although New York's 7th Avenue remains the center of the nation's garment trade, a westward tilt continues. Los Angeles began monopolizing the casual clothing industry in the 1920s with the emergence of the film industry. By the 1940s movie fashion designers such as Adrian and Edith Head were influencing styles nationwide. Los Angeles earned a reputation for popularizing outrageous designs, as when Rudi Gernreich designed topless bathing suits in the 1960s. Today, most designs are stylishly mainline. San Francisco remains the home of the largest California clothing manufacturer, Levi Strauss.

In 1995 almost 120,000 people in Southern California had jobs in more than 4,000 establishments that were in some way related to the garment trade. The industry generated $15 billion in the regional economy, and average annual retail sales rose to $63 billion, exceeding those of New York City.

GATES, DARYL F. (1926–), Los Angeles police chief from 1978 to 1992. He joined the force in 1949 and became Chief William Parker's protégé. After climbing rapidly through the ranks, becoming captain in 1963 and assistant chief in 1969, Gates succeeded Ed Davis as chief in 1978. His antidrug campaign, as well as efficient policing during the 1984 Olympics and visits by several presidents and a pope, brought him much praise. Nevertheless, his career was tumultuous. During his 14-year tenure he was accused of political spying, condoning excessive use of force, and making offensive remarks

---

I had in mind to do something big, and I did.   —Simon Rodia, builder of the Watts Towers, 1950s

---

about Jews, African Americans, Latinos, women, and homosexuals. Although severe criticism was leveled at him when officers shot a black woman named Eulia Love, it was the police beating of Rodney G. King, coupled with criticism of department strategy following the 1992 rioting, that led to his resignation as police chief. In the wake of the critical Christopher Commission Report in 1991 and the subsidence of the riots, Gates was pressured into retiring over the opposition of citizen groups that had organized to support him. His autobiography, *The Chief* (1992), is an account of his stormy years as "top cop," in which he advances the view that most of the city's troubles arose when politicians interfered with the mission of "the thin blue line."

GATEWAY INTERMODAL TRANSIT CENTER, hub of the region's transportation network, located near Union Station at Vignes and Cesar Chavez Streets. The massive undertaking is the work of the Catelus Development Corporation, the principal landowner around Union Station, in conjunction with builders and architects devoted to downtown development, including the developer Nick Patsaouris. Being built in phased increments, the first of which opened in 1995, the center is expected to serve an estimated 100,000 daily commuters using Amtrak, the Metro Red Line subway, the Metrolink system, and a trolley to Pasadena. One of the center's initial components is the East Portal, a glass-domed structure connecting the underground trains to Union Station. A second is the Gateway Tower, the 26-story headquarters of the Metropolitan Transit Authority. Two additional elements of the center will be a sloping walkway on the banks of the Los Angeles River, known as the Arroyo, and a bus plaza. The development is embellished with murals, fountains, sculptures, ornamental fences, benches, and spaces for cultural events. Future plans call for the creation of a new headquarters building for the Metropolitan Water District, a major sports arena, and commercial and residential towers.

GAY AND LESBIAN MOVEMENT in the United States was born in West Hollywood, Hollywood, and Silver Lake in the late 1940s. Originating as a response to police repression and job discrimination, it remained an underground movement in the 1950s, but expanded in the 1960s and then spread to New York and San Francisco. The first gay organization was the Mattachine Society, a Marxist group founded between 1949 and 1951 by Harry Hay, "the father of gay liberation in America," and fashion designer Rudi Gernreich. Hay, who regarded homosexuals as an "oppressed cultural minority," believed they should fight for civil rights but resist assimilation. A tiny group of lesbians known as the Sisters of Bilitis emerged shortly afterward, as did the magazine *One,* published by W. Dorr Legg.

Around the time of the Stonewall Inn battle in Greenwich Village, New York, in 1969, Morris Kight, an anti–Vietnam War activist, founded the Southern California Gay Liberation Front in Los Angeles, which absorbed earlier organizations such as Hay's. As late as 1960, gays and lesbians still suffered routine homophobic violence, exploitation, and discrimination. "Gay bashing" in bars and other public places was common. The AIDS epidemic, which emerged in the late 1970s, added new urgency to the movement, as activists sought medical care and a broad range of civil rights.

Despite continuing homophobia, public policy gradually changed. Although gay rights bills were vetoed by Governors Deukmejian and Wilson, the state attorney general, John Van de Kamp, stated that gays could not be fired from their jobs for engaging in gay rights activities. Since 1979 Los Angeles has had a gay rights ordinance protecting them from job bias. While it has never been fully adjudicated, City Attorney James K. Hahn declared that Los Angeles would enforce the law strictly. The Gay and Lesbian Pride Celebration, an annual parade begun in 1970, currently brings tens of thousands of participants and observers to West Hollywood and Hollywood.

The *Advocate,* a magazine with a circulation of 150,000, is a major voice for the gay community. Three leading activist organizations are the Gay and Lesbian Alliance Against Defamation (GLAAD), ACT UP/L.A., and Queer Nation. After much controversy, in 1991 the Los Angeles Police Department allowed uniformed gay police to recruit new

West Hollywood Gay and Lesbian Parade, 1995. Courtesy West Hollywood Convention & Visitors Bureau.

officers into the force. Although local acceptance of gays has increased, numerous gay-bashing incidents continue to be reported to the Gay and Lesbian Community Services Center.

GAY'S LION FARM, private animal compound near El Monte early in the 20th century. It bred, raised, and trained hundreds of lions for motion pictures, zoos, circuses, and amusement parks.

GEHRY, FRANK O. (1929–), Venice-based architect. Born in Toronto, Gehry moved to Los Angeles, graduated from USC, and took a job at Victor Gruen Associates (which was punctuated by a stint in the U.S. Army). He found himself drawn to urban design, but a stay in Europe rekindled his interest in architecture. In the 1970s and 1980s he developed personal and professional relationships with such artists as Ed Moses, Jasper Johns, Robert Rauschenberg, Billy Al Bengston, and Andy Warhol. More than most architects, Gehry approaches a building as a sculptural object. Labeled a postmodernist, he prefers the metaphor of a "cocktail party" to describe his radical eclectic—"chaotically ordered"—design style, but would like to be thought of as humanistic and optimistic in his objectives. Partly as an offshoot of his childhood wanderings in his grandparents' hardware store, he often uses cheap, commonplace, and unfinished building materials—wire-mesh screens, particle board, corrugated plastic sheeting—that

Frank Gehry. Photo by Eric Sander, courtesy Frank O. Gehry & Associates.

give the appearance of "buildings under construction." Local examples of his work include the Santa Monica Place shopping mall (1981), the Temporary Contemporary art museum (1983), Loyola Law School (1984), and the California Aerospace Museum (1984). The Walt Disney Concert Hall, now under construction at the Music Center, is also his design. His awards for excellence include the prestigious Pritzker Prize, which he won in 1989.

GENE AUTRY WESTERN HERITAGE MUSEUM. *See* Autry Museum of Western Heritage

GERMAN-AMERICAN BUND, Nazi organization, also known as the Friends of New Germany, active in Los Angeles from 1933 to 1941. Arriving from Chicago, its founders infiltrated and eventually dominated the leading local German American community organizations. The Bund's headquarters on 15th Street near Alvarado served as a West Coast distribution point for newly arrived German propaganda literature and as a rendezvous for German Nazi officials sojourning in this country. While most members were German immigrants, some were native born of German descent, and a few, such as Henry Allen of Pasadena, had no German background at all. Led by the West Coast Führer Max Schwinn, the Bund took its orders from Berlin but also maintained active contact with native American fascist groups, such as William Dudley Pelley's Silver Shirts. It promulgated virulent racist, anti-Semitic, and pro-Hitler ideas, while attempting to polish the image of Adolf Hitler's regime. A typical ploy was to drop leaflets from tall buildings onto the city streets. One such "bombing," in Hollywood in 1936, attacked the film industry for being Jewish-dominated. Around 1939, federal and state officials began prosecuting the leading Los Angeles Bundists for violating enemy-agent laws; most of the accused fled the country before the U.S. declaration of war with Germany in 1941.

GERMANS, who in 1990 numbered some 30,000 in Los Angeles, were first represented locally in the person of "Juan Domingo," a German seaman rescued from a wrecked ship in San Pedro Harbor who was listed in the 1836 census. He became a prominent landowner in San Pedro. In the 1850s in the town of Los Angeles proper, other pioneer Germans, such as Charles W. Flugge, John Brehn, and Jacob Kuhrts, listed themselves as bakers, pharmacists, brewers, barbers, boot makers, and carriage builders. In the coming years the community established its own benevolent society, German language school, athletic club (the Turnverein Society), and cultural society (Teutonia-Concordia), as well as an offshoot agricultural colony at Anaheim (German for "home on the Ana [River]"), in Orange County. By 1876 some 2,000 Germans lived in Los Angeles County.

Although German immigration declined precipitously during World War I, by 1930 the Census listed over 120,000 Germans in the county. In the 1930s, some 1,000 exiles from Hitler's Germany found their way to Hollywood, including distinguished musicians, playwrights, novelists, painters, and filmmakers. Novelist Thomas Mann wrote *Dr. Faustus* while in Los Angeles, playwright Bertolt Brecht wrote *The Life of Galileo* (which premiered at the Coronet Theater in 1947), Franz Werfel

---

I am a foresighted man. I believe that Los Angeles is destined to become the most important city in the country, if not in the world. It can extend in any direction, as far as you like; its front door opens on the Pacific, the ocean of the future.

—Henry E. Huntington, railroad magnate

---

wrote *Jacobowsky and the Colonel,* and Alfred Döblin wrote *November 1918.* Max Reinhardt's Hollywood Bowl production of *A Midsummer Night's Dream* was a milestone in Shakespearean production. Fritz Lang continued his career in the film industry, and the Austrian Billy Wilder began to make his name as a director. Other notable German émigrés included philosophers Theodor Adorno, Max Horkheimer, and Hannah Arendt; writer Lion Feuchtwanger; conductors Bruno Walter and Otto Klemperer; and composer Arnold Schoenberg. While in Los Angeles Mann declared that "for the duration of the present European dark age, the center of Western culture will shift to America."

GERNREICH, RUDI (1922–1985), Vienna-born clothing designer who created the topless bathing suit in 1964, the unisex look, and other daring fashions. He arrived in Los Angeles in the 1930s and studied at City College and Art Center. Gernreich, who helped focus international attention on the Los Angeles fashion industry, was also active in the early gay rights movement.

GETTY, J. PAUL (1892–1976), oil magnate and one of the world's richest men. He founded a notable art collection now housed in the J. Paul Getty Museum in Malibu. Born in Minneapolis, he lived in California, attended UC Berkeley, UCLA, and Oxford, and eventually settled in England. A controversial man who tended to be reclusive, he derived his fortune from the Getty Oil Company. The family fortune today is said to be about $3 billion.

GETTY CENTER, 110-acre cultural complex due to open in 1997. The $733 million center is the design of New York architect, Richard Meier. Set on a hill in Sepulveda Pass in Brentwood, the various buildings will include a museum, auditorium, art history and humanities center, restaurant, and art history information program. The museum, a series of buildings surrounding a garden, will contain all of the Getty collections except the classical Greek and Roman treasures, which will remain in the Malibu Getty Museum. The grounds are planned to feature gardens, fountains, and spectacular views. The center will be the new home of the J. Paul Getty Trust, the world's richest private art institution, with an endowment of $4.1 billion. Required by law to spend 4.1 percent of its assets every year, the trust has developed numerous new programs, which will be housed at the center, and awards fellowships to scholars.

GETTY HOUSE, official residence of the mayor of Los Angeles. The 14-room, three-story French Colonial mansion in the Windsor Square area of Hancock Park was privately built in 1921 for $83,000. It has six bedrooms, children's rooms, a library, and a game room. The 1-acre estate contains gardens, a tennis court, and a swimming pool. It was once leased to the movie-star couple Dolores Costello and John Barrymore. The Getty Oil Company purchased the residence in 1957 and leased it to acting coach Lee Strasberg, but in the 1970s donated it to the city. Mayor Tom Bradley and his family lived in Getty House for 16 years, although Mayor Richard Riordan chose to live elsewhere.

GETTY MUSEUM, J. PAUL. *See* J. Paul Getty Museum

GIBSON, MARY SIMONS (1855–1930), reform-minded clubwoman, cofounder of the Los Angeles Woman's Club and Friday Morning Club. Together with her colleagues, she advocated birth control, legal reform in dealing with prostitution, and special education for immigrants. A strong believer in the assimilation of immigrants, she was appointed by Gov. Hiram Johnson to the state immigration and housing commission in 1913.

GIESLER, JERRY (1886–1962), Beverly Hills criminal lawyer. He came from Iowa to Hollywood in 1910; hearing about Clarence Darrow's defense of the McNamara brothers, he decided on a legal career. He graduated from the USC Law School and became an associate of the celebrated trial lawyer Earl Rogers. In 1929 he was catapulted into the limelight when he obtained an acquittal for the theater chain magnate Alexander Pantages, indicted for the statutory rape of a 17-year-old showgirl. This launched Giesler's career as attorney to the rich and famous. He subsequently won acquittals for movie actor Errol Flynn, charged with the rape of two actresses in 1942–1943; mobster Benjamin "Bugsy" Siegel, cited for complicity in the murder of Harry "Big Greenie" Greenberg; stripteaser Lili St. Cyr, arrested for indecent exposure; and movie star Charlie Chaplin in 1944, accused of violating the Mann Act; and successfully represented Shelley Winters and Zsa Zsa Gabor in divorce proceedings.

GILL, IRVING J. (1870–1936), architect. In the first decades of the century Gill developed his own version of the Mission style as a variation of what was known as European International Modern. His sensitivity to natural surroundings and his interest in bringing nature into the home led him to the Arts and Crafts, or Craftsman, movement, though he used stucco rather than wood as his dominant outer surface. Much of Gill's work has been destroyed, including the seminal Dodge House in West Hollywood, built in 1916. Of the examples that still exist, the largest concentration is in the city of Torrance: the Pacific Electric Railroad Station and Bridge; the Roi Tan, Murray, Colonial, and Brighton Hotels; City Hall; Municipal Auditorium; Torrance High School; and Worker's Single-Family Housing.

GILMAN, CHARLOTTE PERKINS (1860–1935), most widely read and prolific feminist writer of her time. New England bred, related to the prominent Beecher and Stowe families, she married artist Charles W. Stetson in 1884. Falling into a deep depression upon the birth of a daughter in 1885, she left her family and moved to Pasadena to recuperate. After an unsuccessful attempt at marital reconciliation in the East, she returned to Pasadena, resumed a friendship with Caroline Severance, and became part of Charles

The Dodge House, West Hollywood, designed by Irving Gill in 1916. Photo ca. 1950 by Julius Shulman, Hon. AIA.

Fletcher Lummis's circle. As Gilman honed her skills as a speaker, writer, and poet, she credited Southern California for the gift of good health. After living in different locations and marrying New York lawyer George Houghton Gilman, she returned to Pasadena in 1934, where she was diagnosed with cancer and committed suicide. Ironically, her unhappy end came in the same city where she had first regained her health and developed her feminist philosophy. Gilman's most famous works are *The Yellow Wall Paper* (1891), a fictionalized account of her bout with mental illness; *Women and Economics* (1898); and *Suffrage Songs and Verses* (1911).

GILMORE COMPANY, A. F., family-owned conglomerate business centered in the Fairfax district. It was founded by Arthur Fremont Gilmore (1850–1918), a farmer who took title to the 256-acre Rancho La Brea in 1880. Later, while drilling for water, he struck oil. By 1905 he had abandoned his dairy cows for oil rigs. When his grandson, Earl

---

Los Angeles is seventy-two suburbs in search of a city.   —Dorothy Parker

---

Bell Gilmore (1897–1964), took over in 1921, the company shifted from drilling to distributing oil and gas. It soon became the largest independent oil marketer in the West, with 1,100 stations in five states. The firm was known for innovative marketing: patrons who pumped their own gas at a "gas-a-teria" saved 5 cents per gallon. Radio commercials and billboards featured the company's Red Lion logo and motto: "Give your car a kick in the gas." The firm was bought out by Mobil Oil in 1943.

At Gilmore Stadium, also in the Fairfax district, Earl Gilmore pioneered the sport of midget auto racing—the progenitor of the Indy 500, which explains his place of honor in the Indianapolis 500 Hall of Fame. Gilmore also promoted the Gilmore Economy Runs, forerunner of today's stock-car racing, and he sponsored a car that won the land speed record in 1939 at Bonneville, Utah. The Farmers Market (1934), Pan Pacific Auditorium (1935), Gilmore Drive-In movie theater (1948), and Gilmore Commercial and Savings Bank (1955) were also creations of this versatile firm.

The company is now headquartered in a secluded part of Farmers Market, in a complex of buildings that include Gilmore Adobe, a structure dating from 1852 that originally had two rooms, a flat roof, and dirt floors. It was the birthplace of Earl Gilmore.

GILMORE STADIUM, in the Fairfax area, was called the "workingman's stadium" because of its low admission price. The multipurpose facility opened in May 1934 at a cost of $100,000 and had 18,000 unobstructed-view seats. Although constructed for midget car racing, it also featured rodeos and wrestling matches. The stadium was home to Los Angeles's first pro football team, the Bulldogs, and doubled as a boxing arena for "Golden Boy" Art Aragon. The Hollywood Stars baseball club of the Pacific Coast League began playing at Gilmore in 1939. The club had originated in San Francisco but moved to Los Angeles. Among its owners were Bing Crosby, Barbara Stanwyck, and Cecil B. De Mille. After winning the league pennant in 1949, 1952, and 1953, the Stars moved to Salt Lake City in 1957. Another memorable occasion at Gilmore Stadium was President Truman's 1948 "stiff upper lip" campaign speech. The stadium was eventually sold to CBS and torn down to make way for a television studio complex.

GLAAD. *See* Gay and lesbian movement

GLASSELL PARK, district of Los Angeles south of Glendale, located east of San Fernando Road. It was named for Andrew Glassell, a prominent attorney who cofounded the Los Angeles County Bar Association in 1878; he acquired land in the area when the Verdugo family's Rancho San Rafael was broken up.

GLENDALE, 7 miles north of downtown Los Angeles, is the third largest city in the county. In prehistoric times, the canyons in the area were occupied by Shoshonean peoples. The village of Tuyungna (Tujunga; the name is a Gabrieleño word meaning "mountain range") was a principal Indian site. Another, in the La Cañada area, still existed in the late 19th century.

In 1784, three years after the 1781 formation of the Spanish *pueblo* of Los Angeles, the governor of California granted much of the hilly area north of the *pueblo* to a soldier, José María Verdugo (originally spelled Berdugo). He took title to the 36,403-

Glendale skyline, 1995. Courtesy Glendale Redevelopment Agency.

acre Rancho San Rafael and raised cattle on the fertile and well-watered pasturage until his death in 1831. Verdugo willed his property to his son, Julio, and daughter, Catalina, who maintained joint ownership until 1861, when Julio took the southern portion and Catalina the northern. Julio lived much of the time at an adobe near present-day Verdugo Road and Acacia Avenue; his sister, who had been blind since childhood and never married, lived with him or at an adobe near what is today Bonita Drive in Verdugo Woodlands. The first Yankee landowner was Joseph Lancaster Brent, a lawyer, who in 1860 bought a parcel from the Verdugos at a spot along the river, in future Atwater.

In 1871 the rancho was divided into 31 parcels among 28 persons, including Benjamin Dreyfus, Rafael Sepúlveda, Andrew Glassell, O. W. Childs, Cameron E. Thom, and Prudent Beaudry. The latter two land developers were destined to become mayors of Los Angeles. Following this division, the future Glendale area was populated largely by farmers who raised sheep or planted wheat, corn, beans, and hay.

The foothill town of Glendale, first known as Verdugo and located between the San Fernando and San Gabriel Valleys, came into being in 1876 with the completion of the Southern Pacific Railroad link between Los Angeles and San Francisco. Local residents selected the new name of Glendale at a town meeting in 1884, rejecting Verdugo, San Rafael, Porto Suelo, Riverdale, Etheldean, and Minneapolis. The official city map of Glendale was recorded in January 1887, during the Boom of the Eighties. In its first generation, Glendale's residents were for the most part conservative orchardists, and

the area emerged as a citrus center. Like many new towns, it languished in the depression of the 1890s.

Modern Glendale emerged at the turn of the century when Leslie C. Brand, a financier, bought 1,000 acres in the Verdugo Mountains for intensive development. Brand, the "Father of Glendale," convinced rail magnate Henry E. Huntington to extend his new Pacific Electric Railway line to Glendale from Los Angeles. The new transportation link assured Glendale's future, and a barbecue feast was held to celebrate its completion, on 2 July 1904. A year later the *Glendale News* began publication, two banks were established, and a Masonic lodge was formed. Brand, who instigated city incorporation in 1906 when the population was 1,100, also dedicated the public library. Bond issues in 1907 and 1908 allowed for the formation of a fire department and public high school. In the census of 1910 the population stood at 2,742. By 1911 voters had approved a new City Hall and library, and in 1912 the Glendale Board of Water Commissioners was established. Three years later, a $248,000 bond issue allowed the city to buy out the independent suppliers drawing water from Verdugo Canyon, Verdugo Springs, North Glendale, and Tropico and to form a consolidated utility. In 1918 the town of Glendale absorbed Tropico, its southern neighbor.

Glendale witnessed explosive growth in the early 1920s, a period of strong population increase throughout Southern California. In 1923 a survey showed that the city's population had tripled in the preceding four years. In 1925 building permits brought in over $10 million, a record for the town. With the number of residents exceeding 60,000 by

1925—having increased by 10,000 in the previous year alone—Glendale proclaimed itself the "Fastest-Growing City in America." In 1926, the neighboring community of Casa Verdugo voted to annex to Glendale. The city was the first Southern California community to adopt the manager-council form of government.

Glendale found itself in a water rivalry with Los Angeles. The larger city enjoyed prior claims to the Los Angeles River basin and had an excess of water from the Owens River, while the smaller city's water supply was less well developed. Los Angeles invited Glendale's residents to consolidate, but they refused. Losing litigation to pump water from the basin, Glendale expanded its boundaries into

---

We have always believed in the future, and it has been at the expense of the past.

—Robert Towne, screenwriter

---

the Verdugo Hills to obtain new water sources. It later annexed land on its western flank in the direction of Burbank, and across its eastern boundary in the direction of Pasadena. The city's boundaries eventually reached 30.6 miles, 13 times their original extent. With the advent of World War II, light industry and residences replaced agriculture as Glendale's mainstay, and by the 1970s 300 industrial plants producing foodstuffs, electronics, house trailers, and pharmaceuticals stood along the city's westside rail line.

Glendale, with a substantial residential community, is able to support a community college and symphony orchestra. It is home to Brand Park, Forest Lawn Memorial Park, and the Glendale Galleria, one of the nation's most successful shopping malls. The city's library has gained renown for its special collections. The 20,000 books at Glendale Central Library on cats is the largest such collection in the world. Few of Glendale's 19th-century structures survive, although since 1964 Glendale's historical society and historic landmarks committee have identified and helped preserve numerous buildings and sites. Of the five adobes associated with the Verdugos, only Catalina's, on Bonita Drive, remains intact and open to the public. Casa Adobe de San Rafael (1865), built by Tomás Sánchez on what is today Dorothy Drive, is owned

by the city of Glendale and maintained as a museum. The Doctor's House, a fine Victorian home, has been moved to the community of Brand Park.

In the era of the freeway, downtown Glendale found itself strategically located 9 miles from downtown Los Angeles in a triangle formed by the Glendale Freeway (Route 2), the Ventura Freeway (Route 134), and the Golden State Freeway (Route 5). At the behest of the business community, the Glendale Redevelopment Agency was established in 1972 to revitalize the downtown business district. This area has since gained commercial vitality, becoming a major site for corporate headquarters. The market value of downtown land has risen from $98 million in 1972 to more than $575 million in 1992. The revitalization project has substantially revived Brand Boulevard. In 1990 the city had a population of 180,000.

GLENDALE AIRPORT, region's first transcontinental aviation facility. The 45-acre field, which was built in 1923 and saw use into the 1950s, was built on a former orange grove. In 1929 it acquired a $3 million Mission Revival–style terminal building. The airport's heyday was in the 1930s, when movie stars and other wealthy travelers used it to take the 16-hour flight to New York. Aviators Charles Lindbergh, Amelia Earhart, and Douglas "Wrong Way" Corrigan landed and took off from Glendale, and William Randolph Hearst and Marian Davies used the field when traveling to Hearst Castle. Howard Hughes built and stored his first plane there. Movie scenes of barnstorming and aviation adventure were filmed at the Glendale field. The airport was the takeoff point for humorist Will Rogers and flying companion Wiley Post on their fateful trip to Alaska in which they both perished. During World War II Glendale was the home base for Lockheed's P-38 fighter plane. Afterward, the field had to yield to the larger Burbank and Van Nuys airports and to Los Angeles International Airport. When the developers of the Grand Central Business Center, an industrial park, took over the grounds in 1959, they closed air operations but salvaged the tower.

GLENDORA, independent residential community at the foot of the San Gabriel Mountains, 20 miles northeast of downtown Los Angeles and halfway between downtown and San Bernardino. The land was home to Indians when the Spaniards arrived in Southern California in 1769. During the

Mexican War (1846–1848) this portion of the San Gabriel Valley was part of Ranchos San José and Azusa. In 1844 the Englishman Henry Dalton purchased Rancho Azusa; he raised sheep, cattle, tobacco, fruit trees, and honey bees on the land during the 1840s and 1850s. Homesteaders further cultivated the area in the 1870s, planting grapes, peaches, apricots, and prunes. The town of Glendora was founded in 1886, spurred by the arrival of the Santa Fe Railroad, the Boom of the Eighties, and the formation of a water company. Completion of the interurban Pacific Electric tracks in 1907 created a second land boom. Increasingly the area's economy was based on growing and packing oranges and lemons. Incorporated in 1911 with 700 residents, Glendora was named by its founder, George Whitcomb, a Chicago manufacturer, who combined the word *glen* with his wife's name, Ledora. The town was "dry" and rock-ribbed Republican.

Following World War II most of the large orchards were divided into small residential lots. While the population rose from 2,800 in 1940 to 3,954 in 1950, Glendora still remained one of the sparsest incorporated areas in the county. In 1969, a four-day torrential cloudburst, which in one three-hour period dropped 2 inches of rain, caused $2 million in damage. In 1987 the city planted a 5-acre grove of oranges in homage to the old days. The Glendora Historical Society maintains a museum and has joined other civic groups in identifying and preserving many historic structures. In 1990 the city's population was 47,800.

GOLDBERG, JACKIE (1945–), teacher and city council member representing the 13th District. From 1983 to 1991 she served as a member of the Los Angeles Unified School District Board. Goldberg is the first openly homosexual council member. Educated at UC Berkeley in the tumultuous 1960s and trained as a teacher, she taught government, economics, and English as a second language at Grant High School in the San Fernando Valley. Her council district, which includes parts of Hollywood, is among the more ethnically diverse and politically progressive; it was formerly represented by 1993 mayoral candidate Mike Woo.

GOLDWYN, SAMUEL (1882–1974), movie mogul during Hollywood's Golden Age. Born in Poland as Samuel Goldfish, he migrated to this country in 1906, became a glove manufacturer, and

in 1910 entered the film industry with his brother-in-law, Jesse Lasky. They moved from the East Coast to Los Angeles, and in 1913 Goldfish (he changed his name around 1920), Lasky, and Cecil B. De Mille opened the Feature Play Company. A merger with the Metro Company took place in 1924; then, with Louis B. Mayer, Goldwyn founded Metro-Goldwyn-Mayer (MGM) in a barn at Vine and Selma Streets in Hollywood. Goldwyn left MGM to join the newly formed United Artists, but maintained his independence as a producer, later forming Goldwyn Pictures Corporation. He hired top talent in the industry to work on his films—including such outstanding writers as Lillian Hellman and Robert Sherwood, because he considered good writing to be especially important—and was an undisputed dictator in an industry rife with dictators. Among the scores of Goldwyn films were *Arrowsmith* (1931), *The Adventures of Marco Polo* (1938), and *The Best Years of Our Lives* (1946), winner of seven Oscars. He was noted for mangling the English language, as in his famous "Include me out."

GOLF, sport said to have originated in Scotland in the 15th century. The first courses in California were built on Santa Catalina Island in 1892, in Pasadena and Riverside in 1894, in Santa Monica in 1896, and in Los Angeles in 1897. The Southern California Golf Association, formed in 1899, held its first annual amateur championship competition at the Los Angeles Country Club in 1900. The "greens" consisted of packed sand and soil that was watered and rolled, allowing the ball to roll freely as in the popular lawn game croquet.

Since 1926 the Los Angeles Open Golf Tournament, sponsored by the Los Angeles Junior Chamber of Commerce, has been the region's star golfing attraction. It has been played on all the major regional courses, including Rancho Park, Los Angeles, Riviera, Hillcrest, and Wilshire, and once in Pasadena at Brookside. Over the years the Los Angeles Open has hosted some of golf's most outstanding players—Harry Cooper, Sam Snead, Byron Nelson, Ben Hogan, Tom Watson, and Arnold Palmer. The National Open was held at Riviera Country Club in 1948. Professional Golf Association (PGA) champions Jerry Pate and Tom Watson consider Hole 10 at Riviera Country Club "one of the greatest par-4 holes in the world."

Women's golf is supported in Los Angeles by the Ladies Professional Golf Association (LPGA) and the Amateur Athletic Foundation of Los Angeles. For its national tour, the LPGA used Calabasas Park in 1976; Rancho Park in 1979; Industry Hills in 1981 and 1982; Oakmont Country Club (Glendale) in 1986 and 1987; and Rancho Park in 1988 and 1989. A Southern Californian, Pearl Sinn of Bellflower, won the U.S. Women's Amateur Championship in 1988. The LPGA established a Junior Golf program in 1989 that attracts children of both sexes, all ages, and all ethnic and racial backgrounds.

During the 1980s Los Angeles County privatized its 20 golf courses: they remain open to the public but are run by private enterprise. Upon entering office, Mayor Riordan suggested privatizing one of the city's 12 golf courses.

GONZALES, RICARDO ALONSO ("PAN-CHO") (1928–1995), Los Angeles–born tennis player, said to be "the best of his generation" and "the father of professional tennis." The barrio youngster spent his early years trying to gain acceptance in the tennis world. In 1948 and 1949 he won two U.S. singles titles and turned professional. The Wimbledon cup, which was open only to amateurs during his peak years in the 1950s, eluded him. In 1969, however, at age 41, he won the longest singles match in Wimbledon history, defeating 24-year-old Charley Pasarell in 112 games. The match lasted five and a half hours and spilled over into a second day. After a career spanning 40 years, Gonzales retired in 1980.

GOOD GOVERNMENT LEAGUE, or "Goo Goos," progressive political association formed early in the century by middle-class professionals—including Edward A. Dickson, associate editor of the *Los Angeles Evening Express,* and attorneys Meyer Lissner, Russ Avery, and Marshall Stimson —to fight machine politics. They had allies in the City Club, another progressive group. In 1904 the league exercised the newly approved recall provision by recalling Councilman James P. Davenport on charges of collusion with the *Los Angeles Times* in a corrupt deal involving the city's printing contract, and five years later they elected George Alexander mayor after forcing the corrupt Arthur C. Harper out of office. The league tried to solve the city's problems by introducing efficient, honest administrative bureaucracy. They broke with socialist forces by seeking to regulate utilities rather than buying them, and by passing an antipicket-

ing ordinance. In 1911, in the wake of the bombing of the *Times* Building the previous year, the Goo Goos allied with their erstwhile enemies, the GOP and *Times* publisher Harrison Otis, to defeat the Socialist mayoral candidate, Job Harriman.

GOODHUE, BERTRAM GROSVENOR (1869–1924), architect of the Los Angeles Central Library (1922–1926). He died before he could see his Egyptian masterpiece completed. Goodhue also designed the Gates Chemistry Laboratory (1917), Gates Annex, and the West Court buildings at Caltech, and influenced the layout and landscaping of the campus.

GOPHER, small nocturnal mammal found in rural residential areas near open rangeland and in piñon-juniper woodland and mountain meadow habitats. Gophers, which burrow underground and eat the roots of plants, are the sworn foe of serious gardeners. The southern pocket gopher is known to scientists as *Thonomys bottae.*

GORMAN, truck stop on I-5 in the mountain pass north of Los Angeles. It was named in 1877 for Henry Gorman, postmaster, who had served in the U.S. Army at Fort Tejón and homesteaded the area in 1864. Only a handful of people reside in this 60-acre commercial strip, though as many as 200 patrons may rent motel rooms on any given night.

GOVERNMENT in Los Angeles County is complicated in that it involves nearly 100 cities, as well as innumerable districts for schools, parks, health services, cemeteries, water, sanitation, planning, and flood, mosquito, and air pollution control. Major regional bodies, including the South Coast Air Quality Management District (AQMD) and the Rapid Transit District (RTD), have been formed to transcend localism. Los Angeles's pattern of overlapping jurisdictions defies logic and resembles a crazy quilt.

The confused governmental picture perennially invites proposals for reform, most of which point to either coordinated local solutions or unification. Prof. Donald Hagman of the UCLA School of Law once proposed a serious plan to dissolve all existing jurisdictions and create "the City and County of Los Orange Angeles," organized around a borough scheme. Other reformers see salvation in smaller, more responsive governments. Further fragmentation is always threatened, and it is not uncommon to find some set of disgruntled San Fernando Valley residents or other demanding secession.

The academic community has a long history of conducting studies that promote bureaucratic reorganization, coordination, integration, or centralization. An early formal effort to foster research in the area of government and public administration was made by the Pacific Southwest Academy, organized in 1927. Perhaps the most fruitful governmental studies were made in the 1950s by the John R. and Dora Haynes Foundation and the Bureau of Governmental Research at UCLA. USC and the Claremont Graduate School have also produced their share of specialized studies. Among nonacademic institutions, the Welfare Planning Council of Los Angeles, now a unit of United Way, was instrumental in conducting important research.

Among published works on Los Angeles government, a benchmark anthology was *Los Angeles: Preface to a Master Plan* (1941), edited by George W. Robbins and L. Deming Tilton. This book resulted from an interdisciplinary symposium and contained many rich insights into public planning; unfortunately, it was rendered useless by the rapid postwar population boom. Another pioneering

---

My next advance was to a small town inhabited by Spaniards, called the town of The Angels. . . . In this place I vaccinated 2500 people.
—James O. Pattie, fur trapper, 1829

---

study, *How the Cities Grew: A Century of Municipal Independence and Expansionism in Metropolitan Los Angeles* (1952) by R. Bigger and J. D. Kitchen, explored incorporation of county cities and the growth of Los Angeles. In 1964 Winston W. Crouch and Beatrice Dinerman issued a memorable report on metropolitan reorganization, *Southern California Metropolis: A Study in Development of Government for a Metropolitan Area* (1964), dealing with the processes by which organized groups have identified and reached decisions on public issues. Henry Reining Jr. and Frank P. Sherwood's *Government Alternatives in Paramount* (1956) concerns smaller communities.

Political scientists have explored numerous other aspects of government structures and processes. Specialized studies have been published on city and county charter reform, the operation of special districts, home rule, municipal consolidation, annexation and government formation, the initiative process, the council-manager form of government (as practiced in Beverly Hills, Long Beach, and Glendale, for example), intergovernmental relations, welfare planning and administration, the Lakewood Plan in which county services are contracted for, and the county's Air Pollution Control District.

GRAFFITI, spray painting of walls, buses, trees, light poles, fences, and other outdoor surfaces as a means of marking territory. The practice reached a crisis level in the 1980s. Some of the graffiti is sprayed by solo "taggers" as an act of ego. In the 1990s the elusive Daniel "Chaka" Ramos left his particular mark 10,000 times, at a cleanup cost of $55,000, before police caught him. Gang members use graffiti to mark their turf in coded messages that sometimes lead to violent encounters.

In 1992 the removal of graffiti cost the city of Los Angeles an estimated $3.7 million, and the Rapid Transit District, $13 million. The city council has banned the sale of spray paint to minors, has offered rewards of $1,000 for information leading to the arrest of taggers, and in 1993 created a civil penalty of $1,000 for graffiti.

Some forms of graffiti have their defenders. Professional muralists and art historians point to the long and honorable tradition of wall painting in Latin America. Raul Gamboa, a self-styled graffiti "writer" who has painted more than 70 walls throughout the area, has honed his craft and perfected his symbolism. He admits that his graffiti is illegal, but claims that it is art.

In September 1991 the Department of Cultural Affairs sponsored a conference to examine the issue. As a means of accommodating graffiti artists, the Department of Public Works has designated certain walls on which young people may paint legally. Most citizens, however, are angry and concerned about the proliferation of graffiti, the assault on private property, and the disfigurement of the city.

In 1995 Calabasas sentenced a 19-year-old to nine months in jail for spraying paint on the Ventura Freeway in Sherman Oaks. He was also fined $34,000 and had to invest 100 hours in community service by removing graffiti from various locations. It was the most severe penalty meted out to that time.

GRAHAM, unincorporated county area near Watts in South Central Los Angeles. It draws its name from a street that ran parallel to the old Pacific Electric Railway lines. In 1990 its population was 22,000.

GRANADA HILLS, residential area of the city of Los Angeles in the northern San Fernando Valley 21 miles northwest of downtown Los Angeles. In 1855 Geronimo Lopez bought land and afterward established Lopez Station and a school in the area (now covered by the Van Norman Reservoir). In 1874 a huge parcel of land that became Granada Hills was purchased by Charles Maclay and George Porter. The name Granada was adopted officially in 1927; it was expanded to Granada Hills in 1942. Major residential development occurred after World War II. Archaeologists have uncovered human remains dating as far back as 1500 B.C. The population in 1990 was 70,000.

GRAND CENTRAL PUBLIC MARKET, downtown retail food emporium. It is located between Broadway and Hill, and 3rd and 4th Streets, on a site vacated by the City of Paris, once Los Angeles's largest department store. The market features over 50 food stalls and serves as many as 25,000 patrons daily, most of them Latinos. When it opened in 1917 it catered to the carriage trade, but as the affluent residents of Bunker Hill moved away the market came to serve a wider clientele. Its greatest volume of sales was recorded in 1944 when 1.2 million people shopped there in a single month. Some market vendors have had stalls at Grand Central for more than 40 years.

GRAND HOPE PARK, 2.5-acre park in downtown Los Angeles, bounded by Olympic Boulevard, Hope Street, 9th Street, and Grand Avenue. Financed by the Community Redevelopment Agency (CRA) to create a hospitable Central City residential neighborhood, the space was dedicated in 1994 after seven years of development and an expenditure of $20 million. The design boasts a 53-foot clock tower, a playground, and a fountain, all enclosed by a wrought-iron fence with 14 gates. The park is managed by Grand Hope Park, Inc., a non-profit organization of local property owners using CRA and private funds.

GRAPE AND WINE INDUSTRY started in the 1830s with the successful production of grapes, wine, and brandy *(aguardiente)* for market distribution. Earlier, the Spanish Franciscans had planted the first grape cuttings at Mission San Gabriel, and in 1824 Joseph Chapman set out 4,000 vines from those cuttings. By 1830, 24 vineyards had been established locally, and Angelenos were producing hundreds of barrels of wine and brandy. In 1831 the French settler Jean Louis Vignes, a native of Bordeaux, bought 104 acres south of Aliso Street and east of Alameda Street and planted El Aliso Vineyard using imported cuttings. A 10-foot-wide grape arbor extended from his adobe down to the river. Within five years he had 40,000 vines and thousands of oak casks, some of which he had fashioned himself. At $2 per gallon for white wine and $4 for brandy, he exported the spirits to Santa Barbara, Monterey, and San Francisco. William Wolfskill, a former fur trapper who became the largest grower in Southern California, with huge orange and walnut groves, also planted a vineyard in 1838 and developed a cellar with a capacity of 60,000 gallons.

In 1859 wine producers had invested over $1 million and were producing 500,000 gallons a year. The previous year the Sainsevain brothers of Los Angeles, a major winemaking company, alone produced 115,000 gallons. The industry was still growing as late as the 1860s. In 1862 the firm of Kohler and Frohling rented the entire basement of City Hall to store more than 100,000 gallons of wines and brandies, including port, champagne, and angelica. These products were shipped all over the world. Wine was also grown in Anaheim by the Los Angeles Vineyard Society, a cooperative formed by Germans from San Francisco. The last commercial vineyard in Los Angeles County was in the northern San Fernando Valley.

GRAUMAN, SID (1879–1950), cinema impresario. His first movie palace, the Million Dollar Theater on Broadway and 3rd Street, opened in 1918 with William S. Hart's *The Silent Man.* He devised the lavish Hollywood "premiere" for introducing new films. The first one occurred on 18 October 1922, when his new movie palace, Grauman's Egyptian Theatre, premiered *Robin Hood,* starring Douglas Fairbanks. While a battery of klieg lights swept the sky over Hollywood Boulevard, a bevy of movie stars emerged from their limousines to the cheers of mobbed fans. Grauman also built the even more opulent Chinese Theatre, farther east on Hollywood Boulevard, and operated the Mayan Theater in downtown Los Angeles. In addition, he was a major distributor to other exhibitors.

GRAUMAN'S CHINESE THEATRE. *See* Chinese Theatre

GREAT DEPRESSION, 1929–1939, brought widespread unemployment and personal hardship to Southern California, although the region experienced a quicker recovery than other parts of the country. For months after the crash of 1929, the chamber of commerce and *Los Angeles Times* diligently denied that the national or local economy had collapsed. Nevertheless, home building and

---

What struck me chiefly on entering this village was the air of cheerfulness, ease and neatness, which, it seemed to me, characterized the inhabitants, and which I had not observed at any of the presidios.
—Auguste Barnard Duhaut-Cilly, French marine officer, 1820s

---

real estate speculation dropped precipitously, and unemployment was rampant as homeless families flocked in from the Great Plains and elsewhere. Some migrants camped in Hoovervilles along the banks, and in the dry bed, of the Los Angeles River. Destitute people overwhelmed the flophouses and soup kitchens run by private charities. The number of people accepting public aid from the county rose from 35,700 in 1932 to 120,000 in 1933, and still stood at 91,000 in 1940.

City hall leadership was poorly equipped for the crisis. The Los Angeles Police Department attempted to stop indigents from entering California by turning them back at the state line, but the short-lived "bum blockade" was a failure. To reduce welfare rolls county officials also rounded up thousands of Mexican families from downtown, often including children born in the United States, and deported them.

On the positive side, the movie industry, which accounted for a large proportion of the job market, prospered greatly in the 1930s. In agriculture,

mild weather helped growers obtain good crops from local orchards and fields to counter threatened starvation. Compared to the rest of the nation, Southern California's recovery was heartening. The completion of Hoover Dam, which assured the delivery of cheap electricity, and the vigor of the airframe industry and rising federal investment in aircraft production when war broke out in Europe further aided the area's relative well-being.

GREATER LOS ANGELES PLANS INCORPORATED (GLAPI), organization formed by 25 powerful downtown leaders in the 1940s to revitalize downtown in the face of growing suburbanization. Their centerpiece project, a publicly financed Bunker Hill opera house, was rejected by voters in 1951 and again in 1953. The strategy therefore continued with private financing, and ultimately succeeded, taking the form of the Music Center.

GREEKS, both nationals and Greek Americans, numbered about 100,000 in Los Angeles as of 1990. One of the earliest Greek pioneers in Los Angeles was "Greek George" Caralampo, a camel driver from Asia Minor who in the 1850s drove a caravan of camels from Fort Defiance in the New Mexico Territory to Fort Tejón in northern Los Angeles County. He became a naturalized citizen in 1876.

The first Greek enclave arose on San Julian Street around 1912, later spreading to Fourth Street near Main, in an area that supported hundreds of Greek restaurants, flower shops, grocery stores, fruit markets, and dairies. Today, many Greeks are concentrated in the vicinity of St. Sophia Greek Orthodox Cathedral at Pico and Normandie. The construction of this cathedral was financed in 1952 by Greek film producer Charles Skouras. Another center of Greek life is in San Pedro. Prominent Greek celebrations occur on the Feast of the Annunciation (March 25), the Blessing of the Waters (January 6), and various other religious holidays.

GREEK THEATRE, Griffith Park amphitheater sited in a natural bowl. Opened in 1929–1930, the 4,600-seat house has seen performances ranging from ballet to rock to drama. A marionette show, mounted by the Federal Theatre Project in the summer of 1937 and attended by over 100,000 people, was a milestone production. Much of the theater's detailing is said to have been designed by its donor, Griffith J. Griffith.

GREENE AND GREENE, architectural firm created by the brothers Charles Sumner Greene (1868–1957) and Henry Mather Greene (1870–1954) of Pasadena. After completing architectural training at Massachusetts Institute of Technology, the Ohio-born brothers traveled to the area in 1893 to visit their parents, who were health seekers, and work on a building commission. The Arts and Crafts, or Craftsman, mode of design captured their imagination. In that vein, in 1902 and 1903 they created the California bungalow style of architecture, which would soon have widespread influence and appeal. In effect, they took the humble bungalow, with its wood construction, boxy shape, exposed beams, and screened porches, and transformed it into a work of high art. The Greene brothers combined a rare talent for design, a keen knowledge of materials, and the ability to gauge a client's needs. They meticulously crafted not only the homes, but also their furniture and decorations. They created scores of beautiful homes, many of which still stand on the eastern side of the Arroyo Seco. The Gamble House (1908), a Greene and Greene masterpiece listed on the National Register, is widely regarded as one of the most beautiful private residences in the nation.

GREEN LINE, modern light-rail train running along the center of the Century Freeway. Service began in 1995 and is planned eventually to connect the cities of Norwalk and El Segundo, with a spur line to nearby Los Angeles International Airport—a total distance of over 23 miles. Part of a network

Green Line Imperial/Wilmington Station, on the Century Freeway. Courtesy Metropolitan Transportation Authority.

operated by the Los Angeles County Metropolitan Transportation Authority, the Green Line is projected to cost $800 million.

GREEN MEADOW, area of South Central Los Angeles south of Manchester Avenue, adjacent to Green Meadows Recreation Center. In 1990 the population was over 50,000.

GREEN VALLEY, secluded Antelope Valley community in the Angeles National Forest. Its original name was La Joya ("The Jewel"). It is located 15 miles west of Palmdale along San Francisquito Canyon Road, 2 miles south of Elizabeth Lake Road. A subdivision in the 1920s created 1,800 lots, each of which was 5,000 square feet. Green Valley now has a population of 850. Limitations on the sewage disposal system create a permanent limit to the community's growth.

GREYSTONE MANSION, elegant 55-room residence in Beverly Hills. It was built in 1927, at a cost of $4 million, by oil magnate Edward Doheny for his son, Edward Lawrence (Ned) Doheny, and his family. It stands on a 415-acre tract on Loma Vista Drive. The Tudor-style building, designed by Gordon Kaufman, takes its name from the somber-looking limestone walls and slate roof. In 1929 the mansion was the scene of a probable murder-suicide when Ned Doheny and his secretary, Hugh Plunkett, were found shot to death in Doheny's bedroom. The mansion then passed into the hands of developer Paul Trousdale, who sold it to the city of Beverly Hills. The grounds were made into a public park, and the gardens have become a particularly popular wedding site. The mansion, with its 46,054-square-foot interior, was temporarily leased to the American Film Institute and subsequently served as an art gallery, but what the permanent use of the landmark structure should be remains a matter of public contention in Beverly Hills.

GRIFFITH, D[AVID] W[ARK] (1875–1948), Kentucky-born pioneer film director and producer whose career spanned the period 1910–1931. He took his troupe of Biograph Players to San Gabriel Mission in January 1909 to film the story of Ramona. The son of a Confederate colonel, he depicted the Civil War and Reconstruction in his epic *The Birth of a Nation* (1915) in a manner highly critical of the Union cause. Griffith's attitude toward the Ku Klux Klan and his stereotypical depiction of black people (portrayed by white actors) continue to make this a highly controversial movie. Technically, he innovated the use of long shots and close-ups, cross-cutting, fade-ins, soft focus, and low-angle shots. For his monumental *Intolerance* (1916), which he made as an antidote to the storm raised over *Birth of a Nation,* Griffith had a Babylonian ziggurat constructed at the corner of Sunset and Hollywood Boulevards, which towered over Hollywood until 1919. Also in 1919, along with Mary Pickford, Douglas Fairbanks, and Charlie Chaplin, he formed United Artists.

Griffith Observatory. Courtesy Los Angeles City Recreation and Parks Dept.

GRIFFITH, GRIFFITH J[ENKINS] (1850–1919), self-made millionaire who, in 1896, donated 3,500 acres to the city for Griffith Park. The land was part of his Rancho Los Feliz and formed the largest urban park in the country. Griffith made his fortune from mining speculation. In 1903, while in a drunken rage, Griffith accused his Catholic wife of conspiring to divert his fortune to the church and shot her. She survived, and he served two years in San Quentin for attempted murder. Upon his release he tried to donate money to the city, but his offer was refused. When he died in 1919 the city finally agreed to accept his gift of $700,000 for an observatory and outdoor amphitheater.

GRIFFITH OBSERVATORY, astronomical museum on the south rim of Griffith Park. It contains a theater and an observatory, built in 1930 and 1935 respectively. On clear nights visitors gather on the terrace for a glorious panorama of the city lights sparkling below. The structure's three domes house a solar telescope, a 12-inch refractor telescope, and a planetarium. Designed by John C. Austin and F. M. Ashley, the observatory constitutes one of the finest examples of 1930s Art Deco design in Los Angeles and is preserved and maintained by the city as a historic-cultural monument. Inside is a science museum, with a Foucault pendulum in the main rotunda, and meeting rooms for astronomy clubs. The observatory was featured in the film *Rebel Without a Cause* (1955).

GRIFFITH PARK, largest municipal park in the nation. Its 5 square miles (4,044 acres) are situated at the eastern end of the Hollywood Hills. Much of the vegetation is native, and some original species of wildlife still roam the park. Experts surmise that Gabrieleño Indians lived and hunted in the Ferndell area, although very little archaeological work has been done to confirm this belief. The land was part of Rancho Los Feliz, awarded in 1796

Griffith Park entrance in the 1920s. Courtesy Robert Weinstein Collection.

to Corp. José Vicente Feliz, one of the soldiers accompanying the original 44 settlers of the *pueblo* of Los Angeles. It remained in the Feliz family until 1863. The land, which was said to have a curse on it, fell into the hands first of Antonio Coronel, and then of Leon Baldwin, who in 1884 sold it to Griffith J. Griffith. Owing to the curse, Griffith was unable to sell the property, and he donated it to the city in 1896 as a "place of recreation and rest for the masses, a resort for the rank and file."

Rising from 325 to 1,625 feet in altitude, Griffith Park has a jumbled terrain of rugged, chaparral-covered hills. In its time parts of the park have been used as a city dump, a sheep pasture, a National Guard airport, a source of firewood, and a rock quarry. It is also intersected by two freeways and bordered by a segment of the concrete-lined Los Angeles River.

While most urban parks are pedestrian oriented, Griffith Park is commonly negotiated by car. Nevertheless, there are 53 miles of hiking trails, as well as bridle paths, tennis courts, four golf courses, a swimming pool, a merry-go-round, miniature train rides, pony rides, and a nature museum display. It is also home to the Griffith Observatory, Travel Town transportation museum, Los Angeles Zoo, and Autry Museum of Western Heritage. Upward of 10 million people use the park yearly. Once sold for $1 an acre, at current market value the estimated worth of the park's land is $2 billion.

GRIFFITH PARK ZOO. *See* Los Angeles Zoo

GROCERY INDUSTRY. Southern California is rated by insiders as the most competitive and innovative retail food marketplace in the nation. Six thousand outlets serving 14 million customers have annual sales of $20 billion. The industry initiated or perfected some of the most important practices in grocery retailing, including the supermarket itself. Chain stores, with Safeway taking the lead, originated in the 1920s but faced competition from independents. Store designs, display signage, and parking lots in the 1920s and 1930s reflected the region's increasing dependency on the automobile. In the 1950s the Southern California industry pioneered the use of piped-in music, spotlights, acoustical ceilings, trading stamps, self-service meat counters, frozen foods, health foods, environmental concerns, and computer technology. The industry has had to adjust to the rise of convenience and discount stores. Since the 1970s corporate

mergers and acquisitions have reduced the number of chains. In terms of the percentage of people who shop at a particular store, the biggest players in Los Angeles and Orange Counties in 1991 were Vons (21 percent), Lucky (18.2 percent), Ralphs (17.9 percent), Alpha Beta (12.9 percent), Hughes (5.3 percent) and Albertson's (5 percent). The major trade organization since 1913 is the Southern California Retail Grocers Association. It prides itself on constructive dealings with unions.

GROWTH became an explosive political issue in the 1980s, as people reacted to rising traffic congestion, unbridled high-rise construction, and growing problems of waste disposal, neighborhood preservation, and street crime. At first limited to upwardly mobile neighborhoods, the anti-growth movement soon took root in other parts of town where the dream of owning a private home in a peaceful neighborhood was coming under increasing threat. The mayor and city council were

---

Crime, pollution, immigration, growth. Is Los Angeles world class or Third World? It's all part of the debate the city is having with itself today.   —Kit Rachlis, editor of *L.A. Weekly*

---

ever more on the defensive in dealing with such issues as the pollution of Santa Monica Bay by the Los Angeles sewer system, traffic congestion in the airport area, overbuilding of shopping malls on the Westside and of office structures on Ventura Boulevard, loss of rural qualities in Topanga Canyon, and air pollution from a proposed LANCER incinerator in a working-class neighborhood near the Coliseum. The growth controversy resulted in the passage of Los Angeles City Proposition U in 1986, which limited commercial development.

GRUEN, VICTOR (1903–1980), architect and principal in Victor Gruen Associates. His designs dot the Southern California landscape; among his most notable works are the Tishman Building (1956), Leo Baeck Temple (1962), Redondo Beach Civic Center (1962), Marina del Rey (1966–1974), Fox Hills Shopping Mall (1973–1976), Pacific Design Center (1975), and Downtown Plaza Building

(1981). Gruen Associates also created the imaginative master plan for the community of Valencia, now incorporated within Santa Clarita.

GRUNION *(LEURESTHES TENUIS)*, small smelts that spawn on sandy beaches in the spring. The miniature surfers appear after the full or new moon during a high tide and ride ashore on high waves. Within 30 seconds the female creates a hole in the sand by swishing her tail and deposits her eggs, which are immediately fertilized by the male, and together they ride back out to sea on the next high wave. Within the short time of their appearance, people waiting on shore attempt to catch the fish and cook them on prepared campfires. (Only hands, not nets, are allowed in fishing for grunion.) The eggs hatch in about two weeks, and the fry wash into the ocean at the next high tide. Grunion are called the "fish that dance at the beach at the full moon."

GUINN, JAMES M[ILLER] (1834–1918), historian. Born in Ohio, Guinn was trained as a teacher at Antioch and Oberlin Colleges, before being wounded in the Civil War. Upon moving to Los Angeles in 1869 to regain his health, he taught school and helped found the Historical Society of Southern California. Guinn edited and contributed to the society's *Annual Publication* and wrote a five-volume *History of California* (1907) that devoted generous space to Southern California.

GUNS have proliferated in the hands of private parties in recent years. In 1991 more than 8,000 people were treated for gunshot wounds in emergency rooms throughout the county, and 1,554 were killed. Of those killed, more than 250 were 19 years of age or younger. On New Year's Eve in 1991, the Los Angeles County Sheriff's Department received an astonishing 777 phone calls reporting illegal gunshots in territory served by deputies. In May 1992, immediately following the violent outbreak that greeted the first Rodney King trial verdict, handgun dealers filed 14,125 permit requests with the state, a 46 percent increase over the preceding year.

Although not all permits are approved (the state rejected 5,859 applications in 1991), enforcement is lax, and background checks tend to be minimal; this means, in effect, that for $30 virtually anyone can easily acquire a gun or permit from any of the county's 3,000 licensed dealers, at wholesale prices. (People who are mentally disabled or have criminal records are forbidden from owning licenses or guns.) In addition to the licensed dealers, others, called "kitchen-table dealers," operate out of their homes, ignoring such state regulations as the 15-day waiting period. Many officials, including Los Angeles police chief Willy Williams, favor tougher laws. Ironically, in the 1970s the city of Los Angeles had refused to issue concealed weapons permits to any private citizen; it was forced by litigation, in 1993, to rescind the ban.

HAAGEN-SMIT, ARIE J. (1900–1977), Caltech biochemist. In 1950, using a laboratory flask, he made the startling discovery that a mixture of hydrocarbons and nitrogen dioxide, exposed to sunlight, produces smog. This experiment proved that auto exhausts were the major source of the polluted air hovering over Los Angeles, more so than any stationary sources.

HACIENDA HEIGHTS unincorporated county area near La Puente, 21 miles east of Los Angeles. The 1990 census counted 52,354 inhabitants.

HAHN, JAMES KENNETH (1950–), Los Angeles city attorney. A graduate of the Los Angeles school system, Hahn received a bachelor's degree in English from Pepperdine University and a J.D. from the Pepperdine School of Law in 1975. While a law student he participated in the creation of a paralegal program for the Family Law Center of the Legal Aid Society. From 1975 to 1979 he worked in the city attorney's office as a prosecutor before leaving to enter private practice. In 1981 he was elected city controller and in 1985 won his first term as city attorney. James Kenneth Hahn is the son of former Los Angeles County supervisor Kenneth Hahn.

HAHN, KENNETH (1920–), longtime county supervisor. Hahn was born in Los Angeles, graduated from Pepperdine, and completed graduate work in education at USC. In 1947, at age 27, he became Los Angeles's youngest councilman ever, and in 1952, at age 32, the youngest county supervisor. He was a mainstay of the board's liberal faction, responsible for a long list of legislative achievements that included the paramedics system, freeway call boxes, the Dodger move from Brook-

lyn to Los Angeles, the rob-a-home-go-to-jail law, Proposition A (1980) supporting rapid transit, the building of the Sports Arena, and the establishment of Martin Luther King Jr. General Hospital after the Watts riot. Hahn retired in 1992.

HAHN, KENNETH P. (1939–), Los Angeles county assessor. Ohio-born, he received a B.A. from Kent State University and has an Advanced Appraisal Certificate from the California State Board of Equalization. A county employee since the end of the 1960s, Hahn has been with the assessor's office since about 1980. He was first elected county assessor in 1990, and won a second election, running as an openly gay candidate, in 1994. As assessor of Los Angeles County, with its population of 9.5 million, and in charge of 2.5 million taxable parcels that provide 21 percent of the county's revenues, he heads an office of more than 1,500 workers. Hahn also serves on a variety of committees and associations; in 1995 he was president of the California Assessors Association, Central/Southern Region. Among his honors is a "Citizen of the Year" award from the Los Angeles Association of Realtors, and the designation of Honorary Director of Aid for AIDS.

HALE, GEORGE ELLERY (1868–1938), astronomer and trustee of Caltech. Born in Chicago, Hale came to Southern California in 1903 under the auspices of the Carnegie Institution to ascend Mt. Wilson and assess its suitability as a site for a telescope. A year later he established the Mt. Wilson Solar Observatory and become its director. He also raised funds for the Palomar Observatory, in San Diego County; helped create the Huntington Library and Art Gallery; assisted in the design of the Pasadena Civic Center; and shaped the de-

velopment of Caltech as one of the world's leading centers of scientific learning.

HAMBURGER, A., & SONS. *See* May, David, II

HAMILTON, CALVIN, city planning director
from 1964 to 1985. Praised as a visionary by some,
Hamilton hoped to control growth by fostering a
few high-density centers and preserving low-density development elsewhere in the city. He advanced the idea of the ill-fated downtown "people
mover" and pedestrian bridges. Detractors criticized him for avoiding controversy and missing
crucial opportunities to humanize the city and control smog, traffic, and urban sprawl. They charged
that he never carried through with his vision, evading making tough decisions in a plan for Hollywood, the placement of the Beverly Center, and
the future of the Mid-Wilshire district. In the end,
Hamilton came under criminal investigation for
using his office to promote his own tourism company, and was embroiled with the city council over
land holdings in Palmdale. He was succeeded by
Kenneth Topping and, more recently, Con Howe.

HAMMER, ARMAND (1898–1990), wealthy oil
executive, art collector, and philanthropist. Born
in New York City, Hammer was a longtime Los
Angeles resident. His early business associations
with Vladimir Lenin fostered trade and improved
political relations between the United States and
the USSR. Hammer's Los Angeles–based Occidental Petroleum was the center of his financial empire. With obsessive zeal he sought city permission
to drill for oil along a 2-acre site on the beach at
Temecula Canyon in Pacific Palisades. Irate local
residents, fearing potential landslides, organized a
group known as No Oil, Inc., to block the drilling.
After 21 years of legal strife—and Hammer's
death—Occidental raised the white flag and abandoned the effort. He created the Armand Hammer
Museum in Westwood to house his art collection.
The museum is now managed by UCLA.

HAM 'N' EGGS, depression-era pension scheme.
It was hatched by local radio commentator Robert
Noble, who proposed tapping the state treasury so
that elderly Californians would receive $30 each
Thursday. He began collecting pennies, nickels,
and dimes for an initiative drive to alter the state
constitution. Two talented admen, Willis and
Lawrence Allen, staged a coup and seized the

movement from Noble. Their hired rabble-rouser,
Sherman Bainbridge, coined the slogan "Ham 'n'
Eggs!" referring to the food the recipients could
buy. It was shouted at large meetings, along with
the slogan "Thirty Thursday!" To garner public
support, the Allens exploited the suicide and funeral of an unfortunate elderly San Diegan, Archie
Price. They eventually collected an astounding
789,000 petition signatures to place the measure
on the ballot. Considered by Carey McWilliams
to be, "by all odds, the most fantastic, incredible,
and dangerous" mass movement of 20th-century
California, Ham 'n' Eggs would have bankrupted
the state. Supported by U.S. senator Sheridan
Downey, it was narrowly defeated in the election
of 1938, and perished the next year in a second
attempt.

HANCOCK, HENRY (1822–1883), landowner.
The New Hampshire lawyer and surveyor came to
Southern California in 1852 and completed a second survey of the city's 35-acre lots several years after his arrival. He acquired Rancho La Brea ("Tar
Rancho") from Antonio José Rocha, a Portuguese
seaman who successfully escaped from an English
ship and became a Mexican citizen. A veteran of
the Mexican War, Hancock rose from captain to
major in the California militia. Despite usually being hard-up for cash, he retained ownership of the
rancho, while his wife, a daughter of "Count"
Agoston Haraszthy, a San Francisco pioneer, managed it. The family fortune was amassed, eventually, through real estate and oil. The Allan Hancock Foundation for Marine Research at USC was
founded in 1905, with funding coming largely
from Henry's son, G. Allan Hancock (1876–1965).
The younger Hancock inherited the property and
in 1916 donated to the county the portion that included tar pits filled with prehistoric bones.

HANCOCK PARK, both a public space on
Wilshire Boulevard and a nearby residential district. The 23-acre Hancock Park on Wilshire Boulevard was donated to the county in 1916 by Maj. G.
Allan Hancock, the oil magnate. It was once part
of Rancho La Brea, a square league of land that
covered most of the Wilshire district and part of
Hollywood. The residential area was developed for
wealthy Angelenos in the 1920s by the Rimpau
brothers, the sons of Theodore Rimpau, a Gold
Rush immigrant from Germany, and his wife,
Francisca Avila. They gained title to the family-

owned Rancho Las Cienegas through the Avilas. Today the residential area, which is bounded by La Brea Avenue, Wilton Place, Melrose Avenue, and Olympic Boulevard, is known as Greater Hancock Park. It includes the neighborhoods of Wilshire Park, Ridge-Wilton, Windsor Village, Fremont Place, Larchmont Village, La Brea–Hancock, Windsor Square, and Hancock Park. The latter encompasses both the Wilshire Country Club and Getty House, the official residence of the mayor of Los Angeles.

HANSEN, HOMER A[LFRED] (1872–1960), physician associated with a famous mountain lodge in Big Tujunga Canyon. On a visit in 1892, the teenager developed a lifelong passion for the area. At the turn of the century doctors diagnosed him as having acute inflammatory rheumatism and gave him one year to live. He retired to the canyon to repair his health, and the outdoor life rejuvenated him. Hansen filed a homestead claim on 93 acres and built a cabin, followed by a 2-story guest lodge. He hosted a wide variety of celebrity guests, including senators, county supervisors, and even the famous criminal attorney Clarence Darrow. His hospitality was legendary. When the cabin was destroyed in the flood of 1926, Hansen rebuilt it, only to see it destroyed again in 1938. Hansen Dam, a flood control dam to control the raging waters of Tujunga Wash, built by the U.S. Army Corps of Engineers near Pacoima in the San Fernando Valley, is named in his honor.

HARBOR, LOS ANGELES, 1781–1899. Identified by Juan Cabrillo in 1542 as "an excellent harbor," for three centuries San Pedro Bay remained little more than an underutilized mud flat. Though sheltered on the west by the Palos Verdes Hills, the bay was exposed to high winds and waves from the south, and part of the inner bay was blocked by a shallow sandbar. The entire spot lay 25 miles from Los Angeles, the nearest *pueblo*. When Richard Henry Dana, author of *Two Years Before the Mast* (1840), landed at San Pedro in 1825 he reported, "We all agreed it was the worst place we had seen yet." Spanish authorities allowed only Spanish ships to engage in trade until 1822, when Mexico took over from Spain. The first known American trading ship at San Pedro, in 1805, was the *Leila Bird* under the command of William Shaler. When the United States seized California there was no deep-water access at San Pedro, and merchants had

to send small boats and rafts to meet cargo-carrying ships at anchor in the bay. Beginning in the 1850s lumber for the burgeoning towns became an important commodity; it arrived chiefly by sea and was off-loaded at San Pedro.

The effort to establish a deep-water port at San Pedro took 50 years of political agitation, federal capital outlay, and visionary local leadership. The first developer was teamster Phineas Banning, who arrived from Delaware in 1851 and set about developing Wilmington. He bought land, dredged the slough to make a primitive landing, and, by 1869, built a railroad line to Los Angeles. Army engineers

---

Fifteen homeboys built the child-care center and the bakery now hires seven homeboys and will employ three times that number when it opens. Jobs reduce crime. Jobs make communities safe.

—Father Gregory J. Boyle, director of Dolores Mission Job Program

---

shifted the mud so that the obstructing sandbar was broken. Harbor improvements began in 1871 with the dredging of the main channel to a 10-foot depth and the building of a breakwater from Rattlesnake (now Terminal) Island to Deadman's Island (removed in 1929). In 1872, when the Southern Pacific (SP) took over the rail line, it extended it southward to San Pedro by 5 miles, raised the freight rates, and, around 1881, dug in to maintain a transportation monopoly in the harbor.

This situation changed when other railroads emerged. One was a line from Santa Monica to Los Angeles, built in 1875 and later incorporated into the SP network. Another was the Santa Fe Railroad, which entered the basin in the 1880s and attempted to develop "Port Ballona" (near today's Marina del Rey). In 1890 Collis P. Huntington of the Southern Pacific tried to block the ongoing development of a harbor in San Pedro in order to boost the fortunes of his own pier at Santa Monica. This ignited a 10-year political battle known locally as the "Free Harbor Contest." Finally, in 1899, Congress voted money for San Pedro, and, after a festive weekend jubilee in the port area on

26–27 April, breakwater construction began that would create the major port of Los Angeles.

HARBOR, LOS ANGELES, SINCE 1900. The opening of the Panama Canal in 1914 created vast potential for Los Angeles, which became the first major port of call for shipping from the East Coast, Europe, and some Central and South American countries. The 1920s were a peak period, with petroleum, cotton, and citrus flowing out and bananas and other products flowing into the port. In 1928 alone, 26 million tons of freight were handled. During the Second World War the navy took over control of the harbor. More than 1,000 ships were built there, including 26 warships, as well as thousands of patrol boats and landing craft. The breakwater was extended after the war, in 1949. In the 1970s cruise ships began to dock at San Pedro, and the main channel was dredged to 45 feet.

The Los Angeles facility, which has adopted the title Worldport L.A. but remains commonly known as Los Angeles Harbor, occupies 7,500 acres of land and water on 28 miles of waterfront. With state-of-the-art container systems, in 1988 the port handled $54.2 billion in cargo, more than any other West Coast port. By 1990 it had bypassed New York as the busiest commercial gateway in the United States. In 1995 it handled 2,518,618 20-foot containers—only 55,209 behind Long Beach, which that year ranked as the largest container port in the nation. (Together the twin ports are the third largest port in the world, behind Singapore and Hong Kong.) More than half of Los Angeles port's revenue, by tonnage, involves the Far East. Automobiles and auto parts, gasoline and jet fuel, steel, footwear, lumber, scrap metal, copper ores, and inorganic compounds are among the major imports.

The port generates over 200,000 jobs regionally, $21 billion in industry sales, and $725 million in tax revenues.

HARBOR CITY, area north of Wilmington, along the "shoestring" addition linking the city of Los Angeles to San Pedro and Wilmington. The original developer, in 1912, was W. I. Hollingsworth, who called the strip Harbor Industrial City to attract industry. When factories failed to materialize, it was renamed Harbor City. About 20,000 people live there, in an area of less than one square mile.

HARBOR DEPARTMENT. *See* Los Angeles Harbor Department

HARBOR-UCLA MEDICAL CENTER, major hospital facility, run as a joint venture by Los Angeles County and UCLA. The facility began when the county purchased the Los Angeles Port of Embarkation Hospital in Torrance from the federal government to provide medical care to the South Bay area. Harbor General Hospital opened in 1947. In 1958 the county signed an operating agreement with UCLA and began hiring full-time faculty members from the medical school to head the hospital departments. The name was changed accordingly. Besides providing basic medical care, the institution engages in extensive research and education.

HARE KRISHNA, religious sect involving Vedic beliefs and stressing devotion to Krishna, an important Hindu god. It was transplanted into this country from India in 1966 and enjoyed a particular vogue in Southern California.

Container cargo, Worldport L.A. Courtesy Worldport L.A.

HARPER, ARTHUR CYPRIAN (1866–?), mayor of Los Angeles from 1906 to 1909. He won praise for initiating plans for a new civic center, but encouraged vice and corruption in city hall. In his run for office he had the backing of the unpopular Southern Pacific Railroad machine. Once elected, Harper fostered a sugar company stock speculation scheme to line his own pockets, and backed private interests who were attempting to steal the city-owned Los Angeles River bed. The rakish Harper also frequented downtown brothels. His blatant misdeeds touched off a recall drive, which forced his resignation and the election of a reform regime.

HARRIMAN, JOB (1841–1925), labor attorney and Socialist leader. Raised in Indiana and trained in the ministry, he settled in Los Angeles in 1886 to cure his tuberculosis. He ran for California governor as a Socialist in 1898, and for U.S. vice president with Socialist presidential candidate Eugene V. Debs in 1900, both times unsuccessfully. Harriman pressed Los Angeles Socialists into a liaison with blue-collar labor, including affiliates of the conservative American Federation of Labor. By garnering strong working-class backing on the Eastside, he came within several hundred votes of being elected mayor of Los Angeles in 1911. In the December runoff election, Harriman faced a coalition of progressives and conservative Republicans who, fearing the Socialist insurgency, backed the moderate candidate George Alexander. Harriman might well have won the mayoral bid had he not been condemned for joining the defense team of the McNamara brothers, who, on the eve of the election, confessed to the previous year's bombing of the *Los Angeles Times* Building. He ran again in 1913, again without success. Discouraged by conventional politics, Harriman took a group of Socialist followers to Llano del Rio in the Antelope Valley and there established a commune.

HARRIS, ELLEN STERN, environmental activist. A native of Beverly Hills, she was executive director of the Fund for the Environment, co-author of Proposition 20, which created the California Coastal Commission, and vice chair of that body when it was first formed. She serves on Beverly Hills commissions and writes on environmental subjects.

HART, WILLIAM S. (1864–1946), silent screen cowboy and author. Born in New York state, he grew up in the Dakota Territory. He came to California in 1914, and made 70 westerns in 11 years. Hart built a home, "La Loma de los Vientos" ("Hill of the Winds"), on the Newhall Ranch in 1925, filling it with antique guns and firearms, Indian artifacts, paintings, sculpture, and personal memorabilia. The 110-acre wilderness estate with its Spanish Colonial home is now the William S. Hart Museum and Ranch, and is administered by the Los Angeles County Museum of Natural History. Hart wrote a considerable body of western fiction and an autobiography, *My Life East and West* (1929).

HARTLEY, FRED L. (1917–1990), successful oil executive. A trained engineer, Hartley joined Union Oil in 1939; he became head of the regional firm in 1964, and began reshaping it into a worldwide giant called Unocal. In 1985 he fought off a hostile takeover by financier T. Boone Pickens Jr. Owing to his leadership, Unocal showed revenues of $11.4 billion in 1989. Hartley retired in 1988. He was also active in local civic and philanthropic affairs.

HARVARD HEIGHTS, neighborhood between Western and Normandie Avenues and Pico and

Job Harriman. Courtesy California State Library.

Washington Boulevards. It was part of the West Adams district, a middle-class area annexed by the city of Los Angeles early in the century. Two-story Craftsman-style Victorian homes still abound there. The estimated population in 1992 was 7,235.

HARVEY MUDD COLLEGE. *See* Claremont Colleges

HATE CRIMES, violence including verbal harassment, physical assault, or damage of the property of others because of their race, religion, or other personal attributes, prosecutable by federal, state, county, and city law. The County Human Relations Commission, noting a rise in such crimes since 1980, established the Network Against Hate Crime in 1984, which brings together voluntary associations as well as government agencies. Prosecutors have since filed numerous actions against

---

In Los Angeles my attention was called by the prayer at dawn . . . to give thanks to God in a loud voice at the break of day. One voice rose above the others, and to it the others responded in the prayer.

—José Arnaz, colonial merchant, 1879

---

organizations espousing white supremacist, anti-Semitic, or antigay ideology, including the Ku Klux Klan, the White Aryan Resistance, and the Fourth Reich Skinheads, a Long Beach–based group. According to federal law agents, after Rodney G. King protested a beating by police, a hate group attempted to kill him. They also attempted to bomb a prominent black church and to incite a race war after the 1992 riots. The human relations commission's 1993 Hate Crime Report indicated a 6.4 percent increase in such crimes in Los Angeles County over the previous year, for a total of 783 —a new high.

HATTEM'S 24-HOUR DRIVE-IN MARKET, first supermarket in Los Angeles. Located at 43rd Street and Western Avenue, the market was built by Isadore M. Hattem, a European Jewish immigrant. The term "supermarket" was evidently coined by the *Southwest Wave,* a community newspaper, in describing the grand opening of Hattem's on 27 December 1927. Hattem combined the self-service operation invented by Piggly Wiggly Stores of Memphis, Tennessee; the Grand Central Market's everything-under-one-roof concept; and a "drive-in" parking lot plan suggested by an architect. The building was Mission Revival architecture, with a red tile roof and a water fountain in front that was stocked with goldfish. The enterprising Hattem is also said to have been the first to use trading stamps in a grocery store.

HAWAIIAN GARDENS, 1-square-mile independent city 18.5 miles southeast of downtown Los Angeles, incorporated in 1964. The town had a population of 11,400 in 1980, and expanded to 13,639 in 1990.

HAWTHORNE, incorporated city 15 miles southwest of downtown Los Angeles. Founded in 1905 and incorporated in 1922, it was named for Nathaniel Hawthorne, author of *The Scarlet Letter.* Hawthorne Airport, located near Los Angeles International Airport, is actively used for small private planes. The town's population in 1990 was 71,300.

HAY, HARRY (1912–), "the father of gay liberation in America." Born into an affluent English family, Hay came to Los Angeles in 1919 and began an acting career in 1933. After joining the Communist Party in 1938, Hay devoted his life to politics. He was called before the House Un-American Activities Committee in the 1940s. In 1950 he and designer Rudi Gernreich founded the Mattachine Society, the forerunner of today's gay movement. In 1978 he founded the Radical Faeries, a gay spiritual movement devoted to fighting the assimilation of gays into straight society. Hay is the subject of a biography by Stuart Timmons, *The Trouble with Harry* (1990).

HAYES, BENJAMIN IGNATIUS (1815–1877), Baltimore-born lawyer and jurist. In 1850 Hayes became the first American-trained lawyer to practice in Los Angeles, and he was soon elected district judge. He toted a shotgun and bowie knife for protection as he rode about the far reaches of Los Angeles County to administer justice. Judge Hayes served in the state legislature and was Southern California's first book collector. He co-authored *Historical Sketch of Los Angeles County*

(1876), a centennial history. He also kept diaries and scrapbooks, some of which were published as *Pioneer Notes* in 1929.

HAYNES, DORA FELLOW (1859–1934),

suffragist leader. She moved from Pennsylvania to Los Angeles in 1887 with her husband, the progressive reformer John Randolph Haynes. Described as "frail, dainty, and quiet," she was nevertheless an active and determined member of the Political Equality League, a suffrage organization. In 1920 she founded the League of Women Voters chapter in Los Angeles, becoming its first president and a lifelong financial backer.

HAYNES, JOHN RANDOLPH (1853–1937),

physician, reformer, and philanthropist. A practicing Philadelphia physician, Haynes moved to Los Angeles in 1887 because of poor health. His timing was fortunate. In the Boom of the Eighties he made a fortune in real estate, banking, mining, and insurance, even as he continued his medical practice.

John Randolph Haynes. Courtesy Security First National Bank Collection, Los Angeles Public Library.

Despite his financial success, Haynes became a confirmed socialist of the English Fabian variety, and in 1899 founded the Christian Socialist Economic League of Los Angeles, a monthly dinner club. Fervidly democratic, he became the first national reformer to advocate direct legislation. In 1903, largely thanks to his long and persistent efforts, Los Angeles acquired charter provisions for the initiative, referendum, and recall vote. Haynes also helped bring about those reforms at the state level through a constitutional amendment in 1911. Widely respected even by his enemies, the leftist progressive served on the city water and power commission, and on the board of freeholders that drafted the 1925 city charter.

HAYS OFFICE, agency formed in 1930 to censor movies in the wake of a series of 1920s scandals involving film celebrities. It was run by former postmaster general Will H. Hays (1879–1954), who in 1922 had been appointed president of the Motion Picture Producers and Distributors Association. Among the scandals, which shaped the industry's image as a sink of immorality, were the death of actor Wallace Reid, the murder of director William Desmond Taylor, the possible murder of filmmaker Thomas Ince, the rape-and-homicide trial of comic actor Fatty Arbuckle, and the shooting of Courtland Dines by the chauffeur of film star Mabel Normand. Hays established the Production Code of 1930 to tone down sexuality in the movies; although it silenced critics by imposing some language and visual restrictions, in reality very little changed. Hays describes the episode in *The Memoirs of Will H. Hays* (1955).

HAZARD, HENRY T. (1844–1914), civic leader and mayor of Los Angeles from 1889 to 1892. Born in Illinois, he arrived with his family in Los Angeles in 1853, after a two-year westward trek from the Midwest via Salt Lake City behind teams of oxen driven by his father. They settled on land 4 miles outside Los Angeles. As a young man Hazard became involved in a variety of civic affairs. During the anti-Chinese riot in 1871 he tried to calm the mob and was rewarded by being shot at. A year later he actively promoted the Southern Pacific Railroad's proposal to enter Los Angeles, and in 1873 helped organize the volunteer fire department. In 1880 Hazard endorsed the division of California into two states, believing it would bring greater political power to Southern California. In the

1880s, with partner George H. Pike, he built Hazard's Pavilion opposite Central Park (today's Pershing Square); it became the city's leading theater. After holding the position of city attorney, Hazard became mayor, serving for three years. He supported the institution of the Fiesta de Los Angeles in 1894.

HAZARD'S PAVILION, theater located at 5th and Olive Streets from 1887 to 1906. The 3-story clapboard building, constructed by Henry T. Hazard and a partner during the Boom of the Eighties, had 4,000 seats and cost an imposing $25,000 to build. The inaugural performance was given by the National Opera Company. As the city's first big concert hall and cultural center, Hazard's Pavilion hosted innumerable performances of opera, drama, ballet, variety shows, and musical concerts, as well as boxing matches, lectures, political meetings, and religious sermons.

Hazard's was replaced in 1906 by Temple Auditorium, a 9-story concrete office and auditorium building constructed by the Temple Baptist Church. It later became known as Philharmonic Auditorium and has since been torn down. Among the featured attractions in these theaters at one time or another were George Gershwin, Mark Twain, Booker T. Washington, Igor Stravinsky, Pavlova, Nijinsky, and Aimee Semple McPherson.

HEALEY, DOROTHY RAY (1914–), Los Angeles Communist Party leader. Born in Denver, Healey joined the Communist movement as a teenager in 1928, eventually becoming a union organizer. In 1933 she led the El Monte berry strike of Mexican and Japanese workers, which spread to fields in Culver City, Venice, and Santa Monica. Healey was active in the Los Angeles chapter of the CIO in the 1940s. In 1945 she headed the Los Angeles branch of the Communist Party, which, next to New York's, was the most important in the country. Arrested along with other Party members in the 1950s, she faced deportation under the Smith Act until the law was declared unconstitutional by the U.S. Supreme Court. In 1966 she ran for Los Angeles County tax assessor, garnering over 86,000 votes. Although she denounced the Soviet invasion of Czechoslovakia and fought with the New York leadership, she maintained her party membership until 1973.

HEAL THE BAY, environmental group devoted to improving the water quality of Santa Monica Bay. It was formed in 1985 in Santa Monica by Dorothy Green and others to protest Los Angeles's daily dumping of millions of tons of partially processed sewage into the Pacific Ocean from the Hyperion Sewage Treatment Plant. The organization had 10,000 members, a budget of $300,000, and was combating other polluters as well. In 1992, in response to the group's lobbying efforts, Los Angeles completed a new $115 million outfall sewer line south of Los Angeles International Airport. Heal the Bay periodically tests the bacteria level of the water at 48 beaches, some of which have repeatedly failed to meet minimum standards.

HEALTH SEEKERS flooded Southern California in the 1870s, 1880s, and 1890s. The halt, the sick, and the lame were drawn to the mild climate of the region by printed accounts in newspapers, letters from residents, and books such as Charles

Glendale Sanitarium, ca. 1910.
Pitt Collection.

Nordhoff's *California for Health, Pleasure, and Residence* (1872). The climate was as benign as the French Riviera's, and railroads offered reasonable fares to the Far West. Although the majority of newcomers suffered from tuberculosis, asthma, and rheumatism, people arrived with myriad ailments. Most were middle class, and some were rich. Many took up residence in specially built sanitariums. To effect a cure, the health seekers hiked, walked, hunted, and maintained special diets. Pottenger Sanitarium in Monrovia was the most famous health spa. In Sierra Madre, a majority of the 2,000 residents were invalids. Barlow Sanitarium in Chavez Ravine, an excellent nonsectarian tuberculosis facility, tended to the poor. Health seekers also flocked to Murietta Hot Springs, Santa Fe Springs, and Temescal Warm Springs to "take the waters."

Initially, local leaders welcomed the invalids, many of whom were wealthy and invested in real estate and other industries. However, dependent sick people drained public finances. At the turn of the century, when the medical profession found that tuberculosis was treatable even in harsh East Coast climates, the health seekers' traffic to Southern California waned.

HEALTH SERVICES DEPARTMENT, LOS ANGELES COUNTY. *See* Los Angeles County Department of Health Services

HEBREW BENEVOLENT SOCIETY, first Los Angeles philanthropic association. It was formed in 1854 by Jewish pioneer Joseph Newmark, Harris Newmark's uncle and an ordained rabbi, to care for the sick and bury the dead. Although Jews were the primary beneficiaries, the society cared for all Angelenos. The organization, which had a women's branch, became known as the Jewish Aid Society of Los Angeles in 1915, Jewish Social Service Bureau in 1929, and, after 1945, Jewish Family Service, now a major component of the Jewish Federation-Council of Greater Los Angeles.

HEIGHT LIMITS. *See* Building height limits

HELLMAN FAMILY, prominent Jewish pioneers. The brothers I. M., Samuel, and Herman Hellman arrived in 1854; their cousins, the brothers Herman M. and Isaias Wolf Hellman, arrived from Bavaria five years later. The most successful family member was Isaias Wolf, who began as a clerk in a dry goods store but soon had his own business. Isaias became a banker, real estate investor, and an influential figure in the city. During the Gold Rush of the 1850s, miners entrusted him with their gold; at one point his safe bulged with $200,000 worth of the precious metal. In 1871 I. W. founded and presided over Farmers and Merchants Bank, with $500,000 in assets. When he died in 1920 the bank's assets exceeded $35 million. Hellman, who owned land in Boyle Heights, subdivided his property and invested in Signal Hill oil with the Bixby family. The Hellmans, along with their relatives in the Harris Newmark family, found easy acceptance in the early Gentile community.

HELMS BAKERY, home-delivery bakery based in Culver City. The firm was founded on Washington Boulevard in 1931 by Paul Hoy Helms, a na-

Helms Bakery building, 1996.
Photo by Lori Shepler.

tive of Pennsylvania. His drivers sold their wares from step-vans that cruised through residential neighborhoods. Helms Bakery was a licensed food provider to the 1932 Olympics. Eventually Helms had a fleet of 300 trucks with regular routes. The drivers' tuneful mechanical whistles summoned children and grown-ups alike to buy fresh bread and pastries. The spread of supermarkets and rising operating costs drove Helms out of business in 1969. The landmark building on Venice Boulevard still bears the original Helms logo.

HENRY E. HUNTINGTON LIBRARY AND ART GALLERY, San Marino research center with a priceless collection of books, manuscripts, and paintings, as well as botanical gardens. It began as the private collections of Henry E. Huntington, builder of the Pacific Electric rail network, and his second wife, Arabella. In 1903 Huntington purchased the 600-acre San Marino Rancho, to which he retired in 1908, devoting himself to his hobbies. In 1919 he deeded his holdings—library, art collection, and gardens—to create the Library and Art Gallery, along with a bequest of $10.5 million. The library, which opened to the public in 1928, houses 3.5 million items documenting British and American culture, including Shakespeare folios, manuscripts of Benjamin Franklin, Thomas Jefferson, and John James Audubon, and a Gutenberg Bible (1455). Scholars come from all over the world to study at the library. The art collection, which reflects the influence and taste of Arabella Hunting-

ton, includes paintings by American portraitist Gilbert Stuart and Gainsborough's *Blue Boy,* purchased in 1922 for $620,000. The gardens contain thousands of species of trees, grasses, shrubs, and flowers on 200 acres. Desert, jungle, Australian, Shakespearean, and Japanese gardens are maintained as separate entities. The center publishes its own books based on research conducted on the premises. Most of the facilities are open to the general public. The estate now comprises 207 acres, of which 150 remain open to the public. The rest of the acreage is given over to service areas.

HERALDO DE MÉXICO. See *El Heraldo de México*

HERITAGE SQUARE, MUSEUM VILLAGE AT, Highland Park sanctuary for orphaned Victorian houses. It originated in 1969 when the Community Redevelopment Agency announced a plan to raze all Bunker Hill structures. Preservationists immediately vowed to rescue the downtown Victorians. The Los Angeles Department of Recreation and Parks gave them 10 acres of land along the Arroyo Seco as a museum site. The first arrival, in 1970, was the Hale House, a Queen Anne–Eastlake mansion (1885) originally situated on N. Figueroa Street. Two Bunker Hill treasures, the Salt Box and the Castle, were also moved there but were, unfortunately, destroyed by arsonists. The square can accommodate 15 buildings; currently 8 Victorian homes, dating from 1876 to about 1899, are on display. They are among the most photogenic buildings in Los Angeles.

The Huntington Art Gallery. Courtesy Henry E. Huntington Library.

Hermosa Beach Street Fair. Bill Alnes Aerial Photography.

HERMOSA BEACH, independent South Bay city 16 miles southwest of downtown Los Angeles. Hermosa (meaning "beautiful"), originally part of Rancho Sausal Redondo, granted by Mexico in 1822, was founded as a residential subdivision in 1901. While the Santa Fe Railroad provided the first transportation from Los Angeles in the 19th century, it was the arrival of the Pacific Electric's Red Cars along Hermosa Avenue after 1900 that made the town accessible as a seaside resort. A pier was built in 1904, but the town's founders attempted to maintain a quiet family atmosphere by forbidding public amusements. The city of Hermosa Beach was incorporated in 1907. The resort's resident population was approximately 600 in 1915, rising to a summer population of 2,000. For some years presidential candidate William Jennings Bryan could be seen, dressed in overalls and a straw hat, fishing from the pier. In 1990 the population of Hermosa Beach was 18,200.

HERNANDEZ, MIKE (1953–), city council member representing the 1st District. The district was created after the U.S. Justice Department threatened to sue Los Angeles under the Voting Rights Act for failing to provide proper representation for Latinos living in the area from MacArthur Park to Mount Washington. An eastside Angeleno, Hernandez formerly worked as a bail bondsman serving undocumented aliens, and was a civic and business leader. Elected in 1990, he advocates better police-community relations and improved social services for his barrio district, one of the poorest areas of the city.

HERTRICH, WILLIAM. *See* Huntington Botanical Gardens

HERZOG, HERMAN (1832–1932), German-born landscape artist. His western sketches and paintings from the 1870s include scenes of Los Angeles.

HIDDEN HILLS, independent town just beyond the western boundary of the city of Los Angeles, 26 miles northwest of downtown, near Calabasas. The 1-mile-square community, with its private streets and guarded gate, was established in the 1950s as a pastoral hideaway by developer A. E. Hanson. The affluent town, which contains only single-family homes, is governed by a city council and a city manager. Restrictive covenants protect the huge lots and prevalent horse corrals. Residents incorporated Hidden Hills in 1961 to stave off a proposed extension of Burbank Boulevard. They have resisted the development of apartments, condominiums, commercial enterprises, and even street lights in the community. The population of Hidden Hills has remained stable for several decades at about 1,700.

HIGHLAND PARK, district along the Arroyo Seco, 6 miles north of downtown Los Angeles. Once called Garvanza, in 1895 its 1.4 square miles became the first major unincorporated territory to be annexed to Los Angeles; Highland Park residents, frustrated by marauding bandits who hid in the arroyo and preyed on travelers, hoped that the city police could secure law and order. Occidental

College made its home in Highland Park from 1887 to 1914, when it moved to Eagle Rock. Three featured historic attractions are the Heritage Square Museum Village, the Southwest Museum, and Lummis House.

HILBORN, WALTER STERN (1879–1976), Boston-born attorney and Jewish leader. After earning a law degree at Harvard and serving as a New York deputy district attorney in 1914, he moved to Los Angeles, where he became a senior member of Loeb and Loeb, with ties to MGM studios. He co-authored a work on small-loan legislation in 1940, and was elected to the executive council of the American Jewish Committee. In 1952 he became director of the Welfare Federation of Metropolitan Los Angeles.

HILLSIDE CONSTRUCTION, or "hill cropping," the preparation of building sites in mountainous areas, has led to an alarming destabilization of fragile terrain in the Santa Monica Mountains. This practice has been an issue west of Sepulveda Pass since the 1970s. Even in older canyons east of the pass, overdevelopment since the 1920s has led to mud slides, a greater potential for devastating fires, and the destruction of wildlife habitat. Utilities are expensive to build and maintain in such areas, and streets are often too narrow to accommodate emergency vehicles. New structures also block the view from older homes both because of their size and because of the planting of trees.

Some improvements have been made in zoning laws in recent years. Additional legislation, pending since 1989, would limit the height of buildings, control their "footprint," make fire sprinklers mandatory, and require ample off-street parking. Passage of these laws has been blocked by both homeowners and developers.

HILL STREET, downtown avenue bordering the east side of Bunker Hill. In the Mexican era it was called Calle de Toros ("Street of the Bulls") and was a site for bullfights. Renamed Hill Street in the American period, it emerged as a residential and commercial street in the latter part of the 19th century. After World War II, Hill Street suffered economic decline. In the 1970s, the section from 7th to 5th Streets became the center of the city's jewelry trade. This trade is now centralized in the 20-story Jewelry Mart facing Pershing Square.

HIMES, CHESTER (1909–1984), African American writer. With a letter of introduction from poet Langston Hughes, Himes came to Hollywood seeking employment as a screenwriter. He was hired at Warner Brothers but encountered racism and was forced to find work in the shipbuilding industry instead. His novel *If He Hollers Let Him Go* (1945), a grim depiction of wartime Los Angeles, reflects the despair and anger caused by bigotry. The central character and narrator, Bob Jones, is a cynical commentator on life, reminiscent of Raymond Chandler's Philip Marlowe. A second novel set in Los Angeles, *Lonely Crusade* (1947), conveys Himes's encounter with racial exclusion. *The Quality of Hurt* (1972) and *My Life of Absurdity* (1976) are autobiographical works. Himes left Los Angeles and moved to New York in 1944. He died in Spain at the age of 75.

HINDUS constituted a very small percentage of the many new religious groups that took shape in Southern California in the 1920s. The number of adherents grew significantly in the 1960s, however, with the increase of immigration from the Indian subcontinent. Most Hindus worship at home, but five or more temples exist in the region, the largest and most elaborate of which is the Sree Venkateswara Temple on Las Virgenes Canyon Road in Calabasas. This nine-domed shrine in the Chola style of architecture stands on a 4.5-acre site and was constructed from 1979 to 1989 by trained Hindu craftsmen according to principles that date back to the 10th century. It receives about 10,000 worshipers monthly.

HISPANICS. *See* Latinos

HISTORICAL RESOURCES FOR LOS ANGELES are scattered abundantly throughout the region, providing for fruitful study and preservation of regional history. The 1991 directory of the California Council for the Promotion of History listed 87 historical organizations, agencies, and museums in Los Angeles County.

The facilities with the most prominent archives maintain professional staffs and publish useful research aids. Among them are the California Collection of the Los Angeles Public Library; the UCLA Department of Special Collections, which includes an extensive oral history collection; the UCLA Film and Television Music Archive and Popular American Music Archive; and USC's Regional Cultural History Collection within the Special Collections division of the library, which contains papers of distinguished members of Congress, the Title Insurance and Trust Company photo collection, and the Los Angeles Chamber of Commerce collection. In Beverly Hills, the movie industry maintains the Margaret Herrick Library of the Academy of Motion Picture Arts and Sciences. San Marino is home to the world-renowned Huntington Library, which includes rich holdings on California. The Los Angeles County Museum of Natural History's Seaver Center has numerous items on Southern California, including tens of thousands of photos. The Southwest Museum in Highland Park is rich in resources about Native Americans. The Southern California Library for Social Studies Research specializes in literature on radical, progressive, labor, and minority movements. And not to be overlooked is the National Archives–Los Angeles Branch in Laguna Niguel, with holdings concerning the federal government's activities in the region.

History museums, many of which are located in historic structures, are another valuable resource. El Molino Viejo ("The Old Mill") Museum in San Marino (remains of the area's first water-powered grist mill) is maintained by the California Historical Society, and the Lummis Adobe is home to the Historical Society of Southern California. Some museums have highly specialized functions. There are historical museums categorized as corporate (Wells Fargo), cultural (Fowler Museum), railway, maritime, and aeronautical. There are even museums devoted to surfing and neon art. The state, the county, the city, and private groups maintain historic parks, such as Drum Barracks Civil War Museum, El Pueblo de Los Angeles Historic Monument, Pío Pico State Historic Park, and Los Encinos State Historic Park.

Also engaged in protecting the past are historical associations and preservation societies. The typical historical society is a membership organization of a few score dedicated people who run a house museum and offer tours. Some publish journals, newsletters, or books highlighting their subregion. Most museums are open to the public, although they may have restricted hours.

HISTORICAL SOCIETY OF SOUTHERN CALIFORNIA (HSSC), region's principal historical society. It was founded in the 1880s by Noah Levering, a former teacher who had studied law

Lummis Home (El Alisal). Photo by Harry Chamberlain, courtesy Historical Society of Southern California.

with Abraham Lincoln, and others. Its mission is to save historical records, mark historic sites, and educate the community as to local heritage. Since 1884 the society has published a respected journal, now titled the *Southern California Quarterly.* The HSSC is headquartered in the landmark Charles F. Lummis home, "El Alisal," in Highland Park, built beginning in 1898. The society presents annual awards for achievement in the field of local history.

HISTORICAL WRITING ABOUT LOS ANGELES, BEFORE 1945. The first "historians" in the region were pioneer American settlers, town boosters, and literary romancers who relied largely on scattered written records and personal reminiscence. Their works showed a marked degree of provincialism and a tendency toward exaggeration. Some books were tinged by the romance of the Spanish missions, as in Helen Hunt Jackson's novel *Ramona* (1884). Historical writing was also influenced by the massive California history books published by Hubert Howe Bancroft in San Francisco. The boosterish lawyers, journalists, physicians, and entrepreneurs who wrote local history were mainly Anglo men whose writings displayed a marked bias in favor of oligarchy and aristocracy. They often ignored or distorted the story of nonwhites.

The first published history about Los Angeles was *An Historical Sketch of Los Angeles County: California from the Spanish Occupancy, by the Founding of the Mission San Gabriel Archangel, September 8, 1781, to July 4, 1876.* It was jointly authored by a trio of pioneers: J. J. Warner, a Connecticut Yankee merchant who arrived in Los Angeles in 1831; Benjamin I. Hayes, a Maryland attorney who came in 1850; and Joseph P. Widney, an Ohio physician who appeared on the scene in 1868, becoming USC's second president. Another early work was Horace Bell's *Reminiscences of a Ranger* (1881), a memorable description of law-and-order issues of the 1850s. Although it made no pretense to historical accuracy, the book contained many valuable anecdotes.

San Francisco–based historian Hubert Howe Bancroft referred to Los Angeles in his monumental seven-volume *History of California* (1884–1890). Many county histories were also issued after 1880. Thompson and West's *History of Los Angeles County, California with Illustrations* (1880), became a major ongoing enterprise, a grab bag of information, not all of it accurate. *An Illustrated History of Los Angeles County . . .* (1889), a collection of biographical sketches issued by the Lewis Publishing Company of Chicago, was probably

---

I like it out here very much, but it's very God damned far away from everything.

—Preston Sturges, movie director

---

written by J. M. Guinn and Henry D. Burrows. Guinn, who took up permanent residence in Anaheim in 1869, was appointed superintendent of Los Angeles schools in 1881. He edited the *Annual Publication* of the Historical Society of Southern California from 1893 to 1913 and produced sizable tomes about his adopted city: *Historical and Biographical Record of Los Angeles and Vicinity . . .* (1901), *A History of California and an Extended History of Its Southern Coast Counties* (1907), and *Southern California, Its History and Its People* (1915), books much influenced by Bancroft.

Harris Newmark's *Sixty Years in Southern California, 1853–1913* (1916) was a prodigious memoir by a German-born Jew, brimming with specific and highly reliable information. John Steven McGroarty's somewhat less dependable *Los Angeles from the Mountains to the Sea* (1921) was one of several works by the California poet laureate, a Pennsylvanian by birth and a lawyer by training. William Andrew Spalding was a journalist who wrote, among other books, *History and Reminiscences: Los Angeles City and County* (1931), while the

banker Jackson A. Graves packed a good deal of local history into his autobiography, *My Seventy Years in California* (1927).

By the 1930s a new generation of writers was making its mark. Boyle Workman's *The City That Grew, 1840–1936* (1936) was the first history written by a native Angeleno, and a civic leader. W. W. Robinson produced a raft of books about Los Angeles beginning in 1931, based on solid research from the files of the Title Insurance and Trust Company. They dealt with various cities, including Los Angeles, Santa Monica, Pasadena, Whittier, and Glendale. His *Ranchos Become Cities* (1939) chronicles the transformation of the old titles into urban developments. A high standard for literary excellence and historical analysis was set by Carey McWilliams's *Southern California: An Island on the Land* (1946). Many regard it as the best book ever written about the region.

HISTORICAL WRITING ABOUT LOS ANGELES, SINCE 1945. In recent years social analysis and critical commentary have added important new perspectives on the past, giving greater breadth to our understanding of local history. Monographs have been written on all manner of specialized topics, from religion to planning and journalism to water development. Investigation into neglected areas has led to the growing literary visibility of racial and ethnic minorities and of smaller communities, as well as to a reassessment of older histories. Conspicuously lacking for a city the size of Los Angeles, however, is a single comprehensive and detailed work.

In a limited space it is possible to mention but a few of the more significant works. Remi Nadeau's *City Makers: The Men Who Transformed Los Angeles from Village to Metropolis During the First Great Boom, 1868–76* (1948) is an example of a history that deals with a neglected era. A solid revisionist view of the Los Angeles Aqueduct controversy is Abraham Hoffman's *Vision or Villainy: Origins of the Owens Valley–Los Angeles Water Controversy* (1981). *The Fragmented Metropolis: Los Angeles, 1850–1930* (1967), by Robert Fogelson, is a path-breaking survey of government structures, and particularly of the planning process. Robert Gottlieb and Irene Wolt produced a large and critical work on journalism, *Thinking Big: The Story of the "Los Angeles Times," Its Publishers, and Their Influence on Southern California* (1977). Intended for the general reader, John Weaver's *El Pueblo Grande: A Nonfic-*

tion Book About Los Angeles (1973), is a delightful compendium of anecdotes. David Clark produced *Los Angeles: A City Apart* (1981), a profusely illustrated history with a brief, factual text. In *L.A. Freeway* (1981), David Brodsly presents a highly appreciative analysis of the freeway system and its impact on local culture. Andrew Rolle's slim volume *Los Angeles* (1981) offers a general survey intended for college freshmen. Gloria Ricci Lothrop's centennial history *Pomona* (1988) is an excellent example of a finely wrought history of a smaller city in Los Angeles County. A notable monograph on local religion is Michael E. Engh's *Frontier Faiths: Church, Temple, and Synagogue in Los Angeles, 1846–1888* (1992). Lionel Rolfe's *Literary L.A.* (1981) presents local writers of fiction in a rich tapestry. Kevin Starr's highly acclaimed series on California cultural history includes the volume *Inventing the Dream: California Through the Progressive Era* (1985), which covers many aspects of Southern California history. Mike Davis, in *The City of Quartz: Excavating the Future in Los Angeles* (1990), provides commentary on social and racial themes.

HISTORIC PRESERVATION MOVEMENT arose initially to save and restore the Spanish missions and other colonial structures. It gradually became more inclusive. The pioneer in the field was Charles F. Lummis, who in 1894 formed the California Landmarks Club. Christine Sterling advanced the cause by tenaciously defending the Plaza area in the 1920s and early 1930s. The Native Sons of the Golden West began naming and preserving landmarks.

In 1962, as bulldozers ripped into old buildings to make way for new roads and commercial development, a committee of architects and civic leaders achieved passage of a Los Angeles ordinance to protect historic and cultural sites. The law established a 360-day moratorium on the destruction of landmarks and created the Los Angeles City Cultural Heritage Commission to oversee the work or preservation. Its first declared monument was the Leonis Adobe in Calabasas. Since then the commission has registered hundreds of sites. The city has also enacted an ordinance penalizing the owners of historic buildings who deliberately neglect their property. On a selective basis the ordinance protects entire historic neighborhoods as well. A citizens group, the Los Angeles Conservancy, formed during the fight to save the downtown public library in the late 1970s, has influenced public policy and heightened public awareness regarding preservation.

Many local historical societies and cities other than Los Angeles have noteworthy preservation programs. Pasadena's Cultural Heritage Commission has an exemplary record of protecting older public buildings and Craftsman-style bungalows. Greene and Greene's Pasadena masterpiece, the Gamble House, is the crown jewel of historic homes. The Arroyo Seco is a declared historic landmark, as are many private residences in its vicinity. The Glendale Historical Society and the city of Glendale have managed to preserve the Doctor's House, a handsome Queen Anne–Eastlake home built in the 1880s, which now stands in Brand Park.

In the 1970s and 1980s public awareness of the need for historic preservation increased. Federal tax laws encouraged private developers to rehabilitate old buildings according to rigorous standards while adapting them for new business uses. Los Angeles city's Community Redevelopment Agency earmarked $100 million for historic preservation in Hollywood, Little Tokyo, and the Central Business District. The county government, by contrast, showed somewhat less commitment to historic preservation, although the County Historical Landmarks and Records Commission has listed over 50 official points of historical interest.

In addition to rescuing old structures, historic preservation works to protect places that have been identified, officially and unofficially, by state and local governments and historical societies as having historic value. The best known involve rancho adobes, missions, exploration routes, film industry sites, commercial buildings, private homes, the site of the first gold discovery in California, and areas related to the Mexican War. The state officially lists locales having anthropological, cultural, military, political, architectural, economic, scientific, and technical importance. Smaller, isolated buildings and sites are designated historic landmarks, while larger sites become historic parks and monuments. The cultural heritage commissions of Los Angeles and Pasadena, as well as local historical societies, identify local landmarks that escape state recognition.

HISTORIC PRESERVATION OVERLAY ZONE (HPOZ), device created by a 1979 Los Angeles city ordinance to protect an entire neighborhood from unwarranted destruction by redevelopment. In any given designated zone, owners are not forced to fix their property, but neither may they make changes that violate the original design and construction elements. No public funds are appropriated for reconstruction. The first HPOZ was Angelino Heights. The effort to create the Carthay zone, near Olympic and Crescent Heights, was spearheaded by Fred Naiditch and other residents to protect the neighborhood's many Spanish Colonial Revival homes erected in the 1920s. Another HPOZ safeguards structures in the Wilton Historic District, along Wilton Place and Wilton Drive between 1st and 3rd Streets. The smallest HPOZ is Melrose Hill, a single block at Marathon Street and North Melrose Hill. The North University Park HPOZ, an area developed in the 1890s but partially demolished in the 1960s, protects Victorians in an area bounded by the Harbor and Santa Monica Freeways and by Jefferson Boulevard and Vermont Avenue.

As of 1995, 7 HPOZs had been approved, and 11 more were under consideration. Among the latter were Beverly-Fairfax, south of West Hollywood; Raymond-Kenwood, Adams-Normandie, and Van Buren Place, all southwest of downtown; Devon-Ashton, east of Westwood; Windward Circle, in Venice; Sorority Row, in east Westwood Village; Miracle Mile South, west of Hancock Park; Carthay Circle, east of Beverly Hills; Lafayette Square, midcity; and Atwater Village, near Glendale.

HISTORY OF LOS ANGELES. *See* Los Angeles city history

HODGES, ALPHEUS P., first mayor of Los Angeles after the Yankee takeover, from 1850 to 1851. A physician, he performed double duty as coroner. The city was then less than 28 square miles in size, with a population of 1,610.

HOLDEN, NATE (1929–), city council member from the 10th District, elected in 1987. A World War II veteran and aerospace engineer, Holden served as a deputy to Supervisor Kenneth Hahn and was president of the California Democratic Council from 1970 to 1974. Holden was elected to the state senate in 1974, remaining until 1978. While on the city council he has served on the transportation, public safety, and governmental relations committees. He is a member of the NAACP and the Urban League.

HOLIFIELD, CHET (1903–1995), Kentucky-born congressman. After riding the rails into Los Angeles at the age of 16, he first became a businessman and then entered politics, winning a seat in the U.S. Congress from the Whittier area in 1942. Holifield held that position until his retirement in 1974. As an original member of the Joint Committee on Atomic Energy, he was an avid believer in the positive uses of nuclear power. During his tenure in Washington he secured federal funds for such projects as bilingual instruction, flood control, and library and hospital improvement.

HOLLYHOCK HOUSE, architectural landmark in Barnsdall Park, also known as Barnsdall House, built between 1917 and 1920. The pre-Columbian-style home was designed by Frank Lloyd Wright for oil heiress and theatrical impresario Aline Barnsdall. It was Wright's first house in Los Angeles. The house gets its name from the flower motif that decorates both exterior and interior spaces. The home was donated to the city in 1927, and in 1963 it was named a historic cultural monument and opened to the public. The interior contains copies of furniture that Wright designed specifically for Hollyhock House. Restoration work is now being carried out by a private foundation.

Hollyhock House, west façade. Photo by Virginia Ernst Kazor, courtesy City of Los Angeles Cultural Affairs Dept.

HOLLYWOOD, name for both a Los Angeles locale, 8 miles west of downtown, and the movie industry. Capt. Gaspar de Portolá's 1769 expedition passed through the canyon that is now at the north end of Sycamore Avenue and encountered resident Shoshonean Indians.

The district, which sits on what was once Ranchos La Brea and Los Feliz, was named in 1886 by Kansans Horace H. Wilcox and his wife, Daeida, transplants to Cahuenga Valley in 1883. The origin of the name is obscure—the holly plant is not native to the area—but may have been suggested by a friend of Mrs. Wilcox's. The Wilcoxes also founded the town, platting it beginning in 1887. Methodists and temperance advocates, they established Hollywood as a dry town. They offered free lots to any who would build churches there—an offer that apparently had great appeal, for many churches were indeed built, including what was then the largest Presbyterian church in the world. When it was incorporated in 1903, one year after Horace Wilcox's death, Hollywood had a population of about 700. The independent city of small wooden bungalows, open fields, and citrus groves was consolidated with Los Angeles in 1910 to assure a larger water supply; by then the population had swelled to some 4,000.

The early straitlaced residents resented the influx of actors, cowboys, and other flamboyant people associated with motion pictures. Actually, Los Angeles's first studios were in the Edendale and Silver Lake districts, but adjacent Hollywood soon became the favored place for early filmmaking. Studios lined Sunset Boulevard and Melrose Avenue, while Hollywood Boulevard became Hollywood's main commercial thoroughfare, as famous in its way as Broadway, in Manhattan. The city pulsed with new life during the Boom of the Twenties as new housing tracts, hotels, restaurants, and studio facilities were opened. Hollywood's population soared to 50,000 in that decade.

Visitors have flocked from all over the world to view the sights of Hollywood. Famous tourist attractions, past and present, have included the Hollywood Bowl; the Hollywood sign (erected in 1923, and originally reading "Hollywoodland"); Grauman's Chinese Theatre, with its cement-embedded hand- and footprints, and the Egyptian Theatre; the corner of Hollywood and Vine; Sardi's; the Brown Derby restaurant and Musso & Frank's Grill; Warner Brothers, Paramount, and the Chaplin Studios; the Hollywood Palladium, the major

showcase for the big bands; and the star-studded Hollywood Walk of Fame, begun in 1960.

To this day, Hollywood is dotted with studios, film labs, costume outfitters, sound and electronic facilities, guild offices, food caterers, and suppliers associated with filmmaking. Yet the movie industry was always located in scattered places throughout Southern California, and the dispersal has continued in recent decades.

Since the 1960s, the district has suffered economic decline and physical blight and lost much of its glamor. The city government, local homeowners associations, and the chamber of commerce have been engaged in attempting to restore the commercial viability of the area and to preserve its residential neighborhoods.

HOLLYWOOD, MOVIES ABOUT, have come in all forms: comedies, melodramas, tragedies, and musicals. The Harold Lloyd comedy *Merton of the Movies* (1924) was one of the earliest, and was remade in 1932 and 1947. A common theme has been the rise and fall of stars. Some of the best known in this genre are *What Price Hollywood?* (1932), which was remade, in different versions, as *A Star Is Born* (1937, 1954, 1976); *Sunset Boulevard* (1950); *The Star* (1952); *The Barefoot Contessa* (1954); *The Goddess* (1958); and *Inside Daisy Clover* (1965). Hollywood also explored its silent film era in such movies as *Hollywood Cavalcade* (1939); Mel Brooks's *Silent Movie* (1976); and the classic *Singin' in the Rain* (1952). The subject of filmmaking and those who create the films are dealt with in the award-winning *The Bad and the Beautiful* (1952); Clifford Odets's *The Big Knife* (1955); *Two Weeks in Another Town* (1962); *The Last Tycoon* (1976), based on the life of Irving Thalberg; and Woody Allen's *Stardust Memories* (1980). *Hollywood Canteen* (1944), filmed during World War II, was filled with stars playing themselves at the famous USO center. Preston Sturges's *Sullivan's Travels* (1941), which questions the role of films in an increasingly dangerous world; *The Way We Were* (1973), concerning the Hollywood blacklist; and Robert Townsend's *Hollywood Shuffle* (1987) all grappled with serious social issues. *The Day of the Locust* (1975), based on what may be the best novel ever written about Hollywood, was a less successful film. Hollywood has continued to picture itself in its own product in such films as *Postcards from the Edge* (1990), *Guilty by Suspicion* (1991), and *The Player* (1992).

HOLLYWOOD ANTI-NAZI LEAGUE, antifascist organization formed in the movie industry during the 1930s as a response to the Spanish Civil War. Its members, who included Fredric March, Florence Eldridge, Donald Ogden Stewart, and Ben Hecht, were harassed for their association with it during the Hollywood Red Scare.

HOLLYWOOD ATHLETIC CLUB, private club on Sunset Boulevard. Designed as an exclusive men's establishment for movie notables, the 9-story building, at the time Hollywood's tallest, opened on New Year's Eve 1923. Olympic gold medalists Buster Crabbe and Johnny Weissmuller, both of them movie Tarzans, trained in its gymnasium and swimming pool. Cornel Wilde was the club's fencing instructor before becoming a movie star. Other habitués of the gym, pool, billiard hall, bar, restaurant, and lodgings were John Barrymore, Errol Flynn, Dick Powell, W. C. Fields, Charlie Chaplin, Clark Gable, Anthony Quinn, Rudolph Valentino, Walt Disney, and John Wayne. As a prank, Wayne once stood on the penthouse level tossing billiard balls at cars passing below. Women, although forbidden above the first floor, were sometimes smuggled in. After World War II the club disbanded. For a time the building stood empty; it then became a Jewish theological seminary and, later, housed the University of Judaism. It was recently carefully refurbished and reborn as an upscale club.

HOLLYWOOD BOULEVARD, Hollywood's main thoroughfare beginning in the 1920s and 1930s, when the industry was in its heyday and the stars still lived in the nearby hills. The intersection of Hollywood and Vine became a fabled crossroads. Adoring fans could catch a glimpse of cowboy idol Tom Mix cruising in a sports car with a hood ornament shaped like Texas steer horns, and Clara Bow, the "It Girl," driving a convertible accompanied by two pet dogs with hair dyed red to match her own. Aspiring stars lodged at Hollywood Boulevard's Roosevelt Hotel or at the Plaza on Vine (Ronald Reagan's hotel when he first arrived from Des Moines) and cut deals with agents quartered in the Taft Building. Notables shopped at I. Magnin Department Store, lunched at Musso & Frank's, dined at the Brown Derby, and danced at the Montmartre Cafe. Gossip columnists referred to the street as "the Golden Road," "Hardened Artery," "Santa Claus Lane," and "Main Street in Slacks."

Today Hollywood Boulevard has lost much of its former appeal. Many properties are run down, and sections of the street appear shabby and uninviting, particularly at night. Hollywood Heritage, the Los Angeles Conservancy, and other groups have made strenuous efforts to identify and refurbish historic structures. In 1986 they succeeded in having the boulevard from Gower to La Brea officially designated a historic district.

In the 1980s a Hollywood redevelopment movement was sparked by the Hollywood Chamber of Commerce, real estate developers, former councilman Michael Woo, and others. Since 1983, major property owners and developers along Hollywood and Sunset Boulevards from Western to La Brea have sought an infusion of Community Redevelopment Agency (CRA) money to improve the local infrastructure and refurbish buildings. In 1987 the CRA proposed to revive commerce and tourism in the film capital by constructing new hotels, office towers, restaurants, and residences, thus imparting to the boulevard some of its former glamour. Some $922 million was earmarked to revitalize 1,107 acres. However, "slow-growth" advocates, wary of high-density development in Hollywood, have become increasingly vocal. Homeowner and tenant groups have launched movements to prevent commercial overbuilding and protect residential values, while preservationists have demanded safeguards for buildings and sites of historical importance.

HOLLYWOOD BOWL, outdoor musical amphitheater in Cahuenga Pass. It was developed by H. Ellis Reed, who chose the spot while hiking in the hills with his father. Calling to each other from deep in the hollow to the rim high above, they were amazed by the clarity of the sound. The amphitheater received its name from benefactor Hugo Kirchhoffer, while funding for the private, nonprofit cultural enterprise was achieved chiefly by Mrs. Artie Mason Carter, Charles E. Toberman, and others. It opened in 1916 with a production of *Julius Caesar*. The all-star cast included Tyrone Power Sr., Douglas Fairbanks Sr., and Mae Murray. The benefactors arranged for the Los Angeles Philharmonic Orchestra to perform outdoor concerts during the summers. Tickets cost 25 cents. The first musical offerings—and Easter sunrise services, which were to become an annual event— took place under primitive conditions in 1922: spectators sat on the grassy slopes, while the per-

Hollywood Bowl, seen from the Goodyear blimp. UPI/Bettmann Archive.

formers used a discarded barn door for a platform. The acoustics were enhanced in 1924 with a shell designed by Lloyd Wright. The shell has been redesigned or replaced three or four times since then. Frank O. Gehry and Associates designed the latest variation, in 1982.

A state law prohibited the county from subsidizing musical or other cultural facilities and events until around 1934, when Supervisor John Anson Ford managed to have the law changed. For a time the Hollywood Bowl organization suffered serious financial strain, but it was rescued in 1951 by Dorothy "Buffy" Chandler. The amphitheater is currently owned by Los Angeles County. It seats 20,000 persons and has standing room for another 10,000. The bowl, with its shell, seating area, and parking, covers 116 acres. It remains world famous for its summertime program, "Symphonies Under the Stars."

HOLLYWOOD CANTEENS, World War II service organizations from 1942 to 1945 designed to raise the morale of men and women in uniform. Thousands of GIs roamed Hollywood on military leave and wandered the streets in hopes of glimpsing celebrities.

The first such establishment was the Hollywood Guild and Canteen, a hostelry run by philanthropist Anne Lehr on Crescent Heights Drive. "Mom" Lehr provided clean beds, free meals, snacks, and live entertainment; she raised funds in the movie studios and arranged for actors and ac-

tresses to provide entertainment. About 1,000 volunteers, mostly women, ran the canteen, while movie stars Mary Pickford, Janet Gaynor, and Myrna Loy coordinated the entertainment. The Hollywood Canteen at Cahuenga and Sunset Boulevard, formed by Bette Davis, John Garfield, and Dr. Jules Stein, was more famous. It attracted the most glamorous stars and the biggest crowds of servicemen and -women. Food and drink were free, and as many as 3,000 GIs might be crowded into the place at one time. Some 6,000 performers, writers, and secretaries played host, dancing with the patrons, mounting skits, giving opera concerts, broadcasting radio shows, and performing comedy acts. On a given night, Marlene Dietrich might be cutting cake, Lana Turner washing dishes, and John Garfield or Betty Grable serving food. The Hollywood Canteen, which inspired a star-studded film of the same name in 1944, was amazingly successful until the day it closed in November 1945.

HOLLYWOOD CHAMBER OF COMMERCE was formed in 1921 by Dr. Allen Shore and others, who started a campaign to convince Hollywood Boulevard merchants to attract attention by leaving their store lights on after 9 P.M. Until then the area was, for all intents and purposes, deserted after nightfall. The boulevard soon attracted large department stores and became an exclusive shopping area. In 1924 the chamber promoted the installation of Christmas trees and street decorations, and initiated the Santa Claus Lane Parade, which, by the 1930s, had evolved into a spectacular display featuring bands, color guards, and floats and vehicles from which Hollywood stars waved to excited crowds lining the thoroughfare. The chamber has maintained the Hollywood sign on the hill and fostered the Walk of Fame—almost 2,000 star-shaped plaques implanted in the sidewalks to honor people in the entertainment industry. Since the 1970s the chamber has been a major player in urban redevelopment planning for Hollywood.

HOLLYWOOD CITIZEN-NEWS, daily paper formed in 1921 by a merger of the *Hollywood Citizen,* a weekly, and the *Hollywood News.* In the 1930s its publisher, Judge Harlan Palmer, a justice of the peace, progressive reformer, and New Deal Democrat, used the paper to attack the corrupt mayor, Frank Shaw. His foes dubbed him a "bluenose" and "longhair" because of the high moral tone of his editorials. Palmer ran for district attorney against the reactionary anti-union incumbent, Buron Fitts, who had the backing of the *Los Angeles Times.* He was instrumental in establishing the City News Service, which supplied news to most local media.

HOLLYWOOD MEMORIAL PARK, most visited cemetery in Los Angeles, founded in 1899 by I. N. Van Nuys and his father-in-law, Isaac Lankershim. Its Jewish counterpart, Beth Olem Cemetery, is on adjoining but separate grounds. Numerous local notables are interred at Hollywood Memorial Park, including newspaper publisher Gen. Harrison Gray Otis and his son-in-law Harry Chandler, among others of the Otis-Chandler clan; public benefactors William Andrews Clark Jr., founder of the Los Angeles Philharmonic, and Col. Griffith J. Griffith, who gave the city land for Griffith Park; and important film figures such as Douglas Fairbanks Sr., Cecil B. De Mille, Peter Lorre, John Huston, and Harry Cohen. The crypt of the silent film star Rudolph Valentino has been a mecca for mourners since his death in 1926.

HOLLYWOOD PARK, racetrack in Inglewood. Established in 1938 by the Hollywood Turf Club and featuring extensive landscaping, it is considered one of the most beautiful tracks in the country. Vast sums of money have been staked there on races such as the Hollywood Gold Cup, California Stakes, and Century Handicap. The track has always attracted the best thoroughbreds in the nation. A monument in the Golden Paddock memorializes Native Dancer (1959–1967), who won three Hollywood Gold Cups. The park's "Lady of the Lake," a woman dressed like a goose, is said to evoke the heraldic emblem of Don Bruno Avila, who once owned a rancho and racetrack in Inglewood. In 1992 track officials announced a $100 million remodeling program that will include the construction of a new 14,000-seat music center on the premises.

HOLLYWOOD RED SCARE, political witch-hunt in the film industry from 1946 to the 1960s. It was spearheaded by the House Un-American Activities Committee (HUAC) during tumultuous hearings in 1947. In the early Cold War years, the committee set itself the task of investigating the film industry and cleansing it of alleged subversives. It subpoenaed actors, writers, and directors who were accused of being Communists or the friends and allies of Communists ("fellow travelers"). Many were in fact leftists who had been active in the Hollywood Anti-Nazi League, an antifascist movement of the 1930s.

The HUAC modus operandi was to ask a subpoenaed witness if he or she was a member of the Communist Party—an unpopular though legal organization—and to request that the names of persons believed to be Communists or Communist

---

When you step in a freezing puddle during a New York November, you think, "You know, it's a little hotter and drier in Santa Monica."

—Paul Reiser, comic

---

sympathizers be supplied to the committee. Those testifying were also asked to name movies they considered subversive (*Gentlemen's Agreement, Forever Amber, Song of Russia, Sister Carrie,* and *Tender Comrade* were among the many cited). Those testifying were divided into "friendly" witnesses (including Robert Taylor, Ginger Rogers, Adolphe Menjou) and "unfriendly" witnesses (of whom the Hollywood Ten were the most prominent).

The Hollywood blacklist cost some 400 people their livelihood or career. The political climate of fear also afflicted public school teachers and other government employees. By the late 1960s, however, blacklisted people came to be regarded as heroes. A nationwide campaign to abolish HUAC, launched in 1956 by Frank Wilkinson and Dorothy Marshall of the Los Angeles–based Citizens Committee to Preserve American Freedoms, finally succeeded in 1969.

HOLLYWOOD REPORTER, daily trade paper of the entertainment industry. It was founded in 1930 by William R. "Billy" Wilkerson, film buff, gambler, and restaurateur (Trocadero, Vendome, La Rue's). When Wilkerson ignored studio public-relations handouts and began to print hard news about the industry, the studios tried to blackball him and even buy him out. In 1936 the paper occupied its own building on Sunset Boulevard, with business offices upstairs, a print shop in the back, and a barbershop and stylish haberdashery in front. Wilkerson, who discovered Lana Turner and was a confidant of Howard Hughes, helped lead the Hollywood anti-Communist crusade of the 1940s and 1950s. When he died in 1960 his widow, Tichi Noble, took over as the *Reporter*'s editor-in-chief and publisher; she ran the daily for 20 more years before selling it to BPI Communications. With news bureaus in New York, Washington, and London, the *Reporter* is read religiously (along with its chief rival, *Daily Variety*) by aspiring and established members of the entertainment industry.

HOLLYWOOD RIVIERA, coastal area annexed to Torrance in 1927. The Huntington Land and Improvement Company and builder Clifford Reid selected the name, suggesting the south of France and the movie industry. They capitalized on the area's proximity to the exclusive Palos Verdes Estates and on the picturesque views, cool summer breezes, and rolling hills. The developers also adopted the Mediterranean architecture of fashionable Palos Verdes; the principal streets they named Paseo de las Tortugas ("Turtle Road") and Calle Mayor ("Main Street"). They built the Hollywood Riviera Club at the edge of the beach and secured perpetual access to the strand for the homeowners. Efforts to lure movie celebrities to Hollywood Riviera failed, although in 1936 Pres. Woodrow Wilson's daughters lived there. In 1992 the community had 10,000 residents and 3,500 homes, some dating back to the 1920s and 1930s.

HOLLYWOOD SIGN, advertising billboard on Mt. Lee, in the hills overlooking the film capital, erected in 1923. The sign is 50 feet high, 450 feet long, weighs 480,000 pounds, and cost $21,000 to construct. It was designed to promote Harry Chandler's real estate development named "Hollywoodland" (the sign's original wording), whose main street was Beachwood Drive. At night the sign was illuminated by 4,000 20-watt bulbs and could be seen from the harbor, 25 miles away. The caretaker lived in a cabin behind the letter *L*. The last four letters were removed by the Hollywood Chamber of Commerce in 1945. Those remaining are made of sheet metal painted white and bolstered by telephone poles. The sign and surrounding land belong to the Los Angeles Department of Recreation and Parks but are maintained by the Hollywood Chamber of Commerce and other community activists. It underwent a renovation in 1978, financed with private funds.

The Hollywood Sign.

HOLLYWOOD STARS, minor league baseball club of the Pacific Coast League that played first at Wrigley Field and later at Gilmore Stadium. Filmdom's George Burns, Gracie Allen, Gary Cooper, Cecil B. De Mille, Walt Disney, and Bing Crosby were among the team's owners. Under manager Fred Haney the club, nicknamed "the Halos," won two pennants. The arrival of the National League Dodgers in Los Angeles put an end to the Stars, who played their last game on 5 September 1957 before 6,354 spectators.

HOLLYWOOD STUDIO CLUB, residence hall founded in 1916 by the YWCA for aspiring young women waiting for work in the movies. The club occupied fine accommodations at Lodi Place. Tenants were provided with sleeping quarters, food, recreational facilities, and reading rooms. The club was a temporary home for thousands of women, including Marilyn Monroe. It closed in the 1960s.

HOLLYWOOD STUDIO MUSEUM, barn used by the Jesse Lasky Feature Play Company, one of the first Hollywood film studios, to make Cecil B. De Mille's *The Squaw Man* (1913). The building originally stood on the corner of Selma and Vine Streets and was part of Paramount Studios until 1919. It was moved to Highland Avenue, across from the Hollywood Bowl, in 1989 as a county project to develop a major film industry museum. The project was largely abandoned. The small museum specializes in showing films of the silent era.

HOLLYWOOD SUBWAY, 1-mile tunnel built in 1924–1925 to relieve downtown congestion caused by the Red Cars and autos. The $15 million hole, which started at Hill and 5th Streets and ended at 1st Street and Glendale Boulevard, allowed the Pacific Electric (PE) Red Cars to shave 15 minutes of travel time off their run to Hollywood, Beverly Hills, Santa Monica, and Burbank. With the decline of the PE ridership it was sealed off and closed in 1955. The cost per mile of today's Metro Red Line under Wilshire Boulevard, projected to run 18 miles, is 45 times greater than that of the old subway tunnel.

HOLLYWOOD TEN, a group of screenwriters and directors who were subpoenaed to appear before the House Un-American Activities Committee (HUAC) in 1947 but invoked their constitutional rights and refused to testify. The ten—Adrian Scott, Ring Lardner Jr., Alvah Bessie, John Howard Lawson, Sam Ornitz, Lester Cole, Albert Maltz, Dalton Trumbo, Herbert Biberman, and Edward Dmytryk—refused to answer questions concerning their own or anyone else's political affiliations, and were held in contempt of court. The studios they worked for fired them. They appealed their case, lost, and each spent a year in jail. After serving his sentence Dmytryk gave names to the committee and regained his job, but the others remained blacklisted. They, along with other blacklisted writers, continued to write scripts under different names, and several won Academy Awards (including Carl Foreman and Michael Wilson for *Bridge on the River Kwai* [1957] and Dalton Trumbo for *The Brave One* [1956]). In recent years the Writers Guild of America has started to restore the proper film credits to these writers.

HOLMBY HILLS, affluent residential area in West Los Angeles situated on the former Rancho San José

Nine of the Hollywood Ten. Courtesy Dept. of Special Collections, University Research Library, UCLA.

de Buenos Ayres. The district was named by rancho owner Arthur Letts Sr., founder of the Broadway Department Store, in honor of his birthplace, Holmby, England. He sold the land to the Janss Investment Corporation for development in 1922. Many stately older residences stand in Holmby Hills. One of the newest additions is producer Aaron Spelling's 56,000-square-foot mansion.

HOMELESSNESS. Originally called the "tramp problem" or "vagrancy problem," homelessness was first noted around 1893 and periodically thereafter, particularly during national economic downturns. Especially in the winter months, unemployed men —"bums"—from the East hopped freight trains headed for Southern California's mild climate. There they gathered around campfires and slept in barns, haystacks, or abandoned shacks. Private charities dealt with the problem.

Homelessness increased dramatically during the 1930s, and again in the 1980s and 1990s, although precise numbers are difficult to determine. A non-profit support agency for the homeless, Shelter Partnership, Inc., estimated that in 1992 there were 68,600 homeless in the county on any given night, many of them children. By contrast, the U.S. Census Bureau counted only 7,706 in the city of Los Angeles and 11,790 in the county in 1992, but conceded that these numbers were low. The *Los Angeles Times* gave a figure of 177,000 for the county in February 1992.

In the United States as a whole in 1990 the number of homeless per 10,000 population was 9.19. Among selected California cities comparative figures were 76.92 in San Francisco, 41.33 in El Monte, 16.47 in Pomona, 10.71 in Long Beach, 1.35 in Torrance, and 0.10 in Thousand Oaks. The recent crisis began when federal housing programs evaporated in the 1980s amid a general economic downturn. Also, some 10,000 downtown housing units have been demolished in recent decades. The efforts of the Community Redevelopment Agency to rehabilitate old homes and apartments, build new housing, and refurbish transient hotels downtown did not keep pace with the increasing homeless population. Many of the homeless now include the working poor and families with children. Some 150 homeless people bathed in the Los Angeles River on a daily basis in the summer of 1990, claiming that, despite the oil, chemicals, and other pollutants, it was safer to go there than to Skid Row.

Some Skid Row workers distinguish among the *houseless,* who need shelter until they obtain jobs; the *disabled,* who can function but need medication, counseling, and a supportive environment; and the *helpless,* who have drug or alcohol addictions or are mentally ill.

The homeless have had a few stalwart champions. Among them are the Union Rescue Mission, which provides temporary shelter; the Shelter Partnership, which has funneled millions of dollars, private and public, into shelters and monitors the distribution of food and goods to those facilities; and the Homeless Outreach Program (HOP), a referral service staffed by former homeless people that provides some downtown social services. The problem of homelessness has been acute in outlying parts of the county as well. In Santa Monica even the liberal governing coalition has been split on how to deal with the hunger, crime, and health problems of the homeless.

In 1993 a homeless community known as Dome City opened on the edge of downtown. Conceived of by homeless advocate Ted Hayes, Dome City (also known as Genesis I, in the hope of inspiring similar clusters) was made up of 18 geodesic dome-shaped units, resembling igloos. It was initially funded by a $250,000 ARCO foundation grant. Residents pay a modest monthly fee from their welfare checks.

HOME OF PEACE MEMORIAL PARK, Jewish eastside cemetery. The 32-acre site at Whittier Boulevard and the Long Beach Freeway is owned by the Wilshire Boulevard Temple. Founded by the Hebrew Benevolent Society, the cemetery's precursor was a Chavez Ravine burial ground dating from 1855. When oil wells and brick kilns began polluting the ravine around 1902, the society exhumed and moved all 360 bodies from the old site to the newly acquired cemetery. The original 360 were subsequently joined by some 50,000 others, including movie notables Louis B. Mayer, Fanny Bryce, and Carl Laemmle.

HOMEOWNERS ASSOCIATIONS, important but underrecognized advocacy groups. The first homeowners association was the Los Feliz Improvement Association, formed in 1916. Some groups are voluntary, but others are mandated by deed provisions. In the 1920s these associations, relying on restrictive deed covenants, helped realtors and developers keep upscale white neighborhoods segregated, successfully blocking African Americans and Asians from 95 percent of available housing. It was not until 1948 that the U.S. Supreme Court overturned such covenants. Homeowners associations have achieved considerable political power in and out of city hall since the 1960s; their support of Proposition 13 helped to turn the state tax tide, and they have waged successful battles to curb unrestricted commercial growth and school busing. The Hillside and Canyon Federation is a particularly well organized and effective umbrella organization.

HOME SAVINGS OF AMERICA, Irwindale banking institution that grew from obscurity during the post–World War II housing boom to become the national giant of the savings and loan industry. Its explosive growth occurred when it was acquired in 1947, for $162,000, by insurance agent Howard F. Ahmanson. He took over a firm with $1 million in assets and four employees working in a single office; by 1988 Home Savings posted $36 billion in assets, with 11,000 employees in 346 offices.

HOPE IN YOUTH, antigang program born after the 1992 riots. The church-backed community organization relies on over 100 social workers to counsel youths, parents, and teachers in Los Angeles's troubled neighborhoods. The first-year budget was $5.4 million.

HOPPER, HEDDA (1890–1966), screen actress and Hollywood gossip columnist. Born Elda Furry, she racked up more than 30 film credits between 1919 and 1966. Most of her films were silents, and she played mainly supporting roles. She played herself in the film *Sunset Boulevard* (1950). Hopper, along with her counterpart Louella Parsons, wielded immense power in the 1930s, 1940s, and 1950s. Using her widely syndicated column like a sword, she could—and did—make and break careers. Since flamboyant hats were her trademark, she called her autobiography *From Under My Hat* (1963).

HORSE RACING was a favored pastime of the Californio rancheros. In the flush Gold Rush year of 1852, José Sepúlveda and Pío Pico raced their steeds for a purse of $25,000 cash and an equal amount in livestock and land. Sepúlveda's Australian mare, Black Swan, came out ahead on the 9-mile course. The "Sport of Kings" has long been tied to gambling. E. J. "Lucky" Baldwin built an active racetrack operation in Santa Anita in the 1870s. When gambling was outlawed in 1907, bookmaking and wagering were likewise forbidden, hobbling the sport for the next quarter of a century. Racing fans could now wager only through illegal bookies, or at Agua Caliente and Tijuana, Mexico.

The sport developed into a multimillion-dollar recreational industry in the 1930s. In 1933 horse race enthusiasts managed to get a bill passed to "promote horse breeding and thereby benefit agriculture." The law established a California Horse Racing Board, limited the take of the tracks for pari-mutuel betting to 8 percent, and earmarked 4 percent to support county fairs, California Polytechnic Schools, and the University of California.

The light in Southern California demands strong colors. Here the sun plays a major role in modeling the texture and surface of buildings, making them sparkle and dance.
—Michael Graves, postmodernist architect

Santa Anita, the first licensed track in Los Angeles County, opened on Christmas Day 1934 and within the first three years had paid out $3.2 million in dividends. An investors group applied for a second racecourse, Hollywood Park, amid fierce opposition from the puritanical Protestant minister "Fighting Bob" Shuler (not to be confused with the Orange County minister). Licensed and running in the summer of 1938, it soon also realized enormous profits.

HORTON, LESTER (1907–1951), dancer. Raised in a working-class Indiana household, Horton never completed high school or had formal dance training. Nevertheless, in 1926 he was hired to choreograph authentic Native American dances for a production of Henry Wadsworth Longfellow's "The Song of Hiawatha." The play caused a sensation and traveled to small theaters as far away as Eagle Rock in Southern California. Horton settled there and helped found the Los Angeles Dance Theater, the first dance theater in the country. It was experimental, modern, and multicultural.

Among Horton's many students were Bella Lewitzky and Alvin Ailey, who went on to found their own modern dance companies and who acknowledge their debt to him.

HOSPITALS today number about 160 in Los Angeles County. The Sisters of Charity opened the first hospital in 1856 and established another, St. Vincent's Sanitarium, in 1888. The latter was among several late-19th-century health institutions that provided a haven for easterners seeking cures for lung diseases. County General Hospital was the first major public hospital, established in 1933, and it remains one of the largest. The National Soldiers Home at Sawtelle was founded in the 1880s, and by 1892 had 741 veterans as residents.

Currently, the major research and teaching hospital is at UCLA. Among the area's largest hospitals and most comprehensive in their coverage are Harbor-UCLA Medical Center, UCLA Medical Center, Cedars-Sinai Medical Center, City of Hope, Children's Hospital, St. Joseph's Hospital, Los Angeles County–USC Medical Center, and the eight facilities operated by the Kaiser Foundation. The Veterans Administration (VA) runs significant facilities in Long Beach, West Los Angeles, and Sepulveda, and the navy maintains a hospital in Long Beach. The two hospitals in the area with the biggest in-patient capacity are the VA hospital in West Los Angeles, with 1,025 beds, and the VA in Long Beach, with 1,000 beds. UCLA Medical Center has 711 beds.

HOTEL AND RESTAURANT EMPLOYEES UNION, an AFL-CIO affiliate, has organized 11,000 workers in Los Angeles (Local 11) and 5,000 in Long Beach and Orange County (Local 681). In 1992 both locals were headed by women: Maria Elena Durazo and Angela Keefe, respectively.

HOTELS. The mainstay of the tourism industry, hotels started out modestly in the 19th century as resting spots for weary travelers passing through the dusty cow town. The Bella Union Hotel, established in the 1850s in the small and quiet *pueblo* of Los Angeles, was a rather crude affair. Pico House, which opened at the Plaza in 1870, was the first inn to boast of deluxe accommodations. Far more elaborate spas opened during the Boom of the 1880s. The first was Hotel Arcadia, named after Doña Arcadia Bandini, wife of Robert Symington

Baker. It was located at the end of a rail line in Santa Monica, of which Baker was cofounder. The finest suburban hotel in the region, the Arcadia stood four stories high on a bluff overlooking the ocean. Pasadena also acquired comfortable hotels that catered to both wealthy visitors and longtime residents. The Beverly Hills Hotel, built in 1911, had the same objective. Attempting to attract wealthy patrons, hoteliers emphasized personal freedom, the glories of the local environment, and elegant comfort.

Additional hotels went up in the 1920s. The Biltmore, overlooking Pershing Square, became the premier downtown lodging house. Some luxury hotels, such as the Ambassador on Wilshire Boulevard and those in Beverly Hills, offered patrons the amenities of rural resorts or country clubs. The Bel-Air Hotel featured rambling, one-story structures and bungalows that gave patrons easy access to swimming pools, tennis courts, gardens, lawns, lounges, and restaurants.

Following expansion of the highway system after World War II, motels catered more and more to families and business persons traveling by car. Chains located near highways and freeways instead of in the heart of town could dispense with the armies of bellboys, waiters and waitresses, formal dining rooms, and central garages that were the hallmark of older hostelries. In the area near Los Angeles International Airport hotel complexes cater to all sizes of pocketbook. Some large chains have created deluxe variations. John Portman's Bonaventure, for example, features a dramatic atrium and structural supports suggestive of freeway construction. Its huge glass cylinders overlooking the freeway in downtown Los Angeles have become a landmark.

HOUSE TYPES in Los Angeles show immense architectural variety, reflecting the continuous waves of settlement and changing social composition of the local population. The first private homes in the Yankee period were Spanish-Mexican adobes. By the 1880s, Queen Anne or Eastlake Victorians—for example, those clustered on Carroll Avenue—were preferred by middle-class families. California bungalows—like those still visible in Hollywood, Pasadena, and Glendale—were designed for working poor, middle class, and rich alike. They became enormously popular early in the century. The Spanish stucco-and-tile (Mission Revival) home also enjoyed great currency. Fol lowing World War II California ranch houses, a favorite design of tract developers, blanketed many new suburban areas. The variety of styles, such as New England saltboxes, French mansards, Swiss chalets, English thatch-roof cottages, and Southern mansions, also reflects the tastes of a community shaped by the movies. Lately the postmodern style has been gaining popularity.

HOUSE UN-AMERICAN ACTIVITIES COMMITTEE. *See* Hollywood Red Scare; Hollywood Ten

HOUSING, PRIVATE, or the single-family detached residence, is an indelible part of the Southern California lifestyle. Los Angeles in 1980 was said "to contain more private houses per capita than any other large city on earth." In the banner year of 1985, 144 firms spent $5.2 million erecting new homes, an increase of 35 percent over expenditures the previous year. Less than a decade later, high land and construction costs and the lack of undeveloped lots portended the end of the dream for many young families. The trend of the 1990s has been toward apartments and condominiums.

During and immediately after World War II, the region's housing shortage was answered by an explosive growth in the number of suburban homes, made possible by the loan programs of the Federal Housing Authority (FHA), the GI Bill of Rights, California veteran financing, and the federal highway program, which encouraged city expansion to outlying regions. In subsequent decades, however, housing costs began to rise above national averages. In 1980, the median rent in the county was $277. In a community where median income was around $24,000, the median purchase price of a house was between $110,000 and $142,000. By September 1991 the median home price in Southern California had reached $221,590, up 6 percent over the preceding year alone. Fewer than half of Angelenos now own their own homes.

In 1991 the Los Angeles City Planning Department determined that, under current zoning practices, the city has space for 1.4 million housing units, of which 1.3 million have already been built. Existing housing stock tends to be older than the national average: in 1984, of 2.8 million housing units in the county, 63 percent were built before 1960, and 20 percent before 1940. Only 48 percent of all units in the county are detached (i.e., single-family homes)—also below the national average.

Stationary prefabricated homes—curiously called "mobile homes"—are relatively abundant; there are some 6,500 spaces in 68 mobile-home parks countywide. As of 1992, the Community Redevelopment Agency had channeled $270 million in low-interest loans to private developers or nonprofit housing organizations to build or rehabilitate 24,000 low- and moderate-income housing units throughout the city.

The U.S. Bureau of the Census defines overcrowded cities as those having 51 percent of their total rental units occupied by more than one person per room. By this measure, Bell Gardens, Maywood, South El Monte, Huntington Park, and Cudahy were overcrowded cities in 1992.

In 1991 Mayor Tom Bradley warned that the 15,000 new homes being built yearly to meet the needs of 30,000 new families still left a troubling housing deficit. According to city housing officials, mortgage and rental prices soared in the 1980s in Los Angeles, contributing to overcrowding and therefore to increasing crime and health problems. The crisis arose from several factors rampant in the 1980s, including a rapid increase in immigration, a slowing in new construction, and inflation. In the recession of the late 1980s to 1990s, the sale price of private homes declined, resulting in the loss of considerable equity to homeowners.

HOUSING, PUBLIC, has been maintained in Los Angeles since the 1930s. In accordance with a 1938 state law the city created a housing authority and, aided by federal loans, launched its first public housing program in 1939. By 1986 Los Angeles operated 32,257 units from Pacoima to Watts. Of this total almost half—15,662—were earmarked for senior citizens. The city also subsidizes the rents or provides funds for repairs of these dwellings, and it maintains some residential units for individuals with physical or mental impairments. The seven-member housing commission is appointed by the mayor and approved by the city council. It acquires land, issues construction bids, sets rent schedules, and deals with the federal government. Among the city's 18 public housing projects are Jordan Downs in Watts; Nickerson Gardens and Imperial Courts in South Central Los Angeles; and Ramona Gardens, Pico Gardens, and Estrada Courts in East Los Angeles. In 1992 the waiting list for these projects, which have on average 100 vacancies a year, reached 20,000.

The construction of public housing rental units

is no longer the preferred method of providing housing for low-income groups. Instead various innovative approaches have been tried to encourage homeownership. The 126-townhouse project in Bell Gardens known as Viñas la Campaña, completed in 1995, is financed in combination by the Roman Catholic and Episcopal churches, government agencies, and the Nehemiah West Housing Corporation, a collective of neighborhood associations. The occupants of Viñas la Campaña need no down payment, and the normal monthly rental fee goes toward the purchase of the houses.

HOYT, MINERVA HAMILTON (1866–1945), desert preservationist, known as the "Apostle of the Cacti." Born in Mississippi, Hoyt moved with her wealthy surgeon husband to South Pasadena in the 1890s. The deaths of her infant son and husband plunged her into deep grief, and she found solace in the southwestern deserts. She began to mount exhibits of desert plants, which caused an international sensation in Great Britain in the 1920s. She also organized the International Deserts Conservation League in 1930. Thanks to her efforts, the once-lowly Joshua tree blossomed as the "Sentinel of the Desert," and in the 1930s Hoyt worked with the Roosevelt administration to create the 825,340-acre Joshua Tree National Monument near Twenty-Nine Palms. A species of cactus, *Mammillaria hamiltonhoytea,* is named in her honor.

HSIEH, FREDERIC O. THOMAS (1933–), Monterey Park land developer. Trained as an engineer, the immigrant from mainland China bought a home in that San Gabriel Valley community in 1972. Visualizing Monterey Park as a world mecca for Chinese, he opened a realty office in 1974 and began buying and selling land, hoping to convert the bedroom community into the nation's first suburban Chinatown. Ads placed in Hong Kong newspapers proclaimed the city as the "Chinese Beverly Hills" and soon attracted $400 million worth of investments for homes, banks, boutiques, restaurants, and regional shopping centers. Hsieh has championed rapid and unfettered urban growth for the San Gabriel Valley. He maintains roots in his native city of Guilin, where he built a $20 million hotel in the 1980s.

HUAC. *See* Hollywood Red Scare; Hollywood Ten

HUBBARD, L. RON. *See* Church of Scientology

HUGHES, HOWARD ROBARD (1905–1976), Texas-born industrialist, landowner, aviator, airline owner, and movie producer. He first attended Rice University and then Caltech. At the age of 19 he inherited the Hughes Tool Company, as well as the oil-drill patent on which the company's success rested. He increased an already substantial family fortune by founding Hughes Aircraft Company in the 1930s, and by purchasing a controlling share of Trans World Airways. He also became a major player in the movie industry. Most of his films—such as *Hell's Angels* (1930), *Front Page* (1931), and *The Outlaw* (1943)—were sensational but fared poorly at the box office. In 1937 Howard Hughes set a transcontinental air record of 7 hours,

---

We halted not very far from the river, which we named the Porciúncula. . . . This plain where the river runs is very extensive.

—Father Juan Crespi, Franciscan missionary and Portolá expedition diarist, 1769

---

28 minutes. In response to the metal shortage during World War II, he designed an experimental plywood seaplane, the *Spruce Goose.* With its 219-foot length and 320-foot wingspan, it was the world's largest plane. In 1947 Hughes flew her for some seconds over the bay on her one and only flight. She was moored in Long Beach in 1964 beside the *Queen Mary* as a public attraction, but was later removed. Late in life, Hughes retired from Los Angeles to Las Vegas, where he bought five hotel casinos. By now a billionaire, he secluded himself in one of his hotels, grew increasingly reclusive and eccentric, and refused to appear in public even to defend himself in massive court cases involving his holdings. Tales of his increasingly bizarre behavior continued to surface years after his death. The film *Melvin and Howard* (1980) is a fictional account of Hughes in his later years.

HUGHES, RUPERT (1872–1956), novelist, playwright, and biographer. Born in Missouri, Hughes was a longtime resident of Los Angeles. His works include *City of Angels* (1941) and a three-volume biography of George Washington (1926–1930). He was Howard Hughes's uncle.

HUGHES AIRCRAFT COMPANY, electronics giant headquartered in Westchester. It originated in the early 1930s when aviator–industrialist–movie producer Howard Hughes formed an aircraft division within the Hughes Tool Company. The company built the *Winged Bullet,* a racing plane that set several speed records, and it developed radio equipment for Hughes's 1937 round-the-world flight that would later result in his entry into the electronics field. During World War II the company developed armaments and two experimental aircraft, including the famous *Spruce Goose,* planned as a giant wooden troop carrier but never actually used.

It is a geometropolitan predicament rather than a city. You can no more administer it than you could administer the solar system.

—Jonathan Miller, British stage director

Beginning in 1947 the Cold War defense contractor was responsible for numerous technological innovations in space and communications, missiles and avionics, air defense, command and control, industrial electronics, and basic research. It began manufacturing radar and started work on an air-to-air guided missile, as well as on measuring devices for nuclear explosions. In the 1960s the company revolutionized communications with satellites and developed applications for the laser. Today Hughes Aircraft is owned by General Motors Corporation and employs tens of thousands of people worldwide. Its Southern California locations are in Westchester, El Segundo, Canoga Park, Manhattan Beach, Long Beach, Van Nuys, and Malibu.

HUMAN RELATIONS COMMISSIONS are maintained by both the county and the city. The county commission, the second in the nation, was formed in 1944 in response to the zoot suit riots the previous year. Both the city and county commissions labored in the 1960s to promote better human relations, civic peace, and intergroup understanding. They continue in their attempts to reduce racially and religiously motivated violence, holding hearings, offering workshops, and producing publications. They issued a joint report in January 1985 on conditions in Watts 20 years after the rioting, finding some improvements but many ongoing dangerous conditions.

HUMMINGBIRDS, tiny, nectar-sipping birds with lightning-speed wings. The best-known variety in Southern California is the Anna *(Calypte anna),* a resident of the foothills, chaparral, and open woodland. The male has an iridescent-green body, brownish wings, and a ruby-red head and throat. Other familiar varieties locally are the Costa, rufous, Allen, and black-chinned.

HUNT, MYRON C. (1868–1952), New England–born architect. Hunt practiced in Los Angeles for 50 years, leaving a considerable legacy that includes the general plan and many of the buildings for Occidental College, the music hall at Pomona College, the Pasadena Rose Bowl, and Huntington Library. His numerous college buildings are in a restrained Mediterranean style.

HUNTING attracted sportsmen from the 1870s until the early years of the 20th century, in an area where Indians had hunted for thousands of years. Coastal wetlands lured migrating birds by the thousands. The call of wild geese could be heard everywhere, and immense flocks of sandhill cranes, now extinct, were seen periodically on a rancho in the southern part of the county. At a routine duck shoot in 1876 sport hunters bagged 1,326 ducks and 28 geese in a single week. Professional market hunters shipped some 10,000 quail that season from Los Angeles, and even in 1890 as many as 100 quail could be killed in one hour in foothill areas. At game stalls in the city, ducks sold five for a dollar in 1871. The 1880s saw the establishment of the Recreation Gun Club, Los Angeles Wing Shooting Club, Ballona Gun Club, and Long Beach Gun Club. Wild boar, bred from escaped hogs a century earlier, were hunted in the mountains. In Pasadena, dogs chased rabbits as parties of spectators galloped behind on horseback or in carriages, in imitation of English chases. It was a gun club, the Valley Hunt Club, that initiated the Tournament of Roses in 1902.

HUNTINGTON, COLLIS P[OTTER] (1821–1900), one of the Big Four rail magnates who built the transcontinental railroad to California. Head of the Southern Pacific Railroad (SP), he became the chief villain in the Free Harbor struggle of the 1880s. While he lobbied Congress for a federal subsidy to build a breakwater in Santa Monica, in order to establish a harbor there and to protect the SP's operation, Los Angeles business and political leaders were pressing hard for development of a harbor at San Pedro. Los Angeles won, thereby inflicting on Huntington a rare defeat. His nephew, Henry E. Huntington, inherited much of his fortune. Henry also married Collis's widow, Arabella.

HUNTINGTON, HENRY E. (1850–1927), developer of the Pacific Electric Railway Company (PE), founded in 1901, and the largest landowner in Southern California. As a young man he worked in San Francisco with his powerful uncle, rail magnate Collis P. Huntington, rising to the position of vice president in the Southern Pacific Company. When Collis died in 1900 Henry inherited much of his uncle's fortune, married his widow, Arabella, and moved to Southern California. A great deal of the San Gabriel Valley was developed by his firm, Huntington Land and Improvement Company.

Henry E. Huntington. Courtesy Henry E. Huntington Library.

His strategy was to purchase rough land, install electric power and rail lines, then contract to build houses for interested homeowners. As his already immense fortune continued to grow he built a palatial mansion in San Marino, in which he housed his fabulous collection of paintings, rare books, and manuscripts. Along with the vast botanical gardens on the property, the collections became the basis of the Henry E. Huntington Library and Art Gallery.

HUNTINGTON BOTANICAL GARDENS, spectacular preserve developed as part of the San Marino estate of Henry E. Huntington. Among the featured attractions are a 12-acre desert garden, a 6-acre Japanese garden, a palm garden, and a Shakespeare garden. The landscaping of the entire 207-acre estate was masterminded from 1904 to 1948 by William Hertrich (1878–1966), a German immigrant hired by the rail magnate to transform a sprawling orchard into private gardens. Given only three months to prepare the Japanese addition for Huntington's new wife, Arabella, he solved the problem by simply buying and installing an entire Japanese tea garden. In addition to doing research and writing, Hertrich scoured the world for unusual and rare plants, and became director of the gardens when they were opened to the public. He served in this capacity from 1928 until his death in 1966.

HUNTINGTON LIBRARY AND ART GALLERY. *See* Henry E. Huntington Library and Art Gallery

HUNTINGTON PARK, independent city south of Vernon, on land once belonging to the family of Don Antonio María Lugo. The town was laid out and named in 1903 by a developer who wished to honor his friend Henry E. Huntington. Incorporation followed in 1906. By 1980 its population was 48,000, and by 1990, 56,000. In recent decades Pacific Boulevard between Randolph Street and Florence Avenue has become a popular *mercado,* or Latino shopping area. On weekends, tens of thousands of shoppers frequent the open-air stores, bridal shops, restaurants, and Spanish-language movie theaters that line the half-mile strip.

HUXLEY, ALDOUS (1894–1963), English writer and member of a famous literary and scientific family who lived in Los Angeles for over two decades. His most famous early works include *Point Counter Point* (1928) and *Brave New World*

(1932), brooding views of modern civilization. Huxley arrived in Southern California in the late 1930s, living first near the Pacific Ocean, then moving to the high desert near Llano, where he spent most of the war years. Here he wrote *After Many a Summer Dies the Swan* (1939), a farcical work about a Southern California oil magnate, Jo Stoyte, who lives in the hills overlooking the San Fernando Valley and becomes obsessed with achieving immortality. The character of Stoyte, based on William Randolph Hearst, is said to have inspired the Orson Welles film classic *Citizen Kane*. *Ape and Essence* (1948), a satire about Los Angeles after a nuclear attack, opens with a scene of mutant survivors warming themselves in Pershing Square by burning books from the public library and engaging in an orgy at the Biltmore. The author, who dabbled in psychedelic drugs and the occult, was active in the Vedanta Society. He researched his books and essays at the UCLA library. Huxley died on 22 November 1963, the day of John Kennedy's assassination.

HYDE PARK, district southwest of downtown, near Inglewood. Although laid out as a town in the 1887 land boom, it was not incorporated as a city until 1921; two years later it consolidated with Los Angeles. The post office and library branch retain the old name of Hyde Park.

HYDROELECTRIC POWER. *See* Electrical power

HYPERION SEWAGE TREATMENT PLANT, city waste facility at Playa del Rey. Hyperion is the largest activated sludge plant in the world, intended to avert 200 million gallons of sewage daily from entering Santa Monica Bay. At first the plant was hailed as a miracle of engineering: "The problem of keeping a great city clean without polluting a river or fouling the beaches, and without robbing the soil of its fertility, has been triumphantly solved," trumpeted novelist Aldous Huxley in 1940. The miracle faded in 1943, however, as filth trickled onto 10 miles of beaches. The plant was enlarged between 1947 and 1951, but within three years again reached capacity.

In 1957 Hyperion was again upgraded, this time with two pipes. The first pipe carried the sludge directly into a submarine canyon. The second pipe, 12 feet in diameter and 5 miles long, mixed with seawater at a depth of 190 feet. This "largest freshwater stream in Los Angeles" was in good repair until about 1987. In that year unrestricted population growth forced the city to undertake a new and even more extensive overhaul, at a cost exceeding $2.3 billion. In 1991 the city undertook yet another upgrade, for an additional $1.6 billion, to treat all wastewater discharged into the bay.

IATSE. *See* International Alliance of Theatrical and Stage Employees

ILGWU. *See* International Ladies Garment Workers Union

ILWU. *See* International Longshoremen's and Warehousemen's Union

IMMIGRATION, FOREIGN, into Los Angeles was relatively light in the last century, but multiplied tremendously after World War II, swelling the population and injecting an extraordinary cultural diversity into the city and county.

The village of Los Angeles was a fairly cosmopolitan place from early on. By the 1850s settlers included English, French, Basques, Spaniards, Mexicans, and Germans, and by the 1870s some 200 Chinese lived in the city as well.

During the late 1800s and early 20th century foreign immigration to Los Angeles was varied, but continued to be light. The new immigrants arrived from Europe, Asia, and Latin America. Natives kept firm control over politics and government, but immigrants found their niches in the region's religious institutions, business communities, fraternal organizations, schools, and work force. Distinctive ethnic communities of Japanese, Chinese, Russian Molokans, and East European Jews had developed throughout the county by the 1930s. Compared to other urban centers in the West, immigrants were assimilated with relative ease in Los Angeles and there was little overt xenophobia.

When the Immigration Act of 1965 opened the door to new immigrants, it initiated dramatic changes in Los Angeles. Of course, statistics concerning populations of recent immigrant settlement in the city and county of Los Angeles are only estimates, and they vary greatly depending on the sources and methods of establishing race and ethnicity. At worst they lack grounding in reliable databases, and at best they are subject to rapid change. The U.S. census showed that by 1980, 21.6 percent of the residents of the Los Angeles–Long Beach area were foreign born—almost double the 11.3 percent figure of 1970. The numbers continued to rise after 1980.

In 1983, the area was home to 3 million people of Latino origin—only Mexico City had a larger number. Los Angeles had about the same number of Canadians as Montreal, as well as 150,000 Armenians, the greatest number of any American city. Persons of Japanese background also numbered about 150,000, and there were estimated to be 100,000 each of Koreans, Chinese, and Israelis, as well as many thousands from Thailand, Vietnam, Iran, Germany, Norway, Great Britain, Hungary, and the Philippines. Waves of Soviet Jews arrived in the 1980s.

In 1985, 75,000 people were naturalized in Los Angeles—one-third of all the immigrants naturalized in the nation that year. The magnitude of the flow of immigration is suggested by the mass swearing-in of citizens: on 4 July 1994, 14,000 immigrants were sworn in as citizens at the Los Angeles Convention Center.

A 1988 census taken by the Los Angeles Unified School District counted 96 different languages represented among school-age children. Los Angeles, the former middle-American mecca, had become a center of unprecedented ethnic, economic, and national range. It supplanted New York City as the nation's major immigrant port of entry, and was taking in newcomers from virtually every nation on earth.

The 1990 U.S. census had its limitations. For example, it lacked information as to the birthplace of the parents of reported individuals. Reliable sources suggested that by 1993 people representing more than 140 countries lived in Los Angeles County, and that approximately 25 percent lacked fluency in English. The County Human Relations Commission estimated that in 1995 fully 40 percent of Los Angeles residents were born outside the United States. It also suggested that as of 1990 only one of every three residents had been born and raised in California.

Some ethnic communities had an astonishingly high proportion of foreign born among them. According to the 1990 U.S. census, of the 1.6 million Mexicans living in the metropolitan region, 63.7 percent were immigrants, with a third having arrived since 1980. To cite but two other cases: of the 178,000 Chinese, 90 percent were immigrants, with 55 percent having arrived since 1980; and of the 159,000 Filipinos, 92 percent were immigrants, with over 50 percent having arrived since 1980.

The process of assimilation in Los Angeles has tended to vary greatly according to the ethnic group. It is generally true, however, that the rapidity with which successful assimilation takes place increases as people move away from highly concentrated areas of their own group. While such neighborhoods have many positive aspects—they offer familiarity of language and customs and a

---

The first truly 20th-century city in America.   —Joel Garreau, journalist

---

sense of safety—they also may slow the process of "Americanization." In this regard the path of assimilation taken by recent arrivals very much resembles that traveled by immigrants earlier in the century. The mass of those immigrants were poor, unfamiliar with the customs and language of the new country, and tended to seek out friends and relatives who lived in concentrated areas among their own. But those who arrived with specialized trades and higher educational and income levels moved directly into the skilled working class or middle class, assuring swifter assimilation and economic success for themselves and their children. However, the problem of illegal entries was not a significant factor in the past.

In 1990–1991 the U.S. Immigration and Natu-

ralization Service, which screens incoming airports, apprehended more than 7,000 people as "excludable aliens." The illegal status of immigrants raised major social and political concerns in the 1990s. According to one count, of the estimated 3.5 million illegal immigrants in the United States, half lived in California, and half of those resided in Los Angeles County. The issue gave rise to a deeply divisive debate. Some people argued that immigration constituted a drain on public funds, increased the population at an unacceptable rate, undermined the strength of the English language as a unifying cultural element, eroded the quality of public education, overburdened health services, and led to an increase in crime. Such beliefs led to the 1994 passage of the state's Proposition 187, which, if upheld by the courts, would deny any public education or welfare to children who are in the state illegally and would limit non-emergency health care and services.

Defenders of the rights of the newcomers asserted that they tended to be self-selected, were usually young, energetic, and hard-working, and were therefore able to provide the backbone of labor for vital enterprises such as textiles, hospitals, electronic assembly, domestic service, agriculture, and food services. They asserted, moreover, that all people had the right to education and medical services, and that such a benevolent approach served the common good.

Los Angeles was increasingly spoken of as the city of the future, the city of the 21st century, the "Fourth World City," the first great metropolis to grapple with problems that were beginning to occur worldwide. Many local leaders hoped to create a model multicultural area: a prosperous and stable core of peoples from all parts of the globe who could maintain their individual ethnic and racial identities while also merging their loyalties and values into those of the larger community. The failures and successes of this ideal would provide important lessons to other metropolises with similarly shifting demographics. The problems and misunderstandings created by so much diversity can be massive, but diversity can also have immensely rewarding and exciting results.

INCE, THOMAS HARPER (1882–1924), pioneer filmmaker. A Rhode Islander by birth, Ince started his career in Los Angeles in 1911. Among other movies, he made the first film version of Eugene O'Neill's *Anna Christie* (1923). His favorite shooting location was Santa Ynez Canyon, where today's Sunset Boulevard ends at the ocean. The site came to be known as "Inceville," although his studios were in Culver City, where his 1916 Triangle Building still stands. In 1924 Ince was stricken ill suddenly and mysteriously on William Randolph Hearst's yacht, the *Oneida*. He was carried off the vessel in San Diego, shipped home by special rail car, and died in his Benedict Canyon home. Among the ship's passengers were newspaper mogul Hearst, his mistress Marion Davies,

---

Here you can change your stripes, give up being a Catholic or come out of the closet, whatever.

—J. S. Holliday, historian

Charlie Chaplin, Chaplin's pregnant fiancée Lita Grey, and Hearst reporter Louella Parsons. Officials attributed Ince's death to heart failure from acute indigestion, but those close to the scene suspected a bleeding ulcer following a wild orgy, or a bullet accidentally inflicted by Hearst, who was said to have aimed a pistol at Chaplin for flirting with Davies. No one will ever know for sure, since the witnesses' testimonies were conflicting and vague. Immediately afterward, Hearst bestowed a trust fund on Mrs. Ince and promoted Parsons—possibly to buy her silence; she became a permanent and powerful gossip columnist for the Hearst papers. The scandal obscured Ince's real importance as an innovator in the industry.

INCOME in Los Angeles, per capita, exceeds that of the rest of the nation, yet poverty and the cost of living are also high. On the positive side, between 1980 and 1990 the median household income in the county rose 18.8 percent, to $34,965 (with adjustment for inflation). The wealthiest communities of Hidden Hills, Rolling Hills, Bradbury, Palos Verdes Estates, and San Marino reported median incomes of over $100,000, for a total rise of 63 percent in the 1980s. Meanwhile, the poorest communities of South Los Angeles, Vernon, Cudahy, Bell, Huntington Park, and Lynwood had increases of less than 5 percent during those 10 years, and a top median figure of $23,000 in 1990. According to a 1989 UCLA study, 15.6 percent of the local population lived in poverty, com-

pared to 13.5 percent nationwide, and that percentage has continued to rise. Middle-class families are also facing problems. To take but two salary examples, an entry-level accountant in California earns $27,500, while an entry-level chemical engineer earns $39,000. Yet the U.S. Labor Department estimates that the average Angeleno household has expenses of $33,482 a year, including $6,000 for transportation. The average renter in 1992 paid $646 a month, compared with a median of $474 for all other metropolitan areas in the nation. The figures indicate that many households are on a break-even basis.

INCORPORATION OF CITIES is controlled ultimately by the state legislature. In 1883, responding to pressures for "local rule," it passed a law providing that citizens could petition their county supervisors for the incorporation of local governments. From then until 1930, 55 new cities were incorporated in Los Angeles County. In 1933 a new law made incorporation more difficult by requiring that the petitioners represent at least 25 percent of the assessed property value of the proposed city. In 1954 the law was again changed and the requirements eased.

Incorporation has typically taken place when civic or business leaders sought a specific objective: to encourage oil drilling (Signal Hill), permit horse racing (Arcadia), keep out a sewage facility (Montebello), improve the road system (Redondo Beach), or close a saloon, as in June 1886, when temperance advocates succeeded in shutting down a tavern on Colorado Street in Pasadena by pressing for incorporation. The watering hole moved south, and in 1889 South Pasadena was incorporated under similar circumstances. Some cities—Beverly Hills, for example—incorporated out of the fear of being gobbled up by a larger neighbor, usually Los Angeles. Additional motivations for incorporation have been the desire of civic leaders to raise revenue, to protect rent control (West Hollywood), or to engage in planning (Calabasas). Sometimes the most strenuous incorporation efforts fail, as has been the case six times in East Los Angeles.

INDEPENDENCE DAY, MEXICAN, is celebrated annually on 16 September, commemorating the date in 1810 when Fr. Miguel Hidalgo y Costilla issued a call in the Mexican town of Dolores for his peasant flock to break from the rule of colonial Spain. The parade usually starts on 1st and Lorena Streets, and ends at Belvedere Park. Over 100,000 people have attended the park entertainments.

INDIANS, AMERICAN. *See* Fernandeño Indians; Native Americans; Tongva Indians

INDIANS, ASIAN, numbered 43,829 in Los Angeles County in 1990. The majority hailed from Gujarat State and the Punjab, with fewer from Goa, Bengal, Bombay, and other areas in India. U.S. immigration quotas prohibited Indian immigration early in the century, although some managed to enter the country via Canada. Courts enforcing Jim Crow legislation regarded Indians as nonwhites and forbade them from owning land. These restrictions ended with the immigration law of 1965, which normalized immigration patterns and encouraged highly trained individuals to come to the United States—a boon for Indian professionals and business owners. The rate of settlement increased rapidly after 1965. The towns of Cerritos and Artesia have had the most thriving Asian Indian communities, although Indian-owned stores, businesses, and homes are located throughout the county. The Sree Venkateswara Temple, a Hindu shrine on a 4.5-acre site in the Malibu Hills, is the largest Chola-style structure in the Western Hemisphere.

INDUSTRIAL WORKERS OF THE WORLD (IWW), radical socialist labor organization formed in Chicago in 1905. The "Wobblies," as they were known, hoped to form "One Big Union." Active locally among San Pedro dock workers around 1912 and among garment workers and maritime hands after World War I, they urged the proletariat to seize and take control of their own workplaces. In 1921 and 1922 Wobblies staged mass meetings to free the "wage slaves" of the local waterfront. Vigilantes and police—claiming to be enforcing criminal syndicalism laws—conducted raids, including a foray into the Bucket of Blood Saloon at 4th and Beacon Streets. The confrontation evolved into a free speech issue and resulted ultimately in the emergence of the local branch of the American Civil Liberties Union.

INDUSTRY took root in Los Angeles in the 1870s, expanded in a series of bursts, and peaked during and after World War II. Manufacturing was pro-moted by aggressive employer groups who sustained an open-shop labor policy, by private capital, and by public subsidies. The subsidies consisted of a harbor developed with federal funds, a supply of abundant water, and cheap electricity provided by the city. Despite a vigorous history, manufacturing began to decline in the 1960s.

Manufacturing originated at the rail yards north of the Plaza, east of Alameda Street, along the tracks that snaked from downtown into Vernon and as far south as the harbor. As trucks replaced trains, and as electric wires were strung everywhere to motivate manufacturing, industries spread throughout the basin. By the early 20th century the geographic locus of industry was decentralized and

---

The cool crisp lines of modernism were softened by the lush vegetation. For so much of L.A. architecture, the garden is a crucial part of the design.

—Thomas Hines, historian

---

scattered. As of the 1920s the mainstay industries were movies and aircraft. They were located on the fringes of settlement, as were shipbuilding yards, auto assembly plants, clothing and pottery factories, and fish canneries. To this day the textile industry exhibits particular vitality, not only in the city's center, but on its outskirts as well. Both movies and aircraft were non-smokestack industries, a distinct advantage in a region that suffers from chronic air pollution.

In the 1920s and 1930s the film industry accounted for the most jobs and income. Oil refining also made a strong showing. Airframe manufacturing, which achieved a moderate level of activity in the 1920s and was boosted by the onset of World War II, became a major enterprise. By 1943 Los Angeles had became "the Pittsburgh of Aircraft," and a modest-sized shipbuilding industry prospered in the harbor area. The area's airplane industry was superseded by aerospace in the postwar period.

In the heyday of manufacturing, most industry was light. As late as 1951 a leading guidebook invited tourists to visit industrial installations, in and near downtown, devoted to light industry: a pottery, brewery, flour mill, meat packing plant, soap manufacturer, coffee processor, tea and spice packer, cookie bakery, walnut packing house, wholesale food terminal, milk processing shed, beverage bottler, rotogravure printer, electrical cable manufacturer, stove assembly plant, stockyards, avocado packing plant, and electrical motor factory. Many of those plants are now extinct. Meanwhile, much of the trucking industry has left Lynwood for the "Inland Empire" of San Bernardino and Riverside Counties.

The largest industrial employers in modern times have been manufacturers of aircraft equipment, apparel and textiles, tools, scientific instruments, electronic equipment, fabricated metal products, industrial machinery, food products, rubber, plastics, furniture, and fixtures, as well as those engaged in the printing and publishing trades. The industrial core of the county in recent decades, located in Vernon and City of Commerce, accounts for as many as 100,000 jobs. There are also lesser concentrations of industry in Huntington Park, South Gate, and Lynwood. Many blue-collar workers live in nearby Bell Gardens, Cudahy, and Maywood, which, however, have no industry to speak of.

Between 1971 and 1992 plant closings in Los Angeles County resulted in the loss of over 22,500 jobs. The 1982 shutting of the General Motors plant in South Gate alone cut 4,500 jobs, and the 1992 closure in Van Nuys cut an additional 2,400 jobs. Other closings and job losses were Ford (2,300 jobs), Weiser Lock (2,100), Chrysler Motors (2,000), Bethlehem Steel (1,600), Goodyear (1,600), Firestone (1,400), Goodrich (1,000), and Max Factor (1,000). These signs of deindustrialization have taken their toll on the region as high-paying jobs have disappeared or been replaced by lower-paying ones. The result has been reduced income, unemployment, and general economic stagnation, particularly in the southeastern part of the county. The racial disturbances of 1965 and 1992 are attributable, at least in part, to this downsizing.

INDUSTRY, CITY OF. *See* City of Industry

INGLEWOOD, independent city 13 miles southwest of downtown Los Angeles. With a 90 percent minority population in 1992, it took pride in its progressive and multiethnic identity. The first Mexican resident in the area was Ygnacio Machado, a soldier's son, who established a rancho and built an adobe in 1834 that still stands at its original location. The town was founded in 1888 by Daniel Freeman, a Canadian, on the former Ranchos Aguaje de la Centinela and Sausal Redondo. Influenced by Nordhoff's *California for Health, Pleasure, and Residence* (1872), Freeman settled where cool sea breezes would help improve his wife's health. He created a farming empire, growing vast amounts of barley. The population exploded during the Boom of the Twenties. Boosters claimed of the period 1920–1925 that Inglewood

---

Los Angeles is the new Ellis Island.

—Kevin McCarthy, demographer

---

was the fastest-growing city in the United States. It was also touted during those years as the "Chinchilla Capital of the World," owing to the commercial farms devoted to those Andean animals. An airport, Mines Field, was carved out in 1927 and turned over to the city of Los Angeles for what eventually became Los Angeles International Airport.

When Inglewood was laid out in 1888 the population was 300; it had risen to 1,200 when the town was incorporated in 1908, and by 1990 had reached 109,600. Inglewood is best known for its aircraft industries and sports centers—Hollywood Park and the Forum. Civic leaders were dismayed when the Hollywood film *Grand Canyon* (1991) depicted their city as a crime-torn ghetto.

INITIATIVE LEGISLATION, form of direct democracy, was pioneered in Los Angeles by progressive reformer John Randolph Haynes. In 1903 this city became the first in the nation to allow initiative charter amendments on the ballot. Los Angeles also was the first city to adopt the referendum and recall—deemed necessary as a means of fighting corruption.

An initiative measure originates through a petition signed by at least 15 percent of the total registered voters in the previous state gubernatorial election. The signed petitions are then brought before the city council, and the members must vote on the proposal. If the council rejects it, the proposal is placed on the ballot. If the voters approve it, the initiative becomes law.

INNER CITY CULTURAL CENTER (ICCC), pioneering multicultural theater group formed in

1966. The brainstorm of C. Bernard "Jack" Jackson, a New Yorker pursuing a music career at UCLA, the theater was born in the aftermath of the Watts riot as an effort to bridge the gaps among racial and ethnic communities. Since 1972 the ICCC has been headquartered in a facility on New Hampshire Avenue and Pico Boulevard that comprises four theaters, a library, and studios. They also use the Ivar Theater in Hollywood. The center has been supported by grants from the National Endowment for the Arts, Ford Foundation, various corporations, and the city's Cultural Affairs Department. It has nurtured the careers of Beah Richards, Paul Winfield, Lou Gossett Jr., George Takei, Nobu McCarthy, Edward James Olmos, and others.

INSECTS buzz, crawl, and fly about all over the basin. Some die off as the habitat changes because of human encroachment, others adapt to change easily. Humans have been fighting various species of insects from the beginning. Fleas (*pulgas* in Spanish) were well known in the Mexican era and, despite endless efforts at eradication, continue to dine on dogs and cats and probably always will. Cockroaches (*cucarachas*) are equally resilient. Termites aggravate homeowners by eating their way through wood-frame buildings. Houseflies are also common warm-weather pests. Less resilient, the El Segundo blue butterfly (*Euphilotes battoides allynii*), which feeds on buckwheat and is endemic to El Segundo Dunes, is an endangered species. The Avalon hairstreak, a small butterfly endemic to Santa Catalina Island and to certain brushy slopes, is also becoming rare. The Mediterranean fruit fly, seen in the Santa Clara Valley in 1880 and Los Angeles County in 1987, has posed a serious threat to agriculture. California agricultural authorities have repeatedly sprayed parts of the basin with malathion in an effort to eliminate the insect.

In 1991 California health authorities warned that the chemical could seriously damage children and people with lung disease.

INTERNATIONAL ALLIANCE OF THEATRICAL AND STAGE EMPLOYEES (IATSE), major film industry union. Organized as a stage theater guild in Los Angeles in 1893, it began asserting itself in filmmaking in 1908, fighting determined employers and engaging in countless jurisdictional disputes with the International Brotherhood of Electrical Workers until a decisive strike settled the balance of power in 1935. The alliance quickly grew to about 12,000 members, becoming an entertainment industry powerhouse, and survived a period in the 1950s when top officers were convicted of bribery and racketeering. The union, an affiliate of the AFL-CIO, has long since cleaned house, and continues to control many crafts associated with the film industry, including film editors, camera operators, sound technicians, costume designers, makeup artists, accountants, publicists, cartoonists, set designers, and art directors.

INTERNATIONAL ASSOCIATION OF MACHINISTS (IAM), labor union associated with the AFL-CIO. The first Los Angeles machinists organization was formed about 1910 but, like the entire labor movement, suffered a crushing blow when union activists were implicated in the bombing of the *Los Angeles Times* Building in 1910. Despite the prevailing anti-union atmosphere and open-shop policy, the machinists union made gains during World War I in both Long Beach and Los Angeles. The IAM Burbank local was organized in the 1930s at the Lockheed-Vega aircraft manufacturing complex; it was highly successful during and after War II in improving working conditions for Lockheed's 30,000 employees. The

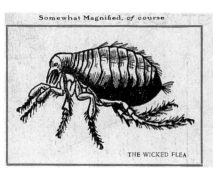

Somewhat Magnified, of course

THE WICKED FLEA

A very prominent, much sought after "Native Son," as described in my recent card to you.
                    Yours,

"The Ubiquitous Flea," a Los Angeles postcard, ca. 1905. Pitt Collection.

IAM has remained a strong element in the passenger airline industry, centered at Los Angeles International Airport.

INTERNATIONAL BROTHERHOOD OF ELECTRICAL WORKERS (IBEW) traces its origins in Los Angeles to 1893. At that time Los Angeles was a small, isolated city of 57,000 residents, just beginning to be served by electrical and telephone lines. A business panic was causing unemployment and wage losses, and employers were resisting unions. Eighteen utility linemen chartered Local 61, predecessor to today's IBEW Local 18. They struck for the first time in 1903, demanding pay increases and an eight-hour day. In 1918, 1,300 linemen lost a strike at Southern California Edison, then the largest electrical utility. Starting a year later and continuing for almost two decades, IBEW clashed with the International Alliance of Theatrical and Stage Employees (IATSE) over union jurisdiction in the movie studios. The feud ended in 1935 with an agreement that, for the most part, favored IATSE. During the Great Depression from 1933 to 1940, when linemen enjoyed steady employment building transmission lines from Boulder Dam on the Colorado River, Local 18 was probably the strongest and most affluent union in the Los Angeles area.

The IBEW supported municipal ownership of electrical utilities, and when the goal became a reality in Los Angeles in the 1920s the union secured another stronghold, the Department of Water and Power (DWP). In a battle over pay and pensions, Local 18 conducted a major strike against DWP in 1974, a three-day walkout in 1980, and a nine-day strike in 1993. Today Local 18, with its 8,000 members, is one of the largest and strongest IBEW locals in the nation. Smaller IBEW locals represent workers in other municipalities. Electricians who wire buildings or manufacture electrical products have maintained separate labor organizations.

INTERNATIONAL BROTHERHOOD OF TEAMSTERS (IBT), union that emerged locally in the 1920s to become one of the most powerful local labor bodies. It supplanted an earlier teamster union formed in 1900, which had almost been wiped out in 1907 by the crusade of the Merchants and Manufacturers Association to maintain an open-shop policy. Although it had regained strength afterward, that union was not yet unified when the ice wagon handlers clashed with their employers in 1918. In the next decade, the drivers of trucks, vans, and cars for laundries, dairies, taxi companies, breweries, bakeries, lumber dealers, and flour and feed hauling firms organized and joined the national IBT. By 1936 the membership numbered 2,000. Teamsters in Los Angeles generally earned lower wages than their counterparts in San Francisco. The local union took part in a violent strike at Los Angeles Harbor in 1937–1938, involving a bitter rivalry with the longshore workers union. More recently the Los Angeles teamsters, which for many years has been headed by national vice president Michael Reilly, conducted major strikes in 1979 and 1994. The latter, a 24-day contest, was the longest in the organization's history.

The Southern California IBT is affiliated with the Joint Council of Teamsters, a regional body that is part of the Western Conference of Teamsters centered in Seattle. Most observers agree that the Western Conference has been free of the corruption and gangsterism that formerly characterized the eastern teamsters union. The IBT often cooperates with the AFL-CIO but has no formal affiliation with that labor federation.

INTERNATIONAL LADIES GARMENT WORKERS UNION (ILGWU), which began organizing in Los Angeles in 1907, was for many years stymied by management's vigorous open-shop policy. The group's first true success was registered in 1933–1934 by Rose Pesotta, a radical ILGWU vice president sent from New York who faced resistance from the male-dominated union leadership. In October 1933, after Congress passed the National Industrial Recovery Act, Pesotta made militant demands on behalf of the mostly Latina women in the work force, touching off one of the few industrywide labor strikes in Los Angeles history. After violent clashes with the police's "Red Squad," the ILGWU achieved some of its objectives. Pesotta returned in 1941–1942 to revitalize the union. By the 1940s the ILGWU had 10 locals in Los Angeles. In an industry that employed 23,000 workers, 12,000 were union members, most of them Mexican and Jewish women. The ILGWU, an AFL-CIO affiliate, enjoys a central place in the garment industry.

INTERNATIONAL LONGSHOREMEN'S AND WAREHOUSEMEN'S UNION (ILWU), AFL-CIO affiliate and dominant labor union in the Los Angeles Harbor. Local 13 of the ILWU, which was established there in 1933, came into its own during the successful Pacific Coast maritime strike of May 1934. Dismal conditions preceded the strike: an unsafe work environment, long hours (some men worked 48 hours without rest), and the instability and insecurity of the daily shape-up for casual labor. Strikers demanded union recognition, a closed shop, union control of the hiring hall, improved safety conditions, job security, and mandatory arbitration. The most militant longshoremen's activity occurred in San Francisco, but on 15 May 1934 a San Pedro unionist was killed in a strike-related demonstration. The union won a major victory and has been a vital force in community affairs ever since.

IRANIANS. Los Angeles represents the largest concentration of Iranians in the United States. This is a recent phenomenon, the majority having arrived after the 1978–1979 revolution in which forces led by the Ayatollah Khomeini toppled the shah. The community is a mix of religious and ethnic groups, including practicing and secular Muslims, Jews, Armenian Christians, Baha'ists, Assyrians, Zoroastrians, and Kurds. Many Iranians live in Palos Verdes, Beverly Hills, Westwood, and West Los Angeles (sometimes referred to as "Little Teheran"), as well as in Santa Monica, Glendale, and western parts of the San Fernando Valley. According to the 1990 U.S. Census, people of Iranian background in Los Angeles County numbered 79,310. The community is relatively affluent and well educated. A 1989 Iranian yellow page phone directory of over 800 pages listed 1,600 Iranian businesses and professionals in the region.

IRISH first arrived in Los Angeles during the Mexican era. The surveyor Jasper O'Farrell, born in Wexford, Ireland, arrived in 1843 in Southern California, where he surveyed 21 Mexican land grants. The 1850 census listed 27 Irishmen. Among the most famous Irish immigrants to Los Angeles were John Gately Downey, a Los Angeles druggist and real estate speculator who in 1859 became governor of California, and the Dubliner William Mulholland, who arrived in 1877 and was later responsible for building the Los Angeles Aqueduct and bringing Owens Valley water to the city. Arriving in 1897, attorney Joseph Scott began a distinguished legal and civic career that spanned 60 years.

The 1930 census listed almost 40,000 Irish residents of Los Angeles County. The heaviest period of Irish settlement began in the 1950s. According to the 1990 census, 56,251 Los Angeles residents were exclusively of Irish ancestry. Santa Monica, with nearly 14,000 persons who listed themselves as entirely or partly Irish, lay claim to being the center of the Irish community of Southern California. Some estimate that the number of those in the county who define themselves as Irish by birth or by descent exceeds a million. The annual Irish Fair and Music Festival in June is the largest such event in the American West. The *Irish Network,* a social and business directory, and the *Irish American Press,* a monthly newspaper, are both published in Los Angeles.

IRON MANUFACTURING. *See* Steel and iron manufacturing

IRWINDALE, independent town 17 miles east of downtown Los Angeles, near Baldwin Park. It was first settled in 1880 by Don Gregorio Fraijo, of Sonora, Mexico. The area soon became home to the many Mexican laborers working on the nearby Rowland and Dalton ranchos, and was known variously as Jackrabbit Town, Cactus Town, Lower Azusa, Sonoratown, and Spanish Town. It became a station on the Southern Pacific line during the Boom of the Eighties. In the next decade it acquired the name of a resident well digger named Irwin, who had installed the first gas-powered water pump and irrigated much of the land.

When incorporated in 1957, Irwindale was intended to blossom as an industrial, rather than a residential, community, focusing largely on rock and gravel companies. Its population has held steady for a decade, standing at 1,050 in 1990.

ISHERWOOD, CHRISTOPHER (1904–1986), prominent English author who moved to California in 1939 after having studied at Cambridge University and lived in Berlin for four years during Hitler's rise to power. His series of sketches *Goodbye to Berlin* (1939) was dramatized by John Van Druten as *I Am a Camera* (1951), and readapted as the musical *Cabaret* (1966). Isherwood settled near Los Angeles and was naturalized in 1946. Part of a group of British expatriates that included novelist Aldous Huxley, he turned to Eastern religions, becoming a believer in Indian mysticism and a follower of Swami Prabhavandanda. Much of his later fiction is set in Southern Cali-

In front of Cavour Italian restaurant, Los Angeles Street, ca. 1928. Courtesy El Pueblo de Los Angeles Historic Monument.

fornia, including *Down There on a Visit* (1962) and *A Single Man* (1964), concerning a lonely middle-aged professor who mourns the death of the man he loves. His autobiographical account is *Christopher and His Kind* (1976).

ISRAELIS in Los Angeles numbered between 100,000 and 200,000 in 1990. They live mostly in the Fairfax area, on the Westside, and in the San Fernando Valley. Many intended to settle here temporarily but, when unemployment rose precipitously in their home country in the 1980s, ended up staying permanently. The Jewish Federation Council attempts to ease their entry into American life. The Israeli community's two weekly newspapers are *Israel Shelanu* (Our Israel) and *Hadshot L.A.* (L.A. news).

ITALIANS first clustered near the downtown Plaza in what is now Chinatown; their community center was Italian Hall on Main Street. Little Joe's Restaurant is a remnant of that old settlement. During this century the Italian community has scattered, maintaining some degree of concentration in the Los Feliz and harbor areas. One of the most famous Italian immigrants was Simon Rodia, a folk artist and intuitive engineer who single-handedly built the Watts Towers between 1921 and 1954. Ethnic Italians in Los Angeles were said to number about 20,000 in 1990.

JACKSON, HELEN HUNT (1830–1885), writer who left a lasting impression on Southern California with her novel *Ramona* (1884). Born in Amherst, Massachusetts, and a friend of poet Emily Dickinson, she enjoyed a modest career as a poet and nature writer. After learning how the government was mistreating western Indians, she published *A Century of Dishonor* (1881), a reformist tract. It aroused enough attention to win her a request from the Department of the Interior to write a report on the needs of California's "mission" Indians. She (with the assistance of Indian agent Ab-

bot Kinney) completed the report in 1883, but the government ignored it. Angered by the snub, Jackson decided to popularize the topic by writing *Ramona,* much as her friend Harriet Beecher Stowe had done for the plight of slaves with *Uncle Tom's Cabin* (1852). She was inspired by information given her by Don Antonio Coronel in Los Angeles and by the physical surroundings she saw in a brief visit to Rancho Camulos, owned by the Del Valle family, in Piru. Although Jackson's novel, about a part-Indian orphan raised in Spanish society and her Indian husband, achieved almost instant success, it failed to arouse public concern for the treatment of local Native Americans. Instead readers accepted the sentimentalized Spanish aristocracy that was portrayed, and the Ramona myth was born. Jackson died a year after her novel was published, never knowing the imprint her book made on the Southern California heritage. The novel *Ramona* has inspired films, songs, and a long-running pageant in Hemet, while the name alone adorns street signs and commercial establishments throughout Southern California.

JACKSON, MICHAEL (1934–), radio talk-show host. Born and educated in South Africa, Jackson lived for some time in London, where he worked for the South African Broadcasting Corporation and the British Broadcasting Corporation. He also hosted television game shows and worked as a disc jockey on Radio Luxembourg before coming to the United States. In Los Angeles he worked for KHJ Radio, KHJ TV, and KNX Newsradio. In 1966 he began his long-running talk show on KABC, for which he received seven Emmy awards and four Gold Mike Awards for outstanding achievement in radio broadcasting. He continues to be a major figure in talk radio.

Helen Hunt Jackson.

JAILS. *See* Prisons and jails

JAMES, GEORGE WHARTON (1858–1923), English-born Methodist minister who became a popular lecturer, author, and local booster. A man of boundless energy, James nevertheless suffered from depression. Accused by his wife of infidelity, he was part of an ugly divorce proceeding and suffered expulsion from his Long Beach pastorate (though he was later reinstated). He became a leading member of the Arroyo Seco set of intellectuals, as author of numerous books extolling the virtues of southwestern deserts, Native Americans, and missions, as well as several guidebooks on the region. From 1912 to 1914 he edited *Out West* magazine. In *Through Ramona's Country* (1908) James explored the origins of the Ramona story, attempting to separate fact from myth.

JANSS INVESTMENT CORPORATION, major Southern California land developer since 1899, founded by Dr. Peter Janss and his son, Dr. Edwin Janss. It developed 47,000 acres in Lankershim in the eastern San Fernando Valley in 1911, and the next year, on 7 December, opened Owensmouth, in the western San Fernando Valley, with a "Monster Free Spanish Barbecue." The company's most celebrated venture began in 1922 when it bought the 3,300-acre Rancho San José de Buenos Ayres, comprising practically all of the property between the National Soldiers Home on the west, Los Angeles Country Club and Beverly Hills on the east, Pico Boulevard on the south, and the foothills on the north. Here the firm laid out Westwood Village, Westwood Hills, and Holmby Hills, and brought UCLA to the site, carefully incorporating it into the overall plan. Janss gave meticulous attention to planning, including the location of

Janss Development, Santa Monica Boulevard and Kelton Avenue, 1922. Courtesy Robert Weinstein Collection.

businesses, residences, schools, fraternities, and churches. Construction started in 1928. To this day the Westwood area is considered a masterful example of systematic suburban development. The firm has had extensive agricultural properties throughout the Southwest and is still active in real estate development in Ventura County.

JAPANESE, TO 1945. Japanese first established a strong presence in the county in the last century, becoming important especially in agriculture. Yet they encountered persistent racial discrimination that culminated, during World War II, in an unprecedented mass imprisonment.

The first Japanese to enter the United States legally, in 1868, settled in Northern California, but when they met powerful anti-Asian sentiment, particularly from San Francisco's labor movement, they began moving southward. In 1890 the Japanese in Los Angeles—mostly males—numbered 1,000. Their life centered on 16 restaurants, stores, and lodging houses, as Little Tokyo began to take shape next to Chinatown. After the 1906 San Francisco earthquake, many Japanese fled to Los Angeles, where they now worked as domestic servants and gardeners to Caucasians and opened businesses catering to their own community. By 1910 they numbered some 9,000, with the figure rising to 20,000 by 1920. Some Japanese farmers had saved enough money to buy or lease land. They first drifted into the town of Moneta, along a rail line in the southern part of the county, and then to the broader farming area now within the boundaries of Gardena, Carson, Compton, Hawthorne, Lawndale, Torrance, Lomita, Inglewood, Long Beach, Harbor City, Palos Verdes, and Dominguez Hills. Here the Japanese *issei* (immigrants) planted flowers, berries, and vegetables.

Among the earliest pioneer landowners at Moneta were Kamesaku Oda and his wife, who arrived from Hawaii. They introduced the Klondike strawberry, which made Moneta a major strawberry center. In January and February 1902 Japanese farmers shipped 22 carloads of strawberries out of Los Angeles, at a value of $500,000. The growers, especially in and around Moneta, formed various business, cultural, educational, and religious organizations, which became the basis of the Japanese community. The annual Gardena Valley Strawberry Festival drew large crowds each year; it was so popular that the 1917 turnout rivaled that of the Pasadena Rose Tournament. During World

War I the Japanese growers cultivated an increasingly wide range of commercial crops.

Organized discrimination against the Japanese, which began in California around 1906, resulted in the state's Alien Land law of 1913, prohibiting Japanese nationals from owning or leasing land. Fortunately, the law was not uniformly enforced, and some farmers were able to assign ownership to their American-born children or to corporations with a majority of American-born Japanese board members. Meanwhile, a federal law limited Asian immigration. Nevertheless, by 1920 the Japanese had become one of Southern California's largest nonwhite minorities. In the 1930s, 90 percent of the produce consumed in Los Angeles was grown by local Japanese farmers.

The Japanese were also entrenched in the fishing industry. A Japanese fisherman discovered abalone in local waters in 1901, which soon led to the creation of a thriving fishing industry at San Pedro, Terminal Island, and Santa Monica. The Japanese were skillful at bargaining collectively with the Caucasian fish packers, but social discrimination in San Pedro around 1906 forced the Japanese to establish a segregated fishing village on Terminal Island. During its 35 years of existence, this ethnic enclave grew from 1,000 to 25,000 people. Although the community no longer exists, old Terminal Islanders still gather for period picnics and reminisce about the past.

On the eve of World War II, 37,000 Japanese lived in Los Angeles County, mainly in the areas of Little Tokyo, Sawtelle (West Los Angeles), and Terminal Island, opposite San Pedro. They experienced isolation, suspicion, and resentment from fellow citizens, owing both to their diligence and to cultural and physical differences. The enforcement of the federal immigration law of 1924 continued to repress their numbers.

When Japan bombed Pearl Harbor on 7 December 1941, many Americans, including key government and military figures, feared that Japanese nationals might be relaying military secrets to the imperial government and engaging in sabotage. (No such occurrence was ever discovered.) The navy's shore patrol arrested fishermen for allegedly signaling to Japanese airmen and naval vessels. On 19 February 1942 rifle-bearing U.S. army soldiers started enforcing Executive Order 9066, a presidential decree evacuating all Japanese nationals and U.S. citizens of Japanese background from the entire West Coast. Although the government as-

Waiting to be interned, 1942. Courtesy Robert Weinstein Collection.

serted that the action was justified by "military necessity," wartime hysteria and racist attitudes played a major role in determining policy. Two-thirds of the victims were American citizens. Most were removed for the duration of the war to an army camp at Manzanar in the Owens Valley, or to a camp at Heart Mountain, Wyoming. (The Owens Valley compound, coincidentally, stood on property owned by the Los Angeles Department of Water and Power.) While some ethnic Japanese were able to avoid imprisonment by moving to the Midwest, most spent the war years behind barbed wire. Many lost all their property in the process, although a noteworthy exception occurred in the Dayton Heights neighborhood near City College on Vermont Avenue. Here Caucasian and African American neighbors protected and maintained the properties of interned Japanese truck farmers, returning them to their rightful owners after the war.

JAPANESE, SINCE 1945. Japanese became reestablished as a major presence in the Los Angeles area after World War II. Those returning from the camps often took up residence in their former communities, such as Sawtelle, Gardena, and Torrance. A high proportion of nisei (second-generation Japanese) entered higher education and went into business and the professions. Few settled in Little Tokyo, although it was a favorite weekend shopping and dining area for the community. Today both Little Tokyo and Gardena remain vital cultural centers, often devoting themselves to traditional culture, an important element especially for older Japanese Americans.

In 1952, with the repeal of the Oriental Exclusion Act of 1924, a wave of immigration occurred.

Eventually, and after years of lobbying and petitioning by internees and their families, the U.S. government voted to make amends to those they had interned, both by means of official apologies and in the form of monetary reparations—though the amount offered—$4.5 million to 2,000 first-generation Japanese immigrants or their heirs—does not approach the estimated $300 to $400 million that was lost by the community as a whole. The city government also made restitution to those who lost their jobs in the wartime relocation. In spite of their ordeal, the Japanese community as a whole has made remarkable educational and financial progress.

By 1990 Los Angeles County had a Japanese population of over 200,000, the largest outside of Japan. About 40,000 were estimated to be Japanese nationals, consisting mainly of two groups. The first is made up of businessmen and their families who were sent by their companies; intending to return to Japan, they live in affluent communities apart from Japanese Americans, tend to lead a traditional Japanese lifestyle, and remain for an average of five years. The second group comprises expatriates who plan to remain in the United States. Visiting students to the United States, most of whom come to Southern California, tend to fall between the two groups. The largest Japanese American newspaper in Los Angeles is *Rafu Shimpo,* with a circulation of 23,000.

Japanese Americans celebrate many public events. Japanese New Year, or Oshōgatsu, on 1 January, and Nisei Week, held in August, are popular festivities in Little Tokyo and West Los Angeles. "Shōgun Santa," a pastiche of Santa Claus and a samurai warrior, has become a Christmas tradition. Girls' Day on March 3 and Boys' Day on May 5 are each celebrated for two days with a range of activities for children. The Buddhist Oban festival, a 1,500-year-old tradition, is held in temples around the city, though in Los Angeles it has become a mixture of the old and the new.

Los Angeles has some 900 Japanese-owned, Tokyo-based businesses, including such familiar names as Sumitomo, Sanwa, and Mitsubishi. But more important over the long run is the influence that Japanese culture has exerted on the area: Japanese-style architecture, food, fashion, and religion are a permanent part of Los Angeles's personality.

JAPANESE AMERICAN CULTURAL AND COMMUNITY CENTER, Little Tokyo facility devoted to advancing the appreciation of Japanese culture. The grounds contain a plaza and rock sculpture designed by Isamu Noguchi, as well as a sunken garden, the "Garden of the Clear Stream." An exhibit hall features traveling exhibits, photos, paintings, and sculptures, while a theater is devoted to the performing arts, lectures, and film. The facility houses organizations devoted to Kabuki, koto playing, flower arranging, and the tea ceremony. Day-long celebrations of festivals such as Children's Day in early May are open to the public.

JARVIS, HOWARD (1902–1986), antitax crusader. Jarvis was a newspaper publisher in his native Utah when he sold out in 1935, moved to California, and became a successful appliance manufacturer. The outspoken Republican brought with him a strong interest in local politics. He would haunt meetings of the Board of Supervisors and other forums to address budgetary and tax matters. In 1962, at age 60, he retired from business and began a full-time tax crusade, urging taxpayer and homeowner associations and owners of apartment houses throughout California to press for legislation limiting property taxes. He insisted that these levies were unfair to people of modest means and

Howard Jarvis. Courtesy Howard Jarvis Taxpayers Association.

only served to nurture parasitical bureaucrats and worthless social services. The drive resulted ultimately in Proposition 13, a constitutional amendment passed by a 62 percent majority on 6 June 1978. A close associate was Paul Gann. With Robert Pack, Jarvis wrote an autobiography, *I'm Mad as Hell* (1979). The Howard Jarvis Taxpayers Association continues his legacy.

JAZZ, FROM 1919 TO 1960, African American musical artform with a lively history in Los Angeles. It emerged locally between 1919 and 1924, when Kid Ory, a Dixieland horn virtuoso, conducted the first all-black jazz recording orchestra in Los Angeles. During Prohibition, in the 1920s, the improvisational music increasingly emanated from hotel lounges, dance halls, speakeasies, and nightclubs in various parts of town. Essentially it was related to the musical style known as swing that was part of the popular dance scene of the late 1920s. Swing and jazz musicians initially supported themselves by wandering among the dancers and passing the hat. In Los Angeles, Les Hite and the California Ramblers pioneered in the band field, along with clarinetist Benny Goodman, who became a sensation at the Palomar dance hall in 1935. Taking his band on tour, Goodman launched the Big Band era throughout the county.

In the 1940s, jazz blossomed on Central Avenue, the center of African American business and entertainment in Los Angeles. Because Los Angeles was then Jim Crow, the music industry was segregated, and black musicians had to form their own union. Bebop and Dixieland were the jazz mainstays, but all existing styles were played. The music blared late into the night at the Brown Bomber, Bird in the Basket, and a dozen other clubs along Central. After dark, middle-class whites came to the clubs, arriving by automobile or Red Car. Jazz also was played in other parts of town. Black musicians performed in the Swanee Inn on Westwood Boulevard, Club Royale at Highland Avenue and Hollywood Boulevard, and at the Hi-De-Ho at Western Avenue and 50th Street. A few clubs also sprang up in the 1940s in Little Tokyo, which was briefly referred to as "Little Harlem" when blacks moved in.

Established musicians arrived from New York and other eastern cities to play or to cut records in Hollywood. Among them were Charlie Parker, Art Tatum, Nat "King" Cole, Louis Armstrong, Lionel Hampton, Teddy Buckner, Howard McGhee,

Kenny Dorham, Ray Brown, Red Callendar, Jimmy Rowles, Oscar Peterson, Barney Kessel, and Shelly Manne, who owned Shelly's Manne Hole on Cahuenga. Other, younger players, born or raised in Los Angeles, who studied music in the public schools, played in neighborhood church bands, or developed on their own in the small local clubs included Charles Mingus, Dexter Gordon, Eric Dolphy, Hampton Hawes, Zoot Sims, and Art Pepper. Los Angeles radio disc jockeys helped popularize jazz, as did the auditorium concerts produced by Norman Granz known as "Jazz at the Philharmonic."

A new jazz era began in 1945, when Dizzy Gillespie brought his sextet—Charlie "Bird" Parker (alto sax), Al Haig (piano), Ray Brown (bass), Stan Levey (drums), and Milt Jackson (vibraphone)—from New York to Billy Berg's Hollywood nightclub. From 1950 to 1960, jazz reached classic dimensions at the small Central Avenue clubs. Bassist Howard Rumsey formed a group, the Lighthouse All-Stars, made up entirely of former Stan Kenton band members: Bob Cooper (tenor sax), Shelly Manne (drums), Jimmy Giuffre (saxophone), Frank Patchen (piano), Milt Bernhardt (trombone), and Milton "Shorty" Rogers (trumpet). They played at the Hermosa Beach Lighthouse Cafe, a converted Chinese restaurant, which soon became a popular jazz scene. When Los Angeles was still Jim Crow, black musicians generally stayed at the Dunbar Hotel, next door to the Club Alabam.

Even as the older blues and Dixieland styles continued, San Francisco and Los Angeles musicians, from the mid-1940s to the early 1960s, developed a new idiom. Called "West Coast Jazz," it was denigrated by some Easterners for being technically fine but unemotional. Some of the names associated with the style were Dave Brubeck, Paul Desmond, Gerry Mulligan, Shorty Rogers, Jimmy Giuffre, Teddy Edwards, Hampton Hawes, and Ornette Coleman.

Wardell Gray, Dexter Gordon, and Teddy Edwards had devoted followings, as did Miles Davis, who created his "Cool Jazz" in Los Angeles in 1949–1950. As the Big Band era faded, musicians gravitated to Los Angeles from the East Coast looking for work in the film studios. Shorty Rogers, a Woody Herman trumpeter, pulled together a popular group that included Art Pepper, a local product. Jazz sessions at the famous Lighthouse lasted from 2 P.M. until 2 A.M. Shelly Manne and Stan Getz also had loyal fans. The innovative Gerry

Mulligan Quartet, which dispensed with piano, became headliners from 1952 to 1954. The Ornette Coleman Quartet burst on the scene in Los Angeles in 1959, and Kid Ory, after having moved elsewhere, returned to perform live and in movies. As Jim Crow laws faded, the racially segregated musicians locals merged in 1951. The jazz scene of the 1950s coincided with the adoption of the 33⅓ RPM long-playing record and the introduction of high-fidelity equipment, which revolutionized the recording industry. One local recording company that featured much big-name talent was Pacific Jazz.

JAZZ, SINCE 1960, continued to produce some headliners on the West Coast. One was trumpeter Carl H. "Doc" Severinson, who played with Tommy Dorsey and Benny Goodman, and in 1967 took over the NBC orchestra on Johnny Carson's *Tonight Show.* Generally, however, jazz suffered its "dog days" during the mid-1960s, when it became swamped by rhythm-and-blues and soul music. Many jazz clubs closed as musicians moved to Europe or worked exclusively in the movie studios. What remained was avant-garde jazz that was extremely vibrant but lacked a popular audience. Horace Tapscott, who formed the Pan-African People's Orchestra and the Underground Musicians Organization, played his own experimental jazz and taught many of the younger musicians who later performed in New York City. In the 1980s, jazz musicians returned from Europe, and coffee shops and new jazz clubs, such as the Jazz Bakery, opened. The Playboy Jazz Festival at the Hollywood Bowl is often sold out. The yearly June event has been hosted by jazz fan Bill Cosby since its inception in 1979. The Los Angeles County Museum of Art hosts jazz concerts on Friday nights year-round.

JEFFERS, [JOHN] ROBINSON (1887–1962), narrative poet associated mainly with Big Sur and Carmel who was born and raised in Los Angeles. The son of a Presbyterian minister, he lived in Highland Park as a youth and studied at Occidental College and USC. He also spent time at Hermosa Beach and Manhattan Beach, and was a tireless hiker in the San Gabriel Mountains. After marrying socialite Una Kuster, Jeffers moved to the untamed headlands of Carmel and built a granite residence, Tor House. He revered nature, and his later poetry struck an anti-urban note. He was also philosophically conservative, and staunchly Republican and anti-Roosevelt in the 1930s. His poem "At Play in Hermosa" describes that beach city as having neither "despair nor hope."

JERDE, JON (1941–), architect. Jerde was educated at USC and went to work for Charles Kober Associates, a firm specializing in shopping malls. His gift is the ability to design spaces that bring people together in the urban setting. His firm, the Jerde Partnership, coordinated the design for the 1984 Olympics, Westside Pavilion on Pico, and Market Place on Figueroa. Leon Whiteson of the *Los Angeles Times* dubs him, along with Frank Gehry, "L.A.'s quintessential architect." He is vice president of the Urban Design Advisory Coalition and a member of the mayor's Design Advisory Panel.

JET PROPULSION LABORATORY (JPL), world's leading planetary exploration laboratory, founded in 1958 by NASA and operated for them by Caltech. The 175-acre Pasadena facility has had a strong military orientation. It is headed by an air force general, who manages an annual budget of over $1 billion. Space vehicles have been launched for encounters with the planets Neptune, Jupiter, Saturn and Uranus, Mercury, Venus, Mars, and the moon. JPL engages in various educational outreach programs.

JEWELRY MART, 20-story twin towers on Hill Street facing Pershing Square housing a large part of the vast jewelry merchandising commerce of Los Angeles. For decades the industry had concentrated nearby, until by 1980 there were 600 or more retail jewelers on a few blocks of Hill Street. Buyers do comparison shopping at small booths in the mart. Much of the merchandise arrives from Lebanon, Iran, Egypt, Israel, and the Far East.

JEWISH FEDERATION-COUNCIL OF GREATER LOS ANGELES (JFC), primary Jewish community organization in Los Angeles County. It is devoted to fund raising, budgeting, planning, and maintaining community services for over 500 affiliated organizations serving half a million. Its origins lie in community organizations formed in the 1930s and 1940s: the United Jewish Welfare Fund, established in 1935 with Judge Isaac Pact as president and Mendel B. Silberberg as general campaign chairman; the Board of Rabbis of Southern California, whose first president, in 1930, was Rabbi Edgar F. Magnin; the Bureau of Education, created in 1938 with Herman A. Bachrack as chairman; and the Jewish Centers Association, established in 1943 with Judge Irving Stalmaster as president. The JFC arose from the 1959 merger of two existing organizations, the Jewish Welfare Federation and the Los Angeles Jewish Community Council.

The JFC provides care for orphans and professional guidance for the unemployed, and sees that medical care, philanthropy, welfare, immigration assistance, war relief, and cultural and religious services are delivered to those needing them. Its specialized agencies that deal with clients directly are the Aviva Center, Jewish Big Brothers Association, Vista Del Mar Child and Family Services, Los Angeles Hillel Council, Jewish Community Centers Association, Jewish Family Service of Los Angeles, Jewish Family Service of Santa Monica, Bet Tzedek Legal Services, Menorah Housing Foundation, Jewish Vocational Service, Gateways Hospital and Mental Health Center, Cedars-Sinai Medical Center, Jewish Free Loan Association, and Jewish War Veterans Service Commission. The umbrella organization has additional structural units, including the Board of Rabbis of Southern California, Youth Department, Jewish Community Relations Committee, Planning and Allocations Department, and Bureau of Jewish Education. The JFC ceased publishing its own news publication in 1985, although since then the *Jewish Journal,* an independent weekly mailed to JFC members, disseminates news and commentary of interest to the Jewish community.

JEWS numbered 550,000 to 600,000 in Los Angeles County in 1983. The combined population is second to that of New York City, but ahead of Tel Aviv. It amounts to nearly 10 percent of American Jews. In 1850, out of 8,624 people in the county, there were 8 Jewish bachelors, from Poland and Germany, engaged in peddling household goods, retail and wholesale merchandising, and banking. These individuals formed partnerships, many of them quite successful. In those days Jews encountered little anti-Semitic sentiment and gained acceptance among Yankee and Mexican Gentiles—though they did not intermarry with Christians. They acculturated quickly, usually learning Spanish and becoming active in the Masonic movement. Jews also participated actively in civic affairs and politics—mostly as Democrats. Solomon Lazard, a French-born merchant, sat on the city council in 1853 and headed the first Los Angeles Chamber of Commerce; Moritz Morris, a vintner, was elected to the council in the 1860s; and Emil Harris, a Polish-born Jew, became police chief in the 1870s.

Harris Newmark, upon his arrival in Los Angeles in 1853, became the first patriarch of the Jewish community. His uncle, Joseph Newmark, followed him the next year. Those Jews already living in the town had been holding sporadic religious services since 1851. After his arrival Joseph Newmark—who was an ordained rabbi, although he had never before served in that capacity—during his first year in Los Angeles organized the Hebrew Benevolent Society and established regular Sabbath services. The first such service was held in the back room of John Temple's adobe.

Residents engaged in the arts and crafts program at the Jewish Home for the Aging in Reseda. Courtesy Jewish Homes for the Aging.

In 1862 Rabbi Abraham Wolf Edelman, who had come to the United States from Poland as a young man in 1851, officiated over the B'nai B'rith congregation's first formal religious service, held in Stearn's Hall (Arcadia Hall). Subsequent services were held in various locations—including the town courtroom, with the permission of Judge Ygnacio Sepúlveda—until in 1873 the congregation built and moved into its own synagogue, a brick building on Fort Street (later Broadway) between 2nd and 3rd.

In 1900 the total Jewish population was an estimated 2,500, and in 1920 it was 20,000. Major immigrant Jewish waves arrived in the period 1920–1970, when Jews became influential in movies, the apparel industry, consumer retail and wholesale trades, the building industry, and the professions. They helped urbanize a community whose outlook had been essentially rural and provincial. The Jewish population reached 70,000 in 1930, and 150,000 in 1940. There was a major influx of Jewish immigrants escaping Hitler, including many artists and filmmakers, and it continued after the war as well.

Around 1910 Jews lived mostly in downtown, close to Bunker Hill and Temple Street, which by then was considered the "Jewish Main Street." Here were located Kaspare Cohn Hospital, the offices of Jewish Federation Charities, Mendelssohn Settlement House, and Olive Street synagogue. In the 1920s and 1930s, with the coming of Jews from Russia, Poland, and Germany, the community moved eastward across the river into Boyle Heights, along Brooklyn and Wabash Avenues, and nearby City Terrace. The Fairfax district currently has the greatest concentration of Jews, including large numbers of Orthodox religious families and Soviet Jews. In the aftermath of the Ayatollah Khomeini's fundamentalist revolution in Iran, a large exodus of Jews left Iran, some 30,000 of whom settled in and around the Beverly Hills area.

JOFFREY BALLET COMPANY, repertory dance company best known for contemporary and experimental work. Its tenure as the resident company at the Dorothy Chandler Pavilion ended after the 1991 season.

JOHNSON, EARVIN ("MAGIC") (1959–), superstar of the Los Angeles Lakers. He was born in Lansing, Michigan, graduated from Michigan State, was picked in the first-round college draft by the

Magic Johnson. Courtesy Los Angeles Lakers.

Lakers in 1979, and played with them for 12 years. A Lansing sports writer gave him his nickname after a 36-point performance in a high school game. He established many team records, including 989 assists, a single-season Laker record. His greatest all-around season was 1986–1987, the year he was voted NBA Man of the Year for his charitable and community services. His remarkable career includes his being named Most Valuable Player (MVP) by the National Basketball Association (NBA) in 1987, 1989, and 1990 as well as All-Star MVP in 1990 and 1992; in addition, he had the most assists (22) in an All-Star game, in 1984. The popular player stunned the nation in 1991 by announcing that he was HIV-positive and was retiring from basketball. He came out of retirement briefly in 1992 and was on the 1992 Olympic "Dream Team." On 30 January 1996 he returned as a Laker player, but retired once again at the end of that season.

JOHNSTON LAKE, small, secluded body of water in Pasadena, fed by streams from the nearby Arroyo Seco. The lake is named for Alexander Campbell-Johnston, a Scot who ran a ranch and winery (San Rafael Winery) there in the 1880s. Catfish, crayfish, and carp were abundant in the 3-acre pond in the 1950s. The area is preserved by local property owners.

JONATHAN CLUB, exclusive downtown club. It was founded in 1895 as a men's club by Republican supporters of William McKinley who greeted one another as "Brother Jonathan," the name George Washington called his friend Jonathan Trumbull. Along with the California Club it ranks among the most prestigious social clubs in Southern California. In the 1970s its membership stood at about 3,500, all men and mostly rising young executives. The club owns a large downtown residence and a beach facility in Santa Monica. When the seaside operation applied for a permit to expand onto state land in 1985, the California Coastal Commission turned them down, citing discriminatory entrance requirements against women, nonwhites, and Jews. The club modified its membership policy in 1987.

JONES, A. QUINCY (1913–1979), Missouri-born architect who practiced in Los Angeles after 1937. He taught at USC from 1951 to 1967 and became dean of the architecture school. He was known for his fine small homes and for his buildings on the University of California campuses of Los Angeles, Riverside, San Diego, and Santa Barbara. Jones contributed to the design of the award-winning Eichler Homes.

JONES, JOHN P. (1829–1912), founder of Santa Monica. The Nevada silver tycoon and former U.S. senator from Nevada laid out the seaside community in 1875, in partnership with Robert Symington Baker. He constructed a pier and initiated construction of a railway to Los Angeles. Finding himself in financial straits in 1877, he sold the rail line to the Southern Pacific Railroad, which shut down the pier. In 1896 Jones and Baker donated 225 acres of land south of what is today the Veterans Administration Hospital to induce interurban rail developers, brothers-in-law Moses Sherman and Eli P. Clark, to construct a commuter line along Santa Monica Boulevard. The arrangement gave birth to Sawtelle and greatly stimulated real estate development in Santa Monica.

JOURNALISM. *See* Newspapers

J. PAUL GETTY MUSEUM, art repository in Malibu founded by oil magnate J. Paul Getty in 1953. It is devoted primarily to Greek and Roman antiquities, Renaissance and Baroque painting, and European decorative art, though in recent years the institution has acquired extraordinary illuminated manuscripts and 20th-century photographs as well. The museum and its collections were originally housed, in 1954, in Getty's home near Pacific Palisades. It was moved to its present 65-acre site in Malibu in 1973. Getty, who moved to England in the 1950s, never actually saw the Getty Museum: the main building, designed by architects R. E. Langdon and E. C. Wilson, opened only in 1974. It is based on the plan of the Villa dei Papiri in Herculaneum, which was buried by an eruption of Mt. Vesuvius in A.D. 79. The site includes gardens with trees, plants, and flowers typical of such a Roman villa. The Getty Foundation has the largest museum endowment in the world. Many millions from that fund are earmarked for the construction

Main Peristyle Garden, J. Paul Getty Museum. Photo by Jack Ross, courtesy J. Paul Getty Museum.

of the Getty Center in Brentwood, a vast new complex for the visual arts that will complement, but not replace, the Malibu institution.

JPL. *See* Jet Propulsion Laboratory

JUDD, WINNIE RUTH (1905–), convicted murderer who was featured in the tabloids as the "Trunk Murderess," "Velvet Tigress," and "Wolf Woman." In October 1931, at the age of 25, she shot two women in Phoenix, dismembered their bodies, and shipped them in trunks on the train she was taking back to Los Angeles. Convicted of murder and sentenced to hang, she was judged insane and confined to the Arizona State Mental Hospital. She managed to escape seven times and was paroled in 1971 to California.

JUDICIAL SYSTEM, as in all California communities, is run exclusively by the county government. The Los Angeles Superior Court, with 22 court locations and 295 judicial officers in 1991, including 238 elected superior court judges, had major jurisdiction in all judicial matters. The Criminal Courts Building on West Temple and Broadway is the nerve center of the Central District of Los Angeles Superior Court, the busiest court in the world's most active criminal justice system. This system, with 34,000 employees, was the second largest employer in the county.

In criminal matters, the district attorney initiates charges and prosecutes offenders. A grand jury inquires into all public offenses committed or subject to trial, and examines the county's financial books. It is composed of 23 court-nominated citizens, with each juror then becoming an officer of the court. A judicial procedures commission works in cooperation with the courts to recommend changes and improvements in judicial procedures to the Board of Supervisors. For Santa Catalina Island, lesser judicial matters are handled by a justice court.

The Municipal Court of California, Los Angeles Judicial District, is the largest court of limited jurisdiction in the nation. It operates 121 courtrooms and handles over 250,000 felony preliminary examinations and misdemeanors, 120,00 civil filings, 77,000 small claims filings, and 900,000 moving and parking citations each year.

The Probation Department is also part of the justice system and works in conjunction with the courts. It is a county agency that handles a case load of some 80,000 adults and 14,000 juveniles annually. As of 1993 the department employed 3,300 probation deputies.

A public defender's office provides legal representation to all persons, including juveniles, who are financially unable to hire their own counsel. The Los Angeles County Sheriff's Department administers the county's police function and operates county detention facilities. The marshal's office serves writs and warrants issued by the courts and provides bailiffs and security within court facilities.

JULIAN, C[OURTNEY] C. (1885–1934), charming and flamboyant oil speculator who breezed into Los Angeles and borrowed huge sums of money for a scheme that destroyed many people in the 1920s—and this in a city notorious for its boom-town real estate, banking, and oil speculators. A Canadian by birth, Julian was an oil roustabout with phenomenal luck. Approximately 40,000 people responded to his breezy newspaper ads by investing in a petroleum company that he said was "certain" to rival the big oil trusts and for which he promised dividends far beyond the company's actual earnings. From 1920 to 1925 he was a celebrity with a lavish lifestyle. When Julian was forced out from his company because of public pressure and government regulations, Julian Petroleum was nevertheless producing oil and solvent. The company was taken over by even wilder speculators. On 7 May 1927 trading in company stock was stopped, and the company collapsed.

The repercussions of the failure were many and varied: the Los Angeles district attorney was sentenced to jail for bribery; a person was murdered in open court; trials for murder, bribery, and embezzlement of the spoils rumbled on into the early 1930s; and 40,000 shareholders lost $150 million. To escape a mail fraud charge, Julian fled to China. He committed suicide at a glittering party in the Astor Hotel in Shanghai 25 March 1934, and was laid in a pauper's grave.

K

KAGEL CANYON, unincorporated community 19 miles from downtown Los Angeles. The area, north of San Fernando, is named for Henry Kagel, a pioneer who claimed government land at the mouth of the canyon.

KAISER PERMANENTE, successful prepaid medical and hospital service. It consists of the eight Kaiser Foundation hospitals and the Southern California Permanente Medical Group, which contract with the Kaiser Foundation Health Plan, Inc., a federally qualified health maintenance organization (HMO).

Kaiser Permanente was established by industrialist Henry J. Kaiser in 1933 when his firm contracted with Los Angeles–area cities to build the Colorado River Aqueduct. The comprehensive medical plan was devised by Dr. Sidney Garfield, a surgeon, to meet the health needs of the construction workers and their families. In the 1940s, when Kaiser moved on to other projects in Washington State and in Fontana and Richmond, California, he recruited Garfield to expand the model. In 1950, at the urging of both the International Longshoremen's and Warehousemen's Union and

Kaiser Permanente, West Los Angeles. Photo by Leonard Pitt.

the Pacific Maritime Association, the Kaiser Foundation Health Plan was extended to workers in Los Angeles Harbor. Major new medical facilities were developed in Los Angeles in 1953, in Harbor City and Panorama City in 1962, in Bellflower in 1965, and in West Los Angeles in 1974.

Kaiser Permanente now serves 12 regions in the United States, coast to coast. The regional unit for Southern California has 10 major medical centers from Bakersfield to San Diego, over 60 medical offices, and 2,300 physicians, serving hundreds of thousands of health plan members. The name Permanente comes from one of Kaiser's early business ventures near Permanente Creek, California.

KAPLAN, SAM HALL (1935–), urban design critic. Originally from New York, Kaplan has practiced, taught, and lectured on public planning and is the recipient of many grants. He is the author of *L.A. Lost and Found: An Architectural History of Los Angeles* (1987). A more recent work, *L.A. Follies: Design and Other Diversions in a Fractured Metropolis* (1989), is a collection of *Los Angeles Times* columns from the 1980s. One of Kaplan's major themes concerns the idea that architects, planners, and builders must create a more humane and livable urban environment.

KELKER, DE LEUW REPORT, comprehensive rapid transit plan for the metropolis. It was prepared in 1925 by Kelker, De Leuw, and Company, a consulting firm hired by the city and county regional planning commissions to address the growing problem of traffic congestion. The firm recommended the creation of a rapid transit network of electric cars that would use subways and elevated tracks in densely urbanized areas but would travel at ground level in outlying regions. They also proposed that street railways and buses serve as feeder lines. The system was to be financed by a combination of bond issues, user fares, and property taxes. Powerful downtown interests turned thumbs down on the plan, opting instead to improve conditions for auto community and to reroute streetcars and existing interurban lines. Their preference for the automobile constituted a consensus, and the Kelker, De Leuw Plan, the most ambitious transit plan ever proposed for Los Angeles, died a quiet death.

KELLER, MATTHEW (D. 1881), Irish-born pioneer. After sojourning in Mexico, Keller arrived in Los Angeles in about 1850 and bought the 13,000-acre Rancho Topanga Malibu Sequit for 10 cents an acre. Don Matteo, as he was called, raised cotton, tobacco, oranges, and grapes, from which he made wine. He rode with the Rangers, an 1850s vigilante group of some 100 men, many of them prominent in the community, and helped form a volunteer fire brigade. In the 1890s his son sold the Malibu property to Frederick Rindge for $10 an acre.

KENNEDY, ROBERT, ASSASSINATION OF. The Democratic presidential candidate was shot on 5 June 1968 at a victory celebration at the Ambassador Hotel, after winning the California primary. He died shortly afterward. A Los Angeles Police Department investigation determined that the sole assailant was Sirhan B. Sirhan, who was tried, convicted, and remains incarcerated.

KERCKHOFF, WILLIAM G. (1856–1929), industrialist. The Indianan was smitten with California while on a camping trip in 1875 and settled in Los Angeles three years later. He bought a lumber company, built a fleet of wooden ships, and supplied ice to the Santa Fe Railroad for shipping oranges. He also became important in the hydroelectric industry, helping to found the Pacific Light and Power Company, a forerunner to the Southern California Gas Company. Kerckhoff was a benefactor to Caltech and UCLA. Kerckhoff Hall, on the Westwood campus, is named in his honor.

KEYSTONE STUDIO. *See* Movie industry, early history (1902–1914)

KIENHOLZ, EDWARD (1927–), rebel avant-garde artist who in the late 1950s helped break the hold of the academic school on painting and sculpture. He was one of the Ferus Gallery group. His sculpture *Back Seat Dodge '38,* exhibited at the Los Angeles County Museum of Art in 1964, featured an actual car body with a young couple making love. It so infuriated a county supervisor that he tried to shut the museum down.

KINDERGARTEN MOVEMENT was established locally in the 1870s by pioneer educator Emma Marwedel, one of the circle who gathered around civic reformer Caroline Severance. In the 1880s pioneer kindergartens were housed in Congregational churches. Marwedel's pupil, Kate Wiggin, went on to San Francisco to establish the state's

---

Freeways, like rivers, age and meander.   —Richard Power

---

first free kindergarten. The theory behind this early-education method, which originated in Germany, was to instruct four-to-six-year-old children by means of stories, games, music, cooperative play, and simple craft activities, thus assisting their transition to primary school education. Early childhood education became a strong point among feminists, urban reformers, and followers of John Dewey's Progressive education movement in Los Angeles at the turn of the century.

KING, RODNEY G. *See* Riot of 1992

KINNEOLA MESA, unincorporated county area in the hills east of Altadena. Abbot Kinney, the developer of Venice of America in 1904, established an estate here in the 1880s. In 1990 the population was 1,300.

KINNEY, ABBOT (1850–1920), New Jersey–born entrepreneur, promoter of cultural uplift, and developer of Venice. While still in his twenties, the widely traveled young man inherited a family fortune derived from cigarette manufacturing. He developed an affection for Southern California while on a trip in 1873, and in 1880 settled on a ranch near Sierra Madre to mend his failing health. He was among the first to cultivate citrus trees in Southern California, and joined the crusade to plant eucalyptus trees. An avid student of Native

Abbot Kinney. Courtesy Photographic Collections, Los Angeles Public Library.

American culture, Kinney was appointed to the post of U.S. Indian commissioner. When Helen Hunt Jackson was requested to write a report on the status of "mission" Indians, Kinney partnered her in the investigation. He was later made head of the State Board of Forestry, an expertise that he picked up on his own through concerted study. A man of wide-reaching intellect, he also wrote pamphlets and articles on sociology, child rearing, sex education, aesthetics, metaphysics, and numerous other subjects.

After 1892 Kinney devoted himself to an ambitious project: the creation of a cultural theme park to be known as Venice of America. At first he had partners, but in 1904 he broke away and proceeded on his own to develop the 1.5-mile coastal area south of Santa Monica. He drained the marshes, dug a network of canals, constructed a breakwater and several piers, and erected facilities for theater, concerts, dance, and lectures, as well as a hotel for tourists. Kinney had gondolas built and imported Italian gondoliers to propel visitors along the Venice canals. He signed up performers in all the arts. Soon, though, having already spent millions of dollars and nearly bankrupting himself, he realized that the public had little use for highbrow cultural events. After waiting months for the au-

diences to swell, Kinney canceled the uplifting programs and turned Venice into a popular amusement park. To fulfill his new goals, Kinney had to go up against his former partners, who now operated a rival pleasure pier in Ocean Park, directly to the north. He incorporated his own development as the independent city of Venice in 1911.

Kinney remained active in business until he died of lung cancer on 4 November 1920. Six weeks later his pleasure pier and all of its attractions were destroyed by fire. His heirs rebuilt parts of the project, though in a different configuration.

KNOLLWOOD, hilly section of Granada Hills in the northern San Fernando Valley area of the city of Los Angeles. The neighborhood takes its name from Knollwood Country Club. Knollwood includes equestrian trails and a bird sanctuary in the former Van Norman Dam reservoir.

KNUDSEN, VALLEY MARY (FILTZER) (1895–1976), civic leader during the 1950s who held dozens of appointive posts. She spearheaded the "Los Angeles Beautiful Movement," which planted trees and otherwise tried to stem urban blight. The *Los Angeles Times* once named her Woman of the Year.

KOENIG, PIERRE (1925–), Modernist architect. Koenig was part of the Case Study homes movement, which had its greatest influence in the 1950s and 1960s, at the time of the postwar building boom. He desired to design homes for people of modest income that were simple, clean looking, and hygienic, reflecting the positive influences of modern technology. The homes featured open kitchens, lofty ceilings, and atriums. His most celebrated creation probably was Case Study House #22, completed in 1960 and immortalized in a famous photograph by Julius Shulman.

KOREANS, as of 1990, numbered approximately 72,000 in the city, 145,000 in the county, and between 200,000 and 300,000 in Southern California as a whole. They form the largest concentration of Koreans outside of Korea and are one of the fastest-growing ethnic groups, with a population of 1 million projected for the early 21st century.

The first Koreans arrived in Los Angeles around 1910, as an offshoot of American Protestant missionary activity in Korea. America's military involvement in Korea during the Cold War led to additional migration, particularly of university students and the wives and children of American GIs. Nevertheless, in 1965 there were only 5,000 Koreans in Los Angeles. A liberalization of the U.S.

I have been given to understand that a very advantageous settlement is established on a fertile spot somewhere in this neighborhood within sight of the ocean, though at the distance of some miles from the coast called Pueblo de los Angeles, "the country town of the Angels," formed in the year 1781. This establishment was looked for in all directions, but nothing was perceived that indicated either habitations or inhabitants.

—Captain George Vancouver, British naval explorer, 1795

---

immigration law, implemented in 1968, allowed a great many more to migrate, often with the blessings of the South Korean government.

Most Koreans became small entrepreneurs—owners of gas stations, neighborhood groceries, liquor stores, and the like. Individual success in the community is attributable in part to an informal network of underground banks, known as *kye,* and also to a willingness to work hard and for long hours.

The community supports four daily newspapers, one of which, the *Korean Central Daily,* has a worldwide circulation of over 2 million. While many Koreans practice Buddhism, about 70 percent enroll in Protestant churches when they arrive. The hundreds of Korean Protestant churches in the region provide a strong social and cultural network.

Acculturation is not without stress. Koreans have experienced a rise in domestic violence, drug abuse, and youth gang activity. The tendency of Korean business people to invest heavily in declining neighborhoods has brought them into bitter conflict with poor black communities. An estimated 2,000 Korean-owned establishments were destroyed during the rioting of April 1992. As a result, some families decided to resettle in Orange County or San Diego. Nevertheless, according to a 1992 *Los Angeles Times* survey 74 percent of Koreans were satisfied with how their lives are going (even after the riots); 36 percent said they were U.S. citizens. Koreans had many more years of education than the county's residents as a whole, and most were much more likely to become professionals or managers than the average population. Most people in the community speak some English as well as Korean.

The annual pace of emigration from South Korea peaked in the mid-1980s (over 35,800 left in 1987 alone) and has declined somewhat since then, although 98 percent of the adult population in Los Angeles was born in South Korea. In the decade 1980–1990 the population has grown by 140 percent. Although Koreatown is the major commercial center, Korean neighborhoods are expanding in several areas, most notably Monterey Park and Garden Grove.

KOREATOWN, fast-growing ethnic community between Normandie Avenue and Hoover Street, north of Pico Boulevard. It emerged as a retail strip, rather than an ethnic neighborhood, since most Koreans have lived elsewhere in the county. Today, however, it houses one-third of all the Koreans living in the county, and it is already larger than Chinatown. Los Angeles posted its first official sign designating this ethnic enclave in 1970 (though in fact most of the area's residents are Latino). The most valuable Korean-owned properties are in the Mid-Wilshire area. These include banks, mini-

Seoul Plaza, Koreatown, 1995. Photo by Dale Pitt.

malls, major office buildings, apartment complexes, hotels, restaurants, and churches. The Wilshire strip is emerging as the "Main Street of Koreatown."

KROTONA, religious colony founded by Albert Powell Warrington, a retired lawyer. Warrington arrived in Los Angeles in 1911 and formed the settlement on a 15-acre hillside plot in the Hollywood Hills. It featured a lotus pond, a vegetarian cafeteria, tabernacles, and a library brimming with works on metaphysics. The center sponsored classes in Esperanto, "Esoteric Interpretation of Music and Drama," and "The Human Aura," as well as studies in physics, chemistry, psychology, and psychic phenomena. Many of Warrington's followers were bright, charming, and accomplished in the sciences and the arts. The Krotona scene is nicely captured in Jane Levington Comfort's novel *From These Beginnings* (1937).

KU KLUX KLAN (KKK), nationwide vigilante organization especially active in Southern California in the 1920s and 1930s. Unlike the post–Civil War Klan, which targeted blacks and their white allies, the revived Klan bashed Catholics, radicals, Jews, labor activists, and "wets" as much as blacks. Despite grass-roots support and backing in the law enforcement community, the incompetently led KKK could not capitalize on its popularity. Today, much diminished in size and influence, the Klan engages in occasional ritualistic activity. In 1983 some members from Lake View Terrace were prosecuted for a cross burning.

KWANZAA, annual African American holiday celebrated for seven days beginning on 26 December and ending on 1 January. The name is Swahili for "first fruits of the harvest." The festivity, initiated in Los Angeles by student activist Maulana (Ron) Karenga in 1966, promotes the principles of community, family, and responsibility. A red, green, and black flag created by Pan-Africanist leader Marcus Garvey is associated with the holiday. It is now celebrated nationwide.

KWOH, STEWART (1948–), Chinese American attorney, considered by many to be the country's most important advocate for all Asians, both American and foreign born. He is the founder of the Asian Pacific American Legal Center of Southern California, which served 15,000 people in 1994. A trusted adviser to Mayor Riordan, and an activist who sits on many boards and commissions in the city and state, Kwoh is regarded as a bridge builder, bringing together people of different and sometimes adversarial backgrounds. He credits his success to his religious values, the influence of the civil rights movement, and his participation in the National Conference of Christians and Jews camp, where he became acquainted with students from all areas of the city.

Stewart Kwoh. Courtesy Stewart Kwoh and APALC.

LABOR UNION MOVEMENT, 1875 TO 1945,
emerged in Los Angeles with the formation of the
typographical union in 1875, but it was shaped by
the battle against an employers' open-shop crusade,
which was particularly intense from about 1880 to
1937. Beginning in the 1880s unions had to confront a determined Harrison Gray Otis, publisher
of the *Los Angeles Times,* and the Merchants and
Manufacturers Association (M & M), who were
bent on maintaining a low wage scale in Los Angeles compared to San Francisco. The employers
resolved to destroy the labor movement, if that
proved necessary. Nevertheless, in the first decade of the 1900s printers, carpenters, painters,
plumbers, teamsters, brewery workers, iron workers, leather workers, and laborers were ripe for organizing. The movement, as a whole, managed to
acquire cohesion, stability, and even occasional political recognition during that period.

Two labor traditions coexisted in Los Angeles.
One, as represented by Arthur Vinette, the popular head of the Carpenters Local 56, involved use
of the political process to express social ideals, advocate a broad program of social reform, and replace the capitalist system with a cooperative or socialist society. The Populist Party of the 1890s
typified this political path, with its advocacy of the
initiative and referendum, eight-hour day, abolition of contract labor, nationalization of mines,
railroads, and telephones, a graduated income tax,
repeal of tramp and labor-conspiracy laws, government work for the unemployed, and abolition
of national banks. The second tradition was a
pragmatic one. It sought collective bargaining contracts with employers that would improve wages
and hours of the craft members, who were, essentially, the native-born white male labor elite. This
craft unionism was represented by the national

leader of the American Federation of Labor (AFL),
Samuel Gompers.

In 1910 labor leaders from San Francisco
launched an organizing drive in Los Angeles that
provoked the wrath of the antilabor M & M. In
the midst of the drive, on 1 October 1910, the *Times*
Building was destroyed by a bomb that killed 20
and injured 17. Two labor officials, the McNamara
brothers, were accused. After first avowing their innocence, they confessed to the crime in December
1911, just before the trial was to begin. This disaster undermined the gains labor had made and
placed it on the defensive in Los Angeles for a
generation.

The union movement languished during the
1920s, but revived during the Great Depression and
New Deal era of the 1930s. In the 1933 El Monte
blackberry and raspberry strike, 1,500 Mexican
workers, led by anarcho-syndicalists, walked off
their jobs demanding a raise in their 9-cents-an-
hour pay. Within weeks they were joined by 5,500
other field workers in Culver City and Santa Monica. The employers, Japanese nationals using leased
fields, worked with the Japanese consul to bring
about a 20-cents-an-hour settlement. Union labor
was employed in the reconstruction of Long Beach
after the 1933 earthquake, in the stretching of the
electrical power lines from Boulder (now Hoover)
Dam to Los Angeles, and in the construction of
extensive flood control projects.

In the 1930s the membership of traditional craft
unions leveled off, while that of industrial unions
gained ground. The new national Committee for
Industrial Organization (CIO) slowly acquired a
foothold among Southern California workers in
oil, auto, steel, rubber, garment making, and aircraft. This trend became pronounced after Congress passed the 1937 Wagner Act granting Amer-

ican unions the right of collective bargaining. A sit-down strike at Douglas Aircraft in March 1937 resulted in 342 arrests, the largest mass arraignment in county history. Despite the new legislation and the friendlier political climate for labor, local employers remained antilabor. The Los Angeles Police Department "Red Squad," acting as the enforcement arm of the M & M, bloodied many heads in 1937 during scores of labor disputes. Longshoremen and oil workers joined the industrial unions. In 1941 the carpenters achieved a master agreement that brought stability to the construction trade for 30 years. Conversely, that same year North American Aviation became a focus of management efforts to halt the drive for unionization. The U.S. Army was called in and broke the strike.

Craft unions were strong in the entertainment industry as well. Movie studio heads began yielding to the demands of unions and guilds in the 1930s and 1940s. Even as these unions fought among themselves for job control, they also wrested major concessions from management. Indicative of the clout exerted by entertainment unions, one of the strongest labor bodies in Southern California in the 1940s was the musicians union.

LABOR UNION MOVEMENT, SINCE 1945, eventually overcame the obstacle of the prevailing open shop. Unions achieved recognition in many key industries, though the road to acceptance was often bumpy. Although labor unions and guilds had by now established themselves in the movie studios, the industry was often the scene of bitter labor strife, not only between unions and studio heads, but also between rival craft unions. They struggled for permanent recognition and improved wages, hours, and benefits for their members. The ugly 1945 contest between the Conference of Studio Unions (CSU) and the International Association of Theater and Stage Employees (IATSE) led to a strike that split the ranks of labor and their supporters. The clash, which had ambiguous results, was renewed in 1946 and 1947. Hundreds of rival picketers threw rocks, shouted, and shoved one another outside the Warner Brothers and MGM studios.

During the Red Scare that followed World War II, the political climate worsened for labor. Antilabor forces portrayed any form of militancy as being tantamount to Communist subversion, and McCarthyism split many unions. In Los Angeles, as in much of the nation, the conservative leadership of the Congress of Industrial Organizations (CIO) expelled major left-led locals.

By contrast, the prosperity of Cold War industry proved a boon to unionism. Unions such as the International Association of Machinists (IAM) and United Auto Workers (UAW) enjoyed considerable vitality in the aerospace and automobile industries in the 1950s and 1960s, and retail clerks secured a strong position in the burgeoning food industry. The independent International Brotherhood of Teamsters also became a powerhouse in the regional economy.

A major organizational event in labor history was the 1956 formation of the Los Angeles County Federation of Labor, a delegate body formed by a merger of the AFL and CIO and covering most of the labor movement (the Teamsters being a notable exception). The executive secretary of the federation from 1975 to 1993, William Robertson, had a seat on the Coliseum commission and was influential enough to be consulted by mayors and council members.

Industrial and white-collar unions continued to gain members in the 1960s and 1970s. The newspaper guild went on strike in 1967, and the teachers union did the same in 1970, both with federation backing. The most notable gains—achieved

---

The wet season is the season in which it can rain but may not; and the dry season is the season in which it cannot rain, but occasionally does.

—Helen Hunt Jackson

---

with and without strikes—were made by teamsters, machinists, teachers, and other white-collar trades. With the recent decline in heavy industry, service industries have became the focus of increased organizing efforts by the labor movement. Retail clerks (food and commercial workers) and hotel and restaurant employees made particular advances.

In the period from the 1970s to the 1990s union membership declined in the construction and industrial sectors, but expanded in the service and government sectors and in certain white-collar fields. The United Teachers of Los Angeles (UTLA) achieved recognition from the Los Angeles Unified School District, one of the largest in the nation; the American Federation of Teachers (AFT) and National Education Association (NEA) represent teachers in different school districts. Some other unions with a steady or rising membership are the United Food and Commercial Workers (UFCW), the Service Employees International Union (SEIU), and the American Federation of State, County, and Municipal Employees (AFSCME). Unions representing nurses have secured contracts in local medical facilities, winning substantial increases in income and benefits. The militant janitorial workers conducted the Justice for Janitors campaign in 1987. They became visible again in 1995 as their contract was about to expire. They are an example of the recent increase in the membership and leadership visibility of women, minorities, and immigrants in the local labor movement.

LA BREA TAR PITS, black bogs in the Wilshire district's Hancock Park. In 1875 amateur paleontologists uncovered the remains of a prehistoric an-

La Brea tar pits. Courtesy Public Affairs Dept., Los Angeles County.

imal that had been trapped in the tar. Oil geologist William W. Orcutt made additional discoveries in 1916, retrieving the first full fossil skull of the saber-toothed tiger ever found. By 1915 the Natural History Museum had collected some 600,000 specimens, the richest trove of Ice Age animal remains anywhere in the world. The 32-acre site containing the pits was once part of a rich oil field owned by G. Allan Hancock; in 1916 he presented it to the county for a preserve soon to be named Hancock Park. There in 1975 the county built the George C. Page Museum of La Brea Discoveries, a branch of the Natural History Museum, to house and interpret the fossil remains of animals trapped in the pits as long as 40,000 years ago.

LA CAÑADA FLINTRIDGE, independent city north of Pasadena and 13 miles from downtown Los Angeles. The first part of the compounded name was given by Catalina Verdugo, who had inherited from her father a portion of Rancho San Rafael, which she called Rancho La Cañada ("Mountain Valley Ranch"). The land was granted to Ignacio Coronel in 1843 and patented by Jonathan A. Scott in 1866. The second part of the name comes from the 700 acres bought by Senator Frank Putnam Flint and subdivided beginning in 1913, as Flintridge. In 1990 La Cañada Flintridge had a population of 19,300.

LACMA. *See* Los Angeles County Museum of Art

LA CRESCENTA, unincorporated hillside area of 4.8 square miles, surrounded by Glendale, La Cañada Flintridge, and the Angeles National Forest, 11 miles north of downtown Los Angeles. It was granted to José María Verdugo in 1787 and patented to Julio Verdugo in 1882. Movie stars Clark Gable and Carole Lombard were among those who built vacation cabins there. The origin of its name is obscure. One suggestion is that it was first used by Dr. Benjamin Briggs, a settler in the 1880s, who looked out his window and saw three crescent-shaped landforms. A more likely suggestion is that the Spanish word *creciente,* meaning flood tide, was used in 1913 in reference to a torrent of water that spilled out of the mountains in a massive rainstorm. On New Year's Day 1934 a flood resulting from an early-morning cloudburst drowned 40 people in the area. The combined population of La Crescenta and adjacent Montrose was over 17,000 in 1990.

LADERA HEIGHTS, unincorporated area situated just north of the San Diego Freeway, north of Inglewood and east of Culver City. In 1990, 6,300 people lived there. It is divided into two areas, the older of which, a product of the 1940s, is called Old Ladera. New Ladera was developed in the 1950s and 1960s.

LAEMMLE, CARL (1867–1939), German-born film pioneer. Beginning as an exhibitor in 1906, he produced *Hiawatha* in 1909, the year he founded Independent Motion Picture Company (IMP). In 1912 IMP became Universal Film Manufacturing Company, then Universal Pictures. In 1915 Laemmle took land that had been a chicken farm

---

Los Angeles is the source and home of more political, economic, and religious idiocy than all the rest of the country together.

—Westbrook Pegler, journalist, 1938

La Fiesta de Los Angeles poster, 1897. Courtesy Seaver Center for Western History Research, Natural History Museum of Los Angeles County.

and opened Universal City in the San Fernando Valley. Laemmle was notorious for hiring family members, regardless of their competence. However, he was also quick to recognize talent and was the first person to tap into the skills of producer Irving Thalberg, placing the Universal lot in the care of the 21-year-old executive while he himself traveled abroad. Today's Laemmle movie theater chain is owned by a branch of the family that entered the field in the 1930s.

LA FIESTA DE LOS ANGELES, street carnival first held from 10 to 13 April 1894 to celebrate the city's Hispanic beginnings, as well as to attract eastern tourists planning to visit the San Francisco fair. Inspired by carnivals at Nice and Monte Carlo, it was the inspiration of business leader Max Mayerberg and the Merchants Association. It consisted of parades, floral battles in Central Park (today's Pershing Square), a grand ball, and firework displays. Also known as Fiesta de las Flores, "Feast of Flowers," it was held annually for 10 years, then languished, and was later revived. Approximately $500,000 was spent on the now 10-day-long festivity in September 1931, when the Great Depression was taking its toll on the city of 1 million

people. Critics feared La Fiesta would turn into "El Fiasco," but the event, held at venues from Long Beach to Santa Monica, attracted 300,000 people to the area, who spent $3 million. In 1989 the merchants association of Broadway again revived the festival in a lively annual Cinco de Mayo celebration, calling it L.A. Fiesta Broadway.

LA HABRA HEIGHTS, independent city on the southeastern boundary of the county, 24 miles from downtown Los Angeles. It lies just north of La Habra, an independent city in Orange County. The population in 1990 was 6,200.

LAKE HOLLYWOOD, attractive body of water in the Hollywood Hills, near the Hollywood sign. It was created by William Mulholland in 1917 as a reservoir for Owens River water delivered by the Los Angeles Aqueduct. The lake, 4 miles in circumference, is a popular circuit for joggers and walkers. The surrounding wooded area was opened to development in the 1920s and 1930s.

LAKE HUGHES–ELIZABETH LAKE, twin communities in Leona Valley, in the northern part of the county. Sandwiched between the San Gabriel

Mountains and Portal Ridge, they are almost completely surrounded by the Angeles National Forest. The two lakes were created in ancient times by the San Andreas Fault. Their first mention in recorded history occurred when San Gabriel missionaries used the valley as part of the Spanish Trail. The rancher Francisco "Chico" Lopez, who discovered gold in Placerita Canyon in 1842, and Gen. Edward F. Beale settled and built adobes in the valley in the early American period, and the area became a stop for the Butterfield stage in 1858. Lake Hughes was named in 1898 for G. O. Hughes, who owned lands adjoining the small lake. In the past century, Lake Hughes–Elizabeth Lake have been devoted to orchards, ranching, farming, and recreation, although several residential tracts were subdivided in the 1920s and 1950s. Developers had created about 350 dwellings by 1984. Future building is restricted owing to seismic activity.

LAKE LOS ANGELES. *See* Desert Buttes

LAKERS, LOS ANGELES. *See* Los Angeles Lakers

LAKEVIEW, unincorporated community in the Palmdale area. It lies west of the Antelope Valley Freeway, 46 miles from downtown Los Angeles. The lake in question is Lake Palmdale, a reservoir for the California Aqueduct.

LAKE VIEW TERRACE, San Fernando Valley community lying within Los Angeles city boundaries near the Hansen Dam recreation area. It is a hillside community of 12,000, made up largely of working-class families. It consists of modest bungalows intermixed with one- or two-acre horse ranches.

LAKEWOOD, "instant city" of 77,000 people near Long Beach, 14 miles south of downtown Los Angeles. It sprouted on bean fields during the suburban boom of the 1950s. The name came from an older community known as Lakewood Village, laid out in 1934 on property owned by the Rancho Los Cerritos Land Company, near a small body of water called Bouton Lake, which would become part of a county golf course. The developer of the new suburb was the Lakewood Park Corporation, owned by Weingart, Boyar, and Taper. Although Long Beach expected to annex the young unincorporated suburb, the residents opted to incorporate as an independent community and to contract with the county for all public services. This arrangement, called the Lakewood Plan, is now utilized by other communities. When incorporated in 1954, Lakewood became the 17th largest city in the state. Lakewood Center Mall was among the first planned regional shopping centers in the nation. In 1990 the city's population was 73,000.

LAKEWOOD PLAN, arrangement whereby an independent city contracts with Los Angeles County for fire, police, library, and other services. The plan arose in 1954 when the newly incorporated city of Lakewood entered into such an agreement, enabling the residents to reduce their property taxes and mandating their treasury to maintain a $300,000 surplus. The Lakewood Plan suited various interests: the Board of Supervisors could ensure existing budget levels; the developers and builders were assured of dealing with the county, where they had significant influence over zoning and land use regulations; and local property owners enjoyed low property taxes. Soon numerous other middle-class areas in the county followed Lakewood's example; by the 1980s, 1.5 million people lived under the Lakewood Plan. Critics, meanwhile, assert that the plan effectively forces the general county taxpayer to subsidize

Lining up for new tract housing in Lakewood, 1951. Courtesy City of Lakewood Public Information Office.

the residents of affluent and middle-class white communities.

LA MIRADA, independent city 20 miles southeast of Los Angeles. In Spanish the name means "the view." It was once part of the vast Rancho Los Coyotes, purchased in 1895 by Andrew McNally of the Rand McNally map firm. The ranch, which specialized in olives and citrus, was subdivided in 1953. The city was incorporated as Mirada Hills on 23 March 1960, but voters changed its name to La Mirada that November. Some residents claim that La Mirada "has everything but a downtown." Its population was 40,400 in 1990.

LANCASTER, largest city in the Antelope Valley, 56 miles from downtown Los Angeles. It encompasses 83.5 square miles of desert and features, in the immediate vicinity, striking vistas of desert plants and shrubs, including the California poppy, Joshua tree, and sagebrush. The area, originally inhabited by Paiute Indians, was first explored by deserters from the Portolá expedition in 1769. It became a supply center for the Southern Pacific Railroad, whose tracks from Northern California entered the valley in 1876. The town of Lancaster was so named a year later, possibly by a real estate developer who hailed from the Pennsylvania township of Lancaster. Lancaster's first hotel was built in 1888. Area farmers raised alfalfa, fruits, nuts, grains, cattle, sheep, and poultry in the early 1900s.

In the 1930s, the U.S. Air Force established a test center that would later be associated with space exploration. The Aerospace Walk of Honor, a series of granite monuments installed along Lancaster Boulevard, pays tribute to Edwards Air Force Base test pilots, including Neil Armstrong, Chuck Yeager, and Tony LeVier. Lancaster was incorporated on 22 November 1977. Homes have sold for about half the price of those in nearby San Fernando Valley. The population shot up 102 percent in the 1980s, reaching a total of 97,300 in 1990.

LANCER (LOS ANGELES CITY ENERGY RECOVERY) PROJECT, city garbage plant proposed to the city council in 1983. It originated in the Sanitation Bureau and had the support of Councilman Gilbert Lindsay and Mayor Tom Bradley, who touted it as a solution to the city's growing solid-waste disposal problem. As proposed, a fleet of 224 diesel trucks operating 24 hours a day would cart away waste to be incinerated at the downtown LANCER installation. An unusual coalition of community activists and environmentalists, including Concerned Citizens of South Central Los Angeles, Greenpeace, the UCLA School of Architecture and Urban Planning, and the Center for Law in the Public Interest, protested that the facility would release highly toxic emissions into the atmosphere. After three years of acrimonious debate, the council killed the proposal.

LANDFILLS, SANITARY. *See* Waste disposal

LAND GRANTS, tracts of land issued by Spain and Mexico as rewards to soldiers or their relatives for military service, to civilians for establishing agricultural villages, and to the Franciscans for their missionary work. Fifty-nine grants were issued in Los Angeles County (with some overlap into Ventura, Kern, and Orange Counties), mostly during the Mexican era (1822–1848). Los Angeles City was itself issued a separate land grant in 1781,

---

The Chinese Theatre is Hollywood: gorgeous, tacky and spectacular. Midwesterners photograph the visiting Japanese, bag ladies try on Marilyn Monroe's handprints.

—Dale Gonyea, musical satirist

---

consisting of 4 square leagues, or 17,172 acres (28.01 square miles). Mission San Fernando, with 116,858 acres, was by far the largest grant. The largest civilian grants ranged from up to 48,000 acres, though most were less than 10,000 acres, and the smallest, Potrero Chico ("Small Grazing Field"), issued to Antonio Valenzuela and Juan Alvitre, was a mere 83 acres. The princely holdings of the Domínguez and Sepúlveda clans blanketed the southern part of the county. According to the original plan of the Franciscan missions, Indian neophytes were entitled to receive land grants, but few did, and most of those were later defrauded by land-hungry settlers.

In time, many grants fell into Yankee hands through sales transactions, donations to lawyers in lieu of fees, forfeiture in tax sales, and marriages between Californio women and Yankee men. Mexican land grants subsequently gave their names to numerous existing sites, such as Ballona Creek, Park La Brea, Encino, and Cahuenga Pass, and their boundaries still define current geographic features: Pico Boulevard, for example, follows the northern edge of Rancho La Ballona. Applicants were supposed to describe grant boundaries accurately, but this rarely occurred, causing confusion later. When land titles were adjudicated under the federal Land Act of 1851, by a land commission that met in California and handed down decisions that could then be appealed in federal courts, the resulting litigation sometimes took decades to resolve. Today the largest single landowner in the county is the federal government, which owns 763,237 acres, or 39.15 percent of the area.

LAND OF SUNSHINE/OUT WEST, Southern California magazine. Founded by Charles Willard and sold within months to Charles Fletcher Lummis, who edited it from 1895 to 1909, it celebrated a life in the sun, the Spanish past, and the arrival

---

Every religion, freakish or orthodox, that the world ever knew is flourishing today in Los Angeles.
— Hoffman Birney, writer, 1930

---

in the Far West of New England gentility. Essentially it was a magazine aimed at women and run by a man. Lummis was a contributor and wrote his own regular column, "The Lion's Den." Margaret Collier Graham of South Pasadena also had a column, and Grace Ellery Channing was an associate editor. Its cover, logo, and page layout displayed the influence of the artist John Gutzon Borglum.

LANDSLIDES and mudslides constitute a perpetual danger to hillside dwellings in Los Angeles County, especially in wet weather. Geologists have mapped 3,800 places where landslides occur. Slippage results from natural faulting and from rainstorms that soften the layers of soil and rock, turning solid ground to mush. Defoliation caused by wildfires, when followed by rainstorms, compounds the problem; the fires weaken root systems, and the residue from the burnt chaparral lubricates the soil, further loosening the soil and encouraging slides.

The San Gabriels, which may rise several feet with every noticeable earthquake, are constantly shedding their outer layer in mudslides caused by heavy rain. While Los Angeles mountainsides can usually absorb a rainfall of up to 6 inches, larger downpours saturate the soil, triggering landslides. This usually occurs when a winter weather system brings two or more storms in a row. Hilly areas altered by cut-and-fill land development, misguided drainage systems, and other forms of human tampering are especially vulnerable.

Landslides also affect coastal areas. A massive slide collapsed parts of Pacific Coast Highway on 4 April 1958, claiming the life of a highway engineer. In March 1995 thousands of tons of dirt again blocked that roadway as a portion of the water-soaked palisades gave way following heavy rains. Since the 1950s slippage in the Palos Verdes hills has caused the loss of more than 150 homes. While city and county building ordinances have tightened somewhat in recent years, the problem of building homes in areas prone to slides continues.

LANG STATION, historic depot on the Southern Pacific line in the Santa Clarita Valley. It was here, on 5 September 1876, that rail officials celebrated the rail connection between Los Angeles and Northern California. The event was made possible by the completion of a 1-mile tunnel through the San Gabriel Mountains, which had been dug by Chinese laborers. The cheering thousands, including the mayors of Los Angeles and San Francisco, applauded as rail magnate Charles Crocker pounded a golden spike with a silver hammer. The site, named for rancher John Lang who once built a hotel at the spot, was later abandoned. The station was dismantled, over preservationists' protests, in the late 1960s.

LANKERSHIM. *See* North Hollywood

LANKERSHIM, ISAAC (1819–1882), German-born agricultural pioneer. A Jew who became a Baptist, Lankershim arrived from San Francisco in 1869 and bought part of Andrés Pico's title to the former Mission San Fernando for $115,000, stocking the land with sheep. Lankershim, in partnership with his son, John B. Lankershim (1850–1931), and his son-in-law, Isaac Newton Van Nuys, formed the San Fernando Farm Association. During a wheat-raising craze that swept California in the 1870s and 1880s, the firm cultivated 60,000 acres of the grain. Lankershim also built the first flour mill in Los Angeles, in 1878.

LA OPINIÓN, largest Spanish-language daily newspaper published in Los Angeles. It was founded on 16 September 1926 by Ignacio Lozano Sr., a Mexican immigrant who had previously run a successful newspaper in San Antonio, Texas. In 1987 circulation exceeded 68,000. *La Opinión* remains a third-generation family-owned and -operated newspaper, although in 1990 it concluded a partnership agreement with the Times-Mirror Company.

LAPD. *See* Los Angeles Police Department

LA PUENTE, incorporated city in the San Gabriel Valley, 16 miles east of downtown Los Angeles. It was the site of the Indian village of Awingna, near the grounds of the present high school. In 1769 Captain Portolá's expedition built a bridge here to cross the muddy *arroyo*. The land occupied by the town was part of 48,470-acre Rancho La Puente ("Rancho of the Bridge"), granted jointly

---

The abundance of jazz music here—some of the best players in the world are here, and if they don't live here they come here to play.

—Chuck Niles, disk jockey

---

to John Rowland and William Workman shortly after their arrival in 1841 on the first overland wagon train to reach Los Angeles. They grew grapes and apples and raised cattle in the 1850s. In 1884 the town was named Puente ("Bridge"); it was altered to La Puente in 1955. The La Puente Historical Society actively promotes preservation. (The carefully restored homes on the Workman-Temple Homestead are located in the nearby City of Commerce.) In 1990 La Puente had a population of 37,000.

LARA FAMILY, one of the 11 founding families of the *pueblo* of Los Angeles in 1781. José de Velasco y Lara was a 50-year-old accountant who came from Spain to Mexico in about 1750, working as an administrator of *haciendas* in Nayarit in the province of Sinaloa. He and his wife, María Antonia Lara, a 24-year-old Indian woman, settled in Los Angeles with their three children. Owing to

problems stemming from a previous marriage, José Lara was forced to return permanently to Mexico. His wife soon died, their son became a soldier in Santa Barbara, and their daughter married a soldier.

LA RAZA UNIDA PARTY, Chicano political party founded in Texas that emerged in Los Angeles in 1971. In 1991 it registered 3,000 voters in the county, but after the next gubernatorial contest the party lost official status as a California party when it failed to win 2 percent of the total vote.

LARCHMONT VILLAGE, Los Angeles neighborhood centered on Larchmont Boulevard between 1st Street and Beverly Boulevard. The developer, Julius LaBonte, established the community before 1920 along a streetcar line, near a mineral hot springs on Melrose Avenue and the residential developments of New Windsor Square, Hancock Park, and Larchmont Heights. The Los Angeles Railway Yellow Cars ran down the middle of Larchmont Boulevard until the 1950s. The street, with its shoe repair store, restaurants, print shop, barbershop, real estate office, hardware store, bookshop, parallel parking for cars, and unhurried pedestrian tempo, has a distinctly small-town, though affluent, midwestern atmosphere.

LA SOCIEDAD HISPANO-AMERICANA DE BENEFICIO MUTUO, a *mutualista* (mutual aid society) formed in 1875 to foster self-help and communal assistance among Mexican families. The society provided business loans to local entrepreneurs, low-cost medical and life insurance, and other social services.

LA SOCIEDAD MUTUALISTA MEXICANA, federation of Mexican fraternal organizations formed around 1918. Its purpose was to unite various groups so as to create a more unified Mexican community in Los Angeles.

LASORDA, THOMAS CHARLES ("TOMMY") (1927–), Pennsylvania-born manager of the Los Angeles Dodgers. He began his professional baseball career in 1945 playing for Concord. A southpaw, he pitched for the Dodgers in 1954 and 1955, and for Kansas City in 1956. Before succeeding Walter Alston as Dodger manager, he spent 11 years as a player, 4 years as a scout, 8 years as a minor league manager, and 4 years as a Dodger coach. As manager, Lasorda led the Dodgers to two World

Championships (1981, 1988) and four National League pennants (1977, 1978, 1981, 1988); they topped the Western Division eight times. In 1996, after 20 years as Dodger manager, Lasorda was forced to retire following a heart attack.

LASUÉN, FERMÍN FRANCISCO DE (1736–1803), Franciscan friar appointed to head San Gabriel Mission in 1772. When a flood destroyed the original ramshackle cluster of huts and killed 10 neophytes, Lasuén moved to a better location (its current site) and transformed the mission into a bustling, successful agricultural station with hundreds of Indian residents and thousands of head of livestock. In 1785 he succeeded Father Junípero Serra as father-president of the missions, and founded nine more missions. Although less well known, Lasuén was as important a figure in California history as Serra.

LATIN AMERICAN CIVIC ASSOCIATION (LACA), Head Start agency in San Fernando founded by community activist Irene Tovar during Pres. Lyndon Johnson's Great Society Program. Now funded by the federal and county governments, LACA provides meals, instruction, and medical and social services to more than 1,000 Latino preschool children. It operates out of a dozen centers in the San Fernando and Santa Clarita Valleys. As many as 18,000 youngsters have benefited from the program.

LATINOS in Los Angeles County number some 3 million people. They make up 35 percent of the general population and in 1990 constituted almost 70 percent of the enrollment in Los Angeles public schools. The rate of increase of the Latino population is dramatic. In the United States as a whole, their numbers rose by more than 50 percent during the 1980s. By the year 2010 they are expected to outnumber Anglos in California. The voting strength of Latinos has shifted in recent years from East Los Angeles to the San Gabriel Valley. Only in a few communities countywide— Monterey Park, Cerritos, Rolling Hills, and Sunland-Tujunga—have their numbers declined in the past decade. Meanwhile, the Latino populations of Long Beach and South Central Los Angeles increased by over 100 percent between 1980 and 1990. The largest proportion of Latinos are of Mexican descent, but many are from El Salvador, Guatemala, Honduras, Nicaragua, Cuba, Puerto Rico, Argentina, Chile, and Peru. Ties to their native homelands, language, and cultures are very strong.

LATINOS IN POLITICS have gained power in the past decade—though not as much as some had predicted. In the late 19th century Cristóbal Aguilar, Antonio Coronel, F. Palomares, Andrés Pico, Manuel Requena, Tomás Sánchez, Prudencio Yorba, and others held elective office or participated actively in party politics in Los Angeles County. In recent times, Edward Roybal broke a political drought for Latinos by gaining election to the city council in 1949, and to Congress in 1962. Julian Nava, elected to the school board in 1967, and Richard Alatorre, voted a seat in the state assembly in 1973, were among the younger Latinos to succeed in politics by the 1970s.

The 1980s did not materialize as the "Decade of

Los Angeles is a city that dared to grow rich and powerful without the help of an adequate water supply, natural harbor, coal, iron ore, forest resources, position on major trade routes and many other resources whose combination is supposed to "create" the site of a city.

—David Clark, historian

---

the Latino," despite predictions to that effect. Among the recurrent problems have been low voter turnout and gerrymandering. Both the city and the county of Los Angeles were sued by the U.S. Justice Department for "diluting" the voting strength of Latinos in the 1980s. The city reapportioned, followed in 1991 by the county; that year Gloria Molina was elected, the first Latina to serve on the Los Angeles County Board of Supervisors. Political advances have been noted in East Los Angeles as well. In the municipality of Bell Gardens, where for 10 years Latinos have constituted a numerical majority, a Latino slate won a significant victory over entrenched Anglo leadership in December 1991. In the towns of Bell, Cudahy, Huntington Park, Maywood, and South Gate, Latino political power is considered overdue. The National Association of Latino Elected and Appointed Officials reports that in 1992 fewer than half of the state's 4.7 million Latino adults were eligible to vote, owing largely to low voter registration or lack of citizenship.

LATINOS IN THE WORK FORCE are dominant in certain areas: restaurants, fast food, apparel manufacturing, hospitals, building maintenance, light industry, roofing, gardening, and agriculture. During the 1980s their numbers rose steadily. Untold thousands are native-born or long-term residents, but many are undocumented immigrants

---

Visitors to Los Angeles, then and now, were put out because the residents of Los Angeles had the inhospitable idea of building a city comfortable to live in, rather than a monument to astonish the eye of jaded travelers.

—Jessamyn West, writer, 1973

("illegals"). (In 1993 government officials estimated that as many as 1 million people of various nationalities were entering the United States illegally each year from Mexico.) Immigration regulations require employers to favor native-born workers, but the rules are poorly enforced. In the 1950s some labor recruitment from Mexico was sanctioned and organized by the *bracero* (guest worker) program, a joint operation of the U.S. and Mexican governments. With the end of that program in the 1960s, methods of recruitment and employment changed. Many workers have been smuggled into the country by *coyotes:* unlicensed labor contractors who demand exorbitant fees and deliver less than they promise.

Currently, between 5,000 and 15,000 Latinos, mainly Mexicans and Salvadorans, hire themselves out as day laborers at sites scattered around the county, including Lankershim Boulevard and Strathern Street in North Hollywood, Pico and Sawtelle Boulevards, and Atlantic and Beverly Boulevards in East Los Angeles. The workers call such places *el mosco* (bugs swarming), in reference to the way men cluster each morning hoping to be

chosen by employers *(patrones)* who drive by looking for temporary workers. These men earn about $5 an hour, or $300 a month, much of which is sent back to their families at home.

L.A. 2000: A CITY FOR THE FUTURE, report issued in 1988 by the Los Angeles 2000 Committee, appointed by Mayor Tom Bradley in 1985. The select panel attempted to identify and resolve major problems: maintaining livable communities and environmental quality; providing effective education and human services; sustaining cultural diversity; improving ground, seaport, and air transportation facilities; and maintaining adequate governance and finance. After studying the problems, the committee proposed many reforms to improve life in Los Angeles. The report, which contained an epilogue by historian Kevin Starr, tended toward optimism based on the belief that managed growth on a regional basis, fostered by an intelligent elite, would solve seemingly intractable problems. However, the implementation of its proposals rested on the repeal of Proposition 13, a political unreality.

LAUREL CANYON, ravine bisecting the Hollywood Hills between Sunset and Ventura Boulevards. Even before Hollywood was annexed to Los Angeles in 1910, motorists used the graded dirt road for scenic excursions into the San Fernando Valley. Lookout Mountain Road, which twisted up Lookout Mountain to a 1908 subdivision with view lots and bungalows, was a favorite turnoff. At the summit stood Lookout Mountain Inn, with a spectacular 270-degree view of the city below. A trackless electric trolley, constructed in 1912, ran every half hour from Sunset to the mountaintop. It was dismantled in 1918 after a fire destroyed the inn.

Laurel Canyon itself was opened to settlement in the 1920s. A parcel known as the Laurel Canyon Addition, 13.6 square miles on the southern slopes of the Santa Monicas, was annexed to Los Angeles in 1923. The road almost became a freeway in the 1960s, and today carries a steady stream of cars daily.

LAUTNER, JOHN (1912–), avant-garde architect. In 1933 he moved from Michigan to Taliesen, Arizona, to work with Frank Lloyd Wright. He arrived in Los Angeles in 1939; there he designed curvilinear, geometrically shaped homes that conform to their sites. Silvertop, built between 1957 and 1963, afforded its owner a view of Silver Lake,

The Chemosphere, Hollywood Hills, designed by John Lautner in 1960. Photo by Julius Shulman, Hon. AIA.

Mt. Baldy, downtown Los Angeles, and the Pacific Ocean. Lautner's most famous creation was the 1960 Malin House, widely known as the "Chemosphere," a circular pod resembling a spaceship poised dramatically atop the Hollywood Hills.

LA VERNE, independent city in the San Gabriel Valley 26 miles east of downtown Los Angeles. Incorporated as Lordsburg in 1906 in honor of the 1884 subdivider, I. W. Lord, the city was renamed La Verne in 1917 to honor yet another promoter. In 1990 La Verne had a burgeoning population of 30,897—up 31 percent in 10 years.

L.A. WEEKLY, alternative newspaper founded in 1978 by Jay Levin, former *New York Post* journalist and former editor of the moribund weekly the *Los Angeles Free Press.* Heavy advertising revenue allows for free distribution. The paper, aimed primarily at a young adult audience, is strong in arts, entertainment, and leisure coverage and has a left-of-center editorial slant. One of the most persuasive voices on the paper for some years was social commentator Michael Ventura. The *Weekly's* circulation was 160,000 in 1992, with an estimated readership of 750,000.

LAWNDALE, independent city 14 miles southwest of downtown Los Angeles, south of Hawthorne and east of Redondo Beach. It was established and named by Charles Hopper in 1905 and incorporated in 1959. In 1990 the population was 27,300.

LAX. *See* Los Angeles International Airport

LEAGUE OF LINCOLN-ROOSEVELT RE-PUBLICAN CLUBS. *See* Lincoln-Roosevelt League

LEAGUE OF WOMEN VOTERS, national civic organization whose Los Angeles division was founded in February 1920, six months before the historic ratification of the national Women's Suffrage Amendment. Suffragist Carrie Chapman Catt had visited Los Angeles in 1919 to establish a league branch. She met with local suffragists, especially Dora Fellow Haynes, who founded and became the first president of the Los Angeles chapter. Not strictly a feminist organization, it is open to all citizens of voting age, regardless of gender. It is nonpartisan regarding specific candidates but does take positions on ballot measures and legislation. The organization's purpose is to promote political responsibility through informed study of major government policy issues. The Los Angeles County division has 15 branches.

LEARN (LOS ANGELES EDUCATIONAL ALLIANCE FOR RESTRUCTURING NOW), reform effort for the Los Angeles Unified School District. It was launched in 1991 by a coalition of business, civic, and educational leaders who hoped to defeat both a proposed voucher system and a plan to break up the school district. LEARN grants greater financial and curricular autonomy for the principals, teachers, and parents of individual schools. In 1993 the experimental program was being phased into 35 selected schools; ultimately it is anticipated that more than 100 schools will join the program.

LEGAL AID FOUNDATION, nonprofit group providing free legal services to low-income persons, concentrating on civil matters related to housing, government benefits, employment, immigration, consumer problems, and law enforcement. Clients must meet federal poverty guidelines. The foundation has operated as many as 14 offices in the area.

LEIMERT PARK, 1-square-mile section of the Crenshaw district of Los Angeles, situated at Leimert and Martin Luther King Jr. Boulevards. Created in 1927 by architect Walter Leimert as an upscale, whites-only bedroom community, it had a golf course and several airstrips, on one of which Howard Hughes learned to fly. The area's commercial center, known as Leimert Park Village, is at 43rd Place and Degnan Boulevard. With its small park, coffeehouse, dance theater, movies, shops, boutiques, and art galleries, the village has developed since the 1970s as a center for African American culture.

Leimert Park banner. Courtesy Leimert Park Planning Commission.

LENNOX, unincorporated area directly east of Los Angeles International Airport. It was named by a resident who came from Lenox, Massachusetts. Previously it had been known as Inglewood Rancho and, for a short time, Jefferson. The population in 1990 was 22,700.

LEONA VALLEY, small unincorporated rural community west of Palmdale, along Elizabeth Lake Road. The community is set in a long, narrow rift valley, also called Leona Valley, created by the seismic activity of the San Andreas earthquake fault. Indians of the Kitanemuk tribe, a Shoshonean-speaking people, inhabited the 35-square-mile valley in historic times. It was part of the Spanish Trail and began to be used for ranching after 1781. Named for Miguel Leonis, a rancher referred to as the "King of Calabasas," Leona Valley is bordered by the Angeles National Forest and the Antelope Valley. The community of country-style homes, pastureland, ranches, and cherry orchards had no sidewalks or traffic lights in 1994 and was home to 1,800 people.

LEONIS, JOHN B[APTISTE] (1872–1953), promoter of the town of Vernon, just south of the city of Los Angeles. He arrived as a teenager in 1887 from the Basque region of France and worked first for his uncle, Miguel Leonis, in Calabasas, then in a winery on Los Angeles Street. In Vernon he established factories and lumberyards beginning in 1905, created a bank in 1919, developed real estate, and helped promote boxing and baseball.

LEONIS, MIGUEL (1829–1889), Basque settler of Calabasas. A sheepman, Leonis arrived from southern France in 1869. He soon acquired property, some through purchase and some through marriage to Espíritu Oden, a daughter of Chief Oden, one of the few Indians to acquire mission land after the secularization of Mission San Fernando. Leonis occupied an adobe on this property in the late 1870s, remodeling it in the Monterey style, developed at the end of the Mexican era, with adobe walls, two stories, and a broad veranda. The physically huge and violent "King of Calabasas" often engaged in pitched battles with neighbors in defense of his property.

LEONIS ADOBE, structure erected in about 1844 by an unknown builder in Calabasas and occupied by the Basque settler Miguel Leonis in the 1870s. The adobe became the first official Los Angeles

City historical landmark. Leonis's widow, Espíritu, lived there from 1889 until her death in 1906. In the 1960s a real estate developer nearly razed the Leonis Adobe for a shopping center. A civic-minded local resident, Kay Beachy, launched a preservation campaign that succeeded in 1965. The historic structure has been maintained and furnished by the Leonis Adobe Association.

LETTS, ARTHUR (1862–1923), successful merchant. Letts founded the Broadway Department Store and later incorporated Bullock's into his chain. He came to Los Angeles in 1896, where he rented a vacant store "practically out in the country" at 4th Street and Broadway. His establishment was so popular that on a single evening in 1903 some 30,000 (of the 130,000 residents of

---

Wracked by floods, droughts, and earthquakes . . . it doesn't matter: nothing is as outrageous as a dream, and a city founded on dreams and scorning prudence is likely to endure forever.   —Brendan Gill, architecture critic

---

Los Angeles) visited it. In June 1915 Letts opened a new nine-story store, with 14 passenger elevators. Patronized by 60,000 people on opening day, it featured a nursery, hospital, writing rooms, restaurants, and even a "silence room" where women suffering exhaustion or strained nerves could retire for complete rest in "absolute silence." In 1919 Letts bought Rancho San José de Buenos Ayres in West Los Angeles for $2 million, which he sold to the Janss Investment Corporation in 1922.

LEWITZKY, BELLA (1916–), modern dance company director. Lewitzky was born in the socialist colony of Llano del Rio in the Antelope Valley. In 1946, together with her mentor Lester Horton, she cofounded the Dance Theater of Los Angeles, and 20 years later she founded the Los Angeles–based Bella Lewitzky Dance Company, which quickly gained international status. In 1995 she startled the dance world by announcing that she would be disbanding her company in 1996, on its 30th anniversary and in her own 80th year,

stating that she felt the need to move on to new projects. Lewitzky has received a Guggenheim Fellowship and numerous awards for excellence. As an educator she has been associated with the California Institute of the Arts, the Idyllwild Arts Foundation, USC, and the California Arts Council.

LIBERTARIAN PARTY, a third party founded in 1971 to uphold the free-market principles of Murray N. Rothbard and Robert Nozick. Its tenets might be described as anarcho-conservative. The party vigorously opposes taxation, labor unions, welfare, government subsidies, and bureaucracy, and favors a pure form of laissez-faire. In 1991 the Libertarians had 12,664 registered voters in the county, and 50,782 statewide.

LIGHT-RAIL TRANSPORTATION. *See* Metro rail system

LILLARD, RICHARD G. (1909–1990), professor of American Studies and English, and an environmentalist. A native Angeleno, Lillard attended Stanford and taught at UCLA, Los Angeles City College, and CSULA. Lillard authored *Eden in Jeopardy: Man's Prodigal Meddling with His Environment—The Southern California Experience* (1966) and *My Urban Wilderness in the Hollywood Hills: A Year of Years on Quito Lane* (1983), a loving chronicle of the natural environment of the Beverly Glen cul-de-sac where he lived in the 1970s. He was part of the hillside neighborhood movement that battled development in the Santa Monica Mountains in the 1970s.

LINCOLN HEIGHTS, area of Los Angeles just east of the Los Angeles River that opened about 1910 as a fashionable residential neighborhood. Earlier, in the 1880s, German and Irish settlers used the area for sheep grazing. Among its early attractions were an alligator farm, an ostrich farm, and the Selig Zoo, a private animal collection used in silent films. The area, originally known as East Los Angeles, took its present name from Lincoln High School, built in 1914. Lincoln Park (originally Eastlake Park), with its small lake, is a favorite local site. The neighborhood's domestic architecture retains the look of 19th-century Los Angeles. A major landmark is the Los Angeles County–USC Medical Center. Ethnically, Lincoln Heights represents a mixture of Latinos, who settled in the 1930s, and Vietnamese Chinese, who began arriving in the

Eastlake (Lincoln) Park, ca. 1908. Pitt Collection.

1970s. It is the site of a major Community Redevelopment Agency project. The population of Lincoln Heights in 1990 was 46,423.

LINCOLN-ROOSEVELT LEAGUE, association of progressive Republicans. Formed in 1907 by attorney Meyer Lissner, *Evening Express* editor Edward A. Dickson, and others determined to overhaul California politics by ending the dominance of the Southern Pacific Railroad, it was founded at a meeting at Al Levy's cafeteria. The coalition helped elect Hiram Johnson as governor (1911–1917), along with a legislature that enacted many fundamental structural reforms.

LINDSAY, GILBERT (1900–1990), first African American member of the city council. Born to a family of Mississippi cotton farmers, he was elected in 1963 by the 9th District, which included the downtown Central Business District. During the Bradley years Lindsay was instrumental in the redevelopment of downtown.

LIPPINCOTT, JOSEPH BARLOW (D. 1941), controversial water engineer who played a pivotal role in creating the Los Angeles Aqueduct, helping William Mulholland develop the Owens River as a source of city drinking water. Before being diverted, the river was slated for a federal reclamation project under his direction. In 1905, two years before construction on the aqueduct began, Lippincott was accused of a conflict of interest in acquiring water rights from local land and water rights owners. The charges involved conspiring with former mayor Fred Eaton and other Los Angeles politicians and real estate interests to steal the water. He vociferously denied the accusations. Recent research tends to point to his innocence. Lip-

Lincoln Park, 1995. Photo by Michael Krakowiak/Marni Pitt.

pincott was also the major consultant in the construction of the Angeles Crest Highway, which got under way in 1919.

LISSNER, MEYER (1871–1930), progressive reformer. In 1907 he helped form the Lincoln-Roosevelt League that catapulted Hiram Johnson into the governor's chair in 1910 and broke the political monopoly of the Southern Pacific Railroad. As a leading "Goo-Goo" (member of the Good Government League) he became an implacable foe of Gen. Harrison Gray Otis, publisher of the *Los Angeles Times.* Lissner, who was Jewish, was subject to occasional anti-Semitic attacks. Otis, for one, denounced him as being "true to the traditions and precepts of his race" and had him cartooned as a dirty, ill-kempt pawnbroker.

LITERATURE (NONFICTION), 1830 TO 1900. Literature developed slowly in the region before the 1890s. Early writers about California, such as James Ohio Pattie (*Narrative,* 1831), Richard Henry Dana (*Two Years Before the Mast,* 1840), Alfred Robinson (*Life in California,* 1846), and William S. Emory and Edward Bryant (*What I Saw in California,* 1848), wrote only briefly about the southern part of the province. With a fervor born of racial and religious bigotry, they drew strong contrasts between Latino and Yankee ways, often disparaging the local people, institutions, and Catholic culture while extolling the natural environment. Sometimes they focused on the region's isolation, crudeness, and lawlessness.

Charles Nordhoff's *California for Health, Pleasure, and Residence* (1872) offered a new, tame and middle-class image of Southern California. The book was masterminded by the Southern Pacific Railroad to lure passengers to the West. The very first literary work of imagination and memory was Horace Bell's *Reminiscences of a Ranger* (1881). This parody, written in the 1870s, described how Yankee vigilantes brought order and discipline to a crime-ridden frontier area. It was also a narrative history of the American era, from roughly 1850 to 1870. Another trend was established by writers who explored the possibility of creating a new Mediterranean culture on the shores of California. Journalist Benjamin Truman's promotional tract *Semi-Tropical California* (1874), written while he was a press agent for the Southern Pacific, was the first of many to advance this idea. The theme was soon echoed by town planners and architects. Another spate of literary works asserted that Southern California represented all of American culture, only more so.

"LITTLE LANDERS," utopian movement of family farmers in Tujunga. They believed that, through careful cultivation, a farm could support a decent life on 1 or 2 acres. The Tujunga colony was founded in 1913 by William E. Smythe, who previously had established colonies in San Ysidro, Hayworth Heath, and Cupertino. Smythe and the utopians were lured by Tujunga land developer Marshall Hartranft, who sold them on the possibilities of irrigating the area between the Verdugo Hills and San Gabriel Mountains. The Little Landers, who fostered enlightened culture, built Bolton Hall, a clubhouse fashioned from local boulders. It became the community's center and included a public library, school, and church meeting hall. The movement waned in the 1920s. When the town of Tujunga was incorporated in 1925, Bolton Hall served as a city hall. Now it is preserved as a Los Angeles City historical monument and functions as a museum.

LITTLEROCK, unincorporated area in the Antelope Valley. The sparsely settled agricultural center, once noted for its extensive rock and gravel pits, is today better known for its pears and peaches. Littlerock's population in 1990 was 1,320. The lack of a viable sewage system limits future population growth. The architectural style and the absence of curbs, gutters, and sidewalks reflect the community's decision to maintain a rural "western" motif. The community is located near the California Aqueduct.

LITTLE TOKYO, Japanese community on 1st Street between San Pedro Street and Central Avenue. By 1900 more than 100 Japanese had congregated in the area, and many more arrived from San Francisco after that city's 1906 earthquake. The name Little Tokyo was first applied in 1908, when an ex-seaman named Kame opened a restaurant on the west side of Los Angeles Street. Before World War II Little Tokyo was home to 30,000 Japanese, most of whom raised or sold produce. In February 1942, when the army interned most Japanese for the duration, other groups, including African Americans, settled in Little Tokyo.

After the war some Japanese returned. In the 1960s the Little Tokyo Redevelopment Project

Little Tokyo Plaza theme tower, 1995. Photo by Michael Krakowiak/Marni Pitt.

was started by the Community Redevelopment Agency, and the area assumed its current appearance. Older residences and stores were demolished in favor of new commercial structures, including four new shopping centers. Tokyo Villa condos, with 128 units, is a successful downtown housing development. While today few of Los Angeles's 100,000 residents of Japanese background actually reside in Little Tokyo, many come to shop, dine, stroll, worship, and attend Japanese cultural events, mingling with tourists and residents of other neighborhoods. The Japanese American Cultural and Community Center's offerings attract people from great distances. The Japanese Union Church and Higashi Honganji, a Buddhist temple, are both active institutions from the original Little Tokyo. The New Otani Hotel and Garden is also a focal point for social and cultural activities.

"LITTLE TWO" FILM STUDIOS. *See* Columbia Pictures Industries; Movie studios; Universal Studios

LITTON INDUSTRIES, $5 billion multiple-industry company formerly based in Beverly Hills, with a major manufacturing facility in Woodland Hills. Litton was founded in 1953 as a small electronics firm, but developed into a military defense contractor with 50,000 employees worldwide. The company was involved in advanced electronics, resource exploration services, industrial automation systems, and marine engineering.

LLANO, small unincorporated Antelope Valley community, 60 miles from Los Angeles. It is the site of the socialist commune known as Llano del Rio, which existed from 1914 to 1917. The site of the colony was 1.5 miles east of present-day Llano on Pearblossom Highway.

LLANO DEL RIO COOPERATIVE COLONY, utopian commune in the Antelope Valley established by Los Angeles Socialist leader Job Harriman after his losses in the mayoral elections of 1911 and 1913. Together with his devoted followers he purchased land known as Llano (Spanish for "river plain"), some 20 miles from Palmdale. Colonization began in 1914. Members built a hotel-clubhouse, engaged in dairy farming and orchard cultivation, built a blacksmith shop, ran a school, published a magazine and newspapers, and debated politics. In the peak year of activity in 1917 more than 1,000 people lived and worked there, enjoying a certain degree of prosperity. A legal snare in their water rights forced the colony's closure. The bulk of the community pulled up stakes in 1917 and drove off to Louisiana. Some of the remaining buildings later attracted English writer Aldous Huxley, who lived there for a time in the 1940s when he was writing *Ape and Essence.*

LOCAL AGENCY FORMATION COMMISSION, agency that screens all proposals for the incorporation of new cities, formation of new special districts, and boundary changes of existing cities and districts. It was created in 1963 under California law and became operational one year later. Although its operating expenses are charged to the county, the commission is not under the authority of the Los Angeles County Board of Supervisors. It holds hearings, issues maps, and establishes the official "spheres of influence" of cities and districts.

LOCKHEED AIRCRAFT CORPORATION, major airplane producer and defense contractor. The firm was established in the 1930s when Robert E. Gross, an investment banker, bought the assets of a failed enterprise, Lockheed Aircraft Company, formed by Allan Lockheed, a self-taught, barnstorming pilot and tinkerer. In a Hollywood garage, Lockheed had produced the Vega monoplane, a craft designed by John K. Northrop. The Vega was tremendously popular among sport flyers such as Amelia Earhart, as well as among business firms. The company faltered during the depression, and Gross was able to buy it out for $40,000. The new Burbank-based firm began marketing the Electra in 1934, and in 1937 produced the twin-engine P-38 "Lightning" fighter for the army air corps. The firm was still small in 1938 when the British government placed an order for 250 combat planes, the largest aircraft order signed to that time. By the time of Pearl Harbor, Lockheed, together with its Burbank subsidiary, Vega Airplane Company, was the nation's largest aircraft producer. During World War II the company produced 20,000 aircraft. After the war it began producing the Constellation, a successful airliner. Among the other aircraft produced by Lockheed were the Electra, the F-104, F-80, L1011, and P2V. From 1940 to 1978 Lockheed owned the airport now known as Burbank-Glendale-Pasadena Airport.

In the 1970s, although the firm faced major troubles and had to be supported by a federal loan guarantee, it remained one of the most important aerospace contractors, developing facilities all over the nation. Since the downsizing of the aerospace industry after 1987 Lockheed's presence in Southern California has diminished.

LOMAX FAMILY. *See* Dunbar Hotel

LOMITA, independent town of 2 square miles near the Palos Verdes Peninsula. The Shoshonean Indian village of Suangna stood there as late as the 1850s. The area was incorporated into Rancho San Pedro, and later subdivided as Rancho Palos Verdes. Ownership of the land was disputed for years by the Sepúlveda and Domínguez families. In the 1860s, after drought curtailed the cattle industry, causing further division of the original ranchos, Nathaniel Narbonne and a Mr. Weston took over ownership. The town of Lomita was first subdivided by the W. I. Hollingsworth Company in 1907, and for a time touted itself as the "Celery Capital of the World." Lomita was incorporated in 1964 and by 1990 had a population of 19,382.

LONG BEACH, second largest city in Southern California, 19 miles south of downtown Los Angeles. The site was long inhabited by Native Americans. A Tongva (Gabrieleño) village called Puvungna (uncovered in 1972 on the CSULB campus) may have been the birthplace of the Indian prophet or god Chinigchinich. The original Spanish land grant of over 300,000 acres, issued in 1784 to Don Manuel Nieto, was called the Nieto Rancho. It was later reduced to 185,000 acres.

The city of Long Beach was founded in 1880 by Englishman William E. Willmore and originally called Willmore City or "American Colony." After Willmore's bid to develop a town failed, a new proprietor, the Long Beach Land and Water Company, took over and successfully developed the city during the Boom of the Eighties. The company incorporated the town in 1888 and advertised it as having California's most exquisite beach. In 1891 the town constructed its first pier.

Baptists built the First Baptist Church in 1893. As a ploy to keep their city dry, the Methodists and

Ocean Avenue, Long Beach, ca. 1910. Pitt Collection.

Long Beach at dawn. Photo by Cynthia Lujan, courtesy City of Long Beach Convention & Visitors Bureau.

other prohibitionists of Long Beach managed to disincorporate the city in 1896, reincorporating it in 1897. Amid growing rancor between "wets" and "drys," the city banned retail liquor, saloons, and gambling; it stayed dry until 1932.

The Arizona-born promoter Charles R. Drake arrived in Long Beach in 1901 and spent the next three decades developing the city into a major seaside resort. Cementing ties with Henry Huntington and his Pacific Electric, Drake brought the Red Car to Long Beach in 1902; that July Fourth saw 50,000 celebrants crowded onto the beachfront. The onset of harbor improvements in 1906 further lifted the fortunes of the resort. Drake's pier, called "Walk of a Thousand Lights," better known as "the Pike," became one of the most famous amusement places in the West.

Long Beach became a favorite haven for retired midwesterners, especially Iowans, who left a strong imprint on the local culture—its architecture, social mores (dancing was banned for a time), and religious preferences. For decades, the annual Iowa picnic at Bixby Park was a featured attraction, attended by thousands of expatriates.

The expansion of naval installations, the presence of navy families, an explosive oil boom, and port development in the 1920s also changed the city's economy and character. The Long Beach oil field, discovered in 1921 and still operating seven decades later with 400 oil and gas wells, has produced over 915 million barrels, with an estimated 11 million still to come. Most important for long-term economic development was the 1925 completion of harbor improvements that allowed the port of Long Beach to accommodate deep-draft ships.

In 1933 a major earthquake severely damaged many masonry buildings in Long Beach. Many were replaced or remodeled to incorporate safety features and more modern architectural styles.

In the 1970s and 1980s part of downtown Long Beach was reshaped by a massive urban renewal project. The city's community redevelopment agency tore down six blocks of older buildings to make way for a $100 million mall and high-rise office towers. Destroyed in the process was the Long Beach Municipal Auditorium (1930–1932), which was replaced by the Long Beach Convention Center. Part of the redevelopment project involved the landscaping of both Long Beach and Ocean Boulevards.

The Port of Long Beach itself has undergone immense expansion since the mid-1880s, mainly through landfill. In 1995 it became the largest container port in the nation—handling 2,573,827 20-foot containers, just beating Los Angeles by 55,209—and ninth largest in the world. The two neighboring ports cooperate, and combined make up the third largest port in the world (behind Singapore and Hong Kong). The ports' success is due largely to their geographic position on the Pacific Rim. In 1995 the two ports brought about $39 billion to the region in revenues. The city of Long Beach receives 10 percent of the port's annual profits, which in 1995 reached $5.5 million. The port also contracts with the city for fire and police protection.

The city's most important institutions include Long Beach City College, California State University Long Beach, the Long Beach Opera, two military hospitals, and the *Queen Mary*, a popular tourist attraction. Harbor workers, navy families, and pensioners, representing many ethnic and racial backgrounds, make up a large part of the population. The large immigrant settlement includes over 50,000 Cambodians, a larger community than anywhere outside Cambodia. The city's total population in 1995 was approximately 450,000.

LONG BEACH EARTHQUAKE, first devastating quake to strike the Los Angeles area after it became a metropolitan center. The temblor struck at 5:54 P.M. on 10 March 1933 along the Newport-Inglewood fault, with the epicenter located 2 miles offshore southwest of Huntington Beach. The quake, which had an estimated force of 6.3 on the Richter scale, struck heavily populated areas, causing 102 fatalities and millions of dollars in damage. Had schools been in session at the time, the loss of life would have been far greater. Scattered looting occurred. Long Beach, Garden Grove, and Torrance were badly damaged. Hardest hit was Compton, much of which sat on ancient water-saturated sediments deposited by overflows of the Los Angeles River. At a time when building codes generally ignored earthquakes, the temblor did major damage to unsupported masonry buildings. About 90 percent of the Compton business district buildings had to be razed. Afterward the state legislature passed the Field Act, upgrading seismic safety standards for schools throughout the state and inspiring many jurisdictions to require masonry reinforcement. The importance of fixing such structures has been amply demonstrated in all subsequent quakes.

LONG BEACH GRAND PRIX, annual street-circuit car race first organized in 1975 by promoter Christopher R. Pook of the Grand Prix Association of Long Beach. Pook, an Englishman who came to the Los Angeles area in 1964, got the idea in 1973 while listening to a broadcast of the Indy 500 race. Since the first Long Beach race the event has become a major attraction both locally and in the world of auto racing. The biggest backer in the 1990s was Toyota Motor Sales, USA. The event, which is sanctioned by the Sports Car Club of America, is one of a series in the PPG Indianapolis 500 Car World Series competition. The legendary A. Unser Jr. has won a record six victories at the Long Beach Grand Prix. The record qualifying speed is 109.639 mph, set in 1996. The 105-lap race uses Seaside Way and Shoreline Drive, in a circuit of 1.59 miles with eight turns. In 1996 the three-day event drew 28 contenders and 88,000 spectators, who filled 18 grandstands, and was broadcast to 110 countries. The main event is preceded by a week of supporting events, including a *concours de promenade,* a charity ball, and a pro-celebrity car race. The combined activities of the entire week attracted more than 200,000 spectators and participants in 1996 and brought a $35 million windfall to Long Beach.

LONG BEACH HARBOR. Development began after the city of Los Angeles won federal support for Los Angeles Harbor in 1901. In 1903 Long Beach civic leaders, seeking additional government assistance, succeeded in arranging a site visit by the U.S. Senate Rivers and Harbors Committee. Meanwhile, C. J. Walker and Stephen Townsend formed a syndicate, Long Beach Land and

Masonry building damaged in Long Beach earthquake, 1933. Courtesy Robert Weinstein Collection.

Navigation, to purchase 800 acres of lowland in order to form a port facility.

In 1909 voters approved a municipal bond issue for harbor improvement. Long Beach Harbor opened officially on 24 June 1911, when a municipally owned pier was completed and the first ship docked there. The vessel, the SS *Santa Barbara,* carried 350,000 board feet of Oregon pine. As the band played, Mayor Charles Windham gripped the freighter's cargo hook and had himself hoisted to the deck. In 1925 the completion of dredging and construction work allowed the first deep-draft vessels to use the harbor.

Twenty-five years after the opening of the harbor, in 1936, oil was discovered in the area. For the next three decades oil pumps provided the city with a greater source of revenue than shipping. The pumping also caused subsidence of the land and lateral shifting over a widespread area, resulting in costly engineering problems. By the 1950s the land was dropping by more than 2 feet a year. Subsidence was buckling pipes, twisting railroad tracks, damaging wharves, and cracking walls and roads. Large-scale injections of water, administered between 1953 and 1958, halted the subsidence, but the efforts to maintain a uniform land surface have cost vast sums over the years that continue to the present day.

Long Beach Harbor shares parts of Terminal Island with the city of Los Angeles. The harbor emerged in 1995 as the leading container port in the country. Together with Los Angeles Harbor it is the most active port on the West Coast and one of the most important centers for international trade, especially in automobiles, petroleum, cement, steel, and containerized goods from Asia, Latin America, and Alaska. The Long Beach Naval Shipyard has been a major military facility since World War II. The California Shipbuilding and Drydock Company is another prominent installation. The harbor provides financing for the Greater Los Angeles World Trade Center in downtown Long Beach and is the site of the popular tourist attraction the *Queen Mary.*

LONG BEACH MUSEUM OF ART, a contemporary museum founded in 1950 and occupying a Craftsman-style building constructed in 1912.

LONG BEACH NAVAL SHIPYARD, naval installation commissioned in 1943 that immediately turned Long Beach into a "navy town." Its chief purpose was to repair and overhaul naval vessels involved in combating submarines and defending against air attacks. Protected against wave action by a mole, the facility covers 347 acres and has six floating drydocks. Counting about 4,000 employees in 1981, it is slated to be shut down in 1997.

LONG BEACH OPERA, founded in 1978, offered its first production, Verdi's *La Traviata,* the following year. The company, which is noted for its nontraditional productions, performs both in the 800-seat Center Theater and the 3,000-seat Terrace Theater. Michael Milenski is general director. The budget for the 1993–1994 season was $1 million. Its 1992 production of Offenbach's *Bluebeard* received exceptionally high critical acclaim.

LONG BEACH PIKE, amusement pier opened in 1902. Its developer, Charles R. Drake, called it the "Walk of a Thousand Lights," but most people affectionately referred to it as "the Pike." It featured a bathhouse, two pavilions, and a band shell, where the nation's first city-supported municipal band played to audiences year-round. The Pike acquired a roller coaster in 1907 and a merry-go-round in 1911, as well as many smaller attractions. Crowds came by Pacific Electric Red Cars to this West Coast version of Coney Island. As late as the 1940s the Pike, by then the West's largest amusement attraction, could draw tens of thousands of fun seekers on a summer's day. It shut down in the next decade, a victim of Disneyland's popularity.

LONG BEACH PRESS-TELEGRAM, a leading newspaper of Los Angeles County. Formed in 1924 when the *Long Beach Press,* founded in 1897, merged with the *Long Beach Telegram,* founded in 1904, it is owned by the Knight-Ridder chain. In 1993 the paper employed 900 workers and had a daily circulation of 125,893.

LONGSHORE UNION. *See* International Longshoremen's and Warehousemen's Union

LOS ALTOS VILLAGE, residential area of eastern Long Beach, near Spring Street and Bellflower Boulevard. It was incorporated into the seaside city of Long Beach in the 1950s and developed by builder Lloyd Whaley.

LOS ANGELES, CITY OF, in 1990 the nation's second largest city in terms of population. It was formed as a Spanish *pueblo* in 1781 by 44 colonists from Mexico and incorporated as a U.S. municipality in 1850, when California entered the union. The population expanded rapidly: from 11,000 in 1880 to 102,000 in 1900, 576,000 in 1920, 1.2 million in 1930, 1.9 million in 1950, 2.8 million in 1970, and 3.4 million in 1990. Its original land area of 28.01 square miles (4 square leagues) has ballooned to 465 square miles in the 20th century, making it geographically the largest city in the nation. Embracing perhaps as many as 100 ethnic, national, and racial groups, the city is today the most socially diverse metropolis in the world.

Los Angeles is governed by a mayor, city council, and numerous commissions, operating under a charter approved in 1925. It is part of the county of Los Angeles, the most populous county in the state. The annual city budget is around $3.8 billion. Los Angeles is richly endowed with natural features, including a mild climate, sprawling beaches, and rugged mountains. Its economy—especially when considered as part of a dynamic region that includes Orange, Ventura, Riverside, and San Bernardino Counties—is vast, varied, and increasingly tied to the economies of the Pacific Rim nations.

LOS ANGELES AND INDEPENDENCE RAILWAY. *See* Railroads

LOS ANGELES AND SAN PEDRO RAILWAY. *See* Railroads

LOS ANGELES AQUEDUCT, system for transporting water to Los Angeles from the Owens River and Mono Basin at the edge of the eastern Sierra Nevada. City water engineer William Mulholland and ex-mayor Fred Eaton conceived of the aqueduct in 1904 while riding a buckboard wagon along the 250-mile path to Owens Valley. Together with members of the Los Angeles establishment they obtained public approval for a bond issue in 1907. Construction—which involved 4,000 workers and innovative technologies, including the caterpillar tractor and a new form of local cement—started in 1909, and the first water flowed into the San Fernando Valley in November 1913. Coursing through open and closed aqueducts, the water was motivated entirely by the force of gravity, without costly pumping, and produced hydroelectric power as it flowed. The rate of flow was 400 cubic feet per second, a volume sufficient to slake the thirst of a city of 2 million people (though in

Aqueduct pipe construction site. Courtesy Los Angeles Dept. of Water and Power.

1910 the city's population was 319,000). Mulholland had the water impounded behind a series of dams in Los Angeles city and county.

The Los Angeles Aqueduct, the longest aqueduct in the world (233 miles), was called one of the engineering wonders of modern times, and Mulholland was hailed as a genius. Nevertheless, the city's tactics in acquiring land and water rights enraged property owners in the Owens Valley, particularly during the 1920s when the Los Angeles Department of Water and Power (DWP) sought to increase the take of water flowing through the aqueduct. In 1924 and 1927 Owens Valley vigilantes dynamited parts of the system. An even more serious event occurred in March 1928 when the St. Francis Dam, in the northern part of Los Angeles County, collapsed, drowning hundreds of people. Mulholland assumed (probably wrongly) that the fault lay with his engineering calculations, and took responsibility. His reputation was ruined. In the 1930s the city extended the aqueduct northward to Mono Lake for a total length of 338 miles. In subsequent decades its main channel was doubled to accommodate even more water.

In recent years California Supreme Court decisions aimed at protecting the ancient Mono Lake, a delicate habitat critical for the survival of certain animal species, have forced the DWP to look elsewhere for some of the water it brings into the city via the Los Angeles Aqueduct.

LOS ANGELES AREA CHAMBER OF COM-MERCE, nonprofit organization promoting business in Greater Los Angeles—that is, Orange, Riverside, San Bernardino, Ventura, and Los Angeles Counties. First organized in the city of Los Angeles in 1888, the chamber fell into disarray after the collapse of the Boom of the Eighties. In October 1890 it was reestablished by a group of leading businessmen wishing to improve sluggish trade: W. E. Hughes, who became president of the organization; Isaac R. Dunkelberger, a former army officer; E. W. Jones; Thomas A. Lewis; S. B. Lewis; Harrison Gray Otis, *Los Angeles Times* publisher; J. V. Wachtel; and William H. Workman, a former Los Angeles mayor.

In the following decades the Los Angeles chamber became arguably the most successful booster organization in the nation. Among the projects it actively promoted were the building of San Pedro Harbor, marketing of citrus fruits throughout the nation, development of Owens Valley water, creation of Union Station, annexation of Wilmington and San Pedro, establishment of a state university campus (UCLA), development of the Union Stockyards, inauguration of commercial airline service, development of a sewer system, building of the freeways, and industrial activity in autos, aircraft, and film; it also championed public education and, naturally, encouraged tourism. The Los Angeles Junior Chamber of Commerce, a related nonprofit volunteer organization for persons between the ages of 21 and 36, was formed in 1924 to promote community service.

Chamber of Commerce wine and walnut display.
Courtesy Robert Weinstein Collection.

LOS ANGELES ATHLETIC CLUB (LAAC), founded in 1880 by prominent men for physical and social recreation. Among the club's early movers-and-shakers were James P. Lankershim (son of Isaac Lankershim), M. H. Newmark, Frederick Eaton, C. L. Coulter, William A. Spalding, William G. Kerckhoff, and W. M. Caswell. The annual membership fee was $5. The gym at Los Angeles and Arcadia Streets had horizontal bars, ladder, springboard, rings, Indian clubs, dumb bells, and boxing gloves. It also featured a billiard room, newspaper rack, and reception room. By 1882 the membership stood at 100. The club held its first public field event on 9 September 1883, at Agricultural Park (today's Exposition Park). In 1889 the club moved to S. Spring Street and within two years had 500 members. Its motto was "Health, Recreation, Grace, and Vigor." The LAAC moved to its current site at 7th and Olive in 1912. The club's membership is now open to women as well as men and numbers some 3,500.

LOS ANGELES BEAUTIFUL, INC. (LAB), civic organization founded in 1949 by Valley M. Knudsen and the Los Angeles Area Chamber of Commerce to improve the visual beauty of Los Angeles. Over the years LAB has promoted parks and open spaces, combated litter, planted trees and flowers, and promoted recycling and conservation activities. It was incorporated as a nonprofit venture in 1964 with a 20-member volunteer board of directors from various sectors of the community. LAB's work is supported entirely by contributions from businesses, foundations, and private individuals. In 1994 it established a new campaign, "Take Pride L.A.," which is directed to eradicating graffiti and supporting student art programs and scholarships that may help counteract the influence of the "tagger" lifestyle.

LOS ANGELES BOARD OF EDUCATION, elective body that governs the Los Angeles Unified School District (LAUSD). Created by the city council in 1853, it remained a part of municipal government until 1937, when it became a special district under state law. Originally it had three members, who were appointed by the council with the mayor's approval; in 1872 it was expanded to five members, and in 1889, to nine. Amendments in 1903 reduced the number to seven members elected at large, a configuration that was reaffirmed in the city charter of 1925. More recently the election basis was changed from at-large to individual districts, a move intended to give the board a more racially and ethnically balanced representation. Board members meet twice weekly and earn $75 per meeting.

The board of education sets policy for 640,000 students and thousands of teachers in what is one of the largest school districts in the nation. In the final analysis, however, it is a creature of the state of California, since the state maintains sovereign power over school finances and curriculum.

LOS ANGELES BUSINESS JOURNAL, weekly newspaper established in 1978 by Cordovan Publishing Company under editor David Rees. Its circulation in recent years has been about 40,000, and its typical reader is an upper- or middle-level manager or business owner. Located in the Miracle Mile district, the *Los Angeles Business Journal* is now owned by California Business Journal Associates.

LOS ANGELES CENTRAL LIBRARY BUILD-ING. *See* Los Angeles Public Library

LOS ANGELES CHAMBER OF COMMERCE *See* Los Angeles Area Chamber of Commerce

LOS ANGELES CHAMBER ORCHESTRA (LACO), professional orchestra formed in 1968, specializing in baroque and classical music. The 15 to 40 musicians perform as many as 25 concerts a year in various venues, including the Dorothy Chandler Pavilion and UCLA's Royce Hall. LACO has served as the official orchestra of the Los Angeles Music Center Opera. The prestigious ensemble, whose annual budget has been as high as $2.1 million, reaches a broad audience through its work with the public schools and radio performances. Its music directors have been Sir Neville Marriner (1969–1978), Gerard Schwarz (1978–1986), Iona Brown (1987–1992), and Christof Perick (since 1993).

LOS ANGELES CITY ARCHIVES, official repository for noncurrent public records. Established by a 1980 city ordinance and housed in a modern facility at Irwin Piper Center, on Ramirez Street, the archives soon contained over 8,000 cubic feet of records originating in more than 30 different city agencies. Among the documents, which are available to the public, are reports, bound volumes, photographs, computer tapes,

maps, and videotapes. The oldest extant records date from 1827. This city agency is administered by the city clerk, as part of the city's overall records management program.

LOS ANGELES CITY ATTORNEY, an official agency divided into two major divisions. The criminal division prosecutes all misdemeanors occurring in the city of Los Angeles. The civil division handles all legal matters involving city departments (including the proprietary harbor, airports, and water and power departments), the city council, and the mayor. The office does not provide legal counsel to citizens. The city attorney is elected at large and serves for four years. Recent officeholders have been Burt Pines, Ira Reiner, Gary Netzer (interim), and James Kenneth Hahn.

LOS ANGELES CITY BALLOT PROPOSI-TIONS consist of ordinance initiatives or charter amendments. They can originate in one of two ways. Most measures are placed on the ballot by a majority vote of the city council, subject to the mayor's veto, which can be overridden. Some ballot propositions start by petitions bearing valid signatures of at least 15 percent of all ballots cast for mayor in the previous election.

LOS ANGELES CITY CHARTER, organizational and administrative framework first adopted in 1925 and frequently amended. From 1850 to 1878 the city operated under an act of incorporation rather than a charter. In 1888—during the Boom of the Eighties, when the population climbed to around 50,000—a board of freeholders drafted a charter that took effect in October 1889. The new framework gave the city council wide legislative powers to control purse strings, set salaries, fix annual tax rates, and approve the budget. It allowed the mayor appointive power, and retained existing citizen boards for health, parks, and police.

Political corruption in city hall and council meddling in the administrative and personnel affairs of the water board and police department caused reformers to draft a second charter. This document, crafted by a board of freeholders in 1923 and adopted by the voters in 1924, took effect in 1925. It bears the stamp of progressive reformer John Randolph Haynes, president of the board of freeholders. The charter was intended to reduce the authority of the council by placing that body's power more in balance with that of the mayor and citizen boards. The net effect was to favor the authority of city commissions. The freeholders considered, but specifically rejected, the city-manager style of government.

LOS ANGELES CITY CHARTER REFORM has been the objective of civic reformers since the 1930s. Attempts to alter the city charter of 1925 have taken the shape of piecemeal ballot amendments, recommendations of an elected board of freeholders, formal proposals of a mayoral commission, and informal suggestions of private civic committees. Efforts to introduce a completely new charter have failed.

Reform movements predate the 1925 city charter. The most successful occurred in 1903, when the city adopted amendments favoring the initiative, referendum, and recall. In 1911 the voters approved a series of amendments that substantially reorganized the government. In 1912 they elected a board of freeholders to draft an entirely new charter but rejected the board's recommendations four years later. In 1923, in response to organized crime and corruption, voters elected a new board of freeholders which produced the charter of 1925, but its effect on corruption was less than decisive.

The 1925 charter rested on a philosophy of checks and balances and featured a weak mayor, a stronger city council, a plethora of civilian commissions, and a host of department heads who often acted autonomously. Operating on an essentially negative philosophy, the freeholders dispersed power in city hall so as to prevent precipitous action and expose overt wrongdoing. By the same token, city government became unnecessarily rigid and slow to meet the needs of a rapidly expanding population. As the framework could not accommodate the increasing demands for new and efficient government services, reformers resorted to piecemeal reforms, which filled the charter with details better left to administrative or legislative action. For example, a city charter amendment was needed to add the "s" in Municipal Arts Council.

The first serious efforts to cope with the deficiencies of the 1925 charter came in 1934, when reformers introduced individual proposals to end the graft and corruption of the Mayor Shaw administration. Subsequently, various public and private groups undertook intensive studies aimed at reform: the Beebe Committee in 1943, the organization known as Government Research, Inc., in 1946, the Little Hoover Commission in 1949–1953,

the respected Town Hall civic organization in 1962–1963, and the League of Women Voters in 1962–1964. In 1969–1971, Mayor Sam Yorty appointed a city commission to critique the existing charter. After extensive deliberation it proposed a comprehensive streamlined charter document for the 1971 ballot. The document threatened to eliminate or shuffle many civil service jobs, alter the salary structure, and modify collective bargaining contracts. Opposition was particularly strong in the Department of Water and Power and public employee unions. The initiative was defeated.

Criticism of the existing charter continues. The most persistent complaint is that it prevents the mayor from exercising full executive authority, as is possible in other big cities. It is further faulted for allowing department heads to serve simultaneously as administrators and commission members; granting the city council both executive and legislative duties; discouraging democratic input on

---

I was in a restaurant . . . when we had a strong aftershock. . . . In 30 seconds, everybody went right back to making their deals. It made me love the spirit of this town, the lack of hysteria.

—John Gregory Dunne, writer

---

vital matters such as zoning and planning; creating confusion as to whether the police department is run by the police chief, the police commission, or the city council; granting to the three proprietary departments—airports, harbors, and water and power—exclusive control over their own revenues, which could best be used for the general good; and creating civil service regulations that are impractical and inflexible. In short, a chorus of critics complains that city hall is marked by bureaucratic buckpassing and legislative gridlock, assuring the dominance of special interests and alienating the electorate. The stalemate is particularly damaging in times of urban crisis and rapid social change.

To some extent state law dictates the method of fundamentally changing the charter. In recent decades the legislature has eliminated the freeholders mechanism, considering it too cumbersome, and ordered that city charter reforms be ini-

tiated either by petition initiative or the action of the city council. It remains possible for change to be initiated by a charter commission. Such a body could be effective only if independently constituted, without allegiance to the mayor, the city council members, or special interests.

In 1996, several conditions led to a groundswell for a new city charter. By then the 1925 charter had become an unwieldy 694 pages, containing over 400 amendments. An embarrassed city council seemed unable to cope with the repair of earthquake damage to the City Hall tower, because no single city agency exercised sufficient power to deal with it. A reform amendment to make department heads more accountable was approved by the voters; it whetted the public's appetite for more fundamental administrative reforms. A threatened secession by the San Fernando Valley crystallized a drive for basic change.

Historically, council members had resisted fundamental charter reform, but in 1996 seven members of that body joined Mayor Richard Riordan in announcing their support for such change. They introduced proposals for creating an independent charter commission to produce a new city charter that would clarify and redistribute civic duties.

LOS ANGELES CITY COMMISSION ON THE STATUS OF WOMEN assists in assuring equal opportunity for women in city government affairs and promotes the general welfare of women in the city. It deals with such issues as child care, discrimination, empowerment, and parenting. Formed provisionally in 1975 and made permanent in 1980, the seven-member commission investigates pay inequities and maintains liaison with citizens' groups. Since 1988 it has worked with the Woman Pioneers Project, a private organization that presents annual awards to outstanding Los Angeles women.

LOS ANGELES CITY CONTROLLER, chief accounting and auditing officer of the city. The post was established in 1878 with the name of city auditor, an appointive position. It became an elective office under the city charter of 1889, and assumed the new name in 1926. Elected every four years, the controller verifies all city financial transactions and estimates future revenues.

LOS ANGELES CITY COUNCIL, main governing body of the city, consisting of 15 members

elected by district. The first council, established in 1850, had 7 members who received no salary. Membership was raised to 15 in 1878. The council's present powers stem from the 1925 city charter, which established 15 districts. By charter amendment in 1953, terms were set at four years. Council members receive a yearly salary of $98,070 (as of 1996), meet at least three days a week (Tuesday, Wednesday, and Friday), and vote on tens of thousands of items yearly. Although the council's decisions are subject to mayoral veto, in general the council has greater collective power than the mayor. For example, the mayor's appointments and removals must be approved by the council; the council has subpoena powers, is authorized to act on contracts, permits, leases, and licenses, and can become involved in planning decisions; it controls city departments; and it has great financial power. Under a city ballot measure passed in June 1991, moreover, the council acquired considerable power over the decision-making authority of city commissions. All council districts are supposed to have approximately equal numbers of residents. Historically, the most important council committees have been public safety, budget and finance, and planning and land use management.

LOS ANGELES CITY-COUNTY CIVIC CENTER, one of the largest government complexes in the world, containing city, county, state, and federal offices, as well as cultural facilities. It sprawls from Figueroa to San Pedro Streets, and from the Hollywood Freeway to 1st Street. It grew over several decades in the early part of the 20th century amid controversies over basic design principles and rivalries among different levels of government.

Planning for the civic center began in 1905 with the establishment of a municipal arts commission, which four years later issued a general plan. In 1918 another city commission was appointed to select a site. The firm of Cook and Hall submitted a detailed civic center plan in 1923. They proposed an axial arrangement focused on Broadway and Main Street and featuring subways and extensive parking areas. Prominent architects protested that the Cook and Hall plan, by retaining auto traffic as usual on six cross streets, would destroy the unity of the center. Architects and planners, including William Woollett in 1925, Lloyd Wright in 1925, and Sumner Spaulding in 1939, contributed alternative schemes, but to no avail. In 1924 a group calling itself the Allied Architects of Los Angeles sub-

Downtown Civic Center, ca. 1940. Pitt Collection.

mitted a design that was more coherent. Through negotiation and compromise the Cook and Hall plan and the Allied Architects plans were melded and finally adopted in 1927.

From a design point of view critics say the civic center is poorly articulated with the rest of downtown. Bisected by six or more major streets, it not only lacks physical unity but also presents an unfriendly environment for pedestrians. Heavy traffic only adds to the confusion. The design and siting of most of the buildings are uninspired. In the end, the lack of a unifying concept robs the civic center of the coherence or distinction that might be expected in a major city. The Los Angeles Mall, with its underground shopping and parking and its Triforium, a high-tech construction with flashing lights that coordinate with music, is a recent attempt to humanize the environment.

Most of the actual civic center construction occurred after 1950. The old Hall of Records, built in 1911 and declared unsafe after the earthquake of 1933, was finally demolished and a new Hall of Administration built in its place. Clearing the new site resulted in the destruction of historic Ferguson Alley, parts of Old Chinatown, and Court Hill, as well as the brusque displacement of many Mexican residents. Today's civic center includes various city buildings: City Hall, the Department of Water and Power headquarters, Parker Center for the Los Angeles Police Department, and the Children's Museum. The county buildings are the Hall of Administration, the Music Center complex (Dorothy Chandler Pavilion, Ahmanson Theatre, and Mark Taper Forum), the Los Angeles County Criminal Courts Building, and the Los Angeles County Law Library. U.S. buildings in the mix are the Federal Courthouse, the Federal Building, and the Post Office. Also present are the Fort Moore Monument and Board of Education headquarters. Some 25,000 people work in the maze of offices, and another 35,000 citizens conduct business there daily.

Civic Center has been beset in recent decades with problems arising from the development of the Red Line, the dispersal of government offices to the suburbs, the deterioration of old buildings, and the overall deficit of office space in downtown Los Angeles. Responsibility for coordinating the rebuilding of the civic center falls under the jurisdiction of the Civic Center Joint Planning Authority, an agency represented by the city, county, state, and federal governments. The planning community has urged this body, which last met in 1982, to resume meetings and address the larger issues.

LOS ANGELES CITY CULTURAL AFFAIRS DEPARTMENT, agency devoted to encouraging the arts. It was formed in 1911 as the Municipal Arts Department, assigned the task of improving the appearance of city buildings and streets. It was completely restructured as the Cultural Affairs Department in 1980, its role now being to encourage citizen participation in the arts. The department, which had 62 full-time employees in 1996, is now responsible for running municipal art galleries, managing the Watts Towers Art Center, maintaining a murals program, encouraging performing arts, presenting free musical events, supporting youth activities, and reviewing the design of all construction on or over public property, such as street lamps and pedestrian walkways.

In the recession year of 1992 the department's budget was $10.3 million, with some funds coming from the city's Community Redevelopment Agency. In 1992 the Endowment for the Arts, op-

erated through the Cultural Affairs Department, awarded 252 grants to arts and community organizations and to individual artists.

The department is advised by the Cultural Affairs Commission, a citizens' arts panel formally established in 1911. The seven commissioners are appointed by the mayor for five-year terms. They advise on the design of all structures built on city property, and recommend which organizations should receive funding through the city budget.

LOS ANGELES CITY CULTURAL HERITAGE COMMISSION, panel established in 1962 as the Cultural Heritage Board to protect endangered historic and cultural landmarks on private property. It was one of the first such bodies in the nation. With its limited statutory powers the commission can order only a one-year moratorium on an endangered structure, allowing private parties to raise funds for purchase, removal, or reconstruction.

In 1958 the local branch of the American Institute of Architects (AIA) formed a committee to save landmarks threatened by rapid city growth, and three years later met with government leaders to explore ways of achieving this goal. An ordinance, passed in April 1962, gave the newly established Cultural Heritage Board the right to identify, survey, and protect legitimate landmarks. Architect William Woollett headed the first board

---

It's the kind of people who come to California—they're the ones who are not satisfied at home. People like that don't give up. . . . If one thing goes wrong, they'll try something else.

—John Weaver, writer

(later named a commission). In 1969 the commission established Heritage Square on parkland along the Arroyo Seco as a haven for Victorian buildings threatened with destruction. By 1994 it had declared nearly 600 sites historic monuments, and it is now empowered to designate Historic Preservation Zones to protect entire neighborhoods. The commission works with the Cultural Heritage Foundation, a private group, to preserve threatened structures. (Unlike the city, the county

has no body or mechanism for promoting historic preservation.)

The commission's first victory was to rescue the Leonis Adobe in Calabasas, built about 1844, from a bulldozer. It then saved the Andrés Pico Adobe, once part of the San Fernando Mission and the second oldest residence in the San Fernando Valley. Soon afterward it would also save Drum Barracks (1862–1866), a Civil War relic in Wilmington; the Rochester House (1887), a three-story Victorian apartment building in the West Adams area; Chatsworth Community Church (1903); the Bradbury Building (1893); Chaplin Studio (1919); Grauman's Chinese Theatre (1927); Angels Flight railway (1901); and the Castle and the Salt Box, the last vintage structures on Bunker Hill. The latter two buildings, carefully removed to Heritage Square in 1969, were burned by vandals a few months later. As of 1989, at least 10 of the city's 460 declared landmarks had been torn down.

LOS ANGELES CITY DEPARTMENT OF AIRPORTS, aviation authority for the nation's second largest city. Created by a 1940 ordinance, with powers broadened by charter amendments in 1947 and 1963, it operates Los Angeles International (LAX), Ontario International, Van Nuys, and Palmdale Regional airports. It is headed by a manager and governed by the five-member Board of Airport Commissioners, appointed by the mayor and approved by the council. The board's policies are executed by an administrative staff and more than 1,500 employees. Drawing upon huge revenues from landing charges, leases, and concessions, it is one of the city's three "proprietary" departments (along with the Harbor Department and Department of Water and Power), which are considerably independent of the council. In 1994 the Department of Airports raised landing fees over the protest of the carriers.

LOS ANGELES CITY DEPARTMENT OF BUILDING AND SAFETY, established by the 1925 charter, enforces all laws relating to construction, repair, or demolition of buildings, enforcement of zoning ordinances, and monitoring of substandard buildings. It is headed by a general manager appointed by the mayor and confirmed by the city council. A five-member Board of Building and Safety Commissioners is advisory to the department and reviews appeals for modifications in building codes. The department has four units:

the Resource Management Bureau conducts research and decides budgetary and financial activities; the Building Bureau enforces regulations; the Conservation Bureau ensures the safety of city buildings; and the Mechanical Bureau enforces ordinances related to the operation of electrical, plumbing, and mechanical apparatus. Seismic regulations were first instituted following the 1933 Long Beach earthquake, and were upgraded in the 1960s, 1971, and 1981 in the aftermath of other temblors.

LOS ANGELES CITY DEPARTMENT OF PUBLIC WORKS, agency charged with public construction. It was established in 1872, with five members of the city council serving as the governing Board of Public Works. In 1905 a charter amendment established a three-member full-time Board of Public Works, and in 1925 the membership was enlarged again to five. The board is operated by the city's only full-time and salaried commissioners, who are appointed by the mayor and need the approval of the city council. The department's 7,000-plus employees work in 13 separate bureaus and are responsible for streets, street lighting, sewers, storm drains, public buildings, and refuse collection.

LOS ANGELES CITY ETHICS COMMISSION, five-member watchdog panel established in 1990 by city charter amendment Proposition H. The commission is intended to oversee lobbying, campaign financing, and ethical conduct by government officials. City council members must disclose campaign gifts in financial statements, and no one may legally contribute more than $500 per election to a city council candidate, or more than $1,000 to a citywide candidate, such as mayor. The commission can issue search warrants and subpoenas while investigating wrongdoing in city offices. The commission's powers are limited and sometimes unclear, but in 1993 it won a major settlement against Evergreen America Corporation, a Taiwanese shipping firm, for a money laundering scheme.

LOS ANGELES CITY FIRE DEPARTMENT has long maintained a national rating of "Class 1." In *pueblo* days, fire fighting was the responsibility of Native Americans. In 1850 the council authorized the formation of a department, but it was not until 1869 that the first informal volunteer organization was formed, with merchants and civic leaders fighting fires in bucket brigades, passing three-gallon leather pails from man to man. The first formal volunteer department emerged in 1871. Anyone discovering a blaze was expected to fire a revolver into the air repeatedly until help arrived. In 1875 the volunteer department began using horses and wagons. The first engine house stood next to City Hall, and fines were collected from people who violated the fire codes.

A professional fire department emerged in 1884, with Walter S. Moore as its first chief. The Plaza Fire House, a rented property, opened that year; it had a 10-mile telegraph alarm system with fire station gongs. The fire fighters—men who exemplified the traditional virtues of "muscle, courage, and steam"—received navy blue uniforms with brass buttons. In those days, defective lamps, stovepipes, and youngsters playing with matches posed the greatest fire dangers.

Improvements proceeded rapidly. Chemicals came into use for fighting small fires in 1891. A 1898 bond issue provided for 12 stations, an improved alarm system, and pensions for the firemen. The first motorized vehicle was purchased in 1908, and the first harbor tugboat in 1917. A two-platoon staffing system was initiated in 1915, replacing the single-shift labor unit. The system changed again beginning in 1960, when each fire fighter went on duty for 72 hours a week, in a three-platoon system. A mountain patrol was created in 1924, and 1927 saw the installation of the first medical rescue ambulance. Elimination of the 150-foot building height limit and the construction of high-rises presented new dangers and challenges to fire fighters. The department received the top rating from the National Fire Underwriters Board for the first time in 1947. The first woman completed training and entered the department as a regular fire fighter in 1979; by 1994, 53 (2 percent) of the 2,700 fire fighters in the city were women.

In 1996 the city employed 3,046 fire fighters and paramedics and 328 civilian workers. City Fire Station 11, located on W. 7th Street west of downtown, responded to more than 20,000 calls in 1990; it was the busiest fire station in the country in that year.

LOS ANGELES CITY GEOGRAPHIC BOUNDARIES. *See* Annexation and consolidation

LOS ANGELES CITY HALL has been at several locations. The first was on the front of a lot on the northwest corner of Spring and Jail (later

The present Los Angeles City Hall. Photo by Michele and Tom Grimm, courtesy Los Angeles Convention & Visitors Bureau.

Los Angeles City Hall, ca. 1910. Pitt Collection.

Franklin) Streets. The second, established in 1850 on Spring Street, was a long, one-story adobe building that served for years as a council chamber, treasurer's office, and residence for a city jailer. The third, a Romanesque structure completed in 1889 on Broadway between 2nd and 3rd Streets, was used for about 40 years and then sold at auction. The current structure at 200 N. Spring Street, designed by Albert C. Martin Sr., John Parkinson, and John Austin, officially opened in 1928. Twenty-eight stories, or 454 feet tall, it was the only building allowed to exceed the height limit of 150 feet (13 stories), and towered over downtown for some years. The main support beams stand in pools of mercury for protection against earthquakes. It cost $9.7 million to build City Hall and to furnish its 912,292 square feet of floor space. The building served as the offices of the *Daily Planet* in the *Superman* television series and has appeared in many films. City Hall South, completed in 1954, added another 138,334 square feet to city office space, and City Hall East added 634,800 square feet, as well as more than 1 million square feet for parking.

Affected by the 1994 Northridge earthquake, the building was largely emptied and its 1,000 workers and numerous departments temporarily dispersed throughout the downtown area to allow for a three-year seismic strengthing project. The move alone will cost the city $22.9 million, while the restructuring will cost an estimated $154 million. Only Mayor Riordan and the city council members retained their offices on the lower floors.

LOS ANGELES CITY HISTORICAL SOCIETY (LACHS), organization established to foster an appreciation of the history of central Los Angeles. It helped form *Los Pobladores,* a group made up of descendants of the founders of Los Angeles; they celebrate the city's founding each 4 September. With the Regional History Center of USC, LACHS is cosponsoring a history computerization project to catalog various data bases concerning Los Angeles.

LOS ANGELES CITY HISTORY. How did the tiny, sequestered *pueblo* of 1781 evolve into one of the world's great metropolises? Considering that the city lacked a natural harbor, had no abundant fuel source or water supply, and was isolated from most of the nation by desert and mountains, its

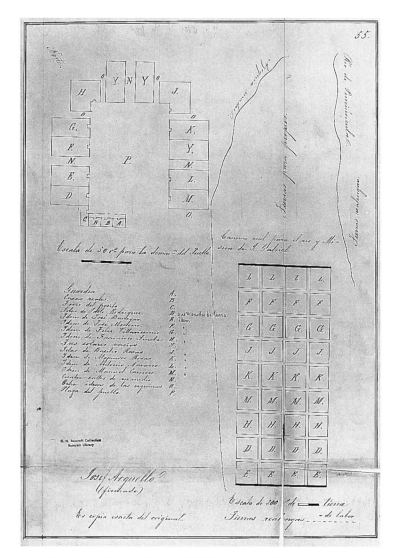

Map of the *pueblo* of Los Angeles, ca. 1783. The letters stand for the following: A, guardhouse; B, royal houses; C, *trozo del posito;* D, Pablo Rodríguez; E, José Banegas; F, José Moreno; G, Félix Villavicencio; H, Francisco Sinoba; Y, vacant; J, Basilio Rosas; K, Alejandro Rosas; L, Antonio Navarro; M, Manuel Camero; N, O, streets; P, plaza. Archives of California, ms. 1767–1846, C-A 2, p. 56, courtesy The Bancroft Library.

growth has been nothing short of miraculous. Three crucial events made Los Angeles what it is today: the acquisition of a rail link, the importation of water from the Owens River, and the development of a major harbor.

For a thousand years prior to the arrival of the Europeans, much of the Los Angeles Basin was home to the Tongva people, Shoshonean-speaking hunters and gatherers who lived throughout the area in scores of villages and numbered between 5,000 and 10,000 when Europeans arrived. Their neighbors to the west, along the Malibu coast, were Chumash people, and to the north, beyond the San Fernando Valley, Tataviam people.

European contact began with a sighting in 1542 by the sea captain Juan Cabrillo. The area was first explored in 1769 by Capt. Gaspar de Portolá and his Spanish land party, which was scouting sites suitable for Franciscan missions and civilian settlements. When Missions San Gabriel and San Fer-

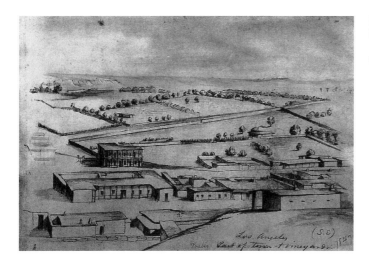

Los Angeles from Fort Moore Hill, William Hutton sketch, 1847. Courtesy Robert Weinstein Collection.

nando were established in the 1770s, the Indian converts came to be called Gabrieleños and Fernandeños. In 1781, during the reign of King Carlos III, a small group of settlers established the *pueblo* of Los Angeles for Spain. It remained a remote outpost of New Spain until 1822, when Mexico broke away and established a new, independent nation. The old Spanish realm of California, including the city of Los Angeles, became a colony of Mexico. The Mexican government designated Los Angeles a city in 1835. Until the 1848 Gold Rush, the community remained the largest settlement in California. The Mexican phase, characterized by rancho life, lasted until the end of the Mexican War, 1846–1848. During those years Southern California was the site of numerous armed skirmishes. At the war's end California became an American province.

In the early years of Yankee rule, from 1850 to 1870, Los Angeles remained an isolated, rough-and-tumble frontier cow town. Murder was a daily event, and bandits and vigilantes dominated the scene. The conflict between Anglos and Mexicans was fierce, particularly in the 1850s. Economic life in these years continued to be shaped by the ranchos, although in 1862 a severe drought destroyed many cattle, undermining the economic base as well as the personal security of the rancheros.

The 1870s were years of economic progress and great change in Los Angeles, despite a business panic that gripped much of the rest of the nation. The completion of the Southern Pacific rail hook-up from Northern California in 1872 ended the isolation that had characterized the region. For a brief period the sheep industry flourished, but it went

under during the drought of 1876–1877. In the mid-1870s the San Fernando Valley became blanketed by huge fields of wheat. Mining operations opened in the San Gabriel Mountains. Large land grants were subdivided, and the new towns of Pasadena, Santa Monica, and San Fernando were laid out. At the same time, however, banditry and lawlessness continued, and the Chinese Massacre of 1871 showed that racism was alive and well in Los Angeles.

The Boom of the Eighties was sparked by the arrival of the Atchison, Topeka, and Santa Fe Railroad in 1885. The Santa Fe became a major town founder and land developer. The excitement sparked by land speculation produced more important changes.

The quarter century from 1890 to 1915 has been described as a golden age in Los Angeles. Richard Lillard called it a "post-frontier, pre-industry, pre-Hollywood, pre-automobile" phase. The city waged the so-called Free Harbor Contest and broke the Southern Pacific's efforts to maintain an absolute transportation monopoly. It also began to import water through an aqueduct from the Owens River valley. The amazing Pacific Electric Red Car lines reached out in every direction. The city's dominant ethnic character was by now Anglo, with the culture very much influenced by the midwestern origin of most newcomers.

Growth and expansion exploded during the 1920s. During this decade Los Angeles received national and international attention, establishing itself as a center for the aircraft and film industries. Hundreds of thousands of Americans arrived by car in what may have been the greatest internal migration in United States history, and Los Angeles, more than any other metropolis, cast its lot with the automobile. Despite its urban character, Los Angeles remained agriculturally wealthy, owing to the widespread cultivation of oranges. The Great Depression of the 1930s saw much want, but a recovery from the economic downturn came with relative speed to Los Angeles.

A new spurt of population growth and industrial expansion during World War II continued into the late 1940s and 1950s. During this period the aircraft industry converted to aerospace work. The freeway era began in 1940 with the Arroyo Seco Parkway (today's Pasadena Freeway) and by the 1960s had expanded greatly as the automobile replaced the Red Car as a vehicle of mass transit. Immigration dramatically altered the town's demography. What had been, in the 1920s, an Anglo town—"the seacoast of Iowa"—now became very much a multiracial, multiethnic city.

Since the 1970s Los Angeles has been heavily involved in Pacific Rim trade enterprises. The national economic recession of the late 1980s and early 1990s struck Southern California particularly hard. Meanwhile, the city faced many challenges: enormous and rapid population growth, crime, immigration on a vast scale, loss of aerospace contracts, and ethnic and racial tensions. Nevertheless, newcomers continued to arrive.

LOS ANGELES CITY MAYOR, chief executive officer of the city. Elected to a four-year term, the Los Angeles mayor must share executive power with both department heads and commissions and a powerful legislative body, the city council. The mayor's greatest policy-making authority lies in the preparation of the city budget. The mayor also exerts influence in the appointment of officials, and has veto power over ordinances passed by the city council.

Before 1850 the chief executive was the *alcalde,* who sat on the *ayuntamiento* (council) and served as both mayor and judge. Among the more prominent *alcaldes* were Guillermo Cota (1827–1828), José Antonio Carrillo (1828–1829), and Stephen C. Foster (1848–1850). The Office of the Mayor and the Common Council were established when the city was incorporated in 1850. In 1869 the mayor

Mayors of the City of Los Angeles

1850–51	Alpheus P. Hodges	1889–92	Henry T. Hazard
1851–52	Benjamin D. Wilson	1892–94	Thomas E. Rowan
1852–53	John G. Nichols	1894–96	Frank Rader
1853–54	Antonio F. Coronel	1896–98	Meredith P. Snyder
1854–55	Stephen C. Foster	1898–1900	Fred Eaton
1855–56	Thomas Foster	1900–1904	Meredith P. Snyder
1856–[a]	Stephen C. Foster	1904–6	Owen C. McAleer
1856–58	John G. Nichols	1906–9[c]	Arthur C. Harper
1859–60	Damien Marchessault	1909[d]	William D. Stephens
1860[b]	Henry Mellus	1909–13	George Alexander
1861–65	Damien Marchessault	1913–15	Henry R. Rose
1865–66	José Mascarel	1915–16	Charles E. Sebastian
1866–68	Cristóbal Aguilar	1916–19	Frederick Woodman
1868–70	Joel H. Turner	1919–21	Meredith P. Snyder
1871–72	Cristóbal Aguilar	1921–29	George E. Cryer
1872–74	James Toberman	1929–33	John C. Porter
1874–76	Prudent Beaudry	1933–38	Frank L. Shaw
1876–78	Frederick MacDougall	1938–53	Fletcher Bowron
1878–82	James Toberman	1953–61	Norris Poulson
1882–84	Cameron Thom	1961–73	Sam Yorty
1884–86	Edward F. Spence	1973–93	Tom Bradley
1886–88	William H. Workman	1993–	Richard J. Riordan
1888–89	John Bryson		

SOURCE: *Los Angeles Times,* 6 Sept. 1988; Los Angeles Public Library.
[a]Served only 4 months.
[b]Died in office.
[c]Resigned.
[d]Interim.

became a member of all council committees and soon afterward also took over the duties of city judge. In 1903 the mayor received even more powers when he was given explicit charge over all boards, departments, and commissions. In 1913, after a season of corruption in the mayor's office, the voters withdrew some appointive powers, and the term of office was reduced from four to two years.

The office now is governed by the charter of 1925. The mayor's appointments, mostly lasting for four years, must be approved by the city council. Many of the officer's day-to-day functions were taken over by the City Administrative Office in 1951. In 1965 the mayor obtained the right to appoint general managers of six departments.

In April 1995 voters passed a series of city reform amendments, including one that increased the power of the mayor and of the city council, while decreasing that of 26 city managers and reversing their civil service protection. The measure gave the power to hire and fire the managers to the mayor, taking it away from citizen commissions.

LOS ANGELES CITY PLANNING DEPARTMENT prepares a general plan for the city. It also processes zoning variances, subdivisions, parcel maps, other land use entitlements, and exceptions to zoning regulations.

The city passed its first zoning ordinance in October 1921, when regional and urban planning was in its infancy and Los Angeles was entering a period of breakneck physical growth and unregulated real estate development. The new law placed all property into five categories: single-family residences, multiple-family residences, businesses, light industry, and heavy industry. In time the basic divisions were simplified to three zones for residential, commercial, and manufacturing use. The ordinance, revised in 1930 and again in 1946, has also had hundreds of textual and thousands of map changes.

In 1941 the city council required the department to draft an overall land use plan. The department began the work but had to postpone it with the outbreak of World War II. In 1965 the effort was renewed when the council, acting on a state mandate, required the department to prepare a comprehensive city plan for Los Angeles. Such a plan was adopted in successive years from 1969 to 1987. Now partly outmoded, the general plan for Los Angeles is undergoing extensive revision.

The City Planning Department is headed by a director of planning—appointed by the mayor and approved by the council—who has authority in zoning matters and advises the mayor and council on planning issues. The department acts as a final review board in zoning cases, making recommendations to the Los Angeles City Planning Commission and the city council. Since 1972 the department also has been charged with preparing environmental impact reports for private-sector projects.

The planning and zoning processes are bewildering to novices, often appearing to be bruising tug-of-war tussles among such players as the council, mayor, planning officials, land developers, environmentalists, and slow-growth activists. Within the department, the Office of Zoning Administration, with members appointed by the director, processes applications for variances, conditional uses, and other zoning entitlements. The Board of Zoning Appeals hears appeals from the zoning administrator's office.

The City Planning Department works in support of the Los Angeles City Planning Commission, a policy-making panel appointed by the mayor and approved by the council. When originally established in 1920, this commission had 52 members and was presided over by pioneer regional planner Gordon Whitnall. The 1925 charter reconstituted the commission, reducing it to five members. The Los Angeles City Planning Commission recommends changes to the general plan; it acts on zoning ordinances, some conditional uses, and other zoning entitlement matters; and it handles boundary matters in cases of an annexation to the city. It coordinates its activities with the traffic, public works, building and safety, and fire departments. Also involved in shaping the general plan is the General Plan Advisory Board, consisting of the general managers of the city departments of fire, police, and building and safety, the Community Redevelopment Agency, and others.

LOS ANGELES CITY TREASURER, custodian of the city's funds, securities, and unsold bonds. From 1850 to 1911 this was an elective post, but it became an appointive position in 1922. The treasurer is responsible for investing surplus city funds that are not immediately needed. The city's receipts and disbursements for 1984–1985 were over $11 billion. The treasurer's financial records are open to the perusal of any city officer.

LOS ANGELES CIVIC CENTER. *See* Los Angeles City-County Civic Center

LOS ANGELES CLIPPERS, National Basketball Association franchise based in the Sports Arena. The team originated in Buffalo and was brought to San Diego in 1981 by Los Angeles–born lawyer and entrepreneur Donald T. Sterling, before moving to Los Angeles in 1984. Former Lakers superstar Elgin Baylor, a vice president since 1986, has been the team's main architect. The head coach since 1989, Bob Weiss, was a player in the 1960s and 1970s. The team acquired Danny Manning in 1988. Other star players have been Ron Harper, Loy Vaught, and Elmore Spencer.

LOS ANGELES COMMUNITY REDEVEL-OPMENT AGENCY (CRA), powerful urban renewal agency, created by state law in 1948, that has reshaped many parts of the city in recent decades, especially downtown. Its stated mission has been to encourage economic development, eliminate blight, revitalize older neighborhoods, build low- and moderate-income housing, and create new employment opportunities. Despite these intentions, it has come under persistent fire from civic reformers.

The CRA has broad powers to acquire, administer, sell, and lease property, including the right of eminent domain and the right to issue bonds and collect taxes. A major source of funding comes through "tax increments," whereby the CRA obtains, for its own uses, all of the property tax proceeds from a project over and above the original assessed value before redevelopment. Other funds derive from federal sources, such as block grants, and the sale of notes and bonds. The CRA budget for 1990–1991 was $352 million. The seven-member governing board is appointed by the mayor and approved by the city council. The administrator, who is responsible for overall functioning, has a staff of about 325 people.

The agency has sculpted a new downtown skyline, paved the way for the renovation of the Central Public Library, expanded the Convention Center, created a new wholesale produce market, and attempted to salvage the low-rent hotels that are the last refuge for the otherwise homeless. It has been responsible for vast increases in the value of real estate.

In all, by 1992 the Los Angeles CRA was working on neighborhood projects affecting 7,000 acres in 9 of the 15 council districts: Adams-Normandie, Beacon Street (San Pedro), Boyle Heights, Bunker Hill, Central Business District, Chinatown, Cren-shaw, Hollywood, Hoover, Lincoln Heights, Little Tokyo, Los Angeles Harbor, Industrial Center, Monterey Hills, Normandie, North Hollywood, Pico-Union, Rodeo–La Cienega, and Watts. The agency hopes to increase the resident population of the downtown area by 100,000 by the year 2010.

From the beginning the CRA came in for criticism for recklessly dismantling 7,000 housing units in the run-down, low-income neighborhood of Bunker Hill. Restructuring of its governing board during the Tom Bradley years forced the agency to work more closely with the city council and a citizens advisory committee. A more persistent charge has been that the tax funds allocated to carry out CRA projects have deprived the public schools and the city and county governments of much-needed general revenue, while favoring wealthy downtown interests. In 1977 San Fernando Valley councilman Ernani Bernardi won a landmark lawsuit forcing the CRA to be terminated by the year 2000. The decision was nullified, however, with a 1993 ordinance that extended the agency's life for an additional 15 years, in exchange for its yielding some revenues for other public purposes.

Numerous other cities in the county have their own community redevelopment agencies. In 1975, the grand total of all redevelopment agency projects completed in Los Angeles County numbered 83.

LOS ANGELES CONSERVANCY, organization supporting research, public education, preservation, and revitalization of historic architecture in Los Angeles. It grew out of a 1978 campaign to save the Los Angeles Central Library Building from demolition.

The 5,000-member conservancy operates on a wide front. It takes up the case of specific buildings threatened with demolition, but goes beyond that with plans for rehabilitation, activities to promote neighborhood preservation groups, and lobbying for city ordinances. Its crusade to save the Wiltern Theatre was a major success story. A corps of trained docents conducts walking tours in the downtown area of the Broadway Historic Theater District, Pershing Square and environs, Spring Street, Little Tokyo, and other neighborhoods. The organization also presents coveted annual awards for the best efforts to recycle old buildings.

LOS ANGELES CONVENTION AND VISITORS BUREAU, quasi-official   countywide booster organization founded in 1921 as the All-Year Club of Southern California. It came into existence when an apartment house owner complained to Harry Chandler, publisher of the *Los Angeles Times,* that her apartments were filled in winter by eastern tourists but vacant in the summer because Americans mistakenly thought that the semitropical region was unbearably hot then. To attract tourists in June, July, and August, Chandler sparked the formation of the downtown association, whose slogan was "Sleep under a blanket every night all summer in Southern California." The bureau's members were hotels, airlines, theaters, restaurants, and other tourist-based businesses. A generous county tax subsidy allowed them to buy advertising space in eastern magazines and newspapers. The ads glorified the year-round sunshine, warm beaches, snow-capped mountains, picturesque deserts, glamorous movie industry, and romantic Spanish past. The campaign was amazingly successful. In 1921, 250,000 tourists visited the area, mostly during the winter months; by 1959–1960 the number had skyrocketed to 4.75 million, with year-round distribution. In addition, the permanent population of the county had risen from 936,000 in 1920 to 2.2 million in 1930. During the depression the "club" reversed its approach when it took steps to discourage "bums" and "Okies" from coming to Southern California. Tourism remained on the back burner during World War II, owing to government-imposed travel restrictions.

Since 1945 the renamed Convention and Visitors Bureau has continued to orchestrate the growth of the tourist industry, though now the county subsidy has stopped completely. The bureau estimates that in 1992 Los Angeles had 25.1 million overnight visitors. The bureau popularized the slogan "L.A.'s the Place." It manages the Los Angeles Convention Center, newly expanded to over 800,000 square feet of meeting and exhibit space.

LOS ANGELES CONVENTION CENTER, conference and exhibition facility designed by Charles Luckman Associates and completed in 1972 at a cost of $43 million. The structure, geared to the automobile, is located on a 63-acre site at the interchange of the Harbor and Santa Monica Freeways. The entire facility was greatly enlarged in 1993. To the existing 234,000 square feet of exhibit space, 350,000 square feet were added, together with such support facilities as new meeting rooms, showrooms, restaurants, offices, and an outdoor plaza. The revamped facility has parking for 6,000 cars. The consulting team for the reconstruction consisted of Pei Cobb Freed and Partners of New York, and Gruen Associates of Los Angeles, whose managing partner, Ki Suh Park, is a Korean-born Angeleno.

LOS ANGELES COUNTY, state's most populous county, created when California entered the Union in 1850. That year it held its first county election, with 377 votes cast. Its boundaries originally encompassed an area of 4,340 square miles along the coast between Santa Barbara and San Diego, but within a year it had grown to 34,520 square miles, reaching from the Tehachapi Mountains in the north to San Juan Capistrano in the south and

Los Angeles Convention Center, 1995. Photo by Michele and Tom Grimm, courtesy Los Angeles Convention & Visitors Bureau.

as far east as the Colorado River. In 1853 the eastern portion became San Bernardino County; the northern part became Kern County in 1866; and in 1889 the southern segment became Orange County. The county now embraces 4,083.21 square miles, 2,686 of which are in unincorporated areas.

Los Angeles County contains 88 incorporated cities—including the largest city in the state—and many large unincorporated areas. Its population has exploded, from 3,530 in 1850 to 101,454 in 1890, 936,445 in 1920, 2.2 million in 1930, 4 million in 1950, 6 million in 1960, 7 million in 1970, and 8.8 million in 1990. In 1996 the county's population was 9,244,600, with 969,400 living in unincorporated areas. The county is governed by one of the most powerful municipal bodies in the country, the five-member Los Angeles County Board of Supervisors. This entity, with its 85,000 employees and annual budgets of about $13 billion, is empowered with both legislative and administrative authority. A budgetary shortfall in 1993 due to shifts in property tax revenues to the state has led to the worst financial crisis in the county's history. Critics often insist that the system has no checks and balances, concentrates excessive authority in the hands of a few, and lacks accountability to constituents.

LOS ANGELES COUNTY AGRICULTURAL COMMISSIONER/WEIGHTS AND MEASURES DEPARTMENT, regulatory agency controlling the growing and handling of food and agricultural products. The office originated as the Board of Horticultural Commissioners in 1881, with one inspector who was devoted solely to beekeeping. The name was changed to Agricultural Commissioner in 1929, when Los Angeles was among the top agricultural counties in the nation. The county's separate Office of Sealer of Weights and Measures, created in 1915, merged with the Agricultural Commissioner in 1984. The combined office enforces state laws regulating the spread of insects, diseases, and animal pests, maintains quality in the handling and sale of food, regulates the use of hazardous pesticides, and protects the consumer by inspecting scales and testing meat, produce, and other edibles for accuracy of weight. The agency produces monthly crop reports, maintains a registry of orchards, and reports on inspections.

LOS ANGELES COUNTY BALLOT PROPOSITION C (1990), measure providing for a half-cent sales tax to support mass transit in the county. It raises about $350 million each year.

LOS ANGELES COUNTY BAR ASSOCIATION, private support group for the legal profession. Founded on 3 December 1878 by 22 civic leaders who hoped to establish a law library consisting of books donated from personal collections and to assist individual lawyers with their practices, it soon declared that its purpose was "to maintain the honor and dignity of the profession of the law, to increase its usefulness in promoting the administration of justice, and to cultivate social intercourse among its members." The first president was Andrew Glassell. A full-time secretary was hired in 1916; he worked out of his own office in the I. W. Hellman Building. The association experienced dramatic growth between 1900 and 1920; in that period it developed an active grievance committee to investigate public complaints and, if necessary, prosecute rogue lawyers. It also monitored judges, exposed sham immigration consultants, and sought tighter requirements for entry into the profession. The association has published its *Bulletin* since 1925. Like many professional organizations, it formerly maintained a strict color bar, specifically rebuffing African American applicants until 1958. Three of its members have risen to preside over the national bar association: Gurney E. Newlin (1928–1929), Lloyd Wright (1954–1955), and Leonard Janofsky (1980–1981). In 1993 there were 38,000 attorneys in Los Angeles County.

LOS ANGELES COUNTY BOARD OF SUPERVISORS, five-member elective body with vast executive, legislative, and quasi-judicial powers (in planning and licensing matters) over persons living in unincorporated parts of the county. With an annual budget of up to $13 billion in a county numbering more than 9 million, it is one of the most powerful municipal governing bodies in the nation.

Between 1850 and 1852 the county was run by the Court of Sessions, consisting of a county judge and two associate justices. The Board of Supervisors, created by state law, was first elected in 1852, with one-year terms in effect until 1862. In 1884 the county was divided into five districts with one supervisor per district, and terms were extended to four years.

The county supervisors have long been accused of being unresponsive to the electorate. In 1991 a

1852
Jefferson Hunt
Julian Chávez
Francis P. Temple
Manuel Requena
Samuel Arbuckle

1853
David W. Alexander
L. Cota
G. A. Sturgess
D. M. Thomas
Benjamin D. Wilson

1854
David W. Alexander
Stephen C. Foster
J. Sepúlveda
Cristóbal Aguilar
S. S. Thompson

1855
David Lewis
Cristóbal Aguilar
Agustín Olvera
Thomas Burdick (J. G. Downey)[a]
James R. Barton
     (David W. Alexander)[a]

1856
David Lewis
Cristóbal Aguilar
Stephen C. Foster
Thomas Burdick
I. B. Winston (Agustín Olvera)[a]

1857
J. R. Scott (Stephen C. Foster)[a]
William M. Stockton
Tomás Sánchez
R. C. Fryer
Manuel Rodríguez (F. Bachman)[a]

1858
Julian Chávez
Francisco O'Campo
Tomás Sánchez
Stephen C. Foster
Francis Mellus (Ralph Emerson)[a]

1859
Stephen C. Foster
Ralph Emerson
Tomás Sánchez
George Alexander
Bernardino Guirado

1860
Abel Stearns
Cristóbal Aguilar
R. B. Moore
Gabriel Allen
Antonio F. Coronel

1861
Benjamin D. Wilson
Morris S. Goodman (T. G. Barker)[a]
Fielding W. Gibson
Julian Chávez
Julius Morris

1862
Julius D. Morris
Benjamin D. Wilson
F. W. Gibson
Cristóbal Aguilar
Vicente Lugo

1864
Asa Ellis
Benjamin D. Wilson
Cristóbal Aguilar
Julius D. Morris
Philip Sichel (M. Krewer)[a]

1866
John G. Downey
M. Krewer
E. H. Boyd
Felix Signoret
E. Polloreno

1868
Wallace Woodworth
G. B. Winston
R. H. Mayes
A. Langenberger (Hugh Forsman)[a]
Henrique Avila

1870
Wallace Woodworth
G. B. Winston
R. H. Mayes
Hugh Forsman
Henrique Avila

1872
1-Francisco Machado[b]
1-S. B. Caswell
2-Hugh Forsman
3-Francisco Palomares
4-A. L. Bush

1874
1-Francisco Machado
1-J. M. Griffith (Gabriel Allen)[a]
2-George Hinds
3-Francisco Palomares
4-Edward Evey

1876
1-John D. Young
1-Gabriel Allen
2-George Hinds
3-J. C. Hannon
4-Edward Evey

1877
1-John D. Young

1-Gabriel Allen (Charles Prager)[a]
2-J. J. Morton
3-J. C. Hannon
4-W. H. Spurgeon

1878
1-John D. Young
1-Charles Prager
2-J. J. Morton
3-J. C. Hannon
4-W. H. Spurgeon (James D. Ott)[a]

1879
1-A. H. Rogers
1-Charles Prager
2-J. J. Morton
3-J. C. Hannon
4-James D. Ott

1880
1-A. H. Rogers
1-W. F. Cooper
2-Charles Prager
3-J. J. Morton
4-Richard Egan

1881
1-A. H. Rogers
1-Charles Prager
2-W. F. Cooper
3-J. C. Hannon
4- Richard Egan

1882
1-A. H. Rogers
1-Charles Prager
2-W. F. Cooper
3-J. C. Hannon
4- Richard Egan

1883[c]
1-L. G. Giraux
2-Charles Prager
3-William M. Osborn
4-D. V. Waldron
5-S. Levy
6-D. Reichard
7-J. H. Moesser

1885[d]
1-James Foord
2-Oscar Macy
3-Milton Lindley
4-George Hinds (J. W. Venable)[a]
5-Jacob Ross

1887
1-W. T. Martin
2-Oscar Macy
3-T. E. Rowan
4-J. W. Venable
5-Jacob Ross

1889
1-W. T. Martin

2-S. M. Perry
3-T. E. Rowan
4-A. E. Davis
5-S. Littlefield (H. C. Hubbard)[a]

1891
1-J. W. Cook
2-S. M. Perry
3-E. A. Forrester
4-A. E. Davis
5-H. C. Hubbard

1893
1-J. W. Cook
2-A. W. Francisco
3-E. A. Forrester
4-James Hay
5-James Hanley

1895
1-W. L. Woodward
2-A. W. Francisco
3-E. S. Field
4-James Hay
5-James Hanley

1897
1-W. L. Woodward
2-R. E. Wirsching
3-E. S. Field
4-A. E. Davis
5-James Hanley

1899
1-O. W. Longden
2-R. E. Wirsching
3-E. S. Field
4-A. E. Davis
5-James Hanley

1901
1-O. W. Longden
2-George Alexander
3-E. S. Field
4-P. J. Wilson
5-James Hanley (C. Patterson)[a]

1903
1-O. W. Longden
2-George Alexander
3-A. J. Graham
4-P. J. Wilson
5-C. E. Patterson

1905
1-O. W. Longden (J. T. Brady)[a]
2-George Alexander
3-A. J. Graham
4-P. J. Wilson
5-C. E. Patterson

1907
1-C. D. Manning
2-George Alexander
3-S. T. Eldridge
4-P. J. Wilson
5-C. E. Patterson

1909
1-C. D. Manning
2-H. D. McCabe
3-S. T. Eldridge
4-C. J. Nellis
5-R. W. Pridham

1911
1-C. D. Manning
2-H. D. McCabe
3-S. A. Butler
4-C. J. Nellis
5-R. W. Pridham

1913
1-C. D. Manning
2-Richard H. Norton
3-S. A. Butler (F. E. Woodley)[a]
4-W. E. Hinshaw
5-R. W. Pridham

1915
1-J. J. Hamilton
2-Richard H. Norton
3-F. E. Woodley
4-W. E. Hinshaw
5-R. W. Pridham

1917
1-J. J. Hamilton
2-R. H. Norton (E. J. Delorey)[a]
3-F. E. Woodley
4-R. F. McClellan
5-Jonathan S. Dodge

1918
1-Prescott F. Cogswell
2-J. H. Bean
3-F. E. Woodley
4-R. F. McClellan
5-Jonathan S. Dodge

1920
1-Prescott F. Cogswell
2-J. H. Bean
3-F. E. Woodley
4-R. F. McClellan
5-Jonathan S. Dodge (Henry Wright)[a]

1922
1-Prescott F. Cogswell
2-J. H. Bean
3-F. E. Woodley
4-R. F. McClellan
5-Henry W. Wright

1924
1-Prescott F. Cogswell
2-J. H. Bean
3-F. E. Woodley
4-R. F. McClellan
5-Henry W. Wright

1926
1-Fred T. Beaty
2-J. H. Bean
3-Sidney T. Graves

4-R. F. McClellan
5-Henry W. Wright

1928
1-Fred T. Beaty
2-Frank L. Shaw
3-Sidney T. Graves
4-R. F. McClellan (John R. Quinn)[a]
5-Henry W. Wright

1930
1-Hugh A. Thatcher
2-Frank L. Shaw
3-J. Don Mahaffey (Harry M. Baine)[a]
4-John R. Quinn
5-Henry W. Wright

1932
1-Hugh A. Thatcher
2-Frank L. Shaw
    (Gordon McDonough)[a]
3-Harry M. Baine
4-John R. Quinn
5-Roger W. Jessup

1934
1-Herbert C. Legg
2-Gordon L. McDonough
3-John Anson Ford
4-John R. Quinn (L. M. Ford)[a]
5-Roger W. Jessup

1936
1-Herbert C. Legg
2-Gordon L. McDonough
3-John Anson Ford
4-L. M. Ford (Oscar Hauge)[a]
5-Roger W. Jessup

1938
1-William A. Smith
2-Gordon L. McDonough
3-John Anson Ford
4-Oscar Hauge
5-Roger W. Jessup

1940
1-William A. Smith
2-Gordon L. McDonough
3-John Anson Ford
4-Oscar L. Hauge
5-Roger W. Jessup

1942
1-William A. Smith
2-Gordon L. McDonough
3-John Anson Ford
4-Oscar L. Hauge
5-Roger W. Jessup

1944
1-William A. Smith
2-Gordon McDonough
    (Leonard Roach)[a]
3-John Anson Ford
4-Raymond V. Darby
5-Roger W. Jessup

1946
1-William A. Smith
2-Leonard J. Roach
3-John Anson Ford
4-Raymond V. Darby
5-Roger W. Jessup

1948
1-William A. Smith
2-Leonard J. Roach
3-John Anson Ford
4-Raymond V. Darby
5-Roger W. Jessup

1950
1-Herbert C. Legg
2-Leonard J. Roach
3-John Anson Ford
4-Raymond V. Darby
5-Roger W. Jessup

1952
1-Herbert C. Legg
2-Kenneth Hahn
3-John Anson Ford
4-Raymond V. Darby
  (Burton W. Chace)[a]
5-Roger W. Jessup

1954
1-Herbert C. Legg
2-Kenneth Hahn
3-John Anson Ford
4-Burton W. Chace
5-Roger W. Jessup

1956
1-Herbert C. Legg (Frank G. Bonelli)[a]
2-Kenneth Hahn
3-John Anson Ford
4-Burton W. Chace
5-Warren M. Dorn

1958
1-Frank G. Bonelli
2-Kenneth Hahn
3-Ernest E. Debs
4-Burton W. Chace
5-Warren M. Dorn

1960
1-Frank G. Bonelli
2-Kenneth Hahn
3-Ernest E. Debs
4-Burton W. Chace
5-Warren M. Dorn

1962
1-Frank G. Bonelli
2-Kenneth Hahn
3-Ernest E. Debs

4-Burton W. Chace
5-Warren M. Dorn

1964
1-Frank G. Bonelli
2-Kenneth Hahn
3-Ernest E. Debs
4-Burton W. Chace
5-Warren M. Dorn

1966
1-Frank G. Bonelli
2-Kenneth Hahn
3-Ernest E. Debs
4-Burton W. Chace
5-Warren M. Dorn

1968
1-Frank G. Bonelli
2-Kenneth Hahn
3-Ernest E. Debs
4-Burton W. Chace
5-Warren M. Dorn

1970
1-Frank Bonelli (Peter F. Schabarum)[a]
2-Kenneth Hahn
3-Ernest E. Debs
4-Burton Chace (James A. Hayes)[a]
5-Warren M. Dorn

1972
1-Peter F. Schabarum
2-Kenneth Hahn
3-Ernest E. Debs
4-James A. Hayes
5-Baxter Ward

1974
1-Peter F. Schabarum
2-Kenneth Hahn
3-Edmund D. Edelman
4-James A. Hayes
5-Baxter Ward

1976
1-Peter F. Schabarum
2-Kenneth Hahn
3-Edmund D. Edelman
4-James A. Hayes
5-Baxter Ward

1978
1-Peter F. Schabarum
2-Kenneth Hahn
3-Edmund D. Edelman
4-James A. Hayes
  (Yvonne Brathwaite Burke)[a]
5-Baxter Ward

1980
1-Peter F. Schabarum

2-Kenneth Hahn
3-Edmund D. Edelman
4-Deane Dana
5-Michael D. Antonovich

1982
1-Peter F. Schabarum
2-Kenneth Hahn
3-Edmund D. Edelman
4-Deane Dana
5-Michael D. Antonovich

1984
1-Peter F. Schabarum
2-Kenneth Hahn
3-Edmund D. Edelman
4-Deane Dana
5-Michael D. Antonovich

1986
1-Peter F. Schabarum
2-Kenneth Hahn
3-Edmund D. Edelman
4-Deane Dana
5-Michael D. Antonovich

1988
1-Peter F. Schabarum
2-Kenneth Hahn
3-Edmund D. Edelman
4-Deane Dana
5-Michael D. Antonovich

1991[e]
1-Gloria Molina
2-Kenneth Hahn
3-Edmund D. Edelman
4-Deane Dana
5-Michael D. Antonovich

1992
1-Gloria Molina
2-Yvonne Brathwaite Burke
3-Edmund D. Edelman
4-Deane Dana
5-Michael D. Antonovich

1994
1-Gloria Molina
2-Deane Dana
3-Michael D. Antonovich
4-Yvonne Brathwaite Burke
5-Edmund D. Edelman

1996
1-Gloria Molina
2-Yvonne Brathwaite Burke
3-Zev Yaroslavsky
4-Deane Dana
5-Michael D. Antonovich

SOURCE: Los Angeles County Board of Supervisors
[a]Persons listed in parentheses were appointed to the position of supervisor to complete the term of the person listed before them.
[b]Numbers (from 1872 on) indicate supervisorial districts.
[c]On 5 September 1882 the county was divided into seven districts.
[d]On 5 August 1884 the county was divided into five districts.
[e]Special election on 19 February 1991, after court-ordered reapportionment.

state court cited it for racially guided gerrymandering and forced it to reapportion district boundaries. Voters have consistently rejected efforts to make the board more accountable by expanding the number of supervisors to seven or nine members or by authorizing an elected executive head. In 1996 county supervisors received a salary of $107,389.92.

LOS ANGELES COUNTY CHARTER, basic framework of county government. The state legislature gave counties the right to formulate their own charters in 1911. A board of freeholders proposed the Los Angeles County document the next year, voters approved it, and it became effective on 2 June 1913. The charter gave the county greater freedom to govern itself, provided for a five-member Board of Supervisors with broad legislative and administrative powers, established three other elective officers—the assessor, who prepares property tax bills; the district attorney; and the sheriff— shaped the other county departments (which are headed by appointed officials), and created a civil service commission. The county charter includes provisions for a merit system for hiring. The charter has been amended by the electorate.

LOS ANGELES COUNTY CHIEF ADMINISTRATIVE OFFICER (CAO), top manager of the county and therefore one of the most powerful public administrators in the nation. The appointive position was created in 1938, during the Great Depression, when county social services were strained to the breaking point. The CAO prepares the budget and makes operational recommendations for the Board of Supervisors, and monitors and controls countywide expenditures. The CAO also analyzes and advocates legislation, coordinates capital projects and asset management efforts, and promotes activities relating to the dissemination of public information about the county. Another major function is to manage employee relations and compensate systems for both union and nonunion employees. In 1994 the holder of this position oversaw 85,000 employees, administered a budget of $13 billion, and earned an annual salary of $178,000.

LOS ANGELES COUNTY CITIZENS' ECONOMY AND EFFICIENCY COMMISSION, body that examines the operations of county government and recommends to the Board of Supervisors methods for improving government economy, efficiency, and effectiveness. Established in 1964, the commission has 21 members, including 4 nominated by the supervisors and the foreman of the previous year's county grand jury. A 1975 ordinance spells out its duties and method of operation.

LOS ANGELES COUNTY DEPARTMENT OF BEACHES AND HARBORS, agency charged with developing and operating county harbors and marinas, as well as maintaining lifeguard services for 30 miles of beaches. The County Board of Supervisors established the marina function in 1954 when it created the Marina del Rey Small Craft Harbor, one of the largest of its kind in the nation. The beaches operation was introduced in 1969, when the supervisors shifted those tasks from the Department of Parks and Recreation. County Beaches and Harbors also has responsibility for safety operations on state waters in county territory.

LOS ANGELES COUNTY DEPARTMENT OF CHILDREN'S SERVICES, unit providing social services to at-risk children and their families. Public services for children have evolved vastly since the Great Depression, when the Los Angeles City Hall directory included a "City Mother" who cared for stray orphans brought in by the police. These matters were soon turned over to two county agencies, the Department of Adoptions and the Child Protective Services Division of the Department of Public Social Services. These were merged in 1984 to create the Department of Children's Services. Its activities are monitored by a citizens' panel, the Commission for Children's Services.

The department handles child abuse issues, adoptions, foster home recruitment, runaway adolescents, and children at risk; provides emergency services and family maintenance; and works on family reunification and permanent placement. One of its major concerns is child abuse, an ancient and persistent problem that has been compounded in urban areas especially by growing poverty, unemployment, and family dysfunction. More aggressive reporting, changing definitions, and cultural differences, rather than an actual rise in mistreatment, may account for many reports of physical, emotional, and sexual abuse, severe and general neglect, and exploitation. In any case, the department's Child Abuse Hot Line received over twice as many calls in 1989 as in 1984, serving more than 60,000 children, 8,741 of whom required immediate response.

Other agencies are involved with children's issues as well. The district attorney's office deals with child support issues, and the Department of Public Social Services handles welfare assistance; in addition, the California Department of Social Services licenses and monitors group care for preschoolers. Moreover, numerous private agencies exist that cope with child abuse and child welfare. In 1984 Children's Services published a directory listing over 1,000 public and private agencies that provide treatment and assistance.

Despite these efforts, the basic needs of many Los Angeles children remain unmet. According to the 1990 U.S. Census, 483,000 children, or 21.4 percent of all children living in Los Angeles County with their families, were below the poverty level, including 31.3 percent of African American children, 28.5 percent of Latino children, 24.7 percent of Native American children, 16.4 percent of Asian–Pacific Islander children, and 15.5 percent of

---

We find ourselves suddenly threatened by hordes of Yankee emigrants, who have already begun to flock into our country, and whose progress we cannot arrest.

—Pío Pico, last Mexican governor, 1846

---

white children. Of these children, 100,000 were receiving Aid to Families with Dependent Children (AFDC) funds. A county planning council report concluded that serious deficiencies exist with respect to children's good health, economic well-being, safety and survival, adult support, and emotional and social support; academic achievement and the readiness of adolescents to participate in the work force were also judged to be wanting.

LOS ANGELES COUNTY DEPARTMENT OF CORONER, agency mandated to inquire into the circumstances of all violent, sudden, or unusual deaths in the entire county. In recent years, an average of one of every four deaths occurring in the county has been a coroner's case. In 1991 alone the coroner investigated 18,068 suspicious or violent deaths, including 2,401 possible homicides, and

performed 6,256 autopsies. The large and overburdened department was overwhelmed with work in 1990, when the homicide rate rose 12.5 percent over the previous year. To deal with the crisis, the Board of Supervisors voted to divide the $150,000-a-year coroner's post into two positions: an administrative manager and a forensic pathologist. The coroners of recent years have been Thomas T. Noguchi, Ronald Kornblum, and, as of 1996, Lakshmanan Sathyavagiswaran, who was appointed in 1992. The budget for fiscal year 1993–1994 exceeded $10 million, which included 145 salaries.

LOS ANGELES COUNTY DEPARTMENT OF HEALTH SERVICES, office responsible for protecting community health by controlling communicable diseases and otherwise maintaining a healthy environment. When formed in 1972 by a merger of the Health Department and the Department of Hospitals, it became the largest public health agency in the nation. In 1989 the county maintained six hospitals and 48 health centers, which supplied less extensive services; the latter were subsequently reduced to 41. Among the comprehensive health centers were El Monte, H. Claude Hudson (Los Angeles), Hubert H. Humphrey (South Central), Long Beach, Edward R. Roybal (Eastside), and Mid-Valley. The county provided around-the-clock emergency services at Los Angeles County–USC Medical Center, Harbor-UCLA Medical Center, Martin Luther King Jr./Drew Medical Center, and Olive View Medical Center.

The county's health care system has been overwhelmed since 1978 by limitations imposed by Proposition 13, economic decline, and budgetary cutbacks—accompanied by rising immigration and unemployment. In 1993–1994, with revenues depleted and a department budget in excess of $4 billion, many new cuts were being proposed, including ones in health clinics and basic services.

LOS ANGELES COUNTY DEPARTMENT OF MENTAL HEALTH, agency charged with caring for severely or chronically mentally ill people who cannot obtain private care. The department, created in 1960 under provisions of the Short-Doyle Act of the California legislature, oversees directly operated facilities and contract agencies. The system provides emergency response, crisis management, case management, social rehabilitation, and acute inpatient care at community clinics. It also serves as a public guardian over mentally ill persons and administers a conservator program for people who are incompetent or gravely disabled by mental illness. Budget cuts severely damaged the system beginning in the 1980s, depriving 30,000 people of services. In 1991–1992 the department cared for 67,714 persons in various modes, including outpatient, case management, acute hospital care, public guardianship, and supplemental residential care. This figure does not cover all persons who suffered from severe mental illness. For example, on any given day in 1991 more than 3,000 psychotic or emotionally disturbed people were incarcerated in county jails rather than in mental health facilities. The 1993–1994 budget of the Mental Health Department exceeded $325 million.

LOS ANGELES COUNTY DEPARTMENT OF PARKS AND RECREATION, agency responsible for the recreational needs of the county's 9 million residents. It was created in 1929 to oversee county recreational camps and several beaches; the latter were subsequently transferred to a separate department.

County Parks and Recreation provides not only for people living in unincorporated areas, but for all residents of Los Angeles County. It maintains 84 parks of various sizes, as well as 18 natural areas for the protection of wildlife and wildflowers—including 5 nature centers—which together make

---

There are 88 cities [in Los Angeles County], and each one is a little fiefdom.
                            —Dan Garcia,
          Los Angeles Planning Commission

---

up 70 percent of its jurisdiction. Among the department's numerous and varied facilities are 334 miles of riding and hiking trails, 13 fishing lakes, and 132 tennis courts. A large area of Santa Catalina Island, the Los Angeles State and County Arboretum, and the Hollywood Bowl Performing Arts Complex are among its major holdings.

The attendance at 32 county swimming pools in 1993–1994 was close to 500,000, and more than 1.7 million people played at its 20 golf courses. The total attendance in all of the department's facilities exceeded 19 million. The department em-

ployed 843 people and operated on a total budget of $63.9 million that year.

In 1993 a budgetary crisis forced the County Board of Supervisors to give this department jurisdiction over facilities formerly administered by the Department of Arboreta and Botanic Gardens, an agency established to develop plant collections and disseminate horticultural and botanical information. Four facilities are involved: the Arboretum, a preserve of 127 acres located in Arcadia, which was purchased jointly by the state and the county in 1947 with funds granted by Harry Chandler; Descanso Gardens, in La Cañada Flintridge, acquired in 1958 and now funded by a private foundation; the South Coast Botanic Garden, an 87-acre reserve in Palos Verdes established in 1961; and the 6.2-acre Virginia Robinson Gardens in Beverly Hills, also run by a private foundation.

LOS ANGELES COUNTY DEPARTMENT OF PUBLIC SOCIAL SERVICES, agency administering the county welfare program. It provides cash assistance, benefits, and other social services to individuals and families who meet specific program requirements. The department is primarily mandated to provide protective services to adults who are neglected and abused, and financial assistance to low-income residents. The welfare program in California (originally referred to as public assistance) began as early as 1855, when the state provided aid for children through institutions and agencies.

The number of people on the public assistance rolls exploded during the Great Depression, rising from 35,700 in 1932 to 120,000 in 1933, and remaining at 91,900 in 1940. In 1936 California established the Aid to Needy Children program under the federal Social Security Act of 1935. To emphasize the need to work with family units, in 1963 the U.S. government changed the name to Aid to Families with Dependent Children (AFDC).

Between June 1988 and March 1992 the county's welfare case load rose 51 percent. In 1991, 1.2 million Angelenos—nearly one in eight persons—were on welfare at some point during the year. The next year one in seven persons in the county, a record 1.3 million, was on welfare at some point, a situation that amounted to a "social emergency" of historic proportions.

The average number of people served each month by the county's welfare program in 1995 was 1,837,402. The numbers broke down into four cash payment programs—Refugee Resettlement Program, 811; In Home Supportive Services, 74,333; General Relief (GR), 91,844; and Aid to Families with Dependent Children (AFDC), 882,646—and two supplemental (non-cash payment) programs —Food Stamp Program, 184,121; and MediCal, 603,644. As of February 1996, payments to those on AFDC varied from one (pregnant) person receiving $299 monthly to a maximum of a family of ten receiving $1,286. The GR payments were $212 monthly. The budget for fiscal year 1995–1996 for direct disbursements, exclusive of administrative costs, was $2.5 billion.

AFDC and GR are major elements of the county's welfare program. The former uses state and federal funds to provide care for needy children in families where one or both parents are absent, disabled, dead, or unemployed. GR serves adults who are not eligible for federal or state assistance. Welfare recipients are limited in the amount of property they may own. Since the mid-1980s the welfare rolls have swelled with unwed teenage mothers and foreign refugees. People in both categories are present in greater numbers in Southern California than in any other region of the nation.

To fulfill its obligations, the county's Public Social Services Department maintains an enormous, complex, and costly program. Headquartered in Rio Hondo, the agency has six general relief offices as well. The department allocates and distributes AFDC and general relief benefits, food stamps, and MediCal. It also runs a workfare program; provides support to Cuban, Haitian, and other immigrants and refugees; investigates and prevents welfare fraud; runs a sheltered workshop program; hears complaints; administers research and maintains statistics; and presents evidence at state and federal hearings regarding welfare matters.

LOS ANGELES COUNTY DEVELOPMENT COMMISSION/HOUSING AUTHORITY, agency responsible for planning, financing, and carrying out the county's housing programs. It represents a blending of two separate departments. The Board of Supervisors created the Los Angeles County Housing Authority to avail itself of federal funds mandated under the National Housing Act of 1937. Almost forty years later, in 1976, the supervisors created the Community Development Department to utilize monies allocated by the U.S. Department of Urban Affairs. The merger of the two agencies took place in 1982.

LOS ANGELES COUNTY DISTRICT ATTORNEY, county prosecutor. The office was established by the state in 1850. Until 1878 it was financed by debt payments, fines, penalties, and forfeitures due the county. It was not a full-time job until 1911. In 1913 the Office of County Counsel was created to provide legal advice to the county.

The district attorney serves a four-year elective term. The office prosecutes individuals charged with felony or misdemeanor crimes and handles specialized felony cases involving narcotics, gang-related crimes, child abuse, consumer and environmental offenses, major frauds, and nursing home abuse. A special bureau was formed in 1976 to enforce family support laws and collect child support payments; other special units assist crime victims and witnesses. The district attorney's office also conducts hearings to resolve neighborhood disputes and hears minor criminal complaints outside the criminal court system. The most recent district attorney, Gil Garcetti, was elected in 1992 and again in 1996. The department budget in 1993–1994 was $130.7 million.

LOS ANGELES COUNTY FAIR, largest county fair in the nation, drawing more than 1 million people each September. It is held on the county-owned Pomona fairgrounds called Fairplex, a 487-acre site with 1.5 million square feet of exhibit space.

The annual 17-day attraction began modestly in 1921 along a railroad siding in downtown Pomona, which was then a major center of citrus production. It later moved to a larger site, thriving under the direction of Pomona councilman C. B. "Jack" Afflerbaugh, who managed it until 1960. In 1933 the Los Angeles County Fair was the first in the nation to feature pari-mutuel horse race betting. The fairground was shut down during World War II, except for a somber period in 1942 when it served as a temporary collection center for Japanese internees who were en route to permanent detention facilities.

Today a monorail circles the grounds, and the fair features fashion shows, a parade, sheep shearing displays, dog shows, draft horses, stage entertainment, competitive exhibits of flowers, honey, dairy products, livestock, home-brewed beers, and more. When the county fair is not in season, Fairplex, which is operated by a nonprofit corporation, hosts such activities as auto drag racing, boat shows, and thoroughbred, quarter horse, and Appaloosa racing with pari-mutuel wagering.

LOS ANGELES COUNTY FEDERATION OF LABOR, delegate labor body of the AFL-CIO. With approximately 600,000 members, it is the second-biggest labor council in the United States. The first Los Angeles Central Labor Council was created in 1884 by six local unions. Today's federation resulted from a 1959 merger of the separate labor councils of the American Federation of Labor (AFL) and the Congress of Industrial Organizations (CIO) in Los Angeles, Pasadena, Pomona, Long Beach, San Pedro–Wilmington, and Santa Monica. Existing AFL organizations were particularly strong in construction and skilled trades. The CIO unions had formed as an amalgam of breakaway industrial unions in 1937, and held their first statewide conference in Los Angeles in August 1938. The CIO represented 50,000 members regionwide who worked in auto, steel, utilities, warehousing, rubber, and maritime industries or belonged to the older craft unions of the AFL. The 1959 Los Angeles merger followed a consolidation of the national AFL and CIO bodies in 1955. The federation deals with public relations, community services, labor education, promotion of union products, lobbying, and labor mutual aid. From 1975 until his retirement in 1992, William Robertson was the federation's executive secretary. After the death of his successor, James M. Wood, in 1996, Miguel Contreras won a special election, becoming the first non-Anglo to head the council.

LOS ANGELES COUNTY FIRE DEPARTMENT, the nation's largest county fire-fighting organization, and one of the largest fire-fighting forces west of Chicago. In 1996 the department had 2,498 uniformed and 793 nonuniformed personnel. The department protects a vast unincorporated area embracing residential and commercial development and forested and chaparral hillside areas. On a contract basis under the Lakewood Plan, it also provides protection for select incorporated cities. One of its specialties is wildfire rescue work. A forestry division fulfills tasks of public education and vegetation management, and tracks and informs the fire department of dangerous weather conditions.

LOS ANGELES COUNTY FORESTER AND FIRE WARDEN, official responsible for watershed fire protection in areas under the jurisdiction of the County Board of Supervisors. The agency originated in 1911 and appointed its first warden in 1914. Despite changes of name, structure, and function over time, the duties of the forester and fire warden—in unincorporated areas and in cities contracting with the county—are to enforce fire laws, inspect hazards, build fire breaks and fire roads, and make educational presentations to prevent dangerous wildfires.

LOS ANGELES COUNTY GRAND JURY, deliberative body that, like all California grand juries, has both criminal and civil responsibilities. In addition to bringing indictments in major crimes, it also oversees the operation of city and county government—a dual role unusual in the United States.

The 1849 California Constitution provided for the establishment of grand juries. In 1879 the new constitution allowed for criminal hearings and preliminary hearings to be held by grand juries before judges in open court. The following year the legislature passed laws requiring grand juries to investigate county government as well. The Los Angeles Grand Jury was established around that time.

Each year 23 citizens from Los Angeles County serve on a grand jury for a period of 12 months, receiving $25 for each day of service. They are nominated and appointed by a committee of superior court judges, after being screened by law enforcement agencies. In criminal hearings the jury weighs the evidence brought by the district attorney's office to determine whether a person should be charged with a crime and required to stand trial in the superior court. The hearings are conducted in strictest secrecy. The standard of proof for this accusatory body is "strong suspicion," as opposed to a trial jury's "beyond a reasonable doubt." Any private citizen may present a complaint in writing to the grand jury. In civil proceedings, the grand jury makes recommendations on ways to improve county government. Its final reports contain open information on its watchdog role, but its findings in criminal proceedings remain secret.

LOS ANGELES COUNTY HUMAN RELATIONS COMMISSION, agency mandated to reduce prejudice, eliminate discrimination, and promote full acceptance of all persons in community life regardless of race, religion, sex, age, national origin, sexual orientation, socioeconomic status, marital status, or physical or mental handicap. It submits its recommendations to the County Board of Supervisors. The commission was established in embryo form in 1941. In 1944, following the zoot suit riots of the preceding year, the county created a joint committee to deal with racial tensions, applying to it the name Committee on Human Relations. For several years it operated as part of the Community Services Department. In 1958 it once again became an independent department.

LOS ANGELES COUNTY METROPOLITAN TRANSPORTATION AUTHORITY (MTA), regional transportation agency. Created by the state in 1993, it is said to be the world's largest public works project. The MTA represented a merger of two previous agencies, the Southern California Rapid Transit District (RTD) and Los Angeles County Transportation Commission (LACTC). The MTA board of directors consists of the Los Angeles mayor, three Los Angeles city representatives, five county supervisors, and four members representing the other cities in the county. Its mission is to provide bus and rail transportation throughout Southern California. It plans, builds, and operates a regional rail system—both light and heavy rail—and plans and operates bus systems covering the five counties of Los Angeles, Orange, San Bernardino, Riverside, and Ventura. Its initial

Gateway Building, MTA Headquarters. Courtesy Metropolitan Transportation Authority.

budget was $3.4 billion. In 1994 it operated the Blue Line and the Red Line (which at that point consisted of a subway link between Union Station and MacArthur Park). By 1995 the estimated cost of subway construction was $5.5 billion, making it the most expensive such project in the country's history. Following the 1994 earthquake, in a further effort to recruit and serve commuters, the fleet of 1,900 MTA buses was rescheduled to accommodate 27 new lines. Metrolink, a commuter train system running on existing tracks, is a separate entity, run by the Southern California Regional Rail Authority. The hub of this new network is the Gateway Intermodal Transit Center, a vast transportation complex adjacent to Union Station. Opened in 1995, the center includes the 26-story office tower of MTA and is expected to serve tens of thousands of daily commuters.

LOS ANGELES COUNTY MUSEUM OF ART (LACMA), area's premier art museum. The facility was founded in 1910 as part of the County Museum of History, Science, and Art in Exposition Park. William Randolph Hearst and J. Paul Getty were important benefactors in the 1930s and 1940s. In 1954 Edward W. Carter, president of the Broadway-Hale Stores, Inc., spearheaded a drive to build a new facility devoted exclusively to art. The art museum split administratively from the Museum of History and Science in 1961, and in March 1965, with gifts of $12 million from Howard Ahmanson, Anna Bing Arnold, the Lytton Foundation, and other patrons, the Los Angeles County Museum of Art opened in Hancock Park. It was an immediate source of community pride. Designed by Pereira and Associates, the building consisted of three pavilions surrounded by a moat. In 1983, after seepage from the adjacent La Brea tar pits created a potentially lethal chemical hazard, the museum complex was completely renovated. During the 1980s the museum received $209 million in donations, mainly for remodeling and new construction.

The museum's holdings number 250,000 individual pieces of art. Today the complex comprises five buildings surrounding a court. The Ahmanson Building contains the permanent collection, on a rotating basis; the Hammer Building houses traveling exhibits; the Pavilion for Japanese Art displays the extraordinary Joe and Etsuko Price Collection, featuring art of the Edo period including netsukes, screens, sculptures, decorative arts, tex-

Los Angeles County Museum of Art. Photo by Spencer Grant / Stock, Boston, Inc.

tiles, and prints; the Bing Center contains a theater and auditorium for lectures, films, and concerts; and the Anderson Building features 20th-century painting and sculpture. In 1986 the Anderson Building became the museum's architectural centerpiece, although critics complained that when viewed from the front the building appears to have devoured, but not fully digested, the previously existing structures.

LOS ANGELES COUNTY MUSEUM OF NATURAL HISTORY opened in Exposition Park in 1913 as the Museum of History, Science, and Art.

The moving force behind it was a museum association founded in 1910. The distinctive building, with fitted marble walls and domed and colonnaded rotunda, is on the National Register of Historic Places. Additional wings opened in 1925, 1930, 1960, and 1976. The museum was divided administratively in 1961 into the Los Angeles County Museum of History and Science and the Los Angeles County Museum of Art. The latter moved to new quarters on Wilshire Boulevard in 1965.

The Museum of Natural History (renamed in 1965) has three main divisions today: (1) Earth Sci-

Natural History Museum, Exposition Park. Courtesy Public Affairs Dept., Los Angeles County.

ences, which oversees collections in mineralogy as well as invertebrate and vertebrate paleontology; (2) Life Sciences, administering holdings 15 million specimens strong in anthropology, botany, entomology, invertebrate zoology, herpetology, ichthyology, mammalogy, and ornithology (a Hall of Birds opened in 1990); and (3) History, which oversees a General Americana section, a transportation and communications section, and the Seaver Center for Western History Research, a rich collection of photos, manuscripts, books, maps, and related treasures.

Among the most popular museum displays are those devoted to animal habitats, dinosaurs, and pre-Columbian art; a gallery of Native American cultures, the Hearst Collection of Navajo Textiles, and a collection of 4,000 baskets are favorites. The museum is fully accredited and has two adjunct facilities: the George C. Page Museum of La Brea Discoveries in Hancock Park, opened in 1975, which displays and interprets the animal remains excavated from the La Brea tar pits; and William S. Hart County Park in Newhall, the former cowboy star's estate, which contains his home furnishings, weapons, and other artifacts. The Peterson Automotive Museum (1994) on Wilshire Boulevard's "Museum Row" is the latest addition to the County Museum complex.

LOS ANGELES COUNTY OFFICE OF EDUCATION, department that serves as liaison among the 82 school districts of the county and with the state of California. It enforces state laws, provides educational leadership, and coordinates existing programs. Although it does not run general public schools, it does operate special education schools and classrooms for handicapped students, wards of the Probation Department, and children enrolled in vocational programs. It also approves changes in school district boundaries. The office was established as the Los Angeles Superintendent of Schools in 1852. In 1856 it became an elected post, but in 1912 reverted to an appointive position. For some time the office functioned under the name of County Board of Education. It became a county department in 1962 and acquired its current name in 1984.

LOS ANGELES COUNTY PROBATION DEPARTMENT, criminal justice agency providing probation services for both adults and juveniles, as required by state and local laws. The department works closely with the courts, investigating cases and supervising individuals on probation, mainly criminals who, instead of being incarcerated, are performing community work. Prevention, reduction, and control of crime are at the core of the department's work. Gang prevention is of particular concern, as is the suppression of crime in the schools. The department established the first juvenile detention home in the county in 1903. Today's 445-bed Juvenile Hall opened downtown in 1912. At the peak of operations in 1980 the department had 3,972 employees, but the staff has been reduced in the past decade. The department is headed by the Chief Probation Officer.

LOS ANGELES COUNTY PUBLIC LIBRARY SYSTEM, one of the largest library jurisdictions in the nation, originated in 1912 as the County Free Library, primarily serving farm communities and cities that lacked library services. It maintained offices in the county's Hall of Records. In 1913 it opened its first library in a small building in Willowbrook; a second library followed in Lancaster, in 1923. The system adopted its current name in 1932.

The system's greatest expansion occurred in the 1950s and 1960s. The 1970s, a decade of tax freezes and Proposition 13, drastically reduced its major source of income, property taxes, and resulted in an increase of funds from the state.

In 1985 the system moved to new headquarters in Downey. By 1992 it served 58 municipalities and unincorporated areas through 91 regional and community libraries, in addition to bookmobiles that visited the county's more remote areas.

The county library system has 5 million books, magazines, video and audio cassettes, and compact discs. Its reference librarians answer 12.3 million questions annually. To meet the diverse interests and needs of its patrons, the system has special collections in Californiana, government publications, Judaica, philately, poetry, drama, and art, and provides special services for the visually impaired. In selecting books the system subscribes to the Library Bill of Rights and the Freedom to Read policies of the American Library Association.

The county's library system comes under the ultimate jurisdiction of the Los Angeles County Board of Supervisors. Owing to the board's revenue shortfall in 1993–1994, the library's budget that year was reduced by 42 percent over the previous year, to $39.5 million, resulting in the closure of 10 service outlets.

LOS ANGELES COUNTY REGIONAL PLANNING DEPARTMENT AND RE-GIONAL PLANNING COMMISSION, agencies administering a general plan to ensure orderly growth, covering land use, housing, and traffic circulation throughout the county, particularly in unincorporated areas.

The county first evinced interest in planning in 1921 and 1922, during an era of unprecedented growth. A group of regional and urban planners sponsored major conferences in Los Angeles to confront the random development of streets and roads, as well as the chaotic regulation of land use. The nation's first regional planning commission was the result, established in 1923. It began zoning land systematically in 1927, and in 1939 the state empowered it to coordinate planning activities for the entire region, not merely the county. The commission produced its first master plans for land use, highways, and shorelines in 1940.

Of the various commission directors, one had particular impact: Milton V. Breivogl, who served from 1953 to 1964. He oversaw the adoption of plans for the Civic Center, North County, and Mulholland Highway, as well as the drafting of a new zoning ordinance.

By 1974 the commission had grown to an enormous size, and the County Board of Supervisors decided to divide it into two separate entities. The first was a new Regional Planning Department, charged with administering a master plan covering highways, freeways, shorelines, parks, airports, and administrative centers. This master plan has affected the growth of business and residential

---

Thought is barred in this City of Dreadful Joy, and conversation is unknown.   —Aldous Huxley, 1926

---

communities and the pattern of transportation and recreation. The department has in its jurisdiction unincorporated areas, including much of the Santa Monica Mountains, Santa Clarita Valley, Antelope Valley, East Los Angeles, West Athens–Westmont, and Hacienda Heights, to name but a few. This domain encompasses some 1,000 square miles and 900,000 residents. The department also handles planning for independent incorporated commu-

nities that contract for its services, and it administers the county's subdivision and zoning ordinances and conducts research, maintaining a huge base of information on economic and social conditions in the county.

The second planning entity, the Regional Planning Commission, serves as a final appeal board in zoning cases. Its five citizen members are appointed by the supervisors and report directly to them. Commission meetings can become acrimonious, with developers, corporate lawyers, and residents maneuvering to shape the master plan or to challenge the zoning for a specific locale.

LOS ANGELES COUNTY REGISTRAR-RECORDER/COUNTY CLERK, appointive official with multiple responsibilities. This merged position dates back to 1850, when the first county recorder, a Californio named Ignacio del Valle, served as the official registrar of titles and of vital statistics. With the adoption of a new county charter in 1913, a separate Registrar of Voters department was established. Meanwhile, the county clerk, an elective position from 1850 to 1913, served both the superior court and the Board of Supervisors on an administrative basis. In 1968 the departments of Registrar and Recorder were combined; the county clerk duties were transferred over in 1991.

Today the registrar-recorder sees to the registration of voters and conducts federal, state, local, and special elections. The office also records legal documents determining ownership of real property and issues birth, death, and marriage certificates. The county clerk performs all nonjudicial and administrative functions for the superior court. These include managing jury selection and court reporters and maintaining the court's records.

LOS ANGELES COUNTY SHERIFF'S DE-PARTMENT, law enforcement body formed in April 1850 with Sheriff George T. Burrill and two deputies. The Los Angeles sheriff, unlike the chief of police, is an elected official. Twenty-five men have held office since the department was formed, six of whom were County Board of Supervisors appointees. Sheriff Sherman Block, reelected in 1994, has been in the position since 1982.

The department has far-flung responsibilities. It serves all unincorporated areas, as well as 42 incorporated cities that have opted to forgo their own police departments and contract with the county under the Lakewood Plan. The department also contracts with the Metro Blue Line and with foreign consuls in Los Angeles, and it staffs the superior courts with bailiffs. Finally, it runs the largest jail in the Western world, Men's Central Jail, with 22,000 inmates. In 1990–1991 the department's budget was $726.6 million, and in 1993–1994, $777.8 million. It employed 11,760 people in 1993–1994 and operated 23 stations in county areas, as well as a headquarters office in Monterey Park. The total force of 7,440 sworn officers as of December 1993 (civilian employees numbered 3,640) included 6,522 men and 918 women, of whom 5,538 were white, 1,228 Hispanic, 659 black, and 195 other. The organization is divided into five administrative divisions: detective, administrative, court services, custody, and technical services.

Like the Los Angeles Police Department, the Los Angeles County Sheriff's Department has recently been charged with misconduct. A 1992 study commissioned by the Board of Supervisors and authored by James G. Kolts, a retired judge, found a pattern of excessive force and lax discipline on the part of sheriff's deputies. Kolts concluded with recommendations for widespread reforms.

LOS ANGELES COUNTY TAX ASSESSOR, elected official who supervises the complex process of assessing property values and collecting taxes. The assessor's job is to maintain a file on every piece of property, including dwellings, factories, stores, orchards, oil wells, schools, and churches— and on every improvement ever made on a piece of property; to reassess property upon transfer or change of ownership and assess the added value for new construction; to manage litigation arising from tax issues; to supervise the mailing of millions of tax bills and posting of returns; and to oversee responses to protests involving assessment excesses or irregularities.

LOS ANGELES COUNTY TRANSPORTA- TION COMMISSION. *See* Metro rail system

LOS ANGELES COUNTY–USC MEDICAL CENTER, nation's largest acute-care hospital and medical teaching facility. In 1885 the county founded the Los Angeles County Hospital on Mission Road as a 100-bed facility. Affiliated with the University of Southern California School of Medicine, it had 47 patients, 6 staff members, and a budget of $4,000. The hospital now has over 2,000 beds, a staff of 10,000, and a budget of $708 million. The current name was acquired in 1968. In 1991–1992 doctors delivered 14,000 babies and laboratories conducted 25 million laboratory tests for 764,00 outpatients. The institution is USC's primary teaching facility and consists of a general hospital, a women's hospital, a pediatric pavilion, and a psychiatric hospital. Some 400 staff physicians assist in the education and supervision of 700 residents-in-training.

LOS ANGELES DAILY JOURNAL, newspaper catering to the legal community of California. Published in the city since 1888, it was created to print official legal notices. It also contains state and national legal news, appellate reports, court calendars, verdicts and settlements, legal advertising, and classified advertising for attorneys. Published by the Daily Journal Corporation, the newspaper's circulation in 1995 was 17,500.

LOS ANGELES DAILY NEWS, independent tabloid founded in 1923 by Cornelius Vanderbilt Jr., millionaire New York socialite. On its first day the *News* scooped its rivals, the *Los Angeles Times* and *Los Angeles Examiner,* with a headline story on the Tokyo earthquake. Nevertheless, the paper could not build sufficient circulation and foundered financially. Three years later, liberal publisher Manchester Boddy breathed new life into the *News,* adopting a livelier style and a strong pro–New Deal editorial posture. In the 1930s Boddy attacked corrupt Mayor Shaw, who was backed by the *Times,* supporting the reformer Fletcher Bowron instead. The feisty staff, with its penchant for lurid headlines (for example, "Ding-Dong Daddy of the D-Car Line," about a philandering streetcar conductor), could not keep the scrappy paper alive, and it died in 1954. Approximately 200,000 negatives and 20,000 photos from the *News* remain on deposit at the UCLA library. In 1981 the *Valley News,* a San Fernando Valley newspaper, assumed the name of *Daily News of Los Angeles.*

LOS ANGELES DEPARTMENT OF WATER AND POWER (DWP), largest municipally owned utility in the nation, delivering all the water and much of the electricity used by the city's residents. The DWP, originally known as the Bureau of Power and Light, resulted from the Owens River (Los Angeles) Aqueduct early in the century.

The need for water prompted the aqueduct project, but the electrical energy generated as a by-product of construction was a major boon in its own right. In 1911 voters authorized an agency to distribute electricity as well as water. The DWP built hydro facilities along the Los Angeles Aqueduct route, at San Francisquito Canyon, Franklin Canyon, and in the San Fernando Valley. By 1939 it had bought out three other utility companies and soon afterward emerged as the nation's largest electric utility.

The Owens River is the source of most DWP water, but the utility also pumps some water from underground wells within city limits. The Department of Water and Power is a founding member of the Metropolitan Water District of Southern California (MWD) and as such also obtains a fraction of state water via the California Water Aqueduct, with the water flowing into the DWP network near Castaic.

The policy-making body for the DWP is the five-member Los Angeles Board of Water and Power Commissioners. As authorized by the 1925 city charter, the commission members are appointed by the mayor and approved by the council. The board was created in 1902 when the city seized the assets of the privately owned Los Angeles Water Company and created a public water utility. This new body served as a tool for an influential Los Angeles elite, which sought a free hand in land development and water acquisition without suffering the "interference" of the city council and mayor. Commissioner Moses H. Sherman, for example, belonged to the land syndicate that owned much of the San Fernando Valley and stood to profit personally if water was brought from the Owens Valley. Only after it had obtained water rights in the Owens area did the commission inform the council of its action. It then supervised the building of the Los Angeles Aqueduct, completed in 1913, and fought the rebellious Owens Valley interests in the 1920s. Despite the conflict of interest and power plays of some commissioners during the aqueduct's development, the board ran an efficient public utility and became the prototype of the powerful, independent city commission.

LOS ANGELES DODGERS, National League baseball team, born a century ago in Brooklyn. First called the "Bridegrooms," owing to the marriage of a player, the team changed its name to the "Trolley Dodgers," after the trolley lines that snaked through Brooklyn. It was finally shortened to "Dodgers."

The 1958 move from New York City to Los Angeles was engineered by the late Walter O'Malley, club president and chief owner. The Dodger deal had numerous local supporters but also occasioned a public protest, since Chavez Ravine, the site chosen for Dodger Stadium, had been slated to become a low-cost, integrated public housing project. In 1959, playing in the Coliseum, the club won its first pennant in 65 years, and drew the three biggest crowds in World Series history, topping out at 92,706. The Dodgers soon became the most successful baseball franchise. In 1962 the club played its first year in the new Dodger Stadium. As part of the National League's Western Division, the Dodgers have played in 11 World Series: in 1959, 1963, 1965, 1966, 1974, 1977, 1978, 1981, 1983, 1985, and 1988. They won the series five times: in 1959, 1963, 1965, 1981, and 1988.

In 1977 the Dodgers became the first club with four players who hit over 30 home runs in one season: Steve Garvey, Reggie Smith, Ron Cey, and Dusty Baker. The next year the team reached a 3 million attendance record, a feat they would repeat five more times. Two Dodger players are represented in the Baseball Hall of Fame: triple Cy Young Award winner Sandy Koufax, who once pitched 18 strike-outs in a single game, and Don Drysdale, who one season pitched 58 2/3 scoreless innings and six consecutive shutouts. Other memorable Dodgers include Don Sutton, Maury Wills, Fernando Valenzuela, Willie Davis, and Orel Hersheiser. Walter Alston managed the team from 1954 to 1976; Tommy Lasorda, who succeeded him in 1977, led the team to six division pennants. Popular radio and TV announcer Vince Scully was the first Dodger employee to receive a salary of $1 million. He was named best sportscaster of the year four times, and was inducted into the broadcast section of the Baseball Hall of Fame.

LOS ANGELES FESTIVAL, arts fair sponsored by the city of Los Angeles. It originated as the Olympic Arts Festival in 1984, and was repeated in 1987, 1990, and 1993, when it lasted 31 days at a cost of $4 million. The theme of the 1993 festival was multiculturalism, with particular focus on African, Middle Eastern, and African American cultures. Presentations were held at 49 venues—theaters, churches, auditoriums, museums, schools, and colleges—and included dance performances, poetry readings, drama, painting exhibits, and film showings.

LOS ANGELES FREE CLINIC, private nonprofit medical facility. It opened in the Fairfax area in 1967 to serve counterculture youths afflicted with drug addictions and sexually transmitted diseases. The clinic now has two centers: one on Beverly Boulevard, which serves adults, most of whom are unemployed, uninsured, homeless, or immigrant, and one on Hollywood Boulevard, which caters to at-risk adolescents. The professional staff serves pro bono. The annual patient load in 1993 was about 30,000.

LOS ANGELES HARBOR. *See* Harbor, Los Angeles; Los Angeles Harbor Department

LOS ANGELES HARBOR DEPARTMENT, city agency responsible for managing and supervising the harbor district. In 1907, on the eve of the consolidation of San Pedro and Wilmington with Los Angeles, the city council officially formed the Port of Los Angeles. At the same time, it established the five-member Board of Harbor Commissioners, giving it control over a Harbor Department. The board members, appointed by the mayor and confirmed by the city council, serve for a term of five years. They control the management of all navigable waters and submerged lands within the city. They even have the authority to regulate commerce, navigation, and fishing in the state-owned tidelands, a function imparted to them by the state in 1911.

The Harbor Department owns the majority of wharves and piers in the harbor area, and disburses leases for industrial sites and oil drilling. One of its major tasks is to establish and enforce rules and regulations governing those assets. Like the Departments of Airports and Water and Power, the Harbor Department is "proprietary"—that is, it controls its own coffers and functions largely independently of the city council.

In 1991 the department netted more than $80 million after expenses, despite the fact that it was operating at only 60–65 percent capacity. It plans to spend $2 billion over the next 30 years on dredging deeper channels and creating new terminals. Opponents contended that the expansion is unwarranted and that the revenues should be used to offset the city's budget deficit.

LOS ANGELES HERALD-EXAMINER, morning daily newspaper founded by William Randolph Hearst in 1903. It was first called the *Los Angeles Examiner* and was intended as a pro-union newspaper, in a town dominated by the anti-union *Los Angeles Times.* After 1932 it occupied a Mission Revival building designed by Julia Morgan, designer of Hearst Castle. By the 1950s the *Examiner* was the largest afternoon daily in the nation. Its stock-in-trade was eye-grabbing headlines, muckraking exposés, sensational stories, color comics, and jingoistic editorials. In 1961 Hearst, who also owned the evening *Herald-Express,* merged the two papers, creating the *Los Angeles Herald-Examiner* and abandoning the morning market to the *Times.* The move proved a strategic blunder. With readers turning to television, the evening market was already in decline.

Aerial view of Los Angeles Harbor, 1980. Courtesy Worldport LA.

From 1967 to 1973 the *Herald-Examiner* was hit by a bitter labor strike. Although the newspaper was doing well, with 750,000 paid subscribers and the largest afternoon circulation of any paper in the country, it still had to compete with the *Times* and television news. Management decided to shake off the Newspaper Guild, the recognized union in the industry. The guild went on strike. Readership and advertising plummeted. Although management eventually settled, the paper never recovered its lost circulation or advertising. The *Herald-Examiner* shut down its presses for good in 1989. The paper's death also wounded the guild.

LOS ANGELES INTERNATIONAL AIR-PORT (LAX), major air facility for the Los Angeles metropolis, and one of the world's busiest and most modern transportation centers. It was created on a Westchester bean field in 1928, when the city leased 640 acres from a private landowner for a period of 50 years at $125,000 per year. A 2,000-foot oiled landing strip and two 100-foot hangars, each with a 20-plane capacity, were built on the south side of the airport. The official dedication of the facility, then known as Mines Field, took place on 7 June 1930. In 1935 the federal government granted a subsidy of $558,000 to improve the airport, and three years later authorized additional work under the Work Projects Administration. The city purchased title to the entire site in 1937 for $2.2 million, thus saving $3 million over the term of the contract. In 1940 the city council created a three-member Board of Municipal Airport Commissioners, and the voters approved a bond issue of $3.5 million in 1941. In 1946 most airline compa-

nies moved their flights and facilities from the San Fernando Valley's Lockheed field, which until then was the region's major airport, to the new, larger field. A year later voters approved a charter amendment giving the airport independent status similar to the Department of Water and Power. The name Los Angeles International Airport was assigned in 1949.

Many of LAX's modern improvements date from the 1950s and 1960s: a new traffic control tower and air freight terminal (1951); the Sepulveda Boulevard underpass (1953); a new, jet-age passenger terminal that was dedicated by Pres. Lyndon Johnson (1959–61); the futuristic saucer-shaped theme building, containing a restaurant, designed by architect William Pereira as an emblem of the "first airport of the jet age" (1962); a joint-powers agreement making Ontario International Airport a part of the Los Angeles regional airport system (1967); and the World Way Postal Center and giant Parking Lot B (1968).

Today, after additional improvements in the 1970s and 1980s, LAX has state-of-the-art terminals, hangars, and service facilities. The new $20 million control tower, which airport officials hope will become a city landmark, rises 289 feet. The airport covers 3,500 acres and provides parking for 20,000 vehicles; each year it guides 500,000 landings and takeoffs, handles 32 million passengers, and loads and unloads 750,000 tons of freight. LAX has produced surplus revenues of $50 million annually.

LOS ANGELES KINGS, ice hockey team based at the Forum in Inglewood. The National Hockey

Theme building and new control tower, Los Angeles International Airport, 1995. Courtesy City of Los Angeles Dept. of Airports.

League affiliate was formed in 1967 by sports pro-moter Jack Kent Cooke, and was later owned by Jerry Buss, Bruce McNall, and, as of 1994, Joseph Cohen. The Kings enjoyed a winning year in the 1974–1975 season, amassing a record 105 points, with legendary Rogie Vachon as goaltender. The crowds remained sparse, causing Cooke to remark, "Now I know why 300,000 Canadians moved here. To get *away* from hockey." Attendance reached a respectable 471,789 in 1984–1985, when the team finished fourth in its five-team division. In 1993 superstar Wayne Gretzky led the Kings into their first Stanley Cup playoffs, against the ulti-mately victorious Montreal Canadians. The fol-lowing year he scored his 802nd career goal, set-ting a new record.

LOS ANGELES LAKERS, National Basketball Association team. Originating in Minneapolis, the team moved to Los Angeles for the 1960–1961 sea-son, and soon dominated the sport. Between 1961 and 1991 they were Western Conference champi-ons 18 times; between 1970 and 1990 they were Pa-cific Division champions 15 times; and after their move to Los Angeles they won the NBA champi-onship 6 times—in 1972, 1980, 1982, 1985, 1987, and 1988.

Among the team's superstars have been Elgin Baylor, Jerry West, Gail Goodrich, Wilt Cham-berlain, Michael Cooper, Kareem Abdul-Jabbar, and Earvin "Magic" Johnson. James Worthy's re-tirement in 1995 represented the end of the great Laker teams of the 1980s. At the end of the 1995–1996 season, with a record of 1,835 wins and 1,103 losses, the team had won 62.5 percent of their games since coming to Los Angeles.

The Lakers' play-by-play broadcaster, the only one in Laker history, is Francis Dayle "Chick" Hearn. Hired in 1961, he has missed only two games, the last one on 20 November 1965. He en-tered the 1994–1995 season having broadcast 2,692 consecutive games. He is one of only three ra-dio/TV people inducted into the Basketball Hall of Fame.

Laker coaches in recent years have been Bill Sharman, who led the team from 1971 to 1976; Jerry West, from 1976 to 1979; Paul Westhead, from 1979 to 1982 (partial); Pat Riley, from 1981 to 1990; Mike Dunleavy, from 1990 to 1992; Randy Pfund, 1993; and Del Harris, 1994 to the present. Jerry West has been general manager for two decades; in 1995 he took over the new position of executive vice pres-

ident of basketball operations. Since 1979 the Lak-ers have been owned by Jerry Buss (a former owner of the Los Angeles Kings hockey team), who also owns their playing arena, the Forum, with its 17,505 seats.

LOS ANGELES MARATHON, sporting event established in 1986. While not the first marathon to be run in the area, it was the first to be backed by the city council. In its inaugural year, 11,000 runners participated in the 26.2-mile race that started and ended outside the Los Angeles Memo-rial Coliseum in Exposition Park. Five years later, in March 1991, more than 20,000 runners com-

Los Angeles Marathon, 1995. Marathon Foto.

pleted the course, including wheelchair racers, and an estimated 1.5 million spectators lined the route. The record time for a man in the Los Angeles Marathon is 2 hours, 10 minutes, and 19 seconds, established in 1988 by Martin Mondragon, from Mexico. The women's record is 2 hours, 26 min-utes, and 23 seconds, established in 1992 by Mad-ina Biktagirova from the Commonwealth of In-dependent States. In 1995 rain did not dampen the enthusiasm of 19,500 runners, 12,500 cyclists (the first time they were invited to enter the Marathon), and numerous wheelchair entrants.

LOS ANGELES MASTER CHORALE AND SINFONIA ORCHESTRA, largest choral en-semble in the United States, and one of the most highly acclaimed. Established by Roger Wagner in 1964, it was the resident chorus for the Music Center and the Los Angeles Philharmonic Orchestra. It presented its first concert, featuring Bach's Mass in B Minor, in January 1965. The Master Chorale has always shared personnel and worked in tandem with a smaller group established by Wagner in 1946, the Roger Wagner Chorale. Depending on the particular engagement, the 32-voice Roger Wagner Chorale, a profit-making group, can be expanded into the 120-voice Master Chorale, a nonprofit ensemble.

Roger Wagner directed the Master Chorale until 1986. He was succeeded by John Currie from 1986 to 1991, and then by Paul Salamunovich. Guest conductors have included Aaron Copland, Margaret Hillis, John Nelson, Robert Page, Helmuth Rilling, Robert Shaw, Alfred Wallenstein, and Richard Westenberg. The Master Chorale has, on occasion, sung with the Music Center Opera.

LOS ANGELES MAYOR. *See* Los Angeles City mayor

LOS ANGELES MEMORIAL COLISEUM, arena completed in 1923 at a cost below $1 million. The Exposition Park facility was the site of both the 1932 and 1984 Summer Olympics, was home to the Dodgers before their Chavez Ravine stadium was completed, and was the site of two football Super Bowl games (I and VII) and the baseball World Series of 1959. It is the home of USC football, the first game having been played in 1923 against Pomona College. UCLA played football in the Coliseum from 1933 to 1981, before shifting to the Rose Bowl. The arena has hosted countless sporting events, meetings, musical concerts, and public celebrations. During the 1960 Democratic con-

vention, John Kennedy and Lyndon Johnson delivered their acceptance speeches in the arena, and in 1987 Pope John Paul II addressed an enthusiastic Coliseum crowd.

Originally the structure seated 76,000 people, but it was enlarged in 1932 to hold 105,000. In what finally proved to be a futile attempt to prevent the departure of the Los Angeles Raiders, a major tenant, the stadium was partially refurbished in 1993 at a cost of $15 million, with additional improvements awaiting an improved budgetary picture. The Coliseum and nearby Sports Arena are governed by a nine-member commission representing the city, county, and state. The Coliseum, an official National Historic Landmark, sustained severe damage in the 1994 Northridge earthquake and is now undergoing major repair and retrofitting.

LOS ANGELES MEMORIAL SPORTS ARENA, multipurpose facility in Exposition Park. Designed by Welton Becket and opened in 1959, the 15,000-seat arena has been used for basketball, boxing, wrestling, circus performances, ice hockey, skating, table tennis, equestrian events, conventions, pop music concerts, and track-and-field meets. The arena hosted the Democratic presidential convention of 1960, when John Kennedy received the party's nomination. It is home to the Los Angeles Clippers of the National Basketball Association. The facility is governed by the Los Angeles Coliseum Commission, made up of representatives from the city and county of Los Angeles, and the state government.

LOS ANGELES MIRROR, tabloid newspaper started by the *Times* in 1948 and named for an ear-

Los Angeles Memorial Coliseum, 1996. Photo by Lori Shepler.

lier paper founded in 1873. Its main mission was to cripple the rival Democratic tabloid, the *Daily News. Mirror* staff adopted an independent posture even toward publisher Harry Chandler and the top brass of the Times-Mirror Corporation. They also took a tough, crime-busting approach to local news that attracted new readers. The policy succeeded in causing the demise of the *Daily News* in 1954. Chandler, who had achieved his objective and was never happy with his own tabloid, closed the *Mirror* down in 1962.

LOS ANGELES MUSIC CENTER. *See* Music Center of Los Angeles County

LOS ANGELES MUSIC CENTER OPERA, performance company formed in 1985. It usually features classical opera—recent offerings have included Donizetti's *Don Pasquale,* Verdi's *Otello,* Gounod's *Faust,* Strauss's *Elektra,* and Mozart's *Don Giovanni*—with occasional modern productions such as George Gershwin's *Porgy and Bess.* In its ninth season the company staged 54 performances at the Dorothy Chandler Pavilion. To defray costs in an era of declining support for the arts, the Los Angeles Opera coproduces with other theaters, including the Houston Grand Opera. Peter Mennings is the company's general director.

LOS ANGELES NAME, ORIGIN OF, has been a subject of historical debate. Some scholars believe the original Spanish name in 1781 was El Pueblo de Nuestra Señora la Reina de los Angeles de Porciúncula. Others suggest that the words *Nuestra Señora* (Our Lady) and *Porciúncula* (from the Latin, meaning "small portion," as in the name of an Italian church beloved by St. Francis of Assisi; also the name given to the Los Angeles River by the Portolá expedition) never appeared officially. If so, the original name was El Pueblo de la Reina de los Angeles, best rendered in English as "The Village of the Queen of the Angels." In time, Spaniards and Mexicans referred to the village simply as El Pueblo de los Angeles. Mexico officially raised its status to that of *ciudad* (city) in 1835, and the California legislature incorporated it as the City of Los Angeles in 1850.

LOS ANGELES ON FILM. Los Angeles tends to be presented as both a city of evil and a city of innocence. Innocent Los Angeles, the place where dreams come true, is much the older theme, pres-

ent from the very beginning of filmmaking. Because movies in the silent era usually were filmed on location, audiences soaked up the city's climate, clean streets, landscaped homes, and sunny beaches, building an early image of a fun-loving, laid-back town. From 1912 on, Mack Sennett's Keystone Kops busily and incompetently chased around in police cars on the uncrowded, tree-lined streets of Los Angeles. Charlie Chaplin, Buster Keaton, and Stan Laurel and Oliver Hardy created their own chaos in that same genial atmosphere, while W. C. Fields drove west with his movie family to begin life as an orange grove owner in *It's a Gift* (1934). The Gidget and Beach Party films of the 1950s and 1960s enhanced the image of a youthful, carefree post–World War II Los Angeles, impressing an entire generation of teenagers. More recent comedies, such as the good-naturedly satirical *L.A. Story* (1991) and *Defending Your Life* (1991), further bolster the already upbeat picture of Los Angeles.

Los Angeles on film has its nightmarish aspect as well: a sun-drenched coastal city with a diseased underbelly. In the *film noir* rendition, the city is dominated by corrupt, loveless people from all classes whose greed drives them to moral depravity and violence. *Film noir* was brought from Europe by directors who fled Hitler's Germany and found refuge in Hollywood, among them Billy Wilder, Otto Preminger, Fritz Lang, and Michael

---

Fattest land I ever saw.

—Harrison Gray Otis,
founder of *Los Angeles Times,* 1874

Curtiz. They and American directors applied the style to books by such authors as James Cain and Raymond Chandler, thereby merging the menacing black-and-white European look with the hardboiled American mystery. The merger produced a spate of movies, many with a Los Angeles background, that offered dramatic, and negative, portraits of the city and its people—most notably, *Double Indemnity* (1944), *Mildred Pierce* (1945), *The Postman Always Rings Twice* (1946), *The Big Sleep* (1946), and *D.O.A.* (1949). This sinister side of the city's personality continued to be explored in *Chinatown* (1974), and even in some more ambivalent science-fiction and futuristic films—*Planet of the Apes* (1968), *Blade Runner* (1982), and *Brother from*

Another Planet (1984). Robert Altman's *Short Cuts* (1993) is a more textured presentation.

Before the mid-1980s only a few films pictured life in the Los Angeles barrios and black ghettoes, including *The Ring* (1952) and *Zoot Suit* (1981). More recent movies—such as *Colors* (1988), *Boyz N' the Hood* (1991), *Grand Canyon* (1991), and *American Me* (1992)—were filmed in the streets of Los Angeles and continue the depiction of the city as a seamy, dangerous place. Not all films of ghetto and barrio life deal with gangs and violence. Both *Stand and Deliver* (1987) and *La Bamba* (1987) are examples of very different, ultimately positive, stories, and Cheech Marin, an East Los Angeles–born actor-director, made *Born in East L.A.* (1987), a comic vehicle about a serious subject: the experiences of Chicanos caught up in an Immigration and Naturalization Service raid.

LOS ANGELES PHILHARMONIC ORCHESTRA, founded in 1919 by financier, art patron, and amateur musician William Andrews Clark Jr. The opening concert, at Trinity Auditorium, featured Dvořák's *New World* Symphony and Liszt's *Les Préludes,* directed by Walter Henry Rothwell. The orchestra performed at the Philharmonic Auditorium, opposite Pershing Square, from 1920 until 1964, when it moved to the 3,201-seat Dorothy Chandler Pavilion. Formerly, too, during the summer months, the 110-member group played at the Hollywood Bowl. The orchestra's sponsor is the Los Angeles Philharmonic Association. Its budget for 1992 was $33 million, the third highest of any orchestra in the nation. The site for the orchestra's new home, the Walt Disney Concert Hall, is near the Music Center.

The world-renowned orchestra has had 10 permanent conductors: Walter Henry Rothwell (1919–1927), George Schneevoigt (1927–1929), Artur Rodzinski (1929–1933), Otto Klemperer (1933–1939), Alfred Wallenstein (1943–1956), Eduard van Beinum (1956–1959), Zubin Mehta (1962–1978), Carlo Maria Giulini (1978–1984), André Previn (1985–1989), and Esa-Pekka Salonen (1992–). (Time gaps in this roster were filled by guest conductors.)

LOS ANGELES POLICE COMMISSION, five-member civilian board that serves as head of the Los Angeles Police Department (LAPD). The commissioners, who meet in open weekly meetings, are appointed by the mayor in staggered five-year terms. The Board of Police Commissioners, as it is

formally known, sets overall policy and exercises executive oversight, whereas the police chief, through the chain of command, controls the day-to-day operations of the LAPD. The commission, established under the city charter of 1925 (an earlier one was established in 1870), was the work of progressive reformers who intended it to represent the citizens in municipal government.

The Police Commission has a number of vital functions, in addition to setting overall policy. It conducts the final review in any mandatory investigation on the use of force—that is, all instances in which an officer has used a firearm. The final determination of whether a shooting meets police policy regarding the use of deadly force rests with the commission. Officer discipline is another board responsibility. Although authority to impose discipline rests exclusively with the chief of police, the commission may, on the filing of a grievance appeal, act as a procedural review body, determining whether a disciplinary matter has been fully examined according to established procedures.

The board also plays a role in reviewing citizen complaints. While it is not authorized to investigate individual complaints, it does monitor the overall system to determine if such complaints are being adequately addressed.

The commission also oversees issuance of a variety of permits for things ranging from parades and athletic events to tow truck operators. The commission has established a Police Permit Panel to assist in this function.

The commission is involved in broad issues relating to police-community relations. In 1992 it favored Charter Amendment F, which grew out of the recommendations of the Christopher Commission investigation of the police beating of Rodney G. King. The commission has embraced the concept of community-based policing and a partnership between the LAPD and the community it serves.

LOS ANGELES POLICE DEPARTMENT (LAPD), 1850 TO 1950, evolved from a one-man marshal's office to one of the biggest and most sophisticated law enforcement agencies in the nation. Through many decades, however, it was troubled by politics and corruption.

From 1851 to 1876, when the city marshal was the top lawman, law and order scarcely existed. Notorious killers and rowdy gunfighters haunted the many saloons, and shootings were an everyday oc-

Los Angeles policemen, about 1900. Courtesy Seaver Center for Western History Research, Natural History Museum of Los Angeles County.

currence. In the 1850s repeated outbursts of Mexican banditry were met not by police action but by gringo-led vigilante justice. During the disastrous anti-Chinese riot of 1871, the police were completely ineffectual.

In 1870 the first police commission was appointed to run the police department; the city marshal still served as chief. A full-fledged police department coalesced in 1876, when the first appointed police chief, J. F. Gerkins, replaced the last marshal, J. J. Carrillo. The next year J. F. Burns, a deputy from the county sheriff's department, doggedly pursued the murderer Stephen "Buckskin Bill" Samsbury from Glendale to Nevada, and then to Baja California. When Burns finally caught and killed his quarry, he preserved the murderer's six-toed foot in mescal as proof of his deed. He was named the city's police chief in 1889.

Although the department gained strength in the 1880s, it was a fertile field for political meddling by the city council and was riddled with corruption well into the early decades of the 20th century. A tug-of-war developed between the police commission and the chief of police, with power shifting back and forth in 1878, 1889, and 1911. The 1925 city charter provided for a chief of police with a lifetime appointment, but placed the department under the control of a five-member Board of Police Commissioners appointed by the mayor and approved by the council.

Even this administrative change failed to bring order to the department. In the 1920s and early 1930s the police force was infamous for condoning and promoting bookmaking, slot machines, prostitution, and wide-open violations of Prohibition. The corrupt officers went unchallenged as long as they protected downtown business interests by keeping the lid on organized labor. Mayor George Cryer attempted reform—for instance, he had Chief Louis D. Oakes arrested in his official car while drunk and in the company of a half-clothed woman—with little effect. The department's nadir was reached during the administration of Mayor Frank L. Shaw (1933–1938), when police lieutenant Earl Kynette, who had tried to stop an investigation into political corruption by bombing the car of a private investigator, was sent to San Quentin Prison. The resignation of Shaw and the installation of Mayor Fletcher Bowron in 1938 finally ended the career of Chief James Davis and the era of flagrant corruption.

LOS ANGELES POLICE DEPARTMENT (LAPD), SINCE 1950, has become the second largest police force in the nation, protecting over 3.4 million people living in a 465-square-mile area. Its mandate is to enforce city, state, and federal laws for the protection of persons and property and for the preservation of community peace. The police chief is responsible for the administration, inspection, and control of the department and for maintaining relations with the city council. The 1925 charter also provides for a five-member police commission to exercise broad citizen oversight, although in practice the chief's voice has generally prevailed.

William H. Parker, police chief from 1950 to 1966, reorganized the LAPD along military lines, thereby achieving a reputation for running a clean and effective force. He deflected occasional criticisms as to the use of excessive force and racial bias by keeping the crime rate in check. The popularity of Jack Webb's television series *Dragnet* (1951–1959, 1967–1970), which was drawn very loosely from LAPD case histories, presented an idyllic version of Los Angeles law enforcement and helped build the department's positive image.

Parker survived the 1965 Watts riots with his reputation intact, although the McCone Commission investigating the disturbance noted the racial imbalance in police hiring and staffing. Police-community relations in minority communities remained strained afterward as civil rights and civil liberties groups repeatedly called for more equitable hiring, as well as the creation of a civilian review board to investigate use-of-force issues. Parker's successors—Thomas E. Reddin (1966–1969) and Ed Davis (1969–1978)—continued to garner considerable community confidence; in contrast, Chief Daryl Gates's often controversial tenure, which began in 1978, proved troublesome enough to force his resignation in 1992. By then the LAPD was being accused by many groups of racial and gender bias and of using excessive force in apprehending suspects.

The racial composition of the force has stirred active public debate since the 1960s. As in all police departments in major U.S. cities, white officers (68.7 percent) were overrepresented on the force relative to the proportion of whites in the city's population as a whole. After the McCone report, the racial composition of the force became more equitable, particularly when LAPD signed a consent decree to hire more officers of minority background. By 1992, Caucasians still represented 59.9 percent of the force, but now African American officers made up 14.1 percent and Latinos 22.3 percent, reflecting an aggressive effort to recruit both groups.

The first woman officer, Alice Stebbins Wells, sworn in in 1910, was a self-taught Pentecostal minister from the Midwest who had lobbied for an ordinance that would allow her to join the force. She patrolled dance halls, but was never permitted to carry a gun.

The role of women on the force became an issue in 1972, when federal legislation forced city police departments to hire women officers. In 1980, of the 171 women officers in the LAPD, only 20 were on patrol. In a discrimination case brought by Fanchon Blake, the court issued a consent decree ordering that within six to eight years 20 percent of the force be composed of uniformed policewomen. By 1995, 16 percent, or some 1,300 of almost 8,000 sworn officers, were women. They still faced strong prejudice from male officers, many of whom believed they would shy away from danger, falter where physical force was needed, and alienate the general public. Instead, a 1994 internal study revealed that the women usually communicated better out on the streets than their male counterparts and tended to draw their guns less often, resulting in a reduction, rather than an escalation, in violent confrontations. Among the 120 officers identified by the Christopher Commission as using excessive force, none were women.

The excessive-force issue came to a head in Los Angeles with the police beating of motorist Rodney King in 1991, the court trial for the officers involved, and subsequent rioting. At the time the department had 8,400 sworn officers (and 2,000 civilian personnel)—the lowest ratio of sworn officers (2) per 1,000 residents and the second lowest ratio of officers (15) per square mile of any force in the country. In 1991 the Christopher Commission cited the department for excessive use of force, racism, and mismanagement at the top levels. After much dissension, Chief Gates resigned, and a 1992 charter amendment established a maximum of two 5-year terms for the chief of police.

The King beating and its aftermath led to demands for a new, community-based, approach to policing. This approach, implemented successfully in other large cities, encourages officers to leave the patrol car and interact with citizens. Willy Williams, the chief hired in 1992, was a strong advocate of the community-based policing model.

The LAPD is divided into 18 geographic divisions, with headquarters in downtown's Parker Center. The LAPD responds to 3 million phone calls yearly, and engages in many aspects of crime prevention, traffic control, and antidrug programs. It has rebuilt its numbers, and in 1996, 8,805 sworn officers were serving the city.

LOS ANGELES PUBLIC LIBRARY (LAPL), one of the biggest and best-regarded library systems in the nation. The library began with the 1872 founding of the blue-ribbon Los Angeles Library Association, whose members included former gov-

The Central Library Building of the Los Angeles Public Library, 1996. Photo by Lori Shepler.

ernors John G. Downey and George R. Stoneman, Judge Ygnacio Sepúlveda, and J. P. Widney, founder of the USC medical school. Officially established by city ordinance on 7 March 1878, the library was housed in City Hall in the 1880s.

The system currently operates out of the Central Library Building on 5th Street, designed by Bertram Goodhue and built in 1926 at a cost of $2.3 million. A librarian and a five-member Board of Library Commissioners appointed by the mayor serve as system administrators. The library has three service divisions—central library, branch library, and technical services—and maintains seven regional divisions, 56 community branches, and two bookmobile units. In 1989 voters approved a $53 million ballot proposition authorizing expansion and repair of branch libraries. (LAPL is sometimes confused with the Los Angeles County Public Library, whose system serves 58 municipalities and unincorporated areas through a system of 91 branch libraries.)

The LAPL has 6.5 million books, over 2 million of which are stored in the Central Library Building. In 1990–1991, the library had a book budget of $5.3 million. It loaned out 10.5 million items and its staff answered 16.8 million questions from pa-

trons. A unique feature of the LAPL—compared, for example, to the New York Public Library—is that most of its downtown collection circulates to the branch libraries.

The Central Library maintains two special collections having to do with Los Angeles in particular. One, maintained by the History Department, comprises 80,000 maps and 1,600 atlases, many of which relate to the history and development of California and Los Angeles. The second is the Security Pacific Historical Photograph Collection, consisting of 250,000 photos of Los Angeles from the 1870s to the 1960s, with emphasis on the 1920s to the 1950s.

On 29 April 1986, an arson fire destroyed 20 percent of the central library collection and suspended service in the 5th Street building. A spirited save-the-books campaign by the Friends of the Library amassed $10 million to replace lost items. A second arson fire occurred that September. The catastrophes came amid prolonged public debate concerning the future of the Goodhue building, which for years had been cited for major fire and safety hazards. After dismissing arguments to raze the structure, the city approved an innovative plan to preserve it. The private development firm of Maguire Thomas Partners agreed to pledge over $125 million toward financing the library construction, in exchange for permission to build a supertower on 5th Street, whose height would exceed the normal zoning limits. A land purchase, incremental tax financing, and in-kind contributions were also involved in the complex financial strategy.

Remodeling began in 1988 and was completed in 1993. A new east wing has been added to the original Central Library Building, with four stories above ground and four stories below, including a parking garage. The library grounds were also landscaped according to a 1920s plan.

LOS ANGELES RAIDERS, professional team of the National Football League (NFL). The Raiders originated in Oakland in 1963 and were brought to Los Angeles in 1982 by head coach and general manager Al Davis. The team's home field is the Los Angeles Memorial Coliseum; their motto is "Commitment to Excellence," and their colors are silver and black. By the end of the 1990 season the Raiders had won 269 league games, tied 11, and lost 130, for a winning average of .656. In world championship Super Bowl games, the Raiders lost to Green Bay in January 1968, but defeated Minnesota in 1977, Philadelphia in 1981, and Washington in 1984. Among the star players of recent years have been Howie Long, Greg Townsend, Don Mosebar, Steve Smith, and Jim Brown. In 1995 owner Davis made a deal to move his team back to Oakland, the first NFL team to return to the city it had deserted.

LOS ANGELES RAILWAY COMPANY (LARy), companion system to the Pacific Electric (PE) network. This narrow-gauge city streetcar line, formed in the 1890s by Moses H. Sherman and Eli P. Clark, handled 90 percent of the rail passengers, far more than the better-known wide-gauge PE. Henry Huntington gained complete control of both lines in 1898.

LOS ANGELES RAMS, professional team of the National Football League (NFL). Owner Dan Reeves moved the franchise from Cleveland to the Los Angeles Coliseum in 1946, where his team played until 1979. (Upon Reeves's death in 1971 ownership passed first to Carol Rosenbloom and then to Rosenbloom's wife, Georgia Frontiere.) Some of the star players of that era were Elroy Hirsch, Roman Gabriel, Deacon Jones, and Roosevelt Greer. The Rams subsequently moved to Anaheim Stadium in Orange County but retained their old name.

LOS ANGELES RIVER, 58-mile stream that is today mainly a cement-lined flood channel. It has undergone amazing changes during its lifetime.

For millennia—since the end of the Ice Age—the Los Angeles Basin was essentially an extensive wetland, interspersed with islands of forested land and dense shrubbery. A river flowed through this expanse; its banks, along which the Indians lived, were lush and green. The waters originated in the San Gabriel and Santa Monica Mountains and converged near what is today Elysian Park, spilling out from there onto the floodplain. Rather than flowing all the way to the ocean, the river sank into the soil, creating the numerous lakes, ponds, and marshes of the vast wetland. This was the panorama described by the first European expedition to the region, that of the Spaniard Gaspar de Portolá, which camped, on 2 August 1769, on the bank of the river, calling it Río Porciúncula.

When, periodically, the water gathered enough volume, it flowed westward into Ballona Creek and emptied into Santa Monica Bay at what is now Marina del Rey (formerly Playa del Rey Inlet). All that changed when, in 1825, a deluge of biblical proportions in Big Tujunga Canyon in the San Gabriel Mountains flooded the plains. The immense downpour forced the river's course into a southerly channel, causing the water to discharge into San Pedro Bay at what is today Wilmington. Mustard plants indigenous to Big Tujunga Canyon washed down with the water and sprouted over the entire Los Angeles Basin.

In 1829 the American fur traders Kit Carson and Ewing Young described the Los Angeles area as "truly a paradise on earth." Early in the 20th century city engineer William Mulholland still described the Los Angeles River as "a beautiful, limpid little stream with willows on its banks." Nevertheless, after 1825, when the river shifted course permanently to empty directly into the Pacific, much

Los Angeles River, looking north from 1st Street Bridge. Photo by Michael Krakowiak/Marni Pitt.

of the lush, green basin went dry. Only a few isolated wetlands remained, at Venice, Bixby Slough, and Bolsa Chica. The plant life became sparser, and some of the area took on a desertlike appearance.

Periodic flooding continued, posing an ongoing danger to human settlement. Major flooding of the Los Angeles River occurred in 1861–1862, 1884, and 1914, when the water flowing into the Pacific equaled the normal flow of the Colorado River. In 1917 voters passed a bond issue and the county formed a flood control district. A deluge in the winter of 1933–1934 led to construction, beginning in 1938, that would set the river's channel in concrete. Today 40 percent of the river is dammed; the Sepulveda Flood Control Dam is the main barrier to the river's flow. Only 17 percent of the streambed remains lined with vegetation; the rest is imbedded in cement. The engineering stemmed further flood damage, but it also prevented the flow of sediment necessary for beaches—and it created a massive eyesore.

Environmentalists have proposed rehabilitating the Los Angeles River. They would blast the cement and restore parts of the riverbed, plant vegetation on the banks, and use the adjacent areas for strolling, biking, and horseback riding. Part of the stream could be used for rafting. Some citizens have already created a riverine garden and nature trail near Cedros Avenue in Sherman Oaks. Others mention the Sepulveda Flood Control Basin in the San Fernando Valley as viable for rehabilitation. In 1994 the Downtown Strategic Plan Advisory Committee, established by Mayor Tom Bradley, suggested rehabilitating the east bank of the waterway from N. Main Street to the Golden State Freeway, to enhance the area's aesthetic quality. Another proposal, to adapt the cement riverbed to carry auto traffic during the dry season, had no real practicality.

The Los Angeles River is one of four rivers in the Los Angeles Basin, along with the San Gabriel, Santa Ana, and Rio Hondo. (The Santa Clara River is outside the basin, but in the county.) The headwaters of the Los Angeles River are Chatsworth Creek and Calabasas Creek, which flow together in Canoga Park. On its path to the ocean the stream is fed by the Tujunga Wash in Studio City and the Arroyo Seco. The river's mouth is at Ocean Boulevard and Harbor Scenic Drive in Long Beach.

LOS ANGELES SENTINEL, largest African American newspaper in Los Angeles, and the second largest in the United States (of 128), with a paid circulation that once reached 56,000 and in 1987 stood at 25,000. It was founded and published by Leon Washington in the 1930s. Although originally intended as an advertising throwaway, the *Sentinel* battled Jim Crow in the job market with the masthead slogan "Don't spend where you can't work." For over three decades it has featured work by the award-winning editorial cartoonist Clint C. Wilson Jr.

LOS ANGELES SONGS. A song about the city was first composed especially for La Fiesta de Los Angeles in April 1894. While a band played, a chorus sang, "People from every zone / Merged here in softest tones / Of God's great world. / Welcome to small and great / Into this golden state, / Into this city gay, welcome today." More contemporary tunes, including "Pico and Sepulveda" and "Make the San Fernando Valley My Home," acquired some popularity during the postwar population boom but were soon forgotten.

Chicago, New York, and San Francisco have acquired official anthems, or at least popular favorites used on ceremonial occasions, but Los Angeles, the capital of the record industry, remains unsung. Local disk jockeys and city hall officials have scoured the local talent in search of a worthy melody. "Angeltown," a city council favorite in 1959, never took hold. In a 1974 contest the Municipal Arts Council screened 729 entries (with lyrics covering such topics as tar pits, smog, and freeways) but failed to find a winner.

During the 1981 celebration of the city's bicentennial the Cultural Affairs Department received more than 1,000 song entries and invited 21 finalists to perform their creations at a special concert at John Anson Ford Theater. These were then winnowed down to 10 top entries, but again no winner was declared. One of the rejected tunes had alternative titles: "L.A.'s the Place," or, "Number One for the Human Race." Randy Newman's popular "I Love L.A." was used in the torch relay at the 1984 Olympics, but the lyrics were hardly appropriate for an official song: "And the people are so friendly when you meet them on the street. / Whether they'll rob, kill, or befriend you is hard to tell, / Ain't that swell." The *Los Angeles Times* called the song a "wicked ode to municipal cynicism and hedonism." The search goes on.

The pop music depiction of Los Angeles is still personified by the Beach Boys, who sang sweetly of fun, hot-rodding, and surfing at Malibu. More recently, pop bands have been less optimistic. The Go-Go's, for example, sing, "We're all dreamers— we're all whores. / Discarded stars / Like worn- out cars / Litter the streets of this town."

The Midniters recorded a number called "Whit- tier Boulevard," and Jan and Dean sang a tune of their own composition that celebrated the "Little Old Lady from Pasadena" ("She's the terror of Col- orado Boulevard . . . "). "Stand and Be Proud," written by former teen idol David Cassidy and his wife, Sue Shifrin, became the anthem of Rebuild L.A., an organization whose mission was to find resources to upgrade the areas hardest hit by the riot of 1992.

In the end, fame and fortune still await the song- smith who does for Los Angeles what "Chicago," "I Left My Heart in San Francisco," and "New York, New York" did for those cities.

LOS ANGELES STAR, first Los Angeles newspa- per, founded 17 May 1851. It was printed in both English and Spanish until 1855, with the two Span- ish pages titled "La Estrella de Los Angeles." In 1855 the Spanish section was transferred to another pa- per, *El Clamor Público,* and the *Star* appeared in English only. The owners, partisan pro-southern Democrats, supported slavery and condemned Lincoln as a "fourth-rate lawyer" and corrupt and worthless politician. The editor, after issuing pun- gent editorials on these and similar themes, was im- prisoned for a time during the Civil War. The pa- per ceased publication in 1879.

LOS ANGELES SUBURBAN HOMES COM- PANY, land syndicate. The company was involved in the biggest Southern California real estate deal: the purchase and subdivision of most of the San Fernando Valley, from Burbank to Tarzana, in the early 1900s. Suburban Homes had a partner in the San Fernando Mission Land Company, formed be- fore Suburban Homes and headed by Harrison Gray Otis and his son-in-law, Harry Chandler. The major partners in Suburban Homes were Otis, Chandler, and a member of the water board, Moses H. Sherman. Thirty-seven other investors were in- volved, most notably financier L. C. Brand, de- veloper H. J. Whitley, Roy Milner, and Otto Brant of Title Insurance and Trust. Together they also purchased another set of properties, the Lanker- shim–Van Nuys holdings, thereby acquiring Isaac Van Nuys as yet another partner. In 1911 the com- bined syndicate subdivided the towns of Van Nuys,

Lankershim (North Hollywood), Marion (Reseda), and Owensmouth (Canoga Park).

A public controversy involving the syndicate arose in 1906 and 1907, when Otis and Chandler were ac- cused of using the *Times* to press for the Owens River water project (begun 1908) in order to gain a per- sonal advantage for their land holdings. The suspi- cion was that they had bought land cheaply in an- ticipation of selling it dearly once Owens River water was delivered. Otis, protesting his innocence, stated that he had resigned from the San Fernando Mis- sion Land Company before the start of the Owens project. In any case, upon the arrival of water Sub- urban Homes realized a profit of $100 million, and San Fernando Mission Land Company earned $5 to $7.5 million. Otis's share became the basis for the Times-Mirror Company fortune.

LOS ANGELES THEATER CENTER (LATC), downtown theater complex from 1985 to 1991 sup- ported by the Community Redevelopment Agency (CRA). The theater originated in Hollywood in 1975 as an offshoot of the Los Angeles Actors' Thea- ter. In 1985 it moved to a new home in a remod- eled bank building on Spring Street and formed

---

Last night there was a great fandango or dance among the Spanyards. They kept it up till nearly day light from the noise.

—Harrison Rogers, fur trapper, 1826

Latino, African American, and Asian American workshop labs. Under artistic director William Bushnell, LATC achieved notable artistic successes with avant-garde and multicultural productions. CRA's failure to create a viable downtown resi- dential-and-commercial neighborhood, however, meant that LATC audiences had to travel to a deeply depressed area. When a $4 million CRA subsidy ran out, the theater was forced to drop its curtain. Today a variety of independent companies, many of them multicultural, rent the theater's fa- cilities for independent productions.

LOS ANGELES TIMES, nation's third largest daily newspaper, with daily and Sunday circulations of 1 million and 1.2 million, respectively. Founded in

Second building of the *Los Angeles Times*, ca. 1900, northeast corner of 1st Street and Broadway. Courtesy Los Angeles Times History Center.

Current headquarters (and fourth building) of the *Los Angeles Times*, corner of 1st and Spring Streets. Courtesy Los Angeles Times History Center.

1881, the small paper was bought and developed by ultraconservative Harrison Gray Otis, a towering figure in Los Angeles history. His son-in-law, Harry Chandler, took the paper over upon his death. Both men were noted for their powerful editorial biases. The newspaper, which is still controlled by the Chandler family, is part of the Times-Mirror Company media conglomerate.

The *Times*'s journalistic reputation was slow to evolve. As late as 1937 the Washington, D.C., press corps voted it the "least fair and reliable" newspaper in the country. A major change occurred in 1960 when Harry Chandler's son, Otis Chandler, took over as publisher. He opened the opinion page to diverse points of view, hired quality professionals, and established new overseas bureaus.

By 1994 the *Times* and its journalists had received scores of awards, including 19 Pulitzer Prizes, journalism's highest honor. Individual Pulitzers have gone to Martin Bernheimer (1982), Howard Rosenberg (1985), Richard Eder (1987), and David Shaw (1991), for criticism; to sports columnist Jim Murray (1990), for commentary; to correspondents William Touhy (1969) and Michael Parks (1987), for international reporting; to Gaylord Shaw (1978), for national reporting; to Philip P. Kerby (1976), for editorial writing; to Bruce Russell (1946) and Paul Conrad (1971, 1984), for editorial cartooning; and to John L. Gaunt Jr. (1955), for news photography.

The paper has also earned several collective Pulitzers. Its earliest, a prize for public service

awarded in 1942, recognized the *Times*'s reaffirmation of the principle of freedom of the press. It has won three awards for local reporting of spot news: in 1966 for coverage of the 1965 Watts riot; in 1993 for coverage of the 1992 riots; and in 1995 for coverage of the 1994 Northridge earthquake. It has also received several Pulitzer Gold Medals: for an investigation into narcotics smuggling across the Mexican border (1960); for a study of malfeasance in public office in Los Angeles (1969); and, in the public service subcategory, for an in-depth series on the Latino community (1984).

In recent decades, *Los Angeles Times* circulation has trailed that of only the *Wall Street Journal* and *New York Daily News*. The paper's regional editions and sections attract a wide audience. In 1992 both the San Fernando Valley edition, with some 257,000 daily readers, and the Orange County edition, with 225,000, appeared seven days a week. South Bay and Ventura editions appeared less often, as did Glendale, Westside, Southeast, Long Beach, and San Gabriel Valley sections.

LOS ANGELES TRIBUNE, title used by several different newspapers over the years. The most important was published by Edwin T. Earl from 1911 to 1919. It had a strong Progressive editorial slant and a circulation of 54,000, or about 10 percent of the city's population. The same name was used for an African American newspaper in the 1940s and 1950s.

LOS ANGELES UNIFIED SCHOOL DISTRICT (LAUSD), nation's second largest school district, formed in 1855 when Schoolhouse No. 1

opened at 2nd and Spring Streets. At the time, the city's population numbered 3,000.

Today the 708-square-mile service area of LAUSD encompasses a population of 4 million. It serves cities other than Los Angeles—Cudahy, Gardena, Huntington Park, Lomita, Maywood, San Fernando, Vernon, West Hollywood, and 19 others—as well as unincorporated county areas. In

---

You can drink in a drive-in saloon, eat in a cafe shaped like a toad, and when you die, they will bury you in a "Happy Cemetery."

—Willard Huntington Wright
[S. S. Van Dine], writer, 1913

1995 the school district employed some 33,127 certificated personnel and 22,267 nonteaching employees. It had 418 elementary schools, 71 middle schools, 50 senior highs, and 5 multilevel schools. In addition to general-curriculum offerings, the district ran 20 magnet schools and 99 additional schools, such as continuation, adult education, and special education, for a total of 663 schools.

In the fall of 1995, the total K–12 enrollment was 649,054 students. Spanish-surnamed students made up 67.2 percent of the total; black (not Hispanic), 14.3 percent; white (not Hispanic), 11.3 percent; Asian, 4.6 percent; Pacific Islander, 0.4 percent; American Indian/Alaskan Native, 0.3 percent; and Filipino, 1.9 percent.

The LAUSD is governed by the Los Angeles Board of Education, a state-authorized body consisting of seven members elected by geographic district for four-year staggered terms. It is managed through eight regional offices, each with its own assistant superintendent. The annual budget for 1995–1996 was $4.44 billion.

Demands for major structural reforms in LAUSD arose in the 1960s and 1970s, when the district entered into an era of seemingly perpetual crisis. In 1989 the demands resulted in a power-sharing arrangement whereby teachers, parents, and staff began participating in school-based policy-making. In an effort to utilize physical resources more efficiently, in 1991 LAUSD placed all of its schools on year-round operation, though it soon scaled back the experiment. In 1993 critics of

LAUSD launched a well-financed campaign to break the district into smaller districts. Also in 1993 Californians voted on a controversial measure authorizing a school "voucher system," which opponents feared would destroy the public school system. The measure was defeated both in Los Angeles and statewide.

LOS ANGELES URBAN LEAGUE, national membership organization seeking improved social and economic opportunities for African Americans and other minorities. The local branch grew out of an organization formed in 1921 by Katherine Barr and other Angelenos who had attended Booker T. Washington's Tuskegee Institute in Alabama. After carefully documenting specific racial inequities in job hiring, health services, and housing in Los Angeles, they developed reform proposals. To further their work they voted to join the national Urban League.

The group's greatest challenge came during the Great Depression when over 50 percent of black Angelenos were on public relief. In World War II the league fostered government fair employment programs, helped the city cope with the zoot suit riots of 1943, and assisted in the formation of the City Human Relations Commission. Afterward it pressed the cause of integration in housing and schools, as well as in police and fire departments and labor unions.

The Los Angeles Urban League, one of more than 100 affiliates, is most active in South Central Los Angeles, Pasadena, and Pomona. Its longtime director has been John Mack, a southern-born civil rights activist since the 1950s. The league's constituency has changed in recent decades, from around 90 percent black in 1970 to 40 percent Latino by the late 1990s. Working in partnership with business, government, and voluntary associations, it serves 100,000 poor and disadvantaged people annually, helping them advance in semiskilled and skilled crafts and in clerical and related fields, especially in the high-tech and service industries.

LOS ANGELES ZOO, Griffith Park animal preserve. It derived from Selig Zoo, a private zoo located in 1885 near Lincoln Park and reconstituted as a city facility in 1912. The new zoo consisted of 15 animals caged in a shady canyon on the eastern face of the Griffith Park hills. Major additions in 1939 included nine cageless compounds surrounded by moats for lions and bears, and new cages for monkeys. These animals were sometimes employed in movies. By the 1950s the collection of 1,000 animals, birds, and reptiles had outgrown the crowded 11-acre site. After a major design study the zoo was rebuilt in a new 114-acre park location—80 acres for zoo and support facilities, 34 acres for parking—and opened on 28 November 1966. The new layout grouped the animals according to the five continents, with geographically appropriate landscaping.

The Los Angeles Zoo now houses 1,200 animals of 400 species. It is involved in programs to save endangered species such as the California condor, chimpanzee, and Indian rhinoceros. Although owned and operated by the city of Los Angeles and managed by the Los Angeles City Recreation and Parks Department, it receives major funding from the Greater Los Angeles Zoo Association, a non-profit membership organization, which also manages visitor services. The zoo's director, Manuel A. Mollindeo, was appointed in 1995.

LOS ENCINOS STATE PARK, 5-acre preserve in the southern San Fernando Valley established through the efforts of Encino resident Maria Steward. The land lay at the center of a 4,400-acre Mexican rancho granted to Don Vicente de la Osa in 1845. An Indian village had existed on the site for hundreds of years before that. Historic structures, including a nine-room adobe, are preserved in the style of the early American era, 1849–1870. In the 1860s and 1870s the rancho house was used as a stagecoach station. A limestone cookhouse, built in 1872, is on the National Register of Historic Places. Artifacts belonging to the "lost village of Encino," a Gabrieleño (Tongva) community mentioned by a member of the Portolá expedition of 1769, are on display at the park as well.

LOS FELIZ DISTRICT, residential area south of Griffith Park. It was named for a land grant cultivated by José Feliz, a soldier and a cofounder of the Los Angeles *pueblo,* who claimed the entire area, including Griffith Park, early in the 19th century. (Indians once inhabited the Ferndell area, now part of the park.) The 6,600 acres that Feliz received were retained by his family until 1863. Horace Bell fabricated the myth of the "Feliz curse," asserting that when Antonio Coronel "robbed" the Feliz family of their land, the disinherited niece, Petranilla Feliz, cursed the land, "causing" damaging fires and floods in the area. In 1884 Griffith J. Griffith assumed ownership of the land. By the 1920s the

neighborhood featured attractive hillside homes, many of them in the Italianate style. Such luminaries as Cecil B. De Mille, W. C. Fields, and Deanna Durbin lived above Franklin Avenue. So many physicians moved to Los Feliz that it was nicknamed "Pill Hill." The neighborhood of single-family homes has retained its stability since the 1920s. With the average home price hovering around $500,000, the lifestyle suggests "old money." In 1990 the Los Feliz district's population was 41,312.

LOS NIETOS, area of Santa Fe Springs. It derives its name from Manuel Nieto, a Spaniard who was granted several land parcels—Los Alamitos, Los Cerritos, Santa Gertrudis, Los Coyotes, and Las Bolsas—in November 1784. The present-day community's name originated in 1867 with the establishment of a post office, and in 1891 was extended to a Santa Fe Railroad station. The 1980 census counted 24,164 people living in Los Nietos and nearby West Whittier.

LOVELL HOUSE, residence in the Griffith Park district designed in 1929, in the International style, by Richard Neutra. Considered one of the great monuments of modern architecture, it features a light-weight steel frame, prefabricated panels, and suspended balconies that seem to embody the vision of the Machine Age. The Lovell House helped establish Neutra's reputation as an architect, but also started a long-standing feud with his associate, Rudolph M. Schindler, who had competed for the contract.

LOWE, THADDEUS S[OBIESK] C[OULIN-COURT] (1832–1913), self-trained chemist, inventor, and entrepreneur. While working for the Union army during the Civil War he originated the nation's first air corps, consisting of five gas balloons and 250 men who performed surveillance work. Lowe later became wealthy by inventing refrigeration equipment for the railroad industry. He left New Hampshire in the 1880s to settle in Pasadena for his health, building a palatial home on Orange Grove Boulevard. He became a major figure in the gas industry in Los Angeles. He also built a rail line up to Mt. Lowe—named in his honor—that presented a breathtaking view of the basin below.

LOYOLA-MARYMOUNT UNIVERSITY, Catholic coeducational institution formed through the merger of Loyola University and Marymount

College in 1973. Loyola arose in 1911 as an outgrowth of St. Vincent's College, which, founded in 1865, was the first college in Southern California. Loyola moved from downtown to the bluffs of Westchester in 1928. Loyola originated in the Jesuit tradition, while Marymount, near downtown Los Angeles, was formed by the Religious of the Sacred Heart of Mary. The beautifully appointed Westchester campus consists of 128 acres overlooking Marina del Rey. It focuses on undergraduate instruction, but offers 19 master's degrees as well and grants the J.D. degree in the Loyola Law School. In 1995 Loyola had 319 full-time faculty and 293 part-timers. Undergraduate enrollment was 4,100, while graduate students numbered 966.

LUCKMAN, CHARLES (1909–), architect. Although Luckman originally trained as an architect, the depression diverted his career into advertising and corporate management. His work caught the attention of Pres. Harry Truman, who called on him to direct the patriotic "Freedom Train" project. Luckman later returned to architecture, designing Houston's Manned Spacecraft Center and New York's new Madison Square Garden. Now retired, he was a partner in the Los Angeles firm of Pereira and Luckman, and a founder of the Luckman Partnership. The latter firm designed the Broadway

Plaza (1972–1973) and the soaring First Interstate Bank Tower (1973). In 1985 his alma mater, the University of Illinois, granted him a special lifetime achievement award.

LUGO FAMILY, wealthiest and most influential family in Southern California during the 1850s. The patriarch, Don Antonio María Lugo, a landowner and cattle rancher, was a familiar figure on the streets of Los Angeles. Sitting astride his horse on a silver-decorated saddle, a sword dangling at his side, Lugo was the quintessential Californio. Three of his sons—José María, José del Carmen, and Vicente Lugo (who built the first two-story home on the Plaza)—received a sprawling land grant in San Bernardino and Yucaipa Valleys in 1842. In May 1849, before he moved to San Bernardino, José del Carmen Lugo became the first *alcalde* and *presidente* of Los Angeles to serve under American rule.

Two sons of José María Lugo—Francisco "Chico" and Francisco "Menito"—were accused of murdering two men in 1851 and prosecuted in Los Angeles in a famous trial. The celebrated case created a high state of racial tension in the *pueblo*. The Lugos were defended by a brilliant young Maryland attorney, Joseph Lancaster Brent, who succeeded in preventing a lynching and ensuring a fair

Lugo family at their adobe, in present-day Bell Gardens. Courtesy Robert Weinstein Collection.

trial. In fact, Brent got the charges dismissed for lack of evidence and is said to have earned the then enormous fee of $20,000.

LUMMIS, CHARLES FLETCHER (1859–1928), celebrated literary and cultural figure. Lummis *walked* all the way to Los Angeles from Cincinnati in 1884, wiring breezy reports ahead to the *Los Angeles Times* while en route. He then served as the paper's city editor and edited *Land of Sunshine* magazine. Lummis established the California Landmarks Club in 1895 to facilitate the preservation of historic buildings, and in 1907 he cofounded the Southwest Museum, an institution devoted to the study of native cultures of the southwestern United States, which opened in 1914. He served as city librarian from 1905 to 1911. His olive-green corduroy jacket and pants and gray sombrero became a personal trademark. With his own hands, assisted by Indian labor, "Don Carlos" built a two-story stone house on the Arroyo Seco beginning in 1898, hauling boulders out of the riverbed and shaping log telephone poles into beams. The house was completed in 1903. Lummis called his home El Alisal ("The Sycamore"). For many years it was a rendezvous for artists, writers, and scientists. El Alisal, also called the Lummis Adobe, is now part of a city park, and serves as headquarters for the Historical Society of Southern California.

LUMMIS ADOBE. *See* El Alisal

LUTHERANS of the region belong mostly to the Southern California (West) Synod of the Evangelical Lutheran Church in America, though some congregations are part of the smaller Missouri and Wisconsin synods. The first Lutheran churches in Southern California were established in 1887–1888, during the Boom of the Eighties. In 1990 the local synod had 160 congregations and some 160,000 members (out of 8 million nationwide). The church has recently realized strong gains regionally among African Americans, Latinos, and Asian Americans. The church, which employs a paid staff and relies on the help of many volunteers, supports homes for the aged, ministries to the poor, and other social services. California Lutheran University in Thousand Oaks enrolls about 3,000 students.

LYNWOOD, independent city 9 miles south of downtown Los Angeles. Its name derives from that of the wife of a local dairy owner, Lynn Wood Sessions. When incorporated in 1921 the town adopted the nickname "All-American City." The attractive suburb, with its artesian well system, tree-lined residential streets, and independent public school system, was settled by the families of many World War II veterans. In the 1960s its commercial base was undermined by the intrusion of the Century Freeway through its center. Lynwood had a population of 61,945 in 1990—a booming increase of 27.6 percent over 1980.

MacARTHUR PARK, public space at Wilshire Boulevard and Alvarado Street, originally called Westlake Park. In the 1860s the area was an unsightly ravine filled with curious alkali cones. Because the city was unable to auction off the 32 acres of land at the terminus of two streetcar lines, even at a price as low as 25 cents an acre, Mayor William Workman decided to develop a lake and a park instead. Boating and afternoon concerts, introduced in 1896, drew families looking for Sunday recreation and sparked nearby real estate developments on what was then the outskirts of town. In the 1930s Wilshire Boulevard cut Westlake Park in two. The park was renamed for World War II hero Gen. Douglas MacArthur in the early 1950s, as part of William Randolph Hearst's abortive campaign to see the general elected president in 1952.

MacArthur Park (formerly Westlake Park), ca. 1908. Pitt Collection.

At ten in the morning the earth trembled. The shock was repeated with violence at one in the afternoon, and one hour afterwards we experienced another. The soldiers went out this afternoon to hunt, and brought an antelope. . . . It was not bad.

—Father Juan Crespi,
Franciscan missionary
and Portolá expedition diarist, 1769

The park now marks the center of the Central American community of Los Angeles, a neighborhood plagued by overcrowding, crime, homelessness, and drugs. In the 1970s the neighboring Otis College of Art and Design spearheaded a discussion of extensive renovation. More recently the prospects for the park's future have been tied to the completion of a Metro Red Line station on the site. The MTA Rapid Transit District envisions the development of restaurants, shops, and entertainment facilities that local residents will patronize. In the 1980s the lake was

MacArthur Park, 1995. Photo by
Michael Krakowiak/Marni Pitt.

drained, the lake bed repaired, and the park
newly landscaped.

**MacDOUGALL, FREDERICK A. (1814–
1878),** physician and mayor of Los Angeles from
1876 to 1878. The son-in-law of Julian Isaac
Williams, a wealthy landowner, MacDougall was
a charter member of the exclusive Los Angeles Social Club, founded in 1869. When MacDougall was
mayor the city was less than 30 square miles in area
and had a population of 11,000.

MACHINISTS UNION. *See* International Association of Machinists

MACLAY, CHARLES (1821–1890), founder of
the town of San Fernando. In the winter of 1873,
while visiting Gen. Andrés Pico at the former San
Fernando Mission, Maclay became intensely interested in buying the 117,000-acre property from
the de Celis family estate, which was being sold in
a sheriff's sale. Maclay and three backers, George
K. Porter, Benjamin F. Porter, and Thomas G.
McLaren, by bribing an intermediary, obtained an
option to buy the property, which comprised the
entire northern half of the San Fernando Valley and
was being offered for $117,500. The quartet was
short of cash and resolved to seek the backing of
Maclay's friend Leland Stanford, head of the
Southern Pacific Railroad. As their option deadline approached, Maclay sailed by steamer to San
Francisco, obtaining Stanford's support with only
minutes to spare before the deadline. Not only did
Stanford back the syndicate, but he also gave
Maclay information as to the future location of a

rail line from the San Fernando Valley to Los Angeles. After reserving a spot for a rail depot, Maclay
laid out the town of San Fernando and quickly auctioned off more than 12,000 lots.

MAFIA. *See* Organized crime

MAGIC CASTLE, membership club featuring
performances by magicians. It was founded in
1963 by brothers Milt and Bill Larson and is housed
in a Victorian mansion on a hilltop in Hollywood.
Famous magicians such as David Copperfield and
Blackstone have appeared there, and it is also a
showcase for new talent. The landmark club has
over 5,000 members.

MAGIC MOUNTAIN, Time-Warner Entertainment Company theme park, founded in 1979 on
200 acres in Valencia and hosting more than 20
million visitors a year. The park features "The
Colossus," one of the largest wooden roller coasters in the country, and 75 other rides and attractions, some of them based on Warner Brothers film
and cartoon characters such as Batman and Bugs
Bunny. The park's official name is Six Flags Magic
Mountain, after the Six Flags chain founded by An-
gus G. Wyne Jr. in Texas in 1961. Other Six Flags
parks are in Atlanta, St. Louis, Houston, New Jersey, and Chicago.

MAGNIN, EDGAR F[OGEL] (1890–1984),
prominent rabbi and, from 1915 on, Jewish community leader. He was a scion of the California clan
that founded the I. Magnin Department Store
chain in San Francisco. The Reform rabbi led the

B'nai B'rith congregation of the new Wilshire Boulevard Temple, at Hobart and Wilshire Boulevards (constructed 1922–1929), until his death. Better known for civic leadership than theology, Magnin sought to improve relations between Christians and Jews, to battle anti-Semitism, and to create racial harmony. He cultivated a wide range of friends in government, the film industry, the Kiwanis Club, and other religious and fraternal organizations.

MAGUIRE THOMAS PARTNERS, nationwide developers and builders based in Los Angeles for the last two decades. The firm is associated with major construction projects, such as Wells Fargo Center, First Interstate World Center, the Gas Company Tower, and Playa Vista, all in Los Angeles; Plaza Las Fuentes, in Pasadena; and the Colorado Place, in Santa Monica.

MAHONY, ROGER M. (1936–), first California-born Roman Catholic cardinal. A North Hollywood electrician's son, Mahony was trained as a social worker and is bilingual in English and Spanish. He attended seminary in San Fernando and Camarillo in the 1950s, was ordained as a priest in Fresno in 1962, became bishop of Fresno in 1975, and archbishop of Los Angeles in 1985. Called a "social liberal and doctrinal conservative," he was both an outspoken proponent of nuclear disarmament and a vigorous opponent of abortion. Although he supported the United Farm Workers union early on, and served for a time as chair of the state Agricultural Labor Relations Board, he has also, at times, taken antilabor positions.

MALDEF. *See* Mexican American Legal Defense and Educational Fund

MALIBOU LAKE, small community in the Santa Monica Mountains, off Mulholland Highway, 7 miles south of the Ventura Freeway, as well as a small lake created when state engineers built Malibou Dam on Malibu Creek in 1923. (The lake, dam, and community retain an earlier spelling of "Malibou.") At first the area attracted Hollywood celebrities and others seeking a nearby vacation spot; later the community became popular for year-round living.

From time to time droughts cause the lake to dry out. In 1961 the inhabitants of Malibu Lake hired a rainmaker, whose efforts proved unsuccessful. Malibou Lake Mountain Club, a gated community, is set in picturesque chaparral, amid live oaks and eucalyptus trees. Malibou Lake's 250 residents have consistently thwarted developers' efforts to introduce condominiums, tract homes, and shopping facilities. The area is almost completely surrounded by the Santa Monica Mountains National Recreation Area.

MALIBU, independent coastal city 26 miles west of downtown Los Angeles. Incorporated in 1990, it extends for 27 miles from the western boundary of the city of Los Angeles to the Ventura County line. A Chumash village called Humaliwu existed here for perhaps 4,000 years, until it came under the jurisdiction of Santa Barbara Mission in the 1790s. The name Malibu is from the Chumash word *umalibo,* probably meaning "where the surf sounds loud," and first appears in connection with a land grant—Topanga Malibu Sequit—issued in 1805. This 13,316-acre rancho comprised a 25-mile stretch of mountains, canyons, and beaches. It had a series of owners—José Tapia, Leon Prudhomme, Matthew Keller, and, as of 1892, Frederick H. Rindge.

May Rindge, Frederick's widow, spent a fortune preventing the Southern Pacific Railroad from laying tracks, and the state of California from constructing a coastal highway, through the land. Instead she built her own private railway near the coast in 1906. Malibu was then considered one of the most beautiful, and perhaps the most valuable, large real estate holdings in the nation. After 17 years of litigation over the issue of a road, the state finally prevailed and started work on Roosevelt (now Pacific Coast) Highway in 1926.

To pay her taxes, Rindge leased lots west of Malibu Lagoon to movie celebrities, and began selling

Malibu coastline. Photo by Beverly Hammond, courtesy the Malibu Visitors' Bureau.

them in the 1930s. Among the buyers of the beachfront property were Jack Warner, Clara Bow, Dolores Del Rio, Ronald Colman, Barbara Stanwyck, and John Gilbert. The beach area became known as the "Malibu Movie Colony," and today is called simply "The Colony." Other locales sharing the name are Malibu Hills, Malibu Junction, Malibu Lake, and Malibu Riviera. Malibu is also the site of the J. Paul Getty Museum. In November 1993 a major firestorm that originated in Calabasas burned many homes and hundreds of acres in Malibu.

MALIBU CREEK STATE PARK, nation's largest wilderness park situated in an urban setting. The creekside portion of the 8,000-acre Santa Monica Mountain preserve was long occupied by Indians, both Tongva and Chumash. The park area was the site of Talepop, a Chumash village that may have existed from A.D. 1000, and lasted into the early 1800s.

The area was part of Rancho Las Virgenes, granted to Domingo Carrillo and Nemisio Domínguez in 1834. People claimed that the bandit Joaquín Murietta visited a Sepúlveda family adobe in the area in 1853. Over the years the land was used in a variety of ways: the Mexican grantees raised cattle, uprooted Civil War veterans farmed, and Angelenos escaping urban pressures came to camp.

In 1901 a group of prominent Pasadenans formed Craig's Country Club, a private organization for professional men, near the creek. The area was also the location of some ranches and second homes for affluent families. With time, more elaborate and permanent homes were built in the oak-dotted hills by citizens such as attorneys John Mott and William Garland, razor baron King C. Gillette, and movie actor Ronald Reagan. Twentieth Century–Fox used the Malibu Creek area as a location for its award-winning film *How Green Was My Valley* (1941), and subsequently purchased some of the land. In 1973 Gov. Ronald Reagan declared the site a state park and had the state purchase land from the studio. Malibu Creek State Park is now part of the Santa Monica Mountains National Recreation Area.

MALLS, SHOPPING, retail commercial centers pioneered in Southern California. They are closely tied to a dependence on the automobile and the development of the suburbs, two typically Southern Californian phenomena.

Although Hollywood's Crossroads of the World (1936) was originally intended as a shopping mall, it was on a much smaller scale than the large shopping centers of today. The first "regional mall" was the Crenshaw Shopping Center, which opened in 1947 at Crenshaw Boulevard and Santa Barbara Avenue (now Martin Luther King Jr. Boulevard). It was later remodeled, expanded to 90 stores, and renamed Baldwin Hills Crenshaw Plaza. Other regional malls were built in the 1960s and 1970s. Among them are Topanga Plaza in Canoga Park, the Sherman Oaks Galleria, the Glendale Galleria, and the Fox Hills Mall in Culver City. The West-

West Covina Fashion Plaza. ©1995 Douglas McCulloh Geographics, courtesy West Covina Redevelopment Agency.

side Pavilion, near Westwood, was built in 1985, its colorful façade influenced by designs used during the 1984 Olympics; it expanded to 170 stores in 1991.

In contrast with the suburbs, downtown Los Angeles has few malls. ARCO Plaza at 5th and Flower Streets, and the Broadway Plaza at 7th and Flower Streets, are the largest.

A typical regional mall is anchored by two or three major department stores and has many smaller stores and movie theaters. It provides a host of fast-food eating places and devotes a substantial area to parking. It advertises to attract targeted customers with known levels of disposable income. Malls sometimes have a large cultural impact, serving, for example, as a meeting place for teenagers as well as older people.

The *Thomas Brothers Guide* for 1991 listed 84 shopping centers in Los Angeles County. Among them are the huge regional malls, as well as more modestly sized venues. In addition, the region has thousands of nameless mini-malls.

MANHATTAN BEACH, independent South Bay city 22 miles southwest of downtown Los Angeles. Its boundaries take in parts of Rancho Sausal Redondo, issued to Antonio Ygnacio Avila in 1822, and Rancho Aguaje de la Centinela. The Santa Fe rail station established in the 1880s where the town eventually grew was known first as Potencia and

---

The business section wore its old Spanish facades like icing on a stale cake.   —Ross Macdonald, mystery writer

---

then as Shore Acres. The town's founder, Stewart Merrill, named the locale after New York's Manhattan Island, in 1902. A fishing pier—built and rebuilt three times in the face of buffeting waves and corrosive salt air—has marked the spot ever since. When the Pacific Electric Red Car line reached Manhattan Beach a year later, the town became a favorite place for swimming and fishing (halibut, yellowtail, and barracuda), from both piers and boats. Its most avid promoter, George Peck Jr., pressed for incorporation in 1912, when the population of the 4-square-mile city stood at 600. Manhattan Beach grew most rapidly in the 1920s, and again in the 1950s. The population has hovered around 32,000 in recent decades.

MANN, THOMAS (1875–1955), distinguished German novelist and essayist. Winner of the Nobel Prize for Literature in 1929, and considered by some to be the greatest novelist of the 20th century, Mann lived in Pacific Palisades from 1942 to 1952. He and his daughter, Erika (an actress and author in her own right, and wife of poet W. H. Auden), came to the United States in 1938 as refugees from Nazism, and he took American citizenship in 1944. Mann protested the internment of "enemy" aliens—i.e., Japanese and Japanese Americans—in 1942. While a Los Angeles resident he wrote *Doctor Faustus* (1947) and *The Holy Sinner* (1951). In 1953 he moved to Switzerland, having openly stated his aversion to investigating committees during the McCarthy period.

MANNING, TIMOTHY (1909–1989), Irishborn bishop. He succeeded Cardinal James F. McIntyre as head of the Los Angeles Roman Catholic archdiocese in 1970, where he remained until retirement in 1985. He moved his quarters from the Wilshire district to downtown's St. Vibiana Cathedral, where he could better address the problems of immigrants and Latinos. In the 1970s and 1980s, Manning attempted to stem the loss of Latino Catholics to evangelical sects such as Assemblies of God.

MANN'S CHINESE THEATRE. *See* Chinese Theatre

MANSON, CHARLES (1937–), mass murderer. Manson's hypnotic hold on drug- and sex-ridden "family" followers led to the gruesome murders of 26-year-old Sharon Tate, film actress and wife of director Roman Polanski, and four guests in her Benedict Canyon home on the night of 8 August 1969. The Manson group also killed a couple in Silver Lake two nights later. There they wrote the words "Healter [*sic*] Skelter," from a Beatles song, in blood on a refrigerator. After a trial lasting almost 10 months, Manson and six others were convicted of first-degree murder. They were sentenced to die, but began serving life sentences when the death penalty was overturned in 1972. Their petitions for parole have been repeatedly denied.

MARCHESSAULT, DAMIEN (1821–1868), mining speculator and mayor of Los Angeles from 1859 to 1860, and again from 1861 to 1865. In 1858 the French pioneer formed a mining company with compatriot Victor Beaudry. A proposal to split California into two states received his active support. While out of office he and another Frenchman, Louis Sansevain, laid wooden water pipes for the city from Macy Street to 1st Street. The hollowed-out pine logs from the San Bernardino Mountains were in a constant state of disrepair. Despondent because of ongoing public controversy over the faulty pipes, Marchessault committed suicide in the city council chamber in 1868.

MARINA DEL REY, unincorporated county-owned development on Santa Monica Bay. Designed in 1958 around the nation's largest artificial small-craft harbor, it opened in 1962. The marina harbor serves 6,000 boats. Leases for the marina's condominiums, apartments, shops, commercial structures, and restaurants generate as much as $24 million in annual revenue for the county. In 1989 a group of Saudi Arabian investors acquired 49.9 percent ownership of Marina del Rey's three hotels. By 1991 the development had 10,642 residents —only 4 percent of whom were children—living in 5,900 housing units, most of them upscale apartments overlooking blue waters and white sails. Plans developed that year involved adding 700 more hotel rooms and 200,000 additional square feet of office space. Residents complain of insufficient parking spaces, pedestrian walkways, and bike trails and an overabundance of high-rise development.

MARINELAND OF THE PACIFIC, theme park and tourist attraction located at Long Point, on the Palos Verdes Peninsula, from 1954 to 1987. Its giant tanks and pools displayed whales, fish, and other aquatic animals. The popular attraction also conducted a marine animal care program. A public outcry failed to halt the closure of Marineland.

MARK TAPER FORUM, Los Angeles County Music Center theater operated by the Center Theatre Group/Mark Taper Forum. It was established as an outgrowth of UCLA's Theater Group, founded by John Houseman. Since its 1967 opening with a memorable presentation of John Whiting's *The Devils,* it has been under the artistic direction of Gordon Davidson. The Taper, whose

---

Hollywood is wonderful. Anyone who doesn't like it is either crazy or sober.   —Raymond Chandler

---

mission is to develop new plays and serve a broad audience, has received virtually every theatrical award, including 18 Tonys, one of which, in 1977, was a special award for theatrical excellence. The 760-seat house, named after the philanthropist who funded the building, boasts a thrust stage. Many of its plays have gone on to successful award-winning runs on Broadway, including *The Shadow Box* (1977), *Children of a Lesser God* (1980), and *Angels in America* (1993–1994). Its regular season, usually consisting of six plays, has some 24,000 subscribers. Among its other activities are the Taper Lab and the Taper Lab New Work Festival, P.L.A.Y. (Performing for Los Angeles Youth), and the Mentor Playwrights and Young Audiences Programs.

Marineland of the Pacific, 1974. Photo by Leonard Pitt.

MARTIN, ALBERT C., AND ASSOCIATES (ACMA), leading architectural and engineering firm, founded by Albert C. Martin Sr. in 1906, and headed since 1945 by his sons, Albert C. Martin Jr. and J. Edward Martin. The elder Martin designed Grauman's Million Dollar Theater (1919) and, along with John Parkinson and John Austin, Los Angeles City Hall (1928). Under the leadership of Martin's sons and grandsons, the firm created the Los Angeles Department of Water and Power Building (1963–1964), the Sears Complex in Alhambra (1971), the 51-story ARCO Plaza Towers (1972), St. Basil's Roman Catholic Church (1974), the downtown Wells Fargo Building (1979), Union Bank Square (1980), Security Pacific Bank World Headquarters (1980), and the Sherman Oaks Galleria (1980).

MARTIN, GLENN L. (1886–1955), airplane designer who arrived in Santa Ana in 1905. He first worked in the auto business, and in 1909 established an airplane factory in an abandoned church. Martin raised capital by working as a stunt pilot for the movies. His planes were used for sport flying and exhibitions, and were the first ones hired for government mail delivery. For a time his associate was Donald Douglas. Martin later moved his factory to Baltimore.

MARTIN LUTHER KING JR./ DREW MEDICAL CENTER, Los Angeles County hospital. It sprang from the ashes of the Watts riot of 1965 to meet the critical medical needs of South Central Los Angeles. The ground breaking ceremony was held in April 1968, and by the time the hospital was dedicated in February 1972 the name had been changed to honor the slain civil rights leader. The hospital's Drew Medical School, an affiliate of the UCLA School of Medicine, named for pioneer African American physician Charles R. Drew, opened in 1970.

MAR VISTA, district near Santa Monica, originally called Ocean Park Heights and then Barnes. The current name, applied in 1904, is Spanish for "view of the sea." A post office bearing that name was established in 1925.

MASCAREL, JOSÉ (1816–1899), mayor of Los Angeles from 1865 to 1866. A French sea captain, Mascarel came to California from Mexico with the Victor Prudhomme party and settled in Los Angeles in 1844. He was married to a Native American woman. In partnership with another Frenchman he acquired a valuable block of land on Commercial Row (today's Commercial Street). During the Civil War Mascarel was a Union supporter in a city that was predominantly Democratic and prosecessionist. While mayor he hosted an official visit from one of President Lincoln's generals, Maj. Gen. Irvin McDowell. The city was then 29 square miles in area and had a population between 4,000 and 5,000. In 1871 Mascarel became a cofounder of Farmers and Merchants Bank.

MASON, BIDDY (1818–1891), ex-slave who became a successful entrepreneur. She was brought to Los Angeles by her owners, a Mormon family, in 1851. In a celebrated 1855 court case she won freedom for herself and her family as well as another slave family. During the Civil War era she held religious services in her home for the small community of free blacks. Working as a nurse and midwife, Mason saved her earnings, bought land, and become a major downtown property owner. Her sons also prospered as landowners. In her Spring Street home in 1872 Biddy Mason helped organize, along with 12 charter members, the First African Methodist Episcopal Church of Los Angeles. A

Biddy Mason.

small park at South Spring, land that once belonged to her, is named in Mason's honor.

MASONIC ORDER. *See* Fraternal societies

MASQUERS CLUB, oldest theatrical club west of Broadway. Founded in 1925 as an all-male society, with a motto of "We laugh to win," the club has been located since 1927 in Hollywood. The first "harlequin" was Robert Edeson. John Barrymore and W. C. Fields were among the club's early members.

MATTACHINE SOCIETY. *See* Gay and lesbian movement

MATTHEWS, MIRIAM (1905–), retired librarian and expert on African American culture in Los Angeles. She has amassed a notable collection of photographs, paintings, and printed works, and is a consultant to the Afro-American Museum.

MAY, CLIFF (1908–1989), self-taught architect. May, a sixth-generation Californian, is considered "the grand master of the California ranch house," a rambling, one-story home with large windows, low-pitched roof, and free access to the outdoors, as exemplified by residences on Riviera Rancho Road, off Sunset Boulevard. Perfected by May from the 1930s to the 1950s, the ranch-house style inspired the design of hundreds of thousands of homes in California. He personally designed about 1,000 homes and produced plans that were used in 18,000 additional homes.

MAY, DAVID, II (1912–1992), department store executive, shopping mall pioneer, and grandson of the founder of the May Company Department Stores. The first Los Angeles May Company was established in 1923 when the Denver-based firm took over A. Hamburger & Sons at 8th Street and Broadway. In 1992 the now St. Louis–based merchandising firm, with 324 stores nationwide, merged with the Robinson's department store chain, to become Robinson's-May.

Named after his grandfather, who founded the firm, David May II helped develop, in the 1940s and 1950s, Crenshaw Shopping Center, the nation's first shopping center. He oversaw the May Company's expansion into numerous other regional shopping centers, and shocked the industry by encouraging rival department stores to open

in the same malls. His interests as civic leader and philanthropist included the Jules Stein Eye Institute at UCLA, Westlake School for Girls, and National Jewish Center for Respiratory Medicine and Immunology.

MAYER, LOUIS B. (1885–1957), film mogul. Born in Russia and raised in Canada, Mayer started out as a rag collector but soon became an exhibitor and distributor of films in New England, then moved to Hollywood and became a producer. In 1924 he helped create the Metro-Goldwyn-Mayer (MGM) studio, and for the next 25 years ran the lot with an iron grip. Mayer was a master at shaping films to popular taste. The short, feisty, cigar-chomping man was also explosive, dictatorial, and sentimental. The "cellulord's" white leather walls were covered with pictures of such friends as J. Edgar Hoover, Herbert Hoover, and Cardinal Spellman. His salary of $1,296,000 made him the highest paid business executive in the nation in 1927.

MAYO, MORROW, journalist and author. Mayo excelled as a writer of historical vignettes and biographical sketches. His best-known work, *Los Angeles* (1933), castigates the city's water policies in the eastern Sierra Nevada in the early 1900s as the "rape of the Owens Valley."

MAYOR OF LOS ANGELES. *See* Los Angeles City mayor

MAYWOOD, incorporated city 8 miles southwest of downtown Los Angeles. It was named by its residents in a popularity contest near the time of its incorporation in 1925. The population grew 28 percent between 1980 and 1990, reaching 27,850.

MCA. *See* Music Corporation of America

McALEER, OWEN C. (1858–?), mayor of Los Angeles from 1904 to 1906. In the 1905 election he had the backing of the Southern Pacific Railroad and the *Los Angeles Times.* By that time the city's area was 43 square miles and its population had topped 100,000. After McAleer visited the Owens River Valley in 1905 he enthusiastically supported the bond issue to obtain its water for Los Angeles.

McCONE COMMISSION, investigative body established in 1965 to examine the causes of the

Watts riot. Appointed by Gov. Edmund G. "Pat" Brown and headed by Pasadena resident John A. McCone, a former CIA head, the commission took extensive testimony and proposed modest changes or improvements in public education, transportation, social services, hospital facilities, and police-community relations. It generally supported the conduct of the police department under Chief William Parker. With the exception of the establishment of Martin Luther King Jr. Hospital, stepped-up employment and training programs, and the strengthening of the police commission, few of its recommendations were enacted.

McCOY, ESTHER (1904–1989), prolific architectural writer on contemporary California architects and architectural styles. Beginning as a poet and fiction writer, McCoy went to Paris in the 1920s, but settled in Southern California in the 1930s. She wrote influential essays and books on Richard Neutra, Rudolph M. Schindler, Craig Ellwood, Charles Greene, and the Case Study Houses.

McGROARTY, JOHN STEVEN (1862–1944), writer and public figure. The Pennsylvania-born attorney was named poet laureate of California in 1933 and represented Los Angeles in the U.S. House of Representatives from 1935 to 1939. He was also a *Los Angeles Times* editorialist for 40 years, and he wrote the five-volume booster history *California of the South* (1933). His most lasting contribution, however, was as author of the *Mission Play.* This highly romantic pageant, depicting the history of the missions, has been performed annually since 1912 at the Mission Playhouse in San Gabriel. McGroarty's former residence in Verdugo Hills is now part of the Los Angeles city park system.

McINTYRE, JAMES FRANCIS ALOYSIUS (1886–1979), Roman Catholic cardinal. A protégé of New York's Cardinal Spellman, McIntyre transferred to Los Angeles and was consecrated as the first cardinal of the western United States in 1953. He became a prolific builder of churches at a time when Catholic immigration to Los Angeles was estimated at 1,000 a week. A man of authoritarian personality and ultraconservative politics, McIntyre was an avid supporter of Sen. Joseph McCarthy and a great ally of Police Chief William Parker. McIntyre resisted the reforms of Vatican II. He purged the Immaculate Heart of Mary teaching order from the archdiocesan schools for op-

posing the Vietnam War and backing civil rights. He was the basis for a character in John Gregory Dunne's novel *True Confessions* (1977), adapted for the screen by Dunne and Joan Didion in 1981.

McNAMARA TRIAL, celebrated 1911 Los Angeles labor case involving John J. and James B. McNamara, midwestern iron worker unionists. The case resulted from the bombing of the *Los Angeles Times* Building, on 1st Street and Broadway, on 1 October 1910. The explosion killed 20 and injured 17. The McNamaras were seized, brought to Los Angeles, and indicted for the crime. While in prison the McNamaras—one of whom was an official of the Bridge and Structural Iron Workers Union—staunchly protested their innocence. The brothers received the backing of the entire labor movement, including Samuel Gompers and the American Federation of Labor. The defense was headed by Clarence Darrow, assisted by Job Harriman, Socialist candidate for mayor in the 1911 election, LeComte Davis, and others.

The case, which appeared to be a frame-up, became a nationwide cause célèbre. In truth, it appears that the McNamaras had chosen dynamite as a weapon of class warfare, intending to frighten, but not to kill, members of the antilabor *Times* organization. As the year progressed the evidence against the brothers—which was assembled by private detective William J. Burns and included a confession by a McNamara associate, Ortie McManigal—began to mount.

Just before the trial—and the mayoral election

The McNamara brothers. California Historical Society, Los Angeles Area Chamber of Commerce Collection, Dept. of Special Collections, USC Library.

—Darrow recommended a change of plea to spare the lives of the accused. The McNamaras confessed. James received a life sentence, and John got 15 years. The confessions destroyed Harriman's political candidacy.

In the course of the proceedings Darrow was accused of attempting to bribe a prospective juror named Lockwood and had to stand trial in Los Angeles. He was eventually acquitted, but the McNamara case caused a deep split between Darrow and the labor movement, and ended for a generation the efforts of Southern California labor to undo employers' strict open-shop policies.

McPHERSON, AIMEE SEMPLE (1890–1944), Canadian-born minister who established the Foursquare Gospel Church and became Southern California's most famous religionist. A convert to Pentecostalism, she lived for a time in China with her missionary husband, who died there. Her second marriage, to Harold S. McPherson, ended in divorce. At age 26 she began an itinerant career as a tent revivalist. Arriving in Los Angeles in 1918 with a sick child, McPherson built and dedicated Angelus Temple in 1923.

The Foursquare Gospel is based on the concepts of the Savior, baptism, healing, and the Second Coming. McPherson adapted show-business flamboyance to preaching and healing and was accused of conducting "religious vaudeville" spectacles. Beautiful, energetic, and charismatic, McPherson acquired a huge and devoted following. Her church at one time had 400 branches, a radio studio, and worldwide missions.

In May 1926 Sister Aimee "disappeared" in the surf at Ocean Park. A month later she reappeared in Douglas, Arizona, claiming she had been kidnapped by three men. A cheering crowd of 100,000 greeted her rose-covered car when she returned to Los Angeles. In reality, she had been with a lover in Beechwood Canyon in the Hollywood Hills. The district attorney, who threatened to prosecute Aimee, her mother, and her lover for conspiracy, dropped the charges at the last minute. Suffering from a severe mood disorder and estranged from her daughter, McPherson suffered a nervous breakdown in 1930. She died of a drug overdose in an Oakland hotel and was buried at Forest Lawn Cemetery. Her International Church of the Foursquare Gospel continues today, although in a diminished form.

McWILLIAMS, CAREY (1905–1980), Colorado-born attorney, journalist, historian, and community activist. McWilliams attended USC Law School, entered law practice in the 1920s, and subsequently served as head defense attorney in the Sleepy Lagoon murder trial. As a literary reviewer for the AAA's *Westways* magazine, McWilliams developed close associations with many literary figures. Among his works are a biography of Ambrose Bierce (1929) and *Factories in the Fields* (1939), a classic study of California agriculture and agricultural labor. His book *Southern California: An Island on the Land* (1946) is generally acknowledged to be the finest interpretive history of the region. He also wrote on such topics as civil rights and anti-Semitism. McWilliams moved to New York in 1955 to become editor of the *Nation* magazine.

MEAT PACKING INDUSTRY, commercial activity centered on Vernon Avenue in the city of Vernon, the location of the Union Stockyards from 1922 to 1963. Despite the demise of the stockyards, 30 to 45 giant packing plants still operate in the area. The animals come from feedlots in the Imperial and San Joaquin Valleys. Farmer John (Clougherty Packing Company), Oscar Mayer, Kal Kan Foods, Pacific Soap, Swift Adhesives, Ver-

Aimee Semple McPherson. Pitt Collection.

non Leather, and Academy Candle are among the big firms operating in Vernon. Trucking facilities are also highly concentrated in the area.

MEChA (MOVIMIENTO ESTUDIANTIL CHICANO DE AZTLÁN), Mexican American student organization formed in the 1960s to promote Chicano studies programs on college campuses. MEChA still exists in many institutions.

MEDITERRANEAN FRUIT FLY (CERATITIS CAPITATA), or "medfly," insidious killer of fruit and vegetable crops, in Los Angeles County since 1987. A program by the California Department of Food and Agriculture to eradicate the medfly by spraying malathion proved highly controversial and inconclusive. An effort to use sterile flies as an alternative has not yet been shown to provide permanent relief.

MEHTA, ZUBIN (1936–), conductor and music director. His father, Mehli Mehta, was a violinist and conductor, and Zubin grew up with music as part of his home environment. Educated in Bombay, Vienna, and Italy, he conducted in Europe and Canada before being hired to lead the Los Angeles Philharmonic Orchestra in 1962. Mehta was hailed for his sensitive rendering of the Romantic composers. In 1978 he left Los Angeles to conduct the New York Philharmonic Orchestra.

MELLUS, HENRY (1810?–1860), mayor of Los Angeles in 1860. Born in Boston, Mellus came to California with Richard Henry Dana in 1835 on the brig *Pilgrim,* later made famous by Dana's *Two Years Before the Mast* (1840). He returned to the East Coast in 1837, then came back again to California as a supercargo. When a business he had established in Gold Rush San Francisco was wiped out by fire in 1851, Mellus again went east, where he lost $250,000 in a bad investment. In 1858 he settled in Los Angeles permanently. The following year he shepherded Dana around Southern California on the author's return visit to the West Coast.

A member of a committee that first attempted to found a public library in 1859 (the goal was realized in 1872), Mellus was elected mayor on 7 May 1860, governing 4,000 people living in a 29-square-mile area. On 8 October 1860 he formally presided when the first telegraph message was received in Los Angeles from San Francisco. Mellus died in office several months later, on 26 December 1860.

MENTAL HEALTH DEPARTMENT, COUNTY OF LOS ANGELES. *See* Los Angeles County Department of Mental Health

MENTRYVILLE, site of the first oil well in California and the longest continuously pumping well in the world. It is located in Pico Canyon in the Santa Susana Mountains, 8 miles from Santa Clarita. Local Indians had long used the surface petroleum as medicine and to seal their huts against the weather. An oil prospector, Alex Mentry, a French immigrant who had worked in the oil fields of Pennsylvania, dug a well there in 1876. This sparked a group of entrepreneurs to form the California Star Oil Works. The drillers and their families created a small canvas-and-wooden town centered around Mentry's two-story house, opening a one-room schoolhouse in 1885. Eventually most of the wells dried up, and the drillers and their families left for more productive sites. The small school remained active until 1932, when the town was deserted. The California Star Oil Works was swallowed up by Standard Oil of California (later, Chevron), but California Star Oil Well No. 4 kept pumping until it finally gave out in 1990. An elderly couple remained behind as self-appointed caretakers of the ghost town of Mentryville, leaving only after the 1994 Northridge earthquake. With Chevron's sale of the surrounding property to the state of California in 1995, Mentryville was expected to be restored as a historic site in the midst of a beautiful public park.

MERCED THEATRE, city's first indoor stage theater. It was built and operated by cabinetmaker and undertaker William Abbott and his wife, Mercedes. Located on Main Street next door to Pico House, the finest hotel in town, it celebrated a gala opening on New Year's Day 1870. The stage and seating area were on the second floor. Plays were performed in both Spanish and English. Cramped backstage quarters, poor acoustics, and a shift of the commercial center southward eventually led to the theater's decline. Today the distinguished Italianate building is part of El Pueblo de Los Angeles Historic Monument. Efforts are being made to restore it and operate it once again as a legitimate theater.

MERCHANTS AND MANUFACTURERS ASSOCIATION (M & M), militant employers organization devoted to the open-shop policy.

Formed in 1896 at the suggestion of Harrison Gray Otis, it involved a merger of two preexisting entities: the Merchants Association and the Manufacturers Association. Among the founders were R. W. Pridham and Felix J. Zeehandelaar. Initially M & M's purpose was to boost general business interests, but soon, at Otis's urging, it began to pursue an aggressive anti-union policy. In 1903 it came to the defense of Hamburger's People's Store, an association member targeted by a costly and effective union boycott. As documented before the La Follette Committee of the U.S. Senate, the M & M members formed company unions, organized labor spies, used blacklists, supplied guards and strike breakers, lobbied for anti-union laws and ordinances, advised union members not to pay their dues, created employer associations whose members agreed never to sign a union contract under penalty of a $10,000 fine, enlisted police cooperation, and promoted back-to-work movements during strikes. It had a huge war chest and was extremely successful in keeping wages and union memberships low until the late 1930s.

MESA FAMILY, one of the 11 founding families of the *pueblo* of Los Angeles in 1781. Antonio Mesa was 38 years old, the son of a black slave and an Indian woman (the 1781 census listed him as being of African ancestry). His wife was Gertrudis López, a 27-year-old *mulata.* They had two daughters, María Paula, 10, and Antonio María, 8. Dissatisfied with life in Southern California, the Mesas soon returned to Alamos, Sonora.

METHODIST EPISCOPAL CHURCH, Christian denomination that first established a presence in Los Angeles in 1850. That year Rev. J. R. Brier, who, with his wife, had survived the passage through Death Valley, preached the first Protestant sermon in Los Angeles. Regular Methodist services were established in 1853 when Rev. Adam Bland leased the El Dorado Saloon and transformed it into a chapel. His wife conducted a girls' school on the premises. In 1866 the congregation moved to a brick building near the courthouse, and in 1868 to a church on Fort Street (now Broadway). Here the Methodist Church licensed its first Chinese Christian minister in the United States, Chan Kin Lung. Chan later became pastor of a local Chinese Methodist church. The Methodist Church South had separate institutions in Los Angeles beginning in the Civil War era, but the branches merged in 1939, when the entire Methodist movement achieved national unity.

METRO BLUE LINE. *See* Blue Line

METRO-GOLDWYN-MAYER (MGM), undisputed leader among the "Big Five" film studios during the heyday of the motion picture industry. The studio emerged in 1920 when theater owner Marcus Loew gained control of the Metro Company, a film distributor. Metro Pictures, as Loew called his new concern, produced two moneymakers, *The Four Horsemen of the Apocalypse* (1921), starring Rudolph Valentino, and *The Prisoner of Zenda* (1922). Worried about Adolph Zukor's growing power in the film industry, Loew joined forces with Louis B. Mayer and Samuel Goldwyn; together they merged with the Goldwyn Company to create Metro-Goldwyn-Mayer in 1924. (Sam Goldwyn then left to found his own company with

First Methodist Episcopal Church, ca. 1909. Pitt Collection.

Metro-Goldwyn-Mayer Studio Gate. Courtesy Turner Entertainment Co.

the understanding that "Goldwyn" would remain part of the studio name.) Within a short time MGM gained immense prestige, thanks in large part to the 25-year rule of autocrat Louis B. Mayer and to the genius of "boy wonder" Irving Thalberg, who had moved from Universal Studios to join MGM.

MGM, whose motto was "More stars than there are in heaven," signed more major actors and actresses to contracts than any other studio, and inched out Paramount to become the undisputed king of Hollywood's court. Located in Culver City, it boasted five lots behind fortresslike walls. One of the lots was the site of the burning of Atlanta for *Gone With the Wind.*

Among its best-known stars were Greta Garbo, Clark Gable, Lionel, Ethel, and John Barrymore, Hedy Lamarr, Lon Chaney, Myrna Loy, Spencer Tracy, Katharine Hepburn, Judy Garland, James Stewart, Elizabeth Taylor, Esther Williams, Nelson Eddy, Jeanette MacDonald, Mario Lanza, Robert Taylor, Gene Kelly, and Lassie. Its many notable movies include *The Big Parade* (1925), *Ben Hur* (1926), *Grand Hotel* (1932), the *Thin Man* series (1934–1947), *Mutiny on the Bounty* (1935), the *Andy Hardy* movies (1937–1958), *Gone With the Wind* (1939), *The Wizard of Oz* (1939), the nine Spencer Tracy–Katharine Hepburn movies (1942–1967), *Lassie Come Home* (1943), *Singin' in the Rain* (1952), *Seven Brides for Seven Brothers* (1954), and *Doctor Zhivago* (1965).

In recent years MGM has experienced consid-

erable internal turmoil. In 1986 financial troubles forced it to sell its fabled Culver City studio to Ted Turner's Turner Broadcasting Company, which sold the studio within the year to Sony Pictures Entertainment. In a brief period the Turner Company sold the MGM name and logo to previous owner Kirk Kerkorian, but retained for itself the entire MGM film library. In addition to Kerkorian and Turner, MGM owners have included Giancarlo Paretti and Crédit Lyonnais, a French bank that also controlled United Artists movie studios. Under U.S. banking laws, Crédit Lyonnais must sell out by 1997.

METRO GREEN LINE. *See* Green Line

METROLINK, regional commuter rail service authorized by a 1990 bond issue and developed by the Southern California Regional Rail Authority. The system uses Union Station as a hub for three rail lines, which run from downtown to Moorpark in Ventura County, Santa Clarita, and San Bernardino. These lines will coordinate with the regionwide Metro rail system of rapid transit, with its Red, Blue, and Green Lines, now partially completed. Pending additional bond authorization, Metrolink will form the basis of a six-county network of long-distance commuter rails.

METROPOLITAN TRANSPORTATION AUTHORITY (MTA). *See* Los Angeles County Metropolitan Transportation Authority

METROPOLITAN WATER DISTRICT

(MWD), world's largest water agency, supplying about 60 percent of the water used between Ventura County and the Mexican border. The Colorado River is the main source of the water. In 1931 voters approved a $220 million bond issue for the Colorado River Aqueduct, which was completed in 1941. The American Society of Civil Engineers regards the aqueduct as one of the seven modern engineering wonders of the United States. Some water is brought from California's northern counties as well, via the Los Angeles and California Aqueducts.

Today the MWD delivers 1.5 billion gallons of water daily to 122 cities in six counties, an area of 5,200 square miles. The biggest single user is San Diego. The MWD has 27 member agencies and is run by a 51-member board headquartered in Los Angeles. The cities in Los Angeles County that depend on its resources are Los Angeles (which gets a small fraction of water from the system), Beverly Hills, Burbank, Compton, Glendale, Pasadena, Long Beach, San Marino, Santa Monica, and Torrance, as well as numerous smaller communities.

Despite its tremendous technical success, the MWD has its share of critics, who say that the utility charges urban water consumers high rates in order to subsidize agricultural users. (About 8 percent of MWD water is used on farms; 92 percent is used for businesses and homes.) This subsidy, they say, encourages farmers to raise such inefficient crops as alfalfa, which would not otherwise be grown in California.

The MWD's role in future water development is problematic. The agency has always assumed endless urban and industrial growth in its service area, but recently has had to face the fact that California's legal entitlement to water from the Colorado River is declining, based on a 1964 U.S. Supreme Court ruling. The MWD favors the development of a peripheral canal at the Sacramento River Delta to augment the flow of northern waters to Southern California. Of late, it also favors water trading among water districts, reclamation, improved agricultural conservation, and other important innovations. A major problem has been Southern California's growth rate of about 350,000 people each year.

METRO RAIL SYSTEM,

integrated transportation network launched in 1990 by the Los Angeles County Transportation Commission (LACTC),

an 11-member board that includes the county supervisors, the mayor of Los Angeles, and five others. The system is the successor to the Red Car lines that were disbanded in the 1960s. Supported by sales taxes approved by the voters in 1980 and 1990, it is intended to relieve traffic gridlock, improve air quality, ease dependence on foreign oil, and generally enhance the area's quality of life. Essentially it is a subway system for the inner city and a commuter rail network for those living outside the downtown area. It is expected to run 300 miles and take 30 years to complete, and will use Union Terminal as a passenger hub. The entire network will eventually reach as far as San Bernardino, Moorpark, and Santa Clarita, the terminuses of the complementary Metrolink system, now under construction. Included in the 30-year plan is a system of light-rail transportation, which began to be implemented after LACTC purchased 175 miles of right-of-way from Southern Pacific in 1990.

Los Angeles has been wrestling with mass transit problems for almost a century. Among the dilemmas facing the commission in the next several decades will be how to provide affordable transportation for the working poor whose jobs are widely dispersed; how to serve residential neighborhoods still spreading out across an already

---

Some Americans despise Los Angeles, just as some Europeans despise America, and for the same reason. Los Angeles, like America, like freedom applied, is strong medicine—an untidy jumble of human diversity and perversity.   —George Will, columnist

---

sprawling landscape; how to lure middle-class commuters from their automobiles; how to deal honestly and efficiently with the contractors, who contribute heavily to political campaigns; and how to ensure sound construction standards in a terrain afflicted by earthquakes, petroleum pockets, and other geological hazards.

The system has several segments, some of which have already been completed. The Metro Blue Line, a 22-mile light-rail line connecting Long Beach to downtown Los Angeles, was opened in 1990.

The Metro Red Line, a heavy-rail subway authorized by Los Angeles County Proposition A in 1980, which allowed a half-cent sales tax for transit improvement, will be the backbone of the entire system. It is being constructed in segments and is now expected to run 18 miles from Union Station along the Wilshire Corridor to Hollywood, and then to North Hollywood in the San Fernando Valley. The segment from downtown to Mac-Arthur Park was completed in January 1993. The Red Line project has been plagued by major management difficulties and severe technical problems, including a dramatic land subsidence on Hollywood Boulevard. In 1995 excavation work began on the planned 2.3-mile tunnel linking North Hollywood with downtown, a project that, barring further mishaps, is expected to be completed by the year 2000.

The Metro Green Line, opened in 1995, is a 23-mile automated light-rail line connecting Norwalk to El Segundo.

Plans are now being drawn up for additional light-rail lines. One such line would run from Pasadena to downtown Los Angeles; another would run from Santa Monica, following Exposition Boulevard for most of the way.

METRO RED LINE. *See* Red Line

MEXICAN AMERICAN LEGAL DEFENSE AND EDUCATIONAL FUND (MALDEF), national civil rights organization with a base of operation in Los Angeles. It was formed in Texas in 1968 to protect the interests of Latinos in education, employment, political access, and immigration. After Congress passed the Civil Rights Acts of 1975 and 1982, MALDEF succeeded in challenging registration laws and at-large voting practices. In 1981 it filed a suit in Los Angeles jointly with the ACLU charging the county with gerrymandering to dilute Latino electoral strength. This case resulted in significant redistricting and, ultimately, in the election of Gloria Molina to the Board of Supervisors. In a 1992 case against the Los Angeles Unified School District, MALDEF achieved more equitable financing for inner-city schools.

MEXICAN AMERICAN MOVEMENT (MAM), short-lived Chicano youth organization that grew out of a YMCA conference in San Pedro in 1934. It held annual congresses, published a newspaper, and tried to create Chicano leadership in education, social work, business, and other professions.

It fought discrimination and juvenile delinquency. Among its movers were Feliz Gutiérrez Sr., Richard Ibanez, and Mary Anne Chavolla. The organization was a forerunner to the Community Service Organization.

MEXICAN AMERICAN POLITICAL ASSOCIATION (MAPA), political organization formed in 1959 to improve Mexican representation statewide. The founding leadership consisted of California Mexicans loyal to the Democratic Party. MAPA's first victory came in 1962 when Los Angeles council member Edward Roybal was elected to the U.S. Congress. Today the association endorses candidates, registers voters, and publicizes the plight of Mexicans in the electoral process. With members from the San Francisco Bay Area to the Imperial Valley, MAPA has strong local roots on the Eastside and in the San Fernando Valley.

MEXICAN LOS ANGELES, 1822-1846, brief historical interlude between the end of Spanish rule and the outbreak of the Mexican War. From the city's beginnings in 1781, however, the bulk of *pueblo* settlers were Mexican colonials, not European Spaniards, making the city culturally Mexican from the start. This would hold true for some years after 1848 as well.

About 650 *gente de razón* ("people of reason," i.e., non-Indians) lived in the *pueblo* of Los Angeles in 1820, and 770 in 1830, when the total non-Indian population of the Los Angeles region was only 1,180. In 1844, 1,841 *gente de razón* and 1,200 Native Americans were counted in the Los Angeles District (from San Fernando to San Juan Capistrano).

The most important change during the period was the secularization of the missions, beginning in 1836. Neophytes either moved to the *pueblo* and were assimilated, or left. The ranchos became more dominant during the secularization process. A parish church was built, and the *zanja* ditches, first dug in the 1780s, revamped. Guillermo Cota was appointed *alcalde* in 1823, followed by José María Avila. Both legal and illegal shipping increased during the period. In 1825 the Los Angeles River overflowed its banks, causing severe flooding. A year later the famous Yankee mountain man Jedediah Smith arrived at Mission San Gabriel. The 1830s saw a significant growth in the hide-and-tallow trade and in trade with foreigners. Two-thirds of all Californians lived in the southern part of the territory, and from time to time bitter north-south political rivalries erupted into fighting. Francisco "Chico" López discovered gold in Placerita Canyon in 1842. As the former mission properties fell into the hands of civil administrators and rancheros, an affluent local elite emerged. Los Angeles soon surpassed Santa Barbara as the region's political and economic center. The position of *alcalde* was abolished and replaced by two *jueces de paz* (justices of the peace).

Among the most important local figures in the Mexican period were José Antonio Carrillo, who served as *alcalde* in 1828–29; the rancher Manuel Domínguez; José Sepúlveda, owner of Rancho San Joaquín; Manuel Requena, vineyard owner; the Yankee Abel Stearns, the largest land and cattle owner of the era; and Governor Pío Pico. In April 1845, on the eve of the war with the United States, Pico transferred the capital of California from Monterey to Los Angeles.

MEXICANS. According to the U.S. Census, people of Mexican origin in Los Angeles County numbered 2,519,514 in 1990. Mexicans—people largely of mixed Spanish and Indian descent—first came to Southern California under the flag of Spain, having been recruited from Sonora and Sinaloa in New Spain (Mexico) beginning in 1781. Although their numbers were small, their language and culture prevailed over those of the local Indian inhabitants. Mexico ruled California from 1822, when Mexican rebels overthrew Spanish rule, until the end of the Mexican War in 1848. Both Mexicans and Mexican Americans remained an important ethnic group even after the Yankee takeover in 1848.

In 1830 the Mexican population of Los Angeles totaled 1,180, of whom 770 lived in the *pueblo* and the remainder in surrounding ranchos and missions. The Indian (Gabrieleño) population of this region was then estimated at slightly less than 2,500. The Mexicans remained in the majority after 1848 but lost political and social dominance. Their numbers increased markedly after the Mexican revolution of 1910.

In the 1860s most Mexicans living in the city of Los Angeles resided just south of 1st Street and around the Plaza area, in a downtown neighborhood called "Sonoratown." During the 1870s they spread east of the river into Boyle Heights. By the 1910s and 1920s, after a migration to the north following the Mexican revolution of 1910, the population had become concentrated north of 3rd Street, near Aliso, and in the Belvedere area of East Los Angeles. By 1930 the Mexican-born population had risen to 368,000 in 1930, compared to 8,000 in 1900.

During the Great Depression federal officials met the problem of declining tax revenues available for public services by expatriating thousands of Mexicans living in Los Angeles—many of whom were U.S. citizens. They were simply given one-way rail tickets to Mexico. During World War II a great many Mexican nationals served in the U.S. military or worked in wartime industries.

Since 1945 Mexicans have become increasingly urbanized and less isolated from the mainstream. With the end of the war and the return of their GIs, they established organizations that reflected a growing political consciousness. Southern California now replaced Texas as the favored place of entry into the United States, and after much struggle political leaders emerged: Edward Roybal, Ju-

La Fiesta de Los Angeles parade, 1896. Courtesy California State Archives.

lian Nava, Richard Alatorre, Art Torres, and Gloria Molina, among others.

Los Angeles is enriched by the presence of Mexican culture through language, food, public celebrations, mariachi and salsa music, craft shows, murals, and religious observances. Cinco de Mayo, a holiday commemorating the 1862 Mexican defeat of French colonial forces at Puebla, is celebrated with more enthusiasm in Los Angeles than in Mexico City. By 1989 one-quarter of the city's population was Mexican, and Los Angeles had the largest concentration of Mexicans outside of Mexico City.

MEXICAN WAR, 1846–1848, begun when the United States, coveting California, provoked fighting on the Texas border; it resulted in significant but inconclusive skirmishing in and around Los Angeles. The war's prelude in California, the Bear Flag rebellion, in June 1846, had few local ramifications. More significant were two naval operations: the seizure of Monterey by a U.S. Pacific naval squadron on 7 July 1846; and the landing of Commodore Robert Stockton in San Pedro Bay, followed by the invasion of Los Angeles by a 400-man army. The town was then the largest Mexican settlement in California, home to 675 adult males. To minimize American reprisals against Mexican civilians, Gov. Pío Pico left Los Angeles, which he had named the territorial capital, for Sonora. Stockton ordered a marine, Lt. Archibald Gillespie, and 50 men to garrison the town. Once established, Gillespie behaved like a martinet. In September Servulio Varela and Leonardo Cota organized a guerrilla force of 300 Mexicans to drive him out. A larger force, which included Capt. José María Flores as *comandante,* as well as José Antonio Carrillo and Gen. Andrés Pico, also took up the fighting at Rancho Chino. On 4 October Gillespie surrendered and left town, giving the Mexican guerrilla force temporary control over all of Southern California. Two days later Capt. William Mervine landed at San Pedro, and on 8 October confronted the Mexicans at the Domínguez ranch house in the Battle of the Old Woman's Gun (named after a weapon dug out of a woman's garden). Stockton returned on 23 October but left immediately for San Diego.

At the Battle of San Pascual (near present-day Escondido) on 6 December, Californios, including many from Los Angeles, confronted a U.S. Army unit led by Gen. Stephen Watts Kearny

that had just arrived from New Mexico. The 600 mounted Southern Californians, armed with lances, inflicted some losses on the Americans but had to fall back in the face of artillery. The final engagements of the war occurred on the San Gabriel River (near today's Montebello) on 8 and 9 January 1847. Stockton recaptured Los Angeles. At Cahuenga on 13 January, Gen. Pico formally capitulated to Lt. Col. John C. Frémont. From a larger historical perspective, all of the above was of relatively little consequence compared to the fighting that went on near Mexico City and the diplomatic maneuvering under way in Washington. The war's official end came with the Treaty of Guadalupe Hidalgo in 1848.

MIGRATION into Los Angeles County occurred in a series of spectacular waves beginning in the 1880s. By the 1990s the region (in U.S. Census terms, the Los Angeles–Long Beach Metropolitan Area) had become the most populous metropolitan area in the country. At first most newcomers arrived from other parts of the United States, but in recent decades the vast majority have come from foreign countries. (It should be noted that while the city of Los Angeles proper is the second largest city in the United States, it contains only 40 percent of the county's population.)

The 1980s and 1990s witnessed a considerable out-migration from Los Angeles County. Those who leave seem to be escaping the perceived problems of ineffectual public schools, traffic congestion, smog, and street crime. Department of Motor Vehicles data, accurate demographic indicators, show that Los Angeles suffered a net loss of 14,367 drivers to other counties and states in 1986; in the year ending 30 June 1991 the number had climbed to 105,672. Studies by the Rand Corporation indicate that Orange, Ventura, and San Bernardino Counties, together with Oregon, Washington, and other nearby states, are common destinations of the departing residents.

MINES FIELD. *See* Los Angeles International Airport

MINI-MALLS began appearing as early as the 1930s, but multiplied rapidly in the 1970s and 1980s when as many as 2,000 were built in the region. The "Father of the Mini-Mall," Tom Layman of T. W. Layman Associates, a Van Nuys–based architectural firm, is said to have designed an estimated 300 of these commercial sites single-handed. They often spring up on corner lots where gas stations or other enterprises have failed—properties already zoned for commercial activity and ready for swift and inexpensive development.

Mini-mall stores are often small franchises and mom-and-pop operations. Typically oriented in an L-shape, mini-malls feature such retail businesses as video rental shops, nail parlors, fast-food restaurants, convenience stores, and doughnut and yogurt shops. At first these shopping facilities were loosely regulated and received much criticism for lacking sufficient trash receptacles, parking spaces, or other amenities for customer convenience, causing litter and traffic gridlock on nearby surface streets. In the 1980s the city enacted more stringent regulations.

MINUTE MEN (MINUTEERS ASSOCIA-TION), Los Angeles urban reform group from 1932 to 1938, organized by irate members of the Los Angeles Junior Chamber of Commerce to combat racketeering, public indebtedness, and corrupt police, judges, and politicians, as well as the region's continuing unemployment. The leaders were Raymond L. Haight, a former state commissioner of corporations, and Roy P. Dolley, an attorney; they headed a central committee of 30–50 Minute Men. The nonpartisan grass-roots organization set about

---

You have to begin with the singular fact that in a population of a million and a quarter, every other person you see has been here less than five years. More than nine in every ten you see have been here less than fifteen years.

—Garet Garrett, writer, 1930

---

documenting corruption in both county government and the cities of Los Angeles, Pasadena, Burbank, Long Beach, Beverly Hills, and Santa Monica. In 1934 they accused District Attorney Buron Fitts of protecting wrongdoers by manipulating the grand jury. When Fitts blocked their efforts they aligned themselves with two other reform groups, Clifford Clinton's CIVIC (Citizens Independent Vice Investigating Committee) and the Municipal

League. With the support of an honest presiding judge, Fletcher Bowron, the reform coalition obtained important grand jury indictments in 1937. A car bombing directed against Harry A. Raymond, an investigator employed by the reformers, finally toppled the corrupt Frank Shaw regime and swept Bowron into office as Los Angeles mayor.

MIRACLE MILE, commercial strip on Wilshire Boulevard, from La Brea to Fairfax Avenues. In the 1920s Wilshire was being extended from downtown, past the new University of California campus in Westwood, all the way to the ocean. Downtown realtor A. W. Ross, recognizing that the automobile was about to decentralize downtown business, started developing the La Brea–Fairfax strip—which he envisioned as the "Fifth Avenue of the West"—in 1921, on 18 acres purchased for $54,000. The name Miracle Mile was applied beginning in 1928. By 1940 Ross's efforts had attracted over 100 upscale retail shops, including B. F. Coulter, Phelps-Terkel, Desmond's, Silverwood's, May Company, and branch stores of other major downtown retailers. The shops tended to cater to motorists rather than pedestrians or public transportation passengers, which meant that their main entrances were not on the street but were accessed from off-street parking lots. By the 1960s the Miracle Mile was fading, losing its trade to more modern suburban shopping malls, and many of the notable architectural creations—variations of the Art Deco style—began to disappear. Today tens of thousands of people live in the houses and apartments in the immediate vicinity, known as the Miracle Mile District.

MISSION HILLS, neighborhood in the San Fernando Valley, located between Pacoima and Granada Hills. Its most famous historical landmarks are the San Fernando Mission, dating from 1797, and the Andrés Pico Adobe, built in 1834. The latter is the home of the San Fernando Valley Historical Society. In 1990 the population was 31,000.

MISSION INDIANS. *See* Fernandeño Indians; Native Americans; Tongva Indians

MISSION PLAY (1912), most popular of all outdoor California pageant plays, even *Ramona*. It was written by John Steven McGroarty, a newsman for the *Los Angeles Times* for 40 years and author of a five-volume booster history, *California of the South*

(1933). His highly romanticized play traces the history of the California missions from 1769 to 1849. Performances were held in the 1,450-seat Mission Playhouse (now known as the San Gabriel Civic Auditorium) on Mission Drive. The original $1.5 million production, backed by Henry E. Huntington, employed 300 actors, mostly amateurs, and utilized singing, dancing, and dialogue. In the initial version, the American conquerors were the villains; a revised version that ends before the arrival of the American army places the blame for declining conditions on the republican Mexican government. Between 1912 and 1929 the play attracted more than 2.5 million spectators.

MISSION REVIVAL ARCHITECTURE, California style dating from the 1890s that became popular locally between 1900 and 1915. It is characterized by white stucco walls, arched openings, tile roofs, and bell towers. The style has been used for railroad stations, resort hotels, schools, churches, apartments, and single-family dwellings. A celebrated example is Grace Brethren Church in Pasadena.

MISSION SAN FERNANDO. *See* San Fernando Rey de España Mission

MISSION SAN GABRIEL ARCHANGEL. *See* San Gabriel Mission

MISSION VIEJA. *See* San Gabriel Mission

MOLINA, GLORIA (1948?–), county supervisor from the 1st District. The East Los Angeles farm worker's daughter rose through grass-roots political action from a position as field representative for Assemblyman Art Torres, to the California Assembly in 1982, to the Los Angeles City Council in 1986, and finally to the Los Angeles County Board of Supervisors in 1991. She was the first Latino elected supervisor in this century, and the first woman ever elected to that post (Yvonne Brathwaite Burke was appointed). Molina entered office after a historic court battle over redistricting, the aim being to undo racial discrimination on the board. She represents a large district that includes East Los Angeles.

MONEY, WILLIAM (1807–1890?), an eccentric Scotsman and first leader of the Reformed Church, a sect that he founded locally around 1841 with 12 converts. The Catholic clergy regarded him as "the most obstinate heretic on the earth." In addition to leading his small flock, he was also the first local book author, publishing *The Reform of the New Testament Church* in 1854. As "Professor Money" he issued economic theories (he was known also as "Bishop Money," a self-bestowed title, or "Doctor Money"). He ran a medical practice of sorts, without having a medical license, and boasted that of 5,000 patients only four had died. He once displayed a map entitled "William Money's Discovery of the Ocean." Married to a Mexican woman and fluent in Spanish, he had some following among local Californios, most of whom considered him a harmless crank. He published a work in Spanish, *A Treatise on the Mysteries of the Physical System and the Methods of Treating Diseases by Proper Remedies.*

MONOGRAM PICTURES CORPORATION, film studio that specialized in horror, crime, and comedy "B" and "C" films in the 1930s and 1940s. Monogram was a subsidiary of Allied Artists, which used the Monogram label to issue lesser, "second-feature" products. Among its players were Frankie Darrow, the East Side Kids, the Bowery Boys, Bela Lugosi, and Charlie Chan. In the 1950s the studio made a few prestigious "A" movies, such as *Friendly Persuasion* (1956).

MONO LAKE CONTROVERSY, dispute between environmentalists and the city of Los Angeles. The tributary streams of Mono Lake, a million-year-old body of water at the base of the eastern Sierra Nevada, have supplied as much as one-sixth of the city's total water supply since the 1930s by means of the Los Angeles Aqueduct. Alarmed by the basin's declining water level, environmentalists formed the Mono Lake Committee in 1978 to challenge Los Angeles's continuing water imperialism. The committee won several landmark California Supreme Court decisions. One, in 1983, ordered that the lake be protected, and a second, in 1989, required the city to free Mono's tributary streams. At issue has been the survival of the brine shrimp in the extremely salty water, and of the California gull nesting grounds on islands in the lake, which with low water levels become accessible to predators. All but admitting total defeat, the DWP appeared ready in 1991 to look elsewhere, principally the San Joaquin Valley, to replace the water it would have drawn from Mono by further pumping. The lake is now part of Mono Lake National Monument.

MONROE, MARILYN (1926–1962), movie superstar. Born in Los Angeles General Hospital's charity ward as Norma Jean Baker, she was baptized by Aimee Semple McPherson at the Foursquare Gospel Church in Echo Park, and lived for a time at the Los Angeles Orphans Home at El Centro Avenue in Hollywood. She became a starlet at 20th Century–Fox, which put her under contract in 1946 and changed her name to Marilyn Monroe. She made more than 15 films in the 1950s, becoming a major sex symbol after appearing in *The Asphalt Jungle* (1950), *Gentlemen Prefer Blondes* (1953), *The Seven-Year Itch* (1955), and *Some Like It Hot* (1959). Her appeal rested not only on her beauty, but also on her ability to project both vulnerability and humor. To many she represents Hollywood's fabled exploitation of young, glamorous actresses.

Monroe married and divorced luminaries Joe DiMaggio and Arthur Miller. As with other film superstars who died young and tragically, such as Rudolph Valentino and James Dean, Monroe's persona has only grown stronger and more mythic with the passing years, and questions continue to be raised as to the manner and cause of her death.

MONROVIA, San Gabriel Valley town incorporated in 1887 and named for its developer, William Newton Monroe (d. 1935). It lies on parts of the former Rancho Santa Anita, purchased by E. J. "Lucky" Baldwin, the high-rolling San Francisco stock gambler. Monroe bought 240 acres from Baldwin in 1875 for $30,000 and proceeded to develop his town, which blossomed with orange groves. Myrtle Street is named for his wife. The teetotaling town leaders prohibited the sale of liquor. In 1903 a local newspaper was founded, and Pacific Electric linked the town with downtown Los Angeles. In 1923 Monrovia adopted a city-manager form of government. The numerous orange groves have long since given way to homes; by 1990 the population stood at 35,761. Monrovians take particular pride in their museums and historic preservation activities. In 1995 the National Civic League, out of regard for Monrovia's downtown revitalization program, crime-cutting campaign, job development policy, and social services for at-risk youths, named the city as one of 10 "All-American Cities."

MONTEBELLO, city of 8 square miles in the San Gabriel Valley, 7 miles east of downtown Los Angeles. It was founded on parts of three ranchos— San Antonio, La Merced, and Paso de Bartolo— and was the site, on 8–9 January 1847, of the Battle of San Gabriel, a Mexican War skirmish involving some 1,000 Californios and U.S. soldiers. In the 1860s Italian-born Alessandro Repetto established a 5,000-acre ranch in the area, part of which Har-

Monrovia land auction, 1886. Courtesy Robert Weinstein Collection.

ris Newmark and Kaspar Cohn, pioneer Los Angeles merchants, took over in 1887. They laid out a townsite originally named Newmark, and in 1900 another part of the rancho was taken over and incorporated by the Montebello Land and Water Company. The community was then little more than a company town run by Simon's Brick Company, "the world's largest brickyard," which was staffed by Mexican laborers from Michoacán. In about 1912 the name Newmark was dropped from the first subdivision, and the entire town became known as Montebello ("beautiful mountain" in Italian).

From the turn of the century Montebello's rich fields bore flowers, vegetables, berries, and fruits. Change came swiftly when oil was discovered in 1917: within three years the wells were producing one-eighth of the state's crude oil. As a ploy to prevent the construction of a sewage dump in the nearby hills, Montebello briefly merged with Monterey Park, but in 1920 it broke away and reincorporated as Montebello. The city had 60,738 residents in 1990.

MONTECITO HEIGHTS, hilltop residential neighborhood in Los Angeles, adjacent to Ernest E. Debs Regional Park. Located east of Mount Washington and near downtown, the community, which began to be laid out in 1917, today has about 4,300 residents, many of whom work downtown.

MONTEREY PARK, 7.7-square-mile incorporated city in the San Gabriel Valley, 6 miles east of downtown Los Angeles, north of the Pomona Freeway. It was part of an 1810 grant belonging to Don Antonio María Lugo, which passed into the hands of Italian immigrant Alessandro Repetto in 1866. Richard Garvey Sr. (d. 1930), a successful miner who became the rancho's final owner when he was still a teenager, began developing the town in 1892. In 1906 the development was called Ramona Acres, after the celebrated novel by Helen Hunt Jackson. Residents voted to incorporate in 1916 as a defensive measure, to prevent neighboring Alhambra, Pasadena, and South Pasadena from converting the area into a sewer farm (i.e., a site for processing sewage for irrigation).

Since the 1970s Monterey Park has emerged as the major Chinese enclave in Southern California. The nation's first "suburban Chinatown," it has the highest concentration of Asians (40 percent of the total population) of any city in the country. The demographics owe much to the Chinese developer Frederic Hsieh, who bought and resold many parcels of real estate to immigrants from Taiwan and Hong Kong. Many Asian immigrants to the United States settle first in Monterey Park. The community has innumerable Chinese restaurants, shops, and services, including three Chinese-language newspapers. Ethnic friction was manifest when a controversial ordinance was proposed to make English the official language of the city and for signs to be printed only in English. A compromise was reached, and the controversy subsided. Monterey Park has been hailed as an "All-American City" for its exemplary efforts to assimilate foreigners. The population grew from 49,000 in 1970 to 60,738 in 1990. The city is not to be confused with Monterey Hills, a Los Angeles neighborhood several miles to the northwest.

MONTROSE, community located partly in Glendale and partly in unincorporated territory. In 1913 it was part of La Crescenta. The name, which was selected by a popular contest, is carried by a post office, but there is no Montrose City Hall. In 1991, the estimated population was 2,088.

MOORE, CHARLES W. (1925–), distinguished architect and architectural writer. He designed the Beverly Hills Civic Center, St. Matthew's Episcopal Church in Pacific Palisades, and co-authored *The City Observed: Los Angeles* (1984). A principal in the firm of Moore Ruble Yudell, he is a former UCLA dean, and in 1991 won the Gold Medal of the American Institute of Architects.

MORENO FAMILY, one of the 11 founding families of Los Angeles in 1781. José Moreno, 22 years old, and his wife, María Guadalupe Pérez, 19, were a *mulato* couple from the town of Rosario, Mexico, who married in 1780 on the eve of their departure for California. In their new home they enjoyed success as wheat farmers and were able to ship surplus grain to San Blas, Baja California. José Moreno died at age 47, but María Pérez Moreno lived to the age of 100, the last of the adult founding *pobladores.* Their eldest son, born in Los Angeles in 1787, lived on a ranch in what is today West Hollywood, in an adobe near Larrabee Street and Santa Monica Boulevard; two palm trees at the entrance to the ranch stood as a local landmark for many years. His daughter, Catarina Moreno, married Gen. Andrés Pico, brother of Gov. Pío Pico.

MORGAN, WALLS, AND CLEMENTS, influential Los Angeles architectural firm from about 1910 to the early 1930s. The principals were Octavius Morgan, J. A. Walls, and Stiles O. Clements, who was trained in the Beaux Arts school in Paris. The firm designed scores of the most visible downtown commercial structures. Their 1928 black-and-gold Richfield Building, since razed, was considered a masterpiece. Their many theaters include the Belasco, Globe, El Capitan, Leimert, Mayan, Pantages, and Warner Brothers Western. Some, such as the Pantages Theater (1911)—now called the Arcade—and the Globe Theater (1921) can still be seen downtown. The firm helped introduce the Spanish and Mexican Churrigueresque architectural styles to Los Angeles.

MORMONS, adherents of the Church of Jesus Christ of Latter-Day Saints, first entered Southern California during the Mexican War. The Mormon Battalion reached Los Angeles in late January 1847 as a special U.S. Army detachment. Members of the church then established a colony in San Bernardino.

The modern organization emerged locally in 1923 with the formation of the Los Angeles stake (equivalent of a diocese) that served 4,000 members countywide, in Los Angeles (West Adams district), Long Beach, Ocean Park, San Pedro, Huntington Park, Hollywood, Highland Park, Glendale,

---

The Pullman cars in the winter used to be full of sick people banished from the East by physicians who did not know what else to do with their incurable patients.

—David Starr Jordan, president of Stanford University

Boyle Heights, Inglewood, Lankershim, Alhambra, and Pasadena. Unlike their experience in the eastern part of the nation and early Utah, Mormons entering Southern California encountered no vocal opposition, and by the 1930s they were the third largest religious denomination in the county, exceeded only by Catholics and Jews. Today they proselytize actively among the many ethnic groups residing in Southern California.

The church is organized into wards (congregations), branches (small congregations), and stakes (dioceses). The regional headquarters is the Mormon Temple in Westwood, located on a 25-acre hilltop parcel acquired in the 1930s. The imposing 200,000-square-foot marble structure, with a 257-foot tower topped by a gilt statue of the angel Moroni, was designed by Edward D. Anderson and constructed in 1956. The temple is a sanctuary used for holy rituals and instruction rather than for everyday worship. Since Mormons believe in the need to baptize every person who has ever lived, they actively inquire into their genealogical roots. On the temple grounds in a separate structure, therefore, the church maintains a family research library that offers Mormons and non-Mormons alike access to the world's largest collection of microfilmed genealogical information.

MOROSCO, OLIVER (1875–1945), theater manager and director who at the turn of the century made Los Angeles into a major center for drama. The former treasurer of San Francisco's Grand Opera House came to Los Angeles in 1899 and took over the struggling Burbank Theater. It became a home for stock productions, touring companies, and vaudeville and opera performances. Morosco revolutionized the theater by employing a stable of 500 actors, directors, writers, and stage hands, and by shaping and reshaping new plays rather than relying only on old favorites.

Morosco built the 1,650-seat Majestic Theater on Broadway at a cost of $250,000, and managed the David Belasco Theatre, as well as a fourth theater, built and named by David's brother, Frederick Belasco. The 1,450-seat Morosco Theater at Broadway and 7th, built at a cost of $500,000, was hailed as the finest theater building in the country when it opened on 6 January 1913. Morosco's fortunes soon declined, owing to the rising influence of movies as popular entertainment and the trend toward smaller theaters.

MORTON, PEARL (18??–19??), celebrated madam. She operated the town's most famous bordello in the Murietta Building at Spring and Temple Streets, within sight of City Hall and the police station, on the site of today's Hall of Justice. Opulently furnished, it was a popular haunt for businessmen and politicians. Morton, her white pet bulldog, and her well-dressed "girls" advertised themselves by riding about town in a horse-drawn open carriage. Men followed in their own buggies.

She was protected by, among others, Mayor Arthur Harper and U.S. senator Stephen White, who were frequent visitors at her establishment. Attorney Earl Rogers lived there for weeks at a time. In 1909 the mayor, accused of a variety of corruptions, including taking payoffs from madams, was forced to resign. The new mayor closed the city's brothels, forcing Morton to leave town and to resume her successful career in San Francisco's Barbary Coast. Actress Ona Munson, who played Belle Watling in *Gone with the Wind,* is said to have been made up to look exactly like Pearl Morton, flaming red hair and all.

MOSLEY, WALTER (1952–), writer of hardboiled mysteries. His African American private eye, Ezekiel ("Easy") Rawlins, appears in three crime stories—*Devil in a Blue Dress* (1990), *A Red Death* (1991), and *White Butterfly* (1992)—set in 1948, 1953, and 1956, respectively. Rawlins's beat is mainly South Central Los Angeles.

MOTION PICTURE AND TELEVISION FUND, charitable fund for elderly and infirm movie and television actors. It was founded in 1921 by Mary Pickford, Charlie Chaplin, and Douglas Fairbanks Sr. Its main mission since 1941 has been to support a retirement home in Woodland Hills;

It rained for ten days and ten nights with hardly an intermission—the river overflowed and changed its bed, moving over nearer the Pueblo. . . . The Indian village of Yang Na was a sea of floating wickiups.

—J. Gregg Layne, historian, commenting on the 1815 flood

---

known as "The Lot," it features cottages for independent living, a 256-bed hospital, and landscaped grounds. Some stars, such as Mary Astor and Burgess Meredith, have lived there, but most of the residents have been gaffers, grips, and other behind-the-scenes studio workers. The fund, which has annual operating expenses of over $30 million, also provides some emergency assistance and other social services.

MOTION PICTURE ASSOCIATION OF AMERICA (MPAA), voice and advocate of the American motion picture and television industry. Founded in 1922, it conducts market research, protects copyrights, lobbies Congress, and fights censorship. In cooperation with the National Association of Theater Owners, MPAA enforces a voluntary movie rating system; the ratings include R (Restricted), PG (Parental Guidance Suggested), and PG-13 (Parents Strongly Cautioned). The association maintains national offices in Sherman Oaks, although its chief executive, Jack Valenti, operates from Washington, D.C. The MPAA's international arm is the Motion Picture Export Association of America (MPEAA).

MOUNTAIN LION (*FELIS CONCOLOR*), wild cat also known as puma or cougar. The beautiful nocturnal hunters have been sighted in the mountainous areas of Beverly Hills, Studio City, Tarzana, and Chatsworth. Naturalists estimate that a dozen or so prowl the area. They once preyed on cattle, but now feed on small game and deer, and occasionally pets that stray, unwisely, from their homes.

MOUNTAINS. As much as the ocean or any other geographical feature, mountains define the Los Angeles Basin by ringing it with high walls. Most of the local mountain ranges were formed by powerful geological forces that are still active.

To the northwest lies the Santa Susana chain, which defines the limits of the western San Fernando Valley. On the north and northeast, the San Gabriel and the San Bernardino Mountains sprawl for some 60 miles. These three ranges were sometimes referred to by the Spaniards as the Sierra Madre. In front of them and running parallel are, from west to east, the Santa Monica Mountains, Santa Ana Mountains, Puente Hills, Repetto Hills, and San Jose Hills. These ranges delineate three inland valleys—the San Fernando, the San Gabriel, and the San Bernardino—and, spread out in front of them, the Los Angeles Plain.

The mountains create a barrier to physical movement, define zones of recreation, provide homesites with spectacular views, affect overall climate and weather, block winter storms, and determine a wide range of microclimates—local rainfall and temperature conditions—within the county. The tallest peak in the city is Mt. Lukens, at 5,074 feet; the tallest in the county is Mt. San Antonio (Old

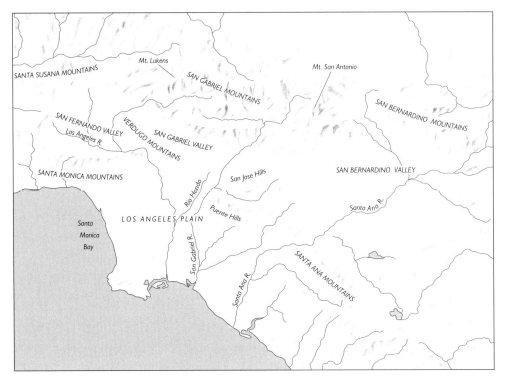

Mountains and other landforms of the city of Los Angeles.

Baldy), at 10,080 feet. Of the total 4,083-square-mile land area of the county, almost half—1,875 square miles—is considered mountainous.

MOUNT BADEN-POWELL, peak in the Mt. Baldy area. It was named to honor Sir Robert Baden-Powell, who founded the Boy Scout movement in 1908.

MOUNT DISAPPOINTMENT, 5,994-foot peak in the San Gabriels. It was so named when a U.S. Army mapping party climbed it in 1875, only to discover a taller and more important peak farther east. It has long been popular among climbers. In 1955 it became a Nike missile base.

MOUNT LOWE, San Gabriel Mountains peak above Altadena, about 4 miles west of Mt. Wilson. It is named for Thaddeus S. C. Lowe, an eccentric scientist and engineer who in 1892 led a party of friends up nearby Oak Mountain. He had served with the aeronautic corps of the U.S. Army during

Mount Lowe Railroad. Pitt Collection.

Circular Bridge, Mt. Lowe R. R. California.

513

the Civil War, using balloons for reconnaissance. In 1893, after four years of construction, Lowe opened the 3,000-foot-long Mt. Lowe Scenic Railway, a narrow-gauge cable line that lifted passengers 1,500 feet in elevation from Mountain Junction into Rubio Canyon. On the first trip, the front car was filled by the Pasadena City Band, which played "Nearer My God to Thee" as the car made its daring way upward through the clouds. On the breathtaking tour, the passengers riding in open-sided cars passed over a curved cantilevered trestle bridge several hundred feet high, from which they had a panoramic view that encompassed distant Santa Catalina Island. At Echo Mountain, on the way to Mt. Lowe, he built a hotel complex and an observatory in 1894. The hotel burned to the ground in 1900. Sold to the Pacific Electric Railway in 1900, the line carried a total of 3.1 million passengers, at $5 a head, until it ceased operating in 1937.

MOUNT LUKENS, highest point in the city of Los Angeles, at 5,074 feet. Rising north of La Crescenta Valley, it was named for Theodore P. Lukens, mayor of Pasadena, a promoter of reforestation.

MOUNT MARKHAM, 5,742-foot peak between Mt. Lowe and San Gabriel Peak, in the San Gabriel Mountains. It is named for Henry H. Markham, a prominent Pasadena resident who served as governor of California from 1891 to 1895.

MOUNT ST. MARY'S COLLEGE, independent Catholic institution primarily for women. Founded in 1925 by the Sisters of St. Joseph of Carondelet, it was temporarily housed at the girls' school St. Mary's Academy, located at Slauson Avenue and Crenshaw Boulevard. In 1927 it purchased 56 acres in the Santa Monica Mountains from the Rodeo Land and Water Company at $4,500 an acre for a campus on Chalon Road. In 1962 the college expanded to a second campus, located on the former estate of Edward L. and Estelle Doheny, in downtown Los Angeles. The old Chalon campus in West Los Angeles continued to offer bachelor's degrees, while the new Doheny campus offered associate and master's degrees. The late Sister Magdalene Coughlin, president from 1976 to 1989, is credited with having built the college into a national model of multicultural education.

MOUNT SAN ANTONIO, also known as Old Baldy, is, at 10,080 feet, the highest peak in Los Angeles County. Located in the San Gabriel Mountains and within the Angeles National Forest, the snow-capped mountain is sometimes visible from as far away as Santa Monica.

MOUNT WASHINGTON, neighborhood above Highland Park off San Rafael Avenue. Sometimes called "the poor man's Bel-Air," it has been favored by artists, writers, and others since the early part of the century. A 1,000-foot cable incline railway ran there beginning in 1909. The late *Los Angeles Times* columnist Jack Smith, a resident, wrote lovingly of the area. On a clear day many homes have a fine view of downtown.

MOUNT WILSON, 5,710-foot peak in the San Gabriel Mountains overlooking Pasadena. Named for Benjamin D. Wilson, an early landowner and mayor of Los Angeles, it is best known as the site of the Mt. Wilson Observatory.

Beginning in 1889 Pasadena entrepreneurs began constructing a toll trail to the mountaintop. That same year Harvard University scientists had a 13-inch telescope installed at the summit, and in 1903 they built an observatory, under the direction of astronomer George E. Hale. Six years later they put in a 60-inch telescope, which was replaced in 1917 by a 100-inch device. Scientists at the observatory, which is now maintained by the Carnegie Institute, have measured the extent of the Milky Way galaxy, but are now often hindered by smog in the atmosphere.

A hotel, built at the summit in 1905 and rebuilt in 1915 after being destroyed by fire, was demolished in 1966. The Mt. Wilson Trail, following a pathway used by Gabrieleño Indians from time immemorial, ascends 8 miles from Sierra Madre to the top of the mountain and is very popular with hikers.

MOVIE INDUSTRY, EARLY HISTORY (1902–1914). The fact that the movie industry became established in Los Angeles was almost accidental. The nation's first cinema, downtown's Electric Theater, opened in 1902, before any movie studio had discovered the area. The American Biograph and Mutoscope Company founded a studio in Los Angeles in 1906. A year later Chicago producer William Selig, influenced by a Los Angeles Chamber of Commerce brochure promising 350 days a year of sunshine, sent actor-turned-director Francis Boggs, along with actors and crew, to finish filming an outdoor scene for *The Count of Monte*

Buster Keaton arrests a policeman. Pitt Collection.

Cristo. Boggs liked Los Angeles and stayed, continuing to work for Selig. He directed *The Power
of the Sultan* (1908), hiring Hobart Bosworth, a
former stage actor recovering from tuberculosis, as
star. Ironically, TB had rendered Bosworth mute.
Sultan, shot outside on a vacant lot at Olive and
7th Streets, adjacent to a Chinese laundry, was the
first dramatic film shot entirely in Los Angeles.
Boggs then rented the roof of a downtown building to make films (both exterior and interior scenes
had to be filmed in natural sunlight). This was
probably the first "permanent" film studio in Los
Angeles. Meanwhile, Selig had moved west and
opened a studio on Alessandro Street.

An influx of new studios in the West began in
1908, spurred by the formation, in the East, of the
Motion Picture Patents Company (MPPC). The
MPPC was made up of such companies as Edison
and Biograph, who owned key patents on film
processes and equipment. Its aim was to destroy
independent movie producers who were filming
without patent rights. These producers, to escape
arrest, imprisonment, and even physical harm, fled
to California.

D. W. Griffith, who in 1909 had come from the
East Coast to film several outdoor scenes in Los Angeles, returned with some of his company (including Mary Pickford) in 1910. He rented a vacant lot at Washington Street and Grand Avenue,
shooting more than 20 films in his first three
months in the area. (The term "lot" as synonymous
with "studio" came from this early practice of renting vacant lots to shoot movies.) The 1910 appearances of the "Biograph Girl," Florence Lawrence,
and the "Vitagraph Girl" anticipated the star system. Earlier films seldom credited actors by name.

In October 1911 the first permanent movie studio opened in Hollywood. English brothers, David
and William Horsley, owners of the New Jersey–based Centaur Company, flipped a coin and
relocated in Los Angeles rather than Florida. Their
studio, at the corner of Sunset Boulevard and
Gower Street (current site of the CBS Building),
had first been a tavern and then a Salvation Army
meeting hall. They bought the building and the
barn in back, for film processing, from Frank
Blondeau, Hollywood's only barber. Their first feature, *The Best Man Wins* (1911), was Hollywood's
first full-length film. Called Nestor Studios, the
Horsley's enterprise was taken over in 1912 by Carl
Laemmle's Universal Pictures.

In 1909 Adam Kessel and Charles Bauman, who
were bookmakers in New York before entering the
movie business, left their East Coast studios and
built an open stage at 1712 Alessandro Street, which
in a few years became the locale of Mack Sennett's
Keystone Company. Thomas Ince, a talented director and an important figure in Hollywood, arrived in 1911 and a year later convinced Kessel and
Bauman to leave the Keystone studio and buy land
in Santa Ynez Canyon. The two men purchased
20,000 acres in a favorite area of Ince's that came
to be known as "Inceville." Ince, meanwhile, established his own studio in Culver City, and by 1913
employed 700 people, had $35,000 worth of build-
ings, and was turning out many films.

By 1912 many people who were to become a permanent part of movie lore had arrived in Los Angeles. Most eastern companies had either moved
to or established branches in Los Angeles. Adolph
Zukor's Famous Players Company was filming
Broadway plays using the stage stars, and Mack

Sennett turned out his first two Keystone films in 1912.

In 1913 Cecil B. De Mille made his first Hollywood film, *The Squaw Man*. De Mille and his partners, Jesse L. Lasky and Samuel Goldwyn, like the Horsley brothers, were escaping the MPPC. *The Squaw Man* was filmed in a rented barn at the Hollywood corner of Selma and Vine. No print survives, but De Mille remade the film in 1918 and again in 1930. In 1913 William Fox, together with other independent producers, initiated an antitrust suit against the MPPC, and by 1917 had broken its power.

Between 1912 and 1914 Mack Sennett, an ex-vaudevillian, was hiring performers with backgrounds similar to his own. The Keystone stable included Roscoe "Fatty" Arbuckle, Mabel Normand, Marie Dressler, Chester Conklin, and their top star, Ford Sterling. When Sterling left, Sennett hired English comic Charlie Chaplin, at a beginning weekly salary of $150. He debuted as a featured player in *Making a Living* (1914), and appeared in 35 more short comedies that year. The "Little Tramp" was introduced in his second short, *Kid Auto Races* (1914), filmed in Venice. He constructed a costume using Arbuckle's pants and hat, Sterling's large shoes worn on the wrong feet, a painted-on moustache, and a walk copied from a London cabbie. Also in 1914 Chaplin and Dressler appeared together in *Tillie's Punctured Romance,* the first full-length comedy ever made.

Lasky, Sennett, Zukor, De Mille, and others were turning out an increasing number of films. Meanwhile, theater owner and exhibitor William Wadsworth Hodkinson was contracting with various producers to distribute their films. As Europe plunged into World War I, that continent's film production slowed. Audiences here and abroad looked increasingly to Hollywood for entertainment. The movie industry had taken root in Los Angeles and would now flourish in the rich soil.

MOVIE STUDIOS were classified in the 1930s and 1940s, and into the 1950s, as the "Big Five" and the "Little Two." The five studios and the men in charge for much of the period were Metro-Goldwyn-Mayer (MGM), run by Irving Thalberg and Louis B. Mayer; RKO Radio Pictures, run by Joseph P. Kennedy and Howard Hughes; 20th Century–Fox, run by Darryl F. Zanuck; Warner Brothers, headed by Jack Warner; and Paramount, run by B. P. Schulberg and Jesse Lasky. The "Little Two" were Columbia Pictures, headed by Harry Cohen, and Universal Studios, run by Carl Laemmle. Trailing behind were such minor companies as Republic Studios and Monogram Pictures. Several highly successful independents produced memorable films as well—the standouts are Walt Disney, David O. Selznick, and Samuel Goldwyn.

The studios' operational scheme was to keep a stable of actors, writers, and directors under contract and control their output. They also tried to command both production and distribution, but

Louis B. Mayer. Courtesy Turner Entertainment Co.

the courts rendered this an illegal restraint of trade in the 1940s. The undisputed leader of the pack was MGM. Although some studios, such as Paramount and Monogram, were located in Hollywood, most were scattered throughout the Los Angeles area: the MGM lot was in Culver City, 20th Century in West Los Angeles, Universal in the San Fernando Valley, and Warner Brothers in Burbank.

In recent decades, a series of corporate mergers, buy-outs, takeovers, bankruptcies, and split-offs has created studio family lineages more convoluted than those of the Greek gods. For example, MGM has sold the Culver City lot and moved elsewhere, and the studio has been divided between Sony and Columbia. According to a *Los Angeles Times* listing of films produced in 1992, the leading studios were Warner Brothers, Disney, Fox, Columbia, Universal, Paramount, and TriStar. The list varies from year to year. Independent organizations now play an increasing role in the industry, and the star stable system has been completely dismantled.

Preservationists have struggled to save the studios' historic structures, sites, and artifacts. A developer recently destroyed a studio building on the corner of Sunset Boulevard and Beachwood Drive originally owned by the pioneer Horsley Studios in 1919. The barn in which De Mille had his first Hollywood office has, however, been moved near the Hollywood Bowl and is preserved by Hollywood Heritage, a volunteer organization headquartered in the historic Wattles Mansion on N. Curson Avenue.

MOVIE THEATERS in Los Angeles have evolved from small storefront nickelodeons, to ornate big-screen movie palaces, to large neighborhood theaters, to small multiplexes in shopping malls. Thomas L. Tally of Waco, Texas, became the first local exhibitor when he opened his "Phonograph and Kinetoscope Parlor" in August 1896 at 311 S. Spring Street. This open-front store contained six viewing machines. Soon Tally acquired a Vitascope projector and renamed his establishment the "Phonograph, Kinetoscope, and Vitascope Parlor." Patrons who feared being in the dark during the day could sit behind a screen and peek through a hole at the projection. In April 1902 Tally opened the Electric Theater at 262 S. Main, the first real movie house, a sit-down theater with 200 seats. Admission cost a dime and each film short was about 50 feet long. His first bill was *Capture of the Biddle Brothers* and *Blizzard Scenes in New York.*

The first theater engineered for sound was the Art Deco cinema in the Avalon casino, on Santa Catalina Island, which opened in 1930. The 1,200-seat theater still exists. Filmmakers De Mille, Mayer, and Goldwyn sailed their yachts there to preview films.

In the early part of the century downtown's Broadway glittered with the lights of movie palaces and vaudeville theaters, some of which have survived thanks to an active preservation campaign. The theaters were famous for their exotic façades, glittering crystal chandeliers, sweeping stairways, and elaborate ladies' and men's restrooms. The Cameo Theater, built in 1910, was the oldest continuously running movie theater in Los Angeles when it closed in 1991. The Globe Theater, which opened in 1913 as the Morosco theatrical chain's Southern California outlet, suffered severe damage

Grand Theatre, 10 cents a ticket. Courtesy Robert Weinstein Collection.

recently when it was converted into a flea market. The Million Dollar Theater, showman Sid Grauman's first Los Angeles picture palace, opened with a premiere of *The Silent Man* (1917); it is now a church. The Loew's State Theater, opened in 1921 as part of a nationwide chain, became the most successful of the downtown movie theaters. The Orpheum Theater, opened in 1926, was the Los Angeles showcase for the popular Orpheum vaudeville circuit, and a favorite venue for performers Will Rogers, Count Basie, Duke Ellington, and Jack Benny. It still has its original Wurlitzer organ. The United Artists Theater, opened by Charlie Chaplin, Mary Pickford, Douglas Fairbanks, and D. W. Griffith in 1927, is now the headquarters of Dr. Gene Scott's vast television ministry. The exotic-looking Mayan Theater on S. Hill Street, which also opened in 1927, has been completely renovated and functions as a nightclub. The Los Angeles Theatre, the most ornate of the palaces, which opened with the premiere of Charlie Chaplin's *City Lights* in 1931, is slated for renovation.

Not surprisingly, Los Angeles helped pioneer the drive-in theater. The first was built in New Jersey, but the second, the Picwood Theater, which opened in the 1930s, was at the corner of Pico and Westwood Boulevards.

MTA. *See* Los Angeles County Metropolitan Transportation Authority

MUDSLIDES. *See* Landslides

MULBERRY TREES were first planted locally in the 1860s by French pioneer Louis Prevost to foster an experimental silk industry. He set out thousands of cuttings in his 50-acre nursery/cocoonery on S. Main Street. When he died in 1869 the enterprise perished with him, though some trees remained as his memorial.

MULHOLLAND, WILLIAM (1855–1935), water czar of Los Angeles. The Dublin, Ireland–born youth spent four years as a merchant seaman, using his leisure time at sea to teach himself mathematics. Later he was an itinerant knife sharpener and lumberjack in Michigan, sold dry goods in Pittsburgh, prospected in mines, and fought Indians in Arizona, before arriving in Los Angeles in 1877 with $10 in his pocket. While laboring as a well digger he taught himself geology and engineering from public library books. He was living

William Mulholland. Courtesy Los Angeles Dept. of Water and Power.

in a shack near Los Feliz and Riverside Drive (near the Mulholland memorial fountain) when, in 1878, he began working as a *zanja* (ditch) laborer for the private water company of Los Angeles. He made his way up to chief engineer and became superintendent in 1886.

The drought of the 1890s convinced Mulholland that Los Angeles would stagnate without a new water supply: "Whoever brings the water will bring the people" became his motto. Fred Eaton, an ex-mayor, approached him with the idea of importing water from the eastern Sierra Nevada. The pair rode by buckboard to Owens Valley in 1904 to survey the route of an aqueduct. Despite a falling-out with Eaton, "the Chief" began acquiring the land and water rights and designing a water delivery system from the Owens Valley. Mulholland met with Pres. Theodore Roosevelt to clear the path through federal property. He then supervised an army of 5,000 workers in the six-year construction of the 233-mile engineering marvel: the Los Angeles Aqueduct. Mulholland also established and headed the Department of Water and Power (DWP), the largest and most efficient municipal water company in the nation at the time. Amazingly, the longest aqueduct in the world worked exclusively by gravity flow. On 5 November 1913, 40,000 spectators cheered as the water roared down into the

San Fernando Valley, and Mulholland delivered one of the shortest ceremonial addresses on record: "There it is! Take it!"

Triumph turned to tragedy on 12 March 1928 when the St. Francis Dam, a DWP installation in the Santa Clara River valley, collapsed, killing 450 people in Los Angeles and Ventura Counties. A jury blamed the beloved hero for the disaster, and he assumed full responsibility, admitting that the calamity probably resulted from a flawed engineering design. The terrible event destroyed Mulholland's reputation and cast him into deep despair. (In 1992 a professional engineering association exonerated him posthumously.) Unquestionably, he was one of the most crucial figures in Los Angeles history, making possible the city's expansion beyond a population limit of 250,000. In the movie *Chinatown,* the character of murder victim Mulray, a figure unwittingly caught up in nefarious water dealings, is based, very loosely, on Mulholland.

MULHOLLAND DRIVE, scenic highway at the crest of the Santa Monica Mountains, named after the legendary water engineer and city builder William Mulholland. Its official opening in 26 December 1924 evoked great fanfare. The occasion was marked by an aerial display, a rodeo show featuring cowboy star Tom Mix, a celebration in the Hollywood Bowl, and a carnival on Vine Street.

The highway winds 21 miles from Cahuenga Pass in Hollywood to the Pacific Ocean at Leo Carrillo State Beach. Much of it passes through undeveloped area in the Santa Monica Mountains National Recreation Area. Turnoffs with picturesque views of the San Fernando Valley, especially at night, have made the road a "lover's lane." Since the 1960s homeowners associations and environmentalists have waged an incessant battle with developers to protect the natural character of the area adjacent to the two-lane serpentine road. Numerous celebrities own homes where the drive passes through affluent Beverly Hills and Bel-Air.

MURALS are so prevalent in Los Angeles that the city has recently been declared the "Mural Capital of the World." The art form has a long lineage, going back in time to local Indians' cave paintings. Murals frequently express radical social commentary. In 1806 the padres of San Fernando Mission conscripted an Indian neophyte to paint religious scenes on the church walls of the San Fernando Mission. The remarkable mural series "The Four-teen Stations of the Cross," attributed to neophyte Juan Antonio and adapted from engravings, can be interpreted as demonstrating the Indians' hostility to the Spanish soldiers, who are depicted as tormentors of the Indians as well as of Christ.

Los Angeles's modern mural era began with Mexican muralist David Alfaro Siqueiros (1896–1974). While living in Los Angeles from May to November 1932, he taught at the Chouinard School of Art and painted "A Workers' Meeting." He was also commissioned to paint a mural on an Olvera Street wall, which he called "Tropical America." When Christine Sterling, the doyenne of Olvera Street, deciphered the symbolism—an American eagle preying on Mexican peasants—she was outraged and had it whitewashed. (It has been restored and will eventually be shown again.) The renowned Marxist muralist also painted a panel on the patio wall of a private Pacific Palisades home titled "Portrait of Present-Day Mexico" that is today valued at $1.5 million.

During the 1930s the federal arts program of the Work Projects Administration (WPA) commissioned painters—including, locally, Howard Warshaw, Huge Balin, and Millard Sheets—to beautify post office buildings and libraries by painting large murals on the walls.

In the 1960s murals began to appear spontaneously on buildings in East Los Angeles and Venice. Some, crafted by nonprofessionals, depicted local scenes and activities, contained messages of social protest, or portrayed aspects of Mexican history. In 1973 the city subsidized the Inner City Mural Program, giving new legitimacy to the art form. In preparation for the 1984 Olympics, Caltrans sponsored murals on some freeways. The Community Redevelopment Agency (CRA) also promoted new murals, but, in an incident reminiscent of the Siqueiros affair, it rejected Barbara Carrasco's wall painting "L.A. History—A Mexican Perspective" owing to its militant depiction of the treatment of minorities. The CRA removed the wall containing the offending work and presented it to the artist. Yet despite occasional dissension, public subsidies continued. In 1991 the city financed ethnic and environmental panels in an art program called "Neighborhood Pride: Great Walls Unlimited." One of them, "The Party at Lan Ting," is Chinatown's first mural, and graces the public library branch at Yale and College Streets.

In all, there are said to be 1,500 murals in Los Angeles—enough for one cultural group to have arranged a special four-hour bus tour to sample them. Interestingly, the fly-by-night graffiti virtuosos who desecrate walls throughout Los Angeles often seem to avoid harming murals.

MURDER CASES have long captured the public imagination, especially if they involved the high and mighty of Los Angeles. Sensational homicides that presented a dark counterpoint to Southern California's otherwise sunny reputation have always received national newspaper coverage. Even a boosterish newspaper such as the *Los Angeles Times* has tended to relish the bizarre details of grim crimes associated with the exotic, the rich, and the famous. Celebrity-studded Hollywood, which middle Americans increasingly viewed as decadent, was subject to especially close public scrutiny in the 1920s and 1930s. The hard-boiled detective novelist Raymond Chandler, who dealt with many strata of Los Angeles society, skillfully cultivated a *noir* image in his popular murder mysteries. A representative sampling of actual, well-publicized crimes might include the following:

Griffith J. Griffith was a wealthy and well-known Los Angeles businessman who in 1896 had donated 3,500 acres of land to the city to create Griffith Park. By 1903 he was an alcoholic unreasonably fearful of the Roman Catholic Church, of which his wife, Christina, a descendant of the Verdugo family, was a member. He accused her, among other things, of conspiring with the pope to kill him, steal his money, and give it to the church. In a drunken rage he shot Christina. The bullet tore out her eye, but she managed to escape. Griffith was defended by the brilliant young attorney Earl Rogers, who offered an early innocent-by-virtue-of-insanity defense. The jury, however, found Griffith guilty, and he was given a two-year sentence; owing to good behavior, he served only one year at San Quentin.

John and James McNamara made headlines in 1910, when the entire nation focused on the bombing of the *Los Angeles Times* Building that killed 20 employees and injured 17. The accused McNamara brothers, union activists, were defended by Clarence Darrow, the country's preeminent defense attorney. Other prominent people involved in the case were Samuel J. Gompers, head of the American Federation of Labor; Job Harriman, Socialist candidate for mayor; journalist Lincoln Steffens; and Gen. Harrison Gray Otis, owner of the *Times.* On 1 December 1911, faced by the over-

whelming evidence against them, the McNamaras confessed in an attempt to save themselves from the death penalty. James received a life sentence, his brother John received 15 years.

Roscoe "Fatty" Arbuckle, a film comic second in popularity only to Charlie Chaplin in 1921, was indicted and tried for the rape and subsequent death of screen hopeful Virginia Rappe during a wild, three-day drunken spree in a San Francisco hotel. After two hung-jury trials (aided, it was said, by studio money), a third jury entered a not-guilty verdict. Arbuckle's career, however, was over.

Clara Phillips, a former chorus girl, learned her husband was having an affair. In 1922 she purchased a claw hammer; after downing drinks in a speakeasy with her best friend, Peggy Caffee, and the rival for her husband's affections, Alberta Meadows, the three women went for a car ride. In a deserted area, Phillips lured Meadows from the car and, to Caffee's horror, bashed her to death

---

Bad taste, to me, is the attempt to express style without humor or mystery, and you can certainly see plenty of that in L.A.　　—Charlie Scheips, project manager for ART-L.A.

---

with the hammer, smashing her face and disemboweling her. The result was so like being mauled by an animal that Clara Phillips became known as the "Tiger Woman." Indicted for the crime, Phillips pleaded her innocence and accused her friend Peggy Caffee of the murder. She was found guilty, however, and sentenced to 10 years to life in prison. On her release, in 1935, Phillips was greeted by hundreds of fans chanting, "Tiger Woman."

William Desmond Taylor was a respected film director. His 1922 demise reads like a classic murder mystery except that the crime was never solved. When the handsome Englishman's valet entered the apartment of the upscale Hollywood court complex ready for the day's work, he discovered his employer's body on the floor, shot to death and neatly arranged. The many suspects included actress Mabel Normand, to whom Taylor had once been engaged and who was addicted to drugs; Mary Miles Minter, an innocent-looking 17-year-old screen actress with whom he was having an affair; her mother, Charlotte Shelby, another Taylor conquest; a disgruntled former valet; Taylor's former wife; and a man with whom Taylor had had a falling out when both were part of a Canadian army regiment. The case was complicated by a possible cover-up orchestrated by Taylor's studio, as Hollywood was still trying to win back public confidence after the Arbuckle scandal. The studio may have suppressed evidence in the apartment involving aspects of Taylor's sexual orientation and, perhaps, evidence pointing to the murderer.

Otto Sanhuber, a bizarre and unlikely murderer, was dubbed the "Bat Man" during the 1922 murder trial for the shooting death of one Fred Oesterreich. In Milwaukee, Wisconsin, in 1903, 17-year-old Sanhuber and 36-year-old Walburga ("Dolly") Oesterreich became lovers. In 1907 she moved Otto into a small attic space directly above the bedroom she shared with her prosperous, solidly middle-class husband, Fred. Otto lived there for 10 years, emerging during the days to make love with Dolly and do her housework. When the Oesterreichs moved to Los Angeles in 1918, Dolly found

---

Angelenos, as all the world knows, are conceived on freeway off-ramps, born in drive-in maternity clinics, reared on surf boards and, at an advanced age, laid to rest in the same cemetery in which they got married.

—John Weaver, writer

---

a home with an attic and moved her lover into it. In 1922, according to testimony given by Sanhuber many years later, he and Fred Oesterreich had an unexpected confrontation, and Oesterreich was shot as the two men struggled with a gun. Dolly hid Otto away, claiming that an intruder had shot her husband. In 1930 Sanhuber, who had continued to live in the attic even after Fred's death, was discovered. He was charged with murder, a charge that was changed to manslaughter because the statute of limitations had taken effect; however, he was released. Instead Dolly Oesterreich was arrested and charged with conspiracy; she was defended by Hollywood attorney Jerry Giesler. The trial ended in a hung jury, and she, like her former lover, was set free. Her fortune lost in 1929, she

opened a supermarket in Beverly Hills and lived a withdrawn life in an apartment over the store.

Paul Bern, Jean Harlow's bridegroom, was recorded as a suicide. Their marriage was only two months old when Bern's perfumed body was found nude in front of his bedroom mirror, a suicide note and gun beside him. The butler who discovered him called MGM moguls Irving Thalberg and Louis B. Mayer, rather than official investigators. It wasn't until two hours after the two men's arrival on the scene that the police were notified. No one knows what transpired during that time. Immediately afterward, talk circulated about the presence in the house of a mysterious dark-haired woman on the previous evening.

Thelma Todd's 1935 demise, which was also officially recorded as a suicide, or accidental death, generated even more speculation than had Bern's. Todd, a popular and glamorous actress, had never given any hint that she was suicidal. The inquest into, and the coroner's re-creation of, her death by asphyxiation while seated in a car in her garage raised more questions than it answered. As in the Taylor murder, the cast of characters involved former lovers and a jealous wife, as well as a possible connection to organized crime. Again, whispered gossip suggested that a cover-up had taken place and money had changed hands.

The cases in the 1920s and 1930s involving the film industry—others entangled such luminaries as actor Wallace Reid and director/choreographer Busby Berkeley—seriously tarnished Hollywood's image. Under attack by both political figures and the public, the industry instituted a self-imposed censorship system, administered by the "Hays Office." It followed the Production Code of 1930, authored by Will H. Hays, former postmaster general and president of the Motion Picture Producers and Distributors Association of America from 1922 to 1945. Although it silenced critics, very little actually changed. Social critics viewed the mayhem as generational. For many, though, the crimes only proved that there is nothing new under the sun.

MURPHY, FRANKLIN P. (1916–1994), civic and business leader. Born in Kansas City, Mo., Murphy was the son of a physician father and a pianist mother. He graduated from the University of Pennsylvania School of Medicine. While in the army he did research on malaria and other tropical diseases. Murphy practiced and taught medicine, and in 1948 became dean of the University of

Kansas School of Medicine, and then chancellor of the university in 1951. In 1960 he came to UCLA as chancellor, where he presided over the addition of 40 new buildings. During his tenure, which ended in 1968, the student body increased from 20,000 to 30,000.

A patron of the arts, Murphy helped create the Los Angeles County Museum of Art and the Music Center. He served as chairman and CEO of the Times-Mirror Company, parent company of the *Los Angeles Times,* from 1968 to 1980, and was a director of numerous other corporations and served on many boards and foundations devoted to education, art, and philanthropy. At UCLA, both the administration building and the sculpture garden are named in his honor.

MURRAY, JIM (1919–), *Los Angeles Times* sports columnist. Born and educated in Connecticut, Murray worked for the *Los Angeles Examiner, Time* magazine, and *Sports Illustrated* before being hired by the *Times* in 1961. Murray is the recipient of numerous awards, including induction into the National Sportscasters and Sportswriters Hall of Fame in 1977. He received the Pulitzer Prize for commentary in 1990, and has authored several books, including *Jim Murray: An Autobiography* (1993).

MUSCLE BEACH, small strand in Santa Monica. Since the late 1930s bodybuilders, gymnasts, and lifeguards have played volleyball and worked out on this patch of sand, to the great appreciation of onlookers. Vic Tanny, Joe Gold, Jack LaLanne, Steve "Hercules" Reeves, and Abigail "Pudgy" Stockton have all flexed their pecs here. Bernard McFadden, pioneer bodybuilder and health food promoter, sponsored physical culture events, including the Mr. America and Mr. Universe con-

Bodybuilders at Muscle Beach. Photo by Phil McCarten/ PhotoEdit.

tests, at the beach. More recently bodybuilders have shifted to Venice Beach, which now claims the name of Muscle Beach.

MUSEUM OF MINIATURES. *See* Carole and Barry Kaye Museum of Miniatures

MUSEUMS, both public and private, have enjoyed a renaissance in recent decades. They have become more specialized, diverse, and numerous, reflecting the increasing population, ethnic diversity, and cosmopolitanism of Los Angeles. A reliable 1990s directory lists more then 200 museums in the Los Angeles region.

The grandparents of local museums are the California State Museum of Science and Industry (1912), the Los Angeles County Museum of Natural History (1913)—both located in Exposition Park, and the latter today being the largest museum west of the Mississippi—and the Southwest Museum in Echo Park, incorporated by Charles Fletcher Lummis in 1907 and completed in 1914. The Cabrillo Marine Museum, established in 1934, is another patriarch, though not quite as old.

Los Angeles rose quickly as a major metropolis, attracting not only wealthy collectors and patrons in the 1960s but also state and federal funding. The Los Angeles County Museum of Art (LACMA) split off from the Natural History Museum and moved to spacious new quarters in Hancock Park on Wilshire Boulevard, where it displayed one of the nation's most valuable art collections. LACMA also acquired a notable satellite in the Fairfax area: the George C. Page Museum of La Brea Discoveries, located beside the La Brea Tar Pits and specializing in Ice Age fossils. Other widely celebrated museum openings of the era involved the Norton Simon Museum of Art (1974), formerly the Pasadena Museum of Modern Art, in Pasadena; the J. Paul Getty Museum (1974), in Malibu; the Museum of Contemporary Art (MOCA), featuring art produced since 1940, which opened on Bunker Hill in the 1970s; and the Temporary Contemporary art museum, a facility administered by MOCA, in Little Tokyo.

Smaller, more specialized museums came into existence as well. They include the Los Angeles Maritime Museum; the Fort MacArthur Military Museum; the Museum of Cultural History at UCLA, as well as UCLA's Wight Gallery; the Armand Hammer Museum of Art and Cultural Center, now associated with UCLA; the Wells Fargo History

Academy of Motion Picture Arts and Sciences, Beverly
 Hills
Adobe de Palomares, Pomona
Alhambra Historical Society Museum, Alhambra
Amateur Athletic Foundation of Los Angeles Library,
 Los Angeles
American Military Museum and Heritage Park, El Monte
American Quilt Research Center, Los Angeles
Andrés Pico Adobe, Mission Hills
Angels Attick, Santa Monica
Antelope Valley California Poppy Reserve Visitors Center,
 Lancaster
Antelope Valley Indian Museum, Lancaster
ARCO Corporate Art Collection, Los Angeles
Armand Hammer Museum of Art and Cultural
 Center/UCLA, Los Angeles
Autry Museum of Western Heritage, Los Angeles
Avila Adobe, Los Angeles
Azusa Historical Society Museum, Azusa
Baldwin Park Museum, Baldwin Park
Banning Residence Museum, Wilmington
Bolton Hall Museum, Tujunga
Bradbury Building, Los Angeles
Brand Library and Arts Center, Glendale
Cabrillo Marine Museum, San Pedro
California Afro-American Museum, Los Angeles
California Center for the Arts Museum, Los Angeles
California Museum of Science and Industry, Los Angeles
Campo de Cahuenga, North Hollywood
Canoga-Owensmouth Historical Museum, Canoga Park
Carole and Barry Kaye Museum of Miniatures,
 Los Angeles
Casa Adobe de San Rafael, Glendale
Casa de Adobe, Highland Park
Catalina Island Museum, Avalon
Centinela Adobe Complex, Los Angeles
Chatsworth Museum, Chatsworth
Children's Museum, Los Angeles
Chinese Historical Society of Southern California,
 Los Angeles
Clark Humanities Museum/Claremont Colleges,
 Claremont
Clarke-Gill Estate, Santa Fe Springs
Craft and Folk Art Museum, Los Angeles
Dibble Museum, City of Industry
Doctor's House, Glendale ·
Drum Barracks Civil War Museum, Wilmington
Duarte Historical Museum, Duarte
Eagle Rock Valley Historical Society Museum, Eagle Rock
El Dorado Nature Center and Museum, Long Beach
Elizabeth Holmes Fisher Gallery/USC, Los Angeles
El Molino Viejo Museum (The Old Mill), San Marino
El Monte Historical Society Museum, El Monte
El Pueblo de Los Angeles City Historical Monument,
 Los Angeles
Ferndell Nature Museum, Los Angeles
Firehouse and Jail Museum, Covina
Firehouse No. 1, Los Angeles
Forest Lawn Memorial Park—Hollywood Hills,
 Los Angeles

Fort MacArthur Military Museum, San Pedro
Fowler Museum of Cultural History/UCLA, Los Angeles
Franklin D. Murphy Sculpture Garden/UCLA,
 Los Angeles
Frederick R. Weisman Museum of Art, Pepperdine
 University, Malibu
Frederick S. Wight Gallery/UCLA, Los Angeles
Frederick's Lingerie Museum, Hollywood
Galleries of the Claremont Colleges, Claremont
Gallery in Motion, Glendale
Gamble House Museum, Pasadena
George Anderson House, Monrovia
George C. Page Museum of La Brea Discoveries,
 Los Angeles
Getty Center, Brentwood
Gilbert Sproul Museum, Norwalk
Glendora Historical Society and Museum, Glendora
Goez Art Studios, Los Angeles
Greystone Park, Beverly Hills
Grier-Musser Museum, Los Angeles
Griffith Observatory, Los Angeles
Grunwald Center for the Graphic Arts/UCLA, Los Angeles
Hancock Memorial Museum/USC, Los Angeles
Hargitt House, Norwalk
Hathaway Ranch Museum, Santa Fe Springs
Herbarium/UCLA, Los Angeles
Heritage Park, Santa Fe Springs
Heritage Square Museum, Los Angeles
Hermosa Beach Historical Museum, Hermosa Beach
Hollyhock House, Los Angeles
Hollywood Bowl Museum, Hollywood
Hollywood Studio Museum, Hollywood
Hollywood Wax Museum, Hollywood
Holyland Exhibition, Los Angeles
Homestead Acre and the Hill-Palmer House, Chatsworth
Huntington Library, Art Collections and Botanical
 Gardens, San Marino
International Buddhist Progress Society, Hacienda Heights
Italian Cultural Institute, Los Angeles
J. Paul Getty Museum, Malibu
Japanese American National Museum, Los Angeles
John Panatier Nature Center, Arcadia
Jonathan Bailey Home, Whittier
Junior Arts Center Gallery, Los Angeles
Korean American Museum, Los Angeles
La Casa Primera de Rancho San Jose, Pomona
La Puente Valley Historical Society Museum, La Puente
Lancaster Museum and Art Gallery, Lancaster
Lannan Foundation, Los Angeles
Latino Museum of History, Art and Culture, Los Angeles
Leonis Adobe, Calabasas
Long Beach Children's Museum, Long Beach
Long Beach Firefighters Museum, Long Beach
Long Beach Museum of Art, Long Beach
Lopez Adobe, San Fernando
Los Angeles Art Association, Los Angeles
Los Angeles Center for Photographic Studies, Los Angeles
Los Angeles Contemporary Exhibitions, Los Angeles
Los Angeles County Medical Association Library,
 Los Angeles

Los Angeles County Museum of Art, Los Angeles
Los Angeles Maritime Museum, San Pedro
Los Angeles Mormon Temple Visitor Center, Los Angeles
Los Angeles Municipal Art Gallery, Los Angeles
Los Angeles State and County Arboretum, Arcadia
Los Angeles Zoo, Los Angeles
Los Encinos State Historic Park Museum, Encino
Lummis Home, El Alisal, Highland Park
Malibu Creek State Park Visitor Center, Malibu
Malibu Lagoon Museum and Adamson House, Malibu
Manhattan Beach Historical Society Collection,
    Manhattan Beach
Mann's Chinese Theatre, Hollywood
Max Factor Museum of Beauty, Hollywood
Maxwell H. Dubin/Alfred Wolf Exhibit Center,
    Los Angeles
McGroarty Cultural Arts Center, Los Angeles
Meridian Iron Works, South Pasadena
Mildred E. Mathias Botanical Garden/UCLA, Los Angeles
Mission San Fernando Rey de España Museum,
    Mission Hills
Mission San Gabriel Arcángel Museum, San Gabriel
Mount Wilson Institute, Pasadena
Muller House, San Pedro
Museum of African American Art, Los Angeles
Museum of Chinese American History, Los Angeles
Museum of Contemporary Art, Los Angeles
Museum of Flying, Santa Monica
Museum of Jurassic Technology, Los Angeles
Museum of Neon Art, Los Angeles
Museum of Television and Radio, Beverly Hills
Museum of Tolerance, Los Angeles
NASA Dryden Flight Research Facility Museum, Edwards
    Air Force Base, Antelope Valley
National Hispanic Museum, Los Angeles
Natural History Museum of Los Angeles County,
    Los Angeles
Neff Home, La Mirada
Norton Simon Museum, Pasadena
Otis Parson Gallery, Los Angeles
Pacific Asian Museum, Los Angeles
Palos Verdes Art Center, Rancho Palos Verdes
Peterson Automotive Museum, Los Angeles
Petterson Museum of Intercultural Art, Claremont
Phillips Mansion, Pomona
Pico Rivera Historical Display, Pico Rivera
Pío Pico Mansion, Whittier
Placentia Canyon Nature Center, Newhall
Point Vicente Interpretive Center, Rancho Palos Verdes
Queen Mary Museum, Long Beach
Radio and Television Museum, Beverly Hills
Ralph W. Miller Golf Library and Museum, City of Industry

Rancho Los Alamitos Historical Ranch and Gardens,
    Long Beach
Rancho Los Cerritos Historic Site, Long Beach
Rancho Santa Ana Botanic Garden, Claremont
Raymond M. Alf Museum of Life, Claremont
Redondo Beach Historical Museum, Redondo Beach
Richardson House and Lizzie's Trail Inn, Sierra Madre
Rose Hills Memorial Park, Whittier
Rowland Museum, City of Industry
SS *Lane* Victory Memorial Museum, San Pedro
Saddleback Butte Park Visitor Center, Lancaster
Salvation Army Western Territorial Museum, Torrance
San Gabriel Historical Association Museum,
    San Gabriel
Santa Monica Heritage Museum, Santa Monica
Santa Monica Historical Society and Museum,
    Santa Monica
Santa Monica Mountains National Recreational Area
    Visitor Center, Calabasas
Santa Monica Museum of Art, Santa Monica
Saugus Train Station and Museum, Newhall
Self-Realization Fellowship Lake Shrine Museum,
    Pacific Palisades
Sepúlveda House, Los Angeles
Skirball Cultural Center and Museum, Los Angeles
South Coast Botanic Garden, Palos Verdes Peninsula
Southwest Museum, Highland Park
Sunland-Tujunga Little Landers Historical Society,
    Sunland-Tujunga
Temporary Contemporary Museum of Art, Los Angeles
Timken Museum of Art, Los Angeles
Topanga State Park Visitor Center, Topanga
Travel Town, Los Angeles
University Art Museum, California State University,
    Long Beach
Virginia Robinson Garden, Beverly Hills
Watts Towers Art Center, Los Angeles
Watts Towers of Simon Rodia State Historic Park,
    Los Angeles
Wells Fargo History Museum, Los Angeles
Western Hotel/Museum, Lancaster
Western Museum of Flight, Hawthorne
Whittier Museum, Whittier
Whittier Narrows Center and Wildlife Sanctuary,
    South El Monte
Will Rogers State Historic Park, Los Angeles
William R. Rowland Adobe Ranch House, Walnut
William S. Hart County Park and Museum, Newhall
Woman's Building, Los Angeles
Woodworth House, Bell Gardens
Workman and Temple Family Homestead Museum,
    City of Industry

Museum of Contemporary Art (MOCA). Photo by Dale Pitt.

Museum; Heritage Square, a parklike setting along the Arroyo Seco providing a refuge for vintage Victorian homes threatened with destruction; the Los Angeles Children's Museum in downtown Los Angeles; the Museum of Tolerance, dedicated to fostering understanding among all people; the Lomita

---

The Pueblo de Los Angeles—the town of the Angels—is not, in its present state, a very angelic place.
    —Charles Nordhoff, travel writer, 1872

Railroad Museum, which focuses on the era of the steam engine; the Long Beach Museum of Art; the University Art Museum on the CSULB campus; the Aerospace Building of the State Museum of Science and Industry in Exposition Park; and the Museum of Flying, located on the former site of the Douglas Aircraft Company in Santa Monica. The subject matter of some of these small museums can be very esoteric, such as the Museum of Neon Art, the Museum of Jurassic Technology, the Fiske Museum of Musical Instruments at the Claremont Colleges, and, open by appointment only, the Air Conditioning and Refrigeration Industry Museum in downtown Los Angeles.

Museums dedicated to preserving the heritage of ethnic groups have proliferated. To name but a few: the California Afro-American Museum in Exposition Park, the Japanese American National Museum in Little Tokyo, the Ruben Salazar Mexican American Hall of Fame in Montebello, the Italian Cultural Institute in Westwood, and the Skirball Cultural Center and Museum in Brentwood.

While many museums had to curtail develop-

mental programs and institute cutbacks in the 1980s and 1990s owing to a reduction in private donations and public funding of the arts, the problem was less severe for a few private institutions. For example, the Autry Museum of Western Heritage, in Griffith Park, was endowed by wealthy film personality Gene Autry. The Museum of Television and Radio opened in 1996 in Beverly Hills. Under construction on a knoll in the Brentwood area of the Santa Monica Mountains was a second J. Paul Getty museum complex. Scheduled for opening before the turn of the century, the Getty Center will feature photographic galleries, conservation laboratories, and a residential facility for visiting scholars in the arts.

A notable museum development in the 1990s was the emergence of "Museum Row" on Wilshire Boulevard. The older, established LACMA and Page Museum were joined, within easy walking distance, by the Carole and Barry Kaye Museum of Miniatures, the Craft and Folk Art Museum, and the Peterson Automotive Museum, the latter administered by the Natural History Museum.

MUSIC, CLASSICAL, began locally with chamber music performed in private homes. The first professional chamber group, the Hayden Quartet, was formed by Harley Hamilton, the city's musical leader in the 1880s and 1890s. He also formed the Woman's Symphony Orchestra, in 1895, and the Los Angeles Symphonic Orchestra, a group that survived for 23 years. It was superseded by the Los Angeles Philharmonic, founded in 1919 by financier, art patron, and amateur cellist William Andrews Clark Jr., who in 1910 had organized the Saint-Saëns Quintet. At the turn of the century two pianists, Alice Coleman and Blanche Rogers, promoted chamber music, the former presenting Pasadena's Coleman Concerts and the latter organizing the Los Angeles Chamber Music Society. In 1910, local music patron Albert C. Blicke formed the Brahms Quartet, bringing musicians from Vienna.

In the 1930s, under conductors Artur Rodzinski and Otto Klemperer, the Los Angeles Philharmonic joined the ranks of major orchestras in the United States. During the summer the Philharmonic played in the Hollywood Bowl, an amphitheater that has been a unique feature of the Los Angeles music scene since 1922. The concert series "Symphonies Under the Stars" has captivated as many as 250,000 people each summer. Other musical performances were staged there as well, including the 1923 debut of Los Angeles baritone Lawrence Tibbett singing the role of Amonasro in *Aida.* In the 1930s the Hollywood Bowl attracted top-flight visiting conductors Eugene Goossens, Bruno Walter, Ernest Bloch, Pierre Monteux, and Leopold Stokowski.

Choral groups, both secular and church affiliated, were part of the musical mix. The earliest choral society was the Euterpe Male Quartet, forerunner of the Orpheus Club. The Women's Lyric Club, established in 1903, lasted for decades. The Los Angeles Oratorio Society was formed in 1912, and the Roger Wagner Chorale, founded in 1964, established a national reputation.

In the 1930s the region attracted European musicians escaping from Hitler such as Otto Klemperer, Kurt Weill, and Ernst Toch. One émigré, the distinguished Austrian composer Arnold Schoenberg, took up residence at UCLA and deeply influenced an entire generation of serious students of music. The USC campus also developed an active music teaching program. The Russian-born composer and conductor Igor Stravinsky was also part of the Los Angeles musical scene, as was Ernst Krenek, who arrived in Los Angeles in 1948.

Classical music in post–World War II Los Angeles made major advances owing to heightened public and private support for the arts. The opening of the Music Center in 1964 not only provided a spectacular new venue for the Philharmonic, but also became home to the new Los Angeles Master Chorale and Sinfonia Orchestra, which immediately became a world-class ensemble. The Music Center sponsors opera, although the city has never supported a major resident company. The year 1968 saw the formation of the Los Angeles Chamber Orchestra. Meanwhile, various communities sponsor their own orchestras, chorales, and chamber groups.

MUSIC, FOLK AND ETHNIC, has been an integral feature of Southern California culture since earliest times. Music played a vital role in the daily life of the local native peoples—more so than among most other North American Indians. Their musical patterns are said to suggest syncopation and to resemble Asian music. Some of the instrumentation employing rattles, flutes, drums, and wooden clappers survived long enough to be recorded by Charles F. Lummis in 1900.

During the colonial epoch, 1781 to 1848, *pobladores* commonly sang Spanish and Mexican folk songs, some of which remained popular for several decades into the American period. Singing was a popular family pastime, and people often composed their own songs or added verses to existing ones. By the 1870s, however, American music had become dominant and traditional melodies were largely forgotten. Fortunately, Lummis not only preserved the music of the Native Americans, but also recorded hundreds of Spanish folk songs sung to him by survivors of the old era.

In more recent years, ethnic and racial contributions to music in Los Angeles have been made by Mexican mariachi players on the Eastside, African American jazz musicians on Central Avenue, and Croatian folk dance groups in San Pedro, to mention only a few.

MUSIC, MOVIE, was shaped by the emergence of the film, radio, and record industries. With the shift to sound, movie studios spared no effort in recruiting instrumentalists, singers, classically trained composers, and even songsmiths from New York's Tin Pan Alley. Among composers who wrote notable film scores are Jerome Kern, George Antheil, George Gershwin, Robert Russell Bennett, Irving Berlin, Bernard Herrmann, Miklós Rósza, Werner Janssen, Sigmund Romberg, Deems Taylor, Max Steiner, Dimitri Tiomkin, Alfred Newman, Henry Mancini, Victor Young, Jerry Goldsmith, Elmer Bernstein, James Horner, Randy Newman, Bruce Springsteen, and Hans Zimmer. Some of the hundreds of serious artists who appeared in feature films or recorded for the studios were Arturo Toscanini, Grace Moore, Tito Schipa, José Iturbi, Amelita Galli-Curci, Gladys Swarthout, Mario Lanza, Jascha Heifetz, and Ezio Pinza.

The Hollywood entertainment industry—both film and radio—also hired talent from the world of ragtime, jazz, and swing. The big bands of the era—with leaders Benny Goodman, Ina Ray Hutton, Duke Ellington, Tommy and Jimmy Dorsey, Louis Armstrong, Harry James, and Glenn Miller—were all featured regularly in films. It was, incidentally, Paul Whiteman, one of the founders of swing, who gave Bing Crosby, of the "Three Rhythm Boys," his first big break. As the movies attracted popular music stars, the stars attracted the record industry. As a result, Los Angeles quickly came to rank second to New York in the production of popular phonograph records.

MUSIC CENTER OF LOS ANGELES COUNTY, cultural complex on Bunker Hill con-

Los Angeles Music Center, facing Dorothy Chandler Pavilion. Photo by Larry Lee, courtesy Music Center of Los Angeles County.

sisting of three theaters, with more to come. The centerpiece of the 7-acre site is the white-marble Dorothy Chandler Pavilion, a 3,200-seat theater that opened in 1965. It is named for "Buffy" Chandler, the civic leader who made the center a reality by obtaining the patronage of two archrivals in the savings-and-loan industry, Mark Taper and Howard Ahmanson. The Mark Taper Forum, with its semicircular thrust stage and 737 seats, has become, since its opening in 1967, one of the leading regional theaters in the nation. The Ahmanson Theatre, opened in 1964, has a proscenium stage, seats up to 2,071, and has featured hundreds of touring-company productions. In 1995 it received a major renovation. The Dorothy Chandler serves as home to the Los Angeles Philharmonic, the Los Angeles Opera, the Los Angeles Master Chorale, and hosts the annual Academy Awards. A plaza connects and unifies the individual buildings. The Jacques Lipchitz sculpture and playful fountain are a favorite meeting place for crowd watching on performance days. Two new facilities, the Walt Disney Concert Hall and the Dance Gallery, both designed by architect Frank Gehry, are planned additions to the complex.

MUSIC CORPORATION OF AMERICA (MCA), entertainment conglomerate. Lew Wasserman founded the firm in the 1920s as a band-booking agency, remaining part owner and active partner in its operations until 1995. In the 1960s MCA acquired Universal Pictures; Alfred Hitchcock's *The Birds* (1963) was its first film production. Films and television have accounted for about half the company's profits, with the other half coming from music distribution, theme park operations, and book publishing. (Universal City is the nation's third largest theme park, after Disney World and Disneyland.) In 1991 the MCA library included 3,000 feature films and more than 8,500 episodes of 140 television series. The company also had a major stake in Cineplex-Odeon, the Canadian-based theater chain, and in the Curry Company, long a major concessionaire for Yosemite National Park.

In 1990 Japan's Matsushita Electrical Industrial Company, Ltd., purchased the firm for $6.13 billion. Five years later Canada's Seagram Company, headed by Edgar Bronfman Jr., acquired 80 percent of MCA from Matsushita for $5.7 billion.

MUSIC GUILD, organization that has sponsored chamber music concerts by visiting national and international groups since the mid-1940s. Based at the Wilshire Ebell Theater and managed by Eugene Golden, the guild was founded by Alfred Leonard and has been sustained by subscriptions. The Music Guild celebrated its 50th anniversary in the 1994–1995 season.

MUSICIANS UNION. *See* American Federation of Musicians, AFL-CIO, Local 47

MUSLIMS, those who worship Allah and his prophet Mohammed. They number in the tens of thousands in Southern California, and represent great political and cultural diversity. The Nation of Islam (Black Muslims), formed in Chicago in the 1930s, maintains a major place of worship at Misjad Felix Bilas, a large mosque in the South Central district, although many followers attend smaller mosques. The current membership in Southern California is estimated to be about 5,000. Most Muslims of Middle Eastern background attend the Islamic Center of Southern California, one of 30 such regional centers. This center established a Muslim Political Action Committee to encourage Muslims to exercise their vote; it also offered public forums to promote better understanding, especially in the wake of the 1990–1991 Gulf War. The Muslim Woman's League of Southern California and Islamic Research Institute are also active in the region.

MWD. *See* Metropolitan Water District

NAACP. *See* National Association for the Advancement of Colored People

NADEAU, REMI (1819–1887), French Canadian pioneer who arrived in Los Angeles, from New England, in 1861 driving a team of oxen. During the silver-mining excitement in the Cerro Gordo region of Inyo County his teamster operation brought tons of silver to Southern California and carted back food and supplies to the miners. By 1873 he operated 80 such teams. He also built the Nadeau Hotel, Los Angeles's first four-story structure and the first building with an elevator. Remi Nadeau's great-grandson and namesake is a local historian.

NAPLES, man-made island on Alamitos Bay, part of Long Beach. It was developed in 1903 by Arthur Parsons and his Naples Land Company on Bixby Slough, a marshy wetland owned by the Bixby family. He envisioned it as a place of canals, bridges,

and gondolas, much as Abbot Kinney dreamed of Venice West. A few homes were built in 1906, just in time for a severe business depression that curtailed operations. The project was finally completed in the 1920s. The island's hotel was operated by Almira Hershey of the famous chocolate family. The canal walls and bridges suffered considerable damage in the 1933 earthquake and had to be rebuilt. Naples today has comfortable residences along the shore, and is home to the Long Beach Yacht Club.

NATIONAL ASSOCIATION FOR THE ADVANCEMENT OF COLORED PEOPLE (NAACP), civil rights organization founded in 1910 and active in Los Angeles since 1913. Its agenda has been to remove the color bar in all public institutions and to achieve equal justice in courts of law. The national head, W. E. B. DuBois, visited Los Angeles when the local chapter was founded.

Naples Island, Long Beach. Photo by M. Burgess, courtesy Long Beach Area Convention & Visitors Bureau.

Citing the color bar in hotels and restaurants, labor union discrimination, and the hardships faced by African American women in industry, he declared that "Los Angeles is not a paradise, much as the sight of its lilies and roses might lead one at first to believe." The national NAACP held its first western convention at the Hotel Somerville on Central Avenue in 1928. In the late 1940s the Los Angeles NAACP's legal battles against restrictive covenants, discrimination in housing, and school segregation met with little success. In 1962 it joined with the American Civil Liberties Union (ACLU) and the Congress on Racial Equality (CORE) to launch a major legal challenge to school segregation. This effort led to long and painful litigation, court-ordered busing, and a powerful backlash against busing, that did not end until the 1970s.

NATIONAL CHICANO MORATORIUM, coalition formed in 1969 by the militant Brown Berets, a Mexican American group of young activists, to oppose the Vietnam War. Headed by UCLA student leader Rosalio Muñoz, it protested the disproportionate number of Mexican youths killed in the war. A march involving 20,000 to 30,000 protesters, on 29 August 1970, culminated in violence at Laguna Park when sheriff's deputies and police tear-gassed and clubbed demonstrators indiscriminately. Much property damage and looting occurred. Tear-gas projectiles killed a 15-year-old boy and newspaperman Ruben Salazar, who was covering the story for the *Los Angeles Times*.

NATIVE AMERICANS occupied the Los Angeles region for thousands of years before the coming of Europeans, and live there still. The most

Native American artist Michael Horse painting a mural of prehistoric horses for the exhibit "Spirit Horses," Southwest Museum. Photo by Topi Arvi, courtesy Southwest Museum.

widespread group in the Los Angeles Basin were the Tongva, a Shoshonean people whom the Spanish colonists called Gabrieleños because of their connection with the Catholic mission of San Gabriel. At any given time the Tongva probably numbered 5,000 to 10,000. Another major Indian group, the Chumash, a coastal people with a large settlement in Ventura and smaller ones in Malibu, occupied the coastal area and the western canyons of the Santa Monica Mountains as long as 10,000 years ago. They lived in the Temescal Canyon area apparently until the late 1800s. Yet a third group, the Tataviam, with some 1,000 people living in 20 villages, resided in the region north of the San Fernando Valley.

In recent decades Los Angeles County, which has attracted Native Americans from outside the state, has acquired the largest Indian population of any county in the nation—some 50,000 to 200,000 in 1990, by various estimates. Of the more than 100 separate peoples represented, the Navaho (Dineh) are the most numerous. Individual nations, tribes, and groups regularly conduct traditional dances and hold powwows or other ceremonies at special gatherings at UCLA, CSUN, and other locations.

The Los Angeles Indian population grew most noticeably before 1980, when the federal government attempted to "terminate" the reservations—that is, to force Indians off the reservations and into mainstream American society. Many who relocated suffered from the stress of urbanization, discrimination, poverty, and lack of social visibility. Approximately 20 percent of Native Americans live below the poverty level. Their fate is determined by a bewildering array of federal agencies: the Bureau of Indian Affairs (BIA); U.S. Senate Select Committee on Indian Affairs; Department of Labor, Health, and Human Services; Department of the Interior; and Department of Housing and Urban Development (HUD).

Although there was no single locale where Native Americans concentrated, many lived in Long Beach and Bell Gardens. In 1976 the 15-member Los Angeles City-County Native American Indian Commission was formed to seek funds for programs that would aid local Native Americans, including advocating legislation and disseminating information. The Southern California Indian Center on W. 6th Street offered social services as well as educational, cultural, economic, and recreational programs.

NATURAL HISTORY. *See* Birds; Chaparral; Mountains; Reptiles; Wildflowers; Wildlife; and individual plants and animals

NATURAL HISTORY MUSEUM OF LOS ANGELES COUNTY. *See* Los Angeles County Museum of Natural History

NAVARRO FAMILY, one of the founding families of the *pueblo* of Los Angeles in 1781. They were José Antonio Navarro, a 42-year-old *mestizo* farmer; his wife, María Regina Navarro, a 47-year-old *mulata;* and their three children, aged 10, 9, and 4. María Regina died in 1785, and a year later José Navarro was punished for adultery; he was eventually exiled to San Jose and San Francisco. The Navarro son, who became a farmer, also served as sexton in the Plaza Church in the 1830s and 1840s.

NAZIS. *See* German-American Bund

NEENACH, rural community west of Lancaster, 73 miles northwest of downtown Los Angeles. It was officially recognized in 1890. The name is probably of Shoshonean origin, but of unknown meaning.

NEGRO ALLEY, notorious street east of the Plaza, running parallel to Main Street and connecting Aliso Street with the Plaza. Known in the Mexican era as Calle de los Negros, this 40-foot-wide, block-long strip was crammed on both sides with shops, saloons, and gambling dens. Men went armed, and violent crimes were commonplace. In October 1871 the alley was the scene of bloodshed during the Chinese Massacre. In the 1870s it was a favorite meeting place for those involved with the Cerro Gordo silver mines in Inyo County. By the 1880s the street had opium dens, houses of prostitution, a joss house, and had become part of Chinatown. The city council changed the name to Los Angeles Street in 1877, and in the early 20th century obliterated the buildings by straightening and widening the street.

NEIGHBORHOODS, in the city of Los Angeles, have historically had amorphous geographic boundaries, elusive names, and fluid ethnic composition. Probably more than in comparable cities, they have been impacted by population booms, changing migration patterns, aggressive real estate development, freeway construction, and transformations in land use.

While some early communities and neighborhoods, such as Sonoratown near the Plaza, have disappeared completely, many others have persisted. Westlake, Boyle Heights, Lincoln Heights, and Fairfax are examples of neighborhoods that have survived but undergone radical demographic changes from shifting migration patterns. Watts went from being a white farm suburb to a predominately black town and is now a community of both Latinos and African Americans. Downtown had thriving residential neighborhoods early in the century, although the introduction of interurban streetcar lines and the decentralization of industry soon gave its working-class residents an opportunity to move to the suburbs. The affluent 19th-century neighborhood on Bunker Hill declined in the 1930s and was eradicated completely by urban renewal efforts in the 1960s. Although the Community Redevelopment Agency has taken strong measures to re-create viable residential neighborhoods in the downtown area, they have yet to succeed.

The naming of neighborhoods has been a haphazard process. It often reflects the whims of tract developers, who favor the names of local ranchos, of their own hometowns or of family members, or romantic literary allusions. On occasion, as in the case of Tarzana, the local residents were allowed to

Negro Alley, late 1880s. Courtesy Photographic Collections, Los Angeles Public Library.

Some Los Angeles City Neighborhoods

Adams	Hollywood	Sepulveda
Angeleno Heights	Hyde Park	Shadow Hills
Arleta	Jefferson Park	Sherman Oaks
Atwater Village	Koreatown	Sherman Village
Bel-Air/Bel-Air Estates	Lake View Terrace	Silverlake
Benedict-Coldwater Canyons	Larchmont Village	South Carthay
Beverly Glen	La Tuna Canyon	South Central
Boyle Heights	Leimert Park	South Vermont
Brentwood/Brentwood Village	Lincoln Heights	Studio City
Carthay Circle	Little Tokyo	Sunland
Central Avenue	Los Feliz	Sun Valley
Central City	Mar Vista	Sylmar
Century City	Mid-City	Tarzana
Chatsworth	Miracle Mile District	Terminal Island
Cheviot Hills	Mission Hills	Toluca Lake
Chinatown	Montecito Heights	Tujunga
Country Club Park	Monterey Hills	Valley Village
Crenshaw District	Mount Olympus	Van Nuys
Cypress Park	Mount Washington	Venice
Downtown Los Angeles	North Hills	Virgil Village
Eagle Rock	North Hollywood	Watts
Echo Park	Northridge	West Adams
El Sereno	Olive View	Westchester
Elysian Valley	Pacific Palisades	Westdale
Encino	Pacoima	West Hills
Exposition Park	Palms	Westlake
Fairfax Village	Panorama City	West Los Angeles
Fashion Village	Park La Brea	Westwood
Glassell Park	Park Mile	Westwood Village
Granada Hills	Pico Union	Wholesale District
Hancock Park	Playa del Rey	Wilmington
Happy Valley	Porter Ranch	Wilshire Center
Harbor City	Rancho Park	Windsor Square
Harbor Gateway	Reseda	Winnetka
Hermon	San Pedro	Woodland Hills
Highland Park	Sawtelle	

SOURCES: Office of the City Clerk, City of Los Angeles; Chief Administrative Officer, County of Los Angeles; *Thomas Guide Los Angeles County Street Guide and Directory* (Irvine, 1995).

choose a name by democratic vote. Since 1962 the Los Angeles City Council has eased the process for changing community or neighborhood names. Homeowners' associations, chambers of commerce, and realty organizations have petitioned with increasing frequency to alter names, usually to protect property values and avoid the stigma of gangs, drugs, crime, or physical blight.

In the 1970s, Los Angeles posted uniform blue-and-white signs to identify over 75 communities. Mounted on light poles, these official placards were based on anecdotal information and custom rather than on professional opinion surveys or old maps. They generally appeared at the center of a given neighborhood, not at the supposed bound-

aries. The designations can be eliminated or altered through community petition, although the process is sometimes long and tortuous. The respected *Thomas Guide* does not include all of them.

Homeowner organizations have contributed to protecting neighborhood interests, especially in middle-class areas where they are mandated by real estate covenants. Elsewhere, neighborhood organizations have coalesced spontaneously, often in response to the threat of commercial overbuilding, street widening, or other public works projects.

From time to time, public-spirited citizens have attempted to revive older subdivision names or to clarify community boundaries in the hopes of empowering local residents, overcoming feelings of alienation, or improving the business climate. Since the 1970s, John Maxon of the Arleta Chamber of Commerce has lobbied in vain before the Los Angeles City Council to gain approval for his meticulously drawn map of the subcommunities of the San Fernando Valley. Gregory Fischer of University Park has crusaded for the revival of nostalgic older tract names. He points out, for example, that the early parcel names for today's Silver Lake—Ivanhoe Hills, Manzanita Heights, Primrose Hill, Sunset Heights, Capitol Hills, Child Heights, and Crestmont—are evocative and might be warmly accepted.

In response to crime, traffic, and parking problems, property owners have increasingly petitioned the city council for permission to erect barricades, fences, or gates that cross public streets. Perhaps the first gated community in the city was Bel-Air, founded by Alphonso E. Bell in the 1920s. The number of gated neighborhoods multiplied in the 1980s, and by 1992 the city council had approved 22 in all; a year later it received 150 more applications. The first older community given permission to install gates was Brentwood Circle, off Sunset Boulevard, in the area near the new Getty Center. The fences are intended to protect homes, condos, and apartments, and to maintain real estate values. Wealthier communities have led the trend toward the iron solution, but even the low-income public housing project Mar Vista Gardens, in Los Angeles, is now surrounded by a fence to deter drug dealers.

Opponents of the physical barriers have argued that marking off and isolating public spaces by race, class, or ethnicity leads to a fortress mentality, political "Balkanization," and cultural isolation. The gates and barriers also pose jurisdictional questions concerning street maintenance and police and fire protection. State courts have disallowed the establishment of new gated communities that force the city to maintain the public roads at the taxpayer's expense but have authorized them where the gated householders pay their own maintenance costs.

Some city areas have instead embraced historic preservation as a way to maintain their neighborhoods. Carthay Circle, near Fairfax Avenue, is a successful example of that trend. The 1990s have seen moves to reverse the perceived decline of residential areas by reinventing community politics and empowering residents at the neighborhood level. In 1996, the mayor and members of the city council began encouraging the formation of neighborhood advisory groups as a surrogate for the grass-root political parties that never existed in Los Angeles. Elected officials tentatively identified about 100 neighborhoods where residents could be convened in special meetings to wrestle with local planning, zoning, transportation, policing, schooling, and economic development issues. Ideally, the assembled neighbors would reach a consensus on how they would like the city to deal with these issues and forward their recommendations to the council. Districtwide and citywide meetings might also consider the broader implications of these issues and make comparable proposals. Adherents of such a plan asserted that even though the nonpartisan neighborhood councils lacked legislative or budgetary power, they might strongly influence public policy, invigorate election campaigns, and improve life in the city's neighborhoods.

NESTOR STUDIOS, Hollywood's first movie studio, opened in October 1911. It was owned by two Englishmen, William and David Horsley, who operated it as the West Coast branch of their New Jersey–based Centaur Company. It occupied the former Blondeau's Tavern, on Sunset Boulevard and Gower Street—the site of today's CBS building—and was taken over by Universal Studios in 1916, when Hollywood was emerging as the center of the film industry.

NEUTRA, RICHARD J. (1892–1970), Austrian-born architect who established a practice in Los Angeles in 1926. Neutra believed that people were happiest when linked closely to their natural environment, an idea that he called "Biological Realism." It was reflected in his use of windows, moats, roofs, and terraces arranged in simple geometric forms, and in his reliance on glass, lightweight steel, and thin concrete walls. Southern California's climate was ideally suited to this concept.

Much of the Neutra vision was first expressed in his design of the experimental Lovell House (1929) on Dundee Drive, located on a slope overlooking Griffith Park area and called "one of the great monuments of Modern Architecture." This home, designed for a wealthy, health-conscious physician, Dr. Phillip Lovell, made Neutra a world celebrity of the International school of architecture, alongside Walter Gropius, Ludwig Mies van der Rohe, and Le Corbusier. He was much sought after by film people (such as screenwriter Anita Loos) and by teachers and scientists (including

The Singleton House, Mulholland Drive, designed by Richard J. Neutra, 1959. Photo by Julius Shulman, Hon. AIA.

Caltech geologist Charles Richter). He was a friend, co-worker, and sometime rival of Rudolph Schindler, another young Viennese architect who practiced locally.

Not all of his efforts went into the design of private homes. Neutra also experimented with mass-produced prefabricated construction, as seen in the Channel Heights Housing Project (1941–1943) for San Pedro war workers. Although this project has since disappeared, scores of modernist Neutra homes and office buildings may still be seen in Palos Verdes, Westwood, and Bel-Air, including his own residence in Silver Lake, which is open to the public.

NEVE, FELIPE DE (1728–1784), New Spain's governor of California, responsible for the founding of Los Angeles. While traveling to the territorial capital of Monterey he was impressed by the coastal plain of the Los Angeles River and decided to make it the site of a civilian *pueblo*. He organized the expedition from Mexico that founded the *pueblo* on 4 September 1781.

NEW AGE MOVEMENT, metaphysical religious movement very popular in Southern California. The region has supported like-minded movements since early in the century. New Age is based on the idea that mankind is on the verge of an extraordinary era that will "yield tremendous advances in human development and social organization." It emphasizes spiritual healing, the mind-body connection, meditation, environmental awareness, and paranormal phenomena. It appeals strongly to people dissatisfied with mainstream religion and who seek community, ritual, and spiritual expression.

NEWHALL, oldest residential community in the Santa Clarita Valley, and a part of the city of Santa Clarita. The town was laid out in 1876 on land donated by Henry Mayo Newhall, a local rancher, along the Southern Pacific Railroad right-of-way. Oil in the surrounding area was once a major factor in the local economy.

NEWHALL LAND AND FARMING COMPANY, stock raising enterprise on Rancho San Francisco near Santa Clarita, founded in 1883 by the sons of Henry Mayo Newhall (1825–1881). The elder Newhall, born in Saugus, Massachusetts, had made a fortune during the Gold Rush in the auction business and railroading and had bought ranchland in what are today Ventura, Santa Barbara, and Monterey Counties. The firm raised horses and cattle on the Santa Clarita ranch, and soon branched out into oil and orange production and, later, real estate development. Despite its name, Newhall Land and Farming did very little farming.

NEWMARK, HARRIS (1834–1916), pioneer merchant and patriarch of the Jewish community. Arriving in 1853, he befriended almost everyone and knew almost everything that went on in town. In old age he published a detailed memoir, *Sixty Years*

Harris Newmark.

in Southern California, 1853–1913, now considered a regional classic. His son, Marco R. Newmark (1862–1959), was a local historian and one-time president of the Historical Society of Southern California.

NEWS FOR AMERICA, maverick Latino political organization formed in the east San Fernando Valley in 1990. Its 100-plus members include professionals, many of them Republicans. Two of the founders are Manuel Hidalgo and management consultant Xavier Hermosillo. NEWS for America believes that the 40 percent of the local population that is Latino can win political and economic power without seeking alliances with either African Americans or Anglos. The group takes credit for ousting an Anglo majority in the city government of Bell Gardens, and for increasing the numbers of Latinos hired at Martin Luther King Jr. Hospital.

NEWSPAPER GUILD, labor organization chartered in Los Angeles in 1937 by journalists of the *Los Angeles Evening Herald-Express, Los Angeles Examiner, Hollywood Citizen-News,* and City News Service. The founding meetings took place at the San Fernando Valley ranch of movie actor Edward Everett Horton, a trade union activist. The group became Local 69 of the American Newspaper Guild, founded in 1933 by New York columnist Heywood Broun. The mother organization was expelled from the American Federation of Labor (AFL) in 1937 for supporting maverick labor or-

ganizer John L. Lewis, whereupon it joined the left-leaning Congress of Industrial Organizations (CIO). Fighting off fierce employer resistance, the local union won recognition by the *Evening Herald-Express, Los Angeles Daily News,* and *Los Angeles Evening News* in 1937. A strike against the *Hollywood Citizen-News* in 1938 was one of the most tumultuous in local labor history. The employer, though a liberal, steadfastly refused to recognize the union. The strikers had the active support of college students, screenwriters, screen directors, typographers, teachers, longshoremen, and auto workers. The battle ended ambiguously, but did succeed in raising weekly wages from $35 to $55.

In later years the independent union re-affiliated with the AFL-CIO. A 1967 strike against Hearst's national flagship publication, the *Los Angeles Herald-Examiner,* tried to preserve union recognition. The protracted contest (it continued until 1973) crippled the paper, however, which shut down its presses for good in 1989. Local 69 remains active today.

NEWSPAPERS, ENGLISH-LANGUAGE, 1851–1945, started modestly in Los Angeles and proliferated slowly. The main purpose of the first papers was to express the publishers' political beliefs, which tended to color both the reporting and the editorials. Only later did advertising become a dominant aspect of newspaper publishing and the reporting achieve a greater degree of fairness. The emergence of high-speed presses and a large, decentralized metropolis, between about 1887 and 1910, nourished the newspaper business in Los Angeles and other cities, though many papers had a short life span. Of the approximately 200 separate newspapers published from the 1850s to 1936, only a score or so covered the entire city or lasted more than a few years. As population grew and circulation increased, newspapers became big business, and the major dailies jockeyed fiercely for customers on the streets, at newsstands, and with home delivery. This rivalry was reflected in competitive editorial columns as well.

The first Southern California paper, the *Los Angeles Star,* appeared on 17 May 1851. Published by pro-southern Democrats, the paper was forced to suspend publication during the Civil War when its editor was charged with treasonous support of the Confederacy. It resumed publication in 1868, and lasted until 1879. The *Los Angeles Daily News,* from 1869 to 1873, was an early rival.

The *Los Angeles Evening Express* appeared in 1871, and the *Los Angeles Daily Herald* in 1873. These merged in 1931 to became the *Los Angeles Evening Herald-Express.* The *Los Angeles Times,* founded in 1881, was eventually destined to dominate the field of journalism, but had major rivals at first. Its editor beginning in 1882 was Harrison Gray Otis, a rock-ribbed Republican. Otis became owner and publisher in 1886. He eventually turned the paper over to his son-in-law, Harry Chandler. E. W. Scripps founded the *Los Angeles Record* in 1895. William Randolph Hearst founded the *Los Angeles Examiner* in 1903, voicing an editorial position opposite to the *Times* on many issues, including labor unions.

In 1923 Cornelius Vanderbilt Jr., the progressive-minded scion of a railroad fortune, began publishing a staid family-oriented tabloid, the *Los Angeles Daily News,* defying blunt warnings from both Hearst and Otis to stay out of the newspaper business. In 1925 Vanderbilt accused his rivals of using bribery and violence to hamstring him. The following year his paper failed and was taken over by Manchester Boddy. Boddy became a New Dealer, presenting a strong contrast to the strict conservatism of the *Los Angeles Times.*

In the 1920s and 1930s the city's morning market was dominated by the *Times* and Hearst's *Examiner.* The evening market was shared by the *Herald-Express,* also a Hearst paper, and the *Daily News* and *Record* (which closed down in 1935), both published by Scripps.

NEWSPAPERS, ENGLISH-LANGUAGE, SINCE 1945, exist in a complex publishing environment. The field has been shaped by such factors as the rivalry between newspapers and television news, the emergence of giant multimedia corporations, a revolution in communications technology, and the proliferation locally of a multiethnic population.

Following World War II the number of metropolitan dailies continued to shrink. In 1948 Norman Chandler launched a new paper, the *Los Angeles Mirror.* Six years later the Times-Mirror Corporation bought the *Los Angeles Daily News* and merged it with the *Mirror,* creating a new tabloid, also called the *Los Angeles Mirror,* thereby reducing the number of dailies to four: the *Times,* the *Examiner,* the *Herald-Express,* and the *Mirror.* Th *Mirror* ceased publication in 1962, leaving the city with three dailies. The number shrank to two

when Hearst, also in 1962, merged the morning *Los Angeles Examiner* with the afternoon *Herald-Express* to create the *Los Angeles Herald-Examiner.* What remained, then, were the *Times,* a morning paper, and the *Herald-Examiner,* an afternoon paper. The latter paper ceased publication in 1989, after a bitter strike by the Newspaper Guild, leaving the *Times* as the ultimate winner in the field of Los Angeles dailies.

Although the *Times* reigned supreme in the region as a whole, individual communities throughout the area still published 21 general daily papers in 1967. Among these, the oldest is the *Santa Monica Evening Outlook,* founded in 1875. The *Long Beach Press-Telegram* has served the southern half of the county and western part of Orange County since 1888. The *Santa Ana Register,* an Orange County paper, covers parts of Los Angeles County as well. The *Los Angeles Sentinel* and the *Wave* serve the African American community. The *California Eagle,* formed in 1910 under black ownership, reached its peak in the 1940s and is no longer published. Today the regional paper with the biggest circulation is the *Daily News,* serving the San Fernando Valley, Glendale, Burbank, the Santa Clarita Valley, and eastern Ventura County.

In addition to the dailies, scores of suburban weekly papers are published as well. In 1981, in a bold attempt to rival the *Times* in the outlying communities, the Hearst Corporation acquired 28 weeklies and 2 dailies in Los Angeles County whose total circulation was 425,000. Alternative-press papers also flourish, the most notable ones being the *L.A. Reader* and the *L.A. Weekly.*

NEWSPAPERS, NON-ENGLISH, have been serving the culturally diverse population of Los Angeles since the 1850s. Usually formed to serve struggling immigrant communities, the papers reflect the cultural nationalism of the mother country and report on the achievements and conflicts encountered daily by their transplanted readers. As business enterprises they are often short-lived. The most numerous by far have been Spanish-language newspapers.

The first such paper was *La Estrella de Los Angeles,* which started out as the Spanish-language page of the Yankee-owned *Los Angeles Star.* The earliest independent Spanish-language journal was *El Clamor Público* (The public outcry, 1855–1859), founded by young Francisco P. Ramírez, a native Angeleno. Also appealing to Californios were *La*

Crónica (The chronicle), a weekly published from 1872 to 1892, and *Las Dos Repúblicas* (The two republics), which had correspondents in California, Arizona, and northern Mexico. *El Joven* (Youth) was published in the 1870s.

In 1991 Los Angeles County had 18 papers written in either Spanish or Spanish and English. The oldest ongoing daily paper and the one with the largest circulation (64,676) is *La Opinión,* published daily by Lozano Enterprises and the Times-Mirror Corporation. The major Spanish-language weekly is *Variedades de la Guía;* published in Van Nuys, it serves Orange and Los Angeles Counties and has a circulation of 218,000. Easter Group Publications publishes several papers—*Eastside Sun, East Los Angeles Brooklyn-Belvedere Comet, Montebello Comet, Monterey Park Comet,* and *Wyvernwood Chronicle*—with a combined circulation of 40,000. Most of the other papers are independents.

The leading paper serving the Chinese community is the *American Chinese News.* In the Japanese community *Rafu Shimpo* (L.A. news) has been a mainstay since 1902, and currently is the only locally published paper in Japanese. The *Korea Times,* founded in 1969, has a daily circulation of 50,000. There have been, or still are, smaller-circulation papers issued in French, German, Greek, Yiddish, and other languages.

NICHOLS, JOHN G. (1813?–1898), merchant and mayor of Los Angeles from 1852 to 1853, and again from 1856 to 1858. He ran the first grocery store, on S. Main Street, and in 1854 built Los Angeles's first brick building. During the *bandido* disturbances of the 1850s Nichols was a prominent member of Dr. Hope's Rangers, a 100-member vigilante police group. As mayor he guided construction of the Bath Street School, one of the city's first public schools. His enlargement of the *zanja* irrigation system resulted in expanded fruit growing and the construction of the Aliso grain mill in 1857. Nichols's home was the site of the first Protestant services in Los Angeles, held in 1859. The population of the city in the 1850s was less than 4,000, and the area about 29 square miles.

NICKERSON, WILLIAM, JR. (1879–1945), pioneering African American entrepreneur. The son of a Texas dirt farmer, Nickerson was an insurance salesman in Houston, Texas, when, in 1919, he launched a successful campaign for black voting rights in that state. Arriving in Los Angeles

in 1921, he saw the potential for providing reasonable insurance to the 16,000 blacks who were forced to pay discriminatory rates because of Jim Crow policies. With associates Norman O. Houston and George A. Beavers, he cofounded and headed Golden State Mutual Life Insurance Company. The firm, which soon branched out into the funeral business, broke new ground for African Americans, becoming the largest black-owned life insurance company in the western United States. The company survived the Great Depression, when it supported 126 employees and had an annual income of over $188,000. Golden State occupied its landmark headquarters at Western Avenue and Adams Boulevard in 1949, and by the 1980s showed an income from nationwide sales of over $40 million a year. At his death Nickerson was an NAACP activist and a member of the Republican Party central committee in Los Angeles.

NICKERSON GARDENS, public housing project in Watts. It is the largest such development in the city, occupying some 68 acres.

NIXON, RICHARD M. (1913–1994), 37th president of the United States, from 1968 to 1974. Nixon was born in Yorba Linda (Orange County) and raised in Whittier (Los Angeles County),

Richard Nixon. Courtesy The Richard Nixon Library & Birthplace.

where he attended Whittier College and practiced law. He first won a seat in Congress as a Republican in 1946, after a bruising battle against New Dealer Jerry Voorhis. Prominent Southern California Republicans backed Nixon's candidacy to the U.S. Senate in 1950, a post he won after a notorious red-baiting campaign against Helen Gahagan Douglas.

In 1952 Nixon was elected vice president on the GOP ticket headed by Dwight Eisenhower. After serving two terms as vice president, he lost two major contests: the 1960 presidential election, which was won by John F. Kennedy (Nixon lost his home county of Los Angeles by 21,157 votes); and the 1962 gubernatorial campaign, in which Edmund G. "Pat" Brown was the victor. Nixon then delivered his memorable, and ultimately inaccurate, exit line to the assembled media at the Beverly Hilton Hotel: "You won't have Nixon to kick around anymore because, gentlemen, this is my last press conference." Nixon shifted his political base to New York and, making a remarkable comeback, was elected U.S. president in 1968 and reelected in 1972. His second term ended in disgrace with his resignation during the 1974 Watergate scandal, the alternative being almost certain impeachment. He and his wife, Pat Nixon, are buried on the grounds of the family home and Nixon Library in Yorba Linda.

NORDHOFF, CHARLES (1830–1901), author of *California for Health, Pleasure, and Residence* (1872), a guidebook that put Southern California on the map. A New York *Tribune* journalist, Nordhoff was hired by the Southern Pacific to trumpet the virtues of Southern California, which was then viewed as a dusty, violent backwater stop on the way to San Francisco. In a series of *Harper's* magazine articles, republished in book form, he touted the benign climate, cheap land, bountiful agriculture, beautiful flowers, interesting architecture, and inviting hotels of the region. This array of virtues quickly spurred tourism and growth throughout Southern California. Nordhoff followed his own advice by moving to the region. He died at Coronado Beach in 1901. His son, Walter Nordhoff, and grandson, Charles B. Nordhoff, were also literary figures.

NORDSKOG, ANDRAE B. (1885–1962), Iowa-born entrepreneur and civic reformer. In the early 1920s Nordskog settled in Santa Monica, where he manufactured phonograph records. After suffering a business reversal he moved to Los Angeles, and later to the San Fernando Valley. Nordskog published the small weekly paper the *Los Angeles Gridiron*. He also, shortly after his arrival, became a crusader in the "water wars" that pitted Los Angeles against the Owens Valley, arguing that a Los Angeles elite was conspiring to cheat Owens

---

[I]n early California] everybody sang; and a great many made their own songs, or verses to other songs.
—Charles Fletcher Lummis, writer

Valley property owners of their water rights. Unfortunately for him, he was subsidized by the Watterson brothers, prominent Owens Valley bankers who were eventually convicted of embezzlement. He also opposed the extension of the Los Angeles Aqueduct into Mono Basin, the construction of Boulder (now Hoover) Dam on the Colorado River, and the granting of extensive powers to the Metropolitan Water District. For a generation Nordskog's contentious views on water strongly influenced the writing of local history.

NORTH HILLS, San Fernando Valley neighborhood 21 miles northwest of downtown Los Angeles. Early residents settled on 1-acre plots, cultivated vegetable gardens and fruit trees, and tended small chicken and rabbit ranches. The area's 1915 name, Mission Acres, was changed in 1927 to Sepulveda, in honor of Fernando Sepúlveda, son of Don Francisco Sepúlveda, who had an adobe at the base of the Verdugo Mountains. The community's largest growth occurred between the 1930s and the 1950s. In 1991, residents who thought a community name change would disassociate them from crime in Sepulveda, prevailed on the Los Angeles City Council to change the name to North Hills.

NORTH HOLLYWOOD, district in the eastern San Fernando Valley, some 10 miles northwest of downtown Los Angeles. It has undergone several name changes. Before being subdivided in 1888 it was known as Toluca Lake (after a city, Toluca, in Mexico), the lake in question being a small body of water bordering the Los Angeles River. When the Los Angeles Suburban Homes Company first subdivided the area around 1911 they named it Lankershim, after Isaac Lankershim, an original owner. It was formally renamed North Hollywood and annexed to Los Angeles in 1923. Dubbing itself the "Gateway to the Valley," North Hollywood is currently undergoing major redevelopment. The project will cost $96 million over 15 years, and is intended to improve business, transportation, and housing. In 1990 the population of North Hollywood was 215,000.

NORTHRIDGE, district in the northwestern San Fernando Valley, 29 miles northwest of downtown Los Angeles, and home to California State University, Northridge (CSUN). Once part of the vast ranching domain of Benjamin F. Porter, in 1908 it became a shipping point on the Southern Pacific Railroad branch line, with the biblical name of Zelzah, meaning "watering place in the desert." Renamed North Los Angeles in 1933, the area acquired a reputation as the horse capital of the valley. Architect Paul Williams built a home for movie star Barbara Stanwyck, who helped start a 125-acre horse breeding farm known as Northridge Farms. Here horse people staged an annual show called the Northridge Stampede. A prominent resident realtor, Carl S. Dentzel (later, director of the Southwest Museum), proposed renaming the community Northridge. When the CSUN campus replaced an orange grove in the 1950s, the surrounding rural area was swiftly transformed into a bedroom community. In 1990 the population stood at 58,971. Northridge made world headlines as the epicenter of a strong 1994 earthquake.

NORTHRIDGE EARTHQUAKE occurred at 4:31 A.M. on 17 January 1994, registering 6.7 on the Richter scale. The fault area near Northridge and in the Santa Susana Mountains was previously unmapped. The temblor caused at least 61 deaths and 6,500 injuries, destroyed or seriously damaged more than 1,000 buildings throughout the Los Angeles Basin, and left 20,000 people homeless. Freeway overpasses collapsed, some of them 20 miles away from the epicenter. The traffic disruption was especially severe in the Santa Clarita Valley. The quake damaged many historic buildings, including Frank Lloyd Wright's Hollyhock House (1917–1920), the Egyptian Theatre (1922), St. Monica's Roman Catholic Church (1925), and the Henry Weaver House (1910), a famous example of the Craftsman style of architecture.

Gavin Canyon Bridge, Santa Clarita, after the Northridge earthquake. Photo by Jayne Kamin-Oncea.

The crisis brought a deployment of the national guard, a visit from Pres. Bill Clinton, who witnessed a severe aftershock, and the most extensive federal earthquake relief effort in the nation's history. With the estimated damage bill running as high as $20 billion, the Northridge earthquake was one of the costliest natural disasters in American history.

NORTHROP AIRCRAFT COMPANY, major defense contractor. Founded in 1932 by aeronautical engineer and designer John K. Northrop (1895–1981), it later became part of Douglas Aircraft. Northrop has maintained several divisions in the county: aircraft manufacturing in Hawthorne and El Segundo, B-52 production at Palmdale and Pico Rivera, and electronics fabrication at Hawthorne. In 1994, because of a merger, the company name was changed to Northrop Grumman Corporation.

NORTH UNIVERSITY PARK, historic district near USC and Exposition Park in Los Angeles. It emerged in the 1890s when a trolley line was completed along Hoover Street to the park, then known as Agricultural Park. The neighborhood's decline began in about 1910, with the opening of the West Adams district. It had decayed noticeably by 1940. In the postwar period multifamily units replaced the bulldozed Victorian-era homes. The North University Park Community Association has fought, with some success, to preserve the remaining old homes in the area between Vermont Avenue and the Harbor Freeway, and between Jefferson Boulevard and the Santa Monica Freeway.

NORTON SIMON MUSEUM OF ART. *See* Simon, Norton

NORWALK, independent city east of the San Gabriel River near Santa Fe Springs and Cerritos. It was called, at various times, New River, Seven Sycamores, Sycamore Grove, Corazón de los Valles ("Heart of the Valleys"), and Corvalles. It was renamed Norwalk in 1877 by the Southern Pacific Railroad, possibly after Norwalk, Connecticut, the former home of a rail official. At the turn of the century much of Norwalk consisted of dairy and sugar-beet farms. Residential development came with the end of World War II. When incorporated in 1957 Norwalk was the fifth largest city in the county. A lingering taste of the old lifestyle can be had by touring the Hargitt House, an 1891 Queen Anne home, and the Gilbert Sproul House, a farmhouse constructed in 1870. Both are now maintained as museums. The town's population reached 94,300 in 1990.

NOSOTROS, Latino media advocacy organization founded by actor Ricardo Montalban in 1970. Its name in Spanish means "Us." It bestows annual Golden Eagle Awards on individuals who improve the image of Latinos in the field of entertainment.

NOT YET NEW YORK, slow-growth organization founded in the 1980s by UCLA Professor Laura Lake and public-interest attorney Barbara Blinderman. It has won a number of victories at the neighborhood level and in regional disputes involving excessive development.

OAK TREE (*QUERCUS* spp.), abundant, visually dramatic, and dominant native tree found in coastal, foothill, hill, and mountain areas. It has both deciduous and evergreen varieties. Its acorn fruit was an important food source for Indians, who ground it into flour and leached it with water to remove bitterness. The scrub oak, a large evergreen shrub with twisting branches, is found on protected slopes of the coastal plain. In the oak woodland environment, in and around chaparral-covered foothills, are several varieties: the coast live

---

> **W**hoso sneers at Los Angeles . . .
> thumbs his nose at a city that will
> eventually be the largest in the world.
> —Basil Woon, travel writer, 1933

---

oak can grow to 65 feet, from sea level to about 3,000 feet; the scrub interior live oak is rarely over 12 feet tall; the canyon live oak, with its light colored bark, can reach 40 feet in height and grows up to elevations of 6,500 feet; the Engelmann oak grows to 50 feet, and has frequently been used for firewood; the valley oak, the largest of the western deciduous oaks, is found below the 2,000-foot elevation. In the mountain areas, the interior coast live oak, a black tree with broad leaves, looms up 75 feet at higher elevations.

Oaks, once numerous in the Topanga–Las Virgenes area, have been seriously depleted by indiscriminate cutting, for firewood and to make way for housing developments, and the lowering of the water table. A county ordinance requires builders to preserve the oldest specimens and replace younger ones, at a ratio of two saplings for each one felled, but giant loopholes in the law have allowed for noncompliance.

OAT MOUNTAIN, unincorporated region in the hilly northwestern part of the county, above Highway 118. In 1991 it was home to fewer than 1,000 residents.

OCCIDENTAL COLLEGE, distinguished liberal arts college. Founded in 1887 in Highland Park, it moved to Eagle Rock in 1914, where it occupies a 120-acre campus. The Mary Norton Lapp Library contains more than 480,000 volumes. Accredited, independent, and coeducational, the college maintains high academic standards. Ninety-five percent of the faculty hold doctorates. The student-to-faculty ratio is 12 to 1, and 75 percent of classes have fewer than 15 students. Occidental College has 1,650 undergraduates, most of whom live in campus residences. More than 75 percent of Occidental's undergraduates go on to attend graduate school.

OCCIDENTAL PETROLEUM. *See* Oil industry

OCEAN PARK, beach community located in the southwest corner of Santa Monica just north of Venice. The boundaries of the less than 1-square-mile neighborhood are Pico Boulevard (north), Lincoln Boulevard (east), and Marine Street (south), with the Pacific Ocean serving as the western boundary. Ocean Park was founded in 1892 as a seaside resort by Abbot Kinney, who also founded Venice. He built a wharf, beachfront promenade, and small bungalows to attract vacationers to what had been sand dunes and marshland. By the turn of the century his effort had realized significant success. In the post–World War II decades the area attracted elderly Jewish immigrants. Pacific Ocean

Bathhouse and beach, Ocean Park, ca. 1909. Pitt Collection.

Park (POP), an amusement park built in 1958 to stimulate commerce, went bankrupt in 1967 and was demolished in 1975. Horace McCoy's *noir* novel *They Shoot Horses, Don't They?* (1935) depicts the seamy life of marathon dancers at a dance hall on Ocean Park Pier during the Great Depression. The film version (1969) starred Jane Fonda and won a supporting actor Academy Award for Gig Young. In 1994 the resident population was about 11,000.

ODYSSEY THEATRE ENSEMBLE, experimental theater group in West Los Angeles since 1969. The Odyssey houses three separate 99-seat equity theaters, allowing for simultaneous performances. Founded by Ron Sossi, the company has achieved much box office success and critical acclaim, staging both traditional and new works. Bertolt Brecht's *Baal;* Henrik Ibsen's *Peer Gynt; The Adolph Hitler Show,* in 1973; *The Chicago Conspiracy Trial,* which ran for 15 months beginning in 1979; *Tracers* (staged in collaboration with Vietnam veterans), in 1980; and *Awake and Sing,* in the 1994–1995 season, were among its most successful productions.

OIL INDUSTRY. The local petroleum fields were known to the Gabrieleño Indians well before the Europeans arrived. They used the thick, sticky substance that oozed from tar and pitch sumps to waterproof their woven baskets. In 1769, Captain Portolá's men were fascinated by the black seepage in the area now known as the La Brea tar pits, and Spanish missionaries and rancheros had to take pains to prevent their cattle from falling into the pits and dying. Later, Americans living in the Mexican *pueblo* used the tar for roofing. In 1850 An-

drés and Pío Pico collected tar seepage and distilled it for oil lamps used in San Fernando Mission.

The first salable petroleum in California was the oil found at Pico Canyon near San Fernando after 1850. In 1859, a whale oil merchant became intrigued by the seepage on the property belonging to Maj. Henry Hancock near Los Angeles. He proceeded to set up a primitive still, with which he produced a semiliquid asphaltum until Hancock drove him off his land. The Pioneer Oil Company—with officers who included Phineas Banning, Benjamin Davis Wilson, Winfield S. Hancock, and John Gately Downey—drilled an oil well near Newhall in 1865. That company was followed in the mid-1870s by the newly formed California Star Oil, which changed its name to Pacific Coast Oil Company and eventually became the Standard Oil Company of California. By now a drilling frenzy was under way, reminiscent of the gold mining mania a few decades earlier. California crude was mostly sold unrefined, as it emerged from the

Oil well, middle of La Cienega Boulevard, near Beverly Boulevard. Courtesy Robert Weinstein Collection.

oil head. Edward L. Doheny discovered oil on 4 November 1892 at 2nd Street and Glendale Boulevard in downtown Los Angeles. His find set off a boom that lasted years. By 1897 the city had 500 derricks, and in 1910 the area near Santa Monica Boulevard and Vermont Avenue was an unruly oil shantytown.

Drilling activity in the county reached new heights in the 1920s, when major finds were made in Whittier, Montebello, Compton, Torrance, and Inglewood. The biggest strikes were in Huntington Beach in 1920, and Santa Fe Springs and Signal Hill in 1921. These three huge fields upset national oil prices and glutted existing storage facilities.

Oil production has continued down to the present throughout the Los Angeles Basin; between 1953 and 1988 some 1,000 wells pumped 375 million barrels of oil from the Los Angeles anticlines. Recently, however, new drilling has become problematic. In 1965 Occidental Petroleum focused its

---

The Valley of Los Angeles can easily hold a million inhabitants, although it now supports less than 20,000.
—Ludwig Salvator, Austrian archduke, 1878

---

attention on a small plot near the coast at the Pacific Palisades. It eventually calculated the existence of an oil field of 25 million barrels and sought permission to pump oil on a 2-acre plot from a structure equal in height to a 15-story building. Meanwhile, a geologist reported to the Santa Monica City Council that an estimated 50 million barrels of oil lay in the tidelands off the coast of Venice and could be pumped from drilling platforms. An aroused local community fought back, eventually forcing Occidental and other drillers to abandon their plans. Oil pumps still operating in the Los Angeles Basin are less unsightly and better camouflaged than in the past.

OKIES, migrants to California from the southern plains states. The derogatory term, a shortening of "Oklahomans," referred to the Dust Bowl farmers forced off their land by the Great Depression and the harsh physical conditions that prevailed during the 1930s. Of those who came to California from Oklahoma, Texas, Arkansas, and Missouri be-

tween 1935 and 1940, some 96,000, or 38 percent, ended up in Los Angeles. They came in old cars and trucks bearing their few possessions and took up residence in any shelters they could find. The exodus was immortalized in John Steinbeck's novel *The Grapes of Wrath* (1939).

The Okies lived in widely scattered parts of the metropolis, with a slight concentration in Bell Gardens. Except for their poverty, they resembled in culture and outlook the many thousands of other midwesterners who flooded into Los Angeles. In 1936 Los Angeles police chief James E. Davis tried to stem their influx by posting 136 uniformed police at the state borders to prevent them from entering. The misguided "bum blockade" proved completely futile. By World War II many of the rural immigrants had improved their lot and found work in blue-collar jobs at Southern California shipyards and aircraft factories.

OLD BALDY. *See* Mount San Antonio

OLIVARES, LUIS (1934–), controversial priest of the historic downtown Plaza church, Our Lady Queen of Angels. He was born of Mexican parents in San Antonio, Texas, earned a master's degree in business administration from Notre Dame University in 1964, and attended the Claretian Seminary in Dominguez Hills. A born social crusader, Father Olivares helped found the United Neighborhood Organization of East Los Angeles, challenged the church hierarchy by championing the cause of farm workers and the poor, opened the door of his church to homeless Central American immigrants, and protested U.S. policy in El Salvador. A diabetic, he contracted AIDS from a needle in a refugee camp in Central America.

OLIVES, fruit grown in Southern California since mission days. The Franciscans at Mission San Fernando set out the first olive grove. In 1894, Robert Widney, a Los Angeles businessman, pioneered the commercial olive growing industry in Sylmar, in the northern San Fernando Valley. He employed Chinese field hands to plant and maintain his orchard, reputedly the largest in the world. Even into the 1960s, olives remained a major industry, and a Sylmar label signified a quality product.

OLMOS, EDWARD JAMES (1947–), East Los Angeles–born screen actor who played the role of El Pachuco in *Zoot Suit* (1981) and Garfield High

Edward James Olmos as El Pachuco in *Zoot Suit*, with Rachel Levario and Mike Gomez, Mark Taper Forum Production. Center Theatre Group/Mark Taper Forum.

School teacher Jaime Escalante in *Stand and Deliver* (1987). By going into the streets and helping cleanup efforts in the wake of the 1992 Los Angeles riots, he inspired many hundreds of Angelenos to turn out and do the same.

OLMSTED-BARTHOLOMEW-CHENEY RE-PORT, private study issued by the city traffic commission in 1924 surveying the causes of traffic congestion, authored by regional planners Frederick Law Olmsted Jr., Harland Bartholomew, and Charles H. Cheney. The report stated that in 1923, 650,000 people were traveling downtown daily by car, as compared to 750,000 who used street rail-

ways. It then proposed a comprehensive integrated pattern of parks and parkways to tie the region together and accommodate the steadily increasing automobile traffic. Despite sound concepts of regional planning, nothing came of the specific proposals contained in the report.

OLVERA, AGUSTÍN (1820?–1876), Mexican settler who arrived in California as part of the unsuccessful Hijar-Padres colony, a company of Mexicans organized to settle the secularized mission lands of Alta California in 1834–1835. By 1841 he was commissioner for the secularized mission of San Juan Capistrano, where he also served as judge. He came to Los Angeles in 1845, fought against the Yankees in the Mexican War, and was one of the signatories to the surrender in January 1847. Olvera later became a farmer in Los Angeles, a judge, county supervisor, and even a presidential elector. Olvera Street, where he once lived, is named for him.

OLVERA STREET, colorful Mexican-style marketplace, part of the city-owned Pueblo de Los Angeles Historic Monument. A powerful tourist magnet since its opening in April 1930, Olvera Street now attracts 2 million visitors yearly. The street's original name, Wine Street, reflected the vineyards and wineries once located nearby. It was renamed in honor of Judge Agustín Olvera, a prominent Mexican who once lived there. In the 1920s when Christine Sterling organized a campaign to save its brick and adobe structures from destruction, the street was a back alley for machine shops. Out of whole cloth she created a lively Mexican *mercado,*

Strolling on Olvera Street, 1995. Photo by Michael Krakowiak/Marni Pitt.

closed to cars and open to tourists. Today the shops and carts are owned by 79 merchants whose wares include souvenirs, crafts, leather goods, jewelry, and clothes. Olvera Street has several bustling restaurants and counts among its other attractions the Avila Adobe, and Sepulveda House, now converted to museum buildings. The street is slated for a major face-lift.

OLYMPIC AUDITORIUM, sports arena at 18th Street and Grand Avenue. Built by boxing promoter Jack Doyle and dedicated in 1924 by boxing great Jack Dempsey, it was the staging area for the boxing and wrestling matches of the 1932 Olympic Games. "Gorgeous George," the blond curly-haired wrestler who sprayed perfume on his body between rounds, fought there in 1948, attracting a new generation of wrestling fans who watched him perform on television. In 1960 Sugar Ray Robinson and Gene Fullmer fought to a draw for the middleweight crown. A later battle between Mando Ramos and Ultimo "Sugar" Ramos, which drew the auditorium's biggest gate receipts ($91,000), was probably its most famous fight. With the decline of boxing's popularity, the landmark Olympic Auditorium closed in 1987 and was nearly demolished, but in the nick of time received a $5 million renovation and reopened in 1994.

OLYMPIC GAMES. Los Angeles was the proud host of the 10th and 23rd Summer Olympiads, held in 1932 and 1984, respectively. Olympic fever began as early as 1912, however, when local youth Fred Kelly won the 110-meter hurdles championship at Stockholm; shortly thereafter civic groups began a campaign for Los Angeles to host the games.

In 1924 the International Olympic Committee (IOC), seduced by the newly completed 76,000-seat Memorial Coliseum, awarded the 1932 games to Los Angeles. In 1928 local leaders, seeing the enormous possibilities for tourism, immigration, and economic development, launched a drive persuading voters to approve a statewide Olympiad bond to enlarge the Coliseum to 105,000 seats.

Arrangements for the 1932 games went forward, despite the economic stress of the Great Depression and the reluctance of some nations to participate amid the international tensions aroused by the Japanese occupation of Manchuria. It was at this time that Olympic Boulevard was named. Over 400,000 visitors passed through the area, and local businesses earned $50 million, in the two-week period of the games.

Two traditions were created at the 1932 Los Angeles games. First was the establishment of an Olympic village to house the participating athletes. Atop Baldwin Hills, carpenters hurriedly hammered together 550 two-bedroom portable bungalows, along with dining halls and a hospital. The second innovation was a victory stand for the winners. A minor uproar occurred when Italian Luigi Beccali, winner of the gold medal in the 1,500-meter run, mounted the victory stand and gave the Fascist salute. Afterward Beccali drank champagne with his party in defiance of Prohibition laws. (He later entered the wine business in New York.)

Almost half a century elapsed before Los Angeles put in a competitive bid to host another Summer Olympiad. The IOC rejected Los Angeles's bid for the 1980 games. In 1981 the California Fiestas Association enlisted Col. William May Garland, a wealthy Los Angeles real estate developer,

Olympic Village, 1932. Pitt Collection.

to lobby their cause in Europe. He won the support of Baron Pierre de Coubertin, guiding spirit of the modern Olympic Games, who had visited California and been favorably impressed. The IOC subsequently approved Los Angeles as the site for the 1984 Olympics.

The games were staged amid great concerns about terrorism and the skyrocketing costs of each new Olympiad, but Mayor Tom Bradley made good on his pledge to provide security and keep the event solvent. In fact, under the direction of Peter Ueberroth the games ended with a surplus of $300 million—in sharp contrast to the 1976 games, which cost Montreal taxpayers $1 billion. Another fear, concerning potential freeway gridlock, also went unrealized as traffic flowed freely thanks to staggered work schedules throughout the city. Among the American gold medal winners in the 1984 games was Jeff Blatnick, Greco-Roman wrestling superheavyweight, who competed even while suffering from Hodgkin's disease.

O'MELVENY, HARVEY K[ILPATRICK] S[TUART] (1823–1890), pioneer attorney. O'Melveny first practiced in Illinois, where he was active in Democratic politics. He came to California during the Gold Rush and, after serving as a circuit judge in Sacramento, arrived in Los Angeles with his family in 1869. He was among the town boosters who convinced the Southern Pacific Railroad to construct its line through Los Angeles in 1876. In 1872 he was elected judge of Los Angeles County. Six years later he helped found the Los Angeles Bar Association, and in 1887 he was appointed to the post of superior court judge.

O'MELVENY, HENRY (1859–1941), attorney. He came to Los Angeles with his family at 10 years of age, graduated from Los Angeles High School, and attended the University of California. Following in the footsteps of his father, Harvey K. S. O'Melveny, he began practicing law in Los Angeles in 1881. After serving as an assistant district attorney, he formed a law firm with Jackson A. Graves in 1885. The partnership earned substantial fees from land deals and litigation during the boom years of 1886 and 1887. In the 1890s its leading clients were the families Domínguez, del Amo, and Watson, who had vast land, oil, and commercial holdings in the southern part of the county. O'Melveny played an important role in the formation, in 1893, of the Los Angeles Title Insurance and Trust Company. During the Free Harbor Contest he joined the league that helped to defeat the Southern Pacific Railroad and establish San Pedro as a harbor. Throughout his career, from 1881 until his death in 1941, O'Melveny maintained a journal concerning the practice of law in Southern California. All 50 volumes were deposited in the Huntington Library and later published as his memoirs.

The firm of O'Melveny and Meyers (formerly Graves, O'Melveny, and Shankland) has grown steadily, and now employs some 400 attorneys. It is headquartered in its own 26-story Bunker Hill tower, with additional offices in London and Tokyo. Warren Christopher was chairman until his appointment as U.S. secretary of state in 1993.

ONE CALIFORNIA PLAZA, 42-story office tower on Bunker Hill. This high-rise, high-tech building, the dominating structure along a corridor of new financial skyscrapers on Grand Avenue, boasts 960,000 square feet of space. It is part of a complex that includes the existing Museum of Contemporary Art. A second tower is planned as a luxury hotel. Many of the law firms and businesses in the building play key roles in Pacific Rim commerce.

OPINIÓN. See *La Opinión*

OPOSSUM (*DIDELPHIS MARSUPIALIS*), marsupial commonly found amid low shrubs or in empty garages and wood piles. It is not native to these parts, having been introduced into California in the early 1900s. Less appealing than Pogo, the lovable comic strip 'possum of Okefenokee Swamp, the real animal, with its pointed nose, naked tail, and pink-tipped ears, is quite homely. Animal Regulation, which gets more complaints about opossums than about any other wild creature, will supply traps and air lift captives to the Angeles National Forest. They do indeed "play 'possum" when threatened.

ORANGES, Southern California's dominant agricultural crop from around 1890 to 1940. The first grove was planted by the mission fathers and Indian neophytes at San Gabriel in 1804. The first commercial crop is credited to William Wolfskill. In 1877 he shipped a boxcar of oranges from his grove on Alameda Street; they arrived in St. Louis a month later in good condition. Five years after-

Orange grove in Los Angeles, 1870s. Courtesy Henry E. Huntington Library.

ward 500 carloads were being shipped annually, and by the early 1920s, 50,000. By 1950 more than 200,000 acres were devoted to the crop in Los Angeles County.

In 1895 growers formed a marketing cooperative, the California Fruit Growers Exchange (since 1952 called Sunkist Growers, Inc.). The exchange extolled the food value of oranges, the beauty of the trees and orchards, the fragrance of the blossoms, and the lifestyle of the grower. The fruit became a symbol of the good life in Southern California, helping to sell land and bring people to the region.

On 5 to 25 acres growers could earn a modest living, with the exchange organizing the work of picking, grading, and storing the fruit. Clever marketing helped growers overcome the costs of land, advertising, labor, and irrigation and increase their profits. Los Angeles soon became the world's leading commercial center for oranges, although Riverside ran a close second.

The product evolved significantly over time. At first the orange variety grown in Los Angeles was thick-skinned, sour, full of pits, and dry. Then came the sweet and tasty Brazilian navel orange, developed after 1878 and sold during the winter, and an improved version of the valencia, which reached the market in the summer months. Although the trees grew well, they needed special conditions of climate, water, and soil to reach maximum yield. Groves were planted widely in an 80-mile belt at the foot of the San Gabriel and San Bernardino mountains. Growers of the cold-sen-

sitive fruit had to use heaters (smudge pots) or large rotary fans (wind machines) to fend off crippling frosts. The industry was also troubled by such pests as scales, spiders, aphids, and, most recently, the Mediterranean fruit fly.

Orange growers benefited greatly from the completion of transcontinental railroad lines after 1886, giving them access to new markets and allowing them to exhibit at fairs in New Orleans, Chicago, and Boston. Joining ranks with Union Pacific Railroad, the fruit exchange targeted Iowa for a pilot advertising campaign. It plastered newspapers and billboards with the Sunkist label, which differentiated the California orange from the Florida orange. It also distributed silver "orange spoons" and other bonus giveaways. Through such promotional efforts growers convinced Americans of the benefits of a daily glass of orange juice, changing breakfast patterns for good. More than that, the orange became a symbol of Southern California. The picture-postcard view of a San Gabriel Valley orange orchard—with its green foliage, white blossoms, and bright-colored fruit, bathed in sunshine and framed against distant snowy mountain peaks—became a scene as familiar to Americans as that of a New England village.

ORD, EDWARD O. C. (1818–1883), U.S. Army lieutenant hired by Los Angeles after the Mexican War to draw up the first city map. On the document submitted in 1849 he identified several hundred adobes, dirt roads, trails, vineyards,

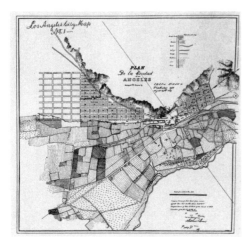

First map of Los Angeles, 1849. California Historical Society, Title Insurance and Trust Photo Collection, Dept. of Special Collections, USC Library.

orchards, and irrigated fields. The main door on the Plaza Church marked the center of the city. For the area north of Main Street (Calle Principal) he indicated city-sized blocks and lots for future development. Legend has it that the lieutenant named Spring Street for the woman he loved, Señorita Trinidad de la Guerra, whom he called *Mi Primavera*—"My Springtime." The former army base Fort Ord in Monterey was named for him.

ORGANIZED CRIME, known popularly as the "Mob," "Mafia," or "Cosa Nostra," emerged in Los Angeles during the corrupt era of Mayor Frank Shaw (1933–1938). Every major movie studio was subject to extortion during the 1930s and 1940s. Crime boss Meyer Lansky placed Benjamin "Bugsy" Siegel in charge of the territory, and Siegel took as his lieutenant the flamboyant Mickey Cohen. Although weakly organized and subservient to Chicago, the Los Angeles contingent was represented at the national Mafia meeting in Appalachia, New York, in 1954. According to FBI sources, the local arm is still controlled from Chicago, and deals in pornography but not drugs. In a 1992 cocaine trafficking trial, however, defendant Ronald A. Lorenzo, charged with doing business in Woodland Hills and Hollywood, was described as a member of the Bonanno crime family of New York. Law enforcement authorities believe that the drug dealings of the Crips and Bloods, as well as of emerging Asian American street gangs, are far more dangerous than those of the Mafia.

ORTEGA, JOSÉ FRANCISCO DE, scout with the Portolá expedition. He surveyed Indian trails and selected campsites near water in the 1769 exploration of the Los Angeles area.

OSTRICH FARMS originated in the United States in Anaheim in 1882, with birds imported from South Africa. By 1910 there were 10 such farms in Southern California. Cawston Ostrich Farm in South Pasadena, located along the Pacific Electric Railway line from downtown Los Angeles, was a major tourist attraction and successful commercial venture. At one time hundreds, perhaps thousands, of birds were raised there. An 1897 magazine advertisement promised children rides on the backs of the birds, while ladies were lured by quality ornamental feathers that could be fashioned into boas, capes, and collars. In the 1930s Cawston's claimed to be the oldest ostrich farm in the nation.

Ostrich farm. Pitt Collection.

OTIS, HARRISON GRAY (1837–1917), newspaper publisher, real estate tycoon, and city booster. A native of Ohio, Otis came to Los Angeles in 1881, became editor of the *Los Angeles Times* in 1882, and took over ownership in 1886. He proceeded to mold the paper as the region's leading business promoter, building the firm into a powerful commercial empire with diverse interests.

Otis shaped the young city of Los Angeles much as a mature schoolmaster shapes an impressionable child—so much so that the city came to be known as "Otistown." He also shaped Republican politics to his own beliefs, crusading against such "pestiferous" reformers as the Good Government League and the Lincoln-Roosevelt League. His decision to back the fight for a "free" harbor (free, that is, of Southern Pacific control) won him many supporters, and his paper many readers. A veteran of the Civil War, he was appointed a brigadier general in the Spanish-American War, went off to battle in 1898, and returned home a hero.

The pugnacious Otis had a virulent hatred for organized labor, and led a highly successful crusade to maintain the open shop. *Times* editorials and news articles took strong antilabor positions; the paper's banner slogan was "True Industrial

Harrison Gray Otis. Courtesy California State Library.

Freedom"—meaning a society completely free of labor unions. By the 1890s the national labor movement had labeled him "the most notorious, most persistent, and most unfair enemy of trades unionism on the North American continent." When two iron workers, John and James McNamara, bombed the *Times* Building in 1910, Otis's antilabor sentiment gained many new advocates in the ensuing hysteria.

Otis's influence extended beyond his labor stance. He also helped bring Owens River water to Los Angeles, was a member of the land syndicates that developed the San Fernando Valley, owned ranchland, and held investments in Mexico. Upon his death, Otis left his private home on Wilshire Boulevard to Los Angeles County, which converted it into an art institute that bears his name. As for the *Times,* the old publisher's mantle passed to his son-in-law, Harry Chandler.

OTIS COLLEGE OF ART AND DESIGN, commercial and studio art school opposite MacArthur Park. It was founded by the county in 1918 in the home bequeathed to it by the late Harrison Gray Otis. The Otis Art Institute, as it was then called, reached a pinnacle of importance from 1953 to 1959, when the painter Millard Sheets was director. In 1978 Otis merged with the Parsons School of Design in New York, but it became fully independent again in 1991, under its current name. The Otis College of Art and Design has a full-time faculty of 23 and a part-time faculty of 225. It enrolls several thousand full- and part-time students, who work toward B.A. and M.F.A. degrees in fashion design, photography, illustration, computer graphics, and environmental design.

OUT WEST MAGAZINE. See *Land of Sunshine/Out West*

OWENS, ROBERT (1806–1865), African American pioneer who settled in El Prieto (Negro) Canyon in the San Gabriel Mountains. Born a slave on a Texas cotton farm, he bought his liberty in 1853, took leave of his slave family, and headed for California. Passing through the town of Los Angeles, where proslavery and antiblack sentiments were rife, Owens settled on unclaimed land in the mountains, between Millard Canyon and the Arroyo Seco. There he cut and hauled wood for a living, saving as much of his earnings as possible. In 1854 he purchased the freedom of his wife and three children and brought them to Los Angeles. Investing in cheap land along Los Angeles and San Pedro Streets, he eventually became the wealthiest African American in Los Angeles. His offspring married into the family of Biddy Mason, another Southern California ex-slave pioneer. The Owens Block on Broadway near 3rd Street was once owned by family members.

OWENSMOUTH. *See* Canoga Park

OWENS RIVER VALLEY, area in Inyo County owned mainly by the Department of Water and Power (DWP) of the city of Los Angeles. Located 230–250 miles northeast of Los Angeles, its main features are Owens Lake, a saline body of water, and the Owens River, whose headwaters lie in the eastern Sierra Nevada. The river supplies the major portion of Los Angeles's drinking water. The valley was first settled in 1861 by hearty pioneers arriving in covered wagons. The small towns of Bishop and Independence, which depend largely on an agricultural and tourist economy, are the valley's main communities.

From 1904 to 1913, the DWP secured water rights and land, and built an aqueduct that became the Los Angeles lifeline. During a series of drought years in the 1920s, Los Angeles sought to squeeze even more water from the valley. This precipitated a bitter struggle between Owens Valley residents and the city of Los Angeles. Owens Valley demanded that the city pay higher prices for the land and for improvements than it was offering, or cease the buying altogether. Vigilantes dynamited the aqueduct several times, spilling the precious liquid onto the desert floor. Population declined, and businesses were ruined in the valley towns of Independence, Lone Pine, and Bishop. In 1925 Los Angeles agreed to some of the demands of Owens Valley landowners and business leaders, but not until 1929 did formal arbitration put an end to the acrimonious "water war."

In 1953 a new controversy arose, when the DWP stripped all the water from the Owens River Gorge, located 10 miles north of Bishop. Years of protest and negotiation finally led to a settlement in 1994, when the department again allowed water to flow into the gorge and restocked the stream with 10,000 fingerling trout. This symbolic act was applauded by locals, especially anglers. Still, some longtime valley residents resented the fact that some 50 miles of the lower river remained dry, and continued to feel victimized by Los Angeles's water imperialism.

To this day, the city of Los Angeles owns about 300,000 acres in Inyo and Mono Counties, an area about the size of the city itself. The ownership continues to rankle some local residents. Yet many conservation-minded people applaud the fact that DWP has stymied intense commercial development and preserved the area in a largely natural or pastoral state. While the valley supports substantial agriculture, its beautiful deserts, mountains, grasslands, and woodlands attract a wide array of campers, climbers, hikers, anglers, hunters, and photographers.

PACHUCO, derogatory term that surfaced in the 1940s, referring to young delinquent Mexicans, or "zoot suiters." It also is a term for the patois of English and Spanish spoken by them and their Caucasian compatriots on the streets of East Los Angeles, Belvedere, and Boyle Heights. In some legal proceedings the courts had to employ anthropologists or sociologists to act as interpreters for Pachuco witnesses who were fluent in neither English nor Spanish.

PACHUCO RIOTS. *See* Zoot suit riots

PACIFIC COAST HIGHWAY (PCH), state roadway that passes through the county intermittently from Long Beach to Malibu. The most scenic portion, extending north from Santa Monica to the Ventura County line, hugs the coastline of former Rancho Malibu. To lay the road, the state waged a long legal battle against Malibu ranch owner May Rindge. Engineers and crews completed the scenic section, called Roosevelt Highway, in 1929. This heavily trafficked part of PCH—a fraction of California Route 1—provides access to beach areas and serves long-distance coastal travelers. It is subject to landslides.

PACIFIC DESIGN CENTER, wholesale marketplace in West Hollywood serving the interior design trade. The massive structure with its striking blue glass exterior was designed by Pelli, Cesar, and Gruen Associates. When it opened in 1975, *Los Angeles Times* architecture critic John Pastier likened it to a whale hiding in a backyard and dubbed it "the Blue Whale." A nine-story green glass extension was later added. The building sits on a 16-acre site, a former Pacific Electric railway yard, and has 200 designer showrooms—1.2 mil-

lion square feet of floor space—the largest such concentration in the West. On display are furniture, fabric, lighting, and floor coverings. Except for a fourth-floor restaurant, the building is not open to the general public.

PACIFIC ELECTRIC RAILWAY COMPANY (PE), interurban rail network that once served much of Southern California. Henry E. Huntington established the PE in 1901 to sell and develop vast tracts of real estate. He bought up and expanded an existing transportation network, built by Moses Sherman and Eli Clark, that linked Los Angeles with Pasadena and Santa Monica. By 1911 PE owned 415 cars and ran them as one-, two- or three-car trains, powered by overhead electrified copper wire. At the company's peak the PE Big Red Cars ran in trains traveling at 40–50 miles an hour on more than 1,000 miles of track. The 50-foot-long Red Cars were made of wood and steel, and painted crimson with gold letters and trim. Huntington also owned a streetcar system (LARy), the Yellow Cars, which made shorter runs for a nickel fare, mostly in downtown Los Angeles. In 1910 Huntington sold the entire interurban line to the Southern Pacific Railroad and devoted himself to his art and book collections at his San Marino estate.

Although the Big Red Cars carried freight, the main cargo was people, whose fares averaged less than a penny a mile. They could travel from the San Fernando Valley to the foothills of the San Gabriels, along the coast from Santa Monica to Newport's Balboa Island, and inland as far as San Bernardino and Redlands. People used the line for work, recreation, and sightseeing. Favorite tourist lines were the Mt. Lowe funicular, the Poppy Car to Monrovia, the Old Mission Trolley trip to Mis-

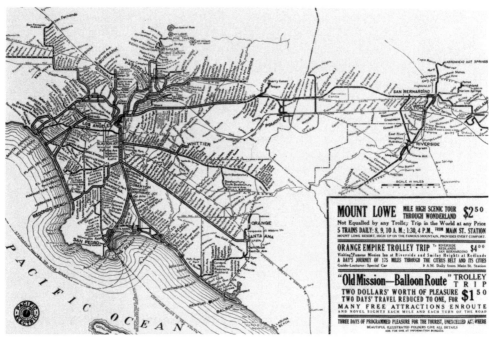

Pacific Electric Railway map, 1912. Courtesy Dept. of Special Collections, University Research Library, UCLA.

sion San Gabriel, the Orange Empire trip to Mission Inn in Riverside, the Tournament of Roses Special, and the "Balloon Trolley Trip" (referring to a circular route made by the trolley), which cost $1 for an entire day's outing. The photogenic cars appeared in the movies, and several studios had their own cars outfitted with special camera booms. In the grand finale of his film *The General* (1927), Buster Keaton demolished 12 obsolete Red Cars on a rail spur in Truckee.

In the 1930s, as automobile traffic increased, PE passengers declined in number, travel time increased, revenues fell, and the trains caused massive clogging of downtown streets because grade separations were lacking. Although rail traffic rose briefly during World War II, it resumed its downward slide when the war ended.

The demise of the Red Car system had several causes. Clearly, the PE could not match the speed, convenience, or flexibility of the car. Yet the company's demise was orchestrated, rather than left to chance. The well-organized auto-freeway lobby had, since the 1920s, actively opposed public subsidies for transportation. A clutch of giant corporations with a stake in cars and buses—General Motors, Standard Oil, Firestone Tire, Phillips Petroleum, and Mack Truck Manufacturing Company—organized a dummy corporation, National City Lines, to buy

up and dismantle mass transit lines throughout the country, including the Red Cars. In 1949 a federal court convicted them and fined them $37,007 for violating the Sherman Antitrust Act—but by then it was too late for the Red Cars. A comic version of this real corporate conspiracy underlies the plot of the animated film *Who Framed Roger Rabbit?* (1988).

The PE was ill even before it was murdered. However, the railway system, which was intended to promote real estate sales, lost money throughout its tenure, and survived only because it was subsidized by the corporation's land operations. By the 1940s and 1950s the technology was growing old, and people preferred cars. In addition, Angelenos harbored a well-founded distrust of corrupt state, regional, and city governments' ability to control a private transportation company or to organize and run a publicly owned mass transit system. The PE owners offered to sell the company to a public agency several times but were rebuffed.

The last Red Car, carrying old-timers, rumbled down the Long Beach line in 1961, marking the end of an era. One car—Big Red Car No. 498—salvaged as a museum piece, welcomes passengers at the Orange Empire Railway Museum in Perris, southeast of Riverside. Some cars were sold in South America, and others were junked. Today, amid growing freeway congestion and the rising cost of mass transportation, memories of the Red Car hold great appeal.

PACIFIC LIGHTING CORPORATION. *See* Southern California Gas Company

PACIFIC OCEAN PARK (POP). *See* Amusement parks and piers

PACIFIC PALISADES, residential community near the ocean, 17 miles west of downtown. Indians lived along its jagged shoreline cliffs and at the mouth of Santa Monica Canyon as much as 10,000 years before the area's first land grants were issued to Francisco Marquez and Ysidro Reyes. Angelenos were using the region as a summer resort in the 1860s. In 1921 a Methodist group formed a colony, "the Chautauqua of the West," for cultural and moral betterment. Led by Rev. Charles H. Scott, the members bought house lots for $1,000 each and constructed homes on the mesa above Potrero Canyon. Desirable suburban real estate developments—Huntington Palisades, Miramar Estates, and Castellammare—soon opened nearby. From the 1920s to the 1940s Pacific Palisades was a popular area for artists, architects, writers, and theater people. Architectural publisher John Entenza encouraged the building of homes in Pacific Palisades that represented the modernist style and the Case Study House program. An enclave of the Self-Realization Fellowship is located off Sunset Boulevard.

PACIFIC PALISADES HIGHLANDS, affluent high-density residential community in the Santa Monica Mountains developed in the late 1960s by Sunset Petroleum Company. A medley of town houses, condominiums, massive Tudor castles, and Spanish haciendas, it received high marks for planning, but low marks for intruding on a wild area of Santa Ynez Canyon.

PACIFIC RIM, the coastal regions bordering the Pacific Ocean. The term is often used in conjunction with trade and commerce specifically. The linkage between Los Angeles and Pacific Ocean nations in this regard was mentioned by historian Carey McWilliams in *Southern California: An Island on the Land* (1946), and novelist Caroline See uses it in her works. Today, California's major trading partners around the Pacific Rim are Japan, Taiwan, South Korea, Mexico, Singapore, Malaysia, Indonesia, Canada, and Australia.

PACIFIC STOCK EXCHANGE, securities exchange headquartered in Los Angeles and San Francisco. Predecessor exchanges were the San Francisco Stock and Bond Exchange, formed in 1882, and Los Angeles Stock and Oil Exchange, founded in 1899. The two exchanges merged in 1957, thanks to the efforts of Thomas P. Phelan (1906–1993) of Los Angeles, the first president of the merged organization. The Pacific Stock Exchange became the first securities exchange in the nation to accept a woman member. Many listings are dually listed with the New York and American exchanges. By 1989 the Pacific Stock Exchange had 551 members, representing the nation's largest brokerage firms. More than 1.7 billion shares were traded that year. The exchange uses a high-tech communications network to record transactions and handles over 1,600 securities.

PACOIMA, east San Fernando Valley area of the city of Los Angeles 17 miles northwest of downtown, established in 1887 along the route of the Southern Pacific Railroad. The name derives from a Gabrieleño (Shoshonean) word possibly meaning "rushing water," a reference to the beautiful canyon to the north, once a favored place for summer homes but now under water. The founder of Pacoima, Jouett Allen, purchased the land from Charles Maclay, who established the town of San Fernando. Industry was forbidden in the original settlement. In 1887 Mrs. E. M. Rose planted seeds obtained from a barrel of Florida oranges. When Pacoima joined Los Angeles to ensure a reliable water supply from the Los Angeles Aqueduct, the area became noted for its citrus fruit, vineyards, and vegetables. It was also known as a place where racehorses were bred. During World War II many African American defense workers took up residence in Pacoima. In 1949 the Hansen Dam Recreational Area was created in the area surrounding a nearby reservoir. In 1990 the population of Pacoima and neighboring Arleta was 92,255.

PADILLA, VICTORIA (1905–1981), horticulturist and teacher, specializing in Southern California flora. Born in San Francisco, Padilla lived most of her life in Los Angeles. She received a bachelor's degree from UCLA in 1927 and a master's degree from USC in 1933. Although not trained in the biological sciences, Padilla became a world-renowned expert on bromeliads, writing three books on that plant family. She also authored

Southern California Gardens (1961), still considered the basic resource for information on native and exotic plants in the area. Until she retired in 1969 Padilla taught music, business, and English. She was active in the Southern California Horticultural Institute.

PAGE, GEORGE C., MUSEUM OF LA BREA DISCOVERIES. *See* La Brea tar pits

PAINTING, TO 1920, was shaped largely by the desire of settlers in Southern California to perpetuate established aesthetic traditions and tastes, rather than to innovate. Ideas regarding painting were derived mainly from concepts taught in leading European art academies.

For at least 8,000 years before Europeans came to Southern California, Tongva people were painting drawings of animals and people on their bodies and on cave walls. Later, under Spanish rule, mission Indians crafted the first known European-style paintings in the area. Among these was "The Fourteen Stations of the Cross," a mural series at San Gabriel Mission attributed to the neophyte Juan Antonio and evidently drawn from engravings shown him by a mission father. Generally, however, the Spanish-Mexican colonial period, from 1769 to 1850, directed aesthetic energies largely to song, dance, costuming, and domestic crafts, rather than to painting.

The Mexican War, the Gold Rush, and the completion of the railroads brought sojourners and settlers to Southern California, some of whom carried sketch pads in their luggage. William Rich Hutton, a U.S. soldier stationed in Monterey, drew vignettes of the *pueblo* of Los Angeles in 1847. William H. Meyers, a naval gunner, did a series on Mexican War skirmishes in Southern California. Skilled portraitists and landscapists passed through Los Angeles, depicting rancho life and mission ruins. Ferdinand Deppe, a Yankee merchant, was an early portrayer of San Gabriel. The first resident artist was French-born Henri Penelon, who in the 1850s painted oil portraits of rancheros and other local citizens.

As the population increased, so did people's interest in painting. The first art schools were founded between the Boom of the Eighties and the turn of the century, including the Los Angeles School of Art and Design, founded by Louisa Garden MacLeod, and USC's college of fine arts. A legion of newspaper illustrators, designers of bird's-eye city views, lithographers, and painters of orange-crate labels also made influential images of the region.

Toward the end of the century health seekers poured into Southern California, and among them were artists and art patrons. Art clubs formed in the 1890s offered classes, sponsored exhibitions, promoted public school instruction, and hosted visiting notables from the art world. Alberta and William McClosky's romantic landscapes, known for "soft and sweet but bright colors," especially gold and rose, were very popular. The French painter Paul DeLongpre, the "Roi des Fleurs" ("King of Flowers"), retired to California in 1898 and lived in a grand house at Cahuenga and Hollywood Boulevards. Tourists by the thousands came to see his gallery of floral still lifes. For many years the center of the Los Angeles art world was the Blanchard Music and Art Building, a downtown private enterprise that opened in 1899 replete with studios, auditoriums, and a gallery.

At the turn of the century painters influenced by the French Barbizon and Impressionist schools set up their easels in the Arroyo Seco, Topanga Canyon, Laguna Beach, Avalon, and outlying desert areas to paint landscapes. Their palettes, which evoked golden grasses and green bushes, as well as the rose, ocher, and gray of dry terrain and foliage, came to be known as the "Eucalyptus School." In 1906 San Francisco painters, uprooted by the earthquake, moved to Southern California

---

I almost agreed to write music for a film [*The Good Earth*], but fortunately asked $50,000, which, likewise fortunately, was much too much, for it would have been the end of me.
    —Arnold Schoenberg, mid-1930s

---

as well. That same year, the *Los Angeles Times* hired its first art critic, and the Los Angeles Art Students' League began offering classes. The rapidly expanding film industry began to recruit painters as set designers, and by 1917 the distinguished stage designer Norman Bel Geddes was working in the Los Angeles theater. Popular artists Elmer Wachtel, an Ohio-born painter who had studied in Europe, and his wife, Marion Kavanaugh Wachtel, were also active in Los Angeles. Two commercial galleries had opened downtown. The early part of the century also saw the birth of the Otis Art Institute.

While the taste of the local public, press critics, galleries, museums, and art schools clung to Impressionism, by 1910 a few young painters returning from Europe and New York were starting to explore ideas derived from "Modernism"—Cubism, Expressionism, Fauvism. Among these pioneers were Rex Slinkard and Stanton Macdonald-Wright, who formed the Modern Art Society in 1916. Macdonald-Wright was also a founder of Synchronism, a trend born in Paris.

PAINTING, 1920–1960, was characterized at first by the continued popularity of traditional styles. The dean of the painting fraternity in the 1920s was William Wendt, a Chicagoan who had come to Los Angeles in 1906. In addition to landscapes, Wendt also produced figure paintings, still lifes, Indian portraits, and other popular western themes. Other painters tended to embrace similar themes. The population boom of the 1920s brought patrons who supported commercial galleries, art clubs, and art schools. Mrs. Nelbert ("Nelly") Chouinard, an instructor at Otis Art Institute, founded the Chouinard Art Institute in 1921, an important institution in the Los Angeles art world.

Beginning in the 1930s, local art was heavily influenced by the ascendancy of Modernism, as exemplified by the developing ideas of Surrealism, Cubism, and Geometric Abstraction. An infusion of European émigré artists, the aesthetics of the cinema, and the social climate of the Great Depression played a defining role as well. Some painters worked for the film studios, particularly in animation. Oskar Fischinger, a German who arrived in Hollywood in 1936 and worked for Disney, made major contributions to the field. The New Deal's Work Projects Administration employed artists to create murals in public places, many of which dealt with subjects of social concern. Diverse painters such as Anton Refrigier, Jackson Pollock, Charles White, and Philip Guston were involved in the movement known as Social Realism. (Guston, a graduate of Manual Arts High School in Los Angeles, studied at Otis in the late 1920s.) Also among the leading modernists of the 1930s and 1940s were Man Ray, Stanton Macdonald-Wright, Lorser Feitelson, Eugene Berman, Millard Sheets,

Granville Redmond, Albert King, and Oskar Fischinger.

The local 1940s art scene was dominated by Rico Lebrun; Francis de Erdeley, a Hungarian immigrant who taught at USC; sculptor and painter Peter Krasnow; Boris Deutch, a Figurative Expressionist; and William Brice. They all received critical acclaim.

Individual artists were still inspired by the region's light, climate, and distinctive landscape. However, they were also influenced by the new material culture, and elements drawn from the culture of cars and freeways, Hollywood studios, and the aerospace industry found their way into their paintings.

In the late 1940s Abstract Expressionism, or action painting, arrived in Los Angeles. This new avenue of Modernism incorporated the mood of upheaval unleashed by World War II, the Holocaust, the dawn of the nuclear age, and the Cold War. It drew upon the art of Picasso, Miró, and the Surrealists, but was more violent. An important outlet for artists was the Copley Gallery in Beverly Hills, run by the painter William Copley, who featured the works of Yves Tanguy, Max Ernst, Man Ray, and others.

Rico Lebrun's *Crucifixion* paintings and drawings, the culmination of a life of work dealing with figurative imagery based on Italian Renaissance ideas, was unveiled at the Los Angeles County Museum of Art in 1957. The younger Los Angeles Expressionists at this time included artists as diverse as Howard Warshaw, Jan Stussy, Martin Lubner, Robert Chuey, and Edward Kienholz.

PAINTING, SINCE 1960, reflected the continuing dominance of Modernism, including Expressionism, as well as the emergence of the loosely defined Postmodernist style. In the 1960s Los Angeles experienced an art boom. In terms of gallery and museum traffic, as well as the sheer output and commerce of painting, the city evolved into one of the nation's leading art centers. Painters were influenced by the advertising industry, a pervasive consumerism, and the celebration of outdoor living.

In Los Angeles the attention of the art world became riveted on the work of the avant-garde artists who exhibited at the Ferus Gallery in the late 1950s to the mid-1960s. Included in this group were some Chouinard graduates: Edward Kienholz, Craig Kauffman, Ed Moses, Robert Irwin, John Mason,

Martin Lubner, "Studio #20," 1983 (oil on canvas, 76⅛" X 99¼"). Collection of the Newport Harbor Art Museum, Gift of Martha Cooley.

and Billy Al Bengstrom. These artists had been snubbed by local galleries and had fought against the hegemony of the New York art world. After gaining Ferus exposure, they remained prominent during the "golden age" of the Southern California art scene.

The advent of the Ferus Gallery and half a dozen others, including the Felix Landau and Frank Perls Galleries, in the late 1950s and 1960s dramatically improved the ability of the Los Angeles public to view works by diverse artists. Meanwhile, universities and other schools—USC, UC Santa Barbara, UCLA, Chouinard, Otis, Cal Arts —encouraged the development of new talent throughout the region. Modernists' canvases found their way into museums and private collections such as those owned by Norton Simon.

Among the few women represented in the galleries were Martha Alf, Vija Celmins, and Jay De-Feo, an Abstract Expressionist whose thickly smeared paintings were hung at the Ferus. The works of sculptor Claire Falkenstein also found exposure from the 1940s to the 1960s.

David Hockney, a transplant from England, was influenced by the outdoor living and bright sunlight of Southern California. His paintings of the Los Angeles landscape and middle-class lifestyle have been in great vogue since the late 1960s. The Ocean Park series by Richard Diebenkorn is another important contribution—and depiction—of the Los Angeles scene.

The local art world of the 1960s and 1970s— which continued to be dominated by Modernism —also witnessed the emergence of the loosely defined "Postmodernist" style, which included Pop art. The leading practitioners locally were Edward Ruscha, Billy Al Bengston, and Lynn Foulkes.

Young activist painters also demanded support for "public art"—murals, sculptures, and paintings —to be integrated into major building projects of the Community Redevelopment Agency. A quartet of Chicano painters known as "Los Four"— Frank Romero, Beto de la Rocha, Gilbert Lujan, and Carlos Almaraz—had works shown at UC Irvine and the Los Angeles County Museum of Art in 1979. They were among the first Chicano artists to achieve national recognition. Other Latino artists featured in galleries and museums during the 1980s and 1990s include sculptor Luis Jimenez and painter Rolando Briseno. The Self-Help Graphics and Art Center in East Los Angeles promotes the work of Latino artists as well, and the city of Los Angeles is assisting in the formation of a California Latino art museum.

By the 1980s and 1990s the art boom had subsided, but art galleries and museums were dispersed throughout the Los Angeles Basin, particularly in affluent neighborhoods. In 1991 *Artscene,* the monthly guide to painting and sculpture, listed 74 venues in West Hollywood and Beverly Hills; 67 on the Westside, including Santa Monica and Venice; 19 in Pasadena and in the eastern part of the county; 18 in downtown Los Angeles; 17 in Hollywood; and 15 in the San Fernando Valley and Glendale.

PALESTINIANS number between 40,000 and 50,000 in Southern California, according to the Arab-American Anti-Discrimination Committee. They began arriving after the 1967 war with Israel and the Lebanese civil war in 1975. Although many are Christian, the majority are of the Muslim faith.

PALMDALE, "gateway city" to the Antelope Valley, 47 miles northwest of downtown Los Angeles. In prehistoric times Indians frequented nearby regions, where water was available. The Spanish colonial governor Pedro Fages passed through the area in 1772, noting the exotic vegetation. In the 1850s the area was served by the Butterfield stage,

but the completion in 1876 of the Southern Pacific Railroad line through valley had a marked impact on the growth of agriculture, commerce, and settlement. The first settlers, in 1886, were German Lutherans who called their new home Palmenthal ("Palm Valley"). The "palms" were really Joshua trees, sometimes known as yucca palms. The name was changed to Palmdale in 1890. The first paved road to Los Angeles was completed in 1921.

By 1930 the town had a population of 6,000. Housing units in the area expanded during the 1930s and into the 1950s to accommodate the personnel of nearby Edwards Air Force Base, a military testing center at Muroc (a.k.a. Rogers) Dry Lake. The 1952 establishment of USAF Plant 42, which employed 6,400, and Lockheed's decision to manufacture the L-1011 (Tristar) in Palmdale brought additional newcomers to the community.

The city was incorporated in 1962; its boundaries encompass 48 square miles, about the area of Long Beach. The desert community derives ample water from underground sources and from the California Aqueduct. In the 1970s Los Angeles acquired 17,000 acres in Palmdale for the site of a new international airport, but the airport never materialized. Civic leaders have long maintained a "progrowth" position. Palmdale's population grew from 12,000 in 1980 to 68,800 in 1990, making it the fastest-growing area in Los Angeles County.

PALMS, Los Angeles city neighborhood north of Culver City, centered at Palms Boulevard and Motor Avenue. It was part of Rancho La Ballona before three midwesterners bought and subdivided

Lake Palmdale. Courtesy City of Palmdale.

the land in 1886, calling it "The Palms." The community was situated alongside a Southern Pacific rail line connecting Santa Monica with downtown Los Angeles. Although Culver City attempted to annex the Palms, residents preferred to be part of Los Angeles, and annexation occurred in 1915. The 1991 population was about 35,000. The photogenic Palms railway station building frequently appeared in feature films, and is now part of the Heritage Square Museum on the Arroyo Seco.

PALM TREE, ubiquitous and emblematic tree. All but one of Southern California's palms are exotics. Although as many as 2,000 varieties have been identified worldwide, the only true native is the California or Washington palm *(Washingtonia filifera)*. It varies in size from about 15 feet to over 70 feet, and its fruit was a food source for the Indian population. Many palms planted in the 1920s and 1930s continue to dominate the streetscape in certain neighborhoods, presenting a familiar Los Angeles scene.

Palm trees. Photo by Dale Pitt.

PALOS VERDES ESTATES, CITY OF, incorporated community 27 miles southwest of downtown Los Angeles on the Palos Verdes Peninsula. It overlooks the ocean from Malaga Cove to Lunada Bay. The name (variously translated as "green trees," "green sticks," or "green masts") is derived from Cañada de los Palos Verdes, a peaceful canyon of willows and grass near today's Harbor Lake, at Pacific Coast Highway and Vermont Avenue, that was owned by the Sepúlveda family after 1827. It was favored by early settlers as a place of repose. The 3,200 acres of land that later became the city were developed as a "millionaire's colony" after 1922 by New York banker Frank A. Vanderlip and an associate, E. G. Lewis. They hired the celebrated Boston firms of Olmsted & Olmsted and Charles H. Cheney to design the project, which comprised Palos Verdes Estates and Miraleste. The designers selected the Spanish (Mediterranean) architectural style, which is permanently preserved in protective clauses of each private deed. Half the area was reserved for parkland and public rights-of-way. Peacocks, introduced to enhance the natural environment, thrived and became a featured attraction of the area. Home building began in 1926 and was substantially completed by 1931.

In 1939, many residents of the unincorporated territory had suffered financial losses in the depression and owed Los Angeles County a total of about $34,000 in back taxes. The Los Angeles County Board of Supervisors threatened to seize the extensive public parkland in lieu of payment, whereupon the homeowners voted—by the narrow margin of 419 to 412—to incorporate as a city and retain control over their open space. Over time, the ornamental birds multiplied and became so noisy that in 1985 the city limited the number of peacocks to 67, deporting the rest. The population of the City of Palos Verdes Estates stood at 13,500 in 1990, down 5 percent from 1980.

PALOS VERDES PENINSULA, highland area separating Santa Monica Bay from San Pedro Bay. It has handsome headlands, rocky beaches, sandy coves, and 13 terraces rising to a height of 1,300 feet, topped by San Pedro Hill at 1,480 feet. In the Ice Age the peninsula was submerged, but later rose as an island and became attached to the mainland. It was home to Indians in prehistoric times, the village of Chowing-na at Malaga Cove constituting one of the largest and richest archaeological sites in California. In Spanish days the peninsula was granted to Juan José Domínguez. After prolonged litigation it fell into the hands of the Sepúlvedas, and subsequently of the Bixby family. The latter sold 16,000 acres to New York banker Frank Vanderlip and a Los Angeles real estate firm. In 1914 this syndicate planned a fashionable and exclusive colony, Palos Verdes Estates, which in turn came into the possession of E. G. Lewis in the 1920s.

Today Palos Verdes Peninsula comprises various jurisdictions: San Pedro (part of the city of Los Angeles) and the cities of Palos Verdes Estates, Rancho Palos Verdes, Rolling Hills Estates, and Rolling Hills. Among its historic landmarks are Point Vicente Lighthouse (1926), Malaga Cove Plaza (1922), Wayfarer's Chapel (1949), South Coast Botanic Garden (1961), and the site of the Portuguese Bend Whaling Station (1820s).

PANORAMA CITY, 5.5-square-mile suburb of Los Angeles located near Van Nuys in the San Fernando Valley. In 1947 developer Fritz B. Burns and Associates bought 1,000 acres from Panorama Dairy and Sheep Ranch and built 3,000 homes and a commercial center on the property. Panorama City Shopping Center opened in 1955, and a Kaiser hospital located there soon afterward. Panorama City's population in 1988 was about 45,000.

PAN PACIFIC AUDITORIUM, meeting hall in the Fairfax area from 1935 to 1972. Designed by Plummer, Wurdeman, and Becket, it embodied in its Streamline Moderne style and its four fin-shaped towers a Buck Rogers futurism reflecting the hopeful spirit of the Chicago World's Fair of 1933. Gen. Dwight D. Eisenhower addressed an audience of 20,000 in the Pan Pacific during the 1952 election campaign, and five years later Elvis Presley performed there before a wildly enthusiastic audience. The annual Ice Capades also attracted a large following. As a meeting place the auditorium was displaced by the downtown Convention Center in the 1970s and stood virtually empty for years. Named to the National Register of Historic Places, it was slated for a $22 million face-lift when destroyed by fire in May 1989. The county plans to reconstruct the façade as it appeared in the 1930s.

PANTAGES THEATER, Hollywood Boulevard movie house. When it opened in 1929, the 2,812-seat theater was advertised as the largest and most ornate movie palace in the region. Now called the Arcade, it has been refurbished for stage productions, primarily musicals.

PARAMOUNT, incorporated city 11 miles south of downtown Los Angeles, between Los Angeles and Long Beach, created in 1948 by a merger of the cities of Hynes and Clearwater. The city was named after its main boulevard at the urging of Frank Zamboni, head of the local Kiwanis Club. Paramount recorded a 30.9 percent population increase between 1980 and 1990, reaching 47,600.

PARAMOUNT PICTURES CORPORATION, one of the "Big Five" movie studios of Hollywood's Golden Age, and today the film studio (now also television) with the longest ongoing tradition. It was formed in 1914 by theater owner William Wadsworth Hodkinson, who bought and exhibited films from production companies such as Adolph Zukor's Famous Players and Jesse Lasky's Feature Play Company. (Hodkinson took the name Paramount from an apartment building he saw in passing, and the snow-capped peak logo from a

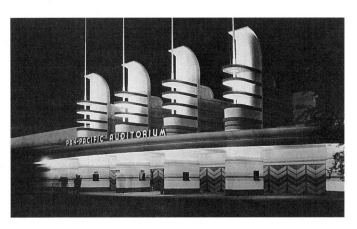

Pan Pacific Auditorium, Plummer, Wurdeman, and Becket, 1935. Courtesy Ellerby Becket.

mountain near his Utah home.) In 1913, Lasky and Cecil B. De Mille had produced *The Squaw Man,* and Lasky soon bought 10 percent of Paramount. Two years later Zukor and Lasky merged their two companies to form Famous Players–Lasky, with De Mille and Samuel Goldfish (later Goldwyn) as major partners. Within a few years Goldwyn sold his share and Hodkinson resigned. Lasky took control and changed the company's name to Paramount Pictures. At the first Academy Awards presentation in 1929 Paramount's *Wings* won as best picture of 1927–1928.

Among Paramount's major stars were Mary Pickford, Douglas Fairbanks, the Marx brothers, Mae West, Cary Grant, Burt Lancaster, Kirk Douglas, and Marlon Brando, and directors included Cecil B. De Mille, D. W. Griffith, Preston Sturges, William Wyler, Ernst Lubitsch, and Billy Wilder. A few of the hundreds of Paramount's acclaimed movies are *A Farewell to Arms* (1932), *Sullivan's Travels* (1941), *Double Indemnity* (1944), *Sunset Boulevard* (1950), *Roman Holiday* (1953), *The Godfather* (1972), *Raiders of the Lost Ark* (1981), and *Beverly Hills Cop* (1984). In 1966 Paramount was taken over by Gulf+Western, which also absorbed Desilu Productions. In 1967 the company began major television operations, including such series as *Gunsmoke, Happy Days, Mork and Mindy, Taxi, The Brady Bunch,* and *The Odd Couple.*

In 1987 Paramount was the largest-grossing film company, and the only major film studio still located in Hollywood.

PARAMOUNT RANCH, park in the Agoura Hills area of the Santa Monica Mountains. It was part of the 8,885-acre Las Virgenes Rancho, granted in 1822 and later homesteaded by Yankee ranchers in the 1860s. Paramount Pictures Corporation bought 2,700 acres in 1927, using the land as a location for movie and TV westerns, such as *The Cisco Kid* and *Bat Masterson,* into the 1950s. The site, which today is protected as part of the Santa Monica Mountains National Recreation Area, includes a replica of the main street of a 19th-century western town. Paramount Ranch is best accessed from U.S. Highway 101 at Kanan Road.

PARKER, WILLIAM HENRY (1902–1966), Los Angeles police chief from 1950 to 1966. Born into a prominent South Dakota family, he came to Los Angeles in 1922 and entered the Los Angeles Police Department in 1927. He served with dis-

tinction in the U.S. Army in World War II, participating in the Normandy invasion. After the war he returned to the blue uniform, and became chief in 1950. Parker helped clean up city hall corruption and professionalized the department along the lines of a quasi-military organization. Although lauded nationally as an honest, efficient, and effective police chief, he was nevertheless strongly criticized by the black community for racial bigotry before and during the Watts riots of 1965. He died while he was still chief of police. Parker Center, the downtown police headquarters, is named for him.

PARKING REGULATION is handled by individual municipalities. At first the automobile, universally regarded as a symbol of personal freedom and urban progress, was exempt from parking limits. This happy situation ended abruptly in the summer of 1919, when a month-long strike of streetcar workers brought tens of thousands of autos into downtown, where they jammed curbside parking spots for hours on end. The chaos only worsened after the strike ended, as the numbers of cars continued to grow. In April 1920 a frustrated city council ordered a stringent parking ban during working hours. This extreme solution brought cries of

Street signs, Los Angeles. Photo by Dale Pitt.

outrage from car dealers, auto owners, and downtown merchants. The council had to modify and then lift the ban in very short order, but it has maintained some degree of public control ever since.

The Los Angeles Department of Transportation issued 3.2 million parking tickets in 1987, twice as many as 10 years earlier. Beverly Hills wrote 350,000, Santa Monica 300,000, and Pasadena 107,000. Regionally, the number of tickets issued was over 6 million—more citations than cars or trucks registered (5.6 million in the county). Ticketing has become more aggressive as cities scramble to supplement declining tax revenues. In Los Angeles, most of the tens of millions of dollars fed into the tens of thousands of parking meters is used to improve traffic control.

PARK LA BREA, apartment project at Fairfax Avenue and 3rd Street begun by the Metropolitan Life Insurance Company in the 1940s and completed after World War II. The 176-acre site contains blocks of two-story garden apartments, built to harmonize in scale with the surrounding neighborhood and occupied in 1946. More prominent are the 12-story towers, whose massive size is suggestive of the Bronx in New York City. The entire complex has 4,213 living units. The grounds present a vista of green lawns, lightly trafficked streets, and a quiet urban environment for people of varying ages, races, and ethnic backgrounds. The estimated population in 1992 was 6,836. Park La Brea is now owned by Forest City Enterprises.

PARKS, maintained by numerous government jurisdictions, numbered 370 in 1991 in Los Angeles County. By area the total public space devoted to parks in Los Angeles is relatively abundant. However, given the enormous size and distribution of the population, as well as the pressing need to protect the natural environment, parkland is generally considered scarce, especially at the neighborhood level.

The federal government leases recreational areas to select users in the Angeles National Forest, although that is a forest preserve rather than a park. The Santa Monica Mountains National Recreation Area, operated by the National Park Service, includes parkland.

The state of California maintains various recreational sites in the Los Angeles area, the most heavily used being beaches. The state also owns thousands of acres in the Santa Monica Mountains, and

it preserves historic sites, such as Los Encinos Park in Encino and Will Rogers State Park in Pacific Palisades.

The county maintains a large network of regional parks, recreation areas, natural areas, nature centers, wildlife and wildflower sanctuaries, and golf courses. Thanks to Supervisor William A. Smith, the greatest expansion of county parks came in the 1930s. By 1959 the Department of Parks and Recreation supervised 140 parks comprising 11,393 acres, as well as 10.5 miles of beaches. Some parks, such as Hancock Park and Descanso Gardens, were made possible by charitable donations. Others were developed piecemeal, including Plummer Park in Hollywood (the result of agitation by the crusty John Anson Ford), Alondra Park, City Terrace Park, John Anson Ford Park, Whittier Narrows Dam Recreational Area, Herbert C. Legg Fishing Lake, and Puddingstone Park. After a careful assessment of needs, the county recently concluded that it is seriously deficient in all park categories.

The Los Angeles City Department of Recreation and Parks has jurisdiction over more than 150 recreation centers and 350 parks totaling 15,098 acres. The first city park was Pershing Square; the largest is Griffith Park. Lately, complaints about drug sales and gang activity in inner-city parks deprived them of financial support, causing them to be regarded as "dead." In 1987 the city began implementing a plan to refurbish the 66 neediest recreation centers and strengthen their security. Under the state's Quimby Act, the city allocates to parks a percentage of money received from real estate developers.

PARKSIDE MANOR, neighborhood in the heart of Watts, bordered by Central Avenue Mary Avenue, and 103rd and 107th Streets. Located on former farmland, the tract, consisting of 240 homes, was developed at the end of World War II, one of the first new housing developments in the Watts area. The "park" in question is Will Rogers Park, immediately to the north.

PARROT, KENT K. (1880–19??), political power broker. Parrot came to Los Angeles from Maine in 1907 and attended USC Law School, where he made lasting connections. In 1913 he entered municipal politics with a group of social-reform progressives that included George E. Cryer. He organized Cryer's successful 1921 mayoral campaign and managed a shifting coalition that backed the mayor until 1929. Because Los Angeles lacked a true political machine, Parrot never became a political boss in the eastern sense. Instead he worked on an ad hoc basis for Cryer, handling appointments, troubleshooting, juggling interest groups, and organizing the mayor's reelection campaigns. Parrot finessed everyone—Democrats, Republicans, labor leaders, mobsters, the irascible Rev. Robert Shuler, the powerful Harry Chandler, and the progressive Dr. John Randolph Haynes. Increasingly, Parrot edged Cryer toward progressivism, supporting municipal ownership of the electrical utility in opposition to the *Los Angeles Times*.

Parrot had a brief fling at controlling state and county politics in 1925 and 1926, but opponents coalesced to defeat the Cryer-Parrot regime in 1929. Although he was seen occasionally at City Hall for several more years, Kent Parrot had no more power after that time.

PARROTS, AMAZONIAN, tropical birds, have been flying free locally since the beginning of the century. In 1913 Lucky Baldwin set them loose on his Arcadia estate; in the 1950s smugglers abandoned their birds when government regulators closed in; and in 1961 homeowners freed the birds from aviaries as the Bel-Air fire approached. The resulting communities of colorful, raucous, wild parrots appear to have adapted successfully to the urban environment. They eat seeds and fruit, and nest only in or near select fruit trees (avoiding ba-

nana and orange trees). The parrots seek out only built-up areas, avoiding wilderness, and roost where they can take cover from the cold. The birds mate in pairs for life. The leading varieties are yellow-headed, red-headed, and lilac-crowned.

PARSONS, LOUELLA (1880–1972), syndicated Hollywood gossip columnist. Parsons came to California from Illinois for health reasons. In 1924 she was a guest on William Randolph Hearst's yacht, the *Oneida,* when director Thomas Ince was stricken mysteriously. Hearst hired Parsons as a journalist immediately after Ince's death, possibly to pay her for her silence. She practically invented the role of syndicated Hollywood correspondent. With an estimated readership of 20 million in the 1930s and 1940s, she and her rival, Hedda Hopper, wielded great power over stars, studios, and the box office. She also had a radio interview program, *Hollywood Hotel,* and appeared in several movie bit parts, playing herself. Her autobiography is titled *Tell It To Louella* (1962).

PASADENA, San Gabriel Valley's principal city, located 10 miles east of downtown Los Angeles. It lies at the base of the San Gabriel Mountains on what was once part of Don Manuel García's Rancho San Pascual. Its first Yankee community emerged in 1873, when Daniel Berry, an Indianapolis teacher-journalist, led a band from Indiana seeking refuge from the harsh midwestern winters. Despite its fertile soil, abundant water, and mild climate, the original "Indiana Colony" col-

Pasadena, September 1885, celebration of the completion of the Santa Fe Railroad, a direct hookup to the East. Courtesy Pasadena Historical Museum and Archives.

lapsed owing to financial troubles. The colonists reorganized as the San Gabriel Orange Grove Association, purchased 1,500 acres of land, and created 100 lots, which were offered for sale. The name Pasadena, chosen by Judge Benjamin S. Eaton and formally applied in 1875, when the city was incorporated, is of obscure origin. It probably comes from the Chippewa language and means "crown or key of the valley."

The town had only 271 permanent residents in 1883. It was connected by railroad to Los Angeles upon the completion of the Los Angeles and San Gabriel Valley Railroad in 1885, and incorporated on 19 June 1886. During the Boom of the Eighties, which caused an enormous rise in tourism, wealthy midwestern and eastern families arrived in luxurious Pullman cars to escape the bitter winter cold. As Pasadena became a popular resort, elaborate hotels were built to accommodate the visitors.

A board of trade (later, chamber of commerce) was organized in 1888. The first "Festival of Roses" parade, on 1 January 1890, featured carriages decorated by members of the fashionable Valley Hunt Club. This first celebration was simple. Participants picnicked, snapped pictures to be sent back East, and adorned their buggies with roses. Today the annual parade, together with the college championship Rose Bowl Game, is a major event, broadcast the world over.

Pasadena became a charter city in 1900 and elected its first mayor in 1901. By then it had become a winter playground for the rich and famous. Wealthy midwesterners settled in lavish homes on "Millionaire's Row" on Orange Grove Avenue. Around the turn of the century Pasadena was the center of the "Arroyo culture," an aesthetic movement featuring the creative work of artists, craftsmen, writers, and architects. The Gamble House, built in 1908 by Charles and Henry Greene for the Gamble family of Cincinnati, was a crowning achievement of this movement. By 1925 the town's main attractions were Throop Polytechnic Institute (later, Caltech), the Pasadena Playhouse, and the Rose Bowl. The city boasted of numerous striking homes designed by distinguished architects; it also had a distinctive civic center, a central library, and a civic auditorium.

The era from 1940 to 1965—the period of World War II and the Cold War—brought major expansion to Pasadena as a center of scientific research and high-tech industry. The main locus of this activity was at Caltech and the Jet Propulsion Laboratory. The 1940 opening of the Arroyo Seco Parkway (today's Pasadena Freeway), with its connection to downtown Los Angeles, promoted a housing boom in the postwar period. The city's population grew by more than 100,000, particularly in the areas of Linda Vista, San Rafael, and Allendale; meanwhile, a new shopping district emerged on South Lake Avenue. Also contributing to the city's cultural riches in this era was the Norton Simon Museum of Art.

Nevertheless, by the 1970s the city was experiencing economic decline, with the original business district sinking to skid row status. Through a major revival effort in the 1990s, combining public and private investment, the area was reborn as Pasadena Old Town, or Old Pasadena. This district, which comprises the 14 blocks bordered by Pasadena Avenue, Walnut, Arroyo Parkway, and Del Mar, includes refurbished buildings, some dating back to the 1890s, that house more than 130 retail establishments, restaurants, and theaters. Some 35,000 visitors stroll through Pasadena Old Town each weekend.

Pasadena's population rose from 30,000 in 1910 to 131,500 in 1990. Changing demographics are apparent in the large groups of African Americans, Asians, Latinos, and Armenians. The city prides itself on its support for human services and efforts to preserve historic buildings.

PASADENA CULTURAL HERITAGE COMMISSION, panel established in 1976 to preserve the city's historic landmarks and districts. The seven-member panel is authorized to place a one-year moratorium on a demolition order for a designated structure or site that is 50 years or older. Since its founding it has so designated 43 cultural heritage sites. One of them is the South Marengo Historic District, with 12 structures at 462–569 Marengo Avenue dating from the early part of the century. At least 37 Pasadena properties are listed on the National Register of Historic Places.

PASADENA DOO DAH PARADE, irreverent offshoot of the Pasadena Tournament of Roses. A predecessor group calling itself the Komical Knights of the Karnival formed a high-jinx parade in 1911, donning clown costumes and strutting up and down Colorado Boulevard the evening before the 1912 Rose Parade.

The idea for today's Doo Dah Parade took shape in August 1977 when a group of revelers at Chromo's Saloon on Colorado Boulevard realized that, owing to the Rose Parade's never-on-Sunday policy, the thoroughfare would be empty of floats on 1 January 1978. They filled the gap themselves, organizing a parade with "no themes, no judging, no prizes." Among the lighthearted, satirical entrants were the Synchronized Briefcase Drill Team, the World Famous Couch Potatoes, Pregnant Nuns, and the Hibachi Marching Barbecue Bank. Other participants depicted lawyers chasing ambulances and the Little Old Lady from Pasadena gulping from a wine bottle as she was wheeled by a clown. The parade became a yearly event and was moved to the first Sunday after Thanksgiving. By the 1980s the event had acquired TV coverage, sponsors, and 40,000 spectators who cheered on some 100 participating groups. As the decade wore on, increasing controversy over antics by new entrants, and vandalism and minor incidents of violence on the part of spectators, dampened enthusiasm. In 1993 the event's organizer, Peter Apanal, attempting to recoup expenses and maintain order, decided to shift the locale to an enclosed area, limit the number of entrants, and charge a spectator fee. His attempt was unsuccessful. The parade moved back to Pasadena's streets, and in 1995 was sponsored by a nonprofit Pasadena arts group.

PASADENA FREEWAY. *See* Freeways

PASADENA PLAYHOUSE, prominent theater that opened in May 1925 on S. El Molino Avenue in Pasadena. It became famous not only for its staged productions but also for its actor training program, which began in 1928 and gained a boost with the advent of talking pictures.

Under the direction of founder Gilmor Brown, the Playhouse was honored in 1937 as California's

Original curtain of the Pasadena Playhouse, by artist Alson Clark, 1925 (still in use). Archives of the Pasadena Playhouse.

state theater. By 1941 the resident company had performed all of Shakespeare's plays and more than 80 previously unproduced dramas. Casts were drawn from the acting school. Film actors associated with the Playhouse include Dustin Hoffman, William Holden, Raymond Burr, and Gene Hackman.

The proliferation of theaters throughout Los Angeles, the establishment of new drama schools—both private and in universities—and the advent of television led to a dwindling audience for the Playhouse, and in 1966 it was forced to close. Twenty years later it reopened, instituted a school for child actors, and launched stage productions.

PASADENA TOURNAMENT OF ROSES. *See* Pasadena; Tournament of Roses

PATRIOTIC HALL, downtown meeting place for veterans organizations. The stately Italian Renaissance–style structure on S. Figueroa Street, dating from 1924–1925, was built expressly for such groups, which have been active locally since the Spanish-American War and World War I. Designed by military engineers, the hall is one of the most solidly constructed steel-reinforced buildings in the county. It also houses county offices that offer services to veterans and nonveterans.

PATTIE, JAMES OHIO (1804–1850?), Yankee mountain man hired by the Spanish mission fathers to inoculate 2,500 Indian neophytes against smallpox. His 1831 *Narrative* is among the first books by an American to comment, rather negatively, on life in Spanish Southern California.

PAULEY, EDWIN W[ENDELL] (1903–1981), University of California regent and UCLA benefactor who gave $1 million as a matching gift to the UCLA Alumni Association for the construction of what became Pauley Pavilion.

PAULING, LINUS CARL (1901–1994), Caltech chemist, world peace advocate, and two-time Nobel Prize winner. Born in Oregon and educated at Oregon State University, Pauling came to Caltech in 1922, where he earned a doctorate in chemistry. He remained at Caltech, as student and professor, for 41 years. In the 1930s Pauling made one of most important discoveries in the history of chemistry when he determined the nature of the chemical bond—how atoms link up to form mol-

Linus Pauling, Nobel Laureate, 1963. Courtesy Caltech.

ecules in both living and nonliving systems. His book on the subject is still a classic in the field. He played a key role in the discovery of the genetic defect that leads to sickle cell anemia. Considered one of the most original and creative scientific thinkers of the 20th century, Pauling won the Nobel Prize for chemistry in 1954. He also authored the book *No More War!* (1958) and spearheaded a petition campaign against atmospheric nuclear testing that was signed by more than 11,000 scientists worldwide. These efforts won him the Nobel Peace Prize in 1962. In 1973 he founded the Linus Pauling Institute of Science and Medicine near Stanford University, where he did much of his work researching and advocating the beneficial properties of vitamin C.

PEACE AND FREEDOM PARTY (PFP), national third party dating from the 1960s. First organized in 1967 during the civil rights and anti–Vietnam War movements, by 1991 it had 16,555 registered voters in the county, and 52,283 in the state. The party is headquartered in Oakland. Its county central committee is elected in the June primary of odd-numbered years, and organizes in January of even-numbered years. It allows people under the age of 18 full voting rights on its established committees.

PEARBLOSSOM, small foothill community in the Antelope Valley, 54 miles from downtown Los Angeles. Its 3,000-foot altitude moderates the desert climate. An ill-fated Quaker colony faltered here in the 19th century. When the Southern Pacific Railroad completed its line in 1876 and fired numerous Chinese laborers, the U.S. government contracted with the local Carter Ranch to retrain the Asians as vegetable farmers. In the late 1920s, J. B. Elliot bought a vast acreage of uninhabited desert land, named it North Pasadena, advertised it as if it had all the amenities of a modern town, and sold numerous lots to the unsuspecting. His enterprise cost him a term in San Quentin. In 1927 a rancher, Guy C. Chase, purchased a quarter section of land, drilled for water, planted a pear orchard, and proposed the name of Pearblossom. More recently the community has attracted aerospace workers and a pumping station for the California Aqueduct.

PENTECOSTALISM, worldwide fundamental movement born in Los Angeles early in the century. Religious historians trace it to William J. Seymour (d. 1929), an African American Baptist holiness preacher who arrived from Texas in 1906. He became pastor of the Azusa Street Mission in the working-class neighborhood east of Alameda Street. His fiery preachings, reported in the *Los Angeles Times* as "weird babble," were publicized by Frank Bartle-

---

Strip away the phony tinsel in Hollywood and you'll find the real tinsel underneath.

—Oscar Levant, pianist and raconteur

---

man, a journalist for the holiness press, who kept a diary of the revival meetings and wrote reports eventually published as *How Pentecost Came to Los Angeles* (1925). Many of Seymour's followers were white. Pilgrims representing many denominations gathered from all parts of the world, especially in the period 1906–1909, and left to sow the gospel from Azusa Street. Associated with Pentecostalism is "speaking in tongues" (glossolalia), which followers maintain is supported by the Bible (John 3:8).

A defining moment in the movement occurred in Los Angeles in 1960, when Pentecostalists at St. Mark's Episcopal Church in Van Nuys split the congregation in two. It was the first mainline church to experience such a rift. An estimated 75 million people, including both Catholic and Protestant denominations, maintain the Pentecostal (and charismatic) tradition. Half of the more than 3,000 students at Fuller Theological Seminary in Pasadena represent Pentecostal or charismatic elements of mainstream churches worldwide. The movement has many adherents in Latin America and in the Latino population of Los Angeles. Oral Roberts, Pat Robertson, and Jim Bakker have been among its leading preachers in the United States. The movement developed along racial lines, with the white-dominated Pentecostal Fellowship of North America remaining separate from the African American Church of God in Christ, the largest Pentecostal denomination. In 1994 a new, interracial fellowship was formed that would embrace as many as 10 million members.

PEPPERDINE UNIVERSITY, Malibu-based institution affiliated with the Church of Christ. Its main unit is Seaver College, a beautiful 830-acre residential campus overlooking the ocean. Classes are also held in West Los Angeles. The university was founded in 1937 by George Pepperdine, a rugged individualist, founder of Western Auto Supply Company, and a Church of Christ congregant. It enrolls 6,800 students in four areas—letters and science, law, business, and management. The professional schools and graduate programs were added in 1970. Two years later the institution moved from its original downtown Los Angeles location to the Malibu campus, which occupies land granted by the Rindge-Adamson family.

PERCIVAL, OLIVE (1869–1945), Illinois-born member of the turn-of-the-century "Arroyo culture." She came to Los Angeles in 1887, living with her mother in Garvanza (now Highland Park) in a cottage called Down-hyl Claim. Her home was open to painters, sculptors, writers, and bibliophiles. Percival's major interests were writing poetry, collecting books, and gardening. She wrote and illustrated *The Children's Garden Book.* Despite her identification with the Arroyo, she was outside the circle of Charles F. Lummis, the doyen of the Arroyo culture, whom she dismissed as a "poseur." An ardent feminist, Percival held memberships in the Los Angeles Women's Athletic Club, the Friday Morning Club, and Daughters of the American Revolution.

PEREGRINE FALCON, endangered raptor that in recent decades was reduced to two pairs in the Los Angeles area. Attempts to save the birds increased the population to more than 77 pairs statewide. The falcon is a small bird, weighing only 2½ pounds. From their aeries on the roofs of Wilshire Boulevard high-rises they swoop down to feed on pigeons and other small birds.

PEREIRA, WILLIAM L[EONARD] (1909–1985), architect. The son of a Chicago printshop owner, Pereira graduated from the University of Illinois and worked for the firm that drafted the master plan for the Chicago World's Fair of 1933.

Pepperdine University. Ron Hall Photography, courtesy Pepperdine University.

Credited with "creating modern architecture in Los Angeles," he was considered the dean of local architects. He and his associates designed Robinson's Department Store in Pasadena (1950), CBS Television City (1952), Los Angeles County Museum of Art (1964), and the Malibu campus of Pepperdine University (1971–1973), as well as creating the master plan for Los Angeles International Airport (1959–1962). In 1942 Pereira shared an Oscar for architectural design work on Cecil B. De Mille's *Reap the Wild Wind* (1942). He received many honors from his profession as well.

PÉREZ, EULALIA ARRILLA DE (D. 1878), midwife *(partera)* and overseer of supplies *(llavera)* at Mission San Gabriel from 1821 to 1835. She lived to be more than 100 years old—in fact, legend has it that she died at age 141! She claimed to be the true recipient of Rancho San Pascual, granted as a reward for her work at the mission. As such she was one of only 66 women in Southern California to receive rancho lands. At the age of 97, while dictating her story to Thomas Savage, who worked for historian Hubert Howe Bancroft, she boasted, "It was I, with my daughters, who made the chocolate, the oil, the candy, the lemonade. I made so much lemonade that some of it was even bottled and sent to Spain."

PERKINS, CHARLOTTE. *See* Gilman, Charlotte Perkins

PERSHING SQUARE the city's oldest park, a one-block space in the middle of downtown bounded by Olive, 5th, 6th, and Hill Streets. When

Pershing Square, 1930s. Courtesy Robert Weinstein Collection.

created in 1866 it was named Central Park; subsequently it has been referred to as Public Square, La Plaza Abaja, City Park, 6th Street Park, and St. Vincent's Park. Finally, on Armistice Day in 1918 it was renamed for the commander of the American Expeditionary Forces in World War I, Gen. John J. "Blackjack" Pershing.

The park is fringed with architecturally significant buildings, including the palatial Biltmore Hotel (1923), the Oviatt Building (1927–1928), and numerous office buildings. Through the 1940s it was alive with strollers, loungers, and soapbox orators. During the 1960s it began attracting more homeless people than downtown workers and tourists, and tens of millions of dollars were spent on underground parking and other "improvements." Yet the homeless population continued to rise, and the park deteriorated until it became an eyesore. In preparation for the 1984 Olympics a downtown business association attempted im-

Pershing Square, 1995. Photo by Michael Krakowiak/Marni Pitt.

provements, but the effort failed. A rehabilitation project was completed in 1994, in which a new, colorfully painted fountain, a café, kiosks, and a 125-foot campanile designed by Mexican architect Ricardo Legorreta were added.

PETERSON AUTOMOTIVE MUSEUM, opened in 1994, is the newest annex to the County Museum of Natural History. The $40 million facility at Wilshire and Fairfax occupies the former Orbach's Department Store and is named for its major donor, Robert E. Peterson, a publisher of automotive magazines. Its purpose is to depict how automobiles affected the life and growth of Los Angeles.

PETREE, NEIL (1898–1991), downtown business executive and civic leader. Born in Missouri and educated at Stanford University, Petree served in World War I before settling in Los Angeles. He rose through the ranks of the Hale Department Stores and similar establishments, becoming president and director of Barker Brothers from 1938 to 1960. Petree was also on the board of directors of many corporations, including Mutual Life, Douglas Aircraft, and Southern California Gas Company. He served as president of the powerful Downtown Businessmen's Association in the 1940s, was a major force in the chamber of commerce and All-Year Club, presided over the Auto Club, and headed the Metropolitan Traffic and Transit Commission. After the Second World War Petree worked with a score of other top executives to see to it that downtown maintained its cultural and commercial position in the face of the booming suburbs. He shaped plans for downtown redevelopment, the freeway system, and the Convention Center. He is also credited with saving the Hollywood Bowl from financial disaster in the 1950s, and helping to elect Norris Poulson as mayor.

PETROLEUM INDUSTRY. *See* Oil industry

PHILANTHROPY, 1850–1900. The philanthropic spirit in Los Angeles was built on a solid tradition of generosity and hospitality nurtured by the Spanish and Mexican missionaries, rancheros, *pobladores,* and early Yankee pioneers. In early Los Angeles, organized charity was associated with ethnic or religious institutions that provided aid on a nonsectarian basis. The city's first charity was the Hebrew Benevolent Society, founded in 1854. In short order this organization was followed by the Catholic Sisters of Charity, who in 1856 established an orphanage for children of all denominations; the German Teutonia-Concordia Society (1859); the organization that built the French hospital (1860); and the Ancient Order of Hibernians, an Irish group founded in 1875. The ex-slave Biddy Mason, who had become a successful businesswoman, was a patron to the poor, and children gained assistance through the Boys and Girls Aid Society, formed in Pasadena in 1888. The Odd Fellows, a fraternal membership organization, became a local institution in the 1870s. Philanthropy also entered the realm of education as the founders of the University of Southern California, originally a Methodist school, turned to Catholics, Protestants, and Jews for financial support.

By the 1880s Angelenos showed themselves to be great joiners of clubs, fellowships, and organizations devoted to charitable and community work. Dorothea Rhodes Lummis, wife of literary lion Charles Fletcher Lummis, established a Society for the Prevention of Cruelty to Children, as

---

They have this narrative about it being the future, and now they have this narrative about the future failing, the dream failing. It is just one of those stories. —Joan Didion

---

well as a Society for the Prevention of Cruelty to Animals. A local branch of the nonsectarian Associated Charities was founded in 1893; in 1902 this group spent $7,900 to help 7,000 people—"hobos," health seekers, and other people suffering in the aftermath of economic hard times. The charity, which maintained a bunkhouse and shop where clothing and discarded furniture were cleaned and mended, was headed by merchant Herman W. Frank.

In 1901 the state stepped in for the first time, appropriating $410,000 to disperse to charities helping the poor. This public assistance tended to reduce somewhat the private donations to local charities.

Charity was the particular realm of women, giving them identity and purpose in an age when outlets for their ambitions and abilities were otherwise limited. Women proved to be talented fund-raisers, a socially acceptable activity, and their goal of making city life more civil was lauded by all. To this end they formed and sustained churches, hospitals, orphanages, libraries, and residence halls for working women. Although child welfare tended to be their greatest single concern, they also engaged in

---

What the city has never come to grips with is, when is enough enough?
—Laura Lake, community activist

---

reform of prisons and the justice system, and sought to control prostitution. One of the earliest women-run charities, founded in 1859, was the Ladies Sewing Society, which established a Protestant church. Other 19th-century philanthropic groups spearheaded by women were the Ladies Hebrew Benevolent Society (1870), Protestant Ladies Benevolent Society (1877), Women's Christian Temperance Union (1883), Ladies Missionary Society, Catholic Ladies Society, News and Working Boys Home Society, German Ladies Benevolent Society (1884), and Orphans Home Society. The Friday Morning Club, formed by Caroline Severance in 1891, pioneered in the kindergarten movement.

PHILHARMONIC AUDITORIUM, assembly hall housed in a nine-story Gothic office building at 5th and Olive Streets. Built by the Temple Baptist Church in 1906, and originally called Temple Auditorium, it seated 2,600. A variety of cultural events took place on its stage, including concerts, theatricals, operas, and even the world premiere of D. W. Griffith's film *The Birth of a Nation* (1915). The hall was home to the Los Angeles Philharmonic Orchestra beginning in 1920. When the Music Center opened on Bunker Hill in 1964, the auditorium brought down its curtain for the last time. The historic building overlooking Pershing Square stood empty for some years before being demolished.

PHILHARMONIC ORCHESTRA. *See* Los Angeles Philharmonic Orchestra

PICKFAIR, Beverly Hills home of the famous movie couple Mary Pickford and Douglas Fair-

banks. Built in 1910 as a six-room hunting lodge on the highest point of land in Beverly Hills, it was bought by Fairbanks in 1919 for $35,000. After enlargement it became a gathering place for Hollywood celebrities. Pickfair had the first private swimming pool in Los Angeles. The home underwent another remodeling when Jerry Buss, owner of the Los Angeles Lakers, bought it in 1980 for $5.4 million (whereupon a waggish journalist rechristened it "Bussfare"). In 1987 Buss sold the residence for $7 million to Pia Zadora and Mishulam Riklis, who initiated a "teardown" reconstruction (near total demolition) at a cost of $11 million.

PICKFORD, MARY (1893–1979), Canadian-born silent screen star. She began acting at the age of five in a Toronto stock company, and later came under the wing of the Belasco Theatre Company in New York, where at one point she played a bit part with Cecil B. De Mille. At 16 she arrived in Los Angeles with filmmaker D. W. Griffith's company and began working in his Biograph Studio, located in a lumber yard on the corner of Grand Avenue and Washington Street. Pickford appeared in *Her First Biscuits* (1909) and played an Indian girl in Griffith's film adaptation of *Ramona* (1910). In one of her lesser-known films, *The Little American,* about the sinking of the *Lusitania,* she had to endure the frigid ocean water off San Pedro clad in an evening dress. By 1913 "America's Sweetheart" was earning $1,000 a week, playing adorable, funny young girls and sweet ingenues. Married first to ac-

"America's Sweetheart," Mary Pickford. Courtesy Robert Weinstein Collection.

tor Douglas Fairbanks, and then to actor Buddy Rogers, Pickford became not only one of the most famous and highest paid Hollywood stars, but also one of the most powerful. She—along with Fairbanks, Griffith, and Charlie Chaplin—was a founder and principal stockholder in United Artists, a company created to distribute their own and other stars' films.

PICO, ANDRÉS (1810–1876), landowner and military commander in Mexican Los Angeles, and brother of Gov. Pío Pico. During the Mexican War, on 6 December 1846, he led the successful attack on U.S. general Stephen Watts Kearny's forces at San Pascual. Fearing Kearny might execute him, he capitulated to John C. Frémont at a treaty conference at Cahuenga Pass on 13 January 1847. In 1853 Don Andrés bought half of the San Fernando Valley from Los Angeles merchant Eulogio de Celis, who seven years earlier had bought the entire 117,000-acre property from Governor Pico. Don Andrés's home, the Pico Adobe, in today's Mission Hills area, was built by mission Indians in 1832, restored in 1932, and bought by the city. Pico Adobe, the second oldest home in the city of Los Angeles, is headquarters of the San Fernando Valley Historical Society.

Andrés Pico. Courtesy Robert Weinstein Collection.

PICO, PÍO (1801–1894), Mexican governor of California and lifelong resident of Los Angeles. Born at San Gabriel Mission of African-Mexican parentage, he served as governor for several weeks in 1832, and again from March 1845 to July 1846. The secularization of the missions was completed during his last term. He was the political rival of José Castro and Juan Alvarado, who were based in Northern California. Pico clearly understood the challenge posed by enterprising incoming Yankees prior to 1846, but lacked the means to resist them.

Don Pío Pico and Doña Nachita Alvarado de Pico, flanked by nieces, ca. 1856. Courtesy Robert Weinstein Collection.

Yankees accused him of recklessly bestowing mission property on his associates on the eve of the Yankee takeover so as to deprive the Americans of land. If true, he certainly refrained from lining his own pockets in the process.

During the Mexican War Pico fled south of the border, returning in 1848. He then maintained several estates in Southern California, including a 33-room home overlooking the Los Angeles Plaza, and an 8,800-acre property, Rancho de Bartolo, in today's Whittier, called El Ranchito (now included in Pío Pico State Park). Near his Plaza home he built a deluxe hotel, the Pico House, which opened in 1870; it remained in his ownership but a short time. When the flooding San Gabriel River destroyed much of his beloved El Ranchito in 1884, Pico put up all his holdings as collateral, borrowed $62,000, and rebuilt it. Nevertheless, at age 91 he lost this and other properties to loan sharks, and died in poverty.

PICO CANYON, gorge in the northwestern part of the county, west of the Golden State Freeway. It was named for Don Andrés Pico, a prominent landowner who, during the Mexican period, collected oil there for use at San Fernando Mission.

The first commercially successful California oil well (Pico No. 4), oil refinery (Star Oil), and oil town (Mentryville) were established there in 1876. The sites, near Newhall, are open to the public.

PICO HOUSE, historic hotel overlooking the Los Angeles Plaza. Built by former governor Pío Pico and completed on 19 June 1870, the three-story building, with its indoor plumbing, dramatic gas lighting, and French restaurant, ranked for a time as the most luxurious hotel in Los Angeles. When the city's commercial center moved south, Pico House rapidly declined. Pico lost his ownership but frequented his former holding until his death. An outstanding example of the Italianate style of architecture, Pico House is listed on the National Register of Historic Places and has been undergoing renovation as part of El Pueblo de Los Angeles Historic Monument since 1953.

Pico House, 1870s. Courtesy Robert Weinstein Collection.

PICO RIVERA, incorporated San Gabriel Valley city, located 14 miles east of downtown Los Angeles. The name Rivera means "between two rivers," and indeed Pico Rivera is lodged between Rio Hondo on the west and the San Gabriel River on the east. It is the location of the ancient Indian village of Awing-na and, subsequently, of Ranchos Paso de Bartolo and Santa Gertrudes. Juan Crispin Perez, who grazed cattle on Paso de Bartolo in 1806, gained title to the land in 1835. In time Pío Pico, the last Mexican governor of California, bought the property and built an adobe that, now restored, still stands in the town of Whittier. By 1886 the area was known as Maizeland because of its corn fields. In 1904 Richard Nixon's father, Frank Nixon, worked as a motorman on the Pacific Electric car line between the towns of Whittier and Rivera (the latter having been created during the Boom of the Eighties). In 1958 the two unincorporated towns

of Pico and Rivera decided to merge in order to avoid being annexed by other cities. At that time orange and avocado groves were already giving way to suburban home tracts. In 1990 Pico Rivera had a population of 59,100.

PICO-UNION, neighborhood in Los Angeles centered near the intersection of Pico and Alvarado Boulevards. It developed late in the last century as a residential middle-class community connected to downtown by the Pico Boulevard streetcar line. At the turn of the century many grand and fashionable Victorian homes graced the area, but as downtown commerce moved west, decline set in. In the 1970s Pico-Union attracted many Central American refugees. Since 1970, the Community Redevelopment Agency has rehabilitated some existing homes and developed many attractive new housing units. The community suffered greatly during the riot of 1992.

PIERCE, C[HARLES] C. (1853–1956), commercial photographer and dealer in photographic supplies. Illness brought Pierce to the mild clime of Los Angeles in the winter of 1886. With his camera he captured street scenes, buildings, neighborhoods, and the people of a growing and rapidly changing city. He also collected the work of other photographers, notably George Wharton James's collection on Indian ethnography. Pierce's 13,500 negatives and 18,650 vintage prints were subsequently acquired by various repositories, including the Huntington Library and UCLA Special Collections.

PILGRIMAGE PLAY, drama celebrating the life of Jesus, performed from 1920 to 1954 at an outdoor theater in Cahuenga Pass. Christine Wetherill Stevenson and Mrs. Chauncy D. Clarke formed the Pilgrimage Play Association and built the special theater, which opened in 1920. The drama's success inspired Cecil B. De Mille's *King of Kings* (1927). The theater structure was destroyed by fire in 1929, rebuilt in 1931, deeded to the county in 1943, and remodeled in 1946; it continued hosting the religious drama until 1954. Protests that public funds were supporting a sectarian drama eventually forced the Board of Supervisors to end the play's performances. The theater, renamed the John Anson Ford Theater after the late supervisor, is now used for Shakespearean drama and musical concerts.

PÍO PICO STATE HISTORIC PARK, in Whittier, preserves an 1870s residence of Pío Pico, last Mexican governor of California. In 1850 Pico bought an 8,800-acre property, which he called El Ranchito ("The Little Rancho"), and built a beautiful adobe where the thriving Pico family entertained lavishly throughout the 1870s. Pico's friend Harriet Russell Strong rescued the structure from oblivion in 1907, and deeded it to the state in 1917. Efforts are under way to restore El Ranchito, located on Pioneer Boulevard, to its original state.

PITZER COLLEGE. *See* Claremont Colleges

PLACERITA CANYON, oak-studded ravine along the Santa Clarita River, east of Newhall. In 1842, six years before the historic gold discovery in Northern California, Francisco "Chico" López made the first confirmed gold discovery in California in this canyon, near the "Oak of the Golden Dream." Hundreds of miners removed thousands of dollars' worth of the precious metal from the gully in the next dozen years or so. The oak is still there. Placerita Canyon is now a rural residential area.

PLAN/LA, coalition of Los Angeles homeowner groups, designed to coordinate lobbying efforts in the areas of tax, property, and planning law. It has been headed recently by westside neighborhood activist Bill Christopher, a member of the Board of Zoning Appeals.

PLANNING, CITY AND REGIONAL, 1900–1945. During the reformist "city-beautiful movement" that swept the nation at the turn of the century, local progressives set about to influence urban design and government policy in the cities of Los Angeles, Long Beach, and Pasadena. The reformers pressed for parks, parkways, promenades, public squares, oceanfront and waterside amenities, and grand architecture, as well as for comfort stations, public baths, and other conveniences for working-class people. They helped bring about a comprehensive zoning ordinance for Los Angeles in 1909, formed a city planning association in 1915, and created the City Planning Commission in 1920. Dana Bartlett, a Los Angeles preacher and settlement house director, was an enthusiastic backer of the movement. His book *The Better City* (1907) is filled with unbounded optimism about the future of Los Angeles.

On the county level the movement produced the Regional Planning Commission in 1923. Early on the commissioners decided to invite a blue-ribbon committee to examine the growing impact of the automobile on the urban environment, and in 1931 hired Frederick Law Olmsted Jr.'s distinguished Boston architecture and planning firm to present a model plan for the future (the Olmsted-Bartholomew-Cheney Report). The firm's imaginative and comprehensive blueprint for the region's parks, parkways, and roads was shelved and forgotten when the Great Depression curtailed government revenues. A decade later, a thoughtful

---

When I remember this desperate, lie-telling, dime-hunting Hollywood I knew only a few years ago, I get a little homesick. It was a more human place than the paradise I dreamed of and found.   —Marilyn Monroe

---

report entitled *Los Angeles: Preface to a Master Plan* (1941), published by Pacific Southwest Academy, contained contributions by reform-minded academics and professionals Clarence A. Dykstra, George W. Robbins, L. Deming Tilton, Constantine Panunzio, Richard Neutra, and Arthur G. Coons, the academy's president. With the advent of World War II this report, too, was set aside. However, the city and county of Los Angeles did adopt a revised plan for a civic center in 1941.

PLANNING, CITY AND REGIONAL, SINCE 1945, has proceeded in the face of monumental problems. These include explosive population growth, virtually exclusive reliance on the automobile as mass transportation, the need to preserve the beauty of the natural environment, the demands of powerful and often unbridled developers, and the requirements of overlapping and conflicting governmental entities. As a result, the planning process often seems like a bruising tug-of-war among government planners, private developers, city councils, the County Board of Supervisors, homeowner and neighborhood associations, and individual property owners.

In 1946 the city of Los Angeles, on the verge of another population surge, adopted a comprehensive zoning ordinance. Robert Alexander, the architect who served as president of the city's planning commission and a driving force behind the ordinance, favored the garden-city approach for Los Angeles, in which suburban communities would be separated by greenbelts. In the case of San Fernando Valley, for example, alfalfa farms and orange orchards would have served as greenbelts. Special interests assailed the plan as a form of Communist subversion and riddled it with zoning variances favoring residential development. By 1960 the greenbelt idea—together with the farms and orchards—had entirely vanished.

Public planning is now carried out piecemeal by a huge and cumbersome bureaucratic apparatus. Government planners are frequently opposed by an aggressive community of builders and developers, and must respond to rapid population growth and demographic and social changes on an emergency basis. The mayor of Los Angeles lacks authority over the planning department, the city council exercises only partial oversight, and since the 1950s the Community Redevelopment Agency (CRA) has seized considerable power from both the planning department and the city council. After ongoing jousting between the CRA and the council over downtown's future, in 1986 the council wrested back some authority from the CRA and gave it to the planning director. Nevertheless, public planning in Los Angeles is weaker than in most big cities.

Private planning efforts, in contrast, have achieved a few notable successes—including Valencia, in Santa Clarita, and Westlake Village, in the western part of the county.

Under state law, each California city is required to draft a general plan treating, among other issues, land use and transportation, and to abide by it through zoning and other regulations. In 1965 Los Angeles began preparing the state-mandated general plan, which was completed in stages and, at each step, tested in court. After an extensive process of citizen review, a general plan, known as the Centers Plan, was adopted by the city council in 1974. It provided for a series of high-density centers connected by public transit, and at the same time assured protection for low-density areas outside these centers. During the next decade specific plans were adopted for 35 separate neighborhoods and communities as well. In 1977 a state law (A.B. 283) required all cities to bring their zoning laws into conformity with community plans. In the 1980s Los

Angeles routinely evaded this law, despite pressure from homeowner organizations. A court order in 1985 speeded up the process, but the evasion continued, until finally Warner Ridge Associates brought a suit concerning a commercial project in Woodland Hills. The state court of appeal in 1992 ordered the city to obey the law. Planners, developers, and slow-growth advocates alike believe that the court order will finally strengthen the planning process.

Professional planners, urban affairs specialists, and architects have all criticized city planning in Los Angeles. They charge that council members, instead of exercising long-term oversight of planning or development, take each new project on an ad hoc basis and act as independent feudal lords. They also claim that the mayor has failed to lead

---

In a great city, City Hall must be a beacon to the people's aspirations.
—Tom Bradley

---

in this matter, that the bureaucracy snuffs out grassroots input at the neighborhood level, that the planning director has evaded making hard decisions and by default has let other agencies do the planning, and that builders have had too free a hand. According to a private management study from 1992, Los Angeles has fewer controls on design than most major cities, fewer qualified staff architects (there is only one landscape architect), weaker regulations, sparser neighborhood guidelines, and, in general, a relatively user-unfriendly urban landscape.

On top of all this, the new countywide rapid transit system poses major planning challenges as well. One of the greatest is how to preserve the neighborhoods of low-density and single-family homes in areas near the projected 52 rail stations that are to be built in the coming decades.

Two decades after the adoption of the Centers Plan, the city of Los Angeles began intensive deliberations to perfect a General Plan Framework. This document, mandated by state and federal law and necessitated by enormous recent population growth, is intended not to affect specific entitlements or alter zoning for any individual property, but rather to shape the city's long-range comprehensive growth strategy. The framework attempts to encourage intensive growth in high-density areas while protecting the single-family-home lifestyle in low-density neighborhoods. By 1995 the City Planning Commission and relevant committees of the city council had approved the document. Once approved by the full council, the framework will be implemented by updating the 35 individual community plans and revising the zoning codes.

PLANNING COMMISSION, COUNTY OF LOS ANGELES. *See* Los Angeles County Regional Planning Department and Regional Planning Commission

PLANNING DEPARTMENT, CITY OF LOS ANGELES. *See* Los Angeles City Planning Department

PLAYA DEL REY, Los Angeles city district on Santa Monica Bay, 14 miles southwest of downtown Los Angeles. It is sandwiched between Ballona Creek and Los Angeles International Airport (LAX). The predecessor community was Port Ballona, planned and built beginning in 1885 by Moye L. Wicks and his associates as a tidewater terminal for the Santa Fe Railroad. Their La Ballona Harbor and Improvement Company brought in a steam dredger and began creating a channel and inner harbor. Work crews constructed a pier for the Santa Fe to accommodate steamers, and the railroad brought in excursion trains that rode on tracks extending to the water's edge. In 1888 the Wicks syndicate ran out of funds and ceased dredging operations. The ocean tides resumed unfettered, and the dream of a port city died.

Playa del Rey, whose name meaning "The King's Beach" was coined in 1902, was associated not with the Santa Fe, but with the Pacific Electric (PE) Railway. The PE, completed by 1910, linked together all of the beach cities from Venice to Manhattan Beach. A $200,000, 50-room hotel built at Playa del Rey became a favorite tourist stop on the Red Car excursion line until it was dismantled when wildcatters struck oil on the beachfront. In 1924 the Dickinson and Gillespie Corporation developed a residential area on the bluffs known as Palisades del Rey.

In recent decades the former seaside resort has undergone development down-scaling. The Red Car lines stopped running in the 1950s, and when nearby LAX was expanded the roar of jetliners overhead drove many residents away. However, oil drilling at the water's edge ended, allowing the coastal stretch to revert to a natural beach. The remaining wetlands at the northern end of Playa del Rey, the Ballona wetlands, have been closed to development and are scheduled to be restored and protected as a bird sanctuary.

PLAYA VISTA, planned community in the city of Los Angeles near Marina del Rey, now under development. Comprising 1,000 acres stretching westward from the San Diego Freeway almost to the ocean, it is the largest undeveloped land area in the city, and one of the largest anywhere in urban America. Once owned by Howard Hughes, the property was acquired by Maguire Thomas Partners in 1989. Playa Vista (meaning "Beach View") represents a $7 billion investment in 5 million square feet of office space, thousands of dwellings, extensive retail space, and several thousand hotel rooms. The developers estimate the total occupancy at 28,000 residents, in addition to 20,000 office workers. The final plans evolved after years of debate involving such issues as noise pollution and traffic gridlock. It is the site of the new Dream-Works studio.

PLAZA, LOS ANGELES, historic downtown public space, located east of Main Street, north of the Hollywood Freeway, and adjacent to another

The Plaza, 1862 (earliest known outdoor photograph of Los Angeles). Courtesy Robert Weinstein Collection.

landmark, Olvera Street. An earlier plaza created by the Spaniards in 1781, at a site northwest of the current one, was destroyed by a flood. The present Plaza, moved to higher ground and laid out in 1818 during the construction of the Plaza Church (completed in 1822), was surrounded by public buildings and the homes of rancheros in the 1830s and 1840s. It retained an amorphous shape for decades, though it was ringed in for Sunday bull fights (the bulls were rarely killed).

The Plaza was the center of town in the 1860s. It officially became a city park in 1869, when the Pico House hotel was being built on the south side. In the coming decades the space was landscaped with topiary plants and given a circular form. During the 1890s the surrounding street formed an outdoor public food market and was often ringed by farmer's wagons. A kiosk was added in 1962.

The neighborhood adjacent to the Plaza has been multiethnic through most of its existence, and was once part of Old Chinatown. Its fortunes fell when the commercial center of Los Angeles moved southward in the 1880s. Today the Plaza is part of the 44-acre Pueblo de Los Angeles Historic Monument.

PLAZA CHURCH. *See* Church of Our Lady Queen of the Angels

PLAZA DE LA RAZA, community arts center located in Lincoln Park. In 1970 film actress Margo (Margo Albert) and union organizer Frank Lopez conceived and founded the cultural facility for Latino arts. In addition to presenting musical and theatrical performances and gallery exhibits, Plaza de la Raza offers classes to neighborhood children and adults, in dance, music, theater, and painting.

POINT DUME, a community at the western edge of the city of Malibu. The name also applies to a state beach and to a massive lava outcropping marking the far western point of Santa Monica Bay, named in 1792 by the English navigator George Vancouver for Father Dumetz of Mission Santa Barbara. The community consists mainly of private beach residences. The Visitors and Convention Bureau has designated Point Dume State Beach as "clothing optional."

POINT FERMIN, cape marking the western boundary of Los Angeles Harbor. It was named by the English navigator Capt. George Vancouver

in 1792 in honor of Father Fermín Lasuén, head of the Franciscan mission system in Alta California. A lighthouse tower built in 1874 still sits atop an Eastlake cottage on city land accessible to the public.

POLITI, LEO (1910–1996), artist, author, and book illustrator. Politi began publishing children's books on local themes in 1938. In 1949 *The Mission Bell,* an illustrated work about San Juan Mission, won the coveted Caldecott Medal for children's literature. Politi lived on Bunker Hill for over 30 years. In the 1950s and 1960s, when the Community Redevelopment Agency slated that neighborhood for total destruction and urban renewal, Politi painted the Victorian buildings as they might have appeared half a century earlier, publishing the illustrations in *Bunker Hill, Los Angeles* (1964). He also issued a collection of watercolors depicting the early parks of Los Angeles, and painted a mural on the Biscailuz Building in El Pueblo Park in the 1970s.

POLITICS, CITY OF LOS ANGELES. Politics in Los Angeles has, since early in the century, been shaped by at least four forces: a nonpartisan electoral process; the dominance of downtown business and civic leaders in city politics from the 1920s to the 1960s; the increasing importance of suburban communities since that time, with a resultant loss of strength in the center; and recent and ongoing shifts of power resulting from immigration and ethnic change.

California Progressives, including adherents in Los Angeles, instituted constitutional reforms in 1913 to counteract corruption and the dominance of the Southern Pacific Railroad. They stripped the Democratic and Republican labels from the ballot in all municipal and county elections, thus undermining the political party systems in most cities. (The labels remained in effect for voter registration, and continued to appear on ballots in state and national election.) As the saying went at the time regarding city hall, "There is no Republican or Democratic way to fill a pothole." Party machines, party bosses, and grass-roots political organizations soon ceased to exist. Although this maximized the opportunities of independent voters and candidates, it crippled local party structures.

A relatively narrow downtown elite strongly influenced political and governmental decisions throughout the first half of the century. The decision to bring water from the Owens Valley is a case in point. In the post–World War II period most major decisions—to create a freeway system, to build a convention center, to establish a music center, to eliminate a subsidy for public housing, to develop a civic center, and how to deal with riots— were initiated or directed by the downtown elite. Men representing department stores, property owners, and banking and corporate interests, such as Asa Call, James Lin Beebe, Neil Petree, and John McCone, worked behind the scenes through ad hoc groups, such as the low-profile Committee of 25, to create the new downtown.

By the 1970s and 1980s the dispersal of population into the suburbs and the creation of commercial centers on the Westside, in the San Fernando Valley, and elsewhere led to new political centers. This shift dissipated the power of the downtown elite. The wealthiest political areas became the Westside and the Hollywood Hills, whose affluent residents donated millions of dollars to local, regional, and national politicians and party organizations.

Changes in the racial and ethnic makeup of the general population have slowly impacted politics as well. In the 1980s the voting population was still mainly white, Anglo, and middle class, although the population as a whole was becoming increasingly nonwhite. A closer examination of ethnicity, income, and political beliefs reveals important local distinctions, however. According to a 1987 study, the northern San Fernando Valley (north of Roscoe Boulevard) was conservative, 67 percent white, mostly Democratic, but with a tendency to switch to Republican. The southern valley was 82 percent white, more liberal and more loyally Democratic. The Westside (west of La Cienega Boulevard) was 75 percent white, long influenced by a large Jewish population and many professionals, but with Democratic registration dropping. The Southside (south of Pico and Venice Boulevards) was 70 percent black, with growing numbers of Latinos, low income, and maintaining continuing Democratic loyalties. The northern inner city, including Mid-Wilshire, Hollywood, Hollywood Hills, Lincoln Heights, Highland Park, Eagle Rock, and Los Feliz, was fast increasing in population, becoming more ethnically diverse and having no distinct racial majority, although liberal and Democratic. The downtown and Eastside was 70 percent Latino, predominantly poor, Democratic and fast growing, but having very low (8 percent)

voter turnout—a circumstance that favors Republican office seekers. In the shoestring areas and south to San Pedro was a conservative area that included older, blue-collar workers and some "empty nesters" living in expensive homes; it was 47 percent white, 39 percent Latino, 8 percent Asian, and 6 percent African American.

Meanwhile, political contributions, "the mother's milk of politics," continue to pour into city hall. The most active contributors in recent years have been the real estate, entertainment, and cable television industries. Between 1983 and 1989, for example, the entertainment industry contributed $1.3 million to the mayor and council. The Los Angeles City Ethics Commission, established in 1990, is responsible for monitoring lobbying and election contributions. No one may legally donate more than $500 to a city council candidate, or over $1,000 to a mayoral candidate.

POLITICS, COUNTY OF LOS ANGELES.
As a legacy of turn-of-the-century Progressivism, politics in the greater county of Los Angeles is still conducted on a nonpartisan basis. Democratic and Republican identities remain, but all county offices are filled by independent candidates backed by ad hoc groups rather than by party organizations. Parties are far weaker than in eastern cities, and the terms "machine" and "party" hold little meaning. County supervisors are generally divided along liberal and conservative lines as they argue such issues as taxation, social service spending, real estate development, and law enforcement, but the partisan labels remain muted.

Registration in the county is still by party affiliation, however, and on the gubernatorial and congressional levels partisan politics do prevail. Law requires parties' central committees to manage partisan campaigns, and the central committees are often dominated by elected officials. Yet even here, politics is fairly decentralized, and voters are often of an independent mind.

In 1965 Los Angeles County gained a much larger representation in state politics than it had previously enjoyed. Until that time, representation in the state's bicameral legislature was by area rather than population. Following a U.S. Supreme Court decision, the districts were established on the basis of "one person, one vote." The representation of what was then the most populous county in the state thus increased from 2 to 14.5 seats.

Since 1958, more voters have registered as Dem-

Registered Voters by Party, by City, 1993

	Democrat	Repub-lican	American Indepen-dent	Green	Liber-tarian	Peace and Freedom	Other	Declined to State	Total No. Regis-tered	% Demo-crat	% Repub-lican	% All Others
Agoura Hills	4,684	5,573	174	46	49	35	46	1,438	12,045	38.89	46.27	14.84
Alhambra	14,786	9,529	331	67	72	124	82	3,471	28,462	51.95	33.48	14.57
Arcadia	7,520	15,498	313	57	83	45	62	2,457	26,035	28.88	59.53	11.59
Artesia	2,887	1,888	61	9	22	18	17	493	5,395	53.51	35.00	11.49
Avalon	671	906	14	10	7	13	1	93	1,715	39.13	52.83	8.05
Azusa	6,918	4,720	239	29	51	87	50	1,497	13,591	50.90	34.73	14.37
Baldwin Park	10,554	4,199	259	24	44	108	48	1,622	16,858	62.61	24.91	12.49
Bell	3,106	1,326	59	2	10	56	15	463	5,037	61.66	26.33	12.01
Bellflower	13,240	9,141	410	31	125	94	52	2,145	25,238	52.46	36.22	11.32
Bell Gardens	3,843	1,069	160	3	21	66	16	637	5,815	66.09	18.38	15.53
Beverly Hills	11,684	5,880	189	65	62	64	76	2,251	20,271	57.64	29.01	13.35
Bradbury	131	356	5	0	2	0	3	50	547	23.95	65.08	10.97
Burbank	21,847	20,354	769	221	220	209	184	5,220	49,024	44.56	41.52	13.92
Calabasas	5,030	4,841	153	56	42	25	45	1,284	11,476	43.83	42.18	13.99
Carson	27,898	7,928	524	39	154	211	87	3,982	40,823	68.34	19.42	12.24
Cerritos	11,474	11,012	258	31	78	81	71	3,206	26,211	43.78	42.01	14.21
Claremont	8,396	8,318	222	230	80	98	66	1,929	19,339	43.41	43.01	13.57
Commerce	3,144	455	42	2	14	20	8	281	3,966	79.27	11.47	9.25
Compton	31,217	1,306	368	11	54	452	81	1,527	35,016	89.15	3.73	7.12
Covina	8,729	9,393	302	38	78	61	58	1,818	20,477	42.63	45.87	11.50
Cudahy	1,822	626	53	3	3	28	9	313	2,857	63.77	21.91	14.32
Culver City	13,178	5,831	268	129	89	103	74	2,375	22,047	59.77	26.45	13.78
Diamond Bar	9,653	13,003	376	41	100	71	53	3,207	26,504	36.42	49.06	14.52
Downey	19,769	16,728	463	49	127	115	84	2,835	40,170	49.21	41.64	9.14
Duarte	3,906	3,482	132	13	37	32	18	921	8,541	45.73	40.77	13.50
El Monte	13,109	6,004	330	32	75	117	49	1,912	21,628	60.61	27.76	11.63
El Segundo	3,422	4,787	192	25	42	15	37	1,208	9,728	35.18	49.21	15.61
Gardena	13,408	4,885	235	29	69	86	42	2,093	20,847	64.32	23.43	12.25
Glendale	24,275	34,960	937	249	300	272	235	6,988	68,216	35.59	51.25	13.17
Glendora	8,488	13,978	375	45	79	66	65	2,311	25,407	33.41	55.02	11.58
Hawaiian Gardens	2,351	782	57	2	14	25	13	288	3,532	66.56	22.14	11.30
Hawthorne	16,954	6,326	416	42	509	176	72	2,581	27,076	62.62	23.36	14.02
Hermosa Beach	5,563	6,025	313	76	121	52	80	2,176	14,406	38.62	41.82	19.56
Hidden Hills	440	615	6	3	8	1	1	95	1,169	37.64	52.61	9.75
Huntington Park	4,665	1,945	116	7	26	79	14	724	7,576	61.58	25.67	12.75
Industry	67	80	4	0	0	3	0	26	180	37.22	44.44	18.33
Inglewood	32,945	3,594	374	34	99	249	77	2,739	40,111	82.13	8.96	8.91
Irwindale	488	96	15	4	0	3	0	47	653	74.73	14.70	10.57
La Cañada Flintridge	3,236	8,961	99	33	47	22	25	1,097	13,520	23.93	66.28	9.79
La Habra Heights	807	2,254	51	8	9	8	6	272	3,415	23.63	66.00	10.37
Lakewood	20,424	16,133	612	58	163	139	80	3,367	40,976	49.84	39.37	10.78
La Mirada	9,730	10,580	341	38	125	61	72	1,901	22,848	42.59	46.31	11.11
Lancaster	15,711	23,326	1,037	63	143	159	136	4,425	45,000	34.91	51.84	13.25
La Puente	7,150	2,281	145	14	40	58	61	880	10,629	67.27	21.46	11.27
La Verne	6,501	8,623	245	42	54	39	43	1,486	17,033	38.17	50.63	11.21
Lawndale	4,884	3,157	211	35	54	58	46	1,183	9,628	50.73	32.79	16.48
Lomita	4,266	4,020	193	30	35	46	38	1,119	9,747	43.77	41.24	14.99
Long Beach	93,083	63,533	2,967	586	800	1,144	536	18,838	181,486	51.29	35.01	13.70
Los Angeles	827,604	340,352	17,122	5,976	5,453	8,328	4,716	129,581	1,339,132	61.80	25.42	12.78
Lynwood	10,141	1,511	175	3	33	106	32	813	12,814	79.14	11.79	9.07

	Democrat	Repub-lican	American Indepen-dent	Green	Liber-tarian	Peace and Freedom	Other	Declined to State	Total No. Regis-tered	% Demo-crat	% Repub-lican	% All Others
Malibu	3,933	3,576	93	79	34	46	53	1,144	8,958	43.90	39.92	16.18
Manhattan Beach	9,338	12,043	316	110	144	55	79	2,783	24,868	37.55	48.43	14.02
Maywood	2,298	860	65	6	11	40	7	453	3,740	61.44	22.99	15.56
Monrovia	6,838	7,116	263	57	73	71	41	1,599	16,058	42.58	44.31	13.10
Montebello	14,984	4,928	216	30	65	123	54	1,838	22,238	67.38	22.16	10.46
Monterey Park	12,381	6,532	240	31	62	101	60	3,135	22,542	54.92	28.98	16.10
Norwalk	22,775	9,296	455	33	110	138	116	2,561	35,484	64.18	26.20	9.62
Palmdale	12,446	15,675	726	37	119	117	79	3,190	32,389	38.43	48.40	13.18
Palos Verdes Estates	2,501	6,242	87	27	32	10	22	916	9,837	25.42	63.45	11.12
Paramount	7,104	2,832	162	8	35	59	26	937	11,163	63.64	25.37	10.99
Pasadena	32,945	23,889	786	297	279	417	266	6,727	65,606	50.22	36.41	13.37
Pico Rivera	17,816	4,057	260	27	78	109	81	1,433	23,861	74.67	17.00	8.33
Pomona	22,840	12,543	629	128	140	319	87	3,674	40,360	56.59	31.08	12.33
Rancho Palos Verdes	8,608	15,294	278	42	109	48	70	2,690	27,139	31.72	56.35	11.93
Redondo Beach	15,384	16,212	765	147	251	153	186	5,233	38,331	40.13	42.29	17.57
Rolling Hills	242	1,050	11	2	0	2	0	112	1,419	17.05	74.00	8.95
Rolling Hills Estates	1,412	3,338	34	4	11	7	14	457	5,277	26.76	63.26	9.99
Rosemead	8,149	3,963	182	29	44	87	45	1,604	14,103	57.78	28.10	14.12
San Dimas	6,573	8,741	276	50	63	51	49	1,762	17,565	37.42	49.76	12.82
San Fernando	4,028	1,227	59	6	21	33	106	440	5,920	68.04	20.73	11.23
San Gabriel	6,257	5,177	146	18	41	60	45	1,475	13,219	47.33	39.16	13.50
San Marino	1,467	5,654	61	19	15	6	14	808	8,134	18.04	69.51	11.35
Santa Clarita	21,936	33,530	1,108	169	244	211	176	6,837	64,211	34.16	52.22	13.62
Santa Fe Springs	5,376	1,575	98	6	29	24	19	495	7,622	70.53	20.66	8.80
Santa Monica	32,299	14,436	630	549	282	294	242	6,453	55,230	58.48	26.14	15.30
Sierra Madre	2,759	3,696	94	40	50	35	32	777	7,483	36.87	49.39	13.74
Signal Hill	1,811	1,526	70	13	24	27	13	559	4,043	44.79	37.74	17.46
South El Monte	3,623	908	43	5	17	27	17	392	5,032	72.00	18.04	9.96
South Gate	10,720	4,623	229	15	69	148	45	1,361	17,210	62.29	26.86	10.85
South Pasadena	5,952	6,096	179	102	68	70	56	1,870	14,393	41.35	42.35	16.29
Temple City	6,307	7,158	205	34	38	49	21	1,466	15,278	41.28	46.85	11.87
Torrance	28,823	32,753	1,101	193	295	211	192	8,075	71,643	40.23	45.72	14.05
Vernon	29	13	3	0	0	1	0	7	53	54.72	24.53	20.75
Walnut	4,963	5,318	181	13	29	47	30	1,749	12,330	40.25	43.13	16.62
West Covina	20,077	15,350	584	61	155	163	100	3,826	40,316	49.80	38.07	12.13
West Hollywood	14,933	3,761	334	154	93	211	117	3,018	22,621	66.01	16.63	17.36
Westlake Village	1,619	2,913	61	16	17	9	37	589	5,261	30.77	55.37	13.86
Whittier	16,950	17,514	479	131	150	112	94	2,895	38,325	44.23	45.70	10.07

SOURCE: County Registrar-Recorder

ocrats in Los Angeles than Republicans. The California Democratic Council (CDC), an influential statewide grass-roots organization, had considerable local support in the 1960s. Third parties, including the Prohibition, Independent Progressive, American Independent, Peace and Freedom, Libertarian, Socialist, and Communist, have appeared on the ballot.

In February 1993 the county registration records, by party, showed a distribution of 1.9 million (54.9 percent) Democrat; 1.1 million (32.3 percent) Republican; 49,292 (1.3 percent) American Independent; 12,125 (0.5 percent) Peace and Freedom; and 14,656 (0.4 percent) Libertarian. Voters are permitted to register "Other," and a disgruntled minority takes advantage of the offer. The registrar maintains a list of some 3,000 "parties" so named, including the "Let's Have a," "Boston Tea," "Halloween," "Hoochie Koochie," "Mickey Mouse," "Anarchist," and "Reefer Raider."

In 1993, 350,827, or 9.7 percent of voters, declined to state any registration preference—a block that partisan party leaders tend to woo seriously at election time. To retain a position on the ballot in California, a political party must garner more than 2 percent of the ballots cast in a gubernatorial election.

POLLUTION. *See* Air pollution

POLO, sport introduced into the eastern United States from England in 1876, and into Santa Monica in 1878. A group of riders with the U.S. Coastal Survey stationed in that city organized the first pickup match with a team of locals led by Manuel Marquez. The Californios, who were skilled horse- men, beat the Yanks on a makeshift field at Ocean Avenue and Hotel Block. Subsequent matches occurred at 8th Street (now Lincoln) Park and in the canyon area along Sunset Boulevard. The sport was favored by society and show people. The Southern California Polo Club of Santa Monica became the best polo team in the West. A league formed in 1906 included teams from Los Angeles, Riverside, Santa Barbara, and Burlingame. Will Rogers, Darryl F. Zanuck, Errol Flynn, Tyrone Power, and other leading screen figures became avid players and spectators in the 1920s and 1930s, and still played the game near Sunset until the area became suburban in the 1940s and 1950s. Professional polo is still played at Will Rogers State Park during the summer months.

POMONA, city on the eastern boundary of the county, 31 miles from downtown Los Angeles. The prehistoric valley, now called Pomona Valley, that lies at the foot of the San Gabriel Mountains and is topped by Mt. San Antonio ("Old Baldy") was once covered with wild grasses, chaparral, scrub oak, and prickly-pear cactus. Most of the region was used seasonally by migratory Shoshonean Indians, although there were a few permanent Indian settlements near a flowing spring at today's Town and San Bernardino Avenues and at Ganesha Park, Indian Hill, and Mud Springs, north of Claremont.

Beginning in 1771 Pomona Valley came under the jurisdiction of Mission San Gabriel. By 1837 the mission had been secularized and Mexican governor Juan Alvarado had granted much of the area, as Rancho San José, to Ygnacio Palomares and Ricardo Vejar for the purpose of raising cattle and horses. Palomares built a home near Ganesha Park,

Pomona street scene, ca. 1910. Pitt Collection.

and Vejar built one near San Jose Creek. The pair were soon joined by Luis Arenas, who settled on the old San Bernardino Road near McKinley Avenue, before selling out to Englishman Henry Dalton. The rancho was subject to Indian raids, drought, and floods. In 1846 the property was divided, with the section that would host the future townsite of Pomona going to Vejar. In the late 1850s the famous Butterfield Stage passed through on its way from San Francisco to St. Louis. About that time, too, Yankees began drifting into the nearby area known as "Willow Grove" (El Monte).

In 1873 the Southern Pacific Railroad was granted a right-of-way through the Pomona area, and the first train puffed in a year later. In 1875 the Los Angeles Immigration and Land Co-operative set up shop with the intention of forming a town

---

It's a great place to live, but I wouldn't want to visit there.

—Mark Twain

---

and raising oranges. On Washington's birthday in 1876 the newcomers greeted an excursion train from Los Angeles and showed off their fields of bright poppies, graded streets, irrigation ditches overflowing with water, and new hotel. The co-op members held a contest and chose the name, Pomona, for the Roman goddess of fruit. Owing to drought, a hotel fire, and a shortage of investment capital, by 1880 the population had reached only 130, although at the beginning of the boom year of 1887 the number had risen to 3,500.

In 1888 Pomona College was established and the town incorporated. Pomona was then the fifth largest city in the county. Cereal king W. K. Kellogg owned a ranch there, where he raised Arabian horses and entertained celebrities in lavish style. In 1932 he turned most of his property over to the state. In 1949 he gave a further 813 acres to California Polytechnic School, Pomona (Cal Poly, now a state university), which took over the care and breeding of the horses. The city, which calls itself "the Gateway to the Inland Empire," has been, since 1922, the site of the Los Angeles County Fair, the largest county fair in the nation.

Since World War II, and the completion of the Pomona Freeway, the city has flourished as a bedroom community. Civic leaders actively pursued a policy of territorial expansion, in competition with the cities of La Verne and Claremont, annexing 3.5 square miles between 1953 and 1961. Pomona's population exceeded 100,000 in 1960, and reached 131,700 in 1990.

POMONA COLLEGE. *See* Claremont Colleges

POMPA, AURELIO, Mexican immigrant to Los Angeles who became an international *cause célèbre* in 1924. Indicted for killing an Anglo co-worker, he pleaded self-defense. Community activists raised money and hired prominent Mexican American lawyer Frank Domínguez for his legal defense. When Pompa was convicted, Mexican president Obregon appealed to California governor Friend W. Richardson for a pardon but was rebuffed. Pompa's execution embittered Mexicans in Los Angeles, who had complained of many injustices. A follower celebrated him in song with a *corrido:* "Farewell, my friends, farewell my village: / Dear Mother, cry no more. / Tell my race not to come here, / For here they will suffer: / There is no pity here."

POPPY, CALIFORNIA (ESCHSCHOLTZIA CALIFORNICA), bright orange native flower, designated the state wildflower in 1903. It once carpeted Altadena, Monrovia, and other parts of the Los Angeles Basin. In the first decade of the 20th

California poppy.

century the "Poppy Car," a special car on the interurban rail line, made tourist excursions to the area. The Altadena fields were reported to be visible from ships in the Catalina Channel. Poppy fields are now best seen in a special preserve in the Antelope Valley during the months of April and May.

POPULATION, CITY OF LOS ANGELES, has grown irregularly, often by leaps and bounds. When founded in 1781 the *pueblo* totaled 44 people; that number reached 650 in 1820, roughly at the end of Spanish rule. The census during the Mexican period counted 770 in 1830, and 1,250 in 1845. The figure stood at 1,610 in 1850, the first census taken during American rule; 4,385 in 1860; 11,183 in 1880; and 50,395 in 1890, at the end of the Boom of the Eighties. At the turn of the century population came to over 102,000. The city experienced expansion in the late 1910s and 1920s, with more than 576,000 in 1920 and 1.2 million in 1930. The 1940s was another major growth period; the city had 1.5 million residents in 1940, and over 1.9 million in 1950. The rate of increase continued to rise in the post–World War II era, with the number reaching over 2.4 million in 1960 and 2.8 million in 1970.

The 1990 Census Bureau figures for Los Angeles have been disputed by some experts, who estimate an undercounting by as much as 4.6 percent. Clearly, though, the densest part of the city is the Rampart district near Westlake Park, an area of 11.7 square miles with a population of 21,430 people per square mile. In West Los Angeles, by contrast, the density is 3,084 per square mile, in an area 64 square miles large.

Birth rates vary according to ethnicity and race. Latinos have the highest birth rate, with 30.2 births per 1,000 people; Asians have a rate of 24.1; African Americans, 20.7; and whites, 11.1.

The 1990 figures suggest that Los Angeles, which has grown by 26 percent in the last decade, is among the fastest-growing metropolitan regions (areas with more than 1 million people), along with Orlando, 53 percent; Phoenix, 40 percent; Sacramento, 34 percent; San Diego, 34 percent; Dallas–Fort Worth, 32 percent; and Atlanta, 32 percent. City planners estimate, however, that the population of Los Angeles actually fell 68,000 between 1991 and 1992, in the wake of an economic downturn and the 1992 riots. The largest declines, approximately 1.4 percent, were registered in the central and southern parts of the city.

Population, 1781–1990		
City of Los Angeles	County of Los Angeles[a]	State of California[b]
1781[c]	44	—	—
1830[d]	770	—	—
1845[e]	1,250	—	—
1850[f]	1,610	3,530	92,597[g]
1860	4,385	11,333	379,994
1870	5,728	15,309	560,247
1880	11,183	33,381	864,694
1890	50,395	101,454	1,213,398
1900	102,479	170,298	1,485,053
1910	310,198	504,131	2,377,549
1920	576,673	936,455	3,426,861
1930	1,238,048	2,208,492	5,677,251
1940	1,504,277	2,785,643	6,950,000
1950	1,970,358	4,151,687	10,643,000
1960	2,481,595	6,038,771	15,863,000
1970	2,811,801	7,055,800	20,039,000
1980	2,967,000	7,477,503	23,780,100
1990	3,485,390	8,769,944	29,976,000

SOURCES: Howard J. Nelson, *The Los Angeles Metropolis* (Dubuque, Iowa: Kendall/Hunt, 1983), p. 136; Los Angeles City Planning Commission, 1959; Los Angeles County Department of Regional Planning, 1991; Los Angeles County Budget, 1990–91.
[a]Figures from 1940 on are estimates as of 1 January.
[b]Figures from 1940 on are estimates as of 1 July.
[c]The *pueblo* of Los Angeles is founded.
[d]During the Mexican period.
[e]The last census of the Mexican period.
[f]American rule begins.
[g]This figure is official but inaccurate.

POPULATION, COUNTY OF LOS ANGELES, reached 8.8 million in 1990—3.7 million more people than in Chicago's Cook County—making it the most populous county in the nation (see census table, Appendix B). The increase between 1970 and 1980 was 5.6 percent, and between 1980 and 1990, 19.1 percent. The state of California in 1993 projected that the county's population would exceed 10.1 million in 1995, 12.9 million in 2000, and 16.2 million in 2040. Interpretations of the actual data vary considerably, striking notes from gloomy to apocalyptic. In 1992 the Southern California Association of Governments predicted that as many as 6 million more people in the county by the year 2021 would have a dire impact on unemployment, traffic congestion, air pollution, and housing. On the other hand, some experts contend that Los Angeles is reaching the end of an abnormal 50-year population boom, and that "normal," or slower, growth is on its way.

PORCIÚNCULA. *See* Los Angeles name, origin of

PORT BALLONA, rail terminus in the 1880s on the site of today's Marina del Rey. Here the Santa Fe Railroad built a rail spur from downtown, brought in a dredger to clear a channel in the slough, and erected a pier to serve oceangoing vessels. When the construction company ran out of funds, however, dredging stopped and the effort failed. In 1899 the railroad developed the town of Redondo Beach instead.

PORTER, GEORGE KEATING (1833–1906), major landowner in the northern San Fernando Valley. Arriving in California from Massachusetts in 1849, Porter spent years as a miner, farmer, and lumberman. With his cousin Benjamin Franklin Porter he formed a prosperous leather manufacturing firm in San Francisco and bought large land parcels throughout the state. One such investment, in 1874, was as a principal backer to Charles Maclay in the development of the city of San Fernando. When he and Maclay had a permanent falling out over that deal, Porter retained ownership of 56,000 acres (much of which he later sold), where he raised cattle, sheep, and grain. In the 1870s and 1880s Porter hired cowboys to protect his watering holes from farmers. The core of the holdings of today's Porter Ranch Development Company is part of the original ranch.

PORTER, JOHN C[LINTON] (1871–1959), used car dealer who was Los Angeles mayor from 1929 to 1933. Porter was born in Iowa and brought to California at age 11. He later worked as a railroad agent for 15 years before entering the auto business. As mayor at the start of the Great Depression, Porter reduced some city salaries but failed in his attempt to cope with the budget crisis. A petition recall drive against Porter failed, however, and he remained in office and presided at the opening of the Olympic games in 1932.

PORTER RANCH, major planned residential and commercial community currently under construction in the northwest corner of the San Fernando Valley. The Porter Ranch Development Company, owned by developer Nathan Shapell, plans to spend some $2 billion to develop the 1,300-acre project, which will have approximately 11,000 occupants. The land is part of the original George Keating Porter ranch. Slow-growth proponents ar-

gue that Porter Ranch will overburden existing water and sewage systems, reduce air quality, and increase congestion in that part of Los Angeles.

PORT LOS ANGELES, mile-long wharf that jutted into Santa Monica Bay from 1890 to 1893. It was created by Collis P. Huntington, head of the Southern Pacific Railroad (SP), in partnership with Sen. John Jones, founder of Santa Monica. "Uncle Collis" launched his project—which was intended to serve SP exclusively—by buying land along the beach, below the palisades; he then tunneled under Ocean Avenue to access the shoreline, and laid tracks as far north as Temescal Canyon, north of Santa Monica Canyon. Here he built a wooden pier, the "Long Wharf," also called "Port Los Angeles." More than 300 vessels were loaded and unloaded there in its first year. Although the wooden structure was heavily buffeted during storms, it successfully competed with shipping at a Redondo landing controlled by the Santa Fe Railroad. During the Free Harbor Contest, Huntington lost his bid for a federal subsidy to build a protective breakwater in Santa Monica Bay when Congress instead allocated the money for a break-

Port Los Angeles Wharf (Santa Monica), ca. 1890. Pitt Collection.

water at San Pedro. In 1908 major steamships stopped calling, in 1910 all shipping ceased, and within a few more years the crashing waves had swallowed up the remains of Port Los Angeles.

PORT OF LONG BEACH. *See* Long Beach Harbor

PORT OF LOS ANGELES. *See* Free Harbor Contest; Los Angeles Harbor Department; Harbor, Los Angeles (1781–1899 *and* since 1900); Long Beach Harbor

PORTOLÁ, GASPAR DE (1723–1786), Catalonian-born captain of dragoons who, in 1769, led the first Spanish land exploration from Baja California into the territories to the north. He had fought in Spain and was serving as governor of Lower California when José de Galvez, visitor general of New Spain, tapped him to lead the expedition as *comandante-militar* of Alta California. He was also appointed first governor of California, in which capacity he served from 20 November 1767 to 9 July 1770. The Portolá expedition that arrived in San Diego originally consisted of two land parties and three ships. Their principal objective was to find Monterey Bay, in central California, which had been previously sighted from sea. Among the participants was the Franciscan father Junípero Serra, who was charged with the task of establishing the first Indian missions in California. For this reason, the expedition is sometimes known as the Sacred Expedition.

The bronzed and bearded Captain Portolá, with his party of 64 men, trekked northward through the Los Angeles Basin from 24 July to 8 August 1769. According to diarist Father Crespi, they crossed the river, stopped at the Indian village of Yangna, experienced five earthquakes, and passed "boiling" tar pits. On 4 August they camped at a Tongva village known as Kurovongna ("place in the sun"), on what is now the University High School campus. They crossed Sepulveda Pass into the San Fernando Valley, and then proceeded north to Monterey and San Francisco Bay. On their return trip to San Diego the Portolá party passed through Los Angeles Basin again in January 1770.

PORTUGUESE BEND, mile-long stretch of coast along Palos Verdes Drive in the city of Rancho Palos Verdes. It was the site of a whaling station in the 1850s, staffed by Portuguese whalers; af-

ter running out of firewood to render gray whale blubber into oil, they were forced to abandon the station in the 1880s.

Portuguese Bend is one of Southern California's most scenic areas, but it is also one of the most unstable geologically. Earth slippage destroyed some 100 homes on the headland in the mid-1950s, and led to new standards for construction. The earth's movement had slowed from one inch a day in 1957 to several inches a year by the 1970s.

POULSON, NORRIS (1895–1982), mayor of Los Angeles from 1953 to 1961. While serving a term in Congress Poulson was drafted by the *Los Angeles Times* and downtown business and civic leaders to run against incumbent mayor Fletcher Bowron. He is remembered for encouraging freeway development, rehabilitating downtown, helping to lure the Dodgers from Brooklyn, initiating racial integration in the police and fire departments, and attempting to pressure the auto makers of Detroit to clean up their engines. Poulson opposed the development of public housing in Chavez Ravine, favoring the construction of a baseball stadium instead. Los Angeles International Airport was expanded during his term, and the Plaza area became a state park. In the course of a reelection bid in 1961 he lost his voice, and was defeated by challenger Sam Yorty.

POWELL, LAWRENCE CLARK (1906–), literary essayist and librarian. Educated in the public schools of South Pasadena, Powell attended Occidental College, UC Berkeley, and the University of Dijon, France. During his youth he intermittently earned his living by playing in dance bands. Powell worked as a librarian for the Los Angeles Public Library before moving to UCLA, where he served 28 years, rising to the post of head librarian. His essays span the fields of literature, history, and bibliography, with a specialty in the literature of California and the Southwest. He is the author of several books, including an anthology, *California Classics: The Creative Literature of the Golden State* (1971). Powell Library at UCLA was named in his honor.

PREHISTORY. Some 400 million years ago, in the Silurian period, Los Angeles lay beneath the sea. Around 150 million years ago, when dinosaurs roamed the earth during the Cretaceous period, the Los Angeles Basin had risen from the sea 350 miles south of its present location and was floating slowly northward, on the edge of what geologists call the Pacific plate. By the onset of the Cenozoic era, over 65 million years ago, the dinosaurs had disappeared. Twenty million years ago Southern California was an active volcanic area, and 5 to 1.8 million years ago the basin, after disappearing under the sea, rose from the ocean again, filled with sediment.

The La Brea tar pits were deposited 12,000–40,000 years ago, trapping diverse species of wildlife, including such large mammals and birds (some of them now extinct or no longer indigenous to the area) as porcupines, ground sloths, camels, deers, cats, cranes, condors, and eagles. The imperial mammoth, a large relative of the elephant,

---

Every American city that is growing now is growing in one and only one fashion: like Los Angeles.

—Joel Garreau, journalist

---

stood 10–13 feet high and weighed in at 8 tons; its tusks were some 15 feet long. A close relative, the mastodon, was half the size. The giant ground sloth had long claws and was coated with coarse, heavy hair. There were many saber-tooth cats, similar in size to the African lion, but with more powerful forelegs and chest, and with large, curved, dagger-like canines (up to 8 inches long).

The first humans arrived in the region over 25,000 years ago. They probably crossed a land bridge connecting the North American and Asian continents, and arrived after a long southward migration. The Museum of Natural History in Exposition Park displays the oldest human remains found in North America: the partial skulls of "Los Angeles Man," said to be about 26,000 years old, and "Laguna Woman," about 18,000 years old.

Ten thousand years ago the coastal and mountain areas of Southern California looked much as they do today, except they were more lush and green. Los Angeles was then a grassy plain laced with flowing streams, small lakes, marshes, and ponds. Junipers and cypresses were scattered widely throughout the area. Many of today's shoreline invertebrate animals also lived then. The people known as Native Americans settled in the area during the most recent epoch, developing a culture

that remained intact until Spanish explorers entered the basin in 1769.

PRESBYTERIANS conducted their first Los Angeles services in 1854 in a carpenter shop on Main Street. The following year services were held in the courthouse at Franklin and Spring Streets, and a congregation was formed. Difficult social conditions in Los Angeles, however, caused the dispirited minister, Rev. James Woods, to leave town. His successor, T. M. Davis, followed his example in 1856. The *Los Angeles Star* remarked on the "truly deplorable state of society" and the "torrent of vice and immorality which obliterates all traces of the Christian Sabbath." The town remained without a Presbyterian preacher until 1859, when a new minister delivered a sermon in the schoolhouse on Bath Street, north of the Plaza. In 1862 Civil War sectionalism divided and again put an end to the congregation, which did not reemerge until 1869. The first Presbyterian church was built in 1883 by the Rev. John W. Ellis at 2nd and Fort Streets. Despite additional factionalism in the 1890s, the church subsequently expanded and grew stronger.

For some time the national Presbyterian church movement was broken into several organizations, the largest of which was the United Presbyterian Church. Through mergers in 1958 and again in 1983, the Presbyterian Church (U.S.A.) was formed. The synod of Southern California and Hawaii, with 365 churches and 110,000 members, is one of the largest religious denominations in the region. Its affiliates appeal especially to the many ethnic and racial minorities in the region. In the 1990s, for example, the True Light Chinese Presbyterian Church of Los Angeles was said to run the only program in the nation designed for second- and third-generation American-born, English-speaking Chinese.

PRISONS AND JAILS in downtown Los Angeles house 25,000 prisoners, the largest incarcerated population of any city in the nation. The first jail—indeed, the first building constructed by the county—went up in 1853. It stood in the center of the lot on the northwest corner of Spring and Jail (afterward Franklin) Streets. Today the system consists of six county and federal facilities, as well as a federal building on Terminal Island and additional detention sites maintained by the Immigration and Naturalization Service. Men's Central

Jail, with 22,000 inmates, is the largest single jail facility in the Western world. The county also operates Peter J. Pitchess Honor Rancho near Saugus, with 6,000 inmates. The overcrowding of jails and prisons has caused the county to search for a new site; the state has also been pressing for a new prison to be located in East Los Angeles. Both projects have been vigorously resisted by community coalitions.

PRODUCE MARKETING (WHOLESALE) takes place entirely at two teeming facilities: Terminal Market on 7th Street, and the 9th Street Market. In an earlier era, from the 1880s to the turn of the century, merchants conducted their colorful haggling from horse carts parked around the downtown Plaza. When space for the rigs gave out, the market moved to its current sites. Today's joint locations make up the second largest produce mart in the world, after New York's. It is one of the few such markets still located in the heart of a major city. The market comes alive each weekday at 2:00 A.M. and remains active until about noon. The fresh produce is unloaded from huge trucks, and bidding commences to set the prices. When the bidding is over, truckers haul the goods off to stores throughout the Los Angeles area and as far away as San Luis Obispo and Phoenix.

The produce trade generates $300 million in gross revenues yearly. Prices vary from hour to hour, as business is conducted by auction. Some 5,000 to 6,000 people earn their living in the market.

Vegetable peddler, Los Angeles Plaza, 1885. Courtesy Robert Weinstein Collection.

PROGRESSIVE MOVEMENT, national reform impulse loosely associated with the presidencies of Theodore Roosevelt (1901–1909) and Woodrow Wilson (1913–1921) and evident locally during the first decades of the 20th century. The proponents, who were white, middle class, and mostly professionals, strove to eliminate political corruption and make government more efficient for the middle classes and more humane for the working poor.

In California the main target of the Progressives was the Southern Pacific Railroad (SP), a transportation monopoly, huge landowner, and political powerhouse. The SP had a hammerlock on the Republican Party, it strongly influenced the Democratic Party and independents, and it exercised unrivaled influence in Sacramento. It also maintained strong leverage on municipal governments. In Los Angeles, the SP had suffered a major defeat in its effort to gain exclusive control over the harbor, and was exposed as conspiring to seize the Los Angeles riverbed for rail lines. Dr. John Randolph Haynes, who sparked approval of the recall amendment to the city charter in 1903, was an early spokesman for Progressive ideas. During the 1906 municipal election campaign the progressive Republican forces, galvanized by Edward A. Dickson, associate editor of the *Los Angeles Evening Express,* together with three attorneys, Meyer Lissner, Russ Avery, and Marshall Stimson, organized the Good Government League (nicknamed the "Goo Goos"), which achieved limited successes at the ballot box. Further flexing their muscles in 1907, this quartet convened a meeting at Al Levy's cafeteria of like-minded reformers from elsewhere in California and formed the Lincoln-Roosevelt League. The league helped elect the reform-minded Hiram Johnson as governor of California in 1911, thereby toppling the SP from statewide political power. That same year the Los Angeles reformers forced the resignation of corrupt mayor Arthur Harper and elected George Alexander to replace him.

Elements of the Progressive movement persisted beyond what is often considered its cutoff year of 1920. In Los Angeles, reformers were responsible for the 1925 city charter, with its strong emphasis on the commission system of government, and in 1924 the Progressive Party was on the California ballot.

PROHIBITION, CA. 1870–1917, movement that emerged when midwestern temperance advocates, or "drys," colonized Southern California.

While founding new towns in the 1880s these reformers succeeded in wiping out the open and relaxed drinking habits of the former Spanish-Mexican *pueblo* and frontier cow town. Before the "licentious" movie actors took over in 1910, champions of temperance established Hollywood as a dry town and set up an active branch of the Women's Christian Temperance Union (WCTU).

The prohibition movement was politically potent for two generations. It achieved its first victory in 1899, when the Anti-Saloon League (formed nationally in 1895) succeeded in limiting the number of saloons in Los Angeles to 200, and in 1904 launched a campaign to banish them entirely. Drys also won an ordinance ordering Los Angeles bars to close at midnight and forbidding drinking and dancing in the same establishment. This caused "wet" Angelenos to seek their entertainment outside city limits. Vernon, south of downtown, became a new oasis for night-life lovers. Jack Doyle's Saloon, boasting "the longest bar in the world," was always packed with patrons, and the Vernon Country Club, established in 1912 and patterned after a San Francisco Barbary Coast saloon and dance hall, attracted rich society people and movie stars to its party atmosphere.

Meanwhile, the Prohibition Party and drys in the mainstream parties gained political strength in Los Angeles. Unlike San Francisco, whose residents were predominantly foreign-born Catholics (only 15 percent were Protestant), Los Angeles had a population that in 1906 was 56 percent Protestant, and most of them were native-born midwesterners who made up the core of the prohibition movement. Hiram Johnson's gubernatorial campaign in 1910 received a boost when he picked Andrew J. Wallace, a wealthy dry leader from Southern California, as his running mate. Los Angeles voted itself completely dry in 1917, two years before the federal prohibition amendment took effect. By then the city had the reputation of being a "dry town," meaning that the Anti-Saloon League was well organized, had succeeded in passing local ordinances, was backed by the *Los Angeles Times,* and had placed its members in important law enforcement posts.

PROHIBITION, 1917–1934. When Congress passed the 18th Amendment and sent it to the states for ratification in 1917, Los Angeles was the largest city in the nation totally without legal drinking parlors. The Prohibition Party was gathering respectable numbers of votes in local elections. From 1929 to 1933 Mayor John C. Porter, for one, had their support. He gained popular approval when, as a member of a U.S. trade delegation to France, he refused to drink a wine toast at a public ceremony in that country.

Nevertheless, in the dry 1920s Los Angeles citizens were far from unanimous on the prohibition question. Huge amounts of illegal liquor were consumed, some of it smuggled from Canada and Mexico, and some produced in moonshine stills tucked away in secret corners of the sprawling

---

L.A. is not a fixed thing. It's a moving target, an elusive energy psyche that is not physical. —Jon Jerde, architect

---

county. People also obtained legal alcohol by filling medical prescriptions for intoxicants at the town's 600 drugstores. Tijuana, with its rampant prostitution, gambling, liquor, and dope dealings, attracted regular car commuters. Few speakeasies operated within city limits during the decade-long "noble experiment," but many arose elsewhere in the county. Culver City roadhouses, for example, were favorite night spots for Angelenos.

The conflict over prohibition peaked in 1924, when county voters elected Asa Keyes, a dry, as district attorney. The police were in disarray, and Keyes proved lenient toward bootleggers. A raid in Chino netted 20,000 gallons of whiskey and corn mash in three 250-gallon copper stills. By the same token, many cases involving bribery, license violations, and even murder went unprosecuted. By now the "noble experiment" was clearly a failure in Los Angeles. City voters approved the adoption of the 21st Amendment, which repealed the 18th. The cause is not dead, however; the nation's largest WCTU chapter remains in Southern California, with 1,500 members dedicated to educating people to the dangers of alcohol.

PROPOSITION 13 (1978), California constitutional amendment limiting taxation. Spearheaded by the United Organizations of Taxpayers, headed by Howard Jarvis and Paul Gann, and backed by a powerful coalition of Los Angeles home and apartment owners, Proposition 13 limits ad valorem taxes on real property to 1 percent of market value, except to pay indebtedness approved by voters. The 1975–1976 assessment is considered the base amount, with annual increases limited to 2 percent. Reassessment occurs after a sale, improvement, or transfer of property. In addition, any future special city taxes would require a two-thirds vote of the electorate. The proposition clearly had a strong impact on public revenues. Although proponents argued that vital services would not be affected, in fact the tax-revolt measure severely restricted the growth of city and county public services, including education.

PROSTITUTION was denounced by the Franciscan missionaries who, as early as 1826, complained of loose women in the *pueblo* of Los Angeles. The Los Angeles town council issued a resolution declaring prostitution an evil to be eliminated, along with gambling and blasphemy. During the 1870s and 1880s the "oldest profession" flourished in Sonoratown, around the Plaza, near the railroad depots, at downtown flophouses, and in Chinatown, where Chinese women were sometimes forcibly exploited.

Although from time to time reformers sought to expose, outlaw, or control prostitution, their attempts were ineffective. In 1897 Mayor Meredith P. Snyder was asked to contain the traffic in the raucous oil shantytown near Santa Monica Boulevard and Vermont Avenue, but he refused, fearing such an action would undermine the lucrative oil industry. In the first decade of the century streetwalkers were in evidence near the many downtown hotels and flats that catered to single males. Prostitution was associated with saloons, gambling, and political corruption. Mayor Arthur C. Harper and his city hall cohorts not only protected vice, but were known to frequent bawdy houses themselves in the City Hall area. A scandal arising from this behavior led to his recall in 1909.

For 30 years, beginning in the 1880s, the Women's Christian Temperance Union lobbied for the licensing of "bawdy houses," as well as for other reforms they believed would support the health and welfare of women and the integrity of the family. A reluctant city council finally responded with the Red Light Abatement Act of 1913, which outlawed houses of prostitution, some of which were located conveniently near the courthouse. During the 1920s prostitution and bootlegging activities were focused on the Plaza area and along the Sunset Strip. A brash council member, Carl Jacobson,

made headlines when he publicly named the places where vice flourished along Sunset. In the late 1940s the *Los Angeles Daily News* published reliable information that the police were protecting prostitutes with the knowledge of Police Chief C. B. Horrall, who was subsequently forced to retire. The city then established an Internal Affairs Division to investigate corruption. The "oldest profession" was again the subject of headlines in 1953. A member of the State Board of Equalization, William Bonelli, was accused in the press of running a saloon empire that involved a "B-girl" operation in downtown Los Angeles. Bonelli fled to Mexico.

Prostitution has been prevalent in all social strata, from the poorest ghetto to the poshest suburb. Expensive call girls continue to ply their trade discreetly out of private homes and large hotels, evading the California law that bans houses of prostitution. Since the 1970s prostitutes, both male and female, have become part of the Hollywood street scene and a matter of growing concern to merchants, residents, and law enforcement officers. In the 1980s many prostitutes who took to the streets were children—strays, runaways, homeless. Prostitution was increasingly associated, on a local and national level, with cocaine trafficking and the spread of AIDS.

PROTESTANT CHURCHES. *See* individual churches and religious groups

PRUDHON, VICTOR, prominent pioneer, probably originally from France. Prudhon came to Northern California in 1834 with the Hijar-Padres colony, a group of doctors, lawyers, teachers, goldsmiths, and artisans recruited for service in California by José María Padres. When the colony disbanded the same year, Prudhon settled in Los Angeles. Starting as a teacher, he became a member and then secretary of the *ayuntamiento*. He also served as personal secretary to Governor Juan Alvarado, rising finally to the level of captain of the provincial militia. Along with other reformers, including Ignacio and Antonio Coronel, Prudhon attempted to improve the *pueblo* by building a school, imposing discipline in cases of antisocial behavior, and encouraging husbands to work and wives to remain at home where they could instruct their children.

Prudhon gained his greatest renown as the founder and president of a vigilance committee of 1836. He and his associates, the first vigilantes in

California, seized and executed María del Rosario Villa and her lover, Gervasio Alipas, for the murder of Villa's husband, Domingo Felix, a reputable citizen. Prudhon left a rare written justification for his actions, professing a passionate desire to maintain virtue and defeat sin.

PUBLIC ART PROGRAM, organized effort to install the artworks of regional artists in and near buildings developed with public funds. The program, fostered by the arts community, particularly encourages the participation of ethnic and women artists. It took root in 1968 when the Community Redevelopment Agency required builders of nonresidential projects in Los Angeles to set aside 1 percent of their total development costs for art. (The cities of Culver City and Santa Monica mandate similar public art requirements.) The program is managed by the Los Angeles City Cultural Affairs Department. The National Endowment for the Arts has contributed materially to the program, as has the Metropolitan Transit Authority with its ambitious $10 million allocation for beautifying the Red Line subway stations. When the builders of large structures on Bunker Hill agreed to pool resources and create an entire museum, the result was the Museum of Contemporary Art. Probably the best-known public artwork in the region is the "Great Wall of L.A.," which depicts aspects of the region's history. The mural, on a half-mile stretch of the Tujunga Wash flood control channel in Van Nuys and North Hollywood, was painted by a number of artists from 1976 to 1983.

PUBLIC WORKS DEPARTMENT, CITY OF LOS ANGELES. *See* Los Angeles City Department of Public Works

PUEBLO DE LOS ANGELES HISTORIC MONUMENT. *See* El Pueblo de Los Angeles Historic Monument

PUTNAM, GEORGE (1914–), the dean of Los Angeles newscasters in terms of longevity. His broadcasting career began in Minneapolis, but he has been a news anchor on Los Angeles radio and television since 1951. Still broadcasting on station KIEV in 1995, Putnam was given that year's Los Angeles Area Governors Emmy Award from the Academy of Television Arts and Sciences.

QUAIL, CALIFORNIA (CALLIPEPLA CALI-FORNICA), fancy-feathered small game birds residing in chaparral areas. They feed on seeds, leaves, and wild fruit. The young are easy prey, for they are unable to fly until half grown. Gabrieleño Indians hunted them as a source of food.

QUARTZ HILL, unincorporated residential and agricultural area at the southern margin of the western Mojave Desert. Earlier called Earl Station or Earl Estates, it took its current name from a prominent lode of silicone oxide at Avenue M and 45th

---

Los Angeles seems endlessly held between these extremes of light and dark—of surface and depth. Of the promise, in brief, of a meaning always hovering on the edge of significance.
—Grahame Clarke, *The American City,* 1988

Queen Mary. Queen Mary Photo.

Street W. The community sprawls along Highway 14, 7 miles southwest of Lancaster. Quartz Hill was first settled by homesteaders, some of whom planted walnut groves. In 1990, with a population of 20,000, the area served as both a bedroom community for the aerospace industry and a retirement community.

QUEEN MARY, tourist attraction permanently moored in Long Beach. The British luxury liner, the fastest and largest ever to sail the North Atlantic, was sold to the city in 1964, moved there in 1967, and opened to the public in 1971. The ship is 1,000 feet long and rises almost 150 feet above the water line. It originally accommodated 2,000 passengers. Of the original 998 rooms, 400 now serve as hotel rooms. The *Queen Mary,* decorated in the Art Deco style, has files filled with archival materials, as well as open displays, detailing the ship's history. In addition to the hotel, the ship contains restaurants, shops, and a popular wedding chapel. Its interiors were used in *The Poseidon Adventure* (1972), as well as other movies.

QUEER NATION. *See* Gay and lesbian movement

QUINTERO FAMILY, one of the 11 founding families of the *pueblo* of Los Angeles in September 1781. Luis Quintero was 55 years old, the son of a black slave father and Indian mother. His wife, María Petra Quintero, was a 40-year-old *mulata.* They and their five children were recruited into the founding expedition in Alamos, Sonora. Quintero would later work as a tailor at the Santa Barbara Presidio. By 1835 the Quintero descendants numbered more than 170 in Southern California.

RACCOON (PROCYON LOTOR), small nocturnal mammal with a black face-mask and black and white tail rings. It usually lives near streams in foothills below 6,000 feet, occasionally wandering into streets, yards, and gardens at lower levels. In the wild, the raccoon feeds on fruit seeds, insects, and frogs.

RACE RELATIONS have had an uneven history in Southern California. Racist sentiments, racial segregation, and outbursts of racial violence have periodically disturbed the social peace. By the same token, efforts to ameliorate racial tension have also been impressive, especially in recent decades.

During the Mexican colonial era, social relations between the colonials and Native Americans quickly developed a strong racial dimension. The *gente de razón* ("people of reason," that is, non-Indians) confined the Indians to the missions or reduced them to peonage on the ranchos and in the *pueblo.* The Indians resisted, stealing livestock and sometimes committing acts of physical violence. In the early 19th century Mexicans became fearful of mission Indian runaways and marauding tribes. They began distancing themselves socially from the native people in their midst. With each succeeding census enumeration, Mexican families of *mestizo* background changed their racial designation to erase, if possible, any connection to their Indian heritage. In the first decades of American rule, the Yankees and upper-class Mexicans continued to brutalize and enslave the native peoples, virtually destroying them and their cultures by the 1880s.

The intense nationalism and race consciousness born during the Mexican War persisted for years. In the 1850s the town was racked by repeated attacks by Mexican *bandidos,* some of whom professed to be taking vengeance for Yankee injustice, as well as counterattacks by vigilantes, some of whom espoused racist sentiments. Peacemakers on both sides urged calm, but murders and lynchings continued to cost scores of lives.

In 1871, when anti-Chinese sentiment climaxed in California, a vicious mob lynched and shot 19 Chinese men near the Plaza. None of the victims was guilty of any wrongdoing. One of 11 white men who attempted to protect the Chinese lost his own life. The Chinese Massacre represented perhaps the extreme of overt racism in 19th-century Los Angeles.

In the late 19th and early 20th centuries, Jim Crow practices became rooted in both custom and law. Los Angeles of the 1920s and 1930s was a town dominated by whites who made little allowance for racial minorities. Many jurisdictions routinely enforced Jim Crow patterns. Glendale, for example, boasted that "no Negro ever sleeps overnight in our city." Anti-Asian sentiment increased in the 1930s as well, and reached new heights at the outbreak of World War II, when all the Japanese of Los Angeles were rounded up from Terminal Island and Little Tokyo and sent to detention camps for the war's duration. Neighborhood confrontations between Anglos and Mexican youths *(pachucos)* in the 1940s erupted into one full-scale conflict, the so-called zoot suit riots of June 1943.

The Watts riot of 1965 came as a thunderclap to many white Angelenos, who believed that black people in Los Angeles lived in reasonably decent circumstances and were more or less content. Any lingering doubt as to the benign quality of race relations was dispelled by the 1992 riot. Racial tensions were doubly alarming because living conditions in the central city had deteriorated, and the city as a whole was more populous and more ethnically and racially diverse. Misunderstandings, often due to language and cultural differences, also pitted Latinos, African Americans, and Asians against one another.

By the same token, racial and ethnic groups have achieved remarkable accommodation in the past century. The National Association for the Advancement of Colored People (NAACP) established a local branch in 1913 and took part in suits for the elimination of racial barriers in housing and education. World War II saw the creation of the Fair Employment Practices Commission by the federal government. In the 1950s, the Urban League and the NAACP convinced the county to establish a Commission on Human Relations, while the Community Service Organization fought for the civil rights of Mexicans.

Race relations have changed dramatically since the civil rights revolution of the 1960s. Under pressure from civil rights groups, legal barriers to housing, education, recreational facilities, hiring, and public accommodations were ended. When a U.S. Supreme Court case broke racial covenants in home deeds in the 1960s, the Fair Housing Council of Los Angeles, a local coalition of whites and blacks, crushed existing racial barriers in real estate sales and apartment rentals. Representation of minorities in city governments and, by the 1990s, on

---

Disaster is not an enduring discomfort—cold weather is an enduring discomfort. Cold weather emptied the Midwest and filled California.   —Kevin Starr, historian

---

the Board of Supervisors has increased. In 1973, with the election of Tom Bradley, Los Angeles became one of the first major cities to have an African American mayor.

No area of race relations was more controversial than school integration. Throughout the Jim Crow era, schools routinely segregated Chinese, Japanese, African American, Native American, and Mexican children. In the decade following the U.S. Supreme Court decision in *Brown v. Board of Education* (1954), Los Angeles civil rights organizations pressed for desegregation in the sprawling Los Angeles Unified School District (LAUSD), with busing proposed as the principal tool to achieve the goal. Fol-

lowing a series of court rulings, LAUSD instituted busing in 1976 but, amid mounting white flight, rapid demographic changes, and opposition from various white and minority communities, ended the program in 1979. The problem of de facto school segregation remains a serious one. Achieving and maintaining unity amid racial and ethnic diversity remains, arguably, the greatest single challenge to community well-being in Los Angeles.

RADER, FRANK (1848–1897), mayor of Los Angeles from 1894 to 1896. The city, then some 30 square miles in area, had between 50,000 and 100,000 people.

RADIO BROADCASTING, HISTORY OF. Los Angeles radio began in 1901, when local ham operators, using crystal sets and headphones, beamed messages between Santa Catalina Island and San Pedro. Commercial broadcasting started in 1922. Soon three stations—KNX, KFI, and KHJ—dominated the local field as part of national networks.

KNX got its real start in 1923 when Guy C. Earl, promotion manager of the *Los Angeles Evening Express,* arranged for his paper to give away 1,000 crystal sets as a gimmick to increase newspaper circulation. This gave KNX an assured audience, and it began advertising a variety of products, even though it had no regularly scheduled programs. By 1925 KNX was earning a healthy profit from sponsors. Supported by Earl's increased involvement in KNX programming, the station managed to broadcast a sensational murder trial—though their reporter was ousted from the courtroom several times. On 1 January 1926 it secretly rigged a feed through the telephone company and broadcast the Rose Bowl game locally by telephone, although KFI had bought the rights from the telephone company. The station later became the Columbia Broadcasting System (CBS) affiliate in Southern California.

KFI was founded in 1922 as a 100-watt station by car dealer Earle C. Anthony as a means of selling his cars. With the cooperation of civic groups, government agencies, and schools, he soon initiated educational and musical programming. In 1924 he aired a live opera—a national first—and presented the West's first on-air live symphony performance. Celebrities, both local and visiting, were interviewed regularly. In 1929 Anthony hired newspaperman José Rodriguez to play new phonograph recordings on the company-owned spinoff

KCEA. This pioneer disk jockey won overwhelming audience approval. KFI also was the first station to broadcast from the Hollywood Bowl. It became part of the Red Network of the National Broadcasting Company (NBC) in 1927. The nation's first coast-to-coast broadcast was NBC's coverage of the 1927 Rose Bowl game between Stanford and Alabama, broadcast by Graham McNamee.

KHJ's founder was Harry Chandler, publisher of the *Los Angeles Times*. Also founded in 1922, the station—whose audio trademark of singing canaries gave instant listener recognition—fostered its owner's conservative ideas through community affairs broadcasts, and created special programming for children. In 1927 Chandler sold KHJ to Don Lee, a car dealer who took the station into the Mutual network.

Radio emerged as an important Los Angeles industry in the 1930s as the medium increased its programming range, its only rival in that period being New York. Hollywood studios released their talent pool for broadcasting once it became clear that radio could help sell films. Radio versions of movies performed by glamorous stars, original dramas, variety shows, comedy series, and documentaries all reached burgeoning audiences. In 1937–1938 CBS built a state-of-the-art broadcasting studio at Columbia Square, on Sunset Boulevard. Not to be outdone, NBC completed its "Radio City," also in Hollywood, at the same time, while the network that would become the American Broadcasting Company (ABC) established local headquarters on Vine Street.

Commercially, news, weather reports, and concerts became radio staples in the 1930s. The airwaves were also used for noncommercial purposes, including police bulletins, airport information, college instruction, ship-to-shore communication, ham and shortwave broadcasting, farm-belt weather reports, and religious sermons.

In the late 1940s and 1950s, as the infant medium of television entered more homes, radio began to lose large numbers of listeners. Comedy stars such as Jack Benny or George Burns and Gracie Allen, comedy shows such as *The Goldbergs,* musical variety revues such as *Your Hit Parade* and *The Lawrence Welk Show,* cowboy series such as *The Lone Ranger* and *Gunsmoke,* and detective shows such as *Dragnet* and *Ellery Queen* all deserted their radio listeners and moved to television.

A quick death was predicted for radio, and the medium certainly languished for a while. However, bolstered by a loyal core audience, aided by the advent of car radios, FM, and stereo, boosting its appeal through a mix of news, music, talk, and increased foreign-language and ethnic broadcasting, Los Angeles radio has retained its spot as the nation's leading market.

RADIO STATIONS numbered 84 in the Los Angeles area in 1991—37 AM and 47 FM—more than in any other metropolitan area. Motorists and young adults are the major targeted consumers, and music is the main fare. Stations specialize to suit every musical taste: country and contemporary country, top 40, classic rock, progressive rock, oldies, rap, hip-hop, big band/nostalgia, jazz, classical, early music, new age, easy listening, light/soft rock, and music delightfully titled middle-of-the-road.

A number of stations air programs that appeal to specific religious and ethnic groups. The 11 stations specializing in Christian programming emanate from Los Angeles County or from a mountain location just outside its boundaries. They include KFRN-AM (Long Beach), KFSG-FM

People, I just want to say, you know, can we all get along?
— Rodney G. King, 1992

(Los Angeles), and KPPC-AM (Pasadena). Some broadcast in Spanish only: KALI-AM, KLVE-FM, KSKQ-AM/FM, and KWIZ-FM. The public-educational format is maintained by KCRW-FM, affiliated with Santa Monica College; KUSC-FM, affiliated with USC; KXLU-FM, affiliated with Loyola-Marymount University; and KPCC-FM, at Pasadena Community College. The only pure classical station is KKGO-FM, although KUSC has classical music in its programming. Most stations broadcast some news, but two maintain an entire news menu: KFWB-AM and KNX-AM. Programming changes are frequent and very fluid. The talk-radio format has captured several stations. Michael Jackson of KABC-AM, who has maintained high ratings for decades, is the acknowledged master.

In terms of wattage, the most powerful stations are KTSJ-AM (250,000), KBIG-FM (150,000), and KPFK-FM (112,000). Some operations manage to stay on the air putting out as little as 250 watts (KPPC-AM).

Although most stations operate independently, some are affiliated with major or minor networks: ABC Radio, NBC Radio, Mutual Broadcasting System, CBS Radio, Family Stations, AP Radio, Cable News (CNN), Sun Radio, American Public Radio, Spanish Broadcasting System (KSKQ-AM), National Public Radio, and the Pacifica network.

RAFU SHIMPO, Japanese daily newspaper (with English pages) founded in Los Angeles in 1903. The name means "L.A. News." The paper survived the wartime internment of Japanese Americans and in 1992 had a circulation of 23,000. The laborious process of handsetting the several thousand syllabic characters and ideograms used in Japanese, which took up to three hours per page, has recently given way to a rapid computerized operation.

RAIDERS, LOS ANGELES. *See* Los Angeles Raiders

RAILROAD MUSEUMS in Los Angeles tend to be small, inadequate memorials to a transportation system that was essential to the growth of Southern California. Griffith Park's Travel Town displays steam and passenger cars. The Lomita Railroad Museum shows memorabilia and artifacts—semaphore signals, whistles, marker lights—as well as a Southern Pacific locomotive and caboose. The Saugus Train Station in Newhall, run by the Santa Clarita Valley Historical Society, features an oil-burning locomotive that once chugged through the area. The Orange Empire Railway Museum in Perris operates streetcars and electric interurban cars, and exhibits locomotives and rail cars. The Pacific Railroad Society, based in San Marino, owns equip-

ment, organizes tours, and is currently seeking financial backing to establish a comprehensive museum of railroad history.

RAILROADS, transportation system that transformed the growth and development of Los Angeles, especially in the 19th century. Almost 200 railroad companies were incorporated in the county, although only a handful were brought to fruition. Railroads carried large contingents of tourists and settlers, improved commerce, fostered agriculture, created new towns, blazed the trail for future freeways, and helped overcome the region's natural isolation—all against a background of fierce corporate and urban competition.

The first rail lines were strictly local. The Los Angeles and San Pedro line, completed in 1869 and facilitating harbor commerce with the *pueblo,* ran from Alameda Street near the downtown Plaza to Wilmington, and later to San Pedro. In the 1870s the Los Angeles and Independence Railway connected Santa Monica to Los Angeles. It was intended to run eventually from Los Angeles to Independence in the Owens Valley, near where its builder, Sen. John P. Jones, had a silver mine in the Panamint Range, but this never happened.

Far more significant were the rails laid by the Southern Pacific Railroad (SP) from San Francisco Bay to Los Angeles, which, upon completion in 1876, gave Los Angeles a transcontinental hookup. The SP absorbed both the earlier lines and added new ones that extended northward to the San Fernando Mission, eastward to Arizona, and southeastward to Anaheim. Where the former downtown orange grove of Don "Guillermo" Wolfskill had stood, the SP built Arcade Station in 1888, occupying it until 1915. Beginning in 1881 the SP ran the *Sunset Limited,* with its comfortable Pullman Palace cars, from San Francisco to New Orleans via

"San Gabriel," first locomotive in Los Angeles, 1868. Courtesy Photographic Collections, Los Angeles Public Library.

Railroad on bridge across
Arroyo Seco, 1885. Courtesy
Robert Weinstein Collection.

Los Angeles. The SP initiated even more deluxe passenger service, the *Golden State Limited* between Los Angeles and Chicago, beginning in about 1903.

The SP's transportation monopoly was broken only by the entry of the Atchison, Topeka, and Santa Fe into the Los Angeles Basin in 1885. This event touched off a competition that led to the lowering of fares from the Midwest to Los Angeles, which in turn marked the start of the Boom of the Eighties, a major event in the expansion of Southern California. The Santa Fe bought land and established numerous new railside communities. At the same time, it mastered the art of deluxe passenger travel: the Santa Fe's *California Limited* from Chicago to Los Angeles offered Pullman service and, in partnership with the Fred Harvey organization, excellent dining car service, as well as hotel accommodations along the way.

Beginning in 1887 work progressed fitfully on a line to Utah to challenge the SP's near stranglehold on transportation within the Los Angeles Basin. This line, begun by a Salt Lake syndicate, became the San Pedro, Los Angeles, and Salt Lake Railroad (SP, LA & SL). It was finally completed in 1905 by William Andrews Clark, the Montana copper king, with the backing of financier and industrialist J. P. Morgan and railroad czar Edward Harriman. Eventually the line was absorbed into Harriman's Union Pacific system.

At the turn of the century landowner May K. Rindge built the Hueneme, Malibu, and Port Los Angeles Railroad from Santa Monica north to Ventura County, to thwart SP efforts to defile her vast landed empire along the Malibu coast. She used her private railroad to ship grain and hides to market, but eventually it was absorbed into the SP network.

Around the turn of the century, too, another form of railroading, the interurban trolley, began to make its mark in Los Angeles. Henry Huntington's Pacific Electric Railway, running its Red Cars on more than 1,000 miles of track, criss-crossed the area from 1895 to about 1960, though the railway was absorbed by SP in 1910.

Early in the century the SP, the Santa Fe, SP, LA & SL, and the Red Car lines all converged on downtown, each maintaining its own terminal and freight yards. The Santa Fe, for example, operated out of La Grande Station, a Moorish-style depot built at a cost of $50,000 in 1893, at 2nd Street and Santa Fe Avenue. The streets of downtown were often jammed with trains, horse-drawn buggies, streetcars, and later, passenger automobiles and trucks—not to mention bewildered pedestrians. This confusion ended when the city forced the lines to build the Union Passenger Terminal on Alameda Street. This 16-track station was the last great passenger terminal constructed in the United States.

The opening of Union Station in 1939 coincided with the arrival of diesel electric power and the modern streamline passenger train, featuring sleek smokeless engines, Pullman sleeping cars, day coaches with comfortable and quiet suspension, cocktail lounges, dining cars where courteous waiters served good food at reasonable prices, clean toilets, and observation lounge cars. The SP adapted these features to the already-existing *Sunset Limited* and *Golden State Limited* trains. The latter regal streamliner went through New Mexico, thus cutting travel time from Chicago from about 65 hours to 40 hours. The SP also operated a popular bargain-rate overnight train, the *Owl,* between Los Angeles and San Francisco. The comparable Union Pacific streamliner was the *City of Los Angeles.*

In the late 1930s the Santa Fe introduced the all-Pullman diesel streamliner, the *Chief,* and improved on it shortly thereafter with an even more opulent train, the *Super Chief.* With its dome observation car, this was probably the world's most deluxe and modern train in the *belle époque* of railroading. For the traveler of average means, the Santa Fe ran the *El Capitan,* which had no Pullmans but featured amazingly smooth-riding double-decker coach cars and excellent food service.

Even in the age of automotive trucking and extensive air travel, the railroads remain important in Southern California. Amtrak, the federally sponsored passenger system established in 1971, utilizes existing private rail lines in Los Angeles and Union Station. Metrolink, the new public transit system, also uses that facility and envisions its service as a major transportation hub. In addition, huge freight trains laden with import and export goods are hauled in and out of Los Angeles Harbor by rail lines regularly. These trains use the Alameda Corridor, an old strip of land stretching from the harbor area to downtown that is now being upgraded. Freight lines continue to provide a major source of revenue in Southern California.

RAINFALL is normally so scarce on a yearly basis that the area is essentially a desert. Although the mountains may receive an annual precipitation of 30–40 inches, the coastal areas average only 10–15 inches. Rain occurs typically from October through April. Apart from occasional thunderstorms over the mountains, summers are dry. The wettest year on record was 1884, when 40.29 inches of rain fell at the civic center; the driest was 1953, with a scant 4.08 inches.

RALPHS GROCERY COMPANY, regional grocery chain, founded in 1879 as Ralphs Bros. Grocers at 6th and Spring Streets. Principal founder George A. Ralphs, a bricklayer, arrived in Southern California in 1872; he went into food retailing after losing his arm in a hunting accident. His brother, Walter, dropped out of the partnership almost immediately. The store branched out to a location at Pico and Normandie in 1911, experimented with self-service and home delivery, and afterward became a chain. In 1926 it set up its own bakery to break the power of the "bread trust," a would-be baking monopoly, and produced bread at 5 cents a loaf. By 1988 the Ralphs chain had 88 stores, and by 1995, 176. In that year Ralphs merged with the Alpha Beta and Food 4 Less Supermarkets (owned by Yucaipa Companies); the end of 1995, therefore, saw 338 grocery stores operating in Southern California under the Ralphs name.

RAMÍREZ, FRANCISCO P. (1837–?), California-born liberal journalist. He began his career in 1853 as compositor of "La Estrella," the Spanish page of the *Los Angeles Star,* the city's first newspaper. In 1855 he founded his own Spanish-language newspaper, *El Clamor Público* (The pub-

Original Ralphs grocery store, 6th and Spring Streets, 1889. Courtesy Robert Weinstein Collection.

lic outcry), a one-sheet weekly that was Los Ange-les's third newspaper, and the first published entirely in Spanish. It sold for $5 yearly. The self-styled champion of the Spanish-speaking popula-tion of California, Ramírez reported on issues that pertained to Mexicans, particularly when they in-volved Yankee racial and cultural oppression. As a Republican and free-soil advocate in a Demo-cratic, pro-southern town, he made enemies. In 1859 Ramírez ran out of money, closed his press, and left for Mexico. Upon his return to Los An-geles in 1864 he served as postmaster and state translator and, in 1872, as editor to the subsequent Spanish-language paper, *La Crónica.*

RAMO, SIMON (1913–), physicist and engi-neer. Born in Utah, Ramo received a Ph.D. at Caltech and worked at Hughes Aircraft Com-pany in the 1940s on airborne radar and air-to-air missiles. While at Hughes he joined up with a bril-liant classmate, Dean Wooldridge, to form Ramo-Wooldridge, a technological firm that developed the engineering for the intercontinental ballistic missile (ICBM). In turn, they merged with Thompson Products to form the now giant cor-poration Thompson Ramo Wooldridge (TRW).

RAMONA, novel by Helen Hunt Jackson pub-lished in 1884 that created a lasting romantic vi-sion of the missions and Old California. Ramona, a part-Indian orphan reared to think of herself as Spanish, falls in love with and marries the Indian Alessandro. Forced to fight Yankees for his place in the sun, he dies at the hands of the villainous Jim Farrar. Although the people and events in *Ra-mona* are fictional, they were based on actual people and places, including Rancho Camulos in the Santa Clarita Valley.

Passionately devoted to the cause of Indian re-form, Jackson hoped that, like Harriet Beecher Stowe's *Uncle Tom's Cabin,* her novel would im-prove the plight of a downtrodden people. She failed in that regard, but her novel did cast a spell over Southern California, evoking an enduring leg-end of the past with the missions as the central sym-bol. The name Ramona became attached to street signs, motels, food stands, movies, song sheets, tourist traps, and several town halls throughout the region. The myth of Ramona and of the missions was later fostered by the writer George Wharton James and others involved with boosting Southern California culture. The Ramona Pageant, an out-

Ramona Pageant play, Hemet. Pitt Collection.

door event staged in Hemet annually since 1923, uses hundreds of locals to act out the melodrama, and draws thousands of viewers.

RANCHO, landed property granted by Spanish and Mexican colonial authorities to encourage

Ranchero.

Ranchos Become Cities

	Year Issued	Present-Day Town, City, or District	Size (in Acres)	Grantee
Aguaje de Centenela	1844	Inglewood	2,219	Ignacio Machado
Azusa	1837, 1841	Azusa	6,596, 4,451	Andrés Duarte, Ygnacio Palomares, Ricardo Vejar
Boca de Santa Mónica	1828	Santa Monica	5,657	Ysidro Reyes, Francisco Márquez
Ciénega o Paso de la Tijera	1843	Crenshaw district, L.A.	4,481	Vicente Sánchez
El Encino	1845	Encino	4,461	Vicente de la Osa
El Escorpión	1845	Calabasas	110	Odan and Manual
El Pueblo de la Reina de Los Angeles	1781	Los Angeles downtown	17,172	
Ex–Mission San Fernando	1846	San Fernando Valley	116,858	Eulogio de Celis
Isla de Santa Catalina	?	Avalon	45,820	Juan Mariá Covarrubias
La Ballona	1822	Culver City	13,920	Felipe and Tomá Talamantes; Agustín and Ygnacio Machado
La Brea	1828	Hancock Park district, L.A.	4,439	Antonio Rocha
La Cañada	1842	La Cañada	5,832	José del Carmen Lugo
La Merced	?	Montebello	2,364	María Casildo Soto
La Puente	1845	La Puente, Hacienda Heights, Industry, Walnut	48,791	John Rowland, William Workman
Los Alamitos	1784	Long Beach	28,027	José Manuel Nieto
Los Cerritos	1784	Western Long Beach	27,054	José Manuel Nieto
Los Feliz	1796	Griffith Park in L.A.	6,647	José Vicente Feliz
Los Palos Verdes	1821	San Pedro, Palos Verdes	13,629	José Dolores Sepúlveda
Paso de Bartolo Viejo	1835	Whittier	8,885	Juan Crispin Pérez
San Antonio	1810	South and east of L.A.	29,513	Antonio María Lugo
Santa Anita	1841	Arcadia, Monrovia	13,319	Hugo Reid
Santa Gertrudis	1784	Downey, Santa Fe Springs	17,602	José Manuel Nieto
San José	1837	Pomona	22,340	Ignacio Palomares
San Pascual	1843	Pasadena, South Pasadena, Altadena	13,694	Manuel Garfias
San Pedro	1784	Compton, Gardena, Wilmington	43,119	Juan José Domínguez
San Rafael	1784, 1789	Glendale, Eagle Rock, La Cañada Flintridge	36,403	José María Verdugo
San Vicente y Santa Mónica	1828	West L.A. area	30,260	Francisco Sepúlveda
Topanga Malibu Sequit	1804	Malibu	13,316	José Bartolomé Tapia

SOURCE: Antonio José Rios-Bustamante and Pedro Castillo, *An Illustrated History of Mexican Los Angeles, 1781–1985* (Los Angeles: University of California, Chicano Studies Research Center, 1986), pp. 18–19.

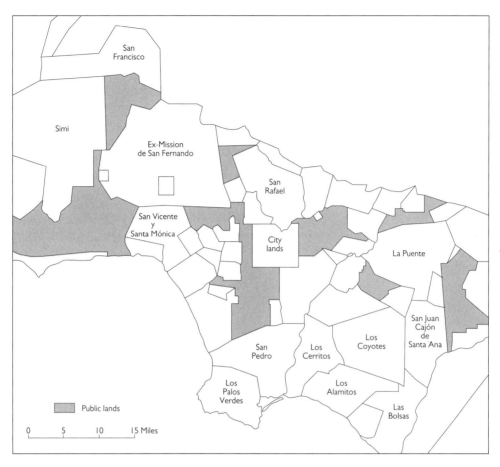

Ranchos, city lands, and public lands in the Los Angeles region, 1848.

civilian settlement, reduce the influence of the missions, and reward soldiers for military service. Though frequently called "Spanish ranchos," most were granted in the Mexican era, after 1836. The title applicants (rancheros) particularly sought locations with access to water and Indian laborers. More than 50 grants were issued in Los Angeles, 11 before 1822 and 39 between 1823 and 1848. The rate of grant-giving increased greatly after mission secularization in 1835. The largest estates were about 48,000 acres; the smallest, 1,000. Rancho titles were issued according to a set pattern: A would-be ranchero drafted a petition for the land, accompanied by a *diseño* (map) and a sketch of the property, however rough. Rarely was the land surveyed. This documentation satisfied the early officials, although it often proved insufficient later in Yankee courts of law. Foreigners could take title only if they were naturalized Mexicans. The ranchero Abel Stearns, a Massachusetts native who married a lo-

cal woman, owned vast estates in the region and may have been the wealthiest man in California. Californio rancheros, who enjoyed a gracious lifestyle, raised more livestock than field crops on their land, and depended on Indian labor to do the hard work.

In the American period title holders were expected to establish their rights under the U.S. Land Law of 1851, which proved difficult. In addition, most Mexican rancheros lost title to their lands in the late 19th century, owing to tax debts, lawyer fees, and fatal droughts. Gambling, borrowing money at 5 percent interest per month, and cosigning friends' loans also contributed to their demise. The Domínguez family was an exception in that it held on to large parcels, some of which remain intact in the southern part of the county. Rancho outlines are visible still today. Wilshire and Pico Boulevards, for example, mark the lines of old landed estates.

RANCHO LOS ALAMITOS, historic site on Bixby Hill Road in Long Beach, with one of the oldest buildings in California. The property comprises 7½ acres of the former rancho of the same name (meaning "ranch of the little cottonwoods"); the site of an Indian *ranchería* (village), it was granted to Manuel Nieto, a retired soldier who had accompanied Captain Portolá in 1769. The rancho home, built in 1806, was later used by Abel Stearns, who bought the property in 1842 as a summer home for his young bride, Arcadia Bandini (she was 14 when they married in 1839). In 1878 it was occupied by Susan and John W. Bixby. On the grounds are a freshwater spring; a profusion of native plants, roses, vines, Moreton Bay fig trees, palms, and pepper trees; a blacksmith shop and barn, complete with farm equipment; Indian artifacts; and an abandoned tennis court dating from the early part of this century. The home is furnished with original Bixby family possessions.

RANCHO LOS AMIGOS MEDICAL CENTER, county medical facility in Downey. Founded as the County Poor Farm in 1887, it was where indigent and chronically ill "inmates" were housed after being removed from Los Angeles County Hospital. The county allocated $300–$500 monthly for groceries and provisions for both the patients and employees. Because it treated World War I veterans, the poor farm gradually evolved into a facility for mentally and physically ill patients. It opened its first mental ward in 1910, its first infirmary wards in 1923, and a separate medical building in 1931. In 1955 the County Poor Farm ceased its indigents' operations, adopted the name Rancho Los Amigos Hospital, and began functioning as a facility for both chronic and convalescent patients. It pioneered in the treatment of polio. The hospital also became a training facility after affiliating with the University of Southern California. Today it offers a wide range of medical services and programs. The current name, Rancho Los Amigos Medical Center, dates from 1984.

RANCHO PALOS VERDES, independent community on Palos Verdes Peninsula 21 miles southwest of downtown Los Angeles. It was incorporated in 1973, and its population reached 41,600 in 1990.

RANCHO PARK, residential and commercial district of Los Angeles centered on Pico Boulevard between Motor Avenue and Sepulveda Boulevard.

Pico Boulevard in this area is the boundary of an old Mexican land grant, hence the name. The area was subdivided for homes and shops in 1922, beginning with the Janss Investment tract north of Pico. After World War II new housing tracts were added, and the city purchased a park with a defunct golf course at Pico and Patricia Avenue, which it called Rancho Park. This spacious city park is now well used, and the golf course has been the site of several Los Angeles Open tournaments. The name Rancho Park was applied to the district as well.

RANCHO SANTA ANA BOTANIC GARDEN, devoted to native California plants and flowering shrubs, especially those indigenous to the southern part of the state. Founded in 1927, the garden is located in Claremont, in the far eastern part of Los Angeles County. It boasts a fine collection of cactuses, succulents, shrubs, and palms, and it specializes in lilacs, whose perfume fills the air from March to May. On display, in an accredited museum, is a demonstration of ways in which Indians used native plants.

RAND CORPORATION, Santa Monica–based "think tank" formed in 1946 by the U.S. Air Force for strategic planning. It became independent in 1948 and began using its scientific methodologies to solve problems for civilian government agencies, including the city of Los Angeles. The name comes from "R and D"—research and development.

RAPID TRANSIT, fixed-rail electric trains running on their own right-of-way. Early in the century the Pacific Electric (PE) Red Cars operated successfully on their own rights-of-way in interurban areas, using city streets downtown. By around 1950 they still cruised speedily in some outlying areas, but were forced to crawl in the auto-clogged civic center. Red Car lines were soon abandoned. The issue became how—and whether—to design a Los Angeles rapid transit to meet the demands of the auto age.

Rapid transit has been a controversial issue ever since the Los Angeles Chamber of Commerce seriously floated a new plan in 1948. The basic concerns have been how to meet construction costs and how to lure motorists from their vehicles. Some planners hoped to incorporate rapid transit into the burgeoning freeway system, but the idea was sidetracked. Currently, with jammed freeways and piecemeal metropolitan rail construction

Artist's vision of future transportation in Los Angeles, 1913. Courtesy Photographic Collections, Los Angeles Public Library, Security Pacific Collection.

under way, rapid transit remains a bone of contention. In 1951 the legislature created the Metropolitan Transit Authority (MTA), which immediately proposed an extensive project for an overhead monorail but then failed to appropriate funds. In 1964 the legislature established the Southern California Rapid Transit District (RTD), with taxing powers and the right of eminent domain to build new transit lines. Four years later, RTD unveiled a plan involving an 89-mile dual rail system, complete with 20 miles of tunnel, serving downtown along five corridors reaching out to Wilshire Boulevard, San Fernando Valley, San Gabriel Valley, Long Beach, and Los Angeles International Airport. The rail lines, according to the plan, would be connected with 115 feeder bus lines, and the $2.5 billion cost would be financed by a half-cent sales tax. The idea had many backers, but the *Los Angeles Times* was not among them. It attacked the plan on grounds that it would provide a windfall for land developers in the transit corridors, benefit downtown inordinately, cost too much to build, and serve too few passengers. Voters rejected it.

In 1974 RTD floated yet another plan, this time to upgrade the existing bus fleet and create a 145-mile fixed rail system. The system would be funded by a one-cent sales tax that would produce $4.7 billion. This proposal received support from the Sierra Club, the *Times,* and even the Southern California Auto Club, but, owing to fears of an economic downturn and the potential effects of a bus driver strike, it, too, died at the polls, especially among voters in Los Angeles and Orange Counties. In 1976 County Supervisor Baxter Ward made a new and innovative proposal, for a 230-mile system that would follow freeways, flood control channels, and use existing railroad rights of way. It lost at the ballot box as well.

Finally in 1978 the voters approved a plan for raising the sales tax and creating a "starter" rapid transit line 15 miles long from Union Station to Hollywood and North Hollywood. This system has been under construction, with the link from Union Station to Alvarado completed in 1993.

RATS probably came with the first Spanish sailing vessel and are by now considered virtually indigenous. They live for about a year, during which time the female produces four or five litters, each made up of four to ten young. Rats weigh about a pound and can grow to 16 inches, including the tail. They carry fleas and are associated with bubonic plague. During the 1920s a serious outbreak of plague afflicted Mexicans in the Plaza area. The brown rat lives at ground level, eats almost everything, forages even during the day, and is destructive. (The Swedish naturalist Carolus Linnaeus named them *Rattus norvegicus,* or Norway rat, as an ethnic joke.) The roof rat lives above ground, travels on wires and fences, and is nocturnal and vegetarian. Rats can be controlled, but have proven impossible to eradicate.

RAVENNA, small rural community near Acton in the Antelope Valley. It was named for Manuel Ravenna, an Italian immigrant who arrived in Los Angeles in 1858 and opened a grocery store and saloon. The enterprising Ravenna commissioned Wells Fargo stage drivers to deliver ice from the mountains to his store. The ice, wrapped in blankets, increased his trade and made him wealthy. In 1861 he formed the Soledad Gold, Silver, and Copper Mining Company, to mine precious ores in Soledad Canyon. In this endeavor he proved less successful. During the 1870s the Southern Pacific

Railroad gave the name Ravenna to a stop along its Soledad Canyon rail line.

RAYMOND HOTEL, first and perhaps most famous Pasadena hotel. Built in 1886 on 25 acres of gardens atop Raymond Hill, it was owned by a Boston travel agency, Raymond and Whitcomb. In its first six months of operation the spa drew 35,000 tourists, many of them chilled-through New Englanders hoping to bask in the warm Pasadena winter sun. Boasting 200 suites and 40 indoor toilets, the Raymond was for a time the most luxurious lodging house in the West.

RAZA UNIDA PARTY. *See* La Raza Unida Party

REAGAN, RONALD (1911–), Hollywood leading man who became president of the United States. Illinois-born and Iowa-bred, Reagan moved to Southern California in 1937. While covering the spring training of the Chicago Cubs as a sports announcer, he took a screen test at Warner Brothers and landed a $200-a-week contract. Reagan's achievements as a performer were unremarkable. He was active, however, in Hollywood Democratic politics; the Screen Actors Guild, where he served as president; and the Music Corporation of Amer-

ica (MCA) when it became an entertainment industry giant. Among his 50 films, *Knute Rockne, All American* (1940) and *King's Row* (1941) were probably the most popular. During World War II Reagan served in Culver City, at the Hal Roach Studios—the U.S. military's official studio—on National and Washington Boulevards, working on propaganda and training films. He emerged from the war a lieutenant.

In 1947 Reagan testified as a friendly witness before the House Un-American Activities Committee. Still an ardent Democrat, he campaigned for Helen Gahagan Douglas during her 1950 Senate race against Richard Nixon. Married and divorced from actress Jane Wyman, he experienced a major turn in his life when he married Nancy Davis in 1952 and began hosting television's *General Electric Theater* in 1954. He soon adopted a conservative philosophy, going on to become Republican governor of California in 1966 and president in 1980. On leaving the presidency after his second term, he retired to his home in Pacific Palisades. The title of his pre-presidency autobiography, *Where's the Rest of Me?* (1965), echoes a line from *King's Row,* when he awakens to find his leg has been amputated. In 1994 Reagan Ronald startled the nation by announcing that he was stricken with Alzheimer's disease.

REAGH, WILLIAM (1911–1992), Los Angeles photographer. For over 50 years the Kansas-born Silver Lake resident, a graphic artist by trade, spent his off-hours recording the city's passing parade in stark black-and-white photos. Seedy old buildings, ragged children, and old people were among his favorite subjects. The California State Library purchased 200 of Reagh's prints.

REAL ESTATE DEVELOPMENT, singularly important business enterprise in Los Angeles, from the 1870s to the present. Until fairly recently land was relatively cheap and abundant, and developers played a crucial role in founding towns, converting land into home lots and commercial centers, developing water supplies, fostering commuter rail lines, establishing street railways, exploiting electricity, popularizing architectural tastes, and securing the single-family-home lifestyle that typifies the region.

In the 19th century, real estate developers were generally lauded for espousing a utopian vision of Southern California and admired for their exu-

Ronald Reagan, *General Electric Theater* television host. Courtesy Ronald Reagan Presidential Library.

berant boosterism. Their role was entwined with the series of real estate booms that created a metropolis out of raw land. Among the leading real estate entrepreneurs were John Temple, Robert S. Baker, Charles McClay, Jonathan S. Slauson, and W. E. Wilmore. Less well known were the land developers associated with the Southern Pacific and Atchison, Topeka, and Santa Fe railroads. The main contribution of developers in the 1870s and 1880s was to convert the old ranchos into towns and home lots.

Probably the most important early-20th-century land entrepreneur was Henry E. Huntington, who built up the San Gabriel Valley, while the single most important real estate syndicate was the Los Angeles Suburban Homes Company, which developed the southern San Fernando Valley at a time

---

I would take to driving around the city at night, through Silverlake, Echo Park, down Temple, where the streetlamps were low and yellow and nippled and the palm trees were high with scrawny fronds.

—Robert Towne, screenwriter

---

when water and suburban rail lines arrived. In the 1920s developers opened the hinterlands to suburban living, establishing such exclusive luxury communities as Palos Verdes. In the building boom that lasted from the late 1940s to the 1960s developers helped create the quintessential middle-class suburban sprawl that is Los Angeles. The Southern California industry was associated with innovations in the escrow and title insurance industries, and in the establishment of suburban malls. Developers influenced public policy, shaped housing and architectural tastes, and molded zoning and building regulations.

In the meantime, the reputation of developers has declined considerably as they have been accused of innumerable social ills: plotting conspiracies to feather their own nest, ignoring the need for low-cost housing, enforcing racial restrictions, bribing elected officials, thwarting the recommendations of trained planning specialists, and destroying the natural environment. They are now frequently embattled with slow-growth advocates

and conservationists. Nevertheless, it is impossible to overstate their importance in defining regional history. It has been, and continues to be, pivotal.

REASON FOUNDATION, Los Angeles–based think tank that endorses privatization in general, and that of Los Angeles International Airport in particular. It favors the voucher system for schools, and, in the aftermath of the 1992 riots, argued for the "empowerment" policies of Jack Kemp. Although linked with the Bush administration, it also supports abortion rights and the legalization of drugs.

REBUILD L.A. *See* RLA

RECALL ELECTIONS, reform pioneered at the municipal level in Los Angeles in 1903. The procedure, which was adopted as a city charter provision, provides for the removal of a public official by popular vote. For the first time anywhere in the nation, the ballot box could be used to purge a mayor or council member for corruption or other wrongdoing. Dr. John Randolph Haynes masterminded this reform; his campaign for direct democracy also included charter provisions for the initiative and referendum. The recall was first invoked in Los Angeles in a 1904 election to oust a corrupt councilman, James P. Davenport. He had voted for a contract awarding city advertising rights to the *Los Angeles Times,* even though the paper's bid was $10,000 higher than that of the nearest competitor. Davenport thus became the first elected official in the United States to be recalled. The recall mechanism also came into play in 1911, when reformers threatened a recall campaign against the corrupt mayor Arthur Harper, forcing his resignation. In that same year, Haynes convinced the California legislature to approve the recall option for the state as a whole. A successful mayoral recall campaign was mounted in 1938 as well, against Frank Shaw.

RECORDING INDUSTRY began thriving in Los Angeles in the 1930s and 1940s. Its course was closely tied to the growth of the film and radio industries. The first local pressing, made in 1921 by two African American songwriters, the Spikes brothers, was a 78 record of the song "Someday Sweetheart." In the 1930s radio personality Al Jarvis was a pioneer in the disk jockey radio format with a show called "Make-Believe Ballroom."

Capitol Records Tower, Hollywood. Photo by Michael Krakowiak/Marni Pitt.

He followed on the heels of KFI's José Rodriguez, who had launched a similar show in 1929. Live radio broadcasts from the Hollywood Palladium, featuring Bing Crosby among others, further stimulated the recording industry. In 1940 Glenn Wallichs founded a record store known as Wallichs' Music City. It attracted crowds of students from Hollywood and Fairfax High Schools and within a year was selling more records than any store west of Chicago. Together with Johnny Mercer and others, Wallichs formed Capitol Records in 1942. By pioneering album design and marketing strategies, the firm became one of the top three in the industry.

By the 1970s Los Angeles was the dominant center for the recording industry, which in 1978 pumped an estimated \$2 billion into the local economy.

RED CAR. *See* Pacific Electric Railway Company

RED LINE, Los Angeles's first subway system. Authorized by a county half-cent sales tax in 1980 and operated by the Metropolitan Transit Authority, the first leg opened on 30 January 1993. Formally known as Metro Red Line, it is considered the spine of the Los Angeles region's proposed 300-mile rail transit system. The Italian-built stainless steel cars are designed to travel as fast as 70 miles per hour and carry up to 169 passengers. By 1996 the Red Line ran from Union Station to Wilshire

Red Line subway. Courtesy Metropolitan Transportation Authority.

and Alvarado Boulevards. A dramatic tunnel subsidence under Hollywood Boulevard in 1994 caused a public outcry for improvements in oversight, safety, and management of the construction phase. The largest public works project in the region's history, the Metro Red Line was planned to extend eventually through Hollywood and into the San Fernando Valley, into East Los Angeles as far as Atlantic and Whittier Boulevards, and west to Pico and San Vicente Boulevards.

REDONDO BEACH, independent South Bay residential and resort city 19 miles southwest of downtown Los Angeles. Founded in 1881 on the former Rancho San Pedro and incorporated a year later, the town drew its name from nearby Rancho Sausal Redondo ("Ranch of the Round Clump of Willows"). The Santa Fe Railroad, whose tracks reached the Redondo site in 1888, was able to load and unload box cars from ships docked at a pier. The Santa Fe planned to develop a deep-water port, but dropped the plan when San Pedro became the major Los Angeles harbor. From 1890 through the 1920s, the splendid Redondo Hotel attracted throngs of vacationers.

The arrival of Henry Huntington's Pacific Electric Railway, in 1905, assured Redondo's place as a major tourist attraction. By the summer of that year some 100 real estate agents were greeting passengers arriving on the Red Cars, which were making 80 round trips daily from Los Angeles. A hot salt-water plunge, built in 1909 with 1,350 dressing rooms, remained a favorite attraction through the 1930s. The first surfing in California was introduced at Redondo, in 1907, by George Freeth, a

---

In the '40s, there was a time of great hope in Los Angeles. It was a big place, it was a countrified place.

—Walter Mosley, mystery writer

---

native of Hawaii. Redondo Beach, whose first pleasure pier was built in 1913, now has three piers: Municipal Pier, Monstad Pier, and a fishing pier sheltered by the King Harbor breakwater. Municipal Pier, which was closed in 1988 because of fires and storms (a few shops were the exception), reopened in 1995, refurbished with a concrete deck and concrete pilings. Redondo Seaport Village is now the city's major commercial attraction. The population, which was 2,395 in 1910, stood at 60,100 in 1990.

RED SQUAD, familiar name of the notorious Intelligence Bureau of the Los Angeles Police Department, established around 1933 by Chief James Davis, headed by Capt. William F. ("Red") Hynes, and protected by Mayor Frank Shaw. Its purpose was to converge upon, beat up, arrest, and disperse labor unionists, Communists, and other radicals during public demonstrations. The squad was disbanded by Mayor Fletcher Bowron after 1938.

REFERENDUM, voting procedure whereby a proposed or existing law is submitted to a direct popular vote. It was installed in the Los Angeles city charter in 1903 along with two other electoral reforms, the initiative and recall. Owing to the vigorous campaigning of the reformer Dr. John Randolph Haynes, Los Angeles became the first city in the nation to adopt these reforms.

REGIONAL HISTORY CENTER, UNIVERSITY OF SOUTHERN CALIFORNIA, main-

tains (along with the Los Angeles City Historical Society) a valuable computer data base and information network, the History Computerization Project. It is available for use by independent researchers.

REGIONAL PLANNING DEPARTMENT, COUNTY OF LOS ANGELES. *See* Los Angeles County Regional Planning Department and Regional Planning Commission

REID, HUGO (1810–1852), Scottish pioneer who arrived from Mexico in 1832. After forming a trading partnership that imported finished goods and exported cattle hides to New England, Reid purchased a large part of Rancho Santa Anita, took a seat on the Los Angeles *ayuntamiento* (council), and was elected a delegate from Los Angeles to the 1849 constitutional convention in Monterey. He was a scholarly man, but because he married Victoria Bartolome'a Comecrabit, an Indian woman who had been a neophyte at Mission San Gabriel, he never achieved full acceptance among the local elites. Helen Hunt Jackon's heroine, Ramona, was based partly on what Antonio Coronel told her about the hardships faced by Hugo and Victoria Reid's daughter. Reid's deep personal interest in Gabrieleño Indians led him, in 1852, to write a commentary about the native people in the *Los Angeles Star*. It was reprinted as *The Indians of Los Angeles County* (1968). The Reid ranch and three-room adobe, built in 1839, later passed through many hands, including E. J. "Lucky" Baldwin's. It is the oldest of the historic buildings on the grounds of what is now the Los Angeles State and County Arboretum.

RELIGION, TO 1890, reflected the complex and overlapping influences of Native American, Catholic, Protestant, Jewish, and Chinese peoples. Until 1769 Indian religion prevailed exclusively. The Tongva observed ancient rituals and cults similar to those of other Shoshonean peoples, including the use of the narcotic jimsonweed in their religious practice. In historical times they created a powerful cult figure, Chinigchinich, who was also adopted by nearby tribes such as the Juaneños (of Mission San Juan Capistrano).

In the 1770s Indian religions began to share the stage with Roman Catholicism. With the establishment of Mission San Gabriel in 1771 and Mission San Fernando in 1797, and of the Los Angeles *pueblo* in 1781, Catholicism became the region's official religion, promulgated by Franciscan missionaries rather than parish priests. Although they vigorously converted the natives to Christianity, the Franciscan fathers allowed the natives to continue following their traditional rites, as long as they also adhered to Catholic observances. Natives outside the missions, meanwhile, held to their traditional ways until the late 1880s.

California was part of the Catholic diocese of Sonora, Mexico, until 1840, when a separate diocese was established in California. The main Los Angeles religious center was the Plaza Church.

To survive in Hollywood, you need the ambition of a Latin American revolutionary, the ego of a grand opera singer, and the physical stamina of a cow pony.   —Billie Burke, actress

---

Even after the Mexican War (1846–1848) the Yankee frontier town, unlike other contemporary frontier towns, remained predominantly Catholic, and continued so for some decades.

The first Protestant minister in Southern California was William Money (Bishop Money), founder in 1841 of the Reformed Church, a local sect with 12 followers. The Catholic clergy regarded Money as "the most obstinate heretic on the earth." At midcentury, orthodox Protestantism began to take root, shaped by the complex forces of isolation, urbanization, voluntarism, and secularism. Protestant congregations were few, small, and dispirited. The first Methodist sermon was preached by Rev. James W. Brier in 1850. The congregation consisted of his own family and Mayor John G. Nichols. Most early Protestant missionaries like Brier gave up and moved on quickly. The first permanent Protestant congregation (Episcopal) was organized in 1865. The first informal Jewish services, held in the rear room of John Temple's adobe in 1854, were intoned by Joseph P. Newmark, a businessman who was also an ordained rabbi. The first formal services attended by the congregation, calling itself B'nai B'rith, were conducted by Rabbi Abraham Wolf Edelman in 1862. The congregation has been ongoing ever since.

Chinese laborers in the 1870s brought their own religious beliefs and worshiped in makeshift joss houses. Protestant evangelicals set about missionizing the Chinese. Once the railroad was completed in 1876, Yankees established many churches. During the Boom of the Eighties alone some 40 churches were built, most of them Protestant. By 1890, 11 denominations had assigned clergy to Los Angeles: Roman Catholic, Jewish, Episcopal, Congregational, Northern Methodist, Southern Methodist, African Methodist Episcopal, Baptist, Presbyterian, Disciples of Christ, and Lutheran (Missouri Synod).

RELIGION, 1890–1945, featured Protestantism, especially Protestant evangelism. By the early 1900s the town counted 231 Christian churches, with a total membership of over 80,000. The mainline sects were strong, and the town considered itself a "model Christian community," with churches, schools, and civic bodies "deeply interested in the best."

The proliferation of religious sects in the early part of the century was attributed to the hospitable climate, the presence of many uprooted and alienated émigrés, and the host of wealthy, leisured individuals arriving from all parts of the globe. By the 1920s the city had attracted many Protestant fundamentalists. It also had an extraordinary collection of fortune tellers, astrologers, occultists, swamis, and psychics, which provoked easterners to regard Los Angeles as a city peopled by the bizarre and eccentric. Several important denominations arose locally during this era: the Foursquare Gospel movement of Aimee Semple McPherson; the Church of the Nazarene; the Pentecostal movement, which was to have worldwide impact; the Hebrew Evangelization Society; and the Christian Fundamentals League.

Other religions also became established in Los Angeles. The Mormons created their first Los Angeles stake (the equivalent of a diocese) in 1923, while the first Japanese and Chinese Buddhist temples were established before the turn of the century.

Religious rivalry and disharmony were common. Mainline churches tended to bash the splinter groups as "cults." Aimee Semple McPherson enraged other Protestant ministers with her unorthodox style, and constantly had to fend off their attacks in public forums and in her radio broadcasts. An outspoken rival, "Fighting Bob" Shuler of Methodist Trinity Church, had his own popular radio ministry in the 1930s; he was noted for his vicious anti-Semitic and anti-Catholic outbursts. Meanwhile, sophisticates complained that Los Angeles was an excessively puritanical, provincial, and narrow-minded city.

Religious architectural styles tended to be traditional, a reflection of the conservative tastes of the city's political and economic leaders. Buildings housing the largest and wealthiest congregations seemed to favor imposing size and Gothic design. By the 1920s the Mid-Wilshire district had a heavy concentration of houses of worship. Located near one another in this area were the First Baptist Church of Los Angeles, Immanuel Presbyterian Church, St. James Episcopal Church, Wilshire Christian Church, Wilshire Methodist Church, Wilshire Boulevard Temple, and First Congregational Church. The latter, with its 5,000 members in the 1940s, was the largest Congregational ministry in the country. It remains today the oldest continuously functioning Protestant church in Los Angeles.

RELIGION, SINCE 1945, has been characterized by increasing diversity—and greater mutual acceptance. A recent telephone book had 70 columns of religious sects and denominations throughout greater Los Angeles. Although revivalists and cultists have drawn the greatest publicity, most people belong to traditional faiths.

Of the mainline religious denominations, Roman Catholics are the most numerous in Los Angeles, with the archdiocese counting 2.37 million

---

Whatever your politics, in L.A. you have to look successful.

—Bob Roth, publisher of *L.A. Weekly*

---

parishioners in 98 parishes in Southern California. The largest Protestants groups are Baptist, Church of Jesus Christ of Latter-Day Saints (Mormon), United Methodist, Presbyterian, Episcopalian, Lutheran, Church of Christ, Reform Church, and Assembly of God (Pentecostal). In 1982 the Baptists claimed 172,777 members, and United Methodists, 84,835. The African Methodist Episcopal Church remains a stalwart of the black community. Although there are about 500,000 Jews in Los Angeles, many consider themselves part of an ethnic group rather than a religion, and attendance

in synagogues is far less than that number. The religious culture of Los Angeles also includes a host of charitable associations and voluntary groups that are associated with established houses of worship.

The city's growing ethnic diversity contributes to religious diversity. Older, established churches are attracting relatively fewer whites and more African Americans, Koreans, Latinos, and Filipinos, especially those of the middle class. Eastern Orthodox congregations are also active among the growing Greek, Russian, and Armenian communities of Los Angeles. Meanwhile, many non-Judeo-Christian religions are springing up. *Santería* (Spanish for "worship of saints"), a traditional Afro–West Indian religion similar to voodoo, is quite active in Los Angeles today. Adherents of Buddhism number in the tens of thousands, as do Islamic worshipers. In 1990 an estimated 70,000 Hindus lived in Los Angeles, most of whom worshiped at home.

RENAISSANCE PLEASURE FAIRE, yearly outdoor fair with an Elizabethan theme. Born of a pageant staged by Phyllis Patterson for the Laurel Canyon Wonderland Youth Center in 1960, it had its first outdoor weekend in 1963. By 1965 the fair was so successful that it moved to a 300-acre site in Agoura and expanded to nine weekends. The fair, which features crafts, foods, and entertainment, all with a Renaissance flavor, attracts as many as 200,000 people, many of them appropriately costumed. In 1987, facing the loss of its lease in Agoura, the fair moved to grounds in San Bernardino County.

RENT CONTROL is mandatory for all dwelling units in the cities of Beverly Hills, Los Angeles, Santa Monica, and West Hollywood, and for mobile-home units in Palmdale. In Los Angeles, rent increases may not exceed the rise in the cost of living, although the owner may pass on to the tenant the cost of certain capital improvements approved by the city. While Santa Monica enforces the most hard-line law, two state laws—the Ellis Act of 1986 and the Costa-Hawkins Act of 1995—help to limit policy at the local level.

REPTILES in Los Angeles County include four poisonous rattlesnakes. The largest, the Pacific rattler, inhabits mountain and foothill regions. The sidewinder, as well as the white and Mojave rattlers, mainly live in the county's desert areas, although they are also seen in mountainous regions up to 8,000 feet. Many other varieties of snakes live in the region, including the California boa, various water snakes, the common kingsnake, and the gopher snake. Although shy, snakes bite when threatened; some 50 bites a year are reported in the Los Angeles area. Bites are generally not fatal if victims remain calm and are treated within six hours. (In fact, more people probably die from bee stings than from snake bites.) Zoologists stress the importance of not killing harmless snakes, as they compete with rattlesnakes for the same food and so control the number of rattlers. The desert tortoise, also found along the edges of Los Angeles's deserts, is an endangered species. Lizards are plentiful in the desert environment and include the horned toad, rough scaled lizard, and desert lizard. Except for the rattlesnakes, reptiles seen in Los Angeles County are not poisonous.

REPUBLICAN PARTY had a weak presence in Los Angeles just after its founding in 1854, but grew into a major party by the end of the century. So strong was Democratic (and proslavery) sentiment in the 1850s, and so feeble the Republican opposition, that on the eve of the Civil War the staunchly Republican editor of *El Clamor Público,* Francisco P. Ramírez, had to close down his newspaper and flee the town. The prospects of the Republicans, using the new name of Union League, gained ground when war erupted and California declared its allegiance to the Union. On 17 April 1865 Phineas Banning, an ardent abolitionist and Republican, organized a Union League funeral procession in Los Angeles in memory of the slain Abraham Lincoln.

The GOP waxed stronger during the Gilded Age, when the dominant politicians were Republicans associated with the Southern Pacific Railroad. In 1884 Edward F. Spence was elected mayor on the Republican ticket. By the time of the 1896 election of President McKinley, the party had become something of a powerhouse.

The conservative *Los Angeles Times* played a commanding role in Republican politics for at least two generations. Its first publisher, Harrison Gray Otis, was the town's leading Republican. Although the party old guard failed to counter the progressive wing of the party from 1911 to 1913, over the long haul the conservative core prevailed.

Legend has it that a faux pas committed by Republican presidential hopeful Charles Evans

Hughes in Long Beach in 1916 cost the party the presidency that year. Hughes, while campaigning in California and staying at a Long Beach hotel, refused to pay a courtesy call on a fellow guest, the progressive Republican governor Hiram Johnson. This slight enraged Johnson, costing Hughes many votes in California, and resulted in Democrat Woodrow Wilson's narrow victory.

When Harrison Otis's son-in-law, Harry Chandler, became publisher of the *Times* in 1917, he also inherited the mantle of Republican kingmaker in Los Angeles. In the 1934 gubernatorial race, the paper pulled out all stops to defeat Socialist-turned-Democrat Upton Sinclair. Norman Chandler, Harry's son, took over the paper in 1945, and likewise accepted the inherited role of Republican potentate. The paper was instrumental in picking

---

Every time I find myself in Los Angeles I wonder what I've done to displease God.

—Lucius Beebe, writer

---

mayors, city council members, and county supervisors. In 1958 the Republican old guard—consisting now of Norman Chandler, *Times* political columnist Kyle Palmer, insurance executive Asa Call, department store executive Neil Petree, and business executive James Lin Beebe—captured city hall by getting Norris Poulson elected mayor. They also set about engineering the rise of Richard Nixon from congressman to senator to vice president. In recent decades, however, the *Times* has refrained from making outright endorsements for president.

In 1993 Los Angeles elected a Republican mayor. Yet if the measure of Republican strength is voter registration, the city of Los Angeles, with a scant 25.4 percent of voters registered GOP, was anything but a Republican town. The party's strongholds lay mostly in the smaller, outlying county communities: Arcadia (59.5 percent), Avalon (52.8 percent), Bradbury (65.1 percent), Glendale (51.3 percent), Glendora (55.0 percent), Hidden Hills (52.6 percent), La Cañada Flintridge (66.3 percent), La Habra Heights (66.0 percent), Lancaster (51.8 percent), La Verne (50.6 percent), Palos Verdes Estates (63.5 percent), Rancho Palos Verdes (56.4 percent), Rolling Hills Estates (63.3 percent), San Marino

(69.5 percent), Santa Clarita (52.2 percent), and Westlake Village (55.4 percent).

Republicans from outlying areas of Los Angeles County have been well represented in Congress, even during the years of Democratic control. Carlos J. Moorhead, first elected in 1972 from Glendale, Burbank, and Pasadena, sat on the judiciary committee during the impeachment hearings of Pres. Richard Nixon, and has served on the commerce committee and a subcommittee on intellectual property. Moorhead is now the dean of the California delegation. David Dreier, representing Covina, Monrovia, Arcadia, and Claremont, entered the House at age 28 in the 1980 Reagan landslide and served on the rules committee. He has become part of Speaker Newt Gingrich's inner circle. Howard P. "Buck" McKeon, whose main electoral base is Santa Clarita, was chosen leader of the 50 Republican freshmen elected to the House of Representatives in 1992.

REPUBLICAN PARTY ORGANIZATIONS include both official and volunteer bodies. The Los Angeles County Central Committee represents the Republican Party officially, with members elected in the June primary of even years. It meets in January of every odd-numbered year to elect

---

The map of Los Angeles is never completed.

—Ben Macomber, journalist, 1923

---

officers, and every third month to conduct business. All meetings are open to the public. The committee is composed of one member from each assembly, senate, and congressional district, as well as six members appointed by the chair. In recent years the Central Committee has been headquartered in South Pasadena.

Republican volunteer organizations date back to the 1930s. The California Republican Assembly is the oldest group, having been organized in 1934. It seeks out candidates and makes endorsements. In 1968 the county committee evolved an especially successful plan to involve professionals and volunteers at the precinct level. One of the most effective political groups in California is the Republican Associates, which is supported entirely by dues from the business and professional communities.

It maintains a comprehensive library of articles on incumbents and on issues. The Lincoln Clubs of Los Angeles County are a fund-raising arm of the county party. The Federation of Republican Women has 35,000 members in 80 clubs countywide. Also active locally are the California Republican League—popular among some young professionals—the California Young Republicans, and the California College Republicans.

REPUBLIC PICTURES CORPORATION, small movie studio founded in 1935 by Herbert J. Yates, a former tobacco executive. It turned out numerous second-billing films and serials when both were a regular part of movie viewing. The products, mainly westerns or pseudo–*film noir,* were generally low budget, quickly shot, and competently assembled. They featured such players as Roy Rogers, John Carroll, and Yates's wife, Vera Hruba Ralston. *Rio Grande* (1950), *The Quiet Man* (1952), and *High Noon* (1952) were among the few major Republic films. In the mid-1950s, when television helped kill off filmdom's second and third features and Saturday serials, the studio joined the enemy and turned to television production.

RESEDA, district in the western San Fernando Valley 30 miles northwest of downtown Los Angeles. Once part of the huge San Fernando Mission, the area was subdivided in 1913 by the Los Angeles Suburban Homes Company, a syndicate formed mainly by Harry Chandler, Harrison Gray Otis, and Moses Sherman. The town's first name was Marian, after Otis's daughter and Chandler's wife, but the post office objected that this conflicted with Mariana, another California community. The name Reseda was therefore selected, meaning "gives comfort" in Latin. The town's first residents, according to the Reseda Chamber of Commerce, were Mr. and Mrs. W. J. Lausen. In the 1930s Reseda was the preeminent lettuce growing area in the United States. The community was served by a rail line along Sherman Way that ended at Reseda Boulevard. The design of Sherman Way was inspired by Paseo de la Reforma, a boulevard in Mexico City that greatly appealed to Chandler. Reseda's population in 1996 was 61,213.

RESTAURANTS historically have catered to the city's ethnic mix, exploited the cornucopia of local farms and orchards, and specialized in informal dining, including, in the automobile age, drive-ins

Brown Derby Cafe. Wilshire
Boulevard, 1930s. Pitt
Collection.

and takeout food places. Mexicans ran the first Los Angeles eateries, called *cafeterías* (coffee shops) but featuring more tavernlike drinking than eating. It was a Frenchman, John La Rue, arriving via San Francisco in the 1850s, who shifted the emphasis to meals. He waited on his customers in a scruffy, mud-floor, one-room restaurant with attached kitchen. Harris Newmark, a guest at the Bella Union Hotel in 1853, paid $9 a week for "three more or less hearty meals a day" at La Rue's. French cuisine continued to be the preference of wealthy residents and visitors. The poshest restaurants were in hotels, a trend established by the Pico House in 1870. In 1876 Victor Dol, another Frenchman, opened the Commercial, which satisfied its patrons' appetites for 25 years.

In 1905, when downtown teemed with out-of-town boardinghouse roomers, Helen Mosher opened the first steam-table cafeteria, on Hill Street between 3rd and 4th Streets. Her motto was "All Women Cooks—Food That Can Be Seen—No Tips." By 1922 Los Angeles had 1,152 restaurants, for a population of some 700,000. In the district south of the Plaza and east of Bunker Hill, 35 cafeterias served the downtown crowd, which now included department store shoppers who came from the suburbs by auto or Red Car. Although novelist Raymond Chandler gave the impression that all Los Angeles restaurants featured stained checkered tablecloths, chianti wine, and greasy food, the food connoisseur Duncan Hines stated that there were "twice as many good eating places in Los Angeles as San Francisco."

Many Los Angeles restaurants have reached landmark status because of their longevity, their clientele, or their special dishes. Among them are Philippe the Original, opened in 1908 near the railroad terminal, post office, and Olvera Street; Cole's P.E. Buffet, in operation since 1908 even though the Pacific Electric Railway is long gone; Musso & Frank's Grill, a renowned Hollywood meeting place since 1919 for literary people and screenwriters, including Hemingway, Faulkner, and Thomas Mann; La Golondrina, opened in 1924, a longtime Olvera Street fixture; El Cholo, one of the best-known Mexican restaurants, dating back to 1927; Canter's Delicatessen, a Jewish deli opened in 1931, originally in Boyle Heights, but a Fairfax Avenue fixture since the 1940s; Clifton's Cafeteria, which opened in 1935, in the depths of the Great Depression, and offered free meals to those who could not afford to pay; and Lawry's Prime Rib in Beverly Hills, dating to 1938, which recently moved lock, stock, and barrel to new and improved quarters. Other surviving restaurants are Pacific Dining Car (1921), Original Pantry (1924), and Les Frères Taix (1927). Some old favorites are now nothing but fond memories, including Perino's, Scandia, Vickman's Cafeteria, Levy's Cafeteria, House of Murphy, Tom Bergen's, Dinty Moore's, and the singular Brown Derby. Chasen's, one of the most famous of the old venerables to close, operated from 1936 to 1995. Encouraged by his friend Harold Ross, editor of the *New Yorker,* actor Dave Chasen opened his restaurant in a corn field at Beverly Boulevard and Doheny Drive; it was soon a favorite and famous haunt for Hollywood stars.

A few eateries—the hot dog–shaped Tail o' the Pup (1938) and the hat-shaped Brown Derby (1926)—were probably more famous for their architecture than for their food.

Individual Los Angeles chefs and restaurants have made notable culinary contributions. Caesar

Cardini probably invented the Caesar salad. The hot fudge sundae was the brainchild of Clarence Clifton Brown, a candy maker from Ohio who opened C. C. Brown's ice cream parlor in 1906. He originally operated from a covered wagon at 7th and Hill Streets but set up shop in Hollywood in 1928; his parlor remained in the family until it closed in 1996. The founder of Philippe restaurant, opened in 1908, claimed credit for serving the original French dip sandwich, a treat that customers still line up for. A short-order cook, Lionel Sternberger, claims to have produced the first cheeseburger sometime in the 1920s in Pasadena. In the 1930s the Brown Derby served up the Shirley Temple cocktail in homage to the world-famous young actress. In more recent years, Wolfgang Puck has joined the ranks of culinary innovation with the designer pizza.

Fast-food restaurants and drive-ins evolved with the automobile culture. Notable fast-food eateries include Harry Snyder's In-N-Out burger stand in Baldwin Park (1948), Mike Phillips Burger King in San Pedro (1970s), Bob's Big Boy in Glendale

[Los Angeles] is in love with its limitless horizontality, as New York may be with its verticality.

—Jean Baudrillard,
French philosopher, 1986

(1936), Carl Kartcher's (Carl's Jr.) burgers in South Los Angeles (1940s), and Denny's in Lakewood (1953). Drive-ins gained particular favor with Los Angeles young people, a love affair that was captured in teen movies of the 1960s and 1970s, in particular *American Graffiti* (1973).

In the past several decades Los Angeles restaurants and chefs have become recognized as the equal of any other city's. In addition, Los Angeles has perhaps the most ethnically diverse restaurants in the world. Mexican, Italian, Jewish, French, "Soul," Thai, Chinese, Indian, Greek, Iranian, and Japanese foods are as familiar and available as hamburgers. As of 1992, Los Angeles listed some 12,000 restaurants.

A historic change occurred when, in 1993, the Los Angeles City Council banned smoking in restaurants, the largest city in the nation to enact such legislation. City council member Marvin

Braude, a former two-pack-a-day smoker, was a major force in getting the law passed. In Los Angeles County each municipality enacts its own smoking regulations. Most cities have smoking and nonsmoking sections in an attempt to satisfy all customers. The restaurant and tobacco lobbies continue to fight the smoking ban in Sacramento.

RICHFIELD BUILDING, downtown architectural landmark. The black-and-gold–sheathed building, designed by Morgan, Walls, and Clements (1928–1929), was considered the greatest example of the Art Deco style in Los Angeles. Sadly, it was demolished in 1968.

RICHTER, CHARLES F. (1900–1985), Ohio-born physicist and seismologist. He received his B.A. from Stanford University and, in 1928, his Ph.D. from Caltech. He taught at the latter institution from 1937 to 1970. In the early 1930s Richter, together with fellow professor Beno Gutenberg, developed a system for measuring the magnitude of earthquakes. His work provides an important basis for more modern studies of seismic energy. His measurement was expressed in whole numbers and decimals, each number representing a ten-fold increase in magnitude.

RIDE, SALLY KRISTEN (1951–), astronaut. In 1968 she graduated from Westlake School for Girls (now Harvard-Westlake School) in Los Angeles. A trained scientist, Ride became, on 18 May 1982, the first American woman to travel in space. Afterward she continued to work for NASA.

RIDGE ROUTE, main highway crossing the Tehachapi Mountains north of Newhall. The current road, Interstate 5, is a fast, smooth, safe highway. In its first incarnation—the Old Ridge Route, constructed in 1914—it was a tortuous 48-mile dirt road. The route was relocated in 1933, renamed Highway 99, and its numerous hairpin turns straightened out. The late 1940s brought another face-lift, to accommodate large trailer trucks, and in 1966–1967 further changes were made to accommodate high-speed motorists. Drivers may still view parts of the Old Ridge Route off of Elizabeth Lake Road.

RIDLEY-THOMAS, MARK (1954–), Los Angeles City Council member, representing the 8th District. The executive director of the Southern

Christian Leadership Conference from 1981 to 1991, he holds a doctorate in social ethics from USC. Elected to the council in June 1991, he was instrumental in introducing police reforms following release of the 1991 Christopher Commission report.

RINDGE, FREDERICK HASTINGS (1857–1905), landowner. The scion of a wealthy Massachusetts family, Rindge visited Southern California several times hoping to improve his health. On a third trip, in 1887, he and his wife, May K. Rindge, settled permanently in the region, purchasing a home in Los Angeles and building another on Ocean Avenue in Santa Monica. A shrewd entrepreneur, Rindge served as a corporate director in various enterprises. He also acquired, in 1891, the 13,316-acre Rancho Topanga Malibu Sequit and continued to buy up additional land until he owned 24 coterminous miles of coastal property. The Rindges took up residence in a palatial Malibu Canyon home and devoted themselves to ranching. With a felicitous pen the Harvard-educated Rindge wrote an illuminating memoir of life on the vast and beautiful estate, *Happy Days in Southern California* (1898).

RINDGE, MAY K. (1866–1941), "Queen of the Malibu." Upon the death of her husband, Frederick Hastings Rindge, in 1905, May decided to keep the estate—arguably one of the most beautiful in the country—intact and resist, by force if necessary, all attempts by outsiders to intrude on her property. She stayed true to her word, fighting off all would-be invaders: homesteaders who, using the estate's private roads, helped themselves to her cattle; the Southern Pacific Railroad, which sought to build a coastal route; and the state of California, which, claiming the right of eminent domain, sought to build Pacific Coast Highway. She erected fences, built a private railroad, maintained her own roads, patrolled the property with an armed escort, and accompanied her lawyers to court. In 1925 a state court ruled in favor of the state highway, and financial problems in the next decade forced her to sell the entire estate in 1940. She died the following year in poverty at her West Adams home, a symbol of a passing California lifestyle.

RIO HONDO, river formed in the flood of 1861–1862, when much of Los Angeles County lay under water. During this deluge the San Gabriel River overflowed its banks, creating a new channel west of El Monte that joined the Los Angeles River a few miles to the south—Rio Hondo. Today it originates in the Norwood Village area of El Monte and flows into the Los Angeles River near Imperial Highway, at the boundary of the towns of South Gate and Lynwood. Next to it, the county created the Rio Hondo Spreading Grounds, where rainwater can percolate into an underground aquifer rather than flowing into the ocean.

RIORDAN, RICHARD J. (1930–), New York–born lawyer and entrepreneur elected mayor of Los Angeles in 1993. He studied with Jesuits at Santa Clara University, received a B.A. in philosophy from Princeton, and earned his law degree from the University of Michigan, ranking first in his class. He built his fortune in the 1970s and 1980s by reorganizing Mattel Corporation and other businesses. A philanthropist devoted to improving public education, Riordan donated millions to introduce computers into the classrooms of Los Angeles schools. He is also a cofounder of the innovative educational programs KIDS, FIRST! and LEARN.

Riordan had virtually no name recognition at the beginning of the mayoral campaign, so he del-

Mayor Richard J. Riordan. Courtesy Office of the Mayor.

uged voters with mailings, financed largely with his own money, and introduced himself door-to-door. Running on the slogan "Tough Enough to Turn L.A. Around," he defeated his opponent, Michael Woo, by an unexpectedly large margin. The problems facing the new mayor included a shrunken budget, an insufficient police force, racial and ethnic Balkanization, and loss of an industrial job base. Riordan was the first Republican and the first Catholic elected mayor in recent times.

RIOT OF 1992, worst American civil disturbance in decades. It began at 6:15 P.M. on 29 April at Florence and Normandie Avenues, after four Los Angeles police officers, on trial for the 3 March 1991 beating of African American Rodney G. King, were acquitted. The battering of King, who had been stopped for speeding, was captured on videotape

---

The times prior to July 1846 . . . halcyon days they were. We shall not see their likes again.

—Thomas Larkin, merchant

---

and broadcast around the world. After hearing the announcement of the acquittal, an angry crowd congregated at the South Central intersection. Police massed in the area, but were ordered to retreat. A camera captured the scene as white truck driver Reginald Denny was dragged from his cab and beaten by young black men as he lay on the ground. He was rescued by a woman and three men, also African Americans, who had been watching television and seen the driver being brutalized. They rushed out to save him, risking their own safety.

Unlike the Watts riot of 1965, the burning and looting that began in South Central Los Angeles spread quickly to other communities, nor were these acts restricted to a single ethnic or racial group. Long Beach, Hollywood, portions of West Los Angeles, and Koreatown were among the areas affected. Korean merchants suffered very heavy losses, an indication of the tensions and tragic cultural misunderstandings that had developed between Korean immigrants and African Americans.

The burning and looting lasted until 5 May, taking an extraordinary toll. When evangelist Wallace Tope Jr., who had been beaten during the riot, died

in a coma in December 1993, he became the last of the 55 people to die in the disturbance. There were over 2,300 injuries, and more than 1,100 buildings damaged, at an estimated cost of $785 million. Rioters caused 623 fires, which overwhelmed the 3,500 fire fighters deployed. A dusk-to-dawn curfew was imposed on the city. Only after the arrival of 9,800 National Guardsmen, 3,300 federal troops, and hundreds more from the FBI and border patrol did the rampage subside, allowing fires to be extinguished. A Rand Corporation analysis reported that, of the approximately 10,000 people arrested, most of them young men, 51 percent were Latino and 36 percent black. Because the looters seen on television were of all ages, races, and both sexes, critics charged that the distribution of arrests proved the police department's inherent racism.

Most analysts traced the explosion of violence to high unemployment, failed education, racism and alienation in the culture generally, strained police-community relations, poor police preparation, and decades of neglect and physical deterioration in the South Central portion of the city. The Bush White House blamed the institutionalized social programs of the 1960s and 1970s, such as welfare. Afterward, enraged rioters, speaking through the media, claimed that it had taken the days of rampage to finally call attention to their needs. Some of these people were members of African American street gangs, an element not present during the Watts riot.

Rodney King, appearing briefly before television cameras, pleaded for calm and healing. Shaking and near tears, he urged, "People, I just want to say, you know, can we all get along . . . ?" Police Chief Daryl F. Gates was criticized for indecision in responding to the crisis and for demonstrating insensitivity to minority communities, a charge he vehemently rejected. A commission was established, headed by the FBI's William Webster, to examine the issue. Mayor Tom Bradley appointed popular businessman Peter Ueberroth to organize and lead Rebuild L.A., to restore and improve the damaged areas with money pledged by both government and private resources. When the organization began to founder owing to broken pledges and internal differences, Ueberroth resigned.

The event struck a critical blow to Los Angeles's reputation as a multiethnic mecca. By the same token, a spontaneous but massive cleanup effort began within hours after the violence had been quelled, with Angelenos arriving, mops in hand, from all parts of the city. One of the unofficial headquarters for planning, prayer, and reconciliation was Rev. Cecil "Chip" Murray's First African Methodist Episcopal church.

RIPSTON, RAMONA (1927–), executive director of the American Civil Liberties Union of Southern California. Ripston was educated at Hunter College in New York, and the University of West Los Angeles School of Law. In 1986 she was a vice president of People for the American Way, and assumed her present post in 1987.

RITCHIE, WARD (1905–), influential book designer and publisher. Ritchie was born in Pasadena and attended Occidental College, where he became interested in the art of fine printing. In 1932 the two men founded Ward Ritchie Press, which became known for its well-designed books and limited editions. Ritchie was an early member of the Zamorano Club, a society of book lovers, and his home was a gathering place for writers and artists. In addition to his own publishing activities, he designed books for Anderson, Ritchie, and Simon, a letterpress printing establishment, and for Silver Lake Press, a lithography firm.

RKO RADIO PICTURES, INC., one of the "Big Five" movie studios of Hollywood's Golden Era. In 1928 the Rockefeller-owned Radio Corporation of America (RCA) bought both the Film Booking Office and Radio-Keith-Orpheum studios, merging them into RKO, which produced its own films and distributed those of other companies.

In 1932, during the difficult days of the Great Depression, RKO verged on bankruptcy. Production head David O. Selznick and respected director George Cukor left to join the more stable MGM. Nevertheless the studio opened the glittery Radio City Music Hall in New York City. The expense of maintaining a permanent orchestra, a line of dancers (the Rockettes), and star-studded live shows (some of them staged by the yet unknown Vincente Minnelli) further eroded the studio's financial standing.

The studio's position improved when Broadway dancer Fred Astaire was put under contract; together with his partner, Ginger Rogers, he created some of the most popular films of the period. RKO also hired such radio names as Norman Corwin and Orson Welles, along with established directors John Ford and Howard Hawks. During the studio's most successful period it released the works of such independent filmmakers as Samuel Goldwyn, David Selznick, and Walt Disney. Cary Grant and Katharine Hepburn were RKO stars, and some of the studio's best-known films were *Cimarron* (1931), *King Kong* (1933), *The Informer* (1935), *Bringing Up Baby* (1938), and *Citizen Kane* (1941).

In those days the RKO studio comprised several units: 14 acres on Gower Street in Hollywood,

---

A lot of our problems come from the fact that there are just so many of us. The population pressure forces us to create these gigantic, monumental constructions that grow beyond human scale.

—Eric Lloyd Wright, architect

---

with 15 sound stages and 40 buildings; a 20-acre lot in Culver City, also with 40 buildings and 11 sound stages; a 110-acre ranch in the San Fernando Valley; and a 40-acre tract for outdoor sets.

By 1948 RKO had suffered several bad years, owing mainly to the rise of television, and owner Fred Oldum sold the studio to Howard Hughes. One story is that Hughes came to RKO only once, inspected the premises, said "Paint it!" and left. Others claim he never visited the lot at all. In any event, he never moved his offices from there. In 1955 Hughes sold out to General Tele-Radio, an entertainment arm of the General Tire and Rubber Company. At the same time, he sold RKO's 740 feature films and 1,100 short subjects to the C & C Super Corporation, ceding them all television rights as well. With this transaction the RKO studio had, for all intents and purposes, ceased to exist.

RLA, private-sector committee established by Mayor Tom Bradley to address the rebuilding of Los Angeles communities damaged in the 1992 riots. Originally called Rebuild L.A., it was led by Peter Ueberroth, hero of the 1984 Los Angeles Olympics, who coordinated four ethnically diverse co-chairs and 63 directors. Their task was to forge a cooperative effort by government, private industry, and community organizations. A private management consultant, McKinsey & Co., estimated that $4–$6 billion in investments would be needed to bring inner-city employment up to overall county levels. Affirming that job creation and job training were the top priorities, and realizing that major federal support would not be forthcoming, RLA set out to secure blue-chip corporate investments. Newly elected mayor Richard Riordan streamlined the leadership and affirmed his support. The group set to work, creating some new jobs and receiving millions in private commitments for urban investment. Nevertheless, one year after its establishment some of the influential directors had departed, banks had made few loans, corporate funding remained meager, federal funding was equally scarce, and only 69 percent of the riot-damaged buildings had been rebuilt. Peter Ueberroth resigned his leadership position in 1993, although he remained on the board. Lodwrick M. Cook, chairman and CEO of ARCO, agreed to take over the helm on the condition that Linda Griego, owner of an upscale downtown restaurant and a former deputy in the Bradley administration, be made CEO.

ROACH, HAL (1892–1992), movie director and studio owner. Roach came to Los Angeles in 1913 from Elmira, New York, and with several hundred dollars established a studio at Washington and National Boulevards in Culver City. He paired Stan Laurel with Oliver Hardy, launched the career of Harold Lloyd, created the *Our Gang* comedy troupe, and made as many as 50 feature comedies a year for over 20 years, among them such classics as *Topper* (1937) and *Turnabout* (1940). During World War II the studio housed the U.S. military office responsible for producing training and propaganda films. Ronald Reagan spent the war at "Fort Roach." The studio was torn down in the 1960s, making way for a car dealership. A plaque in a small park nearby marks the site of the former "Laugh Factory to the World."

ROBERTSON, WILLIAM R. (1916–), labor leader. Born and raised in St. Paul, Minnesota, he joined the hotel employees and restaurant workers in that city, became a union official in Illinois and Idaho, and in 1957 took a union leadership position in the San Fernando Valley. He joined the staff of the Los Angeles County AFL-CIO in 1967, and served as its executive secretary-treasurer from 1975 to 1993, simultaneously serving as an officer of the state AFL-CIO. He played key roles on the Los Angeles Memorial Coliseum Commission, City Recreation and Parks Commission, and on the governing body of United Way–AID.

ROBINSON, ALFRED (1807?–1895), Massachusetts native who settled in Santa Barbara during the Mexican era. He published *Life in California* (1846), a book that helped develop American interest in California. Although it describes Los Angeles only in passing, the volume includes a notable appendix by Fra Gerónimo Boscana describing the religious beliefs of the Gabrieleños and other Indians of Southern California.

ROBINSON, JACKIE (1919–1972), first African American to play major league baseball. Robinson was born in Georgia but reared in Pasadena and attended UCLA, where he excelled in football, basketball, track, and baseball. In 1940 he became the U.S. NCAA long jump champion. He played pro football briefly, but made sports his-

Jackie Robinson, UCLA long-jump champion, 1940. ASUCLA Photography.

tory when he signed with the Brooklyn Dodgers in 1945, breaking a rigid color bar that had existed since the beginning of professional baseball. Robinson was named baseball's Most Valuable Player in 1949.

ROBINSON, JESSE (1912–1993), Compton civil rights leader. Born in Hattiesburg, Mississippi, Robinson came to Southern California when his mother took a domestic job in Beverly Hills. He attended Manual Arts High School, Compton College, UCLA, and worked for 32 years as a postal worker. Robinson chaired the Greater Los Angeles Urban Coalition from 1970 to 1976, and in 1974 headed a county grand jury investigation in Compton.

ROBINSON, W[ILLIAM] W[ILCOX] (1891–1972), historian and writer. Born in Trinidad, Colorado, Robinson moved to Riverside in 1899. He attended USC and UC Berkeley, and served in the military in World War I. He moved permanently to Los Angeles in 1919. While working as a professional property title researcher for the Title Insurance and Trust Company, he developed an extensive knowledge of local history and land development. Possessing a felicitous way with words, he produced readable pamphlets and books on history, including *Ranchos Become Cities* (1939), *Land in California* (1948), *Lawyers of Los Angeles: A History of the Los Angeles Bar Association and of the Bar of Los Angeles County* (1959), *What They Say About the Angels* (1942), *Los Angeles, A Profile* (1968), and *Bombs and Bribery* (1969), a personal recollection of the bombing of the *Los Angeles Times* and McNamara trial. Robinson also wrote poetry, fiction, children's books, and essays.

ROCK, POP, AND RAP MUSIC. Los Angeles entered the rock-and-roll scene in the early 1960s with a group of teenage boys from Hawthorne calling themselves the Beach Boys. They sang about surfing, hot rods, and young love. Spearheaded by Brian Wilson's songs, such as "California Girls," their album *Pet Sounds* influenced, among others, the Beatles. In the mid to late 1960s the folk-rock of the Buffalo Springfield, the Byrds, and the Flying Burrito Brothers coexisted with the diverse musical styles of such groups as the Doors, Frank Zappa's Mothers of Invention, Captain Beefheart, and Arthur Lee and Love. Also performing locally were singer-songwriters Randy Newman, Harry

Rock legend Jim Morrison, lead singer of the Doors, whose hits included "L.A. Woman" (1971).

Nilsson, Van Dyke Parks, and the Canadian-born Joni Mitchell, who frequently sang about her adopted hometown of Los Angeles, the "city of the fallen angels." Her intimate jazz-oriented compositions and sensitive lyrics influenced many subsequent performers. West Hollywood clubs—notably the Roxy, the Whisky-A-Go-Go, and Doug Weston—became increasingly popular venues for performers.

The 1970s produced the softer "El Lay" sound, though again, many styles were in evidence, such as the New Orleans–classic pop blend of Lowell George's band, Little Feat. The "Malibu Mafia"—Fleetwood Mac, Linda Ronstadt, Jackson Browne, the Eagles, Warren Zevon, and others—became staple listening on FM radio. During the latter part of the decade Tom Petty and the Heartbreakers, who began as punk/new wave, and hard rock innovators such as Van Halen became superstar groups, in the latter case thanks to the virtuosity of the lead guitarist, Eddie Van Halen. The quartet the Knack topped the charts with their single "My Sharona," and the East Los Angeles group Los Lobos mixed rock, blues, and Latin folk to become an act with staying power.

Los Angeles was home to a thriving punk rock scene during the late 1970s and early 1980s. Achieving quick fame were acts like X, the Minutemen, and hardcore bands such as Black Flag, the Circle

Jerks, and Fear. During the late 1980s Sunset Strip clubs catered to "hair bands"—groups wearing leather, lace, makeup, and hairspray. Led by Motley Crue and a bevy of others, they gave testimony to the growing dominance of rock video. These bands gave way to "grunge" and "new punk" bands.

The hip-hop style emerged in Los Angeles with the advent of "gangsta" rap artists such as Ice-T, N.W.A., Ice Cube, and Dr. Dre. As a producer, Dre created a Los Angeles sound with recordings that featured the lyrics of his fellow hardcore rapper, Tupac Shakur.

RODEO DRIVE, Beverly Hills' premier commercial street. In 1990 rentals averaged $275 per square foot, placing it among the 10 highest rental streets in the world, along with the Ginza in Tokyo and Fifth Avenue in New York City. Although the architecture is undistinguished, Rodeo Drive is celebrated for its exclusive shops featuring high-fashion clothing, jewelry, art, and home furnishings. Among the notable retailers on the drive are Gucci, Armani, Cartier, Ralph Lauren, and Celine.

RODIA, SIMON (SABBATINO). *See* Watts Towers

RODRÍGUEZ, PABLO (B. 1756), AND MARÍA ROSALÍA RODRÍGUEZ (B. 1755), along with their infant daughter, were an Indian family from Mexico. They were among the original 44 founders of the Los Angeles *pueblo* in 1781.

ROGERS, EARL ANDRUS (1870–1922), celebrated criminal attorney. Born in New York, Rogers began practicing law in 1890 with Stephen M. White, archfoe of the Southern Pacific Railroad. Subsequently Rogers handled many cases originating in the brothels, gambling houses, and saloons of Los Angeles. The publisher of the *Los Angeles Evening Express,* E. T. Earl, hired him in 1909 to secretly investigate corruption in Mayor Arthur Harper's regime. The evidence he uncovered helped topple Harper. Clarence Darrow, considered by many to be the greatest trial lawyer of his day, reserved that accolade for Rogers, his adversary in the investigation of the *Los Angeles Times* bombing. When Darrow was accused of bribing a juror in the McNamara case, Rogers defended him in court, ultimately winning the case. Rogers also defended Griffith J. Griffith when he was charged with attempting to murder his wife. Writer Adela Rogers St. John, Los Angeles's first police reporter, was his daughter.

ROGERS, WILL (1875–1935), Oklahoma-born cowboy, humorist, and movie star who settled in Southern California in 1919. Among his films were *Connecticut Yankee* (1931), *State Fair* (1933), and *David Harum* (1934). He also wrote a newspaper column and had a radio show on which he delivered his sharp social commentaries in a fine western drawl. He lived at first in Beverly Hills, but in 1928, at the height of his career, bought a ranch in Pacific Palisades, where he built a large, comfortable, rambling house. Rogers died in a plane crash in Alaska in 1935, along with pilot Wiley Post. Rogers's wife lived in their home until her death in 1944, at which time the family donated the ranch to the state. It is preserved at Will Rogers State Historic Park. A state beach in Santa Monica is also named after him.

Rodeo Drive and Wilshire Boulevard. Photo by Lori Shepler.

ROLLING HILLS, 3.1-square-mile independent community of semirural estates on Palos Verdes Peninsula, 23 miles southwest of downtown Los Angeles. It is not to be confused with Rolling Hills Estates. Developed by Frank Vanderlip, and incorporated in 1957, it is distinguished by a white rail fence 8 miles long, private streets, and four guarded gates. Its population was 1,950 in 1990, down 8.7 percent since the previous census.

ROLLING HILLS ESTATES, independent community on Palos Verdes Peninsula, 23 miles southwest of downtown Los Angeles. It was developed by A. E. Hanson in 1934 on the former Rancho El Elástico. He had planned to call it "Folded Hills" but changed his mind after the Long Beach earthquake. The developers made an unusual design choice, combining the western ranch motif with the American Colonial and California board-and-batten architectural styles. The semirural community, which was incorporated in 1957, has become a haven for wealthy Southern Californians. The population has hovered around 7,700 for several decades.

ROMAN CATHOLIC CHURCH became established in Southern California in the late 18th century. In 1769 Fr. Juan Crespi, a Franciscan attached to the exploring party led by Captain Portolá, conducted the first mass in the area. During that "Sacred Expedition" he wrote a favorable diary account that led to the founding of Missions San Gabriel in 1771 and San Fernando in 1797. When the *pueblo* was established in 1781, all the original settlers were Catholic. Fr. Junípero Serra, father-president of the Franciscan missions, opposed the settlement, complaining that the civilians might endanger the Indians and missionaries at San Gabriel. He first visited the *pueblo* a year after its founding. The first permanent Catholic church, apart from the missions, was the old Plaza Church; it took four years to build and was dedicated in 1822. In 1837 the *pueblo* council declared that "the Roman Catholic apostolic religion shall prevail throughout this jurisdiction." The first Catholic school was founded in 1851, with 26 students.

Most Angelenos were Catholic in the early 1850s, and Catholics remained dominant until the 1880s, when Protestant dominance grew. The Los Angeles archdiocese that today embraces parts of three counties emerged through a series of geographic and administrative alterations by the Church. A diocese established in 1840 included both Californias, and in 1849 was formally named the diocese of Monterey (later, Monterey–Los Angeles). Ten years later, Bishop Thaddeus Amat removed its seat to Los Angeles. In 1922 the diocese of Los Angeles–San Diego was created, and in 1936 the province

---

Up to the year 1853 I was in good circumstances. Although I did not have money, I had plenty of land and other things of value.

—José del Carmen Lugo, ranchero, 1877

---

of Los Angeles was established within it, renamed the archdiocese of Los Angeles in 1948. In 1976 Pope Paul VI created the new diocese of Orange County and placed Los Angeles, Ventura, and Santa Barbara Counties in another diocese. The importance of Southern California in Catholic affairs is attested to by the fact that in 1953 the archbishop of Los Angeles became the first cardinal in the western United States.

In 1986 there were 284 Catholic parishes in Los Angeles, with 2.6 million members, 1,401 priests, 141 brothers, 2,543 nuns, and 141 deacons. The Church supported 16 hospitals, 1 orphanage, 11 health care centers, 6 day care centers, 5 colleges and universities, 21 seminaries, 55 high schools, and 233 elementary schools.

Before Roger M. Mahony became archbishop of Los Angeles in 1985, the diocese had four archbishops, three of whom became cardinals: John J. Cantwell (1936–1947), James F. McIntyre (1948–1970), and Timothy Manning (1970–1985).

ROSAS FAMILY, one (or actually two) of the founding families of the *pueblo* of Los Angeles in 1781. Basilio Rosas, a 62-year-old Indian, was married to Manuela Hernández Rosas, a 37-year-old *mulata.* They came from the Mexican mining town of Rosario with seven children. One of those children, Alejandro, had married an Indian woman in Sinaloa, which made them a founding family in their own right. Two other of the seven children married Indian women from Los Angeles, and one joined the army at San Diego. Basilio Rosas, the eldest of the founding *pobladores,* died when he was about 90, in 1809. His wife died in 1823 at the age of 80.

ROSCOMARE CANYON, picturesque canyon in the Bel-Air Estates area of the Santa Monica Mountains. Its road connects Sunset Boulevard and Mulholland Drive.

ROSE, H[ENRY] R., police judge and mayor of Los Angeles from 1913 to 1915, when the population was over 300,000 and the area 90 square miles. In the 1913 election the *Los Angeles Times* opposed Rose, while the Socialists and Progressives backed him. The sides were determined by Rose's support of a plan that would distribute surplus Owens River water in a manner favoring individual landowners and penalizing speculators.

ROSE BOWL, Pasadena stadium. Since 1922 it has been associated with the annual New Year's Day college football classic that pits the leading team of the Pacific Coast Conference against that of the Big Ten Conference. Before that year play was at Tournament Park on the Caltech campus, and was called the East-West Game.

As designed by architect Myron Hunt, the original stadium was horseshoe shaped and required 28 miles of lumber for the 57,000-seat viewing stands. After being remodeled numerous times, the Rose Bowl was finally upgraded to accommodate over 106,000 fans. The Tournament of Roses Association, which built and paid for the arena, donated it to the city of Pasadena.

A KFI broadcast of the Rose Bowl game of 1 January 1927 was the first coast-to-coast radio transmission. In the 1940s and 1950s the venue was used for auto racing, and more recently, for swap meets. The stadium is now the home field for UCLA foot-ball. It has also been the site of five professional-football Super Bowl games; the 1993 game was watched by more than 253 million. The stadium hosted the final game of the 1994 World Cup Soccer Championship, reputedly the largest single sporting event in the world. In 1996 the Rose Bowl was home to professional soccer when the Los Angeles Galaxy drew 109,602 fans to its first two games.

ROSECRANS, district near Compton. It was named after the Union army general, William S. Rosecrans, who settled in the area after the Civil War. He served as a Southern California congressman from 1880 to 1884.

ROSEDALE CEMETERY, burial ground on W. Washington Boulevard established in 1884. The general locale, then a suburb of Los Angeles, is now in the Mid-City area. The facility featured the first crematorium in the West and became the resting place for many pioneer families. It has outstanding examples of funerary architecture. In a time when even cemeteries drew the color line, some nonwhite celebrities managed to be buried there, including Oscar-winning actress Hattie McDaniel, jazz pianist Art Tatum, and actress Anna May Wong. Baseball immortal Frank Chance, of the famous Chicago Cubs triple-play combination "Tinker to Evers to Chance," is buried there as well. Across the street is Chapel of the Pines, where movie notables Ann Sheridan, Raymond Massey, and Walter Huston are interred.

ROSEMEAD, independent community in the San Gabriel Valley 11 miles east of downtown Los An-

Rose Bowl game, USC vs. Ohio State. Courtesy Pasadena Convention & Visitors Bureau.

geles, incorporated in 1959. The name means "Rose's meadows" and honors an early Yankee couple, Leonard J. and Amanda Rose, who established a horse farm called Sunnyslope Estate. J. W. Robinson, the department store head, had a large ranch and summer home in Rosemead. Rosemead is 5.5 square miles in area, and its ethnically diverse population totaled 52,000 in 1994.

ROSE PARADE. *See* Pasadena; Tournament of Roses

ROUNCE AND COFFIN CLUB, association of book designers and printers devoted to exhibiting and honoring fine books published in the West. It was founded as a social club in 1931 by Ward Ritchie, Jake Zeitlin, Saul Marks, Gregg Anderson, and Grant Dahlstrom. They were later joined by Merle Armitage, Richard Hoffman, William Cheney, and Joseph Simon.

ROWAN, THOMAS E[DWARD] (1842–1901), mayor of Los Angeles from 1892 to 1894, though in private life he was a real estate agent. During the period he held office the city's area exceeded 30 square miles and its population was more than 50,000.

ROWLAND, JOHN ALBERT (1791–1873?), Missouri-born pioneer. He came to Los Angeles in November 1841 as part of the 25-member Rowland-Workman party. Having lived in New Mexico and married a New Mexican woman, he had become a Mexican citizen, and so was entitled to own land in California. He and his friend William Workman were formally granted the large estate of Rancho La Puente in 1845. They shared unfenced pasture lands and lived in adobes less than a mile apart. The property was later divided. Rowland built a two-story brick structure in 1855 that remains on Gale Avenue in City of Industry.

ROWLAND HEIGHTS, county area near La Puente, named for Yankee pioneer John Rowland. In 1990 it had 42,647 inhabitants.

ROYBAL, EDWARD R. (1916–), New Mexico–born dean of Latino public officials in Los Angeles. Roybal came to the Far West with his family in 1922, and graduated from Roosevelt High School and UCLA before becoming a social worker and community organizer. Although he failed in

Edward Roybal. Courtesy Edward Roybal Institute for Applied Gerontology.

his first city council bid in 1947, the campaign sparked the formation of the Community Service Organization as a base for improving political representation of Mexican Americans. Roybal succeeded in his 1949 run for office, the first Mexican American since 1881 to become a member of the city council. In 1962 he topped that, becoming the first Mexican American elected to the U.S. Congress. As a member of Congress he chaired the House subcommittees on treasury and postal service, and on aging. Representative Roybal opposed the 1986 amnesty law for illegal immigrants, but he actively appropriated funds for expanded medical, welfare, and educational services for immigrants. He retired from politics in 1992.

RTD. *See* Rapid transit

RUBIO CANYON, gorge rising into the San Gabriel Mountains from Altadena. It is named after Jesús Rubio, a native Californian who became an American citizen after the Mexican War and settled in the canyon in 1867.

RUSCHA, EDWARD (1937–), Nebraska-born Pop artist who was part of the rebellious Ferus Gallery group in the 1960s. He has since gained national recognition. Educated at Chouinard Art Institute (now Cal Arts), he is noted for colorful silkscreens that "mirror the dreamlike state" many people find typical of California. Many of his works portray gas stations, parking lots, and street panoramas. *Every Building on the Sunset Strip* (1966) presents an unglamorous tableau of the famous street.

RUSSIANS have arrived in Los Angeles in a distinct series of immigrations. First came the 7,000 or so members of the poor and struggling pacifist sect called Molokans, or "Holy Jumpers." They clustered early in the 20th century on Vignes Avenue and then moved to the east bank of the Los Angeles River, or the "Flats" area of Boyle Heights. The Molokans had fled military conscription in the Russo-Japanese War of 1905, and the majority worked in the lumber trade and shipbuilding. A second group of Russians appeared around 1920, some via China, as escapees from the Russian revolution and civil war. Among them were representatives of an old-aristocratic cultural elite. They settled in and around Hollywood. A Russian Orthodox church built in 1928 in the Silver Lake district gave proof of their presence. By 1940, 25,000 Russians lived in Los Angeles, largely near Brook-

lyn Avenue in East Los Angeles, from State Street to the city's edge. After World War II thousands of former POWs who were freed from German prison camps by U.S. forces decided not to return to the Soviet Union. The fourth and largest migration was that of Russian Jews; arriving beginning in the 1970s, they settled mainly in the Fairfax, West Hollywood, Sherman Oaks, and Studio City areas. In 1991 *Panorama,* a Russian-language weekly founded in 1978, had a readership of 30,000.

RUSTIC CANYON, wooded section of Santa Monica Canyon, south of Sunset and east of Chautauqua Boulevard. In 1887 the state of California established a pioneering experimental forestry station in that natural thicket; University of California specialists conducted research on the growth of the eucalyptus and other trees. In the 1920s the state withdrew, selling the property to the Uplifters Club, a group of wealthy businessmen and writers, who built a clubhouse as a retreat for members. An art colony subsequently formed amid the mixed groves of redwood, oak, and eucalyptus. Today the area is preserved as a beautiful 8-acre city park surrounded by a quiet, affluent neighborhood.

S

SACRED EXPEDITION. *See* Portolá, Gaspar de

ST. FRANCIS DAM DISASTER, collapse of a Los Angeles Aqueduct storage dam in San Francisquito Valley, near Saugus, on the night of 12 March 1928. The disaster is considered by some to be "the greatest American civil engineering failure of the 20th century." The 180-foot-high, 600-foot-long concrete structure, owned by the Bureau of Water Works (later the Department of Water and Power [DWP]), stood on what proved to be unstable soil and crumbled on its first complete filling. The collapse unleashed a tidal wave into the Santa Clara River valley that drowned more than 400 people and destroyed some 1,200 homes before emptying into the ocean near Ventura. It destroyed the reputation of 80-year-old William Mulholland, the dam's designer and the bureau's chief engineer. "I envy the dead," he declared tearfully at the coroner's inquest, while assuming full personal responsibility. The city's out-of-court reparations totaled $15 million. As a result of the tragic error, the state created the first public laws regarding the design, testing, and inspection of dams and the state's handling of wrongful-death suits. Recent studies suggest that geologic conditions unknown to Mulholland, including the permeability of the underlying soil, contributed to the failure. Some rubble from the disaster may be seen by taking San Francisquito Canyon Road past County Detention Camp No. 17, from I-5.

ST. JOHN'S HOSPITAL AND HEALTH CENTER, Santa Monica medical facility opened in October 1942 by the Sisters of Charity, a Catholic order that originated in Leavenworth, Kansas, in 1858. The hospital grew from 89 beds and 40 bassinets into a 521-bed medical center, with

Rubble, St. Francis Dam, March 1928. Courtesy Robert Weinstein Collection.

1,000 physicians in 88 medical specialties and an additional staff of 2,000. The building suffered severe structural damage in the 1994 earthquake, but all patients were removed safely, and rebuilding began immediately.

ST. VIBIANA'S CATHEDRAL. *See* Cathedral of St. Vibiana

SALAZAR, RUBEN (1928–1970), journalist. Born in Juárez, Chihuahua, he moved to Texas as a child, and later to Los Angeles. As a reporter Salazar worked on the *Los Angeles Herald-Express* before breaking into the *Los Angeles Times* with a series of six articles on Mexican Americans. He covered the rebellion in Santo Domingo in 1963 and the Viet-

---

For Asian-Americans, we wear our heritage on our face, and no matter how many generations we're here, people still treat us like foreigners.

—Debra Ching, Chinatown Service Center

---

nam War in 1965. By 1969 his beat was the Los Angeles barrio. When Salazar became news director for KMEX-TV he continued to write an outspoken and controversial weekly column for the *Times*. On 29 August 1970, while Salazar was covering an antiwar rally in East Los Angeles, a gas projectile fired by a sheriff's deputy struck and killed him. Lincoln Park was renamed Salazar Park in his honor.

SALVADORANS took up residence in Los Angeles by the tens of thousands during the 12-year civil war in El Salvador that ended in 1992. Most of the immigrants worked in restaurants, as domestic laborers, or in their own small businesses. As political militants they entered labor unions and challenged immigration laws. By 1990 some 350,000–500,000 Salvadorans resided in the county, with a strong concentration in the Pico-Union district. Thousands fleeing war or natural disasters have applied to remain in the United States under a "temporary protected status" program of the federal government. The passage of California Proposition 187, which threatened the future of illegal immigrants in the state, caused great concern in the community.

SALVATOR, LUDWIG (1847–1915), Austrian archduke who visited Southern California in 1876. He lodged for a while at the Pico House on the Plaza, visiting with local families. *A Flower from the Golden Land* (1929), a favorable memoir of his stay, was the first published work about Los Angeles to gain wide currency in Europe.

SAMOANS are among the 20 or so Asian-Pacific ethnic groups represented in the local population. They gravitated to the fish packing industry on Terminal Island, and to communities in Carson, Long Beach, and Wilmington. More Samoans— approximately 60,000—now live in the Centinela –South Bay area than in American Samoa. Lately, college football coaches have been recruiting Samoan high school graduates. In general, the acceptance of Samoans into the larger society has been relatively free of conflict. Samoans tend to be culturally traditional, with the *matai* (chief) remaining an important arbiter in both community and family affairs.

SAN ANDREAS FAULT, long, dangerous earthquake zone dissecting northern Los Angeles County from northwest to southeast. It ruptured in 1857 with an estimated force of 8.0 on the Richter scale. The results of its powerful geological action over many millennia can be viewed in places such as Tejon Pass along the Golden State Freeway, and the Antelope Valley Freeway near Avenue S. The fault constitutes a major consideration in urban planning from Mendocino County to the Mexican border. Although scientists periodically discuss the probability of another massive rupture within the foreseeable future—one measuring up to 8.3 on the Richter scale—specific predictions remain impossible.

SAN CLEMENTE ISLAND, a 22-mile-long island south of Santa Catalina Island and 17 miles west of Palos Verdes Peninsula. An extension of the Peninsular Mountain Ranges, it rises 599 feet at its highest point. The outcropping was spotted by the explorer Juan Cabrillo in 1542 but was named by the merchant contractor Sebastian Vizcaíno on his voyage of 1602–1603. Sheep were raised there in the 19th century. Los Angeles County owns San Clemente but leases it exclusively to the U.S. Navy as a training center. A wilderness preserve, it protects several endangered species but has no permanent inhabitants.

SAN DIMAS, independent city in the eastern reaches of the county, 29 miles from downtown Los Angeles. Known earlier as Mud Springs and La Cienega ("The Marshland"), it acquired the name San Dimas after the repentant thief crucified with Jesus, perhaps in reference to the bandits who once roamed the area. In 1878 the Teague family began growing lemons in San Dimas, which eventually became home to the largest lemon packaging house in the world. It was a stopping point for early travelers between Los Angeles and San Bernardino, and became a station of the Santa Fe Railroad when a line through the area was completed in 1885. San Dimas's greatest natural features are Puddingstone Reservoir and Frank G. Bonelli Regional County Park. The town features pleasant residential streets with modest, late-19th-century cottages as well as bungalows built somewhat later. The population grew nearly 35 percent in the decade after 1980, reaching 32,300 in 1990.

SAN FERNANDO, independent city in the San Fernando Valley, 20 miles northwest of downtown Los Angeles. The land belonged to Mission San Fernando beginning in the 1790s, and to ranchero Eulogio de Celis in the 1850s. The town was founded by Charles Maclay in 1874. Maclay chartered excursion trains from Los Angeles to bring prospective land buyers to view the townsite and enjoy a free lunch at the former mission. Town lots sold for $10–$25 each, and farm lots were $5–$40 an acre. When the railroad tunnel north of town was completed in 1876, prices soared to $150 an acre. With rails now providing access to markets in San Francisco, wheat raising and flour mills near San Fernando became a major enterprise. In 1880

the Los Angeles Farm and Milling Company produced 500,000 bushels of grain.

Unlike many other municipalities, San Fernando maintained its independence from water-rich Los Angeles, by tapping into its own deep-water wells. The city of San Fernando, incorporated in 1911, became an island completely surrounded by Los Angeles. It was a major center for growing, packing, and shipping olives, citrus fruit, and vegetables. The agricultural activity came to an end after World War II, when suburban homes took over. San Fernando is managed by a city administrator, is the site of a county court house, and is part of the Los Angeles Unified School District. The population increased by 27 percent between 1980 and 1990, reaching 22,500.

SAN FERNANDO REY DE ESPAÑA MISSION, 17th Franciscan mission in the chain of 21 to be founded in Alta California. It was consecrated on 8 September 1797 by Father Fermín Lasuén, successor to Junípero Serra as father-president of the Franciscan missions, and named by him for Ferdinand III, 13th-century king of Castile and León. The mission produced olives, dates, wheat, barley, corn, wine, wool, and leather hides. For years it supplied vast quantities of food to the Los Angeles *pueblo* and to the presidio at Santa Barbara. The neophyte Indian population at San Fernando reached 1,080 in 1819. The mission suffered serious damage in an 1812 earthquake, and further deterioration occurred after mission secularization in the 1830s. The main building was partially restored in 1879, and again in the 1930s. When the 1971 Sylmar earthquake destroyed the mission church, a duplicate was rebuilt on the same site. Despite its

San Fernando Mission. Courtesy Robert Weinstein Collection.

name, the mission is situated in Los Angeles, rather than in the city of San Fernando. The archives of the Los Angeles Catholic archdiocese are located on the grounds.

SAN FERNANDO VALLEY, densely occupied lowlands northwest of downtown Los Angeles, known to locals simply as "the Valley." Except for the cities of Burbank, Hidden Hills, and San Fernando, and the county area of Calabasas, most of it is part of the city of Los Angeles.

A triangle about 24 miles at its base, the valley, when viewed from surrounding mountains—the Simi, San Rafael, and Verdugo Hills, and the Santa Susana, San Gabriel, and Santa Monica Mountains —appears as a sprawling flatland. The first Europeans spotted the area from Sepulveda Pass in

---

The unemployment and relief rolls were in the tradition of the biggest and best; but during those bad years, while things were at half speed, people rediscovered the city.

—Matt Weinstock, columnist, regarding the 1930s

August 1769, when Fr. Juan Crespi, referring to it as "a very pleasant and spacious valley," dubbed it Valle de Santa Catarina de Bononia de los Encinos ("Valley of St. Catherine of Bononia of the Oaks"). In the name of the king of Spain, a mission and two ranchos were established there: Mission San Fernando Rey de España, in 1797; Rancho San Rafael, in 1784; and Rancho Encino, in 1795. The mission, with its hundreds of resident Indians, became noted for its wheat and grapes.

The San Fernando Valley passed into private hands upon the secularization of the mission in the 1830s and the emergence of additional ranchos in the 1840s. Stage lines crossed the valley in the American period. In 1874 the Southern Pacific Railroad (SP) began offering service from Los Angeles to San Fernando. Soon afterward, Isaac Lankershim, his son John B. Lankershim, and his son-in-law I. N. Van Nuys cultivated wheat on a 60,000-acre ranch in the southern portion of the valley.

Real estate developers platted separate commu-

nities such as Zelzah (today's Northridge), Van Nuys, Marian (Reseda), and Owensmouth (Canoga Park) early in the 20th century, particularly after the Pacific Electric Railway entered the area around 1903. Completion of the Los Angeles Aqueduct, bringing Owens River water in 1913, opened the area to numerous truck gardens, vineyards, and citrus and other fruit orchards. It also sparked the annexation of 168 square miles to the city of Los Angeles in 1915, as well as the extinction of many independent smaller towns.

By 1920 about 50,000 acres of valley land were irrigated. Amid the citrus groves there arose airplane factories, movie studios, light industry, commercial strips, and residential tracts. The population doubled between 1930 and 1940, and grew even more explosively following World War II. Had the San Fernando Valley been an independent city in 1970, its population of 1.8 million would have made it the sixth largest city in the nation. Heavily trafficked freeways serve the valley today: the San Diego, Ventura, Golden State, Hollywood, and Simi Valley. The area also remains an SP rail corridor to Los Angeles, from the west and north. From time to time disaffected valley residents have attempted to split from Los Angeles, or create an independent school district.

Pop music helped shape the region's image. "I'm Packin' My Grip," about "making the San Fernando Valley my home," written in 1943 by Gordon Jenkins, was popular during the postwar population surge. Frank and Moon Unit Zappa's tune "Valley Girl," which satirized local "teenspeak," captured the nation's attention with lines like "Barf me out" and "Gag me with a spoon."

SAN FRANCISQUITO CANYON, valley north of Saugus, once part of the former Rancho San Francisco land grant. The name means "little San Francisco." Placer gold was discovered in the canyon by Francisco López in 1842. It is the site of the 1928 St. Francis Dam disaster that claimed hundreds of lives.

SAN GABRIEL 4-square-mile independent city in the San Gabriel Valley. The first settlement was at the Mission San Gabriel, established in its current location in 1776 and secularized in the 1830s and 1840s. The town evolved as an unplanned community in 1842 adjacent to the mission. The families of John Rowland and William Wolfskill, who arrived from New Mexico in 1831, were instrumental in its growth. In the last decade of the 19th century Chinese laborers worked the town's orange groves. Fearing that the town might be swallowed up by Alhambra, residents incorporated San Gabriel in 1913. The residential part of the city north of Las Tunas Boulevard, developed in the 1930s and 1940s, is known as North San Gabriel; it is bordered also by San Marino, Alhambra, and Temple City. North San Gabriel has three grammar schools. Between 1980 and 1990 the population of San Gabriel rose 23 percent, from 30,000 to 37,100.

SAN GABRIEL MISSION, fourth of the 21 Franciscan missions in Alta California, and one of two in Los Angeles County. Known as the "Queen of the Missions," it was founded on an earlier site near the San Gabriel River, now known as Mission Vieja, on 8 September 1771 by Fathers Angel Somera and Pedro Bonito Cambon. Owing to river flooding, the first mission was moved in 1775 to its present location on Mission Drive. The mission's original name was Misión del Santo Arcángel San Gabriel de los Temblores ("Mission of the Holy Archangel St. Gabriel of the Earthquakes"), either

San Gabriel Mission. Photo by Peter Menzel / Stock, Boston, Inc.

because Captain Portolá's expedition had recorded an earthquake there in 1769 or because the mission's original site was on Río de los Temblores (now the Santa Ana River). Architecturally, the mission design was influenced by the cathedral at Córdoba, Spain.

San Gabriel Mission, with an original land grant of 1.5 million acres extending from the mountains to the sea, cultivated extensive vineyards and orchards, and grazed hundreds of cattle and other animals. Neophyte Indians, whose population reached about 1,000 in 1817, supplied the labor power. The mission was secularized by decree in November 1834, although the church building was returned to Church control in 1859. A cemetery containing the remains of 6,000 Tongva (Gabrieleño) Indians testifies to the fact that the Spanish occupiers of California, whatever their intentions, caused devastation to the local Native Americans.

Today's 13-acre mission property was granted by the U.S. government to the Catholic diocese of Los Angeles in 1874. Since 1908 the pastorate has been administered by the Claretian fathers, who restored the church, built a parochial school, and converted the monastery into a museum. The Whittier earthquake of 1987 severely damaged the fragile adobe walls of the main building, forcing temporary closure.

SAN GABRIEL MOUNTAINS, major geographic feature defining the northern perimeter of the Los Angeles Basin. The ancient Indian name was Qui-Qua-mungo. The Spaniards first called the range the Sierra Madre ("Mother Mountain Range"), and then, around 1800, Sierra de San Gabriel. The range was officially called the San Gabriel Mountains in 1927. Major attractions include the Mt. Wilson Observatory, Angeles National Forest, San Gabriel Valley Wilderness Area, Crystal Lake, and 10,080-foot-high Mt. San Antonio ("Old Baldy"). San Gabriel Peak, 6,161 feet in elevation, was so named by a U.S. Army survey team in 1875 because it appeared to dominate the watershed of the west fork of the San Gabriel River. The San Gabriels, among the most rapidly rising mountains in the world, can increase their altitude by two or three feet in a large earthquake.

SAN GABRIEL RIVER, one of four rivers in the Los Angeles Plain, along with the Los Angeles, Santa Ana, and Rio Hondo. It originates in the mountains and empties into the ocean near Naples and Seal Beach in the South Bay. When Captain Portolá's men first encountered the river in July 1769, they declared it "a good channel of water" but were forced to build a bridge over it because it was murky. In 1861–1862 the San Gabriel over-flowed its banks west of El Monte, creating a new channel (Rio Hondo) that linked up with the Los Angeles River. The San Gabriel again flooded its bed in 1914, when 19 inches of rain fell on the San Gabriels during a four-day storm. Long Beach be-came an island. A third major inundation oc-curred in 1938. The river's flow is now regulated by flood control reservoirs, with much of the water (99 percent above Whittier Narrows) saved from being lost to the sea. During storms some water can be diverted onto spreading grounds below Whittier Narrows Dam, where it is allowed to per-colate into the ground through a porous surface, and some is channeled in cement. The stream is also fed by water reclaimed by sewage processing.

SAN GABRIEL VALLEY. The area generally re-ferred to as the San Gabriel Valley is so amorphous and its boundaries so difficult to identify that the U.S. Geological Survey does not recognize it as a separate entity. However, within Southern Cali-fornia the informal description is of a half-moon-shaped valley squeezed between the San Gabriel and Verdugo Mountains, and the San Rafael, Mon-tebello, Puente, and the San Jose Hills. The valley is drained by tributaries of the San Gabriel River.

In Southern California, I found what I had hoped for . . . a good climate for trying something independent of hidebound tradition.

—Richard Neutra, architect

The Tongva (Gabrieleño) Indians occupied the val-ley for millennia. When the Portolá expedition en-tered the area in 1769, it named the valley San Miguel Arcángel, and two years later Mission San Gabriel was established near the San Gabriel River (though it moved in 1775). When the mission was secularized and the mission Indians and property were dispersed, Mexican authorities issued land grants, including Rancho El Rincón de San Pas-cual and Rancho Santa Anita. In the American pe-riod the valley acquired an early reputation as a gar-den spot, and from the 1880s to the 1930s was renowned for its citrus orchards, vineyards, truck farms, and resorts.

More recently the San Gabriel Valley been taken over by suburban homes. The only transconti-nental rail line into Los Angeles crosses its entire length. The valley includes a large portion of the city of Los Angeles, but also is the site of other cities, including San Gabriel, Covina, Pasadena, San Marino, and Alhambra.

SANITARY LANDFILL. *See* Waste disposal

SAN MARINO, 3.75-square-mile independent city in the San Gabriel Valley, 8.5 miles northeast of downtown Los Angeles. It is on land once part of Mission San Gabriel and, later, Rancho San Pas-cual. The first private home built there, in 1878, be-longed to James de Barth Shorb and his wife, on land given by her father, Benjamin "Don Benito" Wilson, as a wedding gift. Shorb's family estate in Maryland was called San Marino, probably after the Italian republic. The railroad magnate Henry E. Huntington bought out the Shorbs in 1903, and razed their home but retained the name. Hunt-ington helped open the valley by developing tract homes and introducing the Pacific Electric Red Car. His legacy, the Henry E. Huntington Library and Art Gallery, where the Shorb home once stood, remains the city's most renowned feature. To avoid being annexed by Los Angeles and to protect their affluent estates, the residents of San Marino in-corporated in 1913. The city discouraged industry and enacted zoning laws prohibiting hospitals and mortuaries. San Marino, whose average house-hold income in 1993 was $146,000, has been con-sistently listed as one of the nation's wealthiest communities. The population of this "old money" town has held steady at around 13,000 in the 1980 and 1990 census tallies.

SAN PEDRO, harbor community that was an-nexed to the city of Los Angeles in 1909. Located 22 miles south of downtown Los Angeles, it is the heart of the most active port on the West Coast. Long before the explorer Juan Rodríguez Cabrillo entered the harbor on 8 October 1542, the area was inhabited by Tongva (Gabrieleño) Indians. Smoke rising along the shore from Indian fires caused Cabrillo to call the site "Bay of Smokes." In 1603 another of Spain's explorers, Sebastián Vizcaíno,

Front Street, San Pedro, ca.
1910. Pitt Collection.

dubbed the inlet San Pedro, in honor of St. Peter, the second-century bishop of Alexandria. In 1784 Spain granted the area that now includes San Pedro to a 65-year-old former soldier, Juan José Domínguez, who wanted to live and pasture horses and cattle at the well-watered location near the new *pueblo* of Los Angeles.

Smuggling became a popular and lucrative harbor activity when colonial authorities allowed only two foreign ships a year to drop anchor there in the 18th century. During the 1820s and 1830s a wooden landing was built on the tidal flats of San Pedro to accommodate American ships in the hide-and-tallow trade. The Yankee entrepreneur Phineas Banning started a harbor improvement drive in the 1860s, and introduced stage and freight lines that connected San Pedro and Wilmington to the city of Los Angeles. The railroad from Los Angeles was completed in 1868. In the 1870s and 1880s the mud flats evolved into a sea port, and the area between the harbor and Palos Verdes Hills became a residential community. The town of San Pedro was incorporated as an independent city in 1888.

In 1890 Congress authorized a subsidy for construction of a breakwater, promising a bright future for the area. On 26 April 1899, with great fanfare, construction barges dropped into place the first rocks for the massive project. In 1908 President Theodore Roosevelt honored San Pedro by sending 16 ships of the "Great White Fleet" steaming into the harbor. The drive of the city of Los Angeles to acquire San Pedro—and Wilmington—eventually overcame stiff local resistance, and consolidation occurred in 1909. San Pedro's extensive dock facilities—now protected by the 2-mile Angel's Gate breakwater, completed in 1912 as the

longest breakwater in the United States—assured San Pedro's standing as a major seaport.

Fort MacArthur was renovated by the War Department as a military post just before World War I. During Prohibition, in the 1920s, the area was again the scene of smuggling as small boats bootlegged illegal whiskey from "mother ships" lying safely outside the 12-mile U.S. coastal limit. San Pedro also became home to shipyards and fish canneries that saw their greatest activity in World War II. These enterprises began declining in the 1960s and had largely disappeared by the 1970s. Meanwhile, the old business district and residential area fell into decay. Aided by the Community Redevelopment Agency, a revival of the area has been ongoing since the 1980s.

Locals pronounce the name of their community "San Peedro." Ethnically, it has long been a melting pot of Slavs, Italians, Serbo-Croatians, Portuguese, Scandinavians, Russians, Greeks, Britons, and Latinos. Its numerous wood-frame buildings represent a variety of styles. Point Fermin Lighthouse (1874), Fort MacArthur (1888), Cabrillo Maritime Museum (designed by Frank Gehry in 1981), and Ports-of-Call Village are among San Pedro's attractions. The district had a population of 77,000 in 1990.

SAN PEDRO, LOS ANGELES, AND SALT LAKE RAILROAD (SP, LA & SL), rail line connecting Utah's capital with the harbor at San Pedro. The corporation was formed in Salt Lake City in 1887 with the backing of William Andrews Clark, the Montana copper king. The line passed through Las Vegas, Nevada, entered Southern California at Cajon Pass in San Bernardino County, wound its way through Riverside County, and connected with the newly improved harbor at San Pedro, a town that would become, in 1909, part of the city of Los Angeles.

The building of the SP, LA & SL, which began in 1892, faced stiff opposition from Collis P. Huntington, head of the Central Pacific–Southern Pacific Railroad, which enjoyed a near-monopoly on transportation in Southern California. This combine fielded its own railroad project to block the Salt Lake line. What started in court as a protracted right-of-way legal contest in 1901 became a violent face-off between rival track-laying teams in Lincoln County, Nevada. The Salt Lake Railroad project had the advantage, however, because of William Clark's connections with J. P. Morgan, Jay Gould, and Edward H. Harriman, owner of the Union Pacific Railroad and virtual czar of American railroading. This financial combination eventually overcame the Southern Pacific opposition, and the final spike was driven in January 1905. The line was eventually absorbed into the giant Union Pacific Railroad system, which to this day plays a considerable role in Southern California commerce.

SAN RAFAEL, 1.5-square-mile section of Pasadena. It is noted for its fine views: the San Gabriels to the north, Arroyo Seco to the east, and Los Angeles to the southwest. A row of elegant mansions stands on San Rafael Avenue, overlooking the arroyo, some of which have appeared in movies. Residents share the wild outdoors with raccoons, skunks, possums, and coyotes.

SANTA ANA WINDS, blasts of air blowing in from the northeastern desert, reversing the normal westerly winds. They resemble the hot sirocco winds that blow from the Libyan desert into southern Europe. The name derives from Santa Ana Canyon in Orange County, through which the winds often pass. These "northers" are most common from late summer to early fall. Although they can cause temperature drops, they usually bring very hot, very dry weather and beautifully clear skies. Santa Anas often fan destructive wildfires. Mystery writer Raymond Chandler wrote that when a Santa Ana—or "red wind"—blows, tensions heighten as "meek little wives feel the edge of the carving knife and study their husbands' necks."

SANTA ANITA PARK, racetrack in the San Gabriel Valley city of Arcadia. It is situated on Rancho Santa Anita, granted by Mexico to Hugo Reid in April 1841 and developed in the 1880s by E. J. "Lucky" Baldwin. The wealthy and flamboyant Baldwin conducted horse racing on his estate until California outlawed the sport early in the 20th century. When the state again legalized racing in 1934, Santa Anita Park became the model for modern thoroughbred racing. It pioneered the development of the automated starting gate, photo finish, and electrical timer. The army commandeered the facility during World War II, temporarily housing thousands of ethnic Japanese in the stable compound before transferring them to a detention camp at Manzanar.

Santa Anita racetrack. Courtesy Santa Anita Park.

SANTA CATALINA ISLAND, resort isle 21.8 miles southwest of San Pedro's breakwater. Catalina is the second largest of the Channel Islands chain that also includes Santa Barbara, San Nicolas, and San Clemente Islands. On clear days it is visible on the horizon from hilly places in the county. The rugged 47,884-acre island is 21 miles long, and it varies in width from ½ mile (at the Isthmus) to 8 miles. Mt. Orizaba, the highest point, rises 2,069 feet. Although various microclimates prevail on the island, summer days seldom rise above 80 degrees, and winter nights rarely fall below 50 degrees. An average year has 267 sunny days, and the average yearly rainfall is 14 inches.

The island was inhabited by Native Americans for at least 4,000 years, and some 40 townsites have been identified. The Luiseños and other groups used it for fishing. The Tongva (Gabrieleño) Indians called it Pineugna. Juan Cabrillo, who landed there in 1542, called it San Salvador after one of his ships. Its modern name was first applied by the explorer Sebastián Vizcaíno in 1602. Both men claimed the island for Spain. In the first decade of the 19th century the island's Gabrieleño population was destroyed, mainly by Russian hunters seeking sea otter pelts. Later the island was widely used by pirates and Yankee smugglers. It took on a more peaceful countenance after a brief gold mining flurry, during the Civil War, came to an end. From the 1850s to almost the turn of the century residents relied on carrier pigeons to carry news between the mainland and the island.

In 1846 Gov. Pío Pico granted the island to an American, Thomas Robbins. After changing hands many times, Catalina was acquired by Phineas Banning's three sons, who formed the Santa Catalina Island Company in 1894 and turned the island into a resort, introducing the famous glass-bottom boats. For $3 million they sold the island in 1919 to the Chicago chewing gum king William Wrigley Jr., who built a home there. Wrigley further developed part of the island as a tourist attraction. In the bay town of Avalon he built a casino in 1929, with a ballroom and cinema, and established the small beach area. Avalon became famous for its luxuriant gardens and trees, fresh sea breezes, glass-bottom boats, yacht harbor, and rare-bird park. Wrigley's baseball club, the Chicago Cubs, used Catalina as a winter training camp until 1951.

Wrigley preserved the rest of the island as a wilderness area, and so it remains to this day. Over 100 varieties of birds, transitory and permanent, have been sighted on Catalina, including the bald eagle. Game fish are plentiful, and the island has native quail, rattlesnakes, ground squirrels, and the Channel Island fox. Among the many animals that have been introduced since Spanish explorer days are deer, goats, pigs, and bison, which have multiplied into a herd that roams the island.

From the 1920s to the 1970s the island was served by the SS *Catalina,* a big white steamer that sailed between Catalina and San Pedro. Catalina is now accessible by smaller boats from Long Beach, San Pedro, and Newport, and by airplane and helicopter. The use of private cars on the island is possible only by obtaining a city permit. Numerous movies and television series have used Santa Catalina as a setting. The stately Wrigley Mansion, a 22-room Georgian structure, is now a bed-and-breakfast inn. The Catalina Island Museum Society has spearheaded the preservation of documents, photos, artifacts, and historic sites and buildings, among them a U.S. Post Office building (1889), a Congregational church (1901), and a library (1904).

In 1974 Los Angeles County, through an easement agreement, was given the right to share in the use of 41,000 acres of Catalina's coastline and interior for purposes of conservation, preservation, and park use, the terms to extend for 50 years. In 1975 a nonprofit foundation, the Santa Catalina Island Conservancy, gained title to over 42,000 acres—about 86 percent of the island. The county and conservancy work together for the benefit of the island.

SANTA CLARA RIVER, Southern California's longest and best preserved water course. It rises in the mountains in Aliso Canyon above Acton and drains an area the size of Delaware before emptying into the ocean at Oxnard, 100 miles away. Its name, applied by Fr. Juan Crespi on the 1769 Portolá expedition, honors St. Clare of Assisi, cofounder of the Franciscan order. Much of the native riparian woodland, described by Crespi as rich in grasses, wild roses, cottonwoods, willows, oak, and grape vines, remains wild. It shelters rare and endangered species of birds (least Bell's vireo, California least tern, and brown pelican) and fish (unarmored three-spine stickleback). The capricious Santa Clara River is dry most of the year, but swells with water during the winter. Land developers, citrus growers, water engineers, and gravel miners would like to tame it with concrete channels and a diversion dam; environmentalists, however, revel in its natural condition and demand that it be left untouched.

SANTA CLARITA, incorporated city in the northwestern part of the county, 26 miles from downtown Los Angeles between highways I-5 and 14. The city combines the communities of Newhall, Saugus, Valencia, and Canyon Country. Among the points of interest are California Institute of the Arts, Placerita State and County Park, and William S. Hart Regional Park. Its population grew 65.8 percent in the 1980s, from 66,700 in 1980 to 110,600 in 1990, making it one of the fastest-growing areas in the state.

SANTA FE RAILROAD. *See* Atchison, Topeka, and Santa Fe Railroad Company

SANTA FE SPRINGS, independent town near Downey, 11.5 miles southeast of downtown Los Angeles. It once formed part of the huge Los Nietos land grant, issued in 1784. The community first emerged in 1873 when J. E. Fulton established a sanitarium there at the site of a sulfur spring. The town received its present name when the Santa Fe Railroad came through in the 1880s. Farming was the main occupation until 1919, when Alphonzo Bell discovered oil near Telegraph Road and Bloomfield Avenue and the area was transformed into an oil boomtown. Santa Fe Springs was incorporated in 1957; in 1990 its population stood at 15,500.

SANTA MONICA, independent bedroom community and seaside resort 14 miles west of downtown Los Angeles. It was probably named by the Portolá expedition on 4 May 1770, the feast day of St. Monica, mother of St. Augustine. The name was first officially recorded on two land grants in 1839: San Vicente y Santa Monica and Boca de Santa Monica. The town was platted in 1875 by Nevada senator John P. Jones, on land owned jointly with Col. Robert S. Baker. Baker (who married the widow Arcadia Bandini Stearns), a sheep rancher, had purchased a large estate—much of the future Santa Monica, West Los Angeles, and Brentwood—from the Sepúlveda family for $55,000. A realtor advertised the new town as "the Zenith City by the Sunset Sea," but a business depression stunted its growth, and by 1880 the population stood at only 350. Nevertheless, the optimistic Baker built the Arcadia Hotel in 1887, naming it after his wife. The large wooden structure overlooked the ocean near the end of a rail line to Los Angeles. The town, a favorite summer resort for Angelenos, began to grow more rapidly during the 1890s. At the turn of the century, Collis P. Huntington and the Southern Pacific Railroad attempted to make Santa Monica into a major seaport. Happily for the town's future as a seaside resort, this scheme failed when San Pedro Harbor was developed as the Los Angeles port.

In the 1920s movie stars built beach homes in Santa Monica, some of which later became clubs, and the city quickly expanded. During Prohibition, water taxis carried men and women out to gambling ships anchored offshore. Douglas Aircraft (later, McDonnell-Douglas) became a major industrial complex in Santa Monica by the late 1930s, remaining so until it closed down in 1974.

Arcadia Hotel, Santa Monica, ca. 1887. Courtesy Robert Weinstein Collection.

Santa Monica Pier. Photo by Michael Krakowiak/Marni Pitt.

The city is also home to the RAND corporation, a major think tank.

Santa Monica was the scene of social activism in the 1970s; it was reflected in the rise of such groups as Santa Monicans for Renters' Rights, a coalition that dominated city politics well into the 1990s. The city instituted rent control, stopped high-rise development, and forced developers to pay for low-cost housing and model social programs. Its policies regarding the homeless, the environment, community-based policing, and height limits on new construction, to name but a few, have sparked vigorous public debate.

Santa Monica Pier, at the foot of Colorado Avenue, has been rebuilt several times since its original construction in 1874. It remains the most elaborate and popular amusement pier on the West Coast. The city also boasts an outstanding city college, a civic center, a major regional library, and Palisades Park, a green strip of land that crowns the top of the ocean cliffs. In 1989 the city opened the Third Street Promenade, a three-block-long open-air pedestrian mall south of Wilshire Boulevard. Flanked by movie theaters, stores, and restaurants, it achieved instant commercial success. The city's 1990 population was 86,900, down by 1,100 since 1970.

SANTA MONICA BAY, body of water defined by Point Dume on the north and Palos Verdes Peninsula on the south, washing the shores of Malibu, Santa Monica, Manhattan Beach, Redondo Beach, and Palos Verdes Estates. The bay was named by the explorer Juan Rodríguez Cabrillo in 1542. Although its waters and beaches

are well used by swimmers, surfers, boaters, and fishermen, they have suffered lately from pollution caused by wastewater discharge, surface runoff, power plant operations, industrial effluents, chemical dumping, and dredging operations. Environmental groups, such as Heal the Bay, have organized to reverse the situation.

SANTA MONICA MOUNTAINS, mountain chain in the Transverse Ranges that rises dramatically from the Oxnard Plain in Ventura County and extends 60 miles into the heart of Los Angeles in the Griffith Park area. The western part remains largely undeveloped, with many parks marked by hiking paths, equestrian trails, and campgrounds. The chain, composed mainly of sandstone, granite, and slate, is intersected by steep canyons—Malibu, Topanga, Sepulveda, and Laurel, among others. A substantial portion is covered by chaparral. Its grasses, flowers, shrubs, and trees provide habitat for the abundant wildlife, which include mountain lions and golden eagles. Much of the area is within the boundaries of the Santa Monica Mountains National Recreation Area.

SANTA MONICA MOUNTAINS CONSER-VANCY, branch of the California Resource Agency established in 1979 to acquire parkland and trails for preservation as well as public recreation in the mountains of Southern California, especially the Santa Monica Mountains. It cooperates with the National Park Service to purchase land for inclusion in the Santa Monica Mountains National Recreation Area. The conservancy has the unique power to purchase private land as soon as it becomes available. Among its major land acquisitions since 1980 have been the Circle X Ranch (1,655 acres), Jordan Ranch (2,308 acres), and Fryman Canyon (59 acres). The body is steered by an executive director and governed by an eight-member board appointed by various agencies of state, county, and city governments and by the National Park Service. The conservancy has a working relationship with the privately operated Mountains Conservancy Foundation.

SANTA MONICA MOUNTAINS NATIONAL RECREATION AREA (SMMNRA), protected zone embracing some 150,000 acres in the Santa Monica Mountains and along the seashore, from Point Mugu in the west to the Hollywood Freeway in the east. The SMMNRA was established by Congress in 1978, in a bill spearheaded by Rep. Anthony Bielenson; it is administered by a coalition of government entities. The area has tremendous

> **W**e live in a city with 105 square miles of poverty. . . . If you don't rebel against this fate, God help you. What's the alternative?
>
> —Tom Hayden

biological, ecological, historical, and aesthetic value. Among the natural features are ancient groves of oak, sycamore, and ash; streams and waterfalls; and hosts of wildlife. Approximately one-third of the area is publicly owned; the rest is in private hands. Some 45 percent of the total area is devoted to open space, including 12,600 acres of federal land and 55,000 acres of other public and private lands. The entire area is managed by the National Park Service. Among the park's amenities are interpretive centers, horse and bicycle trails, and tent and equestrian campsites.

Prior to 1978, land use planning in the area had been neglected, resulting in inappropriate development, spot zoning, and massive grading at critical sites. That year, Congress authorized $155 million for land purchases.

Ten years later, less than half the total amount had actually been appropriated. In 1988 the Wilderness Society called the SMMNRA one of the "ten most endangered national parks in the country,"

along with Yosemite and Yellowstone, mainly because of public neglect and abuse. The original plan called for the acquisition of 80,000 additional acres, but in the meantime major parcels such as Beverly Park Estates in Franklin Canyon and the Currey-Riach tract near Las Virgenes Road were lost to private developers, so that the total has had to be downscaled. A major current objective is to acquire sufficient parkland and trails to create the Backbone Trail, a path navigating the ridgeline of the Santa Monicas from Will Rogers State Historic Park to Point Mugu State Park.

SANTA MONICA MUNICIPAL AIRPORT (CLOVER FIELD), region's oldest airport. Established in 1923 and named after Lt. Greayer Clover, a World War I hero, it was home to the rambling Douglas Aircraft plant. The first round-the-world air expedition was launched from the flying field on 16 March 1924. A pair of Douglas cruisers, whose final destination was Seattle, took off on a 15-day (371-hour), 72-stop trip. The field's most active period was during World War II. In the 1970s the 250-acre facility was almost shut down when nearby homeowners protested the noise of jet engines, but it survived by adopting a program of reduced jet activity, particularly between 11 P.M. and 7 A.M. The airport's Museum of Flying is devoted to the conservation, restoration, and display of historic airplanes.

SANTA MONICA OUTLOOK, oldest continuously published regional newspaper. Founded by L. A. Fisher, it began publication on 13 October 1875 as a four-page weekly. Announcing that it would "skip a week" of publication during the economic slump of 1877, the paper took an extended hiatus and did not reappear until the Boom of the Eighties. The *Outlook*'s ownership changed hands 17 times before it was sold to Ira C. Copley in 1927. It has recently dropped the word "Evening" from its title, since it issues both a morning and an evening edition.

SANTA SUSANA MOUNTAINS, range that divides the Simi and San Fernando Valleys. The mountains, over 1,000 feet in elevation, are apparently named for St. Susanna, a third-century martyr especially celebrated by the Franciscan fathers who colonized California. The Southern Pacific Railroad, employing Chinese laborers, pierced the mountain with a tunnel near Chatsworth in

1902. In 1995 the Chevron Corporation agreed to sell 3,035 acres that it has owned for more than 100 years to the Santa Monica Mountains Conservancy for $4.9 million. The land is proposed as the center of a 6,000-acre preserve, Santa Clarita Woodlands Park. The acreage includes a waterfall, forests, and the remnants of the ghost town of Mentryville, the site of the state's first oil well.

SARTORI, JOSEPH F[RANCIS] (1858–1946), banker and financier. Born in Iowa and educated in law at the University of Michigan, Sartori settled in Monrovia in the 1880s. In 1888 he founded Security Savings Bank in Los Angeles, which eventually became Security Pacific Bank. It merged with Bank of America in 1992. He became a prominent figure in the American Bankers Association and a director of the Federal Reserve Bank in Los Angeles.

SATURDAY NIGHT, stylish and lively magazine published in Los Angeles in the 1920s. It was founded by former Chicagoan Samuel Travers Clover, editor of the *Los Angeles Evening News* and a member of the exclusive California Club. The publication covered the performing and literary

---

We have tried every part of the world, and we find that Los Angeles is the best place to make our pictures.
—Francis Boggs, filmmaker, 1909

---

arts and recreational and sporting life of Southern California. Its appeal was decidedly elitist—the upper-middle-class Republican town-and-country set was its main readership. It presented an image of Los Angeles as the West Coast New York City. Carey McWilliams, a young USC law student who would later distinguish himself as a journalist and historian, wrote its book reviews.

SAUGUS, unincorporated town near Santa Clarita and Magic Mountain. The name—from an Algonquin word meaning "outlet"—was first applied to a Southern Pacific station in 1878 because the site recalled the Massachusetts birthplace of Henry M. Newhall, the most prominent landowner in the region. The name is perfectly appropriate to the California location, however, for it is the outlet of

four canyons. The Saugus Train Station, built more than 90 years ago, was recently removed to Hart Park in Newhall, where it became a museum and the headquarters of the Santa Clarita Valley Historical Society.

SAVINGS AND LOAN ASSOCIATIONS. *See* Banking

SAWTELLE, Los Angeles residential area south of the Sawtelle Veterans Hospital in Westwood. Land barons John P. Jones and Robert S. Baker, founders of Santa Monica in the 1870s, established the new community in 1896. Hoping to spark Santa Monica's growth, Jones and Baker donated 300 acres of land to the federal government for a veterans' home in 1888. They subsequently donated 225 more acres south of the home to Moses Sherman and H. P. Clark, operators of an interurban streetcar line. In exchange Sherman and Clark agreed to extend their line from Pasadena to Santa Monica. They installed the tracks along Santa Monica Boulevard and platted the village of Sawtelle, named after the local banker W. E. Sawtelle. Properties sold briskly in both Sawtelle and Santa Monica. Apartments and homes were built for veterans' wives along Nevada Avenue— "Widows' Row" (now Wilshire Boulevard). Many Japanese families settled in Sawtelle, including many gardeners who developed commercial nurseries, some of which remain in operation. Incorporated in 1906, Sawtelle was consolidated with Los Angeles in 1922. In 1990 the population of the Sawtelle and nearby Brentwood areas was over 44,000.

SAWTELLE VETERANS HOSPITAL. *See* Veterans Administration Hospital, Sawtelle

SCATTERGOOD, EZRA F[REDERICK] (1871–19?), chief electrical engineer on the construction of the Los Angeles Aqueduct and top official of the Department of Water and Power (DWP). On the recommendation of William Mulholland, he was named to head the DWP's burgeoning power bureau in 1907. Local business leaders, bent on developing a private electrical utility, resisted his plans for a full-fledged municipally owned electrical system. Nevertheless, by 1928 Scattergood had built what was then the nation's largest and most highly respected public utility.

SCHINDLER, RUDOLPH M. (1887–1953), Austrian-born architect. He arrived in Los Angeles in 1920, as an associate of Frank Lloyd Wright, to work on Aline Barnsdall's house on Olive Hill. In 1921 he designed the Schindler Studio House on Kings Road in West Hollywood, a residence suggesting the Craftsman style but that gave expression to new and unconventional ideas as well. In a manner reminiscent of Japanese and Hispanic homes, its rooms opened onto an inner court. The house also had a flat roof, sliding doors, concrete slab flooring, and a flow of space that integrated the indoor and outdoor areas. Many of these features subsequently became hallmarks of California residential architecture. Schindler lived in the classic structure with his wife, Sophie, as, from 1925 to 1930, did his associate Richard Neutra, together with his family. The home was much modified after Schindler's death. Today, Friends of the Schindler House, a nonprofit foundation, are restoring it to its original design.

SCHOENBERG, ARNOLD FRANZ WALTER (1874–1951), composer. Born in Vienna, Schoenberg was living in Berlin when Hitler's persecution of the Jews forced him to flee to France and then America. He and his family arrived in Los Angeles in 1934, and in 1941 he acquired American citizenship. Although suffering from asthma and bouts of deep depression, he lectured and taught at USC for a year, and then at UCLA from 1936 to 1944. His compositions, many of them based on a 12-tone scale, ran counter to the tastes of the age.

Although they never won him popular acceptance, musicologists consider him among the greatest musical innovators of modern times. Schoenberg Hall at UCLA is named for him.

SCHOOL DISTRICTS, for elementary and high schools, number 83 in the county. Community colleges are divided into an additional 13 districts. The largest school district, the Los Angeles Unified School District (LAUSD), comprises eight separate regions; it enrolled 610,000 students in 1991. The smallest school district, with 410 pupils, is Hughes–Elizabeth Lake Union Elementary in Lake Hughes.

SCHOOL INTEGRATION. *See* Desegregation of public schools

SCHULBERG, BUDD (1914–), writer of short stories, screenplays, and novels. His father was Paramount film mogul B. P. Schulberg, whose career, in part, inspired the younger Schulberg's novel about Hollywood, *What Makes Sammy Run?* (1941). After the Watts riot of 1965, he conducted a writing workshop for black youths, which resulted in the nonfiction work *From the Ashes: Voices of Watts* (1967). Schulberg's screen credits include *On the Waterfront* (1954) and *A Face in the Crowd* (1957).

SCHWAB'S DRUGSTORE, legendary neighborhood pharmacy and soda fountain that was located at Sunset and Laurel Canyon Boulevards. Both Hollywood hopefuls and established names

The Van Patten House, Silver Lake, designed by Rudolph M. Schindler, 1934–35. Photo by Julius Shulman, Hon. AIA.

met there—though the story that Lana Turner was discovered while sipping a soda there is a groundless myth started by gossip columnist Sidney Skolsky, a Schwab's habitué. On the other hand, it is true that writer F. Scott Fitzgerald suffered a heart attack while buying cigarettes at Schwab's. The store was torn down in 1987 to make way for a shopping mall.

SCI-ARC. *See* Southern California Institute of Architecture

SCIENTOLOGY. *See* Church of Scientology

SCREEN ACTORS GUILD (SAG), professional organization of actors. It was founded in Hollywood in 1933 when actors, working for as little as $15 a day under unregulated conditions, were ordered to take a 50 percent pay cut owing to the depression. A small group of actors formed a self-governing guild to give performers a unified voice in bargaining with producers. The move started a bitter four-year struggle for recognition. In 1937 the young guild, now affiliated with the AFL, won its first union-shop contract, with wage increases, pension and health plans, residuals, regulation of talent agents, and safety standards on the set as the major provisions. The guild members waged a significant fight in 1960 to win residual rights for their television film work, a move necessitated by the growing power and influence of the new medium. The guild's presidents have been Ralph Morgan, Eddie Cantor, Robert Montgomery, Edward Arnold, James Cagney, George Murphy, Ronald Reagan, Walter Pidgeon, Leon Ames, Howard Keel, George Chandler, Dana Andrews, Charlton Heston, John Gavin, Dennis Weaver, Kathleen Nolan, William Schallert, Edward Asner, Patty Duke, and Barry Gordon.

SCREEN WRITERS GUILD. *See* Writers Guild of America, West, Inc.

SCRIPPS COLLEGE. *See* Claremont Colleges

SEAL OF THE CITY OF LOS ANGELES, adopted in 1905, symbolizes the city's history. A lion and a castle represent Spanish control; a beaded boundary implies a rosary, symbolizing the Franciscan mission period; an eagle holding a serpent is drawn from Aztec legend and is a reminder of Mexican control. The Bear Flag suggests the brief California Republic of 1846; the Stars and Stripes indicates the American takeover; and sprays of olives, grapes, and oranges signify the region's garden setting and agricultural history.

SEAL OF THE COUNTY OF LOS ANGELES, adopted in 1957, was designed by Supervisor Kenneth Hahn and executed by painter Millard Sheets. It is dominated by the central figure of Pomona, goddess of fruit trees and gardens, symbolizing the county's agriculture. In her arms she holds a sheaf of grain, an orange, a lemon, an avocado, and some grapes. The waves beneath her feet represent the Pacific Ocean, and the mountains

Seal of the County of Los Angeles.

in the background, the San Gabriels. Panels surround Pomona: the triangle and caliper indicate Los Angeles industry's role in conquering space; the Spanish galleon is Cabrillo's vessel, *San Salvador,* which sailed into San Pedro harbor on 8 October 1542; the cross recalls the historical importance of the Catholic missions; the tuna is a reminder of the county's active fishing industry, and the cow, a champion named Pearlette, stands for the dairy industry; the oil derricks depict the petroleum fields discovered on Signal Hill; the Hollywood Bowl honors the county's cultural achievements; and the movie and the television industries are represented by two stars.

SEAVER CENTER FOR WESTERN HISTORY RESEARCH, historical collection of the Los Angeles County Museum of Natural History. Housed in handsome quarters in the Exposition

Park facility, the center contains rare books as well as photographs and negatives tracing the development of Los Angeles, Southern California, and the West.

SEBASTIAN, CHARLES E[DWARD] (1873–1929), Los Angeles police chief from 1910 to 1915, and mayor from 1915 to 1916. Born in Missouri, Sebastian arrived in Los Angeles before 1900 and worked as a ranch hand and railroad laborer before joining the police force. After serving for 10 years he became chief of police. On the eve of the 1915 mayoral election his political enemies had him formally charged in the beating death of an imprisoned disabled homeless man. When the charge was proven baseless, he found himself accused of contributing to the delinquency of a minor, 16-year-old Edith Serkin, whose sister, Lillian Pratt, was his mistress. Edith, it seemed, had sat in the lobby of downtown's Arizona Hotel while her sister met Sebastian in a room upstairs. After he was acquitted of the second charge, a festive parade was organized in his honor. On 31 May 1915 an unknown assailant shot at Sebastian but missed, whereupon the mayoral candidate was charged with plotting a fake assassination to advance his political career.

Sebastian survived all of these tribulations and was elected mayor. Within a year of taking office, however, he was forced to resign when the *Los Angeles Record* published letters written to his mistress in which he referred to his wife as "the Old Haybag." His wife sued for divorce. Sebastian's fortunes sank steadily after that. He spent the ensuing years at various jobs, the last one as a gas station attendant. He suffered a severe stroke, and was cared for by the faithful Lillian. She could be seen pushing him in his wheelchair along the boardwalk in Venice, where they lived.

SECURITY PACIFIC BANK, major regional banking enterprise until 1992. Originally situated on Main Street, it was founded in 1888 by Joseph F. Sartori as the Security Savings Bank (then changed to the Security and Trust Savings Bank of Los Angeles). The bank managed to survive the Great Depression by having its employees take a 15 percent cut in salary. Eventually the name was changed to Security First National Bank. The modern bank of the 1970s, known as Security Pacific Bank, was the creature of its CEO, Richard J. Flamson III. Under his leadership it expanded from a regional to a world banking institution, with far-reaching investments in Great Britain, Canada, and Australia. Security Pacific faltered for several reasons, including the ill-advised purchase of a failed commercial bank in Arizona in 1985. It was absorbed into the Bank of America in 1992.

SELF-REALIZATION FELLOWSHIP, worldwide religious organization centered in Southern California and dedicated to meditation, tolerance, and cross-cultural appreciation. It has headquarters atop Mt. Washington, and a shrine off Sunset Boulevard in Pacific Palisades. The Mt. Washington quarters are in a hotel building, built in 1908, at the end of a funicular railway line. It was restored in 1925 by Yogi Pramahansa Yogananda and lavishly furnished with artifacts from India. The secluded 10-acre spot in Pacific Palisades features a small, picturesque, spring-fed pond, a "Golden Lotus" archway, a replica of a 16th-century Dutch windmill, and domes of gold. Both shrines are open to the public. The religious belief system, based on Eastern religion, is essentially a Southern California creation.

SELIG, WILLIAM NICHOLAS (1864–1948), pioneer filmmaker who worked in the new medium from 1907 to 1917. As head of the Chicago-based Selig Polyscope Company, Selig dispatched a unit to California in 1907 to complete exterior shots for a one-reel version of *The Count of Monte Cristo*. The team shot 1,000 feet of film in Venice, Laguna Beach, and atop the roof of a Main Street building. Selig's director, Francis Boggs, was taken with

---

The whole place stank of orange blossoms.

—H. L. Mencken, journalist and editor

---

the possibilities of the new location and convinced Selig to open a Los Angeles branch. Selig came west and remained, building a small studio on Alessandro Street, in Edendale, in the Griffith Park area. He also rented a 50 ¥ 50 ¥ 100-foot lot adjacent to the Sing Loo Chinese Laundry on Olive near 7th Street, where he made *The Power of the Sultan* (1908), the first film shot entirely in Southern California. In 1911 Selig built another studio and private zoo on Mission Road in Lincoln Park. The zoo was later dismantled and the animals turned over to the city. A few years later a gardener, seemingly angered or unbalanced by the noise coming from the movie set, shot and killed Boggs and wounded Selig. It was the first of many Hollywood shootings to come.

SENIOR CITIZENS MOVEMENT grew rapidly in Southern California as the population aged. The elderly became an identifiable group in the 1920s, when older farmers retired from the bitterly cold winters of the Midwest to bask in sunny Southern California. Growing numbers of the elderly resulted in more political clout and expanded social services. American retirees made their political debut with the California pension plan movements of the 1930s. The Townsend Plan, which began in Long Beach in 1933, helped nudge the New Deal administration into passing the Social Security Act.

In the 1960s, as the numbers of persons 65 years and older grew nationwide, advocacy organizations became better organized and politically more vocal. The American Association of Retired Persons (AARP), the world's largest membership organization of its kind, established offices in Los Angeles, as did related organizations: the Affiliated Committees on Aging, Asociación Nacional por Personas Mayores, the California League of Senior Citizens, the Gray Panthers, and the National Retired Teachers Association. Their lobbying efforts helped establish the Los Angeles Department of Aging, Area Agency on Aging, California Commission on Aging, and California Department of Aging. The city of Los Angeles is generally considered to be extremely responsive to the needs of the aging.

SENNETT, MACK. *See* Movie industry, 1902–1914

SEPULVEDA, COMMUNITY OF. *See* North Hills

SEPÚLVEDA, YGNACIO (1842–1916), Californio who became a superior court judge. He presided over the inquiry into the vigilante lynching in 1869 of Frenchman Miguel Lachenais—who had killed one man in 1861 and another in 1869—and the Chinese Massacre of 24 October 1871.

SEPULVEDA BOULEVARD, longest road in both the city and county of Los Angeles. Its length within city limits is 26.4 miles, with a slight incursion into Culver City. It stretches 76 miles in the county, from the I-5 in the San Fernando Valley to Willow Street on the border of Long Beach, passing through several cities along the way.

SEPULVEDA CANYON, gap through the Santa Monica Mountains, named for Francisco Sepúlveda, grantee of Rancho San Vicente y Santa Monica in 1839. The canyon, around 500 feet above sea level, was Captain Portolá's entryway into the San Fernando Valley in 1769. Today the San Diego Freeway (I-405) runs through it, the major route between the southern part of the San Fernando Valley and the Los Angeles Basin.

SEPÚLVEDA FAMILY, prominent Spanish-Mexican clan established in Southern California by Francisco Xavier Sepúlveda (1742–1788), a Mexican colonial soldier. One son, Juan José (1764–1808), founded a branch of the family near Redondo Beach and San Pedro; he received title to the 13,629-acre Rancho Los Palos Verdes in 1821. Another son, Francisco (1775–1853), founded a branch in the Los Angeles *pueblo* in 1815, where he served as *alcalde* in 1825. Francisco received title to Rancho San Vicente y Santa Monica (1839), comprising 30,260 acres. Francisco's daughters married

José Sepúlveda, ca. 1890. Courtesy Henry E. Huntington Library.

into the de la Guerra family of Santa Barbara. His son José Andrés Sepúlveda, generally known as José Sepúlveda, inherited Rancho San Joaquín, a huge property running from Tustin to San Juan Capistrano. One of the largest landowners in California, José Sepúlveda was noted for his generous hospitality and elegant dress, as well as his horsemanship and gambling prowess. He was the father of Judge Ygnacio Sepúlveda. The Palos Verdes Sepúlvedas waged a prolonged and debilitating legal feud with the neighboring Domínguez clan over pasturage boundaries. Today a major canyon, a long boulevard, and a community, all in Los Angeles County, bear the name Sepulveda.

SEPULVEDA FLOOD CONTROL BASIN, U.S. Army Corps of Engineers facility on the Los Angeles River in Van Nuys. The project, authorized by Congress in 1937 after a disastrous flood in the valley and completed in December 1941 at a cost of $6.6 million, created a 710-foot-high dam with spillway that restrains water in a basin covering 1,335 acres. Usually only one dam tender is on duty at any given time. The corps, which is responsible for all navigable inland waterways, also controls Santa Fe Dam in Irwindale and Whittier Narrows Dam in Montebello, on the Rio Hondo and San Gabriel River, respectively.

SERRA, JUNÍPERO (1713–1784), founder of the California Franciscan mission chain. Born on the Spanish island of Majorca, Serra had been a professor of philosophy and a missionary in Mexico City before coming to Baja and Alta California. He established nine of the 21 missions and

Fr. Junípero Serra. Pitt Collection.

presided over the entire mission system as father-president until his death. Serra first visited the Los Angeles area in 1782, a year after the founding of the *pueblo*. He had resisted this civilian settlement, feeling that the colonists posed a danger to the well-being of the Indians and missionaries at San Gabriel, and he demanded increased military support for the missions from Mexico. Despite controversies over the missions' mistreatment of the Native Americans, the Catholic Church has deemed Fra Serra "venerable" and is advancing him toward sainthood.

SERVICE EMPLOYEES INTERNATIONAL UNION (SEIU), main labor union for county

Justice for Janitors Strike, April 1995. Photo by Michael Krakowiak/Marni Pitt.

and other public-sector, as well as some private-sector, wage workers. Its origins lie in the 1911 formation of the Los Angeles County Employees Association, which merged with SEIU in 1969. A leading figure in the union's rise to prominence was its secretary-treasurer, George Hardy. Local 660, which currently represents 40,000 county employees who are organized into 22 bargaining units, is the largest labor local in the county. Other, smaller SEIU locals represent janitors, hospital workers, home care workers, and teaching assistants in the city school system. As an AFL-CIO affiliate, SEIU has fought for pension and civil service rights, mutual benefit insurance, medical insurance, and other social and welfare programs. The union conducted successful strikes in 1985 and 1991, and a nurses strike in 1988. In 1987 SEIU Local 399 launched a militant "Justice for Janitors" campaign to raise the wages and benefits of maintenance workers in major office buildings of Los Angeles. That local's membership of 6,000 includes 90 percent of the janitors in the high-rises downtown and in Century City. Most of these workers are resident immigrants.

7TH STREET, city's premier shopping street from 1909 to 1929. Bullock's opened its first Los Angeles department store on 7th and Broadway in 1907, Coulter's followed suit the same year at 7th and Olive, and Robinson's located at 7th and Grand in 1914. Barker Brothers arrived in 1928. The street, together with Broadway, quickly became the heart of downtown and remains a strong retail artery to this day. Broadway Plaza, at 7th and Flower, is a major downtown shopping center. The street's vintage buildings, many with a strong Beaux Arts flavor, include the Union Oil Building (1911); the Los Angeles Athletic Club (1911–1912); Clifton's Silver Spoon Cafeteria (1922); and the palatial Fine Arts Building (1925). Some architectural treasures are being restored, renovated, and recycled for new users.

SEVERANCE, CAROLINE MARIA SEYMOUR (1820–1914), civic reformer. An abolitionist and founder of Boston's New England Women's Club in 1868—the first such in the country—she came to Los Angeles in 1875 with her husband, T. E. Lawrence, a retired banker whose health demanded a milder climate. She immediately set to work in her new home, advancing the cause of women's emancipation, education, and

other rights. "Madame Severance" formed the Los Angeles Women's Club, whose members concerned themselves with the plight of homeless children, helping to establish the Orphans Home Society in 1883 and promoting free kindergartens. Severance introduced the Unitarian movement to Los Angeles in 1877, and four years later she founded the Friday Morning Club, devoted to cultural and social betterment and civic reform. The club ran a lending library, maintained an employment bureau, and conducted classes. The tireless Madame Severance also helped develop the Los Angeles Philharmonic Orchestra, began a city public library system, worked to found a local branch of the University of California (later UCLA), promoted historic preservation, crusaded for woman suffrage, and championed international peace. Following ratification of the suffrage amendment in 1911, she was honored that year by being the first woman to register to vote in California. Severance's home, "El Nido" ("The Nest"), was a social center and meeting place for Los Angeles reformers.

SEWAGE DISPOSAL. Today toilet wastewater is carried by thousands of miles of underground sewer pipes, which prevent the city from being devastated by plagues of cholera and typhoid, to four treatment plants; after processing, the water is discharged into the Pacific.

Needless to say, this situation differs dramatically from that of 19th-century Los Angeles. In the village days of the 1860s Harris Newmark, like most residents, drained his bathtub by means of a wooden pipe that emptied into the nearest *zanja* (irrigation ditch). When public sewers were built in 1875 the system was designed to flush wastes directly onto land in the southern part of the city. Waste disposal became more sophisticated in the 1880s under City Engineer Fred Eaton; then the city used Ballona Creek to carry waste into Santa Monica Bay. Elsewhere, farmers used city waste for fertilizer. Pasadena in 1892 bought a "sewer farm" in neighboring Alhambra, where a prosperous Iowa farmer grew corn and pumpkins. Arcadia maintained individual cesspools until the 1940s, while Pasadena and South Pasadena relied on activated sludge treatment to produce a dried residue useful for agriculture.

Los Angeles completed its efficient Hyperion Sewage Treatment Plant at Playa del Rey in 1894, expanding it in 1908. People using the waters and beaches of Santa Monica Bay soon began complaining of pollution, however, and in 1915 the state ordered a cleanup, which was finally begun in 1922 and finished two years later. Meanwhile, Venice beach had to be quarantined. Eventually Vernon, Culver City, Glendale, San Fernando, Beverly Hills, Santa Monica, and Burbank also hooked into Hyperion. This treatment plant, regarded as an engineering miracle in the 1940s, has been overtaxed in subsequent decades and is now in need of major repairs.

The small Tapia Water Reclamation Facility on Malibu Creek is applauded by engineers as an excellent plant but cursed by surfers and Malibu locals who claim that it emits unhealthy discharges.

A spirit of hatred and revenge took possession of me. I had numerous fights in defense of what I believed to be my rights and those of my countrymen.

—Tiburcio Vásquez, California bandit, statement before his hanging, 1875

Tapia is operated by Las Virgenes Municipal Water District, serving Calabasas, Agoura Hills, Hidden Hills, and other nearby areas.

Each day the city of Los Angeles dumps 360–420 million gallons of wastewater into Santa Monica Bay from the Hyperion plant, while the Los Angeles County Sanitation District dumps an additional 360 million gallons into the ocean off Palos Verdes Peninsula.

Biologists consider that, because of this activity, parts of the offshore area have become significantly altered, providing a less healthy habitat for much of the sea life that dwells there. For example, the 1,500-acre kelp forest that once covered the Palos Verdes shelf disappeared in the 1960s and 1970s—and along with it a home for hundreds of species of fish and invertebrates.

SHARKS, fish species represented along the West Coast by seven varieties. By far the most common in California waters is the white shark *(Carcharodon carcharias),* an endangered species occasionally seen near the shore and in shallow bays. These sharks grow to 20 feet, feed voraciously on smaller

fish and marine mammals, and have been known to attack divers. Scientists study them avidly, attempting to discover why, for example, they do not suffer from virus infections or tumors.

SHAW, FRANK L. (1877–19??), county supervisor and Los Angeles mayor from 1933 to 1938 who was accused of corruption. As mayor he allegedly used relief funds to help maintain himself in public office. He and his brother J. Shaw, also a public official, were convicted of selling civil service jobs. Although supported to the bitter end by the *Los Angeles Times,* Frank Shaw was toppled by a recall movement that brought in Fletcher Bowron as mayor.

SHEEP RAISING, once a major industry, is now dying in the county. Sheep were introduced to California by Iberian colonists. In the 1820s the mission fathers had a flock of 15,000 at Mission San Gabriel. In the county as a whole there were 20,000 in 1858, and 40,000 by 1860, when the price reached $3.50 a head. Sheep replaced cattle when drought destroyed the cattle industry in 1861. Many sheep raisers were French Basques with such surnames as Leonis, Oxarart, Amestoy, and Bastanchury. The Bixby brothers, Llewellyn, Jotham, and Amasa, were also major sheep ranchers. An absolute sheep craze swept the county in 1872–1873, when a dirty, greasy, burry pound of wool sold for an amazing 45 cents.

In this century growers have pastured their animals mostly in the hills above Malibu, and in the San Fernando, San Gabriel, and Antelope Valleys. Most recently the sheepmen have been Spanish Basques, who arrived in the 1950s, or Peruvians and Chileans, who worked under government labor contracts and became independent growers or resident laborers. They lead a nomadic life, often living in car trailers. Suburbanites and environmentalists, beginning with John Muir, have complained that the sheep eat even the roots of plants, destroying all surface growth.

Declining lamb prices, a worldwide glut of wool, and regional drought took a heavy toll after 1986. The animals are now barred by the Bureau of Land Management from access to land in the Mojave Desert, where growers used to graze their animals in the late spring. With only 20 major growers left in the county in 1991, and fewer than 10,000 head, sheep raising has become a rapidly declining enterprise in Los Angeles.

SHEETS, MILLARD OWEN (1907–1989), painter. Sheets was born in Pomona, taught at Scripps College, and was director of the Otis Art Institute (now the Otis College of Art and Design) from 1953 to 1959. He gained international recognition as a water colorist, but was also known for his oils, acrylics, tapestries, mosaics, and murals. Sheets's biographers consider him a "one-man renaissance." His work is featured at the neighborhood offices of Home Savings Bank and at the Scottish Rite Masonic Temple on Wilshire Boulevard.

SHEINBAUM, STANLEY (1913–), civic leader. Raised in New York City during the Great Depression, Sheinbaum graduated from Stanford University in economics. In the 1960s he was an outspoken critic of the Vietnam War, and in 1977 was involved in private Middle Eastern peacemaking as an intermediary between Israel and the Palestinian Liberation Organization (PLO). A former official of the ACLU and regent of the University of California, Sheinbaum was appointed by Mayor Tom Bradley to the police commission in 1991, and presided over it during the heated controversy surrounding the resignation of Chief Daryl Gates. He published *New Perspectives Quarterly,* a political journal.

SHERIFF. *See* Los Angeles County Sheriff's Department

SHERMAN, MOSES HAZELTINE (1853–1932), pioneer interurban streetcar magnate, land developer, and town booster. He arrived in Los Angeles in 1889 with his brother-in-law, Eli P. Clark. Together they built the first interurban streetcar lines, beginning in 1893. With Clark and Harry Chandler, Sherman created a land syndicate that opened up 47,000 acres in Hollywood. He was also part of the private syndicate that opened 108,000 acres in the San Fernando Valley. In 1903 he was appointed to the Los Angeles Water Board, and reappointed in 1909, even though reformers charged him with conflict of interest. Sherman Way in the San Fernando Valley is named after him, as is Sherman Oaks.

SHERMAN OAKS, San Fernando Valley area 14 miles northwest of downtown Los Angeles. Its boundaries run roughly from Coldwater Canyon to Sepulveda Boulevard, and from Magnolia Boulevard to Mulholland Drive. The land passed through the hands of various title holders: the San Fernando Mission, in 1797, followed by Pío and Andrés Pico, Eulogio de Celis, Pío Pico again, the Van Nuys family, the Los Angeles Suburban Homes Company, and Moses H. Sherman, after whom it is named. When Sherman subdivided the first 1,100 acres of the area in 1927 it was known as Cahuenga Park. The price of land was then $780 an acre. In time, the small farms and orchards evolved into residential and commercial tracts. The greatest development took place in the 1930s. Stan Laurel and Oliver Hardy were among the Hollywood personages who lived in Sherman Oaks. Today the population is approximately 50,000, in an area of about 10 square miles. Buildings along the main thoroughfare, Ventura Boulevard, suffered major damage in the 1994 earthquake.

SHERMAN WAY, cross-valley thoroughfare named for Moses H. Sherman. Built at a cost of $500,000, the road was intended to resemble Paseo de la Reforma in Mexico City, a boulevard greatly admired by the developer of Reseda (through which Sherman Way runs), Harry Chandler.

SHIPBUILDING, major industry in the harbor area in the first half of the 20th century. Its peak years were during World War II, when the industry employed as many as 90,000.

The Los Angeles Shipbuilding and Dry Dock Company was established in San Pedro in 1917; it and ancillary companies soon employed 20,000 people. In 1943, after experiencing financial failure

Basically the region is a paradox: a desert that faces an ocean.
    —Carey McWilliams, journalist, 1946

in the Great Depression, the company was taken over by Todd Shipyards, an eastern firm. Todd occupied a 112-acre yard, where it built, repaired, or refitted more than 2,000 ships during World War II alone. More recently it constructed guided-missile frigates, but shut down in 1989.

The largest and most productive Los Angeles shipyard, and one of the biggest in the nation, was the California Shipbuilding Corporation. Calship, as it was known, originated in 1940 on 175 acres on Terminal Island, from which it began launching

Liberty ships in 1941, delivering 15 ships within the year. Eventually this yard, with its 55,000 employees, was rolling one ship into the water each day.

The war also brought activity to Bethlehem Shipbuilding Corporation, which maintained a 40-acre yard and used 3,000 feet of berthing space. Consolidated Steel Corporation, operating in Wilmington and Long Beach, produced many ships during those years as well, launching three on one record-breaking day, 29 May 1944. Meanwhile, scores of smaller firms helped produce submarine chasers, patrol boats, PT boats, landing craft, rescue boats, barges, and tugs in World War II.

SHOESTRING STRIP, ribbon of land 16 miles long and a half-mile wide that was added to Los Angeles in 1906, linking Wilmington and San Pedro to the city proper. It jogged a bit to avoid Gardena Village. The annexation gave Los Angeles a more convenient access to the Pacific Ocean.

SHOPPING MALLS. *See* Malls, shopping; Minimalls

SHORB, JAMES DE BARTH (D. 1895), pioneer settler of San Marino. Upon his arrival in Southern California from Maryland in 1864 he was employed as superintendent of the Philadelphia and California Oil Company. In 1867 he bought the mountainous Rancho Temescal in the northwestern part of the county and began mining on the property. When Shorb married a daughter of Benjamin D. Wilson, "Don Benito" gave the couple land as a wedding gift. Shorb called their estate —the first private home in the area—San Marino, after his family's Maryland estate. In addition to managing Wilson's winery, he developed the Alhambra tract, which he inherited on his father-in-law's death in 1878.

SHRINE AUDITORIUM, theater and conference center at Jefferson Boulevard and Figueroa Street. Designed with Moorish architectural motifs, it is easily identified by its paired domes. Built between 1920 and 1926 at a cost of $2.6 million, the facility is the meeting place and headquarters of the Al-Malaikah Temple, a division of the Ancient Arabic Order of Nobles of the Mystic Shrine, commonly known as the Shriners. When first opened, it was the nation's largest theater complex: the auditorium seats 6,489, while the pavilion can accommodate 7,500 ballroom dancers. The Shrine,

which has long hosted operas, concerts, ballet, and public meetings, contains the Moehler pipe organ, the largest theater pipe organ in the world.

SHRUBS AND PLANTS. *See* Chaparral; Wildflowers; individual plants

SHULER, ROBERT PIERCE ("FIGHTING BOB") (1880–1965), mercurial Methodist preacher. Born in Tennessee and trained as a circuit rider, serving first in Texas, he moved to Los Angeles in 1920. During the 1930s he used his pulpit at Trinity Methodist South Church, together

---

Los Angeles produces less than any other great city of the things that, from a grim, Protestant way of looking at things, anyone really needs. And yet it grows like mad.

—Nathan Glazer, sociologist, 1965

---

with a radio broadcast, to express his hatred of Jews, Catholics, big business, public officials, the bar association, antiprohibitionists, and rival preacher Aimee Semple McPherson. In 1931 the federal government withdrew Fighting Bob's broadcasting license. He ran a tumultuous campaign for the U.S. Senate, and when he lost disappeared from the public eye.

SHULMAN, JULIUS (1910–), architectural photographer. Born in Brooklyn, he moved to Los Angeles with his family in 1920. As a chronicler for some of the region's most important modern architects—Richard Neutra, Gregory Ain, and Rudolph M. Schindler, among others—Shulman established the reputation of Los Angeles architecture beginning in the 1930s. Although lacking formal training, he had a superb eye and taught himself how to use natural light to its best advantage. His 1960 photograph of the Pierre Koenig Case Study House No. 22 overlooking Los Angeles at night became a symbol of the glamor and beauty of the growing modern metropolis. The world-recognized photographer's numerous commendations include a 1969 award for architectural photography from the American Institute of Ar-

Koenig Case Study House. Photo by Julius Shulman, Hon. AIA.

chitects, and a 1995 award from the Los Angeles Cultural Heritage Commission "for revealing the beauty of Los Angeles architecture to the world through photography." A biography by Joseph Rosa, *A Constructed View: The Architectural Photography of Julius Shulman,* was published in 1994.

SIEGEL, BENJAMIN ("BUGSY") (1906–1947), Brooklyn-born underworld boss who came to Hollywood in 1936 as a protégé of mobster Meyer Lansky. Befriended by movie star George Raft and other celebrities, he settled in Holmby Hills and made the "A" list for Hollywood parties. He and Lansky headed the notorious organization known as Murder Incorporated. He was indicted but never tried for the murder of gangster Harry "Big Greenie" Greenberg. Siegel was gunned down on 21 June 1947 while seated in his Beverly Hills living room, in a still-unsolved shooting. He was given too much credit for having "envisioned" the gambling casinos of Las Vegas in the mythic ro-

mantic movie *Bugsy* (1991), with Warren Beatty in the lead role.

SIERRA CLUB, ANGELES CHAPTER, local section of the San Francisco–based conservation organization. After abortive efforts to form a group locally in 1903 and 1909, the club finally emerged in November 1911, with an excursion up the Arroyo Seco. Under the leadership of Philip Bernays, William Patrick Boland, and Judge Clair S. Tappan, the 1,500 members built Muir Lodge in the San Gabriels in 1913. At the Sierra Club's diamond jubilee in 1986, the southern section was represented by 68 separate committees, groups, and sections and 28 task forces. Calling itself the world's largest outings organization, the Sierra Club listed 2,000 organized activities and counted 46,000 members in Southern California. Its numerous activities include rock climbing, skiing, mountaineering, ice skating, natural science, hiking, mule packing, photography, bicycle touring, and river touring. Angeles Chapter (the official name since 1954) pioneered the concept of preparing environmental impact reports (EIRs) to challenge major developments in wilderness areas (with the San Jacinto Tramway project in 1951). In 1971 the chapter organized a successful march to oppose the expansion of Mulholland Highway. On the social side, it was the first Sierra Club section to establish a singles group.

SIERRA MADRE, independent city 2.9 square miles in area at the base of Mt. Wilson. It is 13 miles northeast of downtown Los Angeles. The name means "mother mountain range" in Spanish. At an elevation of 835 feet, it was where Shoshonean Indians began their climb into the mountains. The earliest non-Indian inhabitants were the patients of Sierra Madre Villa Sanitarium, a hotel and cottage complex built in 1875 for tuberculosis victims.

Europe can supply her own wants; we shall supply the wants of Asia. There is nothing that cannot be made and few things that will not grow in Southern California.

—Henry E. Huntington, railroad magnate

The "lungers," who flocked from all over the nation to breathe the recuperative air, sat on the 200-foot-long veranda, or behind its immense sliding glass windows, absorbing the warm sunshine and fragrant mountain breezes. In 1881 patients, recovered patients, and the overflow population created the town of Sierra Madre on a portion of Rancho Santa Anita, bought by Nathaniel C. Carter from E. J. "Lucky" Baldwin. The town was incorporated in 1907. Considered the "Capital of the Sanitarium Belt," Sierra Madre was more closely associated with the migration of health seekers to Southern California than any other city in the region.

The town shares a boundary with the Angeles National Forest, where Mt. Wilson Observatory is located. The Mt. Wilson Trail, following the ancient Indian pathway, ascends 8 miles to the mountaintop.

Each year Sierra Madre celebrates its Wisteria Fête. A wisteria vine, planted in 1894, branches out from a large central trunk. By the 1940s it shaded more than an acre of ground, and it is still growing. The annual event occurs during blooming season, usually the second half of March. By 1940, too, the deep green of orange trees dominated the scene. At that time the population stood at 3,500. It has remained stable at 10,700 since 1980. Outdoor scenes for *The Invasion of the Body Snatchers* (1956) were shot at the Sierra Madre town square.

SIERRA MADRE MOUNTAINS, name applied by the San Gabriel Mission fathers to the steep slopes of the San Gabriels nearest to the Mission, and by Spanish settlers to the entire high wall of rugged mountains surrounding Los Angeles: the Santa Susana, San Bernardino, San Jacinto, and San Gabriel mountain ranges.

SIGNAL HILL, independent community 17 miles south of downtown Los Angeles, on a 2,000-foot slope entirely surrounded by Long Beach. Under Spanish rule the hill was part of Rancho Los Alamitos, granted to José Manuel Nieto in 1784, and was known as Los Cerritos. Later ownership passed from the Temple family to the Bixby family and then became part of Abel Stearns's vast empire. About 2 miles from the ocean, the hill was renamed Signal Hill when an official U.S. mapping party placed a marker on its peak in 1849. Many of Pearl White's silent films were made on site.

Predictions were that the town's lovely view lots would attract wealthy residents. Instead, in June 1921 an oil gusher erupted at Hill Street and Temple Avenue. (Upton Sinclair vividly captured the scene in his 1926 novel *Oil!*) The next morning almost 15,000 people swarmed in to see the gusher. This find, called Alamitos No. 1, together with oil pumped at other nearby sites, made Los Angeles

Cherry Avenue and 21st Street in Signal Hill, looking north, ca. 1924. Courtesy City of Signal Hill.

Cherry Avenue and 21st Street in Signal Hill, looking north, 1995. Photo by Lee N. Duer, courtesy City of Signal Hill.

County the world's fifth largest oil producer. The forest of derricks that sprouted on the 1,400 acres became the richest oil field in U.S. history. The oil brought enormous wealth to investors, but rather than attracting wealthy residents, it turned Signal Hill into a working-class community. Oil, tool, and machine-shop industries flourished.

In recent decades, oil production has lessened and oil operators have dismantled their equipment in anticipation of residential development. The population increased 46 percent in the decade after 1980, standing at 8,300 in 1990.

SILBERBERG, MENDEL B. (1886–1965), co-founder of the firm of Mitchell, Silberberg, and Knupp in 1909 and a prominent Hollywood attorney. Although born into a Christian Science household, he acquired a Jewish identity in adulthood, and in the 1930s became the film industry's liaison to the organized Jewish community. He was an associate of Louis B. Mayer. As head of the Community Relations Committee of the Jewish Federation Council (JFC), Silberberg defended the movie industry against anti-Semitic attacks. He was a prominent Republican among Democrats in the JFC.

SILVER LAKE, small, picturesque residential area north of Echo Park. It is noted for its high concentration of first-rate architecture designed by Rudolph M. Schindler, John Lautner, Richard Neutra, Gregory Ain, and Raphael Soriano. Most of their work dates from the 1920s to the 1940s. Many lucky Silver Lake residents have a rare view of the hills, the reservoir built in 1907, and the city of Los Angeles.

SILVER REPUBLICAN CLUB OF LOS ANGELES, maverick GOP movement that supported the Democrat-Populist candidate William Jennings Bryan for president in 1896. Backed by Edward L. Doheny, William F. Burbank, Henry T. Hazard, and C. F. Edson, the club's activity reflected the popularity of the silver issue in Southern California during the presidential elections of 1892 and 1896. On 5 July 1896 the silver-tongued Bryan, while on a whistle-stop tour of California, made an impassioned two-hour speech in Fiesta Park. The club pulled many voters into the Democratic column, giving Bryan a 400-vote margin in Los Angeles.

SIMON, NORTON (1907–1993), wealthy industrialist and art patron. Simon, the son of a Portland, Oregon, department store owner and him-

Norton Simon, in front of Rembrandt painting. Courtesy Norton Simon Museum.

self a college dropout, bought a defunct Fullerton bottling company for $7,000 and parlayed it into a multinational corporate empire that included Hunt-Wesson Foods, McCalls publishing, and Canada Dry. In 1970 he ran, and lost, in the senatorial primary as a liberal against the conservative Republican incumbent, George Murphy.

Simon became a shrewd buyer of art works in the post–World War II era, using part of his fortune to acquire 12,000 pieces of art, including masterpieces by Rembrandt, Raphael, Cranach the Elder, van Gogh, Picasso, and Cézanne. In 1975, after having searched unsuccessfully for a place large enough to house his collection, he settled on the financially troubled Pasadena Art Museum as a repository. Renamed the Norton Simon Museum of Art, it has become one of the world's important art museums. Upon his death he was survived by his second wife, former movie star Jennifer Jones.

SIMPSON, O[RENTHAL] J[AMES] (1947–), football star and movie actor. Born in San Francisco, Simpson attended the City College of San Francisco and USC, where he played football and was named All-American twice and won the Heisman Trophy. He played professionally for the Buffalo Bills from 1969 until 1978, when he moved to the San Francisco 49ers. At his retirement in 1979 he had racked up 11,236 yards, a ball-carrying record second only to that of Jim Brown. He also won four NFL rushing titles, was selected to the Pro Bowl five times, and in 1985 entered the Football Hall of Fame. The Los Angeles resident worked as a television football analyst and as an actor, beginning with *The Towering Inferno* (1974) and including the *Naked Gun* series from 1988 to 1994. In 1994 Simpson was indicted for the murders of his ex-wife, Nicole Brown Simpson, and her friend, Ronald Lyle Goldman. In a televised trial that captured international attention and ended 474 days after his arrest, the jury—which had been sequestered for 266 days—acquitted Simpson. In a 1997 civil trial, a jury found him liable for the killings and awarded the Brown and Goldman families a total of $33.5 million in damages.

SINAI TEMPLE, Jewish Conservative temple located in Westwood at the corner of Wilshire and Beverly Glen Boulevards since 1961. The congregation was first located, in 1909, in downtown Los Angeles at 12th and Valencia Streets, in a building subsequently occupied by the Welsh Presbyterian

Church in 1925. In 1926 it moved to a new temple at 4th Street and New Hampshire Avenue—the present home of the Korean Philadelphia Presbyterian Church. The first classes of the University of Judaism in Los Angeles were held at the New Hampshire location. Both earlier sites have been named city cultural monuments.

SINCLAIR, UPTON BEALL (1878–1968), prolific socialist writer who moved to Southern California in 1915, lured west by H. Gaylord Wilshire, the eccentric millionaire socialist. Sinclair settled in Pasadena in 1916, a decade after publishing his exposé about the Chicago stockyards, *The Jungle* (1906). That novel not only influenced enactment of the first pure-food-and-drug legislation, but also made Sinclair a world celebrity. His more than 100 books include *The Brass Check* (1919), a barbed look at journalism, especially as practiced by Col. Harrison Gray Otis of the *Los Angeles Times; The Goose Step* (1923), concerning higher education at USC; and *Oil!* (1927), based on the Signal Hill oil boom.

The frail and ascetic-looking figure was a health-food enthusiast, prohibitionist, and, basically, a Christian socialist. Sinclair ran, unsuccessfully, as the Socialist Party candidate for Congress in 1920, for the U.S. Senate in 1922, and for governor in 1926. In 1934 he registered as a Democrat in Beverly Hills and launched a second gubernatorial

> **I** actually went to Forest Lawn to mock and came away humbled. Despite the fairground atmosphere, the beauty of the landscape was touching.   —Lawrence Durrell

campaign under the motto "End Poverty in California" (EPIC). When he won the nomination over George Creel, the *Los Angeles Times*'s Harry Chandler organized California media, business interests, and political officials to combat his candidacy, hiring an advertising firm to mastermind what Chandler termed "a war." Sinclair lost to incumbent Frank Merriam. The campaign was inspired by his own novel, *I, Candidate for Governor, and How I Ended Poverty: A True Story of the Future* (1935).

During the 1923 "Wobbly" free speech strike in

San Pedro, Sinclair was jailed for reading the Declaration of Independence. He was a cofounder of the American Civil Liberties Union, and a staunch defender of women's rights. Although noted more for his polemics than for his literary style, Sinclair's fiction was widely read, including the extremely popular Lanny Budd series, written in the 1940s.

People as diverse as John F. Kennedy, Leon Trotsky, Ramsey Clark, Eric Sevareid, Maxim Gorky, and Mahatma Gandhi attested to having been influenced by Sinclair. His wide circle of friends, acquaintances, and correspondents included Charlie Chaplin, Luther Burbank, Aline Barnsdall, Jack London, Albert Einstein, Eugene Debs, Clarence Darrow, George Bernard Shaw, Winston Churchill, H. L. Mencken, and the socialist razor manufacturer King Gillette. He talked politics with Henry Ford while hiking in the San Gabriel Mountains.

SIQUEIROS, DAVID ALFARO. *See* Murals

SISTERS OF CHARITY, independent community of Roman Catholic women, officially called the Daughters of Charity of St. Vincent de Paul. Tracing their roots back to 1634 Europe, they came to Los Angeles from the eastern United States in 1856 to open an asylum for orphan girls and a school for day students. The Sisters of Charity built the city's first hospital in 1858 and maintained it under a contract with the Board of Supervisors. Today it is known as St. Vincent Medical Center.

SKATEBOARDING, sport said to have originated in Southern California in 1963. After dying out for a time, it surged back, achieving even greater popularity in the 1970s when manufacturers began selling fiberglass boards with polyurethane wheels that allowed greater speed and more athletic moves. Teams, championships, and publications have helped skateboarding evolve into a semiorganized sport.

SKID ROW, squalid 50-block area bordered by Main, 3rd, Alameda, and 7th Streets downtown. Officially named Central City East by the Community Redevelopment Agency (CRA), it contains transient hotels, liquor stores, and shelters for homeless people, but also includes wholesale enterprises in food processing, toys, and electronics. Most of its denizens, felled by unemployment, poverty, mental illness, drugs, or alcohol, are home-

less males, but a growing number are women and even entire families. Social services are inadequate, and the CRA has slated the area for redevelopment according to a twofold plan that would "contain" the homeless—i.e., drive them out of the Central Business District—and provide them with new accommodations and social services in Central City East. A public corporation has purchased single-room-occupancy (SRO) hotels in the new area in anticipation of this event.

SKIRBALL CULTURAL CENTER AND MUSEUM, complex in Sepulveda Pass, completed in 1996, specializing in art and artifacts relating to American Jewish life. Founded in 1875 as a Judaica museum at Hebrew Union College (HUC) in Cincinnati, Ohio, it moved in 1971 to the new Los

---

Great weather and automobiles.
                    —Jamal Wilkes, basketball player

Angeles campus of HUC, adjacent to the University of Southern California. In 1983 HUC evolved a plan to expand the museum by adding a conference and educational center, as well as other amenities. It purchased a 15-acre site in the Santa Monica Mountains, near the campus of the University of Judaism. The Skirball Cultural Center and Museum was designed by architect Moshe Safdie and funded by the Jack and Audry Skirball Foundation, J. Paul Getty Trust, and Roy Disney Family Foundation.

SLAUSON, JONATHAN SAYRE (1829–1905), prominent local entrepreneur. Slauson was a director of the Los Angeles County Bank (formed in 1874), a backer of the Los Angeles and Independence Railroad, a leading Presbyterian layman, and an avid land developer. He organized the Azusa Land and Water Company and, during the Boom of the Eighties, laid out the town of Azusa on a 4,000-acre segment of the old Rancho Azusa, which he purchased from the Yankee settler Henry Dalton. Slauson chose a site that was "practically all sand, gravel, and boulder wash," saying, "If it's not good for a town, it isn't good for anything!" Speculators grabbed up $280,000 worth of lots in one day, and within three months Slauson had pocketed profits of $1.1 million. Azusa, a town created largely from puffery, became a citrus shipping center and had a population of a few hundred in 1890. An inveterate gambler, Slauson backed Thaddeus S. C. Lowe's scheme to manufacture gas from water, and became a member of a land development syndicate formed by Henry Huntington. In 1903 he served on the Los Angeles Board of Education. Slauson Boulevard is named for him.

SLEEPY LAGOON MURDER, homicide case that racked Los Angeles from 1942 to 1944. On 2 August 1942 the comatose body of teenager José Diaz was found close to an open reservoir near Slauson and Atlantic Boulevards, a popular swimming hole for Mexican young people. Diaz died in a hospital without regaining consciousness, and the police initiated a dragnet in which they rounded up 300 Mexican American youths, 23 of whom were eventually arrested on murder charges. Dubbing it the "Sleepy Lagoon Murder," even though there was no proof that Diaz had in fact been murdered, the press featured it on the front page for months, calling it a gangland slaying. Bigotry was rampant and overt. One expert witness from the sheriff's office testified that Mexicans committed cruel crimes because they were Indians. In blatant flagrancy of justice, the district attorney's office refused to allow the defendants to cut their hair or change their clothing during the course of the trial, and the presiding judge declined to instruct witnesses of their rights, declaring that it would take up too much time.

The Mexican American community, together with civil rights organizations, formed the Sleepy Lagoon Defense Committee, which was headed by attorney Carey McWilliams. Although the prosecution failed to establish that a murder had taken place, and the defense maintained that the death was most likely due to an accident, 12 of the defendants were convicted of murder and 5 others were convicted of assault. The U.S. District Court of Appeals overturned the convictions as a miscarriage of justice, citing the lack of evidence, and rebuked the presiding judge for numerous improprieties. All defendants were acquitted and freed in October 1944. By then, eight of the young men had spent two years in San Quentin.

The Sleepy Lagoon case represents the first major victory of the organized Chicano community in Los Angeles. It was the subject of Luis Valdez's play *Zoot Suit* (1978), starring Edward James Olmos as El Pachuco; he reprised the role in the film

of the same name in 1981. Thomas Sanchez's novel *The Zoot Suit Murders* (1978) also revolves around the Sleepy Lagoon case.

SLOW-GROWTH MOVEMENT, grass-roots drive to limit real estate development and protect the quality of city life. In Los Angeles it coalesced in the early 1980s as a revolt of upper-income and middle-class homeowners on the Westside and in the San Fernando Valley against high-rise development. In November 1986 the movement crossed ethnic, racial, geographic, and class lines when it won passage of Proposition U, which cut by half the building density allowed on commercial property and imposed a growth management plan on the city. In 1987 the movement was instrumental in defeating progrowth city council member Pat Russell's bid for reelection, as well as the city's proposed incinerator plant in South Central Los Angeles. A year later, in the aftermath of an overload crisis at the Hyperion Sewage Treatment Plant, the council passed a stop-gap ordinance restricting the number of city sewer hookups.

Slow-growth proponents have also attempted to halt the expansion of Los Angeles International Airport, freeway double-decking, and the extension of light-rail transportation. Although some slow-growth leaders have embraced broad related policies such as family planning, permanent limits on office buildings, the clustering of urban functions by neighborhood, and restriction of foreign immigration, most activists take a pragmatic, case-by-case approach. They found a new and effective tool in the "interim control ordinance," a city council measure that imposes specific limits for individual neighborhoods for a specified number of months or years. Additional ordinances have been passed imposing a variety of other limits. They include density limits for apartments, height restrictions, a moratorium on mini-mall construction, restrictions protecting views and ensuring setbacks, traffic mitigation and parking restrictions, open space provisions, limits on commercial and industrial development, restrictions on auto body shops, and bans on conflicting zoning within a neighborhood.

SMITH, JACK CLIFFORD (1916–1995), syndicated *Los Angeles Times* columnist noted for his witty, literate observations. Born in Long Beach, Smith served in the Marine Corps in World War II and was a combat correspondent in the battle of Iwo Jima. He and his wife, Denise, lived on Mt.

Washington, a neighborhood near downtown Los Angeles that often appeared in his columns. Selected *Times* columns were reprinted in book form in *Jack Smith's L.A.* (1980), and his observations in *Westways* magazine appeared in a work entitled *The Big Orange* (1976). Smith, who relished words and their usage, is responsible for popularizing the name "Big Orange" for Los Angeles, to parallel "Big Apple" for New York City.

SMITH, SARAH BIXBY HATHAWAY (1871–1935), author. She was born on Rancho San Justo near San Juan Bautista in Monterey County. Llewellyn Bixby, Sarah's father, had come from Maine during the Gold Rush. He arrived in Los Angeles in 1896 with his family, and became a prominent landowner. Smith married twice, bore four sons and a daughter, studied painting, and wrote poetry and prose. It was her second husband, Paul Jordan-Smith, the literary editor of the *Los Angeles Times,* who encouraged her writing career. Sarah Bixby Smith's classic memoir *Adobe Days* (1925) describes pioneer life in Northern California and in the *pueblo* of Los Angeles in the American era; it offers vivid personal details of life on Ranchos Los Alamitos and Los Cerritos, two large Bixby-owned estates in Southern California.

SMOG. *See* Air pollution

SNAKES. *See* Reptiles

SNYDER, MEREDITH P[INXTON] ("PINKY") (1859–1937), three-time mayor of Los Angeles. The durable and persistent Snyder, who came to Los Angeles in 1880 and clerked in a furniture store, served as mayor from 1896 to 1898, 1900 to 1904, and 1919 to 1921. A Democrat in a period of Republican ascendancy, he was elected the first time because he favored municipal ownership of the waterworks. In 1898 he lost his reelection bid to Republican Fred Eaton, but staged a comeback in 1900, when waterworks issues again dominated the local scene. In 1904 he opposed a corrupt printing contract between the city and the Republican *Los Angeles Times.* The *Times* retaliated, causing him to lose reelection in 1905. Snyder remained active in civic affairs even while out of office; for example, he vocally supported annexation of the harbor in 1909. His terms spanned a dynamic period in the city's history, with the area mushrooming from 30 to 300 square miles and the population soaring from 100,000 to

500,000. Snyder's cousin, Arthur Kress (1932–), was a Los Angeles councilman during the 1970s.

SOCCER, world's most popular sport. Strongly favored in Latin American and European communities, it is gaining ground with the general Southern California population. The slogan of the American Youth Soccer Organization, "Everyone Plays Soccer," indicates that all team members have an opportunity to participate, and that the game is popular with both boys and girls. The Greater Los Angeles Soccer League, an organization of amateurs, has been in existence since the 1940s. Pasadena's Rose Bowl hosted eight contests of World Cup '94, including the final match between Italy and Brazil. The average attendance for the eight games was 89,478.

In 1996 the Galaxy, a Los Angeles team, played their first professional game in the Rose Bowl. Their first two Bowl games drew a total of 109,602 fans.

SOCIAL AND FRATERNAL CLUBS. *See* Fraternal societies

SOCIAL AND PUBLIC ART RESOURCES CENTER (SPARC), multicultural arts center

Los Angeles Chamber Orchestra, SPARC mural. Photo by Lori Shepler.

formed in 1976 by muralist Judith F. Baca, painter Christina Schlesinger, and filmmaker Donna Deitch. Since 1978 it has occupied the historic Venice Police Station building. Working under contract with the Los Angeles Cultural Affairs Department, SPARC is devoted to fostering a diversity of expression in public art and public monuments. Among its best-known projects are the "Great Wall of Los Angeles," a half-mile long mural along the Tujunga Wash in the San Fernando Valley, and freeway murals honoring the 1994 World Cup Soccer finals.

SOCIALIST PARTY, moderate reform party active in Los Angeles politics from 1902 to 1915. Like the Progressive movement, it pressed for honesty in government, completion of a deep-water harbor, municipal ownership of public utilities, a graduated income tax, female suffrage, and the initiative, referendum, and recall. The party arose amid the concerted antilabor crusade of Harrison Gray Otis and the Merchants and Manufacturers Association, and during the crescendo of labor militancy from 1900 to 1910. Although its membership was small, it enjoyed a large following in the

---

It's a land on the surface of dreams. And then there's a kind of slimy underlayer. The contrast of beauty and possibility and that ugliness and corruption is very powerful.

—Walter Mosley, mystery writer

---

industrial labor movement and among some ethnic groups. The Socialists reached their apogee on 31 October 1911, when their candidate, labor attorney Job Harriman, won the mayoral primary. The party, however, had staunchly defended the innocence of the McNamara brothers, and when the pair pleaded guilty shortly before the mayoral election to bombing the *Los Angeles Times* Building, the Socialists' chances were dashed. Membership and influence declined, though the party did manage to garner 50,000 votes in 1915. The Socialist Party was part of the wider movement whose local leaders and supporters included Upton Sinclair and H. Gaylord Wilshire.

SOCIAL SERVICES. The first major push for government services for the poor occurred during the Progressive Era at the turn of the century when reformers began to press actively for playgrounds, public baths, employment services, and improved housing. Additional services came during the depression, under the aegis of the New Deal, and especially in the 1960s and 1970s, with the enactment of new federal and state programs. Severe cutbacks were made in the 1980s.

The main governmental agency in this field is the Los Angeles County Department of Public Social Services, which, among other functions, handles general relief. Its 1993–1994 budget exceeded $565 million—and in that year general relief payments were reduced by 27 percent from the previous year.

Los Angeles County is especially rich in self-help groups, as well as telephone hot lines and information and referral services, which developed in the 1970s. The most comprehensive information and referral service is United Way's INFO LINE (213-686-0950), a comprehensive 24-hour telephone operation offering assistance in Spanish, Mandarin, Cantonese, Farsi, Armenian, Tagalog, Korean, Portuguese, and Italian.

SOCIEDAD HISPANO-AMERICANA DE BENEFICIO MUTUO. *See* La Sociedad Hispano-Americana de Beneficio Mutuo

SOCIEDAD MUTUALISTA MEXICANA. *See* La Sociedad Mutualista Mexicana

SOKA UNIVERSITY, school in the Santa Monica Mountains National Recreation Area, near Calabasas. Soka University of America, founded in 1987, is a language school for 200 American and Japanese students, employing 15 faculty members. It is basically a liberal arts school focusing on Pacific Rim studies. Situated on 580 acres, it offers free lectures and nature walks to the public. Although the university does not offer religious instruction, it is affiliated with Soka Gakkai Buddhism.

SOLEDAD, sparsely occupied unincorporated area in the Antelope Valley. The nearby rugged hills also bear the same name, which means "solitude" or "loneliness." Early travelers passed through Soledad Canyon and over Soledad Pass en route to the Antelope Valley. It was in that canyon on 6 Sep-

SONY PICTURES ENTERTAINMENT

Chinese laying railroad tracks, Soledad Canyon, ca. 1871. Courtesy Photographic Collections, Los Angeles Public Library.

tember 1876 that the last rails were laid linking Southern California to Northern California and to the rest of the United States.

SOMERVILLE, JOHN ALEXANDER (1882–1973),

first African American dentist in California. A Jamaican by birth, Somerville worked in Redlands, saved money, and entered USC dental school, graduating at the turn of the century. He set up his office at 4th Street and Broadway. He also built Hotel Somerville at 41st Street and Central Avenue, which became the major hotel for black people in Los Angeles. It was the site of the NAACP's national convention in 1928. Somerville lost ownership during the Great Depression, and his property was renamed the Dunbar Hotel, after the celebrated African American poet Lawrence Dunbar.

SONORATOWN, former Mexican downtown residential neighborhood. Mexicans returning from the California Gold Rush in the mid-1850s settled in adobes north of the Plaza Church, along North Main and North Broadway, and on the hilly streets north and west of the Plaza, including Alpine and Buena Vista. The long, low, white-washed adobes were homes and shops to poor, working-class Mexicans, many from the Mexican province of Sonora. The Plaza Church was their cultural anchor. By the early 1900s, however, the arrival of the railroad, the spread of industry and commerce, and the southward spread of real estate development all gradually undermined Sonoratown as a residential neighborhood.

SONY PICTURES ENTERTAINMENT (SPE), Japanese-owned film conglomerate headquartered in the old Metro-Goldwyn-Mayer lot in Culver City. In one of the biggest media acquisitions of recent times, Sony has spent over $6 billion since the 1980s to assemble a film unit comprising Columbia Pictures, TriStar Pictures, Sony Classics, and Triumph Releasing. By acquiring Columbia it inherited a library of 3,000 feature films dating back to the 1920s, including 12 best picture Academy Award winners. Sony Television Entertainment produces and distributes syndicated game shows *(Jeopardy* and *Wheel of Fortune)* and soap operas *(The Young and the Restless* and *Days of Our Lives),* while another arm, Columbia TriStar Television Distribution handles talk shows *(Ricki Lake)* and other daytime and prime-time TV features *(Seinfeld).* SPE also has access to a library of 30,000 episodes of 270 television series, which it distributes worldwide. Its Columbia TriStar Home Video division is a marketplace leader in the home video field. The state-of-the-art studio operation employs 2,500 people working 38 sound stages at the 60-acre facility.

Sonoratown, 1869. Courtesy Robert Weinstein Collection.

SORIANO, RAPHAEL S. (1907–1988), distinguished architect. Soriano practiced in Southern California from the 1930s to the 1950s and was associated with the International style and the Case Study House movement. His residences, apartments, and offices were often designed around factory-produced steel frames. The Shulman House and Studio, a city historical monument in the Hollywood Hills, is one of the few Soriano houses that remains in its original condition.

SOUTH BAY, term used loosely to define part of the coastal area of Santa Monica Bay, from Los Angeles International Airport on the north to Rocky Point or Point Vicente on the south. South Bay communities include El Segundo, Hermosa Beach, Manhattan Beach, Redondo Beach, and Palos Verdes Estates. A chamber of commerce coalition casts a wider net and includes 18 coastal and inland cities and communities from Westchester to Long Beach.

SOUTH CENTRAL LOS ANGELES, 40-square-mile district in the city of Los Angeles between downtown and Long Beach. It is bounded by the city's Wilshire, Westlake, Southeast Los Angeles, and West Adams districts, and by the independent cities of Gardena and Torrance; it also includes the older area of Watts. Early in the century South Central's population was predominantly African American, but since the 1970s it has become more multiracial owing especially to a large influx of Latinos. According to a city council study, the area has 587,000 residents.

SOUTH COAST AIR QUALITY MANAGEMENT DISTRICT (AQMD), regional air pollution control agency formed by the state. In the 1990s conservationists considered it to be the most effective local air quality district in the nation. It was created in 1975. The new district merged the Los Angeles Air Pollution Control District, formed in 1948, with its counterparts in Orange, Riverside, and San Bernardino Counties. The territory covered is the South Coast Air Basin, an area of 13,350 square miles, with 13 million people and 9 million cars. The AQMD's task is to meet air quality goals established by state and federal governments—a heroic goal considering that there are 60,000 sources of pollution in Los Angeles County alone. The agency monitors ozone, the most significant cause of air pollution, as well as other pollutants, such as lead, sulfate,

and sulfur dioxide. It declares smog alerts, and it brings offenders into court, imposing fines ranging from $1,000 to $100,000. It has an operating budget of over $100 million, and a 12-member governing board. In 1986 the AQMD established a comprehensive clean-air plan. By 1991, the cleanest smog season since monitoring began, the agency proclaimed that the improved air quality was a direct

---

We have a tremendous stake in the outcome of things being planned for Los Angeles. . . . The Korean community can play a pivotal role in the social change taking place.
—Edward Taeh Chang,
professor of Ethnic Studies

---

result of the 1986 plan. Vigorous policy enforcement, it says, has reduced air pollution by half, even though the population has increased dramatically. Critics, however, charge that no progress has been made in dealing with invisible gasses.

The chief executive officer of the AQMD since 1987 has been James M. Lents, a Tennessean by birth, who holds two degrees in physics. He is generally regarded as the single most important person shaping air policy in the region.

In 1993 the agency tentatively announced a controversial "smog exchange program," by which polluters who reduce their emissions below specified levels would be allowed to sell their "pollution credit" to others who have not yet installed new emission controls. Environmentalists protested that the trade-off system would allow excessive amounts of sulfur oxides, hydrocarbons, and nitrogen oxides to remain in the air.

SOUTH EL MONTE, incorporated town in the San Gabriel Valley, 10 miles east of downtown Los Angeles. It was formed from land omitted from El Monte when that city was created in 1912. Calling itself "the Hub of the Valley," South El Monte was incorporated in 1958. Its population reached 20,800 in 1990, an increase of more than 25 percent in 10 years.

SOUTHERN CALIFORNIA, geographic region with Los Angeles at its core. The boundaries are generally defined by the Pacific Ocean to the west, the Tehachapi Mountains to the north, the San Bernardino and San Jacinto Mountains to the east, and the Mexican border to the south. Thus Southern California includes the southern part of Santa Barbara County; all of Ventura, Los Angeles, and Orange Counties; and the parts of San Bernardino, Riverside, and San Diego Counties that lie to the west of the mountains. (To confuse matters, the term "Inland Empire" is used for all of San Bernardino and Riverside Counties.)

The term "Southern California" is of fairly recent origin. In the 19th century the area was variously called "California del sur," "the California of the south," "subtropical California," "the cow counties," or "the land south of Tehachapi." The practice of capitalizing the "s" in Southern California became well established in the 1920s. The word "Southland" is used by local newspapers and newscasters as a rough equivalent of "Southern California," but has not gained full currency in scholarly books or popular usage.

In the eyes of geographers, Southern California is distinguished by the fact that it is the only place in the country with a Mediterranean climate. The surrounding mountains, ocean, and deserts have created an insular aura, leading some writers—most notably Carey McWilliams—to describe it as "an island on the land." With a geographic area of 12,000 square miles—about the size of Belgium—it is home to more than half of California's 30 million population.

SOUTHERN CALIFORNIA: AN ISLAND ON THE LAND (1946), classic regional history by Carey McWilliams. The author says, "I did not just happen to write this book: I lived it." It reflects his activist career as journalist and attorney, and describes his association with innumerable local intellectuals.

SOUTHERN CALIFORNIA ASSOCIATION OF GOVERNMENTS (SCAG), regional planning body formed in 1965 to deal with areawide concerns throughout the 38,500 square miles of Los Angeles, Orange, Ventura, Riverside, and Imperial Counties. All cities in the region are eligible for representation, but maintain their local autonomy. SCAG's formation grew out of a requirement that grant applications for federal funding be reviewed by a local body. It has since prepared a master plan involving transportation, airports, and parks and recreation, as well as studies of population, housing, employment, and related issues. The association gathers information on all of these areas, but has faced traditional California resistance to regional government. At times some 20 percent of potential members have boycotted the agency, which they regard as lacking in authority. New Sacramento initiatives to stimulate regional government are pending.

SOUTHERN CALIFORNIA EDISON COMPANY, nation's fourth largest electric utility. With headquarters in Rosemead, it operates outside the boundaries of the city of Los Angeles. In addition to Los Angeles County, it takes in all of Orange County and parts of Ventura, Santa Barbara, and Riverside Counties. It grew out of a combination of predecessors. One was the Edison Electric Company of Los Angeles, founded in 1897, which amalgamated with Henry E. Huntington's Pacific Light

---

If we are a nation of extremes, Los Angeles is an extreme among us. . . . What Los Angeles is to excess, all cities are to some extent.
—Sarah Comstock, writer, 1928

---

and Power Corporation. In 1922 it sold this distribution company to the city of Los Angeles. Other predecessors were Mt. Whitney Power Company, established in 1899, and Nevada Power, Mining, and Milling, established in 1904. Southern California Edison operates some of Hoover Dam's generators, both for itself and for other investor-owned utilities. In 1982 the company received the John and Alice Tyler Ecology-Energy Award as well as the National Wildlife Federation's special conservation award. The company is experimenting with solar and wind energy and desalinization of seawater.

SOUTHERN CALIFORNIA GAS COMPANY, OR THE GAS COMPANY, nation's largest distributor of natural gas. The company was preceded by the Los Angeles Gas Company, founded in 1867, and emerged in 1910 under the name of Southern California Gas Company. It later acquired over 50 additional gas companies, including Southern Counties Gas in 1970.

In 1929 Southern California Gas was itself acquired by a larger entity, the Pacific Lighting Company of San Francisco, known since 1988 as Pacific Enterprises. Southern California Gas remains the largest subsidiary of Pacific Enterprises, and is a monopoly regulated by the state Public Utilities Commission. Most of the natural gas it supplies to Southern California originates 1,200 miles away, in Texas and eastern New Mexico. Highly efficient and relatively pollution free, the fuel is delivered via a pipeline completed in 1946–1947. The Gas Company has 9,000 employees, and serves more than 12 million people in a service area of over 20,000 square miles. The firm is a leader in environmental concerns such as developing pollution-free alternative fuels.

SOUTHERN CALIFORNIA INSTITUTE OF ARCHITECTURE (SCI-ARC), independent architectural training institution founded by Raymond Kappe in 1972. The West Los Angeles–based school, formed with a nucleus of faculty from Cal Poly, Pomona, was originally known as the New School of Architecture. In 1994 it had 450 undergraduate and graduate students and 75 faculty members. It has achieved international renown for its community outreach programs in architectural education, its devotion to redefining the role of the architect in society, and its creative efforts to solve problems such as livable low-cost public housing.

SOUTHERN CALIFORNIA LIBRARY FOR SOCIAL STUDIES AND RESEARCH, independent archives located in South Central Los Angeles. The library specializes in the books, periodicals, and historical documents of the political left since the 1930s. Founded by activist Emil Freed in 1963, it maintains collections, fosters research projects, sponsors exhibits, and hosts social events.

SOUTHERN CALIFORNIA RAPID TRANSIT DISTRICT (RTD). *See* Los Angeles County Metropolitan Transportation Authority

SOUTHERN CALIFORNIA REGIONAL RAIL AUTHORITY. *See* Metrolink

SOUTHERN PACIFIC RAILROAD (SP), historically the most important transportation link for Los Angeles. It was created as a subsidiary of the transcontinental Central Pacific Railroad to build lines from San Francisco to Los Angeles and eastward to the Colorado River. As a condition for serving Los Angeles, the SP demanded that the city pay $600,000 in cash and donate considerable land for rail yards. If its conditions were not met, the SP threatened to lay its tracks elsewhere, bypassing Los Angeles entirely. The railroad gained voter approval in a special election in November 1872. Construction began in the San Joaquin Valley in 1873 and was completed in northern Los Angeles County in 1876. The SP also built other lines out of the city: north to the San Fernando Mission, east to Arizona, and southeast to Anaheim. It absorbed the existing lines of the Los Angeles and Independence and the Los Angeles and San Pedro Railroads.

The SP stimulated agriculture, especially in the marketing of oranges; built towns; encouraged oil drilling and industrial development; made Los Angeles into a tourist mecca; and generally contributed to the prosperity of the region. Yet its determination to maintain a transportation monop-

Southern Pacific Rail Depot, ca. 1916. Pitt Collection.

oly angered many citizens. Collis P. Huntington, SP president, fought hard to prevent the Santa Fe Railroad from entering the Los Angeles Basin, and he attempted to undermine the port at San Pedro to benefit his own hastily built port facility in Santa Monica. In addition, he sought to bribe city hall officials into granting the SP exclusive control over the bed of the Los Angeles River for its tracks. All three efforts failed, amid a growing antirailroad reform movement.

The SP remains, along with the Santa Fe and Union Pacific, one of the three major railroads in Los Angeles. Headquartered in San Francisco, the corporation was bought by investor Philip F. Anschutz in 1991 for $1 billion. Its main business in Los Angeles includes shipping imported automobiles and containerized freight from the Long Beach/Los Angeles Harbor area. The SP's 7,000 miles of tracks, which radiate out into 14 western and southwestern states, are now merged with those of the Denver and Rio Grande Railroad. They are also used by Amtrak, the national passenger rail service.

SOUTH GATE, independent city 7 miles south of downtown Los Angeles, north of Lynwood and west of Downey. The Shoshonean village of Tibahagna was located where the first City Hall was later built. The area was part of the Spanish Rancho San Antonio, granted in 1810, and during the World War I era it was home to Ascot Speedway, an early auto race track. Subdivided for homes in 1917, it was named South Gate Gardens a year later,

---

There's nobody here with any roots. Even the houses are built with mud and chicken wire.

—William Faulkner, early 1940s

---

after the gardens located near the south gate of the Cudahy Packing Company Ranch. The pilot Amelia Earhart learned to fly at South Gate's Kinner Field in 1921. The 7.5-square-mile community was incorporated under the name of South Gate in 1923, and soon acquired key industrial plants, including a General Motors auto assembly plant and a Firestone tire factory. It was the birthplace and childhood home of Glenn T. Seaborg, the Nobel Prize–winning chemist who discovered pluto-

nium and oversaw development of the Manhattan Project during World War II. South Gate and its large blue-collar population lost a valuable job base when the factories closed in the 1970s and 1980s, but has since become one of the fastest-growing areas of Los Angeles. The population increased 29 percent in the decade following 1980, reaching 86,200 in 1990.

SOUTHLAND. *See* Southern California

SOUTH PARK, planned residential and retail area at 9th Street and Grand Avenue surrounding a new 2.5-acre city park. Under development by the Community Redevelopment Agency, the project is intended to revitalize the central city by enticing middle-income residents. After decades of building, the dream has yet to materialize.

SOUTH PASADENA, independent San Gabriel Valley city 3.4 square miles in area, 6 miles northeast of downtown Los Angeles. In 1885 its original settlers built midwestern-style homes and established tidy vineyards and orchards on "surplus" land acquired from neighboring Pasadena.

Much of South Pasadena still resembles a midwestern town, owing in part to slow-growth policies. The city government has resisted condominiums, for example, and for three decades has resisted construction of a 6.2-mile extension of the Long Beach Freeway (I-710), claiming that it would split the town, displace 12 percent of the population, destroy historic homes and neighborhoods, reduce the tax rolls, and increase surface-street congestion along its path.

South Pasadena supports a police department with 31 officers. The town's $3 million civic center combines design elements of traditional Spanish, Mission Revival, and postmodern architectural styles. In 1920 the population was 7,652; by 1995 it had grown to 24,000.

SOUTH SAN GABRIEL, part of the city of Rosemead. It was the site of the original Mission San Gabriel, established on 8 September 1771, before the Franciscan fathers moved it to higher ground in San Gabriel in 1776. South San Gabriel was founded by Richard Garvey Sr., who came to Los Angeles in 1858, worked as a government mail rider, and became a close associate of E. J. "Lucky" Baldwin. In the 1870s he homesteaded the area known as Garvey Ranch; in 1892 he subdivided

4,500 acres for residences in South San Gabriel and Monterey Park, and also organized the Garvey school district.

SOUTHWEST MUSEUM, private institution atop Mt. Washington in Highland Park. Specializing in artifacts and arts and crafts of Native Americans and of the Spanish and Mexican colonial periods of the American Southwest, it was founded by Charles Fletcher Lummis together with other members of the Southwest Society, a branch of the Archaeological Society of America. Construction began in 1910, and the museum opened to the public in 1914. Only 5 percent of its 250,000-piece collection is on display at any given time. The main building is in the Mission Revival style. Also part of the museum complex are La Casa de Adobe, a re-creation of a rancho adobe, and Lummis's private residence on the Arroyo Seco, "El Alisal." After repeated debates about moving to a new site, the museum board has decided to remain at its original historic location.

Southwest Museum. Photo by Larry Reynolds, courtesy Southwest Museum.

SOUTH WHITTIER, county area between Whittier and La Mirada. Its population in 1990 was 49,514.

SPALDING, WILLIAM ANDREW (1852–1941), journalist and business promoter. Spalding arrived in Los Angeles from Kansas in 1874 and worked as a reporter, business manager, and editor on the *Los Angeles Herald-Express* and *Los Angeles Times,* where he helped Harrison Gray Otis fight organized labor. An ardent regional booster, he promoted the development of Pomona, the San Fernando Valley, and Colton, as well as the Sunset orange growers organization. After retirement in the 1930s he wrote a descriptive memoir, *Los Angeles Newspaperman,* which was published posthumously in 1961.

SPANISH-LANGUAGE NEWSPAPERS. *See* Newspapers, non-English

SPANISH (MEXICAN COLONIAL) PERIOD, 1542–1821. Three expeditions of discovery passed through the area early on, ultimately leading to settlement of Alta California. In 1542 Juan Rodríguez Cabrillo, a Portuguese navigator sailing under the flag of Spain, sighted Santa Catalina Island, which he named San Salvador, and San Pedro Bay, which he called Bay of Smokes. In 1602 Sebastián Vizcaíno sailed past, conferring upon Santa Catalina Island its modern name. And in 1769 an exploration was conducted by Capt. Gaspar de Portolá, Father Juan Crespi, and a force of 67 men. Blazing the trail later called El Camino Real, the party passed through the southern part of what is now Elysian Park. Crespi wrote: "a very spacious valley, well grown with cottonwoods and alders, among which ran a beautiful river." The Franciscan fathers established Mission San Gabriel on 8 September 1771 and Mission San Fernando 1797.

The *pueblo* of Los Angeles was settled by Gov. Felipe de Neve in 1781, who methodically recruited Mexicans from Sinaloa and Sonora with inducements of land, money, livestock, and farming implements. A band of Mexican colonials—11 men, 11 women, and 22 children, most of them farmers, laborers, mine workers, and artisans—left Alamos in Mexico in February and arrived at Mission San Gabriel in August. On or about 4 September 1781, de Neve led the small procession, probably accompanied by four soldiers and several Indian neophytes, near the site of the present-day Plaza. Eight of the 23 adults were Indian, 10 were of African descent, and de Neve was from Spain—as a group they mirrored colonial life in Mexico. De Neve had paved the way among the local Indians on an earlier trip; now he staked out 4 square leagues, consisting of a small plaza surrounded by 7-acre fields for cultivation, as well as pastures and royal lands. The family names of the pioneer *pobladores* were Camero, Lara, Mesa, Moreno, Navarro, Quintero, Rodríguez, Rosas, Vanegas, and Villavicencio.

This was the beginning of what some scholars call the "Mexican colonial" period of Los Angeles history. Without ceremony, the settlers set about digging irrigation ditches *(zanjas),* building huts to live in *(jacales),* and planting corn, squash, beans, cilantro, barley, wheat, and melons. In 1788 civilian government was established. The missionaries fought with the local military and civilian authorities for control almost continuously. Settlement increased and crops became abundant, despite occasional attacks by locusts. By 1790 there were over 1,500 grazing animals in the *pueblo*. Ranchos were established in the vicinity, with Juan José Domínguez receiving the first grant, for Rancho San Pedro. *Pobladores* and rancheros often married Native Americans. The Sepúlveda, Verdugo, Nieto, and Yorba families were especially prosperous rancheros. By 1820 the population of Los Angeles had soared to 650 *gente de razón* (non-Indians), making it the largest town in Alta California.

SPANISH PLACE-NAMES exist in great numbers as a permanent heritage of the Spanish and Mexican past. Many have become Anglicized or corrupted, owing in part to Yankees' unfamiliarity with the syntax and spelling of Spanish. For example, Princessa Way in Canyon Country is a false spelling in both Spanish *(princesa)* and Italian *(principessa),* and Murrieta is widely misspelled as Murietta (perhaps a reminder of Marietta, Ohio). The masculine article, *el,* is often linked with a feminine noun (El Vista Court in Montrose), while the

---

Hollywood is a dreary industrial town controlled by hoodlums of enormous wealth, the ethical sense of a pack of jackals, and taste so degraded that it befouled everything it touched.   —S. J. Perelman

---

feminine article, *la,* is sometimes attached to masculine nouns (La Valle Street in Sylmar). Another cause of corruption was the Yankee misunderstanding or ignorance of the meaning of Spanish words. Thus Mesa Peak translates as flat-topped peak, a contradiction in terms, and Arroyo Seco Creek as Dry Creek. Incorrect pronunciation affected the spellings of names as well, often because accents were dropped. Thus, "Portohla High School" and "Crezzpi High School" appear on older maps. Finally, names have been hybridized by real estate promoters to give their tracts a romantic aura. The city of Buena Park wins the prize for pseudo-Spanish street names, especially

through its prolific and imaginative use of "San," including San Rio (Holy River—the Jordan?) and San Calvino (St. Calvin).

SPENCE, EDWARD F[ALLES] (1832–1892), mayor of Los Angeles from 1884 to 1886. A Gold Rush pioneer, he arrived in Los Angeles in 1874 and helped found the Commercial Bank, later known as First National Bank. He was also one of the original founders of the University of Southern California in 1880, and in that same year supported a move to divide California into two states. Spence served as mayor on the eve of the Boom of the Eighties, when the city's population was over 11,000 and its area 29 square miles. His interest in civic affairs continued after he left office. In 1886 he served on the commission that established the city's professional fire department, and he donated money for USC to install a telescope on Mt. Wilson. Upon the former mayor's sudden death, however, the University of Chicago took over ownership of the observatory and installed the great glass on the San Gabriel peak.

SPIELBERG, STEVEN (1947–), Ohio-born filmmaker. At the age of 20, while still attending CSULB, he signed a seven-year directing contract with Universal Studios. His first film was *The Sugarland Express* (1974), followed soon afterward by *Jaws* (1975) and *Close Encounters of the Third Kind* (1977). His films *E.T. The Extra-Terrestrial* (1982) and *Jurassic Park* (1993) were the biggest-grossing films in motion picture history. Among the scores of films credited to him as writer, director, or producer are *The Color Purple* (1985), *Raiders of the Lost Ark* (1981), and *Schindler's List* (1993), for which he received an Academy Award as best director. In 1987 the Academy of Motion Picture Arts and Sciences honored Spielberg with the prestigious Irving G. Thalberg Award. In 1994 he, along with David Geffen and Jeffrey Katzenberg, formed DreamWorks, the newest major multimedia studio.

SPORTS. Five major professional teams—the Dodgers, Kings, Clippers, Lakers, and Galaxy, a new professional soccer team—make their home in the county. The Angels play in neighboring Orange County, as did the Rams until their move to St. Louis in 1995. In addition, numerous colleges and universities in the metropolis have nationally ranked teams. Los Angeles hosted the Olympics in 1932 and 1984. The mild climate encourages outdoor sports and contributes to a recreation-oriented society. Athletic events of all kinds, both amateur and professional, include ice hockey, basketball, tennis, football, baseball, horse racing, yachting, soccer, track and field, auto racing, skiing, swimming, surfing, skin diving, boxing, and wrestling.

SPORTS ARENA. *See* Los Angeles Memorial Sports Arena

SPRING STREET, former financial center known as the "Wall Street of the West" in the 1920s. The area deteriorated in the 1960s as new office towers were constructed on Flower and Grand Streets. Spring Street now borders on skid row and is cut off from the revival efforts on Bunker Hill. However, the city has officially designated it as a historic district, a move that supports efforts to preserve and restore architectural treasures. These include, among others, the Banco Popular (1903) with its stained-glass dome, the Palm Court of the Alexandria Hotel (1906), the I. N. Van Nuys Building (1911), the Art Deco lobby of the Title Insurance Building (1928), the Pacific Coast Stock Exchange (1930), and the bank building subsequently used by the Los Angeles Theater Center (LATC). The Community Redevelopment Agency has poured $50 million into various rehabilitation efforts, such as the LATC, with mixed success. The

Ronald Reagan State Office Building (1991) at Spring and 3rd Streets is a recent addition.

STANDARD OIL COMPANY OF CALIFORNIA (CHEVRON), giant California petroleum corporation. Although headquartered in San Francisco, the company has historic roots in Southern California. The germ of the operation was the Pacific Coast Oil Company, established in the 1870s in Pico Canyon in the Santa Susana Mountains of northwestern Los Angeles County. As the state's first successful commercial oil company, Pacific Coast Oil used imaginative marketing to fight off Standard Oil (Ohio). In 1900 Pacific Coast was bought out by the Rockefeller organization and merged with the assets of Standard Oil (Iowa); six years later a large new integrated enterprise named Standard Oil (California) emerged. In 1911, when the courts shattered the Rockefeller trust, the independent California branch went off on its own, flourishing in the Far West and achieving unsurpassed prominence in the international oil industry. Today Chevron, one of the top 11 industrial corporations in the country and the third largest U.S. petroleum company, maintains oil field research operations in La Habra.

STARR, KEVIN (1940–), cultural and social historian of California. He is author of the series "Americans and the California Dream," which

The intersection of 1st and Spring Streets, ca. 1886. Courtesy Robert Weinstein Collection.

includes, to date, *Americans and the California Dream, 1850–1915* (1973), *Inventing the Dream: California Through the Progressive Era* (1985), and *Material Dreams: Southern California Through the 1920s* (1990). Starr holds that whereas "most cities happen . . . Los Angeles willed itself into being." The series devotes considerable attention to the cultural life of Los Angeles, focusing on the evolution of literary, artistic, political, and business endeavors. A native Californian, Starr taught at USC, and was the principal of a communications consulting firm. In 1994 he was appointed state librarian.

STATE HISTORIC PARKS, under the direction of the State Department of Parks and Recreation, preserve, restore, and interpret sites of historic value in Los Angeles County. The properties are normally acquired through state bond funds and maintained by monies from the state annual budget, as well as by entrance fees, gifts, and donations of historical societies and foundations.

Fort Tejón State Historic Park near Lebec, off I-5, is the site of a military barracks that has been restored to the period of the 1850s. The Los Angeles State and County Arboretum in Arcadia contains a historic area amid its gardens, including the reconstructed dwellings of the Tongva (Gabrieleño) Indians and a Victorian mansion. Los Encinos State Historic Park in Encino preserves the adobes of a 19th-century rancho, previously the site of a Tongva Indian village. Malibu Lagoon State Beach in Malibu contains the Adamson House, once owned by Rhoda Rindge Adamson, daughter of the last owners of Rancho Topanga Malibu Sequit. Placerita Canyon State and County Park in

Newhall embraces the area where gold was discovered in 1842. Will Rogers State Historic Park in Pacific Palisades is the former estate of the beloved humorist, and features his ranch house and stables. In addition, the state maintains a regional office in El Pueblo de Los Angeles Historic Monument, on Main Street, which is owned and governed by the city of Los Angeles.

STEAMSHIPS entered the Southern California transportation scene in 1849, when the steamship *Gold Hunter,* a sidewheeler from San Francisco, anchored in San Pedro Bay. Along with stagecoaches and railroads, steamships carried passengers, freight, and mail between the Bay Area, San Pedro, and San Diego.

Although infrequent at first, regular steamship service started in 1855, when the SS *Senator* began leaving San Francisco on the 5th and 20th of each month. In San Pedro, sandbars blocked steamers from docking at piers. Phineas Banning, "the Father of San Pedro Harbor," maintained tugboats and lighters to transfer passengers and goods from deep-draft vessels anchored offshore.

Merchants and passengers using the steamship option faced great risks. The industry was plagued by poor boiler equipment, unreliable schedules, lack of repair facilities, uncharted coastal waters, irascible crews and captains, and primitive docking facilities in San Pedro Harbor. Accidents were common. Passing through San Francisco Bay on the run from San Pedro in January 1857, the *Sea Bird* was nearly engulfed by a tidal wave unleashed by the powerful Fort Tejón earthquake. In February 1863 Dr. Thomas Foster, a former Los Angeles mayor, was lost off the *Senator,* a ship that would

SS *Harvard* and SS *Yale,* in Los Angeles Harbor, ca. 1912. Pitt Collection.

come to be known as "the floating coffin." Two months later, on 27 April 1863, the boiler of Banning's steamer *Ada Hancock* exploded in San Pedro Harbor, killing 26 people and injuring others, including Banning himself. To allay fears about questionable vessels, the owners sometimes resorted to renaming them to mask their identity.

Beginning in the 1870s steamships had to compete with railroads, but they also served to complement the railroads at dockside. The principal carrier, Pacific Mail Steamship Company, had a fleet consisting of the *Senator, Pacific, Orizaba,* and *Mohongo.* Some steamers served a Southern Pacific Railroad port in Santa Monica Bay, or a port at Redondo Beach, or docked at Newport Landing, south of San Pedro.

In the 1880s much of the lumber for home building came to Los Angeles via San Pedro by steamship from the Pacific Northwest. At the height of the Boom of the Eighties sailors in the coastal trade struck for higher wages. In 1887 the Banning Company, which had purchased Santa Catalina Island and hoped to develop it as a tourist attraction, initiated weekly service from San Pedro to Catalina's city of Avalon. A round-trip ticket cost $4. Steamer service to Catalina has been a constant since that time.

In 1920 pleasure cruises began at Los Angeles Harbor. The Los Angeles Steamship Company acquired the *Yale* and *Harvard,* two World War I surplus naval vessels, and introduced a popular coastal cruise to San Francisco. It also added two confiscated German liners, rechristened *City of Los Angeles* and *City of Honolulu,* and used them for cruises to Hawaii. With the completion of the Panama Canal, the dredging of the harbor, and the improvement of docking facilities, steamers enjoyed an even more hospitable environment at San Pedro and Long Beach. The great Cunard steamer *Queen Mary,* a veteran of 1,001 Atlantic crossings, entered Long Beach Harbor on 9 December 1967 and is now permanently moored as a museum ship.

STEARNS, ABEL (1798–1871), Yankee pioneer in Los Angeles. A native of Massachusetts, Stearns arrived in Los Angeles in 1829 after a stay in Mexico, where he had become a naturalized Mexican citizen. In the *pueblo* he set up shop as a merchant. A homely man, in part because of a facial stabbing inflicted by a disgruntled customer, he was nicknamed Cara de Caballo ("Horse Face"). Stearns was 40 when he married the beautiful 14-year-old

Abel Stearns. Courtesy Photographic Collections, Los Angeles Public Library.

Arcadia Bandini. He built her a spacious residence, "El Palacio de Don Abel," in 1842 on the southeast corner of what are now Main and Arcadia Streets. Soon he reigned as the biggest land owner and rancher in Southern California. At the height of his career Don Abel grazed 30,000 cattle, 2,000 horses and mules, and 10,000 sheep on his princely ranchos of some 200,000 acres. Stearns served a few terms as *alcalde* and judge. Attracted by political intrigue, he helped overthrow California governors Manuel Victoria and Manuel Micheltorena in 1831 and 1845, respectively, and worked with U.S. consul Oliver Larkin in Monterey before the outbreak of the Mexican War. Stearns took part in California's first gold mining flurry, near Newhall in 1842. In 1861, as a member of the state assembly, he helped Southern California acquire a subsidy for a railroad from Los Angeles to San Pedro. He suffered a reversal of fortune in the 1860s when a plague of grasshoppers, a flood, and a subsequent drought destroyed 30,000 head of stock. His annual income fell to $300, and he had to auction off much of his landed empire.

STEEL AND IRON MANUFACTURING existed in Los Angeles from the 1920s until the 1960s, although the region was best known for its "smokeless" industries such as movies and aircraft. Heavy industrial firms served local markets, especially oil drilling, building construction, and shipbuilding. Columbia Steel operated a major installation in Torrance in the 1930s. During the war the biggest steel complex in the West was Kaiser Steel in Fontana, a product of wartime needs. The industry reached its production peak in the 1940s.

STEPHENS, WILLIAM D[ENNISON] (1859–1944), mayor of Los Angeles in 1909 and governor of California from 1917 to 1923. An Ohioan by birth, Stephens worked in Los Angeles from 1891 to 1902 as a salesman for retail grocers M. A. Newmark & Co. He became president of the Los Angeles Chamber of Commerce in 1907 and chairman of the Knights Templar of California in 1908. During his term as interim mayor of Los Angeles in 1909, the 90-square-mile city had over 300,000 people. Stephens served as U.S. congressman from the 10th District from 1910 to 1916. Initially a Republican, he became a Progressive, urging increased taxes on corporations and utilities. In 1917 Progressive governor Hiram Johnson appointed Stephens lieutenant governor of California, and that same year he won the gubernatorial election, serving for six years.

STERLING, CHRISTINE (19??–1963), "Mother of Olvera Street." In 1928, while walking through

Christine Sterling. Courtesy El Pueblo de Los Angeles Historic Monument.

the area, she discovered that a dilapidated building in a dirty back alley was in fact the Avila adobe, the oldest house in Los Angeles. As a person of strong romantic imagination, Sterling focused on converting the one-block stretch off Main Street, a seedy and rat-infested light-industry area, into a lively and colorful Mexican-style *mercado*. Sterling then moved into the Avila adobe when it was slated to be demolished and, gathering powerful supporters like Harry Chandler, spearheaded an effort to preserve the entire Plaza area. She succeeded, at least in part, when Olvera Street was dedicated on 20 April 1930 and became a successful tourist attraction.

STILL, WILLIAM M. GRANT (1895–1978), Mississippi-born dean of African American composers. Still studied violin as a child and attended Wilberforce University and the Oberlin Conservatory of Music, where he trained as a violinist and composer. After playing with such popular musicians as W. C. Handy, Paul Whiteman, and Artie Shaw, he debuted as a classical composer with a work called *Festive Overture.*

Still moved to Los Angeles in 1934. By leading the Los Angeles Philharmonic Orchestra in a performance of his own compositions in 1936, he became the first African American to conduct a symphony orchestra in the United States. Some of his later compositions, such as *The American Scene* (1957), were written for children. Several of his operas have been broadcast on national television. In all, he wrote more than 150 pieces, including operas, ballets, symphonies, chamber works, incidental music for television, and arrangements of folk songs. The city's William Grant Still Community Arts Center in South Central Los Angeles honors his memory.

STIMSON, MARSHALL (1859–1943), attorney and influential Progressive leader. When he was young his family moved from Cambridge, Massachusetts, to Los Angeles. After attending Los Angeles High School he went to Harvard, but returned to practice law in Los Angeles. His first foray into politics occurred in 1898, when he became an officer of the Anti-Saloon League. An optimist with strong convictions about civic activism, he joined like-minded reformers in Levy's Cafeteria to form the Lincoln-Roosevelt League, the goal being to topple Southern Pacific from its political perch. He, Chester Rowell, and Edward A. Dickson personally remonstrated with Hiram Johnson in his home and convinced him to run for governor in 1910. Stimson remained active in state and local politics, supporting Teddy Roosevelt's presidential bid in 1912, joining the ill-fated effort to form the California State Progressive Party in 1913, and later supporting Calvin Coolidge and Herbert Hoover in their runs for president.

STIMSON RESIDENCE, county's sole remaining example of brownstone architecture in the style of Henry Hobson Richardson. Built in 1891 on South Figueroa, near Adams Boulevard, it was designed by architect Carroll H. Brown. One of the city's most interesting buildings, it is currently owned by the Sisters of St. Joseph of Carondolet and is used as part of Mount St. Mary's College.

STONE, EDWARD DURRELL (1902–1978), architect. Active in the 1950s and 1960s, he designed the Ahmanson Center Building (1970) on Wilshire Boulevard, Perpetual Savings Bank Building (1962) in Westwood, and a unified block of handsome buildings on the USC campus.

STRAWBERRY PEAK rises between the Arroyo Seco and Big Tujunga watersheds. At 6,164 feet, it is the grand summit of the San Gabriel Mountains. The peak made news in March 1909 when a gas balloon carrying a party of six Pasadena men was accidentally lofted onto the mountain's crest. The party was stranded there for 72 hours in the midst of a raging snowstorm. They finally made their way to Switzer's Camp, 8 miles away. Strawberry Peak remains a favorite of mountain climbers.

STREETCARS, whether horse-drawn, cable, or electric, performed a yeoman's service until exiled from the city by the automobile. Horse-drawn streetcars appeared in the 1870s as an adjunct to

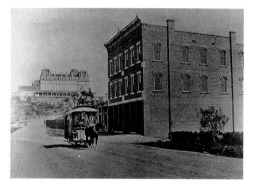

Pasadena's first streetcar, Fair Oaks Avenue, 1886. Courtesy Robert Weinstein Collection.

real estate developments. The first such line, inaugurated on 22 September 1873, was the "Pioneer Omnibus Street Line." It ran from the Plaza along Main Street to Washington Avenue; 12 tickets sold for $1, and two cars ran every half hour, at a pace of 8 miles an hour. Robert Widney installed a line in 1874 on tracks that zigzagged from the Plaza to 6th and Figueroa Streets, where Widney owned a home and property. In 1877 the Aliso Avenue Street Railway crossed a bridge over the river into Boyle Heights. By the end of the 1880s horse-car lines had been laid in Pasadena, Santa Monica, and Pomona as well. Also in the late 1880s, cable cars were replacing horse-drawn transportation in hillside communities, including Bunker Hill and Crown Hill. Running on wooden tracks, the cable cars were noisy and troublesome. Still, after the first line opened in 1885 they contributed to Los Angeles's reputation as having an excellent transportation system. The introduction of the electric car soon doomed the cable cars, which lasted only 80 years.

The man who in 1882 brought electric streetlights to the city, F. H. Howland, also brought the first electric streetcars, in 1887. He developed a line that ran along his 280-acre tract development at

Los Angeles's first trolley train, 1887.

Pico Boulevard and Vermont Avenue, a project he called "The Electric Railway Homestead Association." The car line helped him sell his real estate, although a year later it went bankrupt and had to be shut down.

In 1890, when the much larger cities of Boston and Philadelphia were still in the horse-car age, Los Angeles, with a population of only 50,000, had both cable cars and electric streetcars. That year the brothers-in-law Moses Sherman and Eli P. Clark bought up all existing lines to create a network; by 1891 they had combined five lines into one, called the Los Angeles Railway Company (LARy). Henry Huntington and Isaias W. Hellman bought them out in 1898. At that time 103 yellow LARy streetcars ran on 72 miles of track serving downtown, Eagle Rock, East Los Angeles, Boyle Heights, Vernon, Inglewood, Pico Heights, and other communities. Huntington eventually took sole control of the Yellow Cars, operating more than 525 of them on 172 miles of track. This network connected into his interurban Pacific Electric Railway Company and its "Big Red Cars," giving Los Angeles one of the best urban transportation networks in the country. The combined system suspended operations in 1961.

STREET GANGS. *See* Gangs

STREET LIGHTING. In the Mexican era, a homeowner living on a traveled street in Los Angeles was obliged to hang a lantern outdoors from sundown until 8 P.M. in winter and 9 P.M. in summer. Gas lights later replaced some of the lanterns.

On New Year's Eve 1882, the mayor switched on arc lights perched atop two 150-foot poles at Main and Commercial Streets, and 1st and Hill Streets. He did so despite dire predictions that the light would cause chickens to molt, cows to go dry, and people to suffer color blindness. Within a few years downtown was basking in the glow of 36 lighted poles, except on bright moonlit nights, when the power was conserved.

During World War II Civil Defense authorities enforced brownouts, a policy that darkened most street lights and all store signs. Now streets are lit by some 220,000 fixtures along 7,000 miles of streets in the city of Los Angeles. The illumination is under the jurisdiction of the Bureau of Street Lighting, in the Department of Public Works. Property owners share installation and operation costs by special assessment, averaging $35 per year.

The bureau maintains a mix of incandescent, low-pressure sodium, mercury vapor, metal halide, and high-pressure sodium lamps. Most fixtures burn special, highly efficient 100-watt bulbs.

STREET NAMES are now carefully regulated in Los Angeles. In 1849, the Spanish names were translated. Edward O. C. Ord's map shows that *Loma* became Hill; *Accytuna,* Olive; *Esperanzas,* Hope; *Flores,* Flower; *Chapules,* Grasshoppers; *Alta,* High; *Fortín,* Fort; *Virgenes,* Virgins; *Colejio,* College; and *Corta,* Short. When *Calle de Caridad* was renamed Charity, the Yankee residents, who resented "living on Charity," petitioned the city council, and the street was renamed Grand Avenue in 1886.

Streets are named after a variety of places and people, including landforms (e.g., Hill), surveyors ([Edward O. C.] Ord), historic figures ([Pío and Andrés] Pico), relatives of prominent men (Arcadia [Bandini, daughter of Juan Bandini and wife of Abel Stearns]), war heroes ([Gen. Douglas]

> Los Angeles is probably the most lenient city when it comes to reviewing large [building] projects.
> —Zev Yaroslavsky, Los Angeles politician

MacArthur), ranchos (Los Feliz), trees (Palms), land developers ([H. Gaylord] Wilshire), and a variety of towns in the eastern United States (Melrose). Hollywood names appear on many street signs, such as Edward Everett Horton Way in the San Fernando Valley, named after the actor; Rochester Circle in South Los Angeles, a reference to Jack Benny's fictional sidekick, played by Eddie Anderson, who once lived there; Rue de Vallee, a private driveway in the Hollywood Hills leading to the home of the late singer Rudy Vallee; Trigger Street and Dale Court, on the former Roy Rogers ranch, honoring the cowboy's horse and wife, respectively; and Tara Street, on the old Clark Gable estate, memorializing the fictional plantation in *Gone with the Wind.*

To name a new street, a subdivider or developer must apply to the Department of Public Works and obtain city council approval. Alteration of a name also requires council action, as does even the naming of private streets. Since the 1930s east-west thoroughfares in the city are called streets, and north-south ones are avenues, though numerous exceptions exist. Officially no street name may exceed 16 letters, including spaces, though again there are a few exceptions: Ellison S. Onizuka Street in Little Tokyo, named in honor of the Japanese American astronaut who died in the 1986 *Challenger* explosion, and Gen. Thaddeus Kosciuszko Way, citing a Pole who fought in the American Revolution in 1777 and 1778. Streets may not be named for living persons, although again an exception was made in naming George Burns Road in honor of the comedian's 90th birthday; it is paired with cross street Gracie Allen Drive, named for his late wife.

In Los Angeles County naming follows guidelines established by a county committee. Historic names are preferred, and duplicates are avoided. Streets are not named after commercial organizations, nor are descriptive words such as "Street," "Way," "North," "South," "East," and "West" part of the official name.

Children, and probably many adults, once learned the sequence of downtown streets by memorizing the doggerel "From Main we Spring to Broadway / Then over the Hill to Olive / Wouldn't it be Grand / To pick a Flower at Figueroa?"

STREETS in the city of Los Angeles numbered over 10,000 in 1995, some 1,000 of which were private roads. The *Thomas Brothers Guide* listed 53,000 streets in the county and city combined.

The most universally recognized streets in the city are probably Sunset Boulevard, Rodeo Drive, and Wilshire Boulevard. Los Angeles City's longest street is Sepulveda Boulevard, which runs for 26.4 miles, including a short stretch through Culver City. (In the county it extends 76 miles from the I-5 in the San Fernando Valley to Willow Street near Long Beach, passing through several cities.) By contrast, the city's shortest street, Powers Street, is but 13 feet long. Fargo Street in Silver Lake, pitched at a 32 percent grade, is the city's steepest street. Bruno Street, the only road still paved with its original handmade granite blocks, has been honored as a historic landmark, although the city's oldest street is, appropriately, Main Street. Its original name was Calle Principal.

STRONG, HARRIET WILLIAMS RUSSELL (1844–1929), agriculturist, civic leader, and water developer. Her husband, Charles Strong, whom she married in 1863, bought 220 acres from Pío Pico near the present city of Whittier. After Charles's death in 1883 she planted walnuts and other crops, and came to be known as the "walnut queen" and "pampas lady." She studied marketing and irrigation, becoming an activist for a better water supply system. Strong patented a water storage apparatus, along with other inventions, and was the first woman elected to the Los Angeles Chamber of Commerce. She was an exhibitor at the 1893 World's Columbian Exposition in Chicago. In 1917 Strong came up with the idea of using the Colorado River to irrigate California's southeastern deserts; 11 years later her dream was brought to fulfillment with the Swing-Johnson Act. An active feminist and club woman, Strong founded the Wilshire Ebell Club and was a member of both the Friday Morning Club and the Los Angeles Symphony Association.

STUCCO, form of cement extensively used as a building material in Southern California for both exterior and interior walls. It is applied with a trowel over a lath or wire mesh, and is ideally suited to the mild Southern California climate.

STUDIO CITY, eastern San Fernando Valley district 11 miles northwest of downtown Los Angeles. Originally called Maxwell, it was the home of Republic Studios, which opened in the 1930s and whose stable included Ronald Reagan, Gene Autry, Roy Rogers, John Carroll, and Vera Hruba Ralston. The town also emerged in the 1930s, with a commercial strip along Ventura Boulevard. Studio City, so named in 1928, includes residences built on narrow, winding roads in the hills south of the Los Angeles River and facing the valley. The area has notable architecture, much of it dating from the 1940s and designed by Rudolph M. Schindler.

SUI SIN FAH, pseudonym of Edith Eaton, an English-born author. The daughter of an English father and a Chinese mother, she earned a living as a stenographer but wrote short stories concerning Chinese life in Los Angeles. They were published in the early 1900s during Charles F. Lummis's editorship (1895–1909) of *Land of Sunshine* magazine.

SUNKIST GROWERS, trade name adopted in 1952 by the California Fruit Growers Exchange, a cooperative organization established in 1902 to

Sunkist logo. Courtesy Sunkist Growers.

market oranges. By working closely with the railroad, employing scientific growing techniques, standardizing cleaning and packing, lobbying for protective legislation, and engaging in nationwide advertising, Sunkist played a vital role in selling Valencia oranges and other Southern California citrus. Eventually it controlled 70 percent of the state's citrus crop. The cooperative's boosterism and advertising did much to make Southern California a mecca for settlement and tourism. In 1995 the Van Nuys group was listed as the largest cooperative in California, and the 12th largest in the nation. Revenues in 1993 exceeded $1 billion.

SUNLAND-TUJUNGA, area in the northern San Fernando Valley, between the Verdugo Hills and San Gabriel Mountains, 14 miles north of downtown Los Angeles. The area was originally settled by the Tongva people, and became part of the Tejunga (original spelling) and La Cañada Ranchos. It took its name from the Indian *ranchería* of Tuyungna, which became part of a Mexican land grant in 1840. The Gabrieleño word probably means "mountain range." The area was subdivided during the Boom of the Eighties, but the community collapsed in the bust that followed.

M. V. Hartranft founded a socialist utopian colony in Tujunga in 1907 based on the principles of William Ellsworth Smythe, an irrigationist, social philosopher, and community organizer. Because the colony's slogan was "A Little Land and a Lot of Living," people referred to them as the "Little Landers." Their community center, Bolton Hall (1913), is still standing. Constructed of boulders, it has a wood-beamed interior that architectural critics consider an extraordinary piece of craftsmanship.

Another Tujunga landmark, Rancho Chupa Rosa, was the private residence of John Steven McGroarty, California poet laureate, author of the *Mission Play,* and congressman. The home, built in 1923, and its surrounding 16 acres were acquired by the city after McGroarty's death and converted into a recreation center.

Coronet magazine called Tujunga, with its 1,500-foot elevation, intense sunlight, and fresh mountain breezes, "the most healthy place in the world." It attracted many asthmatics. Tujunga was incorporated in 1925, but decided to join Los Angeles in 1932 to ensure a supply of water.

Adjacent Sunland had joined Los Angeles in 1926. The southwestern part of Sunland is called Shadow Hills; it boasts a number of horse ranches and suggests a rural lifestyle. In 1990 the area, now called Sunland-Tujunga, some 20 square miles in extent, was home to 55,000 people. It was the location for a portion of the movie *E. T. The Extra-Terrestrial* (1982).

SUNSET, boomtown in West Los Angeles. The Los Angeles and Santa Monica Land and Water Company platted the town in 1887 on a portion of the Wolfskill rancho, roughly where the UCLA campus now stands. Although the site was linked to Los Angeles by a nearby steam railway, the town never succeeded as a real estate venture, and ownership of the land reverted to the Wolfskill family.

SUNSET BOULEVARD, major artery running 25 miles along the foot of the Hollywood Hills and Santa Monica Mountains from the downtown Plaza to the Pacific Ocean. Following the path of a centuries-old Indian trail, it today passes through neighborhoods that reflect the amazing social and ethnic diversity of Los Angeles.

The popular aura of Sunset Boulevard arose from its early association with the wealth and glamor of Hollywood. Warner Brothers and other studios were located on Sunset. The boulevard gained particular fame in the 1920s for a 1.7-mile portion known as Sunset Strip. Sandwiched between Hollywood and Beverly Hills, it became a center for speakeasies and dance clubs and a favorite pleasure area for movie stars. Originally in unincorporated county territory, the Strip now lies within the city of West Hollywood, established in 1984.

In the 1930s and 1940s celebrities frequented such Sunset Strip establishments as the Garden of

Sunset Strip, looking east. Courtesy West Hollywood Convention & Visitors Bureau.

Allah Hotel, the Beverly Hills Hotel, Chateau Marmont Hotel, and the street's famous trio of nightclubs, Ciro's (now the Comedy Store); the Mocambo, owned by *Hollywood Reporter* publisher W. R. Wilkerson, where stars came to be seen and photographed; and the Trocadero, which appeared prominently in the film *A Star Is Born* (1937). Some of these landmarks still survive.

In its transition period, Sunset Boulevard was romanticized by the television series *77 Sunset Strip* and the film (and more recently the stage production) *Sunset Boulevard* (1950). During the 1960s the Strip became a haven for hippies and teenage flower children, who clashed periodically with sheriff's deputies and police. Today an array of oversized billboards advertising movies, recordings, stage shows, and other entertainments loom over the street below. Although outdoor cafés, nightclubs, stores, and restaurants flourish and the area remains lively and pedestrian oriented, the high-gloss glamor of the 1920s through the 1950s is a thing of the past.

Long known as "a boulevard of dreams," Sunset now reflects Los Angeles's tremendous ethnic, social, and economic diversity. Beginning at the Plaza, it passes through or near Silver Lake, Echo Park, Los Feliz, East Hollywood, Hollywood, West Hollywood, Beverly Hills, Bel-Air, Westwood, Brentwood, Rustic Canyon, and Pacific Palisades, and ends at Pacific Coast Highway. It crosses or marks the entry of numerous canyons—Temescal, Mandeville, Kenter, Stone, Beverly Glen, Benedict, Coldwater, Laurel, Nichols, and others. All along Sunset, from downtown to the ocean, can be found a dazzling variety of immigrant cultures, including, in Chinatown, just south of the boulevard, a community of Chinese, Vietnamese, and Cambodians; in Echo Park, Mexicans and Central Americans; in Hollywood, Armenians and Soviet Jews; in the Vermont area, Filipinos; and in Brentwood and Pacific Palisades, Europeans, Middle Easterners, and Asians.

SUN VALLEY, 16-square-mile district in the city of Los Angeles near Burbank Airport and Hansen Dam. It is on land once owned by José María Verdugo, and later developed, in the 1880s, by Charles Maclay. An armed bandit once held up a Southern Pacific passenger train that had stopped at a water tower near Sunland Boulevard and San Fernando Road. It is unclear whether the robber, the train engineer, or the brakeman was named Roscoe, but the site was called Roscoe from that time until 1948, when the residents renamed it Sun Valley. Since the early part of the century the region's sand and gravel operations have supplied the basic building materials for tens of thousands of San Fernando Valley homes. Sun Valley has a major shopping center, Canyon Plaza. The area's population in 1990 was 77,110.

SUN VILLAGE, tiny community north of Littlerock, in the Antelope Valley. It was formed as an African American enclave in the 1940s by Melvin Ray Grubbs, an African American lawyer and real estate agent from Chicago, and a white family named Marble, owners of Sun Village Land Corporation and the first Antelope Valley developers to sell to black owners. The rural enclave of Sun Village had 2,000 residents in the 1960s and 1,400 in the 1980s. Immediately west of Sun Village is the protected wilderness area of Little Rock Wash.

SUPERMARKETS. *See* Grocery industry; Hattem's 24-Hour Drive-In Market

SURFING, sport closely associated with the

Southern California beach lifestyle. It was introduced locally in 1907 when Henry E. Huntington and his Pacific Electric Railway brought George Freeth (1883–1918), a young Irish Hawaiian, to Redondo Beach to promote the new rail line. Freeth demonstrated daring feats with an 8-foot, 200-pound board. He later died attempting a rescue at sea and is memorialized by a bust on the Redondo pier. The sport gained new popularity in the 1950s after Bob Simmons, who had attended Caltech, designed a lightweight board made of synthetic materials. Surfing was featured prominently in the *Gidget* and *Beach Party* movies of the late 1950s and 1960s. Legendary "ripper" Greg "Da Bull" Noll published a surfing memoir, *Da Bull: Life Over the Edge* (1992). A devotee nicknamed "Bank Wright" wrote the classic wave analysis, *Surfing California* (1973).

SUYDAM, NELLIE (1877–1946), Glendora diarist and literary figure. Born in Illinois, she came to Los Angeles with her family in 1887. After completing a correspondence course from the typographers union she became a printer, an unusual occupation for a woman. Unhappily married for a time to an alcoholic husband, childless, and plagued by respiratory problems, she tried living in Arizona, but returned to Glendora. She worked intermittently as a newspaper reporter and, more or less steadily, at orange growing. A diary that Suydam maintained from 1892 until before her death offers interesting insights and comments on her gardening, fruit growing, literary efforts, and ordinary family matters.

SVORINICH, RUDY (1960–), city council member representing the 15th District. He owns a paint store and was chief of staff to former assemblyman Gerald Felando. Svorinich, a Republican in a Democratic district, replaced Joan Milke Flores on the council.

SWIMMING, recreation that emerged locally in 1886, when a public pool was built on Fort Street (Broadway), next to City Hall. Admission was 35 cents; Wednesday and Saturday mornings were "ladies only." Santa Monica beaches, a distant 16 miles from downtown by horse-and-buggy, were a treat for summer swimmers and gave rise to bath houses as early as the 1870s. The beaches, fed by streams from Santa Monica Canyon, were much sandier a century ago than they are now. The ocean

bottom sloped out gradually for a mile, encouraging bathing, though the undertow could be treacherous. In the 1880s the bath house owners hired Pedro García, a champion fisherman and swimmer, as a lifeguard. The vogue of the home swimming pool did not arise until the 20th century.

SWITZER, PERRY (1826–1910), adventurer and founder of a resort in the Arroyo Seco. Born in Virginia, he trudged from Ohio to California during the Gold Rush, and came south to Los Angeles in 1854 driving a flock of sheep before him. "Commodore" Switzer, as he was known, settled in Pasadena and became a successful building contractor. The first person to popularize the Arroyo as a public wilderness campground, he created Switzer's Camp, a hostelry above the falls, in 1884. Three years later John Muir proclaimed it a "charming" spot. Renamed "Switzer-land," the camp survived under other ownerships into the 1940s.

SYLMAR, northern San Fernando Valley district, 22 miles northwest of downtown Los Angeles. Early in the century it was an olive growing center and a haven for people recovering from lung diseases. Olive View Medical Center, a county facility, has its roots in a tuberculosis sanitarium established in 1920. Sylmar, a diamond-shaped area

---

I've seen congestion in almost every major city in the world far worse. By comparison, L.A.'s a paradise.

—Tom Bradley

---

of 23 square miles, was annexed to the city of Los Angeles in 1915 to ensure a viable water supply.

The Franciscans planted the first olive trees at nearby Mission San Fernando. The earliest commercial planting was done by Robert Widney, a Los Angeles businessman, around 1894. As the site of the world's biggest olive groves, the area was dubbed Sylmar ("Sea of Trees"). As late as the 1960s olives remained a major industry. Filmmaker D. W. Griffith filmed parts of his epic *Birth of a Nation* (1915) at his Sylmar ranch.

On 9 February 1971, the area suffered a 6.6 earthquake that toppled freeway bridges, bent railroad tracks, and left 64 dead. Although few homes were destroyed, an 850-bed hospital that had opened a month earlier collapsed.

The population has been climbing rapidly in recent decades. In the 1980s it was the fastest-growing area in Los Angeles, and by 1990 residents numbered 59,876. Unregulated growth threatens surrounding open spaces, however, including Wilson Canyon in nearby county territory.

SYLMAR EARTHQUAKE, 6.6 temblor that occurred at 6:00 A.M. on 9 February 1971, at an epicenter 7 miles north of San Fernando (24 miles from downtown Los Angeles). More violent than the Long Beach quake of 1933, it lasted 10 seconds. The force elevated parts of the San Gabriel Mountains by several feet and pressed them south by several inches. It destroyed freeway bridges, damaged a major dam, and shook buildings vigorously in downtown Los Angeles. Sixty-four lives were lost, many in the collapse of a new hospital, and damage totaled $1.5 billion. Only two people perished in private dwellings, a testimony to improved building codes after 1933. Had the shaking occurred a few hours later, when freeways were crowded and schools and offices occupied, many more fatalities would have occurred. The Alquist-Priolo Act, limiting construction of high-occupancy buildings near known faults, was enacted because of the Sylmar quake. The Northridge quake of 1994 also caused damage in the area.

SYNANON, former drug and alcohol rehabilitation organization centered in Ocean Park. Founded in 1958 by Charles E. "Chuck" Dedrich, the center featured encounter sessions as therapeutic treatment for addictions. Other programs attempted to help juvenile delinquents and people suffering from emotional disturbances. After a time the organization took on aspects of a quasi-religious sect with huge economic assets. In the 1970s it became involved in a series of high-profile lawsuits and countersuits, and the organization ceased to exist.

TAPER, S. MARK (1902–1994), financier and philanthropist. Born in Poland and raised in England, Taper quit school at 14 to enter his father's textile business. He amassed several fortunes, the first as a manufacturer of military uniforms. He retired from that occupation at 25, but soon entered the real estate business in London, pioneering, in the 1930s, the development of mass housing. Taper retired again, this time leaving England with his family and taking up permanent residence in Southern California. Resuming his career, he bought cheap land near Long Beach and, with several partners, developed the post–World War II middle-class suburban housing community eventually known as Lakewood. Having constructed 35,000 homes in Los Angeles by 1955, Taper withdrew from the business of home development and began devoting himself full time to several savings and loan banks he had purchased, including the giant First Charter Financial Corporation and American Savings and Loan Association. When approached by Dorothy Chandler for a philanthropic contribution to help build the Music Center, Taper donated $1.5 million. She rewarded him by naming one of its two theaters in his honor. He also made large donations to the Los Angeles County Museum of Art and to UCLA. Although not personally involved with the arts or education, he felt a deep responsibility to return wealth to his community.

TARZANA, district of Los Angeles in the San Fernando Valley, 19 miles northwest of Los Angeles. Edgar Rice Burroughs, author of the *Tarzan* books, first applied the name to the 550-acre ranch he bought from *Times* publisher Harrison Gray Otis in the southern part of the valley in 1919. In 1927 the 300 residents of the surrounding community

held a contest and chose the name Tarzana for this rural place of berry farms and chicken ranches. The post office followed suit in 1930, assigning the name to one of its stations. Today Tarzana is a bedroom community with about 45,000 residents.

TATAVIAM INDIANS were native to parts of Los Angeles County north of the San Fernando Valley. In 1769 they were estimated to have a population of 1,000, dispersed among 20 villages. They appear to have been strongly influenced by their neighbors, the Tongva (Gabrieleño) and Chumash.

TAX ASSESSOR, LOS ANGELES COUNTY. *See* Los Angeles County Tax Assessor

TEACHERS' UNIONS. *See* United Teachers of Los Angeles

TEAMSTERS. *See* International Brotherhood of Teamsters

TECHNOCRACY, social movement that flourished briefly in Southern California during the early years of the Great Depression, especially among the unemployed. It espoused the belief that engineers and technicians should take full charge of the nation's resources, eliminate the price and profit system, and develop a rational and efficient economy that would restore and maintain prosperity. Manchester Boddy, publisher of the *Daily News,* supported the idea enthusiastically and gave it widespread coverage in December 1932. When the New Deal was introduced, technocracy fizzled.

TEHACHAPI MOUNTAINS, range of peaks at the southern end of the Sierra Nevada that swing to the west and divide the Central Valley from the

Antelope Valley, and, generally, Northern from Southern California. Two major gaps in the southern portion are Tehachapi Pass (4,025 feet), through which the Southern Pacific Railroad twists, and Tejon Pass (4,100 feet), where highway I-5 curves through Grapevine Canyon.

TEJON PASS, important northern gateway to Los Angeles County cutting through the Tehachapi Mountains at 4,100 feet elevation. In 1772 Pedro Fages came upon the pass while tracking Spanish army deserters. In 1806 Lt. Francisco Ruiz and a troop of soldiers encountered a badger *(tejón)*—hence the name of the region. In the 1850s the pass was part of the Butterfield stage route. The grade of Interstate 5 at this point is the steepest allowable incline on a major federal highway. An earthquake, estimated at 7.7 on the Richter scale, rocked Tejon in 1857 and was felt sharply in the village of Los Angeles 80 miles away.

TELACU. *See* East Los Angeles Community Union, The

TELEPHONES were first installed locally in the offices of the old River Rail Station in 1882, six years after Alexander Graham Bell's momentous invention. An instrument was also soon installed at the courthouse. On one occasion some bored jurors used it for a prank: they phoned the police with a

---

Rain—the sweetest music to the California ear.
          —Theodore Van Dyke, writer, 1886

---

false report of a riot in progress across the street from the courthouse, then stood laughing uproariously as the bewildered officers deployed on the peaceful street below. An irate judge fined each juror $25 for the antic.

The first phone company was the Home Telephone and Telegraph Company, headed by Alonzo B. Cass, a prominent entrepreneur. For years small companies kept cropping up, only to be merged or acquired by bigger ones. The biggest regional firm was the Associated Telephone Company, which in 1929 combined six small companies operating in Long Beach, Redondo Beach, Covina, Huntington Beach, Laguna Beach, and San

Bernardino. It grew during the 1930s and, especially, during and after World War II, with the influx of new money and the establishment of new households, stores, and defense industries. In 1953 Associated changed its name to General Telephone of California (GTE) and in the next six years increased the number of phones in service from 500,000 to 1 million. It continued to acquire other small companies, including one in Sunland-Tujunga in 1964. In 1985 GTE created a wholly owned subsidiary to handle the newly deregulated business. The company now serves 3.6 million lines. Pacific Bell, based originally in Northern California, is the other giant in the Southern California region.

TELEVISION in the Los Angeles region includes 13 commercial channels: KCBS (2), KNBC (4), KTLA (5), KABC (7), KCAL (9), KTTV (11), KCOP (13), KSCI (18), KWHY (22), KAGL (30), KMEX (34), KVEA (52), and KDOC (56). The four stations associated with national networks are KABC, with the American Broadcasting Company; KCBS, with the Columbia Broadcasting System; KNBC, with the National Broadcasting Company; and KTTV, with Fox Broadcasting. The remainder are independent.

In addition there are four public stations: an independent channel, KVCR (24), which broadcasts from San Bernardino; and three PBS affiliates—KCET (28), with studios in Hollywood; KOCE (50), in Huntington Beach; and KLCS (58), which is managed by the Los Angeles Unified School District.

One station, KTBN (40), is devoted exclusively to religious broadcasting. Several stations also cater to the large multiethnic population of Los Angeles. KMEX and KVEA feature Spanish-language programming exclusively. KMET (38) is a multilingual television station licensed in 1993 and catering exclusively to the 8.9 million residents of Los Angeles county who speak a language other than English at home. It broadcasts in English, French, Hindi, Italian, Korean, Russian, and Spanish, and plans to add Japanese and Tagalog; it also has African and Salvadoran programming. Some 100,000 people watch it every day. The area's oldest foreign-language channel is KSCI, which claims 2 million viewers. This independent station provides programming in more than 14 languages, including Arabic, Armenian, Cambodian, Farsi, French, Hindi, Italian, Japanese, Korean, Spanish,

Tagalog, and Vietnamese. With a potential audience of 5.2 million households in the Los Angeles and San Diego area, KSCI prides itself on being "the nation's leading international broadcaster."

TELEVISION INDUSTRY, now centered mainly in Burbank, Hollywood, and the Fairfax area, got its start in the early 1930s. The pioneer television broadcaster in Los Angeles was Don Lee, who had exclusive California distribution rights for Cadillac cars. Seeking a suitable advertising medium, he used his earnings to create a broadcast network. He and his son, Thomas Lee, together with an electrical engineering student, Harry R. Lubcke, established a studio at 7th and Bixel Streets, having been granted a federal license for experimental station W6XAO-TV. The station went on the air on 23 December 1931, when there were only five receiving sets in the entire city. Lee's operation broadcast regularly for one hour a day, six days a week—eight years before NBC set up its first station on the East Coast. W6XAO-TV used homemade equipment, and established a number of firsts: the first full-length movie ever broadcast on TV, *The Crooked Circle;* the first use of kinescope, a film of a transmitted program, in 1936; the first "simulcast" on radio and TV, also in 1936; the first remote broadcast in the West, in 1940; and the first commercially sponsored telecast in Los Angeles, in 1941.

Regularly licensed commercial broadcasting originated in 1946, when the Federal Communications Commission held hearings, set standards, and granted the first license, to KTLA-TV—which was also owned by an auto dealer. In 1947 Lee's W6XAO-TV entered the commercial field with *Queen for a Day,* a show heard on its sister radio station as well. The remarkably popular children's show *Howdy Doody* debuted in 1947 and lasted until 1960. Soon the Los Angeles area had 12 television stations broadcasting to 14,000 homes. Most shows originated in Los Angeles or New York. In 1948 CBS in New York launched *Talk of the Town,* which became *The Ed Sullivan Show.* Milton Berle's wildly successful *Texaco Star Theater* also debuted in 1948. Popular radio shows migrated to television as well: *The Lone Ranger* (1948), *Arthur Godfrey's Talent Scouts* (1948), *One Man's Family* (1949), *The Goldbergs* (1949), Eddie Cantor's *Colgate Comedy Hour* (1950), and *The Burns and Allen Show* (1950), to name but a few. In 1952, with the televised broadcast of the Republican presidential convention that nominated Dwight D. Eisenhower, the infant medium entered the information age.

Jay Leno interviewing Hugh Grant on the *Tonight Show,* 1995. Photo by Margaret Norton, courtesy NBC, Inc.

The film industry, which had initially viewed television as an inept passing fad, soon became alarmed. In 1946, Hollywood's most profitable year, some 90 million Americans were making weekly pilgrimages to their favorite movie palaces to view films on the big screen. As television programming increased, these same Americans began to buy television sets. Soon NBC built a television studio in Burbank, and CBS established itself in the Fairfax district. Movie attendance fell to half its previous level between 1946 and 1955 as audiences stayed home to be entertained in their own living rooms. Movie theaters were virtually empty on Tuesday nights, when Milton Berle was on the air, and on Saturday nights—the traditional moviegoing night—when Sid Caesar appeared on *Your Show of Shows.* Hollywood's yearly output in the 1930s had averaged 750 feature films; in the 1950s it was down to about 300 and still falling, despite efforts to win back audiences by installing new stereo sound systems, employing such visual techniques as 3-D, and building wide screens that emitted odors.

Hollywood only began to recover in the early 1970s, owing in part to the introduction of multiplex theaters in shopping malls and, even more, to the financial marriage and ensuing interdependence of the television and movie industries. Eventually the small screen proved to be an even greater magnet for bringing hopeful talent to Los Angeles than the big screen had been. Each medium had found its niche. The Hollywood film retained its position as the ultimate entertainment, but television had become the major disseminator of popular culture. In any event, Los Angeles remained firmly in charge of American image-making.

TEMPERATURE in Los Angeles is blessedly moderate most of the time, thanks to the Mediterranean climate. However, temperature varies substantially from place to place, reaching much higher levels in the valleys than at the seashore. Fog, wind, and elevation are also determining factors. Beach cities tend to be 10–15 degrees cooler than downtown Los Angeles. The farther inland one goes, the warmer the temperature becomes. The

---

In a country where sickness was once almost unknown, doctors, dentists, faith-healers, and quacks multiply and increase as the quails of yore.
—Horace A. Vachell, British writer, 1904

---

hottest month, August, averages 82 degrees downtown and 68 degrees at the ocean—only 15 miles away. Daily temperature changes can also be extreme. It is not unheard of for areas in the San Gabriel Valley to reach 100 degrees during the day and fall to 40 or 50 degrees at night. The highest recorded downtown temperature occurred in 1885, when the mercury reached 106 degrees.

Temperatures vary less widely in winter than in summer. The coldest month is January, with mean temperatures above 40 degrees. The snows and winter frosts that occur occasionally at lower elevations once posed a threat to Southern California's agricultural economy. With agriculture no longer a major industry in the area, such winter weather is now more a treat than a threat.

TEMPLE, FRANCIS PLINY FISK ("TEMPLITO") (1820–1880), landowner and rancher. Temple sailed around Cape Horn in 1841 and, upon his arrival in Los Angeles, entered business with his brother John. After marrying Antonia Margarita Workman in 1845 the 5-foot, 4-inch Templito made his home on Rancho Merced in the San Gabriel Valley. He planted an orchard, grapevines, and a garden, which he completely enclosed with a fence—a rarity at that time. He died in poverty in a shepherd's hut located on his own property.

TEMPLE, JOHN (A.K.A. JONATHAN, JUAN) (1798–1866), Massachusetts trader who came to

Los Angeles via Honolulu and San Diego in 1827 and engaged in the hide-and-tallow trade. He opened the first general store in the *pueblo* (on the site of the present Federal Building), encouraging the Californios to use hides as currency. Temple, in partnership with his brother Francis ("Templito"), conducted a brisk trade in *serapes, rebozos,* wine, and other goods, not only in Los Angeles but as far north as Monterey. He became a naturalized Mexican citizen, married Raphaela Cota in 1830, and acquired ownership of Rancho Los Cerritos in 1844, on present-day Signal Hill. Don Juan Temple also bought the property belonging to La Purísima Mission, near Lompoc, when it was secularized. By 1848 he owned an estimated 14,000 head of cattle, 5,000 head of sheep, and 1,000 horses. In the American period he built the first office building in Los Angeles. Temple Street is named for him.

TEMPLE, SHIRLEY (1928–), most famous child movie star and one of the top-ten box office stars from 1934 through 1939. Born in Santa Monica, she started acting at age three in *The Red-Haired Alibi* (1932). *Little Miss Marker* (1934), her first starring role, brought her fame at the age of six. A talented singer and dancer, her infectious dimpled smile and bouncy blonde curls lightened the Great Depression for moviegoers nationwide. Among her films are *Curly Top* (1935), *Heidi* (1937), *The Little Princess* (1939), *Since You Went Away* (1944), and *The Bachelor and the Bobby Soxer* (1947). She received a special Academy Award in 1934. In 1950 Temple retired from show business. As Shirley Temple Black, she later became active in California politics, and subsequently was appointed an envoy to the United Nations, ambassador to Ghana, and chief of protocol of the United States.

TEMPLE CITY, independent San Gabriel Valley city 10 miles east of downtown Los Angeles. It was named in 1923 for Walter P. Temple, town founder and president of the Temple Townsite Company. Its population was 31,100 in 1990.

TENNEY, JACK B[RECKENRIDGE] (1898–1970), state senator who in 1941 headed the legislature's Fact-Finding Committee on Un-American Activities. A piano player and composer ("Mexicali Rose"), he served for a time as president of the Los Angeles musicians union. Originally a left-leaning Democrat, he became a far-right Re-

Los Angeles's first tennis club, 1884. California Historical Society, Title Insurance and Trust Photo Collection, Dept. of Special Collections, USC Library.

publican after losing reelection to that post—a defeat for which he blamed Communists. Like his idol, Congressman Martin Dies, Tenney was prosecutor and judge of witnesses he called to testify in the Un-American Activities hearings. His threat in 1949, during the rise of Cold War anticommunism, to institute a special test oath at the University of California pushed the UC regents into instituting their own "loyalty oath." When in the same year Tenney became too zealous and began red-baiting members of the legislature, he was forced to resign.

TENNIS was introduced in Santa Monica by William Young, its English creator, who moved there in 1879. The first lawn tennis association, the Santa Monica Improvement Club, was established in 1887. The group sponsored an annual tournament that drew players from Riverside, Pasadena, Los Angeles, San Gabriel, and Pomona. The affluent young set, gathering for the week-long round of tennis and polo matches, stayed at the Miramar and Arcadia hotels and the Casino Club, where, between events, they attended social teas, dinner parties, and the gala victory ball. By 1890 there were 15 local tennis clubs. In 1904 May Sutton won the U.S. singles title, and the following year became the first non-English Wimbledon champion. She played doubles with another Southern Californian, Elizabeth Ryan, who won 19 Wimbledon titles. Other great players from around Los Angeles have included Pancho Gonzales, Jack Kramer, Bobby Riggs, Elsworth Vines, Pauline Betz, Louise Brough, Billie Jean King, Tracy

Austin, Arthur Ashe, Michael Chang, and Pete Sampras.

TERMINAL ISLAND, artificial island in the Los Angeles–Long Beach harbor. Originally it was a natural outcropping, first called Isla Raza Buena Gente, and then Rattlesnake Island. A fashionable resort was built at the turn of the century on the southern end. Until about 1916 rich Angelenos flocked to the pleasant beach, called Brighton Beach, with its hotel and restaurant and 200 privately owned cottages. For 5 cents the ferry boat, *Blanche,* carried passengers from the 5th Street landing in San Pedro. The South Coast Yacht Club, forerunner to the Los Angeles Yacht Club, had a landing at Brighton Beach. The club held its first race there in 1902, with boats racing to the buoy near Point Fermin and back.

The name Terminal Island was applied in 1900 when the Terminal Railway built a line from Los Angeles to the island. Harbor dredging, starting in around 1916, transformed the outcropping. Mud was added gradually to Rattlesnake, causing the beach to shrink. The summer playground gave way to Fish Harbor, with scores of fishing boats and 18 canneries. Distressed by the changes, the rich sold their cottages to the Japanese fishermen and packinghouse workers. During the depression squatters claimed some of the broken-down or abandoned cottages.

On 28 February 1942, at the peak of wartime racial hysteria, the navy evacuated the island and shipped most of its Japanese residents to relocation centers. Today the island belongs to the cities of

Los Angeles and Long Beach and to the federal government. Fish Harbor now has only a handful of ships and packinghouses. More prominent on Terminal Island are Long Beach Harbor, Long Beach Naval Shipyard, the *Queen Mary,* a U.S. customs station, and a major federal correctional facility. Until recently it also housed Howard Hughes's *Spruce Goose* airplane (it has since been moved to the state of Oregon). The ferry from San Pedro stopped running when Vincent Thomas Bridge was built. A huge container terminal is located on the island, and the dockyards are lined with cars imported from Asia.

THALBERG, IRVING (1899–1936), Brooklyn-born movie producer. He was the protégé of Carl Laemmle, who appointed him head of Universal Studio from 1919 to 1923. When he was only 22, Thalberg fired director Eric Von Stroheim following a dispute—probably the first time a director was replaced on a film. Dissatisfied at Universal, where he was refused a salary raise to $600, Thalberg moved to Metro-Goldwyn-Mayer (MGM) in 1924, remaining there until 1933. At the age of 26 Hollywood's "boy wonder" became the head of MGM. Much of his success at the Culver City studio rested on literary films such as *The Barretts of Wimpole Street* (1934), *Mutiny on the Bounty* (1935), *Romeo and Juliet* (1936), and on the hiring of the Marx brothers. Novelist F. Scott Fitzgerald modeled Monroe Stahr, the central character in *The Last Tycoon* (1940), after him. Thalberg was married to actress Norma Shearer. He is still considered one of Hollywood's true geniuses.

THEATER, 1781–1917. During the Spanish and Mexican colonial eras, a period of some 70 years, plays were strictly religious, performed at Christmas by the Franciscan missionaries. Commonly acted out on the streets of the *pueblo,* they usually depicted the wise men's journey to Bethlehem and the conflicts experienced along the way, especially the struggle between Satan and the Archangel Michael. *Los Pastores* (The shepherds) incorporated guitar music, songs, and comedy. *La Pastorela* (The pastorale) was written by Padre Florencio of Mission Soledad, perhaps California's first playwright. On Christmas Eve 1861, Don Antonio Bandini starred as Arcángel Miguel. A member of the audience wanted a better look at his paper wings and held her candle too close to the costume. Bandini's clothes caught fire, and the actor playing Satan ex-tinguished the flames. It was *La Pastorela*'s final performance.

In 1848 the first semipermanent stage—an open-air, covered platform with a proscenium arch—was erected at Antonio F. Coronel's adobe near the Plaza, for $5,000. The performances ended abruptly when the actors, U.S. Army soldiers, went AWOL to search for gold. As more Yankees poured into California, religious theater gave way

---

Cheap pedicures, perpetual sun, · guilt-free careerism, seeing Vincent Price at the 7-Eleven, having a back yard, no cockroaches, true love, and Disneyland. Every day is like Saturday.

—Ann Magnuson, performance artist

---

to secular entertainment. Increasingly, beginning in the mid-1840s, outdoor performances were provided by traveling troupes arriving by ship from San Francisco, the theater capital of the West. In 1858 Stearns Hall was built, and the California Minstrels and Burlesque Troupe performed there. Don Juan Temple built a combination auditorium and market that also housed visiting entertainers. The first real indoor theater was erected in 1870 by cabinetmaker-undertaker William Abbott and his wife, Mercedes. Their Merced Theatre's gala opening was on New Year's Day 1870.

Despite these efforts, theater in the provincial city remained largely dependent on traveling troupes, amateur readings, minstrel shows, and one-act plays. Perhaps the best of the community entertainments were the annual "Unitarian Thursdays," Victorian entertainments performed for a decade by members of the Unitarian Church at Union Hall.

Los Angeles's next theater, the second largest on the Pacific Coast, was the 1,200-seat Ozro Childs Grand Opera House, built on Main Street near 1st Street in 1884. The inaugural performance was the 18th-century English comedy *School for Scandal,* by Richard Brinsley Sheridan. Children who had to be held were not allowed in, the mayor addressed the audience, and songs were played during intermission.

By the mid-1880s Los Angeles had become a regular stop for touring theatrical companies. In 1887 a visiting Shakespeare troupe grossed an impressive $17,936 in one week. The Los Angeles Theatre on Spring Street, built in 1888, hosted Maurice Barrymore, Lillian Russell, and Sarah Bernhardt.

A short-lived local professional stock company performed at the Park Theatre (formerly known as Hazard's Pavilion) at 5th and Olive Streets in 1893. The Orpheum opened as a vaudeville house a year later. Subsequent attempts to set up local professional theater companies were largely unsuccessful.

The man who finally put Los Angeles on the theatrical map was Oliver Morosco. In 1899, at age 24, he used a theater built by Dr. David Burbank, a local dentist, to present stock productions, touring shows, vaudeville, and opera. He also founded a successful stock company that remained active for 25 years. In 1904 Morosco leased the David Belasco Theatre, a move that established him as an important theatrical producer.

By the early 1900s Los Angeles audiences were being treated to such productions as *The Prisoner of Zenda, Peck's Bad Boy, The Country Girl, Charley's Aunt,* and numerous Shakespeare plays. Among the stage stars who came to the city were William Gillette, Harry Langdon, George M. Cohan, Lionel Barrymore, and the glamorous French actress Anna Held, who was famous for taking milk baths— which she did, in 1904, at the Nadeau Hotel, the first four-story building in Los Angeles. It was while Sarah Bernhardt was appearing at the Orpheum that she had the seemingly minor automobile accident that eventually led to the amputation of her leg. Polish star Helena Modjeska took center stage in 1906 playing Mary Stuart, even though she had already passed her peak, and her heavy accent was difficult for audiences to decipher. England's most famous actress, Mrs. Patrick Campbell, performed in Los Angeles for several seasons, bringing Henrik Ibsen's *Rosmersholm* to the Belasco Theatre in 1908. The great beauty Ethel Barrymore appeared in Los Angeles frequently, and was an audience favorite. In 1909 Morosco took over ownership of the Belasco and made it very successful. From 1904 to 1915 a dozen playhouses were operating at a profit.

Two early plays with California themes were David Belasco's *Girl of the Golden West* (reworked by Giacomo Puccini as an Italian opera) and *Rose of the Rancho,* a romantic, sentimental piece about a struggle over land during the Mexican period, with a half-Spanish, half-American heroine.

THEATER, 1917–1945. During World War I most local theater companies failed. After the war, actors who had been performing in legitimate theater and vaudeville were drawn to the new movie medium, as were their audiences. Nevertheless, movie actors returned to the stage when they could; as a result, the 1920s and 1930s were a time of renewal for local drama. Of the 90 theaters built between 1921 and 1930, 43 were strictly movie houses, but 47 could be used for either films or stage productions. In 1925 John Barrymore and W. C. Fields helped found the Masquers Club, which remains "the oldest theatrical club west of Broadway."

In 1916 Pasadena theater manager Gilmor Brown moved his Savoy Stock Company into the old Savoy Theater. He replaced the vaudeville performances with new and classic plays. Initially unsuccessful, the theater was saved when a citizens' committee organized the nonprofit Pasadena Community Playhouse Association. In 1925 Brown's company christened the 700-seat Pasadena Playhouse as a showcase for professional performances and theatrical training. The theater's success was assured when it staged the world premiere of Eugene O'Neill's *Lazarus Laughed* in 1928.

Poster, "Follow the Parade," ca. mid-1930s.

The post–World War I theater revival included more frequent appearances by touring companies, the opening of new little theaters, and the rise of independent local productions. The Pilgrimage Play Amphitheatre on Highland Avenue was built as a private venture expressly for the *Pilgrimage Play* (1920), a religious epic depicting the life of Christ. The Ramona Pageant began its annual performances in Hemet in 1923. The Hollywood Bowl was also a creation of the 1920s and enjoyed great success. The Biltmore Theater opened in 1924 with a splashy production of *Sally, Irene, and Mary;* tickets cost $10, and Will Rogers was master of ceremonies. In the next few years the curtain went up in various other new theaters: the El Capitan, the Mayan, the Hollywood Playhouse, the Hollywood Music Box, and the Vine Street Theatre.

In 1927 Morosco's company performed *Abie's Irish Rose* for 33 weeks; the play then headed to New York, where it became, for many decades, that city's longest-running play. Morosco's company then disbanded.

Theater, after many successful seasons from 1928 to 1932, plummeted during the Great Depression. The bigger houses suffered particularly, though a few small theaters managed to keep struggling along. Even the *Pilgrimage Play* and John Steven McGroarty's *Mission Play,* which had been staged in San Gabriel since 1912, ceased to be performed for lack of funds. Exceptions included the Padua Hills Theatre at Claremont, which from 1932 to

It takes a certain kind of innocence to like L.A. . . . When people are not happy, they fight against L.A. and say it's a "wasteland" and other helpful descriptions.   —Eve Babitz, writer, 1974

1975 presented Mexican American actors in productions of modern folk dramas, some of them in Spanish. At the Greek Theatre, Austrian director Max Reinhardt's lavish 1934 production of *A Midsummer Night's Dream* played for four nights to audiences totaling 150,000. He also staged an elaborate 1938 production of *Faust,* at the Pilgrimage Play Amphitheatre. An old-fashioned melodrama, *The Drunkard,* which saw audiences enthusiastically cheering the hero and booing the villain,

opened in 1933 and was a Los Angeles staple for many years.

Puppeteers Harry Burnett, Forman Brown, and Richard Brandon had a successful run starting in the early 1930s. Burnett fashioned the marionettes, many of which caricatured well-known people. The trio performed on Olvera Street in the 80-seat El Torito Theater, then opened their own house, the Turnabout, in 1941, which featured a stage at both ends of the hall. The audience sat in old Red Car seats that could be shifted either way. The first half of the evening was devoted to a puppet show, usually written by Brown; then the audience members turned their seats about so that they faced the opposite stage, where they were treated to a live performance. Elsa Lancaster was a frequent entertainer in this venue. As the nation's only full-time puppet theater, the Turnabout was a huge success until audiences dwindled in the 1950s; the house closed in 1956. Burnett and Brown were the first recipients of lifetime achievement awards from the Los Angeles Drama Critics.

Theater's sagging finances received a boost during the depression when government subsidies were dispersed by the Federal Theatre Project (FTP), a section of the Works Progress Administration (WPA), authorized by Congress on 8 April 1935. Less than 1 percent of the $5 billion allocated to the WPA went to the arts, and only a small portion of that trickled down to theater. Yet in a few short years the FTP produced more than 150 arts productions in Los Angeles alone, including plays by new authors. One production was Elmer Rice's *Judgement Day.* Of 22 companies the FTP sent out nationally of Sinclair Lewis's *It Can't Happen Here,* two played simultaneously in Los Angeles and had successful runs. Paul Green's *Johnny Johnson* played in Los Angeles for six weeks in 1937, and his earlier play, *House of Connelly,* enjoyed a successful revival. Of the FTP's 16 national Negro theatrical units, the Los Angeles group was among the most successful. Their most popular production, which ran for more than a year, was the folk-musical drama *Run, Little Chillun* by Hall Johnson, who lived in Los Angeles. In 1938 the Negro unit put on Christine Ames's *Black Empire,* about Haitian revolutionary leader Henri Christophe. The popular production ran from March to July and was performed in both the Hollywood Playhouse and the Greek Theatre.

A children's theater unit was also based in Los Angeles. Walt Disney was so taken with its staging of *Pinocchio* that, after seeing it eight times, he decided to adapt it as a film. The FTP sent out vaudeville units, which staged some elaborate revues, among them *Follow the Parade* and *Revue of Reviews*. Although modern dance was scarce in Los Angeles, choreographer-dancer Myra Kinch organized a group of some 25 dancers that included young Bella Lewitzky. The theatrical excitement declined in 1939 when Congress dismantled the Federal Theatre Project—a victim of anti–New Deal sentiment.

THEATER, SINCE 1945. The postwar period has seen immense growth in terms of the number of theaters, types of dramatic performances, size of audiences, and critical acclaim for productions. Indeed, in the last 50 years Los Angeles has become the nation's second most important theatrical city.

The expansion that began slowly in the 1950s increased rapidly in the 1960s. Among the city's larger theaters, the Huntington Hartford (now the Doolittle) opened in 1953. The county took over operation of the Pilgrimage Play Amphitheatre, which, reconstituted as the John Anson Ford Theater, was adapted for presentation of various plays and musicals. Undoubtedly, the most important event was the 1964 opening of the 2,300-seat Ahmanson Theatre and the 750-seat Mark Taper Forum, both at the downtown Music Center. The Ahmanson often books touring productions, usually directly from Broadway. The longest-running musical in West Coast history was *Phantom of the Opera,* which played 1,772 performances at the Ahmanson between 1989 and 1993 and was seen by 3 million people. Meanwhile, the Mark Taper Forum

has become one of the country's most influential regional theaters. The offspring of a company started at UCLA by John Houseman, the Taper company came into its own under founding director Gordon Davidson. Hollywood's James A. Doolittle Theater and the Westwood Playhouse, now known as the Geffen Playhouse, are both owned by UCLA. The Pantages Theater in Hollywood and Century City's Shubert Theater host touring companies and independent productions.

The 1970s saw considerable theater expansion. The city-owned outdoor Greek Theatre was reorganized in 1976. A year later the old Pantages movie palace on Hollywood Boulevard was converted into a legitimate equity theater, and a Long Beach theater complex was built, with a 3,000-seat hall for stage productions. In 1985, with financial assistance from the Community Redevelopment Agency (CRA), the Los Angeles Theater Center (LATC) was established and opened in a remodeled bank building on a run-down section of Spring Street. It achieved artistic successes, stressing avant-garde plays and multiculturalism in the employment of actors, writers, and directors, but never acquired a downtown residential audience or financial stability. In 1991, when CRA backing and corporate subsidies dried up, LATC was forced to close down.

Smaller theaters of high quality also flourished in the post–World War II period. The equivalent of New York's Off-Broadway theaters, they usually operated in old, low-rent spaces that were remodeled for stage productions. Although tucked away throughout Los Angeles, the majority were in the Hollywood area: the Circle Theater, the Ring

Anna Deavere Smith in *Twilight: Los Angeles, 1992,* Mark Taper Forum. Photo by Jay Thompson, courtesy Mark Taper Forum.

Theater, the Actors Lab, and the Horseshoe Theater, among others.

Small theaters now grace most communities, and vary from tiny, experimental companies to established institutions. The Theatricum Botanicum, the Cast Theatre, the Burbage Theater, Stella Adler's Academy Theater, the Odyssey Theatre, the Bilingual Foundation of the Arts, the Actors Circle Theater, Theatre/Theater, the East West Players (the nation's oldest Asian American theater group), the Ebony Theater, the Tiffany Theater, and Theatre 40 are but a handful of the numerous dedicated houses that present productions on a shoestring and a prayer.

The little theater scene in Southern California is nourished by the fact that one-quarter of the nation's professional actors live in the region, as well as by the equity-waiver rule, which allows professional actors to work together with amateurs in theaters of 99 seats or fewer.

THEATERS, MOVIE. *See* Movie theaters

THIRD STREET PROMENADE, an outdoor shopping area in Santa Monica, officially opened in September 1989. The city initiated it as an urban renewal project in 1984, establishing the Third Street Development Corporation with $13 million in public funds and raising an additional $250 million in private funds. Two blocks wide and three blocks long, the Promenade runs north and south in the heart of downtown, from Wilshire Boulevard to Broadway. It is closed to auto traffic and features scores of restaurants, movie theaters (17 screens in all), retail shops, and services. At night

especially, it attracts an array of eclectic street musicians and performers. The overall design, which includes strategically situated benches, a fountain, greenery, and access to public parking, has achieved widespread acclaim. Third Street Promenade is managed by Bayside District Corporation and attracts 2 million visitors annually.

THOM, CAMERON ERSKINE (1825–1915), civic leader and mayor from 1882 to 1884. Born in the South, Thom came to Los Angeles in 1854, where he practiced law and became district attorney. During the hectic period of land title confirmations initiated by the U.S. Land Law of 1851 the federal government employed Thom as a land agent. He became wealthy, acquiring a large Glendale property. During the Civil War he served in the Confederate army; when he returned to Los Angeles he found his resources depleted and, with borrowed money, began again.

Thom helped found the Los Angeles Social Club in 1869, and the volunteer fire department in 1873. He was one of the few white men who bravely tried to stop the violence of the Chinese Massacre of October 1871. With newfound wealth he built a residence on Main Street and, in 1876, bought land for a summer villa in Santa Monica from his friend Sen. John P. Jones. During Thom's term as mayor Los Angeles was 29 square miles in size and had a population of 11,000. Elysian Park was one of the fruits of his stint in office. He was later called on to help draft the city charter of 1889.

THRIFTY DRUG STORES, retail chain founded in Los Angeles in 1919 as Borun Brothers Drug

Third Street Promenade, Santa Monica. Photo by Lori Shepler.

Stores. The enterprise shifted to a discount operation in 1929; its first Thrifty Cut-Rate Drug Store, on South Broadway, featured "loss leader" products displayed on rough pine counters. By 1934 the firm had 17 such stores. Following World War II it entered the new shopping malls, adopted aggressive marketing strategies, and by 1989 occupied 575 locations. Thrifty Corporation, which also owned the Big Five sporting goods chain, was for a time a subsidiary of Pacific Lighting.

THROOP POLYTECHNIC INSTITUTE. *See* California Institute of Technology

TIMES-MIRROR COMPANY, diversified communications giant that owns newspapers, magazines, a book publishing firm, television and cable channels, and forest product firms, as well as land. The company was incorporated in 1884 for the purpose of securing ownership of the *Los Angeles Times,* established in 1881, and the smaller *Weekly Los Angeles Mirror,* founded in 1873. In 1886 Harrison Gray Otis became the major shareholder, president, and general manager of the *Times.* In the 1960s Times-Mirror became a public corporation, issuing major bond and stock offerings and adding firms that published art, medical, and scientific books. Its major land holding was Tejon Ranch near Tejon Pass. In 1969 overall corporate revenues reached $466 million, earning profits of $38.6 million. By 1977 the company was the nation's largest publisher.

In addition to publishing the *Los Angeles Times,* Times-Mirror also issues the *Long Island Newsday, Baltimore Sun, Stamford (Connecticut) Advocate,* the *Sporting News,* and *Popular Science,* among others. It owns its own newsprint and forest product firms, and maintains 268,000 acres of timberland in the Pacific Northwest. It is headquartered in downtown Los Angeles at Times-Mirror Square. The company has been a major employer, with a payroll, in peak years, of more than 6,000 people. In the 1990s, after a series of mergers, the media giant became a major player in the "information superhighway."

TITLE INSURANCE AND TRUST COMPANY (TI, OR TICOR TITLE), pioneering real estate enterprise that became the largest land title company in the world. It was born in the depression year of 1893, from a merger of two rival companies with roots in the 1870s: the Abstract and Ti-

tle Insurance Company and the Los Angeles Abstract Company. Its purpose was to provide accurate land title abstracts for transactions in a market rife with speculation and fraud. The leading figures in the company were Otto F. Brant, a native of Ohio; Oliver P. Clark, of Indiana; and William H. Allen Jr., of Illinois. TI issued certificates summarizing the chain of ownership and guaranteeing the accuracy of the links. By selling title insurance it served all who were involved in land sales, including government agencies and the legal profession, and became a major player in the escrow business. By the 1920s TI had become the national giant in the land title field, with offices in many California counties and in the state of Oregon. Its greatest success came with the formation of real estate subdivision trusts that developed the San Fernando Valley. These realty trusts produced a vast fortune for the company. As an offshoot of its enterprises, the company amassed a vast collection of maps and other property documents pertaining to Los Angeles that was more comprehensive than that of any other agency, public or private. Its vast collection of photographs is housed at USC. TI's downtown headquarters at 4th and Spring Streets, built in 1928, was a landmark downtown building. TI was later absorbed by the Chicago Title Insurance Company and ceased to have a presence in the region.

TOBERMAN, JAMES R. (1836–1911), mayor of Los Angeles from 1872 to 1874 and 1878 to 1882. Toberman came to Los Angeles from Texas in 1864, having been appointed by President Lincoln as U.S. revenue assessor, a post he held until 1870. In 1868 he, I. W. Hellman, William Workman, Francis Pliny Fisk Temple, and others founded the Hellman, Temple, and Company bank. In 1872 Toberman defeated the incumbent mayor, Cristóbal Aguilar. Property owners liked him for reducing the city's indebtedness from $30,000 to $25,000 and for lowering taxes. In a dramatic moment, on the evening of 31 December 1882, he touched a button that brought the first electricity to the downtown city streets. During his tenure as mayor the 29-square-mile city had between 5,700 and 11,000 residents.

TOLUCA LAKE, private lake and residential neighborhood in the North Hollywood district of the San Fernando Valley. The small body of water known as Toluca Lake is directly adjacent to the Los Angeles River, south of Riverside Drive. When founded as an independent town in 1888, North Hollywood was called Toluca Lake, after a city in Mexico. Aviator Amelia Earhart built a home there in 1928, maintaining it until her disappearance in 1937. Also named Lankershim for a brief period, the Toluca Lake community, like all of North Hollywood, has been part of the city of Los Angeles since 1923. Entertainer Bob Hope once lived there, and actress Ann Blyth once served a term as honorary mayor.

TOMMY'S, or "The Original Ptomaine Tommy" restaurant, was a popular hamburger place on North Broadway, run from 1913 to 1958 by Tommy DeForest and his wife. DeForest's contribution to the culinary art was the "chili size," a hamburger with a secret-ingredient red chili sauce topped by onions. Among his regulars were movie stars Mae West, Mary Pickford, and Dorothy Lamour. Tommy's closed because of financial troubles, and Tommy died a week later. To this day there are many look-alike restaurants around town, attempting to capitalize on the original name.

TONGVA INDIANS (GABRIELEÑOS), native people who inhabited the Los Angeles area for 1,000 years before the coming of the Europeans and numbered anywhere from 1,000 to 10,000. The Spaniards called them Gabrieleños after their association with Mission San Gabriel. Culturally they were of Shoshonean background and linguistically of the Uto-Aztecan family (distantly related to the Utes, Paiutes, New Mexico Pueblos, Yaquis, and Aztecs). Their small villages were scattered throughout the Los Angeles Basin, along its marshes and waterways and near the ocean. Tongva remains have been found in about 40 county locations, including Encino, Long Beach, West Los Angeles, Pasadena, and Santa Catalina Island. Their village near today's Los Angeles City Hall was called Yangna.

The Tongva were hunters and gatherers whose ample food supply included deer, rabbits, quail, ducks, geese, cranes, gophers, rats, squirrels, reptiles, seafood, plants, and seeds, especially acorns, which was their staple. They never farmed. Acorn processing represents a sophisticated adaptation to the environment, since the oak seed in its natural state contains lethal tannin; it is removed by a process of leaching and boiling.

Tribe members performed hard labor in harvest season, but they had much leisure time and enjoyed

Tongva Indian Rogerio Rocha, born 1801, died 1904. Photo by Charles F. Lummis, courtesy Southwest Museum.

such pursuits as archery practice, cat's cradle, guessing games, and hoop-and-pole sports, often gambling on the outcome. The women crafted exquisite baskets (some are preserved at the Southwest Museum) and carved steatite beads, pipes, and animal likenesses. The men fashioned plank boats and rafts that were sturdy enough to carry them to Catalina and San Nicholas Islands and back. Tongva exerted a strong influence on neighbors and trading partners. Although they had no written language, they possessed a rich oral treasury of stories. They created their own religious rituals and societies, one involving the narcotic jimsonweed. Their powerful god, Chinigchinich, appears to have entered their lore during the mission era.

A friendly and intelligent people, the Tongva ended up toiling for the Spanish colonialists in forced labor on the missions and on the ranchos. Strict confinement in unfamiliar living quarters, an alien work regimen, brutalization by Spanish soldiers, and contagious diseases took a heavy toll on their population. In the 1850s and 1860s the Yankees treated them contemptuously and unjustly, herding them into a ghetto near Commercial and Alvarado Streets for a time. Tongva place-names are numerous and include Pacoima, Saticoy, Cucamonga, Azusa, Cahuenga, and Malibu. They shared territory with the closely related Fernandeños (Mission San Fernando neophytes), who were completely extinguished.

Though nearly eradicated by 1910, Tongva have lately revived their communal life. They now practice native arts, protect traditional sites, and generally attempt to maintain their faith. In 1988 they successfully protested a proposed Marina construction project that would have desecrated an ancient cemetery. In 1991 the tribal council demanded protection of the area surrounding a traditional site on the grounds of University High School in West Los Angeles, where 22,000 gallons of water rise to the surface, feeding a waterfall and 80-foot lagoon. They also resisted an archaeological survey on the CSULB campus, charging that it would disturb sacred ground.

TOPANGA, rural county hamlet in Topanga Canyon in the Santa Monica Mountains, 21 miles west of downtown Los Angeles. The name, a Tongva (Gabrieleño) word, was preserved by the Mexicans as a sector of the Boca de Santa Monica land grant in 1839. In 1940 University of California archaeologists determined that Native Americans occupied the area as long ago as 8,000 years. A few dozen homesteaders settled Topanga early in the 20th century. An inn was opened about 5 miles from the beach in 1900, followed by a general store and post office by 1908. Tent camps sprouted at sea level for bathers, while resort cabins and light-housekeeping

---

A city without boundaries, which ate the desert, cut down the Joshua and the May poles, and dreamt of becoming infinite.

—Mike Davis, historian

---

cottages were opened at higher elevations to accommodate hunters and vacationers. The canyon road—a wagon-and-coach trail that followed the rugged creekbed—wound through a picturesque area of stark peaks, flowing water, stately oaks and sycamores, and flowering hillsides. In 1915, with the advent of the automobile, the road was widened into a three-lane, 14-mile highway. The first real estate development, called Topanga City, lasted only from 1912 to 1922. Further development occurred in the next several decades, when ex-urbanites built more conventional and permanent homes.

Topanga maintains a lifestyle that is rural and informal—even bohemian. Its population in 1985 was 7,000. Sectors of the canyon are included in the Santa Monica Mountains National Recreation Area.

TORRANCE, independent city 19 miles southwest of downtown Los Angeles. Its original owner and namesake, the Pasadena financier and philanthropist Jared S. Torrance, planned it in 1911 as a model industrial city. He bought 3,500 acres of land, part of the former Rancho San Pedro, from the Domínguez family and hired the Boston landscape architectural firm of Olmsted & Olmsted to create a model design. Architects Lloyd Wright and Irving J. Gill were also employed on the project in its early years. Torrance was a major stop on the Pacific Electric Railway. In recent years community activists have encouraged the preservation of numerous buildings dating back to the town's beginnings, as well as of a grassy island known as Madrona Marsh, a nature preserve sheltering rare birds and a rare species of tree frog. The 1990 census showed that the industrial, commercial, and bedroom community of Torrance had a population of 133,100.

TOURISM, leading Los Angeles industry since the completion of the railroads in the 1870s. To lure visitors from around the world, local business leaders advertised the year-round sunshine, spectacular natural surroundings, historic sites, and glamorous Hollywood attractions. Pictures of crowded beaches, orange groves, and snow-capped mountains enticed millions not only to visit, but also to take up permanent residence.

The very term "tourist" may have originated in Southern California. In the 1890s affluent travelers from the East began abandoning their European tours to see the wonders of the Far West. They migrated through a network of Southern California hostelries built especially to satisfy their elegant tastes: the Arcadia in Santa Monica; the Arlington and Potter House in Santa Barbara; the Grand View in Monrovia; the Raymond, Green, Maryland, and Pintoresca in Pasadena; the Coronado near San Diego; the Casa Loma in Redlands; and the Sierra Madre Villa in Sierra Madre.

The railroads and hotels fostered art shows and magazines, and subsidized travel books by novel-

"From the Sea to the Orange Groves" excursion car, at San Gabriel Mission. Courtesy Robert Weinstein Collection.

ists and newspaper reporters. Charles Nordhoff of the *New York Tribune,* who put Southern California on the map with his book *California for Health, Pleasure, and Residence* (1872), was on the payroll of the Southern Pacific. Other enthusiastic troubadours and public relations figures were Maj. Benjamin C. Truman, Charles Dudley Warner, and Charles Frederick Holder, an avid booster for the good life offered by Pasadena.

From the 1920s on, county government exercised its legal right to subsidize private groups dedicated to selling the sunshine and scenery. The Board of Supervisors fed public monies directly to the chamber of commerce and the All-Year Club (today's Visitors and Convention Bureau). Other private promotional groups benefiting from county funds were Roads to Romance (during World War II), the Mission Trails Association, and the Imperial Highway Association, dedicated to connecting Los Angeles, Orange, Riverside, and San Diego Counties by means of better highways. Although no longer dependent on public funds, the Greater Los Angeles Chamber of Commerce and the Convention and Visitors Bureau continue to coordinate publicity and promote research on tourism.

In 1989 tourism generated about $8.74 billion for the Los Angeles County economy, as a record 25.2 million visitors arrived on the scene. By one estimate, 24.8 million visitors passed through Los Angeles in 1993, of whom some 5.2 million were international visitors, with 1.8 million from Latin America, 1.3 million from Europe, and 1.1 million from Asia. The nations sending the most visitors

were Mexico, at 1.6 million; Japan, 503,000; Canada, 432,700; United Kingdom, 375,000; and Germany, 312,000. Notwithstanding the 1992 riot and 1994 Northridge earthquake, more than 22.2 million people visited the county in 1994. The county's most popular tourist attractions include the Venice boardwalk, Beverly Hills, Hollywood, Universal Studios, Magic Mountain, and the *Queen Mary.* Most visitors to Disneyland, which is in Orange County, stay in Los Angeles as well.

TOURNAMENT OF ROSES, Pasadena's world-famous New Year's Day parade, since 1890. The event began modestly when members of Pasadena's Valley Hunt Club, mindful of the terrible blizzard of 1888 that had paralyzed the Northeast, decorated a wagon with flowers and rode in it to celebrate New Year's Day—seeming to indicate to those on the other coast the difference between heaven and hell. Some 3,000 spectators attended this first festivity, which ended in a park and featured foot races, tug-of-war matches, and jousts. In 1894 other organizations entered the parade and decorated their own floats. In 1895 the nonprofit Tournament of Roses Association was established to run the annual parade. They modeled their event after European festivals, specifically Nice's Carnival of Flowers. The parade displayed Pasadena's natural gifts.

In 1900, as if to mark the coming technology of the 20th century, motion pictures recorded the event, and one year later automobiles were introduced and decorated. A football game, played at

Tournament of Roses poster, 1912. Courtesy Pasadena Tournament of Roses Association.

Caltech's Tournament Park, followed the 1902 parade. In 1904 chariot races were held, inspired by the popular *Ben Hur,* and in 1905 Hallie Woods was crowned the parade's first queen. A postseason football game became a supplement to the parade as early as 1916, but the Rose Bowl, which was completed in 1922, built and financed by the Tournament of Roses Association, did not host its first game until 1923. One year later the city of Glendale won the first Sweepstakes Prize for its float, "Fairyland." The parade was described in the nation's very first coast-to-coast radio broadcast by sportscaster Graham McNamee, who went on to announce the game. Czechoslovakia became the first foreign nation to sponsor a float, in 1927, and Mary Pickford had the honor of being the first woman grand marshal, in 1933. The first local telecast of the Tournament of Roses was on KTLA in 1947.

The colorful spectacle of marching bands, floral floats, and equestrian units moving along the 5.5-mile route captured the imagination. In 1989 an average float in the Rose Parade cost $85,000 to assemble and required 100,000 blossoms. Half a million roses are used in each parade, more than a million people line the streets to watch the floats ride by, and many millions more watch on television. In 1987 the event was viewed by 350 million in South, Central, and North America and Europe —the largest international audience to that time. It is now an annual world television spectacular, and the viewing audience grows yearly. In 1993 it was even televised to China via satellite.

TOWNSEND PLAN, pension movement led by Dr. Francis Townsend of Long Beach in 1933–1934. The key demand of the movement was a federal law granting $200 a month to every citizen 60 years and over. The funds would derive from a national sales tax, and the recipients would be compelled to spend the money within 30 days, thereby encouraging an economic revival. The plan was the brainchild of Dr. Francis E. Townsend (1867–1960), a California-born physician who also dabbled in real estate and other enterprises. By 1933 the depression had bankrupted him personally and was causing deep suffering among his patients, many of whom were retired midwesterners. He and a real estate colleague, Robert Clements, incorporated as the Old Age Revolving Pensions, Ltd. (OARP), and formed the Townsend Club to bring about the federally financed pension scheme. In 1934 the influence of the movement was such that John Stephen McGroarty of Los Angeles was elected to Congress, and he took their cause to the nation's capital. The Southern California agitation for an old-age pension garnered national support, and spurred Pres. Franklin D. Roosevelt to introduce the Social Security Act in 1935. Although eclipsed by this New Deal legislation, the Townsend movement was the first of several senior citizens' organizations originating in, or having a strong following in, the region.

TRACK-AND-FIELD SPORTS were introduced into the region by the Los Angeles Athletic Club, established in 1880. Since then year-round track and field activities have been fostered by colleges, universities, and noncollegiate clubs. Excellent physical facilities and superior coaching have allowed such schools as UCLA, USC, and Pepperdine to produce many champions. By 1991 USC had won 26 national titles in the 68-year history of the National College Athletic Association (NCAA) outdoor track-and-field championships, and it had produced several Olympic champions, including Frank Wykoff, Lillian Copeland, Bob Seagren, and Charley Paddock, "the world's fastest human," whose life was portrayed in the film *Chariots of Fire* (1981). USC's crosstown rival, UCLA, has won 8 NCAA championships and has placed in the top five scores of times. Some of the NCAA and Olympic immortals from Southern California are Willie Banks, Greg Foster, Mike Tully, Steve Lewis, Kevin Young, Jackie Joyner-Kersee, Rafer Johnson, Florence Griffith Joyner, and Evelyn Ashford.

TRADE AND COMMERCE, FOREIGN, centered on Los Angeles, impacts greatly on the local and national economies. The principal staging areas are the Port of Los Angeles, the Port of Long

Foreign Trade, Worldport L.A., 1992 (in $)ᵃ

Trade Partner	Inbound Net Revenue	Outbound Net Revenue	Total Net Revenue
Taiwan	13,516,138	4,600,139	18,116,277
Hong Kong	14,543,063	2,406,715	16,949,778
Japan	8,950,368	6,968,006	15,918,374
Republic of Korea	3,592,729	1,587,992	5,180,721
Mexico—			
Passenger	2,567,246	2,547,509	5,114,755
Singapore	3,126,801	897,216	4,024,017
Australia	348,118	1,491,606	1,839,724
Thailand	1,268,190	531,163	1,799,353
Philippines	997,913	498,516	1,496,429
Indonesia	975,287	475,326	1,450,613
China	798,777	254,890	1,053,667
Italy	816,093	203,436	1,019,529
Belgium	541,417	445,402	986,819
Brazil	898,560	82,486	981,046
Chile	685,301	206,600	891,901
Mexico—Freight	798,638	70,948	869,586
Ecuador	573,517	239,445	812,962
India	222,374	551,864	774,238
Malaysia	537,467	197,879	735,346
Laos, Vietnam	167,365	425,602	592,967
New Zealand	296,646	190,969	487,615
Germany	298,058	171,602	469,660
Netherlands	233,418	122,002	355,420
United Arab Emirates	176,649	103,651	280,300
Israel	83,338	174,309	257,647
Spain	131,479	84,096	215,575
United Kingdom	87,336	89,699	177,035
France	84,832	91,721	176,553
South Africa	153,466	2,413	155,879
Argentina	88,688	67,186	155,874
Egypt	5,410	134,935	140,345
Colombia	91,898	37,202	129,100
Panama	84,064	43,892	127,956
Saudi Arabia	21,060	82,675	103,735
Sri Lanka	94,866	6,480	101,346

SOURCE: Worldport L.A.
ᵃExcluding petroleum product in bulk.

Beach, and Los Angeles International Airport (LAX).

Owing to its geographic isolation and to the repressive mercantilist policies of Spain and Mexico, commercial relations between Los Angeles and the outside world from 1781 to 1848 were sporadic at best. The major commerce was the hide-and-tallow trade. Even after California became a state, Los Angeles, an inland town with a useless mud flat for a port, could engage in only limited shipping. Between 1890 and 1914, however, the city constructed a deep-draft harbor and annexed the city of San

Pedro with its dock facilities, thus entering boldly onto the stage of world commerce. This development coincided with events in American history that greatly enhanced West Coast shipping: imperialist adventures in the Philippines and Hawaii, a widening interest in Asian markets, and the completion of the Panama Canal.

Foreign commerce expanded markedly in Los Angeles in the 1920s. It grew even more rapidly after World War II, when the city became a shipping center of the Pacific Rim. In recent decades imports into the city have featured electrical machinery, aerospace equipment, instruments, refined petroleum projects, motor vehicles, and apparel, with the largest volume of goods coming from Japan, Taiwan, South Korea, Hong Kong, and Germany. The chief targets of the export trade have been Japan, South Korea, Australia, Taiwan, and the United Kingdom. In the Western Hemisphere, Canada and Mexico are important trading partners. Los Angeles's leading industries in recent years, such as aerospace, tourism, television/motion pictures, and apparel manufacturing, have strong overseas components. The North American Free Trade Agreement (NAFTA) of 1993 was expected to make a major impact on Southern California trade and commerce.

In 1994 Los Angeles surpassed New York as the nation's leading trade center. That year the amount of goods flowing through the Los Angeles Customs District (which includes the twin ports of Los Angeles and Long Beach, as well as LAX and airports in Ventura County and Las Vegas) amounted to $145.9 billion, a 13.5 percent rise over the previous year. The dramatic increase was due to the Port of Long Beach's position as the country's leading con-tainer port, heightened trade with Pacific Rim areas, a greater number of U.S. exports, and a booming high-tech industry.

TRANSPORTATION. *See* Airports; Automobile; Freeways; Metro rail system; Pacific Electric Railway Company; Railroads

TRANSVERSE RANGES, east-west mountains marking the northern limit of Southern California. Approximately 300 miles in extent, they include the Santa Ynez, Topatopa, Santa Susana, Santa Monica, San Gabriel, and San Bernardino Mountains. They were formed by the movement of the North American tectonic plate as it was pulled loose from the mainland of Mexico.

TREES, once a scarcity in Southern California, are now abundant. Before the Spaniards arrived the Los Angeles plains were a semi-arid region with willow-lined streambeds, some marshy areas subject to flooding, sycamores in deep canyons, and live oaks on some coastal hills. The hillsides were a tangle of chaparral, cactus, and wildflowers such as poppy and evening primrose. The colonists introduced trees for ornament, shade, and orchard crops, but even as late as 1840 only two trees graced the Plaza. Numerous orchards were introduced beginning in the 1880s, only to be eliminated by urban development since the 1950s.

The native trees may be divided as to geographic area: On the *coastal plain and foothills* the oak tree is the most abundant and dominant native tree form. In *riparian areas* the big-leaf maple, a tall, broad-crowned tree, is common, along with spruce, alder, sycamore, cottonwood, and willow. In the

Pepper trees on Adams Boulevard, 1907. Pitt Collection.

wooded foothills the characteristic trees are spruce, pine, juniper, walnut, oak, and the omnipresent manzanita shrub. On the *rocky coast* of Santa Catalina Island, Catalina ironwood, an endangered evergreen, is endemic. At *low mountain elevations* is found a mixture of coniferous and hardwood species, typically yellow pine, Jeffrey pine, incense cedar, white fir, black oak, and live oak. At *higher mountainous elevations* are the lodgepole and limber pines.

Hundreds of species have been introduced into the region, including many varieties of fruit trees. The planting of eucalyptus, a native of Australia, became a crusade in the 19th century. It is now considered naturalized and is among the tallest of local trees. Some 48,000 palm trees grow in the Los Angeles area, most of them imported varieties. Pepper trees from the Old World became a dominant addition to the Southern California landscape in the 19th century as well. The purple-blossomed jacaranda, so prominent in Southern California, was imported from Brazil.

Some individual trees or stands of trees have attained a special status. Among the trees the Cultural Heritage Board has designated as cultural-historic monuments are the coral trees—adopted by the city council as the city's official tree—that offer shade and color on the median strip of San Vicente Boulevard between 26th Street and Brigham Avenue in Brentwood; the 51 sycamore trees south of

Planning in Los Angeles? In the world's eyes that is a self-cancelling concept.   —Reyner Banham, writer

Sunset Boulevard on Bienvenida Avenue that were planted in 1926 as part of the design of that subdivision; the 8 avocado trees on the 4400 block of Avocado Street, which are over a century old; the cedar trees that flank both sides of Los Feliz Boulevard between Riverside Drive and Western Avenue, planted in 1916 by a local homeowners' association and women's club; the stand of 144 deodar trees in Granada Hills on White Oak Avenue between San Fernando Mission and San Jose Street, planted in 1932; a 1,000-year-old oak tree that stands just south of Ventura Boulevard in Encino; and a spreading Moreton Bay fig tree planted in 1875, at 11000 National Boulevard in Mar Vista.

The worst assault on trees occurred after World War II, when commercial orange groves were leveled to make way for suburban housing, at a rate of 1,000 trees per day.

Today, trees of many varieties help purify the air, shelter wildlife, host insects, retain the soil, and supply endless aesthetic appeal and character to the region. Botanists recommend that more trees be planted. One estimate is that a major planting of trees in the San Fernando Valley could reduce the summer temperature by 9 degrees and lower the demand for air conditioning by 44 percent. The shovel-wielding Tree People, a voluntary environmental association devoted to tree planting, backed by the *Los Angeles Times,* prepared for the 1984 Summer Olympics by planting 1 million saplings.

TRIUNFO CANYON, unincorporated area in the far western part of the county. The population rose from 337 in 1980 to 770 in 1990.

TROPICO, portion of Glendale. Located east of the Los Angeles River, it was incorporated as an independent city in 1911, but consolidated with Glendale in 1918.

TROUSDALE ESTATES, luxury residential area in the northernmost part of Beverly Hills. It lies in a canyon along Loma Vista Drive, and was developed after World War II by the Trousdale Company.

TRUMAN, BENJAMIN C. (1835–1916), author and journalist. After a celebrated career in the Union army during the Civil War, Truman settled in Southern California in 1866. He wrote essays, sketches, short stories, and booster books, including his celebrated *Semi-Tropical California* (1874), which he penned while working as a publicist for the Southern Pacific Railroad. His jailhouse interview with the bandit Tiburcio Vásquez, published the same year, was extremely popular.

TRW (THOMPSON, RAMO, WOOLDRIDGE). *See* Aerospace industry

TUJUNGA. *See* Sunland-Tujunga

TURNER, JOEL H. (D. 1888), mayor of Los Angeles from 1868 to 1870. During his tenure the city was 29 square miles in area and had a population of 5,700. In 1869 Turner welcomed Secretary of

State William Seward, whose historic northern journey would lead to the U.S. purchase of Alaska. The Los Angeles Board of Education was formed during Turner's mayoral term.

TUTTLE, RICK (1940–), Los Angeles city controller. Born in Connecticut, Tuttle graduated from Wesleyan University and then, in 1963, volunteered as a civil rights worker in Georgia and Mississippi. He moved to Los Angeles, where he was co-chair of California Young Citizens for Robert F. Kennedy in 1968. He received a Ph.D. in history from UCLA in 1974. Tuttle won a landslide third term as city controller in 1993. As controller he has initiated new programs, and as an active member of the community he has been the recipient of awards from the Anti-Defamation League and the NAACP; has been on the board of directors of the Los Angeles West Chamber of Commerce and of the University Religious Conference at UCLA; and was honored with a Lifetime Membership Award from the Los Angeles Business Council.

20TH CENTURY–FOX STUDIO, one of the "Big Five" movie studios of Hollywood's Golden Era. Hungarian-born William Fox established the company, which was founded in New York, on its current Pico Boulevard location (once the site of Tom Mix's ranch) in 1924, on land purchased from the Janss Investment Corporation. Fox, who like many film moguls started in the movie business as a distributor, was an influential figure in the early development of sound, pioneering the Movietone sound-on-film process. He also was important in the careers of such early stars as Theda Bara. In 1935 the Fox Film Corporation merged with 20th Century Pictures, established two years earlier by Joseph Schenck and Darryl F. Zanuck. Zanuck headed production at 20th Century–Fox from the time of the merger until 1956. He returned six years later as studio president, taking over from Spyros Skouras, who had held that office since 1942.

Fox's and 20th Century–Fox's contract players have included Will Rogers, Linda Darnell, Stan Laurel and Oliver Hardy, Don Ameche, Shirley Temple, Alice Faye, Tom Mix, Betty Grable, Tyrone Power, and Marilyn Monroe. Among the distinguished films to emerge from the studio are *What Price Glory* (1926), *Heidi* (1937), *The Grapes of Wrath* (1940), *How Green Was My Valley* (1941), *The Ox-Bow Incident* (1943), *Gentleman's Agreement* (1947), *A Letter to Three Wives* (1949), *All About Eve* (1950), *The Seven Year Itch* (1955), *The King and I* (1956), *The Sound of Music* (1965), and *M*A*S*H* (1970).

In the early years, the 225-acre studio was largely surrounded by stucco walls that enclosed sound stages, office buildings, stables, and sound equipment and backlot storage. In the 1960s, 20th Century–Fox sold off much of its property. The land adjacent to the studio became Century City, a high-rise complex of malls, offices, apartments, condominiums, hotels, theaters, and restaurants.

The movie and television studio is still active, as part of News Corporation, Rupert Murdoch's media empire. It has moved into other entertainment areas such as home video and international cable channels, and is currently planning a $200 million building expansion at its Pico location.

TYPOGRAPHICAL UNION, LOCAL 174, oldest continuously functioning labor body in the county. Now part of the International Typographical Union (AFL-CIO), the local was founded in 1875. Beginning in 1901 it locked horns with the antilabor publisher Harrison Gray Otis of the *Los Angeles Times.* The union organized an aggressive boycott against the People's Store, demanding that the company stop advertising in the *Times.* The boycott galvanized the local business community into forming the Merchants and Manufacturers Association as part of the antilabor crusade. In 1903 Local 174 persuaded William Randolph Hearst to found the *Los Angeles Examiner* as a prolabor rival to the *Times.* Ironically, a strike against the Hearst-owned *Herald-Examiner,* from 1967 to 1972, became one of the bitterest labor confrontations in the region's history, and led to the paper's demise.

𝒰

UAW. *See* United Auto Workers

UCLA. *See* University of California, Los Angeles

UEBERROTH, PETER VICTOR (1937–), entrepreneur and sports enthusiast. The Orange County resident was founder and CEO of the second largest travel agency chain in the nation. Los Angeles mayor Tom Bradley offered him the post of president of the 1984 Los Angeles Olympic Games Organizing Committee. Ueberroth promised to mount the Summer Olympics at no expense to the city, and he was true to his word: in fact, the spartan 23rd Olympiad produced a surplus of $250 million. This earned Ueberroth an appointment as U.S. commissioner of baseball, a position he held for a short time. In the wake of the 1992 rioting Mayor Bradley again called on Ueberroth, this time to head Rebuild L.A., a private-sector committee established after the upheaval. Its goal was to stimulate the growth of jobs in the inner city. He accepted, but resigned from the position in 1993 stating that he would remain on the board.

UNINCORPORATED COMMUNITIES, districts in county territory unaffiliated with any cities and governed directly by the Los Angeles County Board of Supervisors. All together, these areas contained an estimated 961,800 people in 1994. Most of the unincorporated communities, such as Castaic, Val Verde, Agua Dulce, Marina del Rey, and Diamond Bar, are relatively small and lie on the fringes of the county. A few, such as Willowbrook, are centrally located. The most populous unincorporated district is East Los Angeles, which has been the subject of eight unsuccessful incorporation attempts, from 1925 to 1974. All such areas retain the services of the county.

UNION PACIFIC RAILROAD. *See* Railroads

UNION PASSENGER TERMINAL, the last of the great American railroad stations, built in 1939. The facility on Los Angeles and Alameda Streets came about after a long and bitter political fight that split the business community, newspapers, citizens groups, and the city council. As early as 1911 planners urged the Southern Pacific, Santa Fe, and Union Pacific Railroads to consolidate their scattered terminals into one unified facility at the Plaza. The railroad companies, fearing the plan might lead to more competition, resisted. Backed by the chamber of commerce, they offered an alternative scheme featuring a network of elevated railroads that would connect the separate terminals. The city council, however, with support from the *Los Angeles Times,* Interstate Commerce Commission, and state railroad commission, filed a suit in 1916 demanding a single terminal. The case wound through the courts for 10 years, until finally the issue evolved into a city ballot measure. In 1926 the largest voter turnout in the city's history approved a consolidated terminal in the Plaza area, on the site of the old Chinatown.

Architect Donald B. Parkinson designed a cluster of low, stucco, tile-roofed buildings, combining the Spanish Mission and Moderne styles, that were topped by a 135-foot clock tower. The interior is graced by a vast marble floor and tall arched windows. The station opened on 7 May 1939, and 1.5 million people mobbed the facility in its first three days of operation. It served the extensive demands of wartime rail traffic, but the number of passenger trains soon fell off owing to competition from air transportation and improved highways.

Union Station, a recognized national landmark now used by Amtrak, Metrorail, and Metrolink,

Union Passenger Terminal.
Photo by Lori Shepler.

stands amid 52 acres of valuable land owned by a subsidiary of the Santa Fe Pacific Corporation. The company will retain the station as a transportation hub and also construct on the property new office towers, retail stores, hotels, restaurants, and other major commercial structures.

UNION STOCKYARDS. *See* Meat packing industry

UNITARIANS, early-19th-century Christian religious movement that became established in Los Angeles in 1877. The sect was born as a rationalist response to Calvinism, rejecting the concept of the Trinity, emphasizing freedom and tolerance in religious belief, and championing the autonomy of each congregation. The movement emerged in this country among such New Englanders as Ralph Waldo Emerson and William Ellery Channing.

In March 1877 a group of 30 or 40 transplanted New Englanders met at the home of Caroline Severance, in the West Adams district, to organize a permanent Unitarian congregation. After holding services in a series of temporary meeting places, they built their first church on 7th Street near Broadway in 1889. In 1907 the congregation became, officially, the First Unitarian Church. They moved to W. 8th Street and Vermont Avenue in 1927, occupying a church built by John Severance, Caroline's son. From 1933 to 1948 the congregation's minister was Ernest Caldecott, an outspoken pacifist and social activist. He was succeeded by an equally outspoken liberal minister, Dr. Stephen H. Fritchman, who, from 1949 to 1970, was an outspoken opponent of McCarthyism in Los Angeles. He was succeeded by the Rev. Peter

H. Christiansen. As part of a national merger, the Unitarians and Universalists of Los Angeles fused in 1965. The Pacific Southwest District of the Unitarian Universalist Association has 53 congregations ranging from Santa Barbara to San Diego, with 7,000 members; Los Angeles County alone has a dozen or so churches.

UNITED ARTISTS CORPORATION (UA), moviemaking organization founded in 1919 by film pioneers Mary Pickford, Douglas Fairbanks, Charlie Chaplin, and D. W. Griffith. The original UA plans to produce and distribute its own films were thwarted by the conflicting goals of the principals. Griffith, who preferred to work independently, and Chaplin, who wanted to direct, were

United Artists' Douglas Fairbanks Jr., Mary Pickford, Charlie Chaplin, and D. W. Griffith. Courtesy Seaver Center for Western History Research, Natural History Museum of Los Angeles County.

relatively inactive in the company. Fairbanks and Pickford, the more enterprising partners, hired cameraman Charles Rosher and some of Hollywood's best directors—Raoul Walsh, Ernst Lubitsch, and Maurice Tourneur. Mary Pickford's *Pollyanna* (1920), a studio production, was the first Hollywood film sold on a percentage basis for the artists. Joe Schenck was brought in to run the company in the 1920s. Eventually UA became a distributor and financial backer of independents, rather than a producing studio, losing ground as it tried to operate without facilities or its own stars. The most difficult years were the late 1940s and early 1950s. The studio revived when it again produced its own films, including *The Magnificent Seven* (1961), *Tom Jones* (1963), and the James Bond pictures. The huge monetary loss sustained in making *Heaven's Gate* (1980) helped encourage United Artists to abandon filmmaking. It became exclusively a theater operating chain, with over 400 cinemas in the United States, Puerto Rico, and Hong Kong.

UNITED AUTO WORKERS (UAW), major labor union for the automotive and aircraft industries. The Detroit-based industrial union began major organizing efforts in Southern California at the Long Beach assembly plant of the Ford Motor Company in 1937. Ford refused to grant recognition. That same year, UAW's sit-down strike at Douglas Aircraft Company in Santa Monica ended with mass arrests and no contract. In June 1941 a strike at North American Aviation that idled 11,000 employees was quashed by the National Guard.

The UAW achieved its first major organizational victory in the region in 1944 when the National Labor Relations Board ordered an election at Douglas Aircraft in Long Beach. A year later the union turned its attention to the auto industry, with a 113-day labor contest at General Motors that resulted in a contract. The UAW and the International Association of Machinists were plagued by jurisdictional disputes until 1950, when they agreed to a no-raiding pact. This alliance paved the way for the UAW to gain major contract concessions at Douglas, Ford, and Chrysler. However, a 43-day UAW strike in 1953 at North American Aviation in Long Beach failed. In 1967 the UAW ended a 30-year affiliation with the AFL-CIO.

In more recent decades the union has struggled in vain to keep the region's industrial assembly plants open. In 1994, after substantial membership losses, the union represented 20,000 workers in the greater Los Angeles region, including those at the Long Beach McDonnell Douglas, Rockwell International, and Robertshaw Controls, Inc.

UNITED FOOD AND COMMERCIAL WORKERS (UFCW), a major labor union of retail clerks, butcher workers, and other store employees. A fledgling retail clerks organization led by women laundry workers was formed as early as 1911 and reorganized in 1912, but disappeared amid the triumphant open-shop climate that followed the bombing of the *Los Angeles Times* Building. The current union traces its roots to the Retail Clerks Union, formed in 1937 by militant union organizer Joseph DeSilva. In 1989 AFL-CIO Local 770 had 29,000 members and represented workers in retail food and drug stores, packinghouses, pharmacies, and laboratories. The UFCW pioneered in achieving health benefits for its members that included extensive coverage for dental, orthopedic, mental health, and hospital care.

UNITED NEIGHBORHOOD ORGANIZATION (UNO), barrio association devoted to improving living conditions on Los Angeles's Eastside. Established in 1975 by community organizer Ernesto Cortes, a protégé of Chicago activist Saul Alinsky, it received the support of Los Angeles auxiliary bishop Juan Arzube and Fr. Luis Olivares. Gloria Chavez was the founding president. The organization's objectives included eliminating redlining in the insurance and home loan industries, attracting new major retail stores to the area, introducing a job training program in Monterey Park, securing an extension of Metrorail routes, and registering voters. The UNO has purchased 18 acres of land in South Central Los Angeles on which to build, at a cost of $8 million, the largest nonprofit, low-income housing project in the city.

UNITED TEACHERS OF LOS ANGELES (UTLA), union representing classroom teachers in the Los Angeles Unified School District (LAUSD). The first such organization on the local scene, the Teachers Alliance, collapsed shortly after its birth in 1898, the victim of strong open-shop attitudes among Los Angeles employers. The American Federation of Teachers (AFT), a national organization, issued a charter for Local 77 in 1919, but that affiliate was driven out of operation in the 1920s. Still another AFT affiliate, Local 430, which emerged in the 1930s, had an equally poor success rate. The common belief was that teachers, like firefighters and police, were not entitled to strike.

A Los Angeles organization with ties to both the California Teachers Association (CTA) and the National Education Association (NEA) took root in the 1930s, but with principals, rather than classroom teachers, playing the dominant role. This organization's leading rival was a union associated with the California Federation of Teachers (CFT), which in turn was affiliated with the AFT and the AFL-CIO; this group's membership was restricted to teachers.

In the late 1940s and 1950s McCarthyism prevented teachers unions from gaining strength. Advances again occurred in the 1960s. Under the leadership of CFT president Raoul Teilhet, a former Pasadena educator, public school teachers throughout California fought for collective bargaining to

---

... the land of the innumerate billionaire, where a game of Scrabble is a literary event, where the prevailing values are those of the pocket calculator.   —Martin Amis, British writer

---

improve salaries, retirement benefits, sick leave, and ability to transfer tenure, to guarantee more free time during the workday, to protect probationary teachers, and to reduce class size. A state law finally validated the right of collective bargaining for teachers.

In 1970, after years of feuding, the rival Los Angeles California Faculty Association (CFA) and CFT affiliates merged to become the United Teachers of Los Angeles (UTLA), the sole bargaining agent for teachers in the LAUSD. The merger fused the 2,000-member AFT Local 1021 and the 17,000-member Association of Classroom Teachers of Los Angeles (ACTLA), an affiliate of the NEA. Seeking its first contract and hoping to raise average salaries from $13,650 to $20,000, UTLA conducted a bitter five-week strike in April and May 1970 that affected 650,000 students.

The UTLA remains one of the few hybrid NEA-AFT teachers organizations in the nation and is the second largest teachers union in the country, next to New York City's AFT. Seeking pay raises, UTLA struck for nine days in 1988–1989. By then it represented 32,000 certified employees, including teachers, counselors, advisers, audiologists, nurses, and other nonadministrators. For the last decade UTLA has exercised considerable political clout by endorsing candidates in elections to the Board of Education.

Teachers also achieved bargaining status in school districts other than the city of Los Angeles, among them Pasadena, Long Beach, and Culver City. Instructors in private schools, community colleges, and the state university system sought, and gained, representation as well. In the 1970s the AFT College Guild, Local 1521, emerged as the bargaining agent for the Los Angeles Community College District, while the United Professors of California (UPC) represented the teaching faculty of CSU campuses statewide.

UNITED WAY OF GREATER LOS ANGELES, voluntary association devoted to planning, supporting, delivering, and evaluating human service programs. A charitable alliance known as Associated Charities had emerged in Los Angeles in 1893; by the 1920s, however, philanthropic activities in the metropolis were disorganized, competitive, and ineffective. In 1924 the chamber of commerce and a group of community leaders met to create a better system for gathering and distributing charitable donations. They formed an umbrella organization called the Welfare Federation of Los Angeles. This new federation, consisting of 166 independent social agencies, adopted the name and the fund-raising methods of the Community Chest, an organization established in 1887. The group further agreed on a cooperative and equitable method of distributing any funds collected. The combined Community Chest appeal of 1924, new to Los Angeles, raised an impressive $2.5 million. This was $1 million more than the city had ever raised before, and came from 4,000 percent more givers. The drive became an annual event.

United Way, Inc., created in 1963, was the successor organization to the Community Chest. By then it was raising, from payroll deductions from large employers, some $15.5 million annually. In 1977 it brought in $40.3 million. In 1980 United Way merged with another citywide charity group, AID/United Givers. The combined organization, renamed United Way of Greater Los Angeles and considered the country's most successful United

Way affiliate, collected from 168,000 donors in 1992, and served 8.2 million people; it had 350 member organizations, 50,000 volunteers from corporate, labor, and other organizations, and a paid staff of 220 people. Among the largest recipients of United Way funds were the Salvation Army, YMCA, YWCA, Boy Scouts of America, Girl Scouts of America, Catholic Welfare Bureau, Visiting Nurse Association, and Camp Fire Girls.

UNIVERSAL CITY, island on the land in the San Fernando Valley, 10 miles northwest of downtown Los Angeles. It is home to Universal Studios. This city, which no longer has any residents, is located on land once owned by James B. Lankershim, who harvested enormous fields of wheat on the flatlands and is buried at the north end of nearby Nichols Canyon Road. On 15 March 1915 movie mogul Carl Laemmle bought a former chicken ranch and formally dedicated both the new Universal Studios and the township of Universal City—then a village at the base of the hill near today's Lankershim Boulevard and Cahuenga Boulevard. Universal City also is the site of Campo de Cahuenga, where in 1847 John C. Frémont and Andrés Pico signed a peace ending the Mexican War locally. All but a tiny fraction of the 450-acre Universal City lies in unincorporated county territory; its last two residents departed between the 1980 and 1990 censuses. Most of the property is devoted to the studio, its theme park, and amphitheater. The studio is owned by its Japanese parent company, Matsushita Electrical Industrial Corporation, Ltd., of Tokyo.

UNIVERSAL STUDIOS, one of the "Little Two" studios of Hollywood's Golden Era, along with Columbia Pictures, and one of the oldest continuously operating movie studios. Founded by Carl Laemmle in 1909, it was first called the Independent Motion Picture Company and then, in 1912, became Universal Pictures. In 1915 he founded Universal City on 230 acres of land that had been a chicken ranch. Laemmle lost power in the mid-1930s. When the company foundered financially, it was saved from bankruptcy in 1937 by the popularity of its young singing star Deanna Durbin, and by a turn to low-budget second features.

Universal's stars have included W. C. Fields, Hoot Gibson, Lon Chaney, Donald O'Connor, Doris Day, Rock Hudson, Bela Lugosi, Tony Curtis, and Boris Karloff. It counts among its more notable films *The Hunchback of Notre Dame* (1923),

Phantom of the Opera (1925), *All Quiet on the Western Front* (1930), *Dracula* (1931), *Frankenstein* (1931), *One Hundred Men and a Girl* (1937), *The Bank Dick* (1940), *Watch on the Rhine* (1943), *Shadow of a Doubt* (1943), *Pillow Talk* (1959), *The Sting* (1973), *Jaws* (1975), *E.T. The Extra-Terrestrial* (1982), and *Born on the Fourth of July* (1989). Universal established itself early, and firmly, in television with such series as *Leave It to Beaver, Marcus Welby, M.D., Ozzie and Harriet,* and *Dragnet.*

Universal was acquired in 1962 by the Music Corporation of America (MCA), a company founded in Chicago in 1925 by Dr. Jules Stein as a booking agency for bands and musicians. MCA became an entertainment conglomerate under the stewardship of Lew Wasserman, who maintained a stable of stars, made Universal wealthy, and established a personal fortune once estimated at $220 million. Universal is now a division of MCA, Inc., and the giant of filmdom's production companies. It employs 7,000 people, considerably more than any other studio.

UNIVERSAL STUDIOS TOUR, theme park in Universal City that draws more visitors than any other attraction in Los Angeles County. As early as 1916 Carl Laemmle charged enthralled fans 25 cents for a box lunch and a bleacher seat on a hillside above the filming area, from which vantage point viewers could look down upon their silent film favorites emoting below. When sound arrived and scenes were filmed indoors, these public viewing privileges ended.

The modern Universal tour started modestly in 1964 when sightseeing buses—bringing some 39,000 visitors annually—were allowed to pass through the back lot. Soon Disneyland-style attractions were added. Not surprisingly, they tended to be based on the studio's most popular and spectacular film and television shows. Today, guests on trams experience the drama of a runaway train, the thrills of *Jaws* and *Battlestar Galactica,* a 13,000-pound King Kong, and, ironically, an earthquake. Visitors can also watch as movie stunt people demonstrate their harrowing work. Universal Studios, the nation's third largest theme park after Disneyworld and Disneyland, now draws up to 5 million visitors a year.

UNIVERSITY OF CALIFORNIA, LOS ANGELES (UCLA), one of the nation's premier institutions of higher learning. Its embryo was the

Early view of UCLA's Westwood campus. Pitt Collection.

State Normal School, founded in 1881 and opened in 1882 on the present site of downtown's central library. In 1919 the school moved to Vermont and Heliotrope Avenues (site of the present-day campus of Los Angeles City College) and became the Southern Branch of the University of California, a two-year institution. Third- and fourth-year curricula were quickly added, and the first seniors graduated in 1925. In 1927 it was renamed the University of California at Los Angeles (the "at" became a comma in 1958). Ground was broken for its present campus in 1927, as part of the Janss Development Corporation's plan for Westwood. Classes commenced in 1929.

The master plan for the campus, drawn up by architect George W. Kelham, involved the construction of 10 buildings. The original quad, in place by 1931, was formed by Royce Hall, the library, Haines Hall, and the Physics-Biology Building, all built in the Northern Italian, or "Lombard," Renaissance style. By 1931 the campus had ten buildings and a bridge spanning a small arroyo, with a few additional buildings added during the depression.

Today the beautifully landscaped campus comprises more than 100 buildings on 419 acres. The university grounds also house botanical gardens, art galleries, a sculpture garden, a planetarium, a faculty center, a student center, dormitories, a stadium, and a guest house. The UCLA Medical Center, located on the campus, is among the world's top hospitals. The University Research Library has 3.5 million volumes and vast specialized resources, including 30,000 linear feet of materials in the Department of Special Collections. The prestigious American Council on Education in 1970 named UCLA one of the top 10 universities in the nation, the youngest university ever to be so honored.

In addition to its academic accomplishments the school has an athletic program that is competitive in almost all college sports. The students are known as Bruins, and the school symbol is a bear. The UCLA campus, with 35,230 students and 2,800 full-time faculty in 1992, is the largest in the University of California chain.

UNIVERSITY OF SOUTHERN CALIFORNIA (USC), oldest independent university in the West, instituted by the Southern California Conference of the Methodist Episcopal Church in 1879. The school opened to students in 1880 at Exposition Boulevard near Exposition Park, in a rural mustard field. Many of the original 12 instructors and 53 students journeyed to the campus on horse-drawn streetcars. In its early years the school consisted of a two-story wooden building, Widney Hall, now the oldest university building in Southern California.

Robert Maclay Widney, a lawyer and real estate developer, secured the initial endowment of 309 lots (7.6 acres) for the school campus. The three founders were Ozro W. Childs, a Protestant; John G. Downey, a Catholic; and Isaias W. Hellman, a Jew. The first president, from 1880 to 1887, was Rev. Marion McKinley Bovard, a former Los Angeles Methodist pastor. Robert Maclay Widney and his brother, Joseph P. Widney, a doctor and educator, were the first heads of the board of directors.

The formal denominational connection ended during the term of midwesterner Rufus Bernhard von KleinSmid, who served as president from 1921 to 1946, although by rule half of the trustees must be Methodists.

In the first 10 years of von KleinSmid's leadership nine new buildings were constructed. To the

College of Liberal Arts, USC, ca. 1910. Pitt Collection.

education department, established in 1920, were added departments or schools of dentistry, music, fine arts, marine biology, sociology, philosophy, business, journalism, pharmacy, religion, engineering, cinema, architecture, and public administration. The schools of law and medicine are recognized as outstanding; Los Angeles County–USC Medical Center in Boyle Heights is also the county's oldest medical school. In 1994 chemistry professor George A. Olah, a Hungarian émigré, was the first USC faculty member to win a Nobel Prize.

From the start USC declined to pursue the backing of wealthy benefactors, but relied solely on its faculty, presidents, and trustees for support. President von KleinSmid decided to encourage the football program, which had been inaugurated in 1888, as a means of raising revenue. The school's athletic program is now nationally known in virtually every sport. Its teams have won more national championships—73 men's and 13 women's —than any other university. The football program annually sends more players into the ranks of professional teams than any other. The crosstown rivalry with UCLA is fierce.

In 1992–1993 the campus, which had expanded to 98 acres over the years, enrolled 27,734 students and employed a full-time faculty of 2,201. The school nickname, Trojans, arose in 1912 when *Times* sports reporter Owen Bird wrote that USC athletes at a track meet "fought like Trojans." The "Tommy Trojan" statue on the campus was unveiled on 6 June 1930.

UNOCAL CORPORATION, Los Angeles–based oil company with worldwide operations. The Union Oil Company of California, as it was orig-

inally known, was founded in Santa Paula, Ventura County, in October 1890, but has been headquartered in Los Angeles since 1901. The first Union Oil gas station was opened at the corner of 6th and Mateo Streets in 1913. The company discovered major petroleum fields in Wilmington and Santa Fe Springs, and the latter became a major refinery in 1917, on the eve of America's entry into World War I. The firm pioneered an oil-burning railroad engine in 1894, followed by a safe oil burner for marine engines. "Union 76" gasoline, invoking the patriotic Spirit of '76, was a success with motorists after its introduction in 1932. The corporation has used the name UNOCAL since 1985.

UNRUH, JESSE MARVIN (1922–1987), speaker of the California Assembly. The son of Texas sharecroppers, Unruh represented Inglewood as a Democrat and rose to the post of speaker in Sacramento. He authored the 1959 Unruh Civil Rights Act barring racial discrimination in business and permitting victims to recover damages in court. In 1966 the powerful liberal populist led the Democratic-dominated legislature in opposing Gov. Ronald Reagan's programs, and in 1970 he ran against Reagan, unsuccessfully, in the gubernatorial race. A forceful and controversial speaker, Unruh was popular with those who appreciated his hostility to oil companies, real estate developers, and other monied interests. He served for a time as state treasurer. Unruh, who coined the phrase "money is the mother's milk of politics," could never throw off the aura of bossism that clung to him, nor the epithet of "Big Daddy."

UPLIFTERS RANCH AND SADDLE CLUB, fun-seeking brotherhood founded in 1913 by Harry

Haldeman, fellowship chairman of the Los Angeles Athletic Club, and 19 others. The purpose of the club was "to uplift art, promote good fellowship, and build a closer acquaintance." Members included L. Frank Baum, creator of the Oz adventures, who dedicated *The Scarecrow of Oz* (1915) to the club; filmmaker Hal Roach; and banker Marco Hellman, son of Herman Wolf Hellman, who had arrived in Los Angeles in 1859. They succeeded in conducting their high- and low-jinx activities—including evasion of Prohibition laws—in private by purchasing 8 secluded acres in Rustic Canyon, Santa Monica, in 1920. Here they created a hideaway called Uplifters Ranch. The club members built pastoral cottages, some of which have served as movie sets. All wives were banished from their annual outings, the last of which occurred in 1941. The area is now a residential community.

URBAN LEAGUE OF LOS ANGELES. *See* Los Angeles Urban League

URBAN RENEWAL. *See* Los Angeles Community Redevelopment Agency

USC. *See* University of Southern California

UTOPIAN SOCIETY, depression-era movement that erupted in Southern California in 1933. The society, which was formally incorporated on 20 February 1934 by three former stock-and-bond salesmen, used chain letters to recruit members and adopted secret rituals to bond its members. The society's goal was to cure the Great Depression, restore prosperity, and provide moral uplift. It counted some 500,000 adherents and was holding as many as 250 meetings a night in 1934, when it was finally noticed by the press.

Generally, the movement attracted alienated newcomers to Los Angeles of lower-middle-class background. They usually met in small groups, but one public assembly filled the Hollywood Bowl with 25,000 people. Taking a leaf from Aimee Semple McPherson, Utopian Society groups enacted a series of symbolic minidramas in which Good and Abundance eventually triumphed over Evil and Scarcity. The movement provided a means for people to vent their social and personal frustrations. It also frightened members of the political establishment, who felt more secure when the society fell apart in 1935, after Socialist Upton Sinclair lost the 1934 gubernatorial race. No traces of the society remained.

VALDEZ, LUIS (1941–), Delano-born writer-director. Inspired by Cesar Chavez he joined the United Farm Workers in 1965 and founded Teatro Campesino, an agit-prop street theater, in Northern California. His play *Zoot Suit* (1979) was based on the Los Angeles zoot suit riots of 1943. Edward James Olmos played the role of El Pachuco both on the stage and in the 1981 film version. The film *La Bamba* (1987), which Valdez wrote and directed, was based on the life of rock star Ritchie Valens. *Bandido,* a theatrical account of the life of Tiburcio Vásquez, premiered at the Mark Taper Forum in 1994.

VALDEZ DE VILLA, MARÍA RITA (D. 1800S), ranch owner in what is today Beverly Hills. Of African American background, she was the widow of the Spanish colonial soldier Vicente Fernando Villa. In 1841 she received formal title to the 4,449-acre Rancho Rodeo de las Aguas ("Meeting of the Waters"), granted to her husband in 1820.

Los Angeles represents the ultimate segregation of the unfit.

—Bertrand Russell, British philosopher

Valdez's adobe stood on a picturesque spot near today's Alpine Drive and Sunset Boulevard. At that time 29 people named either Valdez, Vejar, or Villa lived on the rancho. She had a falling-out over access to water and ownership of animals with a cousin named Luciano, and sought relief before the *ayuntamiento.* Luciano received $17.50 and was ordered to stop harassing her. Although Americans stole her land-title papers during the Mexican War,

she filed a successful claim to the rancho in 1852. Two years later, however, poor finances forced Valdez to sell the property.

VALENCIA, modern suburban community in the city of Santa Clarita, 30 miles northwest of downtown Los Angeles. The fully planned community, designed by Victor Gruen Associates, has been under development since 1965. It is home to the California Institute of the Arts and Magic Mountain amusement park, and includes some 9,000 single-family residences. In 1989 Lockheed, Textron, Carpeteria, and other firms occupied 8 million square feet of industrial space in Valencia, together employing 12,000 workers.

VALINDA, unincorporated county area near La Puente. Its population in 1990 was 18,735.

VALLEY VILLAGE, Los Angeles city area in the eastern San Fernando Valley. The neighborhood separated from North Hollywood in 1991, reclaiming an older name that had fallen into disuse.

VAL VERDE, county area in Green Valley, near Saugus. A mining town in 1843, the locale was reborn as Eureka Villa in 1925, and three years later became Val Verde, a resort community for African Americans. In that Jim Crow era, when blacks were denied access to many Los Angeles County parks and beaches, a wealthy Pasadena philanthropist donated her Val Verde land to the county as a picnic spot for blacks. In the 1930s the Works Progress Administration (WPA) built an Olympic-size swimming pool for the community and expanded the park. In 1990 the community had a population of 1,689 residents, of whom 53 percent were Latino and 10 percent African American.

VALYERMO, tiny community of about 35 people in the Antelope Valley near Pearblossom, 62 miles from downtown Los Angeles. The name, meaning "desert valley" in Spanish, was given in 1909 by W. C. Petcher, owner of Valyermo Rancho. In 1912 the U.S. Post Office adopted the name officially. A Catholic retreat is now the major landmark. Valyermo hosts a ceramics festival each spring.

VAN DYKE, THEODORE S[TRONG] (1842–1923), journalist and local booster. A native of New Jersey, Strong came to California for his health in 1875. His *Southern California: Its Valleys, Hills, and Streams; Its Animals, Birds, and Fishes; Its Gardens, Farms, and Climate* (1886) was issued during the Boom of the Eighties. He also wrote a satiric novel, *Millionaires for a Day* (1890), about the boom period. Barring rapacious real estate promoters, too-numerous ground squirrels, and the damaging effects of occasional droughts, Van Dyke loved the region.

VANEGAS FAMILY, Indians from Mexico who were among the original founders of the *pueblo* of Los Angeles in 1781. José Vanegas, 28 years old, was married to María Bonifacia Vanegas, 20, and they had a year-old infant, Cosme Damien Vanegas. José, a successful farmer, served as Los Angeles's first *alcalde,* from 1786 to 1788, and again in 1796. When his wife died in 1821 he moved to San Diego. Cosme received title to Carpinteria Rancho in the Santa Barbara area in 1833.

VAN NUYS, southern San Fernando Valley district of the city of Los Angeles, 16 miles northwest of downtown. It was named after landowner Isaac Newton Van Nuys, a well-known wheat rancher in the area. In the fall of 1909 his family sold 475,000 acres south of today's Sherman Way to the Los Angeles Suburban Homes Company. In 1911 this syndicate developed the property into three townsites, one of them being Van Nuys. The syndicate's chief promoter, William Whitsett, capitalized on two major assets of the area: the water brought by the Los Angeles Aqueduct in 1913, and the convenience to downtown via the Pacific Electric suburban streetcar line. The community, however, was compelled to seek consolidation with the city of Los Angeles in order to acquire the water. In 1928 an airport was established in Van Nuys that remains one of the most active regional fields in the nation. A year later the city of Los Angeles built

a municipal building in Van Nuys to accommodate the growing population, which by 1940 had reached 20,000.

Van Nuys grew considerably after World War II as major housing tracts opened and the industrial base expanded. Anheuser-Busch and Joseph Schlitz breweries, and a Chevrolet assembly plant, since closed, were among the larger firms to locate there. With the coming of the freeways, Van Nuys was served by major on-ramps to the San Diego and Ventura Freeways. Los Angeles Valley College, located on 105 acres on Fulton Avenue, enrolled over 20,000 students. By 1990 an estimated 115,000 people lived in Van Nuys.

VAN NUYS, ISAAC NEWTON (1835–1923), pioneer farmer who moved to Los Angeles in 1865 for health reasons. Along with his father-in-law, Isaac Lankershim, he cultivated 60,000 acres of wheat in the southern part of the San Fernando Valley in the 1870s and 1880s.

VAN NUYS AIRPORT was carved out of walnut and peach groves in 1928 and named Los Angeles Metropolitan Airport. The following year Amelia Earhart lifted off from the strip to set a new world speed record. The airport often appeared in early Hollywood films, such as *Lost Horizon* (1937), and it gained importance in World War II when the military created Van Nuys Army Air Field as a pilot training station. The city of Los Angeles acquired the field in 1949, and it remained a California Air National Guard post until 1985. Renamed in 1957, Van Nuys Airport is the busiest general aviation field in the United States, home to almost 900 aircraft and the site of 1,500 daily takeoffs and landings.

VARIETY, trade paper covering all areas of entertainment worldwide, known as "the Bible of show business." Today's paper represents the 1987 merger of the weekly *Variety,* published in New York City since 1905, and the *Daily Variety,* published in Los Angeles since 1933. Both were founded by journalist Sime Silverman, who established a reputation for acerbic commentary, long investigative pieces, and cutting reviews. Readers could rely on both papers for reliable financial news, show business profiles, stock quotations, advertisements, deal announcements, and box office grosses. The *Variety* papers have shaped American slang with terms such as "boffo" (big box office success), "legs" (a film that is a long-running hit), and "oaters" (Western films). Among *Variety*'s most famous cryptic headlines have been "STIX NIX HICK PIX" (rural audiences reject movies with farm themes) and "WALL STREET LAYS AN EGG" (the stock market crashes). Before the merger, the New York publication boasted a circulation of about 30,000, and the Los Angeles paper, 22,000. The 1987 consolidation occurred when the two papers were sold to the Cahners Publishing Company, a division of Reed Publishing, a British company.

VÁSQUEZ, TIBURCIO (1839–1875), last of the Mexican bandit leaders who roamed Southern California from the 1850s to the 1870s. Along with Joaquín Murrieta and Juan Flores, Vásquez was the most famous *bandido,* and the most durable. Born in Monterey, Vásquez had his first run-in with the law in 1853, at age 14, when he stabbed a lawman during a dispute. The youth escaped into the hills, joined other outlaws, and soon headed a band that was wanted for robberies and murders. The state legislature placed an $8,000 reward on his head. A group of prominent Californio rancheros aligned with Yankee vigilantes and rangers to capture Vásquez, whom they viewed as a serious threat to property, safety, and civil order.

The bandit captain was captured in 1874. He was probably betrayed by one of his own men, Abadon

Tiburcio Vásquez. Courtesy Henry E. Huntington Library.

Leiva, whose wife may have been having an affair with Vásquez. An eight-man posse—which included a Los Angeles police detective, Emil Harris, and a newspaper correspondent—cornered him in the cabin of a local, "Greek George," near present-day Santa Monica Boulevard and Kings Road in West Hollywood. Still shaken by the violence of the 1871 Chinese Massacre, city officials took pains to prevent a lynching, placing Vásquez in a secure cell and surrounding the jailhouse with armed men. Fashionably dressed women brought flowers to the celebrity outlaw, and journalists interviewed him at length.

Vásquez, who claimed to be the father of two children living at Elizabeth Lake, denied ever killing anyone. He had resorted to banditry, he said, to protect his people and rid Southern California of the evil Yankees. In recent years, some supporters have interpreted his career as a form of guerrilla warfare. Vásquez was taken to Tres Pinos and then San Jose in Northern California, where he was tried, convicted for murder, and hanged on 19 March 1875.

Emil Harris went on to become Los Angeles chief of police. The Southern California booster and journalist Benjamin C. Truman, who had interviewed the prisoner in his cell, published an account of these exchanges in *The Life, Adventures, and Capture of Tiburcio Vásquez* (1874). Luis Valdez's musical melodrama *Bandido,* which premiered at the Mark Taper Forum in 1994, is based on the life of Vásquez.

VASQUEZ ROCKS, residential community and park on Highway 14, in Acton, 50 miles from downtown Los Angeles. The name is drawn from a rock outcropping formed by the San Andreas Fault where *bandido* Tiburcio Vásquez reputedly buried ill-gotten treasure. The picturesque area has appeared in innumerable movies since 1905, including most of the westerns of the 1940s and 1950s. The area was used for such feature films as *Gunga Din* and *The Flintstones—The Movie,* and for episodes of the television series *Bonanza, The Big Valley, Star Trek,* and *Murder, She Wrote.* The 745-acre Vasquez Rocks Park is visited by as many as 5,000 tourists yearly. The community's post office is Saugus, and the resident population is under 500.

VEDANTA SOCIETY OF SOUTHERN CAL-IFORNIA, Hollywood-based religious association celebrating the beliefs of the Indian Vedantic texts. Its headquarters are at a beautiful secluded retreat on Vedanta Terrace in Hollywood, established by patron William Mead. The site includes Mead's Craftsman-style house (1901), a domed temple (Little Taj, 1938), a bookstore, meeting room, convent, and monastery.

VENICE, unique beach community south of Santa Monica, 14 miles west of downtown Los Angeles. It has a colorful history and is said to be constantly in search of an identity.

The dominant force in the neighborhood's early history, from its founding in 1904 until 1920, was entrepreneur Abbot Kinney, who established a beachfront theme park called Venice of America and developed real estate along a network of improvised canals. The network consisted of a saltwater lagoon, the Grand Canal, and six tributary canals. The community, strategically located along

---

The ultimate world-historical significance—and oddity—of Los Angeles is that it has come to play the double role of utopia and dystopia for advanced capitalism.
—Mike Davis, historian

---

the Pacific Electric Red Car line, was originally part of the independent city of Ocean Park. Kinney's plans for expansion were thwarted for six years by rival entrepreneurs in that city. He undertook a drive for independent cityhood, and in 1911 succeeded in creating the separate city of Venice south of Navy Street. The move gave him the freedom to develop additional beachfront attractions: a Ferris wheel, a huge hydrogen-filled balloon, a water ride called "The Rapids," a wooden mountain covered with lights that at night seemed to explode like a volcano, and other glittering diversions. Kinney remained active in the theme park and real estate developments until his death in 1920.

In the 1920s and 1930s Venice continued to attract crowds of fun seekers, although the Great Depression took its toll, and the development of an oil field along the shoreline created conflicting usages. Residents voted to merge with Los Angeles in 1925 as a solution to increasing pollution created by

the oil field and other environmental problems. The canals languished, and most had to be filled in.

In 1946 the Kinney real estate firm suffered a major blow when it lost not only its tidelands lease with the city of Los Angeles but also its right to operate Venice Pier. In a parallel development, the Pacific Electric Venice Short Line, which carried commuters to and from downtown Los Angeles, stopped running. These events put an end to the theme park operations.

In the 1950s and 1960s Venice gained new notoriety when Stuart Z. Perkoff, Lawrence Lipton, and other members of the beat generation literary movement frequented the local coffeehouses and saloons to read their poetry and fiction aloud and listen to jazz and folk music. During the decade of the 1960s their presence faded, to be replaced by hippies and flower children, many of them deeply involved in the drug culture. Meanwhile, a small, long-established enclave of Jewish senior citizens clung to its community in Venice.

The 1970s and 1980s witnessed further transitions, including the continued decay of older buildings, the arrival of New Age adherents, and the beginnings of residential gentrification. Pricey shops and chic restaurants opened on Main Street, while merchants and middle-class residents demanded a share of urban renewal funds to refurbish the community. At the same time, Ocean Front Walk—"the Venice boardwalk"—saw the installation of bargain stores, stalls, and street vendors, hawkers, street musicians, mimes, jugglers, and Rollerbladers, and became a famous tourist attraction. The beach itself lured hosts of swimmers, volleyball and basketball players, body builders, and Sunday people watchers.

Venice is in many ways a microcosm of Los Angeles. It is multiethnic and multiracial, and its diverse residents include artists and laborers, young and old, affluent and poor. It is often at the center of public debates related to gentrification, the allure of the beach, crime and drugs, historic preservation, and ocean water quality. A project to restore six of the old canals and four Venetian bridges, which began in the 1960s, was completed in 1993. The census of 1990 counted 39,971 residents.

VENICE CANALS, secluded Los Angeles neighborhood in Venice, between Venice and Washington Boulevards. In 1993 it had 1,200 residents living in 351 homes. The houses flank the six canals that remain from the elaborate network created by

Venice canals. Photo by Michael Krakowiak/Marni Pitt.

developer Abbot Kinney at the turn of the century. The photogenic waterways, small houses, and bridges in this coastal salt marsh area have appeared in countless films. In 1993, after decades of neglect, the city finished overhauling the canals, which are named Grand, Eastern, Linnie, Howland, Sherman, and Carroll. The 18-month restoration project cost $6 million.

VENICE FAMILY CLINIC, private, nonprofit, community-based free medical facility in Venice. Since 1970 it has served Westsiders who lack access to regular health care. The Venice area has only one physician per 18,000 people. The clinic sees 10,500 clients yearly, about 29 percent of whom are homeless. The operating budget is $3.2 million. The clinic has been headed in recent years by Fern

Seizer, a New Yorker whose father produced the *Dr. Kildare* and *Marcus Welby, M.D.* television series.

VENICE OF AMERICA, theme park and resort created by Abbot Kinney between 1904 and 1911. The site was originally owned by the Ocean Park Development Company, a partnership that included Kinney. When the owners had a falling-out in 1904, they flipped a coin for control of the 1.5 miles of dunes and coastal wetlands south of Ocean Park in Santa Monica. Kinney won the toss and set about creating a combination cultural center/seaside resort, hoping to attract renowned artistic performers and to establish an institute for humanistic studies. He persuaded rail magnate Henry E. Huntington to bring his Red Car line to "Venice of America." As soon as the tracks were completed

Venice of America, Grand Lagoon and Midway Plaisance. Courtesy Robert Weinstein Collection.

in 1905, crowds of visitors began arriving. Architects Norman Marsh and C. H. Russell designed the site and its buildings, adopting a Mediterranean look in a complex layout. Within a brief 19 months Kinney's work teams drained the marshes, dug a network of canals, constructed a breakwater, erected theaters for drama, concerts, dance, and lectures, and opened a promenade and pier enhanced by cafés and special attractions. Short-term visitors lodged at the St. Marks Hotel, while middle-class families rented new summer cottages. Despite a raging storm that damaged the developing resort in March 1905, Kinney met his promised July Fourth opening date. International actress Sarah Bernhardt appeared in serious drama, and the Chicago Symphony Orchestra performed. Meanwhile, gondoliers imported from Italy guided passengers along the canals in Venetian gondolas.

To his dismay, Kinney soon discovered that the public was more interested in the popular attractions than in the highbrow cultural events. After investing $1.4 million and nearly bankrupting himself, he ended the uplifting programs, including plans for a university-level think tank, and turned Venice into a full-fledged amusement park akin to New York's Coney Island. Eventually the site would host an indoor saltwater plunge and an array of restaurants, dance halls, roller coasters, fun houses, freak shows, and camel rides. The main attractions were located at the Midway Plaisance, surrounding the Grand Lagoon (today's traffic circle). The "Race Thru the Clouds," dedicated in 1911, was the world's largest roller coaster.

On 29 May 1911, after a six-year struggle with a group of rival Ocean Park pleasure-pier entrepreneurs who had thwarted his expansion plans, Kinney succeeded in establishing Venice as an independent city. In addition to crowds of fun seekers, Venice attracted filmmakers, auto racing enthusiasts, and baseball fans. Nevertheless, the community suffered numerous setbacks. A fire in 1912 destroyed many attractions, and a faulty drainage system created a terrible stench in the canals, which was worsened by oil pumping nearby. The only remedy was to fill in the original lagoon and most of the canals. At this point many middle-class residents abandoned their Venice vacation bungalows. Although the pleasure pier continued to entertain for several decades after Kinney's death in 1920, his original expansive cultural dreams for a highbrow theme park had long since evaporated, and the name "Venice of America" was all but forgotten.

VERDUGO, JOSÉ MARÍA (D. 1831), California pioneer. A corporal in the army of New Spain, Verdugo served at Mission San Gabriel and, upon retirement, received one of the first land grants in California, the 36,000-acre Rancho San Rafael (1784)—the site of present-day Glendale. Settling on the fertile estate in 1799, he and his family raised wine grapes, vegetables, oranges, figs, pomegranates, peaches, apples, and wheat, and hunted grizzly bears, mountain lions, deer, coyote, and quail. Verdugo was buried at Mission San Gabriel, and his land passed to his daughter, Catalina, and son, Julio. The rancho slipped out of family hands during the hard times of the 1860s.

VERDUGO CANYON, an area in northeastern Glendale, bounded by the Verdugo Mountains, Mountain Street, the Glendale Freeway and Oakmont Country Club, and Verdugo Boulevard. The wooded canyon, once part of the Rancho San Rafael, includes the neighborhoods of Verdugo Woodlands, Oakmont, and Montecito Park, and contains 5,000 multiple-unit dwellings and single-family homes. Some of the homes date back to 1915, although the majority were built between the 1920s and 1960s.

VERDUGO CITY, a city that is not a city; rather, it is a vacant, unincorporated 10-acre area in La Crescenta Valley. In 1925 a would-be developer, Harry Fowley, attempted to build a community at the terminus of a railroad on the 15-block area separating Montrose and La Crescenta. He constructed a two-story brick building to house a bank and a newspaper, but never managed to establish any homes. The area was first called Verdugo Park and then, more optimistically, Verdugo City. The post office offers rental boxes but no delivery service. The brick building, which was occupied by a drugstore, was destroyed in the 1971 earthquake.

VERNACULAR ARCHITECTURE. *See* Architecture, vernacular

VERNON, independent industrial city 3 miles south of downtown Los Angeles. It was once part of Rancho San Antonio, granted to the Lugo family in 1810. A Mexican War skirmish, the Battle of La Mesa, was fought there in 1846. Basque settler John Leonis founded the town in 1905—also the year of its incorporation—and his family has remained active in local affairs ever since.

Early in the century Vernon's economy rested on manufacturing, lumbering, food packing, and trucking. In 1927 it had a small resident population but daily attracted 20,000 daytime workers, generating an annual payroll of over $30 million. A championship baseball team, the Vernon Tigers of the Pacific Coast League, also brought many Angelenos to the town. In addition, when the city of Los Angeles began enforcing blue laws against gaming and alcohol consumption, saloon, gambling, and boxing entrepreneurs set up shop in nearby Vernon.

In 1990 Vernon, with 152 residents, was the smallest incorporated city in the county. This number represented an increase of 69 percent over 1980, when only 90 people made Vernon their home. However, 51,000 people worked there daily. While the industrial base has been eroded in recent years, city officials are considering a $500 million redevelopment plan. The city's best-known historic landmark is the "Farmer John Mural" (1957), a romanticized depiction of a pig farm, which covers the wall of a meat packing plant.

VETERANS ADMINISTRATION (VA) HOSPITAL, SAWTELLE, military medical center on federal property in the Sawtelle area of West Los Angeles. It is located on unincorporated county territory. The U.S. government established it as the Pacific branch of the National Home for Disabled Volunteer Soldiers in the 1880s, with a 2,000-bed capacity. John P. Jones and Robert S. Baker, the founders of Santa Monica, donated 300 acres of land and $50,000 for the facility, and the noted architect Stanford White designed it.

Following the Spanish-American War in 1898 the facilities included a library, theater, dining hall, chapel, post office, laundry, and barracks. On a visit to Los Angeles in 1901 President William McKinley toured the grounds. In 1927 the government officially opened the James Wadsworth Hospital at Sawtelle, which eventually housed 4,500 veterans. Although the site contains a few historically significant buildings, as well as a major national cemetery, most original structures have succumbed to the wrecking ball. In 1990 the hospital's permanent population was just over 1,000.

VIDA NUEVA (New life), Spanish-language tabloid newspaper founded in 1991 by the Los Angeles Catholic archdiocese. It is sent free of charge to 110,000 Latino households.

VIEJA MISSION. *See* San Gabriel Mission

VIETNAMESE, one of more than 20 Asian-Pacific peoples in Southern California. The end of the Vietnam War brought a wave of immigrants that caused the county's Vietnamese population to climb from 26,000 in 1980 to 85,000 in 1990. The immigrants are overwhelmingly of rural background. The adults often have a difficult time adjusting, owing to language and cultural problems, and they suffer the lowest average income of all the Asian groups. Many Vietnamese have settled in the Lincoln Heights area and in Orange County. Politically they lean toward the right. They practice both traditional and western religions. The first Vietnamese Buddhist temple was an old apartment building on the edge of Koreatown. The community supports one daily and four weekly newspapers.

Chapel of the early Veterans Administration Hospital. Pitt Collection.

VIEWPARK-WINDSOR HILLS, unincorporated county area south of the Crenshaw district. Its population in 1990 was 11,769.

VIGILANTES, take-charge groups that committed numerous lynchings and other extralegal acts in Los Angeles from 1836 to 1874. The first vigilante action, on 7 April 1836, involved a pair of lovers, María del Rosario Villa and Gervasio Alipas, who were accused of killing María's husband, Domingo Felix. There was, as yet, no tribunal in the area authorized to levy the death penalty. Instead the pair was found guilty by a *junta defensora de la seguridad pública* (defense board of public safety), a committee of 40 or 50 residents, including 14 foreigners, who met at the home of John Temple. The accused were taken from the jail and shot.

San Francisco's vigilante committees of 1851 and 1856 inspired local imitators, who, in fact, executed more people than their northern brethren—32 as compared to 8. The worst vigilante offenses occurred during the 1850s, a time of heightened violence and racial tension. The line between lynchers, vigilantes, volunteer police, mounted volunteer

---

Los Angeles is a city on wheels, where Herbert Hoover's dream of "two cars in every garage" nears fulfillment, even if "two chickens in every pot" does not.
—Oliver Carlson, writer, 1941

---

rangers, and sheriff's posses was poorly defined. Vigilantes preferred to act spontaneously and swiftly rather than to take the trouble to form committees, establish by-laws, or record minutes (as their San Francisco counterparts did). Although their actions were clearly illegal, they went unpunished. Established community leaders usually condoned vigilante action, and when the purpose was to repel Mexican *bandidos,* upper-class Californios like Andrés Pico and Tomás Sánchez rode beside the Yankees to capture and summarily execute the alleged miscreants.

In November 1852 the murder of Maj. Gen. Joshua H. Bean, popular commander of the

mounted rangers and brother of the famous Roy Bean, "the Law West of the Pecos," inspired a major round of vigilante action. Bean's body had been found near San Gabriel Mission. A group of Texans who had settled in El Monte and called themselves the El Monte Rangers rode into Los Angeles to participate in most of the lynchings during the racial strife from 1853 to 1857. The last vigilante action occurred in June 1874 when a Californio named Romo, alias "El Gordo" ("The Fat One"), attempted to rob an El Monte store and was captured and lynched.

VIGNES, JEAN LOUIS (1779?–1862), pioneer Los Angeles vintner. Vignes arrived in 1829 from Bordeaux, France, and, with cuttings brought from France, created a 104-acre vineyard bounded on the north by present-day Aliso Street and on the west by Alameda Street. Vignes built an adobe under the shade of a giant sycamore *(aliso)* tree, which gave the name to his property—Aliso Vineyard. Stretching a quarter-mile from the river to his adobe was a magnificent grape arbor. Vignes, who fashioned his own casks, not only made wine, but also cultivated walnut trees and probably was the first person in the region to grow oranges commercially. Vignes's enterprises brought him wealth, and his success attracted many more wine growers to the area. His nephew was Pierre Sansevain, a renowned vintner in Sunol, Northern California. The Aliso Vineyard was put up for sale in 1851 and became, in the railroad era, an industrial site. Vignes Street is named after Jean Louis.

VILLAGE GREEN, low-cost housing development on Rodeo Road, planned by Clarence Stein in 1940–1941. The project, inspired by the garden suburb of Radburn, New Jersey, is acclaimed architecturally for its comfortable apartments, generous gardens and lawns, and artfully hidden roads, garages, and service areas. It is built on an 80-acre superblock. Originally called Baldwin Hills Village, it was converted to condominiums in the 1970s and renamed the Village Green.

VILLA RIVIERA APARTMENTS, oceanfront landmark in Long Beach. The 16-story apartment house on East Ocean Boulevard was designed by Richard D. King and dates from 1928, when it was the second tallest building in Southern California. It was one of the few major Long Beach buildings to survive the 1933 earthquake.

VILLAVICENCIO FAMILY, one of the 11 original founding families of the *pueblo* of Los Angeles in 1781. Feliz Villavicencio, a 31-year-old Spaniard, was married to the 34-year-old Indian María de los Santos Flores. They brought with them an adopted daughter, Josefa Pinuelas, who married a soldier from Santa Barbara and produced many offspring who remained in Southern California. In 1789 Feliz Villavicencio was accused of adultery with an Indian woman from a nearby village and was placed in the stocks for his misconduct.

VINCENT THOMAS BRIDGE, suspension bridge connecting San Pedro and Terminal Island. Spanning the main channel of Los Angeles Harbor, it is named after a state assemblyman who represented San Pedro for many years. The aesthetically pleasing toll bridge cost $21.4 million to build, was opened in 1963, and carries 20,000 cars daily. The main span is 1,500 feet long and clears the water by 185 feet.

VINETTE, ARTHUR (D. 1906), labor leader and social reformer. Born in Montreal of French Canadian parents, Vinette learned carpentry from his father, a ship's carpenter. He arrived in Los Angeles in 1883, and in the 1880s and 1890s organized the carpenters union and formed a labor federation. As the popular head of the Carpenters Local 56 Vinette not only espoused the labor cause but was also associated with various social-democratic reform movements, including the Knights of Labor, the Nationalist Clubs, the People's Party (Populists), Coxey's Army, and, in 1904, the Socialist Party. Over the years he advocated the initiative and referendum for local government, the eight-hour workday, the abolition of foreign contract labor, the nationalization of mines, railroads, and telephones, a graduated income tax, the repeal of tramp and conspiracy laws, government work for the unemployed, and the abolition of national banks. In 1904 Vinette ran, unsuccessfully, as the Socialist candidate for tax collector.

VISITORS AND CONVENTION BUREAU. *See* Los Angeles Convention and Visitors Bureau

VISTA DEL ARROYO HOTEL, Pasadena historic landmark overlooking the Colorado Street Bridge. From 1882 to 1903 a wooden tuberculosis sanitorium occupied the site; it was supplanted by an imposing Spanish Colonial Revival–style hotel designed by Marston, Van Pelt, and Maybury. Opened in 1903, the Vista del Arroyo served a generation of wealthy easterners. The federal government took it over and turned it into an army hospital from 1943 to 1949. In 1992 it became a U.S. Court of Appeals building.

VISTA DEL MAR CHILD CARE SERVICE was incorporated in 1908 as the Jewish Orphans' Home of Southern California. The private agency opened a home on Mission Road in 1909 to house five children. It moved to Huntington Park in 1912, to West Adams Boulevard in 1924, and to its present site on Motor Avenue in Palms in 1925. The agency, which has a nonsectarian admissions policy, serves 100 resident youngsters between the ages of 6 and 18 and offers day care, adoption, and foster care services to many others. It is funded in part by the Jewish Federation Council of Los Angeles and the United Way.

VON KLEINSMID, RUFUS BERNHARD (1875–1964), president of the University of Southern California (USC) from 1921 to 1946, and chancellor in 1947. Born in Illinois, he trained as an attorney and traveled widely in Latin America. He had become a specialist in criminology and international relations before coming to the university. His first years at USC were plagued by financial problems, although von KleinSmid managed to reorganize and expand the campus in an era of intense competition with UCLA, Caltech, and Stanford. He was responsible for secularizing the university, which was founded by and had maintained close ties to the Methodist church.

VOORHIS, HORACE JEREMIAH (JERRY) (1901–1984), liberal Democratic congressman from Whittier from 1936 to 1946. Voorhis backed Socialist Upton Sinclair's gubernatorial bid in 1934 and was a staunch New Dealer while in Washington. He became the model for the naive, idealistic representative in the movie *Mr. Smith Goes to Washington.* Voorhis was targeted for defeat in 1946 by the Los Angeles Republican establishment. They selected as their candidate the young navy veteran Richard Nixon, who in a controversial campaign used red-baiting tactics to topple the incumbent.

VOTING AND ELECTIONS are handled by the Los Angeles County Registrar-Recorder and city officials. The first election for county offices was held on 1 April 1850, with 377 votes cast. The first city election took place on 1 July 1850, when Dr. Alpheus P. Hodges was elected mayor.

By current laws a citizen may register to vote who will be at least 18 years of age at the time of the upcoming election. Registration is permanent unless a person has moved or changed party affiliation or name. A voter may register up to 29 days prior to the date of the election. In California, statewide general elections and county elections are held on the first Tuesday after the first Monday in November of even-numbered years. Statewide direct primary elections are normally held on the first Tuesday after the first Monday in June of even-numbered years (although a temporary exception occurred in 1996). Municipal elections are normally held on the second Tuesday in April of even-numbered years and on the first Tuesday after the first Monday in March of odd-numbered years. Exceptions are possible, as in the case of recall or special referenda; the presidential primary of 1996 was held on Tuesday, March 26. The legislature reapportions all congressional and legislative seats every 10 years, based on the most recent census report. The outcome affects which party will have the most representatives in Sacramento. In recent years, reapportionment has favored Democrats. The federal Voting Rights Act requires that minority neighborhoods be kept intact, a factor supporting the rise of Latino representation at various levels.

By the 1960s more than 10,000 polling places dotted the county. The cost of renting voting quarters and paying for neighborhood polling boards and janitorial services for a general election exceeded $1 million. Under a 1990 election reform act city council campaigns are conducted with a combination of public and private funds, and the amount that individuals may contribute to candidates is limited.

Voter turnout has suffered a decline. According to the *Los Angeles Times,* the highest voter turnout in a Los Angeles city election in recent decades was 64 percent in 1973, and the lowest, 9 percent in 1983.

VROMAN, ADAM CLARK (1856–1916), Pasadena bookman and photographer. He left Illinois hoping that the California climate would cure his wife's tuberculosis, but the illness was too advanced and she died. Upon her death he opened a bookshop in 1894. By the 1920s it had become the biggest bookstore in the West. Vroman befriended the Arroyo artists. A sensitive photographer, he made eight trips to the Southwest to photograph the Pueblo Indians. He also captured on film the remnants of California mission buildings and Indians.

VULTEE AIRCRAFT COMPANY, major airframe manufacturer located south of Downey before and during World War II. It employed thousands of workers producing planes for the U.S. Army and Navy, and for America's allies. As men left the civilian work force to join the military the plant hired many women workers, who gained immortality as "Rosie the Riveter." Ironically, in the beginning, Vultee management, struggling to adjust to women on the assembly line, claimed that each time men turned to look at a woman walking through the assembly plant it cost the company $250 in productivity.

"Rosie the Riveter," Vultee Aircraft Co., World War II. *Los Angeles Examiner,* Hearst Collection, Dept. of Special Collections, USC.

WACHS, JOEL (1939–), Pennsylvania-born Los Angeles City Council member from the 2nd District. He came to Los Angeles with his family as a child, and graduated from UCLA and the Harvard Law School before winning a council seat in 1971. Reelected four times, Wachs has served on the revenue and taxation and governmental operations committees. He originated the landmark city ordinance banning discrimination against AIDS victims, championed the Santa Monica Mountains National Recreation Area, has supported apartment renters and senior citizens, and advocates support for the arts.

WALK OF FAME, star-shaped plaques featuring the names of entertainers that are set into the sidewalks of Hollywood. The attraction was the brainstorm of Hollywood businessman Harry Sugarman and is sponsored by the Hollywood Chamber of Commerce. Since 1958 the chamber has added the 3-foot-square terrazzo-and-brass sidewalk sections at the rate of about one a month. By 1987, 2,518 plaques had been installed along 37 blocks in the film capital—on Hollywood Boulevard from Sycamore to Gower and on Vine Street from Yucca to Sunset. Each costs about $3,500. They commemorate the greats and near greats of the entertainment industry—including the two canines Rin Tin Tin and Lassie. Among those honored are celebrities in motion pictures, recording, television, live theater, and radio. The public may nominate their favorites, but the names must be approved by a chamber of commerce committee. Devoted volunteers clean and polish the plaques of their favorite stars.

WALNUT, 7.5-square-mile city 23 miles east of downtown Los Angeles, in the far reaches of the county. It originated as part of Rancho Los Nogales ("Ranch of the Walnut Trees"), which was acquired piecemeal from José de la Cruz Lineras by the Vejar family beginning in 1837. The Vejar rancho, a

Julio Iglesias Fan Club, Hollywood Walk of Fame, 1995. Photo by Michael Krakowiak/ Marni Pitt.

center of activity for the surrounding area, became a stop on the Butterfield stage line. When the Southern Pacific arrived in the mid-1870s, the community was called Lemon. Although local growers planted both lemon and walnut trees, the latter was the major agricultural product until the 1930s, when a pest infestation destroyed the walnut orchards. Longtime residents, fearing that the town might be swallowed by West Covina, formally incorporated in 1959. The population rose at the rate of 133 percent between 1980 to 1990, reaching a total of 29,100. Walnut, like Cerritos, was claimed by some to be the most ethnically diverse city in the nation in the 1990s.

WALNUT PARK, unincorporated county area near Huntington Park 6 miles south of downtown Los Angeles. It is part of the 50th Assembly District—the district with the largest Latino population in the state of California, represented on the Board of Supervisors by Gloria Molina. The Walnut Park Community and Merchants Association received a development block grant of $25,000 in 1993 to help enforce zoning restrictions. One locale of interest is the Chili Bowl on Florence Avenue, a fast-food chain founded in the 1930s by Arthur Whizin, who coined the slogan "We cook our beans backwards—you only get the hiccups." As of 1990, the population of Walnut Park stood at 14,722.

WALT DISNEY COMPANY, Burbank-based entertainment empire founded by animator Walt Disney in 1940. The company has three divisions. Disney theme parks and resorts make up the first. These have grown steadily since the opening of Disneyland in Anaheim in 1955 and in recent years have

Los Angeles was a wonderful place to be in the 1950s. The city was wide open for experiment.

—Craig Ellwood, architect

brought in a combined revenue in excess of $2.6 billion. The main facility besides the California venue is Walt Disney World in Florida. The company also earns revenue from a Japanese-owned theme park in Tokyo. Another foreign venture, Euro Disney in France, has been a major disappointment.

Walt Disney Studio is the second major division. Since Walt Disney's personal breakthrough with the animated Mickey Mouse cartoon in 1928 and the astounding popularity of *Snow White* in 1938, films, both animated and live action, have remained a company mainstay, intended not only for theatrical release but also for the home video market. Unlike some other film studios, Disney made a successful transition to television as well.

The third major division is the merchandising wing. It licenses the name Walt Disney, as well as Disney characters, literary properties, songs, and music, to manufacturers, retailers, printers, and publishers worldwide. The trademarked Disney characters evoke a seemingly universal fascination in modern popular culture, and they bring in some $200 million annually. In 1990 the company unveiled its modernist Team Disney Building on the Burbank lot. The seven Disney dwarfs, each 19 feet tall, hold up the roof.

The Walt Disney Company's combined annual revenues from its joint enterprises has exceeded $5 billion, with a net income of over $800 million. When, in 1995, it purchased Capital Cities/ABC Inc., the nation's leading television distributor and network, it created an international entertainment powerhouse whose combined annual sales reached an astounding $20.7 billion.

WALTERIA, residential area in the southern part of Torrance, 22 miles southwest of downtown Los Angeles. It was named for Captain Walters, a former sea captain and owner of a local hotel. In the 19th century sheep and cattle grazed the area, which featured a small lake. Early in the 20th century it became home to 600 residents, mostly Japanese farmers and San Pedro dock workers. In 1952 and 1953, when the area was developed for suburban housing, an almanac listed Walteria as the most healthful spot in the nation.

WALTERS, RITA (1930–), Chicago-born and Kansas-raised city council member representing the 9th District. Walters moved to Los Angeles in 1955, and earned an M.A. degree in business administration from UCLA. She served on the Los Angeles Board of Education for 12 years. A lifelong civil rights advocate, Walters supported school integration, pursued higher-quality education in inner-city schools, and won adoption of a regulation mandating that high school athletes maintain a C average with no failing grades. She was elected to the city council in 1991, the first African American woman to serve on that body. The 9th District, with 230,000 residents, covers parts of Chinatown, Little Tokyo, and South Central Los Angeles.

WAMBAUGH, JOSEPH (1937–), retired Los Angeles Police Department sergeant and successful author. His fiction utilizes his personal knowledge of the city, especially police work. *The Onion Field* (1973), one of Wambaugh's best-sellers, is a vivid account of a highly publicized Los Angeles murder; it was made into a film in 1979.

WARNER, CHARLES DUDLEY (1829–1900), booster for the Southern Pacific Railroad and publicist of the good life in Southern California. In a piece in *Harper's,* "Our Italy" (1890), he explored the area's resemblance to the Mediterranean coast. This article fostered a movement toward architecture and other aspects of culture that evoked the flavor of southern Europe.

WARNER, JACK (1892–1978), Canadian-born film producer who, with his three brothers, founded Warner Brothers movie studio around 1918. He remained a dominant figure in its management until his retirement in 1969. Warner was a pioneer in the technology of film sound, devising processes for musical synchronization (*Don Juan,* 1926) and sound dialogue (*The Jazz Singer,* 1927). Jack, who survived his brothers Harry, Albert, and Sam, published an autobiography, *My First Hundred Years in Hollywood* (1965).

WARNER BROTHERS STUDIO, one of Hollywood's "Big Five" studios, founded around 1918 by Jack, Harry, Albert, and Sam Warner. Their first production, *Open Your Eyes* (1919), was an educational film about venereal disease. Warners also bought the formerly great Vitagraph Studios, which had relocated to Hollywood in 1915 from the East, but it remained an insignificant studio in constant financial crisis, in part because of some of Warner's questionable management decisions. (For example, the studio paid the stocky tenor with the magnificent voice, Enrico Caruso, $250,000 to appear in a silent movie.) At one point in the 1920s, the movie dog Rin Tin Tin saved the studio from bankruptcy; he is rewarded by a star on the Hollywood Walk of Fame.

Warner Brothers gambled and invested in a synchronized sound-on-disc process, which had been rejected by all the other studios. In 1925 they signed a contract with the merged companies of Western Electric and Bell Telephone and set up a Vitaphone production unit. The process, never intended for speech, inserted background music and sound effects into film, thus allowing the live piano accompanist to be replaced by fine music that could be heard in even the smallest rural movie houses. The first film to use the Vitaphone process was *Don Juan,* starring John Barrymore, which premiered on 6 August 1926. The only words spoken were by Will Hays, who introduced both the film and the Vitaphone process. When theater owners balked at buying expensive sound equipment, Warners hired Broadway musical star Al Jolson, who was performing in Sampson Raphaelson's Broadway production of *The Jazz Singer,* to re-create his role on film. It was to be silent except for the songs, but Jolson ad libbed, and some of his dialogue ("You ain't heard nothin' yet!") was left in. The movie opened on 6 October 1927 and was a sensation. Warner Brothers made *The Lights of*

Warner Brothers Studios, Burbank. Pitt Collection.

New York, the first all-talking movie, in 1928. A year later *Variety* wrote that their pioneering sound efforts had thrust "Warner Brothers from the last place to first in the league."

In the 1930s and 1940s Warners often dealt with the causes of social and economic turmoil, in such films as *I Am a Fugitive from a Chain Gang* (1932), *The Petrified Forest* (1936), *The Male Animal* (1942), and *Treasure of the Sierra Madre* (1948). Other major films in the Warner library are *Casablanca* (1942), *Mildred Pierce* (1945), *Key Largo* (1948), *Rebel Without a Cause* (1955), *Giant* (1956), *My Fair Lady* (1964), and *Camelot* (1967). Warner Brothers contract players included Humphrey Bogart, Bette Davis, James Cagney, Edward G. Robinson, Ruby Keeler, Errol Flynn, Olivia de Havilland, John Garfield, Ann Sheridan, Ida Lupino, and James Dean. The Turner Broadcasting Company bought up and controls the Warner Brothers film library from its inception to the year 1949.

Warner Brothers' first location in Los Angeles was on Sunset Boulevard, where KTLA-TV is today. They relocated in 1929 to Burbank and became a major studio under the active leadership of Jack Warner, who retired in 1969. Later, Warner Bros. Pictures, Inc., became part of Time Warner, Inc. In 1990 Warners bought Lorimar Television. The following year Japan's Toshiba Corporation and C. Itoh & Co., Ltd., invested $1 billion in Time Warner. Warner's 108 acres incorporates 33 sound stages and many backlot facilities, which it rents out for movie and television productions.

WARNER CENTER, massive commercial development on the site of movie mogul Jack Warner's ranch in the Woodland Hills area of the city of Los Angeles. It opened in the 1970s and by 1991 consisted of two hotels, a hospital, business parks, office towers, and two shopping malls—a total of 14 million square feet of commercial space on 1,100 acres of land. (By comparison, Century City in West Los Angeles occupies 290 acres and has 12 million square feet of commercial and office space.) According to a Los Angeles Planning Department blueprint issued in 1991, commercial space at Warner Center would double during the coming 20 years.

WARNER-HOLLYWOOD STUDIOS, historic film production facility on Santa Monica Boulevard (not to be confused with Warner Brothers Studio). It was established as the Pickford-Fairbanks

Studios in 1919, was reorganized as United Artists that same year, and was renamed Samuel Goldwyn Studio in 1935, after the producer who came aboard as an independent in 1924. Its plain architecture contrasts with the luster of the many films produced there, among them *Wuthering Heights* (1939), *The Best Years of Our Lives* (1946), and *Guys and Dolls* (1955). In recent years Warner Brothers has been the leaseholder.

WARNER RIDGE, proposed 21.5-acre Woodland Hills commercial and residential development. In 1992 Warner Ridge Partners won an important court battle against the Los Angeles City Council, which had tried to stop the construction of some 690,000 square feet of new office space. The developers charged the council with illegally altering zoning regulations to satisfy those opposed to the development on environmental grounds. Although Warner Ridge Partners won, the 1994 Northridge earthquake led to the withdrawal of a major office tenant and an important financial backer, and the project was placed on hold.

WARTENBERG, HENRY (1830–1879), pioneer who helped organize the area's Jewish community. Born in Poznan, Poland, Wartenberg came to Los Angeles and operated a general store beginning in 1857. He joined the Hebrew Benevolent Society, the Masons, and the Odd Fellows, as well as serving on the county grand jury in 1866, on the city council from 1868 to 1870, and on the volunteer fire brigade. Wartenberg was a member of B'nai B'rith congregation and is buried in the old Jewish cemetery in Chavez Ravine.

WASTE DISPOSAL was, at first, essentially a private concern for each household. Only in the 1880s, with the acceptance of the germ theory of disease, did sanitation come to be viewed as a matter of public concern. Today public sanitation in Los Angeles is concerned with garbage (food waste), solid waste (such as ashes, bottles, and metal cans), and sewage (toilet waste water). Until 1957 the city allowed householders to burn combustible trash in backyard incinerators, but concerns about particulate matter in the air brought an end to that practice.

In recent years population growth has been the biggest problem in waste disposal management, outstripping the best-intentioned policy reforms. In addition, control of industrial waste has been relatively loose.

Sanitary landfills came into their own when the backyard trash incinerators were banned. These scientifically managed dumps are located in canyons, where household waste is mixed with soil; water is captured to prevent contamination of underground drinking supplies. Technology minimizes the noise, dust, and methane gas. Landfills can remain active from 5 to 50 years; they can then be safely converted into sites for housing, parks, golf courses, botanical gardens, and other recreational uses. About 30 such operations currently exist in the county, but Los Angeles communities are running out of nearby dump sites.

Not all landfills are sanitary. Indeed, the toxicity level of some older dumps has reached dangerous proportions. In 1987 the federal Environmental Protection Agency (EPA) identified 10 major hazardous-substance dump sites within Los Angeles County, which it placed on the "Superfund" cleanup list. Highest on the list is the 190-acre Monterey Park landfill, once considered one of the most

---

The transformation going on here [through immigrations] is the very definition of what it means to be an American.   —Jay Mathews, journalist

---

toxic dumps in the country. It reeked of cancer-causing contaminants, including vinyl chloride and trichloroethylene, and was closed in 1984. Since then this landfill has been the subject of a massive lawsuit involving scores of industrial corporations and cities, including Monterey Park, Alhambra, Rosemead, Cudahy, Montebello, Southgate, Maywood, and Lynwood, Temple City, South Pasadena, City of Commerce, Compton, San Gabriel, and Bell. Also identified as having contributed to the dump is Los Angeles County, Caltrans, and private waste-hauling firms. The estimated cost of the cleanup ranges from $500 to $650 million.

The EPA has taken drastic steps to force the cleanup of a contaminated site at a former DDT factory near Torrance. The toxic pesticide was manufactured by the Montrose Chemical company from 1947 to 1982. In 1994 the government ordered the removal of 32 families from their residences nearby while it pursued medical and scientific studies.

As a way of controlling the random dumping of toxins, the city and county sanitation bureaus organize monthly "roundups" at various locations where citizens may bring their dangerous household waste, identified as anything labeled "toxic," "corrosive," "flammable," "irritant," or "poisonous."

In 1995 a state law took effect mandating that all California cities reduce their trash flow by 25 to 50 percent by the year 2000. Los Angeles instituted a gradual recycling program in the 1990s, which by 1995 included most of the city. It was salvaging 300–400 tons of recyclables weekly, using 200 special trucks and over 700,000 recycling bins.

WATER, DRINKING, in the city of Los Angeles comes mainly from the Owens and Colorado Rivers, with only about 12 percent pumped from local aquifers (underground water banks that store runoff).

The first residents in the area—Native Americans, Spanish and Mexican colonials, and Yankee pioneers—found sufficient water in the Los Angeles River and other local streams. Water carts, open ditches, and some pipes constituted the delivery system as late as the 1880s. Luckily, the city of Los Angeles won a court decision in 1899 establishing that, as an offshoot of its Spanish grant in 1781, it had exclusive rights to all water in the Los Angeles Basin. The valleys between the mountains of Los Angeles constituted enormous aquifers, with much of the water flowing naturally to the surface in artesian wells.

Water reservoir in the Plaza, 1869. Courtesy Robert Weinstein Collection.

In 1910 local farmers and fruit growers were operating 1,596 artesian wells in the area, plus thousands of turbine water pumps. The city also collected runoff water under the river at Glendale Narrows. At that point, with some 35,000 meters in operation, the natural supply of water in what was basically a desert environment began to give out. After a number of dry years, residents of the San Fernando Valley were feeling the pinch. Although adequate for a *pueblo* and small city, the water supply was clearly too meager for a major city. Water would have to be imported, by means of legal maneuvering, ingenious engineering, and federal intervention.

The Owens River source was developed between 1909 and 1913 by the city of Los Angeles, via the Los Angeles Aqueduct, amid considerable controversy. In the 1930s the Los Angeles Department of Water and Power (DWP) extended the aqueduct northward to the Lake Mono Basin, thus acquiring additional water for the city. More water was still needed, however, particularly by independent cities such as Pasadena, Santa Monica, and Inglewood, and in the late 1930s the Colorado River Aqueduct was built, delivering water impounded at Parker Dam. Soon after, the state created the Metropolitan Water District (MWD) as a giant water wholesaler.

Los Angeles County residents also obtain some water from the California State Water Project, via the MWD. About 5 percent of the water in use is reclaimed wastewater, with Pasadena, Pomona, and Claremont leading the effort. Seawater desalinization appears to be too expensive to have a viable future in the Los Angeles area. Conservation in aquifers of winter rainfall, a source now lost to the ocean, has excellent prospects; reduced consumption can effect major savings as well, as has been demonstrated during recent droughts. Still, there is pressure to satisfy future needs by obtaining additional water from Northern California via a peripheral canal to be built around the Sacramento Delta.

The DWP prides itself on the high quality of its water supply. The department is currently constructing a string of costly filtration plants in Encino, Hollywood, and Stone Canyon to purify drinking water that has been exposed to toxic underground elements.

WATER BOARDS are established by individual water districts. In the San Gabriel Valley alone, out-side the Los Angeles city limits, there are more than 100 water rights holders, suppliers, and districts, controlling the water supply for 30 communities and 1.5 million people. Seats on these boards are now hotly contested. Board policies can determine an area's rate of economic growth and real estate development, affect the availability and price of water imported by the Metropolitan Water District, and influence the handling of expensive pollution problems.

WATER CONSERVATION grows increasingly important as existing supplies diminish and new sources become problematic. Desalinization of ocean water remains excessively costly. Towing icebergs from the Arctic to Santa Monica Bay is imaginative but impractical. Draining more water from Northern California or the Pacific Northwest is expensive and politically difficult. Although

---

Years before I came to Los Angeles to live . . . I had ridden up and down its mean streets as a passenger sitting alongside Philip Marlowe and Lew Archer.   —Charles Champlin, literary critic

---

sewage water is reclaimed—for use on golf courses, for example—by several cities (53,000 acre feet in Los Angeles and Orange Counties in 1981), it will never be used for domestic purposes. Allowing rainwater to fill underground aquifers would save enormous quantities of water, but conflicts with the goals of flood protection. Meanwhile, the Angeleno lifestyle, with its home appliances, lawns, gardens, and swimming pools, leads to a wasteful per capita rate of 175 gallons daily—although statewide agricultural users employ the most water and have the poorest conservation record. In urban areas, consumption varies according to subregion, season, and income level.

The most successful conservation strategy, the installation of water meters, was accomplished early in the century. Subsequent efforts were at best feeble, until the severe drought of the 1970s, when the Department of Water and Power instituted an intensive educational program to save water, which included such minor adjustments as placing a brick in the toilet reservoir and taking shorter showers. The problem of water remains acute, however, particularly during drought years and with the prospect of continued population growth.

WATKINS, TED, SR. (1922–1993), Watts community activist. Watkins founded the Watts Labor Community Action Committee, on Central Avenue, after the 1965 riot. With labor union backing he set about to create housing, jobs, and a better life for South Central residents. Watkins was expert at acquiring government grants for community projects.

WATSON, JAMES ALEXANDER (1821–1869), American adventurer, as well as an attorney, lawman, and former Texas ranger. In the 1850s this son of Scottish immigrants married María Dolores Domínguez, granddaughter of Juan José Domínguez, the original grantee of Rancho San Pedro. After trying his luck in the Gold Rush, Watson entered politics and became secretary of the Democratic Party Central Committee, Monterey customs collector, and three-time assemblyman from Los Angeles.

WATT ENTERPRISES, Santa Monica–based development company. The firm, founded in 1947 by Ray Watt, has created dwellings for 250,000 families nationwide, as well as industrial buildings, offices, and hotels.

WATTS, town 7 miles south of downtown Los Angeles that was consolidated with Los Angeles in 1926. The area, originally a portion of Rancho Tajuanta, was owned by Anastacio Avila and bought by Charles H. Watts of Pasadena. In 1902 Watts donated 10 acres to the Pacific Electric Company (PE) to create a rail junction for the PE's Long Beach–Santa Ana line. Other PE lines passing through Watts connected with San Pedro and Redondo. In 1907, with 1,400 residents, Watts Junction, as it was known, incorporated as a town. This farming and working-class community, centered at 103rd Street, had a multiethnic population that included Germans, Scots, Mexicans, Italians, Greeks, Jews, Japanese, and African Americans. By 1910 Watts had 1,922 residents, many of whom were involved, at the time of World War I, in the planting of huge sugar beet fields. During the Prohibition era Watts became a haven for bootleggers.

An area of Watts known as "Mudtown" served as an entry point into the region for newly arrived Southern blacks excluded from living in other local communities owing to racial covenants and segregation. Some of the men worked for the Southern Pacific as Pullman porters and waiters. The noted black poet Arna Bontemps lived in Mudtown, as did the young Ralph Bunche and Tom Bradley. By 1926 African Americans seemed poised to dominate the Watts government. That year, to undercut African American voting strength, the Ku Klux Klan moved to annex the independent city to Los Angeles.

The Watts area was familiar to most PE riders from the 1920s to the 1950s as Angelenos passed through the area on a daily commute or sought out a famous eucalyptus grove for Sunday picnics.

All labor is done by Indians recruited from a small rancheria on the banks of the river on the outskirts of the village. These poor wretches are often mistreated, and [do] not always receive in full their daily pay.
—Duflot de Mofras, French visitor, 1841

Riders were intrigued by the curious folk-art towers rising at 107th Street and Santa Ana Boulevard. Created by an Italian immigrant, Simon Rodia, who toiled alone on the project from 1921 to 1954, the landmark Watts Towers eventually become world famous.

The area was heavily settled after World War II. In the summer of 1965 Watts was torn apart by serious rioting. After the upheaval the burned-out commercial strip at 103rd Street and Compton Avenue was marked for massive revitalization by the Community Redevelopment Agency. In 1988 the population of 56,000 was 86 percent African American and 13 percent Latino, with the balance changing rapidly each year. By the mid-1990s the Latino population was approaching the 50 percent range.

WATTS RIOT, or Watts Rebellion as some prefer to call it, refers to the six days of racial violence that occurred in the Watts district of Los Angeles during the summer of 1965. It was triggered when two California Highway Patrol officers tried to arrest a young black motorist for drunk driving. The looting, burning, and killing that reigned from 11 to 17 August destroyed black- and white-owned businesses in an area of 11 square miles, causing property damage of some $40 million. The death toll reached 34, 28 of whom were African Americans. One thousand people were injured. Academics, using sophisticated survey techniques, estimated that 50,000 people participated in the rioting. It took about 22,500 police, sheriffs, and highway patrolmen and 13,900 national guardsmen to quell the violence.

Some called the disturbance a "commodity riot," drawing attention to the pillaging of retail stores. Others called it a "rebellion of rising expectations," noting that it occurred during the national War on Poverty and in a political climate that stressed the rapid amelioration of racial injustice. Most analysts have agreed that the deterioration of living conditions and the shaky status of police-community relations had much to do with the explosion in an area that had been considered one of the "best" slums in the nation. The McCone Commission, appointed by Gov. Edmund G. "Pat" Brown, proposed modest changes in the police department, improvements in public transportation and schooling, and the construction of a major hospital to address some of the root causes of the rioting.

WATTS TOWERS, folk-art masterpiece on 107th Street in Watts. Simon (Sabbatino) Rodia (1873–1965), an Italian immigrant tile setter and stonemason, worked on them single-handed from 1921 until their completion in 1954. He intended them as a tribute to his adopted land, once declaring, "I

Watts Towers. Photo by Peter Menzel / Stock, Boston, Inc.

. . . less a city of angels than a paradise of realtors and a refuge for the rheumatic.

——Paul Jordan-Smith, writer, 1925

---

had in mind to do something big, and I did it." The three towers rise to heights of 55, 97, and 99 feet, supported by web frameworks made of discarded steel reinforced with chicken wire and cement. The surfaces are decorated with pieces of glass, tile, shell, and pottery salvaged by Rodia and by neighborhood children along the railroad tracks, alleys, and empty lots of Watts. Rodia never sought a building permit but had the support of neigh-

bors. With his work completed, he moved to Martinez, in Northern California, where he died in self-imposed obscurity.

In the 1960s the towers were condemned as a safety hazard by city engineers and nearly demolished, but tests demanded by preservationists proved that they were structurally sound. The Cultural Heritage Commission designated the Towers of Simon Rodia, as they are officially called, a city cultural monument, and made them the centerpiece of the Watts Towers Art Center, a city park facility. Rodia's fantasy towers have become emblematic of Los Angeles.

WAUGH, EVELYN (1903–1966), English novelist who worked for a time in Hollywood as a screenwriter. His satirical novel *The Loved One* (1948) is a merciless satire of the funeral industry of Southern California, particularly Forest Lawn Memorial Park. It reflects the author's concern with the decline of religious belief in the modern world. It was made into a film in 1965.

WAYFARER'S CHAPEL, Swedenborgian Christian church that sits on a high cliff near Portuguese

Wayfarer's Chapel, Palos Verdes Peninsula, under construction. Courtesy *Herald Examiner* Collection, Los Angeles Public Library.

Bend on the Palos Verdes Peninsula. Built for $80,000 and opened in 1949, it was designed by Lloyd Wright, the son of Frank Lloyd Wright. The chapel is basically a glass construction that links the inner and outer spaces, and the building is embraced by a grove of trees. Each year half a million visitors pass through the grounds and 750 couples walk down the aisle to be married in the serene chapel.

WEINGART CENTER, downtown agency providing shelter for the homeless on Skid Row. Founded in 1983 with funds from the Weingart Foundation and sustained by additional corporate and private donors as well as public funds, the center is located in the refurbished El Rey Hotel, a former transient hotel in Central City East. The 600-bed lodging house also provides social services to help the homeless become self-supporting.

WEINSTOCK, MATT (1903–1970), journalist. As a boy Weinstock trapped opossums on the site of what would later become the May Company Wilshire. After attending UCLA he broke into journalism by covering high school basketball for the *Los Angeles Daily News,* later rising to the post of managing editor. Excerpts from his sage, slice-of-life newspaper column "My L.A." were reprinted in *My L.A.* (1947) and *Muscatel at Noon* (1951).

WEINTRAUB, ROBERTA (1936–), member of the Los Angeles Board of Education from 1979 to 1993. She served four terms, longer than any other member. A conservative from the San Fernando Valley, Weintraub began her political career as a leader of the anti-busing campaign. In 1994 she ran for a seat on the city council; following her defeat she announced her retirement from politics.

WEISMAN, MARCIA SIMON (1918–1991), art patron and cofounder of the Museum of Contemporary Art (MOCA). Born in Oregon, Weisman—who was the sister of art patron Norton Simon—lived in San Francisco and attended Mills College before coming to Los Angeles. She and her husband, a businessman, amassed a personal collection of 1,000 artworks worth an estimated $100 million. By helping to establish the county's leading museum of contemporary art she made a reality of her passionate belief that painting and sculpture should be viewed in public places.

WELLES, ORSON (1915–1985), actor, producer, and director. Welles gained early fame in New York for his Mercury Players stage productions, including his 1938 radio dramatization of H. G. Wells's *War of the Worlds,* which convinced thousands of panicked listeners that Earth was being invaded by space aliens. Summoned to Hollywood, he made his first film, the classic *Citizen Kane* (1941), at age 26. This movie brought him the undying enmity of newspaper publisher William Randolph Hearst, upon whose life the film was based. Welles followed with *The Magnificent Ambersons* (1942), *The Lady from Shanghai* (1947), *Macbeth* (1948), and *Othello* (1951), among others. He acted in more than 35 films, including *Citizen Kane, Jane Eyre* (1943), *Moby Dick* (1946), *Roots of Heaven* (1958), and *Catch-22* (1970). In *Touch of Evil* (1958) director Welles cast himself as a crooked cop haunting the seamy streets of a "Mexican village"—actually the beach community of Venice.

WELSH PRESBYTERIAN CHURCH, downtown place of worship founded in 1888 by Rev. David Hughes and a handful of Welsh immigrants. An early member was Mary Griffith, sister of Griffith J. Griffith, who donated the land to the city that became Griffith Park. By 1926 the congregation had 400 members and was occupying a former Jewish synagogue built in 1909. The church choir sang in the Academy Award–winning movie *How Green Was My Valley* (1941), filmed at a re-created Welsh village in the Santa Monica Mountains. Its annual May song festival, "Gymanfa Ganu," attracts many visitors.

WEST, NATHANAEL (1903–1940), author. West wrote what many critics believe to be the best novel about Hollywood, *The Day of the Locust* (1939). He worked on the satirical, surrealistic book in 1935 while living in a dingy room in the Parva-Sed Apta (Latin for "small but suitable") apartment hotel on Ivar Street near Yucca. The novel is peopled with a ragtag assortment of Hollywood hopefuls and hopeless: starlets, comics, dwarfs, hucksters, technicians, and former vaudeville performers, as seen through the eyes of newcomer Homer Simpson.

West's sister was married to the writer S. J. Perelman, who became Nathanael's patron and admirer. After a small but impressive literary output that also included *Miss Lonelyhearts* (1933), West was killed in a car crash, together with his wife, Eileen (heroine of the popular book *My Sister Eileen,* by her sister Ruth McKenney). He was 36 years old.

WEST ADAMS, historic Los Angeles district extending from Figueroa Street to Crenshaw Boulevard and from Venice to Jefferson Boulevards. It originated as a wealthy residential area when Los Angeles annexed the Rosedale, Southern, and Western Additions in 1896. The new tracts were called West Adams Heights, Kenwood Park, Garfield Heights, Belvedere Heights, Berkeley Square, and Arlington Heights. The Pacific Electric Red Car lines running along Pico, Adams, and Arlington Boulevards provided residents easy access to downtown and to the beach communities. Busby Berkeley, Theda Bara, "Fatty" Arbuckle, Ethel Waters, Hattie McDaniel, Butterfly McQueen, Leo Carrillo, and other movie notables lived there. White flight began in the 1940s, though the trend was somewhat reversed in the 1970s. The West Adams Heritage Association has been struggling to preserve vintage architecture, which includes Victorian, Colonial Revival, and Craftsman styles.

WESTCHESTER, residential and commercial area of Los Angeles and the site of Los Angeles International Airport. In 1940 Westchester had only 17 homes, with a few more added to house aircraft workers in World War II. Following the war, rapid and massive development took place. In 1948 alone builder Fritz Burns constructed over 5,400 homes, selling most of them for about $7,000 to war veterans working in skilled trades, professions, and civil service jobs. Westchester is the home of Hughes Aircraft and Loyola-Marymount College. The population in 1949 was 30,000; by 1990 it had reached 47,498.

WEST COVINA, town located 20 miles east of downtown Los Angeles. It was incorporated in 1923

West Adams Boulevard, 1920s. Pitt Collection.

by Covina residents who were fighting to prevent establishment of a sewage dump on Glendora Avenue. After World War II its many walnut and orange groves fell before bulldozers to make way for residences. The population was 96,000 in 1990.

WESTDALE, Los Angeles neighborhood near Santa Monica and Culver City. It was formerly part of the Mar Vista district.

WESTERN AVENUE, one of the longest thoroughfares in the city. The north-south artery opened in 1925 as a dirt road connecting Hollywood with San Pedro. Originally used mainly by truck farmers, it lay neglected for a generation and was not fully paved until 1958. Major housing and commercial developments arose along the avenue after World War II. Today, the shops, restaurants, and other institutions on Western north of the Santa Monica Freeway reflect a broad range of national and ethnic associations, including African American, Vietnamese, Korean, Cambodian, Salvadoran, Czech, Afghan, and Hungarian.

WEST HILLS, Los Angeles neighborhood in the San Fernando Valley between Saticoy and Vanowen Streets, west of Shoup Avenue. It had been the western part of Canoga Park since 1931, but in 1987 homeowners prevailed on the city council to make a separate district and apply the new name officially.

WEST HOLLYWOOD, independent city of 1.9 square miles located along Santa Monica Boulevard from Doheny to La Brea Avenue, 9 miles northwest of downtown Los Angeles. Older Jewish residents seeking rent control and gays and lesbians seeking civil rights founded the city in 1984. Fol-

Santa Monica Boulevard, West Hollywood. Courtesy West Hollywood Convention & Visitors Bureau.

lowing incorporation West Hollywood elected the nation's first city council with a gay majority, attracting widespread attention as "Gay Camelot" and "America's First Gay City." The population was stable at 36,100 in 1990. West Hollywood is run by a council and city manager and as of 1991 had an annual budget of $38.6 million.

WESTLAKE, Los Angeles city district, 4 miles west of downtown, surrounding MacArthur Park (formerly Westlake Park). At the turn of the century prominent and wealthy Angelenos built huge mansions within walking distance of the park with its artificial lake. In the 1920s apartments were built for white-collar professionals, winter visitors, and retirees. Since World War II the area has evolved into an economically depressed "inner city" neighborhood, and is occupied by retirees and immigrants of diverse ethnicity, especially Latinos. In 1980, 70,000 people lived in Westlake.

WESTLAKE PARK. *See* MacArthur Park; Westlake

WESTLAKE VILLAGE, city in the far western reaches of the county, 37 miles west of downtown Los Angeles. Once owned by William Randolph Hearst, the land was sold when, contrary to expectations, no oil was discovered. Westlake Village, which borders an artificial lake, was developed by reclusive billionaire shipping magnate Daniel K. Ludwig. After incorporation in 1981, the city adopted ordinances that encouraged water reclamation, protected oak trees, limited hillside development, and provided for rent control and restrictions on signage. Plans in the 1980s to convert the golf course to an industrial park evoked a bitter controversy among residents. The population grew 21.7 percent between 1980 and 1990, when it reached 7,455. Westlake Village neighbors the larger community of Westlake in Ventura County (also developed by Ludwig), part of the city of Thousand Oaks.

WEST LOS ANGELES, vague and shifting designation for parts of Los Angeles to the west of downtown. The 1884 Stevenson map of Los Angeles situated "West Los Angeles" near the site of the future University of Southern California and Exposition Park. A century later, in 1986, the *Thomas Guide* designated it as the area south of Westwood, east of Sawtelle, and west of Century City.

The equally imprecise term "Westside" came into vogue in the 1970s. The *Los Angeles Times* used it as a title for a weekly regional supplement covering the area west of Fairfax Avenue, south of Mulholland Drive, as far west as Malibu, and south to Playa del Rey. Congressman Henry Waxman of the 29th Congressional District says the Westside connotes a relatively affluent population and the influence of the film industry.

WESTPORT HEIGHTS, part of the Westchester neighborhood in the city of Los Angeles. It is located near the I-405 freeway, between Sepulveda and La Tijera Boulevards.

WESTSIDE. *See* West Los Angeles

WESTSIDE PARK, unincorporated Antelope Valley community, flanking both sides of the Antelope Valley Freeway just south of the community of El Dorado. Many residents of the rural area maintain horses on their 2.5-acre homesites.

WESTWOOD, westside district 13 miles west of downtown Los Angeles that includes a residential neighborhood, the UCLA campus, and a retail shopping and theater center. It arose on the breezy, rolling hills of Rancho San José de Buenos Ayres, which was granted to Maximo Alanis in 1840 and later transferred to the Wolfskill family. An early attempt to subdivide and form a community known as Sunset City failed.

In 1925 the new ranch owners, Janss Investment Corporation, developed a master plan that hinged on a decision to donate a generous portion of the property for a new campus of the University of California. Opened in 1929 by Janss, Westwood

Westwood Village, 1995. Photo by Leonard Pitt.

is considered one of the nation's best-planned suburban real estate projects from the early part of the century.

Residential Westwood, comprising affluent homes to the north and east and more modest apartments to the west (the latter area now heavily developed with condominiums), was intended chiefly for faculty, staff, and students. The architecture featured the Spanish Colonial Revival style. The combined neighborhoods of Westwood had a population of 42,658 in 1990.

Westwood Village, the commercial area south of the UCLA campus along Westwood Boulevard, was also designed in the Mediterranean or Spanish Revival style. The distinctive fantasy spires, domes, and minarets of the village served to attract the eye of motorists cruising along Wilshire from downtown to the Santa Monica beach. Although the shopping district retains about 60, or half, of its original buildings, neighborhood community organizations have expressed fear for the future of the historic low-rise structures. The Ralphs grocery building on Westwood and Lindbrook (1929), now a movie theater complex, has been nominated for

Westwood Village, 1940s.

the National Register of Historic Buildings. Westwood has the densest collection of movie theaters anywhere in the world. Also within its boundaries is Westwood Memorial Cemetery, the final resting place for such legendary stars as Marilyn Monroe and Natalie Wood.

The village is slated for major redevelopment. Under an imaginative city council plan approved in 1988, the height limits in the older section would be preserved, but property owners elsewhere in the village would be allowed to build slightly higher buildings. Additional shopping and offices are planned, along with parking.

WHALES, highly intelligent giant mammals of the Cetacea order, closely related to dolphins and porpoises, that can be seen migrating in Pacific waters. Whales swim at a speed of 4–8 knots; they have a poor sense of smell but good vision. Like all marine mammals, they are protected by federal law. Whale watching is a favorite Southern California pastime.

Three varieties of whales are seen locally: The killer whale *(Orcinus orca)* is about 30 feet long and weighs 8 tons. Mostly black with white patches on its head, it has a blunt nose, large pointed teeth, rounded flippers, and a triangular dorsal fin. It feeds on fishes, seals, walruses, and other cetaceans. Orcas hunt in groups but, although called killers, are no more aggressive than other whales. The short-finned pilot whale *(Globiocephala macrorhynchus)* can sometimes be found near Santa Catalina Island. The California gray whale *(Eschrichtius robustus),* a baleen whale, appears in December and January and, from shore, is best viewed from Manhattan Beach's municipal pier. It is about 40 feet in length, mottled gray to black in color, with encrusted barnacles and no dorsal fin. Whale watchers charter special boats from King Harbor, Redondo Beach, to view the pods on their way to birthing lagoons on the west coast of Baja California.

WHEAT, a major crop in the San Fernando Valley from 1874 to 1915. The pioneer planter was Isaac Lankershim, who began growing the grain after noticing how wild oats flourished in what would become the Van Nuys area. He created a syndicate with his son, John B. Lankershim, and son-in-law, I. N. Van Nuys; together they bought up half of the valley (most of it south of Roscoe Boulevard) and planted 10,000 acres of wheat. Horses pulled the massive farm equipment before being replaced by huge steam-driven tractors. Lankershim's wagons carried the crop over Sepulveda Pass to Santa Monica, where it made its way by rail to San Pedro. Wheat was also grown on the Workman Ranch (Canoga Park), the Patton Ranch (Tarzana), the Old Sheep Ranch (centered near today's Sherman Oaks Fashion Square), and the Porter Ranch (northern San Fernando Valley). When the Owens River water flowed into the valley via the Los Angeles Aqueduct, wheat gave way to other crops, including sugar beets, lima beans, melons, pears, apricots, walnuts, grapes, pumpkins, oranges, lettuce, and cabbage, as well as to chicken ranching. In 1919 the Lankershim–Van Nuys syndicate gave up growing the grain and sold off their equipment, ending the wheat era.

Wheat threshing, San Fernando Valley. Courtesy Robert Weinstein Collection.

WHITE, STEPHEN M[ALLORY] (1853–1901), the first U.S. senator who was a native of California. He was a major participant in the "free harbor struggle" against the Southern Pacific Railroad (SP). Born in San Francisco and educated in Santa Clara, White practiced law in Los Angeles beginning in 1874, specializing in admiralty, mining, and land litigation. He helped found the Los Angeles Bar Association in 1878. White was elected county district attorney in 1883 and state senator in 1886, before entering the U.S. Senate in 1893 as a free silver Democrat. The scrappy "Little Steve" championed the creation of a Los Angeles harbor free from the domination of the SP. He stood up to powerful rail magnate Collis P. Huntington by helping to secure a huge federal subsidy for a harbor at San Pedro. The contest to "tame the octopus" sapped his fragile health, however, and he died at the age of 48. Grateful citizens raised $25,000 and commissioned the deaf-mute sculptor Douglas Tilden to create a bronze statue of White, which now stands at Cabrillo Beach.

WHITE FENCE FARMS, residential community in the Antelope Valley with a private street system. The large homes sit on 2-to-3-acre parcels. Residents own horses and farm animals and maintain a rural lifestyle.

WHITLEY, H[OBART] J[OHNSTONE] (1860–1931), Canadian-born land developer. Whitley was educated in Flint, Michigan, and helped develop scores of towns on the Great Plains while working for the Great Northern Railroad. His ideas of community building may have derived from the 19th-century French social philosopher Charles Fourier. In 1909 he was part of a syndicate, the Los Angeles Suburban Homes Company, organized to buy up and develop the southern San Fernando Valley. For a relatively small sum the company acquired 47,500 acres from the Lankershim–Van Nuys family and set about establishing residential communities. Whitley was the original manager of Suburban Homes. The syndicate, which included many of the business and civic elites of Los Angeles, was accused of conspiring to import Owens Valley water at public expense to increase the value of members' private holdings. In any case, Suburban Homes was responsible for creating the communities now known as Van Nuys, Canoga Park (known originally as Owensmouth, in which Whitley was the largest private landholder),

Reseda, Sherman Oaks, Tarzana, and Woodland Hills. In addition, the irrepressible "H. J." developed the fashionable 1920s Hollywood tract known as Whitley Heights, as a result of which some dubbed him the "Father of Hollywood."

WHITLEY HEIGHTS, Hollywood hillside neighborhood developed after 1918 by Hobart J. Whitley. The tract, located between Highland Avenue and Cahuenga Boulevard and designed by Arthur Barnes, featured a variation of the Mediterranean style of architecture. It was home at one time or another to Hollywood greats Rudolph Valentino, Francis X. Bushman, Marie Dressler, Bette Davis, Gloria Swanson, and Tyrone Power. In 1982 the local homeowners association succeeded in having the entire neighborhood placed on the National Register of Historic Homes.

WHITNALL, GORDON (1888–1977), pioneer city planner. He was appointed secretary to the new City Planning Commission in March 1920, and director-manager of the Department of City Planning in 1925. Whitnall, who started drafting the first city plan for Los Angeles, regarded rapid transit as crucial to the city's future.

WHITSETT, WILLIAM PAUL (1875–1965), mining, irrigation, and real estate entrepreneur associated with the development of the San Fernando Valley. Born in Whitsett, Pennsylvania, he attended Southwest State Normal School at, ironically, California, Pennsylvania. Seeking to cure his tuberculosis he moved to Acton, north of Los Angeles, around 1905. Starting out with a small investment, he made a fortune developing land in southeast Los Angeles. In 1911 he turned his attention to the Valley, purchasing from the Suburban Homes Company an undivided half-interest of San Fernando land called Van Nuys and acting as sales manager for the development of that town. At a gala land sell-off in Van Nuys on 22 February 1911, Whitsett opened the bidding at $25 a lot. Within a few days sales had reached $125,000, and they soared to $4.5 million within the next eight months. With the coming of water in 1913 via the Los Angeles Aqueduct, Whitsett successfully promoted one-acre farms where small growers could grow potatoes, raise poultry, or graze dairy cows.

Whitsett was also a banker and civic leader. He founded the Bank of Van Nuys, which later merged with Security Pacific. An active supporter of the development of Owens Valley water, he became a Department of Water and Power commissioner in 1924. He was by then known as "the Father of Van Nuys."

WHITTIER, independent city in the San Gabriel Valley, 12 miles east of downtown Los Angeles. Incorporated in 1898, it is located on a slope of the Puente Hills. In prehistoric times the area was dotted with live oaks, sycamores, and willows near the San Gabriel River. It was close to the Tongva brush-hut village of Sejat or Suka, meaning "place of wild bees." From 1771 until 1834 the future Whittier was affiliated with San Gabriel Mission, and also, for a time, with Rancho Los Nietos. After the secularization of the mission in 1834 it became part of Rancho Paso de Bartolo Viejo, owned and occupied by Pío Pico until several years before his death in 1894. On 8 January 1847 it was the site of a Mexican War skirmish between Californios and Americans, both of whom suffered casualties.

John M. Thomas of Indiana, who arrived in 1859, was an early independent Yankee rancher in the area. The town itself was founded by Acuilla H. Pickering and his wife, Hanna, Quakers sent from Chicago to colonize the Far West. They

---

She had no long-drawn-out period of adolescence. Overnight, so to speak, she turned from a pueblo into a giantess.

—Irvin S. Cobb, humorist, 1926

---

formed the Pickering Land and Water Company, purchased a rancho, and sent for their co-religionists. A party of Quaker colonists, most of them from Indiana, Iowa, and Illinois, arrived en masse in July 1887. They named the region after the 19th-century Quaker poet and reformer John Greenleaf Whittier. It became a place of orange and avocado orchards, and the quiet streets resembled a farm town in the Midwest.

Whittier College, a liberal arts school, was established in 1891. Richard Nixon spent his youth in Whittier, attended the college, and worked in a local law firm. After World War II the city pursued an expansionist policy, annexing 5.8 square miles of territory between 1953 and 1961. In 1990 the pop-

ulation was 77,671. The unincorporated surrounding areas, sometimes thought of as Whittier, accounted for another 50,000 people.

WHITTIER BOULEVARD, important east-west artery starting opposite 6th Street at the Los Angeles River and extending 20 miles to the Orange County boundary. It passes through the communities of East Los Angeles, Montebello, Pico Rivera, Whittier, and La Habra.

The road is associated with every era of human life in the Los Angeles Basin, from Indian to Spanish to Mexican to Yankee. It is part of El Camino Real, the King's Highway, which connected the missions and *pueblos* of Spanish California. The rancho home of Pío Pico, California's last Mexican governor, is protected at Pío Pico State Park. Beginning in the last century, during the early Yankee period, areas on both sides of Whittier evolved from sheep pastures, to orange, lemon, and walnut groves, to suburban housing tracts. As recently as 1947 large stretches of the boulevard were still lined with orange trees.

Segments of Whittier Boulevard in East Los Angeles formerly passed through neighborhoods of Armenians, Italians, Greeks, Jews, and Anglos, but it is now a main artery of the largest Mexican community outside of Mexico City—as its shopping strips, food stores, restaurants, and schools make clear. In the 1970s the boulevard attracted so many "low-rider" youths cruising in customized cars that it was occasionally closed to traffic by police and sheriffs. Mexican American journalist Ruben Salazar was killed during the 29 August 1970 Vietnam moratorium in a Whittier Boulevard café; a park near Indiana Street is now named in his honor. The street is the scene of a popular parade every Thanksgiving Day. In Monterey Park the lettering on the street signs gives way from Spanish to Chinese and Vietnamese. Portions of Whittier Boulevard are undergoing urban redevelopment.

WHITTIER NARROWS EARTHQUAKE, 5.9 temblor that occurred at 7:42 A.M. on 1 October 1987—the first major quake in the Los Angeles area after the damaging Sylmar quake of 1971. A 5.1 aftershock followed three days later. The Whittier quake claimed eight lives, injured more than 200 people, and incurred a cost of $385 million. It damaged more than 100 business structures in downtown Whittier, particularly in the area known as Uptown. The surprising collapse of a freeway support on a road connecting the I-5 and I-605 free-ways led to a program of retrofitting most single-column freeway bridges in California.

WHITTINGTON, "DICK." *See* Dick Whittington Photography

WIDNEY, JOSEPH P. (1841–1938), AND ROBERT M[ACLAY] WIDNEY (1838–1929), Ohio-born brothers who, after becoming success-ful business and civic leaders in the 1860s, were important in the establishment of the University of Southern California (USC). They were on the first board of directors. Joseph was a physician and educator, the city's first health officer, a booster of San Pedro, and a faculty member and second president of USC. He believed fervently in the superiority of the Anglo-Saxon race and the future of Los Angeles, as reflected in his books *Race Life of the Aryan Peoples* (1907) and *The Greater City of Los Angeles* (1938). Robert, Los Angeles's first real estate salesman, became a judge. He championed the introduction of streetcars, electric lights, and other civic improvements.

WIGGIN, KATE DOUGLAS (1856–1923), kindergarten teacher and writer. Born Kate Douglas Smith in Philadelphia, she came west in the 1870s. In 1877 she joined the first Unitarian congregation in Los Angeles, begun in Caroline Seymour Severance's home, and became its organist. For fund-raising purposes Wiggin established "Unitarian Thursdays," consisting of a potluck meal and a dance, one of the few entertainments available in the city at that time. Out of this grew the Women's Alliance, still a feature of Unitarian congregations. While in Los Angeles Wiggin studied kindergarten teaching with pioneer educator Emma Marwedel, and took up that profession in San Francisco. After moving back to New England Wiggin earned literary fame for *Rebecca of Sunnybrook Farm* (1903). Mary Pickford starred in the silent film version (1917), and Shirley Temple in the sound film (1938). Her sentimental novel *Mother Carey's Chickens* (1911) was also made into a film (1938).

WIGGINS, FRANK P. (1849–1924), tireless Los Angeles booster and a cofounder of the Sunkist cooperative. He arrived in Whittier from the Midwest in 1886 as an invalid so weak that he had to be carried off the train on a stretcher. Upon re-

gaining his health Wiggins turned his attention to promoting Los Angeles, organizing large railroad exhibits of agricultural products, most notably oranges, that drew huge crowds. By the time of the Chicago World's Fair in 1893 at least 10 million people had seen his traveling show, "Los Angeles on Wheels." The mustachioed Wiggins joined the chamber of commerce in 1890, and seven years later became its secretary. He tirelessly crisscrossed the country promoting his adopted city. A contemporary once said, "God did much for Los Angeles, but Frank Wiggins did the rest." He helped establish what became known as Frank Wiggins Trade School, now Los Angeles Trade Technical College.

WIGHT ART GALLERY, main art exhibition space of UCLA. Founded in 1952 and one of only 11 accredited museums in Los Angeles County, it is now located in the Armand Hammer Museum in Westwood.

WILDFIRES, normal and recurrent phenomenon of the local landscape, and often more devastating than earthquakes. They are natural to the chaparral-clad hillsides, where many seeds need high temperatures for germination. Native peoples would occasionally deliberately set fires to drive out animals or regenerate the vegetation. While lying off San Pedro in October 1542, Juan Cabrillo saw fires burning that may have been signals, cooking fires, or wildfires. For this reason he called the place the Bay of Smokes.

Unlike earthquakes, urban wildfires are more or less predictable, in that areas of relative susceptibility and seasons of high risk can be identified. Whether by accident or arson, wildfires are bound to occur, often with devastating effect in the canyons where humans live amid dry chaparral, during hot summer or fall days when the Santa Ana winds blow and the humidity is low. Under such conditions a stray spark can easily cause a conflagration. Houses with attic vents, overhanging eaves and porches, large windows, and especially wood-shingle and shake roofs are especially vulnerable. The narrow, winding streets of hillside neighborhoods and an abundance of overgrown brush make fire fighting a nightmare.

Several enormous wildfires have occurred in the past generation. The Bel-Air–Brentwood fire in November 1961 burned for two days, destroyed 484 residences and 21 other buildings, and resulted in insurance losses of $24 million. It was the most costly urban conflagration in North America since the Berkeley, California, blaze of 1923. Fire fighters using 200 vehicles and 135 miles of hose raced from canyon to canyon in rugged terrain, dropped retardant chemicals from 14 air tankers, and still lost control of the wind-driven blaze. Over 6,000 acres were scorched, but no lives were lost. On 27 September 1970 the canyons were ablaze from Newhall to Malibu, and in 1982, 42,000 acres of brush went up in flames in Chatsworth.

A series of fires in November 1993 raged in Los Angeles County in the area from Calabasas to Malibu, in Altadena, and in parts of Ventura and Orange Counties. A six-year drought had left a huge amount of tinder in the form of dead branches, trees, and underbrush in the mountains and canyons. Heavy rains the winter before spurred a lush growth of grasses that dried out as the summer progressed. The conditions were lethal. A dozen small blazes broke out and, fanned by Santa Ana winds, began raging through the mountain passes, erupting into major fires.

In their entirety the conflagrations, which affected six counties, destroyed 720 buildings and burned 152,000 acres. The Calabasas-Malibu blaze alone scorched 35,000 acres and destroyed 200 structures. Arson was suspected in some cases. Miraculously, only two people were killed, although 150 were injured. The resulting insurance claims of $950 million were the second highest on record, exceeded only by the $1.7 billion in claims for the Oakland hills fire of 1991.

How to mitigate the effects of urban wildfires is often the subject of public debate, especially in the direct aftermath of a major blaze. Planting fire-resistant vegetation, thinning the brush more regularly, setting controlled fires, requiring fire-resistant roofs, and establishing special tax districts to create the revenue for fire prevention and fire fighting are among the remedies most often discussed.

WILDFLOWERS. Since earliest times, Indians used native plants and flowers for medicinal purposes, food, hair dressing, and dyeing. Despite urban expansion and agricultural transformation, many scores of wild species still thrive in the Los Angeles region. Best known is the California, or golden, poppy *(Eschscholzia california),* the state flower. The Spaniards called it *dormidera* (drowsy one) because the bright yellow-orange petals open in the sunshine and close at night.

Some plants introduced into the county in historic times now grow wild. The mission padres brought in the yellow-flowered mustard and the white-flowered wild radish, both of which are profuse.

Enjoying wildflowers in Los Angeles County was easier earlier in the century. In the springtime, bright colors carpeted the nearby plains, hillsides, inland valleys, and seashore bluffs. On Sundays a special excursion car of the Pacific Electric Railway took hundreds of passengers to see the poppy fields of Monrovia and other hillside areas.

Wildflowers still bloom near the coast, but urbanization has diminished the profusion. Among the flowers commonly seen are the California poppy, matilija poppy, Indian paintbrush, lupine, ceanothus, iris, and primrose. Beach dunes and sandy slopes play host to yellow- and purple-flowered *mesembryanthemum* (ice plant or Hottentot fig, an exotic species).

Picking wildflowers in the foothills. Courtesy Robert Weinstein Collection.

Some of the most colorful wildflowers spring up in burnt areas, where the fire's heat germinates the seeds. These "fire followers," which include the purple Parry's phacelia, the fuchsia-colored foothill lupine, the golden fire poppy, and the mauve Catalina mariposa lily, generally disappear after the first season of growth, pushed out by other plants.

Today visitors can enjoy an array of wildflowers and native plants at several county preserves, such as Sun Valley's Theodore Payne Foundation Preserve. The location that draws the most visitors is the Antelope Valley Poppy Preserve in Lancaster, which generally boasts a spectacular spring showing of bright orange poppies interspersed with the purple, pink, and violet of thistle, sage, and lupine. Nearby, in an area west of Lancaster, is a 560-acre preserve of Joshua trees, which are actually giant lilies. Desert plants such as yucca, prickly pear, and creosote, usually stark and bare, will bloom unexpectedly in a profusion of colors.

WILDLIFE once roamed the area in great abundance. Even today wild animals persevere in some areas, despite urbanization. The natural diversity of the local deserts, mountains, and valleys created hospitable environments for a variety of animals. Until the 1850s bobcats, coyotes, pronghorn antelope, bighorn sheep, mule deer, quail, and black bears were routinely seen. Occasionally grizzly bears were encountered, whose only predators were humans. Between about 1850 and 1910, however, trappers, hunters, miners, farmers, and developers decimated wildlife throughout the state. Some did so to sell the hides, others to ease the way for agriculture and urbanization. Since the 1930s or so the state and federal governments have enacted stronger laws to protect wild species, in some cases saving them from extinction. Deer, rabbits, gophers, and squirrels have made a strong comeback in both suburban and farming areas.

Richard Lillard recorded seeing abundant wildlife in Beverly Glen in the 1970s, including raccoons, coyotes, California quail, woodrats, opossums, ground squirrels, gopher snakes, red-tailed hawks, deer, Jerusalem crickets, bees, skunks, Anna's hummingbirds, crows, horned lizards, Pacific rattlesnakes, moles, foxes, great horned owls, mockingbirds, thrashers, band-tailed pigeons, scrub jays, towhees, and Brewer's blackbirds. Particularly in dry seasons, coyotes, raccoons, opossums, skunks, rattlesnakes, and mountain lions continue to wander into suburban yards, attracted by gar-

dens, garbage cans, and small pets. Most wild creatures are easily scared off, although coyotes are becoming increasingly immune to humans as the latter invade their territory. Mulholland Drive and the foothills of the Santa Monica Mountains still provide cover for coyotes, raccoons, deer, gray foxes, striped skunks, bobcats, opossums, and California brush rabbits. Whales can be seen off the coast in their annual Pacific migration, as can porpoises and dolphins. The Chatsworth Reservoir is a 1,300-acre refuge for migratory birds and other wildlife, where hundreds of species have been seen at a time.

The Los Angeles County Department of Animal Care and Control, which deals with emergency calls, recommends that small pets not be left to wander at night because of predators. In 1986–1987 the department received 7,776 calls seeking assistance with wild animals; that number rose to 10,355 in 1990–91.

WILDLIFE PRESERVATION. A growing national environmental consciousness has led to the establishment of numerous preservation areas and educational programs and facilities throughout Los Angeles since the 1960s.

The Los Angeles Zoo is actively engaged in wildlife preservation. The Wildlife Way Station in Little Tujunga Canyon, established in 1968, is a private refuge for abused and needy wild animals. The Wilderness Institute in Agoura has promoted wilderness experiences for children. The Whittier Narrows Nature Center and Wildlife Sanctuary is a 325-acre preserve bordering the San Gabriel River in South El Monte. The Audubon Society, one of the oldest conservation groups in the country, promotes bird watching at sites countywide. The U.S. Congress established the Santa Monica Mountains National Recreation Area in 1978 and placed it under the administration of the National Park Service, which helps preserve natural habitats. Thanks to the efforts of biologists, the bald eagle, formerly endangered, has made a comeback on Santa Catalina Island.

WILKERSON, WILLIAM R. See *Hollywood Reporter*

WILKINSON, FRANK (1915–), Los Angeles housing official and civil liberties activist. Born in Michigan, the son of a minister, he came to the region in 1925 and attended UCLA, where he was a Republican youth leader and supported Herbert Hoover for president. In 1936 he took a job with the Citizens Housing Council of Los Angeles, which was devoted to slum clearance and public housing. He managed the first integrated city housing project in Watts in 1942, and became assistant director of housing in 1945. In 1949 he obtained $110 million in federal funds for urban renewal and public housing. During the red scare of the 1950s, his advocacy of public housing and racial integration made him a target of the real estate industry, Police Chief Parker, conservative city

---

The variety of the great mass of tar [in the La Brea tar pits], the movement which one sees in all of them at once, the pitchy smell, the sight of that great lake of strange matter. . . .   —Father Francisco Palóu, Franciscan missionary, 1787

---

council members, and the Un-American Activities Committees of both the state and the House of Representatives. The combined pressure forced Wilkinson from office, destroyed the city housing agency, undermined any new plans for public housing, and contributed to the defeat of Mayor Fletcher Bowron in the next election.

When called before the House Un-American Activities Committee (HUAC) and questioned about his political associations, he refused to reply, asserting his First Amendment rights. He served a jail sentence and subsequently organized a successful nationwide campaign to end HUAC. Afterward, under the Freedom of Information Act, he obtained proof of the years of pointless government investigation into his activities.

WILLARD, CHARLES DWIGHT (1860–1914), writer, major Los Angeles booster, and California Progressive. The Illinois-born Willard arrived in the area in the late 1880s hoping the mild climate would help him recover from tuberculosis. He struggled with the disease for the rest of his life, the task being complicated by the fact that he was medicated with cocaine; his wife finally helped him conquer the addiction in the early 1890s. He worked as a reporter for the *Los Angeles Times* and *Los Angeles Herald* and became managing editor of the *Los Angeles Express*. In 1888 Willard reestablished the Los Angeles Chamber of Commerce, which had collapsed as the Boom of the Eighties ended, and served as its secretary from 1891 to 1897. He founded the Municipal League, a civic organization, as well as the booster magazine *Land of Sunshine* (1894), which he sold within the year to Charles Lummis. He published several popular chronicles: *The Herald's History of Los Angeles* (1901), *History of the Los Angeles Chamber of Commerce* (1900), and *The Free Harbor Contest* (1899).

WILLIAMS, PAUL REVERE (1894–1980), Los Angeles–born African American architect. Much of his remarkable career paralleled the Jim Crow era. He attended Polytechnic High School, USC, and the New York Beaux Arts Institute of Design. Williams worked for the J. C. Austin Company before launching his own practice in 1923. He became the first African American member and fellow of the American Institute of Architects. The prolific Williams is responsible for some 3,000 projects in the United States, Colombia, and France. He designed buildings for UCLA fraternities at a time when their racial policies would have denied him entry. His creations include the Hollywood YMCA, Perino's and Chasen's restaurants, the Elks Lodge at 36th Street and Central Avenue, and the Urban League of Los Angeles; he also worked on the theme building for Los Angeles International Airport. Williams became the "architect to the stars," designing homes for Tyrone Power, William "Bojangles" Robinson, Lucille Ball, Lon Chaney, Barbara Stanwyck, and Frank Sinatra. Also among his clients were U.S. senator Frank P. Flint and Victor Rosetti, president of Merchants Trust. He served on the Los Angeles Planning Commission, and President Hoover appointed him to direct the planning of a memorial in Washington, D.C. In 1953 the NAACP awarded Williams the Spingarn Medal for achievement. His own home, in the Hancock Park district, is a designated historic cultural monument.

WILLIAMS, WILLIE F. (1943–), Los Angeles police chief since 1992. A noted advocate of community-based policing, he began his law enforcement career in Philadelphia in 1964, rising to the top post of police commissioner (chief) in 1988. In 1992 he replaced Los Angeles police chief Daryl Gates, assuming a post that was recently

Chief of Police Willie Williams. Courtesy Los Angeles Police Dept.

limited to a five-year term, with the possibility of a second five-year term, subject to city council approval.

WILLMORE, WILLIAM E[RWIN] (1844–1901), founder of Long Beach. Born in England, Willmore arrived at Wilmington in 1870, where he envisioned a city east of San Pedro and Wilmington. In 1880 an option of 4,000 acres from landowner Jotham Bixby allowed him to create a farm community, called American Colony, which he promoted nationwide as Willmore City. The plan offered farm lots ranging in size from 5 to 40 acres, priced at $12.50, $15, and $20 an acre. Affluent buyers willing to pay $100 an acre also re-ceived 70 established (three- or four-year-old) or-ange trees for each acre purchased. Willmore's plan failed, and he lost his option two years later. When he left the area, Willmore City consisted of only a handful of homes. However, surveys had been made, and street maps had been drawn in 1882. The community was renamed Long Beach and developed by other entrepreneurs, who suc-ceeded in forming a city later that decade.

WILLOWBROOK, unincorporated area near Watts, in South Central Los Angeles, 10 miles from downtown. The county built Martin Luther King Jr. Hospital there in the 1970s. The 1990 popula-tion was 32,772.

WILL ROGERS STATE BEACH, 3-mile-long stretch of sand in Pacific Palisades, established as a state beach in 1930. In 1944 it was named to honor movie actor and "cowboy philosopher" Will Rogers, who lived nearby.

WILMINGTON, harbor community of Los An-geles, 20 miles south of downtown Los Angeles. In prehistoric times the general area was inhabited by Native Americans, and from 1784 to 1804 the for-mer soldier Juan José Domínguez lived on the nearby bluffs, having been granted two extensive ranchos in the area by the Spanish government. The actual town of Wilmington was founded in 1858 by Yankee entrepreneur Phineas Banning af-ter a storm demolished San Pedro wharf, 3 miles to the west. He first called the site San Pedro New Town or New San Pedro, but settled on Wilming-ton, after his birthplace in Delaware. Although sit-uated on a mudflat that hindered ocean com-merce, the port of Wilmington was several miles closer to Los Angeles than rival San Pedro. Ban-

Timm's Landing, Wilmington, 1868. Courtesy Robert Wein-stein Collection.

ning ran a fleet of shallow-draft steamers and barges that drew commerce away from San Pedro. The town came to life during the Civil War, when the Lincoln administration, bent on discouraging Confederate activity in Southern California, spent over $1 million creating a military base, Drum Barracks, in Wilmington. During the war thousands of Yankee soldiers passed through the barracks, now a historical museum, on Carey Avenue.

In 1869 the Los Angeles and San Pedro Railroad, the first railroad in Southern California, connected Wilmington to Los Angeles, 21 miles away. The town fathers incorporated Wilmington in 1872. In 1880 the rail line was extended to the more strategically located San Pedro, stealing most of Wilmington's trade and causing its decline. Wilmington was annexed to Los Angeles in 1909, as part of a move to create a major harbor for the larger city. Its old anchorage facilities were vastly improved and integrated into the booming, sprawling Port of Los Angeles. The discovery of the Wilmington oil field in 1932 created a major new economic enterprise in the area. It still had 1,827 producing wells in 1991, with a cumulative production of 2.3 million barrels and an estimated reserve of over 400,000 barrels. The population of Wilmington was 56,147 in 1990.

WILSHIRE, H[ENRY] GAYLORD (1861– 1927), eccentric entrepreneur and socialist. Wilshire came from a wealthy Cincinnati family whose money derived from banking and oil. The handsome, self-assured, articulate Harvard dropout failed in a family-supported milling enterprise, and moved to California to start over. During the Boom of the Eighties he settled near Anaheim, where he developed a walnut and citrus ranch and founded the town of Fullerton. At the same time, he converted to socialism, becoming an ardent member of the Nationalist movement, a social crusade inspired by Edward Bellamy's utopian novel *Looking Backward* (1887). He launched the Nationalists' weekly newsletter, published in Los Angeles, and was drafted to run for Congress on the Socialist ticket—which he did, unsuccessfully, in 1890. He then left for New York, where he ran, again unsuccessfully, for state attorney general. Wilshire proceeded to London for four years, moving in Fabian Society circles and striking up a lifelong friendship with a relatively unknown Irish socialist, George Bernard Shaw, whom he resembled physically.

Returning to Los Angeles in 1895, Wilshire and his brother bought and developed four blocks in the fashionable Westlake district of Los Angeles— one lot of which he sold to *Los Angeles Times* publisher Harrison Gray Otis, his ideological opposite. The brothers also began developing Wilshire Boulevard, the first thoroughfare from downtown Los Angeles to Santa Monica, and they dabbled in property in Santa Monica, Pasadena, and Long

---

After heavy winter rains mud was from six inches to two feet deep, while during the summer, dust piled up to about the same extent.

—Harris Newmark, merchant, speaking about the 1850s

Beach. After losing another congressional bid in 1900, Wilshire used up his own fortune, and his wife's—a total of $3 million—in bad investments in Kern County and British Guiana. The idiosyncratic Wilshire also promoted a dubious invention, an electric belt called the "I-ON-A-CO," which he claimed could cure practically everything from dandruff to athlete's foot.

Wilshire, a noted conversationalist, public speaker, fashion plate, golfer, and wit, once offered presidential candidate William Jennings Bryan $10,000 to debate socialism. Bryan refused. Most of the radical causes Wilshire espoused, from ending child labor to social security, would become part of the American fabric in future decades.

WILSHIRE BOULEVARD, one of Los Angeles's grandest thoroughfares. It runs 15.5 miles from downtown to the ocean, passing through the cities of Los Angeles, Beverly Hills, and Santa Monica.

This age-old animal trail and Indian path became a road for horses and wagons starting with the Portolá expedition in 1769, served as a rancho boundary in the Mexican era, and was dedicated as an official roadway in 1885. For decades it remained a partially completed dirt road variously named El Camino Viejo ("The Old Road"), Orange Street, 6th Street, Los Angeles Avenue, and Nevada Avenue.

This quintessentially capitalist street derives its name from wealthy socialist H. Gaylord Wilshire, who in the 1890s developed property near West-lake (now MacArthur) Park along the boulevard—which he envisioned as the first thoroughfare connecting downtown with Santa Monica. Wilshire sold these house lots to prominent individuals, including Harrison Gray Otis, publisher of the *Los Angeles Times*.

Wilshire Boulevard underwent major development in the 1920s, when it was extended from MacArthur Park to Vermont Avenue, near the site of the future Bullock's Wilshire. A dozen or more religious institutions were built in the vicinity, including Wilshire Boulevard Christian Church

---

The California flea is unlike, both in appearance and manner, the mother flea of ordinary life. . . . These insects, reared in the rough school of bullocks' hide, boldly faced as they attacked us.

—Frank Marryat, British traveler, 1850s

(1922–1923), Wilshire Boulevard Temple (1922–1929), and Wilshire United Methodist Church (1924). Oil wells pumped within viewing distance of the boulevard, even as apartments and homes were being built. The region's wealthiest country club, the Los Angeles Country Club; the affluent suburbs of Beverly Hills and Westwood Village; the prominent Los Angeles Ebell Club for women; and First Congregational Church, the largest of this denomination's churches in the West, framed the boulevard.

Wilshire provided access to the exclusive gated community of Fremont Place—home of, among other celebrities, A. P. Giannini, founder of the Bank of America. The nearby Ambassador Hotel (1919–1921) was one of the finest hostelries in town. Across the street diners flocked to the Brown Derby Restaurant (1926), built in the shape of a bowler hat. Seven parks bordered Wilshire, including Westlake, Lafayette, and Hancock, with its La Brea tar pits, a major tourist attraction.

In the 1920s realtor A. W. Ross founded the Miracle Mile, running from La Brea to Fairfax, the first shopping area designed specifically for people arriving by auto rather than trolley. It attracted branches of the leading downtown department

stores—Desmond's, Coulter's, I. Magnin, and May Company—and offered patrons ample off-street parking, a refreshing improvement over the car-jammed downtown parking scene. In fact, Wilshire quickly became a street with off-boulevard parking lots. Also instituted in the 1920s were such innovations as the first use of ornamental street lighting, Christmas decorations, synchronized traffic lights, and limited parking areas.

Farther west, Beverly Hills and Westwood presented a vista of expensive shops, modern hotels, including the Beverly Wilshire (1928), and spacious homes. Along open stretches were several airports and race tracks. Westwood's minarets and spires lured motorists headed to the beach. On a large military reservation west of Westwood sprawled the Sawtelle Veterans Hospital and cemetery, dating from the Spanish-American War. By the 1930s Wilshire Boulevard, touted as the "Fifth Avenue of the West," represented Southern California's growing material prosperity and urban aspirations.

Today the Wilshire Corridor is the city's major east-west artery for cars, buses, and the planned rapid transit system. The old Miracle Mile area, now part of the Wilshire District, is undergoing redevelopment. Anchored by the Los Angeles County Museum of Art and the Page Museum of La Brea Discoveries, the area is becoming known as "Museum Row." The Craft and Folk Art Museum has returned to its original site with a new, 25,000-square-foot building. Recent additions include the Carole and Barry Kaye Museum of Miniatures and the Peterson Automotive Museum.

Wilshire remains a primary shopping street in Beverly Hills. In the Westwood area it is bounded by high-rise condominiums and office buildings. The intersection at Gayley Avenue is the busiest anywhere in the Los Angeles region. At its far western end, Wilshire attracts large numbers of shoppers in the city of Santa Monica, some on the boulevard itself, and even more just off, as in the 3rd Street Promenade. That it is the pathway of the Metro subway from downtown signifies the boulevard's continuing importance.

WILSHIRE BOULEVARD TEMPLE, Reform Jewish temple at Wilshire and Hobart Boulevards. It is the home of B'nai B'rith ("children of the covenant") congregation, established in downtown Los Angeles in 1862. Rabbi Edgar F. Magnin officiated at the dedication of the structure in 1929. The building features an immense, mosaic-

Wilshire Boulevard Temple.
Courtesy Wilshire Boulevard
Temple.

inlaid dome, Byzantine columns, Italian marble, rare woods, an enormous rose-colored stained window, and mural depictions of Jewish history by Hugo Ballin. In 1994 the congregation had 2,400 member families.

WILSON, BENJAMIN DAVIS ("DON BENITO") (1811–1878), landowner, civic leader, and merchant, as well as Los Angeles mayor from 1851 to 1852. A transitional figure, Wilson represented and was part of the immense changes that took place in Los Angeles between the 1840s and 1870s. He came to Los Angeles from New Mexico with

---

Los Angeles is not behind other cities of its size in regard to cemeteries, of which there are five.

—Walter Lindley, physician, 1888

---

the Rowland-Workman party in 1841, en route to China. Instead he met and married Ramona Yorba in 1844, heir to family land holdings that included Rancho Santa Ana. Wilson began to buy up parts or all of different ranchos. Among them were Rancho San José de Buenos Ayres (now the site of Westwood and UCLA), Rancho La Jurupa (River-

side), and former Mission San Gabriel lands, including the present sites of Pasadena, Alhambra, San Pedro, and San Gabriel.

"Don Benito" was also an early vintner. In 1859 his 2,500-acre Oak Knoll vineyard produced 20,000 gallons of wine. Some years later his son-in-law, James de Barth Shorb, would establish the city of San Marino on this acreage. In addition to cultivating vineyards, Wilson raised sheep and cattle, established orange and walnut groves, and planted fields of wheat.

While serving as the city's mayor from 1851 to 1852, Wilson organized the first Los Angeles police department. In 1855 President Fillmore appointed him U.S. Indian agent, and in 1869 he began serving one of three terms as state senator. During his tenure he traveled to Washington, at his own expense, to lobby for federal support for a railroad and harbor, projects in which he was deeply involved. He also financed a trail up to "Wilson's Peak" in the 1860s. Mt. Wilson and its observatory are named in his honor. One of Wilson's grandsons was Gen. George S. Patton, a hero of World War II.

WILTERN THEATRE, auditorium in the Pellissier Building at the corner of Wilshire and Western, used originally as a movie theater. Built in 1931 in blue and bronze terra-cotta, it is an Art Deco

masterpiece. On the eve of its demolition in 1982 the building was rescued by the Los Angeles Conservancy and bought by developer Wayne Ratkovich, who restored it according to its original plans. Today it is the site of live theatrical and musical performances.

WINERIES constituted an important industry in 19th-century Los Angeles. The Franciscan fathers planted the first vines in Southern California, a region well suited to grapes. The leading pioneers in the field were Joseph Chapman, whose plants came from mission cuttings in 1824; William Wolfskill, who was the first to attempt commercial agriculture; and Jean Louis Vignes, the most influential of the early vintners. Two dozen wineries were involved in making wine and brandy *(aguardiente)* in Los Angeles in the 1830s. Soon the area was producing more than was needed for local consumption, so that grapes and grape products became the region's first successful agricultural export. In 1859 the Los Angeles Vineyard Society founded a cooperative. That same year, 500,000 gallons of wine were produced in the county.

By the 1860s the area was one of the three leading grape- and wine-producing areas in California, along with Anaheim and Sonoma. Vintners, who made red and white wines as well as champagne, had $1 million invested in vineyards and bottling facilities east of Alameda and south of Aliso. Later, vines were planted in the San Fernando Valley that would produce fruit for more than a century. Vineyard output increased so rapidly that by 1869 the growers' combined production was 4 million gallons. In that year 75 percent of the city's manufacturing workers were involved in some capacity in the making of wine, an indication of its regional importance. Soon afterward, however, vineyards began taking hold in counties to the north, and production in Los Angeles tapered off.

WINNETKA, 18-block San Fernando Valley community bounded by Nordhoff Street on the north, Victory Boulevard on the south, Corbin Avenue on the east, and DeSoto Avenue on the west. Beginning in 1920 the area was known as the Weeks Colony, after a utopian agricultural venture founded by chicken farmer Charles Weeks, a native of Winnetka, Illinois. When he left in 1934, the remaining settlers renamed the community

Winnetka. This name (of Potawatomi Indian origin) was suppressed by the U.S. Post Office when it introduced postal zones in the 1950s, but was revived in the 1980s thanks to the efforts of longtime resident and latter-day honorary mayor Art Hieber. Winnetka has about 12,500 households.

WOLFSKILL, WILLIAM ("GUILLERMO") (1798–1866), Kentucky fur trapper who blazed the Old Spanish Trail from St. Louis to Santa Fe to Los Angeles, where, in 1831, he took up farming. Wolfskill settled east of the *pueblo,* near the river. He planted 2 acres of oranges in 1841 and later expanded them to 2,500 trees on 70 acres, the largest orange grove in the United States. He also successfully grew wine grapes and English walnuts. He planted Australian eucalyptus trees, hoping to harvest them commercially as lumber and firewood. While this experiment failed, the imported trees became popular as wind breaks for orange groves.

WOMAN'S BUILDING, center of feminist artistic activity from 1975 to 1981, located on Spring Street. Its original name was the Feminist Studio Workshop. Sponsoring courses, exhibits, and discussions, Woman's Building programs were devoted to raising women's political consciousness by means of art, especially "performance art." Writer Terry Wolverton and Sue Maberry were the leading figures. The Pasadena Women's Graphic Center was a similar facility.

WOMAN SUFFRAGE MOVEMENT, from 1896 to 1911, received vigorous leadership from the Los Angeles Woman Suffrage League. In November 1896 that group helped organize the first statewide suffrage measure, which they targeted at male voters. The measure failed, though it passed in Los Angeles County. Los Angeles civic leader Caroline Severance reactivated the league as a statewide organization in 1900, this time appealing to the sensibilities of women, who were urged to sway the men. In the crucial state election campaign of October 1911, the dominant Progressives supported a suffrage ballot proposition. The league by then had a strong regional network of clubs. California's most effective suffragist leader at this time was another Angeleno, Katherine Phillips Edson. The constitutional amendment won, and Severance, in 1912, had the honor of being the first woman in California to register to vote.

WOMEN, COMMISSION ON THE STATUS OF. *See* Los Angeles City Commission on the Status of Women

WOMEN, TO 1848. According to the Spanish literary myth of Queen Califia, the first rulers of California were Amazon women who tolerated men for purposes of procreation only. While unaware of this fantasy, native Tongva women wielded considerable influence in their own society, which carried over into the Spanish era. In 1785 Toypurina, a 24-year-old Gabrieleño woman, stirred the chiefs and warriors of six *rancherías* to revolt against the soldiers and mission fathers, an act that led to her arrest.

Among the original *pobladores* who arrived in Los Angeles in 1781 from Sinaloa and Sonora, Mexico, were 11 women. Like their husbands they were of Indian, African American, and mixed racial background. In addition, the native women of California married the Spanish and Mexican colonists. For a time it was estimated that women constituted a majority in the province.

Following the arrival of the Spanish and Mexicans, native women were decimated by malaria, smallpox, and other diseases, and endured frequent sexual harassment. The early 19th century was a particularly harsh time for Indians, and infanticide by neophyte mothers was not unknown. The decline of the female population figured strongly in the drop of the Indian population overall. At the end of the mission era the Fernandeño neophyte Espíritu, in the far western San Fernando Valley, was a rare case of a woman who was supposed to receive land. However, she was never able to overcome the legal obstacles and take possession of her share in the Rancho El Escorpión.

Starting in the 18th century women from Mexico entered the region as wives of soldiers. They tended to marry young and have large families, sometimes as many as a dozen children. Girls and widows in the Spanish and Mexican colonial era commonly worked at the Spanish missions. Women had property rights, and *rancheras* (female ranchers) supervised all aspects of their estates in the absence of their husbands. Girls and women raised on ranchos were often excellent horse handlers.

WOO, MICHAEL (1951–), former city council member representing the 13th District, and mayoral candidate in 1993. A native-born Angeleno, Woo attended UC Santa Cruz and UC Berkeley, specializing in city planning. Elected to the council in 1985, Woo was reelected in 1989 with 71 percent of the vote. He vacated his seat to run for mayor in 1993 but lost to Richard Riordan. On the council he was especially active in planning matters such as the redevelopment of Hollywood, the development of Fryman Canyon, near Laurel Canyon, and the improvement of traffic regulations and pedestrian safety.

WOODEN, JOHN (1910–), basketball coach. With a 40-year career of 885 wins and 203 losses (only 27 of them at UCLA) he has the best record of any basketball coach in history. Born in Martinsville, Indiana, Wooden played guard and captained Purdue University's Big Ten championship teams in 1931 and 1932. After teaching high school, coaching at Kentucky and Indiana, and serving in the navy, he began his UCLA coaching career in 1948. Wooden never had a losing year at the Westwood campus. His teams enjoyed four undefeated seasons (30–0), won an unprecedented 10 NCAA championships, and played in 19 conference championships. Wooden became famous for his calmness, civility, and good sportsmanship—qualities he instilled in his players. Wooden retired in 1975, when he was still a winning coach. Among the players he worked with during his career were Gail Goodrich, Mahadi Abdul-Rahman (Walt Hazzard), Keith Erickson, Kareem Abdul-Jabbar (Lew Alcindor), Larry Farmer, Sidney Wicks, Bill Walton, and Marques Johnson. An athletic hall on the Westwood campus is named in his honor. He is the only person to have been inducted into the National Basketball Hall of Fame as both a player and a coach.

WOODLAND HILLS, residential area in the west San Fernando Valley, 22 miles west of downtown Los Angeles. It was originally part of the San Fernando Mission, established in 1797, and of Rancho El Escorpión. Victor Girard, a former door-to-door rug salesman who typified the get-rich-quick land investment artists of the 1920s, was the chief developer. He sold some 6,000 lots, roughly from today's Mulholland Drive to Ventura Boulevard. Many of the lots were as small as 25 feet in width. He planted 120,000 sycamore, pepper, and pine trees along Canoga Avenue, and formed the townsite of Girard in 1923. He and his associates were instrumental in creating Mulholland Highway in 1924 and forming a country club in

1925. In 1932, during the Great Depression, Girard disappeared under a financial cloud. Movie mogul Jack Warner maintained a ranch on what is today Warner Center, a major commercial complex. The community of Girard was eventually incorporated into Los Angeles, and in 1945 became known as Woodland Hills. The Motion Picture and Television Retirement Fund retirement home, known as "The Lot," is a community landmark.

WOODMAN, FREDERICK THOMAS (1872–1949), mayor of Los Angeles from 1916 to 1919. At that time the city had a population of less than 500,000 and occupied an area of 364 square miles.

WOOLWINE, THOMAS LEE (1874–1925), prosecuting attorney. A native of Tennessee, Woolwine arrived in California in 1896, and served as assistant district attorney in 1907 and 1908. Without the support of his superior, District Attorney John Fredericks, a machine politician, he investigated graft and corruption in the red-light district. When the trail led directly to the offices of Police Chief Edward Kern and Mayor Arthur Harper, Fredericks fired him. The solid evidence of political wrongdoing appeared in the pages of the *Los Angeles Express* and eventually forced Harper's resignation. Voters later elected Woolwine district attorney.

WORKMAN, MARY JULIA (1871–1964), "the Catholic conscience of Los Angeles." A native-born Angeleno, Workman was educated at a Catholic academy in Oakland. Her Roman Catholic mother, Mary Boyle Workman, assisted the work of the Sisters of Charity in Los Angeles, and her Protestant father, William H. Workman, was mayor of Los Angeles from 1886 to 1888. A progressive, Mary Julia Workman devoted herself to furthering the causes of social settlements, municipal reform, and international peace. Inspired by a talk given by Jane Addams, the founder of modern social welfare work among the immigrant poor, Workman worked at the Casa de Castelar settlement house, and in 1901 established the Brownson settlement house on Aliso Street, a Catholic charitable institution. Workman was among the pioneer kindergarten teachers of Los Angeles, embracing the theories of Friedrich Froebel and Kate Douglas Wiggin, and earned a kindergarten teaching certificate from the State Normal School (forerunner to UCLA) in 1905. In 1925 Mayor George

E. Cryer named her to the Civil Service Commission, a rare appointment for a woman.

Like Addams, Workman joined the struggle for world peace in the 1930s, establishing a local branch of the Catholic Association for International Peace. The lifelong social reformer joined the movement to topple Mayor Frank Shaw in 1937, and helped elect the reform mayor Fletcher Bowron. In 1942 she vigorously opposed the internment of the Japanese. Workman is also remembered for helping to strengthen lay organization within the Church during an era of strong ecclesiastical control.

WORKMAN, WILLIAM H[ENRY] (1839–1918), Los Angeles civic leader. The Missouri-born printer arrived in Southern California in 1854, where he became a saddle-and-harness dealer. He served as city councilman, city treasurer, and finally mayor of Los Angeles, from 1886 to 1888. As mayor during the Boom of the Eighties he initiated the paving of Main, Spring, Hill, and Fort Streets, and supported the development of the public library. His uncle, the Englishman William ("Julian") Workman, had come to California in 1841 and was a co-grantee, in 1845, of Rancho La Puente.

WORKMAN AND TEMPLE HOMESTEAD, 6-acre fragment of the 49,000-acre Mexican land grant known as Rancho La Puente. The rancho, in what is today City of Industry, was granted jointly in 1845 to William ("Julian") Workman and John Rowland, who arrived in California in 1841 with the first wagon train of Yankees to migrate to Southern California. Each man built an adobe and started raising cattle. Workman's adobe was built with the labor of 50 Indians. He raised wheat and grapes and produced wine. In 1872 his adobe was expanded into a large Victorian-style home with Gothic Revival trim. The Workman property was purchased by Walter P. Temple in 1917.

Part of the property, Campo Santo Cemetery, established in 1850, is the oldest family cemetery in Los Angeles. It is the burial place of the Temple and Workman families and of Pío Pico, the last Mexican governor of California.

WORK PROJECTS ADMINISTRATION (WPA), federal New Deal agency active in the county from 1935 to 1943 (its name was changed to Works Progress Administration in 1939). The public works division of the WPA created a forestry sta-

tion in the Angeles National Forest that resulted in the planting of thousands of seedlings to preserve the Los Angeles watershed. It also developed the Plummer Park Recreation Center in Hollywood. In Altadena, the WPA paid unemployed workers to build the William Davies Memorial Building, a community complex that included an auditorium, which has featured performances by a local theatrical company for six decades. The Arcadia Park and Golf Course, located on the former Lucky Baldwin estate in the San Gabriel Valley, was a WPA project dedicated in 1938. In Chavez Ravine, near downtown Los Angeles, the agency constructed several Art Deco Moderne buildings for a U.S. Naval and Marine Reserve Training Center. In 1935 the WPA dedicated a clubhouse at Mineral Wells in Griffith Park to the memory of the 29 public relief workers who had lost their lives fighting a wildfire at that spot two years before.

The WPA's Federal Arts Project sponsored numerous artistic ventures, many of which can still be seen today. In 1940, the muralist Barse Miller completed a two-panel spread for the U.S. Post Office building in Burbank featuring aeronautical and filmmaking images suggestive of life in that

For 40 years, corporate America, and I'm part of that, has moved every decent job out of the inner city. I had 300 offices and not one was in the inner city.   —Peter Ueberroth, entrepreneur and civic leader

city; he titled it "People of Burbank." In Long Beach the agency originated 14 art projects to decorate public buildings reconstructed after the 1933 earthquake. One of these is the Polytechnic High School mural, showing dockworkers, sailors, surfers, and other figures representative of the local community. Another, the tile mosaic at Long Beach Municipal Auditorium entitled "Recreation in Long Beach," is said to be the largest mosaic in the world. Likewise imposing is Helen Lundberg's WPA mosaic in Centinela Park in Inglewood. The Los Angeles Board of Supervisors commissioned eight historical murals for their meeting room. They also encouraged a team of WPA artists headed by George Stanley to create the Art Deco fountain at the entrance to the Hollywood Bowl; it features a heroic-sized sculpture of a woman kneeling and playing a harp.

The WPA Federal Theatre Project sponsored drama and puppet show productions. Some neighborhood performances were aimed specifically at ethnic audiences that had never before attended the theater.

The Southern California Writers Project, another WPA offshoot, produced *Los Angeles: A Guide to the City and Its Environs* (1941), which was hailed as the finest travel guide ever produced for the region. Under the supervision of John D. Keyes, teams of writers scoured libraries, conducted interviews, and roamed the highways gathering material for the book. Historians John Caughey and Carey McWilliams, art critic Arthur Millier, and architects Richard J. Neutra and Lloyd Wright, among others, assisted in the project.

WORLDPORT L.A. *See* Harbor, Los Angeles, since 1900

WORLD WAR I saw a surge of patriotism and war mobilization in Los Angeles from April 1917 to November 1918, when the United States was a participant in the conflict. Speakers activated by the federal Committee on Public Information delivered patriotic exhortations in movie theaters and other public places. By June 1917, 42,000 of the county's 1 million residents had enlisted in the armed forces. By the war's end, Angelenos had bought $140 million in Liberty Loans and war stamps, donated $500,000 in relief clothing and food, and sent 7 million pounds of sugar to the front. Local refineries produced 28.7 million gallons of oil for the military. Over 16,000 people worked in the shipyards, and a firm on Terminal Island built 23 8,000-ton ships in 77 days. Following the Great War, veterans organizations fostering patriotism became politically active. An estimated 2,400 veterans of that war still lived in the county in 1990.

WORLD WAR II, from December 1941 to August 1945, saw a major expansion of industry, an influx of population, and an upsurge of social tensions and racism in Southern California.

On 8 December 1941 the military police raided the Japanese community on Terminal Island, arresting many males and forcing the closure of most of their businesses, including the fishing industry. In what was the greatest single violation of civil rights in American history, thousands of Japanese and Japanese Americans were rounded up from Los Angeles in 1942 and interned for the duration of the war behind barbed wire at Manzanar in the Owens Valley.

Military installations, particularly Fort MacArthur and the Long Beach Naval Shipyard, were activated and expanded. From the bluffs overlooking San Pedro dozens of aircraft guns pointed skyward.

Beginning with a blackout on 10 December 1941, civil defense officials began enforcing air raid drills and blackout regulations. Some 65,000 people volunteered to serve as block wardens. Local police distributed incendiary-bomb extinguishers to residents worried about Japanese air attacks. On 23 February 1942 a Japanese submarine

World War I victory parade for the 360th Regiment. Courtesy Robert Weinstein Collection.

Defense plant dedication, Long Beach, 1941. Courtesy Dept. of Special Collections, University Research Library, UCLA.

shelled the coast near Santa Barbara, and three nights later Los Angeles succumbed completely to wartime jitters as sirens blared and anti-aircraft batteries fired at "Japanese bombers" in what turned out to be a false alarm, subsequently dubbed the "Battle of Los Angeles."

With the Los Angeles Japanese gone, Mexicans became the object of racial wrath. For several days in June crowds of GIs roamed the downtown area searching out and beating youths wearing "zoot suits," a style of dress favored by young Latinos. The victims were falsely accused of shirking military duty and assaulting white women.

The county population jumped by more than half a million in less than a decade. The influx created a housing crunch as people crowded into all available homes and apartments, even bedding down in shacks, hallways, and trailer camps. Hotels had no room to spare. GIs taking military leave in the city sometimes had to sleep on public benches, though many Catholic churches converted their basements and classrooms into weekend military dormitories. The newcomers taxed social services, as well as recreation and transportation facilities, to the utmost. Shortages and rationing of gas and tires forced many drivers to park their cars and use public transportation, which meant that the Pacific Electric Red Car lines were always jammed, carrying people to and from home, work, shopping, and recreation.

The shipbuilding and aircraft industries expanded dramatically, providing a high level of em-

ployment and income. The federal government poured millions of dollars into war contracts, particularly in the aircraft industry. Practically overnight, Los Angeles became the Pittsburgh of aircraft. Tens of thousands of workers—skilled and unskilled, white and nonwhite, men and women—flocked to the area seeking employment. For the first time, in 1943, women and African Americans were hired to work at well-paying assembly plant jobs, replacing white male workers who had gone into the military.

The film industry did its share for the war effort, making training films for the military and patriotic feature films to boost civilian morale. Movie stars appeared at war bond rallies and ran the Hollywood Stage Door Canteen, providing GIs with recreation.

Some of the perceived economic and social growth generated in wartime Los Angeles was less than its promoters claimed. Although 186,000 new jobs were created, temporarily, Chicago and New York each gained more. Most women who wanted to stay in the job market were forced out when the war ended and the GIs returned home. Some of the wartime changes had negative effects. Plans for freeways and public housing were scrapped, and beaches became polluted and were not cleaned, because of wartime industry and energy that had to be directed elsewhere. If the war had dramatic social consequences, it produced no perceptible changes in politics.

When the war ended, thousands of GIs who had

served in the Pacific theater passed through Los Angeles on their way home, liked what they saw, and returned with their families in the late 1940s and 1950s.

WORLDWIDE CHURCH OF GOD, Pasadena-based Christian fundamentalist church. Founded in 1947 by Herbert W. Armstrong, who considered himself God's special apostle, the church practiced Saturday worship. In the 1970s it was buffeted by legal suits, family squabbles, internal doctrinal battles, defections, and financial crises, reemerging on solid ground in the 1980s. The elder Armstrong ousted his son, Garner Ted Armstrong, who left to set up his own church in Texas.

WPA. *See* Work Projects Administration

WRIGHT, FRANK LLOYD (1869–1959), architect. Known as the apostle of organic architecture, Wright was lured to Southern California from the Midwest in 1917 by oil heiress Aline Barnsdall to design her Hollywood home. This became the Hollyhock House (1917–1920), a Mayan-esque concrete-block structure featuring the hollyhock as a design motif. Wright received five major commissions in Los Angeles between 1917 and 1923 and worked in the area intermittently as late as the 1940s. The Ennis House (1924), in Hollywood, and "La Miniatura" or Millard House (1923), in Pasadena, are reminiscent of the Hollyhock House. These and other Wright creations, including the Storer House (1923) on Hollywood Boulevard, seem to blend into their hillside locations.

WRIGHT, [JOHN] LLOYD (1890–1972), architect who gradually moved from his first specialty in landscape architecture to designing buildings. The eldest son of Frank Lloyd Wright, he supervised the construction of some of his father's buildings. Lloyd Wright was even more prolific than his father in Southern California, building scores of homes and other structures from the 1920s to the 1960s. A popular favorite is the Wayfarer's Chapel in Palos Verdes (1949–1951).

WRIGHT, WILLARD HUNTINGTON (1889–1939), Southern California literary figure. He was the *Los Angeles Times* literary editor before becoming editor of the sophisticated *Smart Set* magazine, which published him for the first time in 1913. Wright was a mortal foe of the midwestern

puritanism and small-town mentality that characterized Los Angeles early in the century. In 1913 he observed, "Los Angeles is overrun with militant moralists, connoisseurs of sin, experts of biological purity." During the 1920s, using the pseudonym S. S. Van Dine, he began writing the Philo Vance detective novels. Perversely, he used New York, rather than Los Angeles, as the background for his cultured hero's adventures.

WRIGHTWOOD, tiny mountain community astride the Los Angeles–San Bernardino County border, in a long narrow valley formed by the San Andreas Fault. This private reserve area within the Angeles National Forest was developed early in the century to cater to recreation seekers. Today it consists of shops, cafés, motels, and riding stables, and caters to skiers in winter.

WRIGLEY FIELD, baseball stadium in South Central Los Angeles, in use from the 1920s to the 1960s. Early in the century, Chicago chewing-gum magnate William Wrigley Jr. fell in love with Southern California and built a winter home in Pasadena. A baseball devotee, in 1919 he bought the Chicago Cubs baseball team, and then purchased Santa Catalina Island for his team to use as a spring training site. Soon after, he also acquired the minor league Los Angeles Angels ball club as a Cubs

---

[I]n Los Angeles] I felt like a hemophiliac in a razor factory. I worried about my career every day.

—Robin Williams

---

farm team, and, to complete his baseball empire, built a new stadium for the Angels. Located on 9 acres at 41st Place and Avalon Boulevard, and designed by Zachary Taylor Davis, Wrigley Field was built at a cost of $1.1 million. It had 22,457 seats, including concrete bleachers, and was accessible to fans who came by streetcar. The gate fee was less than a dollar. Wrigley then built a new Chicago stadium, patterning and naming it after the smaller one in Los Angeles. The movies *Pride of the Yankees* (1942) and *The Babe Ruth Story* (1948), and parts of *Damn Yankees* (1958), were filmed in Los Angeles's Wrigley Field.

In 1957 Brooklyn Dodgers owner Walter

O'Malley, maneuvering to obtain a baseball franchise and shift his team to the West, purchased Wrigley Field. He subsequently traded the stadium to the city in exchange for land rights in Chavez Ravine, where he built Dodger Stadium. Since the old field needed repair and lacked parking, the city was forced to raze it in 1966, building in its stead the Gilbert Lindsay Community Center and a mental health facility.

WRIGLEY MANSION, in Pasadena, winter home of the Chicago chewing-gum king William Wrigley Jr. and his wife. The three-story Italian Renaissance structure, built in 1914, stands on a 4.5-acre plot on Orange Grove Boulevard, the street once known as "Millionaire's Row." It is now owned by the city of Pasadena and serves as headquarters of the Tournament of Roses. Wrigley's Chicago Cubs baseball team held spring training on Santa Catalina Island, where he had yet another mansion.

WRITERS GUILD OF AMERICA, WEST, INC., film industry labor association formed in February 1933. The charter members were movie writers Kubec Glassman, Courtney Terret, John Bright, Brian Marlowe, Lester Cole, Sampson Raphaelson, Edwin Justus Mayer, Louis Weitzenkorn, Bertram Block, and John Howard Lawson, who became its first president. The group assumed the name of Screen Writers Guild, appropriated from an older social organization, and affiliated themselves with the Authors League. The guild struggled for recognition in an age when film writers—who were listed as "titlists," "adapters," "talk experts," "dialoguists," or "scene-makers," but not as screenwriters—had no control over their product. The new organization had to battle a company union, the Screen Playwrights, formed by producer Irving Thalberg.

In the late 1940s the Writers Guild of America had 1,275 members. The guild's greatest crisis was the blacklist of the 1940s to the 1960s, which cost many members their jobs. Founding guild members Lester Cole and John Howard Lawson were two of the Hollywood Ten.

In 1954 the Screen Writers, Radio Writers, and Television Writers Guilds merged to form the Writers Guild of America, East and West, which moved to achieve a minimum basic agreement with management. Major issues arose over residuals, film credits, and the status of hyphenates (that is, those who combine the status of writer, director, and producer). The guild, often considered the most aggressive of the Hollywood labor and professional associations, conducted major strikes in 1960, 1981, and 1987. Today it has more than 9,000 members nationwide. The organization presents coveted annual awards for writing excellence.

𝒳

XANTUS, JOHN DE VASY (1825–1895), Hungarian-born naturalist. A political refugee, Xantus fled to Gold Rush California and joined the U.S. Army. Already a noted botanist, he became an officer and was assigned to head a survey party to define the Mexican boundary and a railroad route in Southern California. The team left San Francisco in 1857 and arrived at San Pedro aboard the steamer *Senator,* en route to Fort Tejón, north of Los Angeles. As was then typical of a landing at San Pedro, Xantus was forced to disembark in a windstorm onto a small fishing barge and then jump into ankle-deep water to reach solid ground. The party celebrated their arrival at Mission San Gabriel by drinking wine and playing cards with the Franciscan fathers. Los Angeles, a village of 500 souls that, as he put it, "lies on a beautiful plain on both sides of a river of the same name and offers a very pleasing view," appealed to him aesthetically. He was less attracted to some of the local culture. The popular bull-and-bear fights, for example, he found gory and detestable. Before they could start work at Fort Tejón, the Angeleno volunteer soldiers he had hired were arrested for drunken brawling and shooting. His eight wagon drivers included a Norwegian counterfeiter, an escaped Neapolitan galley slave, a Prussian deserter, and an Australian deportee.

The naturalist later explored Baja California; he found the life at Cabo San Lucas, where he fathered several children, far more appealing than that in Los Angeles. Xanthus's book of letters and narrative, *Travels in Southern California* (1859), was not issued in this country until 1976. His botanical collection is housed at the Smithsonian Institution.

Y

YACHTING, elite recreation and sport first organized in the region in 1886 by the Los Angeles Yacht Club. For $2,500 the group bought a handsome craft, the *Rambler,* that it maintained in a slip at San Pedro Harbor. Hancock Banning, son of Phineas—who with his brother William bought Santa Catalina Island to develop as a summer resort—berthed his own 47-foot schooner, *La Paloma,* at the club before moving it to the Catalina Yacht Club, formed in 1892. The *La Paloma* in 1893 outraced a San Diego boat to win honors as the fastest sailing vessel on the West Coast. In addition, the South Coast Yacht Club, organized at Terminal Island in 1901, soon had 40 boats in its docks. In recent decades, Marina del Rey has been the regional center of yachting. Since 1956 the Transpacific Yacht Club has sponsored a race from Point Fermin, north of Los Angeles Harbor, to Honolulu that covers 2,225 nautical miles in 12 to 14 days.

YAKUZA, Japanese crime syndicates involved in drugs, prostitution, gambling, loan sharking, and extortion. Their main California center of operations in the 1920s and 1930s was the third floor of the Tokyo Club on Jackson Street and Central Avenue, in Los Angeles's Little Tokyo. This club alone brought in about $1 million annually from blackjack, poker, dice, and other games. The statewide syndicates were led by the mysterious figure Hideo Yamatoda, who fled Los Angeles when reform mayor Fletcher Bowron was elected in 1937. Yamatoda was tried on gambling charges in absentia. He may have worked for U.S. naval intelligence at the outbreak of World War II.

YAMASHIRO RESTAURANT, whose name means "castle on the hill" in Japanese, was built on N. Sycamore Avenue, Hollywood, in 1914 by Asian craftsmen working for the Bernheimer brothers, wealthy importers of Oriental antiques. It served as a clubhouse for the "in" Hollywood crowd during the heyday of the film industry, and remains popular with tourists and local diners.

YANGNA, Tongva (Gabrieleño) Indian village in Los Angeles, one of scores of native settlements encountered by Captain Portolá in 1769. Its specific location is unknown, but it probably stood in Elysian Park or near the downtown Plaza. The village existed until sometime between 1828 and about 1836, when the inhabitants were moved to a spot near the present-day corner of Commercial and Alameda Streets. In 1845 they were again relocated to land above the river. This site, called *pueblito,* was razed in 1847. By the 1850s the Native Americans were either dying of venereal disease or periodically being arrested for drunkenness, vagrancy, or disorderly conduct and auctioned off for forced labor on the ranchos.

YAROSLAVSKY, ZEV (1948–), elected official. Born in Los Angeles, he grew up in Boyle Heights and studied history and economics at UCLA. Starting with a political base in the Fairfax area Jewish community, Yaroslavsky was elected to the city council in 1975, representing the Westside–San Fernando Valley 5th District. He developed special expertise in budgetary matters, and for some years was considered a potential mayoral candidate. In 1994 Yaroslavsky won election to the County Board of Supervisors to fill the seat of the retiring Edmund Edelman.

YMCA OF METROPOLITAN LOS ANGELES, founded in 1882, is the city's oldest organization serving youth, but is open to everyone. The stated goal of the Young Men's Christian Association is to improve "the spiritual, social, mental, and physical life of youth and adults in accordance with the spirit and teachings of Jesus." The Los Angeles "Y" is affiliated with the World Alliance of YMCAs, which was founded by 12 young men in England in 1844 and now has 15 million members worldwide. In Los Angeles 36,000 contributors give $7 million to the local YMCA annually.

YORTY, SAM[UEL WILLIAM] (1909–), Nebraskan who served as mayor of Los Angeles from 1961 to 1973. Yorty came to Los Angeles in 1927, where he studied law and joined the bar. First entering politics in the 1930s, he was pressed to run for mayor in 1937 until Fletcher Bowron entered the race. By the time he retired from politics four decades later he had run for practically every available office, including president of the United States.

Yorty prided himself on being a political maverick. Initially a left-winger, he moved steadily to the right and became a staunch supporter of the House Un-American Activities Committee—though throughout his time in public service he remained a registered Democrat. His right-wing populism meshed with the political climate of the time. After a stint in the state assembly he was elected to Congress, serving from 1951 to 1955. He backed Republican Richard Nixon for president in 1960 rather than John F. Kennedy, stirring the wrath of Kennedy-Johnson Democrats for the next eight years. He became mayor in 1961, defeating the incumbent, Norris Poulson. In 1969 he defeated challenger Tom Bradley, employing tactics that some considered racist. Bradley defeated Yorty in 1973.

"Mayor Sam" was at one point called "traveling Sam" because he had been out of town 372 days over a three-and-a-half-year period. While in office he initiated the Cultural Heritage Board, reduced city property taxes, and allowed householders to combine their trash and metal garbage rather than keeping them separate, a popular move at the time. He backed the building of the freeways, the Los Angeles Zoo, and the Music Center. He also fostered senior citizens programs.

During his time in the mayor's office Yorty remained at odds with the Kennedy and Johnson administrations. He rejected War on Poverty funds in the 1960s, asserting that "handouts" to the poor would give them false hopes and threaten the middle class with bankruptcy. He worked closely with Police Chief William Parker, and blamed the 1965 Watts riots on civil rights leader Martin Luther King Jr. and others whom he perceived as being leftists.

YOUNG, CHARLES (1931–), UCLA chancellor. Young was born in San Bernardino, served in the Korean War, graduated from UC Riverside in 1955, and earned a Ph.D. in political science in 1960. A protégé of University of California president Clark Kerr, Young became chancellor in 1968 and presided over the campus during a period of rapid expansion and growing academic distinction. During his term UCLA became a $1.5 billion operation and the tenth largest employer in Southern California.

YWCA OF LOS ANGELES, social service agency for women. The Young Women's Christian Association was founded in Great Britain, transplanted to New York City in 1858, and established

Courtyard, YWCA Building, Los Angeles, 1909. Pitt Collection.

in Los Angeles as an offshoot of the San Francisco branch in 1898. It is devoted to the physical, social, spiritual, and educational well-being of young women. The "Y" operated a downtown boarding house in 1905, and in 1916 opened the Hollywood Studio Club, a residence for women attempting to break into the film industry. Today the YWCA provides shelter and counseling services for transient and needy women, operates child care centers, sponsors camping trips, and conducts classes and training programs that encourage women to achieve leadership roles.

ZAMORANO CLUB, society of book lovers. Arthur M. Ellis and William Webb Clary formed the association at the University Club, on 25 January 1928, having been inspired by Washington Irving Way, a Chicago bookman who arrived in 1904. Other founding members were Henry Wagner, Robert Cowan, J. Gregg Layne, Carl Wheat, Don Hill, W. W. Robinson, and Homer Crotty. They installed the club in the Bradbury Building, then moved to the Alexandria Hotel a year later. Named for Agustín Juan Vicente Zamorano (1798–1842), secretary to Mexican governor José M. Echeandía (1825) and the first printer of California, the Zamorano Club has long attracted sellers, designers, printers, and collectors of books. In 1945 it issued *The Zamorano 80: A Selection of Distinguished California Books,* and it still publishes *Hoja Volante,* a highly respected quarterly newsletter.

ZANJA, water ditch. Introduced by Spanish *pobladores* in 1781, the *zanja* technology was expanded into a network and used for irrigation and domestic needs even in the early Yankee period. Water was diverted from the riverbed by a brush weir *(toma)* into a main channel, called the mother ditch *(zanja madre)*. It was then allowed to spread at ground level into other branch channels. The water supply was reasonably steady but easily contaminated. When William Mulholland, the legendary water developer, first came to Los Angeles in the 1870s he had a job tending *zanja* ditches. On Olvera Street the path of the original mother ditch is marked by bricks.

ZANUCK, DARRYL F. (1902–1979), Hollywood producer. The Nebraskan began his career in the 1920s writing for the *Rin Tin Tin* films, and by 1931 he had advanced to head of production for Warner Brothers. In 1933 he cofounded 20th Century Pictures. After the studio merged with Fox Film Corporation two years later, he served as vice president in charge of production for 20th Century–Fox, a position he held until 1956, when he left to become an independent producer. Zanuck returned to 20th Century–Fox in 1962 as studio president. He was involved in various capacities with such notable films as *The Grapes of Wrath* (1940), *How Green Was My Valley* (1942), *All About Eve* (1950), *Viva Zapata* (1952), and *The Longest Day* (1962).

ZAPATA, CARMEN (1927–), Cuban American actress-director who cofounded and heads the Bilin-

Carmen Zapata. Courtesy Bilingual Foundation of the Arts.

gual Foundation for the Arts, promoting theatrical performances for Latino and Anglo audiences.

ZAPPA, FRANK (1940–1993), rock musician and social satirist. Raised near Lancaster, in 1964 he organized the rock band Mothers of Invention. His album *Freak Out* (1966) is one of the landmarks of rock music. "Valley Girl," a record he made in the 1980s with his daughter, Moon Unit, parodied the slang of teenagers in the San Fernando Valley. The song became so popular that "Valley speak" was soon adopted by young people across the country.

ZEITLIN, JACOB ("JAKE") ISRAEL (1902–1987), Los Angeles book dealer and intellectual leader. Zeitlin arrived from Texas in 1925, living in poverty with his wife, Edith. He learned the book trade while working in Bullock's Department Store and in 1927 opened a tiny bookshop on Hope Street, with the help of his friend Lloyd Wright. In 1929 Wright designed a more elaborate shop, also on Hope Street, called "At the Sign of the Grasshopper." It immediately became a meeting place for many of the city's intellectuals. Zeitlin and his friends published *Opinion,* a highbrow magazine with a brief but influential life. From 1929 to 1933 he ran the one-man publishing operation Primavera Press, which issued California classics. He was assisted in this enterprise by his friends Carey McWilliams, Phil Townsend Hanna, Lawrence Clark Powell, and Ward Ritchie, who designed the books.

Zeitlin left the downtown area in 1948 and moved his shop into a large red barn on La Cienega Boulevard, selling rare books, prints, and paintings, and continuing to provide an intellectual center. He presented art exhibits in his shop featuring the works of artists who were to become well known in the 1930s. Lawrence Clark Powell, who worked for him and became a good friend, once said of Zeitlin that he was "born old and wise."

ZELZAH. *See* Northridge

ZONING. The idea of designating urban property areas for specific uses was pioneered in Los Angeles between 1910 and 1930. Existing land uses were chaotic, encouraged wild speculation, and undermined real estate values. Developers demanded zoning to stabilize values, but also feared it might limit appreciation. Reformers generally supported zoning; in their view, the system allowed for modifications through negotiations with developers as well as by council variances.

Pressure by developers, especially in the 1920s, created a city that was vastly over-zoned for apartment, commercial, and industrial uses. Single-family dwellings often received short shrift. Of the parcels actually zoned in 1926, 10 percent were for

---

Earthquakes occur fairly frequently, usually in August.
—Ludwig Salvator, Austrian archduke, 1878

---

single-family homes, 59 percent for residential income (apartments), 13 percent for commerce, and 18 percent for industry. A comprehensive ordinance was established in 1925. It rigidly separated industry from residential areas, with most new factories limited to the downtown area east of Alameda Street.

A second comprehensive law, the work of architect and public housing advocate Robert E. Alexander, was adopted in 1945. It stipulated a series of "garden cities" separated by greenbelts, thus sparing farms and orchards and retaining the existing, more rural way of life in the San Fernando Valley. Developers subverted the law by petitioning for zoning variances. By 1960 they had killed the plan altogether.

Zoning has been found by the California Supreme Court to be a legitimate use of police powers. Since 1978 state law has required zoning ordinances to be consistent with each city's mandated General Plan. In the absence of such consistency, private citizens or developers may bring suit against the city council.

In the present day, zoning is simply a quagmire. City planners complain of wasting valuable time on zoning considerations that should be spent working to preserve open spaces and other amenities. The zoning process, enforced by the Department of Building and Safety, tends to favor developers of giant enterprises. No matter how large a project, or how devastating the environmental impact, a project may proceed as long as it meets certain minimum requirements: the city has no power to stop the process. Many local residents decry their lack of power in important local affairs. The Westside Pavilion in West Los Angeles and the Fujita Building in Encino are two projects that advanced over the objections of local homeowners. As a consequence, slow-growth advocates have proposed that projects over 50,000 square feet in area be considered at public hearings, and that they be subjected to greater zoning restrictions than smaller projects.

ZOO, LOS ANGELES. *See* Los Angeles Zoo

ZOOT SUIT RIOTS, racial confrontations that hit Los Angeles from 3 June to 13 June 1943. The stage had been set for violence by 1942's sensational Sleepy Lagoon murder case, a miscarriage of justice in which nine Mexican American youths were tried for murder and convicted. Although the decisions were later overturned, the case created an atmosphere of racist stereotyping and fear.

In the spring of 1943, American servicemen attacked youthful Mexican—and, to a lesser extent, African American—civilians, particularly males wearing the flamboyant "zoot suit" or "drape shape." These outfits consisted of narrow-cuffed pants pleated at the waist, long wide-shouldered jackets, knee-length key chains, and flat-brimmed hats atop pompadour hairdos. They were worn by Mexican youths—commonly referred to as *pachucos*—as well as by African American and Anglo youngsters, mostly as a show of teenage independence. The first confrontations seemed little

more than harmless barroom scuffles, but on 3 June 1943 the encounters erupted into large-scale rioting. The GIs, mostly navy recruits stationed at a Chavez Ravine radar base, were incited by lurid street rumors and baseless press accounts of Mexicans attacking Anglo women. Charging that the Mexicans were avoiding military service, the young sailors hired taxicabs and cruised downtown to punish the "guilty." They seized their victims from streetcars, movie theaters, and street corners, beat them, stripped them of their clothes, and left them lying on the ground. The police and sheriffs, rather than arresting the perpetrators, arrested the victims. The most serious injury involved an African American who was blinded. While few other serious or permanent injuries occurred and property damage was slight, the ugly racial incidents were widely reported (the Mexican government even lodged a formal protest in Washington, D.C.) and caused long-lasting hostility and resentment.

The court proceedings following the zoot suit violence were sporadic, and the pattern of convictions random, with minimal sentences issued. The newspapers' sensationalist coverage and blatant use of stereotypes only helped foment the racial friction. In fact—and in direct contradiction to the accusations—Mexican Americans were awarded more Congressional Medals of Honor than any

Mexican American youths rounded up in zoot suit riots, June 1943. Courtesy Dept. of Special Collections, University Research Library, UCLA.

other minority group during World War II, with the exception of Japanese Americans.

ZORRO, DON DIEGO DE VEGA, fictional Spanish Californian masked hero loosely patterned on Baroness Orczy's hero in *The Scarlet Pimpernel* (1905). Zorro first appeared in screenwriter Johnston McCulley's short story "The Curse of Capistrano" (1919) and, later that same year, as the hero of a comic strip. In 1920 he reappeared in McCulley's novel *The Mark of Zorro*. The story bears no resemblance to history. Zorro, a Californio aristocrat who was more Old Spain than New World, dedicated himself to fighting corruption in the form of evil officials. The highly romanticized tale of early California depicts the rancheros as upperclass Spaniards and the workers as lowly Mexicans. Two *Mark of Zorro* films were made, the first starring Douglas Fairbanks in 1920, the second with Tyrone Power, from the 1940s.

ZUKOR, ADOLPH (1873–1976), Hungarian-born film mogul. Zukor came to this country at age 15, became partners in a penny arcade with Marcus Loew, eventually developed a chain of theaters, and, in 1912, established a studio to supply films for his movie houses; this he called Famous Players Film Corporation, which eventually became Paramount Pictures. Among his associates and stars were Mary Pickford, Rudolph Valentino, John Barrymore, Cecil B. De Mille, and Jesse Lasky. *The Public Is Never Wrong* (1945) is his autobiography. In 1948 Zukor received a special Academy Award for his service to the film industry.

ZUMA COUNTY BEACH, Malibu's largest beach. With over 100 acres of white sand, it attracts sunbathers, joggers, swimmers, surfers, scuba divers, and anglers. The grunion run at high tide in spring and summer. Private properties front the beach.

APPENDIX A: CHRONOLOGY

ca. 10,000 B.C.	Shoshonean Indians occupy the Los Angeles Basin.
1542	Juan Cabrillo nears Santa Catalina Island, enters San Pedro Bay, and claims land for king of Spain.
1602	Explorer Sebastian Vizcaíno names some Southern California coastal points.
1769	Expedition led by Capt. Gaspar de Portolá passes through Los Angeles; Fr. Juan Crespi reports experiencing earthquakes and describes tar pits.
1771	Fr. Junípero Serra founds Mission San Gabriel.
1776	Mission San Gabriel moved to its present location.
1781	Gov. Felipe de Neve visits site of Los Angeles; colonists leave Mexico for Los Angeles and arrive at Mission San Gabriel; Neve issues proclamation to found El Pueblo de la Reina de los Angeles (26 Aug.); Neve and 11 families—all together, 44 men, women, and children—found Los Angeles (ca. 4 Sept.).
1784	First ranchos granted in Los Angeles area; chapel built near corner of today's Buena Vista St. and Bellevue Ave.
1786	Governor Neve orders survey of *pueblo* land, grants house lot, field, and branding iron to each of original settlers. José Vanegas appointed first *alcalde* (mayor) of *pueblo*.
1790	Population of Los Angeles is 139.
1793	Ranchero Francisco Reyes serves as first black *alcalde*.
1797	Drought curtails cultivation; Fr. Serra founds Mission San Fernando Rey de España.
1800	Population of Los Angeles is 315.
1804	José Bartolome Tapia receives 22 miles of coastal property called Rancho Topanga Malibu Sequit; Alta (Upper) and Baja (Lower) California are separated; Mission San Gabriel plants first orange groves.
1805	First American trading vessel, the *Lelia Byrd* (Joseph Shaler, capt.), arrives at San Pedro and initiates hide-and-tallow trade.
1810	In the town of Dolores, Mexico, Fr. Miguel Hidalgo y Costilla urges the independence of Mexico from Spain; population of Los Angeles is 354.
1812	First elected *ayuntamiento* (common council) established by Spanish decree; severe earthquake damages San Gabriel and San Fernando missions.
1814	Plaza Church cornerstone laid, but construction is delayed.
1815	First foreigner, José Antonio Rocha of Portugal, arrives in Los Angeles; a Russian trader is imprisoned in the *pueblo;* river overflows its banks, invades townsite, and causes much destruction.
1817	Maximo Piña, a retired soldier, establishes the *pueblo's* first school, which closes the next year.
1818	Arrival of first Americans, Thomas Fisher, an African American, and Joseph Chapman, an Anglo; temporary resumption of Plaza Church construction; Avila adobe built; *pueblo* plaza moved to higher ground.

1821	Spanish rule in California gives way to Mexican rule; Plaza Church construction resumes.
1822	News arrives of Mexican Revolution and end of Spanish rule. Plaza Church completed and dedicated.
1825	Flood changes course of Los Angeles River, which now empties into San Pedro Bay.
1826	Town council resolves to eliminate gambling, prostitution, and blasphemy; trapper Jedediah Smith arrives at Mission San Gabriel; San Pedro designated as a port; smuggling occurs at Santa Catalina Island.
1827	Arrival of merchant John Temple, who opens first general store in the *pueblo.*
1828	Hollander Juan Domingo (originally John Groningen) buys the land occupied by Indian village of Yangna and expels the natives.
1829	Arrival of Abel Stearns, merchant and eventually the biggest landowner in Southern California.
1830	Beginning of a movement to secularize the missions; population of Los Angeles is 770.
1831	Provincial rebellion against Gov. Manuel Victoria results in local fighting; Franciscans build a boat to hunt for otter, and launch it in San Pedro.
1832	Town council passes judicial reforms, outlaws the carrying of arms within town limits.
1833	Mexican congress officially secularizes the missions, places them under civil rule.
1834	Beginning of mission secularization.
1835	Mexican congress elevates the *pueblo* to the status of a *ciudad* (city); the region's population, including Indians, is the largest in California; the brig *Pilgrim* anchors off San Pedro with Richard Henry Dana aboard.
1836	Town initiates Indian chain gang for forced labor; a vigilance committee is formed; John March, a physician, settles in the town; region's population is 1,250.
1838	Ignacio Coronel establishes a school that lasts six years.
1839	Rapid mission secularization at San Gabriel fosters growth in area; Vicente Lugo builds first two-story house on the Plaza; Abel Stearns arraigned for smuggling at San Pedro; population of Los Angeles rises to 1,100.
1841	Benjamin D. Wilson and Francis Temple arrive; William Wolfskill plants first commercial orange groves.
1842	Gov. Manuel Micheltorena arrives in Los Angeles, expels Yankees, stays for one month; gold discovered at Placerita Canyon near Saugus.
1843	U.S. Comm. Thomas Ap Catesby Jones is feted in Los Angeles.
1844	Gov. Micheltorena orders establishment of a school.
1845	Local assembly ousts Micheltorena, establishes Pío Pico as governor of California.
1846	Comm. John Sloat proclaims California a U.S. possession; Comm. Robert Stockton lands at San Pedro; Lt. Archibald Gillespie's force of 50 marines occupies Los Angeles, but is later expelled by Capts. José María Flores, José Antonio Carrillo, and Gen. Andrés Pico; area's population is about 5,000.
1847	Los Angeles reoccupied by the Americans under Gen. Stephen Watts Kearny and Comm. Stockton (10 Jan.); Gen. Andrés Pico, Mexican commander in California, capitulates to Capt. John C. Frémont at Cahuenga (13 Jan.).
1848	Treaty of Guadalupe Hidalgo cedes California to the United States (2 Feb.), and province comes officially under military rule; Stephen C. Foster becomes *alcalde;* first meeting of town council under American rule.
1849	Los Angeles ceases to be a U.S. military station; new *ayuntamiento* established, with José del Carmen Lugo as *alcalde* and *presidente;* state constitutional convention in Monterey; Lt. Edward O. C. Ord draws first official city map; city is 28 square miles.
1850	Los Angeles County established, consisting of 4,340 square miles and expanding in one year to 34,520 square miles between San Diego and Santa Barbara; first overland

freight wagon arrives; first county election, with 377 votes cast; legislature incorporates Los Angeles (4 Apr.); California admitted to the Union (9 Sept.); first mayor, Alpheus P. Hodges, and common council are elected; first meeting of *ayuntamiento;* first city hall built; Bella Union Hotel is built; first Methodist service held in Los Angeles; first U.S. census counts 1,610 inhabitants in the city of Los Angeles, including two Chinese men; county population is 3,530.

1851   U.S. land commission sits in Los Angeles to decide the fate of southern rancho titles; first newspaper, the *Star,* begins publication; town council organizes a city police force; first Masonic meeting in Los Angeles; arrival of slave Biddy Mason.

1852   Heavy flood destroys homes, farms, orchards, and water works; Phineas Banning and rancher D. W. Alexander form a stage and freight business between San Pedro and Los Angeles; first election of county supervisors; first school tax and school board established; Peter Biggs, ex-slave, establishes first barbershop; first bricks manufactured.

1853   Vigilante group called El Monte or Los Angeles Rangers formed; forerunner of Board of Education created, called School Trustees; first county building, a jail, constructed; Harris Newmark arrives in Los Angeles.

1854   City establishes an overseer of water, appoints first school superintendent; arrival of Joseph Newmark, who officiates over the first regular Jewish services; new Chinese immigrants are brought to serve as laborers and servants.

1855   Stephen C. Foster resigns as mayor to lead a lynching; first public school building built at Spring and 2nd Streets.

1856   Search undertaken for Mexican bandit Juan Flores; ice cream introduced to Los Angeles.

1857   Powerful earthquake near Fort Tejón; Juan Flores hanged; Wells, Fargo & Co. establishes express office in Los Angeles; Sheriff Barton killed, vigilantes detain 52 Mexicans as guerrilla rebels, execute 11.

1858   Butterfield stage line links Los Angeles to St. Louis and San Francisco; Abel Stearns and Phineas Banning develop Wilmington harbor; Sisters of Charity open a hospital.

1859   First organized charity, Ladies Sewing Society, established; 500,000 gallons of wine produced in county; Damien Marchessault is mayor; oil seeps noted on Capt. Henry Hancock's property.

1860   First telegraph line between San Francisco and Los Angeles; U.S. census counts 4,385 in Los Angeles; county population is 11,333.

1861   Union vs. Confederate demonstrations erupt as Civil War begins; telegraph connects Los Angeles and San Pedro; month-long rain beginning Christmas Eve causes devastating floods, dropping an estimated 50 inches of rain in the region.

1862   Floods destroy city water works; drought starts that spells the end of the cattle industry and ranchero class; construction begins on Drum Barracks in San Pedro.

1863   Smallpox epidemic kills many Gabrieleño Indians; lynch mob hangs Manuel Cerradel as he is en route to San Quentin to serve a 10-year term.

1864   Many bank foreclosures on ranch lands; severe drought year.

1865   Founding of St. Vincent's College (now Loyola-Marymount University), the first institution of higher learning in Southern California; typhoid epidemic; José Mascarel elected mayor.

1866   Kern County created from a portion of Los Angeles County; Cristóbal Aguilar elected mayor; Drum Barracks completed.

1867   Prudent Beaudry buys Bunker Hill for $51 and develops it for affluent Angelenos; winter floods again destroy water works.

1868   Los Angeles water system installed, using iron pipes; the only towns in the county are San Gabriel, Los Angeles, Wilmington, El Monte, and Anaheim.

1869	First bicycle in Los Angeles; Los Angeles–San Pedro Railway built; Secretary of State William H. Seward visits Los Angeles.
1870s	Land boom from completion of railroad results in development of Riverside, Pasadena, Pomona, and Long Beach.
1870	A police commission is created by ordinance; Pico House opens; opening of Merced Theatre; population of the city reaches 5,728, including 172 Chinese; county population is 15,309.
1871	Massacre of 19 Chinese by a vigilante mob brings nationwide notoriety to Los Angeles; public animal pound and volunteer fire department are created; U.S. starts improvements on Wilmington harbor; *Evening Express* begins publication.
1872	Board of public works and superintendent of streets and highways are established.
1873	*Los Angeles Herald* (daily) and *Los Angeles Mirror* (weekly) begin publication; first trolley line in Los Angeles; 100,000 eucalyptus trees imported from Australia.
1874	*Bandido* Tiburcio Vásquez captured and hanged the following year.
1875	Pasadena founded; printers (typographers) form first labor union in Los Angeles; first train of the Los Angeles and Independence Railroad run to Santa Monica wharf.
1876	Southern Pacific Railroad (SP) completes connection between Los Angeles and San Francisco at Soledad Canyon; Cathedral of St. Vibiana completed.
1877	William Mulholland arrives in Los Angeles; city's first weather bureau established.
1878	Odd Fellows hall opens on Spring Street; first local oranges shipped to eastern markets.
1879	Founding of first French-language weekly, *L'Union nouvelle.*
1880	University of Southern California founded; U.S. census counts 11,183 in Los Angeles; county population is 33,381.
1881	Completion of SP link with East Coast; city centennial celebration; completion of State Normal School.
1882	First telephone introduced in Los Angeles; Harrison Gray Otis buys *Los Angeles Times;* downtown lit by electric lights.
1883	J. W. Robinson establishes a dry goods store at Spring and Temple; Historical Society of Southern California founded.
1884	Los Angeles has six labor unions; *Ramona* is published.
1885	Santa Fe Railroad completes a second rail line from the East into Los Angeles, initiating the Boom of the Eighties; city pays fire fighters a salary for the first time; Wilshire Boulevard dedicated.
1886	Raymond Hotel in Pasadena opens.
1887	Peak year of the boom; SP brings 120,000 visitors to Los Angeles; Harvey Wilcox, Kansas prohibitionist, lays out town of Hollywood; first electric streetcars; Orange County carved from portion of Los Angeles County.
1888	Boom of the Eighties collapses.
1889	New City Hall completed on Broadway; "Free Harbor Contest" starts.
1890	Council of Labor formed; printers strike against the *Times;* Los Angeles city population is 50,395; county population is 101,454.
1891	Frederick H. Rindge buys Rancho Topanga Malibu Sequit; Los Angeles has 78 miles of paved streets.
1892	Edward Doheny strikes oil in downtown Los Angeles, sparking major oil boom.
1893	Nationwide depression; Los Angeles labor movement endorses Chinese exclusion; Bradbury Building opens; Southern California Fruit Growers organized; inauguration of Mt. Lowe Railway.
1894	Ebell Club founded; Mt. Lowe observatory built; first Fiesta de Los Angeles; Charles F. Lummis founds Landmarks Club.
1895	Electric car line from Los Angeles to Pasadena constructed.

1896	Coin-operated motion picture machines; Merchants and Manufacturers Associations merge; Griffith J. Griffith donates 3,500 acres to Los Angeles to form nation's biggest urban park.
1897	Long Beach incorporated; S. D. Sturgis builds first automobile in Los Angeles, at cost of $30,000.
1898	Homer Laughlin Building is city's first steel structure.
1899	"Free Harbor Jubilee" celebrates start of breakwater construction.
1900	Start of mail service to Santa Catalina Island via carrier pigeon; Automobile Club of Southern California founded; Los Angeles city population is 102,479; county population is 170,298.
1901	Pacific Electric Railway (PE) incorporated; Angels Flight railway begins operating.
1902	First wireless messages exchanged between mainland and Catalina Island; city board of water commissioners appointed as city takes over water system; Henry E. Huntington moves to Los Angeles.
1903	Council passes antipicketing ordinance; Hearst starts publication of *Los Angeles Examiner;* Los Angeles adopts initiative, referendum, and recall.
1903–1904	Growth of inflexible anti-unionism among management; playground commission established.
1904	Abbot Kinney founds Venice of America.
1905	A third major railroad, the Los Angeles, San Pedro, and Salt Lake (now the Union Pacific), comes to Los Angeles; Pleistocene fossils discovered in La Brea tar pits; town of Vernon incorporated.
1906	Shoestring is annexed to Los Angeles; Beverly Hills founded.
1907	Surfing introduced to California at Redondo Beach; Selig Polyscope Co. films part of *The Count of Monte Cristo* in Los Angeles; Santa Monica adopts a charter; voters approve bond to build Los Angeles Aqueduct.
1907–1927	Peak period for construction of California bungalows in Los Angeles.
1908	First traffic regulations established; Great White Fleet visits San Pedro; Good Government League begins drive to eliminate partisan voting in Los Angeles city elections; *The Power of the Sultan* is first movie shot entirely in Los Angeles.
1909	Wilmington and San Pedro are annexed to Los Angeles; a charter amendment provides for borough form of government in Los Angeles (rescinded 1921); Mayor Arthur Harper, accused of corruption, steps down during recall movement; George Alexander elected; construction begins on Los Angeles Aqueduct.
1910	General strike in Los Angeles; incorporation of Watts; first national air meet held at Dominguez Ranch; bombing of the *Los Angeles Times* Building; Hollywood consolidated with Los Angeles; D. W. Griffith and Mary Pickford arrive in Los Angeles; Los Angeles city population is 310,198; county is 504,131.
1911	Manhattan Beach closes its strand to African Americans; Job Harriman receives plurality in primary election for mayor; confession of McNamara brothers in *Times* bombing; defeat of Harriman and victory of George Alexander; Jacob Riis lectures in Los Angeles.
1912	Filmmaker Mack Sennett creates Keystone Kops; presidential nominee Theodore Roosevelt speaks at Shrine Auditorium; Earle Anthony opens first gasoline service station in Los Angeles; Arroyo Seco is annexed to Los Angeles.
1913	Completion of Los Angeles Aqueduct bringing water from Owens Valley; Los Angeles County Museum of Natural History opens.
1914	Los Angeles builds new port facilities at San Pedro to benefit from the completion of Panama Canal; Southwest Museum opened.
1915	The county, with 750,000 people, leads nation with 55,000 privately owned cars; founding of Universal Studios; D.W. Griffith produces *Birth of a Nation;* 168 square

	miles of the San Fernando Valley annexed to Los Angeles; Los Angeles city population is 435,000.
1916	Football game becomes part of Pasadena Tournament of Roses celebration.
1917	City electric power company installs first pole in the city in direct competition with private power utility.
1918	Ship hulls are built for wartime Emergency Fleet Corp.; local army regiments of the American Expeditionary Force ship out for France; tunnel opens on 2nd St. beneath Bunker Hill.
1919	Santa Fe Springs oil field developed; State Normal School in Los Angeles is upgraded to University of California, Southern Branch; first concert of Los Angeles Philharmonic; William Wrigley Jr. purchases Santa Catalina Island and begins to develop it as a tourist attraction.
1920	Population of Southern California surpasses that of Northern California; first performance of *Pilgrimage Play;* Los Angeles city population is 576,673; county population is 936,455.
1920–1940	Film industry employs from 20,000 to 40,000.
1921	Signal Hill oil strike.
1922	Wilshire Blvd.'s Miracle Mile developed; Los Angeles becomes home of the Pacific Fleet; Rose Bowl constructed; first Easter sunrise service at Hollywood Bowl; KFI, KNX, and KHJ are first Los Angeles radio stations.
1923	Completion of Los Angeles Memorial Coliseum; purchase by Water and Power Commission of additional land in Owens Valley touches off new water war; Aimee Semple McPherson dedicates Angelus Temple; Hollywoodland sign erected; longshoremen's strike; Los Angeles City is enlarged by 19,031 acres through 12 annexations.
1924	City planning department approves 40 new subdivisions a week; Mulholland Highway opens; city has 43,000 real estate agents; Douglas airplanes begin around-the-world trip from Santa Monica airport.
1925	New city charter takes effect; city population reaches 896,000.
1926	Los Angeles annexes Watts; Los Angeles Public Library opens new Central Library; Santa Monica purchases Clover Field for municipal airport.
1927	City annexes Cienega, Annandale, and Fairfax; Grauman's Chinese Theatre opens; Los Angeles becomes the nation's second largest rubber manufacturing center.
1928	St. Francis Dam collapses, killing 400 people; new City Hall is dedicated; Henry E. Huntington Library opens to the public; first Mickey Mouse cartoon.
1929	County Planning Commission issues first comprehensive report on highways; Bullock's opens first branch department store; Pacific Coast (Roosevelt) Highway opens as far as Malibu; UCLA moves to new Westwood campus; San Pedro becomes leading U.S. harbor.
1930	Olvera Street dedicated as historic site; Los Angeles is fifth largest city in the nation, but leads in failed businesses; Mines Field dedicated as city airport; Los Angeles city population is 1,238,048, county population, 2,208,492.
1931	Start of Boulder Dam project; city introduces traffic lights; first experimental television station in Los Angeles; first Clifton Cafeteria; county begins repatriating 12,600 Mexicans; *Los Angeles Evening Herald-Express* formed through merger.
1932	Two inches of snow blanket Los Angeles (15 Jan.); Mayor John C. Porter survives recall election; Tenth Olympiad Summer Games are held at the newly enlarged Coliseum; Tujunga annexed.
1933	Long Beach earthquake (6.3) kills 100 people, causing damages of $60 million; Los Angeles County General Hospital opens; Townsend old-age pension plan movement launched.

1934	Los Angeles's first drive-in movie theater opens; Upton Sinclair loses gubernatorial bid; International Longshoremen's and Warehousemen's Union emerges as powerful labor group.
1935	Griffith Park planetarium dedicated; recovery from Great Depression begins; city population is 1,311,000.
1936	"Bum blockade"; 50 labor strikes involving 10,000 workers; electrical power from Boulder Dam arrives; rapid growth of aircraft production; Douglas produces the first DC-3.
1937	Mayor Frank Shaw is reelected, but is soon investigated for corruption; city council passes new antipicketing ordinance; half of Los Angeles citrus crops ruined by frost.
1938	Mayor Shaw is recalled and Fletcher Bowron elected in special election; 6,000 unemployed people sell 2 million apples; 5-day, 31-inch rain starting Feb. 28 kills 100 people, causes $65 million in property damage; Bowron abolishes the LAPD "Red Squad"; labor union membership rises to 150,000 in county; new Federal Building opens.
1939	Union Station opens with 3-day celebration; total crop production in county reaches $76 million; county is fourth in manufacture of women's apparel and furniture, and second in tires, in the United States; 92 film companies spend $140 million on movie production.
1940	County labor force is 1.2 million; 6-mile Arroyo Seco Parkway (Pasadena Freeway) is first freeway in the West; Los Angeles Harbor is the nation's largest commercial fishing port; city population reaches 1,504,277, county population, 2,785,643.
1941	Colorado River Aqueduct delivers water to Los Angeles; completion of Boulder Dam; backlog of aircraft orders in Los Angeles reaches $1.5 billion; Japan bombs Pearl Harbor (7 Dec.); the city and county of Los Angeles adopt a revised plan for a new civic center.
1942	Pres. Roosevelt issues executive order incarcerating the Japanese; Mexican *braceros* brought in to pick crops in absence of Japanese; the "Battle of Los Angeles" (26 Feb.) war scare; Sleepy Lagoon case.
1943	Zoot suit riots; first officially recognized smog attack.
1944	Los Angeles County labor force is 1.5 million; San Bernardino Freeway opens.
1945	First Japanese released from detention camps; end of World War II; Fletcher Bowron reelected mayor; Los Angeles city population is 1,741,000.
1946	First city comprehensive zoning ordinance; Roger Wagner Chorale founded; Cleveland Rams move to Los Angeles; Richard Nixon defeats Jerry Voorhis for Congress; KTLA is Los Angeles's first licensed commercial television channel.
1947	Hollywood Ten refuse to reveal political affiliations before Congress; dedication of Los Angeles State and County Arboretum; mobster "Bugsy" Siegel gunned down; Black Dahlia murder case; CSU Los Angeles opens with 136 students.
1948	Employment in county exceeds wartime levels; Los Angeles auto manufacturers assemble 650,000 cars; Supreme Court outlaws restrictive covenants; Los Angeles International Airport expands from 860 to 2,518 acres; UCLA begins $38 million expansion program; Community Redevelopment Agency established to repair blighted areas; Hollywood Freeway completed.
1949	Chavez Ravine public housing controversy; UCLA loyalty oath; 43,000 orchard acres give way to suburban development (1949–1959); Ed Roybal elected to city council, first Mexican American to serve since 1881; CSU Long Beach opens.
1950	Construction of four new public buildings at Civic Center begins; city population reaches 1,970,358, county population, 4,151,687.
1951	State establishes Metropolitan Transit Authority; official start of the *bracero* labor program; Lloyd Wright's Wayfarer's Chapel completed; Rams win first NFL championship in Los Angeles; Franklin P. Murphy named chancellor of UCLA.

1952   Richard Nixon elected vice president; Norris Poulson defeats Bowron for mayor; Kenneth Hahn elected as youngest county supervisor; establishment of U.S. Air Force Plant 42 at Palmdale.

1953   California Democratic Council formed; El Pueblo de los Angeles State Monument dedicated; driest year on record, with only 4.08 inches of rainfall; Norris Poulson succeeds Fletcher Bowron as Los Angeles mayor.

1954   City experiences worst smog attack to date (13 Oct.); Simon Rodia finishes Watts Towers; county acquires Descanso Gardens property.

1955   Los Angeles County is third most important agricultural county in United States; integration of city fire department begins on a token basis; Los Angeles city population is 2,190,000.

1956   City council repeals 140-foot building height limit; Los Angeles County Federation of Labor (AFL-CIO) established; founding of CSU Northridge.

1957   San Francisco and Los Angeles stock exchanges are consolidated as Pacific Coast Stock Exchange; home incinerators banned in Los Angeles; Hollywood Stars baseball club disbanded.

1958   Brooklyn Dodgers become Los Angeles Dodgers; Ash Grove night club opens; Harbor–UCLA Medical Center merger; Synanon founded; county registers more Democrats than Republicans for first time.

1959   Soviet Premier Nikita Khrushchev visits Los Angeles; term "aerospace" enters vocabulary; Los Angeles Memorial Sports Arena opens; Dodgers win World Series in Coliseum.

1960   City has 250 miles of freeway; John F. Kennedy nominated for presidency at Democratic convention in Los Angeles; county has 500,000 people of Mexican background; city population reaches 2,461,595; county population is 6,038,771.

1961   Sam Yorty defeats Poulson for mayor; PE and Los Angeles Railway lines are discontinued (1961–1963); destructive Bel-Air wildfire.

1962   *Los Angeles Mirror-News* ceases publication; Dodgers move to Chavez Ravine; Cultural Heritage Commission established; Marina del Rey opened.

1963   *Crawford* school integration case starts; beginning of Bunker Hill renewal project; Dodgers win their second World Series; Gilbert Lindsay becomes first African American member of city council in modern era; Baldwin Hills Dam disaster.

1964   Los Angeles County Music Center opens; Los Angeles is second most populous city in the nation; *bracero* farm labor program ends; Rapid Transit District established; Ahmanson Theater opens.

1965   Los Angeles County Museum of Art opens; Yorty is reelected mayor, defeating James Roosevelt; Watts riots in South Central Los Angeles (11–17 Aug.), toll includes 34 killed, $40 million in damage; Gov. Pat Brown appoints McCone Commission to investigate disturbance; Los Angeles Dodgers win World Series.

1966   Busch Gardens opens in Van Nuys; Ronald Reagan elected governor; new Los Angeles Zoo opens; Bella Lewitzky Dance Company formed.

1967   Long Beach acquires SS *Queen Mary;* emergence of Chicano movement; beginning of Newspaper Guild strike against *Herald-Examiner* (to 1973); Los Angeles Free Clinic opens; Jack Kent Cooke forms Los Angeles Kings; Mark Taper Forum opens.

1968   Presidential candidate Robert Kennedy is assassinated at Ambassador Hotel (5 June); Richard Nixon elected president; Angels Flight railway closes; Los Angeles city has 138 miles of freeway; landmark Richfield Building (1928–1929) demolished.

1969   Yorty is reelected mayor, defeating Tom Bradley; severe damage caused by rains and flooding; Ed Davis becomes chief of LAPD; Irving Gill's Dodge House demolished; Heritage Square museum established; Charles Manson murders.

1970   Judge Alfred Gitelson decision in school desegregation case leads to his defeat for reelection; Los Angeles Unified School District (LAUSD) teachers strike; Los Angeles population reaches 2,811,801; county population is 7,055,800.

1971   Sylmar earthquake (6.6); ARCO twin towers presage new downtown skyline; Chrysler auto plant closes in City of Industry; Chicano Moratorium demonstration to end Vietnam War; California Institute of the Arts opens; Libertarian Party founded.

1972   Martin Luther King Jr. Hospital opens; California Coastal Commission formed; Columbia and Warner Brothers form Burbank Studios; remains of Tongva village uncovered on CSU Long Beach campus; Pan Pacific Auditorium closes; Pepperdine University opens Malibu campus; Lakers win first world championship.

1973   Tom Bradley defeats Sam Yorty in mayoral race; merger creates Loyola-Marymount University; Malibu Creek State Park established.

1974   J. Paul Getty Museum relocated to Malibu; drive to incorporate East Los Angeles fails.

1975   Pacific Ocean Park demolished; South Coast Air Quality Management District (AQMD) formed; Kareem Abdul-Jabbar (Lew Alcindor) becomes a Laker; Pacific Design Center completed; George C. Page Museum of La Brea Discoveries opens.

1976   Los Angeles City-County Native American Indian Commission formed; reorganization of Greek Theatre.

1977   Tommy Lasorda named manager of Dodgers; Bradley reelected mayor; Raiders win Super Bowl championship.

1978   California voters approve Proposition 13 tax amendment; Santa Monica Mountains National Recreation Area created by Congress; first Pasadena Doo Dah Parade.

1979   Pico Rivera Lincoln-Mercury auto plant closes; major Teamsters strike; Magic Johnson drafted by Lakers; busing discontinued by state vote; Jerry Buss buys Lakers, Kings, and the Forum.

1980   Screen Actors Guild strike; year-long commemoration of founding of Los Angeles by 44 settlers in 1781 begins (4 Sept.); Los Angeles city population is 2,967,000; county population is 7,477,503.

1981   Los Angeles bicentennial; first diagnosed cases of AIDS in the county; Bradley reelected to third term.

1982   Bradley loses to George Deukmejian in gubernatorial bid; 423,500 dogs estimated living in city of Los Angeles; Sherman Block elected sheriff.

1983   Weingart Center founded on Skid Row; D.A.R.E. antidrug program installed in LAUSD schools; Temporary Contemporary art museum opened; court decision orders protection of Mono Lake.

1984   Twenty-third Olympiad Summer Games are held in Los Angeles; Los Angeles bookstore sales reach $176 million; Aerospace Museum opens in Exposition Park; major archaeological find at Los Encinos State Historic Park of Tongva village; first Los Angeles Arts Festival; West Hollywood becomes independent city.

1985   Bradley reelected to fourth term; law officials estimate 400 gangs with 45,000 members in the county; environmental group, Heal the Bay, is formed; 75,000 immigrants are naturalized in the county; Los Angeles Music Center Opera is founded; Roger M. Mahony named archbishop of Los Angeles; county population is 8,158,700.

1986   First Los Angeles Marathon; two arson fires devastate Los Angeles Central Library; Bradley loses second gubernatorial bid to Deukmejian.

1987   Decline in aerospace industry; agricultural acreage shrinks from 318,000 in 1942 to 32,000; Whittier Narrows earthquake (5.9); Justice for Janitors campaign; Pope John Paul II speaks in Coliseum; Schwab's Drugstore torn down.

1988   L.A. 2000 Committee issues report; Environmental Protection Agency imposes strong requirements on Los Angeles County; Los Angeles is leading West Coast port, handling $54.2 billion in cargo.

1989   Tom Bradley reelected to fifth term; Southern California Auto Club responds to 3 million calls for roadside aid; 73-story First Interstate Tower completed, tallest in the city; Frank Gehry wins Pritzker Prize; Autry Museum of Western Heritage opens; *Herald-Examiner* ceases publication.

1990   County approves transit tax Proposition C; city installs ethics commission; county median household income is $34,965; Los Angeles city population reaches 3,485,390; county population is 8,769,944.

1991   Gloria Molina is first woman and first Latina elected to Board of Supervisors; Caltech celebrates its centennial; Christopher Commission established to investigate Rodney King incident; median cost of a home in the county is $221,590; LEARN coalition created; LAUSD enrolls 640,000; cleanest smog year since AQMD record keeping was initiated.

1992   Acquittal (29 Apr.) of police officers for beating of Rodney King sets off rioting, which ends on 5 May with toll of 55 deaths, 2,300 injuries, 623 fires, and $785 million in property damage; Police Chief Daryl Gates resigns; Willie Williams is appointed police chief; Bank of America absorbs Security Pacific Bank.

1993   Wildfires burn 152,000 acres countywide, resulting in 2 deaths, destruction of 720 buildings, and $950 million in insurance claims; completion of 17.3-mile Century Freeway; austerity budget of $3.9 billion for city; Central City Association issues 25-year "Downtown Strategic Plan"; CityWalk opens at Universal City.

1994   Northridge earthquake (6.7) results in 61 deaths, 6,500 injuries, 1,000 buildings destroyed or damaged, 20,000 people made homeless, and estimated damages as high as $20 billion; Rose Bowl hosts World Cup soccer matches; Peterson Automotive Museum, Craft and Folk Art Museum, and Museum of Miniatures become part of Wilshire Boulevard "Museum Row"; new multimedia entertainment company, DreamWorks, formed; county population reaches 9,230,600.

1995   UCLA wins its first NCAA basketball championship in 20 years; county budget deficit reaches an estimated $1.2 billion; Port of Long Beach becomes the nation's largest container port; *Los Angeles Times* receives Pulitzer Prize for spot coverage of the 1994 Northridge earthquake; Beverly Hills Hotel reopens, and Chasen's Restaurant closes.

1996   Angels Flight restored; Skirball Cultural Center and Museum opens.

APPENDIX B: 1990 CENSUS POPULATION

Los Angeles County
1990 Census Population, by Age and Race

	White	Black	Native American	Asian	Other	Total (previous columns)[a]	Hispanic[a]
Acton[b]							
Under 18 years	389	10	3	2	17	421	58
18 years and over	964	17	13	10	46	1,050	92
Agoura Hills							
Under 18 years	5,696	86	20	475	92	6,369	386
18 years and over	12,681	152	44	921	223	14,021	857
Alhambra							
Under 18 years	6,208	369	90	7,246	4,782	18,695	8,822
18 years and over	27,335	1,274	261	24,067	10,474	63,411	20,804
Alondra Park[b]							
Under 18 years	1,549	362	24	628	635	3,198	1,117
18 years and over	5,347	719	53	1,706	1,192	9,017	2,245
Altadena[b]							
Under 18 years	4,389	4,813	61	395	1,243	10,901	2,132
18 years and over	16,503	11,738	157	1,391	1,968	31,757	3,887
Arcadia							
Under 18 years	5,972	96	54	3,774	517	10,413	1,311
18 years and over	28,547	278	120	7,548	1,384	37,877	3,835
Artesia							
Under 18 years	2,058	117	23	681	1,454	4,333	2,244
18 years and over	6,595	295	61	1,833	2,347	11,131	3,950
Avalon							
Under 18 years	729	1	2	9	0	741	430
18 years and over	2,148	4	10	15	0	2,177	740
Avocado Heights[b]							
Under 18 years	2,350	52	28	498	1,447	4,375	3,351
18 years and over	5,992	68	61	1,209	2,527	9,857	6,245
Azusa							
Under 18 years	7,156	527	63	626	3,527	11,899	7,989
18 years and over	20,125	1,059	223	2,116	5,911	29,434	14,103
Baldwin Park							
Under 18 years	13,346	643	189	2,441	7,764	24,383	19,160
18 years and over	25,177	1,044	320	6,067	12,339	44,947	29,891
Bell							
Under 18 years	4,377	95	110	138	7,049	11,769	10,883
18 years and over	10,071	265	177	334	11,749	22,596	18,700

	White	Black	Native American	Asian	Other	Total (previous columns)[a]	Hispanic[a]
Bellflower							
Under 18 years	9,952	1,411	162	1,707	2,864	16,096	5,153
18 years and over	33,177	2,463	398	4,528	5,153	45,719	9,623
Bell Gardens							
Under 18 years	5,968	64	171	207	10,621	17,031	15,831
18 years and over	10,203	159	320	338	14,304	25,324	21,244
Beverly Hills							
Under 18 years	4,707	98	10	426	53	5,294	235
18 years and over	24,475	445	49	1,319	389	26,677	1,490
Bradbury							
Under 18 years	141	4	0	44	6	195	19
18 years and over	505	14	1	82	32	634	99
Burbank							
Under 18 years	14,184	429	113	1,610	2,402	18,738	6,329
18 years and over	63,158	1,209	388	4,725	5,425	74,905	14,843
Carson							
Under 18 years	6,720	6,135	146	5,787	4,146	22,934	8,339
18 years and over	22,440	15,818	350	15,185	7,268	61,061	15,074
Cerritos							
Under 18 years	5,323	1,169	44	7,493	732	14,761	1,899
18 years and over	17,222	2,791	134	16,564	1,768	38,479	4,767
Charter Oak[b]							
Under 18 years	1,716	147	9	190	297	2,359	766
18 years and over	5,244	234	46	476	499	6,499	1,244
Citrus[b]							
Under 18 years	1,902	154	30	201	905	3,192	1,833
18 years and over	4,284	189	68	467	1,281	6,289	2,724
Claremont							
Under 18 years	5,282	525	32	754	432	7,025	1,085
18 years and over	21,448	1,099	101	2,011	819	25,478	2,249
Commerce							
Under 18 years	1,281	52	41	31	2,599	4,004	3,740
18 years and over	3,443	43	66	125	4,454	8,131	7,266
Compton							
Under 18 years	3,724	15,872	88	765	12,746	33,195	17,085
18 years and over	5,847	33,726	199	983	16,504	57,259	22,425
Covina							
Under 18 years	8,248	619	50	865	1,136	10,918	3,747
18 years and over	26,439	1,157	171	2,416	2,106	32,289	7,295
Cudahy							
Under 18 years	2,315	104	88	121	6,080	8,708	8,080
18 years and over	4,617	158	128	281	8,925	14,109	12,208
Culver City							
Under 18 years	4,387	858	55	1,003	942	7,245	2,106
18 years and over	22,466	3,168	169	3,666	2,079	31,548	5,561
Del Aire[b]							
Under 18 years	1,432	62	12	184	238	1,928	572
18 years and over	4,979	123	36	518	456	6,112	1,312
Desert View Highland[b]							
Under 18 years	533	23	10	13	97	676	205
18 years and over	1,260	35	21	44	118	1,478	203
Diamond Bar							
Under 18 years	9,153	957	49	4,255	911	15,325	3,028
18 years and over	25,012	2,079	141	9,105	2,010	38,347	6,108
Downey							
Under 18 years	14,339	1,077	150	2,206	4,533	22,305	9,605
18 years and over	51,984	1,991	436	5,864	8,864	69,139	19,964

	White	Black	Native American	Asian	Other	Total (previous columns)[a]	Hispanic[a]
Duarte							
Under 18 years	3,155	641	47	715	1,347	5,905	2,644
18 years and over	9,562	1,209	83	1,702	2,227	14,783	4,516
East Compton[b]							
Under 18 years	343	1,135	3	65	1,575	3,121	1,986
18 years and over	598	2,034	17	90	2,107	4,846	2,646
East La Mirada[b]							
Under 18 years	1,901	28	9	85	271	2,294	774
18 years and over	6,126	68	34	238	607	7,073	1,659
East Los Angeles[b]							
Under 18 years	16,674	112	211	283	24,869	42,149	41,383
18 years and over	36,656	1,660	316	1,308	44,290	84,230	78,301
East Pasadena[b]							
Under 18 years	774	41	12	246	322	1,395	577
18 years and over	3,097	71	22	669	656	4,515	1,161
East San Gabriel[b]							
Under 18 years	1,516	69	10	828	281	2,704	671
18 years and over	6,875	186	32	2,152	787	10,032	1,755
El Monte							
Under 18 years	22,116	413	195	3,549	9,874	36,147	29,388
18 years and over	43,980	634	405	8,940	16,103	70,062	47,603
El Segundo							
Under 18 years	2,548	35	13	167	99	2,862	349
18 years and over	11,232	119	52	597	361	12,361	1,033
Florence-Graham[b]							
Under 18 years	4,793	4,181	62	68	13,285	22,389	18,534
18 years and over	6,883	9,541	110	145	18,079	34,758	25,563
Gardena							
Under 18 years	3,276	3,424	78	3,021	1,720	11,519	3,716
18 years and over	12,757	8,289	194	13,545	3,543	38,328	7,790
Glendale							
Under 18 years	26,201	592	154	6,714	5,416	39,077	10,637
18 years and over	107,069	1,742	475	18,739	12,936	140,961	27,094
Glendora							
Under 18 years	10,883	169	68	824	682	12,626	2,508
18 years and over	31,440	368	187	1,863	1,344	35,202	4,742
Hacienda Heights[b]							
Under 18 years	7,230	329	81	4,211	1,981	13,832	5,458
18 years and over	23,726	771	224	10,072	3,729	38,522	11,305
Hawaiian Gardens							
Under 18 years	2,847	270	48	401	1,270	4,836	3,631
18 years and over	5,532	350	73	884	1,964	8,803	5,447
Hawthorne							
Under 18 years	6,064	5,583	68	2,067	4,253	18,035	7,067
18 years and over	24,102	14,629	258	5,752	8,573	53,314	15,152
Hermosa Beach							
Under 18 years	1,695	36	9	87	72	1,899	223
18 years and over	15,163	175	78	606	298	16,320	1,044
Hidden Hills							
Under 18 years	453	1	0	16	1	471	25
18 years and over	1,189	7	4	32	26	1,258	102
Huntington Park							
Under 18 years	5,388	203	105	257	13,373	19,326	18,495
18 years and over	12,098	391	196	778	23,276	36,739	33,001
Industry							
Under 18 years	72	3	0	6	52	133	101
18 years and over	407	16	1	16	58	498	218

	White	Black	Native American	Asian	Other	Total (previous columns)[a]	Hispanic[a]
Inglewood							
Under 18 years	4,747	15,815	107	702	11,627	32,998	15,943
18 years and over	14,326	41,046	320	2,052	18,860	76,604	26,306
Irwindale							
Under 18 years	174	0	0	7	181	362	316
18 years and over	405	1	0	17	265	688	583
La Cañada Flintridge							
Under 18 years	3,811	17	7	959	62	4,856	254
18 years and over	12,834	64	20	1,438	166	14,522	638
La Crescenta–Montrose[b]							
Under 18 years	3,319	20	22	473	149	3,983	439
18 years and over	11,538	39	56	1,017	335	12,985	1,068
Ladera Heights[b]							
Under 18 years	187	837	3	35	22	1,084	53
18 years and over	2,139	2,797	12	201	83	5,232	187
La Habra Heights							
Under 18 years	1,210	4	2	122	55	1,393	217
18 years and over	4,393	17	21	303	99	4,833	461
Lake Los Angeles[b]							
Under 18 years	2,476	234	18	75	431	3,234	733
18 years and over	3,797	305	40	121	480	4,743	827
Lakewood							
Under 18 years	13,842	942	148	1,925	1,290	18,147	3,497
18 years and over	45,848	1,770	339	4,959	2,494	55,410	7,266
La Mirada							
Under 18 years	7,455	210	58	859	1,162	9,744	3,447
18 years and over	25,403	352	186	2,473	2,294	30,708	7,012
Lancaster							
Under 18 years	22,378	2,522	324	1,126	2,757	29,107	5,452
18 years and over	54,847	4,685	589	2,492	5,571	68,184	9,364
La Puente							
Under 18 years	7,503	468	75	790	3,175	12,011	9,868
18 years and over	16,117	840	165	2,106	5,716	24,944	17,795
La Verne							
Under 18 years	6,452	327	55	638	623	8,095	1,867
18 years and over	19,206	599	123	1,579	1,295	22,802	3,808
Lawndale							
Under 18 years	4,014	736	61	973	1,622	7,406	3,084
18 years and over	12,554	1,537	172	2,336	3,326	19,925	6,275
Lennox[b]							
Under 18 years	3,243	501	29	239	4,521	8,533	7,607
18 years and over	5,936	932	61	440	6,855	14,224	11,871
Littlerock[b]							
Under 18 years	330	26	1	7	83	447	161
18 years and over	711	27	9	12	114	873	241
Lomita							
Under 18 years	3,284	256	32	438	521	4,531	1,240
18 years and over	12,074	310	109	1,324	1,034	14,851	2,516
Long Beach							
Under 18 years	44,680	20,247	740	21,071	22,729	109,467	37,581
18 years and over	206,036	38,514	2,041	37,195	36,180	319,966	63,838
Los Angeles							
Under 18 years	369,442	131,459	4,246	76,124	282,006	863,277	473,821
18 years and over	1,471,740	356,215	12,133	265,683	516,350	2,622,121	917,590
Lynwood							
Under 18 years	4,840	5,166	101	461	12,671	23,239	17,749
18 years and over	10,004	9,486	157	912	18,147	38,706	25,816

	White	Black	Native American	Asian	Other	Total (previous columns)[a]	Hispanic[a]
Manhattan Beach							
Under 18 years	4,828	47	15	294	81	5,265	348
18 years and over	25,144	159	71	1,116	308	26,798	1,297
Marina del Rey[b]							
Under 18 years	241	30	3	24	18	316	38
18 years and over	6,425	281	20	313	76	7,115	283
Mayflower Village[b]							
Under 18 years	851	32	7	131	145	1,166	333
18 years and over	3,119	39	14	379	261	3,812	640
Maywood							
Under 18 years	2,911	36	56	65	7,133	10,201	9,849
18 years and over	5,822	78	105	148	11,496	17,649	16,082
Monrovia							
Under 18 years	5,617	1,158	37	372	1,988	9,172	3,620
18 years and over	19,295	2,468	151	1,249	3,426	26,589	6,557
Montebello							
Under 18 years	6,415	192	101	2,007	7,452	16,167	12,579
18 years and over	21,608	387	178	6,994	14,230	43,397	27,684
Monterey Park							
Under 18 years	2,880	105	43	7,805	2,846	13,679	5,185
18 years and over	13,365	284	155	27,093	6,162	47,059	13,846
North El Monte[b]							
Under 18 years	634	6	2	108	56	806	233
18 years and over	2,115	14	8	312	129	2,578	480
Norwalk							
Under 18 years	13,577	1,058	246	3,334	9,902	28,117	16,320
18 years and over	39,059	2,003	567	8,368	16,165	66,162	28,798
Palmdale							
Under 18 years	17,748	1,771	227	1,042	3,488	24,276	6,266
18 years and over	34,353	2,627	421	1,988	5,177	44,566	8,888
Palmdale East[b]							
Under 18 years	779	69	18	36	207	1,109	300
18 years and over	1,537	60	20	52	274	1,943	391
Palos Verdes Estates							
Under 18 years	2,232	33	3	576	7	2,851	77
18 years and over	9,204	123	12	1,265	57	10,661	321
Paramount							
Under 18 years	6,860	1,969	121	880	6,864	16,694	11,792
18 years and over	16,095	3,129	235	1,863	9,653	30,975	17,206
Pasadena							
Under 18 years	12,591	7,291	133	2,073	6,895	28,983	11,788
18 years and over	62,751	17,661	458	8,605	13,133	102,608	24,124
Pico Rivera							
Under 18 years	9,447	144	116	521	7,560	17,788	16,128
18 years and over	25,335	264	218	1,351	14,221	41,389	33,109
Point Dume[b]							
Under 18 years	377	2	2	11	12	404	27
18 years and over	2,279	22	8	59	37	2,405	111
Pomona							
Under 18 years	21,917	6,786	231	2,985	11,280	43,199	26,603
18 years and over	53,196	12,227	514	5,806	16,781	88,524	40,930
Quartz Hill[b]							
Under 18 years	2,485	186	34	64	229	2,998	449
18 years and over	5,945	178	62	131	312	6,628	579
Rancho Palos Verdes							
Under 18 years	5,866	213	21	2,632	154	8,886	624
18 years and over	25,872	575	79	5,914	333	32,773	1,591

	White	Black	Native American	Asian	Other	Total (previous columns)[a]	Hispanic[a]
Redondo Beach							
Under 18 years	8,155	219	52	800	534	9,760	1,621
18 years and over	44,216	741	259	3,311	1,880	50,407	5,296
Rolling Hills							
Under 18 years	340	8	0	52	7	407	22
18 years and over	1,293	20	0	136	15	1,464	57
Rolling Hills Estates							
Under 18 years over	1,281	13	0	378	19	1,691	96
18 years and over	5,108	48	6	886	50	6,098	243
Rosemead							
Under 18 years	4,627	116	84	5,365	5,485	15,677	9,020
18 years and over	13,673	204	166	12,360	9,558	35,961	16,621
Rowland Heights[b]							
Under 18 years	6,052	837	48	3,695	1,670	12,302	4,304
18 years and over	16,907	1,383	129	8,809	3,117	30,345	8,383
San Dimas							
Under 18 years	6,563	414	45	813	637	8,472	1,911
18 years and over	19,906	807	118	1,961	1,133	23,925	3,701
San Fernando							
Under 18 years	2,481	86	61	75	5,031	7,734	7,069
18 years and over	6,318	180	104	247	7,997	14,846	11,614
San Gabriel							
Under 18 years	3,650	116	54	3,027	2,161	9,008	4,113
18 years and over	14,154	278	145	9,017	4,518	28,112	9,358
San Marino							
Under 18 years	1,731	13	4	1,504	49	3,301	143
18 years and over	6,828	19	8	2,685	118	9,658	512
Santa Clarita							
Under 18 years	26,437	553	167	1,367	2,436	30,960	5,102
18 years and over	70,118	1,142	457	3,240	4,725	79,682	9,669
Santa Fe Springs							
Under 18 years	2,107	132	41	219	1,963	4,462	3,400
18 years and over	6,704	190	76	537	3,551	11,058	7,056
Santa Monica							
Under 18 years	8,538	845	67	995	1,532	11,977	3,334
18 years and over	63,423	3,075	317	4,555	3,558	74,928	8,876
Sierra Madre							
Under 18 years	1,824	27	12	141	52	2,056	291
18 years and over	8,049	65	31	408	153	8,706	759
Signal Hill							
Under 18 years	782	302	18	312	390	1,804	640
18 years and over	4,593	582	55	638	699	6,567	1,182
South El Monte							
Under 18 years	4,510	51	30	331	2,170	7,092	6,401
18 years and over	9,217	51	74	757	3,659	13,758	11,232
South Gate							
Under 18 years	10,688	517	132	412	18,055	29,804	27,161
18 years and over	25,248	920	250	982	29,080	56,480	44,566
South Pasadena							
Under 18 years	2,983	166	29	1,331	357	4,866	879
18 years and over	13,728	579	68	3,755	940	19,070	2,334
South San Gabriel[b]							
Under 18 years	617	19	13	629	818	2,096	1,285
18 years and over	2,029	31	24	1,938	1,582	5,604	2,717
South San Jose Hills[b]							
Under 18 years	2,898	130	35	411	2,741	6,215	5,212
18 years and over	6,048	303	78	884	4,286	11,599	8,302

	White	Black	Native American	Asian	Other	Total (previous columns)[a]	Hispanic[a]
South Whittier[b]							
Under 18 years	9,446	231	130	616	5,004	15,427	9,647
18 years and over	23,807	348	221	1,485	8,226	34,087	15,980
Temple City							
Under 18 years	4,784	75	35	1,770	744	7,408	1,876
18 years and over	17,585	117	79	4,297	1,614	23,692	3,986
Torrance							
Under 18 years	17,498	503	116	7,904	1,152	27,173	3,576
18 years and over	79,646	1,430	423	21,193	3,242	105,934	9,822
Valinda[b]							
Under 18 years	3,554	359	24	643	1,666	6,246	4,199
18 years and over	7,799	608	61	1,405	2,616	12,489	6,677
Val Verde[b]							
Under 18 years	296	35	0	12	285	628	405
18 years and over	574	132	5	18	332	1,061	493
Vernon							
Under 18 years	14	2	0	0	26	42	39
18 years and over	52	3	0	4	51	110	80
View Park–Windsor[b]							
Under 18 years	100	1,885	7	26	51	2,069	87
18 years and over	914	8,440	30	157	159	9,700	315
Vincent[b]							
Under 18 years	2,918	172	21	279	1,031	4,421	2,458
18 years and over	6,744	219	67	695	1,567	9,292	3,795
Walnut							
Under 18 years	4,314	645	42	3,658	822	9,481	2,513
18 years and over	9,665	1,280	60	7,251	1,368	19,624	4,323
Walnut Park[b]							
Under 18 years	1,321	12	30	36	3,399	4,798	4,635
18 years and over	3,426	42	29	116	6,311	9,924	8,931
West Athens[b]							
Under 18 years	230	1,597	15	46	915	2,803	1,168
18 years and over	492	3,978	29	216	1,341	6,056	1,738
West Carson[b]							
Under 18 years	2,065	474	26	974	831	4,370	1,475
18 years and over	9,288	1,519	104	3,297	1,565	15,773	3,146
West Compton[b]							
Under 18 years	159	1,090	5	17	319	1,590	522
18 years and over	340	3,014	8	75	424	3,861	748
West Covina							
Under 18 years	14,227	2,701	142	4,659	4,805	26,534	11,620
18 years and over	43,209	5,502	343	11,863	8,635	69,552	21,633
West Hollywood							
Under 18 years	2,089	144	14	111	199	2,557	471
18 years and over	30,482	1,091	116	1,008	864	33,561	2,682
Westlake Village							
Under 18 years	1,404	7	3	141	18	1,573	72
18 years and over	5,491	49	8	285	49	5,882	241
Westmont[b]							
Under 18 years	603	7,628	34	62	2,797	11,124	3,574
18 years and over	1,126	14,789	61	148	3,796	19,920	4,956
West Puente[b]							
Under 18 years	4,160	277	57	498	1,579	6,571	5,423
18 years and over	8,861	607	89	1,234	2,892	13,683	9,785
West Whittier–Los Nietos[b]							
Under 18 years	3,443	50	39	169	3,711	7,412	6,290
18 years and over	9,943	76	103	424	6,206	16,752	11,725

	White	Black	Native American	Asian	Other	Total (previous columns)[a]	Hispanic[a]
Whittier							
Under 18 years	12,554	445	131	684	6,135	19,949	10,587
18 years and over	44,494	547	331	1,897	10,453	57,722	19,691
Willowbrook[b]							
Under 18 years	1,394	5,343	17	61	4,694	11,509	6,263
18 years and over	2,221	12,753	49	134	6,106	21,263	8,355
Other unincorporated areas							
Under 18 years	34,447	3,508	375	3,339	6,935	48,604	13,197
18 years and over	108,395	10,765	895	8,538	14,946	143,539	28,407
All Cities							
Under 18 years	976,266	249,750	11,120	227,318	574,457	2,038,911	1,013,762
18 years and over	3,539,732	614,961	29,306	653,449	1,016,085	5,853,533	1,896,073
All unincorporated areas							
Under 18 years	136,116	37,108	1,580	20,613	91,782	287,199	159,934
18 years and over	382,989	91,155	3,502	53,105	152,770	683,521	281,473
Los Angeles County Total							
Under 18 years	1,112,382	286,858	12,700	247,931	666,239	2,326,110	1,173,696
18 years and over	3,922,721	706,116	32,808	706,554	1,168,855	6,537,054	2,177,546

SOURCE: Los Angeles County Department of Regional Planning, 1990 Census.

[a]The racial categories white, black, Native American (American Indian, Eskimo, and Aleut), Asian (Asian and Pacific Islander) and others sum to the total. Hispanics (persons of Spanish background) are shown in a separate column; they may be included in any of the five racial groups.

[b]Unincorporated area.

APPENDIX C: INCORPORATION AND CONSOLIDATION OF CITIES

Incorporated Cities in Los Angeles County

	Date of Incorporation	Class[a]		Date of Incorporation	Class[a]
Agoura Hills	8 Dec. 1982	GL	La Verne	11 Sept. 1906	GL
Alhambra	11 July 1903	C	Lawndale	28 Dec. 1959	GL
Arcadia	5 Aug. 1903	C	Lomita	30 Dec. 1964	GL
Artesia	29 May 1959	GL	Long Beach	13 Dec. 1897	C
Avalon	2 July 1913	GL	Los Angeles	4 April 1850	C
Azusa	29 Dec. 1913	GL	Lynwood	16 July 1921	GL
Baldwin Park	25 Jan. 1956	GL	Malibu	28 March 1991	GL
Bell	7 Nov. 1927	GL	Manhattan Beach	7 Dec. 1912	GL
Bellflower	3 Sept. 1957	GL	Maywood	2 Sept. 1924	GL
Bell Gardens	1 Aug. 1961	GL	Monrovia	15 Dec. 1887	GL
Beverly Hills	28 Jan. 1914	GL	Montebello	15 Oct. 1920	GL
Bradbury	26 July 1957	GL	Monterey Park	29 May 1916	GL
Burbank	15 July 1911	C	Norwalk	26 Aug. 1957	GL
Calabasas	5 April 1991	GL	Palmdale	24 Aug. 1962	GL
Carson	20 Feb. 1968	GL	Palos Verdes Estates	20 Dec. 1939	GL
Cerritos	24 April 1956	C	Paramount	30 Jan. 1957	GL
Claremont	3 Oct. 1907	GL	Pasadena	19 June 1886	C
Commerce	28 Jan. 1960	GL	Pico Rivera	29 Jan. 1958	GL
Compton	11 May 1888	C	Pomona	6 Jan. 1888	C
Covina	14 Aug. 1901	GL	Rancho Palos Verdes	7 Sept. 1973	GL
Cudahy	10 Nov. 1990	GL	Redondo Beach	29 April 1892	C
Culver City	20 Sept. 1917	C	Rolling Hills	24 Jan. 1957	GL
Diamond Bar	18 April 1889	GL	Rolling Hills Estates	18 Sept. 1957	GL
Downey	17 Dec. 1956	C	Rosemead	4 Aug. 1959	GL
Duarte	22 Aug. 1957	GL	San Dimas	4 Aug. 1960	GL
El Monte	18 Nov. 1912	GL	San Fernando	31 Aug. 1911	GL
El Segundo	18 Jan. 1917	GL	San Gabriel	24 April 1913	GL
Gardena	11 Sept. 1930	GL	San Marino	25 April 1913	GL
Glendale	15 Feb. 1906	C	Santa Clarita	15 Dec. 1987	GL
Glendora	13 Nov. 1911	GL	Santa Fe Springs	15 May 1957	GL
Hawaiian Gardens	14 April 1964	GL	Santa Monica	9 Dec. 1886	C
Hawthorne	12 July 1992	GL	Sierra Madre	7 Feb. 1907	GL
Hermosa Beach	10 Jan. 1907	GL	Signal Hill	22 April 1924	GL
Hidden Hills	19 Oct. 1961	GL	South El Monte	30 July 1958	GL
Huntington Park	1 Sept. 1906	GL	South Gate	15 Jan. 1923	GL
Industry	18 June 1957	C	South Pasadena	29 Feb. 1888	GL
Inglewood	14 Feb. 1908	C	Temple City	25 May 1960	C
Irwindale	6 Aug. 1957	C	Torrance	1,2 May 1922	C
La Cañada Flintridge	8 Dec. 1976	GL	Vernon	22 Sept. 1905	GL
La Habra Heights	4 Dec. 1978	GL	Walnut	19 Jan. 1959	GL
Lakewood	16 April 1954	GL	West Covina	17 Feb. 1923	GL
La Mirada	23 March 1960	GL	West Hollywood	29 Nov. 1984	GL
Lancaster	22 Nov. 1977	GL	Westlake Village	11 Dec. 1981	GL
La Puente	1 Aug. 1956	GL	Whittier	28 Feb. 1898	C

SOURCE: Executive Office, Los Angeles County Board of Supervisors.
[a]GL = General law; C = Charter.

Incorporated Cities, by Supervisorial District

First District	Second District	Fourth District	Fifth District
Azusa	Carson	Artesia	Alhambra
Baldwin Park	Compton	Avalon	Arcadia
Bell	Culver City	Bellflower	Bradbury
Bell Gardens	Gardena	Cerritos	Burbank
Commerce	Hawthorne	Diamond Bar	Claremont
Cudahy	Inglewood	Downey	Covina
El Monte	Lawndale	El Segundo	Duarte
Huntington Park	Los Angeles (portion)	Hawaiian Gardens	Glendale
Industry	Lynwood	Hermosa Beach	Glendora
Irwindale		La Habra Heights	La Cañada Flintridge
La Puente	*Third District*	Lakewood	Lancaster
Los Angeles (portion)		La Mirada	La Verne
Maywood		Lomita	Los Angeles (portion)
Montebello	Agoura Hills	Long Beach	Monrovia
Monterey Park	Beverly Hills	Los Angeles (portion)	Palmdale
Pico Rivera	Calabasas	Manhattan Beach	Pasadena
Pomona	Hidden Hills	Norwalk	San Dimas
Rosemead	Los Angeles (portion)	Palos Verdes Estates	San Gabriel
Santa Fe Springs	Malibu	Paramount	San Marino
South El Monte	San Fernando	Rancho Palos Verdes	Santa Clarita
South Gate	Santa Monica	Redondo Beach	Sierra Madre
Vernon	West Hollywood	Rolling Hills	South Pasadena
	Westlake Village	Rolling Hills Estates	Temple City
		Signal Hill	Walnut
		Torrance	West Covina
		Whittier	

SOURCE: Executive Office, Los Angeles County Board of Supervisors, August 1994.

Former Incorporated Cities Now Consolidated

	Date of Incorporation	City Consolidated with	Date of Consolidation		Date of Incorporation	City Consolidated with	Date of Consolidation
Barnes City	13 Feb. 1926	Los Angeles	11 Apr. 1927	Sawtelle	26 Nov. 1906	Los Angeles	13 July 1922
Belmont				Tropico	15 Mar. 1911	Glendale	9 Jan. 1918
Heights	9 Oct. 1908	Long Beach	24 Nov. 1909	Tujunga	1 May 1925	Los Angeles	7 Mar. 1932
Eagle Rock	1 Mar. 1911	Los Angeles	17 May 1923	Venice	17 Feb. 1904	Los Angeles	25 Nov. 1925
Hollywood	9 Nov. 1903	Los Angeles	7 Feb. 1910	Watts	23 May 1907	Los Angeles	29 May 1926
Hyde Park	12 May 1921	Los Angeles	17 May 1923	Wilmington	27 Dec. 1905	Los Angeles	28 Aug. 1909
San Pedro	1 Mar. 1888	Los Angeles	28 Aug. 1909				

SOURCE: Executive Office, Los Angeles County Board of Supervisors, 1991.

Unincorporated Areas in Los Angeles County, 1993

Acton	Foothill	Pioneer
Agoura	Franklin	Quartz Hill
Alamitos	Gorman	Ramona
Altadena	Hacienda Heights	Rio Hondo
Angeles Mesa	Howard	Rowland Heights
Antelope	Keystone	Royal Oaks
Athens	La Brea	San Clemente Island
Bandini	La Crescenta	Santa Catalina Island
Bassett	La Rambla	Saugus
Belvedere	Ladera Heights	South San Gabriel
Bonner	Lamanda	South Whittier
Canyon Country	Lennox	Spadra
Castaic	Leona Valley	Sunland
Charter Oak	Littlerock	Topanga
Chatsworth	Llano	Universal
Citrus	Los Nietos	Valinda
Del Sur	Malibu Heights	Veterans Administration Center
Desert	Marina del Rey	Walnut Park
Doheny	Miramonte	West Hills
Dominguez	Moneta	Willowbrook
East Compton	Montrose	Wilsona
East Los Angeles	Neenach	Wiseburn
East Whittier	Ocean View	
Florence	Pearblossom	

SOURCE: Los Angeles County Registrar-Recorder

APPENDIX D: CITY AND COUNTY GOVERNMENT ORGANIZATION

Organization of Los Angeles County Government

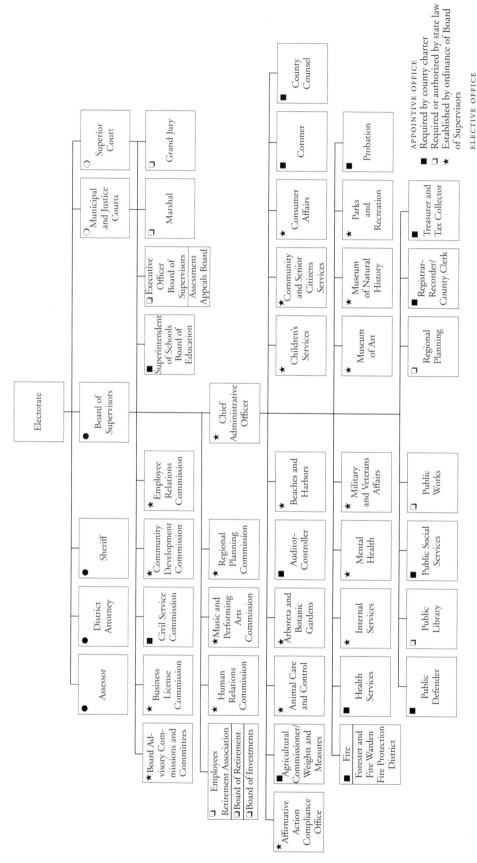

APPOINTIVE OFFICE
■ Required by county charter
□ Required or authorized by state law
★ Established by ordinance of Board of Supervisors

ELECTIVE OFFICE
● Required by county charter
○ Required by state law

SOURCE: Los Angeles County Board of Supervisors

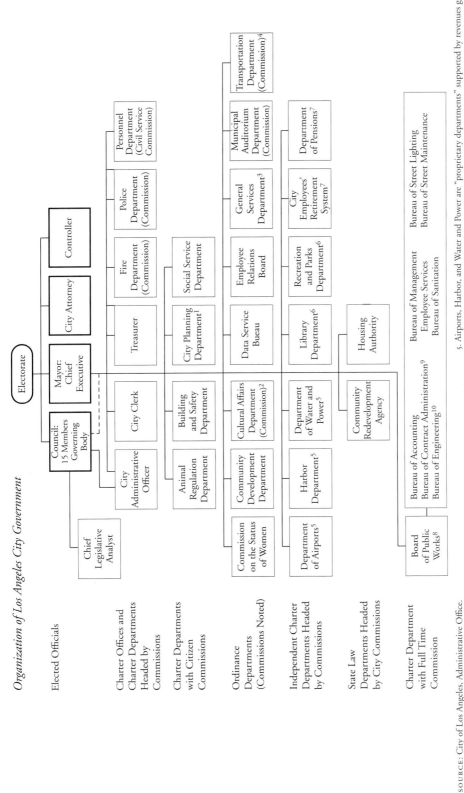

Organization of Los Angeles City Government

SOURCE: City of Los Angeles, Administrative Office.

1. Within the City Planning Department are the City Planning Commission, the Board of Zoning Appeals, and the Office of the Zoning Administrator, all established by Charter. The Environmental Quality Board and Office of Environmental Quality are established by ordinance in this Department.

2. On July 1, 1980, the department incorporated the Municipal Arts Department and portions of Recreation and Parks.

3. On July 1, 1979, this department incorporated the Supplies Department, Bureau of Standards and Bureau of Fleet Services and assumed functions formerly performed by the Public Utilities and Transportation Department, Bureau of Public Buildings, and Bureau of Right of Way and Land. The General Manager General Services fills the Charter position of Purchasing Agent.

4. In 1978–79, this department incorporated the Off Street Parking Agency and the Traffic Department and assumed functions formerly performed by the City Planning Department, Public Utilities and Transportation Department, and Bureau of Engineering.

5. Airports, Harbor, and Water and Power are "proprietary departments" supported by revenues generated by their activities.

6. Library and Recreation and Parks are supported primarily by general City revenues.

7. Pensions and Retirement System are supported by City and employee contributions.

8. The positions of Secretary of the Board of Public Works, City Engineer (Bureau of Engineering) and Inspector of Public Works (Bureau of Contract Administration) are established by Charter. The Chief Accountant Public Works reports to the Secretary of the Board of Public Works.

9. On July 1, 1979, the Bureau of Contract Administration assumed inspections functions formerly performed by the Bureau of Public Buildings.

10. In connection with the establishment of the General Services Department, the Bureau of Engineering assumed functions formerly performed by the Bureaus of Public Buildings and Right of Way and Land.

SELECTED READINGS

Nonfiction

Abdul-Jabbar, Kareem. *Giant Steps.* New York: Bantam Books, 1983.

Abelmann, Nancy, and John Lie. *Blue Dreams: Korean Americans and the Los Angeles Riots.* Cambridge, Mass.: Harvard University Press, 1995.

Acuña, Rodolfo F. *A Community Under Siege: A Chronicle of Chicanos East of the Los Angeles River, 1945–1975.* Los Angeles: Chicano Studies Research Center, 1984.

Anderson, Timothy J., Eudora M. Moore, and Robert Winter, eds. *California Design, 1910.* Salt Lake City: Peregrine Smith Books, 1974.

Apostol, Jane. *El Alisal: Where History Lingers.* Los Angeles: Historical Society of California, 1994.

Atkinson, Janet Irene. *Historical Directory of Los Angeles County.* Rev. ed. Jefferson, N.C.: McFarland, 1987.

Balderama, Francisco E. *In Defense of La Raza: The Los Angeles Mexican Consulate and the Mexican Community, 1929 to 1936.* Tucson: University of Arizona Press, 1982.

Banham, Reyner. *Los Angeles: The Architecture of Four Ecologies.* Harmondsworth, Eng.: Penguin Books, 1971.

Baur, John E. *The Health Seekers of Southern California, 1870–1900.* San Marino, Calif.: Huntington Library, 1959.

Baxter, John. *Sixty Years of Hollywood.* London: Tantivy Press, 1973.

Bell, Horace. *Reminiscences of a Ranger; or, Early Times in Southern California.* 1881; Los Angeles: Anderson, Ritchie & Simon, 1965.

———. *On the Old West Coast.* New York: Harper Perennial, 1992.

Bing, Léon. *Do or Die.* New York: HarperCollins, 1991.

Bowman, Lynn. *Los Angeles: Epic of a City.* Berkeley: Howell-North Books, 1974.

Brodsly, David. *L.A. Freeway: An Appreciative Essay.* Berkeley: University of California Press, 1981.

Brownlow, Kevin. *The Parade's Gone By.* Berkeley: University of California Press, 1968.

Brownlow, Kevin, and John Kobal. *Hollywood: The Pioneers.* New York: Knopf, 1979.

California Coastal Commission. *California Coastal Resource Guide.* Berkeley: University of California Press, 1987.

Cameron, Robert. *Above Los Angeles: A Collection of Nostalgic and Contemporary Aerial Photographs of Greater Los Angeles.* San Francisco: Cameron & Co., 1990.

Caughey, John. *To Kill a Child's Spirit: The Tragedy of School Segregation in Los Angeles.* Itasca, Ill.: F. E. Peacock, 1973.

Caughey, John, and LaRee Caughey, eds. *Los Angeles: Biography of a City.* Berkeley: University of California Press, 1976.

Cerra, Julie Lugo. *Culver City: Heart of Screenland.* Chatsworth, Calif.: Windsor Publications, 1992.

Chang, Edward T., and Russell C. Leong. *Los Angeles—Struggles toward Multiethnic Community: Asian, African American, and Latino Perspectives.* Seattle: University of Washington Press, 1994.

Clark, David. *Los Angeles: A City Apart.* Woodland Hills, Calif.: Windsor Press, 1981.

Cleland, Robert Glass. *The Cattle on a Thousand Hills: Southern California, 1850–1880.* San Marino, Calif.: Huntington Library, 1951.

Crouch, Winston W., and Beatrice Dinerman. *Southern California Metropolis: A Study in Development of Government for a Metropolitan Area.* Berkeley: University of California Press, 1963.

Culbertson, Judi, and Tom Randall. *Permanent Californians: An Illustrated Guide to the Cemeteries of California.* Chelsea, Vt.: Chelsea Green, 1989.

Dakin, Susanna B. *A Scotch Paisano in Old Los Angeles: Hugo Reid's Life in California, 1832–1852.* Berkeley: University of California Press, 1939.

Dash, Norman. *Yesterday's Los Angeles.* Miami, Fla.: E. A. Seemann, 1976.

Davis, Margaret Leslie. *Rivers in the Desert: William Mulholland and the Inventing of Los Angeles.* New York: HarperCollins, 1993.

Davis, Mike. *City of Quartz: Excavating the Future in Los Angeles.* New York: Vintage Books, 1992.

Dumke, Glenn. *The Boom of the Eighties in Southern California.* San Marino, Calif.: Huntington Library, 1966.

Elias, Judith W. *Los Angeles: Dream to Reality, 1885–1915.* Northridge, Calif.: Santa Susana Press, 1983.

Engh, Michael. *Frontier Faiths: Church, Temple, and Synagogue in Los Angeles, 1846–1888.* Albuquerque: University of New Mexico Press, 1992.

Fay, James S., et al., eds. *California Almanac: 5th Edition.* Santa Barbara, Calif.: Pacific Data Resources, 1991.

Federal Writers' Project. *The WPA Guide to California.* 1939. New York: Pantheon Books, 1984.

Femling, Jean. *Great Piers of California: A Guided Tour.* Santa Barbara, Calif.: Capra Press, 1984.

Fine, David, ed. *Los Angeles in Fiction: A Collection of Original Essays.* Albuquerque: University of New Mexico Press, 1984.

Fink, Augusta. *Time and the Terraced Land* [Palos Verdes Peninsula]. Santa Cruz, Calif.: Western Tanager, 1987.

Finney, Guy W. *Angel City in Turmoil: A Story of the Minute*

Men of Los Angeles in Their War on Civic Corruption, Graft, and Privilege. Los Angeles: Amer Press, 1945.

Fogelson, Robert. *The Fragmented Metropolis: Los Angeles, 1850–1930.* Cambridge, Mass.: Harvard University Press, 1967.

Ford, John Anson. *Thirty Explosive Years in Los Angeles County.* San Marino, Calif.: Huntington Library, 1961.

Friedrich, Otto. *City of Nets: A Portrait of Hollywood in the 1940s.* New York: Harper & Row, 1986.

Gader, June Rose. *L.A. Live: Profiles of a City.* New York: St. Martin's Press, 1980.

Gebhard, David, and Harriette Von Breton. *L.A. in the Thirties, 1931–1941.* Layton, Utah: Peregrine Smith, 1975.

Gebhard, David, and Robert Winter. *Los Angeles: An Architectural Guide.* Salt Lake City: Gibbs M. Smith, 1994.

George, Lynell. *No Crystal Stair: African Americans in the City of Angels.* New York: Doubleday, Anchor Books, 1992.

Giesler, Jerry, and Pete Martin. *The Jerry Giesler Story.* New York: Simon & Schuster, 1960.

Gleye, Paul. *The Architecture of Los Angeles.* Los Angeles: Rosebud Books, 1981.

Gordon, Robert. *Jazz West Coast: The Los Angeles Jazz Scene of the 1950s.* New York: Quartet Books, 1986.

Gottlieb, Robert, and Irene Wolt. *Thinking Big: The Story of the Los Angeles Times, Its Publishers, and Their Influence on Southern California.* New York: Putnam, 1977.

Greene, Linda. *A Historical Survey of the Santa Monica Mountains of California: Preliminary Historic Resource Study.* Denver, Colo.: National Park Service, 1980

Greenstein, Paul, Nigey Lennon, and Lionel Rolfe. *Bread and Hyacinths: The Rise and Fall of Utopian Los Angeles.* Los Angeles: Classic Books, 1992.

Gregory, James. *American Exodus: The Dust Bowl Migration and Okie Culture in California.* New York: Oxford University Press, 1989.

Grenier, Judson. *California Legacy: The James Alexander Watson–María Dolores Domínguez de Watson Family, 1820–1980.* Los Angeles: Watson Land Co., 1987.

Grenier, Judson, et al., eds. *A Guide to Historic Places in Los Angeles County.* Dubuque, Iowa: Kendall/Hunt, 1978.

Griswold del Castillo, Richard. *The Los Angeles Barrio, 1850–1890: A Social History.* Berkeley: University of California Press, 1979.

Gudde, Erwin G. *California Place Names.* Berkeley: University of California Press, 1960.

Guinn, James M. *A History of California and an Extended History of Los Angeles and Environs . . . .* 3 vols. Los Angeles: Historic Record Co., 1915.

Halliwell, Leslie. *The Filmgoer's Companion.* 4th ed. New York: Hill & Wang, 1975.

Hancock, Ralph. *Fabulous Boulevard* [Wilshire Blvd.]. New York: Funk & Wagnall, 1949.

Hannaford, Donald, and Revel Edwards. *Spanish Colonial or Adobe Architecture of California, 1800–1850.* New York: Architectural Book Publishing, 1931.

Hart, James D. *A Companion to California.* Berkeley: University of California Press, 1987.

Hayden, Dolores, Gail Dubrow, and Carolyn Flynn. *The Power of Place.* Los Angeles: Power of Place, [1981].

Healey, Dorothy, and Maurice Isserman. *Dorothy Healey Remembers: A Life in the American Communist Party.* New York: Oxford University Press, 1990.

Hendrickson, Joe. *Tournament of Roses: The First 100 Years.* Los Angeles: Brook House, 1971.

Henstell, Bruce. *Los Angeles: An Illustrated History.* New York: Knopf, 1980.

———. *Sunshine and Wealth: Los Angeles in the Twenties and Thirties.* San Francisco: Chronicle Books, 1984.

Hertrich, William. *The Huntington Botanical Gardens, 1905–1949.* San Marino, Calif.: Huntington Library, 1949.

Hine, Robert V. *California's Utopian Colonies.* Berkeley: University of California Press, 1983.

Hoffman, Abraham. *Unwanted Mexican-Americans in the Great Depression: Repatriation Pressure, 1929–1939.* Tucson: University of Arizona Press, 1981.

———. *Vision or Villainy: Origins of the Owens Valley–Los Angeles Water Controversy.* San Francisco: Chronicle Books, 1991.

Hoffman, Tricia, and Nan Fuchs. *Save L.A.* San Francisco: Chronicle Books, 1991.

Hylan, Arnold. *Bunker Hill: A Los Angeles Landmark.* Los Angeles: Dawson's Bookshop, 1976.

Jensen, Joan M., and Gloria Ricci Lothrop. *California Women: A History.* Sparks, Nev.: Materials for Today's Learning, 1988.

Kahrl, William L. *Water and Power: The Conflict over Los Angeles' Water Supply in the Owens Valley.* Berkeley: University of California Press, 1982.

Kaplan, Sam Hall. *L.A. Follies: Design and Other Diversions in a Fractured Metropolis.* Santa Monica, Calif.: Cityscape Press, 1989.

———. *L.A. Lost and Found: An Architectural History of Los Angeles.* New York: Crown, 1987.

Kim, Elaine H., and Eui-Young Yu. *East to America.* New York: New Press, 1996.

Klein, Norman M., and Martin G. Schiesel, eds. *20th Century Los Angeles: Power, Promotion, and Social Conflict.* Claremont, Calif.: Regina Books, 1990.

Kyle, Evelyn Peters. *The Dreams of the Pioneers: A Brief History of the Early Days of Pasadena.* Pasadena: Pasadena Pioneer Association, 1982.

Lantis, David W., Rodney Steiner, and Arthur E. Karinen. *California: Land of Contrast.* Dubuque, Iowa: Kendall/Hunt, 1977.

Leader, Leonard. *Los Angeles in the Great Depression.* New York: Garland, 1991.

League of Women Voters of Los Angeles. *Los Angeles: Structure of a City.* Rev. ed. Los Angeles: League of Women Voters, 1986.

Lillard, Richard G. *Eden in Jeopardy: Man's Prodigal Meddling with His Environment: The Southern California Experience.* New York: Knopf, 1966.

———. *My Urban Wilderness in the Hollywood Hills: A Year of Years on Quito Lane.* Lanham, Md.: University Press of America, 1983.

Littlefield, Douglas R., and Tanis C. Thorne. *The Spirit of Enterprise: The History of Pacific Enterprises from 1886 to 1989.* Los Angeles: Pacific Enterprises, 1990.

Longstreet, Stephen. *All Star Cast: An Anecdotal History of Los Angeles.* New York: Crowell, 1977.

Lothrop, Gloria Ricci. *A Guide to Historical Outings in Southern California*. Los Angeles: Historical Society of Southern California, 1991.

———. *Los Angeles Profiles: A Tribute to the Ethnic Diversity of Los Angeles*. Los Angeles: Historical Society of Southern California, 1994.

———. *Pomona: A Centennial History*. Northridge, Calif.: Windsor Publications, 1988.

Maltin, Leonard. *Leonard Maltin's TV Movies and Video Guide*. Harmondsworth, Eng.: Penguin Books, 1989.

Markinson, Randell. *Greene and Greene: Architecture as Fine Art*. Salt Lake City: Gibbs M. Smith, 1977.

Martinez, Al. *City of Angels: A Drive-by Portrait of Los Angeles*. New York: St. Martin's Press, 1996.

Mayer, Robert, comp. *Los Angeles, 1542–1976: A Chronological and Documentary History*. Dobbs Ferry, N.Y.: Oceana Publications, 1978.

Mayo, Morrow. *Los Angeles*. New York: Knopf, 1933.

Mazon, Mauricio. *The Zoot-Suit Riots: The Psychology of Symbolic Annihilation*. Austin: University of Texas Press, 1984.

McGrew, Patrick, and Robert Julian. *Landmarks of Los Angeles*. New York: Harry N. Abrams, 1994.

McWilliams, Carey. *Southern California: An Island on the Land*. 1946; Santa Barbara: Peregrine Smith, 1973.

Moore, Bebe. *Brothers and Sisters*. New York: G. P. Putnam's Sons, 1994.

Moore, Charles, et al. *The City Observed: Los Angeles*. New York: Random House, 1984.

Mulholland, Catherine. *The Owensmouth Baby: The Making of a San Fernando Valley Town*. Northridge, Calif.: Santa Susana Press, 1987.

Nadeau, Remi A. *City-Makers: The Men Who Transformed Los Angeles from Village to Metropolis . . . 1868–76*. Garden City, N.Y.: Doubleday, 1948.

———. *The Water Seekers*. Santa Barbara, Calif.: Peregrine Smith, 1974.

Nelson, Howard J. *The Los Angeles Metropolis*. Dubuque, Iowa: Kendall/Hunt, 1983.

Newmark, Harris. *Sixty Years in Southern California, 1853–1913 . . . The Reminiscences of Harris Newmark*. Boston: Houghton Mifflin, 1916.

Nunis, Doyce B., Jr., ed. *Southern California's Spanish Heritage: An Anthology*. Los Angeles: Historical Society of Southern California, 1992.

———, ed. *Southern California Local History: A Gathering of the Writings of W. W. Robinson*. Los Angeles: Historical Society of Southern California, 1993.

Nunis, Doyce, and Gloria Lothrop, comps. *A Guide to the History of California*. New York: Greenwood Press, 1989.

O'Connor, Letitia Burns. *Exploring Cultural Resources in Los Angeles*. Los Angeles: Times Mirror Square, 1990.

O'Flaherty, Joseph. *An End and a Beginning: The South Coast and Los Angeles, 1850–1887*. New York: Exposition Press, 1972.

———. *Those Powerful Years: The South Coast and Los Angeles, 1887–1917*. Hicksville, N.Y.: Exposition Press, 1978.

Ostrom, Vincent. *Water and Politics: A Study of Water Policies and Administration in the Development of Los Angeles*. New York: Johnson Reprint Corp., 1972.

Ovnick, Merry. *Los Angeles: The End of the Rainbow*. Los Angeles: Balcony Press, 1994.

Payne, J. Gregory, and Scott C. Ratzan. *Tom Bradley: The Impossible Dream*. Santa Monica, Calif.: Roundtable, 1986.

Pearlstone, Zena. *Ethnic L.A.* Beverly Hills: Hillcrest Press, 1990.

Pitt, Leonard. *The Decline of the Californios: A Social History of the Spanish-Speaking Californians, 1846–1890*. Berkeley: University of California Press, 1966.

Powdermaker, Hortense. *Hollywood: The Dream Factory*. London: Secker & Warburg, 1951.

Powell, Lawrence Clark, and W. W. Robinson. *The Malibu*. Los Angeles: Dawson's Bookshop, 1958.

Queenan, Charles F. *Long Beach and Los Angeles: A Tale of Two Ports*. Northridge, Calif.: Windsor Publications, 1986.

Rand, Christopher. *Los Angeles: The Ultimate City*. New York: Oxford University Press, 1967.

Ray, MaryEllen Bell. *The City of Watts, 1907 to 1926*. Los Angeles: Rising, 1985.

Reavill, Gil. *Los Angeles*. Oakland, Calif.: Compass American Guides, 1992.

Reid, David, ed. *Sex, Death, and God in L.A.* New York: Pantheon Books, 1992.

Rensch, Hero Eugene, et al. *Historic Spots in California*. 4th ed. Stanford: Stanford University Press, 1990.

Rice, William B. *Southern California's First Newspaper: The Founding of the "Los Angeles Star."* Los Angeles: G. Dawson, 1941.

Riddick-Norton, Glenda, comp. *Social Service Resource Directory for Los Angeles County, 1991–92*. Orange, Calif.: Resource Directory, 1990.

Rieff, David. *Los Angeles: Capital of the Third World*. New York: Simon & Schuster, Touchstone Books, 1991.

Robbins, George W., and L. Deming Tilton, eds. *Los Angeles, Preface to a Master Plan*. Los Angeles: Pacific Southwest Academy, 1941.

Robinson, John W. *Los Angeles in the Civil War Days, 1860–1865*. Los Angeles: Dawson's Bookshop, 1977.

———. *The San Gabriels: Southern California Mountain Country*. San Marino, Calif.: Golden West Books, 1977.

Robinson, W[illiam] W[ilcox]. *Lawyers of Los Angeles: A History of the Los Angeles Bar Association and of the Bar of Los Angeles County*. Los Angeles: Los Angeles Bar Association, 1959.

———. *Los Angeles from the Days of the Pueblo, Together with a Guide to the Historic Old Plaza Area . . . .* San Francisco: California Historical Society, 1959.

———. *People versus Lugo: The Story of a Famous Los Angeles Murder Case and Its Amazing Aftermath*. Los Angeles: Dawson's Bookshop, 1962.

———. *Ranchos Become Cities*. Pasadena, Calif.: San Pasqual Press, 1939.

———. *San Pedro and Wilmington: A Calendar of Events in the Making of Two Cities and the Los Angeles Harbor*. 10th ed. Los Angeles: Title Guarantee & Trust Co., 1937.

———. *Southern California Local History*. Los Angeles: Historical Society of Southern California, 1993.

Rolfe, Lionel. *Literary L.A.* San Francisco: Chronicle Books, 1981.

Rolle, Andrew. *California: A History*. 4th ed. Arlington Heights, Ill.: H. Davidson, 1987.

———. *Henry Mayo Newhall and His Times: A California Legacy*. San Marino, Calif.: Huntington Library, 1991.

Romo, Ricardo. *East Los Angeles: History of a Barrio.* Austin: University of Texas Press, 1983.

Schockman, H. Eric, ed. *The Perfecting of Los Angeles: Ethics Reforms on the Municipal Level.* Los Angeles: California State University, Los Angeles, 1989.

Scobie, Ingrid Winter. *Center Stage: Helen Gahagan Douglas, a Life.* New York: Oxford University Press, 1992.

Singleton, Gregory. *Religion in the City of Angels: American Protestant Culture and Urbanization in Los Angeles, 1850–1930.* Ann Arbor: UMI Research Press, 1979.

Sitton, Tom. *John Randolph Haynes: California Progressive.* Stanford: Stanford University Press, 1992.

Smith, Jack. *Jack Smith's L.A.* New York: McGraw-Hill, 1980.

Smith, Sarah Bixby. *Adobe Days, Being the Truthful Narrative of the Events in the Life of a California Girl on a Sheep Ranch and in El Pueblo de Nuestra Señora de Los Angeles. . . .* Cedar Rapids, Iowa: Torch Press, 1925.

Sonenshein, Raphael J. *Politics in Black and White: Race and Power in Los Angeles.* Princeton: Princeton University Press, 1993.

Starr, Kevin. *Inventing the Dream: California Through the Progressive Era.* New York: Oxford University Press, 1986.

———. *Material Dreams: Southern California Through the 1920s.* New York: Oxford University Press, 1990.

Steele, James. *Los Angeles Architecture: The Contemporary Condition.* London: Phaidon Press, 1993.

Steiner, Rodney. *Los Angeles: The Centrifugal City.* Dubuque, Iowa: Kendall/Hunt, 1981.

Sullivan, Neil J. *The Dodgers Move West.* New York: Oxford University Press, 1987.

Thomas Bros. *Guide to Los Angeles, 1994.* Irvine, Calif.: Thomas Bros. Maps, 1994.

Torrence, Bruce C. *Hollywood: The First Hundred Years.* New York: Zoetrope, 1982.

Van Dyke, Theodore S. *Southern California: Its Valleys, Hills, and Streams . . . .* New York: Fords, Howard & Hulbert, 1886.

Vigil, James Diego. *Barrio Gangs: Street Life and Identity in Southern California.* Austin: University of Texas Press, 1988.

Vorspan, Max, and Lloyd P. Gartner. *History of the Jews of Los Angeles.* San Marino, Calif.: Huntington Library, 1970.

Walker, Franklin. *A Literary History of Southern California.* Berkeley: University of California Press, 1950.

Walker, Jim. *The Yellow Cars of Los Angeles.* Glendale, Calif.: Interurbans, 1977.

Weaver, John D. *El Pueblo Grande: A Nonfiction Book About Los Angeles.* Los Angeles: Ward Ritchie Press, 1973.

Weber, Francis J. *Century of Fulfillment: The Roman Catholic Church in Southern California, 1847–1947.* Mission Hills, Calif.: Archival Center, 1990.

Weinstock, Matt. *Muscatel at Noon.* New York: Morrow, 1951.

Wells, Walter. *Tycoons and Locusts: A Regional Look at Hollywood Fiction of the 1930s.* Carbondale, Ill.: Southern Illinois Press, 1973.

Winter, Robert. *The California Bungalow.* Los Angeles: Hennessey & Ingalls, 1980.

Wolf, Marvin J., and Katherine Mader. *Fallen Angels: Chronicles of L.A. Crime and Mystery.* New York: Ballantine Books, 1988.

Workman, Boyle. *The City That Grew, as Told to Caroline Walker.* Los Angeles: Southland Publishing Company, 1936.

Writers' Program of the Work Projects Administration [WPA]. *Los Angeles: A Guide to the City and Its Environs.* New York: Hastings House, 1951.

Xantus, John. *The Fort Tejon Letters, 1857–1859.* Tucson: University of Arizona Press, 1986.

Young, Betty Lou, ed. *Pacific Palisades: Where the Mountains Meet the Sea.* Pacific Palisades, Calif.: Historical Society Press, 1983.

Fiction

The following books vary enormously as to literary merit and represent different genres. Taken together, they offer a glimpse of the way writers of fiction have depicted the area and its people since Helen Hunt Jackson published *Ramona* in 1884.

Allen, Jane. *I Lost My Girlish Laughter.* 1938.

Austin, Mary. *The Land of Little Rain.* 1903.

Baker, Dorothy. *Young Man With a Horn.* 1938.

Baum, Vicki. *Falling Star.* 1934.

Belfrage, Cedric. *Promised Land.* 1938.

Bemelmans, Ludwig. *Dirty Eddie.* 1947.

Bradbury, Ray. *The Martian Chronicles.* 1950.

Brinig, Myron. *Flutter of an Eyelid.* 1933.

———. *Anne Minton's Life.* 1939.

Bukowski, Charles. *Post Office.* 1971.

Cain, James. *The Postman Always Rings Twice.* 1934.

———. *Double Indemnity.* 1936.

———. *Mildred Pierce.* 1941.

Chandler, Raymond. *The Big Sleep.* 1939.

———. *Farewell, My Lovely.* 1940.

———. *The High Window.* 1942.

———. *The Lady in the Lake.* 1943.

———. *The Little Sister.* 1949.

———. *The Long Goodbye.* 1953.

Child, Nellie. *The Diamond Ransom Murders.* 1935.

Connelly, Mark. *The Black Ice.* 1993.

Coo, Bruce. *Mexican Standoff.* 1988.

———. *Death as a Career Move.* 1992.

Corle, Edwin. *Fig Tree John.* 1935.

Davis, Clyde. *Sullivan.* 1940.

Didion, Joan. *Play It as It Lays.* 1970.

Disney, Dorothy. *The Golden Swan Murder.* 1939.

Dunne, John Gregory. *True Confessions.* 1977.

———. *Playland.* 1994.

Ellis, Bret Easton. *Less Than Zero.* 1985.

Ellroy, James. *The Black Dahlia.* 1987.

———. *The Big Nowhere.* 1988.

Elwood, Muriel. *Against the Tide.* 1950.

Fante, John. *Wait for the Spring, Bandini.* 1938.

———. *Ask the Dust.* 1939.

———. *Dago Red.* 1940.

———. *Dreams from Bunker Hill.* 1982.

Fenton, Frank. *A Place in the Sun.* 1942.

Field, Rachel. *To See Ourselves.* 1937.

Fitzgerald, F. Scott. *The Last Tycoon.* 1940.

Freeman, David. *A Hollywood Education: Tales of a Movie Dream and Easy Money.* 1986.

Fuchs, Daniel. *West of the Rockies.* 1971.

Griffith, Beatrice. *American Me.* 1948.

Hallinan, Timothy. *The Man with No Name.* 1973.

Hansen, Joseph. *Death Claims.* 1973.

Haywood, Gar Anthony. *Fear of the Dark.* 1987.

———. *You Can Die Trying.* 1993.

Himes, Charles. *If He Hollers Let Him Go.* 1945.

———. *Lonely Crusade.* 1947.

———. *The Quality of Hurt.* 1972.

———. *My Life of Absurdity.* 1976.

Hornsby, Wendy. *Telling Lies.* 1992.

———. *Midnight Baby.* 1993.

Howe, J. J. *The Mother Shadow.* 1989.

Hughes, Rupert. *City of Angels.* 1941.

Huxley, Aldous. *After Many a Summer Dies the Swan.* 1939.

———. *Ape and Essence.* 1948.

Isherwood, Christopher. *A Single Man.* 1951.

———. *Down There on a Visit.* 1962.

Jackson, Helen Hunt. *Ramona.* 1884.

Karbo, Karen. *Trespassers Welcome Here.* 1989.

Lambert, Gavin. *The Slide Area.* 1951.

Lee, James. *Hollywood Agentry.* 1938.

Lurie, Alison. *The Nowhere City.* 1966.

Luther, Mark Lee. *The Boosters.* 1924.

MacDonald, Ross. *The Moving Target.* 1949.

———. *The Way Some People Die.* 1951.

———. *The Underground Man.* 1971.

———. *The Blue Hammer.* 1976.

MacDonald, William. *California Caballero.* 1936.

McCoy, Horace. *They Shoot Horses, Don't They?* 1935.

———. *I Should Have Stayed Home.* 1938.

Mosley, Walter. *Devil In a Blue Dress.* 1990.

———. *A Red Death.* 1991.

———. *White Butterfly.* 1992.

———. *Black Betty.* 1994.

Nava, Michael. *The Hidden Law.* 1992.

Norman, Marc. *Bike Riding in Los Angeles.* 1973.

O'Flaherty, Liam. *Hollywood Cemetery.* 1938.

O'Hara, John. *Hope of Heaven.* 1938.

Pagano, Joe. *Golden Wedding.* 1943.

Priestly, J. B. *The Doomsday Men.* 1938.

Pugh, Dianne G. *Cold Call.* 1993.

Pynchon, Thomas. *The Crying of Lot 49.* 1966.

Queen, Ellery. *The Origin of Evil.* 1951.

Rechy, John. *City of Night.* 1963.

Roberts, Marta. *Tumbleweeds.* 1940.

Ryan, Don. *Angel's Flight.* 1927.

Sanchez, Thomas. *Zoot-Suit Murders: A Novel.* 1978.

Schulberg, Budd. *What Makes Sammy Run?* 1941.

———. *The Disenchanted.* 1950.

See, Carolyn. *Golden Days.* 1987.

———. *Making History.* 1991.

Shippey, Lee. *Where Nothing Ever Happens.* 1935.

Simon, Roger. *The Big Fix.* 1973.

Simpson, Mona. *Anywhere But Here.* 1986.

Sinclair, Upton. *Oil!* 1926.

Smith, Charley. *Chimney Rock.* 1993.

Storm, Hans Otto. *Count Ten.* 1940.

Tervalon, Jervey. *Understand This.* 1994.

Van Dyke, Theodore S. *Millionaires for a Day.* 1890.

Vidal, Gore. *In Hollywood: A Novel of America in the 1920s.* 1990.

Viertel, Peter. *The Canyon.* 1940.

Wambaugh, Joseph. *The New Centurions.* 1970.

———. *The Choir Boys.* 1975.

Waugh, Evelyn. *The Loved One.* 1948.

West, Jessamyn. *South of Los Angeles.* 1960.

West, Nathanael. *The Day of the Locust.* 1939.

Wilson, Harry Leon. *Merton of the Movies.* 1922.

Wodehouse, P. G. *Laughing Gas.* 1936.

Zeta, Oscar. *The Revolt of the Cockroach People.* 1973.

SELECTED FILMS

The following list is a chronological sampling of films that depict Southern California. The silent movies filmed in and around Los Angeles—especially many of the comedies, such as those featuring Laurel and Hardy, the Keystone Kops, Charlie Chaplin, Buster Keaton, Harold Lloyd, and Charlie Chase—are especially valuable for the glimpse they afford of the city as it looked in the early part of the century.

The Mark of Zorro. 1920, 1940.
Merton of the Movies. 1924, 1932, 1947.
Hollywood Revue of 1929. 1929.
What Price Hollywood? 1932.
It's a Gift. 1934.
Ramona. 1936.
A Star Is Born. 1937, 1954, 1976.
Hollywood Hotel. 1937.
Hollywood Cavalcade. 1939.
Sullivan's Travels. 1941.
Double Indemnity. 1944.
Hollywood Canteen. 1944.
Murder, My Sweet. 1944.
Abbott and Costello in Hollywood. 1945.
Mildred Pierce. 1945.
The Postman Always Rings Twice. 1946.
The Big Sleep. 1946.
DOA. 1949.
In a Lonely Place. 1950.
Sunset Boulevard. 1950.
The Ring. 1952.
Singin' in the Rain. 1952.
The Bad and the Beautiful. 1952.
The Barefoot Contessa. 1954.
Rebel Without a Cause. 1955.
The Big Knife. 1955.
Hollywood or Bust. 1956.
The Goddess. 1958.
Beach Party. 1963.
Bikini Beach. 1964.
Muscle Beach Party. 1964.
Pajama Party. 1964.
Beach Party Bingo. 1965.
How to Stuff a Wild Bikini. 1965.
Inside Daisy Clover. 1965.
The Loved One. 1965.
Ghost in the Invisible Bikini. 1966.
Planet of the Apes. 1968.
They Shoot Horses, Don't They? 1969.
Play It as It Lays. 1972.

The Long Goodbye. 1973.
The Way We Were. 1973.
Chinatown. 1974.
Shampoo. 1975.
Silent Movie. 1976.
The Last Tycoon. 1976.
Annie Hall. 1977.
Big Wednesday. 1978.
California Suite. 1978.
California Dreaming. 1979.
True Confessions. 1981.
Zoot Suit. 1981.
Bladerunner. 1982.
Beverly Hills Cop. 1984.
Brother from Another Planet. 1986.
Down and Out in Beverly Hills. 1986.
Born in East L.A. 1987.
Less Than Zero. 1987.
Stand and Deliver. 1987.
Hollywood Shuffle. 1987.
La Bamba. 1987.
Colors. 1988.
Tequila Sunrise. 1988.
Who Framed Roger Rabbit? 1988.
To Sleep with Anger. 1990.
Postcards from the Edge. 1990.
The Two Jakes. 1990.
Boyz N' the Hood. 1991.
Bugsy. 1991.
Dead Again. 1991.
Defending Your Life. 1991.
Grand Canyon. 1991.
Guilty by Suspicion. 1991.
L.A. Story. 1991.
Scenes from a Mall. 1991.
The Player. 1992.
American Me. 1992.
My Family/Mi Familia. 1995.
Mulholland Falls. 1996.

Designer: Barbara Jellow
Compositor: Integrated Composition Systems
Cartographer: Bill Nelson
Text: 9.5/11.5 Adobe Garamond
Display: Gill Sans, Snell Roundhand
Printer: BookCrafters
Binder: BookCrafters